MW00818261

Hornbook Series and Basic Legal Texts
Nutshell Series

and

Black Letter Series

of

WEST PUBLISHING COMPANY
P.O. Box 64526
St. Paul, Minnesota 55164-0526

Accounting

FARIS' ACCOUNTING AND LAW IN A NUTSHELL, 377 pages, 1984. Softcover. (Text)

Administrative Law

GELLHORN AND LEVIN'S ADMINISTRATIVE LAW AND PROCESS IN A NUTSHELL, Third Edition, 479 pages, 1990. Softcover. (Text)

Admiralty

MARAIST'S ADMIRALTY IN A NUTSHELL, Second Edition, 379 pages, 1988. Softcover. (Text)

SCHOENBAUM'S HORNBOOK ON ADMIRALTY AND MARITIME LAW, Student Edition, 692 pages, 1987 with 1989 pocket part. (Text)

Agency—Partnership

REUSCHLEIN AND GREGORY'S HORNBOOK ON THE LAW OF AGENCY AND PARTNERSHIP, Second Edition, 683 pages, 1990. (Text)

STEFFEN'S AGENCY-PARTNERSHIP IN A NUTSHELL, 364 pages, 1977. Softcover. (Text)

American Indian Law

CANBY'S AMERICAN INDIAN LAW IN A NUTSHELL, Second Edition, 336 pages, 1988. Softcover. (Text)

Antitrust—see also Regulated Industries, Trade Regulation

GELLHORN'S ANTITRUST LAW AND ECONOMICS IN A NUTSHELL, Third Edition, 472 pages, 1986. Softcover. (Text)

HOVENKAMP'S BLACK LETTER ON ANTITRUST, 323 pages, 1986. Softcover. (Review)

HOVENKAMP'S HORNBOOK ON ECONOMICS AND FEDERAL ANTITRUST LAW, Student Edition, 414 pages, 1985. (Text)

SULLIVAN'S HORNBOOK OF THE LAW OF ANTITRUST, 886 pages, 1977. (Text)

Appellate Advocacy—see Trial and Appellate Advocacy

Art Law

DUBOFF'S ART LAW IN A NUTSHELL, 335 pages, 1984. Softcover. (Text)

Banking Law

BANKING LAW: SELECTED STATUTES AND REGULATIONS. Softcover. 263 pages, 1991.

LOVETT'S BANKING AND FINANCIAL INSTITUTIONS LAW IN A NUTSHELL, Second Edition, 464 pages, 1988. Softcover. (Text)

Civil Procedure—see also Federal Jurisdiction and Procedure

CLERMONT'S BLACK LETTER ON CIVIL PROCEDURE, Second Edition, 332 pages,

Civil Procedure—Cont'd
1988. Softcover. (Review)

FRIEDENTHAL, KANE AND MILLER'S HORNBOOK ON CIVIL PROCEDURE, 876 pages, 1985. (Text)

KANE'S CIVIL PROCEDURE IN A NUTSHELL, Third Edition, 303 pages, 1991. Softcover. (Text)

KOFFLER AND REPPY'S HORNBOOK ON COMMON LAW PLEADING, 663 pages, 1969. (Text)

SIEGEL'S HORNBOOK ON NEW YORK PRACTICE, Second Edition, Student Edition, 1068 pages, 1991. Softcover. (Text)

Commercial Law

BAILEY AND HAGEDORN'S SECURED TRANSACTIONS IN A NUTSHELL, Third Edition, 390 pages, 1988. Softcover. (Text)

HENSON'S HORNBOOK ON SECURED TRANSACTIONS UNDER THE U.C.C., Second Edition, 504 pages, 1979, with 1979 pocket part. (Text)

NICKLES' BLACK LETTER ON COMMERCIAL PAPER, 450 pages, 1988. Softcover. (Review)

SPEIDEL'S BLACK LETTER ON SALES AND SALES FINANCING, 363 pages, 1984. Softcover. (Review)

STOCKTON'S SALES IN A NUTSHELL, Second Edition, 370 pages, 1981. Softcover. (Text)

STONE'S UNIFORM COMMERCIAL CODE IN A NUTSHELL, Third Edition, 580 pages, 1989. Softcover. (Text)

WEBER AND SPEIDEL'S COMMERCIAL PAPER IN A NUTSHELL, Third Edition, 404 pages, 1982. Softcover. (Text)

WHITE AND SUMMERS' HORNBOOK ON THE UNIFORM COMMERCIAL CODE, Third Edition, Student Edition, 1386 pages, 1988. (Text)

Community Property

MENNELL AND BOYKOFF'S COMMUNITY PROPERTY IN A NUTSHELL, Second Edition, 432 pages, 1988. Softcover. (Text)

Comparative Law

GLENDON, GORDON AND OSAKWE'S COMPARATIVE LEGAL TRADITIONS IN A NUTSHELL. 402 pages, 1982. Softcover. (Text)

Conflict of Laws

HAY'S BLACK LETTER ON CONFLICT OF LAWS, 330 pages, 1989. Softcover. (Review)

SCOLES AND HAY'S HORNBOOK ON CONFLICT OF LAWS, Student Edition, approximately 1100 pages, November 1991 Pub. (Text)

SIEGEL'S CONFLICTS IN A NUTSHELL, 470 pages, 1982. Softcover. (Text)

Constitutional Law—Civil Rights

BARRON AND DIENES' BLACK LETTER ON CONSTITUTIONAL LAW, Third Edition, 440 pages, 1991. Softcover. (Review)

BARRON AND DIENES' CONSTITUTIONAL LAW IN A NUTSHELL, Second Edition, 483 pages, 1991. Softcover. (Text)

ENGDAHL'S CONSTITUTIONAL FEDERALISM IN A NUTSHELL, Second Edition, 411 pages, 1987. Softcover. (Text)

MARKS AND COOPER'S STATE CONSTITUTIONAL LAW IN A NUTSHELL, 329 pages, 1988. Softcover. (Text)

NOWAK AND ROTUNDA'S HORNBOOK ON CONSTITUTIONAL LAW, Fourth Edition, approximately 1275 pages, August, 1991 Pub. (Text)

VIEIRA'S CONSTITUTIONAL CIVIL RIGHTS IN A NUTSHELL, Second Edition, 322 pages, 1990. Softcover. (Text)

WILLIAMS' CONSTITUTIONAL ANALYSIS IN A NUTSHELL, 388 pages, 1979. Softcover. (Text)

Consumer Law—see also Commercial Law

EPSTEIN AND NICKLES' CONSUMER LAW IN A NUTSHELL, Second Edition, 418 pages, 1981. Softcover. (Text)

Contracts

CALAMARI AND PERILLO'S BLACK LETTER ON CONTRACTS, Second Edition, 462 pages, 1990. Softcover. (Review)

CALAMARI AND PERILLO'S HORNBOOK ON CONTRACTS, Third Edition, 1049 pages, 1987. (Text)

CORBIN'S TEXT ON CONTRACTS, One Volume Student Edition, 1224 pages, 1952. (Text)

FRIEDMAN'S CONTRACT REMEDIES IN A NUTSHELL, 323 pages, 1981. Softcover. (Text)

KEYES' GOVERNMENT CONTRACTS IN A NUTSHELL, Second Edition, 557 pages, 1990. Softcover. (Text)

SCHABER AND ROHWER'S CONTRACTS IN A NUTSHELL, Third Edition, 457 pages, 1990. Softcover. (Text)

Copyright—see Patent and Copyright Law

Corporations

HAMILTON'S BLACK LETTER ON CORPORATIONS, Second Edition, 513 pages, 1986. Softcover. (Review)

HAMILTON'S THE LAW OF CORPORATIONS IN A NUTSHELL, Third Edition, 518 pages, 1991. Softcover. (Text)

HENN AND ALEXANDER'S HORNBOOK ON LAWS OF CORPORATIONS, Third Edition, Student Edition, 1371 pages, 1983, with 1986 pocket part. (Text)

Corrections

KRANTZ' THE LAW OF CORRECTIONS AND PRISONERS' RIGHTS IN A NUTSHELL, Third Edition, 407 pages, 1988. Softcover. (Text)

Creditors' Rights

EPSTEIN'S DEBTOR-CREDITOR LAW IN A NUTSHELL, Fourth Edition, 401 pages, 1991. Softcover. (Text)

NICKLES AND EPSTEIN'S BLACK LETTER ON CREDITORS' RIGHTS AND BANKRUPTCY, 576 pages, 1989. (Review)

Criminal Law and Criminal Procedure— see also Corrections, Juvenile Justice

ISRAEL AND LaFAVE'S CRIMINAL PROCEDURE—CONSTITUTIONAL LIMITATIONS IN A NUTSHELL, Fourth Edition, 461 pages, 1988. Softcover. (Text)

LaFAVE AND ISRAEL'S HORNBOOK ON CRIMINAL PROCEDURE, Second Edition, Student Edition, approximately 1200 pages, December, 1991 Pub. (Text)

LaFAVE AND SCOTT'S HORNBOOK ON CRIMINAL LAW, Second Edition, 918 pages, 1986. (Text)

LOEWY'S CRIMINAL LAW IN A NUTSHELL, Second Edition, 321 pages, 1987. Softcover. (Text)

LOW'S BLACK LETTER ON CRIMINAL LAW, Revised First Edition, 443 pages, 1990. Softcover. (Review)

Domestic Relations

CLARK'S HORNBOOK ON DOMESTIC RELATIONS, Second Edition, Student Edition, 1050 pages, 1988. (Text)

KRAUSE'S BLACK LETTER ON FAMILY LAW, 314 pages, 1988. Softcover. (Review)

KRAUSE'S FAMILY LAW IN A NUTSHELL, Second Edition, 444 pages, 1986. Softcover. (Text)

MALLOY'S LAW AND ECONOMICS: A COMPARATIVE APPROACH TO THEORY AND PRACTICE, 166 pages, 1990. Softcover. (Text)

Education Law

ALEXANDER AND ALEXANDER'S THE LAW OF SCHOOLS, STUDENTS AND TEACHERS IN A NUTSHELL, 409 pages, 1984. Softcover. (Text)

Employment Discrimination—see also Gender Discrimination

PLAYER'S FEDERAL LAW OF EMPLOYMENT DISCRIMINATION IN A NUTSHELL, Second Edition, 402 pages, 1981. Softcover. (Text)

PLAYER'S HORNBOOK ON EMPLOYMENT DISCRIMINATION LAW, Student Edition,

Employment Discrimination—Cont'd
708 pages, 1988. (Text)

Energy and Natural Resources Law—
see also Oil and Gas

Environmental Law—see also Energy
and Natural Resources Law; Sea,
Law of
FINDLEY AND FARBER'S ENVIRONMENTAL
LAW IN A NUTSHELL, Second Edition,
367 pages, 1988. Softcover. (Text)

RODGERS' HORNBOOK ON ENVIRONMEN-
TAL LAW, 956 pages, 1977, with 1984
pocket part. (Text)

Equity—see Remedies

Estate Planning—see also Trusts and
Estates; Taxation—Estate and Gift
LYNN'S AN INTRODUCTION TO ESTATE
PLANNING IN A NUTSHELL, Third Edi-
tion, 370 pages, 1983. Softcover.
(Text)

Evidence
BROUN AND BLAKEY'S BLACK LETTER ON
EVIDENCE, 269 pages, 1984. Softcover.
(Review)

GRAHAM'S FEDERAL RULES OF EVIDENCE
IN A NUTSHELL, Second Edition, 473
pages, 1987. Softcover. (Text)

LILLY'S AN INTRODUCTION TO THE LAW
OF EVIDENCE, Second Edition, 585
pages, 1987. (Text)

MCCORMICK'S HORNBOOK ON EVIDENCE,
Fourth Edition, Student Edition, ap-
proximately 1200 pages, January 1992
Pub. (Text)

ROTHSTEIN'S EVIDENCE IN A NUTSHELL:
STATE AND FEDERAL RULES, Second Edi-
tion, 514 pages, 1981. Softcover.
(Text)

Federal Jurisdiction and Procedure
CURRIE'S FEDERAL JURISDICTION IN A
NUTSHELL, Third Edition, 242 pages,
1990. Softcover. (Text)

REDISH'S BLACK LETTER ON FEDERAL JU-
RISDICTION, Second Edition, 234 pages,
1991. Softcover. (Review)

WRIGHT'S HORNBOOK ON FEDERAL
COURTS, Fourth Edition, Student Edition, 870 pages, 1983. (Text)

First Amendment

Future Interests—see Trusts and Estates

Gender Discrimination—see also Employment Discrimination
THOMAS' SEX DISCRIMINATION IN A NUT-
SHELL, Second Edition, approximately
400 pages, 1991. Softcover. (Text)

Health Law—see Medicine, Law and

Human Rights—see International Law

Immigration Law
WEISSBRODT'S IMMIGRATION LAW AND
PROCEDURE IN A NUTSHELL, Second Edi-
tion, 438 pages, 1989, Softcover.
(Text)

Indian Law—see American Indian Law

Insurance Law
DOBBYN'S INSURANCE LAW IN A NUT-
SHELL, Second Edition, 316 pages,
1989. Softcover. (Text)

KEETON AND WIDISS' INSURANCE LAW,
Student Edition, 1359 pages, 1988.
(Text)

International Law—see also Sea, Law
of
BUERGENTHAL'S INTERNATIONAL HUMAN
RIGHTS IN A NUTSHELL, 283 pages,
1988. Softcover. (Text)

BUERGENTHAL AND MAIER'S PUBLIC IN-
TERNATIONAL LAW IN A NUTSHELL, Second Edition, 275 pages, 1990. Softcover. (Text)

FOLSOM, GORDON AND SPANOGLE'S IN-
TERNATIONAL BUSINESS TRANSACTIONS IN
A NUTSHELL, Third Edition, 509 pages,
1988. Softcover. (Text)

Interviewing and Counseling
SHAFFER AND ELKINS' LEGAL INTERVIEW-
ING AND COUNSELING IN A NUTSHELL,
Second Edition, 487 pages, 1987. Soft-

Interviewing and Counseling—Cont'd
cover. (Text)

Introduction to Law—see Legal
Method and Legal System

Introduction to Law Study
HEGLAND'S INTRODUCTION TO THE STUDY
AND PRACTICE OF LAW IN A NUTSHELL,
418 pages, 1983. Softcover. (Text)

KINYON'S INTRODUCTION TO LAW STUDY
AND LAW EXAMINATIONS IN A NUTSHELL,
389 pages, 1971. Softcover. (Text)

Judicial Process—see Legal Method
and Legal System

Juvenile Justice
FOX'S JUVENILE COURTS IN A NUTSHELL,
Third Edition, 291 pages, 1984. Soft-
cover. (Text)

Labor and Employment Law—see also
Employment Discrimination, Work-
ers' Compensation
LESLIE'S LABOR LAW IN A NUTSHELL,
Second Edition, 397 pages, 1986. Soft-
cover. (Text)

NOLAN'S LABOR ARBITRATION LAW AND
PRACTICE IN A NUTSHELL, 358 pages,
1979. Softcover. (Text)

Land Finance—Property Security—see
Real Estate Transactions

Land Use
HAGMAN AND JUERGENSMEYER'S HORN-
BOOK ON URBAN PLANNING AND LAND
DEVELOPMENT CONTROL LAW, Second
Edition, Student Edition, 680 pages,
1986. (Text)

WRIGHT AND WRIGHT'S LAND USE IN A
NUTSHELL, Second Edition, 356 pages,
1985. Softcover. (Text)

Legal Method and Legal System—see
also Legal Research, Legal Writing
KEMPIN'S HISTORICAL INTRODUCTION TO
ANGLO-AMERICAN LAW IN A NUTSHELL,
Third Edition, 323 pages, 1990. Soft-
cover. (Text)

REYNOLDS' JUDICIAL PROCESS IN A NUT-
SHELL, Second Edition, approximately
310 pages, 1991. Softcover. (Text)

Legal Research
COHEN'S LEGAL RESEARCH IN A NUT-
SHELL, Fourth Edition, 452 pages,
1985. Softcover. (Text)

COHEN, BERRING AND OLSON'S HOW TO
FIND THE LAW, Ninth Edition, 716
pages, 1989. (Text)

Legal Writing and Drafting
SQUIRES AND ROMBAUER'S LEGAL WRIT-
ING IN A NUTSHELL, 294 pages, 1982.
Softcover. (Text)

Legislation—see also Legal Writing and
Drafting
DAVIES' LEGISLATIVE LAW AND PROCESS
IN A NUTSHELL, Second Edition, 346
pages, 1986. Softcover. (Text)

Local Government
MCCARTHY'S LOCAL GOVERNMENT LAW
IN A NUTSHELL, Third Edition, 435
pages, 1990. Softcover. (Text)

REYNOLDS' HORNBOOK ON LOCAL GOV-
ERNMENT LAW, 860 pages, 1982, with
1990 pocket part. (Text)

Mass Communication Law
ZUCKMAN, GAYNES, CARTER AND DEE'S
MASS COMMUNICATIONS LAW IN A NUT-
SHELL, Third Edition, 538 pages, 1988.
Softcover. (Text)

Medicine, Law and
HALL AND ELLMAN'S HEALTH CARE LAW
AND ETHICS IN A NUTSHELL, 401 pages,
1990. Softcover (Text)

JARVIS, CLOSEN, HERMANN AND LEO-
NARD'S AIDS LAW IN A NUTSHELL, 349
pages, 1991. Softcover. (Text)

KING'S THE LAW OF MEDICAL MALPRAC-
TICE IN A NUTSHELL, Second Edition,
342 pages, 1986. Softcover. (Text)

Military Law
SHANOR AND TERRELL'S MILITARY LAW
IN A NUTSHELL, 378 pages, 1980. Soft-
cover. (Text)

Mortgages—see Real Estate Transactions

Natural Resources Law—see Energy and Natural Resources Law, Environmental Law

Office Practice—see also Computers and Law, Interviewing and Counseling, Negotiation

HEGLAND'S TRIAL AND PRACTICE SKILLS IN A NUTSHELL, 346 pages, 1978. Softcover (Text)

Oil and Gas—see also Energy and Natural Resources Law

HEMINGWAY'S HORNBOOK ON THE LAW OF OIL AND GAS, Third Edition, Student Edition, approximately 700 pages, Aug., 1991 Pub. (Text)

LOWE'S OIL AND GAS LAW IN A NUTSHELL, Second Edition, 465 pages, 1988. Softcover. (Text)

Partnership—see Agency—Partnership

Patent and Copyright Law

MILLER AND DAVIS' INTELLECTUAL PROPERTY—PATENTS, TRADEMARKS AND COPYRIGHT IN A NUTSHELL, Second Edition, 437 pages, 1990. Softcover. (Text)

Products Liability

PHILLIPS' PRODUCTS LIABILITY IN A NUTSHELL, Third Edition, 307 pages, 1988. Softcover. (Text)

Professional Responsibility

ARONSON AND WECKSTEIN'S PROFESSIONAL RESPONSIBILITY IN A NUTSHELL, Second Edition, approximately 500 pages, 1991. Softcover. (Text)

ROTUNDA'S BLACK LETTER ON PROFESSIONAL RESPONSIBILITY, Second Edition, 414 pages, 1988. Softcover. (Review)

WOLFRAM'S HORNBOOK ON MODERN LEGAL ETHICS, Student Edition, 1120 pages, 1986. (Text)

Property—see also Real Estate Transactions, Land Use, Trusts and Estates

BERNHARDT'S BLACK LETTER ON PROPERTY, Second Edition, approximately 375 pages, 1991. Softcover. (Review)

BERNHARDT'S REAL PROPERTY IN A NUTSHELL, Second Edition, 448 pages, 1981. Softcover. (Text)

BURKE'S PERSONAL PROPERTY IN A NUTSHELL, 322 pages, 1983. Softcover. (Text)

CUNNINGHAM, STOEBUCK AND WHITMAN'S HORNBOOK ON THE LAW OF PROPERTY, Student Edition, 916 pages, 1984, with 1987 pocket part. (Text)

HILL'S LANDLORD AND TENANT LAW IN A NUTSHELL, Second Edition, 311 pages, 1986. Softcover. (Text)

Real Estate Transactions

BRUCE'S REAL ESTATE FINANCE IN A NUTSHELL, Third Edition, approximately 270 pages, 1991. Softcover. (Text)

NELSON AND WHITMAN'S BLACK LETTER ON LAND TRANSACTIONS AND FINANCE, Second Edition, 466 pages, 1988. Softcover. (Review)

NELSON AND WHITMAN'S HORNBOOK ON REAL ESTATE FINANCE LAW, Second Edition, 941 pages, 1985 with 1989 pocket part. (Text)

Regulated Industries—see also Mass Communication Law, Banking Law

GELLHORN AND PIERCE'S REGULATED INDUSTRIES IN A NUTSHELL, Second Edition, 389 pages, 1987. Softcover. (Text)

Remedies

DOBBS' HORNBOOK ON REMEDIES, 1067 pages, 1973. (Text)

DOBBYN'S INJUNCTIONS IN A NUTSHELL, 264 pages, 1974. Softcover. (Text)

FRIEDMAN'S CONTRACT REMEDIES IN A NUTSHELL, 323 pages, 1981. Softcover. (Text)

Remedies—Cont'd

O'CONNELL'S REMEDIES IN A NUTSHELL, Second Edition, 320 pages, 1985. Softcover. (Text)

Sea, Law of

SOHN AND GUSTAFSON'S THE LAW OF THE SEA IN A NUTSHELL, 264 pages, 1984. Softcover. (Text)

Securities Regulation

HAZEN'S HORNBOOK ON THE LAW OF SECURITIES REGULATION, Second Edition, Student Edition, 1082 pages, 1990. (Text)

RATNER'S SECURITIES REGULATION IN A NUTSHELL, Third Edition, 316 pages, 1988. Softcover. (Text)

SECURITIES REGULATION, SELECTED STATUTES, RULES, AND FORMS. Softcover. 1331 pages, 1991.

Sports Law

SCHUBERT, SMITH AND TRENTADUE'S SPORTS LAW, 395 pages, 1986. (Text)

Tax Practice and Procedure

MORGAN'S TAX PROCEDURE AND TAX FRAUD IN A NUTSHELL, 400 pages, 1990. Softcover. (Text)

Taxation—Corporate

SCHWARZ AND LATHROPE'S BLACK LETTER ON CORPORATE AND PARTNERSHIP TAXATION, Approximately 500 pages, September, 1991 Pub. Softcover. (Review)

WEIDENBRUCH AND BURKE'S FEDERAL INCOME TAXATION OF CORPORATIONS AND STOCKHOLDERS IN A NUTSHELL, Third Edition, 309 pages, 1989. Softcover. (Text)

Taxation—Estate & Gift—see also Estate Planning, Trusts and Estates

MCNULTY'S FEDERAL ESTATE AND GIFT TAXATION IN A NUTSHELL, Fourth Edition, 496 pages, 1989. Softcover. (Text)

Taxation—Individual

HUDSON AND LIND'S BLACK LETTER ON

FEDERAL INCOME TAXATION, Third Edition, 406 pages, 1990. Softcover. (Review)

MCNULTY'S FEDERAL INCOME TAXATION OF INDIVIDUALS IN A NUTSHELL, Fourth Edition, 503 pages, 1988. Softcover. (Text)

POSIN'S HORNBOOK ON FEDERAL INCOME TAXATION, Student Edition, 491 pages, 1983, with 1989 pocket part. (Text)

ROSE AND CHOMMIE'S HORNBOOK ON FEDERAL INCOME TAXATION, Third Edition, 923 pages, 1988, with 1989 pocket part. (Text)

Taxation—International

DOERNBERG'S INTERNATIONAL TAXATION IN A NUTSHELL, 325 pages, 1989. Softcover. (Text)

BISHOP AND BROOKS' FEDERAL PARTNERSHIP TAXATION: A GUIDE TO THE LEADING CASES, STATUTES, AND REGULATIONS, 545 pages, 1990. Softcover. (Text)

SCHWARZ AND LATHROPE'S BLACK LETTER ON CORPORATE AND PARTNERSHIP TAXATION, Approximately 500 pages, September, 1991 Pub. Softcover. (Review)

Taxation—State & Local

GELFAND AND SALSICH'S STATE AND LOCAL TAXATION AND FINANCE IN A NUTSHELL, 309 pages, 1986. Softcover. (Text)

Torts—see also Products Liability

KIONKA'S BLACK LETTER ON TORTS, 339 pages, 1988. Softcover. (Review)

KIONKA'S TORTS IN A NUTSHELL: INJURIES TO PERSONS AND PROPERTY, 434 pages, 1977. Softcover. (Text)

MALONE'S TORTS IN A NUTSHELL: INJURIES TO FAMILY, SOCIAL AND TRADE RELATIONS, 358 pages, 1979. Softcover. (Text)

PROSSER AND KEETON'S HORNBOOK ON TORTS, Fifth Edition, Student Edition, 1286 pages, 1984 with 1988 pocket part. (Text)

Trade Regulation—see also Antitrust, Regulated Industries

McManis' Unfair Trade Practices in a Nutshell, Second Edition, 464 pages, 1988. Softcover. (Text)

Schechter's Black Letter on Unfair Trade Practices, 272 pages, 1986. Softcover. (Review)

Trial and Appellate Advocacy—see also Civil Procedure

Bergman's Trial Advocacy in a Nutshell, Second Edition, 354 pages, 1989. Softcover. (Text)

Goldberg's The First Trial (Where Do I Sit? What Do I Say?) in a Nutshell, 396 pages, 1982. Softcover. (Text)

Hegland's Trial and Practice Skills in a Nutshell, 346 pages, 1978. Softcover. (Text)

Hornstein's Appellate Advocacy in a Nutshell, 325 pages, 1984. Softcover. (Text)

Jeans' Handbook on Trial Advocacy, Student Edition, 473 pages, 1975. Softcover. (Text)

Trusts and Estates

Atkinson's Hornbook on Wills, Second Edition, 975 pages, 1953. (Text)

Averill's Uniform Probate Code in a Nutshell, Second Edition, 454 pages, 1987. Softcover. (Text)

Bogert's Hornbook on Trusts, Sixth Edition, Student Edition, 794 pages, 1987. (Text)

McGovern, Kurtz and Rein's Hornbook on Wills, Trusts and Estates–Including Taxation and Future Interests, 996 pages, 1988. (Text)

Mennell's Wills and Trusts in a Nutshell, 392 pages, 1979. Softcover. (Text)

Simes' Hornbook on Future Interests, Second Edition, 355 pages, 1966. (Text)

Turano and Radigan's Hornbook on New York Estate Administration, 676 pages, 1986. (Text)

Waggoner's Future Interests in a Nutshell, 361 pages, 1981. Softcover. (Text)

Water Law—see also Environmental Law

Getches' Water Law in a Nutshell, Second Edition, 459 pages, 1990. Softcover. (Text)

Wills—see Trusts and Estates

Workers' Compensation

Hood, Hardy and Lewis' Workers' Compensation and Employee Protection Laws in a Nutshell, Second Edition, 361 pages, 1990. Softcover. (Text)

TRUSTS

Sixth Edition

By

George T. Bogert

**HORNBOOK SERIES
STUDENT EDITION**

WEST PUBLISHING CO.

ST. PAUL, MINN., 1987

COPYRIGHT © 1987 By WEST PUBLISHING CO.
　　　　　　　　　　　50 West Kellogg Boulevard
　　　　　　　　　　　P.O. Box 64526
　　　　　　　　　　　St. Paul, Minnesota 55164–0526

All rights reserved ·
Printed in the United States of America

Library of Congress Cataloging-in-Publication Data

Bogert, George Taylor.
　Hornbook on the law of trusts.

　(Hornbook series-Student edition)
　Rev. ed. of: Handbook of the law of trusts / by George Gleason Bogert, George Taylor Bogert. 5th ed. 1973.
　Includes index.
　1. Trusts and trustees—United States.　I. Bogert, George Gleason, 1884–1977. Handbook of the law of trusts.　II. Title.　III. Series.

KF730.B64　1987　　346.7305'9　　87–8302
　　　　　　　　　　347.30659

ISBN 0–314–35139–6

Bogert, Trusts, 6th Ed. HBSE
1st Reprint—1991

This Edition is dedicated to the memory of
George Gleason Bogert
(1884–1977)
Law Teacher and Author of Excellence

*

Preface

The 5th Edition of this Hornbook was published in 1973. Both the text and footnotes require updating by reason of new court decisions and the enactment of new or revised statutes since that date.

As in the past, the primary objective of this 6th Edition is to provide a concise and up-to-date explanation of the laws and rules governing the creation, enforcement, administration and termination of trusts, including voluntary trusts, charitable trusts and trusts created by operation of law, as well as those applicable to similar fiduciary relationships.

The text sections are keyed to corresponding sections in the author's treatise on Trusts and Trustees (rev. 2d edit.), as well as to the Restatements of Trusts, Second, and Property, Second. In addition, numerous references are made to current state statutes relevant to particular subject areas, and to widely adopted state statutes, such as the Uniform Probate Code and other uniform laws, and to federal statutes such as ERISA, that affect trusts.

Specifically, treatment of the following important subjects has been updated and expanded:

The Rule against Perpetuities and similar restrictive property rules have been modified in a number of states by statute (§§ 50–53).

Certain public policy exceptions to the validity of spendthrift trust provisions have been developed, both by statute and by court decision (§ 40).

Changing concepts of trust investments have been enacted in many states (§§ 101–108). In one form or another the prudent investor rule has been adopted in most states. Subject to the prudent investor rule, most trust investment statutes now expressly authorize trust investments in common stocks, real estate interests, and mutual funds.

The care and skill required of a trustee, particularly in making trust investments, appear in some states to extend to other matters of trust administration or management, as illustrated by the provisions of the Uniform Probate Code and recent Minnesota and California statutes. See §§ 93, 106 and 109 (payments to beneficiaries).

The materials relating to the various remedies available to a beneficiary, including the applicable measure of damages recoverable from the trustee for a breach of trust, have been expanded.

See §§ 153–160. Often the beneficiary has a choice of remedies for breach of trust. The remedies discussed include those against the trustee personally (§§ 154–160), remedies including the tracing and recovery of trust property (§§ 161–165), and remedies against a third party participating in a breach of trust (§§ 166–167). Where more than one remedy for a breach of trust is available, the requirement that the beneficiary elect between inconsistent remedies is discussed in §§ 163 and 168.

Cases and statutes dealing with the alteration or modification of trusts have been added in §§ 145–150. The circumstances under which a trust may be modified by the court under deviation principles are examined in § 110 (payments to beneficiaries), and in § 146 (administrative provisions), but deviation principles also cut across other powers and duties in trust administration, such as sales, mortgages and leases (§§ 133–139).

In many states the statutes or court rules governing a trustee's court accountings (§ 142) and the method for determining the amount of his compensation (§ 144) have been revised. As discussed in § 142, nonjudicial and voluntary accounts are authorized by statute in some states.

Important statutory developments in the administration and enforcement of charitable trusts are discussed, including abandonment of the doctrine of charitable immunity from tort liability in many states (§ 129), requirements as to the filing of accounts and reports (§ 142), and provisions regarding enforcement by the state attorney general (§ 156).

Discussion of the trustee's duty of undivided loyalty (§§ 86, 95) has been expanded. The measure of damages for disloyalty is discussed in § 157, and some statutory tendencies towards relaxation of strict loyalty rules are discussed in §§ 95 and 100.

The Index prepared by the author has been revised and expanded to reflect the numerous changes and additions in this Edition.

GEORGE TAYLOR BOGERT

March 10, 1987

WESTLAW Introduction

Bogert's *Trusts, Sixth Edition,* offers a detailed and comprehensive treatment of basic rules, principles, and issues in the law of trusts and similar fiduciary relationships. However, readers occasionally need to find additional authority. In an effort to assist with comprehensive research of the law of trusts and similar fiduciary relationships, preformulated WESTLAW references are included after most sections of the text in this edition. The WESTLAW references are designed for use with the WESTLAW computer-assisted legal research service. By joining this publication with the extensive WESTLAW databases in this way, the reader is able to move straight from the hornbook into WESTLAW with great speed and convenience.

Some readers may desire to use only the information supplied within the printed pages of this hornbook. Others, however, will encounter trust issues that require further information. Accordingly, those who opt for additional material can rapidly and easily gain access to WESTLAW, an electronic law library that possesses extraordinary currency and magnitude.

The preformulated WESTLAW references in this text provide illustrative searches for readers who wish to do additional research on WESTLAW. The WESTLAW references are approximately as general as the material in the text to which they correspond. Readers should be cautioned against placing undue emphasis upon these references as final solutions to all possible issues treated in the text. In most instances, it is necessary to make refinements to the search references, such as the addition of other search terms or the substitution of different proximity connectors, to adequately fit the particular needs of an individual reader's research problem. The freedom, and also the responsibility, remains with the reader to "fine tune" the WESTLAW references in accordance with his or her own research requirements. The primary usefulness of the preformulated references is in providing a basic framework upon which further query construction can be built. The Appendix gives concise, step-by-step instruction on how to coordinate WESTLAW research with this book.

THE PUBLISHER

*

Summary of Contents

*

Table of Contents

Chapter 19. Remedies of Beneficiaries—Tracing the Trust Res—The Bona Fide Purchaser Rule

Chapter 20. Remedies of Beneficiaries— Participation in a Breach— Barring of Remedies

TRUSTS
Sixth Edition

*

Chapter 1

INTRODUCTION AND HISTORY

Table of Sections

DEFINITION OF FUNDAMENTAL TERMS

§ 1. A trust is a fiduciary relationship in which one person is the holder of the title to property subject to an equitable obligation to keep or use the property for the benefit of another.[1]

The settlor of a trust is the person who intentionally causes the trust to come into existence.

The trustee is the person who holds title for the benefit of another.

The trust property is the property interest which the trustee holds subject to the rights of another.

The beneficiary is the person for whose benefit the trust property is to be held or used by the trustee.

§ 1

1. "A trust is an obligation imposed, either expressly or by implication of law, whereby the obligor is bound to deal with property over which he has control for the benefit of certain persons, of whom he may himself be one, and any one of whom may enforce the obligation." Hart, What is a Trust? 15 Law Quart.Rev. 301.

"A trust may be defined as a property right held by one party for the use of another." Keplinger v. Keplinger, 185 Ind. 81, 113 N.E. 292, 293.

See Restatement, Trusts, Second, § 2.

Some definitions of the trust seem concerned rather with the duty or obligation of the trustee, or the right of the beneficiary, than with the trust. The trust in its modern sense is conceived to be the relationship or status in which are concerned certain property and persons, and incidental to which are certain rights and duties. The whole bundle of property, persons, rights, and duties makes up the trust. It is often said that a trustee holds the trust property "subject to a trust," but it would seem to be more accurate to state that he holds it subject to the duties of a trustee.

1

The trust instrument is the document by which property interests are vested in the trustee and beneficiary and the rights and duties of the parties (called the trust terms) are set forth.

The trusts treated herein should not be confused with the business monopolies or combinations called "trusts," or with the offices which are loosely called "positions of trust." The monopolistic trusts were originally so called because the stock of the combining corporations was transferred to technical trustees to accomplish a centralization of control.[2] In common parlance, to be in a position of "trust" or to be a "trustee" often means merely to occupy a station where elements of confidence and responsibility exist.[3] The one trusted in this sense may be in a business relation, or be an agent, a servant, a partner, or a guardian. He is not necessarily in the technical trust relation.

The managers of some corporations are called "trustees" or the "board of trustees". They are not within the meaning of the trusteeships herein treated, although they hold powers subject to an obligation to use them for the benefit of stockholders.

It is not intended that the definitions of the essential terms given at this point shall be final or exhaustive. The detailed nature and incidents of the trust will be developed throughout this book, and the meaning of the elementary terms more fully explained.[4]

A Fiduciary Relation

The relation between trustee and beneficiary is particularly intimate. The beneficiary is obliged to place great confidence in the trustee. The trustee has a high degree of control over the affairs of the beneficiary. The relation is not an ordinary business one. The court of equity calls it "fiduciary", and places on the trustee the duty to act with strict honesty and candor and solely in the interest of the beneficiary.[5] There are many other fiduciary relations, for example, guardianship and executorship.

The Trust Property

It should first be noticed that a specific thing or things and specific property interests therein are always involved in the trust. In some relations men only, or men and property, may be involved, for example, in agency, where A may be the agent of B for the performance of personal services, which have no connection with any property, or no connection with any particular property. But the trust presupposes identified things, tangible or intangible, and ascertained or ascertainable property interests therein, to be held by the trustee. The trust property is sometimes called the trust res, the corpus, or the trust principal or subject-matter of the trust.

2. Jenks, The Trust Problem, 111.

3. See Thompson v. Thompson, 178 Iowa 1289, 160 N.W. 922.

4. For similar definitions, see Restatement, Trusts, Second, § 3.

5. See §§ 86, 95, post.

It is sometimes said that the legal title to the trust property is always in the trustee. His title may be a legal or an equitable one, dependent on the nature of the title which the settlor has seen fit to give him. Thus if the settlor has a fee simple estate in certain lands, and conveys his interest to A to hold in trust for B, A, the trustee, will be seised of the legal estate; yet if the settlor has contracted in writing to buy land for which he has paid the purchase price, but a deed of which he has not yet received, and the settlor transfers his interest in the land to A in trust for B, A, the trustee, will hold merely the equitable title of the contract vendee of the land. It is because of this possibility of legal or equitable ownership that the definition given above merely states that the trustee is a title holder, without regard to the court in which his title will be recognized. In the great majority of trusts the trustee has the legal title to the trust property.

The Trust Parties

It is customary to think of three persons or classes of persons as connected with every trust, namely, the settlor, the trustee or trustees, and the beneficiary or beneficiaries. But if the settlor declares himself a trustee, settlor and trustee are one and the same person, and a trust may exist with only two parties. Because a man cannot be under an obligation to himself, the same individual cannot be settlor, trustee, and beneficiary, and the persons involved in the trust can never be less than two. But a sole trustee may be one of a number of beneficiaries, and one of several joint trustees may be the sole beneficiary.[6]

In some trusts there is no settlor. These are the implied trusts created by law for the purpose of accomplishing justice and are called "constructive" trusts.[7] In these constructive trusts no individual intentionally brings a trust into being. The court gives life to the trust. The acts of one or more persons have caused the court to decree the trust's existence. Such persons are not settlors. Their acts merely afford the reasons which the courts give for declaring the existence of the trust. Hence, in the definition of the word "settlor" given above the word "intentionally" is used, so that the doers of acts which unintentionally result in the declaration of a trust by a court may not be included within the class of settlors. The settlor is also sometimes called the creator of the trust, the donor, or the trustor. Where the trust is created by will the creator is the trustor.

The beneficiary of a trust is the person for whose benefit the trust is created and who is equitably entitled to its advantages. Under older terminology he was called the cestui que trust or the cestui,[8] and this

---

6. See § 35, post.

7. See § 7, post.

8. Pronounced by some as if spelled "cetty kuh trust" and by others as if spelled "cestwe kuh trust." Anderson, Dict. of Law, 162. The words are Norman French. The plural is properly "cestuis

que trust," although frequently spelled "cestui que trustent," "cestui que trusts," or "cestuis que trustent" by the courts. See City of Marquette v. Wilkinson, 119 Mich. 413, 78 N.W. 474, 43 L.R.A. 840. For a discussion of the origin, meaning, and proper form of "cestui que use" and

language is still used by some courts, but corporate fiduciaries and other professional trust men employ the word beneficiary almost exclusively.

The Trust Instrument and Terms

Although in some cases trusts may be, and are, created orally, they are generally based on a written document which describes the trust property, conveys interests in it, names the trustee, names or describes the beneficiaries and fixes their interests. This document generally is called the "trust instrument", and the details as to powers, rights and duties of the trust parties are called the "trust terms".

The Trust Rights and Duties

The trustee holds the property "for the benefit of" the beneficiary. It is unnecessary at this point to consider how the beneficiary may obtain that benefit. The methods vary greatly, according to the terms of the particular trust. In one case the trustee may have no duty other than to hold the property, and the beneficiary may take the benefits directly. In another instance the trustee may be charged with detailed management of the trust assets and the beneficiary may receive the benefits indirectly.

The duties of the trustee may be enforced by the beneficiary. This quality distinguishes the trust in some jurisdictions from certain contracts. Thus if A promises B, for a consideration running from B to A, that he (A) will deliver over certain property to C, C in some jurisdictions might be unable to enforce the performance of A's promise because C is a stranger to the contract.[9] But if A declares himself a trustee of property for C, C everywhere may enforce the trust against A, regardless of privity or of knowledge or consent by C. This quality of enforceability by the beneficiary, notwithstanding a lack of privity, is a characteristic of the trust.

The trustee's obligation is said to be "equitable." Originally it was recognized only by the English court of chancery, which alone administered the rules and applied the principles of equity. Many writers defining the trust make enforceability in a court of chancery or equity a part of their definition. But in the present state of the law it is deemed preferable to define the trustee's obligation as equitable, and to omit any reference to the court in which this obligation may be enforced. In most American states the separate court of chancery has been abolished and both legal and equitable obligations are enforced by the same court, but in a few states the separate court of equity is maintained.[10]

"cestui que trust" see a note by Charles Sweet, Esq., in 26 Law Quart.Rev. 196, in which the views of Prof. Maitland are set forth. The author says: " 'Cestui que use,' therefore means 'he for whose benefit,' and 'cestui que trust' means 'he upon trust for whom,' certain property is held."

9. Williston on Contracts (Jaeger, 3d Edit. 1960) ch. 14; Corbin on Contracts (1963) ch. 41.

10. For a discussion of the effect of constitutional changes on the separate existence of the court of equity, see 1 Pomeroy's Eq.Juris. §§ 40–42. According to

The trustee's obligation is based on equitable principles, whether enforced by a court having both legal and equitable jurisdiction, or by a court having solely equitable functions. In rare cases a court of law enforces the obligation of the trustee to the beneficiary.[11] It seems wiser to omit all reference to the judicial forum of enforcement.

Thus there are three requirements to create a valid private trust. These are (1) an expression of intent that property be held, at least in part, for the benefit of one other than the settlor;[12] (2) at least one beneficiary for whom the property is to be administered by the trustee;[13] and (3) an interest in property which is in existence or is ascertainable and is to be held for the benefit of the beneficiary.[14] The requirement that there be a trustee to administer the trust does not mean that a trust will not come into existence where no trustee is named. A trust does not fail at its inception or thereafter for lack of a trustee since the court will appoint a trustee to administer the trust property for the benefit of the beneficiary.[15]

 WESTLAW REFERENCES

di trust
di(trust /4 defin!)
di settlor
di trustee

A Fiduciary Relation
fiduciary

The Trust Property
di trust property

The Trust Parties
di beneficiary

The Trust Instrument
di trust instrument

The Trust Rights and Duties
di(trustee /s beneficiary /s fiduciary /2 duty relation!)
390k173
trustee /s "legal title" /s trust /2 property res principal corpus
di cestui que trust
marquette +3 wilkinson

ORIGIN OF USES AND TRUSTS

§ 2.   Trusts, in their early development in England, were divided into two classes, namely, special or active trusts, and general, simple,

Clark, Code Pleading (2d ed., 1947), separate courts of chancery were then maintained in New Jersey, Delaware, Arkansas, Mississippi, Tennessee, and Vermont.

11. See § 157, post.

12. See ch. 2, post.

13. See ch. 4, post.

14. See ch. 3, post.

15. See § 29, post.

or passive trusts. The latter were ordinarily called uses. Prior to 1535, uses constituted the more important class of trusts.

Uses were introduced into England shortly after the Norman Conquest (1066 A.D.), although not enforced by the courts until the fifteenth century.

They were patterned after the German treuhand or salman.

They were not based on the fidei-commissum of the Roman law, and have not existed in civil law countries until recently.

The principal objects of their introduction were—

(a) To avoid the burdens of holding the legal title to land, such as the rights of the lord under feudal tenure, the rights of creditors, and the rights of dower and curtesy;

(b) To enable religious houses to obtain the profits of land, notwithstanding the mortmain acts which prohibited their owning land;

(c) To secure greater freedom in conveying land inter vivos (during lifetime);

(d) To obtain power to dispose of real property by will.

The use was a general or passive trust in which the trustee had no active duties, but was merely a receptacle of the legal title for the cestui que use (beneficiary), with a duty to permit the beneficiary to enjoy the property and to convey it as directed by the beneficiary.

The words "use" and "trust" are employed as synonyms frequently by writers and judges. However, there is a distinction in their meanings. Prior to the Statute of Uses (1535) there existed in England a relationship known as a trust. Trusts were of two classes, active or special, and passive, simple, or general. In cases where a trustee held property for some temporary purpose and with active duties to perform, the trust was called active or special. Thus, if A conveyed land to B for ten years, to take the profits of the land and apply them to the use of C, B was an active or special trustee. These trusts were comparatively rare prior to the Statute of Uses. But if the legal title was transferred to one as a holder for the benefit of another, but with no positive duties of care or management, the trust was called general, simple, or passive, or a use. Thus, an enfeoffment of A and his heirs to the use of B and his heirs would create a use or general trust.[1] Uses were far more common than special trusts prior to the Statutes of Uses. Indeed, by the time of Henry V (1413–1422) they were the rule rather than the exception in landholding.[2]

Uses and trusts were introduced into England shortly after the Norman Conquest.[3] The prevalent view is that they were modeled

---

§ 2

1. Bacon, Uses, 8, 9; Sanders, Uses and Trusts, 3–7.

2. Digby, History of Law of Real Property, 320.

3. Ames, Origin of Uses and Trusts, 2 Select Essays in Anglo-American Legal History, 737, 741; Maitland, The Origin of Uses, 8 Harv.Law Rev. 127, 129; Development of Trusts, Hurst, 136 L.T. 76.

after the German treuhand or salman, rather than after the Roman fidei-commissum.[4] Under the Roman law it was not possible to give property by will to certain persons, for instance, persons not Roman citizens.[5] It became customary among the Romans to devise property to one capable of taking it, with a request that he deliver it to a named beneficiary who was incompetent to take directly. This was the creation of a fidei-commissum. The obligation of the devisee to the named beneficiary in this relationship was not at first enforceable in the courts, but later became so. This confidence was analogous in many ways to the English trust or use, but differed in that it arose by will only.

Trusts were not known to the Roman or civil law,[6] although substitutes for them were evolved,[7] and the trust has been adopted by statute in recent years in some countries whose law is founded on the civil law.[8]

"The feoffee to uses of the early English law corresponds point by point to the salman of the early German law, as described by Beseler fifty years ago. The salman, like the feoffee, was a person to whom land was transferred in order that he might make a conveyance according to his grantor's directions." [9]

Reasons for the Invention of Uses and Trusts

It was said by an English lawyer many years ago that the parents of the trust were fraud and fear and that the court of conscience was its nurse.[10] Certain it is that the reasons for the introduction of uses and trusts were not in all cases honorable. The common law of England attached many burdens to the holding of the legal title to land. As the feudal system prevailed when uses arose, the lord was entitled to a "relief," or money payment, when the land descended to an heir of full age; to the rights of "wardship" and "marriage" when the heir was a minor; and to "aids" upon the marriage of a daughter of the lord, the

---

4. Ames, Origin of Uses and Trusts, 2 Select Essays in Anglo-American Legal History, 739, 740; Maitland, The Origin of Uses, 8 Harv.Law Rev. 127, 136. The earlier view was that the use was an evolution of the fidei-commissum. Story, Eq.Juris. §§ 966, 967; Pomeroy, Eq.Juris. §§ 976–978.

5. Digby, History of Law of Real Property, 317.

6. Thus in Louisiana, whose legal system is founded on the civil law, trusts were not recognized (Marks v. Loewenberg, 143 La. 196, 78 So. 444) until 1920 when they were validated to a limited extent. The Louisiana Trust Code of 1964 further extends their validity. See Bogert, Trusts and Trustees (rev. 2d edit.), §§ 2, 7.

7. Lepaulle, Civil Law Substitutes for Trusts, 36 Yale L.J. 1126.

8. For example, trusts have been validated by legislation in Puerto Rico, Cuba, and Mexico. See Bogert, Trusts and Trustees (rev. 2d edit.), §§ 9 (recognition of the trust in foreign countries) and 10 (international estate planning—trust and tax considerations).

Lepaulle, Trusts in the Civil Law, 73 L.T. 226; Patton, Trust Systems in the Western Hemisphere, 19 Tul.L.R. 398; Alfaro, Civil Law Reception of Trusts 2 Comp.L.Ser. 1; Goldschmidt, 3 Inter-Am. L.R. 29.

9. Holmes, Early English Equity, 2 Select Essays in Anglo-American Legal History, 705, 707.

10. Attorney General v. Sands, Hard., 488, 491.

knighting of his eldest son, or when the lord was held to ransom. These burdens, and others of a similar nature, fell upon the holder of the legal title. By enfeoffing another of the legal title and reserving only the use, the tenant escaped such exactions. "The legal ownership, however, represented by the feoffee to uses, was subject to the incidents of tenure, which could be enforced against the land, but by vesting the seisin in two or more feoffees jointly, whose number was renewed from time to time, and the survivor of whom took the whole legal estate, the burdens incident to the descent of land were generally avoided." [11]

So, too, upon the commission of certain crimes the holders of the legal title suffered a forfeiture, which could be avoided by vesting the legal estate in another and retaining only the use. And the common law gave no remedy to a creditor against the interest of the beneficiary of a use. Some dishonest persons escaped payment of their debts by a transfer of land to a feoffee to uses. The incidents of dower and curtesy attached only to the legal estate. A man desiring to prevent the attaching of a dower interest in a prospective wife, could accomplish the result by a conveyance to a feoffee to uses.

Not only was the equitable estate of cestui que use free from dangers and duties, but it could be held by a large and influential class which could not hold the legal estate in lands, for example, religious corporations. The mortmain acts forbade the alienation of land to religious corporations, and thus prevented the religious orders from acquiring directly the real property they needed, and which charitably minded persons often desired to give them. Furthermore, certain of the orders had taken the vows of poverty, and could not consistently hold property in their own names. However, by a conveyance of land to an individual, to be held for the use of the religious order, the monks and friars could have the benefit of the land, though not the seisin. In the opinion of some scholars, the religious bodies were the first to employ the use extensively.[12]

The equitable estate or use was also more easily transferred than the legal estate. The latter could be conveyed by feoffment with livery of seisin, fine, or recovery only. Publicity was essential. The use, on the other hand, could be created and transferred secretly, and with little or no ceremony. This capacity for secret transfer favored fraud on later purchasers of the land and encouraged the employment of the use by the unscrupulous. Likewise the use was capable of being disposed of by will. The legal estate was not so disposable at that period. To be able to control land after death was no doubt a great incentive to the creation of uses.

 WESTLAW REFERENCES

di trust

11. Tiffany, Real Property, 200.

12. Maitland, The Origin of Uses, 8 Harv.Law Rev. 127, 130; Jenks, Short History of English Law, 96.

di use

trust use /s "norman conquest"

Reasons for the Invention of Uses and Trusts
"origin of uses"

USES AND TRUSTS BEFORE THE STATUTE OF USES

§ 3. Originally uses and trusts were not enforceable in any court but were purely honorary. The performance of his duties was voluntary on the part of the feoffee to uses and could not be enforced.

The courts of law did not recognize the claims of the cestui que trust, because no writ existed for that purpose.

Chancery did not originally enforce uses and trusts but began to do so in the early part of the fifteenth century.

Early English law was extremely rigid. Forms and technicalities were strictly observed. The courts of common law gave no remedy unless a writ fitted exactly to the case could be found. The introduction of new remedies through the law courts was a matter of great difficulty.[1] The interests of the beneficiary of a use were not protected by the common law courts, because no writ existed to fit the case. The ecclesiastical courts had no jurisdiction to enforce them. Therefore, for many years uses and trusts existed as honorary obligations but had no legal standing. If the trustee saw fit to deny that he held the property as trustee, and to appropriate it to his own use, he might do so with impunity.[2]

Simple fiduciary relations with respect to money and chattels were early enforced by the common law courts, but these were the so-called "common law trusts," and not uses or equitable trusts. If money was delivered to A, to be paid to B, the common law action of account lay.[3] If a chattel was delivered to another for the use of a third, detinue could be brought by the beneficiary.[4]

But the development of the court of chancery wrought a change. About the time that uses and trusts were arising, it became the custom to petition the king or his council for relief in cases where the law courts gave no remedy. If no writ was available, or if the opponent was powerful enough to prevent justice, the aggrieved suitor besought the king or his council for a special and extra-legal dispensation. Of this

§ 3

1. Spence, History of the Court of Chancery, 2 Select Essays in Anglo-American Legal History, 219.

2. Ames, Lectures on Legal History, 236, 237.

3. Anonymous, Year Book, 6 Henry IV, folio 7, plac. 33; Ames' Cases on Trusts, 2d Ed., p. 1. For a more recent case of this sort see Ripling v. Superior Court In and For Los Angeles County, 112 Cal.App.2d 399, 247 P.2d 117 (1952).

4. Ames, Origin of Uses and Trusts, 2 Select Essays in Anglo-American Legal History, 743.

council the chancellor was a member, and about the time of the reign of Edward I (1272–1307) it became usual to refer these petitions to the chancellor for consideration. The chancellor became the custodian of the king's conscience, and his court the court of conscience. Equity and fairness were supposed to rule there, rather than technicality.

It was natural that beneficiaries who had been injured, due to a failure of their trustees to hold the property for their use, should apply to the chancellor for relief. At some time early in the fifteenth century the justice of these petitions began to be recognized by the chancellor, and uses and trusts were enforced.[5] The chancellors of those days were churchmen, and their consciences were naturally shocked by the unfairness of allowing a trustee to violate an obligation which he had admittedly undertaken. The process by which the chancellor acted was known as a subpoena. It commanded the defendant to do or refrain from doing a certain act. The relief was personal and specific, not merely money damages. Hence it was often said that cestui que trust had a remedy only by subpoena.

 WESTLAW REFERENCES

"king's conscience" /s trust

THE STATUTE OF USES

§ 4. The Statute of Uses provided that wherever any person should thereafter be seised of land to the use of another, the latter should be deemed the legal owner of such lands, and the taker subject to a use should have no interest in the lands.

The object of this statute was to abolish uses by correcting the equitable interest of the cestui que use into a legal interest, and thus—

(a) Prevent the loss of feudal rights by landlords;

(b) Obviate fraud on creditors, alienees, dowresses, and tenants by the curtesy;

(c) Probably to injure the religious orders which were the beneficiaries of uses.

By the beginning of the sixteenth century uses and trusts had come to involve such serious injustices and frauds that parliament was persuaded to act against them. It has been shown that the principal objects of their introduction were to relieve vassals of the burdens of feudal landholding, to enable religious orders to have the benefit of land, to avoid marital estates, and to effect greater freedom in the conveyance of real property. From time to time prior to the Statute of Uses various acts in aid of creditors, purchasers, and landowners

---

5. Ames, Origin of Uses and Trusts, 2 Select Essays in Anglo-American Legal History, 741, 742.

defrauded by uses, and against the holding of lands to the use of religious houses, were enacted by parliament,[1] but they were ineffective. The preamble to the Statute catalogues the evils thought to have been caused by the use in 1535.[2]

Apart from the reasons named in the Statute itself, there was, according to some authorities,[3] the desire on the part of Henry VIII to destroy the monasteries and confiscate their property, which he thought could best be accomplished by abolishing the method by which they held land, namely, the use.

The famous Statute of Uses (27 Henry VIII, c. 10) was enacted in 1535.[4] Its object was to abolish uses, and this it proposed to do by wiping out the estate of the feoffee to uses, and giving to the beneficiary of the use the entire legal estate. The statute "executed the use," in the phrase of the day. Instead of leaving it to the feoffee to uses to transfer the legal title to the cestui que use when the latter required it, the law transferred such interest immediately on the creation of the use.[5] By this "transmutation of the use into possession" it was thought

§ 4

1. Digby, History of the Law of Real Property, 318, 319; Cruise, Uses, 34–37.

2. "Where by the common laws of this realm, land, tenements, and hereditaments be not devisable by testament, nor ought to be transferred from one to another, but by solemn livery and seisin, matter of record, writing sufficient made bona fide, without covin or fraud, yet nevertheless divers and sundry imaginations, subtle inventions, and practices have been used, whereby the hereditaments of this realm have been conveyed from one to another by fraudulent feoffments, fines, recoveries, and other assurances craftily made to secret uses, intents, and trusts, and also by wills and testaments sometimes made by nude parolx and words, sometimes by signs and tokens, and sometimes by writing, and for the most part made by such persons as be visited with sickness, in their extreme agonies and pains, or at such time as they have had scantly any good memory or remembrance; at which times they, being provoked by greedy and covetous persons lying in wait about them, do many times dispose indiscreetly and unadvisedly their lands and inheritances; by reason whereof, and by occasion of which fraudulent feoffments, fines, recoveries, and other like assurances to uses, confidences, and trusts, divers and many heirs have been unjustly at sundry times disinherited, and lords have lost their wards, marriages, reliefs, harriots, escheats, aids *pur fair fitz chivalier* and *pur file marier*, and scantly any person can be certainly assured of any lands by them purchased, nor know surely against whom they shall use their actions or execution for their rights, titles and duties; also men married have lost their tenancies by the curtesy, women their dowers; manifest perjuries by trial of such secret wills and uses have been committed; the king's highness hath lost the profits and advantages of the lands of persons attainted, and of the lands craftily put in feoffment to the use of aliens born, and also the profits of waste for a year and a day of felons attainted, and the lords their escheats thereof. . . ." Preamble to St. 27 Henry VIII, c. 10, as quoted in Digby, History of the Law of Real Property, 347, 348. The statute was repealed by property reform legislation enacted in 1925. 12 & 13 Geo. V, c. 16, sec. 1(7).

3. Jenks, Short Hist. of English Law, 99.

4. For a discussion of the events leading up to its passage, see Holdsworth, Causes Which Shaped the Statute of Uses, 26 Harv.Law Rev. 108.

5. The active portion of the Statute was as follows: "That where any person or persons stand or be seized, or at any time hereafter shall happen to be seized, of and in any honours, castles, manors, lands, tenements, rents, services, reversions, remainders or other hereditaments to the use, confidence or trust of any other person or persons, or of any body politick, by reason of any bargain, sale, feoffment, fine, recovery, covenant, contract, agreement, will or otherwise, by any manner means whatsoever it be; that in every such case all and every such person or persons, and bodies

that this troublesome class of equitable interests would cease to exist, and that all estates in lands would be subject to the same burdens, and the same rules of tenure and conveyance. There would be no uses in land, because the law would change them to legal interests at the instant of their birth.

 WESTLAW REFERENCES

"statute of uses" /s defin!

"statute of uses" /s "henry viii"

THE EFFECT OF THE STATUTE OF USES [1]

§ 5. The Statute of Uses did not have its intended effect because—

(a) **By virtue of its express provisions, and because of the construction given it by the courts of law, certain equitable interests were not converted into legal interests, namely, equitable interests in personal property, active trusts, and uses upon uses;**

(b) **These equitable interests not so converted into legal interests were recognized and enforced by the Court of Chancery as trusts after the Statute of Uses, and form the basis of the modern law of trusts.**

To the common law judges, who alone had to do with legal estates, fell the task of construing the Statute of Uses, and determining when the Statute executed the use and gave to the beneficiary the legal estate. It was evident from the express words of the Statute that uses in personalty were not included. The Statute spoke only of real property. And since it referred only to instances in which the feoffee to uses was "seized," it was readily held that the Statute had no application to interests in real property other than freeholds. Therefore a gift to A of a term for five years or of money or chattels, to the use of B, was not affected by the Statute. The Statute was also held, not to apply to

politick, that have or hereafter shall have any such use, confidence or trust, in fee simple, fee tail, for term of life or for years, or otherwise, or any use, confidence or trust in remainder or reverter, shall from henceforth stand and be seized, deemed and adjudged in lawful seisin, estate and possession of and in the same honours, castles, manors, lands, tenements, rents, services, reversions, remainders and hereditaments, with their appurtenances to all intents, constructions and purposes in the law, of and in such like estates as they had or shall have in use, trust or confidence of or in the same; and that the estate, title, right and possession that was in such person or persons that were, or hereafter shall

be seized of any lands, tenements or hereditaments, to the use, confidence or trust of any such person or persons, or of any body politick, be from henceforth clearly deemed and adjudged to be in him or them that have, or hereafter shall have, such use, confidence or trust, after such quality, manner, form and condition as they had before, in or to the use, confidence or trust that was in them."

§ 5

1. See Restatement, Trusts, Second, §§ 67–73; Holdsworth, IV History of English Law, p. 461, et seq.; Bordwell, 39 Harv.L.R. 466.

active trusts, but only to passive or general trusts. Duties of administration required the legal title in the trustee. Thus, if land was conveyed to A for life, to collect the profits thereof and pay them to B and his heirs, the trust would be active, and the Statute would not execute the use but leave the legal estate in A and the equitable interest in B, separately.

The courts of law also held that the Statute did not affect a use upon a use. It could operate only once. After such operation, its force was spent. Thus if lands were conveyed to A and his heirs, to the use of B and his heirs, to the use of C and his heirs, the Statute was held to transfer the use of B into possession and give him the legal estate, but not to convert the use of C into possession and destroy B's legal estate.[2] This construction has sometimes been thought to be a mere quibble which improperly caused a partial destruction of the Statute.[3] But one scholar pointed out that the use upon a use was held void by the court of chancery before the passage of the Statute of Uses, and that, therefore, the decision of the common law courts in Tyrrel's Case was entirely correct.[4] Where a use upon a use was attempted, the second party named would not be seised of land to the use of the third party, but rather of a use for his benefit, so that logically a case would not be presented for the operation of the Statute as to the second use.[5]

A large number of uses and trusts were thus left unaffected by the Statute of Uses and were recognized and enforced by chancery. The name "trust", after the Statute of Uses, was applied to all the equitable interests so sustained, whether they had before been denominated uses or trusts. Perhaps the court of chancery had no desire to stimulate the enactment of a second Statute of Uses by continuing the name "use." Perhaps it felt that the Statute of Uses had transferred to the law courts jurisdiction over uses.[6] It will be seen that the interests thus supported by chancery after the Statute of Uses, and called "trusts," were composed of the old active or special trusts and that part of the old general trusts or uses which the Statute did not destroy. These interests are the modern trusts which form the basis of the present English and American systems.

 WESTLAW REFERENCES

title property deed trust /100 "statute of uses" /s effect

2. Tyrrel's Case, Dyer 155 (1557).

3. Jenks, Short History of English Law, 100. "By this means, a statute made upon great consideration, introduced in a solemn and pompous manner, by this strict construction, has had no other effect than to add, at most, three words ['to the use'] to a conveyance." Lord Hardwicke, Hopkins v. Hopkins, 1 Atk. 581, 591.

4. Ames, Origin of Uses and Trusts, 2 Select Essays in Anglo-American Legal History, 747 et seq.

5. See Perry, Trusts, 7th Ed., § 301.

6. See 17 Mich.Law Rev. 87, for a discussion of the reasons for the survival of the trust. It is there suggested that the Statute did not contemplate the active trust which was then rare and little developed.

TRUSTS IN THE UNITED STATES

§ 6. The English system of equity jurisprudence, of which the trust was a part, was, with some qualifications, adopted by the colonies and by the original thirteen American states, and now constitutes the foundation on which present day American trust law rests.

Just as the colonists of the thirteen original states adopted substantially entire the common law of England, so they took over with little change the English scheme of equity jurisprudence, a part of which was the system of trusts. The development of chancery in colonial America, however, was slow and difficult. In Massachusetts no equity court existed for any substantial time until 1877.[1] Redress in extraordinary cases was had only through petition to the legislature. In minor cases the legislature doled out to the common law courts meager equity powers, but no inclusive jurisdiction. In Pennsylvania no court of chancery was founded until 1836.[2] The law courts often worked out equitable relief through their own forms. In New York, in 1701, by an ordinance of governor and council, the governor was appointed chancellor.[3] The legislature and people objected to this method of forming the new court and sought its abolition. This movement failed, but the court was thereafter unpopular and little patronized. In Virginia chancery was at first administered by the governor and council and later by the general court and county courts. In the other colonies the governor, aided by his council, usually exercised the powers of a chancellor.[4]

Towards the close of the eighteenth century, when trusts came into more common use in America, the English system had been well developed, and was naturally adopted in substantial entirety by the American colonial and early state chancellors. The first state reports show that, considering the relative poverty and newness of America, trusts were involved in litigation with a fair measure of frequency.[5]

§ 6

1. Chancery in Massachusetts, E.H. Woodruff, 5 Law Quart.Rev. 370.

2. The Administration of Equity through Common-Law Forms in Pennsylvania, S.G. Fisher, 2 Select Essays in Anglo-American Legal History, 810.

3. History of New York, Wm. Smith, Yates' Ed., 385–389; preface to vol. 1, Johns.Ch.Rep.

4. Courts of Chancery in the American Colonies, S.D. Wilson, 2 Select Essays in Anglo-American Legal History, 779.

5. In the following cases, decided before 1800, a trust was discussed or construed:

Connecticut: Bacon v. Taylor, Kirby 368 (1788).

Maryland: State ex rel. Hindman v. Reed, 4 Har. & McH. 6 (1797); Reeder v. Cartwright, 2 Har. & McH. 469 (1790); Swearingham v. Stull's Ex'rs, 4 Har. & McH. 38 (1797); Ridgely v. Carey, 4 Har. & McH. 167 (1798); Dorsey's Ex'rs v. Dorsey's Adm'r, 4 Har. & McH. 231 (1798); Hatcheson v. Tilden, 4 Har. & McH. 279 (1799); Bank of Columbia v. Ross, 4 Har. & McH. 456 (1799).

DEVELOPMENT OF TRUST LAW IN THE UNITED STATES—CODIFICATION—THE RESTATEMENT

§ 7. There has been an increasing tendency in recent years to set forth in trust instruments the rights and duties of the parties and the powers of the trustee and thus to remove the trust from rules laid down by the courts or legislatures.

In addition court-made rules of trust law have been stated or changed by statute in many instances, although there has been no attempt to codify the whole body of trust law.

The American law of trusts has been expounded in the Restatement of the Law of Trusts, adopted by the American Law Institute.

In England a part of the law of trusts has been codified in the Trustee Act of 1925,[1] the Judicial Trustee Act,[2] the Public Trustee Act,[3] the Perpetuities and Accumulations Act of 1964,[4] the Charitable Trusts Act,[5] the Validation of Charitable Trusts Act,[6] the Variation of Trusts Act,[7] and the Charities Act, 1960.[8] However the great body of the English law is still based on judicial decision.

In the United States[9] trust codes have been enacted in some states, for example, in New York[10] (followed in many provisions by Michigan,[11]

New Jersey: Arrowsmith v. Van Harlingen's Ex'rs, 1 N.J.L. 26 (1790); Green v. Beatty, 1 N.J.L. 142 (1792).

New York: Jackson v. Sternbergh, 1 Johns.Cas. 153 (1799); Neilson v. Blight, 1 Johns.Cas. 205 (1799).

North Carolina: Hogg's Ex'rs v. Ashe, 2 N.C. 471 (1797).

Pennsylvania: Kennedy v. Fury, 1 U.S. (Dall.) 72, 1 L.Ed. 42 (1783); Field v. Biddle, 2 U.S. (Dall.) 171, 1 L.Ed. 335 (1792); Knight v. Reese, 2 U.S. (Dall.) 182, 1 L.Ed. 340 (1792); Cox's Lessee v. Grant, 1 Yeates 164 (1792); Fogler's Lessee v. Evig, 2 Yeates 119 (1796); Lee's Lessee v. Tiernan, Add. 348 (1798).

South Carolina: Lindsay v. Lindsay's Adm'rs, 1 Desaus. 150 (1787); Bethune v. Beresford, 1 Desaus. 174 (1790); Stock's Ex'x v. Stock's Ex'r, 1 Desaus. 191 (1791); Gadsden's Ex'rs v. Lord's Ex'rs, 1 Desaus. 208 (1791); Wilson v. Wilson, 1 Desaus. 219 (1791).

Virginia: McCarty v. McCarty's Ex'rs, 2 Va.Col.Dec. 34 (1733); Hill v. Hill's Ex'rs, 2 Va.Col.Dec. 60 (1736); Coleman v. Dickenson, 2 Va.Col.Dec. 119 (1740); Pendleton v. Whiting, Wythe 38 (1791).

§ 7

1. 15 Geo. V, c. 19, 1925.

2. 59 & 60 Vict. c. 35 (1896).

3. 6 Edw. VII, c. 55 (1906).

4. 13 Eliz. 2, c. 44.

5. 15 & 16 Geo. V., c. 27, 1925.

6. 6 & 7 Eliz. 2, c. 53 (1958).

7. 2 & 3 Eliz. 2, c. 58 (1954).

8. 8 & 9 Eliz. 2, c. 58 (1960).

9. As to stages of development, see Scott, 50 Harv.L.R. 60; Keeton, 13 N.Y. U.L.Q.R. 556.

10. See Estates, Powers and Trust Law, enacted by N.Y.Laws 1966, c. 952. The prior law had been in N.Y.—McKinney's Real Property Law §§ 90–117 and N.Y.—McKinney's Personal Property Law §§ 10–23.

11. Mich.C.L.A. §§ 555.1 et seq., 700.501–700.598, 700.767–700.835.

Wisconsin,[12] and Minnesota [13]), in California [14] (followed in many respects by Montana,[15] North Dakota,[16] and South Dakota [17]), Georgia,[18] Indiana,[19] Louisiana,[20] Pennsylvania,[21] Texas [22] and Washington.[23] Somewhat similar "trust acts" have recently been adopted in Illinois,[24] Maryland,[25] Missouri [26] and Oklahoma,[27] but in these states the amount of statutory trust law is relatively small.

An attempt has been made in recent years to codify parts of trust law, for example, in the Uniform Fiduciaries Act,[28] the Uniform Principal and Income Act,[29] the Uniform Trusts Act,[30] the Uniform Trustees' Accounting Act,[31] the Uniform Common Trust Fund Act,[32] the Uniform Testamentary Additions to Trusts Act,[33] the Model Prudent Man Investment Act,[34] the Uniform Trustees' Powers Act,[35] and the Uniform Probate Code.[36] These acts were prepared by the National Conference

12. Wis.A. Ch. 701 (Wis.L.1969, c. 283). The prior law had been at 231.01 et seq.

13. Minn.—M.S.A. ch. 501.

14. West's Ann.Cal.Civ.Code, §§ 715, 852–871, 2215–2289, West's Ann.Cal.Prob. Code § 1120 et seq.

15. Mont.—R.C. Tit. 72, chs. 20–27.

16. N.D.—N.D.Cent.Code ch. 59.

17. S.Dak.Codif.Laws. Tit. 55.

18. Offic. Code Ga.Ann., Tit. 53, chs. 12 and 13.

19. See Indiana Code of 1971, Tit. 30, Art. 4 (Ind.L.1971, P.L. 416).

20. La.—LSA–R.S. 9:1721 et seq., enacted by La.Acts 1964, No. 338.

21. Pa.—See Decedents, Estates and Fiduciaries Code, enacted by Acts 1972, No. 164; 20 Pa.C.S.A. § 101 et seq.

22. V.Tex.C.A., Prop.Code Tit. 9.

23. Wash.—West's RCWA Ins. 11.97–11.106.

24. Ill.Rev.Stat. c. 17, ¶¶ 1651–1690.

25. See Md.Code, Estates and Trusts, Tits. 14, 15.

26. See Mo.—V.A.M.S. ch. 456.

27. Okl.Laws 1941, p. 250; 60 Okl.St. Ann. § 175.1 et seq.

28. See § 167, post. See, for example, Mo.—V.A.M.S. § 456.240 et seq. Though originally adopted in nearly all states, many of the Act's provisions have been replaced by adoption of the Uniform Act for Simplification of Fiduciary Transfers of Securities or by the Uniform Commercial Code.

29. For adoptions of the Act (approved 1931) and the Revised Uniform Principal and Income Act (approved 1962), see § 111, post. As to the major changes made in the Revised Act, see Bogert, 101 Tr. & Est. 787.

30. See, for example, N.Car.G.S. §§ 36A–60 to 36A–84. And see §§ 128, 129, post.

31. Adopted in Kan. and Nev. with modifications. See, for example, Kan. Stats.Ann. 59–1601 to 59–1611. And see § 142, post.

32. See § 105, post. There are now statutes in all states authorizing establishment of common trust funds and more than 34 states have adopted the Uniform Act.

33. See § 22, post. The Act has been adopted in 43 states and the District of Columbia.

34. The Model Prudent Man Investment Act has been adopted, with minor variations, in most states. See § 106, post.

35. See § 88, post. The Uniform Act has been adopted, with or without modification, in 12 states. For the text of the Act and current adoptions, see Bogert, Trusts and Trustees (rev.2d edit.) § 551.

36. Approved by the National Conference of Commissioners on Uniform State Laws and by the American Bar Association in 1960. Article VII of the Code contains a number of provisions regarding the administration of trusts under wills and under living trust agreements. The Code introduced the concept of registration of all trusts with a court, to provide a "home base" court where proceedings by and against trustees can be handled. At this writing the Code has been enacted, with some modifications, in 14 states. For adoptions see 8 Unif.Laws Ann. 75 (with pocket part supplements). For background materials and the text of Article VII, see Bogert, Trusts and Trustees (rev.2d edit.), § 7.

of Commissioners on Uniform State Laws.[37]   Their effects and the extent of their adoption are set forth in later sections.

In 1935 The American Law Institute completed a Restatement of the American Law of Trusts. It set forth the rules of law affecting trust creation and administration as the Institute believed them to exist, and gave illustrations and comments.[38] In 1957 the original Restatement of Trusts was revised and promulgated as Restatement of Trusts, Second. References to the relevant sections of the Restatement, Second, are hereinafter attached in footnotes. In many states the Restatement of Trusts has been annotated with references to the case and statute law of the particular state and these annotations are published in separate volumes.

Three other Restatements published by the American Law Institute have particular relevance to the law of trusts. The Restatement of Restitution [39] contains materials regarding constructive trusts and the remedy of tracing trust property where there is a breach of trust. The Restatement of Property, at this date undergoing extensive revision,[40] contains sections dealing with the creation of trusts and the interests of trustee and beneficiary. The Restatement of Conflict of Laws, Second,[41] was adopted in 1969. Chapter 10 of this Restatement codifies and clarifies rules relating to the validity, construction and administration of multistate trusts which have relationships to more than one state.

In the planning of estates the various uses of personal trusts and their federal and state tax consequences must be considered.[42]

 WESTLAW REFERENCES

"trustee's act"
"charitable trusts act"
"uniform fiduciaries act"
"uniform principal and income act"
"uniform trust act"
"uniform trustee's accounting act"
"uniform common trust fund act"

37. Other Uniform Laws affect trusts. For example, the Uniform Commercial Code which has been adopted in all states (in part by Louisiana) deals with the disposition of the proceeds of collection items held by banks, contract liability on the part of a trustee with respect to negotiable paper, and rules regarding participation in a breach of trust.

38. For comments on the 1935 Restatement, see Arnold, 31 Col.L.R. 800; Scott, 31 Col.L.R. 1266; Isaacs, 8 Am.L.S.R. 424; Butler, 6 Ford.L.R. 228; Vanneman, 34 Mich.L.R. 1109.

39. Currently being revised by the Institute as Restatement of the Law, Second, Restitution.

40. Restatement of the Law, Second, Property, which has been published in part, includes many matters relating to donative transfers, including transfers in trust and powers of appointment.

41. Restatement of the Conflict of Laws, Second, is currently being supplemented and partially revised. See, as to trusts and conflict of laws problems, Bogert, Trusts and Trustees (rev. 2d edit.), Ch. 16.

42. For a discussion of estate and tax planning with trusts, see Bogert, Trusts and Trustees (rev. 2d edit.), Chap. 15.

''uniform testamentary additions to trust act''

''model prudent man investment act''

''uniform trustees' power act''

''uniform probate code''

Chapter 2

CREATION OF EXPRESS TRUSTS—TRUST INTENT—FORMALITIES—CONVEYANCING

Table of Sections

MEANING OF EXPRESS TRUST

§ 8. An express trust is one which comes into being because a person having the power to create it expresses an intent to have the trust arise and goes through the requisite formalities.[1]

In considering the origin of trusts two classes are usually defined. Those trusts which come into being because the parties concerned have formed the actual intent that they shall arise, have expressed that intent in written or spoken words or otherwise, and have made or

§ 8
1. See Restatement, Trusts, Second, § 1.

19

procured the requisite property transfers, are called express trusts. Thus if A executes a writing whereby he declares himself trustee of certain of A's lands for B, using the words "trustee" and "beneficiary", and describing the particular land as the subject of the trust, there is an *express* trust.

But there are certain trusts which do not involve any written instrument or oral expression or other act explicitly showing a trust intent. These latter trusts are usually called *implied,* and are divided into two classes, namely, resulting and constructive. Resulting trusts arise where the courts presume or infer from certain acts that the parties intended a trust to exist, although they expressed no trust intent directly by word or writing. If A pays the purchase price of property to its owner, B, and directs B to convey it to C, and this is done, it is inferred that A desired a trust for his benefit, in the usual case, and this trust is called *resulting.* On the other hand, *constructive trusts* are imposed by chancery on the owners of property as a means of accomplishing justice and preventing unjust enrichment. Constructive trusts are not based on the intent of the parties, either actual or presumed. They are often called involuntary trusts, or trusts ex maleficio. Thus if A, when occupying a fiduciary relation to B, fraudulently obtains B's property, B may have A declared a constructive trustee of the property. Further definition of implied trusts is left to later sections, where their origin is considered.[2] The steps leading to the creation of express trusts will first be described.

 WESTLAW REFERENCES

di trust

WHO MAY CREATE AN EXPRESS TRUST? [1]

§ 9. In order to create an express trust the settlor must own or have a power over the property which is to become the trust property, or must have the power to create such property.

Legal disabilities of a settlor may render his attempt at trust creation void or voidable. If a settlor is illegally induced to create a trust, his act may be void or voidable.

The settlor of a trust has previously been defined as the person who intentionally causes the trust to come into existence.[2]

Who may be the settlor of a trust? What qualifications must the settlor possess in order that equity will recognize and enforce the trust which he has attempted to create?

2. See §§ 71–76, post, as to resulting trusts, and §§ 77–87, post, as to constructive trusts.

§ 9

1. Restatement, Trusts, Second, §§ 17–22, 350.

2. See § 1, ante.

In section 10 to follow the methods of trust creation are described. It appears that those methods involve either (1) making a conveyance of property or obtaining another to make a conveyance, or (2) making a contract or obtaining another to make a contract. It is obvious that if method (1) is used, the settlor must own a transferable property interest or have a power of disposition over such property interest, or he must have the means of contracting with an owner or holder of such a power;[3] and that if method (2) is used the settlor must be able to make a contract, or have the means of inducing a second party to make a contract in favor of a trustee.

The law of persons with respect to disabilities applies to a settlor as it does to all others who attempt to enter into legal relations. Bankruptcy,[4] lack of mental capacity,[5] infancy,[6] and similar situations may either make it impossible for one to create a trust or render his attempt voidable by him.

The law regarding invalidating causes applies to trust settlors and gives ground for ruling invalid an act of trust creation, at the suit of the settlor, or his representative or successors, for example, in the cases of conveyances induced by fraud,[7] mistake[8] or undue influence.[9]

"In general, every person competent to make a will, enter into a contract, or hold the legal title to and manage property, may dispose of it as he chooses, and, sui juris, has the power to create a trust, and dispose of his property in that way . . .."[10] If one may legally convey his property absolutely, he may convey it upon trust, or declare that he holds it upon trust for another.

A person capable of making a contract may create a trust by contracting to pay money to a trustee for a third person.[11]

So too, the beneficiary of a trust (if not restricted as to alienation by way of spendthrift trust[12]) may settle his equitable interest in trust in the same way that the owner of the legal title may create a trust.[13] Thus there may be a trust within a trust.

3. Colman v. Colman, 25 Wn.2d 606, 171 P.2d 691 (1946).

4. In re Shurte, 39 F.2d 100 (D.C.Ill. 1930).

5. Groening v. McCambridge, 282 Mich. 135, 275 N.W. 795 (1937).

6. C.I.R. v. Allen, 108 F.2d 961 (3d Cir. 1939), certiorari denied 309 U.S. 680, 60 S.Ct. 718, 84 L.Ed. 1023 (1940).

7. Kinney v. St. Louis Union Trust Co., 143 S.W.2d 250 (Mo.1940); Gilberti v. Coraopolis Trust Co., 342 Pa. 161, 19 A.2d 408 (1941).

8. Ward v. Waterman, 85 Cal. 488, 24 P. 930; Liberty Trust Co. v. Weber, 200 Md. 491, 91 A.2d 393 (1952); Irish v. Irish, 361 Pa. 410, 65 A.2d 345 (1949). As to subsequent reformation of the trust instrument on the grounds of mistake, see § 148, post.

9. Barnum v. Fay, 320 Mass. 177, 69 N.E.2d 470 (1946). The trust instrument may be set aside when the status of the conveyor is such that a non-trust transfer would be set aside. Kimmell v. Tipton, 142 S.W.2d 421 (Tex.Civ.App.1940).

10. Skeen v. Marriott, 22 Utah 73, 89, 61 P. 296, 300.

11. Fletcher v. Fletcher, 4 Hare 67.

12. See § 40, post.

13. Tierney v. Wood, 19 Beav. 330; Kronheim v. Johnson, 7 Ch.D. 60; Macy v. Hays, 163 Ga. 478, 136 S.E. 517 (1927).

WESTLAW REFERENCES

di settlor

settlor /s "mental capacity" infancy bankruptcy

di(trust /s invalid void voidable /s fraud)

189k49(1)

di(trust /s invalid void voidable /s mistake)

di(trust /s invalid void voidable /s "undue influence")

390k54

120k76 /p trust

120k211(4) /p trust

390k173 /p "undue influence"

390k49

METHODS OF TRUST CREATION [1]

§ 10. The principal methods of trust creation are—

(a) A declaration by a property owner that he holds the property in trust for another, or procuring such a declaration by another;

(b) A transfer by the owner of property (or the holder of a power of appointment over the property) of that property, by deed or will, to another to hold in trust;

(c) Making, or procuring to be made, a contract to pay money or deliver property to another which the payee or transferee is to hold in trust for a third person.

Trust Declarations

If A is the owner of a share of stock in United States Steel Corporation, he may declare in writing or orally that henceforth he holds that stock in trust for his nephew, B, with a duty to pay B the dividends for B's life.[2] This is the creation of a trust by "declaration". The settlor is also the trustee.

If A pays B $1,000 for B's promise that B will hold some of B's stock in trust for C, A is buying a trust declaration by B and A is the settlor of the trust.[3]

Trust Transfers

If A is the owner of stock, he may transfer title to X Trust Company, the stock to be held by it in trust for A's nephew, B, with the duty to pay the income to B for his life. Upon the manifestation of this intent by A, the handing over of the stock certificate, with appropriate endorsement, and the acceptance of the trust by X Trust Company, the

§ 10

1. Restatement, Trusts, Second, § 17.

2. De Leuil's Ex'rs v. De Leuil, 255 Ky. 406, 74 S.W.2d 474 (1934).

3. Guaranty Tr. Co. of N.Y. v. New York Tr. Co., 297 N.Y. 45, 74 N.E.2d 232 (1947).

creation of a trust by "transfer" is completed.[4]

The power to transfer usually arises out of ownership, but may also exist because a power of appointment has been given the settlor. Thus if A leaves property by will to B for life, with a power in B to appoint the property at his death, B may execute a will creating a trust of the remainder interest which he did not own but over which he had a power of appointment.[5]

The courts have agreed that a general power of appointment may be exercised by the donee to appoint in trust, but have disagreed as to whether a special power may be so exercised.[6] Statutes in effect in a number of states specifically authorize the donee of a general[7] or special[8] power of appointment to make a further appointment in trust.

One common way of creating a trust is to leave property by will to another in trust for a third person. Thus a property owner may make a will by which he leaves all his property to B, to hold it in trust for the testator's family. On the death of the testator, with the will unrevoked, title passes to the trustee and the trust begins.[9]

A trust by transfer may also be created by permitting title to pass by intestacy to heirs or next of kin who agree to hold it in trust.[10]

Trusts created by inter vivos arrangements are called "living trusts", and instruments creating them are called "trust agreements".

Contracts in Favor of a Trustee

A may execute a promissory note whereby he agrees to pay $1,000 to B as trustee for C. On the delivery of this note to B for a valuable consideration, a trust will arise.[11] The same result would follow if A agreed to deliver other property to B.

Not only may the settlor create the trust by making a promise to a trustee, but he may secure the making of such a promise by a third person by paying the third party consideration for his undertaking. Thus, A may take out a policy of insurance with the X Insurance Company on his, A's life, and pay the premiums on the policy, and the company may promise to pay the proceeds of the insurance to B as

4. Hinton's Ex'r v. Hinton's Com., 256 Ky. 345, 76 S.W.2d 8 (1934).

5. Union Nat. Bk. of Wilmington v. Wilson, 26 Del.Ch. 170, 25 A.2d 450 (1942). See Restatement, Trusts, Second, § 17.

6. Bogert, Trusts and Trustees (rev.2d edit.), § 43. And see cases cited in Restatement, Property, Second, §§ 19.1 and 19.3 (special power).

7. See West's Ann.Cal.Civ.Code § 1387.1; Colo.R.S. 15–2–301; Conn.G.S.A. § 45–123a; Mass.G.L.A. c. 191, § 11–B; N.Y.—McKinney's EPTL 10–5.1; V.A.Tex. S. Prob.Code, § 112.001(4); West's RCWash.A 11.95.060.

8. See West's Ann.Cal.Civ.Code § 1387.2; Va.Code, 1950 § 55–25.1, as well as the statutes cited in footnote 7, infra.

9. Moss v. Axford, 246 Mich. 288, 224 N.W. 425 (1929). If a husband induces his wife to will property in trust by means of an agreement that the husband will make a reciprocal will, the husband is the settlor of the trust of the wife's property, because he procured the making of it. See § 40, post.

10. Ransdel v. Moore, 153 Ind. 393, 53 N.E. 767, 53 L.R.A. 753.

11. Fogg v. Middleton, 2 Hill's Eq. 591 (here a seal took the place of consideration).

trustee for C, with a duty on the part of B to support C from these proceeds for the life of C. This is the creation of a trust by A as the settlor, through the procuring by A of a contract by X Company in favor of a trustee.[12] The trust will arise when the insurance company issues its policy. These trusts are called "insurance trusts."[13]

 WESTLAW REFERENCES

Trust Declarations

390k1

find 74 ne2d 232

390k153

Trust Transfers

di(transfer! /s property /s creat*** /s trust)

"insurance trust"

EXPRESSION OF TRUST INTENT [1]

§ 11. In order to create an express trust the settlor's intent must be expressed and not merely formed in his own mind. Although it may be expressed (subject to formality requirements later stated) by conduct of the settlor, the use of written or spoken words is the method almost universally employed.

The trust property and the beneficiaries must be described with certainty.

No particular words or phrases need be used, and words of trusteeship are not necessarily conclusive.

The intent to have a trust must not only be formed in the mind of the settlor but must also be expressed by reducing his intent to writing or by communicating it to another.[2] Trusts do not arise out of secret thoughts or drafts of contemplated trust declarations or transfers.

Expressions of vague benevolent or donative intents are not enough,[3] nor are statements of an intent to give a property interest to another by some method other than trust creation,[4] or to convey in

---

12. Shaw v. Johnson, 15 Cal.App.2d 599, 59 P.2d 876 (1936).

13. See § 25, post. And see Bogert, Trusts and Trustees (rev.2d edit.), §§ 235–245, 264.15, 273.40.

§ 11

1. Restatement, Trusts, Second, §§ 23–27.

2. Semple v. Semple, 90 Fla. 7, 105 So. 134 (1925); Bates v. Clark, 349 Mo. 1087, 163 S.W.2d 975 (1942). See West's Ann. Cal.Civ.Code § 2221 ("any words or acts of the trustor"). And see text, infra, at footnote 29.

Ramage v. Ramage, 283 S.C. 239, 322 S.E.2d 22 (1984) (decedent's deed of property to defendants, "to hold in trust," and her codicil directing distribution of the same property by defendants as trustees, showed intent to create a trust of the property; the codicil was the basic trust instrument).

3. Citizens' Tr. & Sav. Bank v. Tuffree, 178 Cal. 185, 172 P. 586; Lanterman v. Abernathy, 47 Ill. 437.

4. Rock v. Rock, 309 Mass. 44, 33 N.E.2d 973 (1941) (imperfect gift of legal interest); Pratt v. Griffin, 184 Ill. 514, 56 N.E. 819; In re Ashman's Estate, 223 Pa.

trust at some time in the future.[5]

No Particular Words Required

If the words used convey the intent to establish a trust, they will have that effect. No formal or technical expressions are required.[6] For example, it is not necessary that the settlor use the words "trust" or "trustee," [7] and the designation of one as a "trustee" does not conclusively show the creation of a trust.[8] The language used may be sufficient, although the person actually intended to be a trustee is called an "executor," [9] an "attorney," [10] an "agent," [11] or a "guardian." [12] If the duties required of the appointed representative are those of a trustee, the party nominated will be held to be a trustee regardless of terminology used.[13] A statement of the motive [14] or purpose [15] of a gift normally does not show an intent to have the donee be a trustee, as where a gift is made to a daughter "so that she can support her children".

Language Must Describe Trust Elements Completely and with Certainty

Acts of trust creation are subject to generally prevailing rules about certainty as a prerequisite to enforceability. Uncertainty and ambiguity in the description of the trust elements may tend to show that no trust was intended; [16] or, even if the intent to create a trust is assumed, it cannot be effective unless certain essential trust elements are properly described, namely, the subject matter, the trust purpose, and the beneficiaries.[17]

Thus if the property to be administered by the trustee is indefinite

543, 72 A. 899; Johnson v. Williams, 63 How.Prac., N.Y., 233.

5. Reynolds v. Thompson, 161 Ky. 772, 171 S.W. 379. But one may provide that a trust shall begin in the future, on the happening of a named event. In re Palmer's Estate, 211 Or. 342, 315 P.2d 164 (1957).

6. In re Heywood's Estate, 148 Cal. 184, 82 P. 755; Anderson v. Crist, 113 Ind. 65, 15 N.E. 9; Blake v. Dexter, 66 Mass. (12 Cush.) 559; Putnam v. Lincoln Safe Deposit Co., 191 N.Y. 166, 83 N.E. 789; Martin v. Moore, 49 Wash. 288, 94 P. 1087. See Offic.Code Ga.Ann. § 53–12–21.

7. Hughes v. Fitzgerald, 78 Conn. 4, 60 A. 694; In re Soulard's Estate, 141 Mo. 642, 43 S.W. 617; Morse v. Morse, 85 N.Y. 53.

8. Bank of Visalia v. Dillonwood Lumber Co., 148 Cal. 18, 82 P. 374; In re Hawley, 104 N.Y. 250, 10 N.E. 352.

9. Angus v. Noble, 73 Conn. 56, 46 A. 278.

10. Mersereau v. Bennet, 124 App.Div. 413, 108 N.Y.S. 868.

11. Anderson v. Fry, 116 App.Div. 740, 102 N.Y.S. 112.

12. Fleck v. Ellis, 144 Ga. 732, 87 S.E. 1055.

13. Ryder v. Lyon, 85 Conn. 245, 82 A. 573; Blake-Curtis v. Blake, 149 Kan. 512, 89 P.2d 15 (1939); Mee v. Gordon, 187 N.Y. 400, 80 N.E. 353, 116 Am.St.Rep. 613, 10 Ann.Cas. 172.

14. Blanchard v. Blake, 91 N.H. 28, 13 A.2d 155 (1940).

15. Witman v. Webner, 351 Pa. 503, 41 A.2d 686 (1945).

16. Pratt v. Trustees of Sheppard & Enoch Pratt Hospital, 88 Md. 610, 42 A. 51.

17. Inglis v. Sailor's Snug Harbor, 28 U.S. (3 Pet.) 99, 7 L.Ed. 617 (1830); Drinkhouse v. German Savings & Loan Soc., 17 Cal.App. 162, 118 P. 953; Tucker v. Countryman, 414 Ill. 215, 111 N.E.2d 101 (1953) (uncertainty as to trust res and interests of beneficiaries).

and incapable of identification, no trust can arise.[18] The residue of the testator's property after the payment of debts, expenses, and legacies is a sufficiently definite subject-matter for a trust,[19] since that is certain which is capable of being made certain. It is not required that the settlor expressly give the trust property to the trustee. If the trust is fully described, the gift of the property to the trustee will be implied.[20] So too, if the description of the beneficiaries is vague [21] the trust will be ineffective. The same result occurs if there is uncertainty as to the purposes of the trust or the size of the interests of the beneficiaries.[22] Vagueness or inadequacy in the description of the trustee is not important, if other trust elements are present, since the court will supply a trustee.[23]

In a few states statutes contain statements as to the content of the settlor's expression which is necessary to trust creation.[24] In other states legislation has been enacted as to the effect of a conveyance to one as trustee, without description of the beneficiaries or other terms of the trust.[25]

Burden of Proof and Character of Evidence Necessary

The burden lies upon the party asserting the existence of a trust to show that the acts of the alleged settlor were sufficient to create a trust.[26] It is frequently stated by courts that the evidence to establish the existence of a trust must be "clear," "convincing," "explicit," and "unequivocal." [27]

On principle it would seem that no stronger evidence should be required to prove the creation of a trust than to prove any other fact in a civil action. However, in many cases the effort to prove a trust involves an attack on a title which by the records or otherwise seems absolute. The public interest in the security of titles is doubtless behind the statements of the courts about the character of evidence

---

18. Mills v. Newberry, 112 Ill. 123, 1 N.E. 156, 54 Am.Rep. 213; Roddy v. Roddy, 3 Neb. 96.

19. Glover v. Baker, 76 N.H. 393, 83 A. 916.

20. Haywood v. Wachovia Loan & Trust Co., 149 N.C. 208, 62 S.E. 915.

21. Condit v. Reynolds, 66 N.J.L. 242, 49 A. 540; Fowler v. Coates, 201 N.Y. 257, 94 N.E. 997.

22. Lissauer v. Union Bank & Tr. Co. of Los Angeles, 45 Cal.App.2d 468, 114 P.2d 367 (1941) (indefinite whether interests for life or absolute).

23. Trustees of McIntire Poor School v. Zanesville Canal & Mfg. Co., 9 Ohio 203, 34 Am.Dec. 436; Appeal of Varner, 80 Pa. 140. See § 29, post.

24. The settlor is required to indicate by acts or words "an intention on the part

of the trustor to create a trust" and "the subject, purpose, and beneficiary of the trust". West's Ann.Cal.Civ.Code, § 2221; Mont.Code Ann. 72–20–107; N.Dak.Cent. Code 59–01–04; S.Dak.Codif.L. 55–1–4.

25. The purport of these statutes is that third parties may rely on the grantee as being the absolute owner or as a trustee with power to sell, and they need make no inquiry as to the terms of the trust. See statutes cited in Bogert, Trusts and Trustees (rev.2d edit.) § 45. See § 133, post.

26. Prevost v. Gratz, 19 U.S. (6 Wheat.) 481, 5 L.Ed. 311 (1821); Russell v. Fish, 149 Wis. 122, 135 N.W. 531.

27. Sheehan v. Sullivan, 126 Cal. 189, 58 P. 543; Lurie v. Sabath, 208 Ill. 401, 70 N.E. 323; Boughman v. Boughman, 69 Ohio St. 273, 69 N.E. 430; Gribbel v. Gribbel, 341 Pa. 11, 17 A.2d 892; Watts v. McCloud, Tex.Civ.App., 205 S.W. 381.

required for the proof of trusts. A rule requiring an extraordinarily high degree of proof has been applied rarely, except in cases where an attempt was made by oral proof to fasten a trust upon property which appeared to be owned absolutely.[28]

Settlor's Conduct May be Proof of Trust Intent

In some cases the settlor's conduct with regard to title to, or possession or enjoyment of property, or his conduct toward the alleged beneficiary, has been held to be sufficient evidence of a trust intent.[29]

 WESTLAW REFERENCES

No Particular Words Required
intent!　/s　creat***　/s　trust　/s　settlor
390k124
390k25(1)
ramage　+3　ramage

Language Must Describe Trust Elements Completely and with Certainty
trust　/s　element　/s　certainty
390k21(2)

Burden of Proof and Character of Evidence Necessary
390k41
"burden of proof"　/s　exist!　/s　trust
di(evidence　/s　trust　/s　clear convincing explicit unequivocal　/s
　　creat***)
390k44(3)

SIMILAR INTENTS DISTINGUISHED—OTHER PROPERTY MANAGEMENT RELATIONSHIPS

§ 12.　The intent to create a trust is to be distinguished from the intent to have some other relationship in which property is to be managed for the benefit of another, for example,

(a) Bailment;

(b) Equitable charge;

(c) Executorship;

(d) Agency;

(e) Guardianship;

(f) Receivership.

28. See Bogert, Trusts and Trustees (rev.2d edit.), § 49. For similar doctrines regarding resulting and constructive trusts, see §§ 72, 78, post.

29. Cazallis v. Ingraham, 119 Me. 240, 110 A. 359, 361 (1920); Eisele v. First National Bank of Edgewater, 102 N.J.Eq. 598

142 A. 29 (1928); Starr v. Starr, 1 Ohio 321; People's Savings Bank v. Webb, 21 R.I. 218, 42 A. 874; Hamner v. Sharp, 58 Tenn. (11 Heisk.) 701; Stearns Coal & Lumber Co. v. Jones, 101 W.Va. 374, 132 S.E. 716. And see Elyachar v. Gerel Corp., S.D.N.Y.1984, 583 F.Supp. 907.

There are many situations in which it is desirable or convenient to have property managed by one for the benefit of another. Several legal relationships have been developed to meet the needs of the parties in varying conditions. A trust is merely one of several of these "property management" relationships. It becomes important to outline the legal differences between these somewhat similar relations so that one may decide which was intended to exist in any given situation and what the legal consequences are. The distinctions between trust and other dispositions of property and legal relationships have relevance in determining the duties and liabilities of one holding property for another as well as the rights of the person intended to be benefitted from the property disposition. The immediately following sections contrast the trust with these other relationships and describe their likenesses and differences.

 WESTLAW REFERENCES

di bailor

di executor

di agent

di guardian

di receiver

BAILMENT [1]

§ 13. A bailment for the benefit of another than the bailee bears a slight, superficial resemblance to a trust but it differs from a trust in that—

(a) **It was developed in the common law actions, whereas the trust was developed in chancery, so that the rights of the beneficiary of a bailment are now legal, while those of the trust beneficiary are equitable;**

(b) **Bailment is not a fiduciary relation;**

(c) **Bailment deals with personal property only, while a trust may involve any kind of property;**

(d) **The bailee has a special, limited property interest, and the bailor has general property, whereas the trustee usually has full ownership subject to the equitable interest of the beneficiary.**

Bailment and trust are in some cases superficially similar. In each the owner of property places it in the control of another, usually for a temporary purpose, and often for the benefit of one other than the transferee. A few definitions of bailment would seem to make it a form of trust.[2]

§ 13

1. Restatement, Trusts, Second, § 5.

2. "Bailment from the French 'bailler,' to deliver, is a delivery of goods in trust, upon a contract, expressed or implied, that

Bailment is a common law institution. It was developed through the common law actions such as detinue, replevin, and trover. Relief for violation of the terms of a bailment is usually given in a court of law.[3] As previously stated, the trust was first recognized by the court of chancery and is enforced almost entirely on equitable principles.

Bailment is a business relation in which the parties deal with each other at arm's length.[4] Bailor and bailee may contract and convey freely with each other and are not in special relations of intimacy or confidence. The trust is a fiduciary relation involving the duty of unselfish loyalty and extreme good faith.

Bailment relates to delivery of personal property by one to another for a temporary purpose, for example, where the general owner of a typewriter delivers it to a friend for safekeeping or use. There can be no bailment of realty. On the other hand the trust subject matter may be any kind of property, real or personal.[5]

It is sometimes said that trust and bailment differ in that a bailee has no "title," whereas the trustee has "legal title." It is more accurate to state that the bailee usually has a special, legal property interest which entitles him to possession and use for a period which is generally relatively short. The larger, general property interest remains in the bailor. In trust the property interest of the trustee is usually legal in nature and much larger than that of the bailee. The trust beneficiary's interest is always equitable. Thus in the normal bailment the total property interest is divided into two types of legal interests, special and general. While in the normal trust full legal ownership is in the trustee, subject to equitable interests in the beneficiaries.

Occasionally it is doubtful whether bailment or trust was intended,[6] but usually a trust intent will appear from the language used and from the formality and relatively long duration of the relationship. Bailments can not be confused with trusts if they are for the sole benefit of the bailee, but there may be a slight chance of confusion if the transferor or a third person is to secure advantages from the property delivered.

the trust shall be faithfully executed on the part of the bailee." Blackstone's Com. 451. The following definition of bailment would seem preferable: "A bailment is the transfer of the possession of personal property, without a transfer of ownership, for the accomplishment of a certain purpose, whereupon the property is to be redelivered or delivered over to a third person." Hale, Bailments and Carriers, 5, 6.

3. Ashley's Adm'rs v. Denton, 1 Litt. 86; Piester v. Ideal Creamery Co., 289 Mich. 489, 286 N.W. 801 (1939).

4. Young v. Mercantile Trust Co., C.C. A.N.Y., 1906, 145 Fed. 39; Taylor v. Turner, 87 Ill. 296.

5. See § 25, post.

6. Brooks v. Davis, 294 Mass. 236, 1 N.E.2d 17 (1936) (bonds delivered by owner to another to be held "in trust" for owner's purposes and then returned; deliveree a bailee, notwithstanding use of trust language).

WESTLAW REFERENCES

di bailment

bailment /s trust

50k23

piester +3 ideal

EQUITABLE CHARGE [1]

§ 14. An equitable charge is distinguished from a trust by—

(a) Its lack of fiduciary relationship;

(b) The presence of beneficial ownership in the obligor.

It is like a trust in that equitable property rights are vested in the beneficiary.

Where an owner conveys property and states an intention that the transferee shall hold it "subject to a charge" to confer benefits out of the capital or income of the property on another, the property is frequently held to be subject to an "equitable charge".

An equitable charge bears many resemblances to a trust. In both relations the holder of the property is vested with a title, generally legal. In both the claimant or beneficiary has property rights enforceable in equity.[2] In both a purchaser of the property with notice of the burden attached will hold it subject to the claim of the beneficiary, but both claims will be cut off by the transfer of the property to a bona fide purchaser. Thus, if A devises land to B, "subject to the payment out of the income of an annuity of $500 to C," B may be intended to take subject to an equitable charge, and if so he will hold subject to equitable rights to $500 income in C, just as if A had devised the land to B "in trust to pay C $500 a year." In the first instance, as well as in the second, X, a purchaser with knowledge of the terms of the devise to B, will take it subject to the burden on the property in favor of C.[3]

But the relations are not equivalent. A trustee is a fiduciary. He alone can perform the duties of the trust. To transfer the trust property to another would be a breach of the trust. In the ordinary case the trustee is expected to retain the trust property and perform the trust duties personally.[4] By contrast, the holder of property subject to a charge is not a fiduciary and has no personal relation to the beneficiary of the charge. He may sell the property to a stranger, and

---

§ 14

1. Restatement, Trusts, Second, § 10.

2. Lofton v. Moore, 83 Ind. 112; Hoyt v. Hoyt, 77 Vt. 244, 59 A. 845. As to trusts see § 37, post.

3. Humphrey v. Hudnall, 233 Ill. 185, 84 N.E. 203; Harris v. Fly, 7 Paige, N.Y., 421. But a purchaser of the land from a holder subject to a charge personally bind-ing on the holder is entitled to have the remedies against the holder exhausted before relief is sought in equity against the property. Kelsey v. Western, 2 N.Y. 500. By express agreement the transferee may assume a personal liability to the beneficiary. Swasey v. Little, 7 Mass. (Pick.) 296.

4. See § 92, post.

pass on the burden of paying the charge, in so far as the encumbrance on the property is concerned.[5] Such an act will not be a breach of any duty to the beneficiary of the charge. And so, too, the holder subject to a charge may deal with the charged property and with the beneficiary of the charge at arm's length and has no restrictions or disabilities about buying a release of the charge.[6] A sale of the trust beneficiary's interest to the trustee, on the other hand normally is voidable by the beneficiary, unless the trustee can show the utmost good faith in the transaction.[7]

In the second place, the holder subject to an equitable charge is a beneficial owner of part of the property whereas the trustee is not. If B receives property subject to a charge of $500 a year in favor of C, and the property produces $1,000 a year, B may retain the surplus $500 for his own use. If B were a trustee of the same property for the purpose of paying C $500 a year, B could not keep the extra $500 (unless an intent to give it to him were found), but would be obliged to hold it for the benefit of the creator of the trust, or for his successors if the settlor were dead. The holder subject to a charge is entitled to all benefits from the property beyond the amount necessary to satisfy the charge. The trustee as such is never entitled to any beneficial use of the trust property.[8]

It is often important to decide whether a relation is a trust or an equitable charge because of the Statute of Limitations.[9] The Statute does not begin to run against the beneficiary's rights until there has been a repudiation of the trust; but the Statute commences to operate against an equitable charge from the time when payments under it become due.

No set formula will always create a charge and refute the notion of a trust. The courts seek the creator's intent, whether it was to make a beneficial gift of the property subject to an encumbrance, or to place upon the recipient of the property a fiduciary relation.[10] Instruments

5. Downer v. Church, 44 N.Y. 647; Korn v. Friz, 128 Wis. 428, 107 N.W. 659.

6. Hayes v. Sykes, 120 Ind. 180, 21 N.E. 1080.

7. See § 96, post.

8. In re West, [1900] 1 Ch. 84; Woodbury v. Hayden, 211 Mass. 202, 97 N.E. 776.

9. Hodge v. Churchward, 16 Sim. 71; McKeage v. Coleman, 294 Ill.App. 232, 13 N.E.2d 662 (1938); Loder v. Hatfield, 71 N.Y. 92; Merton v. O'Brien, 117 Wis. 437, 94 N.W. 340.

10. In the following cases the wording was construed to create an equitable charge: King v. Denison, 1 Ves. & B. 260 (subject to payment of annuities); Hodge v. Churchward, 16 Sim. 71 (paying £ 10 a year); Merchants' Nat. Bank v. Crist, 140 Iowa 308, 118 N.W. 394, 23 L.R.A.,N.S., 526, 132 Am.St.Rep. 267 (support made a lien); Lang v. Everling, 3 Misc. 530, 23 N.Y.S. 329 ("upon the express condition that"); Loder v. Hatfield, 71 N.Y. 92 ("on the following conditions and proviso"); Chew v. Sheldon, 214 N.Y. 344, 108 N.E. 552, Ann.Cas.1916D, 1268 (subject to a duty to support daughter); Dixon v. Helena Soc. of Free Methodist Church of North America, 65 Okl. 203, 166 P. 114 (direction to devisee to pay a legacy).

In the following cases the courts found a trust: Buffinton v. Maxam, 140 Mass. 557, 5 N.E. 519 (for the support of); Baker v. Brown, 146 Mass. 369, 15 N.E. 783 (subject to the condition that); Woodbury v. Hayden, 211 Mass. 202, 97 N.E. 776 (to be used as far as necessary for the support and maintenance of); Powers v. Grand

which are held to create equitable charges often use the words "subject to", "charged with", or "the transferee paying" to another certain sums.

The grantor of land subject to a charge cannot release or destroy the charge, unless he reserved power to do so,[11] a result corresponding to the inability of the settlor to revoke his trust.[12]

The creator of an equitable charge may display an intent to fasten a personal obligation on the recipient of the property, as well as an *in rem* obligation against the property or its income, and such an obligation will then be imposed on a donee accepting the conveyance.[13] It becomes a question of construction whether a personal obligation was intended and accepted.

While a trustee may personally promise that certain payments will be made to the beneficiary of the trust, regardless of the actual yield of the trust property, this is very rarely done. He is usually liable only for income actually earned by the trust property.

An equitable charge is not to be confused with an equitable lien which is created by the court for the purpose of working out justice.[14]

 WESTLAW REFERENCES

"equitable charge"
king +3 denison

EXECUTORSHIP [1]

§ 15. Executorship is similar to trusteeship in that the executor is a fiduciary who holds the title to property for the benefit of others.

It is unlike a trust with regard to

(a) The court of enforcement;

(b) The kind of property held;

(c) The functions to be performed;

(d) The nature of the powers granted.

Lodge, etc., 236 Mo.App. 7, 146 S.W.2d 895 (1940) ("subject to a charge"); Pierce v. McKeehan, 3 Watts & S., Pa., 280 (subject to the maintenance of); Hoyt v. Hoyt, 77 Vt. 244, 59 A. 845 (on condition that).

In the following cases neither an equitable charge nor a trust was held to exist, the recipient of the property taking it absolutely or subject to a condition subsequent; Zimmer v. Sennott, 134 Ill. 505, 25 N.E. 774 (upon condition that); Dee v. Dee, 212 Ill. 338, 72 N.E. 429 (for the benefit of); Crandall v. Hoysradt, 1 Sandf.Ch., N.Y., 40 (for the maintenance of).

11. Logan v. Glass, 338 Pa. 489, 14 A.2d 306.

12. See § 148, post.

13. Commissioner of Internal Revenue v. Smiley, 86 F.2d 658 (2d Cir.1936); Wil-liams v. Nichol, 47 Ark. 254, 1 S.W. 243; Lord v. Lord, 22 Conn. 595; Adams v. Adams, 14 Mass. (Allen,) 65; Redfield v. Redfield, 126 N.Y. 466, 27 N.E. 1032; Logan v. Glass, 338 Pa. 489, 14 A.2d 306 (1940); Meyerson v. Malinow, 231 S.C. 14, 97 S.E.2d 88, 65 A.L.R.2d 194 (gift of stock to sons who were directed to pay widow a monthly sum).

14. As to equitable liens, see Bogert, Trusts and Trustees, (rev.2d edit.), § 32 and § 158, post.

§ 15

1. Restatement, Trusts, Second, § 6. See Keeton, 10 Miami L.Q. 521; Baker, 13 Okl.L.R. 408; 52 Marquette L.R. 303.

Both executors and trustees are fiduciaries.[2] Both occupy positions of high trust and confidence in which they have great control over the affairs of others. The courts require of them unselfish conduct and the highest good faith.[3]

The executor also is like a testamentary trustee in that he holds title to property for others and acquires it by will. When the will is admitted to probate and the executor receives his letters testamentary, he is deemed to have title to the personal property of the testator, dating back to the latter's death.[4] The executor holds this property interest not for himself, but for the creditors and legatees of the testator. A legatee usually has only a right that the executor set off for the legatee certain property or a given sum in satisfaction of his legacy, rather than an interest in any particular property prior to its allocation to him.[5]

The executor (unlike a testamentary trustee) is an officer of the probate court from which he receives his authority.[6] He is named by the testator, just as a trustee may be named by the settlor, but his position is dependent on the action of the probate court in admitting the will to probate and issuing letters to him. He is subject to the direction of that court. Relief against him by legatees or creditors is generally obtained by petition to the probate court. Actions at law or suits in equity are sometimes available to the legatee or creditor, but they are secondary and auxiliary.[7] The trustee is subject to obligations enforceable in a court of equity. Although testamentary trustees often receive approval of their appointments and letters evidencing their authority from a court, they are not usually appointed by the court but rather by the testator.[8]

Courts sometimes make the statement that executors are trustees,[9] but this is not strictly accurate.[10] They are probate fiduciaries who resemble testamentary trustees in some respects.

The Statute of Limitations does not run against the claim of a beneficiary of an express trust until the trustee repudiates the trust.[11] Other statutes of limitation or claim statutes control the claims of

2. Colburn v. Hodgdon, 241 Mass. 183, 135 N.E. 107.

3. Larrabee v. Tracy, 21 Cal.2d 645, 134 P.2d 265 (1943) (duty of executor to legatee).

4. Oulvey v. Converse, 326 Ill. 226, 157 N.E. 245 (1927); Rolfe v. Atkinson, 259 Mass. 76, 156 N.E. 51 (1927).

5. See Brewster v. Gage, 1930, 280 U.S. 327, 50 S.Ct. 115, 74 L.Ed. 457.

6. In re Durel, C.A.9, 1926, 10 F.2d 448.

7. Colt v. Colt, 32 Conn. 422; Andrews v. Hunneman, 6 Mass. (Pick.) 126.

8. See § 33, post. But see In re Barter's Estate, 30 Cal.2d 549, 184 P.2d 305 (testamentary trustee is not such until the probate court appoints him).

9. In re Cooper's Estate, 229 Iowa 921, 295 N.W. 448 (1940); Hardwick v. Cotterill, 221 Ky. 783, 299 S.W. 958 (1927).

10. Hogg v. Maxwell, C.C.A.2, 1915, 143 C.C.A. 389, 229 Fed. 113; In re Armour's Will, 33 N.J. 517, 166 A.2d 376 (1960).

11. See § 170, post.

creditors and legatees against the executor's estate.[12] In the case of creditors there is often a short statutory period, for example, six months, which applies if the executor publishes for claims.

The executor usually holds title to personalty only, although he sometimes has a power of sale over realty. Title to realty passes direct to the devisees. A trustee may hold either realty or personalty.

The executor has a simple temporary function, usually to collect the personal property of the testator, reduce it to money so far as necessary, and pay expenses, taxes, the creditors of the testator and his legatees. This function can generally be performed in a short time, often in a year or a year and a half. A trustee's functions are highly varied. There are many different purposes of trusts and they customarily last for many years or for several lives.

The powers of an executorship, where there are two or more executors, may be vested in each executor;[13] the powers of co-trustees are usually joint and must be exercised by all as a body.[14] Thus in the case of two executors, one may sell estate property and collect the price, without joinder of his associate. In a trust both trustees would be obliged to sign the bill of sale or deed.

Often a will names the same person as executor and trustee and it may become a question as to when he acts in one capacity and when in the other.[15] Normally the executor will complete his work first and then turn over the estate property to himself as trustee, but sometimes the trust administration begins before the executor has presented his account and been discharged.

Even though one is named as executor only, and no reference is made in the will to his acting as trustee, if trust functions are given to him he will be deemed a trustee with regard to those duties.[16] When property is given to an executor to pay debts, he will ordinarily be deemed to take it as executor and not as trustee, unless the provisions for payment are different from those which the law would apply if the will had been silent as to the method of paying debts.[17]

An administrator is like an executor, except that he is named by the probate court and acts in the case of intestacy. He has the same title to property and basically the same functions. In some cases

12. Wilmerding v. Russ, 33 Conn. 67; In re Moore's Appeal, 84 Mich. 474, 48 N.W. 39.

13. Pearse v. National Lead Co., 162 App.Div. 766, 147 N.Y.S. 989. But see, *contra,* Harrison v. Carpenter, 72 Ga.App. 149, 33 S.E.2d 274 (1945); Rabinovitz v. Williamson, 194 Misc. 17, 86 N.Y.S.2d 5 (1948), affirmed 275 App.Div. 841, 86 N.Y.S. 5 (1949) (administrators).

14. See § 91, post.

15. Coudon v. Updegraff, 117 Md. 71, 83 A. 145; Sheffield v. Parker, 158 Mass.

330, 33 N.E. 501; In re Bird's Will, 241 N.Y. 184, 149 N.E. 827 (1925). As to the duties of an executor in transferring property to a testamentary trustee and setting up the trust, see § 97, post.

16. Jones v. Broadbent, 21 Idaho 55, 123 P. 476; Dingman v. Beall, 213 Ill. 238, 72 N.E. 729; Drake v. Price, 5 N.Y. 430; Teel v. Hilton, 21 R.I. 227, 42 A. 1111.

17. Cohn v. McClintock, 107 Miss. 831, 66 So. 217.

statutes vest causes of action in administrators for the benefit of the next of kin in cases where the death of the intestate was caused by wrongful act. Here the administrator is a statutory trustee.[18] The cause of action is not something owned by the intestate during his life and passed on by intestacy. But normally an administrator, like an executor, is a probate fiduciary and not an equity trustee.

 WESTLAW REFERENCES

di executorship
colburn +3 hodgdon
power /s executorship
162k138(1)
162k519(2)

AGENCY [1]

§ 16. Agency resembles trusteeship in that it is a fiduciary relation and may involve the management of property for another person. Some points of difference are:

(a) The principal's rights are ordinarily enforced by courts of law, while the beneficiary's remedies are usually equitable.

(b) An agent is ordinarily not the owner of property for the benefit of his principal, while a trustee always holds the title to property for his beneficiary;

(c) Agency is generally a personal relation, dependent on the agreement and continued existence of both parties; this is not true of trusts;

(d) The agent is a mere instrument in the hands of the principal, and incurs no personal responsibility to third persons for acts done as agent when the agency is disclosed, while the trustee often renders himself personally liable for his official acts.

It is probable that both agency and trust arose from the same ill-defined intermediary relation.[2] Agency was molded by courts of law and received one set of characteristics. The trust was fostered by chancery and developed along different lines. Although now quite distinct, each possesses the element of trust and confidence. Each is a fiduciary relation. Both agents and trustees are placed in positions of

18. Kansas Pacific Ry. Co. v. Cutter, 16 Kan. 568; Howard v. Pulver, 329 Mich. 415, 45 N.W.2d 530 (1951). See Roberts v. Kenna, 241 S.W.2d 680 (Tex.Civ.App.1951) ("not a trustee, but a statutory agent of the probate court").

2. "The germ of agency is hardly to be distinguished from the germ of another institution, which in our English law has an eventful future before it, the 'use, trust, or confidence.'" 2 Pollock & Maitland, History of English Law, 226.

§ 16

1. Restatement, Trusts, Second, § 8; Restatement, Agency, Second, §§ 1, 13, 14B.

intimacy, where it is easy for them to take advantage of those who have trusted them, and therefore are held to a high standard of good faith. Because of this fiduciary element, agents and trustees are under a common prohibition against acting for their private interests when managing the affairs of those for whom they act. For example, neither can purchase the property which is the subject of his dealings, if the principal or beneficiary objects.[3] And they are classed together as "fiduciaries" for many purposes.[4] This common feature has led some authors to confuse the two relationships,[5] and others to call the agent a "quasi trustee";[6] but the distinctions stated below show good reasons for distinguishing them.[7]

It has been seen that an essential feature of the trust is the ownership by the trustee of property for the benefit of the beneficiary. The agent, on the other hand, need own no property. He acts for his principal, and often cares for, or transports, or sells property; but it is ordinarily property to which the title is in the principal alone. Sometimes an agent is vested with title to some of his principal's property with a duty to use it for the benefit of the principal,[8] but this is rare. In such a case he may well be in a double relationship, that of agent and trustee.[9]

A trust is ordinarily indestructible and irrevocable by its settlor, in the absence of a power of revocation expressly reserved.[10] The death of the settlor or of the trustee will not affect the life of the trust.[11] If the latter dies, a new trustee will succeed him. On the contrary, an agency is usually revocable at the option of the principal, unless it is coupled with an interest, and is revoked by the death of either party.[12] The personality of the agent with whom the relation begins is of the essence, and normally no other can be substituted for him. The principal supervises and guides the agent. In contrast, the trust beneficiary usually has little or no control over the trustee.

---

3. Bain v. Brown, 56 N.Y. 285; Copeland v. Mercantile Ins. Co., 6 Mass. (Pick.) 198.

4. As to their fiduciary duties, see for example, §§ 86–87 (constructive trusts) and §§ 95–96 (express trusts).

5. "The terms 'trustee' and 'agent' are frequently used in a loose way, as though those terms marked off absolutely distinct and separate duties and liabilities. All trustees, however, are agents; but all agents are not trustees. A trustee is an agent and something more." Ewell's Evans on Agency, 349.

6. Marvin v. Brooks, 94 N.Y. 71.

7. First Wisconsin Trust Co. v. Wisconsin Dept. of Taxation, 237 Wis. 135, 294 N.W. 868 (1940).

8. Russell v. Webster, 213 Mass. 491, 100 N.E. 637. That a representative to manage property is not given title is often held to show an intent to create agency and not trust. Maihack v. Mehl, 141 N.J. Eq. 281, 57 A.2d 44 (1948).

9. Restatement, Trusts, Second, § 8, Comments a and h; Restatement, Agency, Second, § 14B.

10. § 148, post.

11. § 149, post.

12. Rowe v. Rand, 111 Ind. 206, 12 N.E. 377; Flaherty v. O'Connor, 24 R.I. 587, 54 A. 376. An agency to transfer the principal's property to a trustee is revoked by the death of the principal so that the trust cannot later be completed. Farmers' Loan & Tr. Co. v. Winthrop, 238 N.Y. 477, 144 N.E. 686 (1924).

Furthermore, the agent, contracting in the name of his principal, incurs no personal responsibility for the performance of his contracts.[13] The principal alone is liable. The trustee is personally liable upon contracts made in the performance of the trust unless he expressly excludes liability, though he has the right of indemnity,[14] and neither the settlor nor the beneficiary is responsible on such contracts.[15] The trustee may be personally liable for torts committed in the course of his trust work.[16] The agent is a mere tool or instrument in the principal's hands, but the trustee is a separate, responsible party.

It should be noticed that the principal's rights against the agent are legal rights, and that ordinarily his remedy is in a court of law.[17] The beneficiary's rights are equitable.

Frequent occasions arise for making this distinction between trust and agency.[18]

Corporate fiduciaries are agents when they operate "custodian accounts" for their customers.[19] Here they accept possession of securities belonging to a customer for safekeeping, collect and distribute income, and sell and buy investments either on their own initiative or at the direction of the customer.

An escrow depositary, holding documents and cash for delivery on the performance of conditions, would ordinarily be an agent and bailee or debtor, and not a trustee.[20] His situation is later considered.[21]

In recent years, for tax and other reasons, it has been deemed desirable to make gifts of securities and other property to minors in custodial form, the "custodians" to receive the gifts, manage the property during the minority of the donees, and deliver it to the donees when they reach majority. The powers and duties of custodians have been

13. Restatement, Agency, Second, § 320.

14. Taylor v. Mayo, 110 U.S. 330, 335, 4 S.Ct. 147, 150, 28 L.Ed. 163 (1884); Shepard v. Abbott, 179 Mass. 300, 60 N.E. 782; Hartley v. Phillips, 198 Pa. 9, 47 A. 929. See § 125, post.

15. Everett v. Drew, 129 Mass. 150.

16. See § 129, post.

17. A principal may, however, obtain an accounting from his agent in equity. Warren v. Holbrook, 95 Mich. 185, 54 N.W. 712, 35 Am.St.Rep. 554; Marvin v. Brooks, 94 N.Y. 71.

18. In the following cases the question was one of revocation: Viser v. Bertrand, 16 Ark. 296; Rowe v. Rand, 111 Ind. 206, 12 N.E. 377; Lyle v. Burke, 40 Mich. 499. In others the problem was one of the personal liability of the agent or trustee. Shepard v. Abbott, 179 Mass. 300, 60 N.E. 782; Hartley v. Phillips, 198 Pa. 9, 47 A. 929; Taylor v. Mayo, 110 U.S. 330, 4 S.Ct. 147, 28 L.Ed. 163 (1884).

That the representative is called a "trustee" has not prevented the courts from finding that he was in fact an agent. Viser v. Bertrand, 16 Ark. 296; Rowe v. Rand, 111 Ind. 206, 12 N.E. 377.

Where A sent a check to B payable to the order of B, to be used in paying an assessment against realty, and B deposited it to his own credit and gave a clerk his own check to pay the assessment, and the clerk embezzled the proceeds of this second check, and thereafter A and B died, it was held that B was not a trustee, but a mere agent, and the agency was revoked by death. Title Guarantee & Trust Co. v. Haven, 214 N.Y. 468, 108 N.E. 819.

19. McKay v. Atwood, 10 F.Supp. 475 (W.D.Pa.1934), affirmed 76 F.2d 1014 (3d Cir.1935); Smith v. Simmons, 99 Colo. 227, 61 P.2d 589.

20. Lechner v. Halling, 35 Wn.2d 903, 216 P.2d 179 (1950).

21. See § 27, post.

set forth in a statute which is now adopted in all states and which is called either the Uniform Gifts to Minors Act or the Uniform Transfers to Minors Act. This custodian is an agent with powers fixed by statute, acting for a limited purpose. A trustee or guardian could be used for this purpose but this might involve undesirable expense and complexities.[22]

 WESTLAW REFERENCES

di agency

di(agency /s trust)

308k48

agent /s contract /s name /s principal /s liable

GUARDIANSHIP [1]

§ 17. Guardianship resembles trusteeship in that it is a fiduciary relation involving the management of property for another, but it is distinguished by the difference between the property interests of the two representatives, the status and interests the persons represented, and the origin of the two relationships.

Guardians (sometimes called committees, conservators, or curators) of the property of infants, spendthrifts, persons of unsound mind and other incompetents, resemble trustees by virtue of their fiduciary relation to their wards. Both guardians and trustees control and manage property for others, toward whom the most scrupulous unselfishness, honesty and good faith must be observed. The guardian, when functioning officially, must act solely for his ward and never in his own interest. If a guardian purchases outstanding claims against his ward's property, for example, he can derive no benefit therefrom. The purchase will inure to the benefit of the ward.[2]

A guardian is sometimes said to be a trustee.[3] It would be more accurate to state that he is a court-appointed representative for a person of subnormal capacity who is given powers of management and disposition over the property of his ward, but who does not have the "title" held by the equity trustee.[4] The guardian has possession and powers of disposition, but what is generally called "title" remains in the ward.[5] He is like a court-appointed agent. On the other hand, the

22. See Bogert, Trusts and Trustees (rev.2d edit.), § 15.

§ 17

1. Restatement, Trusts, Second, § 7.

To be distinguished from guardians of the person of incompetents, and guardians ad litem who act for individuals of less than normal capacity in litigation (Schuster v. Schuster, 75 Ariz. 20, 251 P.2d 631 (1952)).

2. Lee v. Fox, 6 Dana, Ky., 171, 176.

3. "The view I take of this case is that the relation of guardian and ward is strictly that of trustee and cestui que trust." Mathew v. Brise, 14 Beav. 341, 345.

4. Matter of Hawley, 104 N.Y. 250, 261, 10 N.E. 352.

5. Rollins v. Marsh, 128 Mass. 116, 118; Seilert v. McAnally, 223 Mo. 505, 515, 122 S.W. 1064, 135 Am.St.Rep. 522; Newton v. Nutt, 58 N.H. 599, 601; McDuffie v. McIntyre, 11 S.C. 551, 560, 32 Am. Rep. 500; Neblett v. Valentino, 127 Tex.

trustee is an owner and manager for others, title to the trust property being in the trustee, subject to an equitable interest in the beneficiary.

The wards for whom guardianships are created are persons of limited legal capacity, but no such requirement exists as to the beneficiaries of trusts.

Guardians are officers of the court that appoints them, or to which they are accountable, generally the probate or equity court.[6] Statutes state which court has the power to appoint, and in many instances prescribe the powers and duties of guardians.[7] Trustees are not usually court officers, even though they may be appointed by a court. They are usually appointed by the settlor.

The powers of joint guardians are held jointly, as are those of co-trustees.[8] The guardian should act in the name of the ward, followed by the words "by _____, guardian".[9] The trustee contracts or conveys in his own name, followed by the words "as trustee under the will of John Brown", or by similar language.

 WESTLAW REFERENCES

di guardianship

196k91/2

390k9

146k18

RECEIVERSHIP [1]

§ 18. **A receiver is not usually a trustee. He is a court officer appointed by the court of equity to manage property which it is seeking to conserve and administer. Neither the court nor the receiver has title to the property, although the court has possession and powers of management and disposition which it exercises through its agent (the receiver). The title remains in the person who is placed in receivership. If the court vests title in the receiver, as is sometimes done, the receiver becomes a court-controlled trustee.**

Receivers are like trustees in that they are fiduciaries, they manage property for others, and are subject to the jurisdiction of the court of chancery.

279, 92 S.W.2d 432 (1936); In re Paulsen's Guardianship, 229 Wis. 262, 282 N.W. 36 (1938).

6. Cobleigh v. Matheny, 181 Ill.App. 170.

7. See, for example, 20 Pa.C.S.A. §§ 5111–5167 (minors) and §§ 5501–5537 (incompetents).

8. Pepper v. Stone, 10 Vt. 427. But see Richardson v. Passumpsic Sav. Bank, 111 Vt. 181, 13 A.2d 184 (1940).

9. Fox v. Minor, 32 Cal. 111, 91 Am. Dec. 566.

§ 18

1. Restatement, Trusts, Second, § 16B.

A trustee in bankruptcy is not an equity trustee of the type herein discussed. He is vested with title to the property of a bankrupt by the bankruptcy court acting, under a federal statute. He is, however, a fiduciary.

When the estate of an insolvent is brought before it, and in other cases, equity sometimes appoints a receiver of the property in order to conserve it for appropriate distribution. Receivers have occasionally been referred to as "trustees".[2] They are undoubtedly fiduciaries governed by the same rules as to good faith and loyalty as trustees.[3] They also resemble trustees in that they are subject to the jurisdiction of a court of equity, and because their function is the management of property for the benefit of others.

But the ordinary receiver is not a trustee of the type herein discussed.[4] He is a court officer and must secure authority from the court for every act he does.[5] The "title" to the property being administered is in the insolvent debtor or other individual who had it prior to the receivership.[6] The creation of the receivership merely indicates that the court has taken the property into its possession in order to guard against wastage or improper usage,[7] and has assumed powers of management and disposition which it will exercise through an officer or agent, the receiver. A trustee is not usually an officer of the court, even though he may have been appointed by a court or his appointment by the settlor may have been approved by a court; his interests in the property he manages are greater than those of the usual receiver and are dignified by the name "title".

A receiver is more like an agent than a trustee. He does not contract or convey as a separate legal entity and is not ordinarily liable on contracts or conveyances.[8] He cannot sue or be sued except with consent of the court.[9] He is usually not held personally liable on his contracts or for torts not involving personal fault.[10] The powers of co-receivers are several and are not vested in them as a board or group,[11] whereas co-trustees usually hold their powers jointly.

Sometimes equity appoints a receiver and vests him with title. Either by court decree, conveyance or statute, the receiver gets all the

2. Byrnes v. Missouri Nat. Bank, 7 F.2d 978 (8th Cir.1925); Dawson v. Detweiler, 299 Mich. 613, 1 N.W.2d 11 (1941).

3. Patterson v. Woodward, 175 Ark. 300, 299 S.W. 619 (1927); Roller v. Paul, 106 Va. 214, 55 S.E. 558.

4. Loft, Inc. v. Guth, 25 Del. 363, 19 A.2d 721 (1941) (sequestrator); Harmon v. Best, 174 Ind. 323, 91 N.E. 19.

5. Strickland v. Williams, 215 Ga. 175, 109 S.E.2d 761 (1959); Nevitt v. Woodburn, 190 Ill. 283, 60 N.E. 500. And see Tobey v. Poulin, 141 Me. 58, 38 A.2d 826 (1944) (sales must be confirmed), petition denied 41 A.2d 376 (1945).

6. Pennsylvania Steel Co. v. New York City Ry. Co., 117 C.C.C. 503, 198 Fed. 721 (2d Cir.1912); Dietrich v. O'Brien, 122 Md. 482, 89 A. 717; Hannon v. Mechanics Bldg. & Loan Ass'n of Spartanburg, 177 S.C. 153, 180 S.E. 873, 100 A.L.R. 928 (1935).

7. In re Marcus, 21 F.2d 480 (D.Pa. 1924) (interference with receiver's control is contempt of court); Callaway v. Security Loan Corp., 249 Ala. 81, 29 So.2d 567 (1947) (property held by receiver not subject to garnishment since in custody of court).

8. McNulta v. Lochridge, 141 U.S. 327, 12 S.Ct. 11, 35 L.Ed. 796 (1891); Avey v. Burnley, 167 Ky. 26, 179 S.W. 1050; International Shoe Co. v. United States Fidelity & Guaranty Co., 186 S.C. 271, 195 S.E. 546 (1938).

9. Massey v. Camden & Tr. R. Co., 75 N.J.Eq. 1, 71 A. 241.

10. Rosso v. Freeman, 30 F.2d 826 (D.C.Mass.1929).

11. Marthias v. Segaloff, 187 Md. 690, 51 A.2d 654 (1947).

interests of the party whose estate is being managed, subject to a duty to manage them for the benefit of creditors, stockholders, or others. Here the receiver would seem to become a court-appointed trustee.[12]

 WESTLAW REFERENCES

di receivership

find 109 se2d 761

323k71

323k74

TRUST INTENT—PRECATORY EXPRESSIONS [1]

§ 19. Usually, if a transferor of property intends the transferee to be a trustee, he directs him to act in that capacity, but sometimes he merely expresses a wish or recommendation that the property given be used in whole or in part for the benefit of another. Words of this latter type are called "precatory" and are generally construed not to create a trust but instead to create at most an ethical obligation.

In a few special cases an intent to have a trust is found.

In weighing the effect of precatory expressions the courts consider the entire document and the circumstances of the donor, his family, and other interested parties.

Sometimes doubts arise as to whether a transferor of property intended the transferee to be a trustee of it because the transferor does not use directions or commands, or describe the donee as a trustee, but instead expresses a hope, wish, or recommendation that the property be used for the benefit of a third person. Such wordings are called "precatory". If, for example, instead of giving property to A "in trust for B," the owner devises it to A "with a request that A care for B from the income of such property," the latter expression of desire is usually held to be merely precatory.[2] In other cases the donor has used the words "desire,"[3] "wish,"[4] "hope,"[5] "recommend,"[6] "in confidence

12. Squire v. Princeton Lighting Co., 72 N.J.Eq. 883, 68 A. 176, 15 L.R.A.,N.S., 657; Mandeville v. Avery, 124 N.Y. 376, 26 N.E. 951 (receiver in proceedings supplementary to execution).

§ 19

1. Restatement, Trusts, Second, § 25.

2. In a few cases, where words of entreaty were alleged or held to have created a trust, the courts have used the phrase "precatory trust". Keplinger v. Keplinger, 185 Ind. 81, 113 N.E. 292; Hunt v. Hunt, 18 Wash. 14, 19, 50 P. 578. But it is submitted that it is more satisfactory to reserve the word "precatory" for the description of the expression to be construed. If the construction is that a trust is created, there is no object in distinguishing it from any other trust by calling it a "precatory" trust. Rigby, L.J., in In re Williams [1897] 2 Ch. 12, 27.

3. In re Browne's Estate, 175 Cal. 361, 165 P. 960; Hardy v. Hardy, 174 N.C. 505, 93 S.E. 976.

4. Sears v. Cunningham, 122 Mass. 538.

5. Van Duyne v. Van Duyne, 15 N.J. Eq. 503.

6. Gilbert v. Chapin, 19 Conn. 342.

that," [7] or "rely." [8] Whether a trust will be found cannot be concluded merely from the particular word or phrase employed.

The basic principle in the construction of precatory expressions is well stated by a distinguished judge. "The primary question in every case is the intention of the testator, and whether in the use of precatory words he meant merely to advise or influence the discretion of the devisee, or himself to control or direct the disposition intended." [9] In order that a trust may be created the settlor must have explicitly or impliedly expressed an intent to impose obligations on the trustee and not merely to give the donee of the property an option to use it for the benefit of another. [10]

The words "request," "desire," and the like, do not naturally import a legal obligation. But the early view in England was that such words, when used in a will, were to be given an unnatural meaning and were to be held courteous and softened statements expressing duties enforceable by the courts. [11] According to that opinion words of request prima facie created a trust. But since the beginning of the nineteenth century the English courts have changed their stand upon this question, and now hold that precatory words do not ordinarily show an intent to have a trust, but that such an intent may be shown by other portions of the instrument or by extrinsic circumstances. [12] The American courts have generally adopted this natural construction of precatory expressions. [13]

When it is alleged that precatory words showed an intent to have a trust, the courts consider the language of the entire instrument and all its provisions, and also the situation of the alleged settlor, his family, and the supposed beneficiaries of the trust at the times the will or other document was executed and went into effect. In view of all these facts and circumstances, was it natural and probable that the donor intended the donee to be bound by an enforceable obligation or was he to be free to use his judgment and discretion? [14]

7. People v. Powers, 83 Hun 449, 29 N.Y.S. 950, 31 N.Y.S. 1131; Buffum v. Town, 16 R.I. 643, 19 A. 112, 7 L.R.A. 386.

8. Blanchard v. Chapman, 22 Ill.App. 341; Willets v. Willets, 35 Hun, N.Y., 401.

9. Finch, J., in Phillips v. Phillips, 112 N.Y. 197, 205, 19 N.E. 411, 8 Am.St.Rep. 737.

10. Ponzelino v. Ponzelino, 238 Iowa 201, 26 N.W.2d 330 (1947).

11. Malim v. Keighley, 2 Ves.Jr. 333; Knight v. Knight, 3 Beav. 148.

This view is sometimes adopted in the case of words addressed to a widow. Knisely v. Simpson, 397 Ill. 605, 74 N.E.2d 695 (1947).

12. "Words of request in their ordinary meaning convey a mere request, and do not convey a legal obligation of any kind,

either at law or in equity. But in any particular case there may be circumstances which would oblige the court to say that such words have a meaning beyond their ordinary meaning and import a legal obligation." Lord Esher, in Hill v. Hill, [1897] 1 Q.B. 483, 486.

13. See, for example, Quickel v. Quickel, 261 N.C. 696, 136 S.E.2d 52 (1964); Burton v. Irwin, 212 Va. 104, 181 S.E.2d 624 (1971). There are decisions in New Jersey and West Virginia following the original English rule. Deacon v. Cobson, 83 N.J. Eq. 122, 89 A. 1029; Bankers' Trust Co. v. New York Women's League for Animals, 23 N.J.Super. 170, 92 A.2d 820 (1952); Hedrick v. Hedrick, 125 W.Va. 702, 25 S.E.2d 872 (1943).

14. See In re Estate of Pearson, 442 Pa. 172, 275 A.2d 336 (1971) (holographic

A failure on the part of the settlor to describe clearly the subject-matter of the supposed trust or the beneficiaries thereof is strong evidence that he did not intend a trust. Unless these elements, trust property and beneficiaries, are definite, the trust will be unenforceable even if it could come into being. A property owner will not be presumed to have disposed of his estate in an ineffectual and useless way. "Whenever the subject to be administered as trust property, and the objects for whose benefit it is to be administered, are to be found in a will, not expressly creating a trust, the indefinite nature and quantum of the subject, as well as the indefinite nature of the objects, are always used by the court as evidence that the mind of the testator was not to create a trust." [15] In many cases the uncertainty as to the property to be affected has influenced the courts to hold that no trust was intended by the precatory words,[16] while the lack of clarity regarding the beneficiaries has had a similar effect in other cases.[17]

If the alleged beneficiary has any moral claim on the supposed creator of the trust, and for this or other reasons the conditions are such that the latter would naturally provide for the former, the courts will tend to construe precatory words as creating a trust. Thus, in one case,[18] where the estate was large and given to the deceased's widow with a request that she care for the deceased's mother and sister for whom no other provision was made, the court held that the precatory words could be construed as showing an intent to have a trust.[19] Any hardship or unnatural result which would be involved in finding a trust or no trust will be influential with the court.[20]

Where a donor first makes an absolute gift of property, without restriction or limitation, and later inserts precatory language in a separate sentence or paragraph, the courts are apt to find that there was no intent to have a trust. Thus if the gift is first made to A "absolutely," [21] or "in his own right," [22] the courts will be inclined to

will). And see In re Kearns' Estate, 36 Cal.2d 531, 225 P.2d 218 (1950) (oral statements by a testator as to intended effect of precatory words not admissible).

15. Lines v. Darden, 5 Fla. 51, 73. Accord: Handley v. Wrightson, 60 Md. 198; Lucas v. Lockhart, 18 Miss. (10 Smedes & M.) 466, 48 Am.Dec. 766.

16. Bryan v. Milby, 6 Del.Ch. 208, 24 A. 333, 13 L.R.A. 563; Coulson v. Alpaugh, 163 Ill. 298, 45 N.E. 216.

17. Seymour v. Sanford, 86 Conn. 516, 86 A. 7; In re Gardner, 140 N.Y. 122, 35 N.E. 439; In re Roger's Estate, 245 Pa. 206, 91 A. 351, L.R.A.1917A, 168. And see Rich v. Witherspoon, 208 S.W.2d 674 (Tex.Civ. App.1948) (trustees to pay former employees of testator such sums as should be fair and within the means of the trust).

18. Colton v. Colton, 127 U.S. 300, 8 S.Ct. 1164, 32 L.Ed. 138 (1888).

19. See also Foster v. Willson, 68 N.H. 241, 38 A. 1003, 73 Am.St.Rep. 581 (a parent); Warner v. Bates, 98 Mass. 274 (a child); Collister v. Fassitt, 163 N.Y. 281, 57 N.E. 490, 79 Am.St.Rep. 586 (a niece).

20. In re Humphrey's Estate, (1916) 1 Ir.Rep.Ch.D. 21 (a trust finding would exclude a posthumous child without reason).

21. Haight v. Royce, 274 Ill. 162, 113 N.E. 71; Riechauer v. Born, 151 Iowa 456, 131 N.W. 705; Williams v. Worthington, 49 Md. 572, 33 Am.Rep. 286; Bacon v. Ransom, 139 Mass. 117, 29 N.E. 473; Noe v. Kern, 93 Mo. 367, 6 S.W. 239, 3 Am.St.Rep. 544; Carter v. Strickland, 165 N.C. 69, 80 S.E. 961, Ann.Cas.1915D, 416; Ringe v. Kellner, 99 Pa. 460; Comford v. Cantrell, 177 Tenn. 553, 151 S.W.2d 1076 (1941) (gift-

22. See note 22 on page 44.

construe later precatory words to have no legal effect. So, too, if to create a trust from the precatory words would be repugnant to other provisions of the instrument which are of undisputed validity,[23] the precatory words will be given no obligatory effect.

Frequently the precatory language is addressed by a testator to his executor as such. In this case the courts are inclined to find an intent to create a trust.[24] If the executor is also a legatee under the will, it may be important to notice whether the request is made to him as executor or as legatee, since in the latter instance the tendency to treat the words as precatory only would apply.[25]

 WESTLAW REFERENCES

di precatory
intent /s trust /s precatory
trust /s intent /s desire wish hope
390k112
409k467

TRUST INTENT—SAVINGS ACCOUNT TRUSTS [1]

§ 20. That one has deposited his money in a financial institution and directed that the account be entitled "in trust" for another does not necessarily prove that the depositor intended to make a gift by means of a present, irrevocable trust. He may have intended to create no trust, but instead to use the beneficiary's name for the purpose of dividing his bank deposits for purposes deemed beneficial to himself. Or he may have intended no present trust, but rather that the account should be held in trust in the future, if left standing until the depositor's death or some other event. Or he may have

to wife to be her absolute estate forever, followed by words of request as to devising the property to other relatives).

22. Frierson v. General Assembly of Presbyterian Church of U.S., 7 Tenn., (7 Heisk.) 683.

23. Clay v. Wood, 153 N.Y. 134, 47 N.E. 274.

24. In re Burris' Estate, 12 Cal.Rptr. 298, 190 Cal.App.2d 582 (1961); In re Moody's Will, 155 Me. 325, 154 A.2d 165, 73 A.L.R.2d 1225 (1959); In re McKay's Estate, 357 Mich. 447, 98 N.W.2d 604 (1959).

25. In re Collias' Estate, 37 Cal.2d 587, 233 P.2d 554; In re Charowhas' Estates, 181 Kan. 322, 310 P.2d 947 (1957).

§ 20

1. Restatement, Trusts, Second, § 58.

In discussions of this subject the phrase "tentative trust" is often used, sometimes as meaning an incomplete trust and in other cases as indicating a complete but revocable trust. Because of its ambiguity the phrase is not recommended.

The words "Totten trust" are often employed because a leading case on the subject is Matter of Totten, 179 N.Y. 112, 71 N.E. 748.

The rules apply to accounts in savings and loan associations as well as in banks. See Fleck v. Baldwin, 141 Tex. 340, 172 S.W.2d 975 (1943), and statutes cited in Bogert, Trusts and Trustees (rev. 2d edit.) § 47.

For law review discussion, see 53 Col. L.R. 103; 29 Conn.B.J. 1; 10 Univ.Fla.L.R. 235; 32 Pa.B.A.Q. 55; 9 Kan.L.R. 46; 53 Ill.B.J. 918; 49 Notre Dame Lawyer 686. And see 64 A.L.R.3rd 187.

intended a present trust of a defeasible interest, subject to a power of revocation in the depositor.

The courts resolve these uncertainties by a consideration of the situation of the depositor and his relation to the supposed beneficiary at the time of the deposit, and the conduct of both parties at the time of and after opening of the account.

Statutes in force in most states establish certain presumptions with respect to ownership and use of such an account and protect the financial institution making payments from the account.

Under the elementary principles concerning the creation of trusts previously stated, it might be assumed that the mere deposit of money in a bank or other financial institution by A to the credit of "A, in trust for B" would lead inevitably to the establishment of a trust. The depositor calls himself a trustee of specific trust property, the claim against the bank. His declaration is communicated to a third party, namely an officer of the bank. The beneficiary is clearly identified. No further formality is required.

However certain practical considerations have led the courts to treat such a deposit as ambiguous and as possibly indicating no real trust intent.[2] The trust form may be used by the depositor to attempt to conceal his property for tax or other reasons,[3] or to avoid a limitation on the size of a single savings bank account,[4] or to secure greater interest,[5] or to split up his bank deposits for the purpose of qualification for federal deposit insurance protection where the dollar amount of a single protected account is limited,[6] or in some other way as indicating an intent to use the beneficiary named in the title of the account as a mere dummy or straw man.[7]

For the purpose of deciding whether the account represents a real or fictitious trust the courts rely on various types of evidence. If the depositor made statements regarding the account at the time of the deposit or later (other than those connected with setting up the deposit), these may be determinative for or against a genuine trust intent.[8] And so too, notice to the beneficiary of the existence of the account given by

---

2. Beaver v. Beaver, 117 N.Y. 421, 430, 431, 22 N.E. 940, 6 L.R.A. 403, 15 Am.St. Rep. 531.

3. Mabie v. Bailey, 95 N.Y. 206; Connecticut River Sav. Bank v. Albee's Estate, 64 Vt. 571, 25 A. 487, 33 Am.St.Rep. 944.

4. Brabrook v. Boston Five Cents Sav. Bank, 104 Mass. 228, 6 Am.Rep. 222 (no trust).

5. Weber v. Weber, 58 How.Prac., N.Y., 255.

6. Cook v. Cook, 331 S.W.2d 77 (Tex. Civ.App.).

7. Stamford Sav. Bank v. Everett, 132 Conn. 92, 42 A.2d 662 (1945) (trust form for mere convenience of depositor).

8. Trust intended: Booth v. Oakland Bank of Savings, 122 Cal. 19, 54 P. 370; Littig v. Vestry of Mt. Calvary Protestant Episcopal Church, 101 Md. 494, 61 A. 635.

No trust intended: Merigan v. McGonigle, 205 Pa. 321, 54 A. 994.

Savings accounts in the name of decedent as trustee for others had been subject to the decedent's full control during his lifetime and therefore were required to be inventoried in decedent's estate. The purported beneficiaries had no knowledge of the accounts until decedent's death. In re Estate of Hoffman, 175 Ohio St. 363, 195 N.E.2d 106 (1963).

the depositor,[9] or delivery of the passbook to the alleged beneficiary [10] tend strongly to show an intent to have an actual trust, as does the fact that the beneficiary was a natural object of the bounty of the depositor or had been favored by him.[11] On the other hand if the beneficiary named was a stranger or remotely related, so that a gift to him was unnatural,[12] or the financial status of the depositor was such that he could not prudently afford to make a gift of the account,[13] the courts will be inclined to hold that there was no real trust intent.

In a few cases, where a married man has created a savings bank trust in favor of one other than his wife but has reserved large powers to himself, and the intent was to deprive his wife of the property to which she would be entitled at the husband's death, it has been held that the trust was "illusory" and merely colorable, and that the account was a part of the estate of the husband at his death and the rights of his widow attached to it.[14]

If a court finds that the intent of the depositor was to create a trust, the question may arise as to the time of the origin of this trust,

---

The depositor may testify as to his intent. Sayre v. Weil, 94 Ala. 466, 10 So. 546, 15 L.R.A. 544.

An admission by the beneficiary named in the account may prevent him from claiming a trust. Barefield v. Rosell, 177 N.Y. 387, 69 N.E. 732, 101 Am.St.Rep. 814.

9. Peck v. Scofield, 186 Mass. 108, 71 N.E. 109; Farleigh v. Cadman, 159 N.Y. 169, 53 N.E. 808.

It is usually held that notice by the depositor to the beneficiary of the existence of the deposit is not necessary to the creation of the trust. In re Podhajsky's Estate, 137 Iowa 742, 115 N.W. 590; Milholland v. Whalen, 89 Md. 212, 43 A. 43, 44 L.R.A. 485.

However, the Massachusetts courts have been inclined to hold that no trust of the account will be found unless the depositor gave notice to the beneficiary or some other person. Cleveland v. Hampden Savings Bank, 182 Mass. 110, 111, 65 N.E. 27. And see Greeley v. Flynn, 310 Mass. 23, 36 N.E.2d 394 (1941); Cohen v. Newton Sav. Bank, 320 Mass. 90, 67 N.E.2d 748, 168 A.L.R. 1321 (1946); Day Trust Co. v. Malden Sav. Bank, 328 Mass. 576, 105 N.E.2d 363 (1952).

10. In re Farrell, 298 N.Y. 129, 81 N.E.2d 51 (1948); Imperatrice v. Imperatrice, 298 N.Y. 549, 81 N.E.2d 95 (1948).

Delivery of the book to the beneficiary is not necessary in order to create a trust. Retention of the book by the depositor-trustee is natural. Milholland v. Whalen, 89 Md. 212, 43 A. 43, 44 L.R.A. 205; Merigan v. McGonigle, 205 Pa. 321, 54 A. 994.

11. Garrigus v. Burnett, 9 Ind. 528 (granddaughter); Farleigh v. Cadman, 159 N.Y. 169, 53 N.E. 808 (adopted daughter); Jenkins v. Baker, 77 App.Div. 509, 78 N.Y.S. 1074 (husband); Merigan v. McGonigle, 205 Pa. 321, 54 A. 994 (person in position of daughter).

12. Rambo v. Pile, 220 Pa. 235, 69 A. 807.

13. Kosloskye v. Cis, 70 Cal.App.2d 174, 160 P.2d 565 (1945); Weber v. Weber, 58 How.Prac., N.Y., 255.

14. For holdings to this effect, see Mushaw v. Mushaw, 183 Md. 511, 39 A.2d 465 (1944); Krause v. Krause, 285 N.Y. 27, 32 N.E.2d 779 (1941); Montgomery v. Michaels, 54 Ill.2d 532, 301 N.E.2d 465 (1973), replaced by Ill.R.S. c. 110½ ¶¶ 601, 602 (fraud test); Sullivan v. Burkin, 390 Mass. 864, 460 N.E.2d 572 (1984).

But see Jeruzal's Estate v. Jeruzal, 269 Minn. 183, 130 N.W.2d 473 (1964) (Totten trusts upheld; test is good faith creation with intent to divest settlor of ownership).

In several states there are statutes to the effect that a revocable trust (including a Totten trust) will be treated as a testamentary disposition insofar as the statutory rights of a surviving spouse are concerned. See, for example, N.Y.—McKinney's EPTL 5–1.1(b)(1); 20 Pa.C.S.A. § 6111. And see Unif.Prob.Code § 2–202; 39 A.L.R.3rd at page 14.

But see In re Halpern's Estate, 303 N.Y. 33, 100 N.E.2d 120 (test of validity whether good faith divestment of property ownership).

whether it was to begin at the time of the deposit or at some future time (for example, the date of the depositor's death). Usually the expectation of the depositor is that he is to have the power during his life to collect interest on the deposit or to withdraw any part or all of the principal for his own use, and that the beneficiary is to get only the balance of the account at the time of the depositor's death. The courts could hold that this intent meant that no interest in the account should pass to the beneficiary until the death of the depositor, and that the creation of the trust amounted to the making of a will and would be invalid unless it met the requirements of the statutes regarding the execution of wills (a signed and witnessed writing).[15] However, the general view has been that if there was a real trust intent, it was intended to vest an immediate interest in the beneficiary, subject to defeasance by a withdrawal of interest or principal during the depositor's life.[16] Thus the transaction usually has not been regarded as testamentary.[17]

It is generally held that if the depositor has not revoked the trust during his life or by his will, the person named as beneficiary is entitled to the balance of the account existing at the death of the depositor.[18] If the beneficiary dies before the depositor and the account is left standing in its original form it may show that no real trust was intended.[19]

The general view that the savings bank trust is not testamentary does not, of course, prevent legislatures from providing that it involves a gift taking effect at the death of the depositor and so is subject to estate or inheritance taxation.[20]

If a court finds that the deposit of money in trust for another shows an intent to have an immediate trust of a defeasible interest, the question may arise whether the depositor had a power to revoke the trust and exercised that power. Contrary to the usual holding that no power of revocation exists unless it is expressly reserved,[21] the courts

---

15. In a few cases the transaction has been held to have been testamentary. See, for example, Reynolds v. Reynolds, 325 Mass. 257, 90 N.E.2d 338 (1950); Malley's Estate v. Malley, 69 R.I. 407, 34 A.2d 761 (1943).

The savings bank trust is often called the "poor man's will", since persons of modest means are able to use it to accomplish the same practical results as those which would be achieved by the making of a will.

16. Wilder v. Howard, 188 Ga. 426, 4 S.E.2d 199 (1939).

17. Bierau v. Bohemian Bldg., Loan & Sav. Ass'n, 205 Md. 456, 109 A.2d 120 (1954); Appeal of Pavlinko's Estate, 399 Pa. 536, 160 A.2d 554; Smith v. Deshaw, 116 Vt. 441, 78 A.2d 479 (1951).

18. Bank of America Nat. Trust & Savings Ass'n v. Hazelbud, 21 Cal.App.2d

109, 68 P.2d 385 (1937); Seymour v. Seymour, 85 So.2d 726 (Fla.1956); Wilder v. Howard, 188 Ga. 426, 4 S.E.2d 199 (1939); Bath Sav. Inst. v. Hathorn, 88 Me. 122, 33 A. 836, 32 L.R.A. 377, 51 Am.St.Rep. 382; Bradford v. Eutaw Sav. Bank of Baltimore City, 186 Md. 127, 46 A.2d 284 (1946); Fiocchi v. Smith, N.J.Ch., 97 A. 283; Fowler v. Bowery Sav. Bank, 113 N.Y. 450, 21 N.E. 172, 4 L.R.A. 145, 10 Am.St.Rep. 479; Petition of Atkinson, 16 R.I. 413, 16 A. 712, 3 L.R.A. 392, 27 Am.St.Rep. 745.

19. Garvey v. Clifford, 114 App.Div. 193, 99 N.Y.S. 555; Rambo v. Pile, 220 Pa. 235, 69 A. 807.

20. Wasserman v. C.I.R., 139 F.2d 778 (1st Cir.1944); Hasbrouck v. Martin, 120 N.J.Eq. 96, 183 A. 735 (1936).

21. See § 148, post.

have usually found that there is an implied power of revocation of savings bank trusts [22] which may be exercised by a change in the title of the account,[23] or by withdrawal of the entire balance,[24] or by an expression of intent otherwise to destroy the trust,[25] for example, by making a will which gives the account to another than the trust beneficiary.[26] Assuming that such a power is impliedly reserved, it would seem that it might be negatived or released by an act of the depositor which indicated an intent to treat the rights of the beneficiary as absolute, for example, by the delivery of the passbook to the beneficiary.[27]

The consequences of a deposit in trust are now often determined by an express stipulation in the contract between the bank and the depositor at the time of the making of the deposit to the effect that, unless notified to the contrary, the bank is relieved from liability by paying the amount of the account to the beneficiary after the depositor has died.[28] Statutes to this effect have been widely adopted.[29] These and other statutes dealing with "multiple party accounts" that are in effect in most states also establish certain presumptions with respect to ownership, use and disposition of such accounts, both during the lifetimes of the parties and on the death of one of the parties.[30]

 WESTLAW REFERENCES

"tentative trust"

"totten trust"

22. Evinger v. MacDougall, 28 Cal. App.2d 175, 82 P.2d 194 (1938); In re Ingel's Estate, 372 Pa. 171, 92 A.2d 881 (1952) (presumptively revocable; burden on beneficiary to show otherwise).

23. Conry v. Maloney, 5 N.J. 590, 76 A.2d 899 (1950); In re Bulwinkle, 107 App. Div. 331, 95 N.Y.S. 176.

24. In re Totten, 179 N.Y. 112, 71 N.E. 748.

25. In re Rodger's Estate, 374 Pa. 246, 97 A.2d 789, 38 A.L.R.2d 1238 (1953) (oral statement to lawyer who drew will).

If the settlor had a power of revocation and became incompetent, the court may direct withdrawals when the settlor is in need. Rickel v. Peck, 211 Minn. 576, 2 N.W.2d 140, 138 A.L.R. 1375 (1942); Ganley v. Lincoln Sav. Bk., 257 App.Div. 509, 13 N.Y.S.2d 571 (1939).

26. In re Schrier's Estate, 145 Misc. 593, 260 N.Y.S. 610 (1932); In re Scanlon's Estate, 313 Pa. 424, 169 A. 106 (1933).

An express gift by will of the account to another than the beneficiary is revocation. In re Beck's Estate, 260 App.Div. 651, 23 N.Y.S.2d 525 (1940). But a gift of the residue of the depositor's estate, without mention of the account, is generally held not to constitute revocation. Brucks v. Home Fed. Sav. & Loan Ass'n., 36 Cal.2d 845, 228 P.2d 545 (1951) (ordinarily the will must expressly mention the account, if there is to be revocation); In re Pozzuto's Estate, 124 Pa.Super. 93, 188 A. 209 (1936) (power not exercised by general residuary clause in will of depositor).

27. In re Farrell, 298 N.Y. 129, 81 N.E.2d 51 (1948); Stockert v. Dry Dock Sav. Inst., 155 App.Div. 123, 139 N.Y.S. 986; Matter of Davis, 119 App.Div. 35, 103 N.Y.S. 946.

28. Walso v. Latterner, 140 Minn. 455, 168 N.W. 353 (rule printed in pass book).

29. For citations to the statutes on this subject, see Bogert, Trusts and Trustees (rev. 2d edit.), § 47. See, for example, Ark. S. § 67–1840; Tenn.Code Ann. § 45–2–704. And see Howard Sav. Inst. v. Kielb, 38 N.J. 186, 183 A.2d 401 (1962) (statutory presumption that depositor intended balance at his death to go to beneficiary is constitutional).

30. See Unif.Prob.Code §§ 6–101 to 6–201, adopted in at least 10 states; and see 20 Pa.C.S.A. §§ 6303–6304.

intent /s creat* * * /s "savings account" /s trust

390k1

390k59(1) /p "savings trust"

find 301 ne2d 465

"poor man's will"

FORMALITY—STATUTE OF FRAUDS [1]

§ 21. In England, prior to 1677, there was no statute making a writing necessary to the creation of trusts.

The seventh section of the English Statute of Frauds, enacted in 1677, required express trusts of real property to be "manifested and proved" by a writing signed by the party declaring the trust.

A great majority of American states have passed similar statutes, though with many minor variations. In a few jurisdictions parol trusts in land are enforceable if proved by clear and convincing evidence.

Implied trusts and trusts of personal property have always been, both in England and America, provable by oral evidence.

In some cases part performance of the trust by the trustee, or action by the beneficiary in reliance on the enforceability of the trust, renders an oral trust of realty enforceable.

The statute makes oral trusts of realty voidable only, not void. Only the trustee or his successor in interest may plead the statute. No one can object to performance of the oral trust by the trustee.

Any writing, however informal, is sufficient to satisfy the statute, if it contains a complete statement of the essential express terms of the trust and is signed or subscribed by the proper party.

Prior to 1677 there was no statute in England specifically concerned with a requirement that trusts be created with any formality. The rules of conveyancing as to real estate imposed indirectly certain requisites as to the method of creating trusts of land.

In 1677 parliament adopted the Statute of Frauds,[2] and its seventh section provided that "all declarations or creations of trusts or confidences of any lands, tenements or hereditaments, shall be manifested and proved by some writing signed by the party who is by law enabled to declare such trust, or by his last will in writing, or else they shall be utterly void and of none effect." This section has been adopted, with modifications, by the majority of American states.[3] The general rule in

---

§ 21

1. Restatement, Trusts, Second, §§ 39–52.

2. St. 29, Chas. II, c. 3. For a discussion of the origin of the statute, see Hening, 61 Pa.Law Rev. 283. See, Law of Property Act of 1925, for the modern sub-stitute for the original statute. 15 Geo. V.C. 20, § 53.

3. A similar section is to be found in the following jurisdictions: Alabama, Alaska, Arkansas, California, Colorado, District of Columbia, Florida, Georgia, Idaho, Illinois, Indiana, Iowa, Kansas, Louisiana,

the United States is that express trusts of real property created by a settlor during his lifetime must be proved or created by a writing.

The eighth section of the English Statute of Frauds expressly exempts from the operation of the seventh section trusts which "arise or result by implication or construction of law." [4] This exception has been generally adopted in the United States. These are the implied trusts, the creation of which is considered later.[5] Thus resulting and constructive trusts are free from any statutory requirement that they be created or proved by written evidence, even though they concern real property.

The seventh section of the English Statute of Frauds applies only to trusts of "lands, tenements and hereditaments," and the American re-

Maine, Maryland, Massachusetts, Michigan, Minnesota, Mississippi, Missouri, Montana, Nebraska, Nevada, New Hampshire, New Jersey, New York, North Dakota, Oklahoma, Oregon, Pennsylvania, Rhode Island, South Carolina, South Dakota, Texas (since 1943), Utah, Vermont, and Wisconsin. For statutory citations, see Bogert, Trusts and Trustees (rev. 2d edit.), § 62.

In other American jurisdictions the seventh section of the statute has not been expressly reenacted, but in some of these states a writing is required nevertheless. This is true in Arizona, Connecticut, Delaware, Hawaii, Kentucky, New Mexico, North Carolina, Ohio, Tennessee, Texas (until 1943), Virginia, Washington, West Virginia, and Wyoming.

In Arizona an express oral trust of realty will not be enforced, although the seventh section of the statute has not been adopted. Rogers v. Greer, 70 Ariz. 264, 219 P.2d 760 (1950).

In Connecticut the court seems to treat parol trusts as unenforceable. Wilson v. Warner, 84 Conn. 560, 80 A. 718. Delaware seems to have no substitute for the seventh section. Rentoul v. Sweeney, 15 Del.Ch. 302, 137 A. 74 (1927); Ross v. Ellis, 34 Del.Ch. 533, 106 A.2d 775 (1954) (parol trust of realty enforceable). In Kentucky apparently a parol declaration of trust is unenforceable, although on a transfer it may be proved by oral evidence that the grantee was to be a trustee. Huff v. Byers, 209 Ky. 375, 272 S.W. 897 (1925).

As to Louisiana, see R.S. 9:1753 (no particular form of words or conduct necessary to manifest an intent to create a trust).

In New Mexico the seventh section seems to be enforced, although not expressly re-enacted. Eagle Mining & Imp. Co. v. Hamilton, 14 N.M. 271, 91 P. 718. As to

the situation in North Carolina, see Lord & Van Hecke, Parol Trusts in North Carolina, 8 N.C.L.R. 152. Oral declarations of realty trusts are unenforceable, but oral agreements by transferees are enforced. Rhodes v. Baxter, 242 N.C. 206, 87 S.E.2d 265 (1955); Roberson v. Pruden, 242 N.C. 632, 89 S.E.2d 250 (1955). In Ohio parol trusts in land seem to be permitted. Mannix v. Purcell, 46 Ohio St. 102, 19 N.E. 572, 2 L.R.A. 753, 15 Am.St.Rep. 562, but see Ohio Rev.Code, § 1335.04. Oral evidence is usable to establish an express trust of realty in Tennessee. Hunt v. Hunt, 169 Tenn. 1, 80 S.W.2d 666 (1935). In Texas no writing was required prior to 1943. Bennett v. McKrell, 125 S.W.2d 701 (Tex.Civ. App.1939), judgment reformed on other grounds, 135 Tex. 557, 144 S.W.2d 242 (1940). But the Texas Trust Act of 1943 required a writing. See V.Tex.C.A.Prop. Code § 122.004. Broden v. Broden, 330 S.W.2d 674 (Tex.Civ.App.1959).

Virginia seems to be free from formality requirements. Fleenor v. Hensley, 121 Va. 367, 93 S.E. 582; 17 Va.L.R. 611. In Washington a section about contracts to convey realty has been held to cover trusts. In re Swartwood's Estate, 198 Wash. 557, 89 P.2d 203 (1939). As to West Virginia, see W.Va.Code, 36–1–4. And see Hoglund v. Curtis, 134 W.Va. 735, 61 S.E.2d 642 (1950) (oral evidence may be used to prove a grantee in an absolute deed was to hold in trust for the grantor or a third person).

In those states where there is no re-enactment of the seventh section the courts often hold that the oral evidence of an express trust of realty must be "clear and convincing". Union Bank & Tr. Co. v. Rice, 279 Ky. 629, 131 S.W.2d 493 (1939); Paul v. Neece, 244 N.C. 565, 94 S.E.2d 596 (1956).

4. St.29 Chas. II, c. 3.

5. See §§ 71, 72 and 78, post.

enactments apply only to trusts of realty. Trusts of leasehold interests in land are within the Statute.[6] In most states trusts of personal property may be created and proved without a writing.[7]

The enforceability of a trust is determined by the nature of the subjectmatter at the time the attempt to create it was made. Thus if the subject matter of an oral trust is originally realty, the trust is unenforceable even though the land is sold and the trustee gets money for it.[8] And if the oral trust had for its subject-matter stocks and bonds, and these are sold and the proceeds invested by the trustee in land, the trust will be enforceable against the land.[9] If one accepts an oral trust of land, and at the same time orally agrees that if he sells the land he will hold the proceeds in trust, many cases hold that there is an enforceable contract to hold personalty in trust which will apply to the sale proceeds if and when received.[10] If an oral trustee of land sells it, and orally admits that he holds the proceeds in trust for another, there is an enforceable trust as to the proceeds, although there would not have been as to the realty. The voluntary declaration is of itself an act of trust creation.[11]

If under the terms of the trust the beneficiary is to have possession of the trust land, and after the creation of the trust the beneficiary does take possession with the consent of the trustee, takes the benefits of the property, and makes improvements or repairs, or pays taxes, some courts hold that the trustee may not thereafter set up the Statute of Frauds.[12] This is sometimes explained by the phrase "part perform-

---

6. Forster v. Hale, 3 Ves.Jr. 696; Skett v. Whitmore, 2 Freeman 280. In accord, see, Weiner v. Mullaney, 59 Cal.App.2d 620, 140 P.2d 704 (1943); Callihan v. Bander, 117 Ind.App. 467, 73 N.E.2d 360 (1947); Smith v. Hainline, Mo., 253 S.W. 1049; Christian Moerlein Brewing Co. v. Rusch, 272 Pa. 181, 116 A. 145 (1922); Hunter Co. v. Fain, 281 S.W.2d 750 (Tex.Civ.App.1955) (oil and gas leases). A trust of a bond and mortgage on real estate is not subject to the statute. Hartman v. Loverud, 227 Wis. 6, 277 N.W. 641 (1938). A trust of the interest of a contract vendee of an enforceable land contract is within the statute. Brooks v. Gillow, 352 Mich. 189, 89 N.W.2d 457 (1958).

7. Noble v. Learned, 153 Cal. 245, 94 P. 1047; People v. Schaefer, 266 Ill. 334, 107 N.E. 617; Bradford v. Eastman, 229 Mass. 499, 118 N.E. 879; Harris Banking Co. v. Miller, 190 Mo. 640, 89 S.W. 629, 1 L.R.A.,N.S., 790; Day v. Roth, 18 N.Y. 448; In re Washington's Estate, 220 Pa. 204, 69 A. 747; Dupont v. Jonet, 165 Wis. 554, 162 N.W. 664.

The Georgia statute requires a writing in order to make enforceable any trust, whether of realty or personalty. Alston v. McGonigal, 179 Ga. 617, 176 S.E. 632

(1934). Statutes enacted in Indiana, Louisiana and Oregon are to the same effect. And see § 11, ante.

8. Alexander v. Spaulding, 160 Ind. 176, 66 N.E. 694.

9. Eadie v. Hamilton, 94 Kan. 214, 146 P. 323.

10. Chace v. Gardner, 228 Mass. 533, 117 N.E. 841; Bork v. Martin, 132 N.Y. 230, 30 N.E. 584, 28 Am.St.Rep. 570, 43 N.Y.St.Rep. 938. But see, *contra*, McGinness v. Barton, 71 Iowa 644, 33 N.W. 152; Glieberman v. Fine, 248 Mich. 8, 226 N.W. 669 (1929); Marvel v. Marvel, 70 Neb. 498, 97 N.W. 640, 113 Am.St.Rep. 792.

11. Westcott v. Sharp, 256 Ala. 418, 54 So.2d 758 (1951); Collar v. Collar, 86 Mich. 507, 49 N.W. 551, 13 L.R.A. 621; Cooper v. Thomason, 30 Or. 161, 45 P. 296.

12. Spies v. Price, 91 Ala. 166, 8 So. 405; Goff v. Goff, 98 Kan. 700, 158 P. 662. For cases of this type, see Stewart v. Damron, 63 Ariz. 158, 160 P.2d 321 (1945); Maddox v. Rainoldi, 163 Cal.App.2d 384, 329 P.2d 599 (1958); Muller v. Sobol, 277 App.Div. 884, 97 N.Y.S.2d 905 (1950) reargument and appeal denied 277 App.Div. 951, 99 N.Y.S.2d 757 (1950); Poe v. Poe, 208 Okl. 406, 256 P.2d 153 (1952).

ance", but may also be said to be based on an estoppel against the
trustee to deny the enforceability of the trust. A similar holding exists
with regard to oral contracts to convey an interest in land. Some
courts also consider that the doctrine of part performance is to be
applied where the trustee for a time carries out the oral trust and later
sets up the Statute of Frauds.[13] His conduct is said to corroborate the
oral evidence that he was a trustee and to make it inequitable that he
should rely on the statute.

The express wording of the English statute and of many of its
American counterparts lead to the belief that oral trusts in land are
null and wholly unenforceable under all conditions. The wording is
that they are "utterly void and of none effect." [14] But in line with the
construction of other sections of the same statute, it has been generally
held that "void" in this connection means "voidable" and that the oral
trust may be carried out or enforced, if the parties are willing and raise
no objection to the lack of written evidence.[15]

Thus, if the trustee desires, he may fail to raise the defense of the
Statute of Frauds, and the trust will be enforced against him; and, if
the trust is completely carried out by the trustee, the validity of acts
performed under it will not be open to question. If a father conveys
realty to a son on an oral promise by the son that he will hold the land
in trust to convey it to his mother after the father's death, and the son
makes such conveyance, the creditors of the son have no standing to
attack the validity of the trust.[16] The son having seen fit to carry it
out, the effect is the same as if the trust had been declared with due
formality. Neither creditors or a trustee in bankruptcy [17] nor a
spouse [18] of the oral trustee has ground for setting aside a conveyance
by such trustee to his beneficiary. If the oral trust is not avoided, it is
as valid as a trust complying with the Statute.[19]

The trustee may avoid performance by refusing to carry out the
trust and by pleading the Statute as a defense if he is sued for
performance of the trust. Only the trustee or those succeeding to his
interest in the trust property can plead the Statute of Frauds.[20]

13. Feeney v. Howard, 79 Cal. 525, 21
P. 984, 4 L.R.A. 826, 12 Am.St.Rep. 162;
Bushner v. Bushner, 134 Colo. 509, 307
P.2d 204 (1957); Pearson v. Pearson, 125
Ind. 341, 25 N.E. 342. But see Andrew v.
State Bank of Blairsburg, 209 Iowa 1149,
229 N.W. 819 (1930). See Harrington, Part
Performance of Oral Trusts, 30 Mich.L.R.
289.

14. St.29 Chas. II, c. 3, § 7.

15. Myers v. Myers, 167 Ill. 52, 47 N.E.
309; Forest v. Rogers, 128 Mo.App. 6, 106
S.W. 1105.

16. Arntson v. First Nat. Bank of Sheldon, 39 N.D. 408, 167 N.W. 760. For a
similar case, see DeVol v. Citizen's Bank,
92 Or. 696, 179 P. 282.

17. Owings v. Laugharn, 53 Cal.App.
789, 128 P.2d 114 (1942); Hays v. Regar,
102 Ind. 524, 1 N.E. 386; Perkins v. Hilton,
329 Mass. 291, 107 N.E.2d 822 (1952).

18. Lehman v. Pierce, 109 Ind.App.
497, 36 N.E.2d 952 (1941).

19. Polk v. Boggs, 122 Cal. 114, 54 P.
536; King v. Bushnell, 121 Ill. 656, 13 N.E.
245; Stringer v. Montgomery, 111 Ind. 489,
12 N.E. 474; Bailey v. Wood, 211 Mass. 37,
97 N.E. 902; Lasley v. Delano, 139 Mich.
602, 102 N.W. 1063; Robbins v. Robbins, 89
N.Y. 251; Blaha v. Borgman, 142 Wis. 43,
124 N.W. 1047.

20. Lach v. Weber, 123 N.J.Eq. 303,
197 A. 417 (1938); Faunce v. McCorkle, 321
Pa. 116, 183 A. 926 (1936). The federal

Although some American re-enactments of the seventh section state that the trust of realty must be "created" or "declared" by a writing, in most states it is sufficient that the trust be "proved" by a writing, and hence a document prepared after the creation of the trust is sufficient.[21] The writing must contain a complete statement of the terms of the trust which were expressly agreed upon.[22] Where there is no identification of the trust res, for example, where the memorandum is defective,[23] but that the length of the trust period is not stated in the memorandum is not important,[24] it being implied that the trust will last as long as necessary to accomplish its purpose.

Since in most states the writing is merely required to "manifest or prove" the existence of the trust, it may be made before, or concurrently with, or after the creation of the trust, and need not be the document that is alleged to create the trust.[25] But there are holdings that the memorandum of the trust must be made before action is brought to enforce it, although this seems illogical.[26]

With respect to the party who has the capacity to make and sign a writing manifesting the trust, and making it enforceable, the memorandum may be made by the settlor before or at the time of the trust creation,[27] and by the trustee before, at the time, or after he receives title.[28] In the case of declarations of trust, it is obvious that only the declarant can execute the memorandum.[29] In the case of inter vivos transfers to trustees, a writing prepared in anticipation of the transfer and signed by either the transferor or transferee should be adequate.[30] A statement of the trust in the instrument of transfer should be sufficient,[31] as should a statement in a separate document prepared and signed by the settlor or trustee at the time of the transfer.[32] Writings

bankruptcy Code (1978) permits a trustee in bankruptcy of a trustee under an oral trust to take advantage of the statute. 11 U.S.C.A. § 541(e). See Dove v. White, 211 Md. 228, 126 A.2d 835 (1956) (failure to plead the statute makes the trust enforceable).

21. For analysis of the wordings of the various American re-enactments, see Bogert, Trusts and Trustees (rev. 2d edit.), § 63. Some states require a mere signature (a signing at any place in the writing), while others require a "subscription" (a signature at the end). Some jurisdictions provide that if an agent signs or subscribes, his authority must be proved by a writing.

22. Marie M. E. Church v. Trinity M. E. Church, 253 Ill. 21, 97 N.E. 262; H. B. Cartwright & Bro. v. United States Bank & Trust Co., 23 N.M. 82, 167 P. 436.

23. Snyder v. Snyder, 280 Ill. 467, 117 N.E. 465.

24. Willats v. Bosworth, 33 Cal.App. 710, 166 P. 357.

25. Gaylord v. Lafayette, 115 Ind. 423, 428, 17 N.E. 899; McClellan v. McClellan, 65 Me. 500; Urann v. Coates, 109 Mass. 581, 585; White v. Fitzgerald, 19 Wis. 504, 511.

26. Lucas v. Dixon, 22 Q.B.D. 357; Huffine v. McCampbell, 149 Tenn. 47, 257 S.W. 80 (1923).

27. Ellison v. Ganiard, 167 Ind. 471, 79 N.E. 450; Johnson v. Candage, 31 Me. 28.

28. Myers v. Myers, 167 Ill. 52, 47 N.E. 309; Williams v. Williams, 118 Mich. 477, 76 N.W. 1039; Baldwin v. Humphrey, 44 N.Y. 609.

29. Emerson v. Galloupe, 158 Mass. 146, 32 N.E. 1118.

30. Hughes v. Davis, 244 Ala. 680, 15 So.2d 567 (1943).

31. Miles v. Miles, 78 Kan. 382, 96 P. 481.

32. Ellison v. Ganiard, 167 Ind. 471, 79 N.E. 450.

signed by the settlor after the transfer should be held unsatisfactory,[33] but the trustee's memorandum at that stage should render the trust enforceable.[34]

"It is not essential that the memorandum relied on should have been delivered to any one as a declaration of trust." [35]   The intent with which the writing was made is immaterial.[36]   Any document which has the requisite signature and description of the trust elements may be used, no matter what its form or purpose.[37]   Indeed, a paper which expressly repudiates the intention of carrying out a trust, but which shows as a whole that the relation of trustee and beneficiary exists, is sufficient.[38]   But the admission that an oral trust exists made in a pleading which sets up the Statute of Frauds, will not be an effective writing.[39]   It is not required that the writing be addressed to the beneficiary or to any particular person.[40]   A signature by initials is satisfactory.[41]

The written evidence may be composed of more than one document.[42]   If they are connected with each other by physical attachment or enclosure in the same receptacle,[43] or by reference to and adoption of one by another,[44] or by clear reference to the same transaction upon the face of each.[45]   Usually a mere reference by a signed document to an unsigned paper, without express repudiation of the accuracy of the unsigned paper, will be held to be an authentication of the latter so that it can be used with the former.[46]

33. Bryan v. Bigelow, 77 Conn. 604, 60 A. 266. But see Lewis v. Curnutt, 130 Iowa 423, 106 N.W. 914.

34. Carrell v. Hibner, 405 Ill. 545, 92 N.E.2d 121 (1950); Holmes v. Holmes, 65 Wash. 572, 118 P. 733.

35. Urann v. Coates, 109 Mass. 581, 584. See also, Viele v. Curtis, 116 Me. 328, 101 A. 966.

36. Kingsbury v. Burnside, 58 Ill. 310, 11 Am.Rep. 67; McClellan v. McClellan, 65 Me. 500.

37. *A letter:* Brackenbury v. Hodgkin, 116 Me. 399, 102 A. 106; Montague v. Hayes, 76 Mass. 609, 10 Gray 609; Malin v. Malin, 1 Wend., N.Y., 625.

A power of attorney: Hutchins v. Van Vechten, 140 N.Y. 115, 35 N.E. 446.

38. Urann v. Coates, 109 Mass. 581.

39. Whiting v. Gould, 2 Wis. 552.

If the trustee in the course of litigation confesses the trust, it becomes enforceable, although oral. Williams v. Moodhard, 341 Pa. 273, 19 A.2d 101 (1941).

40. Bates v. Hurd, 65 Me. 180.

41. Smith v. Howell, 11 N.J.Eq. 349.

42. Tyler v. Granger, 48 Cal. 259; Nesbitt v. Stevens, 161 Ind. 519, 69 N.E. 256;

Stratton v. Edwards, 174 Mass. 374, 54 N.E. 886; Van Cott v. Prentice, 104 N.Y. 46, 10 N.E. 257; In re Greenfield's Estate, 14 Pa. 489.

43. Wiggs v. Winn, 127 Ala. 621, 29 So. 96; Herman v. Edington, 331 Mass. 310, 118 N.E.2d 865 (1954) (envelope and contents read together). Hall v. Farmers' and Merchants' Bank, 145 Mo. 418, 46 S.W. 1000.

44. McClellan v. McClellan, 65 Me. 500; Packard v. Putnam, 57 N.H. 43.

Ramage v. Ramage, 283 S.C. 239, 322 S.E.2d 22 (1984) (decedent's deed of property to defendants, "to hold in trust," and her codicil directing distribution of the same property by defendants as trustees, showed intent to create a trust of the property; the codicil was the basic trust instrument).

45. Ransdel v. Moore, 153 Ind. 393, 53 N.E. 767, 53 L.R.A. 753; Tenney v. Simpson, 37 Kan. 579, 15 P. 512; Gates v. Paul, 117 Wis. 170, 94 N.W. 55.

46. Wood v. Davis, 82 Ill. 311; Wilkinson v. Taylor Mfg. Co., 67 Miss. 231, 7 So. 356; Packard v. Putnam, 57 N.H. 43.

Oral evidence cannot be used to bind several writings together. Their connection must appear from their physical attachment or from their contents.[47] The writing relied on to satisfy the Statute must contain a complete statement of the trust, without the necessity of relying on parol testimony to supply any missing element.[48] The parol evidence rule naturally forbids the admission of oral evidence to vary or contradict the terms of a trust which is evidenced by a writing.[49] But abbreviations, ambiguities or uncertainties in a written instrument creating or proving a trust, and the relation and situation of the parties, may be explained by parol evidence.[50] Oral evidence is receivable to prove that the writing does not contain all the terms of the trust or misstates them.[51] "When the writing relied upon to satisfy the Statute of Frauds has been lost or destroyed, its contents may be shown by parol proof which is reasonably clear and certain in its character . . .. And the same rule should prevail where the party to the suit who is alleged to have signed the writing, and who has or should have possession thereof, fails to produce on notice and denies its existence."[52]

WESTLAW REFERENCES

1677 /s english /s "statute of frauds"

"statute of frauds" /s american

di("statute of frauds" /s trust)

390k921/2

"oral trust"

di("statute of frauds" /s parol /s trust)

find 145 p2d 549

390k21(2)

FORMALITY—WILLS ACTS [1]

§ 22. If a settlor wishes to pass at his death property interests to a trustee and beneficiaries, or merely to a beneficiary, he must do so by a duly executed will.

47. Illinois Steel Co. v. Konkel, 146 Wis. 556, 131 N.W. 842.

48. Cook v. Barr, 44 N.Y. 156; Jourdan v. Andrews, 258 Pa. 347, 102 A. 33. But see Kendrick v. Ray, 173 Mass. 305, 53 N.E. 823, 73 Am.St.Rep. 289.

49. Gale v. Sulloway, 62 N.H. 57; Peer v. Peer, 11 N.J.Eq. 432; Wallace v. Berdell, 97 N.Y. 13.

50. Fox v. Fox, 250 Ill. 384, 95 N.E. 498; Adams v. Canutt, 66 Wash. 422, 119 P. 865. Contrast Lehman v. Pierce, 109 Ind.App. 497, 36 N.E.2d 952 (1941) (land referred to in memo as "the property" and "the farm;" oral evidence to identify property admitted); Laughlin v. March, 19 Wn.

2d 874, 145 P.2d 549 (1944) (document referred to two quarter sections of land owned by declarant near San Diego; oral evidence that declarant owned two quarter sections only in that region not received).

51. Fisher v. Andrews, 94 Md. 46, 50 A. 407.

52. Hiss v. Hiss, 228 Ill. 414, 423, 81 N.E. 1056; Stowell v. Satorius, 413 Ill. 482, 109 N.E.2d 734 (1952); J.A.B. Holding Co. v. Nathan, 120 N.J.Eq. 340, 184 A. 829 (1936).

§ 22

1. Restatement, Trusts, Second, §§ 53–58.

If a settlor executes a trust instrument which reserves many rights and powers to himself, and gives to the beneficiaries fragile or insubstantial interests, a question is raised whether a living trust was in fact created or the transaction amounted to an attempt to make a will. The courts are inclined to treat such dispositions as not testamentary.

Property may be left by will to the trustee of a previously created trust by a mere description of that trust, without setting forth the names and interests of its beneficiaries. In recent years statutes validating this transaction have been adopted, whether or not the donee trust is amendable or revocable.

American statute law requires that if a property owner desires to transfer his title to another at the time of the transferor's death he must go through certain formalities. These rules are laid down in order to prevent disputes over the estates of deceased persons, where opportunity for perjury, forgery and mistake might be involved. The usual provision [2] is that the statement of the intent of the property owner as to the disposition of his property at his death must be in writing, signed or subscribed by him, and witnessed by two or more witnesses who attest to the execution of the will.[3]

It is obvious that if a property owner wishes to create a trust which is to take effect at his death, he must comply with the statutes as to the execution of wills which are often called the Wills Acts.[4] If the settlor wishes to remain the complete owner of the property until his death, and then have a trust begin, the legal and equitable property interests which are then to pass must be transferred by an instrument executed with the formality of a will, and an attempt to vest them in a trustee and beneficiaries by an informal paper or orally will be void and the property will pass by intestacy to the next of kin or heirs of the deceased.[5]

These rules also apply where the legal title is transferred by a will but an attempt is made to pass the equitable interest to the beneficiaries by informal means, as where a property owner executes a will by which he gives property to T in trust for such persons as the settlor may describe in a later writing and leaves a second document with a list of intended beneficiaries not executed as a will. Here the at-

---

2. In some states holographic wills (those in the handwriting of the testator) need not be witnessed. Page on Wills, (Bowe-Parker Rev.), § 20.10.

3. See, for example, Ill.Rev.Stat. c. 110½ § 4–3.

4. The Statute of Wills validated the execution of wills. St. 32 Henry VIII, c. 1. To differentiate this type of statute from those concerned with formalities, it seems best to refer to the latter as the Wills Acts.

By Fla.Stats.Ann. § 689.075(1)(g), where a settlor is made sole trustee the trust instrument is to be executed in accordance with the laws of the jurisdiction in which executed or with the formalities for execution of wills.

5. Reynolds v. Reynolds, 325 Mass. 257, 90 N.E.2d 338 (1950); Matter of Ihmsen's Estate, 253 App.Div. 472, 3 N.Y.S.2d 125 (1938).

tempted express trust is void.[6]

A document which fails as a will for lack of formality may constitute a valid memorandum of a pre-existing trust of part of the testator's property.[7]

Where an insured assigned the policy to such trustees as should be named in the insured's will, to be held in trust for the wife of the insured, and later died leaving a will which named trustees, it has been held that the assignment was testamentary and ineffective for lack of formality,[8] but it would seem arguable that there was a valid inter vivos trust which merely lacked trustees and that they were provided by the will.

When are Instruments Purporting to Create Living Trusts in Fact Testamentary?[9]

The theoretical difference between an inter vivos transfer and a gift by will is clear and easily understood. In the case of a conveyance by a living property owner some interest passes at the time of the delivery of the instrument, although it may be defeasible or determinable on the happening of a future event, or may not entitle the transferee to possession until the death of the transferor. On the other hand, after the making of a will but prior to the death of the testator, he has complete control and ownership of all his property. He may revoke or alter the will, or sell, spend, or give away his property. The donees named in the will have no property interests in the testator's property before his death, but instead have mere expectancies or possibilities. The death of the testator, leaving the will in effect, is a condition precedent to the acquisition of any property interest by the legatees or devisees.

In some cases, where a living settlor has reserved to himself extensive property interests and powers, the heirs and next of kin have claimed that the settlor remained the full owner of the trust property during his life, and that the provisions for its disposition at his death were testamentary, and since not evidenced by the formalities required of a will, were void, so that the property passed as intestate property.[10]

If the settlor merely reserved to himself a *legal* life interest, and transferred to a trustee an interest which was presently vested but entitled the trustee to possession and enjoyment at the death of the settlor, there can be no contention that the transaction is testamentary. The settlor may give to his trustee a future estate or interest, either by

6. Wagner v. Clauson, 399 Ill. 403, 78 N.E.2d 203, 3 A.L.R.2d 672 (1948); St. Mary's School and Junior College v. Winston, 230 N.C. 326, 53 S.E.2d 162 (1949).

As to possible resulting or constructive trusts in this situation, see §§ 75, 85, post.

7. Hiss v. Hiss, 228 Ill. 414, 81 N.E. 1056; Leslie v. Leslie, 53 N.J.Eq. 275, 31 A. 170.

8. Frost v. Frost, 202 Mass. 100, 88 N.E. 446.

9. See Restatement, Trusts, Second §§ 56–57, 360–361.

10. See Ballantine, 18 Mich.L.R. 470; Rowley, 3 Univ.Cin.L.R. 361; Scott, 43 Harv.L.R. 521; Howe, 25 Ill.L.R. 178; Leaphart, 78 Univ. of Pa.L.R. 626; Seftenberg, 5 Wis.L.R. 321.

way of remainder or a springing executory interest. Death of the settlor here is not a condition precedent to vesting, but rather to possession only.[11] And so, also, if the inter vivos instrument merely made the settlor a life beneficiary, there is no ground for claiming that it was a disguised will.[12]

But in many other cases the settlor has provided for himself much greater interests and control, for example, the right to the income of the trust property for his life and to such portions of the trust principal as he may elect to take, or as the trustee may in his discretion decide to turn over to the settlor; and in addition the right to revoke or alter the trust; and the power to give the trustee instructions as to management or to perform personally the acts of trust administration. Here there is some basis for arguing that the settlor remains in substance the owner of the trust property during his life, and that the remainder beneficiaries have no property interests until his death, and hence that the attempt to give them remainders fails because attempted by an informal testamentary disposition. In some earlier cases this contention was accepted.[13]

It is obvious that living trusts of the type just described are intended to take the place of wills, and to do away with the necessity of having the property pass through probate. But this should not be determinative if the trusts in fact involve present gifts of remainder interests, even though such property rights are subject to being destroyed by action of the settlor up until the time of his death.[14] Corporate trustees have been anxious to have these trusts sustained, since they represent a large source of new business.

However the great majority of the decisions in this field have held these trusts to be true living trusts as to the remainder interests and therefore valid, even though not executed with the formalities of wills.[15]

11. Nichols v. Emery, 109 Cal. 323, 41 P. 1089; Candee v. Conn. Sav. Bank, 81 Conn. 372, 71 A. 551.

12. McHenry v. McHenry, 152 Ga. 105, 108 S.E. 522 (1921); Forney v. Remey, 77 Iowa 549, 42 N.W. 439.

13. Dunham v. Armitage, 97 Colo. 216, 18 P.2d 797 (1935); Smith v. Simmons, 99 Colo. 227, 61 P.2d 589 (1936). But see Denver Nat. Bank v. Von Brecht, 137 Colo. 88, 322 P.2d 667 (1958); McEvoy v. Boston Five Cent Sav. Bank, 201 Mass. 50, 87 N.E. 465 (overruled in National Shawmut Bank v. Joy, 315 Mass. 457, 53 N.E.2d 113 (1944)); Warsco v. Oshkosh Savings & Trust Co., 183 Wis. 156, 196 N.W. 829 (1924).

14. See Leaphart, 78 Univ.Pa.L.R. 626; King, 14 Rocky Mt.L.R. 1.

15. Bear v. Millikin Trust Co., 336 Ill. 366, 168 N.E. 349, 73 A.L.R. 173 (1929); Farkas v. Williams, 5 Ill.2d 417, 125 N.E.2d 600 (1955); Leahy v. Old Colony Trust Co., 326 Mass. 49, 93 N.E.2d 238 (1950); Goodrich v. City Nat. Bank & Trust Co., 270 Mich. 222, 258 N.W. 253 (1935); Davis v. Rossi, 326 Mo. 911, 34 S.W.2d 8 (1930); Ridge v. Bright, 244 N.C. 345, 93 S.E.2d 607 (1956); Cleveland Trust Co. v. White, 134 Ohio St. 1, 15 N.E. 627, 118 A.L.R. 475; In re Shapley's Deed of Trust, 353 Pa. 499, 46 A.2d 227, 164 A.L.R. 877 (1946); Westerfeld v. Huckaby, 474 S.W.2d 189 (1971); In re Steck's Estate, 275 Wis. 290, 81 N.W. 2d 729 (1957).

For a statute to this effect, see Wis.S.A. 701.07.

As to savings bank or Totten trusts and the Wills Acts, see § 20, ante.

To the effect that a revocable trust in which broad powers are retained by the settlor is valid and not illusory, see Westerfeld v. Huckaby, 462 S.W.2d 324 (Tex. Civ.App.1970), affirmed 474 S.W.2d 189 (1971); Wis.S.A. 701.07.

Possibly an influential factor in inducing the courts to take this position has been that the trusts have almost universally been evidenced by written instruments of admitted genuineness which have been signed and delivered, and that there is no danger of fraud, perjury or forgery. To deny effectiveness to these documents because they do not purport to be wills and lack witnesses and testimonium clauses may seem to give too much effect to formality and technicality.

Where the res of the living trust is an insurance policy the settlor may reserve the broad powers previously described, and also the power to change the beneficiary in the policy, surrender the policy and take for himself its surrender value, or pledge the policy as security for his personal debts. The general view of the courts has been that the sum total of all these powers does not make the insurance trust testamentary.[16] The beneficiary has a vested interest on the establishment of the trust, even though it is destructible by the insured during his life. His position is not that of the holder of a mere expectancy.

In some cases where the settlor has reserved great powers and interests for himself there has been a claim by his widow that the inter vivos trust was "illusory", that is, in reality no trust at all, and that the husband died intestate as to the property described in the inter vivos trust instrument and the widow was therefore entitled to a statutory share of that property. It has been argued that the so-called trustee was in substance merely an agent of the husband. The authorities are divided on this question.[17]

Gift by Deed or Will to an Existing Trust [18]

Occasionally property is transferred inter vivos to the trustees of a trust which is described in an existing will, the testator of which has not yet died. It would seem that the description in the deed should be

16. Gurnett v. Mutual Life Ins. Co. of New York, 356 Ill. 612, 191 N.E. 250 (1934); Bose v. Meury, 112 N.J.Eq. 62, 163 A. 276 (1932); Gordon v. Portland Trust Bank, 201 Or. 648, 271 P.2d 653, 53 A.L.R.2d 1106 (1954). *Contra,* Bickers v. Shenandoah Valley Nat. Bank, 197 Va. 145, 88 S.E.2d 889 (1955), rehearing denied 197 Va. 732, 90 S.E.2d 865 (1956).

For statutes to this effect, see Ind.Code 30–4–2–5; Wis.S.A. 701.09(3).

A decision in Pennsylvania that such an insurance trust is testamentary (In re Brown's Estate, 384 Pa. 99, 119 A.2d 513 (1956)) has been rendered obsolete by a later statute, and similar legislation has been adopted in several states. See Bogert, Trusts and Trustees (rev. 2d edit.), §§ 103, 239.

17. As supporting the claim of the widow that such a trust may be illusory, see Smith v. Northern Trust Co., 322 Ill.App. 168, 54 N.E.2d 75 (1944); Newman v. Dore, 275 N.Y. 371, 9 N.E.2d 966 (1937); In re

Wittner's Estate, 301 N.Y. 461, 95 N.E.2d 798 (1950); In re Montague's Estate, 403 Pa. 558, 170 A.2d 103 (1961), under the Pa. Estates Act of 1947; Alexander v. Zion's Sav. Bank & Tr. Co., 2 Utah 2d 317, 273 P.2d 173 (1954), opinion adhered to on rehearing 4 Utah 2d 90, 287 P.2d 665 (1955).

Contra: Rose v. St. Louis Union Trust Co., 43 Ill.2d 312, 253 N.E.2d 417 (1969).

And, to the effect that such trusts are not colorable or illusory as to the widow, see Rose v. Rose, 300 Mich. 73, 1 N.W.2d 458 (1942); Smyth v. Cleveland Trust Co., 172 Ohio St. 489, 179 N.E.2d 60 (1961) (overruling earlier Ohio cases).

As to illusory trusts of savings bank accounts see § 20, ante; and as to trusts with intent to defeat or impair the statutory rights of a surviving spouse, see § 48, post.

18. See Evans, 25 Col.L.R. 878; 16 U. of Chi.L.R. 635; Scott, 43 Harv.L.R. 544; Tolan, 46 Mich.L.R. 77.

adequate to identify the beneficiaries as those named in the will as of the date of the execution of the deed, and not those who became the beneficiaries of the testamentary trust at the death of the testator.[19]

Obviously a gift inter vivos to the trustees of an already existing testamentary trust should be held to be adequate as to identification of beneficiaries, and it should not be necessary to name them or describe their interests other than by reference to the will and the trustee under it, or by some other similar method.

Not infrequently, after a man has created a living trust, he makes a will leaving the residue of his estate to the trustee of the living trust for the purposes of that trust, merely naming the trustee and giving the date of the execution of the living trust instrument, without naming the beneficiaries of the living trust and their interests or other trust terms. If the will takes effect, it is held that the residue is added to the property of the living trust. Such a living trust has been named a "pour over" trust, because the res of the testamentary trust is poured over, or into, the previously created living trust.[20]

In some states, where the doctrine of incorporation by reference is applied to wills, and where the will contains a clear identification of the living trust document and shows an intent to incorporate it into the will, the courts have used the incorporation theory as the basis of their decisions.[21]

But in other jurisdictions a different explanation is given for validating the pour over trust, namely, that the reference in the will to the living trust by number, trustee, date of execution or other feature, which removes all uncertainty as to the identity of the living trust and its terms, is an adequate description of the uses to which the "pour over" property is to be put, just as much as if the names and interests of all the beneficiaries of the living trust had been set forth in the will.[22]

If the living trust to which the testamentary gift was made was *amendable* by its settlor, and he changed the trust as to its beneficiaries after the will was executed but before the death of the testator, some courts have held that the testamentary gift must be applied to the

19. Anderson v. Telsrow, 237 Iowa 568, 21 N.W.2d 781 (1946). But see Stalder v. Pacific Nat. Bank of Seattle, 28 Wn.2d 638, 183 P.2d 793 (1947), *contra.*

20. See McClanahan, 47 Cal.L.R. 267; Scott, 37 Tr.Bull. 25; 34 N.Y.U.L.R. 1106.

21. Mastin v. First Nat. Bank of Mobile, Inc., 278 Ala. 251, 177 So.2d 808 (1965); Montgomery v. Blankenship, 217 Ark. 357, 230 S.W.2d 51 (1950); Waterbury Nat. Bank v. Waterbury Nat. Bank, 162 Conn. 129, 291 A.2d 737 (1972); Bolles v. Toledo Trust Co., 144 Ohio St. 195, 58 N.E.2d 381, 157 A.L.R. 1164 (1944); In re Wilson's Estate, 363 Pa. 546, 70 A.2d 354 (1950); Lawless v. Lawless, 187 Va. 511, 47 S.E.2d 431 (1948) (reference to paper but no intent to incorporate shown); In re Brandenburg's Estate, 13 Wis.2d 217, 108 N.W.2d 374 (1961) (draft of will of another held incorporated).

22. Swetland v. Swetland, 102 N.J.Eq. 294, 140 A. 279 (1928); Matter of Rausch's Will, 258 N.Y. 327, 179 N.E. 755, 80 A.L.R. 98 (1932). In the latter case Cardozo, C.J., stated: "A gift to a trust company as trustee of a trust created by a particular deed identifies the trust in describing the trustee, like a gift to a corporation for the uses stated in its charter." And see Wells Fargo Bank & Union Trust Co. v. Superior Court, 32 Cal.2d 1, 193 P.2d 721 (1948).

living trust as it existed when the will was executed, unless the amendment was drawn with the formality of a codicil to a will, since otherwise the testator's property would be transferred informally at his death and thus the Wills Acts would be violated.[23] But in most cases the testamentary gift has been applied to the beneficiaries of the amended trust as they existed at the testator's death, on the theory that such was the intent of the testator as to his donees and that the members of the described class of testamentary beneficiaries could be made to depend on events happening up to the time of the testator's death.[24]

If the living trust to which the testamentary gift was made was *revocable,* and was revoked by its settlor before the will took effect, the testamentary gift necessarily fails since the named donees (takers under the will) are no longer in existence.[25] The testator intended the trustee of the living trust to be the donee for the beneficiaries of that trust. He did not intend those persons who were the beneficiaries of the living trust at the time the will was executed to secure any benefit from the will except through the living trust.

In recent years, in order to resolve conflicting views and make clear the effect of "pour over" wills and trusts, statutes have been adopted in many states.[26] They generally provide that property may be added by will to a trust created in writing before the execution of the will, whether the settlor of such prior trust was the testator or another, and whether it was amendable or revocable; and that, in the absence of express provision in the will of the donor to the contrary, the pour over gift is to be applied by the donee trustee of the previously created trust according to its terms when the testator died and not at the time when the will was executed; and that if the donee trust is revoked the gift to it by will is void.

23. Old Colony Trust Co. v. Cleveland, 291 Mass. 380, 196 N.E. 920 (1935); First-Mech. Nat. Bank of Trenton v. Norris, 134 N.J.Eq. 229, 34 A.2d 746 (1943); Koeninger v. Toledo Trust Co., 49 Ohio App. 490, 197 N.E. 419 (1934).

24. Stouse v. First Nat. Bank, 245 S.W.2d 914, 232 A.L.R.2d 1261 (Ky.1951); Canal Nat. Bank v. Chapman, 157 Me. 309, 171 A.2d 919 (1961); Second Bank-State Street Tr. Co. v. Pinion, 341 Mass. 366, 170 N.E.2d 350 (1960).

25. Bank of Delaware v. Bank of Delaware, 161 A.2d 430 (Del.Ch.1960). But see Fifth Third Union Tr. Co. v. Wilensky, 79 Ohio App. 73, 70 N.E.2d 920 (1946) (testamentary gift to be applied for original trust purposes).

And see Unif.Prob.Code § 2–512.

26. See Bogert, Trusts and Trustees (rev. 2d edit.), § 107, for references to statutes of this type in effect in Delaware,

Louisiana, Missouri, Nebraska, Rhode Island, Virginia and Wisconsin, and to the Uniform Testamentary Additions to Trusts Act adopted in the remaining states and the District of Columbia.

Fleming, 43 Ill.B.J. 906, and 69 Harv. L.R. 1147.

To the effect that a living trust need not be funded during the settlor's lifetime in order to validly receive pour over assets under the settlor's will, see Clymer v. Mayo, 393 Mass. 754, 473 N.E.2d 1084 (1985) (applicable statute, Mass.G.L. C. 203, § 3B, not conditioned upon existence of a trust or trust res but only upon existence of trust instrument). And see Md. ET Law § 4–411. An attempted pour over arrangement that was held ineffective because the living trust was never funded was given effect as an incorporation by reference. Hageman v. Cleveland Trust Co., 45 Ohio St.2d 178, 343 N.E.2d 121 (1976).

No problem as to the Wills Acts arises where testator A makes a gift by a duly executed will to the trustee of a trust created by the previously probated will of B. Either on incorporation theories, or because of adequate description of A's intended beneficiaries by reference to an existing and easily identifiable document (the will of B), A's property should be held to be validly given to the trustee of the trust under the will of B for its beneficiaries.[27]

 WESTLAW REFERENCES

"wills acts"

"statute of wills"   /s   "henry viii"

find 90 ne2d 338

"living trust"

"illusory trust"

162k45

390k153

"poor over trust"

390k14

"poor over will"

DELIVERY OF THE TRUST INSTRUMENT [1]

§ 23. If the trust is created by a written instrument and is to take effect during the life of the settlor, the instrument must be delivered in the sense that the settlor must by some act other than preparing and signing the instrument manifest an intent that it shall take effect. While handing the document to the trustee or beneficiary is the most common way of showing this intent, it is not the exclusive method.

If the trust instrument is a will, it is not necessary to the completion of the trust that the will be placed in the hands of the trustee or of a beneficiary. It must merely have been executed and published as a will and admitted to probate.

Recording of an instrument which declares a trust or transfers property to a trustee is not necessary to trust creation, but may be important to the protection of the interests of the beneficiaries.

While it is possible in almost all states to have personal property trusts created orally, most important trusts of realty or personalty are created by the use of one or more writings. Such a document is called the "trust instrument". It is a paper the legal effect of which is to give the terms of the trust and to transfer an equitable property interest in described property to one or more beneficiaries. It also, in the case of trusts created by transfer, evidences the passing of title to the trustee.

Not infrequently there are two or more trust instruments connect-

27. In re Gregory's Estate, 70 So.2d 903 (Fla.1954); City of Boston v. Curley, 276 Mass. 549, 177 N.E. 557 (1931).

§ 23

1. Restatement, Trusts, Second, §§ 32, 35.

ed with the creation of a single trust,[2] as where an absolute deed is given by S to T and T signs and delivers a separate declaration of trust in favor of B, or where an insurance policy is taken out in favor of T, as trustee, and the terms of the trust are set forth in an agreement signed by the insured and T. What is said here about delivery and recordation applies whether there is one instrument or two or more documents.

If a written instrument is relied upon as one of the elements in the creation of a trust, it must be an operative instrument and not merely a draft or proposed trust instrument, and hence it must be delivered. "Delivery" is here used in its technical sense, as meaning an expression by the party executing an instrument that he desires it to have immediate effect. It is not used in the somewhat common or layman's sense as meaning the placing of the instrument in the hands of another party. While giving another control of the document is the most usual and natural method of showing an intent that the instrument take effect, this state of mind may also be shown by other means, for example, by telling another that the instrument is in effect, or by acting toward another as if he were the beneficiary of the trust described in the instrument.[3]

In numerous cases in which the property owner has declared himself a trustee by formal written document, it has been held unnecessary to give the beneficiary possession of that document.[4] If the declarant has shown an intent to effect a complete trust, his failure to place the instrument stating the terms of the trust in the possession or control of the beneficiary will not be of determining importance. It is in this technical sense only that "delivery" of the trust instrument is required.[5] And when the property owner transfers property to a third person as trustee, the trust deed need not be actually placed in the possession of the trustee,[6] if the settlor has otherwise shown a desire that the deed go into effect, that is, has "delivered" the instrument in a technical sense.[7] While failure to part with possession of the trust instrument is not necessarily fatal to the existence of the trust, it may constitute evidence that a completed trust was not intended and that the settlor had not yet finally determined to create a trust.[8]

It has been held that delivery of a trust instrument is shown by an

---

2. Hoffman v. Gosnell, 75 Md. 577, 24 A. 28; Henderson v. McBee, 79 N.C. 219.

3. McMahon v. Dorsey, 353 Mich. 623, 91 N.W.2d 893 (1958); Halleck v. Halleck, 216 Or. 23, 337 P.2d 330 (1959).

4. Janes v. Falk, 50 N.J.Eq. 468, 26 A. 138, 35 Am.St.Rep. 783; Smith's Estate, 144 Pa. 428, 22 A. 916, 27 Am.St.Rep. 641; In re Eshbach's Estate, 197 Pa. 153, 46 A. 905.

5. Collins v. Steuart, 58 N.J.Eq. 392, 44 A. 467; McArthur v. Gordon, 26 N.E. 459, 801 (N.Y.).

6. Barr v. Schroeder, 32 Cal. 609; Tarbox v. Grant, 56 N.J.Eq. 199, 39 A. 378; Bunn v. Winthrop, 1 Johns.Ch., N.Y., 329; Steele v. Lowry, 4 Ohio 72, 19 Am.Dec. 581; but see Loring v. Hildreth, 170 Mass. 328, 49 N.E. 652, 40 L.R.A. 127, 64 Am.St.Rep. 301.

7. Adams v. Adams, 88 U.S. (21 Wall.) 185, 22 L.Ed. 504 (1874); Huse v. Den, 85 Cal. 390, 24 P. 790; Dohmen v. Schlief, 179 Mo. 593, 78 S.W. 799.

8. Urann v. Coates, 109 Mass. 581, 584.

acceptance by the trustee written upon the trust instrument,[9] by signing and acknowledging it and leaving it to be recorded,[10] or by having it recorded,[11] or by a recital of delivery in the deed coupled with signature, acknowledgment, and recording.[12] Naturally delivery is most commonly shown by proof that the settlor put the trustee or a beneficiary into possession of the trust instrument.[13] A valid delivery of the trust instrument will not be affected by a later return of the instrument to the settlor.[14] A delivery to a third person on behalf of the trustee is sufficient delivery to the trustee.[15]

Where a contract is to be made the subject of a trust, as in the case of insurance policies and promissory notes, there must be delivery of the contract in order to create the contract rights which the trustee is to hold. While possession of the document evidencing the contract need not be given to the trustee, the promisor in the contract must in some way show that he intends the document to be operative, and the best way of doing this is to hand the paper to the promisee. Here delivery is necessary to create the trust property rather than the trust.

Recording of the trust instrument, in the absence of statute, is not essential to completion of the trust.[16] The effect of the recording statutes is the same upon trust instruments as upon other conveyances. A failure to record may make it possible for the title of the beneficiaries to be cut off by a transfer of the same property to a bona fide purchaser who records his deed.[17] The duty of the trustee to obtain the recording of the trust instrument is treated in a later section.[18] The recording of a trust instrument is strong evidence that an operative trust was intended,[19] but it has been held not to be conclusive.[20]

While in a few states statutes [21] expressly require that instruments creating trusts of realty shall be acknowledged and recorded, these acts are not generally held to make such formalities necessary to the creation of a trust,[22] but rather to be concerned only with making a record for the purpose of notice to the public.

9. New South Building & Loan Ass'n v. Gann, 101 Ga. 678, 29 S.E. 15.

10. Lawrence v. Lawrence, 181 Ill. 248, 54 N.E. 918.

11. Walker v. Crews, 73 Ala. 412; Chilvers v. Race, 196 Ill. 71, 63 N.E. 701.

12. Schreyer v. Schreyer, 43 Misc. 520, 89 N.Y.S. 508, affirmed, 182 N.Y. 555, 75 N.E. 1134.

13. Texas Rice Land Co. v. Langham, Tex.Civ.App., 193 S.W. 473.

14. Stone v. King, 7 R.I. 358, 84 Am. Dec. 557; Talbot v. Talbot, 32 R.I. 72, 78 A. 535, Ann.Cas.1912C, 1221.

15. Woodward v. Camp, 22 Conn. 457; Withers v. Jenkins, 6 S.C. 122.

16. Sprague v. Woods, 4 Watts & S., Pa., 192.

17. See § 165, post.

18. See § 99, post.

19. Lawrence v. Lawrence, 181 Ill. 248, 54 N.E. 918.

20. Loring v. Hildreth, 170 Mass. 328, 49 N.E. 652, 40 L.R.A. 127, 64 Am.St.Rep. 301.

21. See Miss.Code § 91–9–1; 60 Okl. Stats.Ann. § 172; R.I.Gen.L. § 34–13–1.

See Board of Trustees v. Odom, 100 Miss. 64, 56 So. 314.

22. Cornelison v. Roberts, 107 Iowa 220, 77 N.W. 1028.

WESTLAW REFERENCES

di delivery

delivery /s "trust instrument"

120k58(4) /p trust

"property owner" settlor /s trustee /s deliver*** /s document
    deed instrument

record*** /s "trust instrument"

CONSIDERATION [1]

§ 24. If a trust is completely created, that the settlor received no consideration for creating the trust will not render it revocable or unenforceable.

A promise to create a trust is governed by the law of contracts and is not enforceable against the promisor unless he received consideration.

A voluntary promise to create a trust, or an incompletely created voluntary trust, is not treated as a declaration of trust.

An incomplete gift of a legal interest in property is not construed to amount to a declaration of trust.

Consideration in the Law of Uses

In the early law of uses a valuable consideration was necessary to raise a use on a bargain and sale,[2] and a blood or marriage relationship was needed to support a covenant to stand seized to uses.[3] In so far as such transactions still have standing in the law of conveyancing these rules still prevail. But most modern conveyances operate as statutory grants and not under the Statute of Uses, so that even in the law of deeds consideration would not seem a prerequisite to a valid conveyance.

Consideration in the Case of Completely Created Trusts [4]

It is well established that no consideration is necessary to make a trust enforceable, if all acts essential to its creation have been performed.[5] Once the owner of the property has placed the equitable interest in the beneficiary, the trust becomes enforceable.[6] The ques-

§ 24

1. Restatement, Trusts, Second, §§ 28–32.

2. Holdsworth, History of English Law, vol. 4, p. 424.

3. Sharington v. Strotton, 1 Plow. 298.

4. Pound, Consideration in Equity, 13 Ill.L.R. 667.

5. Padfield v. Padfield, 72 Ill. 322; Harris Banking Co. v. Miller, 190 Mo. 640, 89 S.W. 629, 1 L.R.A.,N.S., 790; Van Cott v. Prentice, 104 N.Y. 45, 10 N.E. 257; Den-

nison v. Goehring, 7 Pa. 175, 47 Am.Dec. 505.

As to consideration in California and states following the Field Code, see West's Ann.Cal.Civ.Code, § 2222; Mont.Code Ann. 72–20–107, 72–20–108; N.Dak.Cent.Code 59–01–04; S.Dak.Codif.Laws 55–1–5. And see National Bank of Calif. v. Exchange Nat. Bank, 186 Cal. 172, 199 P. 1 (1921); McWilliams, Consideration in the Law of Trusts, 14 Cal.L.R. 188.

6. Stone v. Hackett, 12 Gray, Mass., 227, 230.

tion whether the settlor received value for his transfer is immaterial.[7]

Thus if S owns a bond and orally states that he holds it in trust for his son, B, the trust is binding and irrevocable, notwithstanding that S may have received no consideration for his declaration and that B may not have changed his position at all in reliance on the declaration.[8] And if S conveys a farm to T in trust for B, the fact that B paid nothing for the transfer and that S received no benefit from anyone for the act of trust creation is immaterial.[9] Trust creations are conveyances and the modern conveyance does not require consideration to support it. Although a trustee may make promises to carry out the trust, these are not contracts, and the requirement of the law of contracts that consideration exist in order that promises be enforceable has no application. Most trust creations are by way of gift. The instances where the settlor receives consideration are exceptional.

A trust is "completed" for the purposes of this section when the settlor has performed the acts necessary to vest an equitable interest in the trust property in the beneficiary. It is not "incomplete" merely because the settlor did not succeed in an attempt to pass legal title to a named trustee, since equity will supply the trustee.

Agreements to Create Trusts and Incomplete Trusts

On the other hand, if the property owner has merely agreed to create a trust, or has taken only part of the steps necessary to give the trust existence, or has taken all such steps but some of them in a defective manner, and the beneficiary is a volunteer, equity will not intervene in his behalf.[10] The trust not being in existence, the intended beneficiary can have nothing more on which to rely than a naked promise, or an ineffective gift of the equitable interest, which is of no more significance in equity than at law.[11] "If the deed under which they [the volunteer beneficiaries] claim to be defective and inoperative at law, they cannot have the aid of a court of equity to complete and perfect it, any more than they can have the aid of the court to enforce a promise, or even a covenant, without consideration, to execute a deed."[12]

Thus if S is the owner of bonds and orally promises to transfer them to T as trustee for B, but receives nothing in return for this promise, there is a mere voluntary agreement to transfer property in trust, and equity will not give aid to T or B by forcing S to complete the

7. Hallowell Sav. Inst. v. Titcomb, 96 Me. 62, 69, 51 A. 249.

8. Leeper v. Taylor, 111 Mo. 312, 19 S.W. 955 (voluntary declaration of trust of realty); Frank v. Heimann, 302 Mo. 334, 258 S.W. 1000.

9. Ownes v. Ownes, 23 N.J.Eq. 60.

10. Estate of Webb, 49 Cal. 541; Hamilton v. Hall's Estate, 111 Mich. 291, 69 N.W. 484; Harding v. St. Louis Union Trust Co., 276 Mo. 136, 207 S.W. 68; Austin v. Young, 90 N.J.Eq. 47, 106 A. 395 (voluntary promise to buy land and hold it in trust); Central Trust Co. v. Gaffney, 157 App.Div. 501, 142 N.Y.S. 902; Rousseau v. Call, 169 N.C. 173, 85 S.E. 414.

11. For an example of an incompletely created voluntary trust, see Farmers' Loan & Trust Co. v. Winthrop, 238 N.Y. 477, 144 N.E. 686 (1924).

12. Ames, C. J., in Stone v. King, 7 R.I. 358, 365, 84 Am.Dec. 557.

transfer.[13]   Or if A owns bonds and orally states that he gives them to T
to be held in trust for B, but does not deliver possession of the bonds to
T, and A received no consideration for his act, the gift to T for B is
incomplete, no trust arises, and the court will not compel A to complete
the trust by delivering the bonds.[14]   Promises to create trusts are
subject to the rules of the law of contracts as to enforceability, just as
are promises to perform work and labor or to lend money.   An incomplete act of trust creation by way of transfer is not treated as a
declaration of trust because that was not the settlor's intent.[15]   He
intended the creation of a trust by transfer to a trustee and did not
have in mind making himself a trustee.   If, however, the intended
voluntary beneficiary has sufficiently changed his position in justifiable
reliance on the settlor's agreement to create a trust, the settlor may be
estopped to deny that a trust was created.[16]

Incomplete Gifts of a Legal Interest

Equity's refusal to aid the volunteer precludes declaring implied
trusts in the case of incomplete gifts of the full property interest.[17]   If
the owner of money intended to give A the full ownership therein, but
failed to carry out his intent by delivering the money to A or delivering
a deed of gift, and so the gift of the legal interest failed, there is no
reason why equity should aid the disappointed donee and give him an
equitable estate.   His condition is no worse since the failure to execute
the gift than it was before the intention to make a gift was formed;   the
injustice and unjust enrichment necessary to give rise to a constructive
trust do not exist.   Nor will the court treat the incomplete gift of the
full property interest as amounting to a declaration by the donor that
he was a trustee for the intended donee,[18] since this would be a revision
of the donor's effort instead of carrying into effect his expressed intent.
He never had an intent to be a trustee for the intended donee.

What is Consideration in the Case of Promises to Create Trusts?

The consideration required to support an agreement to create a
trust is the same as that required by the law of contracts to give
enforceability to any other promise.   Although it is stated in some cases
that love and affection or a duty to support are recognized by equity as
sufficient consideration,[19] the weight of modern authority in England

---

13.   Lowry v. McGee, 40 Tenn. 269.

14.   Brannock v. Magoon, 141 Mo.App.
316, 125 S.W. 535.

15.   Colman v. Colman, 25 Wn.2d 606,
171 P.2d 691 (1946).

16.   Dillwyn v. Llewellyn, 4 De Gex, F.
& J. 517; Irwin v. Dyke, 114 Ill. 302, 1 N.E.
913.

17.   Talcott v. American Board Com'rs
for Foreign Missions, 205 Ill.App. 339;
Young v. Young, 80 N.Y. 422, 36 Am.Rep.
634.

18.   In re Hayward's Estate, 57 Ariz.
51, 110 P.2d 956 (1941);   Hebrew Univ.
Ass'n v. Nye, 148 Conn. 223, 169 A.2d 641
(1961);   Detroit Bank v. Bradfield, 324
Mich. 124, 36 N.W.2d 873 (1949);   Cooney v.
Equit. Life Assur. Soc. of U.S., 235 Minn.
377, 51 N.W.2d 285 (1952).

19.   Ellis v. Nimmo, Lloyd & Goold,
temp. Sugden, 333;   McIntire v. Hughes, 4
Bibb, Ky., 186;   Landon v. Hutton, 50 N.J.
Eq. 500, 25 A. 953;   Bunn v. Winthrop, 1
Johns.Ch., N.Y., 329;   Harvey v. Alexander,
1 Rand. 219.

and America denies the validity of such consideration as a basis for the enforcement of an agreement to create a trust.[20]

It is occasionally stated in early cases that a seal will induce equity to carry out an agreement otherwise unenforceable.[21]   But the better view is that chancery will go behind the seal to ascertain the true consideration, and that the presence of a seal will not of itself render a voluntary agreement enforceable.[22]   "It [equity] will doubtless not enforce a contract to create a trust, though it were under hand and seal; and in this respect it carries the doctrine of nudum pactum further than even the law does . . .."[23]   Modern legislation, making the seal merely presumptive evidence of consideration or otherwise altering its common-law effect, has lead equity to recognize even less its esteem for the seal.

If one contracting to create a trust has received consideration for his promise, and then fails to perform, equity will decree a trust or give specific performance of the promise.   "If there be a valuable consideration between the alleged trustee and cestui que trust, then, under the equitable rule that what ought to be done will be considered as done, the court may decree a contract to declare a trust as equivalent to an actual declaration."[24]

If a trust was created for consideration, and the consideration failed, the trust will be voidable.[25]

 WESTLAW REFERENCES

Consideration in the Law of Uses
di consideration
"statute of uses" /s consideration
padfield +3 padfield

Consideration in the Case of Completely Created Trusts
stone +3 hackett

Consideration in the Case of Completely Created Trusts
incomplete /2 trust /s creat***
409k94
390k21(2)
390k1

20. Jefferys v. Jefferys, 1 Craig & P. 137; Phillips v. Frye, 14 Allen, Mass., 36; Matter of James, 146 N.Y. 78, 94, 40 N.E. 876, 48 Am.St.Rep. 774; Keffer v. Grayson, 76 Va. 517, 44 Am.Rep. 171.

21. Caldwell v. Williams, Bailey, Eq., S.C., 175.

22. Selby v. Case, 87 Md. 459, 39 A. 1041; Minturn v. Seymour, 4 Johns.Ch., N.Y., 498; Woodall v. Prevatt, 45 N.C. 199; Black v. Gettys, 238 S.C. 167, 119 S.E.2d 660 (1961) (contract under seal to convey personalty to trustee; lack of consideration provable).

23. Gibson, C. J., in Dennison v. Goehring, 7 Pa. 175, 178, 47 Am.Dec. 505.

24. Janes v. Falk, 50 N.J.Eq. 468, 472, 26 A. 138, 35 Am.St.Rep. 783.

25. In re Ames' Settlement, (1946) Ch. 217 (trust created in consideration of marriage of beneficiary to a certain woman; marriage declared void ab initio and trust failed); Hutchison v. Ross, 262 N.Y. 381, 187 N.E. 65, 89 A.L.R. 1007 (1933).

Incomplete Gifts of a Legal Interest

gift /s implied /2 trust

What is Consideration in the Case of Promises to Create Trusts?

janes +3 falk

390k13

191k4

Chapter 3

CREATION OF EXPRESS TRUSTS—SUBJECT MATTER— TRUSTEE

Table of Sections

THE SUBJECT MATTER OF THE TRUST [1]

§ 25. **Every trust must have some property as its subject matter or res. The trustee's obligation must be to apply defined or ascertainable property to the benefit of another. It cannot be merely to confer benefits from any source chosen by the trustee.**

The settlor's act of trust creation must apply to some interest recognized by equity as capable of ownership and as transferable. Every act of trust creation involves the disposition by the settlor of an interest in the trust property.

The subject matter must be described by the settlor with such definiteness and certainty that the trustee and the court can be sure that the intended trust is being carried out.

While the most common types of property held in trust are bonds, stocks, mortgages, titles to land, and bank accounts, any transferable

§ 25

1. Bogert, Trusts and Trustees (rev. 2d edit.), §§ 111–120; Restatement, Trusts, Second, §§ 74–88.

interest, vested or contingent, legal or equitable, real or personal, tangible or intangible, may be held in trust.

The trust subject matter must consist of a property interest owned by the settlor at the time of trust creation. A mere possibility or expectancy is not a valid trust res. If a settlor tries to create a trust of a property interest which has no present existence, but which he expects to acquire in the future, the transaction cannot amount to a present act of trust creation; but if there was consideration for the act it may be given effect as a contract to hold or transfer the property in trust when and if acquired and as giving the beneficiary equitable rights in the res from the moment of its acquisition. If, however, there was no consideration for the attempted creation of a present trust of a future property interest, no trust will arise when the interest is obtained, unless the settlor expresses his intent to have a trust after he has received the property.

The interest of a beneficiary in an insurance policy is a vested interest (and not merely an expectancy) and so may be the subject matter of a trust, even though it is a defeasible interest.

Necessity for Trust Property

A trust without subject matter is inconceivable. It can no more exist than a trust without a beneficiary.[2] Some property must be identified as the subject matter to be held by the trustee for the beneficiary. The subject matter is often referred to as the trust res, trust property, or trust principal or corpus. In a few cases efforts have been made to prove that a trust existed where no property could be found as the subject matter. Thus in several cases a testator has requested that a certain person be employed by the executors as solicitor or attorney or clerk. It has been held in these cases that the testator's direction did not create a trust because of the lack of subject matter.[3] No sum was left in trust to employ the person named. Nor does any trust arise from a request that the testator's wife and sister should live together.[4]

One criterion for distinguishing debt from trust is that the former relates to no particular subject matter while the latter does. In succeeding sections[5] numerous cases are examined where a trust was claimed to exist instead of a debt, and the discovery of a trust res was of vital importance.

"In general, any right, interest, or thing which may be the subject of property may be granted in trust. Every kind of vested right which

---

2. Gough v. Satterlee, 32 App.Div. 33, 52 N.Y.S. 492.

To the effect that a living trust need not be funded during the settlor's lifetime in order to validly receive pour-over assets under the settlor's will, see § 22, ante.

3. Foster v. Elsley, 19 Ch.Div. 518; Jewell v. Barnes' Adm'r, 110 Ky. 329, 61 S.W. 360, 53 L.R.A. 377; In re

Thistlethwaite, 104 N.Y.S. 264 (Sur.); Matter of Wallach, 164 App.Div. 600, 150 N.Y.S. 302. See Scott, Testamentary Directions to Employ, 41 Harv.L.R. 709. An additional reason is that the courts are hostile to provisions restricting freedom of action by a fiduciary.

4. Graves v. Graves, 13 Ir.Ch. 182.

5. See §§ 27–28, post.

the law recognizes as valuable may be transferred in trust."[6] This property may be an estate in land, a mortgage, a bond, shares of stock, money, a patent right,[7] growing crops,[8] a promissory note,[9] a claim against a bank,[10] an equitable interest,[11] a ship under construction,[12] unaccrued rents and profits,[13] a copyright, trade mark, or trade name,[14] or an interest in a partnership.[15]

If a property interest is by its nature inalienable, obviously no trust can be created in it by declaration or transfer,[16] since every trust creation involves the passage from the settlor to the beneficiary of an equitable property interest in the trust res. In rare cases property rights are disqualified from transfer to a beneficiary or to anyone else.[17] But an inalienable property interest may be held in trust, as where a trustee conveys realty subject to a possibility of reverter or right of reentry and where these interests are still subject to the common law restriction against alienation. This does not mean that they could have been trust property at the creation of the trust. While United States Savings Bonds are inalienable in the sense that the government cannot be compelled to pay to anyone except the purchaser or his beneficiary, the payee may be made a trustee of his right to collect from the government.[18]

Although the settlor usually passes to his trustee a legal and to his beneficiary an equitable property interest of a vested type, the trust res may be a contingent interest and the interest given to the trustee may be an equitable one.[19] It all depends upon the nature of the interest

---

6. Dunn, J., in Burke v. Burke, 259 Ill. 262, 268, 102 N.E. 293, 295. See, also, Haulman v. Haulman, 164 Iowa 471, 145 N.W. 930, 933. Offices are not property. A county clerk could not declare himself trustee of his office. The Buckhurst Peerage, 1893, 2 App.Cas. 1; American Sodium Co. v. Shelley, 51 Nev. 344, 276 P. 11 (1929).

7. In re Russell's Patent, 2 De G. & Jon. 130.

8. Mauldin v. Armistead, 14 Ala. 702.

9. Broughton v. West, 8 Ga. 248; Duly v. Duly, 2 Ohio Dec. 425.

10. McCarthy v. Provident Institution for Savings, 159 Mass. 527, 34 N.E. 1073.

11. Tarbox v. Grant, 56 N.J.Eq. 199, 39 A. 378. In Clark v. Frazier, 74 Okl. 141, 177 P. 589, it was held that a school land certificate entitling its holder to a preferential right to buy the land was an equitable interest which could be the subject-matter of a trust.

12. Starbuck v. Farmers' Loan & Trust Co., 28 App.Div. 272, 51 N.Y.S. 58.

13. Gisborn v. Charter Oak Life Ins. Co., 142 U.S. 326, 12 S.Ct. 277, 35 L.Ed. 1029 (1892).

14. Schellberg v. Empringham, 36 F.2d 991 (D.N.Y.1929); Warren v. Warren Thread Co., 134 Mass. 247.

15. Waddell v. Waddell, 335 Mich. 498, 56 N.W.2d 257 (1953). Such holding must, of course, be subject to the rules of partnership law. Crane on Partnership, sec. 6; 2 Hast.L.J. 24.

16. Thayer v. Pressey, 175 Mass. 225, 56 N.E. 5 (claim against United States before allowance inalienable by statute); In re M.J. Hoey & Co., 19 F.2d 764 (2d Cir. 1927) (seat on stock exchange could not be made res of trust).

17. In re Morse, 247 N.Y. 290, 160 N.E. 374 (1928) (bank stock not good subject matter for voting trust); Clark v. Bayley, 5 Or. 343 (homestead).

18. Katz v. Driscoll, 86 Cal.App.2d 313, 194 P.2d 822 (1948); but see Hatfield v. Buck, 193 Misc. 1041, 85 N.Y.S.2d 613 (1948) (may not be subject of declaration of trust).

19. Ollis v. Ricker, 203 N.C. 671, 166 S.E. 801 (1932) (equity of redemption).

which the settlor has and decides to vest in trustee and beneficiary.

The res of a trust may be a claim against the settlor[20] or against a third person, but difficulties arise if an attempt is made to have a trustee hold a claim against himself[21] or against the beneficiary[22] in trust since the first involves the legal impossibility of the same person being obligor and obligee and the second would seem to result in the forgiveness of the debt.

In the early law an assignee of a chose in action had to sue in the name of the assignor,[23] and in the case of a partial assignment an action at law had to be brought by the assignor for himself and the partial assignee.[24] There has been some argument to the effect that the assignor in these cases is a trustee for the assignee, but this is incorrect.[25] Assignor and assignee are not in a fiduciary relation and their rights are determined by contract principles.[26]

Certainty as to Trust Res

It is obvious that the subject matter of the trust must be certain if a court of equity is to enforce it. An indefinite or uncertain trust res is as fatal to the trust as no subject matter whatever. The subject matter either must be described in the trust instrument or by a formula or method given for identifying it. That which is capable of being rendered certain by action of the trustee under court supervision is sufficiently definite. Thus where a testator provided that after a certain date the trustees might give such portions of the estate as they thought proper to any of the testator's brothers and sisters who might stand in need of the aid, and that the trustees should devote the remainder of the property to the advancement of the cause of temperance or in aid of a manual training school, it was held that the gift in trust for the cause of temperance or the school was void for uncertainty since there was no assurance that any of the testator's property would remain after providing for his brothers and sisters.[27] On the other hand, a legacy in trust of a sufficient sum of money to produce $50 per annum is not void for uncertainty as to subject matter,[28] and a gift to a trustee of such sum out of the testator's residuary estate as was needed

---

20. Rousseau v. Call, 169 N.C. 173, 85 S.E. 414. A check or note by the settlor may be of no value as a trust res, unless given for consideration. In re Burton's Estate, 206 Minn. 516, 289 N.W. 66 (1939); In re Mellier's Estate, 320 Pa. 150, 182 A. 388 (1936).

21. In re McLellan's Estate, 14 Cal. App.2d 271, 57 P.2d 1338 (1936).

22. United States Nat. Bank of Portland, Or. v. Rawson, 150 Or. 358, 43 P.2d 184.

23. Snead v. Bell, 142 Ala. 449, 38 So. 259 (1905); Martin & Garrett v. Mask, 158 N.C. 436, 74 S.E. 343, 41 L.R.A.,N.S., 641 (1912).

24. Cable v. St. Louis Marine Ry. & Dock Co., 21 Mo. 133.

25. See Cook, 29 Harv.L.R. 816, 30 id. 449; Williston, 30 Harv.L.R. 97.

26. Restatement, Trusts, Second, §§ 15, 16; Bogert, Trusts and Trustees (rev. 2d edit.), § 25.

27. Wilce v. Van Anden, 248 Ill. 358, 94 N.E. 42, 140 Am.St.Rep. 212, 21 Ann. Cas. 153.

28. Crawford v. Mound Grove Cemetery Ass'n, 218 Ill. 399, 75 N.E. 998.

to produce an income sufficient to support the testator's widow in comfort would likewise be valid.

When it is said that the trust subject matter must be fixed and specific, it is not meant that the trust property may not change from time to time throughout the life of the trust. It must be specific and identifiable at any given time, but may be changed by the trustee through sale and reinvestment. The subject matter may be a farm at the outset, which the trustee sells and for which he receives a check, which he deposits in a bank and for which he then receives a claim against the bank, which he draws out in order to buy certain bonds, which then become the trust res.

An undivided interest in certain property,[29] or in all the property of the settlor at a certain date,[30] is a sufficiently definite subject matter for a trust. Thus a trust of one half of the net estate left by the testator is valid, since the res will be ascertained in time upon payment of debts, taxes and expenses of the estate.[31]

Attempted Present Trusts of Future Property

If one attempts to create a present trust of a property interest which he does not own, the transaction amounts to a contract to create a trust in the property in question, if and when such property is acquired, provided the element of consideration is present; but if the settlor receives no consideration for his act, the transaction constitutes an unenforceable promise to create a trust in the future.[32] In the case of an attempted present creation of a trust in future property for a consideration, the property, when it comes into existence and is acquired by the settlor, automatically becomes trust property; whereas if there was no consideration no trust arises after acquisition of the property until the owner thereafter manifests an intent to hold it or have it held in trust.[33]

Equity cannot give the attempted present creation of a trust in future property the effect of bringing about a present trust, even though there was consideration for it; but it can give the transaction some effect, namely, that of a specifically enforceable contract to have a trust of the property when and if later acquired.

Two examples will make this point clearer. If a man who expects to gamble on the stock market and to make profits in the year 1988, declares in 1987 that he then holds the expected 1988 profits in trust for his wife and children, the transaction is a voluntary agreement to

---

29. Rollestone v. National Bank of Commerce, 299 Mo. 57, 252 S.W. 394.

30. Helvering v. McIlvaine, 296 U.S. 488, 56 S.Ct. 332, 80 L.Ed. 345 (1936); Rabalsky v. Kook, 87 N.H. 56, 173 A. 803 (1934).

31. Golstein v. Handley, 390 Ill. 118, 60 N.E.2d 851 (1945). The maximum portion of the estate which is deductible under the marital deduction provisions of the tax laws is very commonly the res of a trust. Harlan Nat. Bank v. Brown, 317 S.W.2d 903, 72 A.L.R.2d 1175 (Ky.1958).

32. Bacon v. Bonham, 33 N.J.Eq. 614; Mastin v. Marlow, 65 N.C. 695.

33. In re Barnett, 124 F.2d 1005 (2d Cir.1942); Dyblie v. Dyblie, 389 Ill. 326, 59 N.E.2d 657 (1945).

hold the profits in trust if and when earned during 1988. It is not a present trust in 1987 nor a contract to hold the profits in trust in the future. When the man earns such profits in 1988, they are his until he sets them aside as trust property, as he may voluntarily do. Since they become his when earned, and do not automatically become trust property, he must pay an income tax on them.[34]

If a sister expects to receive property from her brother at his death, either by his will or by intestacy, she is said to have an "expectancy" and not a present property interest. If she purports to assign her expectancy in her brother's property during his life to a trustee for a third person, voluntarily, and later her brother dies leaving her property, she may choose between turning this property over to the trustee and keeping it as her own. She has no obligation to deliver the after-acquired property to the trustee. Her action amounted merely to an unenforceable promise to turn over to the trustee property received from her brother. That the instrument of assignment was under seal makes no difference.[35] The purported assignment did not amount to an actual transfer because there was nothing owned by the sister at that time.

If there had been consideration for the declaration of the trust of the future profits, or for the assignment of the expectancy, a trust would have attached to the profits when realized or to the expectancy when it became a vested interest.[36]

Insurance as Trust Subject Matter

An insurance policy is a valid trust subject matter, even though the insured has reserved the power to change the beneficiary in the policy. The interest of the beneficiary is treated as a chose in action against the insurer which is vested, although subject to being divested and cut off by action of the insured in substituting another person as the beneficiary in the policy, or by permitting the policy to lapse.[37] It is not considered a mere possibility or expectancy.

In many insurance policies the company agrees to hold the proceeds of the policy "in trust" for named relatives on the death of the insured, and to pay the amount due in installments, with interest. These policies are said by the insurance companies to create trusts, but in fact they are merely contracts. The company never agrees to hold particular property in trust, but expects merely to make bookkeeping entries, showing the rights of the beneficiaries.[38] No assets are ever set apart to meet the obligation.

34. Brainard v. Commissioner of Internal Revenue, 91 F.2d 880 (7th Cir.1937), certiorari dismissed 303 U.S. 665, 58 S.Ct. 748, 82 L.Ed.2d 1122 (1938).

35. In re Ellenborough, 1903, 1 Ch. 697.

36. Clark v. Rutherford, 227 Ark. 270, 298 S.W.2d 327 (1957).

37. Cannon v. Nicholas, 80 F.2d 934 (10th Cir.1935); Goldman v. Moses, 287 Mass. 393, 191 N.E. 873 (1934). For a discussion of the various types of insurance trusts and their uses, see § 47, post.

38. Pierowich v. Metropolitan Life Ins. Co., 282 Mich. 118, 275 N.W. 789 (1937); but see Johnson v. New York Life Ins. Co., 75 F.2d 425 (5th Cir.1935); New York Life

While legislation has been adopted in some states to the effect that the proceeds, although not segregated, shall be deemed held in trust by the insurance companies and that the interests of the beneficiaries shall be inalienable and not subject to their debts, and so the appearance of a spendthrift trust is created,[39] the real effect is that the claims against the insurance companies are given protection similar to that of the interests of trust beneficiaries.

Powers of Appointment

Sometimes powers of appointment are given to persons who are directed to exercise the powers for the benefit of others and these powers are called imperative or "powers in trust." Thus a testator owning a fee simple estate in Blackacre may devise a life estate in it to B, with a direction that B appoint the remainder interest in Blackacre, following B's life interest, to the children of B. The question has been raised whether the power of appointment is held strictly in trust and can be the res of a trust. It would seem that such a power can be held in trust and is so held until the death of the donee of the power, but that if the donee dies without fulfilling his duty to appoint, equity will fasten a constructive trust on the property for the benefit of those to whom the donee should have appointed.[40]

 WESTLAW REFERENCES

Necessity for Trust Property

390k1

390k10

di("subject matter" res corpus /s trust /s essential necessary)

money stock patent "promissory note" /s "subject matter" /3 trust

"inalienable trust"

trust /2 res /s contingent

Certainty as to Trust Res

certainty /s trust /2 res

390k13

390k21(2)

Attempted Present Trusts of Future Property

find 59 ne2d 657

Insurance a Trust Subject-Matter

insurance /10 subject res /2 trust

Ins. Co. v. Conrad, 269 Ky. 359, 107 S.W.2d 248 (1937); Van Hecke, Insurance Trusts— The Insurer as Trustee, 7 N.C.L.R. 21.

39. For a collection of statutory references, see Bogert, Trusts and Trustees (rev. 2d edit.), § 240.

40. In re Uihlein's Will, 264 Wis. 362, 59 N.W.2d 641, 38 A.L.R.2d 961 (1953).

Gray, Powers in Trust and Gifts Implied in Default of Appointment, 25 Harv.L.R. 1; Simes, Powers in Trust and the Termination of Powers by the Donee, 37 Yale L.J. 63; Bogert, Trusts and Trustees (rev. 2d edit.), § 116.

DEBT AND TRUST DISTINGUISHED [1]

§ 26. A trust is distinguished from a debt in that the trustee's duties always relates to specific property, whereas the debtor's obligation need not relate to definite property and usually does not.

In addition the relations are distinguishable in that

(a) **Debt arises out of a contract, whereas the trust usually arises from a conveyance;**

(b) **A contract generally requires consideration to make it enforceable, while a trust does not;**

(c) **Sometimes contracts are not enforceable by third party beneficiaries, whereas trusts do not require privity between the trustee and beneficiary;**

(d) **The trustee's obligations are equitable, while the debtor's are legal and any remedies which the creditor may have in a court of equity are auxiliary to the relief given by a court of law;**

(e) **The trustee occupies a fiduciary relation, but the debtor does not.**

The Trust Requires a Definite Subject

The property which the trustee controls for the benefit of his beneficiary is always definite or definable property. A debtor does not usually owe his creditor definite money; he owes him *any* money. If A is a trustee for B, A always owns specific property, for example, the Jones farm or certain Treasury bills, as the subject-matter of the trust. A may have the power under the trust to change the form of the investment, and to buy bonds with the bills originally received; but the bonds then become the specific subject-matter. On the other hand, if A borrows $50,000 from B, it is obvious that A may satisfy his obligation to B by paying any bills or currency. He need not return the identical bills or currency received from B, or their substitutes, in case he invests the money received from B. It is true that one may agree to satisfy contract obligations out of a particular source, as where an employer promises to pay his employee as a salary one half the net sales from a business at the end of each week; but such contracts are rare and merely show that a contract *may* relate to definite property but not that it *must* so relate.

The results of this contrast between trust and debt are striking. If the debtor loses any piece of property through accident, he will not be

§ 26

1. Restatement, Trusts, Second, §§ 12–14.

absolved from payment of his debt; but, if the trust property is lost or destroyed without the fault of the trustee, his obligation is extinguished.[2]

Again, each unsecured creditor is obliged to share pro rata with his fellow creditors all the property of his bankrupt debtor,[3] even though the debtor has in his hands and capable of identification certain specific money lent him or goods sold him. On the other hand, the beneficiary may take from the assets of the bankrupt trustee the specific trust property, if he can identify it.[4]

A debtor, with certain exceptions unnecessary to mention here, may do as he likes with the money he receives from his creditor, or with his property generally. A trustee will be guilty of the crime of embezzlement if he converts to his own use the trust funds.[5] The specific nature of the trust property requires him to keep it separate from private use.

Debt Arises Out of Contract

Debts as here considered are obligations arising from the making of contracts. Hence their enforceability and the methods of their enforcement depend upon the rules of contract law which, for the most part, have been developed by the common law courts. Trust creation is, on the other hand, essentially a conveyance. The creator of the trust conveys an equitable interest to the beneficiary.[6] The transferor to a trustee conveys the legal interest to the trustee and the equitable interest to the beneficiary.[7] It is true that one may create a trust by promising to pay money to another as trustee for a third party, and here rules of contract law will determine whether the trust has a subject-matter of value;[8] nevertheless the promisor is also conveying legal and equitable interests in the chose in action against himself.

Consideration

The contracts out of which the debt arises are, with some exceptions, dependent on consideration for their enforceability.[9] Completely created trusts are enforceable, without regard to the receipt of consideration by settlor or trustee.[10] Thus if A agrees voluntarily to pay $100 to B, the promise may be repudiated by A with impunity in most cases; while if A voluntarily declares himself trustee of a specific $100 bond for B, the latter can enforce the trust despite the lack of consideration in the transaction.

2. Shoemaker v. Hinze, 53 Wis. 116, 10 N.W. 86. In the so-called "unshrinkable" trust, the trustee guarantees the return of the trust capital (In re Cunningham's Estate, 328 Pa. 107, 195 A. 130 (1937)), but this transaction is exceedingly rare and is now prohibited by statute in Pennsylvania.

3. City of Sturgis v. Meade County Bank, 38 S.D. 317, 161 N.W. 327.

4. See § 161, post.

5. People v. Meadows, 199 N.Y. 1, 92 N.E. 128.

6. See § 37, post.

7. See § 32, post.

8. See § 10, ante.

9. Restatement, Contracts, Second, 71–94.

10. See § 24, ante.

Privity

In a few jurisdictions it has been held to be necessary, at least in some cases, to show that the plaintiff was a party to the contract which he seeks to enforce.[11] This idea of privity is foreign to the law of trusts. Chancery enforces trust obligations in favor of beneficiaries who were not parties to the trust instrument and knew nothing of its creation until after the event.[12] Here again the conveyance theory of trust creation is apparent.

Debt a Legal and Trust an Equitable Obligation

As previously stated, the trust is an obligation resting solely on equitable principles, and originally enforceable only in chancery. In a great variety of ways equity will act upon the trustee, and compel him to do or refrain from doing certain acts.[13] The debtor's duties, however, are legal, and are ordinarily enforced by an action to recover the amount of the debt. Equity may, of course, aid the creditor, but the primary method of enforcement is by legal remedies. The courts of law have been largely responsible for defining and enforcing contract rights; whereas chancery first recognized and has fostered and developed the trust.

No Fiduciary Relation in Debt

The debtor's obligations are all self-imposed. He agrees to pay the creditor $100 on January 1st. That is his only duty to the creditor. There is no relationship of trust and confidence between debtor and creditor. The law imposes no obligation on the debtor to deal with the creditor with any more than ordinary fairness. The debtor and creditor may each look out for himself. Neither has a duty to protect the other. They deal with each other at arm's length. In contrast the trustee is a fiduciary, whose obligations are not only those which he has voluntarily assumed by express agreement, but also those which the law imposes on him, whether he will or no. Among those law-imposed duties are the obligations that the trustee act solely in the interest of the beneficiary, treat the beneficiary with the utmost fairness and frankness, conceal nothing from him, and take no advantage of him. To illustrate: A debtor may buy from his creditor any property which the latter will sell him, and which he (the debtor) can pay for. But a beneficiary may avoid a sale of his interest under the trust from himself to his trustee, unless the latter can prove the transaction was absolutely fair and open.[14] Because of this intimacy and control over the beneficiary's affairs, a trustee has been held subject to arrest under some statutes for breach of his duties, where a mere debtor would not

---

11. See Restatement, Contracts, §§ 132, 147. In recent years the privity doctrine has been greatly limited or repudiated. See Restatements, Contracts, Second, § 302 et seq.

12. See § 36, post. And see Bryant v. Russell, 23 Pick. 508.

13. See §§ 153–165, post.

14. See § 96, post.

be.[15]

While it is sometimes loosely said that in the case of a contract to sell land which is specifically enforceable the vendor is a trustee of the land for the vendee and the vendee is a trustee of the unpaid price for the vendor,[16] there is no trust in a strict sense.[17] The vendee has rights enforceable in equity with relation to specific property, as does a trust beneficiary, but there is no fiduciary relation between vendor and vendee and no intent that the vendor shall be a property manager for the vendee.

 WESTLAW REFERENCES

The Trust Requires a Definite Subject
390k21(1)
trust /s require! /s definite definable /s property
390k1

Debt Arises Out of Contract Consideration
390k96
390k357(3)

Privity
di privity

Debt a Legal and Trust an Equitable Obligation
trustee /s compell*** /s perform /s act

No Fiduciary Relation in Debt
"fiduciary relationship" /s debtor /s creditor

BORDERLINE DEBT–TRUST CASES—THE SPECIFIC PROPERTY CRITERION

§ 27. Frequently where insolvency of an obligor has intervened, it is important to determine whether he was a debtor out of whose estate a mere dividend can be recovered, or a trustee from whose estate specific property can be taken. Some of the more important situations involving this controversy are the cases of

   (a) Commercial paper delivered to a bank for collection;

   (b) Money paid to agents;

   (c) Money deposited or paid to enable the deliveree to meet an obligation of the deliveror;

   (d) Security deposits of agents, tenants and servants;

   (e) Funds delivered to be lent or invested by the deliveree for the deliveror;

---

15. Wallace & Sons v. Castle, 14 Hun. 106.

16. Mitchell v. White, 244 Ala. 603, 14 So.2d 687 (1943).

17. Huebener v. Chinn, 186 Or. 508, 207 P.2d 1136 (1949); Restatement, Trusts, Second, § 13; Williston, 9 Harv.L.R. 106.

(f) **Funds delivered to be transmitted for the deliveror or to furnish credit for the deliveror at a distance;**

(g) **Special and general bank deposits;**

(h) **Property conveyed in return for a promise to support the grantor.**

In all these cases the better reasoned decisions hold that if the obligor is to meet his obligation out of particular property he is probably intended to be a trustee of that property, but if he is to perform his duty by the use of any property in his hands which is convenient to him then he is probably intended to be under contract duties only. Since banks and other similar commercial institutions do not usually wish to bind themselves to the earmarking of assets to meet their various obligations, the finding of a trust intent in such cases is rarely justified.

Collection of Commercial Paper [1]

Drafts, checks, and notes are frequently deposited by a customer with his bank for the purpose of having the bank collect the paper from the drawee or maker. Many of these instruments are payable by parties at a distance and hence the instruments have to be sent by the original bank through banking channels for collection. For instance, if A has received from B a check drawn by B in favor of A on the First National Bank of Jonesville and A lives in Brownstown, A will deposit the check to the credit of his account in a Brownstown bank and it will be forwarded by the Brownstown bank through other banks (generally through the Federal Reserve system) to a bank in Jonesville for collection.

The cases of negotiable paper deposited for collection may be divided into two classes, namely: (1) Cases where the paper is uncollected at the time the dispute arises, and the contending parties are the depositor of the paper and the representative of a failed bank; (2) cases where the paper has been collected when the rights of the parties are fixed and the claimants are the same.

The majority of the courts which have considered the first class of cases, namely, those of uncollected paper in the hands of the original intended collector, have directed that the uncollected paper be returned to the forwarder on theories of agency or trust.[2] Little or no attention

§ 27

1. For some law review discussions, see Turner, 37 Yale L.J. 874; Townsend, 39 Yale L.J. 980; 62 Harv.L.R. 905; Bogert, 29 Mich.L.R. 545.

2. Commercial Nat. Bank v. Armstrong, 148 U.S. 50, 13 S.Ct. 533, 37 L.Ed. 363 (1893); Manufacturers' Nat. Bank v. Continental Bank, 148 Mass. 553, 20 N.E. 193, 2 L.R.A. 699, 12 Am.St.Rep. 598; Bank of America v. Waydell, 187 N.Y. 115, 79 N.E. 857; Hazlett v. Commercial Nat. Bank, 132 Pa. 118, 19 A. 55; Second Nat. Bank of Columbia v. Cummings, 89 Tenn. 609, 18 S.W. 115, 24 Am.St.Rep. 618.

There is some ambiguity in the discussion of the relationship here existing. Thus one writer spoke of the collector as an "agent, i.e., trustee" (Ames, Cases on Trusts, 2d Ed., 18, 19), and another called the collector an "agent or trustee" (Tiffany, Banks and Banking, 28).

If the representative of the failed bank collects the item after the bank's insolven-

seems to have been paid to the form of the indorsement to the collector, whether general and unqualified, or restrictive. An unrestrictive indorsement would pass title to the instrument to the collector, and, since ordinarily he would not also be the beneficial owner, he would seem to be properly a trustee. But if the indorsement was restrictive, in that it was "for collection," title would not pass to the collector although he would have power to sue on the instrument, and he would be a mere agent.[3]

As to the second class mentioned above, those cases where the collector has received the proceeds of the collection and the contest is between depositor and collector, it would seem logical that the collecting bank should be regarded as a debtor after collection in most cases, since it does not, in the ordinary instance, intend to keep separate any bills, coins or credit received for the collected paper. The collection is usually accomplished by the giving of a check to the collector by the drawee or in other ways using the item to increase the amount of the collector's credit or decrease the amount of its debts. Cash is not usually delivered to the collector. As a rule the collecting bank expects to pay the depositor from any source which it has conveniently at hand. It expects to have the right to use the proceeds of the collection for its own purposes, and to satisfy its obligation to the forwarder by sending him a check or draft or giving him a book credit. Such incidents are inconsistent with a trust, which is always founded on definite subject-matter. Most courts have held the collector to be a mere debtor after collection.[4]

The American Bankers' Association Bank Collection Code had been adopted in several states [5] and attempted to settle the rights of parties to these collection transactions. It made a bank in possession of uncollected paper an agent, and permitted the forwarder of paper after its collection to obtain payment in full out of the assets of the bank which had collected, even though the proceeds of the collection could not be traced into the property of the failed collecting bank.[6] This statute by its terms applied to all banks, national and state, but was held by the United States Supreme Court [7] to be unconstitutional in so

cy has been adjudged, the forwarder of the item is entitled to a preference to the extent of the amount collected. Hardesty v. Smith, 118 Fla. 464, 159 So. 522; Fine v. Receiver of Dickenson County Bank, 163 Va. 157, 175 S.E. 863, 94 A.L.R. 1393 (1934).

3. Negotiable Instruments Law, § 37; Uniform Commercial Code, § 3–206.

4. Plumas County Bank v. Bank of Rideout, Smith & Co., 165 Cal. 126, 131 P. 360, 47 L.R.A.,N.S., 552; Tinkham v. Heyworth, 31 Ill. 519; North Carolina Corporation Commission v. Merchants' & Farmers' Bank, 137 N.C. 697, 50 S.E. 308; Hallam v. Tillinghast, 19 Wash. 20, 52 P. 329. For a full discussion of the authori-

ties, see Bogert, Collection Items and Failed Banks, 29 Mich.L.R. 545.

5. For example, Alabama, Hawaii, Illinois, Indiana, Kentucky, Maryland, Michigan, Missouri, Nebraska, New Jersey, New Mexico, New York, North Dakota, Oklahoma, Oregon, Pennsylvania, South Carolina, West Virginia, Washington, Wisconsin, Wyoming.

6. For the discussion of the Code, see 43 Harv.L.R. 307, 8 Tul.L.R. 21.

7. Old Company's Lehigh, Inc. v. Meeker, 294 U.S. 227, 55 S.Ct. 392, 79 L.Ed. 876 (1935). In Illinois the entire Code had been held invalid because of the unconstitutionality of that part affecting

far as it attempted to regulate the disposition of the assets of failed national banks, since Congress alone had power over that matter and had acted in regard to it by providing for equal distribution among unsecured creditors.

Under the Uniform Commercial Code which is intended to supercede prior legislation on the subject, and which has been adopted (with some modifications) in all states except Louisiana, a preference is given to the forwarder of a collection item out of the assets of a failed bank which collected before closing but never remitted.[8]

Money Paid to Agents

Where money is paid to one for the use of another, or where the sale proceeds of another's property are held, it is sometimes difficult to distinguish trust from debt. It is often held that such persons as commission agents receiving the proceeds of goods sold,[9] insurance agents collecting premiums,[10] an agent to sell bonds,[11] and a collector of rents [12] are trustees of the money so coming into their hands, when the expectation of the parties is that the agent will keep separate the cash or credit he receives, earmark it as that of his principal, and remit it to his principal. But if he is at liberty to use the proceeds as his own in return for a contract obligation to pay some money to the principal, debt is the normal relationship.[13]

In an escrow transaction, for example, where a buyer of real estate delivers to an escrow agent cash or a check to be handed to the seller at the closing date, the relation between the buyer and the escrow agent would seem to depend on the express or implied understanding as to what the agent was to do with the cash or check pending completion of the transaction. If he was to hold it separate and apart and deliver it or its proceeds to the seller, he would seem to be a bailee if he had mere possession or a trustee if he had title and possession.[14] But if he was to use the cash or check as his own, in return for assuming an obligation to pay a given amount from any of the assets of the escrow agent to the seller at the closing, it would seem clear that he ought to be held to be a debtor and no preference should be given the buyer if the agent fails

---

national banks. People ex rel. Barrett v. Union Bank & Trust Co., 362 Ill. 164, 199 N.E. 272, 104 A.L.R. 1090 (1935). In other states adopting the Code, however, apparently the portion of it relating to state banks is valid.

8. § 4–501(2).

9. Baker v. New York Nat. Exch. Bank, 100 N.Y. 31, 2 N.E. 452, 53 Am.Rep. 150; Boyle v. Northwestern Nat. Bank, 125 Wis. 498, 103 N.W. 1123, 104 N.W. 917, 1 L.R.A.,N.S., 1110, 110 Am.St.Rep. 844.

10. Dillon v. Connecticut Mut. Life Ins. Co., 44 Md. 386; American Surety Co. v. Greenwald, 223 Minn. 37, 25 N.W.2d 681 (1946).

11. Van Alen v. American Nat. Bank, 52 N.Y. 1; Bank of Beaufort v. Commercial Nat. Bank, 207 N.C. 216, 176 S.E. 734 (1934).

12. Grindey v. Smith, 237 Iowa 227, 21 N.W.2d 465 (1946); Farmers' & Mechanics' Nat. Bank v. King, 57 Pa. 202, 98 Am.Dec. 215.

13. Boss v. Hardee, 70 App.D.C. 50, 103 F.2d 751 (1939).

14. Burket v. Bank of Hollywood, 9 Cal.2d 113, 69 P.2d 421 (1937); Smith v. Macbeth, 119 Fla. 796, 161 So. 721 (1935).

before having paid the seller.[15]

Money Delivered to Pay Deliveror's Debt

Frequently a debtor, instead of paying a debt directly, employs a bank or other intermediary to pay it for him and delivers to the intermediary cash or credit for the purpose of procuring the payment of the debt. Thus a person who has drawn a check, or accepted a draft, or signed a note, payable at a given bank,[16] or who owes taxes [17] or the purchase price of property bought or to be bought,[18] may make an arrangement with a bank whereby it agrees to meet his obligation in return for a deposit of cash or commercial paper which he makes. Another example of this situation is that where an obligor on bonds arranges with a local bank to have it provide credit at a distant bank to meet the principal or interest on the bonds.[19]

In all these cases it is unnatural to expect the bank or other intermediary to use the exact cash or credit delivered to it in accomplishing the desired purpose. It is much more natural to construe the transaction as permitting the intermediary to use any of its cash or credit for that purpose and to be able to appropriate the cash or credit delivered to it for any of its own purposes. Banks and similar intermediaries expect freedom to meet their obligations from any assets which are at the time convenient. Hence it would seem reasonable that transactions of this type should be held to create contract relations only, and that the intermediary should not be held a trustee of the cash or credit delivered to it in return for its promise.[20] However, in some cases on more or less satisfactory evidence of an intent to have the very property delivered or its product used to satisfy the obligation of the deliveror, the courts have held that the deliveree was a trustee.[21]

Security Deposits

If an employee or tenant is required by his employer or landlord to make a cash deposit as security for performance of his duties, it is not normally expected that the deposited money will be segregated or deposited in a special bank deposit. It is rather usually intended that the cash or credit deposited can be used as the absolute property of the party with whom it is deposited and that he can satisfy his duty to the depositor by paying any cash or credit of the same amount. The

---

15. Squire v. Nally, 130 Ohio St. 582, 200 N.E. 840 (1936).

16. Furber v. Barnes, 32 Minn. 105, 19 N.W. 728; Bank of Blackwell v. Dean, 9 Okl. 626, 60 P. 226.

17. Gutknecht v. Sorge, 195 Wis. 477, 218 N.W. 726 (1928).

18. Lamb v. Ladd, 112 Kan. 26, 209 P. 825 (1922).

19. Wallace v. Elliott, 87 F.2d 230 (4th Cir.1937); Hershey v. Northern Trust Co., 342 Mo. 90, 112 S.W.2d 545 (1937).

20. Stonebraker v. First National Bank, 76 F.2d 389 (5th Cir.1935); In re Kountze Bros., 104 F.2d 157 (2d Cir.1939); Blakey v. Brinson, 286 U.S. 254, 52 S.Ct. 516, 76 L.Ed. 1089, 82 A.L.R. 1288 (1932); Baiar v. O'Connell, 365 Ill. 208, 6 N.E.2d 140 (1936).

21. Town of La Fayette v. Williams, 232 Ala. 502, 168 So. 668 (1936); Dolph v. Cross, 153 Iowa 289, 133 N.W. 669; Stein v. Kemp, 132 Minn. 44, 155 N.W. 1052.

normal construction is, therefore, contract and not trust.[22]

Funds Delivered for Investment

If cash or credit is left with an attorney, bank or investment counsellor for investment, or to be lent out on bond and mortgage, the relation should be that of debtor and creditor if the investor is to be at liberty to use the funds he receives as his own, and to make the investment from any of his own funds later.[23] However the arrangement should be a trust relation if the funds delivered to the attorney or other party are to be translated directly into a special bank account and then into the investment in the name of the client.[24] The payment of interest by the attorney or bank tends strongly to prove a debt, since interest is a payment for the use of the cash or credit as that of the attorney or bank.[25]

Transmission of Funds—Purchase of Foreign Credit

When a customer delivers to a bank or foreign exchange house cash or a check for the purpose of procuring the transmission of funds to a foreign country and the establishment of credit by cable or otherwise in the customer's favor or for the benefit of another there, the implied understanding is not that the bank will use the cash or credit received by it as the source of the foreign credit to be established, but rather that the bank will treat what it receives as its own property and consider itself under a contract duty to establish the credit for its customer from any source it finds convenient. This is characteristic of contract and not of trust.[26]

Bank Deposits

The relation between customer and bank in the case of a *general* bank deposit, which results in the creation of, or addition to, a checking account, is that of debtor and creditor. The bank becomes the absolute owner of the cash and commercial paper handed to its teller at the time

---

22. Povey v. Colonial Beacon Oil Co., 294 Mass. 86, 200 N.E. 891 (1936); State by Van Riper v. Atlantic City Elec. Co., 23 N.J. 259, 128 A.2d 861 (1957) (public utility security deposits create debt); De Vol v. Citizens' Bank, 92 Or. 606, 179 P. 282, rehearing denied 92 Or. 606, 181 P. 985. By statute these deposits are sometimes declared to be held in trust. Wilson, 34 Col.L.R. 426.

23. Wetherell v. O'Brien, 140 Ill. 146, 29 N.E. 904, 33 Am.St.Rep. 221; Budd v. Walker, 113 N.Y. 637, 21 N.E. 72. See State v. United States Steel Co., 12 N.J. 51, 95 A.2d 740 (1953) (employer made deductions from wages to pay for government bonds; trust created for Statute of Limitations purposes, although no setting apart of any property).

24. Kornbau v. Evans, 66 Cal.App.2d 677, 152 P.2d 651 (1944); Harrison v. Smith, 83 Mo. 210, 53 Am.Rep. 571; Rusling v. Rusling's Ex'rs, 42 N.J.Eq. 594, 8 A. 534; Cavin v. Gleason, 105 N.Y. 256, 11 N.E. 504.

25. Steuber v. O'Keefe, 16 F.Supp. 97 (D.N.J.1936); Pittsburgh Nat. Bank of Commerce v. McMurray, 98 Pa. 538.

26. Equitable Trust Co. of New York v. First Nat. Bk. of Trinidad, Colo., 275 U.S. 359, 48 S.Ct. 167, 72 L.Ed. 313 (1928); Beecher v. Cosmopolitan Trust Co., 239 Mass. 48, 131 N.E. 338 (1921); Legniti v. Mechanics & Metals Nat. Bank of New York, 230 N.Y. 415, 130 N.E. 597, 16 A.L.R. 185 (1921), noted in 19 Col.L.R. 322. See Stone, Legal Problems in the Transmission of Funds, 21 Col.L.R. 507.

of the deposit, and the customer becomes a general creditor of the bank, with no property interest in the cash or paper, or the proceeds of the cash or paper, which he brought to the bank.

This is true whether the funds deposited are ordinary private funds or are public monies, like those of a county treasurer,[27] or are funds held in a fiduciary capacity by the depositor, as in the case of a deposit by an executor or trustee of the funds of the estate or trust.[28] Therefore, in the absence of statute,[29] the public agency or trustee should be a general creditor in case of the failure of the bank, and not preferred on the theory that the bank was a trustee for the depositor.[30]

If the deposit is wrongfully made, however, in that the depositor has no authority to make it, or the bank no authority to receive it, the bank becomes the owner of that which is deposited, subject to a constructive trust in favor of the depositor or those whom he represents,[31] and on the failure of the bank the depositor can take from the assets of the failed bank the trust res or its substitute, if he can find it among the assets on hand at failure.

The term *special* bank deposit is a vague one. It may mean that the depositor has brought money or paper to the bank and deposited it under a label which shows that he intends to use it for a limited purpose, as in the coupon or dividend account cases elsewhere discussed.[32] Or it may mean that the bank, in return for cash or paper delivered to it, undertakes to perform certain acts beneficial to the depositor such as paying his debt to a named creditor, in which case the bank should be held to be a trustee only if it obligated itself to perform its duty out of the funds deposited or their product.[33]

Property Received in Return for Promise of Support

If an owner of a farm or home transfers the property to another in return for the promise by the latter that he will support the grantor during his life, and on the understanding that the grantee is to become the absolute owner of the property on the death of the grantor, it is sometimes claimed that the grantee is a trustee during the life of the grantor, and there is room for this construction where the support was

---

27. City of Fulton v. Home Trust Co., 336 Mo. 239, 78 S.W.2d 445 (1934); State ex rel. Village of Warrensville Heights v. Fulton, 128 Ohio St. 192, 190 N.E. 383 (1934).

28. Corbett v. Hospelhorn, 172 Md. 257, 191 A. 691 (1937); Parker v. Hood ex rel. Central Bank & Trust Co., 209 N.C. 494, 183 S.E. 737 (1936).

29. For references to cases of preferences on statutory or sovereignty grounds, see Bogert, Trusts and Trustees (rev. 2d edit.), § 21.

30. First Nat. Bank in St. Louis v. West End Bank of University City, 344 Mo.

834, 129 S.W.2d 879 (1939); In re State Bank of Elkhorn, 129 Neb. 506, 262 N.W. 15 (1935); State ex rel. Village of Warrensville Heights v. Fulton, 128 Ohio St. 192, 190 N.E. 383 (1934).

31. Screws v. Williams, 230 Ala. 392, 161 So. 453 (1935); Dewey v. Commercial State Bank, 141 Kan. 356, 41 P.2d 1006 (1935).

32. See § 28, post.

33. For discussions of the meaning of "special deposit", see Cardozo, C.J., in 247 N.Y. 52, 55, 159 N.E. 720; 6 Minn.L.R. 306; 10 Tex.L.R. 71; 32 Yale L.J. 411, 851.

to be furnished from the income or principal of the property granted.[34] However the courts are more apt to work out relief for the grantor on the theory of a rescindable contract [35] or an estate on condition subsequent with a right of reentry in the grantor on breach of the promise to support.[36]

 WESTLAW REFERENCES

Collection of Commercial Paper
find 13 sct 533

Money Paid to Agents
52k80(6)
find 69 p2d 421

Money Delivered to Pay Deliveror's Debt
find 76 f2d 389

Security Deposits
"security deposit" /s trust

Funds Delivered for Investment
find 16 f.supp. 97
52k80(7)

Transmission of Funds—Purchase of Foreign Credit
find 48 sct 167

Bank Deposits
"constructive trust" /s depositor
"special bank deposit"

Property Received in Return for Promise of Support
dew +3 requa
property /5 receiv*** /5 support*** /5 grantor

BORDERLINE DEBT-TRUST CASES—THE DEBTOR MAKING HIMSELF TRUSTEE

§ 28. A debtor may, in addition to making himself liable at law on his contract, set up a trust of some of his property to secure the payment of the debt. Examples of cases where it has been claimed that a debtor has created such a trust are to be found where a special bank account has been set up by a corporation to pay dividends to stockholders or interest on bonds, and where an employer creates a payroll bank account from which to pay salaries and wages.

Sometimes it is alleged that one who is admittedly a debtor has set aside part of his property as the subject matter of a trust for the benefit of the creditor, thus giving the creditor an additional remedy beside the

34. Dew v. Requa, 218 Ark. 911, 239 S.W.2d 603 (1951); Norton v. Norton, 50 Cal.App. 483, 195 P. 441 (1920).

35. Oglesby v. Thomas, 245 Ala. 133, 16 So.2d 320 (1944); Payne v. Winters, 366 Pa. 299, 77 A.2d 407 (1951).

36. Hoadley v. Hoadley, 114 Vt. 75, 39 A.2d 769 (1944).

contract claim in a court of law, namely, an equitable claim against the trust property.[1] A corporation which has issued bonds with interest coupons may deposit a sum of money in a bank and entitle the account "coupon account", thus indicating an intention to pay the coupons from that source.[2] Or a corporation which has declared a dividend may make a bank deposit headed "dividend account" and direct the bank to pay from it checks drawn in payment of the dividend.[3] Or an employer who owes his employees salaries or wages may create a payroll account in a bank for the purpose of having such claims paid from this account.[4]

In each of these cases it is a question of fact whether the debtor really intended to declare himself trustee of the property from which it is alleged he agreed that the debt should be paid. If the debtor merely contracted to pay out of particular property, or merely stated his intention to pay out of such property, he did not become a trustee; but if his conduct amounted to an implied declaration that he held the bank account in trust for the purpose of paying the particular creditor or creditors, then such expressed intent should be effective. The question is one of interpretation of the debtor's acts. The tendency has been to treat the dividend account as held in trust for the stockholders,[5] but the coupon and payroll accounts as not held in trust.[6] There seems to be no basis for this distinction. A reasonable construction is that the debtor intends to hold all such special accounts in trust for the creditors,[7] unless he expressly states otherwise, and subject to a power to revoke the trust and use the account for other purposes. The bank in which such an account exists should not be held to be a trustee for the depositor or his creditors [8] since it does not agree to hold any particular assets for the benefit of the depositor or of his special creditors.

§ 28

1. For instances where it was claimed that the debtor had set up a trust fund to guarantee the collection of the debt against him, see In re United Cigar Stores, C.A.2, 1934, 70 F.2d 313; In re Prudence Co., E.D. N.Y.1938, 24 F.Supp. 666.

2. Guidise v. Island Refining Corp., 291 Fed. 922 (D.C.N.Y.1923).

3. Interborough Consol. Corp., In re Petition of H. Content & Co., 267 F. 914 (D.C.N.Y.1920).

4. Northern Sugar Corp. v. Thompson, 13 F.2d 829 (8th Cir.1926). See Killoren v. First Nat. Bank, 127 F.2d 537 (8th Cir. 1942) (employer not trustee of payroll account for employees).

5. Le Roy v. Globe Ins. Co., 2 Edw.Ch. 656; Matter of Le Blanc, 14 Hun 8, affirmed 75 N.Y. 598.

6. Schloss v. Powell, 93 F.2d 518 (4th Cir.1938); Nacional Financiera, S.A. v.

Speyer, 261 App.Div. 599, 26 N.Y.S.2d 865 (1941); Homan v. First Nat. Bank, 316 Pa. 23, 172 A. 647 (1934). And see Ehag Eisenbahnwerte Holding Aktiengesellschaft v. Banca Nationala a Romanisi, 306 N.Y. 242, 117 N.E.2d 346 (1954).

7. See § 2, Uniform Trusts Act, where an attempt is made to solve the inconsistency between the coupon and dividend cases by declaring that all such special accounts are held in trust, unless expressly provided otherwise. For the text of this Act see Bogert, Trusts and Trustees (rev. 2d edit.), § 7.

8. Carnegie-Illinois Steel Corp. v. Berger, 105 F.2d 485 (3d Cir.1939) certiorari denied 308 U.S. 603, 60 S.Ct. 140, 84 L.Ed. 504 (1939); Security Nat. Bank Sav. & Tr. Co. v. Moberly, 340 Mo. 95, 101 S.W.2d 33 (1936).

WESTLAW REFERENCES

debtor /s create set-up /s trust /s creditor

"dividend account"

find 117 ne2d 346

52k119 /p trust

52k153

SELECTION OF THE TRUSTEE—THE EFFECT OF LACK OF A TRUSTEE [1]

§ 29. Ordinarily the trustee is appointed by the settlor, but he may be appointed by the court of equity or the probate court.

Equity will not allow a trust to fail for want of a trustee. If at the beginning of the trust the settlor creates an otherwise complete trust but no trustee is named, or the trustee named is nonexistent or incompetent to accept, or refuses to accept the trust, chancery will supply a trustee, and the settlor's intent to have a trust will be effectuated. The same procedure normally follows where there is a vacancy in the trusteeship during the life of the trust and the settlor has not provided for filling the vacancy.

In rare cases a settlor expresses an intent that the trustee he names shall be the only one capable of administering the trust. Here the trust does fail if the named trustee is deceased when the trust is supposed to begin, or declines to accept the trust. The court does not supply a successor in such a case.

The original appointment of the trustee is ordinarily the function of the settlor.[2] By very definition the settlor is the person who selects the trustee, trust property and beneficiary, and establishes the trust.

In appointing the trustee, the settlor is not under any obligation to consider the wishes of the beneficiary,[3] nor need he use any particular language or describe the trustee as such.[4] It is sufficient if he clearly shows an intent that a trust arise and that a given person shall administer it. For example, that the word "committee," rather than "trustee," was used, is not important, if the intent to create a trust was evident.[5] And so, also, where a will makes a bequest in trust, but no trustee is expressly named to carry out the trust, the executor is often deemed to have been impliedly appointed a trustee for that purpose.[6]

§ 29

1. Restatement, Trusts, Second, §§ 32, 33.

2. Cruse v. Axtell, 50 Ind. 49; Leonard v. Haworth, 171 Mass. 496, 51 N.E. 7.

3. In re Naglee's Estate, 52 Pa. 154.

4. Grant Trust & Savings Co. v. Tucker, 49 Ind.App. 345, 96 N.E. 487.

5. Boreing v. Faris, 127 Ky. 67, 104 S.W. 1022, 31 Ky.Law Rep. 1265.

6. Holbrook v. Harrington, 16 Gray, Mass., 102; Terry v. Smith, 42 N.J.Eq. 504, 8 A. 886; Montfort v. Montfort, 24 Hun, N.Y., 120.

In some instances the original trustee may be appointed by the court rather than by the settlor.[7]

No trust can be administered without a trustee, but the failure of the settlor to select a trustee, or his selection of a trustee who cannot or will not act, is not fatal to the origin of the trust. The identity of the trustee is usually of little importance. Equity will not allow a trust to fail in origin merely for lack of a trustee.[8] Thus if the settlor does all the acts necessary to establish a trust, but fails to name any trustee, the court will supply the deficiency and appoint a trustee to administer the trust. Or if the trustee named by the settlor can never enter upon the performance of his duties, due to the fact that he has died prior to the taking effect of the trust instrument,[9] or because he declines the trust,[10] or because he is disqualified[11] or incompetent,[12] equity will supply a trustee.

The settlor may provide for a substitute or successor trustee if the first one named does not or cannot take;[13] or he may give power to others to supply a trustee, either at the beginning of the trust or a successor trustee thereafter.[14]

Whether A or B is the trustee to administer the trust is not usually important. Any competent and honest man can carry out the intent of the settlor. The important object to be accomplished is the establishment and enforcement of an equitable interest in the beneficiaries, and not the identity of the mere representative or administrator, the trustee. Equity has as a part of its inherent jurisdiction the power and duty to see that trusts are protected and carried out, and the filling of the office of trustee is a part of this function.

Occasionally a settlor picks as trustee the only person in the world who in his opinion is qualified to administer the trust, and expresses an intent that the one named and no one else shall carry out his trust.

7. Bundy v. Bundy, 38 N.Y. 410; In re Weed, 181 App.Div. 921, 167 N.Y.S. 862.

In some states a testamentary trustee is deemed to be nominated by the testator but appointed by the court. See, for example, In re Barter's Estate, 30 Cal.2d 549, 184 P.2d 305 (1947).

8. Kidd v. Borum, 181 Ala. 144, 61 So. 100; Appeal of Eliot, 74 Conn. 586, 51 A. 558; Hitchcock v. Board of Home Missions of Presbyterian Church, 259 Ill. 288, 102 N.E. 741, Ann.Cas.1915B, 1; In re Freeman's Estate, 146 Iowa 38, 124 N.W. 804; Attorney General v. Goodell, 180 Mass. 538, 62 N.E. 962; Penny v. Croul, 76 Mich. 471, 43 N.W. 649, 5 L.R.A. 858; Rothenberger v. Garrett, 224 Mo. 191, 123 S.W. 574; Jones v. Watford, 62 N.J.Eq. 339, 50 A. 180; In re Powell's Will, 136 App. Div. 830, 121 N.Y.S. 779; Goodrum v. Goodrum, 43 N.C. 313; Hill v. Hill, 49 Okl. 424, 152 P. 1122; In re Stevens' Estate, 200

Pa. 318, 49 A. 985; Gidley v. Lovenberg, 35 Tex.Civ.App. 203, 79 S.W. 831.

As to filling vacancies after the trust has begun, see § 32, post.

9. Ex parte Schouler, 134 Mass. 426; Woodruff v. Woodruff, 44 N.J.Eq. 349, 16 A. 4, 1 L.R.A. 380.

10. Carruth v. Carruth, 148 Mass. 431, 19 N.E. 369; King v. Merritt, 67 Mich. 194, 34 N.W. 689; Offutt v. Jones, 110 Md. 233, 73 A. 629.

11. Ogilby v. Hickok, 144 App.Div. 61, 128 N.Y.S. 860.

12. Eccles v. Rhode Island Hospital Trust Co., 90 Conn. 592, 98 A. 129; Childs v. Waite, 102 Me. 451, 67 A. 311.

13. Huch v. Wickersheim, 316 Ill.App. 155, 44 N.E.2d 338 (1942).

14. Baumer v. Johnstown Trust Co., 345 Pa. 51, 25 A.2d 723 (1942).

This is called the nomination of a "personal trustee", and the court of equity respects the expressed desire of the settlor.[15] It is sometimes done where a knowledge of family problems is important and a member of the family is named as trustee. In such a case no substitute can be supplied by the court, and incapacity to take or disclaimer of the trust at the outset prevents the trust from arising. The settlor, or if he is dead his successors, are the owners of the intended trust property.

If a settlor selects a trustee who cannot or will not take title, the *legal* title remains in the settlor in the case of inter vivos trust transfers. In the instance of attempted transfers to such a trustee at the death of the testator, the *legal* title passes to the successors of the testator (his residuary devisees or legatees, or in the absence of a residuary clause to his heirs or next of kin). The legal title is later vested in the court-appointed trustee at the time of his appointment. But in all such cases the *equitable* property interest passes to the intended trust beneficiaries.

 WESTLAW REFERENCES

settlor /s appoint**** /s trustee
trust /s fail*** /s lack /s trustee
390k160(2)

WHO MAY BE MADE A TRUSTEE? [1]

§ 30. Any natural person or corporation capable of taking title to the trust property may be made a trustee of it. That the trustee named has disabilities which prevent him from administering the trust, or handicap in doing so, or which render the trust unenforceable against him, does not prevent the trust from arising, but rather constitutes a ground which may cause the court to prevent the trustee from qualifying or to remove him.

A government or a municipal corporation may be a trustee, as may a private corporation. Trust companies and many banks are qualified to accept and administer trusts.

Foreign corporations are frequently disqualified or handicapped in accepting and administering trusts by reason of statutory restrictions.

An unincorporated association at common law is not a legal person, has not the capacity to receive title to property, and hence cannot be a trustee, but a trust naming such an organization as trustee will not fail for that reason.

The settlor may make himself the sole trustee or one of several trustees.

15. Duer v. James, 42 Md. 492; Loughery v. Bright, 267 Mass. 584, 166 N.E. 744 (1929).

§ 30

1. Bogert, Trusts and Trustees (rev. 2d edit.), § 121 et seq.; Restatement, Trusts, Second, §§ 89–100.

The sole beneficiary of a trust cannot be made the sole trustee thereof; in such case the legal and equitable titles are said to merge. Obligation necessarily involves two parties.

Where the sole beneficiary is one of several trustees, or where the sole trustee is one of several beneficiaries, or where the same group of persons are trustees and beneficiaries, the trust is valid and no difficulty arises. Partial merger is not usually decreed. There is sufficient diversity of personnel to support the equitable obligation.

What persons, natural or artificial, may be named as trustees?

Natural Persons

Any legal entity capable of taking the title to the trust property may be a trustee of it. If he can receive title to it, he can come under an equitable obligation with respect to it, and that is what a trust means. With respect to natural persons (human beings) there is rarely difficulty with regard to the capacity to take title and so to be a trustee.

At common law an alien could not take title to real property by descent, and title obtained by conveyance was subject to being taken from him by the sovereign. Thus he could not be a trustee, if descent were relied upon as a means of conveying title to him, but could be a trustee if title were tendered to him by conveyance.[2] Naturally his disability to hold against the crown made him a very undesirable trustee. In the United States the powers of an alien to take and hold real property have been much enlarged by statute but in some states are not yet complete.[3] But in any event the selection of an alien as trustee will not defeat the origin of the trust, no matter what the disabilities of aliens in that state. These disabilities never extended to personal property.

In some stages of the development of Anglo-American law marital status has affected the power to take or manage property. Married women, even at common law, were capable of becoming trustees, although hampered in the administration of trusts by the rules restricting their dealing with property apart from their husbands.[4] Under modern legislation giving married women power to take, convey, and manage their property as if single, married women may, of course, act without any disability as trustees, and they frequently are appointed.[5] An infant may be a trustee, although subject to the usual disabilities of infancy, in that his contracts and conveyances will be voidable by him

2. See, for example, Beidler v. Dehner, 178 Iowa 1338, 161 N.W. 32; Caparell v. Goodbody, 132 N.J.Eq. 559, 29 A.2d 563 (1942).

3. See Bogert, Trusts and Trustees (rev. 2d edit.), § 126 (statutory references); Kohler, Legal Disabilities of Aliens in the United States, 16 Amer.Bar Ass'n J. 113.

4. Femmes Covert and Spinsters as Trustees, 155 L.T. 106; Still v. Ruby, 35 Pa. 373.

5. Moore v. Cottingham, 90 Ind. 239; Gibbons v. Gibbons, 296 Mass. 89, 4 N.E.2d 1019 (1936); Springer v. Berry, 47 N.E. 330; Schluter v. Bowery Savings Bank, 117 N.Y. 125, 22 N.E. 572, 5 L.R.A. 541, 15 Am. St.Rep. 494; Clarke v. Saxon, 1 Hill Eq., S.C. 69.

when he reaches his majority.[6] Equity, on application, will decree that the infant convey to a new trustee of full capacity.[7] One who is mentally incompetent (insane, an idiot or a lunatic) may be a trustee, although subject to the same incapacities and disabilities as if acting with reference to his own property.[8] His business transactions will be void or voidable. Equity will remove the title from him and vest it in a competent person.[9]

An insolvent[10] or bankrupt[11] person may be a trustee, although equity will ordinarily remove him on application.[12] Such a person has the capacity to hold and manage property, although his financial condition makes it highly dangerous to the beneficiary that he continue in the trust office.

Citizens of the United States are not disqualified to take title to property by reason of the fact that they are not residents of the state where the property is located or where the donor is domiciled. Hence, in the absence of a statute, they may be trustees even though they are not residents of the state under the laws of which the trust is created or is being administered.[13]

Artificial Legal Entities—Governments—Corporations

The sovereign in England may be a trustee, although the beneficiary has no power to enforce the trust against the crown. Statutes[14] have provided against escheat to the crown upon the death of a trustee without heirs, and have also made it possible for the crown to transfer the duties of a trusteeship to another. In England the public trustee is a legal person of statutory origin who is held out as willing to administer trusts not involving the management of a business.[15] He is a public official who is a corporation sole. No such official has been created in the United States.[16]

The federal government may be made a trustee.[17] Both the national government and the state governments cannot be sued without their consents, but this merely renders their trusteeships difficult of enforce-

6. Des Moines Ins. Co. v. McIntire, 99 Iowa 50, 68 N.W. 565; McClellan v. McClellan, 65 Me. 500; Levin v. Ritz, 17 Misc. 737, 41 N.Y.S. 405.

7. Walsh v. Walsh, 116 Mass. 377, 17 Am.Rep. 162. Where infant trustees have conveyed to their beneficiary, equity will confirm this voidable title. Clary v. Spain, 119 Va. 58, 89 S.E. 130.

8. Pegge v. Skynner, 1 Cox, Eq.Cas. 23; Eyrick v. Hetrick, 13 Pa. 488.

9. For a discussion of removal of trustees, see § 160, post.

10. Shryock v. Waggoner, 28 Pa. 430.

11. Rankin v. Barcroft, 114 Ill. 441, 3 N.E. 97.

12. In re Barker's Trusts, 1 Ch.Div. 43.

13. Farmers' Loan & Tr. Co. v. Chicago & A.R. Co., 27 Fed. 146 (C.C.Ind.1886); Roby v. Smith, 131 Ind. 342, 30 N.E. 1093, 15 L.R.A. 792.

14. 39 & 40 Geo. III, c. 88, 1800; 4 & 5 Wm. IV, c. 23, 1834; 13 & 14 Vict. c. 60, §§ 15, 46, 47, 1850.

15. Edw. 7, c. 55 (1906).

16. An exception exists in Colorado as to the public trustee to accept deeds of trust in the nature of mortgages and to foreclose them. Colo.Rev.Stat. 38–37–101, 38–37–140.

17. United States v. Jackson, 280 U.S. 183, 50 S.Ct. 143, 74 L.Ed. 361 (1930); United States v. Getzelman, 89 F.2d 531 (10th Cir.1937), certiorari denied 302 U.S. 708, 58 S.Ct. 27, 82 L.Ed. 547 (1937).

ment and does not prevent them from arising. Boards or courts of claims have been set up by Congress and by many states for the hearing of claims against the government.

A state or one of its officers or departments may be a trustee,[18] as, for example, when the holder of property in trust to establish a home for insane persons,[19] or when taxes are illegally collected,[20] or when money is given for the benefit of the children living in the state,[21] or when the foreshore of the ocean is held for the public,[22] or where land is held for the benefit of soldiers.[23]

"It may be stated as a general proposition of law that, . . . unless specially restrained, municipal corporations may take and hold property in their own right by direct gift, conveyance, or devise, in trust, for purposes germane to the objects of the corporation, or which will promote, aid, or assist in carrying out or perfecting those objects." [24] Instances in which gifts to cities to hold in trust for governmental or other charitable purposes have been sustained are frequent.[25] These trusts are generally in aid of objects which the municipality is under a duty to forward or might well forward. Thus one trust was for the establishment of a hospital for foundlings,[26] another for the purpose of making loans to needy young artificers,[27] and a third for the planting and care of shade trees in the city.[28]

A town or village may become a trustee to carry out purposes for which it was incorporated.[29] "A trust for the support of schools, or of a particular school as a high school, or for any purpose of general public utility is a valid trust. Thus towns can hold property in trust for purposes within the general scope of their corporate existence." [30]

---

18. Preston v. Walsh, 10 Fed. 315 (C.C. Tex.1882).

Sometimes statutes prohibit gifts by will to governments outside the state and so disqualify such governments as trustees. United States v. Burnison, 339 U.S. 87, 70 S.Ct. 503, 94 L.Ed. 675 (1950) (gift to United States; California law changed by chapter 223, L.1951); In re Barter's Estate, 30 Cal.2d 549, 184 P.2d 305 (1947) (foreign government).

19. Yale College's Appeal, 67 Conn. 237, 34 A. 1036.

20. Shoemaker v. Board of Com'rs of Grant County, 36 Ind. 175.

21. Bedford v. Bedford's Adm'r, 99 Ky. 273, 35 S.W. 926.

22. Allen v. Allen, 19 R.I. 114, 32 A. 166, 30 L.R.A. 497, 61 Am.St.Rep. 738.

23. Pinson v. Ivey, 1 Yerg., Tenn., 296.

24. Clayton v. Hallett, 30 Colo. 231, 249, 70 P. 429, 59 L.R.A. 407, 97 Am.St. Rep. 117. Some cities have officers, boards or agencies to administer gifts made to

them in trust, as is the case in Philadelphia and Los Angeles.

25. In re Coleman's Estate, 167 Cal. 212, 138 P. 992, Ann.Cas.1915C, 682; Richards v. Wilson, 185 Ind. 335, 112 N.E. 780; Board of Trustees of Schools for Industrial Education in City of Hoboken v. Hoboken, 70 N.J.Eq. 630, 62 A. 1; McIntosh v. Charleston, 45 S.C. 584, 23 S.E. 943; Maxcy v. Oshkosh, 144 Wis. 238, 128 N.W. 899, 1136, 31 L.R.A.,N.S., 787.

26. Phillips v. Harrow, 93 Iowa 92, 62 N.W. 434.

27. Higginson v. Turner, 171 Mass. 586, 51 N.E. 172.

28. Cresson's Appeal, 30 Pa. 437.

29. Chapman v. Newell, 146 Iowa 415, 125 N.W. 324; Hatheway v. Sackett, 32 Mich. 97; Glover v. Baker, 76 N.H. 393, 83 A. 916; Stearns v. Newport Hospital, 27 R.I. 309, 62 A. 132, 8 Ann.Cas. 1176.

30. Piper v. Moulton, 72 Me. 155, 159, in which case the trust was for educational purposes. In Sargent v. Cornish, 54 N.H.

Doubtless a taxpayer could maintain an action to restrain a public corporation from carrying out a trust which was not concerned with its functions,[31] but the trust would be administered by a substitute trustee.

It is obvious that a private corporation may be a trustee whenever the purposes of the trust are consistent with the objects of the corporation. If carrying out the trust is within the powers granted to the corporation by its charter or certificate of incorporation, then the corporation may validly act as trustee.[32] If to carry out the trust would be beyond the corporate powers of the trustee, then the trust will be established but the stockholders of the corporation may prevent the trust from being administered by their corporation.[33] The ultra vires nature of the trust does not prevent the settlor's act from being effective to create a trust.[34]

In some states archbishops and similar religious officers are given the status of a corporation sole and may be trustees.[35]

The private corporations which are most commonly made trustees are trust companies and banks. When authorized to act as trustee they constitute a class of professional trustees. National banks may be authorized by the U.S. Comptroller of the Currency to act as trustees and many of them have such permits.[36] All trusts companies are authorized to act in a fiduciary capacity, including trusteeship.[37] State banks are in many states also given permission to act as trustees, subject to certain qualifications.[38]

Foreign corporations are frequently prohibited from accepting trusts or are greatly handicapped in qualifying as trustees. Some states permit the foreign corporation to act only if it qualifies to do business in the state; others have a reciprocal statute, permitting foreign corporations to qualify if the state of domicile of the foreign corporation gives corresponding privileges to the local corporations; others flatly forbid foreign corporations from acting as fiduciaries; and in some states the situation seems to be in doubt.[39]

18, the town held property for the purpose of buying and displaying flags for patriotic uses.

31. State v. Higby Co., 130 Iowa 69, 106 N.W. 382.

32. Hossack v. Ottawa Development Ass'n, 244 Ill. 274, 91 N.E. 439; State v. Higby Co., 130 Iowa 69, 106 N.W. 382, 114 Am.St.Rep. 409; White v. Rice, 112 Mich. 403, 70 N.W. 1024; De Camp v. Dobbins, 29 N.J.Eq. 36; Bell County v. Alexander, 22 Tex. 350, 73 Am.Dec. 268; Latshaw v. Western Townsite Co., 91 Wash. 575, 158 P. 248.

33. Cleveland Mtge. & Inv. Co. v. Gage, 144 Fla. 758, 198 So. 677 (1940); Yandell v. Wilson, 182 Miss. 867, 183 So. 382 (1938).

34. Daniel v. Wade, 203 Ala. 355, 83 So. 99; Hayden v. Hayden, 241 Ill. 183, 89 N.E. 347.

35. Chiniquy v. Catholic Bishop of Chicago, 41 Ill. 148; Rine v. Wagner, 135 Iowa 626, 113 N.W. 471.

36. 12 U.S.C.A. § 92a. Prior to 1962 Reg. F issued by the Federal Reserve Board had governed the operation of trusts by national banks. In 1962 Congress transferred these powers to the Comptroller of the Currency.

37. See Bogert, Trusts and Trustees (rev. 2d edit.), § 136.

38. See statutory references in Bogert, Trusts and Trustees (rev. 2d edit.), § 135.

39. For statutory references and discussion, see Bogert, Trusts and Trustees (rev. 2d edit.), § 132.

Unincorporated Associations

The question has frequently arisen whether an unincorporated association may be a trustee. Such a body is not recognized by the law as a legal entity. Examples include labor unions, social clubs, fraternities, and lodges. While under the older orthodox view such an organization cannot receive the title to property and hence could not be a trustee,[40] there are some modern decisions recognizing the association as a de facto trustee,[41] statutes often recognize some associations as legal beings,[42] and in all cases the incapacity of the association to take title does not prevent the trust from beginning but rather merely calls for the appointment of another trustee.

The correct view would seem to be that a trust ought not to fail because an unincorporated association was named as its trustee. Such an association is not a legal entity in the absence of statute. It cannot be under a legal obligation. The title to the trust property was not intended to vest in the members of the association. But even if it be conceded that an unincorporated association is not competent to serve as a trustee, the trust may well be saved under the established principle that equity will not allow a trust to fail for want of a trustee. The better method for dealing with such attempts to create a trust would be to appoint a new trustee.

The Settlor and Beneficiaries as Trustees

The trust settlor often makes himself the sole trustee by a trust declaration, or makes himself one of several trustees by an instrument of transfer. There is no difficulty in giving effect to this intent. In the case of a trust declaration the settlor changes himself from a full owner to a holder of the legal title subject to equities in favor of others.[43] In the case of a transfer there is sufficient diversity between transferor and transferees to support the conveyance.

Frequently a trustee is named as a beneficiary. Does this identity invalidate an attempted creation of a trust? It can be urged that a trust necessarily involves an equitable obligation from trustee to beneficiary and an obligation cannot exist without two separate legal entities; and also it can be argued that the doctrine of merger of an equitable into a legal estate should be applied when the same person owns both estates.

The question may arise in four different situations. T may have been appointed a trustee for himself alone. In such case the sole trustee is also sole beneficiary. There can be no doubt about the result

---

40. Lael v. Crook, 192 Ark. 1115, 97 S.W.2d 436 (1936); Rixford v. Zeigler, 150 Cal. 435, 88 P. 1092, 119 Am.St.Rep. 229; Wittmeier v. Heiligenstein, 308 Ill. 434, 139 N.E. 871 (1923); Douthitt v. Stinson, 63 Mo. 268.

41. Schneider v. Kloepple, 270 Mo. 389, 193 S.W. 834; Parker v. Cowell, 16 N.H. 149.

42. See West's Ann.Cal.Corp.Code § 21200; N.Mex.Stats.Ann.1978, § 53–10–2.

43. Yokem v. Hicks, 93 Ill.App. 667, 670.

in such an instance. The equitable estate merges in the legal and T becomes the owner of the property free of any trust.[44] "The trustee and the beneficiary must be distinct personalities, or, otherwise, there could be no trust, and the merger of interests in the same person would effect a legal estate in him, of the same duration as the beneficial interest designed . . .. That the legal and beneficial estate can exist and be maintained separately in the same person is an inconceivable proposition."[45] An additional reason for the failure of such an attempt at trust creation is that T cannot be under an obligation to himself.

But if the same *group* of persons appointed trustees are also the sole beneficiaries, there is no merger or other difficulty about the origin or continuance of the trust. Thus if A and B are named as trustees for themselves, as trustees they are joint tenants but as beneficiaries they are tenants in common, and this diversity is sufficient to prevent merger. Together A and B can be under an obligation to each beneficiary.[46]

Where T is appointed trustee for T and X, T's legal estate is not the same as his equitable interest. As trustee he holds the entire legal interest, but as beneficiary he has an undivided equitable interest, normally a half interest. In the great majority of the cases the validity of the trust has been sustained and T treated as a normal trustee.[47] No partial merger has been decreed. The obligation running from T to T and X has been deemed sufficient to support the trust. In a few cases the courts have held that a partial merger arose and that T became the absolute owner of half of the property, free of trust, but continued to be trustee as to the balance for the benefit of X.[48] Another view has been expressed in New York, namely, that T may act for X, in the situation described, but is incompetent to act for himself, and that the court will act with respect to trust questions involving the interests of T alone.[49] In a later New York case [50] the Court of Appeals indicated by way of dictum that T would not be competent to act at all when he was appointed as trustee for himself and for X.

If T and X are appointed trustees for T alone, there has been no disposition to treat the act of trust creation as void.[51] The diversity of

44. Nellis v. Rickard, 133 Cal. 617, 66 P. 32, 85 Am.St.Rep. 227; Butler v. Godley, 12 N.C. 94; Danforth v. Oshkosh, 119 Wis. 262, 97 N.W. 258.

As to termination of trusts by merger, see § 151, post.

45. Greene v. Greene, 125 N.Y. 506, 510, 26 N.E. 739, 21 Am.St.Rep. 743.

46. Johnson v. Muller, 149 Kan. 128, 86 P.2d 569 (1939); Sturgis v. Citizens' Nat. Bank of Pocomoke City, 152 Md. 654, 137 A. 378 (1927); Morgan v. Murton, 131 N.J. Eq. 481, 26 A.2d 45 (1942).

47. Tyler v. Mayre, 95 Cal. 160, 27 P. 160, 30 P. 196; Allen v. Hendrick, 104 Or.

202, 206 P. 733 (1922); Fox's Estate, 264 Pa. 478, 107 A. 863.

48. Woodward v. James, 115 N.Y. 346, 22 N.E. 150; Weeks v. Frankel, 197 N.Y. 304, 90 N.E. 969.

49. Rogers v. Rogers, 111 N.Y. 228, 18 N.E. 636.

50. Robertson v. De Brulatour, 188 N.Y. 301, 317, 80 N.E. 938.

51. Restatement, Trusts, Second, § 99. See also Reed v. Browne, 295 N.Y. 184, 66 N.E.2d 47 (1946).

the character of the legal and equitable titles and the obligation of the cotrustees to the beneficiary have been held to obviate any difficulty.[52]

Another contingency is that in which T and X are appointed trustees for T and Y. T here has conflicting interests. He has a private interest as a beneficiary and a representative interest as trustee for Y. A variety of views have been expressed by the courts relative to the effect of such a settlement. The majority of the courts which have had occasion to consider the question have held that the trust was a valid trust and that no merger occurred as to T's interest.[53] "The title held by the trustees is joint, and there is no merger of separate interests in the different trustees arising out of the fact that they are also beneficiaries."[54] Two objections to a merger of the trustee-beneficiary's interests in this situation are urged in a New York case, namely, that the doctrine of merger is aimed at passive trusts only, and that the title of the trustees is joint, whereas the interests of the beneficiaries are separate and several.[55] In a few cases the courts have taken the position that there is a partial merger, and T becomes the absolute owner of part of the property dedicated to the trust.[56] Another position maintained by some courts is that where T and X are named trustees for T and Y the trust is valid, but that T is disabled from acting where his interests as a beneficiary are involved, but may act in all other cases. The noninterested trustees must act alone when the rights of the combination trustee and beneficiary are at stake.[57] As elsewhere noted[58] merger is often regarded by equity as a technical doctrine of property law which ought not to be applied where it will frustrate accomplishment of the intention of the parties.

It can be argued with force that it is undesirable to have one of the beneficiaries act as trustee or co-trustee, since he is thereby put in a position where he may be tempted to favor himself at the expense of his co-beneficiaries. Courts are sometimes persuaded on this ground to refuse to appoint a beneficiary as trustee, or in rare cases to remove him if he had been appointed by the settlor.

Different Types of Trustees; Variations from the Normal

A settlor has great freedom (within the limits mentioned above) in the selection of his trustees. He may appoint a single trustee or two or more co-trustees. He may create different types of trustees, with different functions, as where he appoints a trust company as custodian

52. Bull v. Odell, 19 App.Div. 605, 46 N.Y.S. 306. And see Malone v. Herndon, 197 Okl. 26, 168 P.2d 272 (1945).

53. Dennis v. Omaha Nat. Bank, 153 Neb. 865, 46 N.W.2d 606, 27 A.L.R.2d 674 (1951); Story v. Palmer, 46 N.J.Eq. 1, 18 A. 363; Weeks v. Frankel, 197 N.Y. 304, 90 N.E. 969; Denniston v. Pierce, 260 Pa. 129, 103 A. 557.

54. Burbach v. Burbach, 217 Ill. 547, 550, 75 N.E. 519.

55. Amory v. Lord, 9 N.Y. 403, 412.

56. Bolles v. State Trust Co., 27 N.J. Eq. 308; Craig v. Hone, 2 Edw.Ch., N.Y., 554.

57. Robertson v. De Brulatour, 188 N.Y. 301, 317, 80 N.E. 938.

58. See § 151, post.

trustee to have possession of the trust property, and an individual as managing trustee to make investments, collections and distributions.[59] Or the settlor may choose a trustee in whom title and possession are vested, subject to directory powers in a board of trust managers.[60] Or the settlor may appoint a trustee and an advisor to the trustee whose advice or consent must be obtained before the making of certain decisions.[61] The functions of the trust administration may be distributed, as where one trustee is given control of realty and another of the personal property.[62]

Often the settlor appoints as trustee a relative, friend, or business associate. Or he may appoint a corporate trustee such as a bank or trust company, either as sole trustee or with an individual as co-trustee.[63] In a few localities it is customary to name an individual who holds himself out as a professional trustee. The great complexities and difficulties of present day trust administration with respect to investments, taxation, and property management present a strong argument for the selection of a professional trustee who has available the services of specialists and can give continuity of operation.

 WESTLAW REFERENCES

Natural Person

alien /s disability /s trustee

levin +3 ritz

"mentally incompetent" lunatic idiot insane /s trustee % "dead man's statute" criminal

Artificial Legal Entities—Governments—Corporations

sovereign crown /s trustee /s england

find 50 sct 143

preston +3 walsh

piper +3 mouton

trust /2 company bank /s trustee /s "private corporation"

"foreign corporation" /s act /s trustee

---

59. City of Boston v. Dolan, 298 Mass. 346, 10 N.E.2d 275 (1937); Walker v. James, 337 Mo. 750, 85 S.W.2d 876 (1935); Thomas v. National Bank of Commerce of Seattle, 187 Wash. 521, 60 P.2d 264 (1936).

See N.Y.—McKinney's EPTL 11–1.1(b) (10) (corporate trustee may be given sole custody).

60. Williams v. Williams, 149 Fla. 454, 6 So.2d 275 (1942); Victor v. Hillebrecht, 337 Ill.App. 383, 86 N.E.2d 291 (1949), judgment reversed on other grounds, 405 Ill. 264, 90 N.E.2d 751 (1950), certiorari denied 339 U.S. 980, 70 S.Ct. 1026, 94 L.Ed. 1384 (1950).

61. Gathright's Trustee v. Gaut, 276 Ky. 562, 124 S.W.2d 782, 120 A.L.R. 1403 (1939); United States Nat. Bank of Portland v. First Nat. Bank of Portland, 172 Or. 683, 142 P.2d 785 (1943).

62. See Warner v. Rogers, 255 Ill.App. 78. But co-trustees may not take it upon themselves to distribute their powers between themselves. Caldwell v. Graham, 115 Md. 122, 80 A. 839.

See V.A.Mo.S. § 456.550 (special duties assigned to one or more of several trustees; effect).

63. See Schneck, Choosing a Fiduciary, 109 Trusts & Estates 95. Pugh, 17 Amer.B.A.J. 575; Saltonstall and Carroll, 67 Tr.Companies 136; Pennell, 60 N.Car. L.R. 799.

Unincorporated Associations

"unincorporated association" /s act /s trustee

schneider +3 kloepple

The Settlor and Beneficiaries as Trustees

settlor +5 act +5 trustee

beneficiary +5 act +5 trustee

craig +3 hone

Different Types of Trustees; Variations from the Normal

"gathrights trustees" +3 gaut

Notice to and Acceptance by the Trustee—Disclaimer—Resignation

notice to trustee

notice notify +2 trustee /s creat*** /s trust

Necessity of Acceptance by the Trustee

390k243

find 113 f2d 217

Resignation by Trustee

di(trustee /5 resign!)

390k162

NOTICE TO AND ACCEPTANCE BY THE TRUSTEE—DISCLAIMER—RESIGNATION [1]

§ 31. It is not necessary to the creation of a trust that the settlor notify the trustee that he has created the trust, nor is it necessary for this purpose that the trustee accept the trust and agree to perform his duties under it, unless the trust was intended to be personal.

Every person who is tendered the office of trustee has the power to accept or decline it. Thus acceptance is necessary in order to make a particular person a trustee. Acceptance or disclaimer by the trustee may be express or implied. If no direct position is taken by the trustee, the attitude of the trustee toward the trust property and duties, and toward the beneficiary, will ordinarily be determinative.

Acceptance or disclaimer relates back to the date of execution of the trust by the settlor. Ordinarily it would seem that acceptance or disclaimer should be final and not subject to retraction.

A trustee who has accepted a trust may resign either by complying with the requirements for resignation prescribed by the trust instrument, or by securing the consent of the court of equity. If all the beneficiaries are competent and the trustee presents his resignation to them, upon its acceptance the beneficiaries will not be able to hold the trustee liable for his failure to act as trustee in the future.

Notice to the Trustee

It is well settled that notice to the trustee of the trust creation is

§ 31

1. Bogert, Trusts and Trustees (rev. 2d edit.), §§ 150 (acceptance; disclaimer or renunciation), 511 (resignation); Restatement, Trusts, Second, §§ 35, 106, 354, 378.

not necessary to completion of the trust.[2]   "Although the trustee may never have heard of the deed, the title vests in him, subject to a disclaimer on his part."[3]   This refers to the origin of the trust, and not to the imposition of its burdens on any particular trustee. A trustee, as will appear later,[4] cannot be compelled to accept a trust, but it is not necessary that he know of it or accept it in order that the trust may come into being.

As a matter of course the giving or failure to give notice to the trustee may have some value as evidence of the settlor's state of mind with respect to the completeness of the trust, but it is not conclusive. At least in the case of living trusts, execution of the agreement will signify acceptance and there will be no need to notify the trustee that the trust has been created; upon acceptance the trustee will take possession and begin his duties. If the trustee has not accepted or been notified by the settlor, it is probable that the settlor regarded the transaction as inchoate or incomplete and subject to further deliberation on his part.

Necessity of Acceptance by the Trustee

The validity of an act of trust creation is not affected by the acceptance or rejection of the trust by any particular trustee, except in the rare case where the trust is personal because the settlor has expressed an intent that only the trustee named by him shall be qualified to act.[5] Ordinarily, if a named person declines to accept the trust, another may be substituted for him and the trust carried out without difficulty.[6]

While acceptance is unnecessary to the origin of the trust, this principle should be carefully distinguished from the doctrine that acceptance of the trust is necessary to the vesting of the title to the trust property in any particular trustee and to the fastening of the trust duties upon him. In order that a person may become the owner of the trust property[7] and occupy the position of trustee,[8] he must accept the trust and consent to become a trustee. If he declines, the trust will proceed to execution by another trustee; but it cannot be carried out by him without an express or implied acceptance of its duties on his part.

The trustee may refuse to accept the trust. He cannot be com-

2. In re Way's Trusts, 2 De Gex, J. & S. 365; Thatcher v. Wardens, etc., of St. Andrew's Church of Ann Arbor, 37 Mich. 264.

3. Adams v. Adams, 88 U.S. (21 Wall.) 185, 192, 22 L.Ed. 504 (1874).

4. See note 9, this section, post.

5. Richardson v. Mullery, 200 Mass. 247, 86 N.E. 319.

6. Braswell v. Downs, 11 Fla. 62; Minot v. Tilton, 64 N.H. 371, 10 A. 682; Rhode Island Hospital Trust Co. v. Town Council of Warwick, 29 R.I. 393, 71 A. 644; Cloud v. Calhoun, 10 Rich.Eq., S.C., 358. So held in the case of a charitable trust, in Winslow v. Stark, 78 N.H. 135, 97 A. 979.

7. F.G. Oxley Stave Co. v. Butler County, 166 U.S. 648, 17 S.Ct. 709, 41 L.Ed. 1149 (1897); McFall v. Kirkpatrick, 236 Ill. 281, 86 N.E. 139; Brandon v. Carter, 119 Mo. 572, 24 S.W. 1035, 41 Am.St.Rep. 673.

8. Maccubbin v. Cromwell's Ex'rs, 7 Gill & J., Md., 157.

pelled to undertake the duties of the trusteeship against his will.[9] A trustee cannot accept part of the trust property and duties and reject the remainder. He must accept or reject the whole trust.[10] Acceptance on conditions different from those fixed by the settlor constitutes rejection.[11]

Trustees have no power by agreement among themselves to divide their responsibilities and to limit the liability of any particular trustee to a portion of the trust property.[12] Thus in Caldwell v. Graham,[13] where the trustees divided the trust property among themselves, one taking the realty and the other the personalty, the court declined to excuse one trustee for negligence respecting the property allotted to the other trustee, and said: [14]

> "It was optional with him to accept or decline the trust; but, having undertaken the duty imposed by the will, it was not competent for him to limit his obligations or divest himself of any part of his fiduciary discretion."

If the trust is personal to the named trustee, that is, if the settlor indicated an intent that the trustee named should be the only qualified trustee, then refusal of the trust by that trustee causes the trust to fail.[15] Such an intent by a settlor is very rare.

Acceptance or disclaimer of the trust may be express, as where the named trustee states his position in spoken or written words, or it may be implied from the conduct of the trustee toward the trust property or the beneficiaries. Thus it has been held that an oral acknowledgment by the trustee that he had accepted the trust,[16] failure to object to the trust after knowledge of its existence for some time,[17] taking out letters testamentary when the trustee was also the executor under the will,[18] that the trustee himself wrote the trust deed under which he was appointed,[19] taking control of that deed,[20] joining in its execution,[21]

9. Dailey v. New Haven, 60 Conn. 314, 22 A. 945, 14 L.R.A. 69; Silvers v. Canary, 114 Ind. 129, 16 N.E. 166; Carruth v. Carruth, 148 Mass. 431, 19 N.E. 369.

10. Chase Nat. Bank of City of New York v. Citizens Gas Co. of Indianapolis, 113 F.2d 217 (7th Cir.1940), reversed on jurisdictional grounds, 314 U.S. 63, 62 S.Ct. 15, 86 L.Ed. 47 (1941).

An exception may exist in the case of burdensome and worthless property which the trustee may be permitted to reject and abandon. Bell v. Frankford Trust Co., 154 Pa.Super. 517, 36 A.2d 177 (1944).

11. In re Roth's Will, 291 N.Y. 1, 50 N.E.2d 281, 148 A.L.R. 360 (1943).

12. Bermingham v. Wilcox, 120 Cal. 467, 52 P. 822; In re Stong's Estate, 160 Pa. 13, 28 A. 480; Thomas v. Scruggs, 10 Yerg., Tenn., 400.

13. 115 Md. 122, 80 A. 839, 38 L.R.A.,N.S., 1029.

14. 115 Md. 122, at 127, 80 A. 839, 38 L.R.A.,N.S., 1029.

15. Louisville & N.R. Co. v. Powers, 268 Ky. 491, 105 S.W.2d 591 (1937).

16. Elizalde v. Elizalde, 137 Cal. 634, 66 P. 369, 70 P. 861.

17. Salter v. Salter, 80 Ga. 178, 4 S.E. 391, 12 Am.St.Rep. 249; Roberts v. Moseley, 64 Mo. 507. Standing mute on the statement of the trust was held sufficient in Heitman v. Cutting, 37 Cal.App. 236, 174 P. 675.

18. Coudon v. Updegraff, 117 Md. 71, 83 A. 145.

19. Young v. Cardwell, 6 Lea, Tenn., 168.

20. Hitz v. National Metropolitan Bank, 111 U.S. 722, 4 S.Ct. 613, 28 L.Ed. 577 (1884).

21. Dayton v. Stewart, 99 Md. 643, 59 A. 281.

taking possession of the trust property [22] or exercising control over it,[23] or the performance of any acts which amount to a carrying out of the trust,[24] are all acts on the part of the trustee which show an acceptance of the trust by him.

In some cases doubt has arisen as to whether certain acts amounted to a refusal of the trust by the trustee. It has been held that the failure to qualify [25] or to give a bond,[26] if required by statute or court order, shows a rejection of the trust. But a refusal to act as executor, when the same person is appointed trustee and executor, does not prove a refusal of the trusteeship.[27] Where a trustee refused to take any steps under his appointment for more than two years, or to file a bond, or take possession of or manage the property, and allowed the buildings to become out of repair and untenantable and the land to be sold for the payment of taxes, his acts justified the inference that he had declined the trust.[28]

When the trustee does accept, his title relates back to the time of the creation of the trust, so that he is deemed to have been the owner of the property from the time when the will or deed creating the trust took effect.[29]

The refusal of the trustee to accept the office does not cause the title to the trust property to vest in the beneficiaries,[30] but it instead remains in the settlor (if the trust was created inter vivos) or passes to the heirs or next of kin or residuary legatees of the testator subject to the trust (if the trust was created by will).[31] Equity will then, upon application, appoint a new trustee to execute the trust in the place of the trustee who has declined the trust and transfer the title to him.[32] If two trustees are named in the original settlement, and one rejects the

22. McBride v. McIntyre, 91 Mich. 406, 51 N.W. 1113; Pullis v. Pullis Bros. Iron Co., 157 Mo. 565, 57 S.W. 1095.

23. Freeman v. Brown, 115 Ga. 23, 41 S.E. 385.

24. Patterson v. Johnson, 113 Ill. 559.

25. Sells v. Delgado, 186 Mass. 25, 70 N.E. 1036; In re Robinson, 37 N.Y. 261. Quite often, by statute, failure to qualify within a short time is treated as a declination of the trust. See, for example, Conn.G.S. § 45–83. And see Pungs v. Hilgendorf, 289 Mich. 46, 286 N.W. 152 (1939).

26. Attwill v. Dole, 74 N.H. 300, 67 A. 403. But see Coates v. Lunt, 213 Mass. 401, 100 N.E. 829.

27. Magee v. Magee's Estate, 236 Miss. 572, 111 So.2d 394 (1959); Pomroy v. Lewis, 14 R.I. 349; Garner v. Dowling, 11 Tenn. (Heisk.) 48. But see, *contra*, In re Buelow's Estate, 177 Or. 218, 161 P.2d 909 (1945).

28. Adams v. Adams, 64 N.H. 224, 9 A. 100.

29. Stocks v. Inzer, 232 Ala. 482, 168 So. 877; Daley v. Daley, 300 Mass. 17, 14 N.E.2d 113 (1938); Christian v. Yancey, 2 Pat. & H., Va., 240.

30. Bennett v. Bennett, 217 Ill. 434, 75 N.E. 339, 4 L.R.A.,N.S., 470.

31. Owens v. Cowan's Heirs, 7 B.Mon., Ky., 152; Cushney v. Henry, 4 Paige, N.Y., 345; Goss v. Singleton, 2 Head, Tenn., 67. In an English case, where the trustee under a deed disclaimed, the court said: "Under these circumstances I think that the trust was really created, and that the fact that the trustee subsequently disclaimed did not destroy the trust, but that upon the revesting the settlor himself held in trust. . . ." Mallott v. Wilson, [1903] 2 Ch. 494, 502.

32. Adams v. Adams, 88 U.S. (21 Wall.) 185, 22 L.Ed. 504 (1874); Storr's Agr. School v. Whitney, 54 Conn. 342, 8 A. 141; Richardson v. Essex Institute, 208 Mass. 311, 94 N.E. 262, 21 Ann.Cas. 1158; Stone v. Griffin, 3 Vt. 400.

trust, title to the trust property vests in the other trustee, as if the trustee who declines had not been named.[33]

It would seem that once having accepted the trust the trustee cannot by a later act reject it. Having manifested his intent to assume the trust duties, he can only be relieved of his trust by a resignation or removal, and not by merely casting off the trust upon his own motion;[34] and once having disclaimed the trust the trustee may not thereafter change his mind and accept it.[35]

Even though the trust property is realty the trustee may disclaim orally.[36]

Resignation by the Trustee

Naturally a trustee who has accepted a trust but finds that administration of it has become burdensome or not in the interest of the beneficiaries should be able to rid himself of the trust duties. When and by what method may a trustee resign a trusteeship and be discharged from its obligations? Chancery has the power to accept a trustee's resignation and discharge him from the trust when it deems it fair and equitable to do so. The predominant consideration is the welfare of the beneficiaries.[37] In some states statutory proceedings for resignation are now provided.[38]

Unless the instrument so provides, the mere filing of a resignation with the court, or notification to the beneficiary of an intent to resign, does not constitute resignation. The court must act upon it.[39] It may use its discretion in accepting or rejecting the resignation of a trustee. His resignation will not be accepted as a matter of course, although the unwillingness of the trustee to proceed with the trust is a reason of some force in favor of the acceptance of the resignation. A reluctant trustee is not desirable. Normally, the trustee must allege some cause for his desire to resign,[40] for example, that he is in bad health or that

---

33. In re Kellogg, 214 N.Y. 460, 108 N.E. 844, Ann.Cas.1916D, 1298.

34. Cauhape v. Barnes, 135 Cal. 107, 67 P. 55; Hanson v. Worthington, 12 Md. 418; Drury v. Inhabitants of Natick, 10 Mass. (Allen.) 169; In re Kellogg, 214 N.Y. 460, 108 N.E. 844, Ann.Cas.1916D, 1298; Appeal of Brooke, 109 Pa. 188.

35. In re Van Schoonhoven, 5 Paige, N.Y., 559; In re Kellogg, 214 N.Y. 460, 108 N.E. 844, Ann.Cas.1916D, 1298; In re Estate of Chapman, 258 Wis. 442, 45 N.W.2d 927 (1951). But there is some authority at common law and by statute for permitting a retraction of a disclaimer where action on the disclaimer has not been taken in such a way as to make later acceptance unfair. In re Statler's Will, 81 N.Y.S.2d 916 (Surr.1948), affirmed 276 App.Div. 818, 93 N.Y.S.2d 709 (1949); Brewer v. Brewer, 237 S.W.2d 369 (Tex.Civ.App.1951); In re Cranston, [1949] 1 Ch. 523.

36. In re Robinson, 37 N.Y. 261; Read v. Robinson, 6 Watts & S., Pa., 329.

37. Du Puy v. Standard Mineral Co., 88 Me. 202, 33 A. 976; Bowditch v. Banuelos, 1 Gray, Mass., 220; Young v. Barker, 141 App.Div. 801, 127 N.Y.S. 211.

38. For references see Bogert, Trusts and Trustees (rev. 2d edit.), § 514. See West's R.C.Wash.A. 11.98.029 (resignation without judicial proceedings).

39. Tucker v. Grundy, 83 Ky. 540; In re Miller, 15 Abb.Prac., N.Y., 277; Perkins v. McGavock, 3 Hayw., Tenn., 265.

40. Craig v. Craig, 3 Barb.Ch., N.Y., 76, has been held that the alleged inadequacy of the compensation which the trustee originally agreed to accept is not sufficient ground on which to base the acceptance of a resignation. In re Loree's Trust Estate, 24 N.J.Super. 604, 95 A.2d

his personal business affairs exhaust his time and energy. If it appears that a resignation at that time will be disadvantageous to the beneficiaries, the court may refuse to allow the trustee to resign. An example of such a situation is found in the cases where pending actions brought by the trustee or other unsettled matters render it desirable to retain the trustee in office until the conclusion of the unfinished business.[41]

Ordinarily a court will not force an unwilling trustee to continue. The following have been held to be sufficient grounds for resignation: continuance in office would be inconvenient to the trustee;[42] the trustee is unwilling to continue and that there has been an increase in the amount of the trust property since the original acceptance;[43] the trustee is about to leave the United States;[44] there is serious friction and disagreement between the trustee and the beneficiaries.[45]

A trustee, at any time before the court has taken final action on his resignation, may withdraw it and resume his duties as trustee.[46]

In the proceeding brought by the trustee to obtain his release from the trust, the beneficiaries are necessary parties.[47] The court may impose a condition upon the acceptance of the trustee's resignation, for example, that the trustee account or that he waive his commissions.[48] Before acting the court may require the presentation of a satisfactory accounting showing that the trustee has performed his duties, or, if he violated the trust, that he has reimbursed the trust funds for the resulting loss.[49] Where the resignation is solely for the convenience of the trustee, the court may oblige him to pay the costs of the proceeding.[50] In other instances, where the cause for resignation is not personal with the trustee, the court may direct that the costs be paid out of the trust estate.[51]

The trust instrument may provide the procedure for resignation, for example, that any one of several trustees may resign by filing a written statement of his resignation with the other trustees.[52] In such

435 (1953); Empire Trust Co. v. Sample, 50 N.Y.S.2d 5 (1944).

41. In re Olmstead, 52 App.Div. 515, 66 N.Y.S. 212, affirmed 164 N.Y. 571, 58 N.E. 1090; In re Longstreth's Estate, 12 Phila., Pa., 86.

42. Bogle v. Bogle, 3 Mass. (Allen) 158.

43. Green v. Blackwell, 31 N.J.Eq. 37.

44. Tilden v. Fiske, 4 Dem.Sur., N.Y., 357.

45. In re Bernstein, 3 Redf.Sur., N.Y., 20; Parker v. Allen, 14 N.Y.S. 265 (Sup.). For other cases construing the New York statutes, see In re Cutting, 49 App.Div. 388, 63 N.Y.S. 246; In re Abbot, 39 Misc. 760, 80 N.Y.S. 1117.

46. Dillard v. Winn, 60 Ala. 285. But after action upon the resignation by the

court, even if no successor has been appointed, the resignation may not be retracted. Lednum v. Dallas Trust & Savings Bank, 192 S.W. 1127 (Tex.Civ.App.).

47. Clay's Adm'r v. Edwards' Trustee, 84 Ky. 548, 2 S.W. 147; Riggs v. Moise, 344 Mo. 177, 128 S.W.2d 632 (1939).

48. In re Curtiss, 15 Misc. 545, 37 N.Y.S. 586.

49. In re Carson's Will, 227 Iowa 941, 289 N.W. 30; In re Bernstein, 3 Redf.Sur., N.Y., 20.

50. In re Jones, 4 Sandf.Ch., N.Y., 615.

51. Green v. Blackwell, 31 N.J.Eq. 37; Richmond v. Arnold, R.I., 68 A. 427.

52. Douglas Properties v. Stix, 118 Fla. 354, 159 So. 1.

case no court proceeding will be necessary.

Occasionally there are judicial statements to the effect that the trustee cannot resign without a decree of the court permitting his resignation *or* the consent of all the beneficiaries.[53] "But it is a settled rule of law that a trustee, after he has accepted the office, cannot discharge himself from liability by a subsequent resignation merely. He must either be discharged from the trust by virtue of a special provision in the deed, or will, which creates the trust, or by an order or decree of the court of chancery, or with the general consent of all persons interested in the execution of the trust."[54] Statements sometimes made that a trustee cannot resign without an order of the court *and* the consent of the beneficiaries are clearly inaccurate. The court may accept the resignation, even though the beneficiaries, or some of them, object to resignation.[55]

If all the beneficiaries are competent and, when the trustee presents his resignation to them, they agree that he may resign, they will not be heard later to object to his failure to perform the trust thereafter, but such action will not prevent surcharging the resigning trustee as to previous breaches of trust, or, it would seem, relieve him from a duty to use ordinary care with regard to the safety of the trust property until he has turned it over to a successor.[56] In some states the power of the beneficiaries to accept a resignation is set forth in a statute.[57] Where the beneficiaries are infants, or are otherwise incapable of giving consent to the resignation of the trustee, no resignation based on their consent alone will be valid.[58]

TRANSFER OF TITLE TO THE TRUSTEE— NATURE OF HIS INTEREST—FILLING VACANCIES [1]

§ 32. In order to make a particular person trustee, the settlor must go through whatever acts of formality are required in order to vest that person with the property interest which the settlor intends him to hold in trust.

In the case of declarations of trust, the declarant already owns the property and no transfer of title to a trustee is needed. He ceases to hold for his own benefit and thereafter holds for the benefit of another.

53. Badgett v. Keating, 31 Ark. 400; Henderson v. Sherman, 47 Mich. 267, 11 N.W. 153; Green v. Blackwell, 31 N.J.Eq. 37; Shepherd v. M'Evers, 4 Johns.Ch., N.Y., 136, 8 Am.Dec. 561; Anderson v. Robinson, 57 Or. 172, 110 P. 975; Breedlove v. Stump, 3 Yerg., Tenn., 257.

54. Cruger v. Halliday, 11 Paige, N.Y., 314, 319.

55. In re Nixon's Estate, 235 Pa. 27, 83 A. 687.

56. Williams v. Hund, 302 Mo. 451, 258 S.W. 703; Hart v. Equitable Life Assur. Soc., 172 App.Div. 659, 158 N.Y.S. 1063.

57. See West's Ann.Cal.Civ.Code § 2282.

58. Cruger v. Halliday, 11 Paige, N.Y., 314.

§ 32

1. Restatement, Trusts, Second, §§ 31–34, 88, 103–105, 108, 384, 388.

In the case of a trust creation by way of transfer to a third person, the conveyancing formalities which the settlor must adopt depend upon the time at which title is to pass, the type of property involved, and whether the transfer is voluntary or for a consideration.

If transfer is to occur at the death of the transferor, the law of wills must be consulted; if during the life of the transferor, the law of sales, if consideration is involved, or the law of gifts if the transfer is voluntary, is applicable. As to transfers of personal property the law varies somewhat, dependent on the nature of the interest being passed.

In order to complete a trust and make a certain person trustee, transfer of possession to him is immaterial as such, but it may be necessary in order to pass title.

If two or more persons are named as trustees, a transfer of title to them makes them joint tenants of the trust property unless the settlor provides otherwise. Hence title and the trust powers remain in surviving trustees and the successors of a deceased co-trustee have no interest in the trust property.

In the absence of statute, upon the death of a sole trustee intestate, title to the trust property vests in the trustee's heirs or personal representative, depending upon the nature of the property, whether real or personal. If the deceased sole trustee left a will, title to the trust property, but not the trust office, passes to the devisees or executor named in the will.

By statute in several states, on the death of a sole trustee the title to the trust property vests in the court of equity.

The court has power to fill vacancies caused by the death of trustees or for other reason. It may also increase or decrease the number of trustees.

The size of the property interest passed from settlor to trustee depends upon the needs of the trust. Whatever interest the settlor had passes to the trustee in so far as it is needed by the trustee to enable him to carry out the purposes of the trust. No technical words are required in order to pass such interest.

Since the trustee's title is not a beneficial one and his holding is as a representative only, his property interest is not one which gives his personal creditors any right to take the trust property, nor does his spouse have dower or curtesy or a similar statutory estate.

Vesting of Title in the Trustee

If the settlor declares himself the trustee, the transfer of title is formal or theoretical, but if a third person is to become trustee the transfer is actual and the formalities necessary to convey the title to real or personal property from one to another must be complied with. This usually resolves itself down to the question; how can a gift of this type of property be accomplished?[2] Most trusts are created voluntarily.

For example, if the settlor wishes to transfer title by will, he must follow the local Wills Act as to a written instrument, witnesses, subscription, publication, and other formalities.[3] If the settlor wishes to transfer a fee title to real estate by inter vivos transaction to the trustee, he will usually be required by the law of conveyancing to make, sign (and occasionally, seal), and deliver a deed.

If the trust res is a stock certificate representing shares in a corporation, the normal method of transfer is to indorse the certificate to the trustee and deliver it to him;[4] but it has been held that the transfer may be effected by mere delivery of the certificate with intent to give,[5] or by delivery of an instrument of assignment with a power to complete the transfer on the books of the corporation.[6]

In the case of an intended trust of a bond the most formal method is to deliver the bond and a written instrument of assignment to the trustee, but title may be passed by mere delivery of the bond with donative intent.[7] Usually either delivery of the bond or a deed of gift has been held to be necessary.

Where a settlor wishes to transfer a savings bank account to a trustee, he may vest him with title by delivery of the passbook with an intent to pass title,[8] but this is not true with regard to an ordinary checking account.[9] In the case of either type of bank account, the execution and delivery of a deed of gift is sufficient.[10]

2. See Mechem, Delivery in Gifts of Chattels, 21 Ill.L.R. 341, 457, 568; Williston, Gifts of Rights under Contracts in Writing by Delivery of the Writing, 40 Yale L.J. 1.

See Madison Trust Co. v. Skogstrom, 222 Wis. 585, 269 N.W. 249 (1936) (gift of certificate of interest under a trust); Henderson v. Hughes, 320 Pa. 124, 182 A. 392 (1936) (mortgage); Poirot v. Gundlach, 284 Ill.App. 349, 1 N.E.2d 801 (1936) (non-negotiable chose); Wilson v. Hughes Bros. Mfg. Co., 99 S.W.2d 411 (Tex.Civ.App.1936) (book account).

3. See § 22, ante. A settlor can rely on the statutes regarding descent and distribution of property on the death of its owner intestate as a means of passing property to a trustee. Ransdel v. Moore, 153 Ind. 393, 53 N.E. 767.

4. Uniform Stock Transfer Act, §§ 1 and 22, replaced in all states by Uniform Commercial Code, § 8–309.

5. See Unif.Com.Code § 8–307; Herbert v. Simson, 220 Mass. 480, 108 N.E. 65, L.R.A.1915D, 733; Miller v. Silverman, 247 N.Y. 447, 160 N.E. 910 (1928).

6. Grymes v. Hone, 49 N.Y. 17, 10 Am. Rep. 313. Indorsement without delivery does not constitute an effective transfer until such time as the stock certificate or other instrument of transfer is delivered. For further discussion see Bogert, Trusts and Trustees (rev. 2d edit.), § 142.

7. Pryor v. Morgan, 170 Pa. 568, 33 A. 98. See Uniform Commercial Code, §§ 8–307 to 8–309; Bogert, Trusts and Trustees (rev. 2d edit.), § 142. But see United States v. Chandler, 410 U.S. 257, 93 S.Ct. 880, 35 L.Ed.2d 247 (1973) (mere delivery of U.S. bonds insufficient; reregistration necessary to change ownership).

8. Hellman v. McWilliams, 70 Cal. 449, 11 P. 659; Polley v. Hicks, 58 Ohio St. 218, 50 N.E. 809, 41 L.R.A. 858.

9. Jones v. Weakley, 99 Ala. 441, 12 So. 420, 19 L.R.A. 700, 42 Am.St.Rep. 84; Wilson v. Featherston, 122 N.C. 747, 30 S.E. 325. For illustrative cases, see Bogert, Trusts and Trustees (rev. 2d edit.), § 142.

10. Tarbox v. Grant, 56 N.J.Eq. 199, 39 A. 378. See Havighurst, Gifts of Bank Deposits, 14 N.C.L.R. 129.

While the vesting of title to an insurance policy in a trustee ordinarily will not be achieved solely by making him the beneficiary named in the policy,[11] a formal assignment of the policy to the trustee will vest title in him,[12] and the title may be vested by a parol assignment and a mere delivery of the policy without change of the beneficiary named in the policy.[13]

If the settlor intends to give personal property to the trustee, and relies on a deed of gift rather than delivery of the trust property, he must deliver the deed, that is, indicate his intent to have the instrument take present effect by handing it to the trustee or otherwise.[14]

Whether the trustee must become the holder of a legal or an equitable title to the property before the trust can be complete as to him depends upon the nature of the title which the settlor intends the trustee shall have. Ordinarily the settlor transfers to the trustee the legal title, but occasionally he places in the trustee's hands the equitable title to the property to hold in trust for the beneficiaries.[15] Whatever title the trustee is to have must be given to him before the trust can be said to be completely created as to that trustee. And, as previously shown,[16] acceptance of the tendered title and office is necessary in order to make him a trustee. Nevertheless, if the settlor performs all the acts needed to place title in the trustee and the latter declines to take title, the trust takes effect with a vacancy in the trusteeship; disclaimer of the named trustee has no effect on the validity of the act of trust creation.[17]

Transfer of Possession

In some instances no title to property can be passed without giving possession. The transferee must have possession before he can have title. An oral gift of tangible personal property is an example. Where the creation of a trust is attempted by such a gift, the settlor must give the trustee possession of the trust property before the trust can be completed. The reason lies in the law of gifts rather than in the rules governing the creation of trusts.[18] An alternative to delivery of the thing given is the execution and delivery of a deed of gift. A retention by the settlor of the right to access to the trust property in the hands of the trustees, although the latter are allowed to administer the property without the joinder of the settlor, is sufficient delivery to the trustees

11. Stepson v. Brand, 213 Miss. 826, 58 So.2d 18 (1952); In re Brassell's Estate, 63 Pa.Super. 545.

12. Kendrick v. Ray, 173 Mass. 305, 53 N.E. 823.

13. Miller v. Gulf Life Ins. Co., 152 Fla. 221, 12 So.2d 127 (1942).

See Bogert, Trusts and Trustees (rev. 2d edit.), § 142; and see § 47, post.

14. Murphy v. Killmurray, 324 Mass. 707, 88 N.E.2d 544 (1949), decree affirmed 325 Mass. 247, 90 N.E.2d 305 (1950).

15. Sloane v. Cadogan, 3 Sudgen, Vendors & Purchasers, 10th Ed., Append. 66.

16. See § 31, ante, at ns. 7, 8.

17. Shaw v. Johnson, 15 Cal.App.2d 599, 59 P.2d 876 (1936); In re Edgar's Trust, 200 Minn. 340, 274 N.W. 226 (1937).

18. Wellington v. Heermans, 110 Ill. 564; Brown v. Spohr, 180 N.Y. 201, 73 N.E. 14; Dickerson's Appeal, 115 Pa. 198, 8 A. 64, 2 Am.St.Rep. 547.

and possession by them to make the trust effective.[19]

Where *possession* of the trust property by the trustee is not necessary to the passage of title to the trustee, the trust may well be complete without a delivery of possession to the trustee.[20] "But the validity of the trust is not affected by the failure of the trustee to take possession of the property . . .."[21] Indeed, delivery of the trust property to the trustee does not conclusively show that a trust has been created.[22]

Effect of Death of Sole Trustee

On the death of a sole trustee intestate ownership of the trust property devolves upon the persons entitled to the estate of the deceased. "The general principle is not questioned that trusts of real estate upon the trustee's death devolve upon his heir at law, and trusts of personalty devolve upon the executor or administrator for the preservation of the title, until the appointment of a new trustee. . . .."[23] That the heir becomes the owner of real property[24] held in trust, and the personal representative the owner of personal property,[25] is well recognized. But the heir or representative does not succeed to the trusteeship. His title will be transferred to a court-appointed trustee.

If the deceased sole trustee left a will purporting to dispose of all his property, or of the trust property in particular, it may be held that the title to the trust property passes thereunder to his executor, or to a devisee or legatee, although the office of trustee is not transferred and is vacant.[26]

In several states statutes provide that the title to trust property, upon the death of a sole trustee, vests in the court having general equitable jurisdiction, and require the court to appoint a trustee to carry out the trust to its conclusion.[27]

Sometimes the settlor names a corporate trustee which, prior to or after the beginning of the trust, merges or consolidates with another bank or trust company. While originally there was a tendency to hold that the successor institution did not take the trust intended for its

---

19. Meldahl v. Wallace, 270 Ill. 220, 110 N.E. 354.

20. Cahlan v. Bank of Lassen County, 11 Cal.App. 533, 105 P. 765; Otis v. Beckwith, 49 Ill. 121; Schreyer v. Schreyer, 43 Misc. 520, 89 N.Y.S. 508, affirmed 182 N.Y. 555, 75 N.E. 1134.

21. Young v. Cardwell, 6 Lea, Tenn., 168, 171.

22. Lloyd v. Brooks, 34 Md. 27.

23. Baltimore Trust Co. v. George's Creek Coal & Iron Co., 119 Md. 21, 34, 85 A. 949.

24. Lawrence v. Lawrence, 181 Ill. 248, 54 N.E. 918; Ewing v. Shannahan, 113 Mo. 188, 20 S.W. 1065; Kirkman v. Wadsworth, 137 N.C. 453, 49 S.E. 962.

25. Tyler v. Mayre, 95 Cal. 160, 27 P. 160, 30 P. 196; Lucas v. Donaldson, 117 Ind. 139, 19 N.E. 758; Gulick v. Bruere, 42 N.J.Eq. 639, 9 A. 719; Appeal of Baird, 3 Pa. (Watts & S.) 459.

26. Hartnett v. Langan, 282 Mo. 471, 222 S.W. 403 (1920); Cowles v. Cowles, 89 Neb. 327, 131 N.W. 738.

27. See statutory references in Bogert, Trusts and Trustees (rev. 2d edit.), § 529.

predecessor,[28] it has now generally provided by statute that the successor takes the trust and that there is no vacancy to be filled by the court.[29]

Filling of Vacancies in the Trusteeship

As a part of its general jurisdiction to protect and enforce trusts, the court of chancery has power to appoint a successor trustee. If the settlor has provided no successor or method of appointment to fill vacancies, the power of the court will be exclusive.[30]

On the death of a trustee,[31] or his resignation,[32] or declination [33] of the trust, or when he is unable to administer the trust,[34] or is removed,[35] or, being a corporation, is dissolved,[36] equity may appoint a new trustee. In many states statutes prescribe when and how equity may appoint trustees.[37]

Frequently a sole executor is given the duties of a trustee, and later a vacancy in the executorship occurs. In such a case an administrator with the will annexed is appointed. The general rule is that under such circumstances the administrator with will annexed does not succeed to the position of trustee held by the former executor, but that such administrator is vested only with the duties of the executorship and that a new trustee must be appointed to undertake the separate duties of the trusteeship.[38]

28. Atlantic Nat. Bank of Boston, Petitioner, 261 Mass. 217, 158 N.E. 780 (1927).

29. See Bogert, Trusts and Trustees (rev. 2d edit.), § 531, as to federal and state statutes. And see 23 Ill.L.R. 749; 38 Ill. B.J. 514.

30. Thompson v. Hale, 123 Ga. 305, 51 S.E. 383; Sawtelle v. Witham, 94 Wis. 412, 69 N.W. 72.

31. Allison v. Little, 85 Ala. 512, 5 So. 221; In re Gay's Estate, 138 Cal. 552, 71 P. 707, 94 Am.St.Rep. 70; Cruse v. Axtell, 50 Ind. 49; Weiland v. Townsend, 33 N.J.Eq. 393; Farmers' Loan & Trust Co. v. Pendleton, 179 N.Y. 486, 72 N.E. 508; Thornton v. Harris, 140 N.C. 498, 53 S.E. 341; In re Kane Borough Park Lands Trustees' Appointment, 177 Pa. 638, 35 A. 874; Buchanan v. Hart, 31 Tex. 647; Fisher v. Dickenson, 84 Va. 318, 4 S.E. 737. But if the trust is personal, so that it ends on the death of the trustee, the court will not appoint a successor. Rogers v. Rea, 98 Ohio St. 315, 120 N.E. 828.

32. Vernoy v. Robinson, 133 Ga. 653, 66 S.E. 928; French v. Northern Trust Co., 197 Ill. 30, 64 N.E. 105; Massachusetts General Hospital v. Amory, 12 Mass. (Pick.) 445; Schehr v. Look, 84 Mich. 263, 47 N.W. 445; In re Pitney, 186 N.Y. 540, 78 N.E. 1110.

33. Roberts v. Roberts, 259 Ill. 115, 102 N.E. 239; Greene v. Borland, 4 Metc., Mass., 330; Brush v. Young, 28 N.J.L. 237; Anderson v. Robinson, 57 Or. 172, 110 P. 975; Gamble v. Dabney, 20 Tex. 69.

34. Dean v. Northern Trust Co., 259 Ill. 148, 102 N.E. 244.

35. In re Burk's Estate, 1 N.Y.St.Rep. 316. See § 160, post.

36. Lanning v. Commissioners of Public Instruction of City of Trenton, 63 N.J. Eq. 1, 51 A. 787; Town of Montpelier v. East Montpelier, 29 Vt. 12, 67 Am.Dec. 748.

37. See, for example, West's Ann.Ind. Code 30-4-3-29; Mich.C.L.A. § 555.27; Wis.S.A. 701.16 (testamentary trustee), 701.17 (successor and added trustees). Sells v. Delgado, 186 Mass. 25, 70 N.E. 1036; In re Satterthwaite's Estate, 60 N.J. Eq. 347, 47 A. 226; Roller v. Catlett, 118 Va. 185, 86 S.E. 909.

Some statutes permit the court to transfer the situs of the trust to a foreign jurisdiction to obtain more efficient administration, and to appoint a new trustee. See, for example, Conn.G.S.A. § 45-90; Wis. S.A. 701.23.

38. Stoutenburgh v. Moore, 37 N.J.Eq. 63; Dunning v. Ocean Nat. Bank of City of New York, 61 N.Y. 497, 19 Am.Rep. 293;

Whether or not equity will appoint a trustee to fill a vacancy may be within the court's discretion.[39] Even though a trustee may have been removed, the court may deem it unwise to fill his place. Thus if there is a surviving trustee who is administering the trust successfully, chancery may deem it unnecessary to fill the vacancy; [40] and if the only duty left to the trustees is to transfer the property to the beneficiaries, equity may deem it superfluous to appoint new trustees and may transfer the property itself.[41] The court may increase or decrease the number of trustees in order to secure better administration.[42]

If equity does fill the vacancy, it will select a trustee who will administer the affairs of the trust with fairness and ability. It will not choose a prejudiced or incompetent person. Thus the court will not appoint, as a trustee of a religious charitable trust, a person hostile to the religion to be promoted; [43] nor will the court name as a successor a person who is biased and apt to favor one or more of the beneficiaries as against the others.[44] It is the better practice to appoint a resident of the jurisdiction,[45] but circumstances may justify the choice of a nonresident.[46] The court should consider the wishes of the interested parties in its appointment, though it is not bound to follow them.[47]

Neither a surviving trustee [48] nor a beneficiary [49] has implied authority to fill a vacancy in the trusteeship. Only when expressly empowered by the trust instrument may either of them appoint the successor trustee.

The settlor may prescribe a method of filling vacancies, and this method must be followed unless the court finds it prejudicial.[50] He

In re Sheaffer's Estate, 230 Pa. 426, 79 A. 651.

39. City Council of Augusta v. Walton, 77 Ga. 517, 1 S.E. 214; Ex parte Knust, Bailey Eq., S.C., 489. The discretion warrants the appointment of a trust company as sole trustee, although the instrument provided for several individual trustees. In re Battin's Estate, 89 N.J.Eq. 144, 104 A. 434.

40. Mullanny v. Nangle, 212 Ill. 247, 72 N.E. 385; In re Dietz, 132 App.Div. 641, 117 N.Y.S. 461.

41. Friedley v. Security Trust & Safe Deposit Co., 10 Del.Ch. 74, 84 A. 883; Boyer v. Decker, 5 App.Div. 623, 40 N.Y.S. 469.

42. In re Townsend's Estate, 73 Misc. 481, 133 N.Y.S. 492; Crickard's Ex'r v. Crickard's Legatees, 25 Grat., Va., 410.

43. Glover v. Baker, 76 N.H. 393, 83 A. 916.

44. Waller v. Hosford, Iowa, 132 N.W. 426; In re Welch, 20 App.Div. 412, 46 N.Y.S. 689.

45. Dodge v. Dodge, 109 Md. 164, 71 A. 519, 130 Am.St.Rep. 503.

46. Appeal of Wilcox, 54 Conn. 320, 8 A. 136. For example, where a trust was to be administered in Germany an Iowa court appointed a resident of Germany as trustee. Beidler v. Dehner, 178 Iowa 1338, 161 N.W. 32.

47. Thornburg v. Macauley, 2 Md.Ch. 425; Coster v. Coster, 125 App.Div. 516, 109 N.Y.S. 798; In re Estate of Chapman, 258 Wis. 442, 45 N.W.2d 927 (1951).

In some cases it has been held an abuse of judicial discretion not to follow the desires of the beneficiaries in appointing a trustee. Central Trust Co. of Illinois v. Harvey, 297 Ill.App. 425, 17 N.E.2d 988 (1938); Hodgen's Ex'rs v. Sproul, 221 Iowa 1104, 267 N.W. 692 (1936); In re McCaskey's Estate, 293 Pa. 497, 143 A. 209 (1928). See 42 Harv.L.R. 446.

48. Whitehead v. Whitehead, 142 Ala. 163, 37 So. 929; Mallory v. Mallory, 72 Conn. 494, 45 A. 164.

49. Grundy v. Drye, 104 Ky. 825, 48 S.W. 155, 49 S.W. 469.

50. Tuckerman v. Currier, 54 Colo. 25, 129 P. 210, Ann.Cas.1914C, 599.

may reserve to himself the right to fill vacancies,[51] or may vest such right in the surviving trustees,[52] or in the surviving trustees and the beneficiaries,[53] or in the beneficiaries alone.[54] But in cases where the power to appoint is given the trustee or beneficiary, the court may nevertheless supervise the filling of the vacancy [55] and act if those having the power exercise it improperly or do not exercise it.[56] The creator of the trust cannot vest this power in a court which has no jurisdiction over trusts.[57]

Proceeding for Appointment

The application to the court for the appointment of a new trustee may be made by any one interested financially in the execution of the trust. Thus a beneficiary,[58] or the guardian of an infant beneficiary,[59] may apply, and in the case of a religious charitable trust it has been held that a member of the church to be benefited may make application.[60] In accordance with generally prevailing doctrines, it is usually held that the fact that a person is a citizen and taxpayer in the county where the charity is to be carried on does not show sufficient interest to enable one to apply to the court.[61]

The question of notice upon the application for the appointment of a new trustee is one affected by statute to a large extent, and to the extent not governed by statute the courts have not been in accord upon the subject.[62] In many instances they have held that the notice necessary to be given was entirely in the discretion of the court,[63] while

51. Equitable Trust Co. v. Fisher, 106 Ill. 189.

52. Orr v. Yates, 209 Ill. 222, 70 N.E. 731; In re Cleven's Estate, 161 Iowa 289, 142 N.W. 986; Jacobs v. McClintock, 53 Tex. 72.

53. Griswold v. Sackett, 21 R.I. 206, 42 A. 868.

54. Fuller v. Davis, 63 Miss. 78; Miller v. Knowles, 44 S.W. 927 (Tex.Civ.App.).

55. Bailey v. Bailey, 2 Del.Ch. 95; Yates v. Yates, 255 Ill. 66, 99 N.E. 360, Ann.Cas.1913D, 143. Where the persons given the power to appoint successors do not exercise it, a suit may be brought in equity to obtain an appointment, and it is then too late for the settlor's nominees to act. National City Bank of Cleveland v. Schmoltz, 31 N.E.2d 444 (Ohio App.1934), petition dismissed 129 Ohio St. 158, 193 N.E. 627 (1934).

56. Petition of Stevens, 307 N.Y. 742, 121 N.E.2d 551 (1954); Baumer v. Johnstown Tr. Co., 345 Pa. 51, 25 A.2d 723 (1942).

57. Harwood v. Tracy, 118 Mo. 631, 24 S.W. 214. Thus in Petition of Straw, 78 N.H. 506, 102 A. 628, it was held that the settlor could not give the Supreme Court power to fill vacancies, since such power was vested by statute in the probate court.

58. Cone v. Cone, 61 S.C. 512, 39 S.E. 748.

59. Hallinan v. Hearst, 133 Cal. 645, 66 P. 17, 55 L.R.A. 216.

60. Harris v. Brown, 124 Ga. 310, 52 S.E. 610, 2 L.R.A.,N.S., 828.

Usually the application must be made by the Attorney General. See § 156, post.

61. Harris v. Brown, 124 Ga. 310, 52 S.E. 610, 2 L.R.A.,N.S., 828. Occasionally courts permit a member of the class to be benefitted by a charitable trust to bring suit to compel enforcement of the trust. See Bogert, Trusts and Trustees (rev. 2d edit.), §§ 412, 414.

62. Gray v. Union Trust Co., 213 Ind. 675, 12 N.E.2d 931 (1938), rehearing denied and mandate modified 213 Ind. 675, 14 N.E.2d 532 (1938) (improperly appointed trustees become de facto trustees if they assume charge); State v. Underwood, 54 Wyo. 1, 86 P.2d 707 (if one beneficiary is not notified, only he can avoid the appointment).

63. Dyer v. Leach, 91 Cal. 191, 27 P. 598, 25 Am.St.Rep. 171; In re Earnshaw, 196 N.Y. 330, 89 N.E. 825; Bransford Real-

in other cases notice to all interested parties has been required.[64] Occasionally new trustees seem to have been appointed ex parte.[65] It would seem that normally all beneficiaries are necessary parties to the application,[66] but sometimes this has been denied where their interests are of a future or contingent nature.[67] The heirs of the deceased trustee whose place is to be filled have been called necessary parties,[68] as well as the Attorney General in the case of a charitable trust.[69]

When the new trustee is appointed to fill the vacancy, his title to the trust property is ordinarily acquired by virtue of the order of the court. No conveyance from the retiring trustee is needed in order to vest the property rights in the succeeding trustee.[70] In the early days of chancery practice the court ordered the title-holder to convey to the newly appointed trustee, but nowadays the court has the power to lift the title from one person and vest it in another. Where one is appointed trustee in place of another who has declined the trust, the title to the trust property vests in the appointee as of the date of the inception of the trust by virtue of the doctrine of relation.[71]

Size and Characteristics of the Trustee's Property Interest

A question may arise as to the quantum or size of the property interest conveyed to the trustee. Whether the estate granted to him in trust is a fee, a life estate, or other interest, is determined by the size of the interest owned by the settlor and by the terms of the trust instrument as to conveyancing language and trust purpose. The important principle that a trustee takes such an estate or interest as is necessary to enable him to perform the trust should be observed.[72] If the trust can be administered only through the ownership of a fee simple or absolute interest in personalty, such an interest will be

ty Co. v. Andrews, 128 Tenn. 725, 164 S.W. 1175.

64. Simmons v. McKinlock, 98 Ga. 738, 26 S.E. 88; Clarke v. Inhabitants of Andover, 207 Mass. 91, 92 N.E. 1013.

65. Sullivan v. Latimer, 35 S.E. 422, 14 S.E. 933; Reigart v. Ross, 63 Wis. 449, 23 N.W. 878.

66. In re Earnshaw, Sup., 112 N.Y.S. 197; Henry v. Doctor, 9 Ohio 49; Bolling v. Stokes, 7 S.C. 364.

67. Whallen v. Kellner, 104 S.W. 1018, 31 Ky.Law Rep. 1285; Fitzgibbon v. Barry, 78 Va. 755.

68. In re Abbott, 55 Me. 580; Plumley v. Plumley, 8 N.J.Eq. 511. But see, *contra,* Hawley v. Ross, 7 Paige, N.Y., 103.

69. Lakatong Lodge, No. 114, of Quakertown, etc. v. Board of Education of Franklin Tp., Hunterdon County, 84 N.J. Eq. 112, 92 A. 870.

70. Reichert v. Missouri & I. Coal Co., 231 Ill. 238, 83 N.E. 166, 121 Am.St.Rep. 307; Coster v. Coster, 125 App.Div. 516, 109 N.Y.S. 798; Wooldridge v. Planter's Bank, 1 Tenn. (Sneed) 297. "At common law the appointment of new trustees by parties (not in execution of a special power) did not vest the title in the new trustees without conveyance." Glazier v. Everett, 224 Mass. 184, 187, 112 N.E. 1009 (but common law changed by statute).

71. Parkhill v. Doggett, 135 Iowa 113, 112 N.W. 189.

72. Defrees v. Brydon, 275 Ill. 530, 114 N.E. 336; Cleveland v. Hallett, Mass. (6 Cush.) 403; Wright v. Keasbey, 87 N.J.Eq. 51, 100 A. 172; Brown v. Richter, 25 App. Div. 239, 49 N.Y.S. 368; Holder v. Melvin, 106 S.C. 245, 91 S.E. 97; Montgomery v. Trueheart, Tex.Civ.App., 146 S.W. 284. See Rarick, 8 Okl.L.R. 1, 133, 265.

deemed granted,[73] although the limitations of the deed or will may not clearly show that such an interest was to be transferred. If a life interest will suffice to enable the trustee to perform his duties, such an estate will be deemed vested in the trustee,[74] regardless of the wording of the granting clauses.[75] Ordinarily the legal estate is vested in the trustee,[76] although a trust may be created with an equitable interest as the subject matter.

Probably because of the convenience of the rule of survivorship in the case of co-trusteeships, a transfer to two or more trustees is treated as making them joint tenants, unless the settlor expressly provided that they should hold in some other way, for example, as tenants in common.[77] Therefore, on the death of one co-trustee the surviving trustees hold complete title to the trust property and no interest in that property passes to the successors of the deceased trustee by will or intestacy.[78] Even in states where joint tenancy is generally abolished, it still exists among trustees,[79] and in other states, where all grants to two or more persons are presumed to be to them as tenants in common, there is an exception in the case of trustees and they hold as joint tenants.[80]

The estate of the trustee being held for the benefit of others and not for the advantage of the trustee, his creditors cannot satisfy their claims from the trust property. A judgment against the trustee personally is not a lien upon trust real estate and cannot be collected out of it.[81] Nor can the trustee's estate be made the basis for a claim of dower

73. McFall v. Kirkpatrick, 236 Ill. 281, 86 N.E. 139.

74. In re Spreckel's Estate, 162 Cal. 559, 123 P. 371.

75. In order to convey a fee to a trustee it is not necessary to use the words "and his heirs". Sumter Fert. Mfg. Co. v. Baker, 206 S.C. 446, 34 S.E.2d 681 (1945).

76. Ware v. Richardson, 3 Md. 505, 56 Am.Dec. 762; Welch v. Boston, 221 Mass. 155, 109 N.E. 174, Ann.Cas.1917D, 946.

77. Webster v. Vandeventer, 6 Gray, Mass., 428; Jackson ex dem. Erwin v. Moore, 6 Cow., N.Y., 706. As to the capacity of a corporation to be a joint tenant with an individual, see Bogert, Trusts and Trustees (rev. 2d edit.), § 145.

78. Wilson v. Snow, 228 U.S. 217, 33 S.Ct. 487, 57 L.Ed. 807 (1913); Booth v. Krug, 368 Ill. 487, 14 N.E.2d 645, 117 A.L.R. 1193 (1938).

79. See Bogert, Trusts and Trustees (rev. 2d edit.), § 145; Boyer v. Sims, 61 Kan. 593, 60 P. 309.

80. See, for example, Miss.Code 1972, § 91–9–13; N.Y.—McKinney's EPTL 6–2.2.

81. H.B. Claflin Co. v. King, 56 Fla. 767, 48 So. 37; Taylor v. Brown, 112 Ga. 758, 38 S.E. 66; Cox v. Arnsmann, 76 Ind. 210; Brown v. Barngrover, 82 Iowa 204, 47 N.W. 1082; Emery v. Farmers' State Bank, 97 Kan. 231, 155 P. 34; Feagan v. Metcalfe, 150 Ky. 745, 150 S.W. 988; First Nat. Bank of Catonsville v. Carter, 132 Md. 218, 103 A. 463; Hussey v. Arnold, 185 Mass. 202, 70 N.E. 87; Lee v. Enos, 97 Mich. 276, 56 N.W. 550; Fleming v. Wilson, 92 Minn. 303, 100 N.W. 4; Moran v. Joyce, 125 N.J.L. 558, 18 A.2d 708; Arntson v. First Nat. Bank, 39 N.D. 408, 167 N.W. 760, L.R.A.1918F, 1038; J.I. Case Threshing Mach. Co. v. Walton Trust Co., 39 Okl. 748, 136 P. 769; Eldredge v. Mill Ditch Co., 90 Or. 590, 177 P. 939; Nashville Trust Co. v. Weaver, 102 Tenn. 66, 50 S.W. 763; Davenport v. Stephens, 95 Wis. 456, 70 N.W. 661. This rule applies, even though the trustee is also the settlor of the trust, in the absence of fraud. Wulff v. Roseville Trust Co. of Newark, N.J., 164 App.Div. 399, 149 N.Y.S. 683.

In the early days, when the separation of law and equity was complete, a creditor of the trustee could reach the trust property for the trustee's personal debt in the court of law, but equity would, at the suit of the beneficiary, enjoin the taking of the trust property for that purpose. Giles v.

or curtesy in the spouse of the trustee, in states where those marital estates still exist,[82] or for a similar statutory estate.

The modern rule is that if a sole trustee dies intestate and without heirs, and escheat or the doctrines as to bona vacantia take effect, the crown or state holds for the beneficiaries of the trust.[83]

 WESTLAW REFERENCES

Vesting of Title in the Trustee
di(deliver*** /s title /s vest*** /s trustee)
find 274 nw 266

Transfer of Possession
390k182
meldahl +3 wallace
deliver* /s property res /s trustee /s trust /s creat***
390k1 /p deliver* /s property /s trustee

Effect of Death of Sole Trustee
death /4 "sole trustee"
hartnett +3 langan
find 158 ne 780

Filling of Vacancies in the Trusteeship
death incapacitation resign declin! /3 trustee /s court /s
    appoint /s "new trustee"
orr +3 yates

Preceeding for Appointment
beneficiary /s apply application /s "new trustee"
find 112 ne 1009

Size and Characteristics of the Trustee's Property Interest
find 34 f.supp. 109
51k140(3)
creditor /s claim /s against /s "trust property"
390k151(1) /p claim /s creditor

QUALIFICATION BY THE TRUSTEE

§ 33. Qualification means the performance by the trustee of certain acts required by statute, the court, or the settlor as a preliminary to the beginning of his work as trustee, such as the taking of an oath for the faithful performance of the trust, the filing of a security

Palmer, 49 N.C. 386, 69 Am.Dec. 756. But now this same relief may be obtained in the law action.

Where a trustee becomes bankrupt the legal title to the trust property passes to the trustee in bankruptcy, subject to the trust. In re Heintzelman Constr. Co., 34 F.Supp. 109 (W.D.N.Y.1940).

82. Barker v. Smiley, 218 Ill. 68, 75 N.E. 787; Van Pelt v. Parry, 218 Mo. 680,

118 S.W. 425; Kager v. Brenneman, 47 App.Div. 63, 62 N.Y.S. 339; Hendren v. Hendren, 153 N.C. 505, 69 S.E. 506, 138 Am.St.Rep. 680.

83. See, for example, N.Y.—McKinney's EPTL 7–2.3. St. 47 & 48 Vict. c. 71, § 6; New York Cent. & H.R.R. Co. v. Cottle, 102 Misc. 30, 168 N.Y.S. 463.

bond by which a third person agrees to respond in damages if the trustee is guilty of a breach of trust, or the obtaining of letters of trusteeship from the court which has jurisdiction over the trust.

There are many and diverse statutes regarding qualification. Almost universally it is provided by statute that a corporate trustee need not give a bond if it deposits with a state official securities of a certain value as security for the faithful performance of its trusts.

Directions of the settlor as to qualification will ordinarily be given effect, but he may not override a statutory requirement. The court makes orders regarding qualification, notwithstanding any direction of the settlor, but it will not overrule the settlor unless it is clearly for the best interests of the beneficiaries.

In the absence of statutory control the court of equity has discretionary power to enter such orders about a bond or other acts of qualification as it deems best for the purpose of securing efficient trust administration and protecting the beneficiaries.

The authorities are not harmonious as to the effect of failure to perform required acts of qualification. Some statutes treat such failure as a rejection of the trust; some decisions consider that the trustee has no title or powers until he has qualified; but in other cases failure to qualify is regarded as a breach of duty and as making it unlawful for the trustee to act but not as preventing the trustee from having the title and powers vested in him. In no case does failure to qualify prevent the trust from arising, unless the trust is personal to the named trustee.

"Qualification" is a technical word in the law of trusts and means doing whatever acts are required by the settlor's direction, court order or statute, to be done as a prerequisite to taking possession of the trust property and beginning administration of the trust. The acts, some or all of which are required in some states and with regard to some trusts, are usually: the signing and taking of an oath of office as trustee which is filed with the clerk of the court; the giving of a surety bond signed by one or more third persons by which the sureties agree to respond in damages up to a certain amount for any breaches of trust by the trustee; and the securing from the court of letters of trusteeship which set forth under the seal of the court and the signature of its clerk that the trustee has been appointed and has power to act under a described trust.

In many states trustees are required by statute to give bond for the faithful performance of their duties,[1] in some or all cases, or only where

§ 33

1. See, for example, V.Tex.C.A.Prop. Code § 113.058 (individual trustee). And see Thiebaud v. Dufour, 54 Ind. 320; Sneer v. Stutz, 102 Iowa 462, 71 N.W. 415; Bullard v. Attorney General, 153 Mass. 249, 26 N.E. 691; Gibney v. Allen, 156 Mich. 301, 120 N.W. 811; West v. Bailey, 196 Mo. 517, 94 S.W. 273; In re Keene's Estate, 81 Pa. 133; Kerr v. White, 9 Baxt., Tenn., 161; Lackland v. Davenport, 84 Va. 638, 5 S.E. 540.

the settlor does not excuse the trustee from this duty.[2] Statutes generally provide that corporate trustees are not required to give a bond if they have qualified to administer trusts by depositing, with the state treasurer or some similar official, securities of a described type and of a stated value, which are to stand as security for the faithful administration of all their trusts.[3]

The settlor may provide in the trust instrument that the trustee shall not be obliged to give a bond, and this direction will be respected by the courts in the absence of a clear showing of need for protection of the beneficiaries.[4] And in some instances the consent of the beneficiaries has been held sufficient authority for excusing the trustee from giving security.[5] The settlor may also provide in the trust instrument that the trustee shall give a bond of a certain description and the courts will enforce such directions, unless there is some clear reason why they are highly disadvantageous to the beneficiaries or otherwise unreasonable.[6]

Whether a trustee will be required to give a bond for the faithful performance of his duties ultimately is, in the absence of a controlling statute, in the discretion of the court which has jurisdiction. If the character and situation of the trustee seem to render security necessary, the court may require it. Any interested party may, of course, apply for a court order requiring the giving of a bond. If the trust property does not appear to be in any danger, equity may dispense with the bond.[7] Where the trustee is insolvent or of weak or doubtful financial condition, the court will generally require a bond.[8] If the trustee is a nonresident of the state having jurisdiction of the trust, the court will be inclined to require security.[9] If the trustee has refused to obey an order of the court,[10] or if the beneficiaries are infants,[11] the court may require security of the trustee.

---

2. For the details of many of these statutes, see Bogert, Trusts and Trustees (rev.2d edit.), § 151.

In California a testamentary trustee is "not automatically qualified by his nomination by the testator". He is not trustee until the probate court appoints him. In re Barter's Estate, 30 Cal.2d 549, 184 P.2d 305 (1947). To the same effect, see Wis. S.A. 701.16.

In a number of states the court in its discretion may require a bond of the trustee. See, for example, 20 Pa.C.S.A. § 7111; Va.Code § 26–3; Wis.S.A. 701.16.

See Unif.Prob.Code § 7–304 (no bond required unless required by trust terms,

requested by beneficiary or ordered by court).

5. Dexter v. Cotting, 149 Mass. 92, 21 N.E. 230.

6. Pool v. Potter, 63 Ill. 533.

7. Reeder v. Reeder, 184 Iowa 1, 168 N.W. 122; Munroe v. Whitaker, 121 Md. 396, 88 A. 237; Holcomb v. Coryell, 12 N.J. Eq. 289; Strayhorn v. Green, 92 N.C. 119; Ex parte Conrad, 2 Ashm., Pa., 527; Clarke v. Saxon, 1 Hill Eq., S.C., 69; Dunscomb v. Dunscomb, 2 Hen. & M., Va., 11.

8. Bailey v. Bailey, 2 Del.Ch. 95; In re Deaven's Estate, 32 Pa.Super. 205.

9. In re Satterthwaite's Estate, 60 N.J. Eq. 347, 47 A. 226; Ex parte Robert, 2 Strob.Eq., S.C., 86.

10. Holcomb v. Coryell, 12 N.J.Eq. 289.

11. In re Jones, 4 Sandf.Ch., N.Y., 615.

3. See Bogert, Trusts and Trustees (rev. 2d edit.), § 151.

4. Parker v. Sears, 117 Mass. 513; Liesemer v. Burg, 102 Mich. 20, 60 N.W. 290; In re Kelley's Estate, 250 Pa. 177, 95 A. 401; Kerr v. White, 9 Baxt., Tenn., 161.

It may be an abuse of discretion for the court to require the trustee to give a bond when no reason for apprehension as to safety of the funds exists and the administration of the trust has been entirely satisfactory.[12] While the court may overrule the direction of the settlor regarding the giving or not giving of a bond, it will not do so unless there is clear ground for doing so.[13] Arbitrary action by the trial court in this matter may be corrected by an appellate court.[14]

If the same person is named as executor and trustee, he must give separate bonds for the faithful performance of the duties of each office.[15]

Occasionally it is provided by statute that trustees must qualify by taking an oath that they will administer their office in a legal manner, and by applying for and receiving from the court letters of trusteeship which state the qualification of the trustee and his power to act in the particular trust.[16] Such requirements are, however, no longer common.

If a trustee fails to qualify as required by any controlling authority, it is sometimes held that he is not a trustee and has no powers under the trust,[17] but other courts hold that if the trustee has accepted the trust his failure to qualify does not affect his powers as trustee, although it is a breach of his duty as trustee not to qualify and he cannot legally exercise his powers.[18] Statutes sometimes provide that failure to qualify within a limited period shall be deemed a refusal of the trust.[19] In no case does failure to qualify prevent the trust from being completely created (except in the rare case of the personal trustee).

If a trustee performs an act of trust administration before qualifying and later qualifies, the effect of the qualification on the act in question would seem to depend on the theory adopted in the state on the result of failure to qualify. If qualification is needed to give a trustee any title or powers, then any prior act would be a nullity unless affirmed after qualification.[20] But if a trustee gets his powers without qualification and is merely prohibited from using those powers, then the later qualification might be treated as validating an act that was at

12. Ladd v. Ladd, 125 Ala. 135, 27 So. 924; Berry v. Williamson, 11 B.Mon., Ky., 245; Holcomb v. Coryell, 12 N.J.Eq. 289.

13. Shaull v. United States, 82 U.S. App.D.C. 174, 161 F.2d 891 (1947).

14. Ex parte Kilgore, 120 Ind. 94, 22 N.E. 104.

15. Williams v. Cushing, 34 Me. 370.

16. See Bogert, Trusts and Trustees (rev. 2d edit.), § 151.

By Wis.S.A. 701.16 a trustee is to assume office only upon issuance of his letters.

17. Philbin v. Thurn, 103 Md. 342, 63 A. 571; Chappus v. Lucke, 246 Mich. 272,

224 N.W. 432. In Wisconsin the trustee who accepts but fails to qualify was held to get title but no powers. Madler v. Kersten, 170 Wis. 424, 175 N.W. 779. But see Wis.S.A. 701.16.

18. Pool v. Potter, 63 Ill. 533; Reeder v. Reeder, 184 Iowa 1, 168 N.W. 122.

But see Ohio Rev.Code § 2109.02 (no act valid prior to issuance of letters).

19. Conn.G.S.A. § 45–83; Neb.Rev.St. § 30–1802. And see Pungs v. Hilgendorf, 289 Mich. 46, 286 N.W. 152 (1939); Attwill v. Dole, 74 N.H. 300, 67 A. 403.

20. In re Oliff's Estate, 283 Mich. 43, 276 N.W. 893 (1937).

worst voidable.[21]

In numerous instances there is no provision by statute, court order, or trust instrument for the performance by the trustee of any act preliminary to the beginning of his trust administration, and hence no "qualification" is required and the trustee may proceed with his work as soon as he acquires title and possession.

 WESTLAW REFERENCES

Qualification   /5   trustee
find 184 p2d 305
di(trustee   /s   require*   /s   post   /s   bond)
390k160(2)
trustee   /s   qualif!   /s   oath
find 224 nw 432
390k200(1)

---

21. Little v. Little, 161 Mass. 188, 36 N.E. 795.

Chapter 4

CREATION OF PRIVATE EXPRESS TRUSTS—THE BENEFICIARY

Table of Sections

NECESSITY OF BENEFICIARY—DEFINITENESS [1]

§ 34. In order to create a private trust the settlor must name or otherwise describe a beneficiary of his trust. The attempted trust will fail if no beneficiary is identified, or the beneficiary provided is not a legal entity, or if the description of the beneficiary is vague and indefinite.

The beneficiary does not have to be identified at the date of trust creation. It is sufficient if the instrument gives a formula or description by which the beneficiary can be identified at the time when enjoyment of his interest is to begin.

A private trust may exist for all the members of a class, or for such class members as are selected by the trustee in his discretion, or for such members as meet certain requirements; but a trust for any persons selected by the trustee is invalid.

§ 34

1. Restatement, Trusts, Second, §§ 2, 66, 112. Requirements as to the beneficiaries of charitable trusts are considered in § 55, post.

It is fundamental that every private trust must have a beneficiary.[2] One might as well speak of a contract with but one party as to talk of a private trust without a beneficiary. In the words of Fowler, Surrogate, "to constitute a trust not charitable in nature there must always be a definite person, entitled to enforce the trust or power in trust in equity, and this beneficiary must be ascertained or ascertainable. . . ."[3] Trust creation constitutes a conveyance of an equitable interest in property. There can be no conveyance without a person to receive the interest to be conveyed. There can be no equitable ownership without an owner. Trust creation also involves the establishment of an obligation from trustee to beneficiary. An obligee must be a legal person.

The beneficiary must be described by name, relationship to the settlor, or in such other way that the court can be sure who are the person or persons the settlor intended to benefit.[4] If the trust is to be enforceable, the court must be able to assure itself that the beneficiaries seeking enforcement are the persons intended by the settlor and that the persons to whom the trustee may have given the benefits of the trust property are rightfully entitled to them. If a trust instrument is vague or indefinite in its naming or description of the beneficiary, equity cannot enforce the trust,[5] just as uncertainty in an essential part of any legal instrument renders the courts powerless to give it effect. Thus a trust for certain persons or any of them is too indefinite.[6] But the beneficiaries may be described as a class, for example, the children of A at a given time,[7] and the members of the class will be presumed to have equal interests as beneficiaries.[8] The beneficiaries may also be such members of a class as are selected by the trustee, either in his absolute discretion, or in accordance with a standard fixed by the settlor.[9] Thus a trust for the settlor's grandchildren, with power in the trustee to select any grandchildren he wishes as recipients of the bounty, is valid,[10] as would be a trust for such of the grandchildren as

2. Eldridge v. See Yup Co., 17 Cal. 44; Filkins v. Severn, 127 Iowa 738, 104 N.W. 346; Boskowitz v. Continental Ins. Co., 175 App.Div. 18, 161 N.Y.S. 680. A declaration of trust by a realty owner, the beneficiaries to be such persons as later buy interests under the trust, is void. Kaufman v. Federal National Bank, 287 Mass. 97, 191 N.E. 422 (1934).

A trust to prevent named persons from obtaining the property is not valid. Gross v. Moore, 68 Hun 412, 22 N.Y.S. 1019, affirmed 141 N.Y. 559, 36 N.E. 343.

3. Matter of Catlin, 97 Misc. 223, 227, 160 N.Y.S. 1034.

4. Barkley v. Lane's Ex'r, 6 Bush., Ky., 587; Isaac v. Emory, 64 Md. 333, 1 A. 713; German Land Ass'n v. Scholler, 10 Minn. 331, Gil. 260; First Presbyterian Soc. of Town of Chili v. Bowen, 21 Hun, N.Y., 389; Appeal of Dyer, 107 Pa. 446.

5. Oral evidence will not be admitted to prove the testator's intent as to who were to be the beneficiaries, where the will was ambiguous or silent on that point. Gore v. Bingaman, 29 Cal.App.2d 460, 85 P.2d 172 (1938); Ray v. Fowler, 144 S.W.2d 665 (Tex.Civ.App.1940).

6. Wright v. Pond, 10 Conn. 255.

7. Heermans v. Schmaltz, 7 Fed. 566 (C.C.Wis.1881).

8. Loring v. Palmer, 118 U.S. 321, 6 S.Ct. 1073, 30 L.Ed. 211 (1886); Cowan v. Henika, 19 Ind.App. 40, 48 N.E. 809.

9. In re Davis' Estate, 13 Cal.App.2d 64, 56 P.2d 584 (1936); Atwater v. Russell, 49 Minn. 57, 51 N.W. 629, 52 N.W. 26; Lundie v. Walker, 126 N.J.Eq. 497, 9 A.2d 783 (1939); Hughes v. Jackson, 125 Tex. 130, 81 S.W.2d 656 (1935).

10. Gunn v. Wagner, 242 Iowa 1001, 48 N.W.2d 292 (1951).

the trustee considers most worthy and deserving or in need.[11]

But a trust to pay the income to any persons in the world, in the discretion of the trustee, is not a valid private trust, the element of vagueness and indefiniteness being considered too great.[12] An unlimited power to spend and distribute is often construed as showing an intent to make the donee not a trustee but rather a full owner of the property.[13]

The beneficiaries may be described otherwise than by naming them,[14] for example, to include all the blood relations of a certain party,[15] or all the employees of a named corporation at a certain time.[16] "It is well settled that any description of parties in an instrument of this kind is sufficient, from which the court and jury, aided by a knowledge of surrounding facts and circumstances, are able to say with reasonable certainty that some and what particular persons were intended. It is not necessary that the parties should be described by their names. . . ."[17] It is sufficient that the beneficiaries become ascertained and definite at the time their enjoyment of the trust property is to commence, and it is not required that their names be known or knowable at the date the trust instrument goes into effect.[18]

Sometimes there is a close question of fact as to whether the settlor's description of the beneficiary is clear and capable of being applied with certainty. Examples are found in the cases where a fund is left in trust for the settlor's friends,[19] or close friends,[20] or best friend,[21] or for such person as has given most care to the settlor in his last years[22] or during his final sickness.[23]

11. Applegate v. Brown, 168 Neb. 190, 95 N.W.2d 341 (1959); In re Simard's Estate, 98 N.H. 454, 102 A.2d 508 (1954).

12. Morice v. Bishop of Durham, 9 Ves. 399; Davison v. Wyman, 214 Mass. 192, 100 N.E. 1105; Forster v. Winfield, 142 N.Y. 327, 37 N.E. 111; In re Dormer's Estate, 348 Pa. 356, 35 A.2d 299 (1944).

See also Inland Rev. Com'rs v. Broadway Cottages Trust, [1954] 3 All Eng.R. 120.

13. In re Sargavak's Estate, 41 Cal.2d 314, 259 P.2d 897 (1953); Hodgson v. Dorsey, 230 Iowa 730, 298 N.W. 895, 137 A.L.R. 456 (1941); Weiss v. Broadway Nat. Bank, 204 Tenn. 563, 322 S.W.2d 427 (1959).

14. Turner v. Barber, 131 Ga. 444, 62 S.E. 587.

15. Heilig v. Daniel, 203 Or. 123, 275 P.2d 854 (1954).

16. Board of Directors of Ajax Electrothermic Corp. v. First Nat. Bank, 33 N.J. 456, 165 A.2d 513 (1960).

17. Sydnor v. Palmer, 29 Wis. 226, 241.

18. Heyward-Williams Co. v. McCall, 140 Ga. 502, 79 S.E. 133; Ludlow v. Rector, etc., of St. Johns Church, 144 App.Div. 207, 130 N.Y.S. 679; Ashhurst v. Given, 5 Watts & S., Pa., 323. And see Union Trust Co. of Pittsburgh v. McCaughn, 24 F.2d 459 (D.C.Pa.1927) (trust of insurance policy for beneficiary to be named in will of insured when enjoyment of proceeds would commence, held valid description); National Shawmut Bank v. Joy, 315 Mass. 457, 53 N.E.2d 113 (1944) (trust for lives of named persons, then for appointees by will of one of them or for his next of kin).

19. Clark v. Campbell, 82 N.H. 281, 133 A. 166, 45 A.L.R. 1433 (1926) (too indefinite).

20. In re Rowlands' Estate, 73 Ariz. 337, 241 P.2d 781 (1952) (too vague).

21. Early v. Arnold, 119 Va. 500, 89 S.E. 900 (void).

22. Farley v. Fullerton, 145 Kan. 760, 67 P.2d 525 (1937) (valid); Moss v. Axford, 246 Mich. 288, 224 N.W. 425 (1929) (valid);

23. See note 23 on page 124.

In deciding whether these phrases are too indefinite the courts consider the actual situation of the settlor and those claiming to be beneficiaries at the time the trust was established.

Problems in the construction of trust instruments as to the descriptions of beneficiaries have given rise to much litigation, for example, whether a description of the beneficiaries as the "issue", or "descendants", or "children" of a named person includes adopted children.[24]

If a private trust is otherwise perfectly created voluntarily, but no adequate provision is made for a beneficiary, and the settlor does not provide otherwise, the legal title passes to the trustee but, as later shown, the equitable interest results to the settlor or his successors.[25] Different problems, discussed elsewhere [26], are raised where a trust is for members of an indefinite class, or for indefinite or general purposes, or is for specific noncharitable purposes, and the trustee fails to apply the property as directed.[27]

 WESTLAW REFERENCES

trust /s definite /s beneficiary

390k1 /p beneficiary

390k25 /p "ascertainable beneficiary"

75k19 /p "ascertainable beneficiary"

390k21(2)

find 241 p2d 781

find 87 a2d 290

WHO MAY BE A BENEFICIARY? [1]

§ 35. Any legal entity recognized by law as capable of taking the title to property and of being an obligee may be made the beneficiary of a private trust.

Only a person who is intended by the settlor to acquire benefits through the operation of the trust is a beneficiary.

The settlor may select as beneficiary of his trust any legal entity capable of taking the title to property and becoming the obligee of an equitable obligation which the trustee must assume. "Equity subjects trusts to the same construction that a court of law does legal estates. A donee must have capacity to take, whether it is attempted to convey

---

In re Utter's Estate, 173 Misc. 1069, 20 N.Y.S.2d 457 (1940) (valid); In re Long's Estate, 190 Wash. 196, 67 P.2d 331 (1937) (person who rendered greatest service to testator during declining period, held void).

23. In re Umberger's Estate, 369 Pa. 587, 87 A.2d 290 (1952).

24. For a large amount of material on this subject, see Bogert, Trusts and Trustees (rev. 2d edit.), § 182.

25. See § 75, post. And see Restatement, Trusts, Second, § 411.

26. See § 75, post.

27. See Restatement, Trusts, Second, §§ 416–418.

§ 35

1. Restatement, Trusts, Second, §§ 114–127.

title directly to the party himself, or to another in trust for him." [2] The beneficiary must be a human being or a corporation or other artificial legal entity.[3] The settlor may name several co-beneficiaries, and ordinarily selects income beneficiaries whose interests are to be followed by remainder beneficiaries.

That the person selected as beneficiary possesses disabilities with regard to management of his property or the making of contracts or conveyances is immaterial with respect to his capacity to be a trust beneficiary. Under the common law the disability of an alien to hold real property obtained by conveyance could prevent his continuing to be the beneficiary of a trust of realty but did not prevent the origin of the trust for him.[4] But modern statutes have often decreased or extinguished this disability to take and hold.[5] Since the assumption of control of many countries by communist governments, it has become customary to impound a gift to a citizen of such a country when he would have no benefit from it if it were paid to him.[6] That Indians are under some disabilities with regard to property holding and management does not prevent them from being trust beneficiaries.[7] Married women have always been valid beneficiaries.[8] Prior to their emancipation trusts for them were very common and useful in giving them the benefit of property free from control by their husbands.

Trusts for infants,[9] the mentally incompetent,[10] and persons judicially declared to be drunkards or spendthrifts [11] are, of course, valid, and constitute useful methods of assuring their support and protection. In one state the view had prevailed that trusts should not be sanctioned except for those who were below normal capacity and therefore could not manage their property.[12]

A person yet unborn may be described in a trust instrument as the

2. Trotter v. Blocker, 6 Port., Ala., 269, 305.

3. Notwithstanding the view that one sentenced to imprisonment for life is "civilly dead", trusts for such persons are generally sustained. See Bogert, Trusts & Trustees (rev. 2d edit.), § 164.

4. Leggett v. Dubois, 5 Paige, N.Y., 114, 28 Am.Dec. 413; Hubbard v. Goodwin, 3 Leigh, Va., 492.

5. For example, see N.Y.—McKinney's Real Property Law, § 10 ¶ 2. Even before the change in New York, it was held that under the statute providing that a beneficiary took no interest in the lands, but merely a right against the trustee, an alien might be a beneficiary of land. Marx v. McGlynn, 88 N.Y. 357. And see § 37, ante.

6. See, for example, N.Y.Surr.Ct.Procedure Act, § 2218.

7. Indians may be the beneficiaries of a trust. Chippewa Indians of Minnesota v. United States, 301 U.S. 358, 57 S.Ct. 826, 81 L.Ed. 1156 (1937), rehearing denied 302 U.S. 772, 58 S.Ct. 3, 82 L.Ed. 599 (1937).

8. Wells v. McCall, 64 Pa. 207; Yard v. Pittsburgh & L.E.R. Co., 131 Pa. 205, 18 A. 874.

9. Turner v. Barber, 131 Ga. 444, 62 S.E. 587.

10. McCartney v. Jacobs, 288 Ill. 568, 123 N.E. 557, 4 A.L.R. 1120 (1919).

11. See § 40, post.

12. In Georgia a statute permitted trusts for incompetents only, with one exception. See former Ga.Code.Ann. § 108–114. Armour Fertilizer Works v. Lacy, 146 Ga. 196, 91 S.E. 12; Clark v. Baker, 186 Ga. 65, 196 S.E. 750. This statutory limitation was removed in 1950. See Offic.Code of Ga.Ann. §§ 53–12–2, 53–12–3.

beneficiary of a trust to come into effect upon his birth,[13] but such a person cannot be the sole beneficiary of a present trust. If the unborn person is the sole beneficiary, the trust does not have existence until the described person is born. If a man declares himself trustee of described property for his first born child at a time when he has no children, no trust arises at the time due to the lack of a beneficiary, but if and when he later has a child the trust comes into being.[14] The same would be true of a trust for a corporation to be formed later.[15]

It is shown elsewhere that trusts for the welfare of animals generally, because of indirect benefit to mankind, are regarded as charitable.[16] But trusts having particular animals as beneficiaries are not charitable and as private trusts cannot be regarded as enforceable, since animals are not legal persons who can sue in a court of equity.[17] Yet it would seem that this object of the donor could be achieved by giving the animals and a sum of money to the trustee so that caring for them would be beneficial to him,[18] or by making a gift for the maintenance of the animals with a provision for a reverter or gift over in case the trustee ever neglected them (assuming that any gift over were so limited as not to violate the Rule against Perpetuities).[19] An English court has held valid a trust for specified horses and dogs on the theory of an honorary trust,[20] that is a trust where the carrying out of the obligation rests with the honor of the trustee though not enforceable by any plaintiff. The theory is that such a trust for a purpose not contrary to public policy may be voluntarily performed by the trustee, and that the settlor or his successors are not entitled to claim the property unless the trustee threatens to use it for his own benefit. American courts have not generally recognized honorary trusts, al-

13. Easton v. Demuth, 179 Mo.App. 722, 162 S.W. 294; Folk v. Hughes, 100 S.C. 220, 84 S.E. 713. There is no difficulty if the trust is for the settlor's present children and such others as may be born to him later. Here the existing children are adequate beneficiaries for the trust at the beginning, and the class opens up to let in afterborns. The beneficiaries need not be constant throughout the life of a trust but may change due to deaths, births and other events.

14. Morsman v. Commissioner of Internal Revenue, 90 F.2d 18, 113 A.L.R. 441 (8th Cir.1937), certiorari denied 302 U.S. 701, 82 L.Ed. 542 (1937). And see Carson v. Carson, 60 N.C. 575; Ashhurst v. Given, 5 Watts & S., Pa., 323. See Fratcher, 47 Mich.L.R. 907.

See Carmichael Tile Co. v. Yaarab Bldg. Co., 182 Ga. 348, 185 S.E. 504 (trust for creditors who later construct building).

15. Salem Capital Flour Mills Co. v. Stayton Water-Ditch & Canal Co., 33 Fed. 146 (C.C.Or.1887).

16. See § 61, post.

17. In re Renner's Estate, 358 Pa. 409, 57 A.2d 836 (1948). And see 17 Minn.L.R. 563; 42 Yale L.J. 1290.

18. In re Searight's Estate, 87 Ohio App. 417, 95 N.E.2d 779 (1950).

19. Betts v. Snyder, 341 Pa. 465, 19 A.2d 82 (1941). But see In re Filkins' Will, 203 Misc. 454, 120 N.Y.S.2d 124 (1952).

20. In re Dean, 41 Ch.Div. 552. On this same theory a trust to promote fox hunting has been held valid, in the sense that the trustee may carry it out. In re Thompson, [1934] 1 Ch. 342.

But see Re Astor's Settlement Trusts, (1952) 1 All Eng.R. 1067 (such a trust invalid where no remaindermen ascertainable and so no possible pressure to have the honorary trust carried out); Re Shaw, (1957) 1 All Eng.R. 745 (trustee of noncharitable trust not allowed to carry out trust under supervision of residuary legatees).

though urged to do so.[21]

A trust to close a house,[22] or to keep a clock in repair,[23] being for the benefit of an inanimate object, lacks a proper beneficiary, and fails, unless it can be treated as for the benefit of the owner of the object.[24]

A trust to erect or care for a monument lacks a living beneficiary, and may be held to fail as a private trust,[25] but there are decisions supporting such a trust.[26] It brings no financial benefit to any living person, and the sentimental satisfaction which it may produce in living relatives of the deceased is not an adequate basis for a private trust. Its aspects as a charitable trust are discussed elsewhere.[27] If the gift is for the construction of a monument to the donor or his family, it may be regarded as a valid provision for funeral expenses.[28] Trusts to keep up a cemetery lot or a cemetery raise the same difficulty of the lack of a beneficiary, if regarded as private trusts,[29] but they are often treated as charitable by virtue of statutes.[30]

While in early case law there was some tendency to treat trusts for the purpose of having masses said as private trusts and void for lack of a beneficiary since for the benefit of the dead,[31] they were often supported as gifts to the clergy who were to say the masses,[32] and are now generally regarded as charitable since they are for the performance of a religious ceremony.[33]

The federal government [34] or a state [35] or municipal corporation [36] may be a beneficiary, as may a private corporation.[37] If accepting the benefits of the trust is beyond the powers of the governmental agency or private corporation, there may be objection to its continuance but no

21. Ames, 5 Harv.L.R. 389; Scott, 65 Pa.L.R. 527. But see Gray, 15 Harv.L.R. 510. In the cases of trusts for slaves there was some tendency to regard the trusts as honorary because slaves were not legal persons. American Colonization Soc. v. Gartrell, 23 Ga. 448; Shaw v. Ward, 175 N.C. 192, 95 S.E. 164. And see In re Searight's Estate, 87 Ohio App. 417, 95 N.E.2d 779 (1950) (honorary trust for animal allowed to be carried out).

22. Brown v. Burdett, Wkly.Notes, 1882, 134.

23. Kelly v. Nichols, 17 R.I. 306, 21 A. 906.

24. In re Zoller's Estate, 373 Pa. 451, 96 A.2d 321 (1953); Bliven v. Borden, 56 R.I. 283, 185 A. 239 (1936).

25. Gilmar's Legatees v. Gilmer's Ex'rs, 42 Ala. 9.

26. In Pennsylvania cemetery upkeep trusts are supported as private trusts, the lack of a beneficiary being supplied by the power of the orphans' court to supervise and enforce such a trust. In re Devereux' Estate, 48 Pa.D. & C. 491.

27. See § 59, post.

28. Gilmer's Legatees v. Gilmer's Ex'rs, 42 Ala. 9.

29. Matter of Johnson's Will, 5 N.Y.S. 922, 1 Con.Surr. 518.

30. See § 59, post.

31. Festorazzi v. St. Joseph's Cath. Church, 104 Ala. 327, 18 So. 394.

32. Seda v. Huble, 75 Iowa 429, 39 N.W. 685.

33. See § 58, post. And see Ackerman v. Fichter, 179 Ind. 392, 101 N.E. 493 (trust for souls of particular individuals would be private trust).

34. Neilson v. Lagow, 53 U.S. (12 How.) 98, 13 L.Ed. 909 (1851).

35. Lamar's Ex'rs v. Simpson, 1 Rich. Eq., S.C., 71.

36. In re Sayre's Will, 179 App.Div. 269, 166 N.Y.S. 499.

37. Adams v. Perry, 43 N.Y. 487; Frazier v. St. Luke's Church, 147 Pa. 256, 23 A. 442.

obstacle to its origin exists. A joint stock company [38] and a tribe of Indians [39] have been held qualified as beneficiaries.

"At common law, it is true, a deed of conveyance to an unincorporated voluntary association was bad for lack of a capable grantee, and cases will be found which hold that, where the grantee could not take directly, he or it cannot take through the medium of a trustee. But from this grew an abuse which equity was prompt to remedy. So that it is now recognized that a valid grant may be made to trustees for such an unincorporated voluntary association, and that such title will descend in perpetuity." [40] While, according to the strict common law view, the fact that an unincorporated association is not a legal entity rendered an attempted private trust for it void, many courts recently have sustained such trusts as for de facto legal entities,[41] or sustained them without discussion of the qualification of the beneficiary.[42] If the association is charitable in nature, its lack of legal personality is not a difficulty.[43]

The settlor may be the sole beneficiary or one among other beneficiaries.[44] The possibility that a trustee may also be a beneficiary has been discussed elsewhere.[45]

The beneficiary of a trust is the one intended by the settlor to receive the benefit of the trust property from the trustee, and not one who in the course of the trust administration will incidentally receive an advantage.[46] Thus where a trust is created to support a mentally incompetent pauper, the town where the pauper resides is not a beneficiary of the trust and cannot sue to enforce it, although the execution of the trust would relieve the town of the burden of support-

---

38. Hart v. Seymour, 147 Ill. 598, 35 N.E. 246.

39. Ruddick v. Albertson, 154 Cal. 640, 98 P. 1045.

40. Ruddick v. Albertson, 154 Cal. 640, 644, 98 P. 1045. See also In re Clarke, [1901] 2 Ch. 110; In re Drummond, [1914] 2 Ch. 90; Austin v. Shaw, 10 Mass. (Allen) 552; Sangston v. Gordon, 22 Grat., Va., 755, *accord.* The older view is represented by Kain v. Gibboney, 101 U.S. (11 Otto) 362, 25 L.Ed. 813 (1879); German Land Ass'n v. Scholler, 10 Minn. 331, Gil. 260; King v. Townshend, 141 N.Y. 358, 36 N.E. 513. A trust for an unincorporated village was sustained in Miller v. Rosenberger, 144 Mo. 292, 46 S.W. 167. And see Furniture Workers' Union Local 1007 v. United Brotherhood of Carpenters and Joiners of America, 6 Wn.2d 654, 108 P.2d 651 (1940) (labor union valid beneficiary).

41. Glidewell v. Glidewell, 360 Mo. 713, 230 S.W.2d 752 (1950).

42. Austin v. Shaw, 10 Allen 552; Douthitt v. Stinson, 73 Mo. 199. If the settlor's intent was that the members of

the association from time to time should be the beneficiaries, there is no difficulty. Modern Woodmen of America v. Tulsa Modern Woodmen Bldg. Ass'n, 264 P.2d 993 (Okl.1953).

43. See § 66, post.

44. Lawrence v. Lawrence, 181 Ill. 248, 54 N.E. 918; Colvin v. Martin, 68 App.Div. 633, 74 N.Y.S. 11; Appeal of Ashhurst, 77 Pa. 464.

45. See § 30, ante.

Merger of the interest of a sole trustee who is the sole beneficiary may prevent the origin of the trust. Shope v. Unknown Claimants, 174 Iowa 662, 156 N.W. 850; Lee v. Oates, 171 N.C. 717, 88 S.E. 889, Ann.Cas.1917A, 514. But an expressed intent to the contrary may prevent merger. Highland Park Mfg. Co. v. Steele, 235 Fed. 465, 149 C.C.A. 11 (4th Cir.1916); Bowlin v. Citizens' Bank & Trust Co., 131 Ark. 97, 198 S.W. 288, 2 A.L.R. 575.

46. Brennan v. Vogler, 174 Mass. 272, 54 N.E. 556; Sapp v. Houston Nat. Exch. Bank, 266 S.W. 141 (Tex.Com.App.1924).

ing the poor person.[47]

 WESTLAW REFERENCES

di beneficiary

beneficiary /s "legal entity" /s capable /s tak*** /s title

alien /3 beneficiary /3 trust

infant child*** /s beneficiary /s trust

insane "mentally incompetent" /5 beneficiary /5 trust

drunkard /s beneficiary /s trust

spend thrift /s beneficiary /s trust

indian /s beneficiary /s trust

unborn /s beneficiary /s trust

animal horse cat dog pet /s beneficiary /s trust

"inanimate object" /s beneficiary /s trust

trust /s care /4 cemetery monument

trust /s saying /4 masses

settlor +3 "sole beneficiary" +3 trust

390k154

NOTICE TO AND ACCEPTANCE BY THE BENEFICIARY [1]

§ 36. Notice to the beneficiary by the settlor that the latter intends to create a trust, or has created one, is not necessary for the purpose of completing the trust, although in some cases failure to give notice may show that the settlor did not have an intent to create a present trust but was merely contemplating future creation.

It is not necessary that the settlor obtain the acceptance of the trust by the beneficiary in order that the settlor may complete his part in the process of trust creation.

But in order that the named beneficiary may be the owner of an equitable interest in the trust property and the holder of an equitable claim against the trustee, the beneficiary's acceptance of the trust must be shown. The relationship cannot be forced on the beneficiary without his approval.

Thus a person named as beneficiary of a trust has the power within a reasonable time after he is notified of the settlor's acts of trust creation to accept or reject the trust. Acceptance or disclaimer must be of the whole trust, it is final, and it relates back to the date of trust creation.

Trust creation involves a conveyance of an equitable property interest to the beneficiary. There is no requirement in the law of wills

47. Town of Sharon v. Simons, 30 Vt. 458. A parent who would be financially benefited by the carrying out of a trust for his minor child has no standing to sue to enforce the trust. City Bank Farmers Trust Co. v. Macfadden, 274 App.Div. 1039, 85 N.Y.S.2d 791 (1949), affirmed 299 N.Y. 711, 87 N.Y.S.2d 124 (1949), reargument denied 300 N.Y. 461, 88 N.E.2d 531 (1949).

§ 36

1. Restatement, Trusts, Second, § 36.

or inter vivos conveyancing that for one to become a conveyee he must have knowledge of the conveyance at or before the time the instrument becomes effective. One may become a property owner without being conscious of the fact. That the settlor did not inform the beneficiary of his acts of trust creation before or at the time of performing them does not prevent completion of the trust.[2] For example, if an owner of bonds during his life clearly indicates that he holds them in trust for his son, the fact that his son did not know of the trust declaration until after his father's death a year later does not prevent the court from finding that a trust was completed.[3]

In some cases failure to inform the beneficiary about the trust may be of some probative effect in showing that the settlor did not intend the trust should be effective immediately but rather regarded it as incipient or tentative.[4]

Nor, in order that the settlor's work of trust creation be complete, is it required that he procure from the beneficiary an agreement that the latter is willing to be a beneficiary and to accept the benefits of the trust.[5] If, for example, the settlor has performed all the conveyancing acts needed to pass title to a trustee and the beneficiary but dies before the beneficiary learns of the transaction, the successors of the settlor cannot claim the property on the ground that the trust was incomplete and the settlor died owning the trust property. If the beneficiary wished to accept the trust after the settlor's death, he could not be prevented from doing so.[6]

However, acceptance of the trust by the beneficiary is necessary for completion of the trust so far as the beneficiary is concerned. The settlor's acts of trust creation involve an attempt to convey equitable

---

2. In re Hovland's Estate, 38 Cal.App. 2d 439, 101 P.2d 500 (1940); Clark v. Callahan, 105 Md. 600, 66 A. 618, 10 L.R.A.,N.S., 616.

3. De Leuil's Ex'rs v. De Leuil, 255 Ky. 406, 74 S.W.2d 474 (1934). And see Johnson v. Amberson, 140 Ala. 342, 37 So. 273; O'Brien v. Bank of Douglas, 17 Ariz. 203, 149 P. 747; Lewis v. Curnutt, 130 Iowa 423, 106 N.W. 914; City of Marquette v. Wilkinson, 119 Mich. 413, 78 N.W. 474, 43 L.R.A. 840; Janes v. Falk, 50 N.J.Eq. 468, 26 A. 138, 35 Am.St.Rep. 783; In re Smith's Estate, 144 Pa. 428, 22 A. 916, 27 Am.St.Rep. 641; Fleenor v. Hensley, 121 Va. 367, 93 S.E. 582.

See United States v. Chandler, 410 U.S. 257, 93 S.Ct. 880, 35 L.Ed.2d 247 (1973) (mere delivery of U.S. bonds insufficient; reregistration necessary to change ownership).

The courts of Massachusetts had shown a greater tendency than those of any other state to require notice to the beneficiary. In Boynton v. Gale, 194 Mass. 320, 323, 80 N.E. 448, the court said: "Whatever may be the doctrine elsewhere, it is settled in this state that a mere declaration of trust by a voluntary settlor, not communicated to the donee and assented to by him, is not sufficient to perfect a trust, especially when the property is retained by him subject to his own control." But later cases do not require notice. New England Trust Co. v. Sanger, 337 Mass. 342, 149 N.E.2d 598 (1958).

4. Casteel v. Flint, 112 Iowa 92, 83 N.W. 796; Gobeille v. Allison, 30 R.I. 525, 76 A. 354.

5. In re Pilot Radio & Tube Corp., 72 F.2d 316 (1st Cir.1934); Barr v. Schroeder, 32 Cal. 609; Plaut v. Storey, 131 Ind. 46, 30 N.E. 886. Some courts have held that acceptance is to be presumed where the trust is of financial advantage to the beneficiary. In re Duwe's Estate, 229 Wis. 115, 281 N.W. 669 (1938). And, to the same effect, see V.Tex.C.A.Prop.Code § 112.010.

6. O'Brien v. Bank of Douglas, 17 Ariz. 203, 149 P. 747.

property interests to the beneficiary, and no man can be forced to become the owner of any property interest by inter vivos or testamentary transfer without his consent. Naturally most property transfers are of financial advantage to the transferee and are generally accepted, but the property may be of little value, worthless, or have burdens attached to it,[7] or the intended donee may dislike the donor and be unwilling to benefit by his attempted generosity.[8] Corresponding to the constitutional right not to have property taken without due process of law, there is the common law privilege not to have one's property ownership increased by others without voluntary acceptance of the tendered property interest.[9]

Thus one informed that he has been named as trust beneficiary in a deed or will has the option of acquiescing in the relationship or of declining.[10] He has a reasonable time to make up his mind and need not act immediately.[11] Statutes authorizing disclaimer of various types of property interests are in effect in all states but to avoid federal transfer tax liability or to secure federal tax advantages from a disclaimer the requirements of Internal Revenue Code § 2518 must be met. A person named as a beneficiary must accept or disclaim the property interest in its entirety, and may not attach conditions or qualifications to his action.[12] An infant beneficiary's expression of acceptance or rejection is not final until he has reached his majority.[13]

It would seem that acceptance or disclaimer by the beneficiary should be final and not subject to retraction in case of a change of mind

7. Some courts state that there is no presumption of acceptance of an "onerous" trust, that is, one where the subject-matter involves unusual burdens, even if there is a presumption of the acceptance of the ordinary trust. Roop v. Greenfield, 352 Pa. 232, 42 A.2d 614 (1945) (trust was realty with no value above mortgage).

8. In re Suter's Estate, 207 Misc. 1002, 142 N.Y.S.2d 353 (1955) (beneficiary rejected trust for "moral and political reasons").

9. Bailey v. Worster, 103 Me. 170, 68 A. 698; Cunniff v. McDonnell, 196 Mass. 7, 81 N.E. 879.

10. Statutes now provide that a beneficiary may disclaim his beneficial interest, usually under either a testamentary or a nontestamentary instrument. See, for example, Ill.Rev.Stat. c. 30, ¶¶ 211–213, c. 110½, § 2–7. Minn.Stats.Ann. §§ 501.211, 525.532; S.Dak.Codif.Laws 43–4–28 to 43–4–35. Collins v. Lewis, 60 N.J.Eq. 488, 46 A. 1098; Irving Bank Columbia Trust Co. v. Rowe, 213 App.Div. 281, 210 N.Y.S. 497 (1925). A beneficiary of a testamentary trust may renounce during the life of the

settlor. In re Bishop's Trust, 123 N.Y.S.2d 887 (1953).

For numerous other statutes giving a beneficiary the right to disclaim, see Bogert, Trusts and Trustees (rev. 2d edit.), § 171. A disclaimer qualified for federal tax purposes must meet the requirements of § 2518 I.R.C. See Bogert, Trusts and Trustees (rev. 2d edit.), §§ 171, 278.

11. The time to accept or reject does not run until the beneficiary knows of the creation of the trust. Roop v. Greenfield, 352 Pa. 232, 42 A.2d 614 (1945).

12. In re Hotchkys, 32 Ch.D. 408; Bacon v. Barber, 110 Vt. 280, 6 A.2d 9, 123 A.L.R. 253 (1939). A conditional acceptance is a rejection. Arnold v. Jones, 77 Tenn. (9 Lea) 545. But see In re Morrisey's Estate, 16 Misc.2d 421, 182 N.Y.S.2d 508 (1958) (income beneficiary permitted to reject right to have trust capital invaded).

13. Jervis v. Wolferstan, 18 Eq. 18; Hooton v. Neeld, 12 N.J. 396, 97 A.2d 153 (1953); Bacon v. Barber, 110 Vt. 280, 6 A.2d 9, 123 A.L.R. 253 (1939).

on his part.[14] Disclaimer by a beneficiary may well accelerate the enjoyment of remainder interests following that of the disclaiming beneficiary,[15] but equity will not apply acceleration where to do so would defeat the intention of the settlor.[16] It may be express, as where explicit notice of refusal is given to the settlor or the trustee; [17] or it may be implied, as where the beneficiary does not directly take a position but indicates his attitude by accepting checks for trust income or by refusing to reply to the trustee's letters for a long period.[18] That the res of the trust is real property does not make it necessary that acceptance or disclaimer by the beneficiary be in writing.[19]

Acceptance relates back to the time of the completion of the settlor's acts of trust creation, so that the beneficiary is deemed to have been such from the beginning; and the same theory applies to disclaimer so that after rejection of the trust by the beneficiary the settlor (or if he is dead, his successors) are treated as having been the full owner of the property during the whole period, notwithstanding the attempted trust.[20]

 WESTLAW REFERENCES

beneficiary +3 notice inform** +3 trust

390k25(1) /p beneficiary +3 notice +3 trust

find 93 sct 880

beneficiary +3 accept +3 trust

find 42 a2d 614

409k717

191k47(2)

191k24

NATURE OF BENEFICIARY'S INTEREST [1]

§ 37. While legal scholars have disagreed as to whether the right of a beneficiary is in personam, in rem, or partly both, the

14. Perkins v. Isley, 224 N.C. 793, 32 S.E.2d 588 (1944); Jourdan v. Andrews, 258 Pa. 347, 102 A. 33; Blackwell v. Virginia Trust Co., 177 Va. 299, 14 S.E.2d 301 (1941) (after acceptance of benefits, no disclaimer allowed).

15. Brunton v. International Trust Co., 114 Colo. 298, 164 P.2d 472 (1945); Bross v. Bross, 123 Fla. 758, 167 So. 669 (1936). See Bogert, Trusts and Trustees (rev. 2d edit.), § 172.

16. St. Louis Union Trust Co. v. Kern, 346 Mo. 643, 142 S.W.2d 493 (1940); Trustees of Kenyon College v. Cleveland Trust Co., 130 Ohio St. 107, 196 N.E. 784, 99 A.L.R. 224 (1935).

17. Lytle's Ex'r v. Pope's Adm'r, 50 Ky. (11 B.Mon.) 297.

18. White v. White, 107 Ala. 417, 18 So. 3; Libby v. Frost, 98 Me. 288, 56 A. 906; Redfield v. Critchley, 252 App.Div. 568, 300 N.Y.S. 305 (1937), affirmed 277 N.Y. 336, 14 N.E.2d 77 (1938), reargument denied 278 N.Y. 483, 15 N.E.2d 73 (1938) (failure to cash checks not necessarily rejection of trust).

19. Townsend v. Tickel, 3 B. & Ald. 31; Coleman v. Burns, 103 N.H. 313, 171 A.2d 33 (1961).

20. Jervis v. Wolferstan, 18 Eq. 18; Stoehr v. Miller, 296 F. 414 (2d Cir.1923); Stevens v. Stevens, 121 Ohio St. 490, 169 N.E. 570 (1929).

§ 37

1. Restatement, Trusts, Second, §§ 130–131.

modern tendency is to give the beneficiary's right incidents which make it not only a right against the trustee to have the trust carried out but also the equivalent of equitable ownership of the trust res.

Some statutes purport to declare that a trust beneficiary takes no estate or interest in the trust property, but these acts have been construed in such a way as to give them only a limited effect.

In some trusts of realty where the property is to be held by the trustee for sale, the settlor directs that the beneficiaries shall have no interest in the land but rather interests in the proceeds only. These clauses are given effect on the theory that the realty is equitably converted into personalty. The directions of the settlor as to the nature of the beneficiary's interest are also respected in other trusts.

Whether the beneficiary's rights are in rem or in personam has been the subject of much discussion among legal scholars. Rights in rem have been defined as: "Rights residing in persons, and availing against other persons generally. . . . The duties which correlate with rights *in rem* are always *negative;* that is to say, they are duties to forbear or abstain." And rights in personam have been thus described: "Rights residing in persons, and availing *exclusively* against persons specifically determinate. . . . Of the obligations which correlate with rights *in personam, some* are negative, but *some* (and *most*) are *positive;* that is to say, obligations to do or perform." [2]

Is the beneficiary the owner merely of a claim against the trustee to have the trust carried out, or is he the equitable owner of the trust property; or do his rights combine both a right against the trustee and an ownership of the trust res, good against the world? The theory of a right in personam is supported by Holland,[3] Maitland,[4] Langdell,[5] Ames,[6] and some later writers,[7] the equitable title hypothesis is maintained by Salmond,[8] while several authors have argued that the beneficiary has both a right against the trustee and an ownership of the trust res.[9]

The terminology used by the courts will be of little guidance. Some have called the right of the beneficiary an "equitable estate," [10] some an "equitable fee," [11] others an "equitable title," [12] and others

2. 1 Austin on Jurisprudence, 5th Ed., 370, 371.

3. Jurisprudence, 13th Ed., 246 et seq.

4. Equity, 111–155.

5. Brief Survey of Equity Jurisdiction, 1 Harv.Law Rev. 59, 60.

6. Cases on Trusts, 2d Ed., 244–281.

7. See, for example, Harlan F. Stone, The Nature of the Rights of the Cestui que Trust, 17 Col.Law Rev. 467.

8. Jurisprudence, 278–282.

9. Roscoe Pound, 26 Harv.Law Rev. 462; Houston, The Enforcement Decrees in Equity, 138; Scott, 17 Col.Law Rev. 269; Whitlock, 1 Cal.Law Rev. 215.

10. Leigh v. Laughlin, 211 Ill. 192, 71 N.E. 881; Appeal of Fowler, 125 Pa. 388, 17 A. 431, 11 Am.St.Rep. 902; Citizens' Nat. Bank v. Watkins, 126 Tenn. 453, 150 S.W. 96; Hutchinson v. Maxwell, 100 Va. 169, 40 S.E. 655, 57 L.R.A. 384, 93 Am.St. Rep. 944.

11. Durant v. Muller, 88 Ga. 251, 14 S.E. 612; Reardon v. Reardon, 192 Mass.

12. See note 12 on page 134.

"absolute ownership in equity," [13] or even an "equitable lien"; [14] while other judges have described the right as only a right to enforce the trust against the trustee.[15]

The advocates of the in personam position claim:

(a) The rights of the beneficiary are not enforceable against the whole world, since a bona fide purchaser of the trust res from the trustee is excepted, and therefore, from the very definition of a right in rem, the beneficiary's right cannot be in rem. In reply it is said that many rights admittedly in rem are cut off by transfers to bona fide purchasers, for example, in cases of sales in market overt, sales of realty where a second deed is recorded before the first, negotiations of negotiable paper, sales by a fraudulent vendee of personal property, sales by a seller left in possession of personal property, sales by agents having apparent authority to sell, and sales by conditional vendees of goods when the contract has not been filed or recorded. It is also answered that where the trust res is an equitable interest in property and the trustee sells it to a bona fide purchaser, the right of the beneficiary is not cut off, showing that at least in that instance the beneficiary has a right in rem. It is further alleged that the bona fide purchaser rule regarding trusts is based on the respect of equity for the legal title and on the commercial expediency of having property easily transferable, that is, such rule is a mere exception to the general rule that the beneficiary has a right to the trust res enforceable against all the world.

(b) It is said that equity acts in personam, and the beneficiary's right, being admittedly equitable, must be in personam; to which the reply is that the nature of a right is not necessarily determined by the nature of the remedy given for its enforcement, and that modern statutes generally give equity power to act in rem, and to transfer title or possession directly in case the trustee refuses to obey a decree.[16]

(c) The impossibility of two persons owning the same thing is also urged as favorable to the in personam theory. To this reply has been made that one may be the legal owner of property and another the equitable owner, and that both law and equity regard the trustee as the legal owner and the beneficiary as the equitable owner.

448, 78 N.E. 430; Cornwell v. Orton, 126 Mo. 355, 27 S.W. 536; Davis v. Heppert, 96 Va. 775, 32 S.E. 467.

12. Hallowell Sav. Inst. v. Titcomb, 96 Me. 62, 51 A. 249; Mathias v. Fowler, 124 Md. 655, 93 A. 298.

13. Ex parte Jonas, 186 Ala. 567, 64 So. 960; Ellsworth College of Iowa Falls v. Emmet County, 156 Iowa 52, 135 N.W. 594, 42 L.R.A.,N.S., 530.

14. In re Hart's Estate, 203 Pa. 503, 53 A. 373.

15. Hunt v. Hunt, 124 Mich. 502, 83 N.W. 371; Bennett v. Garlock, 79 N.Y. 302, 35 Am.Rep. 517; Cheyney v. Geary, 194 Pa. 427, 45 A. 369.

16. See Huston, The Enforcement of Decrees in Equity, Appendix, for a list of statutes giving chancery power to act in rem and to transfer title.

(d) Finally, it is urged that the duties which the trustee owes the beneficiary are positive and characteristic of rights in personam, while the obligations to the holder of a right in rem are always negative, merely to refrain from action. The answer is that the trustee has positive duties of management, and also negative duties to refrain from treating the trust res as his private property or from acting in his own interest, and that these latter duties also attach in relations with the general public.

In support of the contention that the beneficiary's rights are in rem or rights of ownership, it has been urged: (a) if the trust res is realty, curtesy and dower attach to the beneficiary's interest; (b) his interest descends to heirs at law or personal representatives, dependent on whether the trust res is realty or personalty; (c) if the res is real, escheat operates on the beneficiary's rights; (d) the beneficiary's powers of alienation show him to be an owner of the res; (e) a transferee of the trustee does not take the property free from the trust; (f) creditors of the beneficiary may take the trust res; (g) a trust may be created without consideration, thus partaking more of the nature of a grant than of a contract; (h) the modern tendency is to preserve the rights of the beneficiary even after the trustee is barred by the Statute of Limitations; and (i) the trustee's interest is purely formal and gives rise to no beneficial incidents to his wife as a dowress, to his creditors, or to the state in case of forfeiture or escheat.

The situation would seem to be summarized by the statement that while the right of the beneficiary was originally purely in personam against the trustee, it has become increasingly a right in rem and is now substantially equivalent to equitable ownership of the trust res.[17] The beneficiary, of course, also has rights in personam against the trustee. Speaking of a transfer by the beneficiary of his interest under the trust, the Supreme Court of the United States has stated: "The assignment of the beneficial interest is not the assignment of a chose in action but of the 'right, title, and estate in and to the property'." [18]

Statutory Declarations as to Nature of Beneficiary's Interest

In several states there are statutes purporting to adopt the in personam theory and to declare that the whole estate in the trust property is vested in the trustee and that the beneficiary is the owner of no interest or estate in the trust property.[19] While in some cases these statutes have been given an interpretation which gives them the

17. See cases cited in §§ 38–39, post, as to the incidents of the beneficiary's interest. See Gordon v. Gordon, 6 Ill.2d 572, 129 N.E.2d 706 (1955) (trust of Illinois realty; nonresident beneficiary had real property interests for jurisdictional purposes).

18. Hughes, C.J., in Blair v. Commissioner of Internal Revenue, 300 U.S. 5, 57 S.Ct. 330, 81 L.Ed. 465 (1937). And see Brown v. Fletcher, 235 U.S. 589, 35 S.Ct. 154, 59 L.Ed. 374; Jones v. Jones, 344 Pa. 310, 25 A.2d 327 (1942).

19. For example, in California, Michigan, Minnesota, Montana, New York, North Dakota, South Dakota, and Wisconsin. For statutory citations, see Bogert, Trusts and Trustees (rev. 2d edit.), § 184.

effect their literal wording would seem to require,[20] in other cases they seem to have been ignored by the courts.[21]

Settlor's Direction as to Nature of Beneficiary's Interest

Where the subject matter of the trust is realty to be held for sale, the trust instrument sometimes provides that the interest of the beneficiary shall be considered personal property and that he shall have no interest in the realty but merely in the proceeds of the realty and its income. Such clauses are respected and enforced by the courts.[22] These cases can be explained by the application of the doctrine of equitable conversion,[23] namely, that equity regards the realty as changed into personalty by the direction to sell and the settlor's provision therefore merely recognizes the true legal situation. The reasons for inserting such clauses are often connected with taxation, ease of transfer, and freedom of the beneficiary's interest from marital estates such as dower and curtesy. The mere direction to sell realty would cause the application of equitable conversion and make the beneficiary's interest personalty, even if there were no declaration by the settlor that the beneficiary's interest should be treated as personalty.[24] The doctrine would also operate if there was a direction to invest money in realty, so that the beneficiary's interest would be treated as realty.[25] Even in trusts where the trustee is under no duty to sell realty or invest in it, the settlor's statement as to the nature of the interest of the beneficiary has been respected.[26]

 WESTLAW REFERENCES

right /2 beneficiary /s rem personam
beneficiary /s "equitable owner" /s "trust property" res
75k49
di(equitable /2 owner title /6 trust)

Statutory Declarations as to Nature of Beneficiary's Interest
find 64 sct 384

20. Archer-Shee v. Garland, 144 L.T. 508 (New York beneficiary has chose in action for tax purposes); Demorest v. City Bank Farmers Trust Co., 321 U.S. 36, 64 S.Ct. 384, 88 L.Ed. 526 (1944) (construction of mortgage salvage statute); Marx v. McGlynn, 88 N.Y. 357 (alien beneficiary of real property trust).

21. Title Ins. & Trust Co. v. Duffill, 191 Cal. 629, 218 P. 14 (1923) (contract to convey); Lynch v. Cunningham, 131 Cal. App. 164, 21 P.2d 154 (1933) (beneficiary has a leviable interest); First & American Nat. Bank of Duluth v. Higgins, 208 Minn. 295, 293 N.W. 585 (1940) (interest of beneficiary devisable); Hull v. Rolfsrud, 65 N.W.2d 94 (N.D.1954) (not to be literally applied for alienation purposes).

22. Ephraim v. Metropolitan Trust Co. of California, 28 Cal.2d 824, 172 P.2d 501 (1946); Duncanson v. Lill, 322 Ill. 528, 153 N.E. 618 (1926).

23. Harrison v. Kamp, 395 Ill. 11, 69 N.E.2d 261 (1946); In re Hustad's Estate, 236 Wis. 615, 296 N.W. 74 (1941).

24. Wollard v. Suller, 55 N.M. 326, 232 P.2d 991 (1951).

25. Ridgley v. Pfinstag, 188 Md. 209, 50 A.2d 578 (1946).

26. Conway v. Adams County, 171 Neb. 677, 107 N.W.2d 418 (1961), rehearing denied, opinion clarified 172 Neb. 94, 108 N.W.2d 637 (1961) (fractional interests in gas production payments; ad valorem tax liability).

Settlor's Direction as to Nature of Beneficiary's Interest
find 172 p2d 501
390k112 /p intent*** /s settlor trustor
390k140(1) /p intent*** /s trustor settlor
390k153

INCIDENTS OF THE BENEFICIARY'S INTEREST [1]

§ 38.   The beneficiary's equitable interest under the trust may be for a definite period or during a named life, or an absolute interest; it may be contingent or vested, subject to a condition precedent or subsequent, determinable, possessory or non-possessory.   A settlor may make some beneficiaries primary or preferred and others secondary beneficiaries.

Co-beneficiaries hold as tenants in common, unless the settlor has expressed an intent that they take some other form of co-ownership. Where man and wife are co-beneficiaries their interests may be community property.

A beneficiary owes a co-beneficiary a duty not to take part in a breach of trust by the trustee and not to profit from such breach.

The interest of the beneficiary is inheritable and devisable and transferable inter vivos (if not limited by a spendthrift clause); and may be subject to dower or curtesy, escheat, a homestead claim, the rule in Shelley's Case, income or property taxation, and liability for debts (if not protected by a spendthrift clause).

If the interest of a beneficiary is subject to an equity, a transferee of the interest must submit to the enforcement of the equity, whether or not he is a bona fide purchaser.

In many states statutes make transfers of the interests of some or all trust beneficiaries voidable unless they are manifested by a writing.

Some courts hold that priority between two successive transferees of the same beneficiary's interest is determined by priority in time of the assignments, while other courts give priority in right to the assignee who first notifies the trustee of his assignment.

Interest of Various Types

Generally speaking the settlor may carve out of his property interest and give to the beneficiary of his trust any one of the various types of estates or property interests recognized by the law.[2]   Thus he may provide that the beneficiary's interest is to continue for a period of years, for the life of the beneficiary or of some other person, or is to be the full and complete equitable interest in the trust property.   He may stipulate that the beneficiary is to have an interest that is contingent or

---

§ 38
1. Restatement, Trusts, Second, §§ 128, 132–163.

2. Tapley v. Dill, 358 Mo. 824, 217 S.W.2d 369 (1949) (estate tail).

subject to a condition precedent,[3] or is vested but is to be subject to being divested upon the happening of a condition subsequent,[4] or is to be automatically terminated upon such event.[5] In nearly all cases the interests of beneficiaries are non-possessory, since the trustee is to have control of the trust assets, but it is legally possible to direct that a beneficiary is to have possession.[6]

In rare cases, for example, where trusts are created for creditors of the settlor, various classes of beneficiaries are provided for, some being preferred and first entitled to payment, and others being secondary and to receive what is left after the first class has been satisfied.[7] Such provisions correspond to those for preferred and common stock in the case of corporations.

Where there are two or more beneficiaries entitled to enjoyment at the same time, and not in succession to each other, they are treated as tenants in common,[8] unless the settlor has made them joint tenants,[9] or where joint tenancy has been abolished, has provided for survivorship rights,[10] or made them tenants by the entireties.[11] Where a man and wife are made co-beneficiaries, they may hold their interest as community property in states where that system exists, or as separate property.[12]

Co-beneficiaries are in a fiduciary relation to each other and owe each other a duty not to seek for themselves exclusive benefits or advantages. If the trustee has committed a breach, for example, and one beneficiary gets a conveyance or mortgage from the defaulting trustee, he may be obliged to hold it for the benefit of all beneficiaries.[13]

A co-beneficiary also owes his fellow beneficiaries the duty not to assist the trustee in committing a breach of trust and not to accept any benefit from a breach.[14] Thus if a beneficiary persuades the trustee to

---

3. Griffin v. Sturges, 131 Conn. 471, 40 A.2d 758, 156 A.L.R. 972 (1944) (son to get income if he ceases to use liquor).

4. Lassiter v. Bank of Dawson, 191 Ga. 208, 11 S.E.2d 910 (1940) (gift over if beneficiary does not claim gift within named time).

5. Taylor v. McClave, 128 N.J.Eq. 109, 15 A.2d 213 (1940) (interest to cease on remarriage of beneficiary); Cox v. Fisher, 322 S.W.2d 910 (1959) (interest to be forfeited if beneficiary contests will).

6. Lincoln Bank & Trust Co. v. Lane, Ky., 303 S.W.2d 273 (1957) (privilege of occupying realty at nominal rent); Frye v. Burk, 57 Ohio App. 99, 12 N.E.2d 152 (1936).

7. Milbank v. J.C. Littlefield, Inc., 310 Mass. 55, 36 N.E.2d 833 (1941).

8. In re Cavanaugh's Will, 95 N.Y.S.2d 383 (Surr.1950).

9. Edmonds v. Commissioner of Internal Revenue, 90 F.2d 14 (9th Cir.1937),

certiorari denied 302 U.S. 713, 58 S.Ct. 32, 82 L.Ed. 551 (1937).

10. Wallace v. Wallace, 168 Va. 216, 190 S.E. 293 (1937).

11. Akin v. First Nat. Bank of Winston-Salem, 227 N.C. 453, 42 S.E. 518.

12. McFaddin v. C.I.R., 148 F.2d 570 (5th Cir.1945).

13. Bodman v. Martha's Vineyard Nat. Bk., 330 Mass. 125, 111 N.E.2d 670 (1953) (co-beneficiary excluded others from possession); In re Du Plaine's Estate, 185 Pa. 332, 39 A. 947, 40 L.R.A. 552; Spencer v. Harris, 70 Wyo. 505, 252 P.2d 115 (1953) (accepting gift of trust property from trustee).

14. Piff v. Berresheim, 405 Ill. 617, 92 N.E.2d 113 (1950). Mere consent to a breach does not violate any duty to a co-beneficiary unless the consenting beneficiary profits from the breach, according to some authorities. Newton v. Rebenack, 90 Mo.App. 650; Blair v. Cargill, 111 App.Div.

buy an illegal investment, or sells to the trustee such an investment, he is guilty of a wrong to his co-beneficiaries, and his interest under the trust may be impounded for the purpose of indemnifying his co-beneficiaries.[15]

If a beneficiary is also a trustee, his wrongful conduct as trustee affects his interest in the trust as beneficiary. He comes under an obligation to his co-beneficiaries to replace, out of his share of the trust property, the damages which have flowed from his breach of trust.[16]

Death of the Beneficiary Intestate

The interest of a beneficiary passes to his heirs at law or personal representatives, dependent on whether the subject matter of the trust is realty or personalty, if the beneficiary dies intestate and his interest is to continue beyond his life.[17] These decisions support the argument that the beneficiary has a property right in the trust property, since the nature of the latter determines the course of devolution of the beneficiary's interest.

Escheat

The early rule in England was that the interest of a beneficiary did not escheat to the crown, but that the trustee held the property free from the trust.[18] A statute now provides for escheat of the beneficiary's interest.[19] In America the interest of the beneficiary, if it continues after his death, whether the trust res be real or personal, passes to the state on the death of the beneficiary intestate without heirs or next of kin.[20] This result is often proclaimed by statute, and the Uniform Act for the Disposition of Unclaimed Property Act, which has been widely adopted, governs interests under trusts and produces a similar result.[21] While technically escheat applied to realty only, an analogous doctrine with regard to bona vacantia or personalty without an owner has been applied.

853, 98 N.Y.S. 109. But see Ehlen v. Baltimore, 76 Md. 576, 25 A. 917.

15. Furniss v. Zimmerman, 154 N.Y.S. 272, 90 Misc. 138; Jones v. Lynch, 137 S.W. 395 (Tex.Civ.App.) As giving a trustee a lien on the interest of a beneficiary who requested him to make an illegal investment, for the purpose of reimbursement, see Davis v. Woods, 273 Ky. 210, 115 S.W.2d 1043 (1938).

16. Belknap v. Belknap, 5 Allen, 87 Mass. 468; Stanley v. United States Nat. Bank, 110 Or. 648, 224 P. 835 (1924).

17. Shackleford v. Elliott, 209 Ill. 333, 70 N.E. 745; Doran v. Kennedy, 122 Minn. 1, 141 N.W. 851; Boone v. Davis, 64 Miss. 133, 8 So. 202; Bredell v. Collier, 40 Mo. 287; Courts v. Aldridge, 190 Okl. 29, 120 P.2d 362 (1941); Cordon v. Gregg, 164 Or.

306, 97 P.2d 732 (1940), petition adhered to on rehearing 164 Or. 306, 101 P.2d 414 (1940); Lamb v. First Huntington Nat. Bank, 122 W.Va. 88, 7 S.E.2d 441 (1940); Sutherland v. Pierner, 249 Wis. 462, 24 N.W.2d 883 (1946).

18. Burgess v. Wheate, 1 Wm. Blackstone, 123.

19. St. 47 & 48 Vict. c. 71, § 4.

20. In re Williams' Estate, 37 Cal.App. 2d 181, 99 P.2d 349 (1940); Matthews v. Ward, 10 Gill. & J., Md., 443; Johnston v. Spicer, 107 N.Y. 185, 13 N.E. 753; In re Linton's Estate, 198 Pa. 438, 48 A. 298.

21. For references to such statutes, see Bogert, Trusts and Trustees (rev. 2d edit.), § 187.

Curtesy and Dower

If a wife has been the beneficiary of a fee simple interest in real property, her widower may be given curtesy in the trust res in states where this estate still exists.[22] This can only be on the theory of an equitable fee in the trust realty. If she owned a mere claim to have the trust enforced, her interest would be personal property, regardless of the subject matter of the trust, and so not subject to curtesy. If the wife's interest as beneficiary had been a separate estate in equity, the prevailing view is that curtesy arises in favor of the surviving husband [23] unless a contrary intent appears in the trust instrument.[24] The exclusion of the husband from any interest in or control of the property is deemed to be limited to the period of coverture.

The widow of a beneficiary having a fee interest was not entitled to dower in England [25] until the passage of a statute.[26] In America a few states have followed the old English rule and refused the widow dower,[27] but either by virtue of statute or by common law the right of dower still attaches to the estate of the beneficiary in some American states.[28] That dower attaches as an incident to the beneficiary's right where the res is real property shows the tendency of modern law to treat his interest as a property right in the res.

Homestead

An equitable owner of land may establish a homestead in his interest.[29] The cases arising have generally been those of contract vendees, but there seems to be no reason to differentiate the beneficiary of a trust.[30] If so, the rule is strong evidence that his interest is treated as a property right in land when the trust res is land.

Rule in Shelley's Case

Where a trustee holds in trust for A for life, with a remainder in trust for A's heirs, the rule in Shelley's Case may apply so that A will

---

22. Richardson v. Stodder, 100 Mass. 528; Donovan v. Griffith, 215 Mo. 149, 114 S.W. 621, 20 L.R.A.,N.S., 825, 128 Am.St. Rep. 458, 15 Ann.Cas. 724; Cushing v. Blake, 30 N.J.Eq. 689; Parham v. Henley, 224 N.C. 405, 30 S.E.2d 372 (1944); Lowry's Lessee v. Steele, 4 Ohio 170; Carson v. Fuhs, 131 Pa. 256, 18 A. 1017; Tillinghast v. Coggeshall, 7 R.I. 383; Norman's Ex'x v. Cunningham, 5 Grat., Va., 63. But see In re Grandjean's Estate, 78 Neb. 349, 110 N.W. 1108, 15 Ann.Cas. 577.

23. Luntz v. Greve, 102 Ind. 173, 26 N.E. 128; Cushing v. Blake, 29 N.J.Eq. 399; Ege v. Medlar, 82 Pa. 86. *Contra:* Jones v. Jones' Ex'r, 96 Va. 749, 32 S.E. 463.

24. Jamison v. Zausch, 227 Mo. 406, 126 S.W. 1023, 21 Ann.Cas. 1132; McCul-loch v. Valentine, 24 Neb. 215, 38 N.W. 854.

25. D'Arcy v. Blake, 2 Sch. & Lef. 387.

26. St. 3 & 4 Wm. IV, c. 105.

27. Seaman v. Harmon, 192 Mass. 5, 78 N.E. 301; Hopkinson v. Dumas, 42 N.H. 296.

28. Jones v. Glenn, 248 Ala. 452, 28 So.2d 198 (1946); Fletcher v. Felker, 97 F.Supp. 755 (W.D.Ark.1951) (Ark. law).

29. Allen v. Hawley, 66 Ill. 164; Hewitt v. Rankin, 41 Iowa 35; Tarrant v. Swain, 15 Kan. 146; Jelinek v. Stepan, 41 Minn. 412, 43 N.W. 90; Smith v. Chenault, 48 Tex. 455.

30. Anderson v. Anderson, 70 S.D. 165, 16 N.W.2d 43 (1944).

become the owner of an equitable fee.[31] Some courts have held that the rule is not to be applied in the case of active trusts, where to apply it would defeat the testator's intent,[32] and the rule has been abolished in many states.[33]

Taxability

It is elementary that income received by a beneficiary under a trust is subject to income taxation. In addition his interest in the trust principal or in the right to future income may be subjected to ad valorem taxation.[34]

Power to Alienate

In the absence of provisions in the trust instrument or statutes to the contrary,[35] the beneficiary may alienate his interest as freely as he might a legal estate or interest.[36] "The law, however, is perfectly settled that the estate of a cestui que trust may be conveyed as well as any other." [37] He may join with the trustee and transfer the whole title, legal and equitable.[38] The consent of the trustee is not necessary to the conveyance by the beneficiary of his interest, unless the trust instrument provides otherwise.[39] The beneficiary may convey to a co-beneficiary,[40] or to the trustee,[41] although in the latter case the transac-

31. Sutliff v. Aydelott, 373 Ill. 633, 27 N.E.2d 529 (1940); Cushing v. Blake, 30 N.J.Eq. 689; Boyd v. Small, 56 N.C. 39; Carson v. Fuhs, 131 Pa. 256, 18 A. 1017; Danner v. Trescot, 5 Rich.Eq., S.C., 356. The rule does not apply unless the life estate and the remainder are both legal or both equitable. Appeal of Van Syckel, 319 Pa. 347, 179 A. 721 (1935).

32. Berry v. Williamson, 11 B.Mon., Ky., 245; Porter v. Doby, 2 Rich.Eq., S.C., 49.

33. See, for example, Md. ET Law, § 11–104; 20 Pa.C.S.A. § 6117.

34. Trust Co. of Norfolk v. Commonwealth, 151 Va. 883, 141 S.E. 825. The beneficiary owns a property interest in the res and not merely a personal claim. Commonwealth v. Stewart, 338 Pa. 9, 12 A.2d 444 (1940), affirmed 312 U.S. 649, 61 S.Ct. 445, 85 L.Ed. 1101 (1941).

35. As to the validity of a clause in the trust instrument to the effect that the beneficiary's interest shall not be alienable, and for references to statutes in some states which make the interests of beneficiaries of some trusts non-transferable, see § 40, post.

36. Hiss v. Hiss, 228 Ill. 414, 81 N.E. 1056; Martin v. Davis, 82 Ind. 38; Parkhill v. Doggett, 150 Iowa 442, 130 N.W. 411; Boston Safe Deposit & Trust Co. v. Luke, 220 Mass. 484, 108 N.E. 64, L.R.A.1917A,

988; Freeman v. Maxwell, 262 Mo. 13, 170 S.W. 1150; Jenkinson v. New York Finance Co., 79 N.J.Eq. 247, 82 A. 36; Cherry v. Cape Fear Power Co., 142 N.C. 404, 55 S.E. 287; Henson v. Wright, 88 Tenn. 501, 12 S.W. 1035; Mortimer v. Jackson, 155 S.W. 341 (Tex.Civ.App.); Burnett v. Hawpe's Ex'r, 25 Grat., Va., 481; Mangan v. Shea, 158 Wis. 619, 149 N.W. 378. The power of alienation is not handicapped by the contingent nature of the beneficiary's interest. Brown v. Fletcher, 253 Fed. 15, 165 C.C.A. 35 (2d Cir.1918). But see Kahn v. Rockhill, 132 N.J.Eq. 188, 28 A.2d 34 (1942), affirmed 133 N.J.Eq. 300, 31 A.2d 819 (1943) (remainder interest contingent as to person not assignable).

A beneficiary may sell or give away part of his income interest. Blair v. Commissioner of Internal Revenue, 300 U.S. 5, 57 S.Ct. 330, 81 L.Ed. 465 (1937).

37. Elliott v. Armstrong, 2 Blackf., Ind., 198, 208.

38. Jones v. Jones, 111 Md. 700, 77 A. 270.

39. Foster v. Friede, 37 Mo. 36.

40. Murry v. King, 153 Mo.App. 710, 135 S.W. 107.

41. Sprague v. Moore, 130 Mich. 92, 89 N.W. 712; People's Trust Co. v. Harman, 43 App.Div. 348, 60 N.Y.S. 178.

tion will be voidable by the beneficiary unless it was entirely fair and at arm's length.[42] This power of alienation exists in the beneficiary of an implied as well as an express trust.[43] Some courts have gone so far as to allow the beneficiary to vest absolute title to the trust res in another free and clear of the trust,[44] but this seems erroneous if the trust is active. The interest of the beneficiary may also be devised,[45] mortgaged or pledged,[46] and made the subject of a gift,[47] or transferred to a trustee to hold under a sub-trust.

A right accruing to the beneficiary under the trust which is purely personal in character, and is intended for his sole benefit, cannot be assigned.[48] Examples include a right to occupy the trust property and use it for grazing and pasturage,[49] and a right to exercise of the trustee's discretion in applying the residue of the estate,[50] or a right to demand principal of the trust.[51]

Transfer by a Beneficiary of an Interest Subject to Equities

If a beneficiary who transfers his interest under the trust had held that interest subject to an equity in favor of another person, the assignee of the interest takes it subject to the equity, and the fact that the assignee may not have known of the equity and may have paid full value for the interest received does not permit the assignee to hold free of the equity. The bona fide purchaser rule does not apply to the purchase of an equitable interest and that is what a beneficiary has.[52] Thus if the assigning beneficiary has joined the trustee in committing a breach of trust, or aided him, an equity arises in favor of the co-beneficiaries that the wrongdoing beneficiary's interest be taken to satisfy the damage, and a buyer of the interest of such a beneficiary, however innocent, will take subject to such equity.[53] Or if one who is both trustee and co-beneficiary commits a breach of trust, a *later* assignee of the interest of such trustee-beneficiary must submit to the collection of the damages out of the assigned interest.[54] If the assign-

42. See § 96, post.

43. Sinclair v. Gunzenhauser, 179 Ind. 78, 98 N.E. 37, 100 N.E. 376; Buck v. Swazey, 35 Me. 41, 56 Am.Dec. 681; Osgood v. Eaton, 62 N.H. 512.

44. Monroe's Trustee v. Monroe, 155 Ky. 112, 159 S.W. 651; Packer v. Johnson, 1 Nott & McC., S.C., 1. Thus in Smith v. Witter, 174 N.C. 616, 94 S.E. 402, real property was held to be alienable by a widow without the joinder of the trustee, where the trust had been a married woman's trust.

45. Newhall v. Wheeler, 7 Mass. 189.

46. Riordan v. Schlicher, 146 Ala. 615, 41 So. 842; Tillson v. Moulton, 23 Ill. 648; Stump v. Warfield, 104 Md. 530, 65 A. 346, 118 Am.St.Rep. 434, 10 Ann.Cas. 249; Perrine v. Newell, 49 N.J.Eq. 57, 23 A. 492; Newton v. Jay, 107 App.Div. 457, 95 N.Y.S.

413; Brown v. Ford, 120 Va. 233, 91 S.E. 145.

47. Henderson v. Sherman, 47 Mich. 267, 11 N.W. 153.

48. Lincoln Bank & Trust Co. v. Lane, 303 S.W.2d 273 (1957) (right to occupy realty at nominal rent not transferable).

49. Davis v. Harrison, Hawaii, 153 C.C.A. 133, 240 Fed. 97 (9th Cir.1917).

50. True Real Estate Co. v. True, 115 Me. 533, 99 A. 627.

51. Merchants Nat. Bank v. Morrissey, 329 Mass. 601, 109 N.E.2d 821 (1953).

52. See § 165, post.

53. Ehlen v. Baltimore, 76 Md. 576, 25 A. 917.

54. American Surety Co. v. Vinton, 224 Mass. 337, 112 N.E. 954.

ment by the combination trustee and beneficiary was made *before* the breach of trust was committed, the result is the same, since the purchasing party knows, or should know, that his assignor is a trustee and that there is a contingent equity hanging over his interest as beneficiary to make good the damage. This latter case may also be affected by the possibility of collusion between a trustee who intends to commit a breach and the assignee of his interest as beneficiary. At any rate such assignee is deemed to know that he cannot get by transfer any greater rights than the assignor would have had if he had continued to own his interest under the trust until settlement of his affairs as trustee.[55]

If a beneficiary of a testamentary trust owed the testator, the trustee has a duty to collect the debt out of the interest given to the beneficiary, and this constitutes an equity against his share.[56]

Statute of Frauds

In a number of states the interest of the beneficiary of a trust of realty or personalty can be assigned only in writing,[57] but in other jurisdictions a writing is required only if the trust subject matter is realty.[58]

Priorities between Successive Transferees

In many states the law is that successive transfers by the beneficiary of his interest take effect in the order of their making.[59] In other jurisdictions the controlling feature is the time of notice to the trustee of the assignment, so that a second assignment of the same interest will be superior to a prior one if the second assignee notified the trustee of his assignment before the first assignee gave notice.[60] A qualification to this rule has been suggested, to the effect that priority of notice is not determinative unless the second transferee can prove that he inquired as to a prior assignment before taking his transfer, and so was misled by the failure of the first assignee to give notice.[61] Thus if B, a trust beneficiary, first sells his interest to X, and later assigns the same interest to Y, whether X or Y is entitled to enforce the trust in the

55. Belknap v. Belknap, 5 Mass. (Allen) 468.

56. Brown v. Sperry, 182 Miss. 488, 181 So. 734; In re Freudmann's Estate, 23 Misc.2d 763, 192 N.Y.S.2d 993 (1959).

57. See references collected in Bogert, Trusts and Trustees (rev. 2d edit.), § 190. Section 9 of the English Statute of Frauds required a writing for the transfer of the interest of any beneficiary.

58. See Bogert, Trusts and Trustees (rev. 2d edit.), § 190.

59. Lexington Brewing Co. v. Hamon, 155 Ky. 711, 160 S.W. 264; Putnam v. Story, 132 Mass. 205; Central Trust Co. v. Weeks, 15 App.Div. 598, 44 N.Y.S. 828; Meier v. Hess, 23 Or. 599, 32 P. 755; Restatement, Trusts, Second, § 163.

60. Adamson v. Paonessa, 180 Cal. 157, 179 P. 880; Lambert v. Morgan, 110 Md. 1, 72 A. 407, 132 Am.St.Rep. 412, 17 Ann.Cas. 439; Canton Exchange Bank v. Zazoo County, 144 Miss. 579, 109 So. 1 (1926). The leading English case establishing this rule is Dearle v. Hall, 3 Russ. 1. And see Law of Prop.Act of 1925, § 137.

61. Salem Trust Co. v. Manufacturers Finance Co., 264 U.S. 182, 44 S.Ct. 266 (1924); Moorestown Trust Co. v. Buzby, 109 N.J.Eq. 409, 157 A. 663 (1932).

place of B depends on which of the rules described above is followed in the state in question.

 WESTLAW REFERENCES

Interest of Various Types

tapley +3 dill

beneficiary /5 interest /5 contingent (subject +2 ''condition precedent'')

409k658

409k681(2)

find 40 a2d 758

Death of the Beneficiary Intestate

beneficiary /3 dies death /4 intestate

Escheat

di escheat

Curtesy and Dower

di dower

di curtesy

curtesy /10 trust

dower /10 trust

Homestead

di homestead

homestead /10 trust

Rule in Shelley's Case

''rule in shelley's case'' /5 trust

Taxability

trust /5 ''ad valorem taxation''

371k80

Power to Alienate

beneficiary /5 alienate /5 interest

interest /5 beneficiary /5 devise* mortgage* gift pledge*

Transfer by a Beneficiary of an Interest Subject to Equities

find 112 ne 954

Statute of Frauds

di(''statute of frauds'' /s trust)

390k921/2

Priorities Between Successive Transferees

dearle +3 hall

AVAILABILITY OF BENEFICIARY'S INTEREST
TO CREDITORS [1]

§ 39. **In the absence of valid direction by the settlor or by statute to the contrary, the interest of the beneficiary is, with rare exceptions, liable to be taken by a creditor for the payment of the beneficiary's debts, either at law or in equity.**

In passive trusts the creditor may resort to an execution in an action at law.

In the case of active trusts a suit in chancery was originally and still is in some jurisdictions the exclusive method of collection. It is based on an allegation that there are no assets from which collection can be had at law.

The modern tendency of court and legislature has been to make the beneficiary's interest available either by execution, attachment, garnishment, or proceedings supplementary to execution. The machinery for collection varies from state to state.

In the absence of a valid direction by the settlor to the contrary,[2] or a statute providing otherwise, or the peculiar nature of the beneficiary's interest found in rare cases,[3] a creditor of the beneficiary can secure satisfaction of his claim out of the interest of the beneficiary.[4] The methods available vary from state to state and are dependent in large part on statutes.

If a trust is passive, under the Statute of Uses or a modern equivalent the legal title to the res passes to the beneficiary, and it can be taken for his debts by an execution in an action at law.[5] There is provision to this effect in an English statute [6] and in American counter-

---

§ 39

1. Restatement, Trusts, Second, §§ 147–148. See Bogert, Trusts and Trustees (rev. 2d edit.), § 193.

2. As to spendthrift clauses making the interest of the beneficiary unavailable to creditors, see § 40, post.

Under federal Bankruptcy Code § 541(b) only a general power of appointment that is presently exercisable by the beneficiary is treated as property in the estate of the bankrupt beneficiary.

3. As to discretionary, support, blended, and protective trusts, see §§ 41–44, post. Where a trust is for the benefit of a husband and wife as tenants by the entirety, there is nothing available for a creditor of the husband or wife alone. M. Lit, Co. v. Berger, 225 Md. 241, 170 A.2d 303 (1961).

4. Taylor v. Harwell, 65 Ala. 1, 13; Heath v. Bishop, 4 Rich.Eq., S.C., 46, 50, 55 Am.Dec. 654.

The creditors of a beneficiary of an unexercised general power of appointment created by another normally cannot reach the appointive assets. See Restatement, Property, Second, § 13.2, citing the general rule and statutory exceptions thereto in effect in a few states. There is a division of authority among the states as to whether assets appointed by a beneficiary pursuant to the exercise of a general testamentary power created by another can be reached by creditors of the beneficiary against his estate. See Restatement, Property, Second, § 13.4. Where the beneficiary exercises a general power inter vivos the beneficiary's creditors may be able to reach the appointive assets under a theory analogous to a fraudulent conveyance. Ibid., § 13.5.

5. Loughney v. Page, 320 Pa. 508, 182 A. 700 (1936).

6. St. 29 Car. II, c. 3, 1677.

parts.[7] Although resulting trusts are passive, this procedure for the collection of the debts of the beneficiary is not followed with regard to them.[8]

If a trust is active, under early law it was natural that courts of law should not direct an execution against the equitable interest of the beneficiary, since they did not recognize that interest and regarded the trustee as the sole owner.[9] However this attitude toward the unavailability of legal remedies has changed and increasingly statutes or the courts permit the interest of the beneficiary to be made subject to execution, attachment or other legal remedy without resort to equity proceedings.[10]

Courts of equity will subject the interest of the beneficiary to the payment of his debts. This has been done by the so-called "creditor's bill" without the aid of statute, where reliance can be had on the doctrine that equity acts where the remedy at law is non-existent or inadequate; [11] and in some states the right to maintain a creditor's bill has been provided by statute.[12] In New York and several other states a judgment creditor is given the right by statute to obtain trust income in excess of the beneficiary's needs for support and education or a certain percentage or dollar amount.[13] In some cases it has been held that a condition precedent to the maintenance of this suit is proof that an execution at law has issued and been returned unsatisfied,[14] but in

7. See, for example, Mass.G.L.A. C. 236 § 1; N.Car.G.S. §§ 1–315, 1–316. For judicial decisions achieving the same result, see: Pitts v. McWhorter, 3 Ga. 5, 46 Am.Dec. 405; Moll v. Gardner, 214 Ill. 248, 73 N.E. 442; Lummus v. Davidson, 160 N.C. 484, 76 S.E. 474; Loughney v. Page, 320 Pa. 508, 182 A. 700 (1936); Bristow v. McCall, 16 S.C. 545; Smitheal v. Gray, 1 Humph., Tenn., 491, 34 Am.Dec. 664.

8. Goodbar v. Daniel, 88 Ala. 583, 7 So. 254, 16 Am.St.Rep. 76; Mayer v. Wilkins, 37 Fla. 244, 19 So. 632; Gray v. Chase, 57 Me. 558; Anderson v. Biddle, 10 Mo. 23; Richardson v. Mounce, 19 S.C. 477; *Contra:* Tevis v. Doe, 3 Ind. 129; Peterson v. Farnum, 121 Mass. 476.

In some states, where A pays the consideration for land and has the title taken in the name of B, by statute no trust results for A, but there is a statutory trust for the creditors of A. Thus they obtain their remedy by a bill in chancery as statutory beneficiaries. N.Y.—McKinney's EPTL 7–1.3. McCartney v. Bostwick, 32 N.Y. 53. See § 74, post.

9. Feldman v. Preston, 194 Mich. 352, 160 N.W. 655, 658; Noyes v. Noyes, 110 Vt. 511, 9 A.2d 123 (1939).

10. See, for example, Ky.Rev.Stat. 381.180; Miss.Code 1972, § 89–1–43; Humphrey v. Gerard, 83 Conn. 346, 77 A.

65; Realty Exchange Corp. v. Phoenix Title & Trust Co., 15 Ariz.App. 199, 487 P.2d 420 (1971).

11. Burke v. Morris, 121 Ala. 126, 25 So. 759; Jennings v. Coleman, 59 Ga. 718; De Rousse v. Williams, 181 Iowa 379, 164 N.W. 896; Presley v. Rodgers, 24 Miss. 520; McGregor-Noe Hardware Co. v. Horn, 146 Mo. 129, 47 S.W. 957; Smith v. Collins, 81 N.J.Eq. 348, 86 A. 957; Bergmann v. Lord, 194 N.Y. 70, 86 N.E. 828; Lummus v. Davidson, 160 N.C. 484, 76 S.E. 474; Egbert v. De Solms, 218 Pa. 207, 67 A. 212; Leake v. Benson, 29 Grat., Va., 153.

12. For statutory references, see Bogert, Trusts and Trustees (rev. 2d edit.), § 193.

13. See N.Y.—McKinney's EPTL 7–3.4 (income in excess of that necessary for the education and support of beneficiary). To the same effect see West's Ann.Cal.Civ. Code § 859; Conn.G.S.A. § 52–321; Mich. Comp.L.A. § 555.13; Minn.Stats.Ann. § 501.14; Mont.Code Ann. § 72–24–210; N.D.Cent.Code 59–03–10; 60 Okl.St.Ann. § 140.

14. See Burke v. Morris, 121 Ala. 126, 25 So. 759; Sefton v. San Diego Trust & Savings Bank, Cal.App., 106 P.2d 974; Binns v. La Forge, 191 Ill. 598, 61 N.E. 382; Cohen v. Dwyer, 134 N.J.Eq. 350, 35 A.2d 709 (1944); Trotter v. Lisman, 199 N.Y.

other jurisdictions it is sufficient to prove inadequacy of the legal remedy otherwise (for example, by showing insolvency or bankruptcy of the debtor),[15] and in other states no showing of the lack of a legal remedy is demanded.[16] The creditor secures an equitable lien on the interest of the beneficiary by starting his suit.[17]

The interest of a beneficiary passes to his trustee in bankruptcy [18] or receiver [19] and they can realize upon it for the purpose of paying creditors.

In many states garnishment or trustee process is available to the creditor, so that he can secure an order of the court requiring the trustee to pay the debt out of the property which is due the beneficiary.[20] Attachment is also usable in some states [21] as well as proceedings supplementary to execution in which equitable assets can be discovered and applied.[22] Sometimes statutes permit the use of an execution at law.[23]

497, 92 N.E. 1052; Rucks-Brandt Construction Corp. v. Silver, 194 Okl. 324, 151 P.2d 399 (1944).

15. De Rousse v. Williams, 181 Iowa 379, 164 N.W. 896.

16. Barry v. Abbot, 100 Mass. 396. See also Heffernan v. Bennett & Armour, 63 Cal.App.2d 178, 146 P.2d 482 (1944); Heaton v. Dickson, 153 Mo.App. 312, 133 S.W. 159. And see Huntington v. Jones, 72 Conn. 45, 43 A. 564.

17. Wickwire Spencer Steel Co. v. Kemkit Scientific Corp., 292 N.Y. 139, 54 N.E.2d 336, 153 A.L.R. 208 (1944); Cannon Mills, Inc. v. Spivey, 208 Tenn. 419, 346 S.W.2d 266 (1961).

18. Bankruptcy Code, 11 U.S.C.A. § 541. In re Reynolds, 243 Fed. 268 (D.C. N.Y.1917); Horton v. Moore, 110 F.2d 189 (6th Cir.1940), certiorari denied 311 U.S. 692, 61 S.Ct. 75, 85 L.Ed. 448 (1940), rehearing denied 311 U.S. 728, 61 S.Ct. 173, 85 L.Ed. 474 (1940); Jenks v. Title Guaranty & Trust Co., 170 App.Div. 830, 156 N.Y.S. 478; In re Cunningham's Estate, 340 Pa. 265, 16 A.2d 712 (1940).

19. Showalter v. G.H. Nunnelley Co., 201 Ky. 595, 257 S.W. 1027 (1924).

20. Henderson v. Sunseri, 234 Ala. 289, 174 So. 767 (1937); Bare v. Cole, 220 Iowa 338, 260 N.W. 338 (1935) (if definite sum due); Estabrook v. Earle, 97 Mass. 302 (if trust revocable and controllable by beneficiary at will); Warner v. Rice, 66 Md. 436, 8 A. 84; Meier v. Blair, 287 Mich. 13, 282 N.W. 884 (1938) (if definite sum due); Cowan v. Storms, 121 N.J.L. 336, 2 A.2d 183 (1938); Brearley School v. Ward, 201 N.Y. 358, 94 N.E. 1001, 40 L.R.A.,N.S., 1215, Ann.Cas.1912B, 251. *Contra:* Plunkett v. Le Huray, 4 Har., Del., 436;

McLeod v. Cooper, 88 F.2d 194 (5th Cir. 1937) (Fla. law), certiorari denied 301 U.S. 705, 57 S.Ct. 938, 81 L.Ed. 1359 (1937), rehearing denied 302 U.S. 773, 58 S.Ct. 5, 82 L.Ed. 599 (1937); Dunham v. Kauffman, 385 Ill. 79, 52 N.E.2d 143, 154 A.L.R. 90 (1943); Ross v. Ashton, 73 Mo.App. 254 (unless trust deed is fraudulent); Willis v. Curtze, 203 Pa. 111, 52 A. 5; Oglesby v. Durr, Tex.Civ.App., 173 S.W. 275; Knettle v. Knettle, 190 Wash. 395, 68 P.2d 218 (1937) (as to right to future unaccrued income).

And see statutes and cases set forth in Bogert, Trusts and Trustees (rev. 2d edit.), § 193.

21. See, for example, Mo.—V.A.M.S. § 513.090; Ohio Rev.Code § 2333.01.

Fidelity Trust & Safety Vault Co. v. Walker, 116 Ky. 381, 76 S.W. 131; Baumann v. Ballantine, 76 N.J.L. 91, 68 A. 1114; Riverside Trust Co. v. Twitchell, 342 Pa. 558, 20 A.2d 768 (1941). *Contra:* Fairfax v. Savings Bank of Baltimore, 175 Md. 136, 199 A. 872, 116 A.L.R. 1334 (1938); Feldman v. Preston, 194 Mich. 352, 160 N.W. 655.

22. Cornelius v. Albertson, 244 N.C. 265, 93 S.E.2d 147 (1956). And see West's Ann.Cal.Code Civ.Proc. § 708.110 et seq.; N.Y.—McKinney's CPLR 5223–5227.

23. See, for example, Ky.Rev.Stat. § 381.180; Ohio Rev.Code § 2333.01.

By St. 1 & 2 Vict. c. 110, execution at law against an equitable interest in land was allowed, and where the judgment debtor has the entire equitable interest in personal property it has been held that such interest may be reached by legal execution. Stevens v. Hince, 110 L.T.R. 935.

In some instances the court enforces the claim against the beneficiary by directing a judicial sale of the interest of the beneficiary in the trust and the application of the proceeds of the sale toward the payment of the debt;[24] but in other cases the court in its discretion orders the trustee to pay the debt from property due the beneficiary.[25]

Where the interest of the beneficiary is contingent or subject to a condition precedent, or is otherwise subject to a qualification which makes it vague or speculative in nature and value, so that a sale of it would benefit the creditor not at all or to a trifling extent, the court has refused to direct a sale,[26] but it will be no objection to the taking of the beneficiary's interest that it is liable to be defeated or lessened by the happening of a condition subsequent, for example, where the birth of children may decrease the share of the debtor.[27]

 WESTLAW REFERENCES

beneficiary /2 interest /10 creditor

find 131 p2d 734

44k60

390k135

44k58

189k32

SPENDTHRIFT CLAUSES [1]

§ 40. A spendthrift trust is one in which, either because of a direction of the settlor or because of a statute, the beneficiary is unable to transfer his right to future payments of income or principal and his creditors are unable to subject the beneficiary's interest to the payment of their claims. Such a trust does not involve any

For court construction of general statutes so as to accord this remedy to a creditor, see Reed v. Munn, 80 C.C.A. 215, 148 Fed. 737 (8th Cir.1906); Hempstead v. Dickson, 20 Ill. 193, 71 Am.Dec. 260; Maxwell v. Vaught, 96 Ind. 136; Hutchins v. Heywood, 50 N.H. 491; Girard Life Ins. & Trust Co. v. Chambers, 46 Pa. 485, 86 Am. Dec. 513.

24. Taylor v. Harwell, 65 Ala. 1; Berning v. Berning, 320 Ill.App. 686, 51 N.E.2d 997 (1943); Southern Nat. Life Ins. Co. v. Ford's Adm'r, 151 Ky. 476, 152 S.W. 243; McGregor-Noe Hardware Co. v. Horn, 146 Mo. 129, 47 S.W. 957; McKimmon v. Rodgers, 56 N.C. 200.

25. Huffman v. Chasteen, 307 Ky. 1, 209 S.W.2d 705 (1948). The procedure may be said to be discretionary with chancery. "And consequently the estate, whether it consist of land or personal property, may be subjected and sold, or if practicable and to the interest of the parties, the rents,

interest, or profits may be subjected and applied by a court of equity to payment of debts of the cestui que trust." Marshall's Trustee v. Rash, 87 Ky. 116, 118, 7 S.W. 879, 12 Am.St.Rep. 467.

26. Anglo California Nat. Bank of San Francisco v. Kidd, 58 Cal.App.2d 651, 137 P.2d 460 (1943) (interest contingent until beneficiary reached age 30); Yancey v. Grafton, 197 Ga. 117, 27 S.E.2d 857 (1943); Russell v. Milton, 133 Mass. 180; Adams v. Dugan, 196 Okl. 156, 163 P.2d 227 (1945); Myer v. Thomson, 35 Hun, N.Y., 561; B.F. Goodrich Co. v. Thrash, 15 Wn.2d 624, 131 P.2d 734 (1942).

27. First Nat. Bank of Spartanburg, S.C. v. Dougan, 250 Fed. 510 (D.C.Ga.1918).

§ 40

1. Bogert, Trusts and Trustees (rev. 2d edit.), §§ 222–227; Restatement, Trusts, Second, §§ 149–159; Griswold, Spendthrift Trusts.

restraint on alienability or creditors' rights with respect to property after it is received by the beneficiary from the trustee, but rather is merely a restraint with regard to his rights to future payments under the trust.

An attempted transfer of his right to future income by the beneficiary of a spendthrift trust does not give the assignee a right to compel the trustee to pay income to him, but if the assignment has not been repudiated by the beneficiary the trustee may treat it as an order to pay to the assignee and the trustee will be protected in making payments to the assignee until the order is revoked, unless the instrument directed payment into the hands of the beneficiary alone.

Spendthrift clauses are void, as creating an unlawful restraint on alienation and as against public policy, in England and in a few American states. In the majority of the American states such clauses are valid, either to an unlimited extent or subject to some statutory restrictions. Where the spendthrift clause is declared invalid, the remainder of the trust is enforced.

Meaning of "Spendthrift Trust"

" 'Spendthrift trusts' is the term commonly applied to those trusts that are created with a view to providing a fund for the maintenance of another, and at the same time securing it against his own improvidence or incapacity for self-protection. Provisions against alienation of his interest by the voluntary act of the beneficiary, or the taking of it by his creditors, are usual incidents of such trusts." [2] They provide for a right in a beneficiary to future income or principal of the trust, but also that his right to receive these payments in the future shall not be transferable by him or liable to be taken for payment of his debts.

Thus if A transfers to B, as trustee, $100,000 in bonds to hold in trust for X, with a provision that B shall pay to X the net income of such bonds, but that X shall not have the power to transfer his right to receive such income, and that the creditors of X shall not have the power to reach the right to future income in the hands of the trustee, the trust is a spendthrift trust. A settlor may consider such a trust desirable, where provision is to be made for an inexperienced, incompetent or wasteful person. If such person had the power to dispose of his right to receive the income from the trust, his incapacity or carelessness would lead him to anticipate his income and convey to money lenders and creditors the right to receive future income as it became due. If the incompetent or spendthrift can be restricted so that he can do nothing with the income until it is paid into his hands by the trustee, then the beneficiary is more likely to be protected, at least to some extent, against want.

It has never been the object of the spendthrift trust to restrain the beneficiary from spending income or principal after it has been paid to

---

2. Wagner v. Wagner, 244 Ill. 101, 111,
91 N.E. 66, 18 Ann.Cas. 490.

him by the trustee, or to restrain his creditors from taking trust income or principal from him after he has obtained it from the trustee. The sole object of these trusts is to prevent anticipation of trust income or principal by assignments of the right to receive future income or principal or from attempts by creditors of the beneficiary to reach such right.

The beneficiary of a spendthrift trust does not, however, need to be a spendthrift or incompetent or subnormal in any way. A spendthrift clause is often found in carefully prepared trusts in the United States.

The ordinary spendthrift clause spells out with clarity the intent of the settlor to prohibit transfer of his interest by the beneficiary and the inability of a creditor to reach that interest.[3] But occasionally such an intent is implied.[4] In some states the interests of some beneficiaries are made inalienable by statute,[5] and in others there are statutory provisions that the interest of a beneficiary of a trust created by another for him may not be taken by a creditor.[6] Thus the spendthrift clause may be limited, in one of these states, either to a prohibition against voluntary assignment of a beneficial interest or to a denial of rights of creditors to that interest.

Arguments for and against Validity of Spendthrift Trusts

There has been much debate as to whether the courts should enforce spendthrift clauses. It has been contended by some courts that an equitable life or fee interest involves alienability as an inherent characteristic, that a clause against transferring equitable interests is repugnant to their very nature,[7] that legal estates for life or in fee cannot be encumbered by restraints on alienation and there is no reason why equitable interests should be different;[8] that spendthrift trusts tend to encourage the weak or improvident to continue to be wasteful, and that such trusts mislead and defraud creditors of beneficiaries.[9]

---

3. For typical spendthrift clauses, see Bogert, Trusts and Trustees (rev. 2d edit.), ch. 59.

4. In re Moulton's Estate, 233 Minn. 667, 46 N.W.2d 667 (1951); Mercantile Nat. Bank v. Wilson, 279 S.W.2d 650 (Tex.Civ. App.1955), error refused n.r.e.

5. See, for example, Minn.Stats.Ann. §§ 501.14, 501.20. As to the necessity for an express spendthrift clause in California, see Bogert, Trusts and Trustees (rev. 2d edit.), § 222.

6. See, for example, Ill.Code of Civ. Proced., Rev.Stat. c. 110, ¶ 2–1403 (replacing Ill.Rev.Stat. c. 22, ¶ 49); West's RC Wash. A 6.32.250. And see ReQua v. Graham, 187 Ill. 67, 58 N.E. 357; Miller v. Miller, 203 Tenn. 590, 315 S.W.2d 101

(1958); Seattle First Nat. Bk. v. Crosby, 42 Wn.2d 234, 254 P.2d 732 (1953).

7. Brandon v. Robinson, 18 Ves.Jr. 429.

8. Restraints on alienation of legal life and fee interests are treated as void at common law because of the public interest in freedom of transfer. Streit v. Fay, 230 Ill. 319, 82 N.E. 648; Lathrop v. Merrill, 207 Mass. 6, 92 N.E. 1019. But clauses restraining the alienation of estates for years are valid. Eldredge v. Bell, 64 Iowa 125, 19 N.W. 879.

9. See Gray, Restraints on Alienation, §§ 134–277a; Scott, Control of property by the dead, 65 Univ. of Pa.L.R. 632, 642; Griswold, on Spendthrift Trusts.

On the other hand it has been urged that the donor of property to a trust beneficiary should be able to attach to it such incidents as he pleases; that equitable interests are legally possible even though inalienable, as is shown by the cases holding valid a clause against anticipation in relation to the married woman's separate estate; that there is no undesirable check on alienation of the trust property since the trustee can usually sell it free of the trust even though the beneficiary cannot transfer his interest; that spendthrift trusts are necessary to the protection of inexperienced and incompetent persons; that creditors should not be misled by the appearance of wealth which a beneficiary may show because the creditors can always inquire into the source of such income, demand a statement of assets as a condition to giving credit, secure a credit report, and find wills and deeds in the public records when spendthrift trusts have been created by them; that creditors can collect in time by taking the income after it has been paid over to the beneficiary; and that if a gift of an equitable estate until attempted alienation or until bankruptcy is good, spendthrift trusts should be allowed.[10]

English and Minority American View as to Validity of Spendthrift Trusts

The English courts have consistently opposed such trusts [11] on the grounds mentioned above, and have held spendthrift clauses void. They have, however, permitted "protective trusts" [12], which to some extent achieve the results of a spendthrift trust.

The first contests over the validity of these trusts were fought in the United States during the latter half of the nineteenth century. Professor John Chipman Gray [13] led the forces which sought to persuade the American courts to follow the lead of the English decisions, and these efforts were successful in a few states.[14]

The attitude which the American courts following the English rule have taken is well expressed by Ames, C.J., speaking for a Rhode Island court: "It is quite clear that it was the intention of the testator to make

10. For discussions, see Costigan, 22 Cal.L.R. 471; Griswold, Spendthrift Trusts, §§ 1–36.

11. Brandon v. Robinson, 18 Ves. 429; Graves v. Dolphin, 1 Sim. 66.

12. See § 44, post.

13. Gray, Restraints on Alienation.

14. In Brahmey v. Rollins, 87 N.H. 290, 179 A. 186 (1935), it was held that a trust to pay an annuity to a beneficiary, where the trustee had no discretion as to the amount, could not be encumbered with a clause against creditors taking the right to future income, regardless of the validity of the clause as far as voluntary alienation was concerned. And see N.H.Rev.Stats. Ann. 498:8, 498:9.

In Ohio the Supreme Court has ruled to the effect that spendthrift trusts are not allowed. Sherrow v. Brookover, 174 Ohio St. 310, 189 N.E.2d 90 (1963); Wallace v. Smith, 2 Handy, Ohio, 78; Hobbs v. Smith, 15 Ohio St. 419. See prior *dictum* apparently favorable to spendthrift trusts in Stanley v. Thornton, 7 Ohio Cir.Ct.R. 455. White, Spendthrift Trusts in Ohio, 2 Cinc. L.R. 333.

Spendthrift trusts were declared invalid in Tillinghast v. Bradford, 5 R.I. 205. See Newport Trust Co. v. Chappell, 40 R.I. 383, 101 A. 323.

Apparently no problems as to the validity and effect of spendthrift trusts have arisen in Alaska, Idaho, New Mexico and Wyoming.

an alimentary provision for his son during life, which should give him all the advantages of an estate in fee, without the legal incidents of such an estate—alienability, unless by will, and subjectiveness to the payment of the son's debts. Such restraints, however, are so opposed to the nature of property—and, so far as subjectiveness to debts is concerned, to the honest policy of the law—as to be totally void, unless, indeed, which is not the case here, in the event of its being attempted to be aliened, or seized for debts, it is given over by the testator to some one else. This has been the settled doctrine of a court of chancery, at least since Brandon v. Robinson, 18 Ves. 429; and its application to such a case as this is so honest and just that we would not change it if we could. Certainly no man should have an estate to live on, but not an estate to pay his debts with. Certainly property available for the purposes of pleasure or profit should be also amenable to the demands of justice." [15]

Majority American View

In most American states, however, spendthrift trusts are allowed, either without qualification or subject to some statutory restrictions.[16] In many states such a trust may be created for any beneficiary as to any amount of principal or income.[17]

---

15. Tillinghast v. Bradford, 5 R.I. 205, 212.

16. See statutes and cases collected in Bogert, Trusts and Trustees (rev. 2d edit.), § 222, at ns. 60, 94. A dictum by Justice Miller, in Nichols v. Eaton, 91 U.S. (1 Otto) 716, 23 L.Ed. 254 (1875), had great influence in persuading state courts to accept spendthrift trusts.

17. See Bogert, Trusts and Trustees (rev. 2d edit.), § 222, n. 94, for current law in all states. For example, see:

Alabama.—By Ala.Code 1975, § 19–3–1 spendthrift trusts of principal and income for relatives are validated. In Alabama the English rule had been observed with some qualifications. A beneficial interest could not be given to one so that it was incapable of being reached by his creditors, unless such interest was conferred and was to be enjoyed jointly with others, and was also incapable of severance from the interest of such others. Bell v. Watkins, 82 Ala. 512, 1 So. 92, 60 Am.Rep. 756. See also, Rugely v. Robinson, 10 Ala. 702.

Arkansas.—The dicta were unfavorable until the decision in Bowlin v. Citizens' Bank & Trust Co., 131 Ark. 97, 198 S.W. 288, 2 A.L.R. 575, which announced that spendthrift trusts were valid.

Connecticut.—Conn.G.S.A. §§ 52–321, 52–327 (support trusts).

Delaware.—12 Del.Code § 3536 (but income beneficiary may assign up to 50% of his income interest to the state or to charity).

District of Columbia.—Fearson v. Dunlop, 21 D.C. 236 (1800). See Utley v. Graves, 258 F.Supp. 959 (D.D.C.1966) (remanded by 127 U.S.App.D.C. 235, 382 F.2d 451 (1967), the Court of Appeals stating that trust income would be available to the beneficiary's creditors for "necessaries").

Georgia.—Offic.Code Ga.Ann. § 53–12–25 (if by deed, must be recorded); Moore v. Sinnott, 117 Ga. 1010, 44 S.E. 810.

Hawaii.—Welsh v. Campbell, 41 Hawaii 106.

Illinois.—Hopkinson v. Swaim, 284 Ill. 11, 119 N.E. 985. See Ill.Code of Civ. Proced., Rev.Stat. c. 110, ¶ 2–1403, making all trusts created by one other than debtor-beneficiary free from creditors' rights.

Indiana.—McCoy v. Houck, 180 Ind. 634, 99 N.E. 97; Gavit, Spendthrift Trusts in Indiana, 3 Ind.L.J. 525. And see West's Ann.Ind.Code 30–4–3–2.

Iowa.—Merchants' Nat. Bank v. Crist, 140 Iowa 308, 118 N.W. 394, 23 L.R.A.,N.S., 526, 132 Am.St.Rep. 267; Horack, Spendthrift Trusts in Iowa, 4 Iowa Law Bul. 139.

Kansas.—Kan.Stat.Ann. 58–2404. See Everitt v. Haskins, 102 Kan. 546, 171 P. 632. But see Koelliker v. Denkinger, 148

Kan. 503, 83 P.2d 703 (1938), judgment modified on rehearing on other grounds, 149 Kan. 259, 86 P.2d 740 (1939) (interest in statutory spendthrift trust held subject to attachment and garnishment). And see Spendthrift Trusts—Validity in Kansas, 9 Washburn Law Journal 75.

Kentucky.—By Ky.Rev.Stat. § 381.180, restraints on voluntary and involuntary alienation are made valid as to income and principal, except amounts needed for support of wife and children and alimony.

Louisiana.—LSA–R.S. 9:2002–2007.

Maine.—Roberts v. Stevens, 84 Me. 325, 24 A. 873; Tilton v. Davidson, 98 Me. 55, 56 A. 215.

Maryland.—Plitt v. Yakel, 129 Md. 464, 99 A. 669.

Massachusetts.—Broadway Nat. Bank v. Adams, 133 Mass. 170, 43 Am.Rep. 504; Boston Safe Deposit Co. v. Collier, 222 Mass. 390, 111 N.E. 163, Ann.Cas.1918C, 962.

Mississippi.—Cady v. Lincoln, 100 Miss. 765, 57 So. 213. See Miss.Code 1972, § 89–1–43.

Missouri.—See V.A.M.S. § 456.080. And see Kessner v. Phillips, 189 Mo. 515, 88 S.W. 66, 107 Am.St.Rep. 368, 3 Ann.Cas. 1005.

Montana.—Code Ann. §§ 72–24–205 and 72–24–210. See Lundgren v. Hoglund, 711 P.2d 809 (1985).

Nebraska.—Weller v. Noffsinger, 57 Neb. 455, 77 N.W. 1075; Summers v. Summers, 177 Neb. 365, 128 N.W.2d 829 (1964).

Nevada.—Nev.Rev.Stat. 166.010–166.160.

New Jersey.—Moore v. Moore, 137 N.J. Eq. 314, 44 A.2d 639 (1945). The law has been affected by a statute permitting garnishment of a certain percentage of the trust income. See N.J.S.A. 2A:17–50, 2A:17–57. Cowan v. Storms, 121 N.J.Eq. 336, 2 A.2d 183 (1938).

New York.—By N.Y.—McKinney's EPTL 7–1.5, express trusts to receive income from property or to apply or pay it to any person are made spendthrift, but statutory exceptions are provided. Creditors may reach that portion of a beneficiary's income interest in excess of income needed for his education and support under N.Y.— McKinney's EPTL 7–3.4 and CPLR 5526. The income beneficiary may assign to persons he is obligated to support. N.Y.— McKinney's EPTL 7–1.5(d). If not prohibited by the instrument the income beneficiary may assign all income in excess of

$10,000 a year to certain relatives or to certain representatives of a minor. N.Y.— McKinney's EPTL 7–1.5(b)(1). In Matter of Vought, 25 N.Y.2d 163, 303 N.Y.S.2d 61, 250 N.E.2d 343 (1969), reargument denied 25 N.Y.2d 959, 305 N.Y.S.2d 1027, 252 N.E.2d 864 (1969), it was held that a settlor may provide that the trust remainder is to be inalienable. For New York law prior to September 1, 1967, the effective date of N.Y.—McKinney's EPTL, see Bogert, Trusts and Trustees (rev. 2d edit.), § 222.

Nevada.—Nev.Rev.Stat. 166.010 et seq.

North Carolina.—Early North Carolina decisions invalidated spendthrift clauses (Dick v. Pitchford, 21 N.C. 480), but a statute has now validated them to a limited extent. See N.Car.G.S. § 36A–115. For prior law see N.Car.G.S. § 41–9 (for support of relative for life; income limited to $500 annually). See Bank of Union v. Heath, 187 N.C. 54, 121 S.E. 24 (1924).

Oklahoma.—60 Okl.St.Ann. § 175.25.

Oregon.—Winslow v. Rutherford, 59 Or. 124, 114 P. 930.

Pennsylvania.—See 20 Pa.S. § 6112. And see In re Minnich's Estate, 206 Pa. 405, 55 A. 1067. An act of 1945 providing that spendthrift trust income beneficiaries may release their interests in favor of remaindermen was valid as to trusts existing at the time the act went into effect. In re Borsch's Estate, 362 Pa. 581, 67 A.2d 119 (1949).

Rhode Island.—R.I.Gen.Laws 1956, § 34–5–10.

South Carolina.—Early South Carolina decisions opposed to spendthrift trusts (Heath v. Bishop, 4 Rich.Eq. 46, 55 Am. Dec. 654; Wylie v. White, 10 Rich.Eq. 294; Ford v. Caldwell, 3 Hill. 248) have been overruled by later cases. Albergotti v. Summers, 203 S.C. 137, 26 S.E.2d 395 (1943); Breeden, U.S.C. Selden Soc.Yr.Bk. 19.

South Dakota.—See First Northwestern Trust Co. of South Dakota v. I.R.S., 622 F.2d 387 (8th Cir.1980).

Tennessee.—See Tenn.Code Ann. § 35–50–113. And see Jobe v. Dillard, 104 Tenn. 658, 58 S.W. 324.

Texas.—V.T.C.A., Prop.Code § 112.035. And see Nunn v. Titche-Goettinger Co., 196 S.W. 890 (Civ.App.).

Vermont.—White's Ex'r v. White, 30 Vt. 338.

Virginia.—Va.Code 1950, § 55–19 (support trusts, $500,000 limit). The rule in Virginia had remained in doubt for many

In a leading early case [18] on the validity of spendthrift trusts, the Massachusetts court argued that the intent of the settlor was clear and should be carried out where not contrary to public policy; that the power to alienate was not an inherent incident of equitable estates; that there was no violation of public policy since creditors should not be deceived; that a donor ought to be able to do directly what he can do indirectly by making an interest determinable on attempted alienation; and that a donor should be able to limit his gift in any way not against the public interest.

In a small group of states [19] spendthrift trusts are given limited validity by statutes which provide that "where a trust is created to receive the rents and profits of real property, and no valid direction for accumulation is given, the surplus of such rents and profits, beyond the sum necessary for the education and support of the person for whose benefit the trust is created, is liable to the claims of the creditors of such person, in the same manner as other personal property which cannot be reached by execution." [20] In construction of these statutes it has been held that the education and support to which the beneficiary is entitled is that to which he has been accustomed and to which persons of his class are used.[21] In deciding what is necessary for support, luxuries and extravagances will not be considered.[22] Income being received by the beneficiary from other sources may be taken into account, but not what he could earn if he would work where he refuses

years. See Hutchinson v. Maxwell, 100 Va. 169, 40 S.E. 655, 57 L.R.A. 384, 93 Am. St.Rep. 944, and Honaker v. Duff, 101 Va. 675, 44 S.E. 900.

Washington.—RCWA 6.32.250 & 11.96.150. And see Milner v. Outcalt, 36 Wn.2d 720, 219 P.2d 982 (1950), noted in 26 Wash.L.R. 141.

West Virginia.—W.Va.Code, 36–1–18. And see Kerns v. Carr, 82 W.Va. 78, 95 S.E. 606, L.R.A.1918E, 568.

Wisconsin.—W.S.A. 701.06.

18. Broadway Nat. Bank v. Adams, 133 Mass. 170, 43 Am.Rep. 504.

19. *California.*—West's Cal.Ann.Civ. Code, § 859; Seymour v. McAvoy, 121 Cal. 438, 53 P. 946, 41 L.R.A. 544; Canfield v. Security-First Nat. Bank, 13 Cal.2d 1, 87 P.2d 830 (1939). See 40 Cal.L.R. 441. Prior to 1872 spendthrift trusts were valid without limit in California. Under § 859 it appears there must be an express spendthrift clause if partial protection against creditors is to ensue. Houghton v. Pacific Southwest Trust & Sav. Bank, 111 Cal. App. 509, 295 P. 1079 (1939). See also West's Ann.Cal.Civ.Code § 867.

Michigan.—Mich.C.L.A. §§ 555.13, 555.19. Cummings v. Corey, 58 Mich. 494, 25 N.W. 481.

See Fratcher, 51 Mich.L.R. 509.

Minnesota.—Minn.Stat.Ann. §§ 501.14, 501.20. Erickson v. Erickson, 197 Minn. 71, 267 N.W. 426 (1936). See Bunn, 18 Minn.L.R. 493; 35 Minn.L.R. 682. See In re Moulton's Estate, 233 Minn. 286, 46 N.W.2d 667 (1951) (statutory sections inapplicable to inter vivos trusts; income interest could not be assigned to wife under a property settlement).

Montana.—Mont.Code Ann. § 72–24–210. See also Mont.Code Ann. § 72–24–205.

North Dakota.—N.Dak.Cent.Code 59–03–10.

South Dakota.—S.Dak.Codif.L. 43–10–12 and 43–10–13.

See also *Conn.*—C.G.S.A. § 52–321; Okl.—60 Okl.St.Ann. § 140; *Wis.*—Wis. S.A. 231.13.

20. West's Ann.Cal.Civ.Code § 859.

21. Magner v. Crooks, 139 Cal. 640, 73 P. 585; Williams v. Thorn, 70 N.Y. 270.

22. Canfield v. Security-First Nat. Bank of Los Angeles, 13 Cal.2d 1, 87 P.2d 830 (1939).

to do so.[23] These statutes and their construction have been criticized.[24] In California and New York the statute has been applied to trusts of personal property as well,[25] but not in Minnesota and Wisconsin.[26]

In other states limitations are placed on the spendthrift trust by statutory provisions that the principal of such a trust cannot exceed a certain sum,[27] or that only a certain amount of trust income can be protected by a spendthrift clause,[28] or that the beneficiaries of spendthrift trusts must be close relatives for whose support the settlor would have a moral obligation.[29]

A model statute on spendthrift trusts, limiting their income to $5,000 a year, permitting creditors to garnishee 10% of all income over $12 a week, preventing a right to principal from being subjected to a spendthrift provision, and excepting claims for support and other meritorious claims from the usual rule, has been substantially adopted in two states.[30]

In a general way it may be said that the trend of the last forty years has been to limit and qualify spendthrift trusts, either by statute or by judicial decisions which create exceptions of the types described at a later point.[31] The spirit of nineteenth century individualism which originally validated these trusts is meeting opposition of a socially-minded character.

Special Cases—Exceptions

It should be noted that a property owner may not create a spendthrift trust in his own favor. If he attempts to do so, the trust is valid but the spendthrift clause is void as to the present and future creditors of the property owner [32] and the settlor is able to transfer his interest.[33] To hold otherwise would be to give unexampled opportunity to unscru-

23. Smith v. Smith, 51 Cal.App.2d 29, 124 P.2d 117 (1942); Wetmore v. Wetmore, 149 N.Y. 520, 44 N.E. 169, 33 L.R.A. 708.

24. Gray, Restraints, 2d Ed., preface, xi.

25. Canfield v. Security-First Nat. Bank of Los Angeles, 13 Cal.2d 1, 87 P.2d 830 (1939); Williams v. Thorn, 70 N.Y. 270; In re Williams, 187 N.Y. 286, 79 N.E. 1019.

26. See Erickson v. Erickson, 197 Minn. 71, 266 N.W. 161 (1936); Williams v. Smith, 117 Wis. 142, 93 N.W. 464. See also Lundgren v. Hoglund, 711 P.2d 809 (1985).

27. Va.Code 1950, § 55–19 (principal not to exceed $500,000).

28. Tenn.Code Ann. § 35–50–113.

29. *Arizona.*—A.R.S. § 14–104 (can be created by parent for child who is actually a spendthrift) was not reenacted, but see Arizona Bank v. Morris, 1968, 6 Ariz.App. 566, 435 P.2d 73 (1967).

Connecticut.—C.G.S.A. § 52–321 (good only for beneficiary or his family and to extent necessary for support).

See also Shelley v. Shelley, 223 Or. 328, 354 P.2d 282 (1960) (recovery of creditor limited to what is reasonable, considering all factors).

30. La.—LSA–R.S. 9:2002–2007; 60 Okl.St.Ann. § 175.25.

31. See text at footnotes 32–47, post, this section. For a review of developments see 53 Harv.L.R. 296, 64 Colum.L.R. 1323.

32. See, for example, Ala.Code 1975, § 8–9–7; West's Ann.Ind.Code 30–4–3–2; N.Y.—McKinney's EPTL 7–3.1; Va.Code 1950, § 55–19.

Nelson v. California Trust Co., 33 Cal. 2d 501, 202 P.2d 1021 (1949); Hexter v. Clifford, 5 Colo. 168; De Rousse v. Williams, 181 Iowa 379, 164 N.W. 896; Wenzel v. Powder, 100 Md. 36, 59 A. 194, 108 Am.

33. See note 33 on page 156.

pulous persons to shelter their property before engaging in speculative business enterprises, to mislead creditors into thinking that the settlor still owned the property since he appeared to be receiving its income, and thereby to work a gross fraud on creditors who might place reliance on the former prosperity and financial stability of the debtor. In some cases there would be an actual intent to defraud or hinder creditors but it would be secret and could not be proved.

The courts have made some other exceptions to the validity of spendthrift trusts on grounds of public policy. Claims of this type are income tax claims,[34] claims for necessaries furnished the beneficiary,[35] or on account of debts due the settlor,[36] and tort claims against the beneficiary.[37]

There have been numerous efforts to subject the spendthrift trust beneficiary's interest to claims for alimony payable to his divorced wife, or to claims of his wife and minor children for support. It has been urged that an exception should be made in favor of such claimants on grounds of public policy, in that the state is interested in requiring a husband and father to perform his legal duty to provide for his wife and

St.Rep. 380; Cunningham v. Bright, 228 Mass. 385, 117 N.E. 909; Jamison v. Mississippi Valley Trust Co., Mo., 207 S.W. 788; Schenck v. Barnes, 156 N.Y. 316, 50 N.E. 967, 41 L.R.A. 395.

See Mackason's Appeal, 42 Pa. 330, where it is said that to permit a spendthrift trust for the settlor "would revolutionize the credit system entirely, destroy all faith in the apparent ownership of property, and repeal all our statutes and decisions against frauds".

33. See, for example, Offic.Code Ga. Ann. § 53–12–25; Ky.Rev.Stat. § 381.180.

Byrnes v. Commissioner of Internal Revenue, 110 F.2d 294 (3d Cir.1940); Liberty Trust Co. v. Weber, 200 Md. 491, 90 A.2d 194 (1952) (opinion modified on another point); Merchants' Nat. Bank v. Morrissey, 329 Mass. 601, 109 N.E.2d 821 (1953); City Bank Farmers Trust Co. v. Kennard, 1 N.Y.S.2d 369 (1937). The spendthrift clause does not make the trust subject to attack by the settlor-beneficiary. The clause is invalid but the trust without the clause is valid. Liberty Nat. Bank v. Hicks, 84 U.S.App.D.C. 198, 173 F.2d 631, 9 A.L.R.2d 1355 (1948).

34. In re Rosenberg's Will, 269 N.Y. 247, 199 N.E. 206, 105 A.L.R. 1238 (1935). And see Fetting v. Flanagan, 185 Md. 499, 45 A.2d 355 (1946) (estate tax claim).

See Ky.Rev.Stat. 381.180(6)(c).

The interest of the beneficiary is subject to seizure by the Attorney General under

the Enemy Alien Act. Matter of Schneider's Estate, 140 Cal.App.2d 710, 296 P.2d 45 (1956), appeal dismissed 352 U.S. 938, 77 S.Ct. 263, 1 L.Ed.2d 235 (1956).

35. See, for example, West's Ann.Cal. Civ.Code § 859; 60 Okl.St.Ann. § 175.25; Wash.—RCWA 11.96.150 (necessities and support of minor children). See Sherman v. Skuse, 166 N.Y. 345, 59 N.E. 990.

It is sometimes held that the support of an incompetent in a state institution is a "necessary": In re Lackmann's Estate, 156 Cal.App.2d 674, 320 P.2d 186 (1958). But see City of Bridgeport v. Reilly, 133 Conn. 31, 47 A.2d 865 (1946).

And see Va.Code 1950, § 55–19.1 (beneficiary receiving public assistance; state may obtain trust income and principal upon court reformation of trust).

36. McKeown v. Pridmore, 310 Ill.App. 634, 35 N.E.2d 376 (1941); Matter of Foster's Estate, 38 Misc. 347, 77 N.Y.S. 922. *Contra,* Brown v. Corn Exch. Nat. Bank & Trust Co., 136 N.J.Eq. 430, 42 A.2d 474 (1945) (opinion modified on other grounds).

37. Davies v. Harrison, 3 Pa.Dist. & Co. R. 481. On the general subject, see Griswold, 43 Harv.L.R. 63. In Blakemore v. Jones, 303 Mass. 557, 22 N.E.2d 112, 123 A.L.R. 1317 (1939), a trustee-beneficiary of a spendthrift trust had committed a breach of trust. It was held that his interest as beneficiary could not be reached to satisfy the damage claim. See 57 Dick.L.R. 220; 28 Notre Dame L. 509.

children and that a clause permitting him to avoid his obligations should be held to be void.

Some courts have held that the living expenses of a wife and children are a part of the beneficiary's own support so that giving the wife and children rights to future payments is in substance enforcing the trust for the beneficiary.[38]

There has been a division among the authorities with respect to this subject, some holding that support claims could be collected, notwithstanding a spendthrift clause,[39] and others taking the position that such an exception should be made only by the legislature.[40] The case for alimony to the divorced wife seems much weaker. Her claims do not rest on the common law duty of the husband, but rather on the divorce decree.[41] In some states the matter has been settled by statute in favor of the wife and children.[42]

While some authorities contend that the spendthrift trust can protect only the beneficiary's right to future *income,* and not his right to *principal* in the future,[43] more recent authorities support these trusts as to both principal and income.[44]

The restraint imposed by a spendthrift trust may be limited to continue for the life of the beneficiary or any part of it or for a period of years.[45] There seems to be no reason why a settlor may not attach a restraint upon voluntary alienation by the beneficiary, but omit any restriction on the rights of creditors; or prevent creditors from reaching the beneficiary's interest but permit transfer of it by the beneficiary.[46] However, one restraint without the other is very dubious protec-

38. Seattle First Nat. Bank v. Crosby, 42 Wn.2d 234, 254 P.2d 732 (1953).

39. Wife, J.B.G. v. Husband, J.B.G., 286 A.2d 256 (Del.Ch.1971); Shelley v. Shelley, 223 Or. 328, 354 P.2d 282 (1960); In re Moorhead's Estate, 289 Pa. 542, 137 A. 802, 52 A.L.R. 1251 (1927); In re Stewart's Estate, 334 Pa. 356, 5 A.2d 910 (1939).

40. Schwager v. Schwager, 109 F.2d 754 (7th Cir.1940); Hitchens v. Safe Deposit & Trust Co. of Baltimore, Md., 193 Md. 62, 66 A.2d 97 (1949); Bucknam v. Bucknam, 294 Mass. 214, 200 N.E. 918, 104 A.L.R. 774 (1936); Erickson v. Erickson, 197 Minn. 71, 266 N.W. 161 (1936).

41. See In re Bucklin's Estate, 243 Iowa 312, 51 N.W.2d 412 (1952); Swink v. Swink, 6 N.C.App. 161, 169 S.E.2d 539 (1969).

42. See, for example, West's Ann.Cal. Civ.Code § 859 (alimony and child support); Conn.G.S.A. § 52–321 (alimony and child support); Mo.—V.A.M.S. § 456.080 (support of spouse and children); N.J.S.A. 2A:17–56.8 (alimony); 20 Pa.C.S.A. § 6112; Wis.S.A. 701.06(4) (claims for child support).

43. Potter v. Couch, 141 U.S. 296, 11 S.Ct. 1005, 35 L.Ed. 721 (1891). See Restatement, Trusts, Second, § 153 (restraint valid if principal payable to the beneficiary at a future time, but not if payable immediately or payable after the death of the beneficiary).

44. Mellon v. Driscoll, 117 F.2d 477 (3d Cir.1941), certiorari denied 313 U.S. 579, 61 S.Ct. 1100, 85 L.Ed. 1536 (1941); Kelly v. Kelly, 11 Cal.2d 356, 79 P.2d 1059, 119 A.L.R. 71 (1938); Snyder v. O'Conner, 102 Colo. 567, 81 P.2d 773 (1938); Medwedeff v. Fisher, 179 Md. 192, 17 A.2d 141 (1941); Erickson v. Erickson, 197 Minn. 71, 266 N.W. 161 (1936); Singer v. Singer, 150 Tex. 115, 237 S.W.2d 600 (1951).

45. Von Kesler v. Scully, 267 Ill.App. 495.

46. Hodam v. Jordan, 82 F.Supp. 183 (E.D.Ill.1949); Henson v. Wright, 88 Tenn. 501, 12 S.W. 1035; Holmesburg Bldg. Ass'n v. Badger, 144 Pa.Super. 65, 18 A.2d 529 (1941).

tion, and the express mention of one may possibly be deemed to carry the other restraint by implication.[47]

Application of Spendthrift Trust Rules

The result of the rules of law just stated may be illustrated by a practical application. Suppose that A, the owner of a farm, conveys it to X, as trustee, to hold for the benefit of the son of A, who is a spendthrift and profligate. The trust instrument directs that the entire net income shall be paid over to the son in semi-annual instalments. It also provides that the son shall have no power to transfer his right to future income and that the right to such income shall not be liable for the debts of son. In those states in which a spendthrift clause is held void, the provisions with respect to anticipation and the rights of creditors will be disregarded, the son will be allowed to assign his rights, and his creditors may attach his right to future income. On the other hand in the majority of American states, where spendthrift trusts are allowed without limit, the settlor's directions will be respected; the son can create no present rights in another by means of an assignment of his right to receive future payments, and the creditors of the son have no remedy against such funds until they are paid into son's hands. They cannot compel the trustee to pay any of the income to them directly. In states following the doctrine that "surplus income" alone is available for creditors, evidence will be taken as to the amount needed to support the beneficiary in the manner in which he has been accustomed and any excess of trust income over that sum will be awarded the creditor.

The rules about spendthrift trusts govern trusts to apply income to the benefit of a beneficiary (as by purchasing shelter, food and clothing for him), as well as to trusts to pay money directly to the beneficiary.[48]

There has been a difference of opinion among the courts as to whether trust income which has been received by the trustee, and credited to the beneficiary but not paid to him, is protected by a spendthrift clause against creditors, some courts granting protection [49] and others denying it.[50]

It should be noted that an attempt by a spendthrift beneficiary to assign his right to future income may be treated by the trustee as a direction to pay the income to the assignee as an agent or similar representative of the beneficiary, and that until such direction is

47. Young v. Handwork, 179 F.2d 70 (7th Cir.1949), certiorari denied 339 U.S. 949, 70 S.Ct. 804, 94 L.Ed. 1363 (1950), rehearing denied 339 U.S. 991, 70 S.Ct. 1021, 94 L.Ed. 1392 (1950); Partridge v. Cavender, 96 Mo. 452, 9 S.W. 785; Shankland's Appeal, 47 Pa. 113.

48. Sand v. Beach, 270 N.Y. 281, 200 N.E. 821 (1936).

49. Travelers Bank & Trust Co. v. Birge, 136 Conn. 21, 68 A.2d 138 (1949);

Huestis v. Manley, 110 Vt. 413, 8 A.2d 644 (1939).

50. Jarcho Bros. Inc. v. Leverich, 240 App.Div. 783, 265 N.Y.S. 919 (1933); Sproul-Bolton v. Sproul-Bolton, 383 Pa. 85, 117 A.2d 688 (1955) (unless settlor expressly stated accrued income was to be protected).

See discussion and cases cited in Bogert, Trusts and Trustees (rev. 2d edit.), § 227.

revoked by the beneficiary the trustee will be protected in paying income to the assignee, although he need not do so.[51] However this principle does not apply if the trust instrument requires the trustee to pay the trust income directly into the hands of the beneficiary.[52] A purported present assignment of trust principal by a spendthrift beneficiary has been held to amount to a contract to assign the principal when received, if the assignment is for consideration, and damages can be recovered for the breach of this contract and collected out of property which has been delivered to the beneficiary by the trustee.[53]

If the beneficiary of a spendthrift trust is adjudicated a bankrupt, his right to future payments under the trust does not pass to the trustee in bankruptcy[54] in states where such a trust is valid without limit. If the trust purported to protect the beneficiary against creditors but did not prohibit voluntary alienation of his interest by the beneficiary, it has been held that the respect which the Bankruptcy Act accords state exemptions prevents the trustee in bankruptcy from claiming the beneficiary's interest on the ground that it was one which he "could by any means have transferred",[55] but it would seem that this situation was changed by a 1938 amendment of the Bankruptcy Act.[56]

There is nothing against public policy in making a gift which is to take effect on the acquisition by the donee of a discharge in bankruptcy, or on his becoming solvent or paying all his debts.[57] Whether the trustee in bankruptcy of such a donee will have any rights with regard to the interest given is to be determined by the terms of the U.S. Bankruptcy Code.[58]

 WESTLAW REFERENCES

Meaning of "Spendthrift Trust"
di spendthrift
di spendthrift trust

51. In re Easton's Estate, 13 N.Y.S.2d 295 (Sur.1939); In re Keeler's Estate, 334 Pa. 225, 3 A.2d 413, 121 A.L.R. 1301 (1939).

52. Ryan v. Ryan, 353 Mo. 289, 182 S.W.2d 301 (1944) (personal receipt required).

53. Kelly v. Kelly, 11 Cal.2d 356, 79 P.2d 1059, 119 A.L.R. 71 (1938).

54. Danning v. Lederer, 232 F.2d 610 (7th Cir.1956); Medwedeff v. Fisher, 179 Md. 192, 17 A.2d 141, 138 A.L.R. 1313 (1941). However, if the beneficiary's interest is voluntarily alienable, though not subject to creditors' claims, the interest may pass to his bankruptcy trustee. See Young v. Handwork, 179 F.2d 70 (7th Cir. 1949), certiorari denied 339 U.S. 949, 70 S.Ct. 804, 94 L.Ed. 1363 (1950), rehearing denied 339 U.S. 991, 70 S.Ct. 1021, 94 L.Ed. 1392 (1950).

55. Eaton v. Boston Safe Deposit & Trust Co., 240 U.S. 427, 36 S.Ct. 391, 60 L.Ed. 723 (1916).

56. Former (1898) Act, 11 U.S.C.A. § 110(a)(5), as amended, gave the trustee in bankruptcy interests of the bankrupt which were inalienable before bankruptcy but became alienable or gave rise to powers to acquire alienable interests. For current (1978 Code) provisions, see 11 U.S.C.A. § 541(c).

57. Hull v. Farmers' Loan & Trust Co., 245 U.S. 312, 38 S.Ct. 103, 62 L.Ed. 312 (1917); Newport Trust Co. v. Chappell, 40 R.I. 383, 101 A. 323.

58. 11 U.S.C.A. § 110(a)(7) (1898 Act, as amended). For current (1978 Code) provisions, see 11 U.S.C.A. § 541(c).

spendthrift /2 clause trust /s intent! /s settlor trustor
390k112 /p intent! /s settlor trustor

Arguments For and Against Validity of Spendthrift Trusts
"spendthrift trust" /s valid ★ ★ ★
390k12

English and Minority American View as to Validity of Spendthrift Trusts
"english rule" /s spendthrift
"protective trust"
brandon + 3 robinson

Majority American View
spendthrift /10 statute
390k152

Special Cases—Exceptions
spendthrift /10 settlor /5 benefit
spendthrift /15 defraud ★ ★ ★ cheat ★ ★ ★ rinder ★ ★ ★ /2
    creditor
spendthrift /15 tax /2 claim
spendthrift /15 tort /2 claim
spendthrift /15 alimony "child support"

Application of Spendthrift Trust Rules
"spendthrift trust" /5 rule
find 232 f2d 610

DISCRETIONARY TRUSTS [1]

§ 41. If a trustee has discretion whether to pay or apply income to or for a beneficiary, or to pay or apply nothing, the interest of the beneficiary before the trustee elects to pay or apply a given amount is not assignable or reachable by his creditors. If, however, the trust has no spendthrift clause in it, and a trustee of such a trust has received notice of an assignment by the beneficiary, or has been served with process by a creditor of the beneficiary attempting to reach the beneficiary's interest, and the trustee thereafter pays or applies trust property to or for the beneficiary, he will be liable to the assignee or creditor for the amount paid or applied.

Sometimes the settlor provides that the trustee shall pay to or apply for the beneficiary only so much of the income or principal of the trust as the trustee sees fit to use for that purpose, and that the remainder of the trust income or property shall be used for another purpose. This is a true "discretionary trust," in the sense that there is a discretion to give the named beneficiary some benefits under the trust or to give him nothing. The technical meaning of the phrase in this connection should be carefully noted, since every trust involves some discretionary powers in the trustee.[2] Here obviously the beneficiary

---

§ 41
1. Restatement, Trusts, Second, § 155.

2. The existence of mere discretion in the trustee as to the time and method of

cannot force the trustee to use any of the trust property for his benefit,[3] nor should anyone taking under him, such as a transferee or creditor, be in any better position.

In a suit to compel the trustee to pay or apply, the trustee could reply that he had elected not to pay or apply.[4] Therefore the nature of the trust gives the beneficiary no interest subject to assignment or to the claims of his creditors, before the time when the trustee has elected to pay or apply some of the trust property for the beneficiary.[5] Alienation and attachment are prevented, not by an express prohibition in the trust instrument but by the character of the interest given the beneficiary.[6]

If, however, the trustee does elect to pay trust income to the beneficiary, or to apply it for his benefit, then the beneficiary has a property interest which, if not protected by a spendthrift trust clause prohibiting alienation or taking by creditors, is assignable and reachable by creditors. If the beneficiary does assign, or creditors seek to take, in advance of the election by the trustee to pay or apply, and later the trustee chooses to pay or apply, the trustee will be liable to the assignee or creditor for the amount paid or applied if he had notice of the assignment or had been served with process by the creditor;[7] he then had a duty to pay to the transferee or creditor the amount which he had elected to pay to the beneficiary. The assignment or attachment is deemed to affect future payments or applications if and when the trustee in his discretion elects to make them.

A settlor may attach a spendthrift clause to a discretionary trust, in which case, even after the trustee has decided to pay or apply something to or for the beneficiary, the beneficiary cannot transfer his interest and the creditor is unable to reach it. Or the settlor may provide that his trust shall be "discretionary" in a technical sense, but that if a creditor seeks to obtain any interest in the property the trust shall become a spendthrift trust, and thereafter the complete or partial protection afforded by the law of the state as to spendthrift trusts is to apply.[8] Or the settlor may create a spendthrift trust with a provision that it is to change to a discretionary trust if any creditor of the

payments does not make a trust "discretionary" in the technical sense here considered. In re Nicholson's Estate, 355 Pa. 426, 50 A.2d 283, 172 A.L.R. 450 (1947).

3. Clarke v. Clarke, 246 Ala. 170, 19 So.2d 526 (1944).

See N.Car.G.S. § 36A–115(b)(1) (beneficiary's interest not alienable).

4. In re Tone's Estate, 240 Iowa 1315, 39 N.W.2d 401 (1949). Sometimes, although there is absolute discretion, the intent to furnish support to the beneficiary is found, and a decision not to pay or apply anything for his benefit is deemed an abuse of discretion and is corrected by court action. Constanza v. Verona, 48 N.J.

Super. 355, 137 A.2d 614 (1958); State v. Rubion, 158 Tex. 43, 308 S.W.2d 4 (1957).

5. Funk v. Grulke, 204 Iowa 314, 213 N.W. 608 (1927); Foster v. Foster, 133 Mass. 179; Todd's Ex'rs v. Todd, 260 Ky. 611, 86 S.W.2d 168 (1935); Calloway v. Smith, 300 Ky. 55, 186 S.W.2d 642 (1945). And see N.Car.G.S. § 36A–115(b)(1).

6. Calloway v. Smith, 300 Ky. 55, 186 S.W.2d 642 (1945).

7. In re Coleman, 39 Ch.D. 443; Canfield v. Security-First Nat. Bank, 13 Cal.2d 1, 87 P.2d 830 (1939); Hamilton v. Drogo, 241 N.Y. 401, 150 N.E. 496 (1926).

8. Canfield v. Security-First Nat. Bank, 13 Cal.2d 1, 87 P.2d 830 (1939).

beneficiary seeks to reach his interest,[9] or is to become a trust for the members of the beneficiary's family.[10] A settlor cannot create a discretionary trust for himself and thus protect his interest from creditors.[11]

 WESTLAW REFERENCES

"discretionary trust"
find 87 p2d 830

SUPPORT TRUSTS [1]

§ 42. In a trust where the trustee is directed to spend only so much of the income as is necessary for the education and maintenance of the beneficiary, and to spend the income only for those purposes, the interest of the beneficiary is neither assignable by him nor reachable by his creditors. This is because of the nature of the beneficiary's interest and not because of any direct prohibition against voluntary or involuntary alienation. Payment to a transferee or creditor would not accomplish the support or education of the beneficiary which the settlor provided every payment by the trustee must accomplish.

If a trustee is directed to spend trust income and/or principal for the benefit of a certain beneficiary, but only to the extent necessary to educate and support him, and only when the payments will accomplish those purposes, the nature of the beneficiary's interest makes it neither transferable by him nor reachable by his creditors. The trustee is directed to disburse the trust property only if his payments will achieve a certain result, namely, the education or support of the beneficiary. Paying money to an assignee of the beneficiary or to his creditors will not accomplish the education or support of the beneficiary. Therefore the nature of the trust involves a restraint on voluntary or involuntary alienation of the beneficiary's interest.[2] The beneficiary could not force the trustee to make any payment or application unless it would result in his support or education, and his creditor or transferee is in no better position. Apparently no attention is paid to the fact that the transferee or creditor may have furnished support or education to the beneficiary in the past and may be claiming reimbursement.

Such a trust should be distinguished from one where the trustee is to pay a fixed amount for the education and support of the beneficiary,

9. Duncan v. Elkins, 94 N.H. 13, 45 A.2d 297 (1946).

10. See § 44, post.

11. Greenwich Trust Co. v. Tyson, 129 Conn. 211, 27 A.2d 166 (1942).

§ 42

1. Restatement, Trusts, Second, § 154.

2. In re Keeler's Estate, 334 Pa. 225, 3 A.2d 413, 121 A.L.R. 1301 (1939); Keyser v. Mitchell, 67 Pa. 473; Seattle First Nat.

Bank v. Crosby, 42 Wn.2d 234, 254 P.2d 732 (1953). And see Jones v. Coon, 229 Iowa 756, 295 N.W. 162 (1940); 1956 Wash. U.L.Q. 106.

If the trust is a support trust until the beneficiary reaches 25, and then the principal is to be paid to him, his income rights cannot be reached by a creditor but his interest in the principal may be taken. Epstein v. Corning, 91 N.H. 474, 22 A.2d 410 (1941).

or is to pay all the income of the trust for such purposes. Technically these latter trusts are not "support" trusts since the beneficiary has a right to money which he will himself apply for his education or support. The words "education and support" in such a case are used merely to show the motive of the settlor and not to show the results which the trustee must accomplish by his payments or applications.[3] The beneficiary is entitled to the stated amount of trust property, whether it is more or less than the sum needed to support and educate him. In these trusts the beneficiary's rights may be alienated or taken by creditors unless protected by a spendthrift clause.

Decisions holding that a given trust is a technical support trust are rare.[4] There is a tendency to treat some trusts as spendthrift which might reasonably be termed support trusts.[5] In states which give unrestricted validity to spendthrift trusts, there would seem to be little need for the support trust, since the former accomplish more than the latter by way of protection; but in jurisdictions where the spendthrift trust is of limited effect, or is not permitted, the support trust may be used as a substitute.

 WESTLAW REFERENCES

"support trust"

BLENDED TRUSTS [1]

§ 43. If a trust is for the benefit of described persons as a group and no member of the group is intended to have a right to any individual benefits separate and apart from the others, then no member has an alienable interest or one which his creditors can reach.

If a trust is established for a described group of persons, for example, for the benefit of a man and his wife and children, with a direction to the trustee to pay or apply the trust income for the benefit of this group,[2] the group is the beneficiary and the interests of the members of the group are so inseparably blended that no one of them can be said to have any individual interest. Each payment or application must work a group benefit. If there are six persons in the group, it cannot be said that each one has a one-sixth interest in the trust. The whole interest is vested in the group. Here, therefore, no transfer by one of the members will give the transferee a right to any trust income

3. Meade v. Rowe's Ex'r., 298 Ky. 111, 182 S.W.2d 30 (1944); Sparhawk v. Cloon, 125 Mass. 263; Young v. Easley, 94 Va. 193, 26 S.E. 401.

4. See Matter of Dodge's Estate, 281 N.W.2d 447 (Iowa 1979). And see N.Car. G.S. § 36A–115(b)(2) (beneficiary's interest not alienable).

5. In re McGregor's Estate, 130 N.J. Eq. 5, 19 A.2d 865 (1941); Albergotti v. Summers, 203 S.C. 137, 26 S.E.2d 395 (1943).

§ 43

1. Restatement, Trusts, Second, § 161.

2. See In re McGregor's Estate, 130 N.J.Eq. 5, 19 A.2d 865 (1941).

in the hands of the trustee, and no creditor of any member can collect trust income from the trustee.[3]

Naturally if the group unites in transferring its interest, and there is no spendthrift clause, the transferee will be entitled to receive the future benefits of the trust, and if there is a creditor of the whole group he may reach the right to future income unless it is protected by a spendthrift or support clause.[4]

Decisions recognizing blended trusts are extremely rare.[5]

 WESTLAW REFERENCES

"blended trust"

PROTECTIVE TRUSTS

§ 44. **The phrase "protective trust" has been used in England to describe a trust of an ordinary type which, on attempted alienation of his interest by the beneficiary or attempted attachment by his creditors, becomes a discretionary trust to apply the income for the benefit of any one or more or all of the group consisting of the original beneficiary and his spouse and issue, or if he has no spouse or issue, for the original beneficiary and his prospective next of kin.**

If the trustee elects to use the income for the benefit of the group as such, or for the members of it other than the original beneficiary, the latter has no interest which is voluntarily or involuntarily alienable, even though, as a practical matter, he may gain advantages from the group.

The so-called "protective trust" to some extent takes the place of the spendthrift trust which is not permitted in England. In it a gift is made to a trustee to pay or apply income for the benefit of a named person until that person seeks to transfer his interest under the trust, or his creditors seek to take it, at which time the trustee is to apply the income for the maintenance and support, or otherwise for the benefit, of all or any one of a group consisting of the original beneficiary and his spouse and issue, or if he has no spouse or issue, for the original beneficiary and his prospective next of kin, during all or part of the life of the original beneficiary.[1] This is in substance an ordinary trust, determinable on attempted voluntary or involuntary alienation, with a gift over to the same trustee on a discretionary trust for application for

---

3. Bell v. Watkins, 82 Ala. 512, 1 So. 92, 60 Am.Rep. 756; Linn v. Downing, 216 Ill. 64, 74 N.E. 729; Russell v. Meyers, 202 Ky. 593, 260 S.W. 377; Talley v. Ferguson, 64 W.Va. 328, 62 S.E. 456, 17 L.R.A.,N.S., 1215.

4. Donalds v. Plumb, 8 Conn. 447; Campbell v. Brannin, 8 B.Mon., 47 Ky. 478.

5. See Bogert, Trusts and Trustees (rev. 2d edit.), § 230. King v. York Trust

Co. of York, 278 Pa. 141, 122 A. 227 (1923) (blended trust for settlor and family held valid as against his creditors). And see N.Car.G.S. § 36A–115(b)(3) (protective trust).

§ 44

1. In re Bullock, 60 L.J.Ch. 341; Scott, Protective Trusts, Harv.Legal Essays, 1934, p. 419.

the benefit of the original beneficiary and his family. By legislation [2] such a protective trust can be accomplished without giving the details of it in the trust instrument but merely by a statement that the property is given to the trustee on a protective trust for A for life or for a lesser period.[3]

The nature of the interests of the members of the group of beneficiaries as a practical matter give them protection against improvidence or misfortune. The trustee in his discretion may exclude any member of the group. It is not until the trustee has determined to apply income for a particular member that there is any interest which is alienable or subject to debts. By electing to apply the income for the living expenses of the members of the group other than the original beneficiary, benefits are apt to flow to the latter through the generosity of the other members. Thus the protective trust takes the place, at least to a certain extent, of the spendthrift trust which the English courts have not considered valid.

Protective trusts, labelled as such, have rarely been before the American courts.[4] But if a settlor desires to do so, he can provide for a shift from a spendthrift or non-spendthrift trust for an individual to a discretionary trust for a group, when there is an attempted voluntary or involuntary alienation by the original beneficiary.

 WESTLAW REFERENCES

"protective trust"

---

2. English Trustee Act, 1925, § 33.

3. For examples of their use, see In re Baring's Settlement Trusts, (1940) 1 Ch. 737; Re Hall, [1943] 2 All.Eng.R. 7453; Re Gourju, [1942] 2 All.Eng.R. 605; Re Richardson's Will Trusts, (1958), 1 All.Eng.R. 538, noted in 74 L.Q.R. 182.

4. See N.Car.G.S. § 36A–115(b)(3) (beneficiary's interest in protective trust inalienable). In re Morris' Will, 197 Misc. 322, 97 N.Y.S.2d 740 (English protective trust valid in New York as to New York realty). And see § 43, ante.

Chapter 5

THE CREATION OF PRIVATE TRUSTS—PURPOSES— RESTRICTIONS ON SETTLOR

Table of Sections

TRUSTS CLASSIFIED AS TO PURPOSE [1]

§ 45. Trusts are classified as to purpose as—

(a) Private or charitable; and

(b) Active or passive.

A private trust is for the financial benefit of identified or identifiable persons.

A charitable trust has as its object the conferring of social benefits on the public.

In an active trust the trustee has affirmative duties of management and administration.

In a passive trust the trustee is a mere holder of the legal title and has no duties of administration.

§ 45

1. Restatement, Trusts, Second, §§ 1–4, 67–73, 348. An active trust may be created for any lawful purpose. See §§ 47 and 49, post.

Private and Charitable Trusts

With respect to the purposes for which trusts may be created there are two large classes. A trust may be private in its purpose, having as its beneficiaries certain identified or identifiable persons who are to receive financial advantages from it. A trust created by a father for the benefit of his son is of this variety. Or a trust may have as its purpose the accomplishment of advantages to society.[2] Such a trust is called a public or charitable trust. If A bequeathed money to T, as trustee, to invest it and apply its income in aid of needy retired clergymen, the trust would be public or charitable. The public is to be benefited by the encouragement of religion and the relief of want through the distribution of aid to elderly, poor ministers to be selected by the trustees. The clergymen who receive money or other financial advantages are not the beneficiaries of this trust but are only the instrumentalities through which the benefits are distributed to society.

Active and Passive Trusts

Trusts are also distinguished with respect to their active or passive nature. "Where the trustee is not merely the recipient of the title for the use of the beneficiary, where he has a duty to perform in relation to the property which calls for the exercise of judgment or discretion, it is an active trust, and is not affected by the Statute of Uses."[3] On the other hand if title is vested in one as trustee for another but the settlor prescribes no duties as to management and distribution of the benefits to the beneficiaries, the trust is called "passive" because of the lack of any affirmative duties of administration.[4]

 WESTLAW REFERENCES

Private and Charitable Trusts
"private trust"
charitable public /2 trust /5 defin!

Active and Passive Trusts
"active trust" /5 defin!
"passive trust" /5 defin!

---

2. As to the purposes which equity regards as technically "charitable", see §§ 54–64, post. They are not confined to almsgiving or the relief of poverty, the meaning given by some laymen to the word "charity".

3. Webb v. Hayden, 166 Mo. 39, 48, 65 S.W. 760.

4. McGookey v. Winter, 381 Ill. 516, 46 N.E.2d 84 (1943); In re Friedheim's Estate, 344 Pa. 542, 26 A.2d 341 (1942). As to the passive trustee's law-imposed duties to protect the property and convey according to the direction of the beneficiary before the Statute of Uses, see Restatement, Trusts, Second, § 69. These duties are not placed upon the passive trustee after the adoption of the Statute.

WHEN TRUST IS PASSIVE—EFFECT OF PASSIVITY [1]

§ 46. In general a trust will be treated as active if its terms give the trustee the power and duty to perform acts of management or administration which involve discretion; and it will be treated as passive if the trustee is to perform no acts of administration at all, or only minor acts that are mechanical or formal in nature.

The English Statute of Uses attempted to abolish uses, which were equivalent to modern passive trusts, by providing that wherever uses of freeholds were created the Statute would execute the use and transfer the legal estate from the feoffee to uses to the cestui que use.

In many American states the Statute of Uses is considered a part of the common law. In other states statutes abolishing passive trusts and transferring the legal title to the beneficiary have been adopted. On one ground or another it is generally held that the creation of a passive trust of real property results in the conveyance of the legal title directly to the beneficiary. The trustee takes nothing, or if he secures a title it is immediately transferred to the beneficiary.

Although the original Statute of Uses and its successors apply to real property only, the American courts have generally held that passive trusts of personalty are executed by an automatic transfer of the title to the beneficiary, either by analogy to the Statute of Uses or because equity treats a trust without a purpose as terminable or terminated.

The following trusts are not generally treated as executed by the Statute of Uses or a similar statute, even though they are passive: trusts to preserve contingent remainders; resulting, constructive, charitable and married women's separate use trusts; and the use upon a use.

What Trusts Are Passive?

Passive trusts are also sometimes called simple,[2] dry,[3] naked,[4] formal,[5] or executed [6] trusts.

§ 46

1. Restatement, Trusts, Second, §§ 67–73.

2. Atkins v. Atkins, 70 Vt. 565, 41 A. 503.

3. Commonwealth v. Louisville Public Library, 151 Ky. 420, 152 S.W. 262.

4. Wilkinson v. May, 69 Ala. 33.

5. Dyett v. Central Trust Co., 64 Hun 635, 19 N.Y.S. 19.

6. Woodward v. Stubbs, 102 Ga. 187, 29 S.E. 119; Kronson v. Lipschitz, 68 N.J. Eq. 367, 60 A. 819; Kay v. Scates, 37 Pa. 31, 78 Am.Dec. 399. Unfortunately the term "executed trust" is also used by some courts to mean a trust completely created. Lynn v. Lynn, 135 Ill. 18, 25 N.E. 634; Gaylord v. City of Lafayette, 115 Ind. 423, 17 N.E. 899; Morris v. Linton, 74 Neb. 411, 104 N.W. 927. The confusion of terminology is increased by an occasional use of the phrase as meaning a trust fully outlined and planned by the settlor as distinguished from one where the details of administration are left to the trustee. Saunders v. Edwards, 55 N.C. 134, 2 Jones, Eq. 134.

A passive trust is one which the trustee has no duties, or only the duty to perform a mechanical or formal act as distinguished from a discretionary one. Thus where a testatrix bequeaths $50,000 to A, to be kept in trust for A by her daughter, the bequest may amount to a passive trust and A will be entitled to the payment of the legacy free from any trust.[7] And where land is conveyed to one in trust without setting out the nature of the trust,[8] or where the purpose of the original trust has already been accomplished,[9] the trust will be treated as a passive trust.

A trust to permit the beneficiary to enjoy the trust property directly, with right to possession vested in him, and with taxes and other obligations to be borne by him, is generally regarded as passive.[10] Where the trustee's only duty is to execute and deliver a deed to beneficiaries, some courts have held the trust active, whether until the date for conveyance or prior to that time,[11] but there are authorities to the contrary.[12]

A trust to pay over the gross income to the beneficiary has been regarded by some courts as passive,[13] although the duties of collection would seem important obligations. Naturally a trust to distribute net income is active, involving important duties with regard to the payment of expenses.[14] Such powers as those of sale, lease, investment and discretionary distribution of trust property naturally mark a trust as active.[15]

The Statute of Uses—Effect in the United States

The reasons for the enactment and the effect of the Statute of Uses have been previously explained.[16] It provided, in substance, that whenever any person should be seised of real property to the use of another by reason of any conveyance, the person to whom the use was given should thereafter have the legal title and the feoffee to uses should take no interest.[17] The use of that day was practically equivalent to the modern passive trust. The feoffee to uses was a mere holder of the

7. Guild v. Allen, 28 R.I. 430, 67 A. 855.

8. Brown v. Harris, 7 Tex.Civ.App. 664, 27 S.W. 45.

9. Rector v. Dalby, 98 Mo.App. 189, 71 S.W. 1078. As to the automatic or court-decreed termination of these trusts, see § 150, post.

10. Alford v. Bennett, 279 Ill. 375, 117 N.E. 89; Everts v. Everts, 80 Mich. 222, 45 N.W. 88; Verdin v. Slocum, 71 N.Y. 345; Hannig v. Mueller, 82 Wis. 235, 52 N.W. 98.

11. Appeal of Clark, 70 Conn. 195, 39 A. 155; McFall v. Kirkpatrick, 236 Ill. 281, 86 N.E. 139; Martling v. Martling, 55 N.J. Eq. 771, 39 A. 203.

12. O'Reilly v. Balkwill, 133 Colo. 474, 297 P.2d 263 (1956); Jacoby v. Jacoby, 188 N.Y. 124, 80 N.E. 676; Sheridan v. Coughlin, 352 Pa. 226, 42 A.2d 618 (1945); Strong v. Gordon, 96 Wis. 476, 71 N.W. 886.

13. Dixon v. Dixon, 123 Me. 470, 124 A. 198 (1924); Kay v. Scates, 37 Pa. 31.

14. Grossenbacher v. Spring, 108 Kan. 397, 195 P. 884.

15. Hart v. Seymour, 147 Ill. 598, 35 N.E. 246; Pugh v. Hays, 113 Mo. 424, 21 S.W. 23; In re Barnett's Appeal, 46 Pa. 392.

16. See §§ 3–5, ante.

17. St. 27 Henry VIII, c. 10, 1535. See Digby's History of the Law of Real Property, 5th Ed., p. 347.

legal title. The Statute of Uses abolished uses and rendered impossible thereafter passive trusts of freehold estates.

The Statute of Uses is regarded as a part of the common law of a majority of the American states.[18] "The Statute of Uses being in force in England when our ancestors came here, they brought it with them as an existing modification of the common law and it has always been considered a part of our law." [19]

In several states there are statutes directly abolishing passive trusts and declaring that attempts to create them result in passing the legal title directly to the beneficiary.[20]

On one ground or another, either because of the operation of the Statute of Uses or a local statute having an effect similar to that of the Statute of Uses, or because of a rule of equity that it will not permit or continue the doing of a useless thing, an attempt to create a passive trust is generally held to result either in the direct passage of the title to the trust property to the beneficiary, or in the passage of the legal estate to the trustee for an instant only, to be passed on immediately to the beneficiary.[21]

Application of the Statute of Uses

The Statute of Uses, by its express wording, is confined to real property, and in a few states it has been construed to have no applica-

18. For a collection of authorities to this effect, see Bogert, Trusts and Trustees (rev.2d edit.) § 208.

19. Marshall v. Fisk, 6 Mass. 24, 31, 4 Am.Dec. 76. And see Alford v. Bennett, 279 Ill. 375, 117 N.E. 89. In some states, although the Statute of Uses has never been in force, the result accomplished by the Statute is achieved by direct action of a court of equity, decreeing that the legal title is in the beneficiary of the passive trust. Farmers' & Merchants' Ins. Co. v. Jensen, 56 Neb. 284, 76 N.W. 1054, 44 L.R.A. 861; Helfenstine's Lessee v. Garrard, 7 Ohio 276.

In a few states the Statute of Uses is not regarded as in effect, nor is there any similar statute. Estate of Fair, 132 Cal. 523, 60 P. 442, 64 P. 1000 (attempt to create a passive trust is void); Noyes v. Noyes, 110 Vt. 511, 9 A.2d 123 (1939).

20. See, for example, West's Ann.Ind. Code 30–4–2–9. For a collection of references to such statutes, see Bogert, Trusts and Trustees (rev.2d edit.), § 206.

21. Huntington v. Spear, 131 Ala. 414, 30 So. 787; Teller v. Hill, 18 Colo.App. 509, 72 P. 811; Slater v. Rudderforth, 25 App. D.C. 497; Smith v. McWhorter, 123 Ga. 287, 51 S.E. 474, 107 Am.St.Rep. 85; Smith v. Smith, 254 Ill. 488, 98 N.E. 950; Allen v. Craft, 109 Ind. 476, 9 N.E. 919, 58 Am.Rep. 425; Commonwealth v. Louisville Public Library, 151 Ky. 420, 152 S.W. 262; Hamlin v. Mansfield, 88 Me. 131, 33 A. 788; Brown v. Reeder, 108 Md. 653, 71 A. 417; Simonds v. Simonds, 199 Mass. 552, 85 N.E. 860, 19 L.R.A.,N.S., 686; Everts v. Everts, 80 Mich. 222, 45 N.W. 88; Thompson v. Conant, 52 Minn. 208, 53 N.W. 1145; Van Vacter v. McWillie, 31 Miss. 563; Jones v. Jones, 223 Mo. 424, 123 S.W. 29, 25 L.R.A.,N.S., 424; Fellows v. Ripley, 69 N.H. 410, 45 A. 138; Melick v. Pidcock, 44 N.J.Eq. 525, 15 A. 3, 6 Am.St.Rep. 901; Jacoby v. Jacoby, 188 N.Y. 124, 80 N.E. 676; Hallyburton v. Slagle, 130 N.C. 482, 41 S.E. 877; Smith v. Security Loan & Trust Co., 8 N.D. 451, 79 N.W. 981; Fogarty v. Hunter, 83 Or. 183, 162 P. 964; In re West's Estate, 214 Pa. 35, 63 A. 407; Darling v. Witherbee, 36 R.I. 459, 90 A. 751; Breeden v. Moore, 82 S.C. 534, 64 S.E. 604; Brown v. Hall, 32 S.D. 225, 142 N.W. 854; Turley v. Massengill, 7 Lea, Tenn., 353; Henderson v. Adams, 15 Utah 30, 48 P. 398; Sims v. Sims, 94 Va. 580, 27 S.E. 436, 64 Am.St.Rep. 772; Blake v. O'Neal, 63 W.Va. 483, 61 S.E. 410, 16 L.R.A.,N.S., 1147; Holmes v. Walter, 118 Wis. 409, 95 N.W. 380, 62 L.R.A. 986.

tion to personal property.[22] But the rule of the Statute has generally been applied to personal property, on the theory that the reason of the rule was equally applicable or that equity would not keep alive a useless trust.[23]

The Statute of Uses and its American counterparts have no application to resulting [24] and constructive [25] trusts. In a few states they are held not to apply to uses created by devise.[26] It has no application to trusts to preserve contingent remainders.[27] Trusts to provide a separate estate for married women were generally excepted from the operation of the Statute of Uses prior to the passage of the Married Women's Property Acts,[28] but in states having adopted such legislation there has been a conflict on the question.[29] It has been urged that the fact that the beneficiary is a married woman, minor, or incompetent shows an implied intent to give the trustee duties of management, but in several cases this argument has been unsuccessful.[30] Charitable trusts for the public in general are not subject to the Statute,[31] probably due to the lack of any entity as a beneficiary capable of taking title; but a charitable trust for an incorporated institution or municipal corporation is subject to the Statute if passive.[32]

22. See, for example, Chicago Title & Trust Co. v. Mercantile Trust & Savings Bank, 300 Ill.App. 329, 20 N.E.2d 992 (1939); Smith v. Smith, 254 Ill. 488, 98 N.E. 950; Slevin v. Brown, 32 Mo. 176; In re Lowitz' Estate, 360 Pa. 91, 61 A.2d 342 (1948). In these states apparently a decree of the court is needed to pass the title to the personal property from the passive trustee to the beneficiary.

23. Bowman v. Long, 26 Ga. 142; Prince de Bearn v. Winans, 111 Md. 434, 74 A. 626; Reed v. Browne, 295 N.Y. 184, 66 N.E.2d 47, 165 A.L.R. 1061 (1946). And see Bellows v. Page, 88 N.H. 283, 188 A. 12; Security National Bank v. Sternberger, 207 N.C. 811, 178 S.E. 595, 97 A.L.R. 720; McDowell v. Rees, 22 Tenn.App. 336, 122 S.W.2d 839 (1938).

Where under a land trust the beneficiary has power to manage the trust real property and to direct the trustee to sell, the trust will not be executed to defeat the trustee's title. West's Ann.Ind.Code 30–4–2–9.

The Statute of Uses did not operate to vest title to trust real estate in the beneficiary of the land trust. His equitable interest was personal property and the trustee was given active duties to deal with the title to all real estate upon the direction of the beneficiary and to sell real property remaining in the trust at its direction. Chicago Title & Trust Co. v. Mercantile Trust & Savings Bank, 300 Ill.App. 329, 20 N.E.2d 992 (1939).

24. Moore v. Spellman, 5 Denio 225; Strimpfler v. Roberts, 18 Pa. 283, 57 Am. Dec. 606. The statutes reenacting the Statute of Uses generally except resulting and constructive trusts.

25. Zimmerman v. Kennedy, 405 Ill. 306, 90 N.E.2d 756 (1950).

26. Bass v. Scott, 2 Leigh, Va., 356; Blake v. O'Neal, 63 W.Va. 483, 61 S.E. 410, 16 L.R.A.,N.S., 1147. But see, *contra*, Restatement, Trusts, Second, § 72.

27. Vanderheyden v. Crandall, 2 Denio, N.Y., 9; Kay v. Scates, 37 Pa. 31, 78 Am.Dec. 399.

28. Richardson v. Stodder, 100 Mass. 528; Walton v. Drumtra, 152 Mo. 489, 54 S.W. 233.

29. Statute not applicable; Bailey v. Nave, 329 Ill. 235, 160 N.E. 605 (1928). Statute applicable: Smith v. McWhorter, 123 Ga. 287, 51 S.E. 474; Allen v. Craft, 109 Ind. 476, 9 N.E. 919.

30. Burnham v. Baltimore Gas & Elec. Co., 217 Md. 507, 144 A.2d 80 (1958); Phillips v. Gilbert, 248 N.C. 183, 102 S.E.2d 771 (1958) (incompetent son); Pilkington v. West, 246 N.C. 575, 99 S.E.2d 798 (1957) (married woman).

31. Huger v. Protestant Episcopal Church, 137 Ga. 205, 73 S.E. 385; In re Stewart's Estate, 26 Wash. 32, 66 P. 148, 67 P. 723.

32. Schenectady Dutch Church v. Veeder, 4 Wend., N.Y., 494; Commonwealth v. First Nat. Bank, 46 Pa.D. & C. 619.

WESTLAW REFERENCES

What Trusts are Passive?
390k136
di(dry simple naked formal /4 trust)

The Statute of Uses—Effect in the United States
"passive trust" /s "statute of uses"
390k136 /p "statute of uses"

Application of the Statute of Uses
"statute of uses" /s "personal property"
390k131
"married women's property act"

ACTIVE PRIVATE TRUSTS—POSSIBLE AND COMMON PURPOSES [1]

§ 47. Private trusts in real and personal property may be created for any purpose which is not against the law or public policy.

The most common trust purpose is the management, conservation, and distribution of property for the benefit of the settlor and/or his relatives.

In addition, trusts serve many business purposes, for example, securing or paying creditors of the settlor, assisting in the management and sale of real estate, facilitating the sale of investments in securities, providing a means of operating businesses, and liquidating the affairs of insolvent corporations.

Trusts are often used in the management and distribution of property for the primary purpose of minimizing income, estate, inheritance, and gift taxation.

For What Purposes May a Private Trust Be Created?

A private trust may be created for any purpose which does not contravene the common law or some federal or state statute [2] or public policy.[3] Numerous examples of trusts for illegal purposes are given in a later section.[4]

Naturally the purpose for which the trust is founded must be certain. A trust instrument which is indefinite as to its objectives can no more be enforced than an indefinite contract.[5] But the trust instrument need not provide for every possible contingency.[6]

§ 47

1. Restatement, Trusts, Second, § 59.

2. A trust designed to carry out a void act of a legislature has an invalid purpose. Disston v. Board of Trustees of Internal Improvement Fund, 75 Fla. 653, 79 So. 295.

3. A trust having the object of suppressing a criminal prosecution is void. Bettinger v. Bridenbecker, 63 Barb., N.Y., 395.

4. See § 48, post.

5. Angus v. Noble, 73 Conn. 56, 46 A. 278; Sheedy v. Roach, 124 Mass. 472, 26 Am.Rep. 680; Gueutal v. Gueutal, 113 App.Div. 310, 98 N.Y.S. 1002.

6. In re Hoffman's Will, 201 N.Y. 247, 94 N.E. 990.

For What Purposes Are Private Trusts Usually Created?

The most common purpose of an express private trust is the distribution of an estate among the members of the owner's family and his friends, with provisions for collection and payment of income to life or term beneficiaries, conservation of the principal of the trust, and the ultimate transfer of the principal to relatives, friends, or charity. This is sometimes called a "family trust".[7] It is often established by will, but frequently created by deed during the property owner's life, the former being called a testamentary trust and the latter a "living trust".[8] Frequently the settlor is himself the sole beneficiary or one of the income beneficiaries of the living trust during his lifetime.

Other common purposes of private trusts include: (1) the management of the settlor's property for him, with the consequent escape from business problems and responsibilities;[9] (2) the protection of the beneficiaries against misfortune or wastefulness, with the use of a spendthrift clause which could not be attached in the case of a gift of the legal interest;[10] (3) securing the custody and preservation of insurance during the life of the insured and the collection and investment of the proceeds on maturity of the policies;[11] (4) furnishing security to lenders, as in the case of the "corporate trusts" where the trustee holds a mortgage for the benefit of bondholders;[12] (5) paying creditors of the settlor, as in the case of an assignment for their benefit made to a trustee,[13] or in the case of an insolvent corporation, where the corporate property is vested in a liquidating trustee for the purpose of enabling him to conserve, sell, and distribute to creditors who hold certificates of beneficial interest;[14] (6) trusts as an adjunct to the marketing of investments, as where there is an investment trust of securities or of real estate and shares in this trust are sold to the investing public,[15] or

---

7. See Sturman, Importance of the Family Trust, 17 The Practical Lawyer 69; Breckinridge, The Family Trust, 28 Ill.L.R. 1062; Budner, Some Basic Reasons for the Use of Trusts, 110 Trusts & Estates 346.

8. See MacLeod, Living Trust Agreements, 106 Trusts & Estates 1105; Goff, Living Trusts, 18 Ohio L.R. 353.

9. Eipper v. Benner, 113 Mich. 75, 71 N.W. 511.

10. See § 40, ante.

11. Gordon v. Portland Trust Bank, 201 Or. 648, 271 P.2d 653 (1954). See Phillips, Life Insurance Trusts, a Recapitulation for the Draftsman, 81 U.Pa.L.R. 284, 408. Books on insurance trusts have been published by Horton, Scully, and Shattuck. See also Bogert, Trusts and Trustees (rev. 2d edit.), §§ 235–245.

12. See Davis, Corporate Trusts; Bogert, Trusts and Trustees (rev. 2d edit.), §§ 250–251; Chicago Title & Trust Co. v. Rogers Park Apts. Bldg. Corp., 375 Ill. 599, 32 N.E.2d 137 (1941).

In many states a "trust deed" for security purposes takes the place of the common law mortgage. As to its relationship to the ordinary trust, see Bogert, Trusts and Trustees (rev. 2d edit.), § 29, and First Nat. Bank of Atlanta v. Southern Cotton Oil Co., 78 F.2d 339 (5th Cir.1935); Touli v. Santa Cruz County Title Co., 20 Cal.App.2d 495, 67 P.2d 404 (1937); Kidd, Trust Deed and Mortgages in California, 3 Cal.L.R. 381.

13. International Brown Drilling Corp. v. Ferguson Trucking Co., Inc., 141 Colo. 250, 347 P.2d 773 (1959).

14. See Bogert, Trusts and Trustees (rev. 2d edit.), § 2534; Cronheim v. Tennant, 30 N.J. 360, 153 A.2d 22 (1959).

15. See Bogert, Trusts and Trustees (rev. 2d edit.), § 249; Lutz v. Boas, 39 Del. Ch. 585, 171 A.2d 381 (1961) (duties of managers of mutual fund). By P.L. 86–779, a Real Investment Trust Act was adopted by Congress in 1960 and similar state statutes have also been passed. See

where there is a "land trust" and the purchase and development of the realty is obtained by the sale of certificates of interest in the realty; [16] (7) the "subdivision trust", where a tract is purchased and held for sale for the benefit of those who furnish capital and are reimbursed as lots are sold; [17] (8) the voting trust, where corporate shares are placed in a trust by several stockholders so that they can be voted for desired corporate management and development purposes; [18] (9) the so-called "Massachusetts" or "business" trust, where the assets of a business enterprise are transferred to a trustee for the purpose of having him manage and develop it, in which case the trust takes the place of a corporation and the trustees are similar to directors and officers and the beneficiaries to corporate shareholders; [19] (10) a trust to carry on the business of a decedent, either indefinitely for profit or to wind up the enterprise and pay off creditors and legatees; [20] (11) pension or profit sharing trusts for employees of a corporation, the fund being raised by contributions of the employer and sometimes its employees, where the objectives are retirement income and disability or death benefits, and occasionally stock purchase rights; [21] (12) trusts created by court decree in order to work out a result which litigation shows to be desirable; [22] (13) trusts created by a legislature in order to achieve a purpose which is deemed to be in the public interest; [23] (14) trusts which are created for a wife or children incident to a separation of husband and wife or pursuant to a divorce decree.[24]

26 U.S.C.A. § 856 et seq.; N.Y.—McKinney's Real Prop.Law § 96(7).

And see Robinson, Investment Trust Organization and Management; Steiner, Investment Trusts; Iowa-Des Moines Nat. Bank & Trust Co. v. Dietz, 225 Iowa 566, 281 N.W. 134 (1938).

16. Horney v. Hayes, 11 Ill.2d 178, 142 N.E.2d 94 (1957); Davis v. Fraser, 307 N.Y. 433, 121 N.E.2d 406 (1954), reargument denied 308 N.Y. 736, 124 N.E.2d 716 (1954).

17. Lane Title & Trust Co. v. Brannan, 103 Ariz. 272, 440 P.2d 105 (1968); Ditis v. Ahlvin Construction Co., 408 Ill. 416, 97 N.E.2d 244 (1951); Bogert, Trusts and Trustees (rev. 2d edit.), § 249. See MacChesney, Practical Real Estate Law; Bingham & Andrews, Financing Real Estate; Piff v. Berresheim, 405 Ill. 617, 92 N.E.2d 113 (1950); Cleveland Trust Co. v. Commissioner, 115 F.2d 481 (6th Cir.1940), certiorari denied 312 U.S. 704, 61 S.Ct. 809, 85 L.Ed. 1137 (1941).

18. Smith v. Biggs Boiler Works Co., 33 Del.Ch. 183, 91 A.2d 193 (1952); Bogert, Trusts and Trustees (rev. 2d edit.), § 252. See Cushing, Voting Trusts; Wool Growers Serv. Corp. v. Ragan, 18 Wn.2d 655, 140 P.2d 512 (1943), rehearing denied 18 Wn.2d 655, 141 P.2d 875 (1943).

19. See Sears, Trust Estates as Business Companies, 2d Ed.; Dunn, Business Trusts; Bogert, Trusts and Trustees (rev. 2d edit.), § 247. For a comparison of express trusts and corporations as business organizations, see Wilgus, 13 Mich.Law Rev. 71, 205.

20. In re Ginter's Estate, 398 Pa. 440, 158 A.2d 789 (1960); Bogert, Trusts and Trustees (rev. 2d edit.), § 571 et seq.

21. George v. Haber, 343 Mich. 218, 72 N.W.2d 121 (1955); Bogert, Trusts and Trustees (rev. 2d edit.), § 255. These trusts are given tax advantages under the Internal Revenue Code and under some state tax statutes. They are also frequently exempted from rules regarding accumulations and perpetuities.

22. See Allen v. Burkhiser, 125 N.J. Eq. 524, 6 A.2d 656 (1939) (to conserve estate pending contingencies).

23. Visser v. Koenders, 6 Wis.2d 535, 95 N.W.2d 363 (1959). For examples, see Bogert, Trusts and Trustees (rev. 2d edit.), § 246.

24. Leighton v. Leighton, 91 Me. 593, 40 A. 671. Bogert, Trusts and Trustees (rev. 2d edit.), §§ 234, 246.

In deciding whether and how to create a trust, tax considerations are very important. A primary object of many trusts is to minimize or avoid income, estate, inheritance, and gift taxes.[25] The subject of "estate planning" has become of increasing importance.[26]

A large amount of life insurance is held in trust under so-called "insurance trusts." If the insured makes a trustee the beneficiary of the policy but transfers no fund to meet the premiums on the policy, the trust is called "unfunded"; whereas if the settlor-insured not only makes the policy payable to a trustee, but also transfers to the trustee bonds or stocks yielding income from which the trustee will be able to meet the premiums on the policy as they become due, the trust is referred to as "funded". Trusts of insurance for the benefit of relatives of the settlor are called "personal" insurance trusts, while those connected with the operation of partnerships and corporations are called "business" insurance trusts.[27] Due to the fact that insurance payable to another than the executor or administrator of the insured is generally not subject to the debts of the insured,[28] and may be exempt from estate or inheritance taxes in the estate of the insured,[29] there are practical advantages in the creation of insurance trusts beyond the ordinary benefits which come from insurance.

 WESTLAW REFERENCES

For What Purposes May a Private Trust be Created?

"private trust" /4 purpose

For What Purposes Are Private Trusts Usually Created?

"family trust"

"living trust"

"corporate trust"

"subdivision trust"

di("voting trust")

"massachusetts trust"

"business trust"

di("insurance trust")

funded unfunded /1 trust

---

25. See Bogert, Trusts and Trustees (rev. 2d edit.), ch. 15.

26. See Robinson, Saving Taxes in Drafting Wills and Trusts, 2d Ed.; Bogert, Trusts and Trustees (rev. 2d edit.), §§ 231–255, 261–287, 291–301; Shattuck, An Estate Planner's Handbook; Nossaman and Wyatt, Trust Administration and Taxation (2d Edit.Rev.); Rollison, Cases and Materials on Estate Planning; Casner, Estate Planning.

27. For discussions, see Horton, Some Legal Aspects of Insurance Trusts; Shat-tuck, Living Insurance Trusts; Hanna, Some Legal Aspects of Life Insurance Trusts, 78 Pa.L.R. 346; Fraser, Personal Life Insurance Trusts, 16 Cornell L.Q. 19; Bogert, Trusts and Trustees (rev. 2d edit.), §§ 235–244, 253, 264.15.

28. See Bogert, Trusts and Trustees (rev. 2d edit.), §§ 243, 264.15.

29. See Bogert, Trusts and Trustees (rev. 2d edit.), §§ 241, 264.15, 273.40, 286.

ACTIVE TRUSTS—ILLEGAL PURPOSES [1]

§ 48. **Examples of trusts with illegal purposes are found where the object is to defraud creditors of the settlor or to deprive his spouse of marital rights, or to encourage immorality or the violation or evasion of a statute, or to secure results which are contrary to public policy.**

A party injured by an illegal trust may have it set aside, as in the case of a trust to defraud creditors.

If the validity of a trust with an illegal object is not attacked by the injured person, and there are innocent beneficiaries of the trust, they may secure its enforcement, if such relief does not accomplish the illegal objectives of the settlor.

Generally a beneficiary of an illegal trust cannot enforce it, where a decree in his favor would mean achieving the illegal objectives of the settlor.

Usually the settlor of an illegal trust is not allowed to recover the trust property from the trustee, either as beneficiary or on the theory of failure of the illegal trust, since the settlor does not come into court with clean hands and equity discourages others from entering into similar transactions.

In some cases, however, equity has returned the property to the settlor where it found that he was guilty of less reprehensible conduct than the trustee, or where no harm to third persons has happened or could happen. In a few cases, innocent successors of the settlor by intestacy or will have been allowed to recover the trust property, even though their predecessor could not have done so.

If a trust has both legal and illegal objectives, it is a question of construction whether the two are inseparably connected so that the illegal cannot be stricken and the legal provisions enforced without doing violence to the settlor's primary intentions.

Illegal conditions precedent and subsequent attached to a beneficiary's interest are declared void and the trust is enforced without the objectionable clauses.

Examples of Illegal Trust Purposes

The most common type of a trust for an illegal purpose is that where the settlor transferred property to a trustee to hold for the settlor or others so as to prevent creditors of the settlor from collecting their claims out of the property.[2] In other cases the illegality consisted

§ 48

1. Restatement, Trusts, Second, §§ 60–65, 422.

2. Pattison v. Pattison, 301 N.Y. 65, 92 N.E.2d 890 (1950). For general treatment of the subject, see Bump, Fraudulent Conveyances; Glenn, Creditors' Rights and Remedies, and The Law of Fraudulent Conveyances. And see the Uniform Fraudulent Conveyances Act and other statutes referred to in Bogert, Trusts and Trustees (rev. 2d edit.), § 211.

By statute in some states it is provided that a settlor retaining the absolute power of revocation is to be deemed the absolute owner of the trust assets as to his creditors.

of a transfer by a husband or wife in order to prevent his or her spouse from acquiring marital property rights such as a statutory share or dower or curtesy in property, where there was a justifiable expectation on the part of the spouse that one or more marital rights would be obtained.[3]

Obviously if the purpose of the trust is to secure for the settlor immoral sexual relations with the beneficiary,[4] or to encourage evasion or violation of a statute,[5] the trust is for an illegal purpose; and the same is true where the purpose is to accomplish other objectives contrary to public policy.[6]

See, for example, Ala.Code § 35–4–290; West's Ann.Ind.Code 30–1–9–14; Kan.Stat. Ann. § 58–2414. And see § 148, post.

3. In several states there are statutes to the effect that a revocable trust (including a Totten trust) will be treated as a testamentary disposition insofar as the statutory rights of a surviving spouse are concerned. N.Y.—McKinney's EPTL § 5–1.1(b)(1); 20 Pa.C.S.A. § 2203. To the same effect see Unif.Prob.Code § 2–202, substantially adopted in Alaska, Colo., Idaho, Me., Minn., Mont., Neb., N.J., N.Dak., S.Dak., and Utah. See Statutory Note to Restatement, Property, Second, § 13.7. And see 39 A.L.R.3d at p. 14; 49 A.L.R.3rd 521; 64 A.L.R.3rd 187.

The rules in § 13.7, Restatement, Property, Second, treat a power to revoke as a general power of appointment and permit the appointive assets to be treated as owned assets of the deceased settlor-donee in determining the rights of the donee's surviving spouse where the power was exercisable by the settlor alone. The section appears to follow Sullivan v. Burkin, 390 Mass. 864, 460 N.E.2d 572 (1984).

In states where no statute specifically covers the matter, courts have reached differing conclusions. See, for example, the following:

Revocable trust found to be a *fraud* on marital rights *or a testamentary disposition,* so that trust assets are subject to the statutory rights of the surviving spouse: See, for example, Sullivan v. Burkin, 390 Mass. 864, 460 N.E.2d 572 (1984) (post Jan. 23, 1984); In re Estate of Collins, 84 Cal. App.3d 928, 149 Cal.Rptr. 65 (1978); Ackers v. First Nat. Bank of Topeka, 192 Kan. 319, 387 P.2d 840 (1963) opinion clarified; rehearing denied 192 Kan. 471, 389 P.2d 1 (1964); Sherrill v. Mallicote, 57 Tenn.App. 241, 417 S.W.2d 798 (1967).

Revocable trust assets *not included* in decedent's estate for purposes of determining statutory rights of surviving spouse: See, for example, Johnson v. LaGrange State Bank, 73 Ill.2d 342, 22 Ill.Dec. 709, 383 N.E.2d 185 (1978) (other than Totten trust assets); Leazenby v. Clinton County Bank & Trust Co., 171 Ind.App. 243, 355 N.E.2d 861 (1976); Horn v. First Security Bank of Utah, 548 P.2d 1265 (Utah 1976).

And compare Restatement, Trusts, Second, § 57, Comment e (surviving spouse not entitled) with Restatement, Property, Second, § 13.7 (revocable trust assets subject to statutory rights of surviving spouse).

Where the surviving spouse is not made the beneficiary, a Totten or savings account trust is included in the estate of the deceased donor-spouse in determining the statutory rights of the surviving spouse, whether by statute or by court decision. See, for example, Montgomery v. Michaels, 54 Ill.2d 532, 301 N.E.2d 465 (1973); Mushaw v. Mushaw, 183 Md. 511, 39 A.2d 465 (1944).

For references to other cases, see Bogert, Trusts and Trustees (rev. 2d edit.), §§ 211, 233; Restatement, Property, Second, Reporter's Note to § 13.7.

4. Dannells v. United States Nat. Bank of Portland, 172 Or. 213, 138 P.2d 220 (1943).

5. Dunn v. Dunn, 1 A.D.2d 888, 149 N.Y.S.2d 351 (1956) (procure veteran's loan unlawfully); Caldwell v. Tucker, 246 S.W.2d 923 (Tex.Civ.App.1952) (old age pension). In re Robbins' Estate, Cal.App., 16 Cal.Rptr. 412, a trust to aid minor Negro children whose parents had been imprisoned as a result of conviction of a political crime was held void because it encouraged violation of the law; but the Supreme Court reversed this judgment by a vote of four to three. 57 Cal.2d 718, 21 Cal.Rptr. 797, 371 P.2d 573 (1962).

6. Woodall v. Peden, 27 Ill. 301, 113 N.E. 608 (obstruction of criminal prosecution); Giddings v. Giddings, 167 Or. 504, 114 P.2d 1009 (to bring about collusive divorce).

In the case of mutual benefit insurance issued by fraternal and similar orders, legislation authorizing the insurance often provides that it may be issued only in favor of described close relatives of the insured. In a few instances the insured has had the policy issued to a relative within the permitted class, on an understanding that the benefits are to be passed on to persons outside the permitted class. It would seem here that there is an attempt to secure evasion of a civil statute, although the policy behind it is perhaps not very important and the creation of the trust is not a serious wrong. Some courts have refused to enforce a trust for the beneficiary,[7] while others have given relief in cases where the next of kin of the insured raised no objection or urged a decree for the beneficiary.[8]

Effect of Illegal Trust Purpose

If the illegal trust is attacked by a person injured thereby, the court will set it aside, as in the case of trusts to hinder or defraud creditors, where the creditor may obtain a decree that the trust is void and the property still belongs to the settlor,[9] or in the case of an illegal trust for an alien, set up in violation of statute, where the state may attack the transaction.[10]

If the injured persons, however, do not attack the trust created for the benefit of innocent persons, and their claims can be enforced without enabling them to profit from the illegality, the court will grant them performance of the trust. For example, where a property owner transfers his assets in trust for his children in order to keep the property away from his creditors, but the creditors never attack the trust, and the trustee then refuses to give the benefits of the property to the children, the children should be able to secure enforcement if they had no part in the creation of the trust.[11]

If, however, suit is brought by a beneficiary of the illegal trust, and granting him enforcement would advance the accomplishment of the unlawful objectives of the settlor, then equity generally refuses relief.[12] The clean hands doctrine may be held applicable; equity refuses to be a party to achieving an illegal purpose, and the court leaves the parties to

---

7. Gillam v. Dale, 69 Kan. 362, 76 P. 861; O'Brien v. Mass. Catholic Order of Foresters, 220 Mass. 79, 107 N.E. 400. And see Jones v. United States, 61 F.Supp. 406 (D.Mass.1945) (war risk insurance).

8. Clark v. Callahan, 105 Md. 600, 66 A. 618, 10 L.R.A.,N.S., 616; Kerr v. Crane, 212 Mass. 224, 98 N.E. 783.

9. Brundage v. Cheneworth, 101 Iowa 256, 70 N.W. 211, 63 Am.St.Rep. 382; Branchfield v. McCulley, 192 Or. 270, 231 P.2d 771 (1951), rehearing denied 192 Or. 270, 235 P.2d 334 (1951). The trustee may not attack the trust as fraudulent regarding creditors. Henderson v. Segars, 28 Ala. 352.

10. Osterman v. Baldwin, 73 (6 Wall.) 116, 18 L.Ed. 730 (1867); Vlahos v. Andrews, 362 Ill. 593, 1 N.E.2d 59 (1936); Faulk v. Rosecrans, 264 P.2d 300 (Okl. 1953) (state may attack trust which had object of illegally qualifying for old age assistance).

11. Thompson v. Finholm, Sup., 77 N.Y.S.2d 78 (1948), affirmed 274 App.Div. 992, 85 N.Y.S.2d 314 (1948).

12. Pace v. Wainwright, 243 Ala. 501, 10 So.2d 755 (1942); In re Xydias' Estate, 92 Cal.App.2d 857, 208 P.2d 378 (1949); Murphy v. Murphy, 308 Ky. 194, 213 S.W.2d 601 (1948).

the tainted transaction where they are, in order to discourage others from entering into similar schemes. Thus if a debtor transferred property to a trustee in order to keep it away from creditors, with an understanding that the trustee should give income and ultimately the principal to the settlor as beneficiary, with a few possible exceptions noted below the courts turn a deaf ear to the settlor-beneficiary who seeks a decree against his trustee.[13]

Nor is the settlor in any better position if he sues on the theory of a resulting trust for him upon the failure of the express illegal trust.[14] The same arguments usually influence the court to deny him relief. The same problem arises in connection with the purchase money resulting trust, discussed in a later section, where A pays for land and has the deed run to B with the intent to defraud A's creditors and to secure the return of the property later; similar treatment is accorded A by the courts.[15]

In some cases, however, the courts have been inclined to make exceptions to the general rule noted above. One of these is illustrated by the doctrine of *"pari delictu"* or equal guilt. If the trustee who was supposed to hold for the settlor for the illegal purpose is considered by the court to be much more blameworthy than the settlor, the court may be induced to grant relief to the settlor.[16] Thus if an uneducated, ignorant debtor is induced by the solicitations of a business man of experience and skill to put his property into the hands of the latter, to hold for the former, in order that creditors of the former may be prevented from collecting, and the plan originated in the mind of the trustee, and especially if he made false statements in order to secure the deed, equity may well regard the trustee as having committed a greater fault than the settlor and may decree an enforcement of the trust for the settlor, assuming the creditors have not attacked it.[17]

Again, in some cases where it was sought to defraud creditors by creating a trust for the debtor, it may be that there were no debts, or the debts were paid from other assets of the debtor or by the aid of friends, or that the property conveyed was not available for the collection of debts, so that no creditor of the settlor suffered loss by reason of the establishment of the trust. Here some courts have been inclined to decree a return of the property to the settlor.[18] They apparently consider an unsuccessful attempt to defraud creditors as not highly

13. In re Durham's Estate, 108 Cal. App.2d 148, 238 P.2d 1057 (1951); Scott v. Sites, 41 So.2d 444 (Fla.1949).

14. Fisher v. Keeler, 142 Neb. 728, 7 N.W.2d 659 (1943); Smart v. Baroni, 360 Pa. 296, 61 A.2d 860 (1948). See § 75, post.

15. See § 74, post.

16. Gray v. Gray, 246 Ala. 627, 22 So. 2d 21 (1945); Coleman v. Coleman, 48 Ariz. 337, 61 P.2d 441, 106 A.L.R. 1309 (1936); Fischer v. Ostby, 127 Cal.App.2d 528, 274 P.2d 221 (1954).

17. Carpenter v. Arnett, 265 Ky. 246, 96 S.W.2d 693 (1936).

18. Berniker v. Berniker, Cal.App., 174 P.2d 668 (1946), affirmed 30 Cal.2d 439, 182 P.2d 557 (1947); Cook v. Mason, 353 Mo. 993, 185 S.W.2d 793, 157 A.L.R. 942 (1945); Zak v. Zak, 305 Mass. 194, 25 N.E.2d 169 (1940); Hanscom v. Hanscom, 186 Or. 541, 208 P.2d 330 (1949); Wantulok v. Wantulok, 67 Wyo. 22, 214 P.2d 477 (1950), rehearing denied 67 Wyo. 22, 223 P.2d 1030 (1950).

blameworthy, or possibly regard the fault as cured by later repentance; or possibly the courts are influenced by a desire to prevent a windfall to the trustee. They are more concerned with the equities of the particular case than with establishing a policy that will deter other fraudulently minded persons from setting up similar trusts.

But other courts, and it would appear with better reason, decline to give relief to the unsuccessful debtor.[19] They regard his intent as just as blameworthy as that of the successful defrauder. They are convinced that the deterrent effect of the rule is more important than attempting to do equity in the particular case, and that there will be deterrence to fraudulently minded debtors if they know that they can secure no relief under such trusts, whether any harm comes to creditors or not. To tell the debtor that he can get his property back if no harm comes to any creditor is to insure him some advantage from such a trust. If creditors are cheated, he has the satisfaction of bringing that about, even though it does not give him any financial gain, and he has the possibility of getting the property back after the storm has blown over, if the trustee does not set up the illegality. And if no harm results to creditors he is just as well off as he was before he made the attempt.[20]

A few courts have given special consideration to innocent successors of the fraudulently minded settlor, for example, his executor or administrator, or his heirs, next of kin, or takers under his will.[21] Certainly no blame attaches to such persons and it can be argued that they ought not to be visited with the sins of their predecessor. If, however, the rule is considered primarily as one to deter wrongdoing and not to adjust the rights of the parties after attempted or accomplished unlawful conduct, it would seem that strict adherence would require a refusal of relief to innocent successors.

If the trust instrument has but one purpose and that purpose is invalid, it is obvious that the entire trust must fall. But in many instances a trust has several purposes. If one of these purposes is valid and the others invalid, will the entire trust fail? The answer depends upon whether the purposes are separable or are inextricably connected. If the valid purpose is independent of the invalid, if the two can be separated and the valid enforced without doing violence to the settlor's main intent, then the valid purpose may be enforced and the invalid stricken.[22] But if, on the other hand, the valid purpose and the invalid purpose are so connected that to enforce one without enforcing the

19. In re Great Berlin Steamboat Co., 26 Ch.D. 616; Menard v. Menard, 295 Mich. 80, 294 N.W. 106 (1940); Pattison v. Pattison, 301 N.Y. 65, 92 N.E.2d 890 (1950).

20. See the excellent discussion by Lockwood, C.J., in MacRae v. MacRae, 37 Ariz. 307, 294 P. 280 (1930).

21. Hurwitz v. Hurwitz, 78 U.S.App. D.C. 66, 136 F.2d 796, 148 A.L.R. 226 (1943); Finnegan v. La Fontaine, 122 Conn. 561, 191 A. 337 (1937). But see, *contra*, Patterson v. Koerner, 220 Miss. 590, 71 So. 2d 464 (1954); Loe v. Downing, Mo., 325 S.W.2d 479 (1959).

22. Younger v. Moore, 155 Cal. 767, 103 P. 221; Amory v. Trustees of Amherst College, 229 Mass. 374, 118 N.E. 933; Culross v. Gibbons, 130 N.Y. 447, 29 N.E. 839; Appeal of Ingersoll, 86 Pa. 240.

other would doubtless produce a result at variance with the settlor's principal objectives, then the entire trust must be declared void because of its partial invalidity.[23]

The settlor may attach to the gift of the equitable interest a condition precedent, so that the gift is not to take effect unless a certain event happens, or a condition subsequent that if a certain event occurs the interest of the beneficiary is to be reduced or forfeited entirely. For example, the instrument may provide that a son of the settlor is to become a beneficiary if he secures a divorce from his present wife, or that an unmarried son is to lose his interest under the trust if he marries a person of a certain race or religion.

These conditions are enforced only if they are not contrary to public policy, and they are declared illegal if deemed against the public interest. When they are decreed to be illegal the gift takes effect without regard to them, that is, the donee takes a present interest notwithstanding the fact that the condition precedent has not happened, or takes an absolute interest even though the condition subsequent has occurred.[24]

As illustrative of conditions which may be held void as against public policy it should be noted that the common law has a well-defined interest in preserving freedom of marriage and of religion, and in the preservation of the family relation.[25] Hence provisions in trust instruments which provide that a beneficiary shall have no interest under the trust unless he obeys the instructions of the settlor regarding marriage [26] or unless he adopts a certain religion,[27] or unless he divorces his wife,[28] may be held illegal as against public policy.

Questions of conflict of laws may become involved when the validity of a trust is being determined. The settlor may have been domiciled in one state, the trustee may be doing business in a second state, the instrument may have been executed in a third state, and the trust property may have been located in a fourth state. The laws of these states may differ as to whether or when a trust is illegal and what the effect of illegality is. Such problems are dealt with under the heading

---

23. Hofsas v. Cummings, 141 Cal. 525, 75 P. 110; Kelly v. Nichols, 17 R.I. 306, 21 A. 906.

24. Winterland v. Winterland, 389 Ill. 384, 59 N.E.2d 661 (1945); Fleishman v. Bregel, 174 Md. 87, 197 A. 593 (1938).

25. Girard Trust Co. v. Schmitz, 129 N.J.Eq. 444, 20 A.2d 21 (1941) (donee to have no social relations with close relatives).

26. In re Liberman, 279 N.Y. 458, 18 N.E.2d 658, 122 A.L.R. 1 (1939). But see In re Rosenthal's Estate, 204 Misc. 432, 123 N.Y.S.2d 326 (1953), order reversed 283 App.Div. 316, 127 N.Y.S.2d 778 (1954), appellate order affirmed 307 N.Y. 715, 121 N.E.2d 539 (1954) (condition against marriage to a gentile not applicable).

27. In re Devlin's Trust Estate, 284 Pa. 11, 130 A. 238 (1925). But see United States Nat. Bank v. Snodgrass, 202 Or. 530, 275 P.2d 860 (1954) (condition against embracing named religion or marrying person of that religion held valid); In re James' Estate, 273 Wis. 50, 76 N.W.2d 553 (1956) (condition subsequent against raising children in certain faith held valid). See Crane, 6 Hast.L.J. 351.

28. Winterland v. Winterland, 389 Ill. 384, 59 N.E.2d 661 (1945); Dwyer v. Kuchler, 116 N.J.Eq. 426, 174 A. 154 (1934).

of trusts and problems of conflict of laws.[29]

 WESTLAW REFERENCES

Examples of Illegal Purposes
find 92 ne2d 890
186k298(1)
trust /s defraud /s creditor
trust /s immoral /2 purpose
trust /s illegal /2 purpose

Effect of Illegal Trust Purpose
illegal /2 trust /4 (set +2 aside) void
"illegal trust" /5 beneficiary
trust /s void /s "public policy"
find 213 so2d 316

ACTIVE TRUSTS—STATUTORY RESTRICTIONS ON TRUST PURPOSES

§ 49. **In a few states early legislation limited the purposes for which trusts of realty could be created, but these restrictions have been removed. In Georgia trust purposes in the case of trusts of any kind of property had been limited to the protection of minors, mentally incompetents, and persons of bad habits, and to the improvement of the trust property.**

While an attempt to create a trust of real property in these states for a purpose not named in the statute did not result in the creation of a trust, the instrument was enforced as a power in trust if otherwise lawful.

These statutes placed no limitation on the purposes for which trusts of personal property could be created.

In all states a trust may now be created for any lawful purpose.

In New York, in an early revision of the statutes, the legislature limited the purposes for which express trusts of realty could be established to four, and this system was followed in California, Montana, North Dakota, Oklahoma and South Dakota.[1] By later statutes the restriction was abandoned in these states.[2] The theory of the founders of this system was that all trusts, except those involving active administration and requiring the holding of the legal title, should be abolished

---

29. See Bogert, Trusts and Trustees (rev. 2d edit.), ch. 16; Restatement, Conflict of Laws, Second, Chap. 10 (Trusts); Beale, 45 Harv.L.Rev. 969; Cavers, 44 Harv.L.Rev. 161; Swabenland, 45 Yale L.J. 438; Scott, 99 Tr. & Est. 186; Leflar, 37 Tr. Bull. 55.

§ 49

1. N.Y.Real Prop.L. §§ 91, 96. The statutes of five other states had provisions very similar to those of the 1830 New York statute. West's Ann.Cal.Civ.Code § 857; Mont.—R.C.1947, § 86–105; N.Dak.—Rev. Code 1943, 59–0312; Okl.Rev.L.1910, § 6662; S.Dak.Code 59.0301;

2. West's Ann.Cal.Civ.Code § 2220; Mont.R.C. 72–20–106; N.Y.—McKinney's EPTL 7–1.4; N.Dak.C.C. 59–01–03; 60 Okl. St.Ann. § 175.2 S.Dak.Codif.L. 55–1–1.

because they rendered uncertain the record title to land and might result in fraud and confusion. If the legal title were really necessary or highly convenient to a manager of realty, said these reformers, a trust should be allowed; but in cases where a trust was an unnecessary formality and the work desired to be done could be done equally well by means of a power, the trust should be abolished.

The trusts originally allowed fell into four main classes: those to sell real property for the benefit of creditors; those to sell, mortgage, or lease for the benefit of annuitants or other legatees, or to pay off a charge; those to collect income and apply it to the use of beneficiaries; and those to collect rental income and accumulate it for persons entitled to receive accumulations. To accomplish these purposes the trust form was deemed necessary or convenient. To accomplish other purposes sometimes reached by trusts, it was felt by the reformers that powers in trust would be equally efficacious and convenient and more conducive to an orderly system of recordation of titles.

The statutes of these states provided that if an attempt was made to create a trust in land for an unauthorized purpose, the trustee was to take no estate as a trustee. However if the trust directed the performance of an act which could lawfully be performed as a power in trust, the instrument was to be given effect as a power in trust.[3]

Thus under this statutory system, if A devised real property to B for the purpose of having B partition the property between C and D, the will would fail to create a valid trust because a trust to partition real estate was not provided within this statutory scheme, but the direction of A would be enforced as a power in trust. The legal title would pass to A's heirs or devisees, but B would have the power to partition the property between C and D.

These statutes did not apply to personal property. Trusts of personal property might be created in these states for any lawful purpose.[4]

In California and Oklahoma these four types of real property trusts were the only ones originally permitted, but later statutes removed such restrictions,[5] and hence a trust is permitted for any legal purpose. In Michigan, Minnesota and Wisconsin statutes name the four purposes set forth in the original New York statute but also permit trusts of real or personal property for any other lawful purpose, thus negativing any

---

3. N.Dak.Cent.Code 59–03–13; S.Dak. Codif.Laws 43–10–9. To the same effect, see Mich.C.L.A. §§ 555.14 and 555.15; Minn.Stat.Ann. §§ 501.01, 501.11; Wis. S.A.1949, 231.01, 231.11, 231.12. See n. 6, infra, for current statutes.

For construction of some of these statutes, see Randall v. Constans, 33 Minn. 329, 23 N.W. 530; Hawley v. James, 5 Paige, N.Y., 318; Selden v. Vermilya, 3 N.Y. 525; Townshend v. Frommer, 125 N.Y. 446, 26 N.E. 805; Murphey v. Cook, 11 S.D. 47, 75 N.W. 387.

4. See, for example, Rev.Code Mont. 1947, § 86–206. And see In re Schwartz, 145 App.Div. 285, 130 N.Y.S. 74; Hammerstein v. Equitable Trust Co. of New York, 156 App.Div. 644, 141 N.Y.S. 1065.

5. West's Ann.Cal.Civ.Code § 2220; 60 Okl.St.Ann. §§ 171, 175.1 et seq.

real restriction.[6] Recently New York has abandoned its statutory restrictions on the purposes of real property trusts and now permits the creation of an express trust "for any lawful purpose." [7]

In Georgia, in the case of executed trusts, the legal title passed to the beneficiary, if he was capable of taking and managing property, but executed or executory trusts of all kinds of property were limited to those for the benefit of minors, incompetents, and persons of bad habits, or for the purpose of improving the trust property. In the case of trusts for other purposes the legal title passed to the beneficiary and the trust was destroyed.[8] By statute enacted in 1950 Georgia now permits an active trust for any purpose.[9]

In all states an active trust may be created for any lawful purpose.[10]

 WESTLAW REFERENCES

statut*** /s restriction /s trust

RULE AGAINST REMOTENESS OF VESTING

§ 50. The common law rule against remoteness of vesting, generally called the Rule against Perpetuities, is that "no interest is good unless it must vest, if at all, not later than twenty-one years after some life in being at the creation of the interest."

This Rule restricts the creator of every private trust by requiring him to provide for the certain vesting of all contingent interests under or following his trust not later than twenty-one years after the end of some life or lives in being at the time the trust instrument goes into effect.

This Rule is in effect in nearly all states. The effect of violating the rule is that the gift of the remote contingent interest is void.

There has been a recent tendency to codify the Rule though often with modifications, and most statutes exempt employee benefit trusts from its operation.

The rule against too remote vesting of contingent interests, commonly called the Rule against Perpetuities, has been stated as follows: "No interest is good unless it must vest, if at all, not later than twenty-one years after some life in being at the creation of the interest." [1] A child en ventre sa mere is regarded as a life in being for the purposes of

---

6. Mich.C.L.A. § 555.11; Minn.Stat. Ann. §§ 501.01, 501.11; Wis.S.A. 701.02.

7. N.Y.—McKinney's EPTL 7–1.4.

8. Ga.Code.Ann. §§ 108–111, 108–112, 108–114; Sanders v. First Nat. Bank, 189 Ga. 450, 6 S.E.2d 294 (1939); Love v. McManus, 208 Ga. 447, 67 S.E.2d 218 (1951).

9. Ga.Code §§ 108–111.1. See Offic. Code Ga.Ann. 53–12–2, 53–12–3.

10. Statutes in many states so provide. See, for example, West's Ann.Cal.Civ.Code § 2210; N.Y.—McKinney's EPTL 7–1.4.

§ 50

1. Gray, The Law of Perpetuities (4th edit.). As to a similar rule, the rule against the undue suspension of the power of alienation, see § 51, post.

the rule.[2] This rule, it will be seen, has to do only with the date at which property interests must vest in *interest*. They must not remain contingent for too long a period, that is, for longer than the continuance of lives in being at the time the instrument takes effect and twenty-one years thereafter. "The rule governs both legal and equitable interests, and interests in both realty and personalty." [3] The rule does not apply to vesting in *possession,* that is, to the right of a property owner to go into possession of the property.

No attempt is made here to treat the Rule against Perpetuities with any fullness. It is covered by treatises on property and future interests.[4] But a warning must be given as to its importance in the drafting of trust instruments. Nearly every complicated family trust is affected by it. This Rule has been in force in nearly all American states.[5]

The rule against remoteness of vesting may affect the settlor of a trust in three ways which are of interest here. First, if he provides that the trust is to begin if a named event occurs, and the happening of this event is uncertain, so that the legal interest of the trustee and the equitable interests of the beneficiaries are contingent at the time the instrument goes into effect and are to become vested, if at all, at a future date, this date must be certain not to be more remote than twenty-one years after the expiration of named or described lives in being. Thus a trust to begin if and when an orchestra is established in a certain city,[6] or if and when a gravel pit is worked out [7] or if and when mortgages are paid off out of rents,[8] is a trust the origin or

2. Long v. Blackall, 7 Term R. 100.

3. Gray, The Law of Perpetuities (4th edit.).

4. For a complete treatment of the Rule, see Simes & Smith, The Law of Future Interests (2d edit. 1956); Restatement, Second, Property, §§ 1.1–1.6 (1983). Powell, The American Law of Property. And see Bogert, Trusts and Trustees, (rev. 2d edit.), §§ 213, 214.

5. For a collection of statutes and other authorities, see Bogert, Trusts and Trustees (rev. 2d edit.), § 214. The common law Rule has been adopted by court decision in about 19 states. See, for example, Colorado Nat. Bank v. McCabe, 143 Colo. 21, 353 P.2d 385 (1960). As possible exceptions, see Locklear v. Tucker, 69 Idaho 84, 203 P.2d 380 (1949); Idaho L.1957, c. 54; Becker v. Chester, 115 Wis. 90, 91 N.W. 87. See also Rundell, 19 Mich.L.R. 235; Dede, 42 Marq.L.R. 514.

As recently stated by the Court of Appeals in New York, an owner's power in New York to dispose of property is limited by three rules. The first two are statutory and, enacted as the Rule against Perpetuities, are set forth in N.Y.—McKinney's EPTL 9–1.1(a) and (b), to the effect that no estate in property is valid "(1) if the instrument conveying it suspends the power of alienation for a period longer than lives in being at the creation of the estate plus 21 years and (2) unless it must vest, if at all, before expiration of the same period." (Court's words). The Court added that the third rule "regulating dispositions is established by common law and invalidates conveyances which impose unreasonable restraints on alienation." Metropolitan Transportation Authority v. Bruken Realty Corporation, 67 N.Y.2d 156, 501 N.Y.S.2d 306, 492 N.E.2d 379, 381 (1986). A preemptive right or option agreement granted in a commercial transaction was held under the circumstances to be a reasonable restriction on the alienability of the business property.

6. In re Dyer, 1935, Vict.L.R. 273.

7. In re Wood, [1894] 3 Ch. 381. See, also, Overby v. Scarborough, 145 Ga. 875, 90 S.E. 67; Ewalt v. Davenhill, 257 Pa. 385, 101 A. 756; Rhode Island Hospital Trust Co. v. Peck, 40 R.I. 519, 101 A. 430.

8. In re Bewick, [1911] 1 Ch. 116.

vesting of which is contingent, and the gift to the trustee and beneficiaries is void because their interests are not so limited as to be sure to vest within the permitted period. It is not certain when, if ever, the orchestra will be founded, the gravel pit will be worked out, or the mortgages paid off; and there is no assurance that such event will occur within the lives of any particular persons living when the trust instrument went into effect or within twenty-one years from that date.

On the other hand, a trust to begin if an uncertain event should happen before the death of the survivor of A and B, who were living when the trust instrument was executed, or if the event should occur before or at the end of twenty-one years from the date of such execution, or before both A and B had died and twenty-one years had expired after their deaths, would be a valid trust under the rule.[9]

Secondly, even though the trust is to begin at once or within the permitted period, there may be contingent equitable interests given to the beneficiaries under the trust, and, if so, these must be made to vest within the permitted period. Thus a trust to provide support for the widow of the settlor and her then living or afterborn children for a period of thirty years, and then to pay the income of the property to the then living lineal descendants of the settlor, would create remote equitable interests in the latter class of persons.[10] Their interests would be contingent since it could not be said until the end of thirty years who would be such descendants. The period during which this contingency was to last was thirty years, a gross period too long under the rule, and not in any way connected with the period of lives necessarily in being when the trust was created. The courts, under the strict common law rules of construction, do not give effect to the trust for the maximum possible gross period, twenty-one years, and lop off the excess period of nine years. The whole gift is void.

On the other hand, a trust to begin at the death of the testator and last during the lives of his children living at his death for the purpose of paying income to such children, and on the death of the last surviving child of the testator to pay income for twenty-one years to the descendants of the testator living at the time of the death of the last surviving child, would be valid, since the interests of such descendants, although contingent because of uncertainty as to the identity of the descendants, would become vested when the last surviving child of the testator died, which would be at the end of lives in being when the will took effect.[11]

Thirdly, it should be noticed that all contingent interests following trust estates are subject to the rule against remoteness and may drag

9. In re Lewis' Estate, 349 Pa. 571, 37 A.2d 482 (1944).

10. Anderson v. Williams, 262 Ill. 308, 104 N.E. 659, Ann.Cas.1915B, 720; Ortman v. Dugan, 130 Md. 121, 100 A. 82; Clark v. Union County Trust Co., 127 N.J.Eq. 221, 12 A.2d 365 (1940).

11. In re Harrison's Estate, 22 Cal. App.2d 28, 70 P.2d 522 (1937).

the trust down with them if they violate the rule.[12] For example, if a trust is created to last for seventy-five years, and contingent legal remainders are provided to follow the trust term, it is obvious that these contingent interests violate the rule against remoteness even though all interests under the trust are vested. The remainders need not vest within lives in being and twenty-one years. In fact they are sure to vest only at the end of a period of years, not in any way connected with lives and greater than the permissible gross period of twenty-one years. Hence, of course, the remainders to take effect and vest at the end of the trust are void for remoteness. It may well be that the falling of these remainders will so destroy the scheme of the testator that it will be necessary, in order to prevent an unjust disposition of the property, to further declare the trust for the term of seventy-five years void. This was done in a Pennsylvania case. The trust was considered valid in itself, but it was destroyed due to its inseparable connection with an unlawful contingent legal remainder.[13] Whether a seventy-five year trust runs afoul of another rule, that a private trust must be of limited duration, is considered in a later section.[14]

On the other hand, although there is a remainder following the trust which is too remote and therefore void, the trust may be separable and may stand alone. In many cases the only effect of the violation of the rule against remoteness by a contingent legal remainder is that the remainder is void. The trust preceding the remainder is enforced.[15]

The separability of valid and void interests under the Rule against Perpetuities cannot be treated here.[16] Sometimes the void carries down with it the valid, and sometimes the two are separated and the valid portion of the trust enforced. The result depends upon the intimacy of connection of the two provisions, the effect of separation, and the actual or presumed intent of the settlor as to what he would have desired to have happen had he anticipated the partial invalidity of his dispositions.[17]

Recent statutes have had considerable effect on the Rule.[18] Some amount merely to a codification of the rule which had previously depended on case law or had been in doubt.[19] Others modify the Rule

12. Johnston v. Cosby, 374 Ill. 407, 29 N.E.2d 608 (1940); Bankers Trust Co. v. Garver, 222 Iowa 196, 268 N.W. 568.

13. In re Johnston's Estate, 185 Pa. 179, 39 A. 879, 64 Am.St.Rep. 621.

14. See § 52, post.

15. Beers v. Narramore, 61 Conn. 13, 22 A. 1061 (1891); Dime Savings & Trust Co. v. Watson, 254 Ill. 419, 98 N.E. 777 (1912); Camden Safe Deposit & Trust Co. v. Guerin, 87 N.J.Eq. 72, 99 A. 105 (1916).

16. See Bogert, Trusts and Trustees (rev. 2d edit), § 213.

17. Story v. First Nat. Bank & Trust Co. in Orlando, 115 Fla. 436, 156 So. 101

(1934); McEwen v. Enoch, 167 Kan. 119, 204 P.2d 736 (1949); First Nat. Bank v. Rice, 101 N.J.Eq. 520, 139 A. 396 (1927).

18. For references to these statutes, as well as to court decisions, see Bogert, Trusts and Trustees (rev. 2d edit.), § 214. And see Leach, 67 Harv.L.R. 1349; Schuyler, 56 Mich.L.R. 683, and 65 N.W.L.Rev. 3.

19. See, for example, Ala.Code 1975, § 35–4–4; Ariz.R.S. § 33–261; West's Ann. Cal.Civ.Code § 715.2; West's Fla.S.A. § 689.22; Offic.Code Ga.Ann. § 44–6–1; West's Ann.Ind.Code 32–1–4–1; Mich.C.L. A. § 554.51; Mont.C.Ann. § 70–1–408; N.Y.—McKinney's EPTL 9–1.1; Ohio Rev.

by providing that where a contingent interest is created and it may or may not vest within the period of the rule, depending on future events, the validity of the interest shall not be decided until the future events occur, and the interest is to be valid if actual occurrences prove that it vested at a date which was not remote.[20] This is the so-called "wait and see" rule.[21] The common law cases invalidated the interest, if at the date of its creation it might vest remotely. Other statutes provide rules of construction which are aimed at preventing the failure of contingent interests under the rule.[22] Many statutes exempt employee benefit[23] and charitable[24] trusts from the operation of the Rule.

 WESTLAW REFERENCES

di("rule against perpetuities")

298k6(1)

409k447 /p "rule against perpetuities"

298k4(3)

298k4(1)

390k21(2) /p "rule against perpetuities"

298k4(15)

298k4(6)

298k4(4)

338k1 /p "rule against perpetuities"

RULE AGAINST UNDUE SUSPENSION OF THE POWER OF ALIENATION

§ 51. In several states there are statutes which make void any attempt to suspend the power of alienation for longer than a fixed period, and this rule is sometimes called a Rule against Perpetuities.

Some of these statutes apply to dispositions of realty alone, but others apply to instruments affecting realty or personalty.

The permitted period of suspension of the power of alienation varies. In some states two lives in being had been the limit, in others

Code § 2131.08; Wyo.Stat.1977, § 34–1–139.

20. See, for example, Ky.Rev.Stat. 381.216; Ohio Rev.Code § 2131.08(C); 20 Pa.C.S.A. § 6104; 27 Vt.Stat.Ann. § 501. See also West's Wash.—RCWA 11.98.130. For case law to the same effect, see First Portland Nat. Bank v. Rodrique, 157 Me. 277, 172 A.2d 107 (1961); Sears v. Coolidge, 329 Mass. 340, 108 N.E.2d 563 (1952); Merchants Nat. Bank v. Curtis, 98 N.H. 225, 97 A.2d 207 (1953).

And see Simes, 52 Mich.L.R. 179.

21. The "wait and see" rule has been enacted in 15 states and adopted in Rest., Second, Property, § 1.4.

22. Conn.G.S.A. §§ 45–95 to 45–96; Fla.S.A. § 689.22(5); N.Y.—McKinney's EPTL 9–1.3.

For statutory provisions authorizing the court to reform the instrument and to apply cy pres, see Offic.Code Ga.Ann. § 44–6–1(b); 60 Okl.St.Ann. §§ 75, 76; V.Tex.C.A. Prop.Code § 121.004.

23. See, for example, Conn.G.S.A. § 45–100; Idaho Code § 51–111; Mo.—V.A.M.S. § 442.555; V.Tex.C.A. Prop.Code §§ 5.043, 112.036. For other statutory citations see Bogert, Trusts and Trustees (rev. 2d edit.), §§ 214, 255.

24. See, for example, Ark.Stat. § 50–201; N.Car.G.S. § 36A:49; V.T.C.A. Prop. Code § 112.036.

any number of lives in being. In some jurisdictions a short period of years may be added to the measuring lives or used as an alternative to lives.

These statutes affect the creation of private trusts whenever, by the settlor's direction or by statute, any interest under the trust is made inalienable. The period for which the interest is rendered inalienable must not exceed that allowed by the statute. If it does, the act of trust creation is invalid.

"The absolute power of alienation is suspended when there are no persons in being by whom an absolute fee or estate in possession can be conveyed or transferred." [1]

The revisers of the New York statutes who prepared the Revision of 1830 inserted sections to the effect that the power of alienation of interests in realty should not be suspended for a longer period than during the lives of two named or described persons who were in being when the property disposition went into effect, and that any conveyance in contravention of this prohibition should be void. [2] Later this rule was extended to provisions for the suspension of the absolute ownership of personal property. [3] The object was to facilitate the transfer of property interests and to prevent them from being kept in a static condition and out of commerce for a lengthy period.

In several other states similar provisions regarding suspension of the power of alienation were adopted, [4] some of them applying to realty only [5] and others to both realty and personalty. [6] Some statutes set the permitted period at not more than two lives in being, [7] while others allowed suspension for any number of lives in being, [8] and others added a period of years to the measuring period. [9]

In recent years these statutes have been repealed in some states [10]

§ 51

1. Definition set forth in N.Y.—McKinney's EPTL 9–1.1.

2. Formerly § 103, Real Property Law.

3. Underwood v. Curtis, 127 N.Y. 523, 28 N.E. 585; Formerly Pers.Prop.L., § 15.

4. Arizona, California, District of Columbia, Idaho, Iowa, Kentucky, Michigan, Minnesota, North Dakota, Oklahoma, South Dakota and Wisconsin. For references to the history and development of the statutes, see Bogert, Trusts and Trustees (rev. 2d edit.), § 219.

5. Arizona, Michigan (before repeal in 1949); Minnesota, and Wisconsin (before July 1, 1925).

6. California, Iowa.

7. Arizona, Michigan, Minnesota, and Wisconsin.

8. California, District of Columbia, Idaho, Indiana, Iowa, Kentucky, Montana, North Dakota, Oklahoma and South Dakota.

9. In Arizona, District of Columbia, Iowa, Kentucky and Oklahoma twenty-one years could be added to the lives period, and in Wisconsin thirty years could be added. In California a twenty-five year period could be used as an alternative to the lives in being period, as to instruments executed before 1951.

10. See, for example, Ind.Code 32–1–4–1; Ky.Rev.Stat. § 381.215 (repealing the suspension of the power of alienation rule and substituting the common law rule against remoteness); Mich.C.L.A. § 554.51; N.Y.—McKinney's EPTL 9–1.1 (lives in being and 21 years). For other statutes, see Bogert, Trusts and Trustees (rev. 2d edit.), § 219.

and greatly modified in others.[11]

In construction of these statutes it was held that private trusts may suspend the power of alienation illegally in any one of three ways: (1) because the instrument prohibits the trustee from selling the trust property for a given period;[12] or (2) because the settlor forbids the beneficiary from transferring his interest (spendthrift provisions);[13] or (3) because a statute makes the interest of the beneficiary of some trusts inalienable by him. As shown in an earlier section,[14] in some states the legislature has provided that the interest of a beneficiary of a trust to collect and pay over income shall be inalienable, and this has given ground for invalidation of a large number of trusts where the duration was not limited to the statutory period. These statutes did not apply to charitable trusts.[15]

There has been a difference of judicial opinion as to whether the existence in the trust instrument of a power of sale in the trustee prevented the statute from applying to a restraint on the alienation of the interest of the beneficiary, some courts arguing that such a power of sale made the property of the trust marketable free of claim by the beneficiary, and that the fact that the beneficiary could not sell or give away his interest in the trust property as it existed from time to time was immaterial.[16] A power in the settlor, beneficiaries or trustee to terminate the trust at any time would seem to render harmless and outside the statute a suspension of the power of the beneficiary to transfer his interest.[17]

The construction of these statutes (often included within or called the Rule against Perpetuities) is a matter of considerable complexity and detail which cannot be discussed here.[18] In the preparation of

---

11. See, for example, West's Ann.Cal. Civil Code § 715.2 (period changed to lives in being plus twenty one years plus any period of gestation actually involved); Idaho Code § 55–111 (lives in being plus twenty-five years); Mont.Code Ann. § 70–1–406 (lives in being plus twenty one years plus period of gestation actually involved); N.Dak.Cent.Code 47–02–27 (lives in being plus twenty-five years).

See also Turrentine, 9 Hast.L.J. 262; Evans, 28 So.Cal.L.R. 111; Fraser & Sammis, 4 Hast.L.J. 101.

12. Williams v. Williams, 73 Cal. 99, 14 P. 394; Fowler v. Duhme, 143 Ind. 248, 42 N.E. 623; Van Tyne v. Pratt, 291 Mich. 626, 289 N.W. 275 (1939); Haug v. Schumacher, 166 N.Y. 506, 60 N.E. 245.

13. See § 40, ante.

14. See § 38, ante.

15. Lowell v. Lowell, 29 Ariz. 138, 240 P. 280; In re Cleven's Estate, 161 Iowa 289, 142 N.W. 986; Allen v. Stevens, 161 N.Y. 122, 55 N.E. 568.

16. As holding that a power of sale in the trustee did not take a trust out of the rule, see In re Maltman's Estate, 195 Cal. 643, 234 P. 898 (1925); Otto v. Union Nat. Bank of Pasadena, 38 Cal.2d 233, 238 P.2d 961 (1951); In re Perkins' Estate, 245 N.Y. 478, 157 N.E. 750 (1927); In re Tower's Estate, 49 Minn. 370, 52 N.W. 27; Atwood v. Holmes, 224 Minn. 157, 28 N.W.2d 188 (1947); In re Walker's Will, 258 Wis. 65, 45 N.W.2d 94 (1950).

17. In re Zeb's Estate, 67 Idaho 567, 189 P.2d 95 (1947); Robert v. Corning, 89 N.Y. 225; Morgan v. Keyes, 302 N.Y. 439, 99 N.E.2d 230 (1951).

18. See Rest., Second, Property, § 1.1. For some discussion, see Powell, 25 Col. L.R. 989; Whiteside, 13 Cornell L.Q. 31, 167; Kharas, 13 N.Y.U.L.Q.R. 191; Goddard, 22 Mich.L.R. 95; Rundell, 4 Wis.L.R. 1; Hohfeld, 1 Cal.L.R. 305; Anderson, 1 Ida.L.J. 73; Fraser, 3 Minn.L.R. 320, 4 id. 318, 8 id. 185, 295, 9 id. 314; Kulp, 7 Okl. St.Bar J. 7.

trust instruments careful attention should be given to any applicable statute of the type discussed herein, and to its construction by the courts.

The effect of an attempt to provide for a suspension of the power of alienation for too long a period usually is that the whole disposition is void,[19] but in some cases the invalid can be separated and stricken and the remainder of the will or deed given effect.[20]

An example of the operation of one such statute may be given. Under New York law prior to 1958,[21] every trust to collect and pay over income of realty or personalty by statute suspended the power of alienation in a technical sense because alienation of the beneficiary's interest was forbidden by statute. Therefore no trust of this type could be created unless its duration was limited to the period of two lives in being. Thus if S left property by will to T in trust to collect and pay over the income to B and his successors for twenty-five years,[22] or during the lives of X, Y and Z (all in being when the will went into effect),[23] the trust was void because it suspended the power of alienation for a gross period of twenty-five years, or in the second case for three lives in being, whereas the maximum period was two lives in being and no period of years was allowed. But if the duration of the trust had been limited to the lives of B and X (both in being when the will took effect), the suspension would have been for a permitted period and the trust would have been enforced. As to trusts created after the effective date of the 1960 amendment to the New York statute, the permitted period of suspension is lives in being and a term of twenty-one years.[24]

 WESTLAW REFERENCES

"undue suspension" /s power /s alienation

RULE AS TO THE DURATION OF PRIVATE TRUSTS [1]

§ 52. While there is some authority for the view that a private trust which is not limited in duration to lives in being and/or twenty-one years is void, it is generally held that such a trust need not be so limited if it is destructible by the parties or the court, and that a provision for indestructibility is valid only for the period of the Rule against Perpetuities.

19. In re Chittick's Will, 243 N.Y. 304, 153 N.E. 83 (1926); In re Durand's Will, 250 N.Y. 45, 164 N.E. 737 (1928).

20. Nellis v. Rickard, 133 Cal. 617, 66 P. 32; Harrison v. Harrison, 36 N.Y. 543.

21. N.Y.—McKinney's Real Prop.Law § 42.

22. Kalish v. Kalish, 166 N.Y. 368, 59 N.E. 917. And see Application of Chapman, 168 Minn. 1, 211 N.W. 325 (1926).

23. In re Halsey's Will, 286 N.Y. 154, 36 N.E.2d 91 (1941).

24. N.Y.—McKinney's EPTL 9–1.1(a) (2).

§ 52

1. Restatement, Trusts, Second, § 62, Comments *n* and *o*.

Is there a common law rule that private trusts must be limited in duration to the period of the rule against remoteness of vesting, namely, to lives in being at the time the trust commences and/or a period of twenty-one years?

If there is such a rule it has nothing to do with vesting of contingent interests or with restraints on the alienation of property, but rather is founded on the idea that it is against public policy to permit the transferor of property to control the way in which the transferee may enjoy his property for too long a period, to require the transferee to enjoy his property indirectly and through a trust instead of directly as a full owner. Such a rule would seem based on the notion that a donor should be able to dictate to his donees who follow immediately, but not to successive donees who belong to the second or later generations following the donor.

Some of the earlier cases seem to hold that a common law rule limiting all private trusts in duration to the period of the Rule against Perpetuities does exist and that the effect of violating it is to give the right to the settlor or his successors to have the trust declared void [2] or that the excessive period beyond the limits of the rule is void and the trust is valid otherwise.[3] But other decisions, including most of the recent cases, are contrary and hold that there is no such rule and that a private trust for any period is unassailable by any one, no matter what the provisions as to its duration, so long as all interests under and

2. Alexander v. House, 133 Conn. 725, 54 A.2d 510 (1947) (perpetual trust); Bigelow v. Cady, 171 Ill. 229, 48 N.E. 974; Tillman v. Blackburn, 276 Ky. 550, 124 S.W.2d 755 (1939); Barnum v. Barnum, 26 Md. 119, 90 Am.Dec. 88; Amory v. Trustees of Amherst College, 229 Mass. 374, 118 N.E. 933; Mercer v. Mercer, 230 N.C. 101, 52 S.E.2d 229 (1949); Williams v. Herrick, 19 R.I. 197, 32 A. 913.

3. Armstrong v. Barber, 239 Ill. 389, 88 N.E. 246; In re Shallcross' Estate, 200 Pa. 122, 49 A. 936.

See Restatement, Property, §§ 378, 381 (even though trust indestructible because beneficiaries cannot terminate it since its purpose unaccomplished, it is not subject to attack by the settlor or his successors for too long duration; but provision for perpetual indestructibility is void as against the beneficiaries, indestructibility for the lives of the beneficiaries is valid, and as to indestructibility for other periods not covered by the rule no position taken).

In § 2.1 of Restatement, Property, Second, a rule limiting the duration of a trust was adopted with the following "justification":

". . . The rule of this section places a limit on the period of time that the creator of a trust is allowed to force the effectuation of the material purpose of the trust, when the continued accomplishment of such purpose is against the wishes and desires of the current beneficial owners of the trust property. Some limit is desirable in order to prevent the possible undesirable social consequences of the views of persons long removed from the current scene influencing unduly the wishes and desires of those living in the present." (Comment a).

". . . Regardless of the type of trust involved, the time when the trust will be destructible, even though thereby a material purpose of the creator of the trust will be defeated, is after the period of the rule has, in fact, expired. . . ." (Comment c).

§ 62, Comment o, Restatement, Trusts, Second, is cited in support.

See Simes & Smith, Future Interests, §§ 553–559 (except in case of honorary trusts, successors of settlor can not attack trust for too long indestructibility; but beneficiaries can strike out indestructibility provision if it is to last for longer than period of rule).

following it are vested.[4] Some of these cases lay no stress on whether the trust was destructible by trust parties or by the court on application of the beneficiaries, or was indestructible. Other authorities, however, have made a distinction between private destructible trusts and private indestructible trusts, and have held that the rules about duration do not apply to destructible trusts. As will be shown later,[5] private trusts are often terminable by the trust parties or by the court on application of the beneficiaries. These trusts are called "destructible." Other trusts are held to be indestructible, so that the trust parties cannot terminate the trust, nor can the beneficiaries secure a court order of termination and distribution of the trust property, even though all beneficiaries are competent and apply for such an order. It is argued that the duration fixed by the settlor for a destructible trust is unimportant, since there is in reality no fixed status or inalienability.

In those cases differentiating between destructible and indestructible trusts on the question, holdings that a destructible trust does not have to be limited in duration are common and natural.[6]

A trust may be indestructible for any one of a number of reasons. In the first place, even if all its beneficiaries are ascertained, in being, competent, and have vested interests, a rule of law may make the trust indestructible if the purpose of the settlor in establishing the trust has not been accomplished.[7] Secondly, the trust may be indestructible because a joinder of the beneficiaries in applying for termination cannot be secured because of the status of one or more beneficiaries, for example, that some are minors or may be born in the future and have contingent interests.[8] Thirdly, the trust may be indestructible because of the nature of the beneficiaries, as where there is no person to benefit financially from the trust and the trust is not charitable. Examples are found in the cases of trusts for cemetery upkeep, animals, unincorporated associations and the like, and there are holdings that the entire trust is void and not merely the provision about its duration.[9]

---

4. Loomer v. Loomer, 76 Conn. 522, 527, 57 A. 167; Deacon v. St. Louis Union Trust Co., 271 Mo. 669, 197 S.W. 261; In re Johnston's Estate, 185 Pa. 179, 39 A. 879; Guarantee Trust Co. v. Latz, 119 N.J.Eq. 194, 181 A. 645.

And see Colo. Nat. Bank v. McCabe, 143 Colo. 21, 353 P.2d 385 (1960); Bardfeld v. Bardfeld, 23 N.J.Super. 248, 92 A.2d 854 (1952); Finch v. Honeycutt, 246 N.C. 91, 97 S.E.2d 478 (1957); Schmidt v. Schmidt, 261 S.W.2d 892 (Tex.Civ.App.1953).

But see Kelly v. Womack, 153 Tex. 371, 268 S.W.2d 903 (1954).

See Cal.L.1959, c. 470, adding § 771 to the Civil Code (trust not invalid because extending beyond lives and twenty-one years; clause against terminability ineffective). See 41 Cal.L.R. 549.

5. See §§ 150–152, post.

6. Cook v. Horn, 214 Ga. 289, 104 S.E.2d 461 (1958); Wechter v. Chicago Title & Trust Co., 385 Ill. 111, 52 N.E.2d 157 (1943); Howe v. Morse, 174 Mass. 491, 55 N.E. 213; Schellentrager v. Tradesmens Nat. Bank and Trust Co., 370 Pa. 501, 88 A.2d 773 (1952).

7. See § 152, post.

8. See § 152, post.

9. Restatement of Property, § 378 (honorary trusts and trusts for unincorporated associations); Simes & Smith, The Law of Future Interests (2d edit. 1956); Carne v. Long, 29 L.J.Ch. 503 (for unincorporated club); In re Moore, [1901] 1 Ch. 936 (upkeep of tomb); Mason v. Bloomington Lib. Ass'n, 237 Ill. 442, 86 N.E. 1044; Lounsbury v. Trustees of Square Lake Bur. Ass'n, 170 Mich. 645, 137 N.W. 513. See

In a few states there are statutes limiting the duration of private trusts, usually the maximum period allowable under the Rule against Perpetuities.[10] Trusts to provide employees with retirement, disability and sickness benefits are commonly exempted from any rule regarding trust duration.[11]

In many cases where the court has to decide whether a certain purpose is charitable the question is important for the reason that a charitable trust may be perpetual or of indefinite duration, while a noncharitable trust with indefinite beneficiaries, if valid at all, is indestructible and must be limited in duration to lives in being and twenty-one years.[12]

When the law is in some confusion, both as to case law and as to opinions of experts in the field of future interests,[13] it behooves the draftsman of a trust to take a conservative view and assume no risks. Practically all private trusts can achieve the legitimate purposes of the settlors in the period of one generation and a minority thereafter. It is believed that the great majority of well-drawn trust instruments expressly limit the duration of private trusts to named lives in being and/ or a period of years not more than twenty-one.

 WESTLAW REFERENCES

rule /s limit*** /s length duration /s "private trust"
destructible /2 trust
indestructible /2 trust

---

also Smith, 30 Col.L.R. 60; Clark, 10 Mich. L.R. 31.

10. See Offic.Code Ga.Ann. § 44–6–1; La.LSA–R.S. 9:1831, 9:1833; Nev.Rev.Stat. 166.140 (spendthrift trusts). And see Ill. Rev.Stat., c. 30, § 195.

11. See, for example, Offic.Code Ga. Ann. § 53–2–10B; V.Tex.C.A. Prop.Code § 121.004. For similar statutes see Bogert, Trusts and Trustees (rev. 2d edit.), § 255.

12. See § 65, post. And see Mason v. Bloomington Library Ass'n, 237 Ill. 442, 86 N.E. 1044; Lounsbury v. Trustees of Square Lake Burial Ass'n, 170 Mich. 645, 129 N.W. 36; In re Stephan's Estate, 129 Pa.Super. 396, 195 A. 653 (1937); Bliven v. Borden, 56 R.I. 283, 185 A. 239 (1936).

13. See Gray, Rule against Perpetuities, 3rd Ed., § 121i; Kales, Future Interests, §§ 658–661; 19 Harv.L.R. 604; 20 Harv.L.R. 202; 2 Ill.L.R. 281; Fraser, 9 Minn.L.R. 314, 326; 34 Mich.L.R. 553; 4 U.Pitts.L.R. 157; Scott, Control of Property by the Dead, 65 Pa.L.R. 632; Cleary, 43 Yale L.J. 393; Schuyler, 28 Chi.Bar Rec. 369. See also 7 Baylor L.R. 402; 24 Tenn. L.R. 1021.

And see Restatement, Property, Second, § 2.1, discussed in footnote 3, supra. The Reporter's note to § 2.1 states that "commentators agree that a private trust cannot remain indestructible for a period longer than a life or lives in being and 21 years."

RULES REGARDING THE DURATION OF TRUSTS PROVIDING FOR THE ACCUMULATION OF TRUST INCOME [1]

§ 53. If the terms of a trust require the trustee to add income to the principal of the trust, instead of distributing it, there is a provision for accumulations.

At common law there is no rule limiting the period during which accumulations may be directed in a private trust, but the ownership of the accumulations must be vested within lives in being and/or twenty-one years under the Rule against Perpetuities.

Under a statute passed in England in 1800, and under legislation in many American states, limitations were placed upon the time during which accumulations may be made; and in a few states there were statutes providing that the accumulation must be for the benefit of a minor.

During recent years the American statutes have been greatly revised, the modern tendency being to allow accumulations during lives in being and/or twenty-one years.

The rules about accumulations apply to implied as well as express provisions, but are limited in most cases to directions to accumulate and do not include clauses merely authorizing the trustee in his discretion to accumulate income.

If a settlor provides for an accumulation for a period of too great length, where possible the courts strike down the provision as to the excessive period only, and permit it to stand for the maximum legal period.

Income invalidly directed to be accumulated is by some statutes payable to the person who would have received it if there had been no provision for accumulation, but by other statutes it is payable to the holder of the "next eventual estate".

A direction that income shall be used to increase the value of trust property, for example, by paying off an encumbrance, amounts to a provision for an accumulation; but instructions to pay premiums on insurance held by the trustee, or to create a sinking or reserve fund to meet future trust expenditures, or to add stock dividends to trust capital, are generally held not to be within the accumulation rules.

Recent statutes except pension and profit-sharing trusts from the operation of accumulation rules.

A trust for accumulations is one where the trustee is directed to set apart income and use it to purchase new trust investments or to

---

§ 53

1. Restatement, Second, Property, § 2.2; Restatement, Trusts, Second, § 62, Comment *t*.

Bogert, Trusts, 6th Ed. HB—8

This section deals only with private trusts. As to accumulation provisions in charitable trusts, see § 70, post.

increase the value of existing trust investments, instead of paying it out to income beneficiaries.[2] The question may arise whether there is, or ought to be, any rule of law restricting a settlor of a private trust with respect to such trusts and limiting the period during which accumulation of income may be made. These provisions deprive the current beneficiaries of the privilege of spending trust income and may tend to concentrate property in the hands of one family or other group and so tend to build up large fortunes. It may be argued that it is against public policy to permit unlimited provisions for accumulation.

In Thellusson v. Woodford[3] a settlor directed his trustee to accumulate income and add it to capital during the lives of nine persons who were in being when the trust began, and at the death of the last survivor of these nine persons to transfer the capital to the eldest male lineal descendant of the settlor's son, Peter, who was then living. It was held that the trust was valid, since the accumulations and the other trust property were to vest at the end of lives in being and so the Rule against Perpetuities was satisfied, and there was no rule limiting the time during which accumulations could be directed.

The large size of the fortune involved in Thellusson v. Woodford and the lengthy period of accumulations caused so much comment and apprehension that Parliament shortly thereafter enacted a statute which has been called the Thellusson Act[4] which permitted accumulations during any one of four periods, namely, the life of the donor, twenty-one years after the donor's death, the minorities of any persons living at the donor's death, and the minorities of persons who would be entitled to the income if no provision for accumulation had been made. This statute was amended by the Accumulations Act of 1892,[5] and the whole law of accumulations was consolidated in the property legislation of 1925.[6] The theory of these statutes was that (with certain exceptions) it is against the public interest to withhold current income from enjoyment by the generation in being when the income is earned, and that the piling up of large fortunes in the hands of one trust or one family is against public policy.

It would seem the doctrine of Thellusson v. Woodford became a part of the common law and that an accumulation could be directed to occur over any period and for the benefit of any person, so long as ownership of the accumulated sum was sure to vest within the period of the Rule against Perpetuities.[7] Thus a direction to add income to

2. Where a settlor has provided that income shall be withheld until a beneficiary reached a certain age and then paid to him, in some cases the trust has been described as one for "accumulation", although there was no express or implied provision for increasing the principal of the trust and the term seems to have required a mere delay in the payment of income. This is true with regard to the early New York statute and its construction.

3. 4 Vesey 227, 11 Ves. 112. See Keeton, 23 Sol. 233, 282.

4. 39 & 40 Geo. III, c. 98 (1800).

5. 55 & 56 Vict., c. 58 (1892).

6. 15 & 16 Geo. V, c. 20, §§ 164–166 (1925).

7. Gertman v. Burdick, 75 U.S.App. D.C. 48, 123 F.2d 924, 152 A.L.R. 645 (1941), certiorari denied 315 U.S. 824, 62 S.Ct. 917, 86 L.Ed. 1220 (1942); Equitable

principal for twenty-five years and then pay all the trust property over to B, a person living when the trust took effect, would be valid in most states, since ownership of the accumulations is vested in B from the start and there is no contingent interest involved.

Illinois and Pennsylvania originally adopted the Thellusson Act,[8] but later adopted statutes [9] which make changes in the law as to trusts created after the dates of their enactment.

The group which revised the statutes of New York in 1830 believed that accumulations should be restricted to an even greater extent than was provided by the Thellusson Act. They permitted accumulations of the income of both real and personal property only for the benefit of an infant and during the period of his infancy.[10] New York law was later changed to permit accumulation of income within the time allowed by the Rule against Perpetuities.[11]

California, Indiana, Michigan, and Montana originally followed the early New York statute [12] but later adopted special rules which varied from the New York standard.[13] In Arizona,[14] Minnesota,[15] and Wisconsin [16] the same type of statute had been adopted, except that it applied to the income of realty only, but more recent statutes have changed the rules in Minnesota and Wisconsin.[17] Alabama also has a special

Trust Co. v. Ward, 29 Del.Ch. 206, 48 A.2d 519 (1946); In re Hustad's Estate, 236 Wis. 615, 296 N.W. 74 (1941). But see Wilson v. D'Atro, 109 Conn. 563, 145 A. 161 (1929).

8. See Ill.Rev.Stat.1933, ch. 30, § 153; 20 Pa.S. § 301.6. And see Simes, 7 Univ. of Chi.L.R. 409; Schnebly, 26 Ill.L.R. 491.

9. See Ill.Rev.Stat., c. 30, § 153 (accumulations permitted for lives in being and twenty-one years, both in the case of deeds and wills). And see Schuyler, 65 N.W.L. Rev. 3.

See 20 Pa.C.S.A. §§ 6106, 6107.

As to prior law, see sections 6, 7, and 8 Pa. Estates Act of 1947, 20 Pa.S. §§ 301.6 to 301.8 (life of settlor, minority and for benefit of the minor, for an incompetent); Pa.L.1955, p. 1073 (valid if to cease within period of Rule against Perpetuities). For construction of the 1947 statute, see In re Wheelock's Estate, 401 Pa. 193, 164 A.2d 1 (1960). Charitable and employee benefit trusts were excepted from the rules of the 1955 amendment.

10. N.Y.—McKinney's Real Property Law, § 61 and Personal Property Law, § 16 (prior to revisions in 1959 and subsequent years). And see S Dak.CL 51–0304 to 51–0307.

11. See N.Y.—McKinney's EPTL 9–2.1.

12. See West's Ann.Cal.Civ.Code § 724; Ind.L.1945, c. 216 (life of settlor,

twenty-one years from date of trust, twenty-one years from death of settlor, or ten years beyond a minority of a minor beneficiary in being and for his benefit); Mich. C.L.A. §§ 554.37—554.38, Mich.L.1949, No. 227 (for minority and for benefit of minor or thirty-three years from death of settlor).

13. West's Ann.Cal.Civ.Code §§ 723–726 (for lives in being or twenty-five years, if instrument executed prior to 1951; for lives in being and twenty-one years, plus a period of gestation actually involved, as to instruments executed after the effective date of Cal.L.1951, c. 1463); Ind.Code 32–1–4–2 to 32–1–4–6; Mich.C.L.A. § 554.36. Another subsequent adoption, and also the current statute in Montana, is R.C. § 70–1–414 to 70–1–418 (period permitted same as for suspending power of alienation).

14. Ariz.—A.R.S. § 33–238, repealed by Laws 1963, Ch. 25. For current law, see Ariz.Rev.Stat. §§ 33–239, 33–240 (common law Rule against Perpetuities period).

15. Minn.—M.S.A. § 500.17, prior to amendment in 1965.

16. Wis.St.1949, §§ 230.37–230.39.

17. See Minn.Stat.Ann. § 500.17 (amended by Minn.L.1965, c. 682), by which accumulations of income from realty are to be governed by the same law governing accumulations of income from personal property; Wis.S.A. 230.37 (revised by

statute on the subject.[18]

In California, Indiana, Michigan, New York, North Dakota, and Wisconsin, statutes have recently been adopted which make important amendments to the law of accumulations, and in general permit accumulations if limited to the period of the Rule against Perpetuities (lives in being and/or twenty-one years), but they generally apply only to trusts created after the several effective dates of the statutes.[19]

While there had been some tendency to apply accumulation restrictions to clauses merely permitting or authorizing a trustee in his discretion to accumulate income,[20] the prevalent view is that only *directions* to accumulate are controlled by the statutes and many of the statutes expressly so provide.[21]

Accumulation clauses may be implied as well as express, but the courts are reluctant to make such implication.[22] The fact that a settlor made express provision for the use of only a part of the trust income does not necessarily show an implied intent that the excess income shall be accumulated.[23]

If an accumulation clause is valid except that it requires too long a period of accumulation, the courts will, if possible, cut off the excessive portion of the accumulation provision and permit enforcement of the provision for the maximum possible period.[24] Thus if a minority is the maximum period, and the clause in question provides for an accumulation until the beneficiary reaches thirty, the court will allow accumulation until the beneficiary reaches twenty-one and merely strike down as invalid the portion having to do with accumulations from twenty-one to thirty.[25]

Under the Thellusson Act, where there is an invalid direction for accumulation, the income was to be paid to the person "who would have

Wis.L.1957, c. 561); for current law, see Wis.S.A. 701.21(2)).

18. Ala.Code 1975 § 35–4–252 (for ten years or for minority of a beneficiary).

19. West's Ann.Cal.Civ.Code, § 724; West's Ann.Ind.Code 32–1–4–2 to 32–1–4–6; Mich.C.L.A. § 554.36; N.Y.—McKinney's EPTL 9–2.1; N.Dak.Cent.Code 47–03–02; Wis.S.A. 701.21 (accumulation of any duration permitted).

20. Re Robb's Will Trusts, (1953) 1 All Eng.R. 920.

21. See, for example, West's Ann.Cal. Civ.Code, §§ 723–725; N.Y.—McKinney's EPTL 9–2.1.

See Ramage v. First Farmers & Merch. Nat. Bank, 249 Ala. 240, 30 So.2d 706 (1947); In re Bailey's Estate, 241 Minn. 143, 62 N.W.2d 829 (1954); In re Wilson's Will, 182 Misc. 698, 45 N.Y.S.2d 167 (1943);

In re Smith's Will, 253 Wis. 72, 33 N.W.2d 320 (1948).

22. Bridgeport-City Trust Co. v. Beach, 119 Conn. 131, 174 A. 308 (1934); May v. Marx, 299 Ill.App. 442, 20 N.E.2d 359 (1939).

23. Hartford-Conn. Trust Co. v. Hartford Hospital, 141 Conn. 163, 104 A.2d 356 (1954); In re McKeown's Estate, 384 Pa. 79, 119 A.2d 76 (1956); In re Gallagher's Estate, 231 Wis. 621, 282 N.W. 615 (1938).

24. See, for example, Ill.Rev.Stat., c. 30 § 153; N.Y.—McKinney's EPTL 9–2.1(b).

And see Walliser v. Northern Trust Co. of Chicago, 338 Ill.App. 263, 87 N.E.2d 129 (1949); In re Edwards' Estate, 190 Pa. 177, 42 A. 469.

25. In re Byers' Will, Surr.Ct., 17 N.Y.S.2d 704 (1940).

been entitled thereto if such accumulation had not been directed".[26] Under the original New York Act and most current statutes such income is payable to the person "presumptively entitled to the next eventual estate".[27] In some states it has been held that in the case of testamentary trusts such income may be treated as passing by intestacy.[28]

A direction that income is to be used to pay off mortgages or other encumbrances on the trust property is clearly a technical accumulation, since it withholds income from distribution in the ordinary course and uses it in such a way as to increase the value of the capital of the trust.[29] Directions for spending income on improvements of trust realty should also be treated as provisions for accumulation, but the same would not be true of provisions for repairs and other maintenance of original value.

While there has been some argument to the effect that using income to pay premiums on life insurance held in trust is an accumulation, since such payments build up the surrender value of the policy, the better view is that the premium payments merely preserve the policy and prevent it from lapsing, and hence are like repairs to real estate.[30]

It is clear that a provision for the temporary withholding of income for the purpose of creating a reserve or sinking fund to meet future payments of income or to pay future expenses of the trust is not an accumulation clause, since such funds are formed by reasonably prudent trustees in the usual course of trust administration, do not increase the value of trust capital, and since it is not prudent to pay out every cent of income at stated intervals.[31]

A direction to add stock dividends to trust principal has not been treated as an accumulation provision, even though all or a part of the dividend might for some purposes be considered by some courts as trust income.[32]

For the purpose of encouraging the establishment of pension, and profit sharing trusts by corporations for the benefit of their employees, statutes have exempted such trusts from the operation of the rules

26. Carlberg v. State Sav. Bank & Trust Co., 312 Ill. 181, 143 N.E. 441 (1924).

27. See Ariz.R.S. § 33–240. This rule is continued in N.Y.—McKinney's EPTL 9–2.3. Compare 20 Pa.C.S.A. § 6107 (to person in whom the interest in the principal or income has vested).

The term "next eventual estate" means the estate which takes effect at the termination of the directed accumulation, whether a possessory or non-possessory estate. In re Saddington's Will, 260 App.Div. 135, 21 N.Y.S.2d 80 (1940).

28. Murphy v. Northern Trust Co., 17 Ill.2d 518, 162 N.E.2d 428 (1959).

29. Hascall v. King, 162 N.Y. 134, 56 N.E. 515.

30. In re Meyer's Estate, Sur., 119 N.Y.S.2d 737 (1953).

31. Matter of Bavier, No. 1, 164 App. Div. 358, 149 N.Y.S. 728; In re Smith's Estate, 385 Pa. 416, 123 A.2d 623 (1956).

32. Equitable Trust Co. of N.Y. v. Prentice, 250 N.Y. 1, 164 N.E. 723, 63 A.L.R. 263 (1928); In re Maris' Estate, 301 Pa. 20, 151 A. 577 (1930). But see In re Warden's Trust, 382 Pa. 311, 115 A.2d 159 (1955).

limiting income accumulations.[33]

 WESTLAW REFERENCES

accumulation /2 trust /2 income
thellusson thelluson +3 woodford
thellusson thelluson +1 act

---

33. See, for example, the current statutes of Illinois, New York and Pennsylvania previously cited in this section.

Chapter 6

CHARITABLE TRUSTS

Table of Sections

DEFINITION OF CHARITABLE TRUST [1]

§ 54. A charitable trust is a trust the performance of which will, in the opinion of the court of chancery, accomplish a substantial amount of social benefit to the public or some reasonably large class thereof.

It is immaterial that the settlor had personal motives in creating the trust, if the trust has charitable effects, but the purpose must not include profit-making by the settlor, trustees, or others.

§ 54

1. Restatement, Trusts, Second, §§ 348, 368, 375, 376.

The creation and use of a charitable trust, whether by will or inter vivos arrangements or by formation of another entity such as a charitable corporation or foundation, has been greatly complicated by the enactment of the federal Tax Reform Act of 1969 and subsequent federal legislation. See Bogert, Trusts and Trustees (rev. 2d edit.), Chap. 15.

A charitable trust is to be distinguished from an absolute gift to a charitable corporation.

A trust for "benevolent" objects may be declared a valid charitable trust, if the word "benevolent" is used as a synonym of "charitable," but not if "benevolent" is construed to mean any object which indicates merely good will toward mankind or mere liberality.

A charitable trust is frequently called a public trust,[2] or merely a charity.[3]

Judicial Definitions

Courts and legislatures have been disinclined to limit themselves by a definition of a charitable trust, but instead have given specific examples of admitted charitable purposes and then referred to the "accomplishment of other purposes" . . . "beneficial to the community".[4] Some rather vague abstract definitions have been given.

"A charity, in the legal sense, may be more fully defined as a gift, to be applied consistently with existing laws, for the benefit of an indefinite number of persons, either by bringing their minds or hearts under the influence of education or religion, by relieving their bodies from disease, suffering, or constraint, by assisting them to establish themselves in life, or by erecting and maintaining public buildings or works, or otherwise lessening the burdens of government."[5] "It [a charitable trust] includes everything that is within the letter and spirit of the Statute of Elizabeth, considering such spirit to be broad enough to include whatever will promote, in a legitimate way, the comfort, happiness, and improvement of an indefinite number of persons."[6] "The word 'charity,' as used in law, has a broader meaning and includes substantially any scheme or effort to better the condition of society or any considerable part thereof. It has been well said that any gift not inconsistent with existing laws, which is promotive of science or tends to the education, enlightening, benefit, or amelioration of the condition of mankind or the diffusion of useful knowledge, or is for the public convenience, is a charity."[7]

Requisites of the Charitable Trust in General

Private trusts have been shown to have as their objectives the furnishing of financial benefits to human beings or corporations. This is not true of the charitable trust. In such trusts the purpose is to bring social benefits to some portion of the public. While money may be paid out by the trustee to or for various persons, the purpose is not

2. Appeal of Eliot, 74 Conn. 586, 51 A. 558.

3. In re Centennial & Memorial Ass'n of Valley Forge, 235 Pa. 206, 83 A. 683.

4. Eng. Charities Act, 1960, 8 & 9 Eliz. 2, ch. 58, § 46.

5. Gray, J., in Jackson v. Phillips, 14 Allen, Mass., 539, 556. See Restatement,

Trusts, Second, § 368 (What Purposes Are Charitable).

6. Harrington v. Pier, 105 Wis. 485, 520, 82 N.W. 345, 50 L.R.A. 307, 76 Am.St. Rep. 924.

7. Wilson v. First Nat. Bank of Independence, 164 Iowa 402, 145 N.W. 948, 952, Ann.Cas.1916D, 481.

to enrich them financially but rather is to advance the public interest in a spiritual, mental, or physical manner. For example, if the trust is to relieve poverty and cash is paid out by the trustee to B, a poor man selected by the trustee, the trust is charitable because the relief of suffering and want is of social benefit, and the fact that B may receive cash or goods in course of administration of the trust is not because the settlor desired to benefit B financially but because the settlor wished to forward the cause of the relief of the impoverished, in which the state is interested. B is not a beneficiary of such a trust. Society is the beneficiary.[8] B is merely the instrumentality through which the public interest is promoted. "While human beings who are to obtain advantages from charitable trusts may be referred to as beneficiaries, the real beneficiary is the public and the human beings involved are merely the instrumentalities from whom the benefits flow." [9]

The social interest needed to qualify a trust as technically charitable must be substantial and not trifling or insignificant.[10] Charitable trusts are accorded by the law a very favorable situation as to taxation and given special privileges in many other ways. In order to justify a court of equity in validating a trust as charitable and thus sanctioning certain social disadvantages (such as freedom from taxation), the court must be convinced that there will be social advantages which will more than counterbalance the social disadvantages. A trust to aid one boy or girl to secure an education may be held to fail as a charity because of lack of a substantial amount of public benefit.[11] The size of the class through whom the community advantages are to flow may be determinative.[12] Or a trust may be deemed to provide some social advantages but also disadvantages to the public which more than offset the community gains, as in the case of a trust to propagandize against vivisection.[13]

While the courts favor charitable trusts and will strive to support them and to find a charitable intent wherever possible,[14] the court must

8. In re Petroleum Research Fund, 15 Misc.2d 23, 507, 184 N.Y.S.2d 413, 421 (1958); McKee's Estate, 378 Pa. 607, 108 A.2d 214 (1954). "The beneficiary of charitable trusts is the general public to whom the social and economic advantages accrue." In re Pruner's Estate, 390 Pa. 529, 136 A.2d 107 (1957).

9. In re Freshour's Estate, 185 Kan. 434, 345 P.2d 689 (1959).

10. Johnson v. De Pauw University, 116 Ky. 671, 76 S.W. 851, 25 Ky.Law Rep. 950; Kent v. Dunham, 142 Mass. 216, 7 N.E. 730, 56 Am.Rep. 667; Masonic Education and Charity Trust v. City of Boston, 201 Mass. 320, 87 N.E. 602.

In Pape v. Title & Trust Co., 187 Or. 175, 210 P.2d 490 (1949), it was held that a trust to furnish self-supporting women with a home in order to provide them with companionship and comforts lacked substantial social benefit.

11. Estate of Huebner, 127 Cal.App. 244, 15 P.2d 758 (1932).

12. See § 55, post, as to trusts to aid relatives of the settlor or employees of a named corporation.

13. National Anti-Vivisection Society v. Inland Rev. Com'rs (1947) 2 All Eng.R. 217.

In deciding whether a charitable trust is void for illegal objects, the court will consider whether social benefits from it outweigh the harm from the encouragement of crime. In re Robbins' Estate, 57 Cal.2d 718, 21 Cal.Rptr. 797, 371 P.2d 573 (1962).

14. Board of Directors of City Trusts of City of Philadelphia v. Maloney, 78 U.S. App.D.C. 371, 141 F.2d 275 (1944), certiorari denied 323 U.S. 714, 65 S.Ct. 40, 89 L.Ed. 574 (1944); Woodstown Nat. Bank & Trust

scrutinize the alleged charity and weigh its social benefits. It cannot accept without examination the settlor's view that the trust is charitable.[15] It must consider the amount of social advantage which will come from it. In these days of search for sources of tax revenue and consequent efforts to evade or avoid taxation, the courts are careful to make sure that a doubtful trust which is alleged to be charitable is not a mere tax avoidance device.

In some cases the charitable intent of the settlor is inferred from the nature of the work of the donee to whom property is given, as where funds are transferred to a church authority and an implication is found that the gift is to be used for religious purposes, although this is not expressly stated.[16]

The American courts do not require that the social benefit be local or domestic and support a charity for the inhabitants of a foreign country.[17] However in some states tax exemption is granted for a gift to a foreign charity only if there is a reciprocal exemption.[18]

The motive of the donor is not important in determining whether a certain gift is charitable.[19] The effect of administration of the gift is the vital matter. The settlor may have had as his principal purpose the glorification of himself or his family or the satisfaction of his vanity in making a gift for the operation of a hospital, but if the relief of disease and suffering is to be brought about by the gift the trust is charitable and the motives of the settlor are treated as minor and immaterial.[20] Thus it is immaterial that the donor described his gift as "a memorial" for himself or others.[21]

The purpose of the settlor of a charitable trust must not be to enrich others, even though he incidentally seeks to confer some public

Co. v. Snelbaker, 137 N.J.Eq. 256, 44 A.2d 210 (1945).

15. Hardage v. Hardage, 211 Ga. 80, 84 S.E.2d 54 (1954) (aid to dependents of blood relatives of settlor; class too narrow); Medical Society of S.C. v. South Carolina Nat. Bank, 197 S.C. 96, 14 S.E.2d 577 (1941) (settlor's view that her home and collection of furniture and bric-a-brac would be beneficial to the public as a museum overruled by the court).

16. In re Norman, [1947] 1 Ch. 349 (to editors of missionary society to be used as they saw fit); In re Flinn, [1948] 1 Ch. 241 (to archbishop to be used in his discretion); In re Small's Estate, 244 Iowa 1209, 58 N.W.2d 477 (1953) (gift to religious authorities; aid of religion implied).

17. Bogdanovich v. Bogdanovich, 360 Mo. 753, 230 S.W.2d 695 (1950); Martin v. Haycock, 140 N.J.Eq. 450, 55 A.2d 60 (1947).

18. See MacGregor v. Commissioner of Corporations and Taxation, 327 Mass. 484, 99 N.E.2d 468 (1951). And see Bogert, Trusts and Trustees (rev. 2d edit.), § 286.

19. In re Coleman's Estate, 167 Cal. 212, 138 P. 992, Ann.Cas.1915C, 682; Haggin v. International Trust Co., 69 Colo. 135, 169 P. 138, L.R.A.1918B, 710; French v. Calkins, 252 Ill. 243, 96 N.E. 877; Richardson v. Essex Institute, 208 Mass. 311, 94 N.E. 262, 21 Ann.Cas. 1158. In re Robbins' Estate, 57 Cal.2d 718, 21 Cal.Rptr. 797, 371 P.2d 573 (1962) (purpose to aid dependent children; motive may have been to encourage the commission of crime of political nature).

20. In re Smith's Estate, 181 Pa. 109, 37 A. 114.

21. Woodstown Nat. Bank & Tr. Co. v. Snelbaker, 136 N.J.Eq. 62, 40 A.2d 222 (1944), affirmed 137 N.J.Eq. 256, 44 A.2d 210 (1945).

benefits.[22] "It is not charity to aid a business enterprise", as a distinguished judge has stated.[23] A trust to aid a private hospital and thus benefit its stockholders is not charitable, although the operation of such an institution will undoubtedly help the sick and suffering; [24] and the same would be true of a trust to advance the interests of a private school run by a stock corporation or to aid a bank or insurance company. The settlor in his instrument must exclude the notion that he intends to aid a money-making business,[25] but this can be done inferentially, as where he makes no provision for the disposition of any profits.[26] However, a trust otherwise charitable is not rendered noncharitable because it is to charge fees, provided such income goes to aid in the operation of the charity and is not paid out as profits to stockholders or others in a similar position.[27]

A charitable trust is not confined to alms-giving. It includes relief of the poor, but also connotes the social advancement of rich and poor in education, religion, culture, and civilization. "It [a charitable trust] is not confined to mere alms-giving, or the relief of poverty and distress, but has a wider signification, which embraces the improvement and promotion of the happiness of man." [28]

If a gift is made to a charitable corporation for any or all of its purposes, with the intent that full title shall vest in the corporation, subject only to the duty of the corporation to use the gift within the purposes of its charter, no trust is created.[29] The property will be devoted to charitable purposes, but not through the medium of a trust. Trust law regarding investments and accountings, for example, will not apply. The corporation can be compelled to apply the property to its corporate purposes through a quo warranto suit by the attorney general.[30] It is sometimes difficult to determine whether the intent of a donor to a charitable corporation was to have the corporation act as trustee or to have it own the property outright.[31]

22. Re Leverhulme, [1943] 2 All Eng. 143; Sussex Trust Co. v. Beebe Hospital of Sussex County, 25 Del.Ch. 172, 15 A.2d 246 (1940).

23. Cardozo, J., in Butterworth v. Keeler, 219 N.Y. 446, 449, 114 N.E. 803.

24. Stratton v. Physio-Medical College, 149 Mass. 505, 21 N.E. 874.

25. Matter of Shattuck's Will, 193 N.Y. 446, 86 N.E. 455.

26. Mitchell v. Reeves, 123 Conn. 549, 196 A. 785 (1938); Trust Co. of Georgia v. Williams, 184 Ga. 706, 192 S.E. 913 (1937); In re Frasch's Will, 245 N.Y. 174, 156 N.E. 656 (1927).

27. Parks v. Northwestern University, 218 Ill. 381, 75 N.E. 991, 2 L.R.A., N.S., 556; Harter v. Johnson, 122 S.C. 96, 115 S.E. 217 (1922). And see Morgan v. National Trust Bank of Charlestown, 331 Ill.

182, 162 N.E. 888 (1928) (interest may be charged on student loans).

28. New England Sanitarium v. Inhabitants of Stoneham, 205 Mass. 335, 342, 91 N.E. 385.

And see Buchanan v. Kennard, 234 Mo. 117, 136 S.W. 415, 420, 37 L.R.A., N.S., 993, Ann.Cas.1912D, 50. Godfrey v. Hutchins, 28 R.I. 517, 68 A. 317.

29. Bradley v. Hill, 141 Kan. 602, 42 P.2d 580 (1935); Greek Orthodox Community v. Malicourtis, 267 Mass. 472, 166 N.E. 863 (1929); Matter of Hart, 205 App.Div. 703, 200 N.Y.S. 63 (1923).

30. St. Joseph's Hospital v. Bennett, 281 N.Y. 115, 22 N.E.2d 305 (1939).

31. Zabel v. Stewart, 153 Kan. 272, 109 P.2d 177 (1941) (to church; no words of trust used); Rohlff v. German Old People's Home, 143 Neb. 636, 10 N.W.2d 686 (1943).

Occasionally a settlor describes the purpose of his trust as "benevolence". Some courts have construed this word to mean a disposition merely to seek the well-being and comfort of others and so not to be necessarily equivalent to "charitable." [32]

The Massachusetts court, speaking through Justice Gray, has said: [33] "The word 'benevolent,' of itself, without anything in the text to qualify or restrict its ordinary meaning, clearly includes not only purposes which are deemed charitable by a court of equity; but also many acts dictated by kindness, good will, or a disposition to do good, the objects of which have no relation to the promotion of education, learning or religion, the relief of the needy, the sick or the afflicted, the support of public works or the relief of public burdens, and cannot be deemed charitable in the technical and legal sense."

In a number of cases where the gift has been to "charity *and* benevolence," it has been held that the use of "benevolence" was merely as an explanatory term, amplifying the meaning of "charity," and that therefore the trust was a valid charitable trust.[34] In cases where the gift was to "charitable or benevolent" objects, there has been a marked difference of opinion as to whether the gift could be sustained as a charitable trust. Some cases have held that the use of "benevolent" was to be qualified by its connection with "charitable," and that it was practically synonymous with "charitable." [35] "Whatever, therefore, may be the meaning, in the law of Massachusetts, of the word 'benevolence' by itself, there can be no doubt that, when used in connection with 'charity,' as in this will, it is synonymous with it; and the connecting 'or' must be taken in the sense of defining and limiting the nature of the charity intended, and of explaining one word by the other." [36] In other cases it has been held that the use of the words "benevolent or charitable" indicates an intent to provide for purposes not technically charitable, in other words, for purposes consistent only with a private trust. Hence in these cases it has been held that the trust is for a mixed charitable and private purpose, with no separation of funds to be applied to each, and therefore the whole trust must fail if of perpetual duration.[37]

It is submitted that the word "benevolent" in a trust instrument should be given a reasonable construction for the purpose of ascertaining the meaning which the settlor intended to give to it. If the other gifts and statements in the instrument and the surrounding circum-

32. Read v. McLean, 240 Ala. 501, 200 So. 109 (1941); Cochran v. McLaughlin, 128 Conn. 638, 24 A.2d 836 (1942); Boyd v. Frost Nat. Bank, 145 Tex. 206, 196 S.W.2d 497 (1946).

33. Chamberlain v. Stearns, 111 Mass. 267, 268.

34. De Camp v. Dobbins, 29 N.J.Eq. 36; People v. Powers, 147 N.Y. 104, 41 N.E. 432, 35 L.R.A. 502; In re Dulles' Estate, 218 Pa. 162, 67 A. 49, 12 L.R.A.,N.S., 1177.

35. Lutheran Home, Inc. v. Board of County Commissioners, 211 Kan. 270, 505 P.2d 1118 (1973); Saltonstall v. Sanders, 11 Allen, Mass., 462; Weber v. Bryant, 161 Mass. 400, 37 N.E. 203; Pell v. Mercer, 14 R.I. 412.

36. Saltonstall v. Sanders, 11 Allen, Mass., 462, 470.

37. In re Macduff, [1896] 2 Ch. 451; Smith v. Pond, 90 N.J.Eq. 445, 107 A. 800.

stances show that he meant by "benevolent" the equivalent of "charitable," then it would seem proper to declare the trust a valid charitable trust. The modern tendency is toward considering the word "benevolent" as a synonym of "charitable." [38]

In an English case [39] the trust was for "purposes charitable or philanthropic." The court held the trust invalid as a charitable trust and said: "Then what is the meaning of the word 'philanthropic'? He means by that something distinguished from charitable in the ordinary sense; but I cannot put any definite meaning on the word. All I can say is that a philanthropic purpose must be a purpose which indicates good will to mankind in general." But another court has treated philanthropy as equivalent to charity.[40]

Gifts have been held charitable when they provided for the "well being of mankind",[41] or for "humanitarian" purposes,[42] or for "public welfare" objectives.[43] But the use of the words "utilitarian",[44] "liberality",[45] or "deserving" or "worthy" [46] have been held not to show a charitable intent.

 WESTLAW REFERENCES

Judicial Definitions
di charitable trust
"charitable trust" /5 defin!

Requisites of the Charitable Trust in General
"charitable trust" /s society /s beneficiary
charitable /2 trust /s social public /2 benefit interest
75k49
75k10 /p "charitable trust" /s public social /2 interest
find 371 p2d 573
75k4
"charitable trust" /5 purpose

38. Smith v. United States Nat. Bk. of Denver, 120 Colo. 167, 207 P.2d 1194 (1949); In re Snell's Will, 154 Kan. 654, 121 P.2d 200 (1942); Moore v. Sellers, 201 S.W.2d 248 (Tex.Civ.App.1947). And see Scott, Trusts for charitable and benevolent purposes, 58 Harv.L.R. 548.

And see N.Y.—McKinney's EPTL 8–1.1 ("disposition of property for religious, charitable, educational or benevolent purposes").

Many other statutes treat "charitable" and "benevolent" as having the same connotation. See Mich.C.L.A. § 554.351; Minn.—M.S.A. § 501.12; W.Va.Code, 35–2–1; Wyo.Stats., § 34–5–114.

For a decision construing the state constitution and a tax statute to this effect, see Lutheran Home, Inc. v. Board of County Commissioners, 211 Kan. 270, 505 P.2d 1118 (1973).

39. In re Macduff, [1896] 2 Ch. 451, 464.

40. Thorp v. Lund, 227 Mass. 474, 116 N.E. 946.

41. In re Scholler's Estate, 403 Pa. 97, 169 A.2d 554 (1961).

42. Pace v. Dukes, 205 Ga. 835, 55 S.E.2d 367 (1949).

43. C.I.R. v. Upjohn's Estate, 124 F.2d 73 (6th Cir.1941).

44. In re Woodgate, 2 T.L.R. 674.

45. Morice v. Bishop of Durham, 9 Ves. 399, 10 Ves. 521.

46. Re Gillingham Bus Disaster Fund, (1958) 1 All Eng.R. 37; affirmed (1958) 2 All Eng.R. 749. But see In re Funk's Estate, 353 Pa. 321, 45 A.2d 67, 163 A.L.R. 780 (1946) ("worthy" held charitable).

di(charitable   /s   purpose   /s   gift)

371k241.1(1)   /p   "charitable   purpose"

75k30

75k37(6)

75k37(1)

75k1

gift   /s   charitable   /s   intent

INDEFINITENESS—PURPOSE AND BENEFICIARIES [1]

§ 55. It is often stated by the courts that indefiniteness of beneficiaries is not an objection in the case of a charitable trust and in fact that charitable trusts must have indefinite beneficiaries. These statements are based on the misconception that the persons to or for whom the trustee applies the trust fund are its beneficiaries. They are in fact merely the conduits through whom benefits flow to the public which is the real beneficiary. Although the persons through whom the public is to receive charitable benefits are usually unidentified when the trust is created, and are usually to be selected by the trustee later, it is not believed that this characteristic is vital. The important requirement is that an appreciably large amount of social benefit accrue. This may come about in rare cases through a trust for a large group of identifiable persons, but usually it can only come through having the benefits pass to a large class whose membership is not fixed and who are to take over a long period.

The furnishing of educational or eleemosynary benefits to the relatives of the settlor is not generally regarded as a charitable object.

Trusts set up by group contributions to a mutual aid fund are private in their nature.

If the settlor states the purpose of his trust in such vague language that a court cannot tell whether it is charitable or noncharitable, no enforceable trust is created.

Trusts to aid charity in general or one particular type of charity without any description of methods are sufficiently definite, since the trustee has a power of selection among charitable purposes.

The courts have sometimes stated that indefiniteness of beneficiaries is not only not a defect in the case of a charitable trust but also that charitable trusts must have indefinite beneficiaries, and that a charitable trust cannot exist for persons who are known and defined at the time the trust begins.[2] Thus under this view a trust to aid the poor of Jonesville, a hamlet of 50 people, indefinitely into the future, would undoubtedly be good, although there might at present be only one poor

§ 55

1. Restatement, Trusts, Second, §§ 364, 375.

2. Averill v. Lewis, 106 Conn. 582, 138 A. 815 (1927); Russell v. Allen, 107 U.S. 163, 167, 2 S.Ct. 327, 27 L.Ed. 397 (1883).

family in the village. The persons to be aided would be those to be selected by the trustees for years to come out of now existing persons and those to be born. However a trust to aid John Brown and his wife and children, who constituted a small group of poor persons, would be invalid as a charity, although it might be a good private trust.

These statements ignore the fact that the human beings who are aided by the administration of a charity are not technically beneficiaries but rather the intermediaries through whom an advantage to the public is achieved. The state or community or public is the beneficiary. The important element is not the definiteness or indefiniteness of the persons to be aided, but rather the amount of social benefit which flows to the public. If the group is small, and consists of named living persons, aid of them will bring about a relatively small amount of social benefit, and the court will not be justified in calling the trust charitable and giving it all the special privileges which charitable trusts have, such as tax exemption. But if the group is reasonably large, even though its members are identifiable and a list of them could be made, then provisions for them may cause sufficient social advantage to make the trust charitable.[3] Thus a trust to aid sufferers from a certain flood, fire, or mine explosion has been treated as charitable.[4] An investigation would disclose to the trustee at the beginning of the trust all the persons who were eligible to receive help in such a case, and thus the human beings to be affected would be definite or identifiable. Yet their large number and the character of the aid to be rendered gives the state an interest sufficient to justify calling the trust charitable.

While it has been established in England that a trust to relieve poor relations of the settlor is charitable,[5] and this doctrine has been unwillingly followed in later cases, the contrary position has been taken by the American courts in many cases because of the lack of substantial public benefit,[6] and the same position has been taken with regard to a trust to educate descendants of the testator.[7] Here the class to receive benefits might be large in number, if the trust were to continue for

---

3. Harrison v. Barker Annuity Fund, 90 F.2d 286 (7th Cir.1937); Dwan, Charities for definite persons, 82 U.Pa.L.R. 12.

4. Pease v. Pattison, 32 Ch.D. 154; In re Northern Ontario Fire Relief Fund, 11 Dom.L.R. 15; Kerner v. Thompson, 365 Ill. 149, 6 N.E.2d 131 (1936); Boenhardt v. Loch, 56 Misc. 406, 107 N.Y.S. 786, affirmed 129 N.Y.App.Div. 355, 113 N.Y.S. 747, affirmed 198 N.Y. 631, 92 N.E. 1078. But see, *contra*, Doyle v. Whalen, 87 Me. 414, 32 A. 1022, 31 L.R.A. 118.

5. Holding such trusts for the relief of poverty charitable, see: Isaac v. De Friez, Amb. 595; In re Scarisbrick, [1950] 1 Ch. 226 (but not charitable to distribute the principal at the death of the settlor's children among their poor relatives).

6. Stanton v. Stanton, 140 Conn. 504; Hardage v. Hardage, 211 Ga. 80, 84 S.E.2d 54 (1954); Kent v. Dunham, 142 Mass. 216, 7 N.E. 730.

7. Holding such trusts for education charitable, see Griffith Flood's Case, Hob. 136 (to educate one person of the donor's blood from time to time in the future); Swasey v. American Bible Society, 57 Me. 523 (to educate one pious relative for the ministry). But see, *contra*, In re Compton, [1945] Ch. 123 (to educate the descendants of three named persons); Jones v. Webster, 133 Ohio St. 492, 14 N.E.2d 928 (1938) (to educate the descendants of the testator indefinitely into the future); Ross v. Stiff, 47 Tenn.App. 355, 338 S.W.2d 244 (1959).

many generations, so that the amount of social advantage would be substantial. However some courts have been impressed with the lack of public spirit on the part of the settlor and with the fact that the settlor might well have been seeking tax avoidance by giving his trust a surface appearance of a charitable nature.

If the members of a large group make contributions toward a common fund, to be administered by trustees, the income and principal to be used to furnish help to the contributors or their relatives if they are sick, disabled, or out of work, the courts do not treat the trust as charitable [8] but rather as a private trust or as giving contractual rights in the nature of insurance. They lay stress on the fact that the beneficiaries in effect have purchased their benefits. It is sometimes said that in the case of a true charitable trust those to be aided must be "suppliants" [9] and must take their benefits gratuitously. This seems to lay undue stress on the source of the funds, and insufficient emphasis on the effect which the trust would have on the community.[10]

If any conveyance or contract or other legal transaction is so uncertain in its terms that its meaning cannot be ascertained by a court, the court will declare it void for uncertainty and will not enforce rights claimed under it. A trust, private or public, is no exception to this rule. If the court cannot tell what the settlor meant to be done by the trustee, it cannot tell whether the trustee has performed his duty, it cannot direct the trustee, and it will decline to sustain the trust. It may be doubtful whether the settlor intended a charitable or a private trust, or what type of charitable aid he desired to secure.[11]

This rule against vagueness and uncertainty of purpose has been variously stated by the courts. The New York Court of Appeals has said that a charitable trust "may be so indefinite and uncertain in its purposes as distinguished from its beneficiaries as to be impracticable, if not impossible for the courts to administer." [12] Thus a trust to pay the income to "such highly evolved individuals, with much occult knowledge who are ceaselessly working for the advancement of the Race and the alleviation of the suffering of Humanity, as to him, my said executor and trustee may seem worthy, and be deemed wise", has been held void on account of uncertainty.[13]

8. Burke v. Roper, 79 Ala. 138; In re Henderson's Estate, 17 Cal.2d 853, 112 P.2d 605 (1941); In re Hobourn Aero Components Ltd.'s Air Raid Distress Fund, [1946] 1 Ch. 194.

9. In re Sharp's Estate, 71 Pa.Super. 34, 37; In re Lowe's Estate, 326 Pa. 375, 192 A. 405 (1937).

10. Burke v. Roper, 79 Ala. 138; Coe v. Washington Mills, 149 Mass. 543, 21 N.E. 966; Powers v. Home for Aged Women, 58 R.I. 323, 192 A. 770, 110 A.L.R. 1361 (1937).

11. Re Warre's Will Trusts, (1953) 2 All Eng.R. 99 (to charitable organization to be disposed of according to a scheme to be framed by it, held too indefinite). The courts are reluctant to strike a trust down as too indefinite and go to great lengths to spell out a charitable objective and required certainty. In re Small's Estate, 244 Iowa 1209, 58 N.W.2d 477 (1953) (vague description of type of religion to be aided).

12. In re Shattuck's Will, 193 N.Y. 446, 451, 86 N.E. 455. Compare N.Y.— McKinney's EPTL 8–1.1(a) (a charitable trust is not "invalid by reason of the indefiniteness or uncertainty of the persons designated as beneficiaries").

13. In re Carpenter's Estate, 163 Misc. 474, 297 N.Y.S. 649 (1937).

The following directions concerning charitable trusts have been held to be sufficiently definite as to purpose and class and, therefore, to create enforceable trusts: to the vestrymen of a church, to be used as they deem best for the interests of the church; [14] to be devoted perpetually to human beneficence and charity; [15] for the support of the poor of a certain county; [16] for the diffusion of useful knowledge and instruction among the institutes, clubs or meetings of the working classes,[17] to be used in the dissemination of the gospel at home and abroad; [18] in trust to be used purely and solely for charitable purposes, for the greatest relief of human suffering, human wants, and for the good of the greatest number; [19] to the cause of Christ, for the benefit and promotion of true evangelical piety and religion; [20] for the propagation of the Christian religion among the heathen.[21]

In a few states statutes require more than the normal amount of definiteness in a gift to charity.[22] In some decisions a rather illiberal attitude has been shown on the subject of certainty; [23] in these instances the court or legislature has required that the settlor give more details and plans of administration than are ordinarily required. Normally, methods of attaining charitable objectives can be left to the discretion of the trustee and need not be outlined by the settlor.[24]

It is well settled that a gift to charity or a trust for charity,[25] without any further description, or a trust for one type of charity in general, for example, a trust for the poor or a trust to aid in educational work, is not indefinite or vague.[26] The trustee has power to apply the property to specific objects. The general description is sufficient to enable the court to decide whether the trustee's administration is

14. Biscoe v. Thweatt, 74 Ark. 545, 86 S.W. 432, 4 Ann.Cas. 1136.

15. In re Hinckley's Estate, Myr.Prob., Cal., 189.

16. Heuser v. Harris, 42 Ill. 425.

17. Sweeney v. Sampson, 5 Ind. 465.

18. Attorney General v. Wallace's Devisees, 7 B.Mon., 46 Ky. 611.

19. Everett v. Carr, 59 Me. 325. "To be spent in charity in Italy and New York City" is not too indefinite. Stewart v. Franchetti, 167 App.Div. 541, 153 N.Y.S. 453.

20. Going v. Emery, 16 Pick., Mass., 107, 26 Am.Dec. 645.

21. Phillips Academy v. King, 12 Mass. 546. A gift "for missions and like good objects" is valid. Coffin v. Attorney General, 231 Mass. 579, 121 N.E. 397.

22. Offic.Code of Ga.Ann. 53–12–75; Ky.—K.R.S. § 381.260. And see Stoeer v. Meyer, 285 Ky. 387, 147 S.W.2d 1041 (1941) (trustee to pay funds to such educational or charitable institutions in a town in Germany as the highest official of that place

designated, held too uncertain under the statute).

23. Wentura v. Kinnerk, 319 Mo. 1068, 5 S.W.2d 66 (1928); Woodcock v. Wachovia Bank & Trust Co., 214 N.C. 224, 199 S.E. 20 (1938) (to such corporations or associations as will best promote the cause of preventing cruelty to animals).

24. Shannon v. Eno, 120 Conn. 77, 179 A. 479 (1935); Taylor v. Trustees of Jesse Parker Williams Hospital, 190 Ga. 349, 9 S.E.2d 165 (1940); Powers v. First Nat. Bank of Corsicana, 138 Tex. 604, 161 S.W.2d 273 (1942).

25. Kirwin v. Attorney General, 275 Mass. 34, 175 N.E. 164 (1931); Anderson's Estate, 269 Pa. 535, 112 A. 766 (1921). See Bunn's Estate, 33 Cal.2d 897, 206 P.2d 635 (1949) (funds to be distributed to a worthy charity to be selected by executor, held valid charitable gift).

26. Grant v. Saunders, 121 Iowa 80, 95 N.W. 411, 100 Am.St.Rep. 310; Whicker v. Hume, 7 H.L.C. 124 (to advance learning all over the world).

proper. If the gift is "to charity" or "to the poor", it is implied that the testator must have contemplated a trust as a means of administration.[27]

 WESTLAW REFERENCES

75k21(1) /p beneficiary /5 large unascertain! indefinit! unknown identif! certain!

charitable public /3 trust /s beneficiary /s fixed short limited /3 number class duration time period

75k7 /p famil! relative

charitable public /2 trust /s social societ** /3 benefit

purpose intent intention** intend! /5 vague! ambigu! uncertain** indefinit! /s trust /10 enforc! unenforcea! non-enforcea! sustain*** uph*ld

HISTORY OF CHARITABLE TRUSTS—STATUTE OF CHARITABLE USES

§ 56. Prior to 1601 charitable uses were recognized and enforced by the English Court of Chancery. In 1601 the English Statute of Charitable Uses was enacted. It enumerated some of the more important charities then in force and provided for their better protection and enforcement.

The Statute of Charitable Uses is considered to be a part of the common law in some states, but in most states charitable trusts have depended for their enforcement entirely on the general jurisdiction of equity over all trusts. In a few jurisdictions statutes are required to give validity to charitable trusts. In some states the law with regard to the validity and limitations of charitable trusts has been codified. The net result is that charitable trusts are recognized and enforced in all states, with very slight exceptions described below.

In 1601 the English Parliament enacted a statute which has come to be known as the Statute of Charitable Uses.[1] Prior thereto the court of chancery had recognized and enforced many charitable trusts.[2] The Statute recited that property had been given for certain enumerated charitable purposes and that the trustees of the charities were, in many cases, neglecting the performance of their duties, and it then proceeded to provide for the enforcement of these charitable trusts by the appoint-

---

27. In re Finkelstein's Estate, 189 Misc. 180, 70 N.Y.S.2d 596 (1947); In re Jordan's Estate, 329 Pa. 427, 197 A. 150 (1938).

§ 56

1. St. 43 Eliz. c. 4. The preamble enumerated the following as some of the purposes for which charities had been established at that time: Relief of aged, impotent, and poor people, maintenance of sick and maimed soldiers and mariners, schools of learning, free schools, and scholars in universities, repair of bridges, ports,

havens, causeways, churches, seabanks and highways, education, and preferment of orphans, relief, stock or maintenance of houses of correction, marriages of poor maids, supportation, aid and help of young tradesmen, handicraftsmen, and persons decayed, relief and redemption of prisoners and captives, aid of any poor inhabitants concerning payments of fifteens, setting out of soldiers, and other taxes. 7 Pickering's English Statutes, p. 43.

2. See Charities in Tudor and Stuart times. Keeton, 26 Sol. 181.

ment of commissioners by the Lord Chancellor or the Chancellor of the Duchy of Lancaster. These commissions might be issued to bishops of the established church or to other persons and were to authorize the issuance of orders for enforcement.

It seems to have been the view of some courts, manifested in early decisions, that the Statute of Charitable Uses *validated* charitable trusts and that they had no life separate and apart from that statute and its successors.[3] Since in some states the statute had been expressly repealed or had been declared not a part of the common law, under this view charitable trusts could not be created. This question was carefully considered by Mr. Justice Story in Vidal v. Girard's Ex'rs,[4] where there was a gift by a resident of Pennsylvania to the City of Philadelphia for the establishment of a school for orphans, and the courts of that commonwealth had held that the Statute of Charitable Uses was not in effect. Mr. Justice Story showed that charitable uses were known and supported prior to the Statute of Charitable Uses, and that the statute merely recognized the existence of such uses and provided for their enforcement. He referred to the views of English judges which supported his contention and also to the then recent report of the Commissioners of Public Records in England, in which a collection of early chancery cases involving charitable trusts was made. Of these early cases, prior to the Statute of Charitable Uses, he said: "They establish in the most satisfactory and conclusive manner that cases of charities where there were trustees appointed for general and indefinite charities, as well as for specific charities, were familiarly known to, and acted upon, and enforced in the court of chancery. In some of these cases the charities were not only of an uncertain and indefinite nature; but, as far as we can gather from the imperfect statement in the printed records, they were also cases where there were either no trustees appointed, or the trustees were not competent to take." [5] To the report of this case is attached a schedule of early cases in chancery, showing the existence and enforcement of charitable uses prior to the Statute of Elizabeth.[6]

That charitable uses were not validated by the Statute of Charitable Uses, but had an independent existence in chancery apart from that statute, has been recognized by the courts of most states.[7] In some

---

3. Philadelphia Baptist Ass'n v. Hart, 17 U.S. (4 Wheat.) 1, 4 L.Ed. 499 (1819) (gift by will of resident of Virginia where Statute of Charitable Uses was not in force, to aid young men to obtain an education for the ministry, held void); Gass v. Wilhite, 2 Dana, Ky., 170, 26 Am.Dec. 446; Dashiell v. Attorney General, 5 Har. & J., Md., 392, 9 Am.Dec. 572; Griffin v. Graham, 8 N.C. 96, 1 Hawks 96, 9 Am.Dec. 619.

4. 43 U.S. (2 How.) 127, 11 L.Ed. 205 (1844).

5. 43 U.S. (2 How.) 127, 194, 11 L.Ed. 205 (1844).

6. 43 U.S. (2 How.) 127, 155, 11 L.Ed. 205 (1844).

7. Carter v. Balfour Adm'r, 19 Ala. 814; In re Hinckley's Estate, 58 Cal. 457; Beall v. Fox's Ex'rs, 4 Ga. 404; Grimes' Ex'rs v. Harmon, 35 Ind. 198, 9 Am.Rep. 690; Miller v. Chittenden, 2 Iowa 315; Going v. Emery, 33 Mass. (16 Pick.) 107, 26 Am.Dec. 645; Chambers v. St. Louis, 29 Mo. 543; Griffin v. Graham, 8 N.C. (1 Hawks) 96, 9 Am.Dec. 619; Landis v. Wooden, 1 Ohio St. 160, 59 Am.Dec. 615; Zimmerman v. Anders, 6 Watts & S., Pa.,

states the courts declare that the Statute is a part of the common law,[8] although it would seem to be a remedial statute which made use of enforcement machinery not available in the United States (as, for example, officers of the established church) and hence that the Statute was not suited to this country.

In other states the view is that the Statute is not in force but that charities are valid by reason of the general powers of equity to enforce all trusts.[9] In Virginia, West Virginia, and Maryland the courts were early led into error by the decision of the United States Supreme Court in Philadelphia Baptist Ass'n v. Hart,[10] and held that charitable uses depended for existence on the Statute, and that the Statute not being in force in those jurisdictions no charitable trusts could exist.[11] Thus gifts to charity could only be made by outright gifts to charitable corporations. This early mistake has been rectified by legislation sanctioning most charitable trusts.[12]

In New York the English Statute of Charitable Uses was repudiated in 1788.[13] The Revised Statutes of 1830 authorized only four classes of express trusts in land and did not mention charitable trusts.[14] It became a question whether charitable trusts had any existence after the adoption of the Revised Statutes. On the one hand, it was claimed that no charitable trust could exist, since the Statute of Charitable Uses was not in force and since the Revised Statutes made no provision for charitable trusts. On the other, it was maintained that the original jurisdiction of chancery over charitable trusts, irrespective of the Statute of Elizabeth, ought to enable the courts to support charitable trusts. The dispute went on for many years, the courts at first leaning to the view that charitable trusts could be supported under equity's general jurisdiction, but later taking a definite stand that charitable trusts were not possible in New York in view of the statute of 1788 and the Revised Statutes of 1830.[15] The only method by which a charitable

218, 40 Am.Dec. 552; Hopkins v. Upshur, 20 Tex. 89, 70 Am.Dec. 375.

8. Haggin v. International Trust Co., 69 Colo. 135, 169 P. 138, L.R.A.1918B, 710; Dickenson v. Anna, 310 Ill. 222, 141 N.E. 754, 30 A.L.R. 587 (1923); Klumpert v. Vrieland, 142 Iowa 434, 121 N.W. 34; Peirce v. Attorney General, 234 Mass. 389, 125 N.E. 609 (1920); Buchanan v. Kennard, 234 Mo. 117, 136 S.W. 415, 37 L.R.A., N.S., 993, Ann.Cas.1912D, 50.

9. For example, the District of Columbia, Nebraska, Ohio, Pennsylvania, South Carolina and Tennessee. See Bogert, Trusts and Trustees (rev. 2d edit.), § 322.

10. 17 U.S. (4 Wheat.) 1, 4 L.Ed. 499 (1819). The decision was later repudiated by the Supreme Court in Vidal v. Girard, 43 U.S. (2 How.) 127, 11 L.Ed. 205 (1844).

11. Gallego's Ex'rs v. Attorney General, 30 Va. [3 Leigh] 450, 24 Am.Dec. 650;

American Bible Soc. v. Pendleton, 7 W.Va. 79; State v. Warren, 28 Md. 338.

12. Va.Code, 1950, §§ 55–26 to 55–34; W.Va.Code, §§ 35–2–1—35–2–9; Md.Code 1957, art. 23, §§ 256–270, ET Law §§ 4–409, 14–301 to 14–302. See also, 4 Howard, 1 Md.Law Rev. 105; 25 Va.L.R. 109; 39 Va.L.R. 121. See Miller v. Mercantile Safe–Deposit & Trust Co., 224 Md. 380, 168 A.2d 184 (1961) (outline of history in Md.); Moore v. Perkins, 169 Va. 175, 192 S.E. 806 (1937); Beatty v. Union Trust & Deposit Co., 123 W.Va. 144, 13 S.E.2d 760.

13. Laws 1788, c. 46; Beekman v. Bonsor, 23 N.Y. 298, 307, 80 Am.Dec. 269.

14. See § 49, ante.

15. Williams v. Williams, 8 N.Y. 525; Bascom v. Albertson, 34 N.Y. 584; Holmes v. Mead, 52 N.Y. 332; Holland v. Alcock, 108 N.Y. 312, 16 N.E. 305, 2 Am.St.Rep. 420.

object could be accomplished during this period was by a gift to a charitable corporation absolutely, either by a donation to a corporation already in existence or to one to be formed.[16] The failure of a large charitable gift by the will of Samuel J. Tilden [17] caused so much discussion and criticism that in 1893 the legislature passed what was known as the Tilden Act, which restored the English system of charities as in force before the American Revolution.[18]

In Michigan, Wisconsin, and Minnesota the history of charitable trusts was somewhat similar to that of New York. Early legislation in these three states repudiated the Statute of Elizabeth and also adopted practically verbatim the New York chapter on uses and trusts, which declared that only four enumerated real property trusts were valid which made no mention of charitable trusts.[19] In Michigan and Minnesota this was held to prohibit charitable trusts both as to real and personal property.[20] In Wisconsin, as a result of this legislation, charitable trusts of realty were held to be impossible,[21] but gifts of personalty in trust for charitable uses were allowed because the Statute had no application to personal property.[22] Later legislation in Michigan and Wisconsin validated all charitable trusts by statutes modeled after the Tilden Act of New York.[23] A general charitable trust act in Minnesota was declared unconstitutional because of a defect in its title,[24] but a later act established the validity of all such trusts.[25]

In Mississippi a constitutional provision restricting gifts to charity [26] has been repealed.[27]

16. Wetmore v. Parker, 52 N.Y. 450; Cottman v. Grace, 112 N.Y. 299, 19 N.E. 839, 3 L.R.A. 145; Riker v. Leo, 115 N.Y. 93, 21 N.E. 719; Bird v. Merklee, 144 N.Y. 544, 39 N.E. 645, 27 L.R.A. 423.

17. Tilden v. Green, 130 N.Y. 29, 28 N.E. 880.

18. Laws 1893, c. 701. Allen v. Stevens, 161 N.Y. 122, 55 N.E. 568; Murray v. Miller, 178 N.Y. 316, 70 N.E. 870; Trustees of Sailors' Snug Harbor in City of New York v. Carmody, 211 N.Y. 296, 105 N.E. 543. N.Y.—McKinney's Real Property Law § 113, and N.Y.—McKinney's Personal Property Law, § 12, in effect prior to September 1, 1967, and the sources of the present statute. For current law, see— McKinney's EPTL 8–1.1.

19. Mich.Rev.St.1846, c. 63; Wis.Rev. St.1849, c. 57; Minn.—M.S.A. § 501.01 et seq.

20. Methodist Episcopal Church of Newark v. Clark, 41 Mich. 730, 3 N.W. 207; Shanahan v. Kelly, 88 Minn. 202, 92 N.W. 948.

21. Danforth v. City of Oshkosh, 119 Wis. 262, 97 N.W. 258.

22. Dodge v. Williams, 46 Wis. 70, 1 N.W. 92, 50 N.W. 1103.

23. Mich.Pub.Acts 1907, No. 122, formerly Mich.How.Ann.St.1912, § 10700, but repealed by Mich.Pub.Acts 1915, No. 280, which re-enacted sections 10700 and 10701, How.Ann.St.1912, and added the sentence, "Every such trust shall be liberally construed by such court so that the intentions of the creator thereof shall be carried out whenever possible," and validates all gifts under the former statute. See Mich.C.L.A. §§ 554.351, 554.352; In re Brown's Estate, 198 Mich. 544, 165 N.W. 929; Wis.S.A. 231.11(6, 7); Williams v. Oconomowoc, 167 Wis. 281, 166 N.W. 322. See Zollman, 8 Marquette L.R. 168; 10 id. 177.

24. Minn.L.1903, c. 132; Watkins v. Bigelow, 93 Minn. 210, 100 N.W. 1104.

25. Minn.L.1927, c. 180. See Minn. S.A. § 501.12. See E.S. Thurston, Charitable Gifts in Minnesota, 1 Minn.Law Rev. 201; Dwan, 14 Minn.L.R. 587.

26. Miss. Const. §§ 269, 270, provided that gifts of land to any religious corporation or to trustees for charity, and gifts of personal property to religious trustees, were void. Gifts of personal property to non-religious charitable trusts were valid.

27. See note 27 on page 216.

In the remaining states charitable trusts have from the beginning been enforced, either because of the adoption of the Statute of Elizabeth or the common law of England, or because of the enactment of statutes which declare the enforceability of charitable trusts,[28] or merely on the basis of equity's general jurisdiction.[29]

The enumeration of charitable purposes in the Statute of Charitable Uses is not considered exclusive, even in those states where that statute is adopted as a part of the common law. The list given in the statute is merely illustrative of charitable trusts theretofore established. Many other analogous and similar purposes are allowed as valid charitable objects. The Statute merely set forth some of the more common charities then in force.[30] "From the foregoing authorities, it clearly appears that the statute cannot be looked to as the sole test of what is public charity, but that 'many other uses, not named, and not within the strict letter of the statute, but which, coming within its spirit, equity and analogy, are considered charitable.' " [31]

Old Ladies' Home Ass'n v. Grubbs' Estate, 191 Miss. 250, 199 So. 287 (1940); Wells, 12 Miss.L.J. 526.

27. Const. Art. 14, § 269, repealed by L.1940, c. 325. See Bell v. Mississippi Orphans Home, 192 Miss. 205, 5 So.2d 214 (1941).

28. Conn.Gen.St.Ann. §§ 45.79, 45.80; Official Code Ga.Ann. § 53–12–70 to § 53–12–77; Ky.R.S. 381.260; Md.ET Law, § 14–301; N.C.—G.S. §§ 36A–49, 36A–52. For construction see Westport Bank & Trust Co. v. Fable, 126 Conn. 665, 13 A.2d 862 (1940); Shrader v. Erickson's Ex'r, 284 Ky. 449, 145 S.W.2d 63 (1940). As to the statute in La. (La.–R.S. 9:2271 et seq.), see Succession of Maguire, 228 La. 1096, 85 So. 2d 4 (1955).

29. Carter v. Balfour's Adm'r, 19 Ala. 814; In re Hinckley's Estate, 58 Cal. 457; Doughten v. Vandever, 5 Del.Ch. 51; Erskine v. Whitehead, 84 Ind. 357; Beidler v. Dehner, 178 Iowa 1338, 161 N.W. 32; Miller v. Tatum, 131 Ky. 490, 205 S.W. 557; Succession of Meunier, 52 La.Ann. 79, 26 So. 776, 48 L.R.A. 77; Preachers' Aid Soc. of Maine Conference of Methodist Episcopal Church v. Rich, 45 Me. 552; Bills v. Pease, 116 Me. 98, 100 A. 146, L.R.A.1917D, 1060; Sanderson v. White, 18 Pick., Mass., 328, 29 Am.Dec. 591; Thorp v. Lund, 227 Mass. 474, 116 N.E. 946, Ann. Cas.1918B, 1204; Catron v. Scarritt Collegiate Institute, 264 Mo. 713, 175 S.W. 571; In re Nilson's Estate, 81 Neb. 809, 116 N.W. 971; In re Hartung's Estate, 40 Nev. 262, 160 P. 782; Gagnon v. Wellman, 78 N.H. 327, 99 A. 786; Board of Education of City of Albuquerque v. School Dist. No. 5 of Bernalillo County, 21 N.M. 624, 157 P. 668;

Hagen v. Sacrison, 19 N.D. 160, 123 N.W. 518, 26 L.R.A., N.S., 724; Landis v. Wooden, 1 Ohio St. 160, 59 Am.Dec. 615; Pennoyer v. Wadhams, 20 Or. 274, 25 P. 720, 11 L.R.A. 210; In re Close's Estate, 260 Pa. 269, 103 A. 822; Rhode Island Hospital Trust Co. v. Olney, 14 R.I. 449; Shields v. Jolly, 1 Rich.Eq., S.C., 99, 42 Am.Dec. 349; Gibson v. Frye Institute, 137 Tenn. 452, 193 S.W. 1059, L.R.A.1917D, 1062; Hopkins v. Upshur, 20 Tex. 89, 70 Am.Dec. 375; United States v. Late Corporation of Church of Jesus Christ of Latter-Day Saints, 8 Utah 310, 31 P. 436; Burr's Ex'rs v. Smith, 7 Vt. 241, 29 Am.Dec. 154; Sussmann v. Young Men's Christian Ass'n of Seattle, 101 Wash. 487, 172 P. 554.

See Smith, 1 Ga.Bar J. 16; 11 Mont. L.R. 96; 3 Southwestern L.J. 168; Wheeler, 15 Tulane L.R. 177; Young, 43 Ill.L.R. 623; 13 Okl.L.R. 354; Fisch, American Acceptance of Charitable Trusts, 28 Notre Dame L. 219; The charitable trust as a giving device, Vestal, 1957 Wash.U.L.Q. 195; Symposium on charitable trusts (with particular reference to Ohio), 18 Oh.St.L.J. 149; Craig, Charitable Trusts in Iowa, 9 Drake L.R. 90; 7 De Paul L.R. 84 (Ill. developments).

30. Clayton v. Hallett, 30 Colo. 231, 70 P. 429, 59 L.R.A. 407, 97 Am.St.Rep. 117; Strother v. Barrow, 246 Mo. 241, 151 S.W. 960; Haynes v. Carr, 70 N.H. 463, 49 A. 638; In re Kimberly's Estate, 249 Pa. 483, 95 A. 86; Harrington v. Pier, 105 Wis. 485, 82 N.W. 345, 50 L.R.A. 307, 76 Am.St.Rep. 924.

31. Buchanan v. Kennard, 234 Mo. 117, 136 S.W. 415, 420, 37 L.R.A., N.S., 993, Ann.Cas.1912D, 50.

Since the adoption of the Statute of Charitable Uses several statutes on the subject have been adopted in England,[32] culminating in the Charities Act of 1960 [33] which was the result of a parliamentary inquiry begun in 1950 that produced an extensive report on the history and status of charities in England.[34] All of these statutes have been chiefly concerned with machinery for enforcement.[35] They have not been intended to validate charities.

 WESTLAW REFERENCES

"statute of charitable uses"

vidal +3 girards

"tilden act"

"statute of elizabeth"

RELIGIOUS PURPOSES [1]

§ 57. Provision for the support of religious institutions, workers, activities and services is regarded as of public benefit and is therefore charitable.

It is the function of the court and not the settlor to decide whether a gift qualifies as religious. No clear-cut definition of religion has been given by statute or decision.

While all the churches and sects which have large followings in the United States have been held to qualify as religious, it is not clear to what extent the courts will sanction the support of other religious beliefs as charitable.

It seems probable that a trust to combat all religions would be held void as against public policy, and clearly this would be so if the so-called religion practiced immoral or criminal acts.

While the Statute of Charitable Uses mentioned only one purpose which would nowadays be classed as religious, namely the repair of churches, this was explained by the draftsman of the statute as caused by the uncertainty in 1601 as to what would be from time to time the established religion, since it depended on the beliefs of the king, and hence trusts founded to aid one religion might be declared void in a

---

32. Mortmain and Charitable Uses Act, 51 & 52 Vict. c. 2, 1888; Charitable Uses Act, 54 & 55 Vict. c. 73, 1891; Charitable Trust Acts 1853 to 1925, 15 & 16 Geo. V, c. 27. In addition a Charities Procedure Act and a Charitable Donations Registration Act were adopted in 1812, 52 Geo. III, cc. 101 and 102: and a comprehensive Charitable Trusts Act was passed in 1853. 16 & 17 Vic., c. 137.

33. 8 & 9 Eliz. 2, c. 58. See Keeton, 20 Sol. 31.

34. See Report of the Nathan Committee, discussed in Bogert, 29 N.Y.U.L.R. 1069. The Report outlines the history of legislation and charitable enforcement in England.

35. See § 156, post, as to methods of enforcement under this and other legislation.

§ 57

1. Restatement, Trusts, Second, § 371.

later reign.[2] But thereafter, when the Church of England was made the established church, trusts for its purposes were declared charitable in many decisions, and although trusts to advance dissenting protestants, Roman Catholic and the Jewish religion were for many years denied any charitable quality and were sometimes classified as "superstitious",[3] this situation was changed by the Toleration Acts of the nineteenth century.[4]

In the United States there has never been any doubt that the advancement of religious enterprise is charitable.[5] Many of the statutes validating charities or providing for their enforcement mention religion.[6] A charitable trust may bring religious benefits to the community in a large variety of ways. For example, it may provide a site for the erection of a house of worship;[7] or for its repair,[8] or for the construction of a parsonage;[9] for the support of a particular church or denomination;[10] for the maintenance of a course of sermons;[11] to pay the salary of the pastor of a church;[12] for the support of home or foreign missions;[13] for the education of young men in the ministry;[14] for the dissemination of religious books;[15] for the aid of a Sabbath school or other religious educational institution;[16] for the benefit of a Young Men's Christian Association;[17] or to provide homes or pensions for retired religious workers and their families.[18]

A trust to aid religion, without specifying what religion or how the aid is to be furnished, is a valid charity, although admittedly giving

2. See Sir Francis Moore's exposition of the statute as given in Duke, Charities, 1805 ed., p. 125.

3. See §§ 58, 147, post. West v. Shuttleworth, 2 My. & K. 684.

4. As to dissenters, see Shrewsbury v. Hornby, 5 Hare 406; Attorney General v. Cock, 2 Ves. 273.

As to Catholics and Jews see St. 8 & 9 Vict. c. 59, § 2; St. 3 & 4 Wm. IV, c. 115; In re Michel's Trusts, 28 Beav. 39; Bradshaw v. Tasker, 2 My. & K. 221.

5. In re Small's Estate, 244 Iowa 1209, 58 N.W.2d 477 (1953) (advancement of fundamentalist doctrine); Buchanan v. Willis, 195 Tenn. 18, 255 S.W.2d 8 (1953) (new testament teachings only); Goetz v. Old Nat. Bk. of Martinsburg, 140 W.Va. 422, 84 S.E.2d 759 (1954) (must be for specific religious organizations).

6. For statutory references, see Bogert, Trusts and Trustees (rev. 2d edit.), § 376.

7. Little v. Willford, 31 Minn. 173, 17 N.W. 282; Mott v. Morris, 249 Mo. 137, 155 S.W. 434.

8. French v. Calkins, 252 Ill. 243, 96 N.E. 877.

9. Sandusky v. Sandusky, 261 Mo. 351, 168 S.W. 1150.

10. Smith v. Gardiner, 36 App.D.C. 485; Attorney General v. Town of Dublin, 38 N.H. 459; Congregational Unitarian Soc. v. Hale, 29 App.Div. 396, 51 N.Y.S. 704.

11. Attorney General v. Rector, etc., of Trinity Church, 9 Allen 422, 91 Mass. 422.

12. Prettyman v. Baker, 91 Md. 539, 46 A. 1020.

13. Hitchcock v. Board of Home Missions of Presbyterian Church, 259 Ill. 288, 102 N.E. 741, Ann.Cas.1915B, 1.

14. Field v. Drew Theological Seminary, C.C.Del., 41 F. 371.

15. Simpson v. Welcome, 72 Me. 496, 39 Am.Rep. 349.

16. Morville v. Fowle, 144 Mass. 109, 10 N.E. 766.

17. Goodell v. Union Ass'n of Children's Home of Burlington County, 29 N.J. Eq. 32.

18. Hood v. Dorer, 107 Wis. 149, 82 N.W. 546.

great latitude to the trustee,[19] and the same is true where the trustee is expressly given discretion to select methods or objects.[20]

The burden is on the court to decide whether the institutions, ideas, and practices which the settlor has sought to make the basis of a charitable trust are religious.[21] The courts have not bound themselves by any clear-cut definition of religion. In several constitutional and tax cases courts have expressed the view that belief in a divinity is essential to a religion,[22] and it may be argued that in addition to a system of ethics or morals this element is a prerequisite, but this view has not received judicial sanction. It seems clear that the settlor cannot create or adopt a set of practices and theories and describe them as his religion, and thus bind the courts to approve a trust for their advancement as charitable. Examples might exist where nudism and sun worshipping, or opposition to the slaughter of animals and consequent vegetarianism, were merely the hobbies of the settlor.

Gifts to the numerous denominations and sects of protestant Christianity have been held charitable,[23] as have donations in aid of the Roman Catholic [24] and the Jewish religions.[25] Whether trusts in support of Mohammedanism and the oriental and other religions, which have relatively small followings in America, would be treated as charitable is an undecided question. The right of all citizens to freedom of speech and religion argues for them,[26] but the result might depend on the breadth of vision and tolerance of the particular court considering the question.[27]

In Thornton v. Howe,[28] the nature of the religion which equity

19. Thompson's Estate, 282 Pa. 30, 127 A. 446 (1925).

20. In re Geppert's Estate, 75 S.D. 96, 59 N.W.2d 727 (1953).

21. In re Hummeltenberg, (1923) 1 Ch. 237 (training of spiritualistic mediums not charitable); Re Coats' Trusts, (1948) 1 Ch. 1, 340. See Glover v. Baker, 76 N.H. 393, 420, 83 A. 916, where the court said: "Mrs. Eddy had the constitutional right to entertain such opinions as she chose, and to make a religion of them, and to teach them to all others; . . . .. Whether her opinions are theologically true, the courts are not competent to decide."

22. Davis v. Beason, 133 U.S. 333, 10 S.Ct. 299, 33 L.Ed. 637 (1890) (alleged illegal establishment of a religion); Berman v. United States, 156 F.2d 377 (9th Cir.1946) (draft act); Washington Ethical Soc. v. District of Columbia, 84 Wash.L.R. 1072 (tax exemption). But see Fellowship of Humanity v. Alameda, 153 Cal.App.2d 673, 315 P.2d 394 (1957) (humanism).

23. In addition to all the larger denominations and sects the courts have approved trusts for Christian Science, the Swedenborgians, and the Shakers. Gass v.

Wilhite, 2 Dana, Ky., 170, 26 Am.Dec. 446; Glover v. Baker, 76 N.H. 393, 83 A. 916; In re Kramph's Estate, 228 Pa. 455, 77 A. 814.

24. Mannix v. Pursell, 46 Ohio St. 102, 19 N.E. 572.

25. Glaser v. Congregation Kehillath Israel, 263 Mass. 435, 161 N.E. 619 (1928).

26. See Potter v. United States, 79 F.Supp. 297 (N.D.Ill.1946) (gift to reading room of "I am" society in Chicago, which was in aid of a peculiar and unusual religion, held charitable for tax purposes); In re Grand, (1946) 1 Dom.L.R. 204 (gift under a trust to Bahai Temple of Chicago charitable).

See also Briggs v. Hartley, 19 L.J. Ch. 416 (prize for best essay on natural theology held not charitable); Korsstrom v. Barnes, 167 Fed. 216 (W.D.Wash.1909) (theosophy not religion); In re Stephan's Estate, 129 Pa.Super. 396, 195 A. 653 (1937) (upkeep of spiritualistic camp not religious charity).

27. For the older, more conservative view, see Turley, J., in Green v. Allen, 5 Humph. 170.

28. 31 Beav. 14.

would support as a charity was considered. A testatrix created a trust to aid in the propagation of the writings of Joanna Southcote, a person who believed that she was with child by the Holy Ghost and had received divine revelations. The court sustained the trust as being in aid of the Christian religion, notwithstanding that a great part of the writings of Joanna Southcote appeared to the court foolish and profitless. The court said, by way of dictum, that "the Court of Chancery makes no distinction between one sort of religion and another. . . . Neither does the court, in this respect, make any distinction between one sect and another. It may be that the tenets of a particular sect inculcate doctrines adverse to the very foundations of all religion, and that they are subversive of all morality. In such a case, if it should arise, the Court will not assist the execution of the bequest, but will declare it to be void; . . .. But if the tendency were not immoral, and although this Court might consider the opinions sought to be propagated foolish or even devoid of foundation, it would not, on that account, declare it void, or take it out of the class of legacies which are included in the general terms of charitable bequests." [29]

If the advancement of religion is for the public interest, it would seem that a trust aimed at weakening or destroying religion would be non-charitable, but the decisions on the subject are not conclusive.[30] In an early Supreme Court decision,[31] in which the settlor had provided that no clergymen were to be admitted to the grounds of a school for orphan boys which he was establishing and that no religious instruction should be given therein, Mr. Justice Story, by way of dictum, considered this problem and the argument that the trust was anti-religious. He seems to have been of the opinion that a charitable trust which repudiated or attacked the Christian religion would not be sustained, saying: "It is unnecessary for us, however, to consider what would be the legal effect of a devise in Pennsylvania for the establishment of a school or college for the propagation of Judaism, or Deism, or any other form of infidelity. Such a case is not to be presumed to exist in a Christian country, and therefore it must be made out by clear and indisputable proof. Remote inferences, or possible results, or speculative tendencies, are not to be drawn or adopted for such purposes. There must be plain, positive, and express provisions, demonstrating, not only that Christianity is not to be taught, but that it is to be impugned or repudiated." [32]

---

29. 31 Beav. 14, 19–20.

30. Bowman v. Secular Society Ltd., [1917] A.C. 406 (absolute gift to society the purpose of which was to do away with the Christian religion, held valid); Zeisweiss v. James, 63 Pa. 465 (trust for discussions in infidel society not charitable); Manners v. Philadelphia Library Co., 93 Pa. 165 (dictum that trust to propagate atheism or infidelity would be void); Knight's Estate, 159 Pa. 500, 28 A. 303 (gift to league for discussions criticising the Christian reli-gion held charitable under the Mortmain Act, the court saying: "In its broadest sense religion comprehends all systems of belief in the existence of beings superior to, and capable of exercising an influence for good or evil upon the human race".). See 31 Harv.L.R. 289; 3 Kans.City L.R. 12.

31. Vidal v. Girard, 43 U.S. (2 How.) 127, 11 L.Ed. 205 (1844).

32. 43 U.S. (2 How.) 127, 198, 199, 11 L.Ed. 205 (1844).

Clearly a trust to support a religion which had immoral or illegal practices as a part of its system would be void. Examples might exist in the cases of polygamy, human sacrifice, or the teaching of doctrines which would lead to hate and violence by one section of the community against another.

It is sometimes held that a gift to a clergyman or other church official, to be used in his discretion, without mention of any particular objectives, should be interpreted as meaning that the money was to be spent for religious work and that the gift was to the donee in his official capacity and not as a private individual.[33]

In England it is held that in order that a trust for religion shall be held charitable it must involve the bringing of religious benefits to the public or some class of it, and must not be merely a case of private religious exercises and devotions, open only to clergy, monks, nuns, or others of similar position.[34] Under this view not all religious trusts are charitable. The distinction is between public or social religion and secret or private religious exercises.

 WESTLAW REFERENCES

"charitable trust" /s religious /2 benefit purpose

75k13

thornton +3 howe

GIFT TO PROCURE THE SAYING OF MASSES [1]

§ 58. While in early English law trusts for masses were void as for "superstitious uses", recent decisions have supported them as charitable because they are in aid of religion.

In the United States a few early cases held trusts for masses void as private trusts without living beneficiaries, but present day cases treat them as charitable, or as amounting to a gift to the priest who is to say the mass, or as providing for funeral expenses.

In England trusts for the purpose of having masses said were for

It was held that the clauses under attack were not anti-religious but merely intended to preserve scholars from the distractions of the religious arguments which were then common.

33. In re Flinn, [1948] 1 Ch. 349; Roller v. Shaver, 178 Va. 467, 17 S.E.2d 419 (1941).

34. In re Delaney, L.J. 71 Ch. 811 ("There is, in truth, no 'charity' in attempting to improve one's own mind and save one's own soul."); Commissioners of Charities v. M'Cartan, [1917] 1 Ir.R. 388; Gilmour v. Coats, (1949) L.J.R. 1034 (House of Lords) (for benefit of a Carmelite convent where nuns live in seclusion and devote

themselves to contemplation, prayers and meditation); In re Warre's Will Trust, (1953) 2 All Eng.R. 99 (conduct of a "retreat" not charitable because of lack of public benefit). And see Old South Society v. Crocker, 119 Mass. 1, 24.

§ 58

1. Restatement, Trusts, Second, § 371, Comment *g*.

See also Curran, 7 Notre Dame Lawy. 42, 5 De Paul L.R. 246; O'Brien, 3 Jurist 416, 4 id. 284; O'Brien & O'Brien, 48 Dick. L.R. 179, 17 So.Cal.L.R. 144, 23 Fordham L.R. 147, 25 Boston U.L.R. 260.

many years held void as for "superstitious uses,"[2] since no religion except the Church of England was recognized; but in 1919 the House of Lords held[3] that legislation adopted in 1829 had validated them, and later decisions have treated them as charitable because they provide for religious services in the Roman Catholic Church.[4] In Ireland there were decisions to the effect that they were valid as honorary trusts, though not legally enforceable,[5] but that since they were not charitable they had to be limited in duration to the period of the Rule against Perpetuities.[6]

The doctrine of superstitious uses never had any force in America, where freedom of worship is guaranteed to all. The New York Court of Appeals, in discussing a case where a gift for masses had been made, said that "in this state, where all religious beliefs, doctrines, and forms of worship are free, so long as the public peace is not disturbed, the trust in question cannot be impeached on the ground that the use to which the fund was attempted to be devoted was a superstitious use. The efficacy of prayers for the dead is one of the doctrines of the Roman Catholic Church, of which the testator was a member; and those professing that belief are entitled in law to the same respect and protection in their religious observances as those of any other denomination. These observances cannot be condemned by any court, as matter of law, as superstitious, and the English statutes against superstitious uses can have no effect here."[7]

In the early days of litigation on the subject a few American courts took the position that trusts for masses were invalid, since they were not charities, and since there was no living beneficiary to enforce them as private trusts.[8] An Alabama court thus expressed its view: "The bequest, in the present case, is, according to the religious belief of the testator, for the benefit alone of his soul, and cannot be upheld, as a public charity, without offending every principle of law by which such charities are supported. . . . It is not valid as a private trust, for the want of a living beneficiary. A trust in form, with none to enjoy or

2. In re Fleetwood, 15 Ch.Div. 596; In re Blundell, 30 Beav. 360.

3. Bourne v. Keane, 121 L.T.R. 426.

4. In re Caus, (1934) 1 Ch. 162.

5. Reichenbach v. Quin, 21 L.R.Ir. 138; Perry v. Tuomey, 21 L.R.Ir. 480. For a similar decision, see Elmsley v. Madden, 18 Grant's Ch. 386.

6. Dillon v. Reilly, Ir.R. 10 Eq. 152; Beresford v. Jervis, 11 Ir.L.T.Rep. 128. *Accord,* Re Zeagman, 37 Ont.L.R. 536.

7. Holland v. Alcock, 108 N.Y. 312, 329, 16 N.E. 305, 2 Am.St.Rep. 420 (holding that the trust was intended as a charity but was invalid because no charitable trusts were allowed at that time). Provi-

sion could be made for masses at this time by a contract made during the life of the donor between him and a priest or church. Gilman v. McArdle, 99 N.Y. 451, 2 N.E. 464.

8. Festorazzi v. St. Joseph's Catholic Church of Mobile, 104 Ala. 327, 18 So. 394, 25 L.R.A. 360, 53 Am.St.Rep. 48; McHugh v. McCole, 97 Wis. 166, 72 N.W. 631, 40 L.R.A. 724, 65 Am.St.Rep. 106. But this latter case seems overruled by In re Kavanaugh's Will, 143 Wis. 90, 126 N.W. 672, 28 L.R.A., N.S., 470. In Minnesota a trust for masses was declared invalid under the peculiar statutory condition then prevailing. Shanahan v. Kelly, 88 Minn. 202, 92 N.W. 948.

enforce the use, is no trust." [9]

In most American states trusts for the purpose of having masses said for the soul of the settlor, or for the souls of his family or another group, are held valid as charitable trusts. They are deemed to be trusts for the purpose of having religious services performed, and the performance of such services is said to be of public benefit and not merely beneficial to the souls of the deceased persons.[10]

"The nature of the mass, like preaching, prayer, the communion, and other forms of worship, is well understood. It is intended as a repetition of the sacrifice on the cross, Christ offering Himself again through the hands of the priest, and asking pardon for sinners as He did on the cross, and it is the chief and central act of worship in the Roman Catholic Church. It is a public and external form of worship—a ceremonial which constitutes a visible action. . . . The bequest is not only for an act of religious worship, but it is an aid to the support of the clergy. Although the money is not regarded as a purchase of the mass, yet it is retained by the clergy, and, of course, aids in the maintenance of the priesthood." [11]

In one state it has been suggested that a trust for the purpose of having masses said for the benefit of all souls is valid as a charitable trust, but that a trust for masses for the souls of particular individuals might be a private trust. In a case in which the masses were to be "for the repose of all poor souls" the court said: "It [the mass] is common, and public to all, as a religious ceremony, and is therefore a religious or pious use, and is a public charity, as distinguished from a private charity, which it might be if restricted to masses for the souls of designated persons." [12]

Occasionally a trust for masses is held to be a valid private trust,[13] a result which seems indefensible. In some cases it has been held that a gift to a named priest or church for the purpose of having masses said does not create any trust, but merely amounts to an absolute gift, with a request as to its disposition.[14] In a Kansas case the words of gift were: "I give and bequeath to Rev. James Collins, for mass for his grandfather's and grandmother's soul." The court said: "The will does not undertake to create a trust. The language in which it is made is

9. Festorazzi v. St. Joseph's Catholic Church of Mobile, 104 Ala. 327, 330, 18 So. 394, 25 L.R.A. 360, 53 Am.St.Rep. 48.

10. In re Hamilton's Estate, 181 Cal. 758, 186 P. 587 (1919). Burke v. Burke, 259 Ill. 262, 102 N.E. 293; Coleman v. O'Leary's Ex'r, 114 Ky. 388, 70 S.W. 1068; In re Schouler, 134 Mass. 426; Kerrigan v. Tabb, N.J.Ch., 39 A. 701; In re Morris, 227 N.Y. 141, 124 N.E. 724 (1919); Appeal of Rhymer, 93 Pa. 142, 39 Am.Rep. 736; In re Kavanaugh's Will, 143 Wis. 90, 126 N.W. 672, 28 L.R.A., N.S., 470.

11. Hoeffer v. Clogan, 171 Ill. 462, 469, 470, 49 N.E. 527, 40 L.R.A. 730, 63 Am.St. Rep. 241.

12. Ackerman v. Fichter, 179 Ind. 392, 101 N.E. 493, 496, 46 L.R.A., N.S., 221, Ann.Cas.1915D, 1117.

13. Moran v. Moran, 104 Iowa 216, 73 N.W. 617, 39 L.R.A. 204, 65 Am.St.Rep. 443; Wilmes v. Tiernay, 187 Iowa 390, 174 N.W. 271, discussed in 5 Iowa Law Bul. 253.

14. Harrison v. Brophy, 59 Kan. 1, 51 P. 883, 40 L.R.A. 721; Sherman v. Baker, 20 R.I. 446, 40 A. 11, 40 L.R.A. 717.

advisory, persuasive, expressive of desire, 'precatory,' as called in the law of wills; but the passing of the gift is not conditioned upon the performance of the act enjoined. Upon the conscience of the donee alone is laid the duty of performing the sacred service named." [15] A gift of a sum to be expended immediately for masses for the settlor and his family may also be regarded as a valid direction to pay funeral expenses.[16]

 WESTLAW REFERENCES

trust /s saying /2 masses
harrison +3 brophy

CEMETERIES AND MONUMENTS [1]

§ 59. A direction by a testator that his executor spend a reasonable sum for the construction of a monument to the testator or for a family monument is regarded at common law as a valid provision for the payment of funeral expenses. Some statutes so provide and even extend the rule to cover decoration of graves and the purchase of a perpetual care contract.

At common law a trust for the erection of a monument to the testator, his family, or others, was not regarded as charitable, unless the monument was for an individual or group whose character and achievements were such that their glorification would bring great advantages to the public. As a private trust it would bring no financial benefit to living persons and, being indestructible, would be void as a "perpetuity" if not limited in duration to lives in being and twenty-one years.

In many states statutes have been adopted which permit perpetual trusts for the upkeep of private lots or cemeteries, as well as public cemeteries, on the theory that the social advantages coming from the decent disposition of the remains of the deceased and the marking and care of graves justify treating such trusts as charitable.

Some of these statutes permit such perpetual trusts only in case a cemetery association or other described corporate entity is made trustee, but other statutes contain no such restriction.

There is some authority at common law that trusts for the upkeep of *public* cemeteries are charitable.

Family Monuments—Funeral Expenses

The erection of a monument to a deceased person, or to him and his family, is generally regarded as a part of his funeral expenses. The executor or administrator is justified in expending a reasonable portion

---

15. Harrison v. Brophy, 59 Kan. 1, 2, 51 P. 883, 40 L.R.A. 721.

16. Chelsea Nat. Bank v. Our Lady Star of the Sea, Atlantic City, 105 N.J.Eq. 236, 147 A. 470 (1929).

§ 59

1. Restatement, Trusts, Second, §§ 124, 374, Comment *h.*

of the funds coming into his hands for the purpose of the decent interment of the deceased and for the construction of a monument above his grave, even though the will is silent on the subject. Naturally provisions in wills directing executors to perform such acts and bequeathing definite sums of money to the executors for that purpose, or giving the executors discretion as to the amount to be spent therefor, are valid, and will be enforced by the courts.[2] "We are of opinion that it is legal for a testator to provide in his will for the purchase and erection of a monument to be placed at his grave; that such expense would be a proper and legitimate part of the funeral expenses. In the absence of such a provision in the will, the probate court would be authorized in making provision for the purchase and erection of a suitable monument at the grave of the testator, the amount or cost of which should be regulated by the value of the estate." [3]

Some courts declare this rule and even extend it to include provisions for the decoration of the family lot with flowers and the making of a contract with a cemetery association for the perpetual care and upkeep of the lot and for markers or monuments.[4]

Trusts for the Construction of Monuments

At common law a trust for the construction of a monument to someone other than the testator and his family was not regarded as charitable.[5] The state had no substantial interest in the execution of such a design, since it would merely bring sentimental satisfaction to a small group of friends or relatives of the person to be celebrated.[6] An exception was made with regard to monuments for public men who have performed great services to the community and who possessed characters worthy of emulation, as in the case of national heroes, statesmen or soldiers. Here the trust is treated as charitable in that the monument will cause succeeding generations to keep in mind and imitate the traits of the person or persons to whom the monument was dedicated.[7]

2. Bell v. Briggs, 63 N.H. 592, 4 A. 702; Detwiller v. Hartman, 37 N.J.Eq. 347; In re Frazer, 92 N.Y. 239; Fite v. Beasley, 12 Lea, Tenn., 328.

3. McIlvain v. Hockaday, 36 Tex.Civ. App. 1, 2, 81 S.W. 54. To the same effect, see Wood v. Vandenburgh, 6 Paige, N.Y., 277, 285.

4. Bankers Trust Co. v. Hess, 2 N.J. Super. 308, 63 A.2d 712 (1949); In re Paddock's Will, 53 N.Y.S.2d 265 (1945); In re Poole's Will, 235 Wis. 625, 293 N.W. 918 (1940).

5. In re Byrne's Estate, 98 N.H. 300, 100 A.2d 157 (1953).

6. Bockel v. Fidelity Development Co., 101 S.W.2d 628 (Tex.Civ.App.1937).

7. Gilmer's Legatees v. Gilmer's Ex'rs, 42 Ala. 9 (confederate generals); Society of Cal. Pioneers v. McElroy, 63 Cal.App.2d 332, 146 P.2d 962 (1944) (Cal.Pioneers); Eliot v. Trinity Church, 232 Mass. 517, 122 N.E. 648 (Phillips Brooks); In re Smith's Estate, 181 Pa. 109, 37 A. 114 (union generals in Civil War); Matson v. Caledonia, 200 Wis. 43, 227 N.W. 298 (1929) (World War veterans).

And see Butin's Estate, 81 Cal.App.2d 76, 183 P.2d 304 (for citizens who have worked for welfare of county); In re Barnard's Estate, 170 Misc. 875, 11 N.Y.S.2d 115 (1939) (for Gold Star Mothers of America).

As a private trust a gift for the purpose of having a monument built has two defects, namely, that it brings no financial benefits to the living,[8] and if perpetual or of indefinite duration it may be held to violate the rule previously noted [9] to the effect that indestructible private trusts must be limited in duration to the period of the Rule against Perpetuities.[10] The first objection may be avoided by treating such a trust as honorary in jurisdictions which recognize such trusts,[11] but the second criticism cannot be overcome, since very evidently there are no beneficiaries who can demand from equity the termination of the trust and hence it is indestructible, even in jurisdictions permitting destruction where all beneficiaries are competent and unite in a demand.[12]

Trusts for the Maintenance of Cemetery Lots and Cemeteries

What has been said above regarding the common law attitude towards trusts to have monuments constructed applies also to trusts to provide upkeep and maintenance either for a single cemetery lot or for an entire private cemetery. At common law they generally were not regarded as involving substantial benefit to society and hence were not technically charitable.[13] As private trusts they lacked living beneficiaries who were to be financially benefited.[14] But the ground generally relied on for a declaration of their invalidity was that they were to last indefinitely and so involved a "perpetuity",[15] that is, an indestructible private trust not limited in duration to a period of lives in being and/or twenty-one years.[16] "The law is well settled in this country that

---

8. Kingsley v. Montgomery Cem. Co., 304 Ill.App. 273, 26 N.E.2d 613 (1940); Whiting v. Bertram, 51 Ohio App. 40, 199 N.E. 367 (1935).

9. See § 52, ante.

10. If the expenditure is sure to be made within a life in being, the trust is not objectionable on this ground. Leonard v. Haworth, 171 Mass. 496, 51 N.E. 7.

11. Re Jones, 79 T.L.R. 154; Mussett v. Bingle, W.N., 1876, 170. And see Palethorp's Estate, 69 Pa.D. & C. 500.

12. See § 152, post.

13. In re Essig's Estate, 167 Pa.Super. 66, 74 A.2d 787 (1950); Rhode Island Hosp. Trust Co. v. Proprietors of Swan Point Cemetery, 62 R.I. 83, 3 A.2d 236 (1938); Travis v. Randolph, 172 Tenn. 396, 112 S.W.2d 835 (1938).

14. Matter of Johnson's Will, 5 N.Y.S. 922, 1 Con.Surr. 518. In Pennsylvania such trusts have been supported as private trusts, the power of the orphans' court to supervise and enforce trusts offsetting the lack of a beneficiary. In re Devereux's Estate, 48 Pa.D. & C. 491. See 60 Dick. L.R. 264.

15. If the upkeep trust is limited to the period of the rule the trust may be supported as an honorary trust, where that doctrine is accepted. Lloyd v. Lloyd, 21 L.J.Ch. 596; Pirbright v. Salwey, W.N. [1896] 86.

To the effect that a donee is not authorized to apply trust property to upkeep purposes beyond the period of the Rule, see Restatement, Trusts, Second, § 124, Comment f.

16. Johnson v. Holifield, 79 Ala. 423, 58 Am.Rep. 596; In re Gay's Estate, 138 Cal. 552, 71 P. 707, 94 Am.St.Rep. 70; Burke v. Burke, 259 Ill. 262, 102 N.E. 293; Piper v. Moulton, 72 Me. 155; Lounsbury v. Trustees of Square Lake Burial Ass'n, 170 Mich. 645, 129 N.W. 36; Hilliard v. Parker, 76 N.J.Eq. 447, 74 A. 447; Sherman v. Baker, 20 R.I. 446, 40 A. 11, 40 L.R.A. 717; Drennan v. Agurs, 98 S.C. 391, 82 S.E. 622; Pope v. Alexander, 194 Tenn. 146, 250 S.W.2d 51 (1952); McIlvain v. Hockaday, 36 Tex.Civ.App. 1, 81 S.W. 54. See Clark, Unenforceable Trusts and the Rule against Perpetuities, 10 Mich.Law Rev. 31, in which the thesis is maintained that trusts of this sort should be held valid if "limited in duration to a period not

a perpetual trust cannot be created to take care of a private burial lot, unless the creation of such trust is authorized by statute." [17] "Our law does not permit the creation of trusts in perpetuity, except for charitable or public purposes. It has been repeatedly determined in this court that a trust for the purpose of keeping in repair the burial place of testator is a purely private trust, and is not a trust the object of which is a charity." [18]

In a few states the view has been maintained that a trust for the perpetual care of a private grave, monument, or cemetery lot or cemetery is a charitable trust. This is apparently on the theory that the public is benefited by the encouragement of reverence for the dead and that such sentiments improve the morals of members of the community. [19]

Statutory Validation of Perpetual Cemetery Trusts

In most states the maintenance of cemeteries is now provided by statutes allowing gifts to be made to cemetery associations or other described corporations, to be held in trust for the perpetual care of an entire cemetery or of any lot or monument. [20] And a gift to *any trustees* for the care or maintenance of a public cemetery or any private lot or monument is made a charitable trust by statute. [21] Whether these statutes expressly declare that such a trust is charitable or not, their theory is that there is social advantage in providing for the sanitary and respectful disposal of the remains of deceased persons, in marking their last resting places, and in maintaining cemetery grounds in orderly and ornamental condition. Most of the statutes apply to all cemeteries, both public and private.

Even at common law there was some authority that the maintenance of a *public* cemetery was a charitable purpose. [22] "That the

longer than twenty-one years after lives in being at the creation of the trust."

17. Mason v. Bloomington Library Ass'n, 237 Ill. 442, 446, 86 N.E. 1044, 15 Ann.Cas. 603, discussed by Kales in 5 Ill. Law Rev. 379.

18. Hilliard v. Parker, 76 N.J.Eq. 447, 448, 74 A. 447.

Care includes the placing of flowers on graves at periodic intervals. Gallagher v. Venturini, 124 N.J.Eq. 538, 3 A.2d 157 (1938); Rhode Island Hospital Tr. Co. v. Proprietors of Swan Point Cemetery, 62 R.I. 83, 3 A.2d 236 (1938).

19. Fitzgerald v. East Lawn Cemetery, 126 Conn. 286, 10 A.2d 683 (1940) (chapel in private cemetery); Ford v. Ford's Ex'r, 91 Ky. 572, 16 S.W. 451; Webster v. Sughrow, 69 N.H. 380, 45 A. 139, 48 L.R.A. 100; Opinion of the Justices, 101 N.H. 531, 133 A.2d 792 (1957). In Trustees of Methodist Episcopal Church of Milford v. Williams, 6 Boyce, Del., 62, 96 A. 795, such a

gift was upheld without a statement of reasons; and to the same effect see Delaware Trust Co. v. Delaware Trust Co., 33 Del.Ch. 443, 95 A.2d 569 (1953).

20. See, for example, N.Y.—McKinney's EPTL 8–1.6 (deposit in trust in bank). For a collection of statutory references on this subject, see Bogert, Trusts and Trustees (rev. 2d edit.), § 377. The authorized trustees sometimes include municipal corporations or public officers, churches, and banks and trust companies.

As to the effect of a gift to an entity which is not a "cemetery authority" see In re Pfund's Estate, 93 Cal.App.2d 444, 209 P.2d 52 (1949) (gift to a lodge void as a perpetuity).

21. See, for example, N.Y.—McKinney's EPTL 8–1.5.

22. Collector of Taxes of Norton v. Oldfield, 219 Mass. 374, 106 N.E. 1014; Stewart v. Coshow, 238 Mo. 662, 142 S.W.

providing and maintenance of a suitable place for the burial of the dead is one of public use and benefit is not open to question. A decent respect for the memory of the dead is a universal characteristic of civilized society." [23] If the graveyard was connected with a church, the trust may be supported as a religious charity.[24]

 WESTLAW REFERENCES

Family Monuments—Funeral Expenses

erect*** /5 monument /s "funeral expenses"

Trusts for the Construction of Monuments

trust /s construction erection /s monument

Trusts for the Maintenance of Cemetery Lots and Cemeteries

trust /s maintenance /s cemetery burial /2 lot

Statutory Validation of Perpetual Cemetery Trusts

statute /s "cemetery trust"

EDUCATION [1]

§ 60. Trusts for the education of a substantial portion of the public are charitable. This may be done by providing for the establishment or support of schools, colleges, universities, libraries, art galleries, museums or similar institutions; or by aiding students, teachers, or research workers; or by the publication and distribution of books; or in any other practicable manner.

Education need not be furnished free of charge but fees charged must not be for the profit of the owners or operators of the educational institution but rather used to pay the costs or to extend educational work.

An educational charitable trust need not be confined to poor persons, since the spread of knowledge to any large group is beneficial to society.

While generally equity will not strike down an intended educational charitable trust because it disapproves of the settlor's project or of the ideas which he seeks to advance, in rare cases, where his plan is clearly without merit, the court decrees that the trust is not charitable.

It is elementary law that trusts for education are charitable. "Not only are charities for the maintenance and relief of the poor, sick, and impotent charities in the sense of the common law, but also donations for the establishment of colleges, schools, and seminaries of learning, and especially such as are for the education of orphans and poor

283; Bliss v. Linden Cemetery Ass'n, 81 N.J.Eq. 394, 87 A. 224.

23. Chapman v. Newell, 146 Iowa 415, 125 N.W. 324, 327.

24. In re Vaughn, 33 Ch.D. 187; Green v. Hogan, 153 Mass. 462, 27 N.E. 413; Driscoll v. Hewlett, 132 App.Div. 125, 116 N.Y.S. 466, affirmed 198 N.Y. 297, 91 N.E. 784.

§ 60

1. Restatement, Trusts, Second, § 370.

scholars." [2]

Illustrations of Educational Charities

The range of educational benefactions which are valid as charitable trusts is wide. A trust to aid education in general in ways to be selected by the trustee is charitable.[3] Trusts are valid as charitable if for the purpose of founding or maintaining a school [4] or college; [5] or for the purpose of aiding or supporting public schools,[6] or to procure a site [7] or erect a building for a school; [8] or for the purpose of employing more teachers [9] or paying higher salaries to those already employed; [10] or to aid needy students in obtaining an education [11] as where loans [12] or prizes [13] are to be given, or to found scholarships [14] or award medals for good work in educational institutions; [15] or for the foundation or maintenance of libraries,[16] historical societies,[17] schools, laboratories, or museums dedicated to the advancement of science or art; [18] or for the education of certain classes of persons, for example, Indians [19] or the

2. Story, J., in Vidal v. Mayor, Aldermen and Citizens of Philadelphia, 43 U.S. (2 How.) 127, 11 L.Ed. 205 (1844). The preamble to the Statute of Charitable Uses mentioned as charitable purposes the maintenance of "schools of learning, free schools, and scholars in universities" and the "education and preferrment of orphans". Many American statutes describe education as a charitable purpose. See Bogert, Trusts and Trustees (rev. 2d edit.), § 375.

3. Whicker v. Hume, 7 H.L.Cas. 124 (to advance learning all over the world); Sweeney v. Sampson, 5 Ind. 465 (education of working classes).

4. Grand Prairie Seminary v. Morgan, 171 Ill. 444, 49 N.E. 516; Sears v. Chapman, 158 Mass. 400, 33 N.E. 604, 35 Am.St. Rep. 502; Keith v. Scales, 124 N.C. 497, 32 S.E. 809; Price v. Maxwell, 28 Pa. 23; Kelly v. Love's Adm'rs, 20 Grat., Va., 124.

5. Connecticut College for Women v. Calvert, 87 Conn. 421, 88 A. 633, 48 L.R.A., N.S., 485; Alfred University v. Hancock, 69 N.J.Eq. 470, 46 A. 178; In re Stewart's Estate, 26 Wash. 32, 66 P. 148, 67 P. 723.

6. Smart v. Durham, 77 N.H. 56, 86 A. 821; In re John's Will, 30 Or. 494, 47 P. 341, 50 P. 226, 36 L.R.A. 242.

7. Baldwin's Ex'rs v. Baldwin, 7 N.J. Eq. 211.

8. Meeting St. Baptist Soc. v. Hail, 8 R.I. 234.

9. Webster v. Wiggin, 19 R.I. 73, 31 A. 824, 28 L.R.A. 510.

10. Price v. Maxwell, 28 Pa. 23.

11. In re Curtis' Estate, 88 Vt. 445, 92 A. 965. It is not necessary that the trust be to aid poor students only. Hoyt v. Bliss, 93 Conn. 344, 105 A. 699.

12. Pattillo v. Glenn, 150 Fla. 73, 7 So. 2d 328 (1942) (loans at interest).

13. Worcester County Trust Co. v. Grand Knight of Knights of Columbus, 325 Mass. 748, 92 N.E.2d 579 (1950).

14. In re Miller, 149 App.Div. 113, 133 N.Y.S. 828.

15. In re Bartlett, 163 Mass. 509, 40 N.E. 899.

16. Franklin v. Hastings, 253 Ill. 46, 97 N.E. 265, Ann.Cas.1913A, 135; Minns v. Billings, 183 Mass. 126, 66 N.E. 593, 5 L.R.A., N.S., 686, 97 Am.St.Rep. 420. That a library and lecture room is to have a dance hall attached does not vitiate the charity, even if it were assumed that the furtherance of dancing is not a charitable purpose. Gibson v. Frye Institute, 137 Tenn. 452, 193 S.W. 1059, L.R.A.1917D, 1062.

17. Missouri Historical Soc. v. Academy of Science, 94 Mo. 459, 8 S.W. 346.

18. Richardson v. Essex Institute, 208 Mass. 311, 94 N.E. 262, 21 Ann.Cas. 1158; Farmers' Loan & Trust Co. v. Ferris, 67 App.Div. 1, 73 N.Y.S. 475; Almy v. Jones, 17 R.I. 265, 21 A. 616, 12 L.R.A. 414. And see Sessions v. Skelton, 163 Ohio St. 409, 127 N.E.2d 378 (1955) (art gallery).

See Citizens Fidelity Bank & Trust Co. v. Isaac W. Bernheim Foundation, 305 Ky. 802, 205 S.W.2d 1003 (1947) (park with arboretum and sanctuary for birds and animals).

19. Magill v. Brown, Fed.Cas. No. 8,952; Treat's Appeal, 30 Conn. 113.

poor or orphans;[20] or for education in certain branches of study, for example, in preparation for the ministry;[21] or in preparation for admission to the Naval Academy,[22] or in the domestic and useful arts;[23] or for the distribution of books,[24] or the diffusion of knowledge[25] or the creation of a lectureship,[26] or for social service work among young men and boys,[27] or for the erection of a monument in a public park dedicated to and in support of music,[28] or to establish a circulating library of phonograph records,[29] or for the promotion of research.[30]

It is not essential that the instruction to be given in the educational institution should be gratuitous, provided that any fees charged are used to pay operating expenses and not for the profit of stockholders.[31] A trust to assist a private school which is operated by a corporation run for profit is not charitable.[32] That the gift aids members of the public in obtaining an education is sufficient, even though they are obliged to bear part of the expense themselves.[33] Nor is the poverty or wealth of the persons to receive the educational benefits of importance.[34] The state is benefited by the spread of knowledge and culture among the members of any large group, regardless of their financial position.

A settlor may limit the class to be educated as he desires, so long as some substantial social benefit will result,[35] and if, in the case of gifts to a state or an agency, he does not deprive persons of their constitutional

20. Moore's Heirs v. Moore's Devisees, 4 Dana, Ky., 354, 29 Am.Dec. 417; Crow ex rel. Jones v. Clay County, 196 Mo. 234, 95 S.W. 369; Kinnaird v. Miller's Ex'r, 25 Grat., Va., 107.

21. Trustees of Washburn College v. O'Hara, 75 Kan. 700, 90 P. 234.

22. Taylor v. Columbian University, 226 U.S. 126, 33 S.Ct. 73, 57 L.Ed. 152 (1912).

23. Webster v. Morris, 66 Wis. 366, 28 N.W. 353, 57 Am.Rep. 278.

And as to musical education, see Re Levien, (1955) 3 All Eng.R. 35 (training singers and organists); Re Delius' Will Trusts, (1957) 1 All Eng.A. 854 (to promote the appreciation of a certain composer).

24. Pickering v. Shotwell, 10 Pa. 23.

25. Sweeney v. Sampson, 5 Ind. 465.

26. Richardson v. Essex Institute, 208 Mass. 311, 94 N.E. 262.

27. Starr v. Selleck, 145 App.Div. 869, 130 N.Y.S. 693.

28. Rhode Island Hospital Trust Co. v. Benedict, 41 R.I. 143, 103 A. 146.

29. In re Futterman's Estate, 197 Misc. 558, 95 N.Y.S.2d 876 (1950).

30. Speer v. Colbert, 200 U.S. 130, 26 S.Ct. 201, 50 L.Ed. 403 (1906) (historical research); Rotch v. Emerson, 105 Mass. 431 (agricultural and chemical improve-

ments); Lackland v. Walker, 151 Mo. 210, 52 S.W. 414 (botany and allied sciences); In re Frasch's Will, 245 N.Y. 174, 156 N.E. 656 (1927) (chemical research). And see Re British School of Egyptian Archeology, (1954) All Eng.R. 887 (conduct excavations in Egypt).

31. Parks v. Northwestern University, 218 Ill. 381, 75 N.E. 991, 2 L.R.A., N.S., 556.

32. Re Leverhulme, [1943] 2 All Eng. R. 143; Putman's Estate v. Gideon, 232 Mo.App. 460, 119 S.W.2d 6 (1938).

33. Burke v. Burke, 259 Ill. 262, 102 N.E. 293.

34. In re Pierce's Estate, 245 Iowa 22, 60 N.W.2d 894 (1953) (loans not confined to aiding those in financial need or who would not otherwise attend school or college).

35. Howard Savings Inst. of Newark v. Peep, 34 N.J. 494, 170 A.2d 39 (1961) (limited to protestant gentiles; riction void when college charter prohibited discrimination and Amherst College the only possible trustee); Humphrey v. Board of Trustees, 203 N.C. 201, 165 S.E. 547 (1932) (education of a single inmate of a home, to be selected periodically); Champlin v. Powers, 80 R.I. 30, 90 A.2d 787 (1952) (loans to students who were self-supporting, unmarried and did not have an automobile).

rights to equal protection of the laws.[36]

Must Chancery Approve the Educational Plan of the Settlor?

Sometimes settlors select very peculiar means of advancing education, or the ideas and theories which they seek to spread are of doubtful soundness or merit. Equity is lenient in approving as charitable trusts those encouraging the knowledge which the settlor believes would be for the best interests of mankind. It does not act as a censor and pass as charitable only those trusts which accord with the beliefs and social views of the chancellor. By and large it permits a man to use a charitable trust to secure converts for his notions, even though the majority of mankind would regard his views as freakish.[37]

However, in rare cases where the evidence shows that it is clear that no social advantage will come from the operation of the supposed educational trust, the court will declare it noncharitable,[38] as where the settlor left her home and its contents for a museum and expert evidence showed that the objects in the home were of dubious artistic merit,[39] or where money has been left to publish notes of the settlor [40] or a diary [41] and it is found that the writings had no philosophical or historical value.

WESTLAW REFERENCES

Illustrations of Education Charities

75k12

trust /s charity charitable /s education

36. In re Girard College Trusteeship, 391 Pa. 434, 138 A.2d 844 (1958) (gift to Philadelphia for school for poor, white orphan boys). In the Girard College case, the court eventually held that even though it was administered by private trustees the College had become public in nature. The trustees were enjoined from denying admission to Negro male orphans solely on the ground they were not white. See Commonwealth of Pennsylvania v. Brown, 270 F.Supp. 782 (E.D.Pa.1967), affirmed 392 F.2d 120 (3d Cir.1968), certiorari denied 391 U.S. 921, 88 S.Ct. 1811, 20 L.Ed.2d 657 (1968). See also Evans v. Newton, 382 U.S. 296, 86 S.Ct. 486, 15 L.Ed.2d 373 (1966), on remand 221 Ga. 870, 148 S.E.2d 329 (1966) (gift to establish city park for whites only); Green v. Connally, D.C.D.C., 330 F.Supp. 1150 (D.D.C.1971), affirmed 404 U.S. 997, 92 S.Ct. 564, 30 L.Ed.2d 550 (1971); Commonwealth v. Board of Directors, 353 U.S. 230, 77 S.Ct. 806, 1 L.Ed.2d 792 (1957), rehearing denied 353 U.S. 989, 77 S.Ct. 1281, 1 L.Ed.2d 1146 (1957) (unconstitutional in case of city-operated trust to exclude Negro boys).

37. Re Price, (1943) 2 All Eng.R. 505 (promote anthroposophical society); Vineland Trust Co. v. Westendorf, 86 N.J.Eq. 343, 98 A. 314, affirmed 87 N.J.Eq. 675, 103 A. 1054 ("furtherance of the broadest interpretation of metaphysical thought").

38. A trust created by the will of George Bernard Shaw to propagandize in favor of the creation of a larger alphabet was held invalid, but by compromise a portion of the fund was allowed to be used for experimentation in the subject. Re Shaw, (1957) 1 All Eng.R. 745, (1958) 1 All Eng.R. 245.

39. Medical Society of South Carolina v. South Carolina Nat. Bank of Charleston, 197 S.C. 96, 14 S.E.2d 577 (1941).

40. Wilber v. Asbury Park Nat. Bank & Trust Co., 142 N.J.Eq. 99, 59 A.2d 570 (1948), affirmed 2 N.J. 167, 65 A.2d 843 (1949).

41. State ex rel. Emmert v. Union Trust Co. of Indianapolis, 227 Ind. 571, 86 N.E.2d 450, 12 A.L.R.2d 836 (1949).

Must Chancery Approve the Educational Plans of the Settlor?

find 138 a2d 844

75k21(4)

RELIEF OF POVERTY [1]

§ 61. The relief of poverty is a charitable object. Included in this object are trusts to provide food, clothing, shelter and the other necessities of a comfortable life to those who are in want.

The term "eleemosynary" has been generally applied to two types of charitable trusts, namely, those to relieve poverty and those to promote health and aid the sick. There is great public interest in preventing want and suffering among human beings everywhere, and therefore a trust to provide the necessities of life to those who lack the means of comfortable existence is charitable.[2]

A trust of this type may merely provide for benefits to the poor generally, and leave to the discretion of the trustee the selection of those who are to be aided.[3] Or it may limit assistance to the poor of a particular group so long as it is of sufficient size to involve a substantial social benefit,[4] as where it is confined to the poor of a particular locality, foreign [5] or domestic,[6] or to the poor in a particular occupation [7] or class.[8] Examples are found in cases where the trust was to aid in establishing young men in a trade or business,[9] or to aid in procuring housing for those who lacked means,[10] or to set up or aid a pension fund

---

§ 61

1. Restatement, Trusts, Second, § 369.

2. The Statute of Charitable Uses listed as charitable the "relief of aged, impotent and poor people", the "maintenance of sick and maimed soldiers and mariners", the "preferment of orphans", procuring the "marriages of poor maids", the "supportation, aid and help of young tradesmen, handicraftsmen and persons decayed", the "relief or redemption of prisoners or captives", and the aid of "poor inhabitants" in paying taxes.

For American statutes including the relief of poverty and sickness among valid purposes of charitable trusts, see statutes referred to in Bogert, Trusts and Trustees (rev.2d edit.), § 373.

3. In re Brown's Estate, 140 Cal.App. 677, 295 P.2d 566 (1956) (relief of human misery); Altman v. McCutchen, 210 S.W.2d 63 (Mo.1948) (alleviation of human suffering).

4. As to trusts for needy relatives of the settlor, see § 55, ante.

5. Klumpert v. Vrieland, 142 Iowa 434, 121 N.W. 34.

6. Strong's Appeal, 68 Conn. 527, 37 A. 395; Trim's Estate, 168 Pa. 395, 31 A. 1071.

7. Holmes v. Coates, 159 Mass. 226, 34 N.E. 190 (disabled soldiers and sailors); In re Pattberg's Will, 282 App.Div. 770, 123 N.Y.S.2d 564 (1953), affirmed 306 N.Y. 835, 118 N.E.2d 903 (1954) (unemployment relief fund of union).

8. Beardsley v. Selectmen of Bridgeport, 53 Conn. 489, 3 A. 557 (to aid worthy, deserving, poor, white, American, Protestant, Democratic widows and orphans of Bridgeport). As to widows or orphans, see De Bruler v. Ferguson, 54 Ind. 549; Rader v. Stubblefield, 43 Wash. 334, 86 P. 560, 10 Ann.Cas. 20. And see, as to poor children, Eccles v. Rhode Island Hospital Trust Co., 90 Conn. 592, 98 A. 129; Swasey v. American Bible Soc., 57 Me. 523.

9. Franklin's Adm'x v. City of Philadelphia, 2 Pa.Dist.R. 435; Clevenger v. Rio Farms, 204 S.W.2d 40 (Tex.Civ.App.1947) (aid of farmers).

10. Bader Realty & Inv. Co. v. St. Louis Housing Authority, 358 Mo. 747, 217 S.W.2d 489 (1949) (slum clearance housing); Webster v. Wiggin, 19 R.I. 73, 31 A. 824, 28 L.R.A. 510. But see other cases

for retired employees.[11]

The settlor may prescribe the method by which he intends that the poor are to receive food, clothing, shelter, and other necessities of a comfortable existence.[12] He may direct the trustee to make payments of money to selected poor persons,[13] or to distribute to them in kind the necessities of a comfortable living,[14] or to make payments to an existing institution which aids the poor, or to establish a new institution for that purpose.[15] Such an institution may not be operated for profit, but may make charges to help in meeting operating expenses.[16]

Those to be aided by a charitable trust of this type need not be destitute or paupers,[17] but they must lack some of the elements of comfortable existence. A trust to increase the well being of those who are able to care for themselves, or to provide them with luxuries, has liberal and generous objectives but not charitable purposes.[18]

 WESTLAW REFERENCES

trust /s (relie** /2 poverty) eleemosynary

PROMOTION OF HEALTH AND AID TO THE SICK, DISABLED OR AGED [1]

§ 62. The promotion of health, the treatment of the sick, and assistance to the disabled, handicapped or aged are charitable purposes, without regard to the financial status of the persons benefited.

There is great public interest in the prevention and cure of disease, the relief of suffering, and in assistance to those who are disabled or

where the housing was not limited to the poor and the gift was held noncharitable; Harvey v. Campbell, 107 F.Supp. 757; Re Sanders' Will Trusts, (1954) 1 All Eng.R. 667.

11. Harrison v. Barker Annuity Fund, 90 F.2d 286 (7th Cir.1937); Craven v. Wilmington Teachers' Ass'n, Del.Ch., 47 A.2d 580; In re Barbieri's Estate, 8 Misc.2d 753, 167 N.Y.S.2d 962 (1957).

12. A gift for the poor is charitable even though the settlor directs that a preference as to benefits be given to his relatives. In re Guggenheimer's Estate, 168 Misc. 1, 5 N.Y.S.2d 137 (1938).

13. Sherman v. Shaw, 243 Mass. 257, 137 N.E. 374 (1922) ($100 annually to each of ten poor boys to be selected by the trustee).

14. Hilliard v. Parker, 76 N.J.Eq. 447, 74 A. 447 (to buy fuel for most needy unmarried woman in the borough).

15. Green's Adm'rs v. Fidelity Trust Co. of Louisville, 134 Ky. 311, 120 S.W.

283, 20 Ann.Cas. 861; Amory v. Attorney General, 179 Mass. 89, 60 N.E. 391; Trustees of Sailor's Snug Harbor in City of New York v. Carmody, 211 N.Y. 286, 105 N.E. 543; In re Daly's Estate, 208 Pa. 58, 57 A. 180.

16. Jensen v. Maine Eye & Ear Infirmary, 107 Me. 408, 78 A. 898, 33 L.R.A., N.S., 141.

17. In re Estate of Nilson, 81 Neb. 809, 116 N.W. 971; Kitchen v. Pitney, 94 N.J. Eq. 485, 119 A. 675 (1923).

18. Eliot's Appeal, 74 Conn. 586, 51 A. 558; Bramblett v. Trust Co. of Georgia, 182 Ga. 87, 185 S.E. 72 (1936) (home for "gentlewomen" not charitable); Pape v. Title & Trust Co., 187 Or. 175, 210 P.2d 490 (1949).

§ 62

1. Restatement, Trusts, Second, § 372. See Bogert, Trusts and Trustees (rev. 2d edit.), § 374.

handicapped or have attained old age. Trusts for these objectives are, therefore, charitable.

The methods by which public health can be promoted are, of course, numerous. Examples are found in research into the causes of certain diseases and the cures for them,[2] aid in the education of doctors or nurses,[3] and the establishment of retirement homes.[4]

Other methods open to the settlor are the aid of an existing hospital or home or other institution;[5] the establishment of a room or bed therein;[6] provision for the payment of the expenses of treatment and of medicines;[7] and the establishment of prizes for those who make important contributions to the practice of medicine or surgery.[8]

Trusts of this class may also be established to assist the blind or persons otherwise disabled or handicapped,[9] or to aid in the care of the aged by establishing a home for them or by other means.[10]

In none of the cases in this group must aid be limited to the poor.[11] The state is interested in the health and physical welfare of all its citizens.

If an institution is aided, it must be one which is not run for profit,[12] although it may make charges to assist in paying its operating expenses.[13]

 WESTLAW REFERENCES

charitable /2 trust /s sick ill disabled handicapped aged elderly

---

2. Hinson v. Smyer, 246 Ala. 644, 21 So.2d 825 (1945); In re Masson's Estate, 142 Cal.App.2d 510, 298 P.2d 619 (1956).

3. In re Carlson's Estate, 187 Kan. 543, 358 P.2d 669 (1961); Royal College v. St. Marylebone Corp., (1958) 1 All Eng.R. 129, affirmed (1959) 3 All Eng.R. 663.

4. See Case v. Hasse, 83 N.J.Eq. 170, 93 A. 728 (vacations in the country for poor children); White v. Newark, 89 N.J.Eq. 5, 103 A. 1042 (fresh air fund for the poor).

5. Noble v. First Nat. Bank of Anniston, 241 Ala. 85, 1 So.2d 289 (1941); Floyd v. Smith, 303 Mich. 137, 5 N.W.2d 695 (1942).

6. Hayden v. Connecticut Hosp. for Insane, 64 Conn. 320, 30 A. 50.

7. Raser v. Johnson, 9 Ill.App.2d 375, 132 N.E.2d 819 (1956).

8. Sheen v. Sheen, 126 N.J.Eq. 132, 8 A.2d 136 (1939) (prize annually for outstanding doctor in the country).

9. In re Somerville's Estate, 12 Cal. App.2d 430, 55 P.2d 597 (1936) (dogs to guide blind); In re Schikowsky's Estate, 155 Kan. 815, 130 P.2d 598 (1942) (disabled veterans).

10. Pacific Home v. Los Angeles, 256 P.2d 36, subsequent opinion, 41 Cal.2d 844, 264 P.2d 539 (1953); Miranda v. King, 11 N.J.Super. 165, 78 A.2d 98 (1951).

11. Dingwell v. Seymour, 91 Cal.App. 483, 267 P. 327 (1928); French v. Calkins, 252 Ill. 243, 96 N.E. 877; Allen v. Stevens, 161 N.Y. 122, 55 N.E. 568.

Homes for the aged are charitable, though not limited to poor persons, since all aged persons need medical care and nursing, and such an institution is for the relief of suffering and the preservation of health, and not for the furnishing of the necessities of life. See In re Henderson's Estate, 17 Cal.2d 853, 112 P.2d 605 (1941).

A trust to provide care for minor children whose parents are in jail is charitable, even though there is no requirement that the children be in poverty. In re Robbins' Estate, 57 Cal.2d 718, 21 Cal.Rptr. 797, 371 P.2d 573 (1962).

12. Scripps Memorial Hospital v. California Employment Commission, 24 Cal.2d 669, 151 P.2d 109, 155 A.L.R. 360 (1944).

13. McClure v. Carter, 202 Va. 191, 116 S.E.2d 260 (1960).

TRUSTS FOR COMMUNITY BENEFIT— "GOVERNMENTAL" PURPOSES [1]

§ 63. Trusts to make the life of a community safer, more comfortable and happier are charitable. They have been sometimes called "governmental" since they furnish to citizens those advantages often supplied by national, state or local governments.

A trust to bring about improvement in the constitutional or statutory law in an orderly manner is charitable, but the advancement of the cause of a political party is not charitable.

There is an important class of charitable trusts which do not fall within the categories previously mentioned. They are sometimes called "governmental" trusts. Although their limits are not clearly defined, they involve benefits to all the inhabitants of a community by making life safer, more comfortable, or happier. To some extent they supplement the work which governmental agencies do or could perform.

Thus trusts for the purpose of assisting in the payment of public debts,[2] or to relieve citizens from tax burdens,[3] or for the benefit of the inhabitants of a given municipality,[4] unincorporated area,[5] or state,[6] are valid charitable trusts of this variety. And a trust to pay the general expenses of a town,[7] or to provide a townhouse [8] or a courthouse,[9] is a trust of this class.

Further illustrations of these charitable trusts may be found in trusts to repair bridges and highways,[10] to provide a fire engine and fire house,[11] to assist a fire company,[12] to aid a life-saving station,[13] to

---

§ 63

1. Restatement, Trusts, Second, §§ 373–374.

2. Girard Trust Co. v. Russell, 102 C.C.A. 592, 179 Fed. 446 (1910).

3. Attorney General v. Busby, 24 Beav. 299.

4. Trustees of New Castle Common v. Megginson, 1 Boyce, Del., 361, 77 A. 565, Ann.Cas.1914A, 1207 ("Any gifts to and for a general public use or lessening the burdens of government are valid as charitable trusts and uses."); Garrison's Estate, 391 Pa. 234, 137 A.2d 321 (1958).

But see In re Hayward's Estate, 65 Ariz. 228, 178 P.2d 547 (1947) (trust for any purpose deemed by the trustees beneficial to the town of Paonia or the Paonia schools not charitable because the first objective might include noncharitable objects).

5. In re Langeloth's Trust, 200 Misc. 551, 102 N.Y.S.2d 978 (1951), affirmed 278 App.Div. 944, 105 N.Y.S.2d 396 (1951).

6. Franklin's Adm'x v. Philadelphia, 2 Pa.Dist.R. 435.

Some more recent statutes validate trusts for the state or its subdivisions to enable them to perform governmental functions. See, for example, N.Mex.Stat. Ann.1978, § 33–6–1 et seq.; N.Y.—McKinney's EPTL 8–1.2.

7. Collector of Taxes of Norton v. Oldfield, 219 Mass. 374, 106 N.E. 1014.

8. Coggeshall v. Pelton, 7 Johns.Ch., N.Y., 292, 11 Am.Dec. 471.

9. Jensen v. Nelson, 236 Iowa 569, 19 N.W.2d 596 (1945); Stuart v. Easton, 21 C.C.A. 146, 74 Fed. 854, (3d Cir.1896).

10. Town of Hamden v. Rice, 24 Conn. 350; Blackford v. Anderson, 226 Iowa 1138, 286 N.W. 735 (1939).

11. Magill v. Brown, Fed.Cas.No. 8,952 (1833).

12. Bethlehem Borough v. Perseverance Fire Co., 81 Pa. 445.

13. Richardson v. Mullery, 200 Mass. 247, 86 N.E. 319.

provide a fountain for furnishing drinking water[14] or for ornamental purposes,[15] and to construct a children's playhouse and playground in a public park.[16]

Trusts for laying out and improving streets,[17] planting shade trees,[18] beautifying grounds,[19] constructing or improving parks,[20] making agricultural or horticultural improvements[21] or providing municipal improvements,[22] are valid charitable trusts, because of their enhancement of human comfort and happiness and the aesthetic pleasure which they give the residents of the cities or towns concerned.

In Oklahoma, by recent statute, a trust may be created to furnish public utility services and thereby take the place of a municipality. Under this statute trusts to furnish gas, electricity, water, and airport services have been sustained.[23]

Trusts to foster patriotism are sustained as charitable trusts,[24] as are trusts to provide for the public defense in time of war,[25] or for training sailors or members of the merchant marine.[26] The promotion of peace,[27] or international good will and harmony between various classes,[28] is a charitable object.

The question has arisen whether a trust for the purpose of procuring a change in the constitution or statutes of the nation or a state is a valid charitable trust. In a Massachusetts case[29], the view was taken that a trust for the purpose of obtaining laws granting the suffrage to women was not a valid charitable trust on the ground that it was against public policy to discredit or criticise the established governmental system, but in the same case a trust to create public sentiment

14. Roach's Ex'r v. Hopkinsville, 13 Ky.Law Rep. 543.

15. Hosmer v. Detroit, 175 Mich. 267, 141 N.W. 657.

16. Board of Assessors v. Cunningham Foundation, 305 Mass. 411, 26 N.E.2d 335 (1940); In re Smith's Estate, 181 Pa. 109, 37 A. 114.

17. Beck v. Philadelphia, 17 Pa. 104.

18. Appeal of Cresson, 30 Pa. 437.

19. Penny v. Croul, 76 Mich. 471, 43 N.W. 649, 5 L.R.A. 858.

20. In re Bartlett, 163 Mass. 509, 40 N.E. 899; Burr v. Boston, 208 Mass. 537, 95 N.E. 208, 34 L.R.A., N.S., 143. Trusts for establishing an ornamental gate (Haggin v. International Trust Co., 69 Colo. 135, 169 P. 138, L.R.A.1918B, 710), or a tabernacle (Lightfoot v. Poindexter, Tex.Civ.App., 199 S.W. 1152), in a public park, have been held valid charitable trusts.

21. Rotch v. Emerson, 105 Mass. 431.

22. Trustees of New Castle Common v. Megginson, 1 Boyce, Del., 361, 77 A. 565, Ann.Cas.1914A, 1207; Franklin's Adm'x v. Philadelphia, 2 Pa.Dist.R. 435.

23. Board of County Com'rs v. Warram, 285 P.2d 1034 (Okl.1955). See 62 Okl. St.Ann. § 651 et seq. and 60 Okl.St.Ann. § 176 et seq.; Harrison v. Barton, 358 P.2d 211 (Okl.1960).

24. Sargent v. Town of Cornish, 54 N.H. 18 (for the exhibition of national flags). See § 59, ante, as to trusts to establish monuments for national heroes.

25. Re Driffil, [1949] 2 All Eng.R. 933.

26. In re Corbyn, [1941] 1 Ch. 400.

27. In re Peck's Estate, 168 Cal.App.2d 25, 335 P.2d 185 (1959) certiorari denied 361 U.S. 826, 80 S.Ct. 74, 4 L.Ed.2d 69 (1959), rehearing denied 361 U.S. 903, 80 S.Ct. 205, 4 L.Ed.2d 160 (1959); Parkhurst v. Treasurer and Receiver General, 228 Mass. 196, 117 N.E. 39. Query whether the establishment of a world government may be the objective of a charitable trust. Turner v. Rust, 228 Ark. 528, 309 S.W.2d 731 (1958).

28. Mills v. Montclair Trust Co., 139 N.J.Eq. 56, 49 A.2d 889 (1946).

29. Jackson v. Phillips, 14 Allen 539.

against Negro slavery was declared a valid charity, although the abolition of slavery would require extensive changes in the law. However later cases have distinguished between attempts to improve the law and subversion or violation of it, and have held that trusts to secure peaceful and orderly change are in the public interest.[30] Such trusts bring about discussion of proposed improvements and will in some cases result in needed reforms, and so should be regarded as of great advantage to the public. So, in an Illinois case,[31] it was held that a trust for the purpose of obtaining the passage of laws giving women the right to vote was a valid charitable trust. And in a New Jersey decision [32] a trust for the dissemination of the writings of Henry George was upheld, although these writings advocate a radical change in the method of landholding in the United States and characterize the present system as unjust. Judge Beasley, made the following statement: "I cannot perceive for what reason it is incompatible with judicial position to aid, if invested with such power, in the circulation of the works of a learned and ingenious man, putting under examination and discussion any part of the legal system. It would not seem to me that, as a judge, I was called upon to discard the use of means in the development of the law, which, in every other science, are regarded as absolute essentials." In a Washington case [33] a gift to propagate socialism was sustained as a valid charity. If the gift were for the purpose of bringing about revolution or change by violent means or disobedience of the law, it is held illegal and not charitable.[34] It is charitable to attempt to secure the enforcement of the law, for example, the statutes relating to the use of liquor or narcotics.[35]

Although it would seem that political parties seek to improve government in accordance with the beliefs of their members, and hence that a trust for the benefit of a political party would result in political education and could result to some extent in the adoption of valuable new ideas, it has been generally held that such trusts are not charitable.[36]

 WESTLAW REFERENCES

trust /s "community benefit"
trust /s "public park"

30. Collier v. Lindley, 203 Cal. 641, 266 P. 526 (1928); Taylor v. Hoag, 273 Pa. 194, 116 A. 826.

31. Garrison v. Little, 75 Ill.App. 402.

32. George v. Braddock, 45 N.J.Eq. 757, 18 A. 881, 6 L.R.A. 511, 14 Am.St.Rep. 754.

33. Peth v. Spear, 63 Wash. 291, 115 P. 164.

34. Matter of Estate of Robbins, 57 Cal.2d 718, 21 Cal.Rptr. 797, 371 P.2d 573 (1962) (a trust to aid the children of parents who were imprisoned on account of political crimes did not have the purpose of encouraging law violation).

35. Haines v. Allen, 78 Ind. 100; Gaston County United Dry Forces v. Wilkins, 211 N.C. 560, 191 S.E. 8 (1937).

36. In re Grossman's Estate, 190 Misc. 521, 75 N.Y.S.2d 335 (1947) (Socialist Labor Party); Boorse Trust, 64 Pa.D. & C. 447. "Political propaganda masquerading as education is not education within the Statute of Elizabeth." Re Hopkinson, [1949] 1 All Eng.R. 346.

trust /s "aesthetic pleasure"

trust /s plant*** /3 tree

MISCELLANEOUS ALLEGED CHARITIES [1]

§ 64. The following have been held to be noncharitable objects: aid to private social clubs or lodges; the conferring of benefits by way of mere generosity, liberality or hospitality; the care of inanimate objects of personal property or of homes or estates; the expenditure of money to satisfy a mere whim or caprice of the testator; the advancement of sport.

The following objects have been held charitable: to furnish public recreation and amusement; for settlement work, eugenics, and experiments in cooperative living; to aid the young in getting married and setting up housekeeping or getting started in a trade or business; for the purpose of conserving natural resources and scenery; to provide for homeless domestic animals and prevent cruelty to them.

There are a number of purposes which perhaps lie near the borderline of charity and do not fall clearly into any of the classes above described. The decisions in these cases may be cited to show the general attitude of the court toward substantial community benefit.

Trusts to further social life in a relatively small group, as in the case of a private club, have not been regarded as charitable.[2] The same view is taken regarding trusts for the benefit of lodges and fraternal orders.[3] Although these groups may perform a certain amount of eleemosynary or educational work, that is not their primary objective, and the cultivation of friendships and the performance of rites is not of public interest.

Merely giving money out of good will, friendliness and generosity, without regard to the need of the donee or the effect of the gift is not charitable;[4] nor is a provision for hospitality without regard to the need of those to be entertained, where the object is merely to show a kindly spirit and to increase the comfort of the guests.[5]

It is clear that trusts to preserve and care for inanimate objects

---

§ 64

1. Restatement, Trusts, Second, § 374.

2. In re Barnett, 24 T.L.R. 788; Re Topham, [1938] 1 All Eng.R. 181.

3. In re Porter, [1925] 1 Ch. 746; In re Mead's Trust Deed, (1961) 2 All Eng.R. 836 (labor union); Veterans of Foreign Wars v. Kunz, 125 Cal.App.2d 19, 269 P.2d 882 (1954); Claim of Phillips, 282 App.Div. 911, 124 N.Y.S.2d 763 (1953); Mason v. Perry, 22 R.I. 475, 48 A. 671.

4. In re Pleasants, 39 T.L.R. 675 (candy for all children in parish under 14); Goodell v. Union Ass'n of Children's Home of Burlington County, 29 N.J.Eq. 32 (Christmas gifts to all scholars in Sunday school); Shenandoah Valley Nat. Bk. v. Taylor, 192 Va. 135, 63 S.E.2d 786 (1951) (gifts to school children at Christmas and Easter).

5. Re Corelli, [1943] 2 All Eng.R. 519; In re Swayze's Estate, 120 Mont. 546, 191 P.2d 322 (1948).

such as a clock or a picture,[6] or to conserve and keep up a home or estate,[7] are not charitable, although they may be of financial benefit to owners of these types of property. As private trusts they would usually fail because of their indefinite duration and indestructible character.

Eccentric testators sometimes set up trusts to achieve sentimental caprices which they have formed, usually involving a perpetuation of the name of the donor and some public recognition of him after his death. There is no social interest in the execution of such directions.[8]

The earlier English cases had held there was no great public interest in encouraging sports such as yacht racing,[9] fishing,[10] and fox hunting,[11] and hence gifts for those objects were not charitable.[12] The later trend, both in England [13] and the United States [14] is that trusts to provide recreation, games, and amusements are charitable in that they promote health and are conducive to public happiness and contentment.

Trusts to support settlement work among the underprivileged,[15] to foster education in and the practice of eugenics,[16] to aid experiments in methods of co-operative living,[17] to assist the young in getting started in married life [18] or in a trade or business,[19] to conserve natural resources and preserve objects of natural beauty so that they may be enjoyed by the public,[20] and to protect minority groups in their legal rights,[21] are charitable.

6. In re Gassiot, 70 L.J.Ch. 242; Kelly v. Nichols, 17 R.I. 306, 21 A. 906; 18 R.I. 62, 25 A. 840, 19 L.R.A. 413.

7. Smith v. Heyward, 115 S.C. 145, 105 S.E. 275 (1920). If a house is of great historic interest, its maintenance as a museum may make its upkeep charitable. Smith v. Powers, 83 R.I. 415, 117 A.2d 844 (1955).

8. Detwiller v. Hartman, 37 N.J.Eq. 347 (to provide band to march to testator's grave on his birthday and holidays and play dirges); In re Palethorp's Estate, 249 Pa. 389, 94 A. 1060 (to furnish a guide in cemetery to lead visitors to the grave of the donor).

A trust to establish a memorial to the testator in the form of a statue or similar object is not charitable. Re Endacott, (1959) 3 All Eng.R. 652.

9. In re Nottage, [1925] 2 Ch. 649.

10. In re Clifford, 81 L.J.Ch. 220.

11. In re Thompson, [1934] 1 Ch. 342.

12. Inland Rev. Com'rs v. Glasgow Police Ath. Ass'n, (1953) 2 All Eng.R. 747 (athletic games and general pastimes in police organization).

13. Recreational Charities Act, 1958, 6 & 7 Eliz. 2, c. 17 (provide facilities for recreation and other leisure-time occupa-

tions charitable, if in the interests of social welfare).

14. Linney v. Cleveland Trust Co., 30 Ohio App. 345, 165 N.E. 101 (1928); Gibson v. Frye Institute, 137 Tenn. 452, 193 S.W. 1059, L.R.A. 197D, 1062. And see Re Dupree's Trusts, [1944] 2 All Eng. R. 443 (encourage chess tournaments and give prizes; held charitable).

15. Starr v. Selleck, 145 App.Div. 869, 130 N.Y.S. 693, affirmed 205 N.Y. 545, 98 N.E. 1116.

16. Collier v. Lindley, 203 Cal. 641, 266 P. 526 (1928).

17. Gass v. Wilhite, 2 Dana, 32 Ky. 170 (Shakers); Peth v. Spear, 63 Wash. 291, 115 P. 164 (communistic community).

18. In re Cohen, 36 T.L.R. 16 (to aid deserving Jewish girls in getting married).

19. Trustees of Smith Charities v. Inhabitants of Northampton, 10 Allen, 92 Mass. 498.

20. Noice v. Schnell, 101 N.J.Eq. 252, 137 A. 582, 52 A.L.R. 965 (Err. & App.1927) (maintain and develop Hudson River Palisades).

21. In re Murphey's Estate, 7 Cal.2d 712, 62 P.2d 374 (1936) (safeguard rights of Jews, develop homeland in Palestine, and secure equality to them).

Trusts to provide food and shelter for homeless domestic animals [22] or to prevent cruelty to them [23] have been held charitable, on the theory that they encourage the development of qualities in the public which are characteristic of a civilized community and not because they have a beneficial effect on the animals.[24]

It has been held [25] that a trust to provide a game refuge for all wild animals (including those hostile to man) is not charitable. This would seem of doubtful soundness since there is considerable community benefit in protecting many species from extinction and in preserving animal life in its natural condition where it may be studied by scientists or the general public.

In an English case it was held [26] that a trust to combat vivisection of animals was not charitable, because any prevention of cruelty to animals that the trust might involve would be more than offset by the social disadvantage of handicapping research workers in the development of medicine and surgery.

A trust to support a single animal, or a small group of animals, is not charitable, because of the small amount of social interest involved.[27] Its status as a private enforceable [28] or honorary [29] trust is considered elsewhere.

 WESTLAW REFERENCES

noncharitable /2 trust
find 62 p2d 374

MIXED TRUSTS—CHARITABLE AND NONCHARITABLE OBJECTS [1]

§ 65. A mixed trust is one where the purpose is to accomplish charitable objects and also to achieve noncharitable results.

If a single fund is given to a trust for mixed purposes, but expressly or by implication the settlor states the proportion of principal to be used for each purpose, equity will treat the trust as if it

---

22. Shannon v. Eno, 120 Conn. 77, 179 A. 479 (1935); Siidekum v. Animal Rescue League of Pittsburgh, 353 Pa. 408, 45 A.2d 59 (1946).

23. In re Douglas, 35 Ch.Div. 472; Woodcock v. Wachovia Bank & Trust Co., 214 N.C. 224, 199 S.E. 20 (1938).

And see In re Coleman's Estate, 167 Cal. 212, 138 P. 992, Ann.Cas.1915C, 682 (providing a drinking fountain for animals).

24. In re Wedgwood, 84 L.J.Ch. 107; Re Moss, (1949) 1 All Eng.R. 495.

25. In re Grove-Grady, [1929] 1 Ch. 557.

26. National Anti-Vivisection Society v. Inland Revenue Commissioners, [1947] 2 All Eng.R. 217. But see Old Colony Trust Co. v. Welch, 25 F.Supp. 45 (D. Mass.1938).

27. In re Forrester's Estate, 86 Colo. 221, 279 P. 721 (1929); Willett v. Willett, 197 Ky. 663, 247 S.W. 739, 31 A.L.R. 426 (1923).

28. In re Bradley's Estate, 187 Wash. 221, 59 P.2d 1129 (1936). See § 35, ante.

29. In re Dean, 41 Ch.D. 552.

§ 65

1. Restatement Trusts, Second, §§ 398, 420, 421.

were two separate trusts and will enforce each part to the extent which the rules about charitable and private gifts permit.

If separation of the principal fund of the mixed trust is not possible, the trust must satisfy the requirements of both the law of charities and of private trusts in order to be valid.

If a mixed trust is destructible by the trustee, its indefinite duration is not an objection to it.

If a perpetual trust has charitable objects and also is to provide noncharitable cemetery or tomb upkeep services, there is authority for enforcing the charity and ignoring the portion having to do with the cemetery or monument.

If property is given to charity, subject to a charge for private purposes, and the latter is void, the trust for charity may be enforced free of the charge.

If a trust is mixed, and the whole of it or the private part is limited in duration to lives in being and/or twenty-one years, there is no objection to it on the ground of duration.

If a trust is for charity and also for indefinite purposes, and no separation of principal is possible, the whole trust fails for uncertainty.

Sometimes a settlor creates a single trust for the purpose of conferring social benefits on the community and also to accomplish noncharitable purposes, such as the distribution of money to friends or relatives of the settlor without regard to their need. These trusts are usually called "mixed trusts".[2] The question arises whether the validity of such a trust is to be determined by the rules of law governing the creation of charitable or of private trusts. These rules are different. For example, a charitable trust can be of indefinite duration,[3] while an indestructible private trust must be limited in its operation to lives in being and/or twenty one years.[4] Sometimes gifts to charity are governed by mortmain statutes which limit the amount of such gifts by will or require that the will be made a certain time in advance of the death of the testator,[5] while there are no such restrictions as to gifts to private persons. A trust is not mixed merely because certain human beings are named as preferred recipients of its benefits, so long as all must qualify from the point of view of need.[6] Thus a trust to aid the needy in Jonesville, with special preference being given to any needy persons named Jones living in that town, would not be a mixed trust.

2. The trust is not mixed where the noncharitable portion of the gift is void (Succession of Maguire, 228 La. 1096, 85 So.2d 4), or where the noncharitable benefits are incidental, as where a trust to furnish pensions to employees incidentally relieves employers of the burden of contributing to a pension fund. In re Tarrant's Estate, 38 Cal.2d 42, 237 P.2d 505 (1951); Newcomb v. Boston Protective Department, 151 Mass. 215, 24 N.E. 39.

3. See § 69, post.

4. See § 52, ante.

5. See § 67, post.

6. Darcy v. Kelley, 153 Mass. 433, 26 N.E. 1110; Matter of MacDowell's Will, 217 N.Y. 454, 112 N.E. 177.

If the settlor has expressly stated an intent that a certain part of the trust principal is to be devoted to charity and the remainder to private or other noncharitable purposes, the case is easy. The single trust for practical purposes amounts to two trusts and each part can be judged separately.[7] Thus if the settlor provides that one half of the trust principal shall be used to aid the needy of his home town, and the other half to make gifts in the discretion of the trustee to the testator's children, regardless of their financial condition, while the trust may be in form a single trust, in essence there are two separate trusts, one charitable and the other private.

Due to their favorable attitude toward charities, the courts will seek to find a means of separation of the principal on the basis of the settlor's intent.[8] Sometimes evidence will be taken as to what principal sum is needed to accomplish the noncharitable objects and it will be held that the testator must have desired a separation on that basis.[9]

If the court can find no express or implied intent of the settlor as to separation of the trust principal, and no other means of dividing the mixed trust into two parts or of striking out or ignoring the invalid part, the validity of the trust will be decided by applying to it the rules regarding the creation of both charitable and private trusts.[10] Thus if the settlor has made an excessive gift to a mixed trust under the mortmain statutes, the excess gift will be invalid, as where the statute makes void a gift of more than half of the testator's estate to charity when close relatives survive and the testator gives his entire estate to a mixed charitable and private trust. Here it would seem the gift should be valid as to one-half of the estate only.

And so too, the validity of the trust from the point of view of its duration will be determined by the rule that private indestructible trusts must not last longer than lives in being and/or twenty-one years.[11] If the whole trust, or the private portion of it, is certain to end within lives in being when the trust started and/or twenty-one years thereafter, the mixed trust should be treated as valid from this point of view.[12] Certain cases where mixed trusts with minor and temporary private purposes have been declared valid are perhaps explainable on

7. Amory v. Trustees of Amherst College, 229 Mass. 374, 118 N.E. 933; Pope v. Alexander, 194 Tenn. 146, 250 S.W.2d 51 (1952); Frost Nat. Bank v. Boyd, 188 S.W.2d 199 (Tex.Civ.App.1945), affirmed 145 Tex. 206, 196 S.W.2d 497, 168 A.L.R. 1326 (1946).

8. The English courts have been inclined in some cases to divide the fund equally if one charitable purpose and several private objects were named. Salusbury v. Denton, 3 K. & J. 529; Hoare v. Osborne, 1 Eq. 585.

9. Smart v. Durham, 77 N.H. 56, 86 A. 821; In re Palethorp's Estate, 249 Pa. 389, 94 A. 1060.

10. Re Corelli, [1943] 2 All Eng.R. 519; Rhode Island Hosp. Trust Co. v. Proprietors of Swan Point Cemetery, 62 R.I. 83, 3 A.2d 236 (1938); Allred v. Beggs, 125 Tex. 584, 84 S.W.2d 223 (1935); Reagh v. Dickey, 183 Wash. 564, 48 P.2d 941 (1935);

11. Estate of Dol, 186 Cal. 64, 198 P. 1039 (1921); Wilce v. Van Anden, 248 Ill. 358, 94 N.E. 42; Goetz v. Old Nat. Bank of Martinsburg, 140 W.Va. 422, 84 S.E.2d 759 (1954);

12. Davenport v. Davenport Foundation, 36 Cal.2d 67, 222 P.2d 11 (1950); Moskowitz v. Federman, 72 Ohio App. 149, 51 N.E.2d 48 (1943); In re Doering, [1949] 1 Dom.L.R. 267.

the ground that the private portion was certain to run out at the end of a few lives in being.[13]

If a mixed trust is destructible by the trustee or the beneficiaries, its duration should not be an objection to it.[14]

In some cases the courts, in their desire to sustain the charitable portion of a mixed trust, have stricken the noncharitable part and enforced the charitable part, as in the case of a perpetual trust for charity and also for tomb or cemetery upkeep, where the latter purpose is not regarded as charitable. Here the courts have directed the trustee to carry out the charitable objects, and have ignored or stricken the other parts of the trust or left them to consideration under the doctrine of honorary trusts.[15] A similar doctrine has been applied in a few cases of gifts in trust for charity, subject to a duty in the nature of a charge on the trustee to make payments for noncharitable purposes, where the latter direction has been held invalid or unenforceable and the whole property has been treated as devoted to charity.[16]

If a trust is for charity and certain other purposes of an indefinite sort which may have been intended by the settlor to be charitable or may have been intended to be for private benefit, and there is no basis for separation of the trust principal, the whole trust may fail for uncertainty.[17] The court cannot ascertain what the settlor meant and what performance of the trust is intended.

In England there has been an important statutory provision as to mixed trusts in recent years. The Nathan Report to Parliament of 1952 recommended legislation to validate them,[18] and by the Charitable Trusts (Validation) Act of 1954 [19] imperfect trust provisions were defined as those where the trust property can be used either for charitable or noncharitable purposes. Imperfect trust provisions taking effect before or after Dec. 16, 1952, are to be considered as having been for charitable purposes only, but trustees who made payments based on the invalidity of such a trust prior to 1952 are protected, and a short Statute of Limitations is provided as to attacks on imperfect trusts

---

13. In re Los Angeles County Pioneer Soc., 40 Cal.2d 852, 257 P.2d 1 (1953) (incidental social purposes); In re Hart's Estate, 151 Cal.App.2d 271, 311 P.2d 605 (1957) (domestic animals of testator to be left in public park); Woodstown Nat. Bank & Trust Co. v. Snelbaker, 136 N.J.Eq. 62, 40 A.2d 222 (1944), affirmed 137 N.J.L. 236, 44 A.2d 210 (1945); Wright's Estate, 284 Pa. 334, 131 A. 188 (1925).

14. In re Taylor, [1940] 1 Ch. 481; In re Sir Robert Peel's School, L.R. 3 Ch. 543.

15. In re Norton's Will Trusts, [1948] 2 All Eng.R. 842; St. Paul's Church v. Attorney General, 164 Mass. 188, 41 N.E. 231. For a good summary of the English law on the entire subject, see In re Coxen, [1948] 1 Ch. 747.

16. Buchanan v. Kennard, 234 Mo. 117, 136 S.W. 415, 37 L.R.A.,N.S., 993; Walker Estate, 21 Pa.D. & C. 512. And see Jones v. Habersham, 107 U.S. (17 Otto) 174, 2 S.Ct. 336, 27 L.Ed. 401 (1883).

17. Hunter v. Attorney General, [1899] D.C. 309; Estate of Sutro, 155 Cal. 727, 102 P. 920; Grigson v. Harding, 154 Me. 146, 144 A.2d 870 (1958); Chamberlain v. Stearns, 111 Mass. 267.

18. For a discussion of this report, see Bogert, 29 N.Y.U.L.R. 1069.

19. 2 & 3 Eliz. 2, c. 58.

created before 1952.[20]

 WESTLAW REFERENCES

75k12 /p "mixed trust"

"mixed trust"

75k13 /p "mixed trust"

THE CREATION OF A CHARITABLE TRUST [1]

§ 66. The requirements previously stated with regard to the creation of private trusts apply in most instances to the establishment of a charitable trust, for example, the existence of a competent settlor, the use of one of the various methods available for trust creation, the clear expression of a trust intent, and obedience to formality requisites.

Instead of identifying persons or corporations as beneficiaries, the settlor of a charity must describe a purpose which is of substantial public benefit.

The failure to name any trustee for the charitable trust, or the selection of a trustee who lacks capacity or refuses to accept the trust, is not fatal to the origin of the trust. The court fills the vacancy. Many corporations and governmental units are granted power by statute to administer charitable trusts. Community trusts and charitable foundations have capacity to accept such trusts and are often used by settlors.

Subject to some statutory restrictions as to amount of a charitable gift and the time of its making when a will is involved,[2] any owner of transferable property or person holding a power of appointment over it may create a charitable trust of it by will or deed. If he lacks capacity, for example because of insanity or infancy, his attempt may be void or voidable.

If the creation of the trust is by the will of the settlor, the document must satisfy the local wills statute as to formality.[3] Oral and informal statements by the settlor as to his intent will not be received,[4] except that they may be used to explain ambiguities in the will.[5] The settlor may add property to an existing charitable trust by giving an adequate description of the donee trust.[6]

---

20. For construction of the act, see Vernon v. Inland Rev. Com'rs, (1956) 3 All Eng.R. 14; In re Harpur's Will Trusts, (1960) 2 All Eng.R. 237; Re Mead's Trust, (1961) 2 All Eng.R. 836.

§ 66

1. Restatement, Trusts, Second, §§ 349–358, 363.

2. See § 67, post.

3. Poole v. Starke, 324 S.W.2d 234 (Tex.Civ.App.1959).

4. First Portland Nat. Bank v. Kaler-Vaill Mem. Home, 155 Me. 50, 151 A.2d 708 (1959); Battle's Estate, 379 Pa. 140, 108 A.2d 688 (1954).

5. In re Momand's Will, 7 A.D.2d 280, 182 N.Y.S.2d 565 (1959).

6. In re Freund's Estate, 33 Misc.2d 6, 226 N.Y.S.2d 620 (1962); In re Brandenburg's Estate, 13 Wis.2d 217, 108 N.W.2d 374 (1961).

If the charitable trust is to be created by deed, the instrument must be completely filled out, signed and delivered,[7] and if the subject matter is realty the Statute of Frauds must be satisfied. Under the parol evidence rule oral evidence will not be received to vary or contradict the terms of the deed.[8]

Charitable trusts are sometimes created by public subscriptions for community causes.[9]

The settlor may create the charity by the use of a power of appointment, or by making or purchasing the making of a contract in favor of the trustee,[10] or by passing the property to the trustee by intestacy.

In his act of trust creation the settlor must describe a purpose which is of substantial public interest.[11] His objective may not be illegal.[12] The instrument must state definitely that a charitable purpose is to be attained, and not a noncharitable one or a mixed purpose.[13] But, as previously shown,[14] trusts for charity merely, or for one type of charity in general, are not objectionable. If the settlor uses words of desire and request as to the results to be achieved by his donee, a question of fact arises as to whether the language was merely precatory and created no trust.[15] The presence or absence of words of trusteeship in the conveyance is not necessarily determinative as to the existence of an intent to have a trust, although it may be of substantial probative effect.[16]

The distinction between an absolute gift to a charitable corporation, to be used for one or more of its corporate purposes, and a gift to it to hold as a trustee for charity, has been previously discussed.[17] Much litigation has arisen as to whether one or the other of these two intents was exhibited by a donor. There are no general rules for solving this

---

7. Miller v. Bowers, 163 Ohio St. 421, 127 N.E.2d 201 (1955) (deed not signed or registered with state attorney general).

8. Forbes Road Union Church v. Incorporated Trustees, 381 Pa. 249, 113 A.2d 311 (1955).

9. Niles Post No. 2074 v. Niles Mem. Hosp. Ass'n, 65 Ohio App. 238, 29 N.E.2d 631 (1936).

10. In re White's Estate, 340 Pa. 92, 16 A.2d 394 (1940).

11. See §§ 57–64, ante.

12. A trust to aid the children of convicted criminals would be void if construed as for the encouragement of law-breaking, but not if merely for the aid of such minor children who are separated from their parents. In re Robbins' Estate, 57 Cal.2d 718, 21 Cal.Rptr. 797, 371 P.2d 573 (1962).

13. Kilfoy v. Fritz, 125 Cal.App.2d 291, 270 P.2d 579 (1954); Hoenig v. Newmark, 306 S.W.2d 838 (Ky.1957).

14. See § 55, ante.

15. Lanham v. Howell, 210 Miss. 383, 49 So.2d 701 (1951), certiorari denied 342 U.S. 834, 72 S.Ct. 57, 96 L.Ed. 631 (1951); Bankers Tr. Co. v. New York Women's League, 23 N.J.Super. 170, 92 A.2d 820 (1952); In re Burton's Estate, 17 Misc.2d 948, 187 N.Y.S.2d 831 (1959).

See Dickson v. United States, 125 Mass. 311 ("wishing to contribute my mite toward suppressing the rebellion and restoring the Union I give . . . to the United States"); Matter of O'Regan's Will, 62 Misc. 592, 117 N.Y.S. 96 (to executors with request that part be used for masses and rest given to charity).

16. First Univ. Soc. of Bath v. Swett, 148 Me. 142, 90 A.2d 812 (1952); In re Mott's Will, 9 Misc.2d 1018, 171 N.Y.S.2d 403 (1958).

17. See § 54, ante.

question. The use of words of trusteeship will generally be conclusive, but a statement that the property given was to be used as a part of an endowment fund is not necessarily determinative.[18] The settlor's expression of an expectation that the property will be used by the charitable corporation for one or more charitable purposes may be held to show merely a motive for an absolute gift; [19] or it may be construed as giving the corporation an estate on condition subsequent or a determinable fee, so that failure to apply the property for charity will give the settlor a power of termination or forfeiture or will cause the property to revert to the settlor.[20] The settlor may make a gift in which the interest of the donee is to be subject to an equitable charge in favor of charity.[21]

The settlor should select and identify a trustee who is competent to take and administer the trust for charity, but, as in the case of private trusts, his failure to do so is not a bar to the origin of the trust but merely gives a basis for the appointment by the court of a qualified trustee.[22] The trustee for charity has the power to disclaim and thus create a vacancy, which the court fills [23] as it does in the case of the death or resignation of a sole trustee.

There is much statute law on the subject of the capacity of corporations, private, governmental, or municipal to accept and carry out charitable trusts.[24] Laws limiting or negating the power of certain corporations are discussed in the next section.[25]

If property is given to a trustee for the benefit of a charitable corporation or unincorporated association, the latter may be a conduit through whom benefits are to flow to the public and thus said to be a subtrustee.[26] It is not a beneficiary of the trust in a strict sense.

A relatively modern institution is available to a settlor who is seeking a trustee for charity, namely, the community trust, in which property is held and managed by corporate trustees subject to direc-

18. Gately v. El Paso County Bar Ass'n, 137 Colo. 599, 328 P.2d 381 (1958); In re Munson's Estate, 238 Minn. 358, 57 N.W.2d 22 (1953); Carlock v. Ladies Cem. Ass'n, 317 S.W.2d 432 (Mo.1958). See Town of Winchester v. Cox, 129 Conn. 106, 26 A.2d 592 (1942) (to town to be used as a park; trust created); Bradley v. Hill, 141 Kan. 602, 42 P.2d 580 (1935) (to lodge for needy members and for aid to crippled children; held absolute gift).

19. De Kay v. Board of Education, 20 Misc.2d 881, 189 N.Y.S.2d 105 (1959).

20. Moore v. Wells, 212 Ga. 446, 93 S.E.2d 731 (1956); Application of Mareck, 257 Minn. 222, 100 N.W.2d 758 (1960). See Longcor v. Red Wing, 206 Minn. 627, 289 N.W. 570 (1940) (to city for use as a public auditorium; held gift on condition subsequent); Kelly v. Wilson, 204 Miss. 56, 36 So.2d 817 (1948) (to schools so long as it

used property for a school; held determinable fee).

21. Merritt v. Bucknam, 78 Me. 504, 7 A. 383.

22. American Bible Soc. v. Wetmore, 17 Conn. 181; In re Shand's Estate, 275 Pa. 77, 118 A. 623 (1922).

23. First Nat. Bank of Chicago v. Elliott, 406 Ill. 44, 92 N.E.2d 66 (1950); In re Scott's Estate, 240 Iowa 35, 34 N.W.2d 177 (1948); Gifford v. First Nat. Bank, 285 Mich. 58, 280 N.W. 108 (1938).

24. See Bogert, Trusts and Trustees (rev. 2d edit.), § 328, for typical statutory references. Many apply to states and their agencies and to all sorts of municipal corporations.

25. See § 67, post.

26. In re Thronson's Estate, 243 Wis. 73, 9 N.W.2d 641 (1943).

tions as to its disposition for charity to be given by a distribution committee, if the donor has not specified a particular type of charity. These trusts have been established in many cities and constitute useful means of making gifts, large or small, to community charitable purposes.[27] Another type of management for charity is the charitable foundation, a large number of which have been established by wealthy families to achieve public benefits of types described in the trust instrument.[28]

 WESTLAW REFERENCES

di("charitable trust" /s creat***)

75k30

75k6 /p creat*** /s "charitable trust"

75k10 /p creat*** /s "charitable trust"

STATUTORY LIMITATIONS AS TO SETTLORS AND TRUSTEES OF CHARITABLE TRUSTS [1]

§ 67. In some states the legislatures have placed restrictions on settlors of charitable trusts designed to make sure that the settlor is competent at the time he makes the gift and that the gift is not unfair to his close relatives. These so-called Mortmain Acts make void devises and bequests to or for charity unless made by a will executed a certain length of time before the death of the testator, or make voidable gifts to charity in excess of a certain proportion of the estate of the testator if he left certain named classes of close relatives.

The invalidity of a gift where the will was executed too close to the date of the testator's death can be raised by his residuary beneficiaries or by his next of kin or heirs. Only a member of one of the classes protected by the statute can raise the question of the invalidity of that portion of the gift which is in excess of the statutory limit.

In creating a charitable trust a settlor may also be handicapped by lack of capacity on the part of his chosen trustee to receive title to the trust property, due to statutory prohibitions, limitations in the charter of the corporation selected as trustee, or lack of legal capacity on the part of the trustee. Equity stands ready, however, to supply a new trustee, if the one named by the settlor turns out to have such a disability.

27. See Bogert, Trusts and Trustees (rev. 2d edit.), § 330, and 41 Amer.Bar.A.J. 587.

28. See Bogert, Trusts and Trustees (rev. 2d edit.), § 331, and Andrews, Philanthropic Foundations. There are said to be more than 15,000 of these foundations (trusts and corporations) with combined assets estimated in excess of 15 billion dol-

lars. For a discussion of the great effect of the federal Tax Reform Act of 1969 upon the use and operations of foundations, see Bogert, Trusts and Trustees (rev. 2d edit.), Chap. 15.

§ 67

1. Restatement, Trusts, Second, § 362.

Restrictions on Gifts to Charitable Corporations and for Charitable Uses in England

Two types of statutory restrictions on charitable gifts existed until recently in England. The first was a prohibition against the gift of land to charitable and other corporations. "The purpose of these statutes in restricting the accumulation of landed property in mortmain—in the dead hand of perpetual corporations—was, on the one hand, to prevent the disinheriting of heirs and the loss of various dues to the feudal lord, and on the other, to prevent these corporations from becoming too powerful by the accumulation in their hands of what was then the main source of wealth, landed property." [2] A statute in 1888 prohibited conveyances of land to or for a corporation without a license in mortmain from the Crown.[3] These restrictions were removed by the Charities Act of 1960,[4] on the recommendation of the Nathan parliamentary committee.

The second statutory restriction was made by the so-called Georgian Statute of Mortmain, adopted in 1736,[5] to the effect that no gift of land should be made for charitable uses, except by deed executed at least twelve months before the death of the grantor, before two witnesses, to take effect immediately, and to be enrolled within six months of its making. This act "was designed to meet the danger of undue pressure on the dying to make dispositions in favor of religious or other charitable foundations".[6] Obviously it prohibited gifts by will for charitable uses. The substance of this statute was continued in the Mortmain and Charitable Uses Act of 1888.[7] Another act in 1891 permitted gifts of land by will for charitable uses, but required the land to be sold within one year from the death of the testator, unless the time was extended by a court or the Charity Commissioners.[8] These mortmain provisions were repealed by the Charities Act of 1960 [9] on the ground that they involved "an anachronism in the conditions of the twentieth century".[10]

Restrictions in the United States

In the United States only a small number of states have felt the need for restrictions on donors to charity, either as to the time of the gift or the amount, and mortmain statutes in six states and the District of Columbia have either been repealed or held unconstitutional.[11] In

---

2. Report of Nathan Committee regarding charitable trusts, p. 61.

3. 51 & 52 Vic., c. 42. See Wills Act, 1837, 7 Wm. IV and 1 Vic. c. 26 (devises to corporations permitted).

4. 8 & 9 Eliz. 2, c. 58.

5. 9 Geo. 2, c. 36.

6. Report of Nathan Committee, p. 65.

7. 51 & 52 Vic., c. 42.

8. 54 & 55 Vic., c. 73.

9. 8 & 9 Eliz. 2, c. 58.

10. Report of Nathan Committee, p. 65.

11. Repealed: West's Ann.Cal.Prob. Code §§ 40–43; Iowa Code Ann. § 633.266; N.Y.—McKinney's EPTL § 5–3.3; Ohio R.C. § 2107.06; 20 Pa.C.S.A. § 2507.

And see R.C.Mont.1947, § 72–11–334 (held repealed by the Montana adoption of the Uniform Probate Code; Estate of Holmes, 183 Mont. 290, 599 P.2d 344 (1979)).

several jurisdictions devises and bequests to charitable corporations or in trust for charity are declared invalid unless the will was executed a substantial time before the death of the testator, the period varying from thirty days to one year.[12]

In several other states the statute requires that the gift to charity be executed prior to a specified date before the testator's death and places a limit on the fraction of the estate that can be given to charity.[13] The object is to prevent gifts to charity being made by a testator at a time when he is weakened in mind and body, unable to deliberate calmly regarding the ethical claims of his family upon him, and when he may be subject to improper influences from representatives of charities.[14]

If the gift is made by a will executed too close to the date of the testator's death or which leaves too large a portion of the estate to charity, it may be held void so that the gift property or excess amount would pass as provided by the statute, which usually states that it may be claimed by the successors of the testator, that is, by his residuary legatees or devisees, or if he had no residuary clause in his will by his heirs or next of kin.[15]

If a testator makes a gift to charity by a will executed in due time under these statutes, but later he makes a codicil to the will, or revokes it and executes a substitute will, in either case at a date which is closer to the death of the testator than the statute allows, the original gift to charity is held to take effect as a timely gift to the extent of its original amount, unless reduced or revoked by the later codicil or substitute will. The reaffirmation of the original gift by the codicil or new will is not regarded as making the validity of the gift depend on the time when the codicil or new will was executed.[16]

If a testator attempts to avoid the statute by making an absolute gift on an oral agreement that the property is to be held for charity, and he dies within the named period, the constructive trust which would arise for charity if the donee should fail to carry out his oral agreement will not be decreed, nor will voluntary execution of the oral trust by the donee be permitted, and the successors of the testator may claim the property.[17] But no evasion is involved if the testator makes

Held unconstitutional: D.C.Code 1981, § 18–302 (In re Small's Estate, 346 F.Supp. 600 (D.D.C.1972), Estate of French, 1976, 365 A.2d 621).

12. West's Fla.S.A. § 732.803; Idaho Code § 15–2–615.

13. Official Code Ga.Ann. § 53–2–10; Miss.Const. § 270, Miss.Code § 91–5–31.

14. For background materials and the text of current and former statutes, see Bogert, Trusts and Trustees (rev. 2d edit.), § 326.

15. In re Estate of Graham, 63 Cal. App. 41, 218 P. 84 (1923); In re Coleman's Estate, 66 Idaho 567, 163 P.2d 847 (1945).

16. In re Herbert's Estate, 131 Cal. App.2d 666, 281 P.2d 57 (1955); McGuigan's Estate, 388 Pa. 475, 131 A.2d 124 (1957). But see, *contra*, In re Pratt's Estate, 88 So.2d 499, and In re Blankenship's Estate, 122 So.2d 466 (Fla.1960), construing an amendment which was intended to change the result in the Pratt case. And see 15 U.Miami L.R. 309.

17. Matter of O'Hara's Will, 95 N.Y. 403; Schultz' Appeal, 80 Pa. 396; Flood v.

an absolute gift, the donee does not learn of the testator's intent that he hold for charity until after the testator's death, and then learns of an orally expressed desire that the donee shall apply the gift to charitable objects.[18] Such a donee becomes an absolute owner and may then voluntarily declare himself a trustee for charity, because of respect for the testator's desires but not because of any duty to do so.

In these states the legislatures have been concerned with protecting close relatives of a testator against excessive generosity to charity and have given such relatives an opportunity to have gifts for charity declared invalid; if the aggregate gifts constitute more than a certain fraction of the testator's property or the will making the gifts was executed within a certain period prior to death, and if the testator left certain described close relatives, the gifts may be invalidated by the relatives in whole or in part.[19] Here again draftsmen of charitable gifts by will should be alert to the possibility of such statutory limitations in the state of the testator's domicile and in the states where he owns realty. For example, the excessive part of a gift for charity may be claimed by the protected classes of relatives,[20] but the permitted portion of the gift is valid.[21] By consents given in advance, or by failure to object after the death of the testator, an excessive gift for charity may be allowed to take effect.[22] The power to object to the gift is not transferable.[23]

Settlors should also inquire into the capacity of any corporation which they have selected as trustee to take title to property of the amount and kind which is intended as the trust property. Sometimes by reason of limitations in the charter, or because of statutory law,[24] a corporation is forbidden to receive title to property greater in value than a named amount,[25] or is prevented from taking title to any property (as sometimes in the case of a foreign corporation),[26] or is restricted as to the amount of property of a certain kind which it can

---

Ryan, 220 Pa. 450, 69 A. 908. See Leaphart, 79 Univ. of Pa.L.R. 253.

18. O'Donnell v. Murphy, 17 Cal.App. 625, 120 P. 1076; Bickley's Estate, 270 Pa. 101, 113 A. 68 (1921). And see In re Sanderson's Estate, 58 Cal.2d 522, 25 Cal.Rptr. 69, 375 P.2d 37 (1962), where there were precatory words in the will addressed to the donee who was to receive an absolute gift in case the gift to charity failed because the will was executed within thirty days of the death of the testator.

19. Official Code Ga.Ann. § 53–2–10 (one-third but no application to the extent the estate exceeds $200,000); Miss.Code § 91–5–31 (one-third).

20. See, for example, Official Code Ga. Ann. § 53–2–10 (spouse or descendants).

21. Ibid.

22. Monahan v. O'Byrne, 147 Ga. 633, 95 S.E. 210; Trustees of Amherst College v. Ritch, 151 N.Y. 282, 45 N.E. 876, 37 L.R.A. 305.

23. In re Sanderson's Estate, Cal.App., 20 Cal.Rptr. 651.

24. See Bogert, Trusts and Trustees (rev. 2d edit.), § 327.

25. See Bogert, Trusts and Trustees (rev. 2d edit.), § 327, for references to statutory restrictions. See also Jones v. Habersham, 107 U.S. (17 Otto) 174, 2 S.Ct. 336, 27 L.Ed. 401 (1883); Chamberlain v. Chamberlain, 43 N.Y. 424.

See Maguire v. Loyd, 193 Va. 138, 67 S.E.2d 885 (1951) (church limited to $100,000 of personalty).

26. Stork v. Schmidt, 129 Neb. 311, 261 N.W. 552 (1935).

take (as in the case of religious corporations and land-holding).[27] Selection of a trustee with one of these disabilities is undesirable since it may make the transfer of legal title to the trustee wholly or partially invalid. However, equity will supply a competent trustee, and the gift of the equitable interest to charity will not be affected.[28]

According to a majority of the decisions, a transfer of property to a corporation outright or in trust which in violation of a statutory limitation is not void but constitutes a voidable conveyance to which the state can object.[29]

Difficulties may also arise if the intended trustee for charity is an unincorporated association. The capacity of such a group to take title varies somewhat from state to state.[30] If a disability to receive ownership exists, it will not cause the failure of the charitable trust but will result in the necessity of application for the appointment of a trustee by the court.[31]

 WESTLAW REFERENCES

Restrictions on Gifts to Charitable Corporations and for Charitable Uses in England

di mortmain

"georgian statute of mortmain"

"charities act of 1960"

Restrictions in the United States

find 365 a2d 621

bequest /s 30 thirty /2 days /s death

"mortmain statute"

75k40 /p "mortmain statute"

409k13(2) /p "mortmain statute"

THE RULE AGAINST REMOTENESS OF VESTING

§ 68. With one exception, the Rule against Perpetuities having to do with the vesting of contingent interests applies to gifts in trust for charity, to gifts to charitable corporations, and to gifts following

27. See, for example, Ill.Rev.Stat. c. 32, § 171. And see Spradlin v. Wiman, 272 Ky. 724, 114 S.W.2d 1111 (1938); Evangelical Luth. Synod v. Hoehn, 335 Mo. 257, 196 S.W.2d 134 (1946) (religious corporations to hold realty for described purposes only).

28. Appeal of Eliot, 74 Conn. 586, 51 A. 558; Chase v. Dickey, 212 Mass. 555, 99 N.E. 410.

29. Union Nat. Bank v. Matthews, 98 U.S. (8 Otto) 621, 25 L.Ed. 188 (1878); In re Darlington's Estate, 289 Pa. 297, 137 A. 268 (1927).

30. See, for example, N.Mex.Stat.Ann. 1978, § 51–18–2 (unincorporated association has capacity to receive as trustee); Vaughn v. Pansey Friendship Prim. Bapt. Ch., 252 Ala. 439, 41 So.2d 403 (1949); In re Merritt's Estate, 273 App.Div. 79, 75 N.Y.S.2d 828 (1947); State v. Sunbeam Reb. Lodge No. 180 of Hermiston, 169 Or. 253, 127 P.2d 726 (1942).

See § 35, ante, as to the capacity of an association to be the beneficiary of a private trust.

31. Craven v. Wilmington Teachers' Ass'n, 29 Del.Ch. 180, 47 A.2d 580 (1946); In re Rowell's Estate, 248 Wis. 520, 22 N.W.2d 604 (1946).

charitable trusts. The wording of the gift must be such that the contingent gift will become vested, if it ever vests, at a date measured by lives in being and/or twenty-one years.

The exception exists in the case of a gift to or in trust for one charity, followed by a contingent gift to or in trust for a second charity, to take effect on the happening of a certain event. In this case the event need not be one certain to occur within a time measured by lives in being and/or twenty-one years, but may be limited to happen at a remote or uncertain future time.

Certain rules of the common or statute law relating to property must be considered by the settlor of a charitable trust, in order that he may be sure that his directions will be carried out by the courts. These restrictions will be considered in the next succeeding sections.

The statement is frequently found in the decisions that the Rule against Perpetuities does not apply to charitable trusts. "It is common knowledge that the rule as to perpetuities does not apply to property given to charities." [1] But, for the reason that "the Rule against Perpetuities" has in some cases been an ambiguous phrase, these statements have caused much confusion of thought. In some instances the Rule against Perpetuities means, to the court using it, the rule against remoteness of vesting; [2] in other cases it means a rule against suspending the power of alienation; [3] and in other instances it may have meant a rule regarding the duration of trusts. [4] As has been said by a Maine court: [5] "The statement is often found in the books that the law against perpetuities does not apply to public charities. But the statement is misleading. It is undoubtedly true that the principle of public policy, which declares that estates shall not be *indefinitely inalienable* in the hands of individuals, is held inapplicable to public charities. But it must be remembered that the rule against perpetuities, in its proper legal sense, has relation only to the time of the vesting of an estate, and in no way affects its continuance after it is once vested."

With respect to the application of the rule against too remote vesting to charitable trusts, four situations may arise: (1) there may be a gift to or in trust for charity, followed by a contingent gift over to a private person; (2) there may be a gift to a private person, followed by a contingent gift to or in trust for charitable uses to take effect if a certain event occurs; (3) an instrument may provide for the vesting of

§ 68

1. Lindley, L.J., in In re Tyler, [1891] 3 Ch. 252, 257. See also, Trustees of New Castle Common v. Megginson, 1 Boyce, Del., 361, 77 A. 565, 570, Ann.Cas.1914A, 1207; Bauer v. Myers, 157 C.C.A. 252, 244 Fed. 902 (1917).

For statutes to this effect, see West's Ann.Cal.Civ.Code § 715 (no perpetuity allowed except for "eleemosynary purposes"); Conn.G.S.A. § 47–2; Ill.Rev.Stat. c. 32,

§ 185; Mich.C.L.A. § 554.351. Statutes in most states provide generally that charitable gifts or interests are exempt from the Rule, and that employee benefit funds and charitable gifts are exempt from the Rule.

2. See § 50, ante.

3. See § 51, ante.

4. See § 52, ante.

5. Whitehouse, J., in Brooks v. Belfast, 90 Me. 318, 324, 38 A. 222.

property in a trustee for charitable purposes at a future time; (4) provision may be made for a gift to or in trust for one charity which is to end on the happening of a certain event, the property then to be given to or held for the benefit of another charity, either by the same trustee, or by a new trustee.[6]

The first situation is illustrated by the case of In re Bowen.[7] In that case property was given in trust to establish schools in named parishes, but if the government should at any time establish a general system of education the charitable trust was to end and the property to go over to certain private persons. The gift over might take effect at any time in the future. The vesting of the property in the private persons was not certain to occur at a time measured by lives in being and/or twenty-one years. That the gift over followed a charitable trust was no reason why the ordinary rule against remoteness should not be followed. This is the view taken by those American courts which have considered the question.[8]

In the second situation, that of a gift to an individual followed by a contingent gift over to charity to vest at a future day, the courts are likewise unanimous in holding that the charitable gift must be limited so as to vest, if ever, at a time which satisfies the rule against remoteness, or it will be void.[9] Thus in Village of Brattleboro v. Mead,[10] the gift was to the testator's son absolutely, with a provision that, if the testator's indefinite line of heirs should fail at any time in the future, the property should be used for the establishment of an industrial school in the village of Brattleboro. It was held that the gift for the school was void as too remote, since the vesting of it was not measured by the period fixed by the rule against remoteness.

In the third situation are cases where no present gift to charity is made but provision is made for a possible future gift to trustees for charity or to a charitable institution, if a described event happens, for

---

6. See Restatement, Property, Second, § 1.6 (Donative transfers—charitable gifts); Gray, Rule against Perpetuities, 3d Ed., §§ 589–628; Simes & Smith, The Law of Future Interests (2d edit. 1956). On the English cases, see Sanger, Remoteness and Charitable Gifts, 29 Yale Law J. 46.

7. [1893] 2 Ch. 491.

8. Starr v. Minister and Trustees of Starr Methodist Protestant Church, 112 Md. 171, 76 A. 595; Proprietors of Church in Brattle Square v. Grant, 69 Mass. (3 Gray), 142, 63 Am.Dec. 725; Rolfe & Rumford Asylum v. Lefebre, 69 N.H. 238, 45 A. 1087. And see Re Engels, [1943] 1 All Eng. R. 506 (gift for church, with gift over if services in German were not held in the church).

But if the provision is merely that the charitable trust is to end upon the happening of a certain contingency and that the

property is then to revert to the settlor's next of kin, this possibility of reverter is not void under the rule against remoteness, even though it may take effect at a time not measured by lives in being and twenty-one years. Hopkins v. Grimshaw, 165 U.S. 342, 17 S.Ct. 401, 41 L.Ed. 739 (1897).

9. Merritt v. Bucknam, 77 Me. 253; Merrill v. American Baptist Missionary Union, 73 N.H. 414, 62 A. 647, 3 L.R.A., N.S., 1143, 111 Am.St.Rep. 632, 6 Ann.Cas. 646; In re Penrose's Estate, 257 Pa. 231, 101 A. 319. And see Re Wightwick's Will Trusts, [1950] 1 All Eng.R. 689 (gift over to charity when vivisection is made illegal); Claiborne v. Wilson, 168 Va. 469, 192 S.E. 585 (gift to churches on indefinite failure of issue of testator).

10. 43 Vt. 556.

example, if a symphony orchestra is ever established in Melbourne, Australia,[11] or if a hospital is organized in a named town.[12] Here the gift to charity is contingent until the occurrence of the event, and, since there is no way of computing the time which will elapse and no guaranty that the condition precedent to the gift will ever transpire, there is an obvious provision for a contingent interest which is not certain to vest within the period of the rule and the gift is void.[13]

If there is any ground for finding that the donor intended the gift to vest in charity immediately, there is no illegality in providing for the beginning of its enjoyment at a later date,[14] as where the trustee is to hold for charity until a corporation which can administer the gift can be formed,[15] or is to accumulate the income until the principal reaches a certain figure and then to employ income for the charitable purpose.[16]

The only case in which the Rule against Perpetuities makes an exception regarding charitable trusts is in the fourth situation mentioned above. Where provision is made for the transfer of property from one charity to another at a future time, the rule does not apply. The possible remoteness of the event is not important. Thus in Christ's Hospital v. Grainger [17] property was given in 1624 to the town of Reading, in trust for the poor of the town, with a clause that, if the town neglected to perform the trust, the property should go over to the City of London in trust for Christ's Hospital. The court held that the gift over was not objectionable, saying: "In this case there is a gift in trust for one charity, and, on the happening of a certain contingency, a gift in trust for another charity. There is no more perpetuity created by giving property to two charities, in that form, than by giving it to one. The evil meant to be guarded against by the rule of law against perpetuities is the making of the property inalienable." This view has been generally accepted in England and America.[18]

In situations one to three, neither courts nor legislatures have felt that the undoubted public advantages of charitable trusts have been sufficiently important to offset the economic disadvantages coming

11. In re Dyer (1935) Vict.L.R. 273.

12. Malmquist v. Detar, 123 Kan. 384, 255 P. 42 (1927).

13. Chamberlayne v. Brockett, 1872, 8 Ch.App. 206; Jocelyn v. Nott, 44 Conn. 55.

14. Henderson v. Troy Bank & Trust Co., 250 Ala. 456, 34 So.2d 835 (1948); Smith v. United States Nat.Bank of Denver, 120 Colo. 167, 207 P.2d 1194 (1949); Thomas v. Bryant, 185 Va. 845, 40 S.E.2d 487, 169 A.L.R. 257 (1946).

15. Dykeman v. Jenkines, 179 Ind. 549, 101 N.E. 1013; Codman v. Brigham, 187 Mass. 309, 72 N.E. 1008; Matter of Juillard's Estate, 238 N.Y. 499, 144 N.E. 772 (1924); Hunter's Estate, 279 Pa. 349, 123 A. 865 (1924); Thomas v. Bryant, 185 Va. 845, 40 S.E.2d 487 (1946).

16. Ingraham v. Ingraham, 169 Ill. 432, 48 N.E. 561; Curtis v. Maryland Baptist Union Ass'n, 176 Md. 430, 5 A.2d 836 (1939).

17. 16 Sim. 83.

18. Tumlin v. Troy Bank & Tr. Co., 258 Ala. 238, 61 So.2d 817 (1950); Storrs Agr.School v. Whitney, 54 Conn. 342, 8 A. 141; MacKenzie v. Trustees of Presbytery of Jersey City, 67 N.J.Eq. 652, 61 A. 1027, 3 L.R.A., N.S., 227; McClure v. Carter, 202 Va. 191, 116 S.E.2d 260 (1960). And see Williams v. Williams, 215 N.C. 739, 3 S.E.2d 334 (1939); Moore v. Sellers, 201 S.W.2d 248 (Tex.Civ.App.1947) (transfer from one set of trustees to another set at indefinite future date, where same charity involved).

And see Va.Code 1950, § 55–13.3(C).

from the existence of remote, contingent, future interests which by their nature were either legally nontransferable and incapable of being destroyed, or as a practical matter, were inalienable and indestructible.

In the case of a gift from one charity to another, where an exception is made, the situation as to alienability and other property status is not changed by the gift over. Tying up property indefinitely through two charitable trusts is no more objectionable than restriction of the property by means of one charitable trust.[19]

 WESTLAW REFERENCES

"rule against perpetuities" /s charity "charitable trust"
298k4(15)
"christ's hospital" +3 grainger

RULES REGARDING SUSPENSION OF THE POWER OF ALIENATION AND DURATION OF TRUSTS

§ 69. The statutory rules existing in some states which limit the period for which the power of alienation can be suspended, and the alleged common law rule as to the maximum possible duration of indestructible trusts, do not apply to charitable trusts. They may be made perpetual or of indefinite duration or to last for any desired length of time.

Attention has been called at an earlier point [1] to the statutory rules in some states which provide that the power of alienation of real or personal property may not be suspended for longer than certain periods measured by lives in being or a short term of years, and it has been shown that settlors of private trusts are restricted in trust creation by these rules. Due to statutes in these same states many private trusts automatically make the interest of the beneficiaries of such trusts inalienable and therefore the duration of such trusts must be limited in time.

Since the equitable interest in the trust property in the case of charitable trusts is vested in the public and is practically, if not theoretically, inalienable, it might be supposed that these statutory rules about the invalidity of too great suspension of the power of alienation would apply to charitable trusts and would limit the period for which they could be created. However this is not the law. The great benefit to society arising from charitable trusts has been deemed a sufficient basis for exempting them from the application of these statutes, so that in this group of states charitable trusts to last for an indefinite period or to be perpetual are without doubt valid, either

19. Jones v. Habersham, 107 U.S. (17 Otto) 174, 185, 2 S.Ct. 336, 27 L.Ed. 401 (1883); Storrs Agr. School v. Whitney, 54 Conn. 342, 345, 8 A. 141.

§ 69

1. See § 51, ante.

because of judicial decision[2] or on account of an express statutory exception in their favor.[3]

A somewhat similar question arises where the settlor of a charitable trust forbids the trustee from alienating the trust res. Such a restraint as to an absolute legal life or fee interest would be void as against public policy.[4] But the prevalent view is that it is valid as to the legal estate held for charity[5] on the grounds that the rule of public policy should not apply in the case of a charity and that if it should become expedient that such a restraint be broken the court can always sanction such action.[6] The same is true of the common law rule,[7] held to exist in some states, that the duration of an indestructible trust must be kept with the period of the Rule against Perpetuities, namely, lives in being and/or twenty-one years. This rule has never been applied to charitable trusts.[8] The social benefits coming from enforcing charities have been regarded as outweighing the disadvantages arising from the static condition of the charitable trust property over a long period. If the trust is for charitable and noncharitable objects, and there is no possibility of separating the trust property to be allotted to each, the trust may be held void if it is to last indefinitely.[9]

 WESTLAW REFERENCES

charity "charitable trust" /s suspen! /s "power of alienation"

298k8(1) /p charit!

length duration /6 charitable /2 use trust

---

2. In re Coleman's Estate, 167 Cal. 212, 138 P. 992, Ann.Cas.1915C, 682; Dykeman v. Jenkins, 179 Ind. 549, 101 N.E. 1013, Ann.Cas.1915D, 1011; Wilson v. First Nat. Bank of Independence, 164 Iowa 402, 145 N.W. 948, Ann.Cas.1916D, 481; Penny v. Croul, 76 Mich. 471, 43 N.W. 649, 5 L.R.A. 858; Allen v. Stevens, 161 N.Y. 122, 55 N.E. 568; Harrington v. Pier, 105 Wis. 485, 82 N.W. 345, 50 L.R.A. 307, 76 Am.St.Rep. 924.

3. In some states there are statutes expressly relieving charitable trusts from the rules about suspension of the power of alienation and the duration of trusts. See, for example, West's Ann.Cal.Civ.Code § 715; D.C.Code 1981, § 45–302; N.Y.— McKinney's EPTL 8–1.2; 60 Okl.St.Ann. § 175.47; Wis.S.A. 700.16.

4. See § 40, ante.

5. Catholic Bishop of Chicago v. Murr, 3 Ill.2d 107, 120 N.E.2d 4 (1954); Seif v. Krebs, 239 Pa. 423, 86 A. 872.

6. Gray, J., in Odell v. Odell, 10 Allen 1, 6.

7. See § 52, ante.

8. In re Pierce's Estate, 245 Iowa 22, 60 N.W.2d 894 (1953); In re Trust Estate of Woods, 181 Kan. 271, 311 P.2d 359 (1957); Dexter v. Gardner, 7 Allen, Mass., 243; Farmers' & Merchants' Bank of Jamesport v. Robinson, 96 Mo.App. 385, 70 S.W. 372; Smart v. Durham, 77 N.H. 56, 86 A. 821; Hilliard v. Parker, 76 N.J.Eq. 447, 74 A. 447; Stanly v. McGowen, 37 N.C., 2 Ired. Eq., 9; In re Smith's Estate, 181 Pa. 109, 37 A. 114; In re Geppert's Estate, 75 S.D. 96, 59 N.W.2d 727 (1953); Franklin v. Armfield, 2 Sneed, Tenn., 305; In re Lemon's Estate, 47 Wash.2d 23, 286 P.2d 691 (1955). And see Miller v. Flowers, 158 Fla. 51, 27 So.2d 667 (1946); Collins v. Lyon, Inc., 181 Va. 230, 24 S.E.2d 572 (1943). See Bogert, Trusts and Trustees (rev.2d edit.) § 351.

9. Davenport v. Davenport Foundation, 36 Cal.2d 67, 222 P.2d 11 (1950); Goetz v. Old Nat. Bank, 140 W.Va. 422, 84 S.E.2d 759 (1954).

THE RULE AGAINST ACCUMULATIONS

§ 70. At common law in the United States, a direction to a trustee for charity to accumulate income is valid if it is to be for a period which is regarded by the court of equity as reasonable.

To some extent accumulations for some or all charities are governed by statute.

Attention has previously been directed to the so-called rule against accumulations, which provides that in the case of private trusts the income of property shall not be accumulated and added to principal, except for a restricted period and in some states for the benefit of certain persons.[1] An important question is whether this rule applies with equal force to charitable trusts. May a settlor direct that the income of property be accumulated for the benefit of a charity with any greater freedom than he may provide for accumulations for his own children? May a testator direct that half the income of the property given to charity shall be accumulated and added to the principal until it reaches a fixed sum or until it is adequate to accomplish the settlor's purpose? Frequently the settlor leaves a relatively small sum but has great ambitions for his charity. If he can add net income to the trust fund for a long period, he may be able to enlarge the trust fund until it is sufficient to accomplish the benefaction he had in mind.

In England accumulations for charity were originally affected only by the Rule against Perpetuities and the rule that the beneficiary of a vested interest could demand a termination of the trust and management of his own property by himself. If the ownership of the accumulation was not vested, provision must be made for vesting within lives in being and twenty-one years.[2] If the accumulation was vested in a charity, that charity could call for payment of the income and ignore the accumulation provision.[3] The Law of Property Act of 1925 permitted accumulations for charity for not more than twenty-one years.[4]

In the United States, where not excepted by statute, provision must be made for vesting income accumulations for charity within lives in being and/or twenty-one years under the Rule against Perpetuities.[5]

In states where there are statutes governing accumulations and the statute does not except charitable trusts, it would seem that they are subject to the same limitations as private trusts;[6] but occasionally a

§ 70

1. See § 53, ante.

2. Martin v. Margham, 14 Sim. 230; In re Monk, [1927] 2 Ch. 197.

3. Wharton v. Masterman, [1895] A.C. 186. See In re Blake, (1937) 1 Ch. 325 (charity not entitled under Property Act of 1925, where successors of settlor have contingent interests in accumulations).

4. § 164; Berry v. Geen, [1938] A.C. 575; In re Blake, [1937] 1 Ch. 325.

5. Porter v. Baynard, 158 Fla. 294, 28 So.2d 890 (1946); Perkins v. Citizens & Southern Nat. Bank, 190 Ga. 29, 8 S.E.2d 28 (1940).

6. Thurlow v. Berry, 247 Ala. 631, 25 So.2d 726 (1946). The Illinois Thellusson Act seemed to apply to accumulations for charity. Summers v. Chicago Title &

limited [7] or general exception [8] is made in favor of charitable trusts. Recently legislatures have excepted from the operation of accumulations rules trusts for the benefit of employees.[9]

In most states there are no statutes expressly covering the matter of accumulations for charity. The attitude of equity in such cases was discussed in St. Paul's Church v. Attorney General,[10] where the trustees were directed to accumulate half the pew rents indefinitely, unless they spent them for charitable purposes. The court, in holding the provision valid, said: "There would be great public danger in allowing an accumulation indefinitely for a charitable purpose that was not to be carried out within some definite time. Such a purpose would be practically no charitable purpose at all. On the other hand, however, there are cases where the income from property might be directed to be accumulated to form a fund, the income of which fund was to be annually applied to charitable purposes, as in the case at bar. Such an accumulation, it is evident, is less objectionable, as the income from the accumulating fund is constantly being applied to the charity year by year in larger amount. There seems to be no more objection to such an accumulation than to the holding of property constantly increasing in value for the benefit of the charity. We are of opinion, however, that the proper course is to hold that the limits of an accumulation for the benefit of charity are subject to the order of a court of equity. By this method of solving the difficulty, on the one hand an unreasonable and unnecessary trust for accumulation can be restrained, and on the other hand a reasonable accumulation can be allowed to carry out the intention of the benefactor and to secure the accomplishment of the trust in the best manner."

This view, that the validity of a provision for accumulations for charity will be decided by the court's view of its reasonableness in the light of all the circumstances and especially the probable length of time it requires, has been followed in many cases.[11] Thus in Woodruff v.

Trust Co., 335 Ill. 564, 167 N.E. 777 (1929); but see Stubblefield v. Peoples Bank of Bloomington, 406 Ill. 374, 94 N.E.2d 127 (1950) (rule does not apply to charities). An exception was made for cemetery upkeep trusts. Ill.Rev.Stat. c. 21, §§ 21, 60. See Simes, 7 Univ. of Chi.L.R. 409; Schnebly, 26 Ill.L.R. 491.

7. See Wis.S.A. 701.21(3) (accumulation directed or authorized for charity subject to supervision of court as to "reasonableness, amount and duration"). For prior law, see Wis.S.A. 230.37 (accumulation of income of realty for charitable corporation limited to 21 years). And see N.Y. EPTL 8–1.7, 9–2.1(c) (subject to control of court).

8. In Pennsylvania accumulations for charity were excepted from the statute under the Estates Act of 1947, 20 P.S. § 301.6. For the current statute to the

same effect, see 20 Pa.C.S.A. § 6106 (when in trust for any charitable purpose).

9. Ill.Rev.Stat., c. 30, § 153; Mo.—V.A.M.S. § 456.070; N.Y.—McKinney's EPTL 9–2.1. And for similar statutes, see Bogert, Trusts and Trustees (rev. 2d edit.), § 216.

10. 164 Mass. 188, 203, 204, 41 N.E. 231.

11. Codman v. Brigham, 187 Mass. 309, 72 N.E. 1008, 105 Am.St.Rep. 394; Ripley v. Brown, 218 Mass. 33, 105 N.E. 637; Collector of Taxes of Norton v. Oldfield, 219 Mass. 374, 106 N.E. 1014; Frazier v. Merchants Nat. Bank of Salem, 296 Mass. 298, 5 N.E.2d 550 (1936) (income from capital of $117,000 to accumulate for a hospital until capital reached $1,000,000, held valid); Brigham v. Peter Bent Brig-

Marsh,[12] where the testator had given $400,000 to trustees to establish a children's home, he directed that $10,000 of the income of this $400,000 should be accumulated annually and added to the principal for a period of one hundred years. This was held by the Connecticut court to be a reasonable accumulation for charity.

In New York it had been held that the general statute relative to accumulations, which prohibited accumulations except during a minority and for the benefit of a minor, applied to charitable trusts, and that a provision for the accumulation of the income of a fund for the benefit of a charitable corporation, pending the organization of that corporation, was invalid.[13] But by statute limited exceptions were made.[14] An accumulation might be directed for education to occur until a sufficient sum was raised to accomplish a given charitable object, and the sufficiency of the sum was to be determined by the regents of the University of the State of New York. Likewise an accumulation to make up a deficiency in the capital sum was allowed, and an accumulation might be provided as to the income of not more than one-fourth of a gift in trust for any charity (the sum not to exceed $50,000), the accumulation to continue until the sum had been raised to $100,000.

In 1961 the New York law relating to accumulations for private and charitable purposes was completely revised in accordance with recommendations made by the New York Law Revision Commission. The statute applied to all existing trusts, as well as those thereafter created. Accumulations for charity are valid, but subject to the supervision of the Supreme Court or the Surrogate's Court. Subject to court supervision, trustees for charity may now accumulate income "to the extent necessary to carry out the purposes of the trust" when not expressly or impliedly forbidden by a statute in force at the time of accumulation or by the trust instrument.[15]

ham Hospital, 67 C.C.A. 393, 134 Fed. 513 (1st Cir.1904).

The will of Benjamin Franklin provided for accumulations for one hundred years in connection with trusts for charity in Boston and Philadelphia. These directions are being carried out and are recognized as valid. Boston v. Doyle, 184 Mass. 373, 68 N.E. 851; Franklin's Estate, 150 Pa. 437, 24 A. 626.

See also Waterbury Trust Co. v. Porter, 131 Conn. 206, 38 A.2d 598 (1944) (income of $30,000 to accumulate until sufficient to establish a school; in 35 years fund had reached $196,000; $750,000 would be required; accumulation ordered discontinued); Perkins v. Citizens & Southern Nat. Bank, 190 Ga. 29, 8 S.E.2d 28 (1940); Girard Trust Co. v. Rector, 30 Del.Ch. 1, 52 A.2d 591 (1947) (capital $160,000; income to be accumulated until sufficient to build and maintain chapel and parish house;

held reasonable); Conway v. Third Nat. Bank & Trust Co. of Camden, 119 N.J.Eq. 575, 182 A. 916 (1936); Penick v. Bank of Wadesboro, 218 N.C. 686, 12 S.E.2d 253 (1940); Schreiner v. Cincinnati Altenheim, 61 Ohio App. 844, 22 N.E.2d 587 (1939).

See Asche v. Asche, 41 Del.Ch. 481, 199 A.2d 314 (1964) (reasonable accumulation period need not be confined to the period of the Rule against Perpetuities).

12. 63 Conn. 125, 26 A. 846, 38 Ann.St. Rep. 346.

13. St. John v. Andrews Institute for Girls, 191 N.Y. 254, 83 N.E. 981, 14 Ann. Cas. 708.

14. N.Y.—McKinney's Real Property Law § 61; N.Y.—McKinney's Personal Property Law § 16.

15. N.Y.—McKinney's EPTL 8–1.7, 9–2.1(c).

Prior California law, limiting accumulations to lives in being or twenty-five years, was amended in 1959 to make the permissible period lives in being and/or twenty-one years, and no exception or qualification was made with regard to charities.[16]

 WESTLAW REFERENCES

"rule against accumulations"   /s   charit!
298k9(6)

See L.1961, c. 866, amending R.P.L., § 61 and P.P.L., § 16, and inserting new §§ 61a, R.P.L., and 16a, P.P.L.

16. Cal.L.1959, c. 470, amending § 724 of the Civil Code.

Chapter 7

ORIGIN OF RESULTING TRUSTS

Table of Sections

IMPLIED TRUSTS [1]

§ 71. The phrase "implied trust" is usually employed in American legal terminology to mean either a resulting trust or a constructive trust.

A resulting trust exists because of inferred or presumed intent of a property owner, as distinguished from a trust based on intent which is directly and clearly expressed.

A constructive trust is a remedial device of the court of equity for taking property from one who has acquired or retains it wrongfully and vesting title in another in order to prevent fraud or unjust enrichment. It is not based on intent of the parties, but rather is created by the court in order to achieve an equitable result.

In previous sections [2] the creation of express trusts has been considered. The origin of resulting and constructive trusts, which are sometimes called implied trusts, will now be considered.

While there has been some difference of opinion as to the meaning to be given the phrase "implied trust",[3] it is generally used by the

---

§ 71

1. For a definition of a resulting trust, see Restatement, Trusts, Second, Chap. 12, Introductory Note. The term "implied trust" is not used in the Restatement. See also Restatement, Restitution, § 160.

2. See, §§ 8–70, ante.

3. Messrs. Lewin and Perry, the authors of texts on the subject of trusts, intro-

duced some confusion into the classification of trusts by giving to the phrase "implied trusts" a peculiar meaning. They defined as "implied" those trusts which exist because of language used by the parties which does not clearly create a trust, but is construed by the courts to have that intent. Under this definition implied trusts arose from ambiguous or doubtful language used by the parties, which was

courts and writers to include all trusts other than the private and charitable express trusts described in the preceding sections. Express trusts depend for their existence on the intent of a property owner which is directly and expressly stated. Implied trusts, on the other hand, either depend on implied or presumed intent of a property owner or are not concerned with intent at all.

The phrase "resulting trusts" has been employed generally to cover cases where the court decrees a property holder to be a trustee, either because it finds there has been an implied intent that he be such or because of a presumed or fictional intent.[4] Discussion of the classes of resulting trusts and illustrations of them will make this meaning clearer.

The "constructive trust", according to general usage, is not based on expressed intent that it exist, or even on implied or presumed intent. It is a court-created trust, fastened on a wrongdoing property holder in order to prevent his unjust enrichment and for the purpose of giving the property to the one rightfully entitled to it. It is a mere piece of remedial machinery, similar to an execution or an injunction. Its characteristics and the causes for its origin will be discussed in later sections.[5]

There is little reason in logic for grouping resulting and constructive trusts together under the single heading of "implied trusts". The classification of trusts has been discussed by several able writers.[6] Undoubtedly a desirable division would be that of Professor Costigan, between "intent-enforcing" and "fraud-rectifying" trusts. Within the former class would fall: (1) cases where the parties have clearly expressed an intent to have a trust exist; (2) cases in which the parties have used ambiguous language which the court construes as showing a trust intent; and (3) cases in which the parties have expressed no intent by words, but have performed acts from which the court infers that a trust was intended. In this latter case the court declares that as a

held by the courts to disclose an actual trust intent. See Lewin, Trusts, 14th Ed., 16, 82; 1 Perry on Trusts, 7th Ed., § 112. These authorities have led several American courts into the classification of trusts into four groups, namely, express, implied, resulting, and constructive. See Kayser v. Maugham, 8 Colo. 232, 6 P. 803; Plum Trees Lime Co. v. Keeler, 92 Conn. 1, 101 A. 509, Ann.Cas.1918E, 831; Weer v. Gand, 88 Ill. 490; Stevens v. Fitzpatrick, 218 Mo. 708, 723, 118 S.W. 51; Olcott v. Gabert, 86 Tex. 121, 127, 23 S.W. 985; Gottstein v. Wist, 22 Wash. 581, 590, 61 P. 715.

But the prevailing view in America is that implied trusts should be defined to include resulting and constructive trusts and that trusts based on construction of ambiguous language should be called express trusts. Eaton v. Barnes, 121 Ga. 548,

49 S.E. 593; Heil v. Heil, 184 Mo. 665, 675, 84 S.W. 45; Lovett v. Taylor, 54 N.J.Eq. 311, 34 A. 896; Gorrell v. Alspaugh, 120 N.C. 362, 366, 27 S.E. 85; McCoy v. McCoy, 30 Okl. 379, 121 P. 176, Ann.Cas.1913C, 146.

4. In Oklahoma the phrase "resulting trust" seems to be used to cover the case of an implied understanding on the part of an absolute grantee that he should hold for the grantor. Owens v. Hill, 190 Okl. 239, 122 P. 801. This is a local usage.

5. See §§ 77–87, post.

6. See Maitland, Equity, pp. 75–76; "The Classification of Trusts as Express, Resulting and Constructive," G.P. Costigan, Jr., 27 Harv.Law Rev. 437; "Resulting Trusts and the Statute of Frauds," H.F. Stone, 6 Col.Law Rev. 326.

result of these acts a trust exists. To the second class, that of "fraud-rectifying," would be assigned those cases now usually classed as constructive or involuntary trusts, in which the parties have expressed no intent to have a trust, nor does the court presume that any such intent existed, but the court uses the trust as the most convenient method of working out justice and preventing one party from unfairly enriching himself. But it seems undesirable in this text to attempt reclassification.

 WESTLAW REFERENCES

di resulting trust

di constructive trust

"implied trust"   /5   defin!

RESULTING TRUSTS—THE STATUTE OF FRAUDS [1]

§ 72. By section eight of the English Statute of Frauds and its American successors, resulting trusts are exempt from the provisions of the Statute of Frauds, and may be proved by oral evidence, whether the subject is realty or personalty.

Section eight of the original English Statute of Frauds [2] provided that section seven (which required proof or manifestation of a trust of realty to be by written evidence) should not apply to resulting trusts. This was a reasonable exception, since, as will be shown later, such trusts are by their very nature based on inferred or fictional intent which could never be written, and hence a requirement of a writing would have amounted to abolishing resulting trusts.

All American Statutes of Frauds make a similar exception,[3] so that resulting trusts may be founded entirely on oral evidence, whether the subject matter of the trust is real estate or personal property. In the case of one type of resulting trust, the purchase money resulting trust, the courts are cautious about accepting oral evidence and require clear and convincing proof, as will be later shown.[4]

 WESTLAW REFERENCES

"resulting trust"   /s   "statute of frauds"

390k62   /p   "statute of frauds"

390k631/2

§ 72

1. Restatement, Trusts, Second, § 406.

2. St. 29 Charles II, c. 3, 1677.

3. See Bogert, Trusts and Trustees (rev. 2d edit.), § 67.

In Pennsylvania the statutes require an acknowledged and recorded declaration of a resulting trust or an action of ejectment begun by the beneficiary in order to make the trust valid against creditors of or bona fide purchasers from the titleholder, after a certain period. Rochester Trust Co. v. White, 243 Pa. 469, 90 A. 127.

4. See § 74, post.

VOLUNTARY CONVEYANCES [1]

§ 73. It was a doctrine of early English equity that a common law conveyance, for which no consideration passed and in which no use was expressed, was presumed to create a resulting use in favor of the grantor. Uses or trusts of this variety are now obsolete, because of a change in the presumption from that of trust to that of gift.

In the early history of the English common law practically all land was held to uses. It was almost universal to mention in conveyances the use to which the property conveyed was to be held. Wherever A conveyed land to B by a common law conveyance (feoffment with livery of seizin, fine, or recovery) without consideration, and no statement was made as to who was to have the use of the property, chancery presumed that the universal custom of holding to uses would be followed, and that a use was intended for the benefit of A, the person naturally entitled to the profits of the property.[2] It was presumed that A did not intend to give away his property, and, if any use were to exist, it would seem natural that it should exist in favor of A. This use was called a resulting use. Later, when the Statute of Uses was enacted, and uses were recognized as trusts, chancery continued to enforce A's rights in the form of a resulting trust which was not executed by the Statute.[3]

Changes in conveyancing have made instruments of transfer without a consideration named and use described exceedingly rare. The old common law forms of conveyancing were superseded by conveyances operating under the Statute of Uses, in which there is no room for a presumption of a trust in favor of the grantor. The conveyances by lease and release and bargain and sale almost always mentioned a consideration or named the person for whose use the land was to be held. The conveyance by bargain and sale relied for its operation on the raising of a use in the grantee. Hence such a conveyance without mention of a use was impossible. Modern conveyances in the form of grants always state that consideration passed, or name the use, or do both, and hence leave no room for presumptions as to the identity of the person who is entitled to the use of the property. The statement of consideration in a deed may not be contradicted by oral proof that no consideration passed, if such evidence would prevent the operation of the deed.[4]

"The old common-law conveyances operated to pass the title without the machinery of a declaration of uses, and where no use was declared, and in the absence of an actual consideration paid, the courts raised a resulting trust in favor of the grantor. But modern conveyances, of which the one in hand is a sample, operate under the Statute

§ 73

1. Restatement, Trusts, Second, § 405.

2. Digby, History of Real Property, 5th Ed., 329, 355; Bacon, Uses, 217.

3. § 46, ante.

4. Where even nominal consideration is recited in a deed which was actually voluntary, there is no presumption of a resulting trust for the grantor. Mills v. Mills, 261 Ky. 190, 87 S.W.2d 389 (1935); Key v. Kilburn, 228 S.W.2d 731 (Mo.1950).

of Uses, and contain an express declaration of uses, and it is contrary to first principles to permit this declaration to be contradicted by parol, except in cases of fraud, accident or mistake." [5]

In discussing this type of resulting trust in 1854 the Supreme Court of New Hampshire stated: [6] "And here we are struck with the circumstance, that we have found no modern case on this subject. . . . As the recital of consideration is now universal in all deeds, and as a use is generally expressed, we find in the rules thus referred to a satisfactory reason for the want of any recent decisions upon this subject."

Furthermore, the presumption of a trust for the grantor on a voluntary conveyance has changed to a presumption of a gift to the grantee, where no consideration or use is mentioned.[7] According to current thought, if a grantor expects a trust for himself or others he will state it in the deed, and if he does not do so, the natural inference is that he desired to make a gift. The holding of property under a trust is now the exception, and not the rule as it was in the middle ages in England. The resulting trust of this nature is, therefore, generally held to be nonexistent.[8] Naturally, if any consideration passed,[9] or any use [10] was stated in the habendum clause of the deed, no trust can result to the grantor. A statute declaring that all conveyances shall pass a fee, unless a contrary intent clearly appears in the conveyance, prevents the occurrence of resulting trusts of this class.[11] The English Property Act of 1925 [12] expressly negatives the existence of this type of a resulting trust.

Under the early common law, when resulting trusts of this class arose, the presumption of a trust in favor of the grantor could always be overcome by parol evidence that a gift was intended. The duty of a man to support his wife and children raised a presumption that a voluntary conveyance to wife or child was by way of gift, and not with the intent that wife or child should hold as a resulting trustee.[13] And under current law, where the presumption is in favor of a gift if no use is declared, oral evidence may be used to prove that no gift was

5. Lovett v. Taylor, 54 N.J.Eq. 311, 318, 34 A. 896.

6. Graves v. Graves, 29 N.H. 129.

7. Collins v. Collins, 46 Ariz. 485, 52 P.2d 1169 (1935); Fooshee v. Kasenberg, 152 Kan. 100, 102 P.2d 995 (1940); Hojnacki v. Hojnacki, 281 Mich. 636, 275 N.W. 659 (1937); Niemaseck v. Bernett Holding Co., 125 N.J.Eq. 284, 4 A.2d 794 (1939); Marston v. Myers, 217 Or. 498, 342 P.2d 1111 (1959).

8. Leman v. Whitley, 4 Russ.Ch. 423; Tainter v. Broderick Land & Investment Co., 177 Cal. 664, 171 P. 679; McClenahan v. Stevenson, 118 Iowa 106, 91 N.W. 925; Philbrook v. Delano, 29 Me. 410; Groff v. Rohrer, 35 Md. 327; Bartlett v. Bartlett, 14 Gray, Mass., 277; Taylor v. Thompson, 88 Mo. 86; Hogan v. Jaques, 19 N.J.Eq. 123, 97 Am.Dec. 644.

9. Verzier v. Convard, 75 Conn. 1, 52 A. 255; Gould v. Lynde, 114 Mass. 366; Jackson v. Cleveland, 15 Mich. 94, 90 Am. Dec. 266; Farrington v. Barr, 36 N.H. 86.

10. Donlin v. Bradley, 119 Ill. 412, 10 N.E. 11; Salisbury v. Clarke, 61 Vt. 453, 17 A. 135.

11. Campbell v. Noble, 145 Ala. 233, 41 So. 745.

12. § 60(3).

13. Christ's Hospital v. Budgin, 2 Vern. 683; Jennings v. Sellick, 1 Vern. 467; Groff v. Rohrer, 35 Md. 327.

intended so that a trust will result for the grantor.[14]

 WESTLAW REFERENCES

"voluntary conveyances"
"english property act of 1925"

PURCHASE MONEY RESULTING TRUSTS [1]

§ 74. **Where one pays the consideration for a transfer of real or personal property, but has the title taken in the name of another, it is presumed or inferred that the payor intended the grantee to be a trustee for the payor.**

This presumption is rebuttable by proof that the payor of the consideration intended a gift to the grantee, either of part or all of the property. The presumption may also be confirmed by evidence that the parties expressly agreed that the payor should have an equitable interest, and such agreement does not make the trust express.

If the payor of the consideration is the husband or parent of the grantee, there is a presumption that the transfer of the property was by way of gift or advancement.

The consideration paid must be money or other property of the alleged beneficiary at the time of the conveyance, if a trust is to exist. If money is lent to the payor by the grantee or another at the time of, or before, the deed, a resulting trust is presumed for the payor; but if the consideration is lent the grantee and paid on his behalf there is no basis for a resulting trust.

The consideration must be paid or agreed to be paid by or for the resulting trust claimant at or before the time when the property is conveyed.

If only a part of the price is paid by or for the resulting trust claimant, he is presumed to have intended a trust of a proportionate part of the property for himself, and not a gift or loan.

In seven states resulting trusts of this kind are abolished or modified by statute.

General Theory of Purchase Money Resulting Trusts

The most important class of resulting trusts arises where A buys property from B and at A's direction a conveyance is made from B to C without any expression in the deed as to the intended effect. In such a case it has generally been held for many years that, subject to the qualifications later mentioned, a trust results, with C as the trustee and A as the beneficiary.[2] Such transactions are very common but are not

---

14. Collins v. Collins, 46 Ariz. 485, 52 P.2d 1169 (1935); Nichols v. Nichols, 170 S.W.2d 558 (Tex.Civ.App.1942).

§ 74

1. Restatement, Trusts, Second, §§ 440–460.

2. Spradling v. Spradling, 101 Ark. 451, 142 S.W. 848; Leroy v. Norton, 49

to be recommended in view of the large amount of litigation which they have caused. The rule is the same whether realty or personalty is involved.[3]

These trusts are "intent enforcing" trusts, based on a finding by the courts that in view of the relationship of the parties their acts express an intent to have a trust, even though they did not use language to that effect. "Such a trust is implied in fact. Strictly speaking, as we shall presently see, it may be and is an intended trust; but the intention is inferable, as has been said, from the conduct of the parties and the lack of family relationship."[4] "On account of the improbability of a gift to a stranger, the law implies that the one who holds the title, without having paid any value for it, is a trustee for the one who in fact paid the purchase price."[5] Persons who pay for property generally expect to get value in return. If the title to property is placed by the payor in another person, the most natural way for the payor to get value is to have the grantee be a trustee for him. Human experience shows that gifts to persons who are not in a close family relationship are rare. Although it is sometimes said that the trust is "presumed" or created by the courts,[6] in reality the courts make a finding that a trust was intended and created and so should be enforced.[7]

In California, Georgia, Montana, North Dakota, Oklahoma, and South Dakota there are statutes declaratory of the usual rule of equity with respect to purchase money resulting trusts.[8]

Effect of Unlawful Purpose

If the purpose of the payor of the consideration in having title placed in the name of another was to evade some rule of the common or statute law, the courts will not assist the payor in achieving his

Colo. 490, 113 P. 529; Lander v. Persky, 85 Conn. 429, 83 A. 209; Pittock v. Pittock, 15 Idaho 426, 98 P. 719; Masters v. Mayes, 246 Ill. 506, 92 N.E. 945; Ratliff v. Elwell, 141 Iowa 312, 119 N.W. 740, 20 L.R.A., N.S., 223; Buck v. Pike, 11 Me. 9; Euler v. Schroeder, 112 Md. 155, 76 A. 164; Brown v. Alexander, 118 Miss. 848, 79 So. 842; Plumb v. Cooper, 121 Mo. 668, 26 S.W. 678; Cowles v. Cowles, 89 Neb. 327, 131 N.W. 738; Mershon v. Duer, 40 N.J.Eq. 333; Summers v. Moore, 113 N.C. 394, 18 S.E. 712; Creed v. President, etc., of Lancaster Bank, 1 Ohio St. 1; De Roboam v. Schmidtlin, 50 Or. 388, 92 P. 1082; Asam v. Asam, 239 Pa. 295, 86 A. 871; Butler v. Rutledge, 2 Cold, Tenn., 4; Burns v. Ross, 71 Tex. 516, 9 S.W. 468; Larisey v. Larisey, 93 S.C. 450, 77 S.E. 129; Fisk v. Patton, 7 Utah 399, 27 P. 1; Flanary v. Kane, 102 Va. 547, 46 S.E. 312.

3. Kirk White & Co. v. Bieg-Hoffine Co., 6 Cal.App.2d 188, 44 P.2d 439 (1935); Gowell v. Twitchell, 306 Mass. 482, 28 N.E.2d 531 (1940); Reetz v. Olson, 146 Neb. 621, 20 N.W.2d 687 (1945).

4. George, J., in Jackson v. Jackson, 150 Ga. 544, 104 S.E. 236, 237 (1920).

5. Howe v. Howe, 199 Mass. 598, 602, 85 N.E. 945, 127 Am.St.Rep. 516.

6. Ward v. Ward, 59 Conn. 188, 195, 22 A. 149; In re Estate of Mahin, 161 Iowa 451, 466, 143 N.W. 420.

7. See Costigan, 27 Harv.L.R. 437; Stone, 6 Col.L.R. 326.

8. West's Ann.Cal.Civ.Code § 853; Official Code Ga.Ann. § 53–12–26; Mont. Code Ann. 72–24–104; N.Dak.Cent.Code 59–01–06; 60 Okl.St.Ann. § 175.137; So. Dak.Codif.Laws 55–1–10. The California statute reads as follows: "When a transfer of real property is made to one person, and the consideration therefor is paid by or for another, a trust is presumed to result in favor of the person by or for whom such payment is made."

improper purpose by enforcing a resulting trust for him.[9] This is in accordance with the "clean hands" doctrine. The court generally refuses to give aid to claims from rights arising out of an illegal transaction. Examples of the application of this doctrine are to be found where the payor could not lawfully take title to land in his own name and he used the grantee as a mere dummy to hold for him and enable him to evade the land laws,[10] or where the objective was the avoidance of income tax liability or forfeiture for engaging in criminal activity,[11] or to evade the law with regard to the certificates of title for automobiles [12] or federal legislation regarding aid to those in military service who wish to buy homes.[13] In many cases the payor is in debt, fears that if he has the title put in his name his creditors will discover the land and take it from him, and so invests his money in land and has the deed run to a friend or relative.[14] Here the payor has been usually denied a resulting trust decree,[15] and his creditor has been able to reach the property in the hands of the voluntary grantee.[16] So common is such attempted fraud on creditors that some statutes create a rebuttable presumption that a payor who has title run to another does it for the purpose of delaying or defrauding his creditors.[17]

The view has been expressed that where a payor had an illegal objective and the grantee refused to convey the property to him, and a suit for a resulting trust is brought, the court should weigh the gravity of the attempted illegality and of the possible unjust enrichment of the grantee, and grant or refuse enforcement of the resulting trust on the basis of that comparison.[18]

9. Houlton v. Prosser, 118 Colo. 304, 194 P.2d 911 (procure continuance of illicit sexual relations); Culley v. Carr, 137 N.J. Eq. 516, 45 A.2d 850 (1946) (avoid liability for support of wife and children).

10. Miller v. Davis, 50 Mo. 572; Murphy v. Johnson, 54 S.W.2d 158 (Tex.Civ. App.1932). As to an alien who is ineligible to hold title to land, who pays for land and has title put in the name of a citizen, see Koyoko Nishi v. Downing, 21 Cal.App.2d 1, 67 P.2d 1057 (1937) (state alone can object); Oyama v. California, 332 U.S. 633, 68 S.Ct. 269, 92 L.Ed. 249 (1948) (statutory presumption that payor was attempting to evade alien land law held unconstitutional).

11. Yeiser v. Rogers, 19 N.J. 284, 116 A.2d 3 (1955).

12. In re Case's Estate, 161 Ohio St. 288, 118 N.E.2d 836 (1954).

13. Towner v. Berg, 5 App.Div. 481, 172 N.Y.S.2d 258 (1958).

14. Harrell v. Fiveash, 182 Ga. 362, 185 S.E. 327 (1936); De France v. Reeves, 148 Iowa 348, 125 N.W. 655.

15. Harrell v. Fiveash, 182 Ga. 362, 185 S.E. 327 (1936); Turner v. Eford, 58 N.C. 106.

16. Lafkowitz v. Jackson, 13 F.2d 370 (8th Cir.1926); Hutchins v. Heywood, 50 N.H. 491.

17. See, for example, N.Y.—McKinney's EPTL 7–1.3, and statutes in Mich., Minn. and Wis., cited in Bogert, Trusts and Trustees (rev. 2d edit.), § 463.

18. Restatement, Trusts, Second, § 444; Thompson v. Steinkamp, 120 Mont. 475, 187 P.2d 1018 (1947). Some of the exceptions made with regard to illegal express trusts have also been made with regard to purchase money trusts for an illegal object. Stamper v. Stamper, 227 Ind. 15, 83 N.E.2d 184 (1949) (no actual harm to creditors possible); Sines v. Shipes, 192 Md. 139, 63 A.2d 748 (1949) (trust claimant less guilty than trustee); Summers v. Moore, 113 N.C. 394, 18 S.E. 712 (no actual harm done).

Inference of Intent to have Trust may be Rebutted or Corroborated

The ordinary inference from the payment of the price and the form of the deed may be contradicted or confirmed by evidence of the conduct of the parties before, at the time of, and after the conveyance, as well as by proof of the situation and relationship in which they stood.[19] Relevant facts include any express statements by the payor or grantee,[20] the occupation and enjoyment of the property and the taking of its profits,[21] the making of improvements,[22] and the bearing of the burdens of ownership such as property or income taxes.[23] For example, if after the delivery of the deed the grantee took possession, collected income, and paid taxes and mortgage interest, with the knowledge and without the objection of the payor of the price, a strong case is made that the usual inference is not to be applied and that the payor intended no trust but intended to have made a gift.[24] On the other hand, if the payor occupied and enjoyed the property the inference that a trust for him was intended is strengthened.[25]

The normal inference may be confirmed in part and rebutted in part, as where the payor provides that he is to have life use of the property only and that the person taking title is thereafter to be the full owner.[26]

Effect of Express Agreement for Trust for Payor

In a great many cases the payor and grantee have a conversation about the transaction before the money is paid and the deed taken, and it is agreed between them that the payor is to have the benefit of the whole property or of part of it. The question has arisen whether such an understanding amounts to an agreement for an express trust for the payor and hence will be unenforceable, if not in writing, in the case of real estate. A few courts have been inclined to give the agreement that effect.[27] But the majority of the decisions treat the promise of the grantee that the payor shall have some or all of the benefits of the property as merely confirmatory of the presumption which ordinarily

19. Tryon v. Huntoon, 67 Cal. 325, 7 P. 741; Livermore v. Aldrich, 59 Mass. (5 Cush.) 431; Irvine v. Marshall, 7 Minn. 286, 7 Gil. 216; Baldwin v. Campfield, 8 N.J.Eq. 891; Warren v. Steer, 112 Pa. 634, 5 A. 4. The presumption has been overcome where the payor of the consideration was indebted at least morally to the grantee for maintenance in old age (Morford v. Stephens, Mo., 178 S.W. 441), where there was long-continued acquiescence by the payor of the consideration in the use of the property by the grantee (Akin v. Akin, 276 Ill. 447, 114 N.E. 908), and where an employer paid the consideration for a house in which her secretary lived, the object being to reward services (Reizenberger v. Shelton, 86 N.J.Eq. 92, 97 A. 293).

20. Knouse v. Shubert, 48 Cal.App.2d 685, 121 P.2d 74 (1941).

21. Kellow v. Bumgardner, 196 Va. 247, 83 S.E.2d 391 (1954).

22. Vreeland v. Dawson, 55 N.J.Super. 456, 151 A.2d 62 (1959).

23. Harrison v. Cruse, 233 Ark. 237, 343 S.W.2d 789 (1961).

24. Adams v. Adams, 348 Mo. 1041, 156 S.W.2d 610 (1941).

25. Tiemann v. Welsh, 191 Md. 1, 59 A.2d 628 (1948); Collins v. Curtin, 325 Mass. 123, 89 N.E.2d 211 (1949).

26. Larisey v. Larisey, 93 S.C. 450, 77 S.E. 129.

27. Montgomery v. Craig, 128 Ind. 48, 27 N.E. 427; Partridge v. Berliner, 325 Ill. 253, 156 N.E. 352 (1927); Keown v. Keown, 230 Mass. 313, 119 N.E. 785.

governs, and therefore as merely giving added strength to the resulting trust and overcoming any possible evidence which might rebut the presumption of an intent to have a trust for the payor.[28]

If A pays the price of land and has a deed made to B upon an oral understanding that B is to hold for C, and the trust for C is unenforceable because of the Statute of Frauds, it has been held that there is a resulting trust for A, since there was no intent to give the property to B and when the oral trust for C is removed there is room for the inference of an intent to have a trust for A.[29]

Title in Name of Another with Consent of Payor

A prerequisite for this type of resulting trust is that the title shall have been taken in the name of one other than the payor with the *consent* of the payor. It is only then that the payor will expect the grantee to be a trustee for him. If A's money pays for land but without his consent the deed is made out to someone else, there is no room for presuming that A wanted that person to be a trustee for A. This is the situation where A orders the deed to be made out to himself, but the grantor violates instructions and makes it out to B; or where B is a servant or agent who has A's money and without the consent of A uses the money to buy realty and has the deed run to B.[30] In such cases there is substantially a conversion of A's money and a good basis for a constructive trust in A's favor based on the wrong to him and the prevention of unjust enrichment of B at A's expense,[31] but it is erroneous to call this a purchase money resulting trust. However, in a number of cases the courts call the trust in this case "resulting".[32]

It may be supposed that payor and grantee agreed that the title to the property to be purchased should be taken in the names of both payor and grantee; that is, that the deed should run to them as tenants in common or as joint tenants. In such a case, if one party takes the title in his own name, without the knowledge or consent of the other, although half the price was paid by the other, a trust has been held in

---

28. Viner v. Untrecht, 26 Cal.2d 261, 158 P.2d 3 (1945); McCollum v. McCollum, 202 Ga. 406, 43 S.E.2d 663 (1947); Padgett v. Osborne, 359 Mo. 209, 221 S.W.2d 210 (1949); Godzieba v. Godzieba, 393 Pa. 544, 143 A.2d 344 (1958).

An express agreement that the payor was to have an interest smaller than his payment would ordinarily give to him is usually treated as in part confirming a resulting trust and in part rebutting it. Edwards v. Tenney, 65 Idaho 784, 154 P.2d 143 (1944); Long v. Huseman, 186 Md. 495, 47 A.2d 75 (1946). An express agreement that the payor was to have a greater interest in the property than his payment would justify would seem an attempted express trust as to the excess, and should produce a resulting trust proportionate to the part of the price paid. Wilson v.

Warner, 89 Conn. 243, 93 A. 533; Wimberly v. Kneeland, 293 S.W.2d 526 (Tex.Civ. App.1956).

29. In re Davis, 112 Fed. 129 (1902), affirmed 118 F. 266; Wells v. Wells, 216 Ga. 384, 116 S.E.2d 586 (1960).

30. Dean v. Roberts, 182 Ala. 221, 62 So. 44; Smith v. Wright, 49 Ill. 403; Crosby v. Rogers, 197 Ga. 616, 30 S.E.2d 248 (1944); Jurewicz v. Jurewicz, 317 Mass. 512, 58 N.E.2d 832 (1945).

31. Stromerson v. Averill, 22 Cal.2d 808, 141 P.2d 732 (1943); Randle v. Grady, 224 N.C. 651, 32 S.E.2d 20 (1944).

32. Carrillo v. O'Hara, 400 Ill. 518, 81 N.E.2d 513 (1948); Hill v. Peterson, 323 Mass. 384, 82 N.E.2d 11 (1948); Pizzo v. Pizzo, 365 Mo. 1224, 295 S.W.2d 377 (1956).

some cases to result in favor of the one paying part of the consideration whose name was not mentioned in the deed.[33] It is submitted that in this class of cases there is actual wrongdoing by the party taking title and that the threatened unjust enrichment of the party taking title at the expense of the payor should be a basis for a constructive trust.[34]

In some cases the payor causes the deed to be made out to himself and another as joint tenants or tenants by the entirety. Here it would seem that the payor has shown an intent that he should have a share of the property only, and that the other person should be a donee of the remaining interest, and there are cases to this effect.[35] If the co-grantee is the wife or child of the payor, the argument for a gift of a partial interest is strengthened.[36]

Effect of Family Relationship Between Payor and Grantee

If the payor of the consideration is related to the person to whom title is conveyed in such a way that a gift is extremely natural, as a contribution toward the support of the grantee, or out of love and affection, or as an advancement in anticipation of death, the presumption of a resulting trust does not prevail, but the presumption of an advancement or gift is established.[37] Thus if H, the husband of W, pays the consideration for a conveyance of property to W, there is a presumption that H intended to give this property to W, because of the duty which H has to support W, and because of the frequency and naturalness of gifts from husband to wife.[38] But this presumption of gift may be overcome by oral proof that no gift was intended, and that a trust in favor of the husband was the object.[39]

33. Ahrens v. Simon, 101 Neb. 739, 164 N.W. 1051; Skehill v. Abbott, 184 Mass. 145, 68 N.E. 37; Puckett v. Benjamin, 21 Or. 370, 28 P. 65; O'Donnell v. McCool, 89 Wash. 537, 154 P. 1090.

34. Longley v. Patton, 264 Ala. 235, 86 So.2d 820 (1956); Askins v. Easterling, 141 Colo. 83, 347 P.2d 126 (1959); Laude v. Cossins, 334 Mich. 622, 55 N.W.2d 123 (1952).

35. Socol v. King, 36 Cal.2d 342, 223 P.2d 627 (1950); Walker v. Walker, 369 Ill. 627, 17 N.E.2d 567 (1938); Ferguson v. Stokes, 269 S.W.2d 655 (1954).

36. Knight v. Wingate, 205 Ga. 133, 52 S.E.2d 604 (1949); Bowling v. Bowling, 252 N.C. 527, 114 S.E.2d 228 (1960).

37. The question whether the title-taker is a natural object of the bounty of the payor is basic. Weisberg v. Koprowski, 17 N.J. 362, 111 A.2d 481 (1955).

38. Goelz v. Goelz, 157 Ill. 33, 41 N.E. 756; Sunderland v. Sunderland, 19 Iowa 325; Spring v. Hight, 22 Me. 408, 39 Am. Dec. 587; Edgerly v. Edgerly, 112 Mass. 175; Ilgenfritz v. Ilgenfritz, 116 Mo. 429,

22 S.W. 786; Olsen v. Best, 167 Neb. 198, 92 N.W.2d 531 (1958); McGee v. McGee, 81 N.J.Eq. 190, 86 A. 406; Egerton v. Jones, 107 N.C. 284, 12 S.E. 434; Coe v. Coe, 75 Or. 145, 145 P. 674; Watkins v. Watkins, 393 Pa. 284, 142 A.2d 6 (1958); Kennedy v. Kennedy, Tex.Civ.App., 210 S.W. 581. Improvements put on wife's land with husband's money do not inure to his benefit by way of resulting trust. Nelson v. Nelson, 176 N.C. 191, 96 S.E. 986; Anderson v. Anderson, 177 N.C. 401, 99 S.E. 106.

39. Perryman v. Pugh, 269 Ala. 487, 114 So.2d 253 (1959) (express agreement of wife and management and improvements by husband); Jackson v. Jackson, 150 Ga. 544, 104 S.E. 236; Scanlon v. Scanlon, 6 Ill. 2d 224, 127 N.E.2d 435 (1955) (husband paid all taxes and for improvements); Towles v. Towles, 176 Ky. 225, 195 S.W. 437; Price v. Kane, 112 Mo. 412, 20 S.W. 609; Woodward v. Woodward, 89 Neb. 142, 131 N.W. 188; Shotwell v. Stickle, 83 N.J. Eq. 188, 90 A. 246; Flanner v. Butler, 131 N.C. 155, 42 S.E. 557, 92 Am.St.Rep. 773; Toney v. Toney, 84 Or. 310, 165 P. 221; Wallace v. Bowen, 28 Vt. 638.

It would seem that this presumption of a gift should extend to a person believed by the payor to have been his wife, although not actually so.[40] The case of a woman to whom the payor was merely betrothed would seem more doubtful.[41] If a husband pays for property and has title placed in the names of himself and his wife as tenants by the entirety or joint tenants, the presumption of a gift to the wife of a one-half interest should apply.[42]

So too, if the payor of the consideration is the parent of the grantee of the property, or a person in loco parentis, equity presumes that the payor intended to make a gift or advancement to the child, and not to raise a trust, because the grantee is a natural object of the bounty of the payor.[43] However, this presumption of gift is rebuttable by evidence that the parent intended a trust and did not have in mind a gift, or by the conduct of the parties after the making of the deed.[44] It applies regardless of the ages or sexes of the parties,[45] although where a gift from an aged parent to a child would render the parent penniless such fact may aid in rebutting the presumption of a gift.[46] It would seem that the presumption of a gift should normally apply where the property is paid for by funds owned by the parents jointly.[47]

Since, in the early days of the development of the common law, the wife was economically inferior and had legal disabilities with regard to taking, holding and managing property, and normally did not make gifts to her husband, the law presumed that if she paid for property and

---

40. Santos v. Santos, 32 Cal.App.2d 62, 89 P.2d 164 (1939); Fowler v. Scott, 8 N.J. Super. 490, 73 A.2d 278 (1950); Texido v. Merical, 132 Misc. 764, 230 N.Y.S. 605. Where the parties live together as husband and wife but know that they are not legally married and make no claim of legal marriage, the presumption of a trust intent has been applied in favor of the man who bought property in the name of the woman. Bohaker v. Koudelka, 333 Mass. 139, 128 N.E.2d 769 (1955); Wosche v. Kraning, 353 Pa. 481, 46 A.2d 220 (1946); but see, *contra*, Creasman v. Boyle, 31 Wn.2d 345, 196 P.2d 835 (1948).

41. As presuming a gift, see Kimbro v. Kimbro, 199 Cal. 344, 249 P. 180; Adams v. Adams, 213 Ga. 875, 102 S.E.2d 566 (1958); but as presuming a trust, see Lufkin v. Jakeman, 188 Mass. 528, 74 N.E. 933.

42. Goldman v. Finkel, 341 Mass. 492, 170 N.E.2d 474 (1960); In re Schlesinger's Estate, 22 Misc. 810, 194 N.Y.S.2d 710 (1959).

43. Euans v. Curtis, 190 Ill. 197, 60 N.E. 56; McGinnis v. McGinnis, 159 Iowa 394, 139 N.W. 466; Clark v. Creswell, 112 Md. 339, 76 A. 579, 21 Ann.Cas. 338; Page v. Page, 8 N.H. 187; Wheeler v. Kidder, 105 Pa. 270; Miller v. Blose's Ex'r, 30 Grat., Va., 744.

The same rule has been applied where the deed was to a son and his wife. Grichuhin v. Grichuhin, 44 Wn.2d 914, 272 P.2d 141 (1954).

The majority of the cases apply the presumption of a gift where a mother is the payor and a child the grantee, but some courts take the view that a trust for mother is to be presumed. Harris v. Cassells, 202 Cal. 648, 262 P. 319; Eckert v. Eckert, 152 Iowa 745, 133 N.W. 112; Paulson v. Paulson, 50 R.I. 86, 145 A. 312.

44. Hartley v. Hartley, 279 Ill. 593, 117 N.E. 69; Rankin v. Harper, 23 Mo. 579; Peer v. Peer, 11 N.J.Eq. 432; Elrod v. Cochran, 59 S.C. 467, 38 S.E. 122; Shepherd v. White, 10 Tex. 72; Clary v. Spain, 119 Va. 58, 89 S.E. 130.

45. Gomez v. Cecena, 15 Cal.2d 363, 101 P.2d 477 (1940) (mother and adult son); Hill v. Lamoreaux, 132 N.J.Eq. 580, 30 A.2d 833 (1943) (father and daughter); In re King's Estate, 49 Wyo. 453, 57 P.2d 675 (1936) (father and adult son).

46. Long v. Huseman, 186 Md. 495, 47 A.2d 75 (1946); Shong v. Farmers & Merchants State Bank, 70 N.W.2d 907 (N.D. 1955).

47. Godzieba v. Godzieba, 393 Pa. 544, 143 A.2d 344 (1958).

had it conveyed to her husband, she expected him to be trustee for her and did not intend a gift. This presumption sometimes prevails,[48] but it can be rebutted by evidence that a gift was intended, as shown by the agreement of the parties or their conduct with relation to the property.[49] The tremendous increase in the amount of property held by women, and the changed relationship between man and wife, have led many courts to the view that the presumption should be that of gift from wife to husband.[50]

A child's payment of the consideration for a deed taken in the name of the parent is presumed to result in a trust in favor of the child.[51] Where the payor of the consideration was the uncle or aunt [52] or brother or sister [53] of the grantee, or other relative,[54] a trust has been held to result, there being no presumption of a gift.

Source and Form of Payment

It is essential that the money or other consideration furnished for the conveyance shall have been the property of the person who claims to be a beneficiary of a resulting trust.[55] If partnership or community property is paid to the grantor for a conveyance which is not made to

48. Shaw v. Bernal, 163 Cal. 262, 124 P. 1012; Loften v. Witboard, 92 Ill. 461; Southern Bank of Fulton v. Nichols, 235 Mo. 401, 138 S.W. 881; Mayer v. Kane, 69 N.J.Eq. 733, 61 A. 374; McCormick v. Cooke, 199 Pa. 631, 49 A. 238; Chalk v. Daggett, Tex.Civ.App., 204 S.W. 1057. Prior to the Married Women's Acts, a wife's money became her husband's property and hence the purchase of property by him with the money formerly held by her as separate property created no resulting trust for her. Brooks v. Brooks, 275 Ill. 23, 113 N.E. 919.

But a gift of a co-ownership interest has been presumed where the wife paid the consideration and had the title taken in the names of both husband and wife. See Jones v. Wright, 230 Ark. 567, 323 S.W.2d 932 (1959); Doyle v. Doyle, 268 Ill. 96, 108 N.E. 796; Haguewood v. Britain, 273 Mo. 89, 199 S.W. 950; Rayher v. Rayher, 14 N.J. 174, 101 A.2d 524 (1953). This seems correct, because the indication by the payor of the consideration that she was to have a certain interest in the property, namely, that of a tenant by the entirety, warrants the presumption that she did not expect to receive any greater interest.

If the payor is not the wife of the grantee, although she is living with him as such, the presumption of a trust intent would normally apply, whether she knew or did not know of the non-existence of a valid marriage. Lamar v. Lamar, 263 Ala. 391, 82 So.2d 558 (1955); Burleigh v. Miller, 209 Md. 57, 120 A.2d 378 (1956).

49. Cisel v. Cisel, 352 Mo. 1097, 180 S.W.2d 748 (1944).

50. Bingham v. National Bank of Montana, 105 Mont. 159, 72 P.2d 90, 113 A.L.R. 315 (1937); Peterson v. Massey, 155 Neb. 829, 53 N.W.2d 912 (1952); Hummel v. Marshall, 95 W.Va. 42, 120 S.E. 164.

51. Champlin v. Champlin, 136 Ill. 309, 26 N.E. 526, 29 Am.St.Rep. 323; Harlan v. Eilke, 100 Ky. 642, 38 S.W. 1094; Detwiler v. Detwiler, 30 Neb. 338, 46 N.W. 624; Weisberg v. Koprowski, 17 N.J. 362, 111 A.2d 481 (1955); O'Neill v. O'Neill, 227 Pa. 334, 76 A. 26.

52. Gowell v. Twitchell, 306 Mass. 482, 28 N.E.2d 531 (1940); Kuncl v. Kuncl, 99 Neb. 390, 156 N.W. 772; Harris v. McIntyre, 118 Ill. 275, 8 N.E. 182; Fitzpatrick v. Fitzpatrick, 346 Pa. 202, 29 A.2d 790 (1943). But see Dahl v. Simonsen, 157 Or. 238, 70 P.2d 49 (1937) (payor is in the position of a parent).

53. Niland v. Kennedy, 316 Ill. 253, 147 N.E. 117; Lanning v. Goldsberry, 177 Kan. 419, 280 P.2d 954 (1955); Summers v. Moore, 113 N.C. 394, 18 S.E. 712.

54. Ryan v. Ryan, 267 Ala. 677, 104 So.2d 700 (1958) (mother-in-law).

55. Crawford v. Manson, 82 Ga. 118, 8 S.E. 54; Shaw v. Shaw, 86 Mo. 594; Eisenberg v. Goldsmith, 42 Mont. 563, 113 P. 1127.

the partnership or community, a trust results in favor of the entity which furnished the consideration.[56] Hence where A has lent money to B and B has purchased property with the money and taken title in his own name, there is no ground for a resulting trust in A's favor. The money furnished for the property had become B's by virtue of the loan, and it cannot be said that A furnished the consideration for the conveyance to B.[57]

On the other hand, if the payor of the consideration for the conveyance has received it as a loan from the grantee of the property, a trust will arise in favor of the payor. If A borrows $500 from B and later pays this money to C, who, in return therefor and at A's request, conveys land to B, a presumption of a resulting trust arises. The money furnished was A's money. It had ceased to be the property of B because of the loan from B to A.[58] In this case, if the lender stipulates he is to hold title as security for the collection of the loan, he is both a resulting trustee for the borrower and a mortgagee, and may refuse to give the borrower a deed until he is reimbursed for the loan.[59]

It is obvious that the payor of the consideration, who claims the resulting trust in his favor need not himself have delivered the consideration to the grantor. It is sufficient if his money was paid by another for him to the grantor, with his consent.[60]

The property transferred by the resulting trust claimant to the grantor must have been all or a part of the price agreed upon as consideration for the deed.[61] It usually takes the form of cash or a check, but it may consist of the giving of a note,[62] the performance of services,[63] or the release of a claim against the grantor,[64] if any of these acts had been provided as part of the price in the contract for conveyance.

Time of Payment of the Price

Whether a purchase money resulting trust should be enforced depends on the facts and circumstances existing when the conveyance

---

56. Korziuk v. Korziuk, 13 Ill.2d 238, 148 N.E.2d 727 (1958); Stone v. Sample, 216 Miss. 287, 62 So.2d 307 (1953).

57. Pain v. Farson, 179 Ill. 185, 53 N.E. 579; Reminger v. Joblonski, 271 Ill. 71, 110 N.E. 903; Kennerson v. Nash, 208 Mass. 393, 94 N.E. 475; Phillips v. Phillips, 81 N.J.Eq. 459, 86 A. 949; In re Gorham, 173 N.C. 272, 91 S.E. 950; Aaron Frank Clothing Co. v. Deegan, Tex.Civ.App., 204 S.W. 471. *A fortiori,* if money is given to A by B and property is purchased by B with the money, no resulting trust arises in A's favor. Metropolitan Trust & Savings Bank v. Perry, 259 Ill. 183, 102 N.E. 218.

58. Bates v. Kelly, 80 Ala. 142; Caruthers v. Williams, 21 Fla. 485; Reeve v. Strawn, 14 Ill. 94; Weekly v. Ellis, 30 Kan. 507, 2 P. 96; Dryden v. Hanway, 31 Md.

254, 100 Am.Dec. 61; Howe v. Howe, 199 Mass. 598, 85 N.E. 945, 127 Am.St.Rep. 516; Rogan v. Walker, 1 Wis. 527.

59. Otts v. Avery, 234 Ala. 122, 173 So. 844; Viner v. Untrecht, 26 Cal.2d 261, 158 P.2d 3.

60. Breitenbucher v. Oppenheim, 160 Cal. 98, 116 P. 55.

61. Wilkinson v. Masoner, 200 Ark. 337, 139 S.W.2d 23 (1940).

62. Allen v. Garman, 201 Okl. 146, 202 P.2d 1073 (1949).

63. Dougherty v. Calif. Kettleman Oil Royalties, 9 Cal.2d 58, 69 P.2d 155 (1937).

64. Hinshaw v. Russell, 280 Ill. 235, 117 N.E. 406.

was made and the intent to be attributed to the resulting trust claimant in view of those circumstances.[65] The rights of the parties are fixed as of that date. If the claimant pays part or all of the price before the deed is given or at the time of its execution and delivery, there is no difficulty in imputing to him an intent to obtain a resulting trust, assuming that the parties are not closely related and that there are no rebutting or contradictory facts.[66]

If, on the other hand, the claimant has paid all or part of the price *after* the conveyance became effective, the result should depend on whether this payment was made in fulfillment of an obligation assumed by the claimant before or at the time of the execution of the deed, *or* was made voluntarily or pursuant to an arrangement entered into *after* the conveyance. In the former case the claimant can reasonably be presumed to have a resulting trust, since he has bound himself to pay part or all of the price, and when he performs that promise his rights should be the same as if he had paid at the time of the deed.[67] He gave the grantee the benefit of his credit which has proved to be good. But in the latter case the claimant cannot reasonably be held to have had an intent to secure a resulting trust for himself at the time the deed was given, because he had done nothing which would give him any basis for claiming such a trust. He had no power to fasten an equity on the property at that date.[68] "The cases which declare the unavailability of subsequent payments have reference to such as are made pursuant to arrangements concocted after the conveyance had been made and consummated."[69] It is necessary that the obligation to pay be incurred by the alleged beneficiary at the time of the conveyance, whether the obligation is evidenced by a writing or not.[70]

Purpose of the Payment

The inference of a trust intent applies only where a payment is made toward the purchase price of the property. Payments for improvements on the property,[71] or to discharge taxes,[72] or to pay off

65. Long v. King, 117 Ala. 423, 23 So. 534; Pickler v. Pickler, 180 Ill. 168, 54 N.E. 311; Lee v. R.H. Elliott & Co., 113 Va. 618, 75 S.E. 146; Whiting v. Gould, 2 Wis. 552. Payment before the conveyance is satisfactory. Guin v. Guin, 196 Ala. 221, 72 So. 74.

66. Alexander v. Tams, 13 Ill. 221; Westerfield v. Kimmer, 82 Ind. 365; Warner v. Morse, 149 Mass. 400, 21 N.E. 960; Ostheimer v. Single, 73 N.J.Eq. 539, 68 A. 231; Appeal of Cross, 97 Pa. 471; Guest v. Guest, Tex.Civ.App., 208 S.W. 547; Beecher v. Wilson, 84 Va. 813, 6 S.E. 209, 10 Am. St.Rep. 883; Bowen v. Hughes, 5 Wash. 442, 32 P. 98.

67. Hooks v. Hooks, 264 Ala. 66, 84 So. 2d 354 (1955); McKindley v. Humphrey, 204 Ark. 333, 161 S.W.2d 962 (1942); Car-

roll v. Markey, 321 Mass. 87, 71 N.E.2d 756 (1947); Green v. Green, 237 S.C. 424, 117 S.E.2d 583 (1960).

68. Hanley v. Hanley, 14 Ill.2d 566, 152 N.E.2d 879 (1958); Davis v. Roberts, 365 Mo. 1195, 295 S.W.2d 152 (1956).

69. Lounsbury v. Purdy, 16 Barb., N.Y., 376, 380. See "Subsequent Payments under Resulting Trusts," Grinnell, 1 Harv. L.R. 185.

70. Wrightsman v. Rogers, 239 Mo. 417, 144 S.W. 479. See Yetman v. Hedgeman, 82 N.J.Eq. 221, 88 A. 206.

71. Johnson v. Johnson, 210 Ga. 795, 82 S.E.2d 831 (1954); Wenzelburger v. Wenzelburger, 296 S.W.2d 163 (1956).

72. Samson v. Wentworth, 108 N.J.Eq. 247, 154 A. 761.

mortgages [73] are not a basis for this type of resulting trust claim, because they do not have the proper objective and also because generally they are made after the deed was delivered and not pursuant to an agreement made at or before the time of purchase.

Payment of Part of the Price

In many instances the resulting trust claimant has paid a part of the price and seeks a decree that he is the beneficiary of a trust of an undivided interest in the property, based upon his contribution to the purchase price.

A few American courts have laid down the rule that a part payment, in order to create a resulting trust, must have been an "aliquot part" of the purchase price and paid for a corresponding interest in the property. The word "aliquot," as used in this connection, means "a 'particular fraction of the whole,' as distinguished from a general contribution to the purchase money." [74] "There is no doubt of the correctness of the doctrine that where the purchase money is paid by one person, and the conveyance taken by another, there is a resulting trust created by implication of law in favor of the former. And where a part of the purchase money is paid by one, and the whole title is taken by the other, a resulting trust pro tanto may in like manner be created. But in the latter case it is believed that the part of the purchase money paid by him in whose favor the resulting trust is sought to be enforced must be shown to have been paid for some specific part or distinct interest in the estate, for 'some aliquot part' as it is sometimes expressed; in other words, for a specific share, as a tenancy in common or joint tenancy of one-half, one-quarter, or other particular fraction of the whole, or for a particular interest, as a life estate, or tenancy for years, or remainder in the whole, and that a general contribution of a sum of money toward the entire purchase is not sufficient." [75]

To require an express agreement for a resulting trust as to a definite part of the property is contrary to the fundamental theory of such trusts that the agreement is implied in fact and does not have to be reduced to explicit language.

Mathematically, an "aliquot part" of the price means a part which is contained in the whole price an even number of times, as, for

73. Hanley v. Hanley, 14 Ill.2d 566, 152 N.E.2d 879 (1958).

74. Skehill v. Abbott, 184 Mass. 145, 147, 68 N.E. 37. In Hinshaw v. Russell, 280 Ill. 235, 117 N.E. 406, "aliquot" was said to mean "a definite and distinct interest, as opposed to an indefinite and unascertainable one," and not a part contained in the whole a certain number of times without remainder.

75. Hoar, J., in McGowan v. McGowan, 80 Mass. (14 Gray) 119, 121, 74 Am. Dec. 668. See, also, Feingold v. Roeschlein, 276 Ill. 79, 114 N.E. 506; Pollock v. Pollock, 223 Mass. 382, 111 N.E. 963; Druker v. Druker, 308 Mass. 229, 31 N.E.2d 524 (1941). For cases following the Massachusetts rule in so far as it requires an express agreement for a particular part, see Staton v. Moody, 208 Okl. 372, 256 P.2d 409 (1952); Cutroneo v. Cutroneo, 81 R.I. 55, 98 A.2d 921 (1953).

example, $500 paid out of a total price of $2,500, where the part goes into the whole five times. But there seems no reason for inferring an intent to have a trust where the payment is one-fifth of the price but denying such an inference when the claimant paid two-fifths. In both cases it is natural to infer that he did not intend to give the grantee the benefit of the payment, but rather instead expected to get something for his money, namely, an equitable interest in the property.[76] Nearly all the cases decree a resulting trust based on a part payment, regardless of the size of the payment and the fraction of the price paid.[77]

If the amount of money contributed by the claimant is uncertain, no trust can result in his favor. The portion of the property claimed as the subject matter of the trust must be a fixed share.[78] It is sufficient, however, to prove that at least a certain fraction or sum was paid, even if the payor cannot prove the exact amount of his payments.[79]

In some cases members of the same family, living in the same household, have contributed to the purchase of a home in the name of one of the members, the transaction has run over a period of years, and no records of the amounts contributed by each have been kept. In such a case a resulting trust must be denied to each contributing member on the ground of failure to prove a definite part payment,[80] unless the general equities of the situation lead a court to hold that there is a presumption that the contributions were equal and that resulting trusts of fractional interests should be decreed on that basis.[81]

In a few cases it has been held that the payment of an uneven fraction of the purchase price, as for example, $1,251.16 out of a total of $9,500, with no agreement regarding an interest in the property to be obtained by the payor, does not give rise to a resulting trust in favor of the payor, but instead indicates a loan or gift.[82] But in other cases such

76. Gerety v. O'Sheehan, 9 Cal.App. 447, 449, 99 P. 545; Fox v. Shanley, 94 Conn. 350, 109 A. 249; Neathery v. Neathery, 114 Va. 650, 656, 77 S.E. 465.

77. Moultrie v. Wright, 154 Cal. 520, 98 P. 257; Price v. Hicks, 14 Fla. 565; Crawford v. Manson, 82 Ga. 118, 8 S.E. 54; Frasier v. Findlay, 375 Ill. 78, 30 N.E.2d 613 (1940); Derry v. Derry, 98 Ind. 319; Johnson v. Johnson, 96 Md. 144, 53 A. 792; Baumgartner v. Guessfeld, 38 Mo. 36; Warren v. Tynan, 54 N.J.Eq. 402, 34 A. 1065; Morey v. Herrick, 18 Pa. 123; McGee v. Wells, 52 S.C. 472, 30 S.E. 602; Shoemaker v. Smith, 30 Tenn. 81, 11 Humph. 81; Neill v. Keese, 13 Tex. 187.

78. Harton v. Amason, 195 Ala. 594, 71 So. 180; Olcott v. Tope, 213 Ill. 124, 72 N.E. 751; Tenczar v. Tenczar, 332 Mass. 105, 123 N.E.2d 359 (1954); Platts v. Platts, 134 Mont. 474, 334 P.2d 722 (1959); Cutler v. Tuttle, 19 N.J.Eq. 549.

79. Helzer v. Hughes, 182 Or. 205, 185 P.2d 537 (1947); Zahorsky v. Leschinsky, 394 Pa. 368, 147 A.2d 362 (1959).

80. Balzano v. Balzano, 135 Conn. 584, 67 A.2d 409 (1949); Shelby v. Shelby, 357 Mo. 557, 209 S.W.2d 896 (1948).

81. Stewart v. Bowen, 224 Ark. 275, 273 S.W.2d 540 (1954); Paluszek v. Wohlrab, 1 Ill.2d 363, 115 N.E.2d 764 (1953); Fidelity & Dep. Co. v. Stordahl, 353 Mich. 354, 91 N.W.2d 533 (1958); Finley v. Keene, 136 N.J.Eq. 347, 42 A.2d 208 (1945); Helzer v. Hughes, 182 Or. 205, 185 P.2d 537 (1947). "Where the court is satisfied that both parties have a substantial beneficial interest and it is not possible or right to assume some more precise calculation of their shares, I think equality almost necessarily follows." Rimmer v. Rimmer, (1952) 2 All. Eng.R. 867.

82. Koehler v. Koehler, 75 Ind.App. 510, 121 N.E. 450; McGowan v. McGowan, 80 Mass. (14 Gray) 119, 74 Am.Dec. 668; Storm v. McGrover, 189 N.Y. 568, 82 N.E.

payment of an uneven fraction of the purchase price, without express agreement, has been held to create a resulting trust.[83] Whether the payment was a loan or gift to the grantee, or a part payment of the price, should be a question of fact to be determined by the particular facts of the case. The presumption may be stronger in favor of an intended trust where all or a large part of the consideration constituting an even fraction has been paid. But there seems to be no reason why a small, odd fractional part payment should not give rise to a presumption of some force that a trust was intended for the payor, leaving open the possibility of rebutting this presumption by evidence that a gift or loan was intended. That the payment was very small or of an odd amount may be of some slight effect as tending to rebut the presumption of a trust and to support the argument for a loan or gift.

Clear Evidence Required for Proof

Since purchase money resulting trusts affect record titles and apparent ownership, and there is a public interest in the security of titles and in the ability of parties to deal on the faith of the appearances of public records, the courts have announced that clear and convincing evidence will be required in order that a claimant may get a decree that such a trust exists. Oral evidence alone may be enough, but whatever the type of proof it must be strong and unequivocal evidence.[84] A resulting trust will be denied where the evidence is conflicting.[85]

Statutes Abolishing or Restricting Purchase Money Resulting Trusts

In Kentucky, Michigan, Minnesota, New York, and Wisconsin there are statutes that abolish resulting trusts of this variety as to realty, unless the title was taken in the name of another than the payor without the payor's consent, or by a grantee who, in violation of a trust, purchased the property with the money of another.[86] Indiana and Kansas also abolish the purchase money trust, unless one of the two exceptions mentioned in the last sentence is found, or there was an oral agreement that the grantee should be a holder for the payor of the consideration.[87]

160; O'Donnell v. White, 18 R.I. 659, 29 A. 769.

83. Lowell v. Lowell, 185 Iowa 508, 170 N.W. 811; Chadwick v. Felt, 35 Pa. 305; Neathery v. Neathery, 114 Va. 650, 77 S.E. 465.

84. Powell v. Race, 151 Fla. 536, 10 So. 2d 142 (1942); Wiley v. Dunn, 358 Ill. 97, 192 N.E. 661; Bisceglia v. Bisceglia, 340 Pa. 293, 17 A.2d 182 (1941).

85. Williams v. Ellis, 323 S.W.2d 238 (Mo.1959); Palmisano v. Gagliano, 1 Wis. 2d 435, 85 N.W.2d 398 (1957).

86. Ky.—K.R.S. § 381.170; Mich. Comp.L.A. §§ 555.7–555.10; Minn.—

M.S.A. § 501.07; N.Y.—McKinney's EPTL 7–1.3; Wis.Stats.Ann. 701.04.

For construction, see Musial v. Yatzik, 329 Mich. 379, 45 N.W.2d 329 (1951); Drees v. Gosling, 208 Minn. 399, 294 N.W. 374. And see Evans, 20 Ky.L.J. 383, Gilmer, 42 Ky.L.J. 455.

87. West's Ann.Ind.Code 30–1–9–6; Kan.Stats.Ann. §§ 58–2406 to 58–2408, 67–406 to 67–408.

For construction, see Kimmick v. Linn, 217 Ind. 485, 29 N.E.2d 207 (1940); Gantz v. Bondurant, 159 Kan. 389, 155 P.2d 450 (1945). And see 24 J.B.A.Kan. 104.

It should be observed that these statutes do not apply to personal property. Hence the common law applies the inference when one pays for personalty and has the instrument of conveyance run to another.[88] Partnership realty being deemed personalty, if a partner uses partnership money to buy land and takes the title in his own name, a trust will result to the other members of the firm, even in those states which have abolished resulting trusts of this type in real property.[89]

The New York Revisers gave as reasons for the adoption of the statute abolishing this type of resulting trust as to realty that without it the prohibition of formal trusts except for limited purposes would be nugatory, that such resulting trusts were in many cases founded on a desire to defraud creditors, and that they marred the title recording system of the state by permitting off-the-record titles.[90]

Some constructions of these statutes are noteworthy. Thus it has been held that if A pays the purchase price of land and directs B, the seller, to convey the land to C upon an oral understanding that the conveyance is to be for the benefit of D, the statute does not apply, and a trust results in D's favor.[91] The statute denies the resulting trust to the payor only. However, it would seem that the trust for D should properly be called express and be subject to the Statute of Frauds. And so too, if the payor of the consideration and the grantee are in a confidential relation towards each other, the courts are quick to seize upon that fact as a basis for a constructive trust, even though the statute prohibits a resulting trust.[92] The statutes have no bearing on constructive trusts. And in some cases the payment and an oral agreement for a trust for the payor,[93] or plus part performance by the payor,[94] or coupled with a recognition of the trust by the grantee,[95] have been held to give a basis for enforcing a resulting trust.

Conditions Precedent to Enforcing the Trust

The resulting trust claimant is entitled to a decree that the trust exists and that the trustee convey to the claimant, if the proof is adequate,[96] or the court may declare the title to be vested in the beneficiary.[97] Any profits taken from the property by the resulting trustee and other value from the use of the property must be accounted

---

88. Baker v. Terrell, 8 Minn. 195, 8 Gil. 165; Bork v. Martin, 132 N.Y. 280, 30 N.E. 584, 28 Am.St.Rep. 570; Tobin v. Tobin, 139 Wis. 494, 121 N.W. 144.

89. Fairchild v. Fairchild, 64 N.Y. 471.

90. See Notes to N.Y.Rev.Stat., vol. 1, p. 722. See also Siemon v. Schurck, 29 N.Y. 598, 610, 611.

91. Siemon v. Schurck, 29 N.Y. 598.

92. Gethsemane Lutheran Church v. Zacho, 253 Minn. 469, 92 N.W.2d 905 (1958); Jeremiah v. Pitcher, 26 App.Div. 402, 49 N.Y.S. 788, affirmed 163 N.Y. 574, 57 N.E. 1113; Masino v. Sechrest, 268 Wis. 101, 66 N.W.2d 740 (1954).

93. Wittner v. Burr Ave. Development Corp., 222 App.Div. 285, 226 N.Y.S. 124.

94. Waters v. Hall, 218 App.Div. 149, 218 N.Y.S. 31.

95. Foote v. Bryant, 47 N.Y. 544.

96. Schlessinger v. Mallard, 70 Cal. 326, 11 P. 728; Magee v. Magee, 233 Mass. 341, 123 N.E. 673. It is not necessary that the claimant prove a demand for a conveyance and a refusal. Poepping v. Monson, 138 Mont. 38, 353 P.2d 325 (1960).

97. Shoemaker v. Smith, 30 Tenn. 81.

for by him.[98] The claimant must do equity, as where he is required to indemnify the resulting trustee against liability on a mortgage which was given to the seller of the property for part of the price,[99] or to reimburse the title-holder for taxes,[1] insurance,[2] and repairs.[3]

 WESTLAW REFERENCES

General Theory of Purchase Money Resulting Trusts
"purchase money resulting trust"

Effect of Unlawful Purpose
find 194 p2d 911
harrell +3 fiveash

Inference of Intent to have Trust may be Rebutted or Corroborated
tiemann +3 welsh
390k633/4 /p "resulting trust"
390k89(1) /p "resulting trust"

Effect of Express Agreement for Trust for Payor
find 116 se2d 586
390k17(3)
390k79
390k65 /p "express trust"

Title in Name of Another with Consent of Payor
find 295 sw2d 377
390k72 /p "resulting trust"
390k79 /p "resulting trust"

Effect of Family Relation
bohaker +3 koudelka

Source and Form of Payment
breitenbucher + oppenheim

Time of Payment of the Price
find 152 ne2d 879
390k371(2)
390k62
390k77

Purpose of the Payment
samson +3 wentworth

Payment of Part of the Price
390k79
"resulting trust" /s part /5 payment consideration

Clear Evidence Required for Proof
"resulting trust" /s clear /2 evidence

98. Drath v. Armstrong, 224 Ala. 661, 141 So. 634; McCafferty v. Flinn, 14 Del. Ch. 307, 125 A. 675.

99. Weisberg v. Koprowski, 17 N.J. 362, 111 A.2d 481 (1955).

1. Jones v. Gore, 141 Cal.App.2d 667, 297 P.2d 474 (1956); Shong v. Farmers & Merchants State Bank, 70 N.W.2d 907 (N.D.1955).

2. Godzieba v. Godzieba, 393 Pa. 544, 143 A.2d 344 (1958).

3. Meyer v. Meyer, 285 S.W.2d 694 (Mo.1956).

390k89(5)

Statutes Abolishing or Restricting Purchase Money Resulting Trust

statute /s abolish*** restrict*** /s "purchase money resulting trust"

Conditions Precedent to Enforcing the Trust

condition /3 precedent /s "resulting trust"

FAILURE OF EXPRESS TRUST [1]

§ 75. Whenever an express private trust is gratuitously created, and it fails or is declared void for any reason except illegality of objective, there is a resulting trust for the settlor, or for his successors if he is dead, provided that the settlor has not expressly or impliedly made a different disposition of the equitable interest under the trust. The same rule applies in the case of a charitable trust, where there is no application of the cy pres doctrine. If the settlor created the express trust for an illegal purpose and it is held to be unenforceable on that account, generally a resulting trust will not be decreed in favor of the settlor.

Where an express private trust is created gratuitously and it fails for any reason, a problem arises as to the disposition of the trust property. Shall the trustee be allowed to retain it for his own benefit? This is a result for which no argument normally can be found, since the settlor usually intends the trustee to get no advantage from the trust except his compensation. Usually the only defensible result is to return the property to the settlor or his successors, either on the theory that he would have intended that result if he had thought of the question, or on the basis of fair play and justice. Surely no one other than the settlor has any equitable or moral claim to the property, assuming that he has not provided in the trust instrument his intent for a different disposition of the property.

The courts declare this return to the settlor, or if he is deceased, to his successors in interest, and they often do it on the theory of a resulting trust.[2] Sometimes they decree the existence of the resulting trust without explanation of its theory, or they state that it occurs by "operation of law"; or is based on the "implied" or "presumed" intent of the settlor, or the intent which the settlor would have had if he had contemplated the situation, or on an "inference of law" and not on the intent of the settlor.[3] It has also been suggested that the theory is the same as that behind the purchase money resulting trusts, namely, an inference of an intent that the trustee was not to keep the property and a carrying out of what the court finds would probably have been the

---

§ 75

1. Restatement, Trusts, Second, §§ 411–429.

2. Blake v. Dexter, Mass., 12 Cush. 559; Broadrup v. Woodman, 27 Ohio St. 553.

3. Re Gillingham Bus Disaster Fund, (1958) 1 All Eng.R. 37.

intent of the settlor.[4]

Thus if a settlor of a private trust transfers property inter vivos or by will to named trustees, as a gift, but fails to describe the beneficiaries at all or describes them in an uncertain way,[5] or the trust is at inception, or becomes, impossible of being carried out,[6] the usual result is that the trust property results to the settlor if he is living, or to the successors of the settlor who would take the kind of property which was the subject matter of the trust.[7] Personalty goes to his next of kin, and realty to his heirs, or if he left a residuary clause the residuary devisees and legatees are the beneficiaries of the resulting trust.[8]

It is sometimes said that the result of the failure of a testamentary trust is that the property passes by intestacy.[9] It is submitted, however, that a more complete statement of the result is that the will is given effect to pass the legal title to the trustee named therein, but that the trustee holds such legal title in trust for the heirs or next of kin, assuming there is no residuary clause. To speak of intestacy in such a case is to declare the will void. The will takes effect and the trustee gets the legal title, but the trustee must hold it for the benefit of the heirs or next of kin or residuary donees, and the same decree which declares the resulting trust will doubtless direct a conveyance by the resulting trustee to the beneficiary of such resulting trust, the resulting trust being passive.

The same result occurs if there is a failure of an express charitable trust, voluntarily created, if the cy pres rule is not in force in the state, or even if cy pres is recognized in the state if the settlor's charitable intent was construed to have been limited. There is a resulting trust for the settlor if living, or for his successors if he is deceased. These matters are discussed more fully in a later section.[10]

If consideration is paid by the trustee or another for the transfer in

4. Restatement, Trusts, Second; see Introduction to chapter on resulting trusts.

5. In re Ralston's Estate, 1 Cal.2d 724, 37 P.2d 76, 9 A.L.R. 953; Huxley v. Security Trust Co, 27 Del.Ch. 296, 33 A.2d 679; Pedrick v. Guarantee Trust Co., 123 N.J. Eq. 395, 197 A. 909.

6. Hansen v. Bear Film Co., 28 Cal.2d 154, 168 P.2d 946 (1946); First Nat. Bank of Brunswick v. Stewart, 215 Ga. 141, 109 S.E.2d 606 (1959).

7. Clark v. McCue, 242 Mich. 551, 219 N.W. 653; McElroy v. McElroy, 113 Mass. 509; Trunkey v. Van Sant, 176 N.Y. 535, 68 N.E. 946.

For statutes see Bogert, Trusts and Trustees (rev.2d edit.), § 468.

See also Minn.Stat.Ann. § 501.195, negating a resulting trust where the settlor showed an intent to divest himself of all interest and reserved no power of revoca-

tion, in which case the trust is to result to the state.

8. Bunker v. Jones, 86 U.S.App.D.C. 231, 181 F.2d 619 (1950) (residuary legatees); Dodson v. Winn, 341 Mass. 345, 169 N.E.2d 898 (1960) (heirs where there was no residuary clause); Commerce Nat. Bank of Toledo v. Browning, 158 Ohio St. 54, 107 N.E.2d 120 (1952) (under residuary clause).

9. In re Fair's Estate, 136 Cal. 79, 68 P. 306; Wilce v. Van Anden, 248 Ill. 358, 94 N.E. 42, 140 Am.St.Rep. 212, 21 Ann. Cas. 153; In re Eaton's Estate, 160 Mich. 230, 125 N.W. 85; Miller v. London, 60 N.C. 628.

10. See § 147, post. And see First Univ. Soc. of Bath v. Swett, 148 Me. 142, 90 A.2d 812 (1952) (trust for particular church only and it closed); Rohlff v. German Old Peoples' Home, 143 Neb. 636, 10 N.W.2d 686 (1943) (narrow charitable intent).

trust, and the trust fails, the trustee retains the property as his own,[11] and no trust results to the settlor, since he has received the value of the property and would be unjustly enriched as against the trustee if allowed to keep the consideration and get back the property. He cannot reasonably be said to have intended a return of the property, after having been paid its value, if the trust failed. He must be deemed to have intended that the trustee retain the property as his own.

The settlor may prevent the trust from resulting to him or his successors by expressing in the trust instrument an intent that in case of failure of the trust the beneficial interest shall vest in the trustee or another person.[12] But an expression of an intent to disinherit a named person, without naming any donee to take upon the failure of an express trust, does not prevent the person intended to be excluded from taking by way of resulting trust as an heir or next of kin.[13]

An exception has been made in the case where the express private trust created was unenforceable because the settlor attempted to accomplish an illegal act through the trust, as where he conveyed property to a trustee to defraud his creditors. Here the express trust will not be enforced, nor will a trust result to the settlor, since either trust would aid in the accomplishment of the illegality.[14] However, the exceptions made in the case of illegal express trusts, which permit recovery of the property by a settlor-beneficiary who was less guilty than the trustee,[15] or by the innocent successors of the guilty settlor, may possibly be extended to the case of this resulting trust.[16] And it has been suggested that the court should not refuse a resulting trust where the illegality was of a relatively unimportant nature.[17]

As to whether a resulting trust arises when a gift is to a donee for distribution among members of an indefinite class, or for indefinite or general purposes, or for specific noncharitable purposes, the cases cited in a previous section generally decree such a trust,[18] but the view of the Restatement differs.[19]

11. Trustees of Methodist Episcopal Church v. Trustees of Jackson Square Church, 84 Md. 173, 35 A. 8 (to trustees for church void because charitable trusts not enforced at that time. "When there is consideration for the conveyance and it is made upon a trust which is void for uncertainty, or otherwise fails, then the grantee takes the beneficial interest.").

12. In re Foord, [1922] 2 Ch. 519; Woodbury v. Hayden, 211 Mass. 202, 97 N.E. 776. Sometimes there is a finding of an implied gift on the failure of the express trust. In re Haber's Will, 281 App.Div. 383, 119 N.Y.S.2d 843 (1953), aff'd 306 N.Y. 706, 117 N.E.2d 804 (1954); Flynn v. Palmer, 270 Wis. 43, 70 N.W.2d 231 (1955).

13. In re Brown's Estate, 362 Mich. 47, 106 N.W.2d 535 (1960); Gross v. Moore, 68 Hun 412, 52 N.Y.St.Rep. 657, 22 N.Y.S. 1019, affirmed 141 N.Y. 559, 36 N.E. 343.

14. See § 48, ante. And see Stone v. Lobsien, 112 Cal.App.2d 750, 247 P.2d 357 (1952); Caines v. Sawyer, 248 Mass. 368, 143 N.E. 326.

15. Carpenter v. Arnett, 265 Ky. 246, 96 S.W.2d 693 (1936).

16. Hurwitz v. Hurwitz, 78 U.S.App. D.C. 66, 136 F.2d 796 (1943).

17. Restatement, Trusts, Second, § 422.

18. See § 34, ante.

19. See Restatement, Trusts, Second, §§ 416–418.

WESTLAW REFERENCES

di("express trust" /s void fail***)

390k72 /p "express trust"

390k62 /p "express trust"

390k68

390k65 /p "express trust"

WHERE RES OF EXPRESS TRUST PROVES EXCESSIVE [1]

§ 76. Where an express private trust is created gratuitously, and the res or subject matter of the trust proves to be larger in amount than is necessary to accomplish the purposes of the trust, and the settlor has not expressly or impliedly disposed of the surplus, there is a resulting trust of the excess for the settlor or his successors.

It sometimes happens that the settlor conveys to the trustee a larger amount of property than is needed to carry out the objects which the settlor has stated. For example, a testator gives $500,000 to T, as trustee, to provide for the living expenses of his widow during her life from income or principal, and then to support his brother, B, during his life; the widow and brother died after the testator but before the trust property was exhausted. Thus a fund is left on hand with no provision in the will for its disposition.[2] Or a public subscription is made to provide a fund to aid the sufferers from a certain disaster, the purposes are not charitable, and the trustees report that they have a balance on hand after giving all the assistance needed.[3] In such a case it would obviously be unfair, and contrary to any reasonably inferred or presumed intent of the settlor, where the trust was created for no consideration, to permit the trustee to use the excess for his own benefit, if no intent to this effect is expressed in the trust instrument.[4] The settlor generally expects the trustee to act in a representative capacity only and not to have any profit from the trust except his commissions. There are no beneficiaries of the express trust named for this portion of the trust principal.[5] The only choice which has merit is to return the excess property to the settlor, or if he is deceased, to his successors, on

---

§ 76

1. Restatement, Trusts, Second, §§ 430–439.

2. Scott v. Powell, 86 U.S.App.D.C. 277, 182 F.2d 75 (1950); Union Nat. Bank of Pasadena v. Hunter, 93 Cal.App.2d 669, 209 P.2d 621 (1949); Tapley v. Dill, 358 Mo. 824, 217 S.W.2d 369 (1949); Smith v. Pratt, 95 N.H. 337, 63 A.2d 237 (1949).

3. Re Gillingham Bus Disaster Fund, (1958) 1 All Eng.R. 37; In re Hobourn Aero Components Ltd's Air Raid Distress Fund, (1946) 1 Ch. 194. But see Cunnack v. Edwards, (1896) 2 Ch. 679 (contributions made to fund to provide for widows of contributors; balance distributed as bona vacantia to the Crown, since contributors received protection in the nature of insurance and had no equity in a refund).

4. Jorgensen v. Pioneer Trust Co., 198 Or. 579, 258 P.2d 140 (1953); In re Zoller's Estate, 373 Pa. 451, 96 A.2d 321 (1953).

5. But see In re Shotwell's Trust, 60 S.D. 553, 245 N.W. 251 (trust to distribute property to A who died before distribution completed; A had absolute interest and there was no excess to be distributed to the settlor's successors).

the argument that this would have been desired by the settlor had he anticipated the situation, and furthermore that return will satisfy the conscience of the chancellor.[6]

If the trustee gave consideration for the creation of the trust, there is no resulting trust as to excess property, and the trustee retains the excess as his own. A return of any part of the trust property to the settlor or his successors would enrich him without cause, since he has already received the value of the trust property, and it would be contrary to his intent to make a sale of the property.

If the settlor expressly or impliedly gave the surplus of the express trust funds to another, no trust results to the settlor or his successors.[7] For example, the settlor may be found to have intended that the trustee should retain as his own any property remaining after satisfaction of the express trust purposes.[8]

In the case of a charity, cy pres usually disposes of excess principal, but if not there will be a resulting trust for the settlor or his successors. If cy pres is not to be applied, either because the doctrine is not in effect or because the settlor's charitable intent was limited, then, as explained in a later section, there is room for an implication that the settlor wanted the property returned to him or his successors.[9]

 WESTLAW REFERENCES

find 51 ne2d 456

---

6. Jordan v. Jordan, 193 Minn. 428, 259 N.W. 386; In re Mooney's Estate, 131 Neb. 52, 267 N.W. 196; Lillard v. Lillard, 63 Ohio App. 403, 26 N.E.2d 933 (1939).

In the case of testamentary trusts, if there is a residuary clause it determines the beneficiaries of the resulting trust; but otherwise the settlor's heirs take realty and his next of kin take personalty. In re Welsh's Will, 1 Misc.2d 440, 145 N.Y.S.2d 727 (1955); In re Devereux' Estate, 48 Pa. D. & C. 491. If the settlor is living he takes under the resulting trust. In re Jackson's Trust, 351 Pa. 89, 40 A.2d 393 (1945); First Nat. Bk. of Bryan v. White, 91 S.W.2d 1120 (Tex.Civ.App.1936).

In some cases words of resulting trust are not used, but the equitable interest is said to "pass by intestacy", where the trust was created by will and no express disposition of the excess was made. Old Colony Trust Co. v. Johnson, 314 Mass. 703, 51 N.E.2d 456 (1943); Skovborg v. Smith, 8 N.J.Super. 424, 72 A.2d 911 (1950).

7. See Brock v. Hall, 33 Cal.2d 885, 206 P.2d 360 (1949); 37 Cal.L.R. 701, 23 So. Cal.L.R. 425.

8. In re Foord, [ ] 2 Ch. 519; Re McGinnis, [ ] 2 Dom.L.R. 522 (gift for masses with direction that donees might retain for themselves any balance left over).

9. See § 147, post. Security Trust Co. v. Willett, 33 Del.Ch. 544, 97 A.2d 112 (1953).

Chapter 8

CREATION OF CONSTRUCTIVE TRUSTS

Table of Sections

DEFINITION—THEORY OF CREATION [1]

§ 77. **Constructive trusts are created by courts of equity whenever title to property is found in one who in fairness ought not to be allowed to retain it. They are often based on disloyalty or other breach of trust by an express trustee, and are also created where no express trust is involved but property is obtained or retained by other unconscionable conduct. The court merely uses the constructive trust as a method of forcing the defendant to convey to the plaintiff. It treats the defendant as if he had been an express trustee from the date of his unlawful holding.**

Plaintiff as the wronged party generally has one or more alternative remedies open to him, and must elect between them and a constructive trust. In order to secure a constructive trust he is not required to show the inadequacy of legal remedies, but he must do equity by performing such acts as the court in its discretion decides are necessary in order to do justice to the defendant.

§ 77

1. Restatement, Restitution, § 160; Restatement, Trusts, Second, § 1, Comment *e*. See Bogert, Trusts and Trustees (rev. 2d edit.), ch. 24.

Constructive trusts do not arise because of the expressed intent of a settlor. They are not "intent-enforcing" trusts, but in a general way may be called "fraud-rectifying" trusts,[2] if the word "fraud" is used in the sense of any kind of wrongdoing and not confined to an intentional false representation.

It would seem preferable to treat these trusts as *created* by courts of equity, rather than to regard them as being brought into being as a result of acts of the parties.[3] Whenever equity finds that one has title to property, real or personal, originally acquired by any kind of wrongdoing or, although innocently obtained, now held under such circumstances that retention of the title will result in unjust enrichment, equity may declare such title-holder to be the trustee of a trust constructed by it for the purpose of working out justice, which is merely a convenient means of remedying a wrong.[4] It is not a trust in which the trustee is to have duties of administration lasting for an appreciable period of time, but rather a passive, temporary trust, in which the trustee's sole duty is to transfer the title and possession to the beneficiary.

The decree establishing the constructive trust amounts to a holding that the defendant ought to be treated as if he had been a trustee for the plaintiff from the time the defendant began to hold the property unconscionably. The constructive trust does not exist merely because of the wrongful holding, but requires a court decree for its origin and this decree is retroactive in effect to the date when the unlawful holding began.[5]

For example, if A, an agent of P, converts money which belongs to P and buys land in the name of A with the converted money, one remedy available to P is to have A declared by the court of equity to be a constructive trustee of the land for P, and a decree to that effect will mean that he is deemed to have been such a trustee from the time he took title to the land.[6]

2. See Costigan, 27 Harv.Law Rev. 437.

3. Parker, C.J., in International Refugee Organization v. Maryland Drydock Co., C.A.Md., 179 F.2d 284 ("it does not exist . . . until it is declared by a court of equity as a means of affording relief"); Healy v. C.I.R., 345 U.S. 278, 73 S.Ct. 671, 97 L.Ed. 1007 (1953), rehearing denied 345 U.S. 961, 73 S.Ct. 935, 97 L.Ed. 1380 (1953) (it is "a fiction imposed as an equitable device for achieving justice"). But sometimes the constructive trust is declared to be created by the parties and merely recognized as existing by the courts. Shearer v. Barnes, 118 Minn. 179, 136 N.W. 861. See Scott, 71 L.Quart.R. 39.

4. "A constructive trust is the formula through which the conscience of equity finds expression. When property has been acquired in such circumstances that the holder of the legal title may not in good conscience retain the beneficial interest, equity converts him into a trustee. . . . A court of equity in decreeing a constructive trust is bound by no unyielding formula." Cardozo, C.J., in Beatty v. Guggenheim Exploration Co., 225 N.Y. 380, 386, 389, 122 N.E. 378. Dean Pound has referred to this type of trust as "specific restitution of a received benefit in order to prevent unjust enrichment." 33 Harv.L.R. 420, 421.

5. Loomis v. Roberts, 57 Mich. 284, 23 N.W. 816; McCabe v. Cambiano, 212 S.W.2d 237 (Tex.Civ.App.1948).

6. Jones v. Carpenter, 90 Fla. 407, 106 So. 127. See §§ 81, 86, post.

The right to a constructive trust is generally an alternative remedy. The wronged party has a choice between a trust and other relief at law or in equity. He has a right to the constructive trust from the time of the wrongful holding, but he may elect not to take advantage of it, and he is the beneficiary of such a trust only from the date when he secures a court decree to that effect. Thus in the case above, P could sue A for the recovery of the amount of money wrongfully taken, or he could elect to have a constructive trust imposed on the land, but he could not get both types of relief.[7]

Although there has been some difference of opinion, the better view would seem to be that the party seeking a constructive trust does not have to prove that he has no adequate remedy at law.[8]

A constructive trust must have definite subject matter, just as an express trust must meet this requirement.[9] It cannot be based on mere possession of property,[10] or on breach of contract where no ownership of property is involved.[11]

If a person has a cause of action for the establishment of a constructive trust and he dies, his right to obtain the trust passes to his successors by intestacy or by will, and if the property is realty his heirs or devisees may secure a decree, or if the res is personalty his next of kin or legatees may secure the constructive trust.[12]

A wronged party seeking the aid of a court of equity in establishing a constructive trust must himself do equity.[13] The court will exercise its discretion in deciding what acts are required of the plaintiff as conditions precedent to the securing of a decree. For example, if the defendant has obtained title to property of the plaintiff by means of fraud, the plaintiff will be required to return any consideration received from the defendant,[14] just as he would if he proceeded on the theory of rescission. And if the defendant has, during his period of wrongful retention of the property, expended money for the preservation or protection of the property, for example, by paying taxes or the principal or interest on a mortgage,[15] reimbursement may well be required of the

7. Shearer v. Barnes, 118 Minn. 179, 136 N.W. 861.

8. City of Boston v. Santosuosso, 298 Mass. 175, 10 N.E.2d 271 (1937); Brown v. Father Divine, 260 App.Div. 443, 23 N.Y.S.2d 116 (1940).

"Delinquent fiduciaries may not insist upon being left in possession of property wrongfully obtained on any theory that they could be compelled to pay damages by an action at law." Coane v. American Dist. Co., 298 N.Y. 197, 81 N.E. 87, 90.

9. Bradford v. Chase Nat. Bank of City of N.Y., 24 F.Supp. 28 (S.D.N.Y.1938), affirmed 105 F.2d 1001 (2d Cir.1939), 309 U.S. 632, 60 S.Ct. 707, 84 L.Ed. 900 (1940); Buettner Bros. v. Good Hope Miss. Bapt. Ch., 245 Ala. 553, 18 So.2d 75 (1944).

10. Ordahl v. Johnson, 341 Ill.App. 277, 93 N.E.2d 377 (1950).

11. Witmer v. Brosius' Estate, 184 Kan. 273, 336 P.2d 455 (1959) (difference between constructive trust and quasi-contract illustrated); Wier v. Kansas City, 356 Mo. 882, 204 S.W.2d 268 (1947).

12. Housewright v. Steinke, 326 Ill. 398, 158 N.E. 138; Goodwin v. McMinn, 193 Pa. 646, 44 A. 1094.

13. In re McCrory Stores Corp., 12 F.Supp. 267 (S.D.N.Y.1935); Wilkins v. Wilkins, 144 Fla. 590, 198 So. 335.

14. Sykes v. Reeves, 195 Ga. 587, 24 S.E.2d 688 (1943). And see § 79, post.

15. Rathbun v. Hill, 187 Kan. 130, 354 P.2d 338 (1960); Weber v. Jefferson County, 178 Or. 245, 166 P.2d 476 (1946).

plaintiff. If the defendant has made improvements or performed services in managing the property, some courts have been induced to require the plaintiff to compensate the defendant to the extent that the plaintiff will secure a benefit from these acts if he secures a constructive trust, especially in cases where the defendant was not an intentional wrongdoer but rather acted under mistake or ignorance.[16]

A plaintiff may not secure a constructive trust where he and the defendant were engaged in an illegal transaction at the time of the alleged wrongdoing of the defendant toward the plaintiff.[17]

The decree establishing the constructive trust will require the defendant to deliver possession and convey title to the property and to pay to the plaintiff profits received or rental value during the period of wrongful holding, and otherwise to adjust the equities of the parties after taking an accounting.[18]

The major problem of great importance in the field of constructive trusts is to decide whether, in the numerous and varying fact situations presented to the courts, there is a wrongful holding of property and hence a potential unjust enrichment of the defendant.[19] An attempt will be made in subsequent sections of this chapter to consider some of the more important instances in which constructive trusts have been created or seriously considered.

Constructive trusts are sometimes called "trusts ex maleficio," "ex delictu," "involuntary trusts," [20] or "trusts in invitum."

 WESTLAW REFERENCES

di constructive trust

"fraud—rectifying trust"

390k91

"constructive trust" /s creat*** /s equity

find 336 p2d 455

16. Weiss v. Storm, 126 So.2d 295 (Fla. App.1961); Ryan v. Pflath, 18 Wn.2d 839, 140 P.2d 968 (1943). For cases denying compensation for management, see Peoples First Nat. Bank & Trust Co. v. Ratajski, 399 Pa. 419, 160 A.2d 451 (1960); Joerres v. Koscielniak, 13 Wis.2d 242, 108 N.W.2d 569 (1961).

17. Frank v. Blumberg, 78 F.Supp. 671 (E.D.Pa.1948); Hyde Park Amusement Co. v. Mogler, 358 Mo. 336, 214 S.W.2d 541 (1948); Araiza v. Chapa, 319 S.W.2d 742 (1958).

18. Dietz v. Dietz, 244 Minn. 330, 70 N.W.2d 281 (1955); Waterbury v. Nichol, 207 Or. 595, 298 P.2d 211 (1956); Dominick v. Rhodes, 202 S.C. 139, 24 S.E.2d 168 (1943).

19. While most constructive trusts are based on loss to the plaintiff as well as gain

by the defendant, the former element is not essential. For example, in cases of disloyalty by a fiduciary resulting in a gain to him, it is not necessary to show that if the defendant had not committed his wrongful act the plaintiff would have been better off financially. Schaffer v. Schaffer, 17 Misc.2d 592, 183 N.Y.S.2d 882 (1959). And see § 86, post.

20. See West's Ann.Cal.Civ.Code §§ 2223, 2224. "One who gains a thing by fraud, accident, mistake, undue influence, the violation of a trust, or other wrongful act, is, unless he has some other and better right thereto, an involuntary trustee of the thing gained, for the benefit of the person who would otherwise have had it." Code, § 2224.

"trusts ex maleficio"

"ex delictu"

"involuntary trusts"

STATUTE OF FRAUDS—CLEAR PROOF REQUIRED [1]

§ 78. The Statute of Frauds has no application to constructive trusts. They are created by equity, whether the evidence on which they are based is oral or written, and whether the property involved is real or personal. However, equity requires that the constructive trust claimant prove his case by clear and convincing evidence.

By the express provisions of the eighth section of the English Statute of Frauds [2] trusts arising "by the implication or construction of law" are not subject to the Statute of Frauds. The American statutes have universally adopted this exception,[3] and decisions that no written evidence is necessary as a basis for constructive trusts are numerous.[4]

However, due to the public policy in favor of the security of titles, the courts are reluctant to disturb record title or other apparent ownership, and hence they require the case for a constructive trust to be proved by "clear and convincing evidence".[5] In practically all cases of suits to establish constructive trusts the defendant appears to the world, by virtue of records, deeds, wills, or otherwise, to be the full and complete owner of the property. The plaintiff is seeking to get a decree that this appearance of ownership is false and that the defendant is to be adjudged a mere trustee for the plaintiff. Hence the courts reject the claim if the evidence is vague, conflicting or otherwise dubious.[6] Some courts have gone to the extent of requiring proof beyond a reasonable doubt or conclusive evidence,[7] but this would seem to be unreasonable in a civil suit.

 WESTLAW REFERENCES

"constructive trust" /s clear convincing /2 evidence

find 89 ne2d 732

§ 78

1. Restatement, Trusts, Second, § 40, Comment *d*.

2. St. 29 Chas. II, ch. 3, 1677.

3. See § 21, ante.

4. De Mallagh v. De Mallagh, 77 Cal. 126, 19 P. 256; Larmon v. Knight, 140 Ill. 232, 29 N.E. 1116, 33 Am.St.Rep. 229; Pratt v. Clark, 57 Mo. 189; Brannin v. Brannin, 18 N.J.Eq. 212; Wood v. Rabe, 96 N.Y. 414, 48 Am.Rep. 640; Schrager v. Cool, 221 Pa. 622, 70 A. 889; Fairchild v. Rasdall, 9 Wis. 379.

5. Leake v. Garrett, 167 Ark. 415, 268 S.W. 608; Gordon v. Kaplan, 99 N.J.Eq. 195, 138 A. 195; Helzer v. Hughes, 182 Or. 205, 185 P.2d 537 (1947).

6. Hill v. Irons, 160 Ohio St. 21, 113 N.E. 243; Arbolino v. Arbolino, 89 R.I. 307, 152 A.2d 541 (1959).

7. Henrichs v. Sundmaker, 405 Ill. 62, 89 N.E.2d 732 (1950) ("so strong, unequivocal and unmistakable as to lead to but one conclusion"); Knight v. Rowland, 307 Ky. 18, 209 S.W.2d 728 (1948) (so clear as to leave no reasonable doubt in the mind of the court); Beach v. Beach, 207 S.W.2d 481 (Mo.1947) (such good proof as "to exclude every reasonable doubt from the chancellor's mind").

390k91

390k110 /p "constructive trust"

FRAUDULENT MISREPRESENTATION OR CONCEALMENT [1]

§ 79. Where property is obtained by intentional misrepresentation of a material fact, its holder may be charged as a constructive trustee for the defrauded person.

Fraud in the sense of misrepresentation is a well-known ground of equitable jurisdiction.[2] "It is a well-settled rule of equity that a misrepresentation constitutes fraud relievable in equity only when (a) it is untrue; (b) the party making it knew, or should have known, it to be untrue, and it was made by him to induce the other party to act or omit to act; (c) it induced the other party to act or omit to act; and (d) it relates to a material fact."[3]

The cases in which equity has held a fraudulent transferee as a constructive trustee are numerous.[4] They may involve affirmative assertion of the truth of a material fact,[5] or concealment of the existence of a material fact when there was a duty to speak.[6] The state of the transferee's mind is a material fact and may be a basis for a constructive trust, as where the transferee promises to use the property for certain purposes beneficial to the transferor but intends at the time of the transfer to keep it for himself.[7] The defrauded party may also proceed on the theory of setting aside or rescinding the transfer[8] which is substantially equivalent to obtaining a constructive trust; or he may elect to sue for damages at law on a deceit theory.

§ 79

1. Bogert, Trusts and Trustees (rev. 2d edit.), § 473; Restatement, Restitution, §§ 166–171, 185. As to fraud on creditors, spouse and others, see Bogert, op. cit. infra, §§ 475 and 477 (forgery).

2. "That courts of equity have concurrent jurisdiction with the law courts to grant relief from the consequences of fraud and misrepresentation is a proposition too firmly established in the jurisprudence of this state to be now questioned." Taylor v. Mullins, 151 Ky. 597, 599, 152 S.W. 774.

3. Culver v. Avery, 161 Mich. 322, 126 N.W. 439, 442.

4. Hays v. Gloster, 88 Cal. 560, 26 P. 367; Batty v. Greene, 206 Mass. 561, 92 N.E. 715, 138 Am.St.Rep. 407; Nesbitt v. Onaway-Alpena Til. Co., 202 Mich. 567, 168 N.W. 519; Valentine v. Richardt, 126 N.Y. 272, 27 N.E. 255; Tetlow v. Rust, 227 Pa. 292, 76 A. 22; Blakeslee v. Starring, 34 Wis. 538.

5. Reiter v. Carroll, 210 Ark. 841, 198 S.W.2d 163 (1946); Bell v. Bell, 210 Ga. 295, 79 S.E.2d 524 (statement as to marital condition); Lloyd v. Phillips, 272 App.Div. 222, 71 N.Y.S.2d 103 (1947).

6. Bankers' Trust Co. v. Patton, 1 Cal. 2d 172, 33 P.2d 1019 (1934); New York Life Ins. Co. v. Nashville Trust Co., 200 Tenn. 513, 292 S.W.2d 749 (1956) (insured disappeared and concealed from insurance company fact that he was not dead and so induced the company to pay the family of the insured as beneficiaries of the policy).

7. Mack v. Marvin, 211 Ark. 715, 202 S.W.2d 590 (1947); Le Cain v. Becker, 58 So.2d 527 (Fla.1952); Crowley v. Crowley, 219 Minn. 341, 18 N.W.2d 40 (1945). And see § 84, post.

8. Howard v. International Tr. Co., 139 Colo. 314, 338 P.2d 689 (1959), certiorari denied 361 U.S. 916, 80 S.Ct. 258, 4 L.Ed. 2d 184 (1959); State v. State Bank of Omaha, 128 Neb. 705, 260 N.W. 195.

If a person secures property of a decedent by fraud on the probate court through false statements or concealments, he may be charged as a constructive trustee for the person who should have received the property by intestacy or will.[9] Examples are found where the defendant concealed the existence of a will or of relatives of the decedent. Sometimes statutes regarding the finality of court decrees in probate matters have been deemed to prevent the imposition of a constructive trust in these cases.[10]

Where property has been conveyed to an innocent grantee, due to the fraud of a third person, such innocent grantee may be decreed to hold the property under a constructive trust [11] if he was not a purchaser for value. The acquisition of title was the result of a wrongful act, and it is immaterial whether the fraud was that of the grantee or of another.

MISTAKE, UNDUE INFLUENCE OR DURESS [1]

§ 80. Where a conveyance of property is induced by mistake, undue influence, or duress, the transferor may have the transferee declared a constructive trustee.

If by mistake of fact title is conveyed to one other than the intended grantee, or the wrong property is conveyed to the intended grantee, or the conveyor is otherwise induced to act by reason of mistake, the grantee may be declared by equity to hold the legal title under a constructive trust for the grantor.[2] "But there is another principle, recognized in equity, that when one person, through fraud or mistake, obtains the legal title and apparent ownership of property, which in justice and good conscience belongs to another, such property is impressed with a use in favor of the equitable owner." [3] Sometimes the result is expressed in terms of setting aside the transfer, or relief is obtained by procuring a decree reforming the instrument of conveyance so that it expresses the intent of the parties. In these cases the conveyance is not void. The transferor actually intended a transfer but the circumstances which caused his mind to operate are such that the court of equity considers it unfair that the grantee retain the property.

---

9. Honk v. Karlsson, 80 Ariz. 30, 292 P.2d 455 (1956); Purinton v. Dyson, 8 Cal. 2d 322, 65 P.2d 777, 113 A.L.R. 1230 (1937); Phillips v. Ball, 358 P.2d 193 (Okl.1960).

10. See, for example, Ohio R.C. § 2107.10. And see Pico v. Cohn, 91 Cal. 129, 25 P. 970; Stevens v. Torregano, 192 Cal.App.2d 105, 13 Cal.Rptr. 604 (1961).

11. Ruhe v. Ruhe, 113 Md. 595, 77 A. 797; Zimmer v. Gudmundsen, 142 Neb. 260, 5 N.W.2d 707 (1942); Saar v. Weeks, 105 Wash. 628, 178 P. 819.

§ 80

1. Bogert, Trusts and Trustees (rev. 2d edit.) § 474; Restatement, Restitution, §§ 163–171.

2. Andrews v. Andrews, 12 Ind. 348; Loring v. Baker, 329 Mass. 63, 106 N.E.2d 434 (1952) (mistake as to appointment of transferee as guardian); Lamb v. Schiefner, 129 App.Div. 684, 114 N.Y.S. 34; Reed v. Reed, 287 P.2d 889 (Okl.1955) (scrivener inserted wrong name in deed); In re Bangor Trust Co., 317 Pa. 495, 178 A. 290.

3. Cole v. Fickett, 95 Me. 265, 270, 49 A. 1066.

The same doctrine is applied where a transferor of property is induced to make the conveyance by "undue influence" exerted upon him. This phrase means conduct by the transferee or another which constitutes such domination over the will of the transferor as to destroy his power of independent action,[4] as where the transferee by argument and discussion brings pressure to bear on the transferor. In cases of conveyances by way of gift to a person in a confidential or fiduciary relation there may be a presumption of undue influence, as is shown later.[5]

If the conduct of the transferee goes beyond persuasion in urging the transferor to make the conveyance, and includes violence or threats of violence or restraint of the person of the transferor or other injury, there is an even stronger case for charging the transferee as a constructive trustee on the ground of duress.[6]

If one obtains the property of another by will or intestacy by preventing the making or revoking of a will by reason of constraining the decedent, or by preventing him from consulting a lawyer, or otherwise frustrating his intended disposition of his property, the wrongdoer should be made a constructive trustee for the person who would have received the property if the decedent had been allowed to act freely.[7]

  WESTLAW REFERENCES

"constructive trust" /s mistake

"constructive trust" /s "undue influence"

"constructive trust" /s duress

390k91 /p duress mistake "undue influence"

---

4. Akin v. Evans, 221 Md. 125, 156 A.2d 219 (1959); In re Walther's Will, 6 N.Y.2d 49, 188 N.Y.S.2d 168, 159 N.E.2d 665 (1959); Kuehn v. Kuehn, 11 Wis.2d 15, 104 N.W.2d 138 (1960).

5. In re Metz' Estate, 78 S.D. 212, 100 N.W.2d 393 (1960); and see §§ 86, 87, post.

6. As to the meaning of duress, see Black's Law Dictionary. See Jersey City v. Hague, 18 N.J. 584, 115 A.2d 8 (1955) (politicians and office holders extorted money from city employees; city may recover on constructive trust theories for benefit of the victims).

And see Olson v. Washington, 18 Cal. App.2d 85, 63 P.2d 304 (1936); Smith v.

Stratton, 302 Mass. 17, 18 N.E.2d 328 (1938); Mullin v. Mullin, 119 App.Div. 521, 104 N.Y.S. 323.

7. Monach v. Koslowski, 322 Mass. 466, 78 N.E.2d 4 (1948) (donee prevented testator from changing will); Latham v. Father Devine, 299 N.Y. 22, 85 N.E.2d 168, 11 A.L.R.2d 802 (1949), reargument denied 299 N.Y. 599, 86 N.E.2d 114 (1949) (donee prevented execution of second will); Pope v. Garrett, 147 Tex. 18, 211 S.W.2d 559 (1948) (heirs prevented execution of will). *Contra*, Ledwidge v. Taylor, 200 Ark. 447, 139 S.W.2d 238 (1940); Moneyham v. Hamilton, 124 Fla. 430, 168 So. 522; Bohleber v. Rebstock, 255 Ill. 53, 99 N.E. 75.

PRODUCT OF LARCENY OR CONVERSION [1]

§ 81. If personal property is stolen, embezzled, or misappropriated and used to purchase other property in the name of the criminal or converter, a constructive trust in favor of the wronged party may be imposed on the property which is the product of the wrongful conduct, so long as it remains in the hands of the wrongdoer or his transferee who is not a bona fide purchaser.

Another illustration of the use of the constructive trust as a remedy in the case of the wrongful obtaining or retention of property is found in the case of thieves, embezzlers, and persons claiming under them. Clearly if one obtains property through the medium of a crime, he ought not to be allowed to retain it as against the injured party. The thief does not get title to the thing stolen (except in the special case of larceny through false representation). Thus if an employee steals his employer's funds, the employer does not need the aid of a constructive trust in order to recover his money. He is still the owner of it and the thief has nothing but possession. But if the thief takes the stolen money to a used-car lot and buys an automobile, he acquires title to the car, because the dealer had title and intended to pass it. Surely the employee would be unjustly enriched if he were allowed to retain his ownership of the car. Here equity steps in and takes the title and gives it to the employer by decreeing the employee to be a constructive trustee for the employer with a duty to transfer possession and title to him.[2]

The attitude of equity is the same where there is an appropriation of the property of another which does not amount to a crime but rather merely to the tort of conversion.[3] The converter will not get title to the thing converted until a judgment has been recovered against him and been collected,[4] but he may be able to secure property from a third person by delivering to him the converted property. In such a case the remedy of a constructive trust as to the product of the converted

§ 81

1. Bogert, Trusts and Trustees (rcv. 2d edit.), § 476; Restatement, Restitution, §§ 128–138.

2. National Mahaiwe Bank v. Barry, 125 Mass. 20; Lamb v. Rooney, 72 Neb. 322, 100 N.W. 410, 117 Am.St.Rep. 795; Lightfoot v. Davis, 198 N.Y. 261, 91 N.E. 582, 29 L.R.A.,N.S., 119, 139 Am.St.Rep. 817, 19 Ann.Cas. 747. See 35 Mich.L.R. 798.

In Newton v. Porter, 69 N.Y. 133, where a thief of negotiable securities had sold them and invested the proceeds in a bond and mortgage, the court, speaking through Andrews, J., said: "The thieves certainly had no claim to the securities in which the proceeds of the bonds were invested as against the plaintiff. . . . If the avails remained in their hands, in money the direct proceeds of the sale, can it be doubted that she could reach it? . . . That she could assert an equitable claim to the money, I have no doubt. And this equitable right to follow the proceeds would continue and attach to any securities or property in which the proceeds were invested, so long as they could be traced and identified, and the rights of bona fide purchasers had not intervened."

3. Burton v. Burton, 332 Mich. 326, 51 N.W.2d 297 (1952); Ogilvie v. Smith, 215 S.C. 300, 54 S.E.2d 860 (1949).

4. Miller v. Hyde, 161 Mass. 472, 37 N.E. 760.

property should be available, for example, where a bailee [5] or pledgee [6] uses the property entrusted to him for his own benefit and thereby acquires property from a third person.

The same equity to secure a constructive trust exists against a third party to whom the wrongdoer has transferred title to the property, unless this person has given value for it without notice of the wrongdoing and has thus secured the protection of the bona fide purchaser rule which is later discussed.[7] Thus if a thief buys insurance payable to his wife with the stolen money, and she is a donee, the proceeds of the policy can be charged with a trust.[8]

One who, without right, takes possession and control of the property of a deceased or incompetent person, and proceeds to manage it, may also be treated as a constructive trustee or, as it is sometimes stated, a "trustee de son tort".[9]

 WESTLAW REFERENCES

"constructive trust" /s larceny

"constructive trust" /s stolen embezzled misappropriated /2
    property

390k95

"constructive trust" /s conversion

PROPERTY OBTAINED BY HOMICIDE [1]

§ 82. Where one obtains property by wrongfully and intentionally killing the owner, a constructive trust may be decreed as to the property obtained.

It sometimes happens that a prospective heir, devisee, legatee, surviving joint tenant, dowress, or tenant by the curtesy, intentionally kills the person through whom he expects to obtain a property right, and is convicted of the crime of murder or manslaughter. The question arises whether the murderer should be allowed to retain the property which came to him by intestacy, through the operation of a will, or otherwise. His act brought into play a rule of law or a conveyance which would normally have given him property rights. Does the fact that the criminal act which precipitated the will, the statutes of

5. Parker v. Lloyd, 321 Mass. 126, 71 N.E.2d 899; Bank of Brookings v. Aurora Grain Co., 45 S.D. 113, 186 N.W. 563.

6. Detroit Trust Co. v. Struggles, 283 Mich. 471, 278 N.W. 385; People's Pittsburgh Tr. Co. v. Saupp, 320 Pa. 138, 182 A. 376.

7. Hyde v. Atlanta Woolen Mills Corp., 204 Ga. 450, 50 S.E.2d 52 (1948); and see § 165, post.

8. Brown v. New York Life Ins. Co., 152 F.2d 246 (9th Cir.1945); Jansen v.

Tyler, 151 Or. 268, 49 P.2d 372 (1935); and see § 162, post, for illustrations of this doctrine, where the primary problem is one of tracing the stolen money.

9. Johnston v. Johnston, 256 Ala. 485, 55 So.2d 838 (1951); Miske v. Habay, 1 N.J. 368, 63 A.2d 883 (1949).

§ 82

1. Bogert, Trusts and Trustees (rev. 2d edit.), § 478; Restatement, Restitution, §§ 187–189.

descent, or other disposing cause, prevent the usual effect of the death of the murdered man?

A few legalistic decisions, handed down during the early development of the subject, held that the murderer might retain what he had gained through his crime, on the ground that the statutes of intestacy and of wills contained no express exception for this case and the courts were not justified in creating an implied exception.[2] The Wills Act provided that if a testator made a will with due form and then died, the donees named in that will should take according to it. If exceptions were to be made, application should be to the legislatures and not to the courts. In some of these cases it was argued that to deprive the murderer of the property would be to impose attainder or forfeiture of property for the commission of a crime, a result which is expressly forbidden by law. In many of the states which followed this line the legislatures later intervened to prevent the murderer from retaining the property.[3]

In some decisions the courts have held that the murderer takes no interest, legal or equitable, from the one murdered, because the law does not permit instruments or statutes to operate in favor of one guilty of such a heinous crime.[4] No man should be allowed to procure an advantage from his own wrong. The legislatures must have intended to exclude the murderer, although they did not expressly mention him.

A third position taken by a number of courts is that the murderer acquires the property interest which he would have taken under the will, by intestacy, or otherwise, if he had been innocent of all wrong, but that the court of chancery imposes on his property interest a constructive trust in order to prevent his unjust enrichment at the expense of the innocent successors of the deceased.[5] This seems sound. The murderer has set in motion instruments or laws which have brought him financial gain. To permit him to retain such property would be repugnant to the court of chancery.

2. Wall v. Pfanschmidt, 265 Ill. 180, 106 N.E. 785, L.R.A.1915C, 328, Ann.Cas. 1916A, 674; Kuhn v. Kuhn, 125 Iowa 449, 101 N.W. 151, 2 Ann.Cas. 657; McAllister v. Fair, 72 Kan. 533, 84 P. 112, 3 L.R.A.,N.S., 726; Eversole v. Eversole, 169 Ky. 793, 185 S.W. 487; Gollnik v. Mengel, 112 Minn. 349, 128 N.W. 292; Shellenberger v. Ransom, 41 Neb. 631, 59 N.W. 935, 25 L.R.A. 564; Wilson v. Randolph, 50 Nev. 371, 261 P. 654; Owens v. Owens, 100 N.C. 240, 6 S.E. 794; Deem v. Milliken, 53 Ohio St. 668, 44 N.E. 1134; Carpenter's Estate, 170 Pa. 203, 32 A. 637, 29 L.R.A. 145, 50 Am.St.Rep. 765; Murchison v. Murchison, Tex., 203 S.W. 423.

3. See, the numerous statutes cited in Bogert, Trusts and Trustees (rev. 2d edit.), § 478.

4. Weaver v. Hollis, 247 Ala. 57, 22 So. 2d 525 (1945); Garwols v. Bankers' Trust Co., 251 Mich. 420, 232 N.W. 239; Perry v. Strawbridge, 209 Mo. 621, 108 S.W. 641, 16 L.R.A.,N.S., 244, 123 Am.St.Rep. 510, 14 Ann.Cas. 92; Riggs v. Palmer, 115 N.Y. 506, 22 N.E. 188, 5 L.R.A. 340, 12 Am.St. Rep. 819; In re Tyler's Estate, 140 Wash. 679, 250 P. 456, 51 A.L.R. 1088; In re Wilkins' Estate, 192 Wis. 111, 211 N.W. 652, 51 A.L.R. 1106.

5. Bates v. Wilson, 313 Ky. 572, 232 S.W.2d 837 (1950); Duthill v. Dana, 113 A.2d 499; Sherman v. Weber, 113 N.J.Eq. 451, 167 A. 517; Ellerson v. Westcott, 148 N.Y. 149, 42 N.E. 540; Parks v. Dumas, 321 S.W.2d 653 (Tex.Civ.App.1959).

The beneficiaries of the constructive trust imposed on the murderer should be those persons who would have taken by intestacy or will or otherwise from the murdered person, as if the murderer had predeceased the one whom he murdered. For example, if a father leaves a will giving to his son all the father's property, and the son murders the father, the successors of the father by intestacy (excluding the son) should be able to take the property from the son on constructive trust theories;[6] and if the father's will gave a farm to the son and the residue of his estate to X, and the son murdered his father, X should obtain the farm.[7]

In many states there are statutes which prevent the murderer from taking or retaining the property of the murdered person.[8] These statutes vary from state to state. All apply to taking by intestacy or will, and some to taking as a surviving spouse, remainderman, surviving joint tenant or tenant by the entirety, or otherwise. Most require that the excluded person shall have been convicted of wrongfully and intentionally causing the death of the property owner. None apply to negligent killing.[9] It is not necessary that the killer shall have committed the crime for the purpose of acquiring the property. Thus the statutes apply if he commits suicide immediately after killing the property holder, showing that his motive for the crime was not a mercenary one.[10] They do not apply to an insane slayer,[11] or to one who kills in self defense.[12]

If two persons are joint tenants or tenants by the entirety and one of them murders the other, and the generally prevailing constructive trust doctrine is to be applied, a question arises as to what shall be the subject matter of this trust. Some courts have applied the rather legalistic common law theory with regard to the nature of the interests of such tenants and the effect of survivorship, and have held that each tenant is the owner of the whole property by reason of the form of the conveyance and that his rights are not increased by survivorship, and hence that the murder did not benefit the survivor and he should be

6. Bates v. Wilson, 313 Ky. 572, 232 S.W.2d 837 (1950); Duthill v. Dana, 113 A.2d 499 (Me.1955); Prichett v. Henry, 287 S.W.2d 546 (Tex.Civ.App.1955).

7. Re Peacock, 2 All Eng.R. 98 (1957); In re Wilson's Will, 5 Wis.2d 178, 92 N.W.2d 282 (1958) (beneficiaries should be determined by deciding "how the wishes of the testatrix would best be carried out under the fact situation which has resulted from the murder").

8. See numerous references in Bogert, Trusts and Trustees (rev. 2d edit.), § 478.

For an exhaustive study of the case and statute law and a draft of a proposed model act to cover all possible situations, see Wade, 49 Harv.L.R. 715.

For recent statutes, see West's Fla.S.A. § 732.802; Ill.Rev.Stat. c. 110½, ¶ 2–6; N.J.S.A. 3A:2A–83; Wis.S.A. 632.485.

9. As to reasons for excluding negligent killing, see In re Houghton, (1915) 2 Ch. 173.

10. Whitney v. Lott, 134 N.J.Eq. 586, 36 A.2d 888 (1944); Parker v. Potter, 200 N.C. 348, 157 S.E. 68; In re Gatto's Estate, 74 Pa.D. & C. 529.

11. Anderson v. Grasberg, 247 Minn. 538, 78 N.W.2d 450 (1956); Eisenhardt v. Siegel, 343 Mo. 22, 119 S.W.2d 810 (1938).

12. Colton v. Wade, 33 Del.Ch. 479, 95 A.2d 840 (1953).

able to retain the property.[13]   But the better view seems to be that for practical purposes the death of one tenant does enlarge the survivor's interest from the right to equal enjoyment during the joint lives and from the possibility of acquiring complete ownership by survivorship to unqualified full ownership.[14]

It would seem that in these cases the courts should ascertain the extent of the murderer's property rights before and after the murder and fasten the constructive trust on any increased benefits certainly or probably flowing from the commission of the crime.   While both tenants are living each is entitled to enjoy the property and take one-half of its benefits for the period of their joint expectancies which can be computed by mortality tables.   The date when the joint tenancy will be extinguished by the death of one tenant cannot be forecasted with accuracy, but the mortality tables will give the junior tenant a greater chance of survival.   If H and W are tenants by the entirety, and H has an expectancy of ten years and W of fifteen years, the probable benefit which H will obtain from the property is the income of it for ten years. In all probability he will not become the survivor and receive the absolute title in severalty.   If H murders W in such a situation, it would seem that a fair result would be to charge H with a constructive trust as to the one-half of the income which should have gone to W during the ten year period, to permit H to retain the other half of the income during that period, and to make him a constructive trustee of the fee or absolute interest.[15]   Some cases, however, permit the murderer to keep a one-half interest in the property and confine the constructive trust to the other half interest, regardless of the relative expectancies of the parties.[16]   This seems unduly favorable to the murderer.

If the beneficiary named in an insurance policy kills the insured intentionally, and thus causes the policy to mature by his wrongful act, he is not allowed to collect the policy.   The proceeds go to the estate of the insured.[17]

 WESTLAW REFERENCES

> "constructive trust"   /s   property   /3   homicide murder manslaughter
>
> find 78 nw2d 450
>
> 390k95

---

13. In re Foster's Estate, 182 Kan. 315, 320 P.2d 855 (1958); Anderson v. Grasberg, 247 Minn. 538, 78 N.W.2d 450 (1956).

14. See cases and statutes cited in Bogert, Trusts and Trustees (rev. 2d edit.), § 478.

15. Colton v. Wade, 32 Del.Ch. 122, 80 A.2d 923 (1951); Neiman v. Hurff, 11 N.J. 55, 93 A.2d 345 (1952). In re Perry's Estate, 256 N.C. 65, 123 S.E.2d 99 (1961).

16. Bradley v. Fox, 7 Ill.2d 106, 129 N.E.2d 699 (1955); National City Bank of Evansville v. Bledsoe, 237 Ind. 130, 144 N.E.2d 710 (1957).

17. National Life Ins. Co. of Montpelier, Vt. v. Hood's Adm'r, 264 Ky. 516, 94 S.W.2d 1022 (1936); In re Greifer's Estate, 333 Pa. 278, 5 A.2d 118 (1939). But see Minasian v. Aetna Life Ins. Co., 295 Mass. 1, 3 N.E.2d 17 (1936) (beneficiary may collect where he unintentionally killed insured, although he was convicted of manslaughter).

BREACH OF UNENFORCEABLE CONTRACT TO CONVEY [1]

§ 83. Ordinarily the breach of an oral contract to convey realty by deed or will is not ground for charging the promisor or his successor as a constructive trustee, where he sets up the Statute of Frauds and refuses to perform his contract. To decree a constructive trust in such a case would usually constitute an evasion of the Statute. The promisee can be protected adequately by a return of any consideration he may have paid for the voidable promise to convey.

However, in the case of the breach of some such voidable contracts the constructive trust is occasionally used to prevent unjust enrichment, as in the case of a contract to leave property by will in return for personal services which have been rendered and the value of which is not computable in money. More frequently specific performance of the contract is decreed.

Where real property is sold at a judicial sale for the collection of a debt, and an oral promise is made by a person to the debtor to bid in the property and later convey it to the debtor, a breach of such promise is often made the basis for a constructive trust, without any clear reason being stated. In these cases the inability to measure the financial detriment to the promisee may be an influential factor, or it may be that the conduct of the promisor is regarded by chancery as so highly reprehensible as to require exceptional treatment.

In some cases it has been urged that a constructive trust should be imposed on a person who makes and breaks an unenforceable contract to convey. The Statute of Frauds provides that contracts to convey interests in land are not enforceable against objection where they are not in writing and no memorandum was signed by the seller. Should the owner of land who has made an unenforceable contract to convey be made a constructive trustee for the one to whom he promised to convey it, if he refuses to carry out the contract?

In deciding these questions the courts are naturally concerned with two objectives; first, to support the Statute of Frauds and not to permit the use of the constructive trust as a means of evasion of the Statute; and second, not to allow the unjust enrichment of a person who has set up the Statute of Frauds and refused to carry out a contract.

In the case of the ordinary contract which is completely executory there is no difficulty. If A owns land and orally promises to sell it to B, and there is no memorandum of the contract, and no part performance by B by way of payment of the price or otherwise, there is surely no ground for charging A as constructive trustee of the land for B when A

§ 83

1. Bogert, Trusts and Trustees (rev. 2d edit.), §§ 479–480, 484, 487, 494; Restatement, Restitution, § 181.

refuses to perform his contract.[2] To make A a constructive trustee for B and under a duty to convey to B would be a complete evasion of the Statute of Frauds and would give B the benefit of a bargain which the legislature has said he should not get. The retention of the realty is not enrichment, and certainly not unjust enrichment, because the legislature has said that A may be freed from all duties under the contract if he desires to rely on the Statute.

If, however, B has paid A all or a part of the price of the land, and A avoids the contract on the ground of the Statute, it is certainly not equitable for A to retain the payment if he is not going to perform his sale contract. Ordinarily this payment will be in money or other property of fixed value and the return of it to B will adjust the rights of the parties satisfactorily.[3] There is no need for a constructive trust of the realty because B can be made whole by giving him back his money or other consideration paid.

In certain cases, on the other hand, the value of the consideration paid by the promisee is not easily determined or it is otherwise impossible to place the promisee in the situation he was in before the making of the contract, and hence a constructive trust of the land or specific performance of the contract may be considered necessary in order to work out justice. One of the instances of this latter sort, which frequently appears in the reports, is that of a person who promises to leave real property by will to another if the latter will furnish the promisor for the rest of his life with a home, companionship, nursing, or other personal services. Such arrangements are often made between an elderly person and a younger relative.[4] Here, if the promisee furnishes the home and personal services but the promisor fails to devise the property to the promisee, a claim for a constructive trust in favor of the promisee and against the successors of the promisor is sometimes made. In some instances, it is felt that the value of what the promisee has furnished can be momentarily measured and that a recovery of this amount should be allowed, although the contract was unenforceable because of the Statute of Frauds.[5] The basis for recovery would seem to be quasi-contractual. Yet in other cases, where the courts have felt unable to put a valuation on the care and services because of their personal and intangible nature, they have been in-

---

2. Mazzera v. Wolf, 30 Cal.2d 531, 183 P.2d 649 (1947); Stein v. Stein, 398 Ill. 397, 75 N.E.2d 869 (1947); McIlwain v. Doby, 238 Miss. 839, 120 So.2d 553 (1960); Clark v. Lovelace, 102 N.H. 97, 151 A.2d 224 (1959); Arndt v. Matz, 365 Pa. 41, 73 A.2d 392 (1950).

3. Murray v. Behrendt, 399 Ill. 22, 76 N.E.2d 431 (1948); Morrison v. Farmer, 147 Tex. 122, 213 S.W.2d 813 (1948).

4. See Sparks, 40 Cornell L.Q. 60, 39 Minn.L.R. 1, 53 Mich.L.R. 1, 215, 20 Mo. L.R. 1; Rheinstein, 30 N.Y.U.L.Rev. 1224.

The fourth section of the Statute of Frauds (regarding contracts to convey an interest in land) applies to these contracts, and in several states there are statutes requiring contracts to devise or bequeath to be in writing. See Bogert, Trusts and Trustees (rev. 2d edit.), § 480.

5. Head v. Schwartz's Ex'r, 304 Ky. 798, 202 S.W.2d 623 (1947); In re Anderson's Estate, 348 Pa. 294, 35 A.2d 301 (1944); In re Rosenthal's Estate, 247 Wis. 555, 20 N.W.2d 643 (1945).

duced to grant the application for a constructive trust,[6] or to decree specific performance of the contract against the successors of the promisor, notwithstanding the lack of all formality.[7]

Another typical case may be explainable on similar reasoning. If A, a mortgagor or judgment debtor whose land is about to be sold at judicial sale, is induced by B to refrain from bidding at the sale or making any effort to salvage his equity in the property, by reason of an oral promise of B to appear at the sale and bid in the property, hold it for A, and later convey it to A on being reimbursed for his (B's) expenditures, the transaction is essentially an informal contract to convey an interest in land and is subject to the Statute of Frauds.[8] Where B breaks his contract, after purchasing the realty at the public sale, some courts hold that the enforcement of a constructive trust against B and in favor of A would be an evasion of the Statute of Frauds and hence refuse to decree such a trust.[9] However there is a considerable body of authority to the effect that B should be made a constructive trustee in such a case, especially where he has obtained the property at less than its market value and where the oral agreement between A and B was known at the sale and discouraged bidding by others.[10] The basis for these latter holdings may be that A has surrendered something which is not capable of clear valuation, namely his chance to protect his equity of redemption by bidding or seeking a loan or getting others to bid for him, and hence that, although A should be reimbursed for this loss, it is not possible to reimburse by a money judgment and a constructive trust is the only available remedy. It may also be these decisions are founded on a view taken by equity, although not clearly stated, that the conduct of B is of an especially reprehensible character, that some relief must be given, and the court will afford this remedy by calling B a constructive trustee, vaguely stating that his conduct was "fraud".[11] Or it may be urged that B should be estopped

6. Wager v. Marshburn, 241 Ala. 73, 1 So.2d 303 (1941); Monarco v. Lo Greco, 35 Cal.2d 621, 220 P.2d 737 (1950); Rubalcava v. Garst, 53 N.M. 295, 206 P.2d 1154 (1949); Vandiver v. Stone, 149 Or. 426, 41 P.2d 247 (1935).

7. Bowles v. White, 206 Ga. 433, 57 S.E.2d 547 (1950); Hatcher v. Sawyer, 243 Iowa 858, 52 N.W.2d 490 (1952); Shives v. Borgman, 194 Md. 29, 69 A.2d 802 (1949); Wright v. Dudley, 189 Va. 448, 53 S.E.2d 29.

8. See Bogert, Trusts and Trustees (rev. 2d edit.), §§ 487, 543(C), 543(D). The agreement may also be regarded as a contract to be a trustee of the realty for the promisee, with one of the trust duties being the obligation to execute a deed to the promisee.

9. Emerson v. Ayres, 196 Ark. 791, 120 S.W.2d 16 (1938); Walter v. Klock, 55 Ill. 362; Kellum v. Smith, 33 Pa. 158; Wood-ard v. Cohron, 345 Mo. 967, 137 S.W.2d 497 (1940); Lancaster Trust Co. v. Long, 220 Pa. 499, 69 A. 993; Stafford v. Stafford, 29 Tex.Civ.App. 73, 71 S.W. 984.

10. Booth v. Mason, 234 Ala. 601, 176 So. 201; Price v. Reeves, 38 Cal. 457; Rives v. Lawrence, 41 Ga. 283; Arnold v. Cord, 16 Ind. 177; Eadie v. Hamilton, 94 Kan. 214, 146 P. 323; Griffin v. Schlenk, 139 Ky. 523, 102 S.W. 837; Northcraft v. Martin, 28 Mo. 469; Dickson v. Stewart, 71 Neb. 424, 98 N.W. 1085, 115 Am.St.Rep. 596; Day v. Devitt, 79 N.J.Eq. 342, 81 A. 368; Rush v. McPherson, 176 N.C. 562, 97 S.E. 613; Beegle v. Wentz, 55 Pa. 369, 93 Am. Dec. 762; Jenckes v. Cook, 9 R.I. 520; Haywood v. Ensley, 8 Humph., Tenn., 460; Chandler v. Riley, Tex.Civ.App., 210 S.W. 716; Harras v. Harras, 60 Wash. 258, 110 P. 1085.

11. See Ryan v. Dox, 34 N.Y. 307, 318–319.

from setting up the Statute.

 WESTLAW REFERENCES

"constructive trust" /s "statute of frauds" /s "real property"

185k119(2) /p "real property" /s "constructive trust"

390k921/2 /p "real property" /s "constructive trust"

BREACH OF ORAL TRUST OF REALTY— RETENTION OF PROPERTY [1]

§ 84. Where land is conveyed by absolute deed under an oral promise by the grantee that he will hold in trust for the grantor, or for a third person, and the grantee later refuses to carry out the oral trust on the ground that it is voidable under the Statute of Frauds, and retains the property for his own benefit, the great majority of American courts refuse to make the grantee a constructive trustee for the grantor or for the intended beneficiary of the oral trust, giving as a reason that to construct a trust in such a case would circumvent the Statute of Frauds.

The English courts and a minority of American courts grant the decree for a constructive trust for the intended beneficiary of the oral trust, because they regard it as dishonest for the grantee to withhold the land from the intended beneficiary by setting up the Statute of Frauds.

If the grantee obtained the land by misrepresentation of the state of his mind as to intended performance of the oral trust or other false statement and later refuses to perform the trust, the court will enforce a constructive trust against him.

If the grantee was in a confidential or fiduciary relation with the grantor at the time of the deed and the oral promise to hold in trust, the grantee is usually made a constructive trustee for the intended beneficiary of the oral trust on account of the wrong involved in the violation of the relationship by repudiation of the promise.

If A is the owner of real property and conveys it to B in reliance on an oral promise by B that he will hold the land in trust for A or for C, and the deed is on its face absolute, the Statute of Frauds prevents A or C from enforcing the express oral trust. A or C sometimes attempts to secure a decree from chancery that B is a constructive trustee for A or C, either on the ground of the breach of the oral express trust, or on the ground of wrongful retention of the property by B for his own benefit after he has relied on the Statute of Frauds. Most of the American decisions which have considered this claim deny it and give as a reason

---

§ 84

1. Bogert, Trusts and Trustees (rev. 2d edit.), §§ 495–499; Restatement, Restitution, §§ 180, 182, 183. And see Restatement, Trusts, Second, §§ 44 and 45, where the black letter sections take no position on the question whether a trust should be constructed where there is no confidential relation and no fraud, but the comments advocate a constructive trust.

that the granting of the decree would nullify the Statute of Frauds, that equity is bound to respect that statute just as much as is a court of law, and that to plead the Statute of Frauds is permitted by the legislature and thus cannot be a reprehensible or "fraudulent" act.[2] This view is expressed as follows in one of the early leading cases:[3] "It is annihilation of the statute to withdraw a case from its operation because of such violation or repudiation of an agreement or trust it declares shall not be made or proved by parol. There can be no fraud if the trust does not exist, and proof of its existence by parol is that which the statute forbids. In any and every case, in which the court is called to enforce a trust, there must be a repudiation of it, or an inability from accident to perform it. If the repudiation is a fraud, which justifies interference in opposition to the words and spirit of the statute, the sphere of operation of the statute is practically limited to breaches from accident, and no reason can be assigned for the limitation."

In England and a few American states it is held that after the oral trustee has refused to carry out his trust in reliance on the Statute of Frauds, if he retains the property for himself he will be attempting to enrich himself unjustly and to perpetrate a wrong on the intended beneficiary and that he ought to be charged as a constructive trustee for the intended beneficiary,[4] whether it be the grantor or a third person.

2. Brindley v. Brindley, 197 Ala. 221, 72 So. 497; Wright v. Young, 20 Ariz. 46, 176 P. 583; Robertson v. Robertson, 229 Ark. 649, 317 S.W.2d 272 (1958); Ussery v. Ussery, 113 Ark. 36, 166 S.W. 946; Von Trotha v. Bamberger, 15 Colo. 1, 24 P. 883; Verzier v. Convard, 75 Conn. 1, 52 A. 255; Mills v. Mills, 112 So.2d 298 (Fla.App. 1959); Fowley v. Braden, 4 Ill.2d 355, 122 N.E.2d 559 (1954); Westphal v. Heckman, 185 Ind. 88, 113 N.E. 299; Dunn v. Zwilling, 94 Iowa 233, 62 N.W. 746; Andrew v. Andrew, 114 Iowa 524, 87 N.W. 494; Horsley v. Hrenchir, 146 Kan. 767, 73 P.2d 1010 (1937) (special opinion by Allen, J., urges that the rule should be changed); Ryan v. Williams, 92 Minn. 506, 100 N.W. 380; Ferguson v. Robinson, 258 Mo. 113, 167 S.W. 447; Dailey v. Kinsler, 31 Neb. 340, 47 N.W. 1045; Lovett v. Taylor, 54 N.J.Eq. 311, 34 A. 896; Wheeler v. Reynolds, 66 N.Y. 227; Braun v. First German Evangelical Lutheran Church, 198 Pa. 152, 47 A. 963; Elick v. Schiller, 150 Tex. 363, 240 S.W.2d 997 (1951); Krouskop v. Krouskop, 95 Wis. 296, 70 N.W. 475. See also, Stone, "Resulting Trusts and the Statute of Frauds," 6 Col.Law Rev. 326; Ames, "Constructive Trusts Based upon the Breach of an Express Oral Trust of Land," 20 Harv. Law Rev. 549; Costigan, 12 Mich.L.R. 423, 515, 28 Harv.L.R. 237, 366; Scott, 37 Harv.

L.R. 653; McWilliams, 16 Cal.L.R. 19; Redmond, 20 Neb.L.R. 160.

3. Patton v. Beecher, 62 Ala. 579, 592, 593.

4. Davies v. Otty, 35 Beav. 208, 213 ("it is not honest to keep the land"); Rochefoucauld v. Bonstead [1897] 1 Ch. 196; Orella v. Johnson, 38 Cal.2d 693, 242 P.2d 5 (1952) ("the grantee will be unjustly enriched, if he is allowed to repudiate his promise and retain the property"); Chandler v. Georgia Chemical Works, 182 Ga. 419, 185 S.E. 787, 105 A.L.R. 837; Becker v. Neurath, 149 Ky. 421, 149 S.W. 857; Kent v. Klein, 352 Mich. 652, 91 N.W.2d 11 (1958); Huffine v. Lincoln, 52 Mont. 585, 160 P. 820; Johnson v. Johnson, 201 Okl. 268, 205 P.2d 314 (1949) (called "resulting"); Schutz v. Schutz, 56 Wn.2d 969, 354 P.2d 694 (1960).

In Massachusetts, if the grantee on oral trust for the grantor will not carry out the trust he may be sued by the grantor for the value of the land. Cromwell v. Norton, 193 Mass. 291, 79 N.E. 433, 118 Am.St.Rep. 499.

And see § 16, Uniform Trusts Act, which provides that there shall be a constructive trust for the grantor. The Act has been adopted in La., Nev., N.M., N.C., Okl., S.D. and Tex.

As a matter of principle, it may be said that parol agreements to hold in trust are of two classes, namely those in which a refusal to enforce the promise will result in the unjust enrichment of the promisor, and those in which the failure to enforce the promise will not cause unjust enrichment of the promisor. If B agrees, voluntarily, to hold in trust for A real property which at the time of the promise belongs to B, and B later declines to carry out his agreement, the refusal of the courts to enforce B's promise will not result in B's being unjustly enriched at the expense of A. But if A voluntarily transfers real property to B, in consideration of an oral promise by B to hold such property in trust for A, and B later repudiates his promise and seeks to hold the real property for his own benefit, failure of the courts to compel B to convey to A will result in the unjust enrichment of B at the expense of A.

In cases where unjust enrichment would result equity should create a constructive trust. This will not be enforcing the original oral express trust, but will be creating an implied trust for the sole purpose of preventing unjust enrichment. The original oral express trust might call for the collection of the rents and the delivery of them and later the capital to the settlor and others, or merely to others. The constructive trust would be a mere passive trust, on the basis of which equity would decree a reconveyance of the property to the settlor. It would require a grantee pleading voidability of his oral promise to hold in trust to return the consideration which he received for making such promise. It would require him to restore the grantor to his former position, if the grantee decided not to go forward with performance of his voidable promise. The holding suggested in cases of unjust enrichment would be in accord with the stand taken by the courts with respect to other agreements, voidable because not complying with the Statute of Frauds. Money paid and the reasonable value of services rendered, under a contract avoided because of the Statute of Frauds, may generally be recovered in quasi-contract.[5]

Actual Fraud at the Time of the Promise

If the grantee, who has agreed to hold the real property in trust for the grantor or another, has a fraudulent intent at the time he makes the promise, then equity will declare the promisor a constructive trustee, notwithstanding that the promise was oral and the Statute of Frauds requires trusts in land to be manifested or proved by a writing.[6]

5. Johnson v. Maness, 241 Ala. 157, 1 So.2d 655 (1941); Cook v. Doggett, 2 Allen, Mass., 439; Herrick v. Newell, 49 Minn. 198, 51 N.W. 819; Erben v. Lorillard, 19 N.Y. 299; Wells v. Foreman, 236 N.C. 351, 72 S.E.2d 765 (1952); Ellis v. Cary, 74 Wis. 176, 42 N.W. 252, 4 L.R.A. 55, 17 Am.St. Rep. 125.

6. Doswell v. Hughen, 266 Ala. 87, 94 So.2d 377 (1957); Von Trotha v. Bamberg-er, 15 Colo. 1, 24 P. 883; Lantry v. Lantry, 51 Ill. 458, 2 Am.Rep. 310; Gregory v. Bowlsby, 126 Iowa 588, 102 N.W. 517; Grote v. Grote, 121 App.Div. 841, 106 N.Y.S. 986; Meek v. Meek, 79 Or. 579, 156 P. 250; Putnam v. Heissner, 220 S.W.2d 701 (Tex.Civ.App.1949).

He has misrepresented the state of his own mind. He impliedly stated that his mind contained an intent to perform the oral trust. In fact his mind was guilty and contained an intent to violate the oral trust. Misrepresentation of any material fact at the time of the transfer ought to entitle the grantor to a constructive trust.[7] The trust should be for the grantor, even though the oral trust was in favor of another.[8] Active solicitation of the conveyance by the grantee under the oral trust may be considered evidence of an intent to defraud the grantor and break the oral promise,[9] when it is followed by an immediate repudiation of the obligation after title was obtained,[10] but the mere fact of repudiation ought not to be evidence of a fraudulent intent at the time of delivery of the deed.[11]

Confidential Relation Between Promisor and Promisee

A further exception to the majority rule denying a constructive trust on the basis of the breach of an unenforceable express trust of realty is found in the case of confidential or fiduciary relations existing between promisor and promisee.[12] Many courts have been eager to avoid the hardship which the Statute of Frauds imposed upon promisees under oral agreements. Equity is well known to be the protector of confidential relations. It has been able to hold, therefore, that while the mere breach of the voidable promise alone might not be a wrong sufficient to warrant judicial relief, the breach and retention of the property in violation of a confidential relation would be.[13] Whatever is obtained for himself by a confidant through abuse of his confidential relation ought to be decreed by equity to be held for the promisee imposing confidence. The trust should be constructed for the promisee and not for any other intended beneficiary of the oral trust.[14] What is

---

7. See § 79, ante.

8. However the cases usually decree a constructive trust for the intended beneficiary of the oral express trust, either the grantor or another. Crabtree v. Potter, 150 Cal. 710, 89 P. 971; Crossman v. Keister, 233 Ill. 69, 79 N.E. 58, 8 L.R.A.,N.S., 698; Ciarlo v. Ciarlo, 244 Mass. 453, 139 N.E. 344.

9. Fischbeck v. Gross, 112 Ill. 208; Lipp v. Lipp, 158 Md. 207, 148 A. 531.

10. Levine v. Schofer, 184 Md. 205, 40 A.2d 324 (1944).

11. Bucher v. Murray, 212 Ga. 259, 91 S.E.2d 610 (1956). But see Dowd v. Tucker, 41 Conn. 197.

12. As to the meaning and rationale of confidential and fiduciary relations, see § 95, post, in discussion of the doctrine of loyalty. The important features are dominance of one party over another by reason of family or business relationship, and/or superiority on account of age, health, experience, education or other factors.

13. Bradley Co. v. Bradley, 165 Cal. 237, 131 P. 750; Stahl v. Stahl, 214 Ill. 131, 73 N.E. 319, 68 L.R.A. 617, 105 Am.St.Rep. 101, 2 Ann.Cas. 774; Newis v. Topfer, 121 Iowa 433, 96 N.W. 905; Staab v. Staab, 160 Kan. 417, 163 P.2d 418 (1945); Knox v. Knox, 222 Minn. 477, 25 N.W.2d 225 (1946); Moses v. Moses, 140 N.J.Eq. 575, 53 A.2d 805, 173 A.L.R. 273 (1947). Jeremiah v. Pitcher, 163 N.Y. 574, 57 N.E. 1113, affirming 26 App.Div. 402, 49 N.Y.S. 788; Marston v. Myers, 217 Or. 448, 342 P.2d 1111 (1959); Metzger v. Metzger, 338 Pa. 564, 14 A.2d 285, 129 A.L.R. 683 (1940); McAdams v. Ogletree, 348 S.W.2d 75 (Tex. Civ.App.1961); Miller v. Miller, 32 Wn.2d 438, 202 P.2d 277 (1949).

14. Jones v. Jackson, 195 Or. 643, 246 P.2d 546 (1952). However, the cases generally give relief to the intended beneficiary of the oral trust, whether the grantor or a third person, and not to the grantor as grantor. Laurincella v. Laurincella, 161 Cal. 61, 118 P. 430; Metzger v. Metzger, 338 Pa. 564, 14 A.2d 285, 129 A.L.R. 683 (1940); Jaeger v. Sechser, 65 S.D. 38, 270

a confidential relationship is not well defined. The courts retain discretion to whether to apply the concept and refuse to bind themselves by any strict definition. Proof of a confidential relation requires more than proof of the existence of trust and confidence by the grantor in the grantee. There must be some superiority of position on the part of the grantee. To hold that the doctrine will be invoked whenever the grantor has confidence in the grantee would be to extend the rule to all transfers on oral trust, since every grantor must rely on the grantee to carry out his agreement.

For example, where a son received real property from his mother under an oral promise to hold the same for the benefit of the mother and the promisor's brothers and sisters, a repudiation of the promise was held to give rise to a constructive trust for the mother and brothers and sisters.[15] The fact of close relationship and the natural trust placed by the mother in her son enabled the court to find a confidential relation. Although no actual fraud in the making of the promise was shown, and although the breach of the oral promise to hold in trust was not a legal wrong, the court found a basis for a constructive trust in the violation of the confidential relationship.

If land is conveyed by A to B on oral agreement to pay A or C money to come from the sale of the land or from another source, there ought to be no difficulty in enforcing performance of the promise by B, since there was no agreement to hold the land in trust, but rather merely a contract to pay money which is not subject to the Statute of Frauds.[16]

In a few cases where A has conveyed to B on oral trust for A or C, and B has in part carried out the trust, or A or C has acted on the faith of the enforceability of B's promise, the courts have decreed B to be a constructive trustee for the intended beneficiary, giving "part performance" as a reason.[17] This might well be treated as the basis for making the oral express trust enforceable, and hence for avoiding all need of relying on a constructive trust as a remedy.[18]

There is also some authority that if the deed from A to B on oral trust was made in contemplation of the death of A, a breach by B may be made a ground for a constructive trust.[19] The rationale here may be that the deed is in substance a will and that the liberal rule applied to

---

N.W. 531; Haws v. Jensen, 116 Utah 212, 209 P.2d 229 (1949).

15. Goldsmith v. Goldsmith, 145 N.Y. 313, 39 N.E. 1067. And see Cardozo, J., in Sinclair v. Purdy, 235 N.Y. 245, 139 N.E. 255, and Foreman v. Foreman, 251 N.Y. 237, 167 N.E. 428.

16. Waterman v. Morgan, 114 Ind. 237, 16 N.E. 590; Tirrell v. Appleton, 274 Mass. 393, 174 N.E. 682; Maca v. Sabata, 150 Neb. 213, 34 N.W.2d 267 (1948).

17. Flannery v. Woolverton, 329 Ill. 424, 160 N.E. 762; Goff v. Goff, 98 Kan.

201, 158 P. 26; Thierry v. Thierry, 298 Mo. 25, 249 S.W. 946; McKinley v. Hessen, 202 N.Y. 24, 95 N.E. 32 (promisee had paid carrying charges, taxes, insurance, repairs and for improvements).

18. See § 21, ante.

19. Allen v. Myers, 5 Cal.2d 311, 54 P.2d 450 (1936); Wellman v. Wellman, 206 Iowa 445, 220 N.W. 82; Messick v. Pennell, 182 Md. 531, 35 A.2d 143 (1943); Bell Holt McCall Co. v. Caplice, 119 Mont. 463, 175 P.2d 416 (1946).

gifts by will on oral trust may therefore be applied.[20]

 WESTLAW REFERENCES

find 242 p2d 5

390k96

Actual Fraud at the Time of the Promise

find 91 se2d 610

120k211(3)

Confidential Relation Between Promisor and Promisee

find 342 p2d 1111

390k103(2) /p "constructive trust"

GIFT BY WILL OR INTESTACY ON ORAL TRUST [1]

§ 85. If a property owner is induced to make an absolute gift by will by reason of reliance on an oral promise by the donee that he will apply all or part of the property to the use of another described person, and, after the will has taken effect upon the death of the testator, the donee refuses to perform his promise, the transaction cannot result in the creation of an express trust because of the Wills Act, but the donee may be made a constructive trustee for the intended beneficiary. The same result exists where the promisee is induced to die intestate on the faith of an oral agreement by his heir or next of kin.

A promise by one joint donee of property does not ordinarily bind the other donees, but it may have that effect if made on behalf of all.

If the recipient by will or intestacy promises to hold for others to be later described by the donor, and no description is communicated to the donee until after the donor's death, the donee will hold as a resulting trustee for the heirs, next of kin, or residuary legatees or devisees of the donor, and no trust will result or be constructed for the intended beneficiaries.

If a gift is stated on the face of a will to be to a donee as trustee, but no description of the beneficiaries appears in the will, and the donee verbally agreed to hold for beneficiaries who were orally or otherwise informally described by the testator to the donee, the successors of the testator can enforce a resulting trust in their favor against the donee.

20. See § 85, post.

§ 85

1. Bogert, Trusts and Trustees (rev. 2d edit.), §§ 498–501; Restatement, Restitution, §§ 184, 186; Restatement, Trusts, Second, §§ 55, 359.

The Problem Stated

It very frequently happens that a property owner who expects his property to pass at his death by will or intestacy to a certain person desires that the latter hold part or all of the property for someone else and expresses this wish at some time before his death but not by a paragraph of his will. Later the owner dies and the property passes to the party who was expected to take it, but the donee refuses to carry out the desire of the deceased and seeks to hold the property for himself. Thus if A, the owner of a farm, makes a will giving it absolutely to B, and informs B prior to the death of A that B is expected to hold the farm for the benefit of C and B agrees to this, and later A dies leaving the will in effect and the will is admitted to probate, but B thereupon declines to give C any benefit from the farm, there is a situation typical of the problems discussed in this section.

The statutes regarding the execution of wills, sometimes called the Wills Acts, provide (with some exceptions) that a property owner cannot pass his property at his death to another without a written instrument, signed by the testator and executed in the presence of witnesses. The stated desire of the property owner, A, indicates an intent that at the moment of his death the legal title to his property shall pass to B and the equitable title to C. He has satisfied the formal requirements with regard to transferring to B the legal interest, but his intent with regard to the transfer of the equitable interest at his death is manifested either orally or in a document not complying with the Wills Act applying to both realty and personalty. Obviously an *express* trust for C cannot be enforced without a clear violation of the Wills Act, because to do so would be to enable A to pass an equitable interest to C at the death of A by virtue of mere conversation or informal papers.

The question which has given rise to much litigation is whether equity ought, in the case assumed, to make B a constructive trustee for C. Has B obtained, or does he retain, the property by unfair and unconscionable means? Is his retention of it for his own benefit merely an assertion of the validity of the Wills Act and an insistence on respect for it? Can it be reprehensible conduct to demand that the courts enforce a statute adopted by the legislature? Even if one admits that B is guilty of unethical conduct, can he be made a constructive trustee for C without in substance repealing in part the statute as to the formalities necessary for the making of a will?

Certain Cases Excluded

Before proceeding to the discussion of the problem just stated, it is necessary to exclude certain fact situations. (1) If B did not learn of A's desire that B hold for C until after A's death, and hence there was no reliance by A on any express or implied promise of B to A to hold for C, B may hold for his own benefit.[2] The gift to him was absolute on the

---

2. Estate of Holt, 61 Cal.App. 464, 215 P. 124; Boynton v. Gale, 194 Mass. 320, 80 N.E. 448.

face of the will and at the time it vested in interest (A's death) B's conscience was not affected with any equity that he hold for someone else. A was not induced to make the gift by any implied or express promise of B.

(2) If B did not promise to hold the property given him for C, but rather to pay C money or deliver other property to C from any source selected by B, the case is one of a third party beneficiary contract made during the lives of A and B and no Wills Act problem arises.[3]

(3) If C can prove that at the time B made the promise to A that he would hold for C, if the property were left to B at the death of A, B had a dishonest state of mind in that he then did not intend to hold for C, B has obtained the property of A by misrepresentation of the state of his own mind, and a constructive trust should be imposed on B under principles previously discussed.[4]

(4) If A and B were in a fiduciary or confidential relation to each other at the time the gift was made and the promise given, then, even if relief could not be worked out otherwise, B should be subject to a constructive trust because of the violation of this relationship.[5] Because equity customarily gives relief in these cases on other grounds, it has not found it necessary to employ the confidential relation concept.

Absolute Gift by Will on Oral Trust for Described Party

The most common case of the type under discussion is that where A makes a will in favor of B, or leaves a will previously made in favor of B in effect, on the basis of an oral promise by B to use the gift property for the benefit of C. A dies leaving the will in effect and B acquires the property but refuses to recognize any rights in C. It is assumed that at the time B made the promise he intended to perform it, and that this honest state of mind continued until the death of A. The courts are nearly unanimous in holding B a constructive trustee for C,[6] giving as reasons that A relied on B's promise, that the operation of the Wills Act is not obstructed or interfered with since title passes to B as stated in the will,[7] but that equity acts on B's title after the will has given it to him, and that this result is necessary in order to prevent "fraud".[8] "Trusts, in cases of this character, are impressed on the

3. Moore v. Ransdel, 156 Ind. 658, 59 N.E. 936; Gaullaher v. Gaullaher, 5 Watts 200.

4. Vance v. Grow, 206 Ind. 614, 190 N.E. 747; In re Stirk's Estate, 232 Pa. 98, 81 A. 187.

5. See § 87, post.

6. De Laurencel v. De Boom, 48 Cal. 581; Rice Stix Dry Goods Co. v. W.S. Albrecht & Co., 273 Ill. 447, 113 N.E. 66; Orth v. Orth, 145 Ind. 184, 42 N.E. 277, 44 N.E. 17, 32 L.R.A. 298, 57 Am.St.Rep. 185; Baylies v. Payson, 5 Allen, Mass., 473; Hooker v. Axford, 33 Mich. 453; Barrett v. Thielen, 140 Minn. 266, 167 N.W. 1030; Crinkley v. Rogers, 100 Neb. 647, 160 N.W.

974; Williams v. Vreeland, 29 N.J.Eq. 417; Casey v. Casey, 161 App.Div. 427, 146 N.Y.S. 348; Winder v. Scholey, 83 Ohio St. 204, 93 N.E. 1098, 33 L.R.A., N.S., 995, 21 Ann.Cas. 1379; Church v. Ruland, 64 Pa. 432; McLellan v. McLean, 39 Tenn. 684, 2 Head. 684.

And see Ames, 20 Harv.L.R. 549; Stone, 6 Col.L.R. 326; Costigan, 12 Mich.L.R. 423, 513, 28 Harv.L.R. 237, 366; Scott, 37 Harv. L.R. 653; McWilliams, 16 Cal.L.R. 19.

7. Winder v. Scholey, 83 Ohio St. 204, 93 N.E. 1098; Church v. Ruland, 64 Pa. 432.

8. Trustees of Amherst College v. Ritch, 151 N.Y. 282, 45 N.E. 876.

ground of fraud, actual or constructive, and the basis or ground upon which fraud is imputed is that of holding the estate of testator against conscience." [9] The court here uses "fraud" as meaning generally reprehensible conduct and not as indicating misrepresentation of fact.

The promise of B may be express or implied. Silence by B when directly informed by A of his intent that B shall hold for C amounts to a promise.[10]

Proof of reliance by A on the promise of B is needed. If it appears that A would have given the property to B even if B had not acquiesced in A's statement of his desires, there is no case for a trust for C. A's intent to have C benefited must have been expressed to B before A's death, agreed to by B, and been an inducement for leaving the will in effect or for making it originally.[11]

The same principles apply to gifts by intestacy or otherwise by operation of law upon the death of the owner.[12] Thus if A fails to make a will because B, his sole heir, agrees orally to hold the land to be inherited in trust for C, and after B has obtained title he repudiates any obligation to C, a trust is constructed for C; and the same is true where A revokes a will and dies intestate on the strength of reliance on such a promise of B. Often a husband and wife agree on the disposition of their property by making a joint will or reciprocal separate wills to the effect that on the death of either his or her property is to pass to the survivor for life with a power to consume principal, and that at the death of the spouse who is the last to die the residue of the property is to be passed by will to children or other named relatives. If the surviving spouse does not keep this promise, but instead leaves the residue to others than the designated beneficiaries, it is generally held that the latter are entitled to a decree imposing a constructive trust on the residue property for their benefit.[13] If the intent as to the disposition of the residue is set forth in a duly executed will, an express trust may be enforced; and if such intent is stated orally or otherwise informally the trust should be constructive, in accordance with other cases of a similar nature previously discussed which do not have the joint or mutual will element.

The cases hold that the beneficiary of the constructive trust should be the person described in the oral statement of the deceased and in the implied or express agreement of the donee as the one who was to receive the benefit of the property given.[14] While undoubtedly taking

9. Powell v. Yearance, 73 N.J.Eq. 117, 67 A. 892, 896.

10. Wiseman v. Guernsey, 107 Neb. 647, 187 N.W. 55; Brook v. Chappell, 34 Wis. 405.

11. Vance v. Grow, 206 Ind. 614, 190 N.E. 747; Bennett v. Littlefield, 177 Mass. 294, 58 N.E. 1011.

12. Barrett v. Thielen, 140 Minn. 266, 167 N.W. 1030; Tyler v. Stitt, 132 Wis. 656, 112 N.W. 1091, 12 L.R.A., N.S., 1087.

13. Brewer v. Simpson, 53 Cal.2d 567, 2 Cal.Rptr. 609, 349 P.2d 289 (1960); Jennings v. McKeen, 245 Iowa 1026, 65 N.W.2d 207 (1954); Price v. Aylor, 258 Ky. 1, 79 S.W. 350.

14. Sick v. Weigand, 123 N.J.Eq. 239, 197 A. 413; O'Boyle v. Brenner, 303 N.Y.

the property from the donee is necessary in order to prevent his unjust enrichment, the imposition of a trust for the intended beneficiary of the agreement between the donor and donee amounts to an evasion of the Wills Act governing the execution of wills.[15] The donor, by oral or other informal means, is enabled to make a gift of property taking effect at his death. It can be argued that a more desirable result would be to prevent unjust enrichment by having a trust for the successors of the donor and thus permitting strict enforcement of the Wills Act. However, such a statute has as its only purpose insuring the genuineness of alleged dispositions to take effect at death, and that object is assured by the application of the "clear and convincing" evidence rule with regard to the establishment of constructive trusts.

Absolute Gift by Will on Oral Trust for Party to Be Described

Occasionally A makes a will in favor of B and exacts from B a promise that B will hold for a party later to be named by A, but A dies without having communicated to B the name of the beneficiary.[16] It is here held that B is a constructive trustee of a trust without a beneficiary at the death of A, and that there is a resulting trust for the successors of A,[17] just as in the case of an express trust without beneficiaries.[18] The status of B is fixed by the situation at the death of A. At that moment B was under an obligation not to hold for his own benefit and to hold for someone other than the successors of the testator, and the court would decree him a constructive trustee for the intended party if it could but it is impossible to do so. Hence the resulting trust for the successors of A.

Absolute Gift to Joint Donees on Promise of One

Where an absolute gift is made by will to several persons as tenants in common or joint tenants, and one of them has made a promise to hold the property for the benefit of another, it would seem that his property interest alone should be affected by a constructive trust, if there is repudiation of any obligation by all the donees, unless he was expressly or impliedly authorized to act for all and purported to act for them, or the others ratified his act when they learned of it.[19]

572, 104 N.E.2d 913 (1952); McGinn v. Gilroy, 178 Or. 24, 165 P.2d 73 (1946).

15. This position was taken in Washington. Brown v. Kausche, 98 Wash. 470, 167 P. 1075.

16. Delivering to the donee a sealed envelope, to be opened on the death of the donor, which contains a paper on which the name of the beneficiary has been written may be held to constitute notice to the donee of a described person and so sufficient basis for a constructive trust. In re Keen, (1937) 1 Ch. 236.

17. In re Boyes, 26 Ch.D. 531.

18. See § 34, ante.

19. Powell v. Yearance, 73 N.J.Eq. 117, 67 A. 892; Heinisch v. Pennington, 73 N.J.Eq. 456, 68 A. 233; Fairchild v. Edson, 154 N.Y. 199, 48 N.E. 541, 61 Am.St.Rep. 609; Trustees of Amherst College v. Ritch, 151 N.Y. 282, 45 N.E. 876, 37 L.R.A. 305; Winder v. Scholey, 83 Ohio St. 204, 93 N.E. 1098, 33 L.R.A., N.S., 995, 21 Ann.Cas. 1379. See In re Stead [1900] 1 Ch. 237, and authorities there collected.

Trust on Face of the Will—Terms Oral

In many cases A, the testator, has stated in his will that B is to hold the property in trust, but has not given in the will any clue to the identity of the beneficiaries, and has relied on oral or other informal instructions made known and agreed to by B during A's life. Here a controversy arises between A's heirs or next of kin, or his residuary donees under his will, on the one side, and the beneficiaries informally named by A, on the other. The former claim under a resulting trust, on the theory that by the will an express trust without a beneficiary is created; the latter claim as constructive trust beneficiaries on the ground that they are in just as good a position as if the will had made an absolute gift to B on its face. The English cases [20] and a few American decisions [21] decree a constructive trust for A's intended beneficiaries. However the larger number of American cases hold in favor of the resulting trust claimants, the successors of A.[22] The latter holdings rely on the argument that if a property owner wishes to have his property pass to others than his heirs at his death, he must give it to those others by a formally executed will, that the will in the case supposed gives the legal title to B but neither excludes the heirs of A as possible donees of the equitable interest nor gives it to others, and therefore the latter are entitled to the benefit of the intestacy laws.

 WESTLAW REFERENCES

The Problem Stated
"wills acts"

Certain Cases Excluded
boynton   +3   gale
vance   +3   grow

Absolute Gift by Will on Oral Trust for Described Property
"oral trust"   /s   will   /s   beneficiary
baylies   /3   payson

Absolute Gift by Will on Oral Trust for Party to be Described
"re boyes"

Absolute Gift to Joint Donees on Promise of One
"re stead"   /p   "secret trust"

Trust on Face of the Will—Terms Oral
parrish   +3   gamble

---

20. Blackwell v. Blackwell, [1929] A.C. 318; Re Rees' Will Trusts, [1950] Ch. 204.

21. Curdy v. Berton, 79 Cal. 420, 21 P. 858; Linney v. Cleveland Trust Co., 30 Ohio App. 345, 165 N.E. 101.

22. Parrish v. Gamble, 234 Ala. 220, 174 So. 303; Wagner v. Clauson, 399 Ill. 403, 78 N.E.2d 203, 3 A.L.R.2d 672 (1948); Oliffe v. Wells, 130 Mass. 221; Lawless v. Lawless, 187 Va. 511, 47 S.E.2d 431 (1948).

BREACH OF EXPRESS TRUST—DISLOYALTY [1]

§ 86. If a trustee of an express trust acquires property by a breach of trust, for example, by a violation of his duty of undivided loyalty to the beneficiary, a constructive trust may be imposed on such property. This doctrine applies to other fiduciaries and to persons who occupy a confidential relation.

In a later section [2] the duty of loyalty is stated, the reasons for its existence are explained, and illustrations of disloyalty are given. If a trustee violates this duty and thereby obtains for himself a property interest, it may be taken from him by the use of a constructive trust which is founded on any kind of fraudulent or unconscionable conduct.[3] Other remedies may also be available, for example, a judgment for the payment of money, the setting aside of a transaction, the removal of the disloyal trustee, or the forfeiture of his compensation.[4] The constructive trust may be applied not only to the property originally obtained by disloyalty, but also to its products and proceeds,[5] and it may be used against persons who succeed the disloyal trustee as the owner of the products of the disloyalty if they are not bona fide purchasers.[6]

In the application of this remedy it is immaterial that the trustee acted innocently because of his ignorance of the rule or his belief that his conduct did not amount to disloyalty.[7] It is unnecessary to prove that the obtaining of the property by disloyalty damaged the beneficiary, since it is sufficient to show the receipt by the trustee of property acquired by breach of his duty.[8]

As is hereinafter shown [9] the duty of loyalty extends to many

§ 86

1. Bogert, Trusts and Trustees (rev. 2d edit.), § 543 et seq.; Restatement, Trusts, Second, §§ 205, 206; Restatement, Restitution, §§ 138, 190–201.

2. See § 95, post.

3. Healy v. C.I.R., 345 U.S. 278, 73 S.Ct. 671, 97 L.Ed. 1007 (1953), rehearing denied 345 U.S. 961, 73 S.Ct. 935, 97 L.Ed. 1380 (1953); Industrial Indemnity Co. v. Golden State Co., 49 Cal.2d 255, 316 P.2d 966 (1957), certiorari denied 356 U.S. 927, 78 S.Ct. 715, 2 L.Ed.2d 758 (1958). While nearly all the cases showing an application of this principle involve disloyalty, the constructive trust may be used as a remedy to prevent unjust enrichment of the trustee as a result of any breach of trust. Akers v. Gillentine, 191 Tenn. 35, 231 S.W.2d 369 (1948); Morris v. Morris, 195 Tenn. 133, 258 S.W.2d 732 (1953) (breach of duty as to investments).

See § 77, ante.

4. Continental Ill. Nat. Bank & Tr. Co. v. Kelley, 333 Ill.App. 119, 76 N.E.2d 820 (1948); George Washington Mem. Park Cem. Ass'n v. Memorial Dev. Co., 141 N.J. Eq. 47, 55 A.2d 675 (1947); Lewis' Estate, 349 Pa. 455, 37 A.2d 559 (1944).

5. See § 161, post.

6. Farrington v. Jacobs, 132 F.2d 745; McConnell v. Dixon, 68 Wyo. 301, 233 P.2d 877 (1951).

7. Winger v. Chicago City Bank & Trust Co., 394 Ill. 94, 67 N.E.2d 265 (1946); Bank of Mill Creek v. Elk Horn Coal Corp., 133 W.Va. 639, 57 S.E.2d 736 (1950). If a competent and well advised beneficiary consents to the disloyal act, the transaction may be rendered invulnerable, not because of the good faith of the trustee but because of the beneficiary's consent to an otherwise unlawful act. Spring v. Hawkes, 351 Pa. 602, 41 A.2d 538 (1945).

8. In re Bond & Mtg. Guar. Co., 303 N.Y. 423, 103 N.E.2d 721 (1952); Slay v. Burnett, 143 Tex. 621, 187 S.W.2d 377 (1945).

9. See § 95, post.

fiduciaries other than trustees, such as executors, guardians, corporate directors, agents, partners and joint adventurers, and attorneys; the remedy of the constructive trust may be used against them where they have obtained a personal benefit by breach of the duty.[10]

In addition, the duty and the remedy exist with respect to persons who are in a "confidential relation", a term having no exact definition but involving dominance and superiority because of such elements as close family relationship, a long continued practice of entrusting business matters to a confidant, and differences in age, health, and education.[11] For example, if an aged and infirm father lives with a son who advises and assists his father in business matters, it may well be held that they are in a confidential relation.[12]

Examples of the use of a constructive trust as a remedy for breach of the duty of loyalty may be found in cases where a trustee as an individual purchases the trust property [13] or a claim against it (for example, a mortgage),[14] or where the trustee sells his individual property to the trust as an investment,[15] or where a trustee employs himself to render services needed by the trust (for example, legal advice or property appraisement),[16] or where a trustee holds a lease which is about to expire and secures a renewal for himself instead of for the trust,[17] or where an agent to purchase property for his principal with the money of the principal buys for himself and pays for the property out of his own funds,[18] or where a partner or joint adventurer in oil properties buys for himself property which should have been acquired for the joint enterprise.[19]

 WESTLAW REFERENCES

trustee /s requir*** /s property /s breach /s "constructive trust"

10. Rothman v. Wilson, C.C.A.Or., 121 F.2d 1000 (attorney); Bainbridge v. Stoner, 16 Cal.2d 423, 106 P.2d 423 (1940) (director of corporation); Schneider v. Schneider, 347 Mo. 102, 146 S.W.2d 584 (1941) (partner).

11. Le Blanc v. Atkins, 387 Ill. 360, 56 N.E.2d 770 (1944); Groves v. Groves, 248 Iowa 682, 82 N.W.2d 124 (1957); Hamberg v. Barsky, 355 Pa. 462, 50 A.2d 345 (1947).

12. McDonald v. Miller, 73 N.D. 474, 16 N.W.2d 270 (1944).

13. Bogert, Trusts and Trustees (rev. 2d edit.), §§ 543(A), 543(C). And see Vrooman v. Hawbaker, 387 Ill. 428, 56 N.E.2d 623 (1944); Faust v. Murray, 245 Wis. 643, 15 N.W.2d 793 (1944).

14. Bogert, Trusts and Trustees (rev. 2d edit.), § 543(D). And see Persons v. Russell, 212 Ala. 506, 103 So. 543; McKinney v. Christmas, 143 Colo. 361, 353 P.2d 373 (1960); Chiswell v. Campbell, 300 Pa. 68, 150 A. 90.

15. Bogert, Trusts and Trustees (rev. 2d edit.), § 543(E). First State Bank v. Catron, 268 Ky. 513, 105 S.W.2d 162 (1937); St. Paul Trust Co. v. Strong, 85 Minn. 1, 88 N.W. 256.

16. Broughton v. Broughton, 5 De G.M. & G. 160; Gamble v. Gibson, 59 Mo. 585; In re Lundberg's Estate, 197 N.Y.S.2d 871 (Sur.1960) (employing self as real estate broker).

17. Pratt v. Shell Petroleum Corp., 100 F.2d 833 (10th Cir.1938), certiorari denied 306 U.S. 659, 59 S.Ct. 775, 83 L.Ed. 1056 (1939); Joslin v. Astle, 59 R.I. 182, 194 A. 703.

18. Stromerson v. Averill, 22 Cal.2d 808, 141 P.2d 732 (1943); Stephenson v. Golden, 279 Mich. 710, 276 N.W. 849 (1937).

19. Horne v. Holley, 167 Va. 234, 188 S.E. 169 (1936). See Bogert, Trusts and Trustees (rev. 2d edit.), § 488.

BREACH OF DUTY IN DIRECT DEALING WITH BENEFICIARY [1]

§ 87. If a trustee or other fiduciary, or a person in a confidential relation, enters into a transaction with the beneficiary or other person represented, by way of sale, gift, release or otherwise, he may be charged as a constructive trustee of any property obtained thereby, unless he can prove that he performed the duty placed upon him by equity to make full disclosure of the relevant facts and law and to act otherwise with the utmost fairness.

In later material [2] dealing with the duties of the trustee, attention is called to his duty to make full disclosure and to treat the beneficiary with the utmost fairness when there is a direct conveyance, contract, or other transaction between trustee and beneficiary. It is there shown that this duty extends to all fiduciaries and likewise to persons in a confidential relation. Many illustrations are given of the breach and performance of this duty and the consequences of each. It is stated that the burden of proving the fairness of the transaction rests upon the trustee when the beneficiary attacks it, and examples are given of adequate evidence by the trustee with respect to discharging the burden. This duty is similar to the duty of loyalty in the administration of the trust but does not seem to be a branch or subdivision of the loyalty rule. It is rather a duty arising from the superiority and dominance of the fiduciary and the danger of overreaching or undue influence.

At this point only the remedial aspects of the situation are discussed, in order to show that one form of relief available to the beneficiary or other person represented is to have the trustee or other representative declared a constructive trustee of any property obtained through a transaction where there was a breach of the duty to make full disclosure and to act fairly.[3] This is clearly a type of inequitable conduct which ought to be a ground for imposition of a constructive trust. Other remedies may be available, for example, obtaining a money judgment against the wrongdoing trustee where he has transferred to a bona fide purchaser the property which he inequitably obtained.[4] Many of the cases decreeing a return of the property which

§ 87

1. Bogert, Trusts and Trustees (rev. 2d edit.), § 544; Restatement, Trusts, Second, § 170.

2. See § 96, post.

3. Phillips v. Willis, 31 Del.Ch. 5, 63 A.2d 171 (1949); McCartney v. McCartney, 8 Ill.2d 494, 134 N.E.2d 789 (1956); Maddox v. Maddox, 151 Neb. 626, 38 N.W.2d 547 (1949); In re Bond & Mtg. Guar. Co., 303 N.Y. 423, 103 N.E.2d 721 (1952).

4. Piff v. Berresheim, 405 Ill. 617, 92 N.E.2d 113 (1950).

was inequitably obtained speak of avoiding or setting aside the transaction.

Thus if a trustee buys the interest of one of the beneficiaries under his trust for an inadequate price, without telling the beneficiary facts which the trustee knew but the beneficiary did not know regarding the value of the interest being sold, and later the trustee realizes a profit on the transaction, this gain may be taken from the trustee through the remedial device of the constructive trust.[5]

One of the most common illustrations of the application of the rule and the constructive trust remedy is that of a gift of his interest by the beneficiary to the fiduciary or a person who occupies a confidential relation, for example, where a client makes the attorney who drew his will a beneficiary under his will. Here, if the donor or his successors attack the gift, the burden is on the donee to prove full disclosure and fair play, and if he cannot do so he may be made a constructive trustee or the gift may be set aside.[6]

 WESTLAW REFERENCES

find 134 ne2d 789

390k365(5)

---

5. Hardy v. Hardy, 217 Ark. 305, 230 S.W.2d 11 (1950); Phillips v. Willis, 31 Del. Ch. 5, 63 A.2d 171 (1949); Maddox v. Maddox, 151 Neb. 626, 38 N.W.2d 547 (1949); Cluzel v. Brown, 133 N.J.Eq. 156, 29 A.2d 864 (1943).

6. Howland v. Smith, 9 A.D.2d 197, 193 N.Y.S.2d 140 (1959), appeal dismissed 7 N.Y.2d 988, 199 N.Y.S.2d 495, 166 N.E.2d 503 (1960); Newkirk v. Stevens, 152 N.C. 498, 67 S.E. 1013; In re Lobb's Will, 177 Or. 162, 160 P.2d 295 (1945).

Chapter 9

THE POWERS OF THE TRUSTEE—IN GENERAL

Table of Sections

EXPRESS AND IMPLIED POWERS [1]

§ 88. A trustee's powers are said to be "express" if they are granted to him in the trust instrument, by court decree, or by statute, and in clear, direct language. They are called "implied" if they are not set forth in the trust instrument in so many words, but are deemed by equity to have been intended by the settlor because convenient or necessary to the accomplishment of his trust purposes.

In well drawn trust instruments a large number of powers of the trustee are stated.[2] Thus the trustee is often given powers to sell the original trust property, to invest the proceeds of any property sold, and to collect the income of the trust property and pay it over to the beneficiaries. These powers are called "express powers" because they are clearly and directly granted to the trustee. Their existence is not left to any inference or implication. Corporate trustees often recommend to draftsmen of trust instruments that every power which may conceivably be necessary or desirable be expressly granted in order to give them freedom to act quickly in all emergencies, without the delay and expense involved in applying to the court for authority,[3] and trust instruments which they help to draw commonly make such provisions.

§ 88

1. Bogert, Trusts and Trustees (rev. 2d edit.), § 551 et seq.; Restatement, Trusts, Second, §§ 186–196.

2. For examples of powers customarily granted, see Bogert, Trusts and Trustees

(rev. 2d edit.), § 1031 et seq. (forms of trust instruments and clauses).

3. For a discussion of the recommended and usual powers, see Bogert, Trusts and Trustees (rev. 2d edit.), § 551 et seq.

The court has the power to grant to a trustee a power which is highly convenient or necessary to the proper execution of the trust but which the settlor did not expressly give to the trustee.[4] And the court may permit the trustee to deviate from the settlor's directions as to powers and duties, as is shown in a subsequent section.[5]

Sometimes legislatures provide that trustees shall have a specific power,[6] or that all trustees shall have very broad and general enumerated powers unless the settlor provides otherwise.[7] It may also be provided by statute that a trustee shall not have a specific power, for example, the authority to use a discretionary power in his own favor where he is both trustee and a beneficiary.[8]

But the fact that a certain power is not expressly stated in the trust instrument or in any court order or applicable statute does not prove that the power in question does not rest in the trustee. If the existence of the power is highly convenient or necessary in order to enable the trustee to carry out the purposes of the trust, it is inferred that the settlor intended to grant the power so that his trustee might not be handicapped or frustrated in securing the results which the settlor intended to accomplish.[9] Such a power is called "implied".

Thus if a settlor leaves improved real estate to a trustee, with a direction to collect the income of it and pay it over to his children for their support, and the instrument contains no power to lease the realty, one may easily be implied since that is the normal way of getting income from improved real estate.[10] And trustees to operate a ranch for the benefit of a family may well be found to have implied power to borrow money to pay operating expenses when climatic conditions make the property unproductive in some years.[11] Where a trustee is directed to distribute principal among numerous remainder beneficiaries, and part of the trust property consists of real estate, and the operation of it by numerous co-owners or its partition into very small tracts would be highly disadvantageous to the beneficiaries, a power to sell the realty and pay the remaindermen in money may well be

4. Wallace v. Julier, 147 Fla. 420, 3 So. 2d 711 (1941) (power to incorporate the trust).

5. See §§ 146, 147, post.

6. For statutes that specifically grant trustees the power to vote corporate stock, see Bogert, Trusts and Trustees (rev. 2d edit.), § 551.

7. The Uniform Trustees' Powers Act, adopted by the National Conference of Commissioners on Uniform State Laws in 1964, provides a large number of customary powers and has been adopted, with or without some modification, in 12 states. See, for example, Miss.Code §§ 91–9–101 to 91–9–119. In other states there is similar legislation which either directly confers certain powers upon the trustee or permits the trustee to incorporate the statutory

powers by reference. For a statute of the former type, see Wash.—RCWA 11.98.070. For a statute of the latter type, see N.Car. G.S. § 32–36.

For references to all state trustee powers statutes see Bogert, Trusts and Trustees (rev. 2d edit.), § 551.

8. See, for example, N.Y.—McKinney's EPTL 10–10.1; Va.Code 1950, § 55–7; Wis. S.A. 701.19.

9. Kipp v. O'Melveny, 2 Cal.App. 142, 83 P. 264.

10. Hutcheson v. Hodnett, 115 Ga. 990, 42 S.E. 422; City of Richmond v. Davis, 103 Ind. 449, 3 N.E. 130.

11. Purdy v. Bank of America Nat. Trust & Savings Ass'n, 2 Cal.2d 298, 40 P.2d 481 (1935).

implied.[12]

 WESTLAW REFERENCES

di express

di implied

"uniform trustees' powers act"

MANDATORY AND DISCRETIONARY POWERS [1]

§ 89. A settlor may direct his trustee to perform a certain act of trust administration and thereby create a power and impose a duty to use the power. Such a power is called "mandatory" or "imperative".

The settlor may also authorize the trustee to do or to refrain from doing a certain act, or to use his judgment as to when or how a power should be used, in which case the power is described as "discretionary".

The court will order the trustee to exercise a mandatory power, or hold him liable for failure to do so, but it will not direct the holder of a discretionary power to act in any particular way or set aside a decision made by him in the use of that power, unless there has been an abuse of the discretion.

Even if the settlor provided that the trustee should have "full and uncontrolled" discretion, the exercise of the power is subject to court supervision and will be upset if the court finds that the trustee acted in disregard of the settlor's purposes.

A settlor may express an intent that the trustee shall in any event perform a certain act in the course of his administration, and may direct the trustee to do the act in question. The trustee's power to perform this act is called "imperative" or "mandatory". For example, if the settlor directs the trustee to sell trust realty as soon as possible and invest the proceeds in bonds, the power to sell is a mandatory one. There is a duty as well as a power.[2] If the trustee fails to use his mandatory powers at the time required by the trust instrument, he is guilty of a breach of trust, and one of the remedies available to the beneficiary is to secure a court order that the trustee exercise the power in question.[3] Or the court may compel the trustee to pay damages for delay in using the power or for total failure to exercise it.[4] The court might give other relief, for example, remove the trustee and appoint one who would exercise the power.

---

12. Vansant v. Spillman, 193 Ky. 788, 237 S.W. 379 (1922); Robinson v. Robinson, 105 Me. 68, 72 A. 883, 32 L.R.A.,N.S., 675, 134 Am.St.Rep. 537; Parker v. Seeley, 56 N.J.Eq. 110, 38 A. 280.

§ 89

1. Restatement, Trusts, Second, §§ 186, 187, 382.

2. Williams v. Gardner, 90 Conn. 461, 97 A. 854; Osborne v. Gordon, 86 Wis. 92, 56 N.W. 334.

3. Stuart v. Chaney, 71 Colo. 279, 206 P. 386 (1922); Congdon v. Congdon, 160 Minn. 343, 200 N.W. 76 (1924). And see § 155, post.

4. See § 157, post.

A settlor may leave to the judgment of his trustee the question whether a certain act should be done or not, in order to carry out the trust. The authority to do such an act is called a "discretionary" power, because it rests in the discretion of the trustee whether the act is done or not. For example, if a settlor creates a trust for his widow and directs that the income be paid to her and also such part of the principal as in the judgment of the trustee is necessary for her comfortable support, the power to pay principal is a discretionary power. It may or it may not be exercised according to the trustee's decision.[5] The discretion may also relate to the time and manner of performing a certain act of trust administration, for example, when the principal of the trust shall be distributed and the trust terminated,[6] or whether trust property shall be distributed in kind or in the form of cash.[7]

The courts are often called upon to pass upon the action or inaction of the trustee with respect to his discretionary powers, or the choice made by the trustee with regard to time, amount, and manner of payments made, or his decision as to the allocation of an item of receipts or expenses to principal or income. The general attitude of the courts has been that they will not upset the decision of the trustee, if it was made in good faith after consideration of the intent of the settlor as to the purposes of the trust and the circumstances of the beneficiaries at the time,[8] even if the court would have taken different action or believes that a reasonable man would have come to a contrary conclusion.[9] The settlor selected the trustee and intended that the beneficiaries should be content with his honest decision. For example, in a case [10] where a trustee was given discretionary power to deliver part or all of the principal of a trust fund to a daughter of the settlor when the trustee thought it wise to do so, and the daughter had had mental trouble but had recovered her health and insisted that the trustee deliver the trust property to her but the trustee declined to do so, the court refused to interfere with the decision since there had been an honest exercise of discretion and there was no evidence of bad faith. And the court will not grant a petition by the trustee for instructions as to how to exercise a discretionary power, but instead will direct the trustee to use his own judgment.[11]

5. Whitaker v. McDowell, 82 Conn. 195, 72 A. 938, 16 Ann.Cas. 324; Safe Deposit & Trust Co. v. Sutro, 75 Md. 361, 23 A. 732.

6. Buchanan v. Patterson, 6 N.Y.2d 40, 159 N.E.2d 661 (1959).

7. In re Fiedler's Estate, 55 N.J.Super. 500, 151 A.2d 201 (1959).

8. In re Sam's Estate, 219 Iowa 374, 258 N.W. 682 (1935); Wight v. Mason, 134 Me. 52, 180 A. 917 (1935); Marburg v. Safe Dep. & Tr. Co., 177 Md. 165, 9 A.2d 222 (1939).

9. In re Ordean's Will, 195 Minn. 120, 261 N.W. 706 (1935); Williams v. Hund, 302 Mo. 451, 258 S.W. 703 (1924); In re Vohland's Estate, 135 Neb. 77, 280 N.W. 241 (1938).

10. Watling v. Watling, 27 F.2d 193 (6th Cir.1928).

11. Camden Safe Deposit & Tr. Co. v. Read, 124 N.J.Eq. 599, 4 A.2d 10 (1939); In re Murphy's Will, 1 App.Div. 737, 146 N.Y.S.2d 848 (1955).

If the trustee refuses to consider whether or not to use his discretionary power, naturally the beneficiary may obtain a court order that the trustee determine what to do, rather than merely ignore the problem involved;[12] and similar intervention may occur where the trustee made his decision without considering relevant information and so acted arbitrarily.[13]

The discretion given the trustee may be to determine the existence of facts and then to use his powers accordingly, as where the trustee is granted power to decide when the life beneficiary acquires good business judgment and is able to manage property prudently; and when the trustee decides that this situation has come about he either is empowered in his discretion to end the trust and turn over the principal to the beneficiary, or is directed to do so. Here the court will not ordinarily upset the decision of the trustee as to the ability and habits of the beneficiary.[14] The trustee's decision as to the existence of the condition precedent will be determinative, unless the court finds, on one ground or another, there has been an abuse of discretion.[15]

Occasionally, however, the court finds that the trustee has not acted in good faith and with consideration of the purposes of the trust, but has instead acted arbitrarily, in bad faith, capriciously, maliciously, or from other improper motive.[16] Here the court finds that there has been "an abuse of discretion", and it either will direct the trustee to reconsider his action, or will instruct him as to how he should make a new decision.[17] Thus if a trustee has discretionary power to pay the widow of the settlor such part of the income of the trust as he thinks necessary for her comfortable support, the trust produces $15,000 annual income, and the widow is an invalid needing special medical care and hospitalization, but the trustee refuses to provide such care and pays out only $5,000 a year to the widow, the court would almost

12. Klug v. Klug, [1918] 2 Ch. 67; In re Sullivan's Will, 144 Neb. 36, 12 N.W.2d 148 (1943).

13. In re Murray, 142 Me. 24, 45 A.2d 636 (1946) (power to pay principal when needed for support; payment made on demand of beneficiary without consideration of need).

14. Robison v. Elston, 113 Ind.App. 633, 48 N.E.2d 181 (1943) (power to pay principal when beneficiary suffered misfortune or disaster); In re Sams' Estate, 219 Iowa 374, 258 N.W. 682 (1935) (when beneficiary obtained an education and became a good citizen); In re Filzen's Estate, 252 Wis. 322, 31 N.W.2d 520 (1948) (when trustee satisfied that beneficiary could manage property).

15. Viall v. Rhode Island Hosp. Tr. Co., 45 R.I. 432, 123 A. 570 (1924).

16. Conlin v. Murdock, 137 N.J.Eq. 12, 43 A.2d 218 (1945) (discretion as to amounts to be paid to sister of settlor; trust fund of $60,000; only $50 a month being paid for support of aged and destitute sister); Stallard v. Johnson, 189 Okl. 376, 116 P.2d 965 (1941) (fund of $20,000; abuse of discretion to pay only $15 a month to aged widow as beneficiary who needed medicines and medical attention).

The trustee abuses his power if he uses it for his own benefit or for the advantage of a third person. In re Ahrens' Estate, 272 App.Div. 472, 71 N.Y.S.2d 462 (1947), appeal dismissed 297 N.Y. 600, 75 N.E.2d 271 (1947); In re Briggs' Estate, 150 Pa. Super. 66, 27 A.2d 430 (1942).

17. Gardner v. O'Loughlin, 76 N.H. 481, 84 A. 935; Stallard v. Johnson, 189 Okl. 376, 116 P.2d 965 (1941).

certainly find an abuse of discretion and direct a larger payment.[18]

In some cases the trust instrument gives the trustee "uncontrolled and absolute discretion" to do or refrain from doing certain acts or to decide certain questions. While here the trustee is probably somewhat less subject to the review and control of the court, the words are not given their literal meaning.[19] It is said that the trustee must act "in the state of mind contemplated by the testator", which would seem to mean he must give some consideration to the fundamental purposes of the trust. Extraordinary decisions preventing accomplishment of a primary purpose of the settlor will not be tolerated.[20] But if the trustee has used his judgment in good faith and has considered the settlor's objectives and the effect of his action on the beneficiaries, the court will not overturn the trustee's decision and direct a different result.[21]

A power is not discretionary when the trustee is directed to perform a certain act if and when a described event happens, and the occurrence of the event is to be determined by external standards and not by the judgment of the trustee. The trustee has a duty to find out whether the event has transpired, and if it has come to pass the power of the trustee becomes mandatory.[22] For example, the trustee may be instructed to pay over the principal of the trust to the beneficiary when he is judicially declared to be sane.[23]

If co-trustees have a discretionary power and cannot agree on the decision to be made under it, the court will not ordinarily settle the

---

18. Strawn v. Caffee, 235 Ala. 218, 178 So. 430 (1938). And see Coker v. Coker, 208 Ala. 354, 94 So. 566 (1922) (trust for support of widow; no payments made and trustee permitted beneficiary to be maintained in an insane asylum in another state).

19. Any attempt by the settlor to exclude the court from considering the decisions of the trustee has been held void. Keating v. Keating, 182 Iowa 1056, 165 N.W. 74; Taylor v. McClave, 128 N.J.Eq. 109, 15 A.2d 213 (1940); Heyer v. Bullock, 210 N.C. 321, 186 S.E. 356 (1936). "His discretion was to be 'absolute and uncontrolled'. That does not mean, however, that it might be recklessly or willfully abused." Cardozo, J., in Carrier v. Carrier, 226 N.Y. 114, 123 N.E. 135 (1919).

20. Helvering v. McCormack, 135 F.2d 294 (2d Cir.1943); Conway v. Emeny, 139 Conn. 612, 96 A.2d 221 (1953); Vest v. Bialson, 365 Mo. 1103, 293 S.W.2d 369 (1956) (full power over investments did not permit speculative or hazardous investments).

21. Robinson v. Chance, 213 F.2d 834 (3d Cir.1954); Offutt v. Offutt, 204 Md. 101, 102 A.2d 554 (1954); Dumaine v. Dumaine,

301 Mass. 214, 16 N.E.2d 625 (1938) (full power to decide whether receipts to go to income or principal; no interference with a decision of trustee that capital gains should be income, since the discretion had been used after serious and responsible consideration and there was no arbitrary, dishonest, or fraudulent conduct or bad faith).

The trustee's discretionary power to decide whether receipts or accretions are to be treated as principal or income, and whether expenses are to be charged to principal or income, may not be used to shift beneficial interests between the income beneficiary and the charitable remainderman. Old Colony Trust Co. v. Silliman, 352 Mass. 6, 223 N.E.2d 504 (1967). For possible federal estate tax effects of such broad discretionary powers, see Bogert, Trusts and Trustees (rev. 2d edit.), § 275.5.

22. The court may intervene if it believes that the event has occurred but the trustee has decided otherwise. Russell v. Hartley, 83 Conn. 654, 78 A. 320.

23. Elward v. Elward, 117 Kan. 458, 232 P. 240; Appeal of Davis, 183 Mass. 499, 67 N.E. 604.

dispute and direct the trustees to act in one way or another,[24] but will rather direct a reconsideration by the trustees, and if they remain deadlocked for a long time it may remove one or all of the trustees.[25]

 WESTLAW REFERENCES

trustee /2 power /s mandatory imperative

find 146 nys2d 848

di(discretionary /2 power /s trustee)

162k80 /p trustee

PERSONAL POWERS AND POWERS ATTACHED TO THE TRUSTEESHIP [1]

§ 90. A settlor may make the power to act as trustee or a power to perform a particular act of trust administration personal to one trustee or to a group of co-trustees, or he may provide that a power shall be exercisable by any occupant of the trusteeship at any time. The former type of power does not pass to a successor, while the latter does.

Due to the disadvantages of personal powers in the performance of most trusts, the courts rarely find an implied intent that powers are personal.

A settlor may make a power to perform an act of trust administration personal to the originally named trustee,[2] or to him and his successors by a particular method,[3] or to the co-trustees who are nominated by him at the beginning of the trust,[4] which means that no other trustee or trustees can exercise the power. Or he can show an intent that the trustee or trustees whom he names and all their successors shall be able to exercise the power, in which case the power is said to be attached to the office of the trusteeship.[5] The ability of the settlor to make the entire trusteeship personal to one trustee or one group of trustees has been previously discussed.[6]

24. Occasionally the court does direct the trustees what to do. See In re Briggs' Estate, 139 Cal.App.2d 802, 294 P.2d 478 (1956); In re Kitzinger's Will, 86 N.Y.S.2d 514 (Sur.1948).

25. McCarthy v. Tierney, 116 Conn. 588, 165 A. 807 (1933); Woodard v. Mordecai, 234 N.C. 463, 67 S.E.2d 639 (1951).

§ 90

1. Restatement, Trusts, Second, §§ 195, 196.

2. Tilley v. Letcher, 203 Ala. 277, 82 So. 527; Sherry v. Little, 341 Mass. 224, 167 N.E.2d 872 (1960) (personal power vested in one co-trustee).

3. United States Trust Co. v. Poutch, 130 Ky. 241, 113 S.W. 107 (original trustee and any successor appointed by him).

4. Dillingham v. Martin, 61 N.J.Eq. 276, 49 A. 143 (to use principal when deemed expedient); In re Towers' Trust, 8 Misc.2d 430, 164 N.Y.S.2d 449 (1957).

5. Jacobs v. Wilmington Trust Co., 9 Del.Ch. 400, 80 A. 346 (use income for daughter until 30 and pay her such part of principal as deemed best after her marriage); Duncan v. Elkins, 94 N.H. 13, 45 A.2d 297 (1946) (pay or apply income); In re Doe's Will, 232 Wis. 34, 285 N.W. 764 (1939) (apply principal to aid of widow).

6. See § 29, ante.

If the settlor does not spell out his intent with definiteness, the question is sometimes raised as to whether he impliedly made a power personal. There are no clear-cut criteria for answering this inquiry.[7] The court will determine the settlor's meaning from a consideration of the nature of the power, the objects to be accomplished by its use, whether the trustee or trustees originally selected had special qualifications which made them and them alone suitable donees of the power, and other relevant facts with relation to the settlor, trustee, and beneficiaries.[8]

If the trustee is a close relative of the settlor and the power relates to family matters and is to be exercised in the near future, an intent to have the power personal to the original trustee may be natural.[9] On the other hand, if the trust term is long (for example, several lives of relatively young persons) and the sole trustee named is an elderly man, and it is probable that it will be advantageous to use the power from time to time throughout the trust, the implication of an intent to have the power attached to the office is strong.[10]

Since declinations, deaths, resignations, and removals of trustees are frequent, if the continuance of the power throughout the life of the trust is highly desirable, the courts are disinclined to find that the settlor intended the power to be personal and thus exposed to extinction.[11] A personal power is a handicap to efficient trust administration. Hence the cases where it has been adjudged that a power or a trusteeship was personal to the originally appointed trustee are rare.[12]

7. In re White's Will, 135 Misc. 377, 238 N.Y.S. 559 (1929) (suggesting some relevant factors); In re Smith, (1904) 1 Ch. 139. All depends on the expressed or implied intent of the settlor. Bratton v. Trust Co. of Ga., 191 Ga. 49, 11 S.E.2d 204 (1940); Watling v. Watling, 27 F.2d 193 (6th Cir.1928).

8. Booth v. Krug, 368 Ill. 487, 14 N.E.2d 645 (1938) (not personal because settlor must have imposed special confidence in trustee). A gift of a power to a trustee "and successors" shows an intent to attach the power to the office. In re Warner's Will, 240 Minn. 540, 61 N.W.2d 840 (1953). Where the trustee is a corporation the power is generally held not to be personal. In re Canfield's Estate, 80 Cal.App. 2d 443, 181 P.2d 732 (1947); In re Boutwell's Estate, 112 Vt. 159, 22 A.2d 157 (1941).

9. Security Co. v. Snow, 70 Conn. 288, 39 A. 153 (mother trustee to make optional payments to daughter); Gilmore v. Gilmore, 201 Ga. 770, 41 S.E.2d 229 (1947); Welch v. Wachovia Bank & Tr. Co., 226 N.C. 357, 38 S.E.2d 197 (1946) (both trustees and distributees were relatives of settlor).

10. Munsey v. Laconia Home for the Aged, 103 N.H. 42, 164 A.2d 557 (1960); In re Walker, 292 N.Y. 19, 53 N.E.2d 378 (1944) (trustees 51 and 57 and payments were to be made over a maximum period of 22 years). Where the trust has a long term and a discretionary power of sale is given, it is natural to hold that it is not intended to be personal to the individuals originally named as trustees. Penn v. Pa. Co., 294 Ky. 271, 171 S.W.2d 437 (1943); Maryland Cas. Co. v. Safe Dep. & Tr. Co. of Baltimore, 115 Md. 339, 80 A. 903.

11. Doe ex dem. Gosson v. Ladd, 77 Ala. 223; Vernoy v. Robinson, 133 Ga. 653, 66 S.E. 928; Yates v. Yates, 255 Ill. 66, 99 N.E. 360, Ann.Cas. 1913D, 143; Moore v. Isbel, 40 Iowa 383; Hicks v. Hicks, 84 N.J. Eq. 515, 94 A. 409; Forman v. Young, 166 App.Div. 815, 152 N.Y.S. 417; Kadis v. Weil, 164 N.C. 84, 80 S.E. 229; Wilson v. Pennock, 27 Pa. 238.

12. In the following cases the power was held personal and not capable of exercise by a successor: Luquire v. Lee, 121 Ga. 624, 49 S.E. 834; French v. Northern Trust Co., 197 Ill. 30, 64 N.E. 105; De Lashmutt v. Teetor, 261 Mo. 412, 169 S.W. 34; Dillingham v. Martin, 61 N.J.Eq. 276, 49 A.

In some cases a presumption is made that a power is attached to the office,[13] and sometimes statutes set forth this presumption or provide that the power passes to successors unless the settlor expressly made it personal to a particular trustee.[14]

As has been shown elsewhere,[15] a trusteeship and all powers attached to it pass to a successor trustee in cases of declination, failure to qualify, death, resignation, dissolution of a corporate trustee, and removal. And when there is a co-trusteeship and for any of those reasons one trustee withdraws, the surviving trustees normally have all the powers which were vested in the original group.[16] On the other hand, if the trusteeship or any power under it was personal to a trustee or group of co-trustees, the trust or the power is destroyed when the personal trustee or trustees (or the holder or one of the holders of the personal power) never accepts the trust or ceases to act.[17]

 WESTLAW REFERENCES

"personal power" /s trustee
find 61 nw2d 840

POWERS OF CO–TRUSTEES USUALLY HELD JOINTLY [1]

§ 91. Where trust powers are vested in two or more trustees of a private trust, and the settlor does not indicate an intent to the contrary, the powers are ordinarily held jointly by the trustees and all must unite in their exercise. An attempt by one co-trustee to use a power is void as to the trust, unless ratified by the co-trustees.

A majority of the trustees of a charitable trust may usually exercise any power.

When a settlor names two or more trustees of a *private* trust and gives them powers, expressly or impliedly, he is deemed to intend that they shall hold and exercise those powers jointly and not severally, unless he expressly provides otherwise. He is regarded as intending

143; Smith v. Floyd, 124 App.Div. 277, 108 N.Y.S. 775; Young v. Young, 97 N.C. 132, 2 S.E. 78.

13. In re Smith, [1904] 1 Ch. 139; Bray v. Old Nat. Bk. in Evansville, 113 Ind.App. 506, 48 N.E.2d 846 (1943); Boardwalk Nat. Bank v. Morlock, 14 N.J.Super. 443, 82 A.2d 215 (1951); Irving Tr. Co. v. Burt, 290 N.Y. 382, 49 N.E.2d 493 (1943).

14. See Bogert, Trusts and Trustees (rev. 2d edit.), § 533, for references to statutes to this effect. The Uniform Trusts Act contains a provision to this effect; see, for example, N.Car.G. § 36A–38.

15. See §§ 29, ante, and 91, 149, post. And see Maryland Casualty Co. v. Safe

Deposit & Trust Co. of Baltimore, 115 Md. 339, 344, 80 A. 903, 905, Ann.Cas.1913A, 1279.

16. Parsons v. Boyd, 20 Ala. 112; Haggart v. Ranney, 73 Ark. 344, 84 S.W. 703; Weeks v. Frankel, 197 N.Y. 304, 90 N.E. 969; Hughes v. Williams, 99 Va. 312, 38 S.E. 138.

17. Boone v. Clarke, 3 Cranch, C.C. 389, Fed.Cas.No.1,641; Dillard v. Dillard, 97 Va. 434, 34 S.E. 60.

§ 91

1. Restatement, Trusts, Second, §§ 194, 383.

that in all the important acts of trust administration the beneficiaries shall receive the benefit of the judgment and discretion of all the trustees named.[2] This rule is harmonious with the implication that the settlor intends co-trustees to hold the title to the trust property as joint tenants.[3] Thus co-trustees must join in such acts as the execution of a deed, lease or contract, and in decisions to buy or sell trust investments. Occasionally, one co-trustee has been permitted by the court to act for the trust, in a case of an emergency in order to prevent threatened loss.[4] In the absence of a statute or trust provision to the contrary, a majority of three or more trustees has no power to act or to compel the minority to join in action.[5] As shown later, the rule is different as to the power to perform so-called "ministerial acts" of trust administration, where one co-trustee or an agent may be used.

An attempt by one co-trustee to act for the trust in an important matter will be void as far as the trust is concerned,[6] as where one of two trustees purports to release a mortgage held by the trust as an investment.[7] Personal liability of the trustee may result, for example, where a co-trustee makes a contract for the improvement of the trust realty and he is held to be bound individually but the co-trustees in their representative capacity are not obligated.[8] However, as later shown, if performance of such an illegal contract increases the value of the trust property, there may be trust liability on quasi-contractual grounds.[9] And, in addition, the action of the trustee in trying to act for the trust may be validated by subsequent ratification of the act by the other co-trustees.[10]

If a settlor desires to do so, he may permit a majority of three or more co-trustees to act for the trust,[11] or he may vest one trust power in one co-trustee and another authority in the other co-trustee, as where he entrusts the management of real estate to one and the disposition of

2. Learned v. Welton, 40 Cal. 349; Dingman v. Boyle, 285 Ill. 144, 120 N.E. 487; City of Boston v. Robbins, 126 Mass. 384; White v. Watkins, 23 Mo. 423; Carr v. Hertz, 54 N.J.Eq. 127, 33 A. 194; Fritz v. City Trust Co., 72 App.Div. 532, 76 N.Y.S. 625, affirmed 173 N.Y. 622, 66 N.E. 1109; Morley v. Carson, 240 Pa. 546, 87 A. 713. This rule is codified in some states: see West's Ann.Cal.Civ.Code, § 2268; Ia.Code Ann. § 633.76. And see Bogert, Trusts and Trustees (rev.2d edit.), § 554.

3. See § 32, ante.

4. See, for example, as to taking an appeal from a decision affecting the trust: Tree v. Continental Ill. Nat. Bank & Tr. Co., 346 Ill.App. 509, 105 N.E.2d 324 (1952); In re Luckenbach's Will, 303 N.Y. 491, 104 N.E.2d 870 (1952).

5. American Sec. & Trust Co. v. Frost, 117 F.2d 283 (D.C.Cir.1940), certiorari denied 312 U.S. 707, 61 S.Ct. 829, 85 L.Ed.

1139 (1941); Cooper v. Federal Nat. Bk., 175 Okl. 610, 53 P.2d 678 (1935).

6. Coleman v. Connelly, 242 Ill. 574, 90 N.E. 278; Nichols v. Pospiech, 289 Mich. 324, 286 N.W. 633 (1939); Brown v. Donald, 216 S.W.2d 679 (Tex.Civ.App.1949) (deed by one of two trustees conveys no interest).

7. Coxe v. Kriebel, 323 Pa. 157, 185 A. 770.

8. Downey v. 282 Beacon St. Trust, 292 Mass. 175, 197 N.E. 643 (1935); Cornett v. West, 102 Wash. 254, 173 P. 44.

9. See § 128, post.

10. Hill v. Peoples, 80 Ark. 15, 95 S.W. 990; In re Gibbons' Estate, 132 Neb. 538, 272 N.W. 553 (1937).

11. Hersh v. Rosensohn, 127 N.J.Eq. 21, 11 A.2d 75 (1940); In re Luckenbach's Will, 303 N.Y. 491, 104 N.E.2d 870 (1952).

the other investments to a second trustee.[12]

The inconvenience that sometimes comes from the necessity of getting unanimous action from a group of trustees, where there may be differences of opinion or one trustee may be absent or sick, has caused a few jurisdictions to enact statutes permitting a majority of the trustees to act for the trust.[13]

The power of a co-trustee to delegate to a fellow trustee the performance of an act of trust administration is considered in the next section,[14] in connection with the whole topic of delegation and the employment of agents and servants.

In the case of *charitable* trusts numerous co-trustees are often used and the difficulties of getting all to unite in a decision and to sign papers carrying out the transaction are greater than in the instance of the usual private trust where the employment of more than three trustees is rare. Accordingly, unless the settlor of a charitable trust expresses a different intent, he is deemed to have intended impliedly that a majority of the group of co-trustees should have power to act for the trust.[15]

If under the terms of a trust unanimous action is required of co-trustees, and a majority propose action which a minority trustee considers unwise he may protect the trust by refusing to join, and may be allowed to procure an injunction against an attempt by the majority to enter into the transaction.[16] But if the refusal indicates mere obstinacy, or, even though it occurs in good faith, if a deadlock in the administration exists, the court may instruct the trustees or remove one or more.[17]

If a majority of the co-trustees are empowered to act, and a minority trustee considers proposed action highly detrimental to the trust, he should seek to prevent the performance of the act,[18] and has no duty to join with the majority. However some statutes require the minority trustee to join the majority, but relieve him from all liability for the consequences of the act if he protested to the majority trustees against the transaction.[19]

12. People ex rel. Courtney v. Botts, 376 Ill. 476, 34 N.E.2d 403 (1941). And see French v. Northern Trust Co., 197 Ill. 30, 64 N.E. 105; Sheets v. Security First Mortgage Co., 293 Ill.App. 222, 12 N.E.2d 324 (1937).

13. See, for example, 20 Pa.C.S.A. §§ 7133, 3328. For references to other statutes, see Bogert, Trusts and Trustees (rev. 2d edit.), § 554. § 11 of the Uniform Trusts Act permits a majority to act. This Act has been adopted in La., Nev., N.M., N.C., Okl., S.D. and Tex. To the same effect see § 6 of the Uniform Trustees' Powers Act.

14. See § 92, post.

15. Boston v. Doyle, 184 Mass. 373, 68 N.E. 851.

16. Crane v. Hearn, 26 N.J.Eq. 378.

17. Story v. Palmer, 46 N.J.Eq. 1, 18 A. 363.

18. Zaring v. Zaring, 219 Ind. 514, 39 N.E.2d 734 (1942).

19. See, for example, § 11 of the Uniform Trusts Act; West's Ann.Ind.Code 30–4–3–4.

WESTLAW REFERENCES

co-trustee /s title /s property /s "joint tenants"
find 104 ne2d 870
390k239 /p joint several /2 authority

DELEGATION OF TRUST POWERS—INACTIVE CO–TRUSTEES [1]

§ 92. A trustee may delegate the exercise of a trust power to an agent or servant in those cases where a reasonably prudent owner of property of the same type as the trust property who was acting for objectives similar to those of the trust would employ assistance. In the case of such highly important transactions as would be managed personally by a property owner following customary business practices, the trustee must personally make the decisions and perform the acts involved.

Delegation may be made to a co-trustee in the cases where a third party agent could be used.

A co-trustee owes a duty to be active in the performance of the trust. If he turns over to a fellow trustee important trust functions he is guilty of an illegal attempt at delegation.

A trustee owes his beneficiary the duty of using reasonable care in employing, instructing and supervising a co-trustee or agent to whom he legally delegates the use of a trust power.

The acts of one to whom a trust power is legally delegated bind the trustee in his representative capacity, but in the case of an illegal attempt at delegation the acts of the agent bind the trustee in his individual capacity only.

It is obvious that no trustee can reasonably be expected to perform personally every act of trust administration. Such a method of operation would make the trustee's work so burdensome that few would accept trusteeships. Many duties of the trustee require special skills and knowledge which the trustee does not possess, so that he could not be expected to perform such work without advice and aid.

In deciding what part of his work the trustee must do by his own hand and what part he may delegate to others, at least two different rules have been suggested. The first is that the trustee may assign to employees "ministerial" powers but may not delegate the performance of "discretionary" acts.[2] This is a vague rule and not believed to be accurate or desirable. There are few, if any, acts of trust administration which are purely mechanical and which do not entail the use of some judgment and discretion. The rule might be better expressed by stating that powers involving little discretion can be delegated to

---

§ 92

1. Restatement, Trusts, Second, §§ 171, 184.

2. Morville v. Fowle, 144 Mass. 109, 10 N.E. 766; Belding v. Archer, 131 N.C. 287, 42 S.E. 800.

others, but those requiring the use of skill or judgment must be exercised by the trustee personally. Furthermore, the importance of the act is not the sole guide. In addition the special knowledge which the act requires and whether the trustee possesses such special skill are relevant.

A preferred method of stating a standard is that which makes delegation a matter of usual business practice among ordinarily prudent business men managing property such as the trust subject-matter for the ends which are to be accomplished by the trust, namely, usually the production for a time of a constant flow of income and the conservation of the capital fund for later owners. When a property manager having such objectives would act through others if an absolute owner, he may do so when he is a trustee.[3] The trustee who is considering delegating should familiarize himself with business practices with relation to the power in question, the amount of judgment and ability which the exercise of the power requires, whether special skills are needed (as, for example, in the case of tax, accounting and legal work), and whether the trustee himself has the ability to exercise the power easily.[4] The trustee is not entitled to spend trust funds in unnecessarily employing an agent to do work for the trust.[5]

In applying the rule of ordinarily prudent business practice to typical trust transactions, it would seem that in the case of a power to sell realty the trustee should retain for his personal use the power to fix the sale price and the terms of the contract and deed, but that he might employ a realtor to seek a purchaser and to negotiate with possible buyers.[6] With regard to improved realty held for lease the trustee should fix rentals and general standards to be used in selecting tenants, but might use a real estate management firm to conduct interviews with proposed tenants, secure signatures to leases, and collect rents.[7] As to investments, the trustee should make decisions on

3. North American Trust Co. v. Chappell, 70 Ark. 507, 69 S.W. 546; Chicago Title & Trust Co. v. Zinser, 264 Ill. 31, 105 N.E. 718, Ann.Cas.1915D, 931; Morville v. Fowle, 144 Mass. 109, 10 N.E. 766; Fowler v. Coates, 201 N.Y. 257, 94 N.E. 997; In re Bohlen's Estate, 75 Pa. 304.

Story stated the rule as follows: "When a trustee acts by other hands, either from necessity or conformably to the common usage of mankind, he is not to be made answerable for losses." Eq.Jur., sec. 1269.

To the same effect, see Lord Hardwicke, Ex parte Belchier, Ambler 218, 219.

4. Gillespie v. Smith, 29 Ill. 473, 81 Am.Dec. 328; Annis v. Annis, 61 Iowa 220, 16 N.W. 97; Turnbull v. Pomeroy, 140 Mass. 117, 3 N.E. 15; Sinclair v. Jackson ex dem. Field, 8 Cow., N.Y., 543; Belding v. Archer, 131 N.C. 287, 42 S.E. 800; Olcott v. Gabert, 86 Tex. 121, 23 S.W. 985.

And see Milbank v. J.C. Littlefield, Inc., 310 Mass. 55, 36 N.E.2d 833 (1941) (breach to permit attorney to draw checks and indorse paper); West v. Hapgood, 141 Tex. 576, 174 S.W.2d 963 (1943) (may delegate to attorney preparation and execution of release decided upon by trustees).

5. See § 143, post. In re Smythe's Estate, 6 Misc.2d 130, 36 N.Y.S.2d 605 (1942).

6. Saunders v. Webber, 39 Cal. 287; Hibernian Banking Ass'n v. Roseboom, 214 Ill.App. 324; Gates v. Dudgeon, 173 N.Y. 426, 66 N.E. 116.

7. Schofield v. John R. Thompson Co., 109 F.2d 432 (6th Cir.1940); Ross v. Freeman, 21 Del.Ch. 44, 180 A. 527; United States Nat. Bank of Omaha v. Alexander, 140 Neb. 784, 1 N.W.2d 920 (1942).

sales and purchases but might employ a broker to seek purchasers or buyers on the terms fixed by the trustee.[8] A trustee holding corporate stock should decide whether to vote the stock by proxy with or without instructions or personally, after a consideration of the amount of the stock, the importance of the questions arising at the meeting, the place of the meeting and similar factors.[9] A trustee faced with legal or tax problems might seek advice from the outside, assuming he did not possess the special knowledge required.[10] Secretarial or bookkeeping work could be delegated.[11] It would surely be a breach of trust to delegate to another all or the major part of the trust work.[12] The propriety of employing assistance should be affected by the facilities and skills possessed by the trustee. For example, a corporate trustee which has real estate, tax, and investment departments, staffed by experts, should be able to delegate less freely than an individual trustee. In the case of a corporate trustee the use of officers and regularly employed servants does not amount to delegation.[13] A corporation cannot act except through such agents. However, if the corporation uses for its trust work persons not regularly on its payroll, there would seem to be technical delegation.[14]

Assuming that a trustee is justified in delegating the performance of a certain act for the trust, he must exercise reasonable prudence and care in employing the assistant. He must make a reasonable investigation as to the honesty and efficiency of the agent or servant, must give him adequate instructions, must supervise and check the performance of the work delegated, and in the case of advice must exercise his own judgment as to its soundness, so far as he is able.[15] If the delegation

8. Washington Loan & Trust Co. v. Colby, 71 App.D.C. 326, 108 F.2d 743 (1939); In re Kohler's Estate, 348 Pa. 55, 33 A.2d 920 (1943). For a case sanctioning delegation by an individual trustee to a trust company of possession, collection, and distribution duties, see Casani's Estate, 342 Pa. 468, 21 A.2d 59 (1941).

9. Spotts, 79 Trusts & Estates, 289; People ex rel. Courtney v. Botts, 376 Ill. 476, 34 N.E.2d 403 (1941).

The voting of stock by a trustee by proxy is now very widely validated by statute. See references in Bogert, Trusts and Trustees (rev. 2d edit.), §§ 551, 556; and see § 8, Uniform Trusts Act.

10. McClure v. Middletown Trust Co., 95 Conn. 148, 110 A. 833; Patterson v. Old Dominion Trust Co., 156 Va. 763, 159 S.E. 168 (1931). And see Wharton's Estate, 47 N.J.Super. 42, 135 A.2d 187 (1957) (trustee should not employ an attorney to do investment or administrative work).

11. Walter-Southland Institute v. Walker, 222 Ark. 857, 263 S.W.2d 83 (1953)

(keeping records); Broeker v. Ware, 27 Del. Ch. 8, 29 A.2d 591 (1942) (clerk and administrative details).

12. Meck v. Behrens, 141 Wash. 676, 252 P. 91.

13. Stockwell v. Barnum, 7 Cal.App. 413, 94 P. 400; Chicago Title & Trust Co. v. Zinser, 264 Ill. 31, 105 N.E. 718, Ann.Cas. 1915D, 931; New England Trust Co. v. Paine, 317 Mass. 542, 59 N.E.2d 263, 158 A.L.R. 262 (1945).

14. McClure v. Middletown Trust Co., 95 Conn. 148, 110 A. 838.

15. Robinson v. Harkin, 2 Ch. 415 (1896); Re Whiteley, 33 Ch.D. 347; Cox v. Williams, 241 Ala. 427, 3 So.2d 129 (1941) (failing to check on work of lawyer); White v. Citizens' Trust & Sav. Bk. of Los Angeles, 46 Cal.App.2d 418, 116 P.2d 117 (1941) (supervising real estate agent); Steward v. Traverse City State Bank, 187 Mich. 387, 153 N.W. 793.

makes it prudent to bond the agent or servant, such action would be obligatory on the trustee.

A co-trustee may delegate the exercise of a trust power to a fellow trustee to the same extent and under the same conditions applicable as in the case of a third person acting as agent.[16] He must follow the practice of ordinarily prudent business men.

A co-trustee has a duty to be active in the administration of the trust as to those functions where usual prudent business practice would dictate personal management instead of action through employees.[17] He violates this duty if he turns over to a fellow trustee the whole administration or important portions of it, when he makes the transfer by active conduct in delivering possession and title to the trust property or by express consent to delegation of a power,[18] as well as in the case where he is passive and inactive and permits the fellow trustee to take control and operate the entire trust or use important powers under it.[19] In many cases a settlor chooses as co-trustees a bank or trust company and one or more relatives of the settlor, and the tendency of the individual trustees is to leave to the skilled professional trustee all or a major part of the work of the trusteeship. This amounts to delegation and it may result in a breach of trust and to impose liability to the beneficiaries, if the active trustee has mismanaged the property or stolen it.[20] Furthermore, even if the delegation to the co-trustee is held

16. Caldwell v. Graham, 115 Md. 122, 80 A. 839; Landow v. Keane, 10 N.Y.S.2d 267 (1939); In re Stong's Estate, 160 Pa. 13, 28 A. 480.

17. For statutory statements of this duty, see Mo.—V.A.M.S. 456.540; Wash.—RCWA 11.98.016. See Bogert, Trusts and Trustees (rev.2d edit.), §§ 584, 589.

18. Barroll v. Foreman, 88 Md. 188, 40 A. 883; Brown v. Phelan, 223 App.Div. 393, 228 N.Y.S. 466 (1928); but see Purdy v. Lynch, 145 N.Y. 462, 40 N.E. 232; Jones' Appeal, 8 Watts & Searg. 143.

19. Fox v. Tay, 89 Cal. 339, 26 P. 897; In re Mild, 25 N.J. 467, 136 A.2d 875 (1957); In re Pessano's Estate, 180 Misc. 829, 45 N.Y.S.2d 873 (1943). But other cases are *contra*. See Stowe v. Bowen, 99 Mass. 194; State v. Guilford, 18 Ohio 500.

20. See Bogert, Liability of an Inactive Trustee, 34 Harv.L.R. 483. The decisions are conflicting, apparently due at least in part to the view of some courts that the attempt to impose liability on the inactive trustee is an effort to make him liable for the wrongdoing of the active co-trustee, whereas others take the more realistic position that the inactive trustee was himself guilty of wrongdoing because he permitted the active co-trustee to place himself in a position where he could commit a breach of trust.

The opinion of a Tennessee court was forcefully put by Turley, J., in Deaderick v. Cantrell, 10 Yerg 263, 272, as follows: "Two trustees are appointed to execute a trust, the final operation of which is not to be completed for years; they undertake to execute it; they are intended as checks on each other, have an equal control over the fund, are mutually bound to attend to the interest of the trust, and shall one be permitted to go to sleep and trust everything to the management of his cotrustee, and when, in the course of ten or fifteen years, the fund having been wasted, and his co-trustee insolvent, he is called upon to make it good, shall he be heard to say that he had implicit confidence in his companion, and permitted him to retain all the money, and appropriate it as he pleased, and that he ought not therefore to be charged? Surely not; it is neither law nor reason."

"A trustee is responsible for the wrongful acts of a cotrustee to which he consented, or which by his negligence he enabled the other to commit, but for no others." West's Ann.Cal.Civ.Code § 2239.

And see Mont.Code Ann. 72–20–211; N.D.Cent.Code 59–01–19; S.D.Codif.Laws 55–2–11.

to be proper, there is a duty on the part of the delegating trustee to keep track of the work of the trustee to whom he made the delegation in order to learn whether he is acting honestly and efficiently and to take steps to protect the beneficiaries if necessary.[21] This is especially true where there has come to the notice of the delegating trustee suspicious or incriminating circumstances in connection with the administration of the active trustee.[22] "It is the duty of one trustee to protect the trust estate from any misfeasance by his cotrustee, upon being made aware of the intended act, by obtaining an injunction against him; and, if the wrongful act has been already committed, to take measures, by suit or otherwise, to compel the restitution of the property, and its application in the manner required by the trust." [23]

Robertson, L.P., in Millar's Trustees v. Polson,[24] has graphically described the position of the inactive trustee in this situation: "It is, of course, disagreeable to take a cotrustee by the throat; but if a man undertakes to act as a trustee he must face the necessity of doing disagreeable things when they become necessary in order to keep the estate intact. A trustee is not entitled to purchase a quiet life at the expense of the estate, or to act as good-natured men sometimes do in their own affairs in letting things slide and losing money rather than create ill feeling."

The terms of the trust instrument or of a court order may determine the legality of an act of delegation.[25]

In some states statutes have sanctioned delegation in described transactions.[26]

If a trust power is delegable, and the trustee who delegates it uses reasonable prudence and care in delegating it and in supervising and investigating the work of the agent, the trustee is not liable to the beneficiaries for negligence of the agent in exercising the power or for his embezzlement of the trust funds which are properly placed in his care.[27] In the case of a legal delegation of a trust power, third persons dealing with the trustee through the agent exercising the power secure the same rights as if the act in question had been performed personally by the trustee who made the delegation.[28] Thus if the trustee had a

21. Kaufman v. Kaufman's Adm'r, 292 Ky. 351, 166 S.W.2d 860, 144 A.L.R. 866 (1942); In re Rambo's Estate, 327 Pa. 258, 193 A. 1 (1937).

22. Bermingham v. Wilcox, 120 Cal. 467, 52 P. 822; Matter of Niles, 113 N.Y. 547, 21 N.E. 687; Pim v. Downing, 11 Serg. & R., Pa., 66. And see Ralston v. Easter, 43 App.D.C. 513; In re Howard, 110 App. Div. 61, 97 N.Y.S. 23, affirmed without opinion 185 N.Y. 539, 77 N.E. 1189.

23. Crane v. Hearn, 26 N.J.Eq. 378, 381. See also Elmendorf v. Lansing, 4 Johns.Ch., N.Y., 562.

24. 34 Sc.L.R. 804.

25. Henshie v. McPherson & Citizens State Bank, 177 Kan. 458, 280 P.2d 937 (1955) (power to allocate trust functions among themselves).

26. See English Trustee Act of 1925. And see statutes referred to in Bogert, Trusts and Trustees (rev. 2d edit.), § 556.

27. Barry v. Barry, 198 Miss. 677, 21 So.2d 922 (1945); Donaldson v. Allen, 182 Mo. 626, 81 S.W. 1151; Dodge v. Stickman, 62 N.H. 330. And see Heilman, 52 Dick. L.R. 255; Hirst, 66 U.S.Law Rev. 146.

28. Telford v. Barney, 1 G. Greene 575; Gray v. Lincoln Housing Trust, 229 Mich. 441, 201 N.W. 489 (1924); Ewing v.

power of sale and could delegate to an attorney the execution and delivery of a deed on his behalf, and the attorney acted in that way, title to the trust property would pass. If there was a valid delegation of the power to make a contract, the delegating trustee is bound by an agreement made by his agent; and if property management is legally placed in the hands of an agent, a tort of the agent committed during the course of his work may create liability against the delegating trustee.[29] If the trust power is properly delegable but the trustee does not use reasonable care in granting power to an agent to use the power on behalf of the trust, it would seem that the trustee's liability to third persons should be the same as if the trustee had personally exercised the power. Thus if a trustee properly delegates to a real estate management firm the power to collect rents from tenants of the trust property, but the trustee is negligent in investigating the character and efficiency of the management firm, and the agent steals rents which are paid to him by the tenants, the tenants are relieved of their liabilities and the receipts given them are binding on the trustee in his representative capacity. But the trustee is liable to the beneficiaries for negligence in selecting the agent.[30]

If the trust power is not legally delegable but the trustee attempts to delegate it, he is liable to the beneficiaries for damages caused by his wrongful act, for example, where the agent negligently injures the trust property or embezzles trust funds.[31]

An act under an illegal delegation of a trust power does not bind the trustee in his representative capacity or the beneficiaries, but may create liability against the trustee in his individual capacity.[32] For example, if a trustee improperly gives to an agent power to set the sale price of trust real estate and to execute a deed of it on behalf of the trustee, the deed ought not to pass title to the trust property but covenants in it should bind the trustee personally.

 WESTLAW REFERENCES

"inactive trustee"

trustee /s delegat*** /S trust /2 power deaderick
    +3 cantrell

Wm. L. Foley, Inc., 115 Tex. 222, 280 S.W. 499 (1926).

29. See §§ 125, 129, post.

30. Cox v. Williams, 241 Ala. 427, 3 So.2d 129 (1941); White v. Citizens Nat. Tr. & Sav. Bank, 46 Cal.App.2d 418, 116 P.2d 117 (1941).

31. Fry v. Tapson, 28 Ch.D. 268; Hirst, 66 U.S.Law Rev. 146.

32. Downey Co. v. 282 Beacon St. Trust, 292 Mass. 175, 197 N.E. 643 (1935).

Chapter 10

DUTIES OF THE TRUSTEE—IN GENERAL

Table of Sections

DUTY TO USE ORDINARY SKILL AND PRUDENCE [1]

§ 93. In the management of the trust the trustee is bound to display the skill and prudence which an ordinarily capable and careful man would use in the conduct of his own business of a like character and with objectives similar to those of the trust. But if the trustee, in advance of accepting the trust, has represented to the settlor that he possessed unusual capacities he will be required to display that amount of ability, and if a trustee actually has greater than normal abilities he will be expected to use them in the performance of the trust.

Ordinary care, skill and prudence are normally required of trustees in the performance of all their duties, unless the trust instrument provides otherwise.[2] One statement of the rule is "that trustees are bound in the management of all the matters of the trust to act in good faith and employ such vigilance, sagacity, diligence and prudence as in general prudent men of discretion and intelligence in like matters employ in their own affairs. The law does not hold a trustee, acting in accord with such rule, responsible for errors of judgment." [3] "All that

---

§ 93

1. Bogert, Trusts and Trustees (rev. 2d edit.), § 541 et seq.; Restatement, Trusts, Second, § 174.

2. Bourquin v. Bourquin, 120 Ga. 115, 47 S.E. 639; Litchfield v. White, 7 N.Y. 438, 57 Am.Dec. 534; Belding v. Archer, 131 N.C. 287, 42 S.E. 800; Gilbert v. Sut-liff, 3 Ohio St. 129; Appeal of Jones, 8 Watts & S., Pa., 143, 42 Am.Dec. 282; Cunningham v. Cunningham, 81 S.C. 506, 62 S.E. 845; Davis v. Harman, 21 Grat., Va., 194; Hutchinson v. Lord, 1 Wis. 286, 60 Am.Dec. 381.

3. Collin, J., in Costello v. Costello, 209 N.Y. 252, 261, 103 N.E. 148.

equity requires from trustees is common skill, common prudence, and common caution." [4]

However some recent statutes hold a trustee to a higher standard of care.[5] For example, the Uniform Probate Code [6] requires the trustee to "observe the standards in dealing with the trust assets that would be observed by a prudent man dealing with the property of another." This standard of care is that of a prudent man who is a trustee for another.

The requisite standard of care includes at least two different qualities: the element of initiative or effort, and the element of skill or judgment. The element of initiative includes such acts as seeking qualified professional assistance where necessary for the proper and efficient administration of the trust.[7] As to the element of skill, recent authorities, both statutory and judicial, are practically united in holding that the existence of higher skill imposes a duty to exercise it.[8]

If the trustee has not used the skill of an ordinarily capable man, it is of no avail to him that he acted in good faith or unintentionally violated his trust.[9] The degree of ability required is the same whether the trustee was or was not to receive compensation for his work.[10] A grant of wide discretionary powers in the trust instrument does not reduce the standard to be applied to the trustee's conduct.[11] A trustee cannot escape liability by proving that he used the same skill and prudence in managing the trust as he did in his own business.[12] He must measure up to the external standard of the skill and prudence of the ordinarily capable business man.

4. Appeal of Neff, 57 Pa. 91, 96. "A trustee, whether he receives any compensation or not, must use at least ordinary care and diligence in the execution of his trust." West's Ann.Cal.Civ.Code, § 2259. And see Official Code Ga.Ann. § 53–13–51; La.—R.S. 9:2090; Mont.Code Ann. § 72–23–302; N.D.Cent.Code 59–02–06; S.D. Codif.L. 55–3–10. And see Restatement, Trusts, Second, § 174 ("such care and skill as a man of ordinary prudence would exercise in dealing with his own property").

5. See, for example, N.Car.G.S. § 36A–2; Wash.—West's RCWA 11.100.020.

6. Unif.Prob.Code § 7–302, adopted in Alaska, Ariz., Fla., Me., Mich., Neb., N.Mex., N.Dak. (individual trustees), S.Dak. and Utah.

7. The trustee has a duty to obtain advice where a reasonably prudent man would do so, and will be protected in acting upon it if he uses reasonable care in selecting the advisor and in checking and following his advice. Appeal of Davis, 183 Mass. 499, 67 N.E. 604 (1903); Miller v. Proctor, 20 Ohio St. 442 (1870); Appeals of During,

King and Miller, 13 Pa. 224 (1850) (Gibson, C.J.). ("When a trustee has to steer his course among the rocks and shoals of his duty, he would be justly chargeable with the consequences of disaster, did he reject the services of a professional pilot, and act of his own head.") But cf. Borden's Trust, 56 A.2d 108, 358 Pa. 138 (1948) ("Acting upon advice of counsel is a factor to be considered in determining good faith, but is not a blanket of immunity in all circumstances.") (dictum).

8. See footnote 17, post.

9. St. Paul Trust Co. v. Strong, 85 Minn. 1, 88 N.W. 256; Moeller v. Poland, 80 Ohio St. 418, 89 N.E. 100.

10. Speight v. Gaunt, 9 A.C. 1; Switzer v. Skiles, 3 Gilman 529, 8 Ill. 529, 44 Am. Dec. 723.

11. Appeal of Davis, 183 Mass. 499, 67 N.E. 604 (1903).

12. Knox v. Mackinnon, 13 App.Cas. 753; Learoyd v. Whiteley, 1887, 12 A.C. 727.

The reasonably prudent and skillful man whom the trustee must emulate is one who seeks objectives in property management similar to the purposes of the trust.[13] These are normally safety of principal and such income as is consistent with security of the trust principal. The trustee should not follow in the footsteps of a reasonably prudent speculator or of a person who is interested only in growth of principal.

There has been some suggestion [14] that professional or corporate trustees such as banks and trust companies should be required to show greater skill and diligence than natural persons, since the former are professional fiduciaries and generally have numerous employees who are specialists in various departments of trust work, whereas the latter are often amateurs without great experience or facilities. While it would appear that the demands on them should not be above normal merely because they are corporations,[15] they may actually be held to a higher standard, either because they have secured the trust because of representations that they were unusually competent and should be expected to give the service which they claimed they would give,[16] or because of the rule that every trustee, corporate or not, has a duty to give to the trust work whatever skill and prudence he actually possesses.[17]

Whether the service of the trustee has measured up to the required amount of skill and prudence is to be determined by a consideration of the situation at the time the act in question was performed and not from events which later transpired.[18] If the trustee makes an investment which under then current economic conditions was reasonably prudent, there is no basis for liability in the fact that the investment has failed and that the beneficiary claims the trustee should have been able to foresee the danger.

A trustee does not conclusively show that he has used reasonable care when he consults an expert, such as a lawyer or investment

13. Thayer v. Dewey, 185 Mass. 68, 69 N.E. 1074; King v. Talbot, 40 N.Y. 76.

14. See 30 Col.L.R. 1162, 1172; 29 Mich.L.R. 125; Surrogate Slater in In re Clark's Will, 136 Misc. 881, 242 N.Y.S. 210 (1930). The Court of Appeals, in reversing the decision of the trial court in the Clark case, based its holding on a finding of the use of reasonable care and did not discuss the question of the special duties of professional trustees. 257 N.Y. 132, 177 N.E. 397 (1931).

15. *Dictum* in Cobb v. Gramatan Nat. Bank & Trust Co. of Bronxville, 261 App. Div. 1086, 26 N.Y.S.2d 917 (1941), reargument denied 262 A.D. 745, 28 N.Y.S.2d 157 (1941); Linnard's Estate, 299 Pa. 32, 38, 148 A. 912 (1930); In re Trust of Bailey & Regar, 29 Pa.D. & C. 215. And see 16 Univ. of Chi.Law Rev. 579.

16. Estate of Beach, 15 Cal.3d 623, 125 Cal.Rptr. 570, 542 P.2d 994 (1975), certiorari denied 434 U.S. 1046, 98 S.Ct. 891, 54 L.Ed.2d 797 (1978); Ferrell v. Ellis, 129 Iowa 614, 105 N.W. 993; Liberty Title & Tr. Co. v. Plews, 142 N.J.Eq. 493, 60 A.2d 630 (1948); In re Killey's Estate, 457 Pa. 474, 326 A.2d 372 (1974). And see Brown v. Shyne, 242 N.Y. 176, 151 N.E. 197, 44 A.L.R. 1407 (1926); In re Allis' Estate, 191 Wis. 23, 209 N.W. 945, 210 N.W. 418 (1926).

17. Tannenbaum v. Seacoast Tr. Co., 125 N.J.Eq. 360, 5 A.2d 778 (1939).

To this effect, see Unif.Prob.Code § 7–302. And see N.Y.—McKinney's EPTL 11–2.2(a)(1) (fiduciary having "special investment skills"); N.Car.G.S. § 36A–2; Wash.—West's RCWA 11.100.020.

18. In re Whiteley, 33 Ch.D. 347, 355; Green v. Crapo, 181 Mass. 55, 62 N.E. 956.

counsellor, and then follows the advice given.[19] It may have been unreasonable to take advice from the party in question, or the advice may have been such that a reasonable man, in complying with his duty to evaluate the advice and consider the reasons given for it, would have known that it was not good advice.[20] The trustee cannot bear the burden of proving the required skill and prudence by showing that he followed a practice which the settlor used.[21] That he consulted the beneficiaries and acted as they suggested may have some effect in establishing proper performance of the trust, or it may prevent the beneficiaries from claiming that a breach has occurred.[22]

 WESTLAW REFERENCES

trustee /s act duty /3 ordinary common /2 care skill prudence

390k182 /p trustee

390k171

390k173

EXCULPATORY OR IMMUNITY CLAUSES [1]

§ 94. **A settlor may reduce the amount of skill and prudence required of his trustee by a provision in the trust instrument, as where he excludes liability for errors of judgment or for any conduct other than a willful breach. Such provisions are called exculpatory or immunity clauses.**

While the courts are hostile to such directions, and sometimes give them a strict or unnatural construction which limits their effect, the clauses are generally enforced, except to the extent that they attempt to relieve the trustee from liability for breaches of trust committed recklessly, intentionally, or in bad faith.

In recent years many corporate trustees have come to regard such clauses as undesirable from the points of view of public relations and ethics, and therefore do not encourage their use.

Sometimes a settlor inserts in his trust instrument a provision relieving the trustee from liability for described breaches of trust. These clauses have the effect of permitting a trustee to exercise less than the degree of care and prudence described in the next preceding section, because they provide that he shall not be liable for every failure to use ordinary skill and ability but rather only in cases of certain aggravated and severe breaches of trust. Such provisions have

19. In re Fensterer's Estate, 79 N.Y.S.2d 427 (Sur.1948); Stirling's Estate, 342 Pa. 497, 21 A.2d 72 (1941).

20. In re Allen's Estate, 35 Hawaii 501; Miller v. Proctor, 20 Ohio St. 442; Freeman v. Cook, 41 N.C. 373; Borden's Trust, 358 Pa. 138, 56 A.2d 108 (1948).

21. Waterman v. Alden, 144 Ill. 90, 32 N.E. 972.

22. Mertz v. Owen, 191 Okl. 77, 126 P.2d 720 (1942).

§ 94

1. Restatement, Trusts, Second, § 222.

commonly been called "exculpatory" or "immunity" clauses.[2]

The cases show a wide variety of wording of these exculpatory clauses. In some cases the statement has been that the trustee should not be liable for certain types of breaches deemed less blameworthy than others, for example, for errors of judgment, mistakes committed in good faith, or for acts of agents or servants. In other instances the phraseology has been that there should be no liability except for certain breaches deemed especially reprehensible, for example, willful and intentional breaches, acts of bad faith, dishonesty, acts of gross negligence, and the like.

The courts have not looked with favor on these clauses,[3] perhaps on the theory that they are dictated by the trustee and are subtly unethical, in that there is an inconsistency between the performance which the trustee led the settlor to expect when the trust was procured and accepted and the reduced standard allowed by the exculpatory clause.

In some cases the courts have given a rather tortured construction to the language of a clause and so limited or nullified the provision. Thus in a New Jersey case,[4] where the clause limited liability to a "willful and intentional" breach, the trustee accepted as a trust investment a second mortgage on realty. This was a breach of trust, but the trustee acted in good faith. It was held that he had committed a "willful and intentional" breach because he knowingly made the investment, although he did not know the investment to be non-legal. But some courts have given a more natural construction to the phrase "willful default", namely, that it refers to an act which the trustee knew was a breach of trust when he committed it.[5]

Most of the decisions have given effect to exculpatory clauses, on the theory that it was within the settlor's power to prescribe the trustee's duties and liabilities,[6] so long as he did not violate public

2. See Payne, 19 Cornell L.Q. 171; Shinn, 42 Yale L.J. 359, 2 Ga.B.J. 21; Kramer, 36 Mich.L.R. 996.

3. See, for example, Perling v. Citizens and Southern National Bank, 250 Ga. 674, 300 S.E.2d 649 (1983) (exculpatory clauses are to be strictly construed).

"His lordship said that he should have been glad to find a case warranting the conclusion, that a duty having been undertaken, any words qualifying such duty should be nugatory; but such could not be held to be the law." Wilkins v. Hogg, 8 Jur.N.S. 25, 26. In Birmingham Trust & Sav. Co. v. Ansley, 234 Ala. 674, 176 So. 465 (1937), a beneficiary who did not know of an exculpatory clause when he accepted the trust was held not bound by it.

4. Tuttle v. Gilmore, 36 N.J.Eq. 617. And see Conover v. Guaranty Trust Co., 88 N.J.Eq. 450, 102 A. 844 (clause excused trustee for mistakes of judgment; held this

did not relieve him from liability for an error in determining what his powers were).

5. New England Trust Co. v. Paine, 320 Mass. 482, 70 N.E.2d 6 (1946) (trustee overinvested in railroad stocks at a time when they had good financial standing; clause limited liability to "wilful default"; trustee protected since there was a mere error of judgment); In re Howard, 110 App.Div. 61, 97 N.Y.S. 23, aff'd 185 N.Y. 539, 77 N.E. 1189 (held a "willful default" to intentionally allow trust funds to come into the hands of a co-trustee after knowledge of his default).

6. See Crabb v. Young, 92 N.Y. 56, where Ruger, C.J., stated: "The testator had an absolute right to select the agencies by which his bounty should be distributed and to impose the terms and conditions under which it should be done. . . . The court has not the right to increase the

policy by sanctioning reckless or dishonest conduct.[7]

Sometimes a settlor names co-trustees and provides that the liability of each shall be limited to the property which he receives or to acts which he personally performs. English courts have not been friendly to clauses in trust instruments excusing trustees from liability except for property actually received by them, and have construed such clauses to mean that the trustee is liable for what he ought to have received, as well as for what he actually did have in his hands.[8] A provision in the trust deed or will that each trustee shall be liable only for his own defaults does not protect an inactive trustee from liability for allowing a co-trustee to have exclusive possession or control. Such negligence is a default as much as a positive breach would be.[9] In Walker v. Walker's Ex'rs [10] the settlor's direction that one trustee should have exclusive possession of the trust property was held to excuse the inactive trustee from liability for the loss of such property. But in Graham v. Austin [11] an attempt by the settlor to restrict the liability of a trustee to a part of the property was not allowed to have effect. The hostility of the courts to a settlor's directions that a trustee's liability shall be limited to the property he actually obtains was further shown in Caldwell v. Graham,[12] where such a clause was somewhat remarka-

---

measure of their responsibility or impose obligations from the burden of which he has in his will so carefully protected them."

7. Browning v. Fidelity Trust Co., 162 C.C.A. 391, 250 Fed. 321 (3d Cir.1918) (no liability for acts of agents or employees or for its own acts unless done in bad faith; trustee not held liable for releasing a mortgage improperly when knowledge of the impropriety was known to one employee but not communicated to the releasing officials); Warren v. Pazolt, 203 Mass. 328, 89 N.E. 381 (liability limited to cases of wilful neglect or default; trustee excused for unlawful investment made in good faith); Crabb v. Young, 92 N.Y. 56 (no liability except for wilful default, misconduct or neglect; trustee not held liable for error of judgment in taking a mortgage with inadequate security); Hazzard v. Chase Nat. Bank, 159 Misc. 57, 287 N.Y.S. 541 (1936), affirmed 257 App.Div. 950, 14 N.Y.S.2d 147 (1939), affirmed 282 N.Y. 652, 26 N.E.2d 801 (1940) (trustee not to be liable except for gross negligence or bad faith; not held liable for permitting settlor to substitute worthless securities in place of valuable ones); Gardner v. Squire, 49 N.E.2d 587 (Ohio App.1942) (to be liable only for "malfeasance"; not held for failing to sell or distribute trust assets); Gouley v. Land Title Bank & Trust Co., 329 Pa. 465, 198 A. 7 (1938) (to be liable only for wilful and intentional breaches; not held for failure

to foreclose a mortgage after default on it). And see Countiss v. Whiting, 306 Ill.App. 548, 29 N.E.2d 277 (1940) (not to be liable for acts done in "good faith"; does not protect trustee for erroneously paying trust property to himself as an "heir" when he was not an heir); Digney v. Blanchard, 226 Mass. 335, 115 N.E. 424 (bad faith to repair trust property contrary to terms of trust); In re Olmstead, 52 App. Div. 515, 66 N.Y.S. 212, affirmed 164 N.Y. 571, 58 N.E. 1090 (gross negligence to turn over insurance proceeds to another on unsecured promise to replace building).

8. Mucklow v. Fuller, Jacobs 198; Bone v. Cook, McClelland 168; Brumridge v. Brumridge, 27 Beav. 5.

9. Marriott v. Kinnersley, Tamlyn 470; Dix v. Burford, 19 Beav. 409. See Mo.— V.A.M.S. § 456.550 (special duties assigned to one or more of several trustees; effect).

10. 88 Ky. 615.

11. 2 Grat., Va., 273.

12. 115 Md. 122, 80 A. 839, 38 L.R.A., N.S., 1029.

A clause excluding liability for the acts of agents or servants of the trustee does not protect a corporate trustee from responsibility for an act which it commits through its officers or employees. White v. Citizens Nat. Tr. & Sav. Bank, 46 Cal.App. 2d 418, 116 P.2d 117 (1941).

bly construed to provide merely against liability for depreciation of the property while in the trustee's hands.

To permit a trustee to hide behind an exculpatory clause and to avoid liability for bad faith, dishonesty, willful breach, and gross negligence would be against public policy, since it would encourage highly reprehensible or even criminal conduct.[13] Hence such clauses are void to the extent that they attempt to relieve the trustee from liability for breaches of these types.

Exculpatory clauses are not usually inserted at the suggestion of the settlor or his counsel. They are often demanded by trustees, commonly by corporate trustees, as a condition precedent to acceptance of the trust. The ethics of the demand by corporate trustees for the insertion of an exculpatory clause seems dubious, to say the least. After advertising great skill and ability, and impliedly promising to use all that care and capacity in any trust where it is chosen trustee, the bank or trust company should not insist that the draftsman of the trust instrument hold the trustee to a lower standard of performance. There is an inconsistency between the efforts of the new business department and that of the advisors to the draftsman. Apparently this argument has been appreciated by many corporate trustees in recent years, and in the interest of public relations and higher ethical standards the use of the immunity clause has greatly decreased.[14]

The validity of exculpatory clauses has been to some extent affected by statute.[15] Under an English statute they are given widespread approval,[16] but by federal [17] and New York [18] legislation their use is

13. In Browning v. Fidelity Trust Co., 162 C.C.A. 391, 250 Fed. 321, 325 (3d Cir. 1918), it was said that "the law, dictated by considerations of public policy, determines a point beyond which the parties cannot agree to relieve a trustee from liability for breach of a trust duty. For instance, a trustee cannot contract for immunity from liability for acts of gross negligence or for acts done in bad faith. Such contracts are invalid because repugnant to law." And see New England Trust Co. v. Paine, 317 Mass. 542, 59 N.E.2d 263 (1945) (no protection against acts of bad faith, intentionally committed breaches, acts performed in reckless indifference to the welfare of beneficiaries, or acts producing a profit to the trustee).

14. "Provisions designed to lower the standard of care, skill, prudence, or diligence are not praiseworthy." Stephenson, Drafting Wills and Trust Instruments, § 13.23.

15. By West's RCWA 11.97.010 a settlor may relieve the trustee of any and all statutory duties, restrictions and liabilities except the duty to act "in good faith and with honest judgment." To the same ef-

fect see Vernon's Ann.Tex.Prop.Code § 113.059. By statute in some states a court is given the power to relieve the trustee of statutory restrictions or duties. See, for example, Mich.C.L.A. § 700.830; Mo.—V.A.M.S. § 456.570; Mont.R.C., § 72–21–204; N.Car.G.S. § 36A–80.

Settlor may relieve trustee from any and all statutory duties, restrictions and liabilities: West's Ann.Ind.Code 30–4–3–32(a) and (b) ("of liability for breach of trust"; certain exceptions).

See also Unif.Trusts Act, §§ 17 (settlor), 19 (court); Unif.Trustees' Powers Act, § 5(a) (court).

And see West's Ann.Cal.Civ.Code § 2261(a)(2) (settlor can expand or restrict prudence standard in § 2261(a)(1)).

16. The Trustee Act of 1925 provides in § 30(1): "A trustee shall be chargeable only for money and securities actually received by him notwithstanding his signing any receipt for the sake of conformity, and shall be answerable and accountable only for his own acts, receipts, neglects, or de-

17.–18. See notes 17–18 on page 341.

limited or prohibited.

 WESTLAW REFERENCES

trustee /s reliev*** exclud*** /s liability /s error /2 judgment

trustee /s exculpatory immunity /2 clause

find 250 f 321

TRUSTEE'S DUTY OF LOYALTY [1]

§ 95. The trustee owes a duty to the beneficiaries to administer the affairs of the trust solely in the interests of the beneficiaries, and to exclude from consideration his own advantages and the welfare of third persons. This is called the duty of loyalty.

If the trustee engages in a disloyal transaction, the beneficiary may secure the aid of equity in avoiding the act of the trustee or obtaining other appropriate relief, regardless of the good faith of the trustee or the effect of the trustee's conduct on the beneficiary or benefit to the trustee.

In enforcing the duty of loyalty the court is primarily interested in improving trust administration by deterring trustees from getting into positions of conflict of interests, and only secondarily in preventing loss to particular beneficiaries or unjust enrichment of the trustee.

One of the most important duties of a trustee is that of undivided loyalty to the beneficiaries. While he is administering the trust he must refrain from placing himself in a position where his personal interest or that of a third person does or may conflict with the interest of the beneficiaries.[2] All his conduct which has any bearing on the

faults, and not for those of any other trustee, nor for any banker, broker, or other persons with whom any trust money or securities may be deposited, nor for the insufficiency or deficiency of any securities, nor for any other loss, unless the same happens through his own wilful default."

17. See Employee Retirement Income Security Act of 1974, 29 U.S.C.A. § 1110 ("any provision in an agreement or instrument which purports to relieve a fiduciary from responsibility or liability for any responsibility, obligation or duty under this part shall be void as against public policy").

Trust Indenture Act of 1939 (15 U.S. C.A. § 77ooo (d)) (trust indenture not to relieve trustee from liability for its own negligence or willful misconduct except that it may relieve from liability for errors of judgment in cases where the trustee was not negligent in ascertaining the pertinent facts, and may relieve the trustee where he

acts in good faith on the direction of a majority in amount of the security holders).

18. N.Y.—McKinney's EPTL 11–1.7 (attempted grant to executor or testamentary trustee or successor of "exoneration of such fiduciary from liability for failure to exercise reasonable care, diligence and prudence" void as contrary to public policy).

§ 95

1. Restatement, Trusts, Second, §§ 170, 206. See also Bogert, Trusts and Trustees (rev. 2d edit.), §§ 543–543(V).

And see Scott, 49 Harv.L.R. 521, 37 Cal. L.R. 539; Clapp, 3 Md.L.R. 221; Niles, 91 Tr. & Est. 734; 25 Univ.Chi.L.R. 382.

2. Enslen v. Allen, 160 Ala. 529, 49 So. 430; City of Chicago v. Tribune Co., 248 Ill. 242, 93 N.E. 757; Teegarden v. Lewis, 145 Ind. 98, 40 N.E. 1047, 44 N.E. 9; In re Carmody's Estate, 163 Iowa 463, 145 N.W. 16; Niblack v. Knox, 101 Kan. 440, 167 P.

affairs of the trust must be actuated by consideration of the welfare of the beneficiaries and them alone. He is in a position of such intimacy with those he is representing and has such great control over their property that a higher standard is established by the court of equity than would prevail in the case of an ordinary business relation.[3]

It is a well-known quality of human nature that it is extremely difficult, or perhaps impossible, for an individual to act fairly in the interests of others whom he represents and at the same time to consider his own financial advantage. In most cases, consciously or unconsciously, he will tend to make a choice which is favorable to himself, regardless of its effect on those for whom he is supposed to be acting. Sometimes no harm will come to the beneficiaries because the trustee is unusually conscientious or the selfish action of the trustee does not work an injury to the beneficiary. But it is highly dangerous to fiduciary administration that the personal interests of the trustee come into play. Often actual harm will come to the beneficiaries. For the sake of protecting them against this risk equity forbids the disloyal transaction and does not consider its actual merits or effects which in many cases may be concealed.[4]

The rule applies to conduct by the trustee which is in the interest of a third party, as well as to the case where his personal interest is involved. If the trustee was motivated by a desire to enrich a third person, the transaction is subject to attack on the ground of disloyalty.[5] Thus if a trustee has realty for sale, and sells it to X for the purpose of enabling X to make a profit on a resale, even though T is not to obtain any financial advantage and even though the sale was otherwise

741; Patterson v. Booth, 103 Mo. 402, 15 S.W. 543; Ludington v. Patton, 111 Wis. 208, 86 N.W. 571. The loyalty rule is stated in the statutes of Mont., N.D. and S.D.; see Bogert, Trusts and Trustees (rev. 2d edit.), § 543. And the Uniform Trusts Act, §§ 5 and 17, codifies parts of the rule.

In some states the trustee's duty of loyalty has been expressed in part by statute. See, for example, West's Ann.Cal.Civ.Code §§ 2229, 2232 2233; West's Ann.Ind.Code 30–4–3–7; Iowa Code, § 633.155.

The settlor may not relieve the trustee of liability for breach of his duty of loyalty: La.—R.S. 9:2206.

And as to trust departments of national banks, see Reg. § 9.12 issued by the U.S. Comptroller of the Currency (self-dealing).

3. "Many forms of conduct permissible in a workaday world for those acting at arm's length, are forbidden to those bound by fiduciary ties. A trustee is held to something stricter than the morals of the market place. Not honesty alone, but the punctilio of an honor the most sensitive, is then the standard of behaviour." Cardozo,

C.J., in Meinhard v. Salmon, 249 N.Y. 458, 464, 164 N.E. 545, 546 (1928).

4. Chancellor Kent, in speaking of the purchase by a trustee of the trust property, said: "However innocent the purchase may be in the given case, it is poisonous in its consequences. The cestui que trust is not bound to prove, nor is the Court bound to judge, that the trustee has made a bargain advantageous to himself. The fact may be so, and yet the party not have it in his power, distinctly and clearly, to show it. There may be fraud, as Lord Hardwicke observed, and the party not be able to prove it. It is to guard against this uncertainty and hazard of abuse, and to remove the trustee from temptation, that the rule does and will permit the cestui que trust to come, at his own option, and without showing actual injury, and insist upon having the experiment of another sale." Davoue v. Fanning, 2 Johns.Ch. 252, 261.

5. North Baltimore Bldg. Ass'n v. Caldwell, 25 Md. 420, 90 Am.Dec. 67; Harrison v. Manson, 95 Va. 593, 29 S.E. 420.

unexceptionable, the sale would be vulnerable under the loyalty rule.[6]

It is sometimes stated that equity "forbids" disloyal transactions, and this might lead to the implication that such acts are void. This, however, is not the case. The beneficiary has the choice of objecting to them, or of treating them as binding and effective. He may set aside the transaction as against the trustee and others (assuming no bona fide purchaser has come into the picture). Or he may elect to take the benefit of the disloyalty and assert his right to one of the remedies available. Thus if a trustee sells trust property to himself and thereby puts himself in a position where his personal interest to get the property at the lowest and best terms conflicts with his representative interest to sell for the highest figure, the beneficiary may affirm the transaction and treat the price paid as trust property and the property sold as belonging absolutely to the trustee; or he may set aside the sale, and get a decree that the property be restored to the trust on the return to the trustee of the price he paid; or he may take from the trustee any profit he may have made on a resale of the property.[7]

Whether the trustee acted in good faith and with honest intentions is not relevant,[8] nor is it important that the transaction attacked was fair and for an adequate consideration so that the beneficiary has suffered no loss as a result of the disloyal act.[9] It is not material that the trustee himself made no profit from the disloyal act, although in most cases he has benefited. Thus if a trustee employs an agent and permits him to enter into transactions beneficial to the agent while he is engaged in the trust work, the trustee may be held liable for the amount of the agent's gain even though the trustee did not share in it.[10]

In applying the loyalty rule the court of equity is not primarily concerned in preventing unjust enrichment and working out the equities of the parties in the individual case, although it does consider that problem in framing its decree. It is principally desirous of procuring a result which will keep all trustees out of temptation and thus conduce to the ethical and efficient administration of trusts.[11]

The loyalty doctrine applies to all persons in a fiduciary or confidential relation, for example, to executors, administrators, guardians, agents, partners, promoters and directors and officers of corporations,

---

6. Noonan's Estate, 361 Pa. 26, 63 A.2d 80 (1949).

7. Taussig v. Chicago Title & Trust Co., 171 F.2d 553 (7th Cir.1948); Beckley v. Munson, 22 Conn. 299; Pomeroy v. Bushong, 317 Pa. 459, 177 A. 10 (1935).

8. Slay v. Burnett, 143 Tex. 621, 187 S.W.2d 377 (1945).

9. In re Kline, 142 N.J.Eq. 20, 59 A.2d 14 (1948).

10. In Mosser v. Darrow, 341 U.S. 267, 71 S.Ct. 680, 95 L.Ed. 927 (1951), a trustee in reorganization for two business trusts which were holding companies for the securities of many corporations hired X and Y to help run the trust and agreed that they might trade in the securities of the corporations. This they did and bought such securities at a discount and sold them to the trust for retirement at a profit to X and Y. Although the trustee had made no profit, he was held liable to the trust for the profits made by X and Y, since he had participated in disloyalty.

11. That the rule is primarily based on prevention and deterrence and is not primarily remedial, see In re Bond & Mtg. Guar. Co., 303 N.Y. 423, 103 N.E.2d 721 (1952).

public officers, and to those who, by reason of family relationship, age, health, education, or experience, have a superiority and dominance over others who trust them with business affairs and are, therefore, deemed to occupy a "confidential relation." [12]

Equity will not permit the loyalty rule to be circumvented by any subterfuge. Indirect disloyalty is just as objectionable as direct.[13] Hence the trustee cannot avoid the operation of the doctrine by dealing with a person who is in collusion with him (a straw man); [14] or with one who has an identity of economic interest, for example, a wife; [15] or with a corporation in which the trustee owns all or nearly all of the stock.[16]

Corporate fiduciaries may violate the rule if they deal with affiliated or subsidiary corporations where there is a high degree of common interest and control.[17]

Agents and employees of the trustee,[18] and officers of a corporate fiduciary,[19] are also affected by the loyalty rule.

Illustrations of Application of Loyalty Rule

It is a violation of the trustee's duty of loyalty when he purchases the trust property on a private [20] or judicial sale,[21] or as trustee leases trust property to himself individually,[22] or purchases for himself a

12. Strates v. Dimotsis, 110 F.2d 374 (5th Cir.1940), certiorari denied 311 U.S. 666, 61 S.Ct. 24, 85 L.Ed.2d 427 (1940) (administrator); Tansey v. Oil Producing Royalties, Inc., 36 Del.Ch. 472, 133 A.2d 141 (1957); Continental Bank & Tr. Co. v. American Assembling Mach. Co., 350 Pa. 300, 38 A.2d 220 (1944) (receiver). See § 86, ante, dealing with fiduciary relationships other than trusts, and Restatement, Second, Agency, §§ 387–398, as to agents.

13. Hartman v. Hartle, 95 N.J.Eq. 123, 122 A. 615; In re Fulton's Will, 253 App. Div. 494, 2 N.Y.S.2d 917 (1938).

14. Presbyterian Church v. Plainfield Tr. Co., 139 N.J.Eq. 501, 52 A.2d 400 (1947) (attorney of trustee).

15. Toombs v. Hilliard, 209 Ga. 755, 75 S.E.2d 801 (1953).

16. Wallace v. Malooly, 4 Ill.2d 86, 122 N.E.2d 275 (1954).

17. Kinney v. Lindgren, 373 Ill. 415, 26 N.E.2d 471 (1940); In re Lewisohn, 294 N.Y. 596, 63 N.E.2d 589 (1945), motion denied 295 N.Y. 935, 68 N.E.2d 37 (1946). "Complete loyalty to the trust does not mean almost complete loyalty nor does undivided loyalty permit slightly divided loyalty. . . . It is necessary that every possible temptation be removed from the trustee." In re Carter's Estate, 6 N.J. 426, 78 A.2d 904 (1951). But in other cases the identity of interest has not been sufficient to cause application of the rule. In re

Comstock's Will, 219 Minn. 325, 17 N.W.2d 656 (1945); Old Settlers Club v. Haun, 245 Wis. 213, 13 N.W.2d 913 (1944).

And see Cornet v. Cornet, 269 Mo. 298, 190 S.W. 333; Shanley's Estate v. Fidelity Union Trust Co., 108 N.J.Eq. 564, 138 A. 388, 5 N.J.Misc.R. 783 (1927).

18. Donovan & Schuenke v. Sampsell, 226 F.2d 804 (9th Cir.1955), certiorari denied 350 U.S. 895, 76 S.Ct. 152, 100 L.Ed. 787 (1955).

19. Greenfield Sav. Bank v. Simons, 133 Mass. 415; Gilbert v. McLeod Infirmary, 219 S.C. 174, 64 S.E.2d 524 (1951).

20. Presbyterian Church of Flemington v. Plainfield Trust Co., 139 N.J.Eq. 501, 52 A.2d 400 (1947); Munsey v. Russell Bros., 31 Tenn.App. 187, 213 S.W.2d 286 (1948). The rule applies to a sale by co-trustees to one of them. Waterbury v. Nicol, 207 Or. 595, 296 P.2d 487 (1956).

21. Fisher v. Grady, 131 Fla. 1, 178 So. 852 (1937); Giese v. Terry, 388 Ill. 188, 57 N.E.2d 462 (1944); Marshall v. Carson, 38 N.J.Eq. 250. There are, however, authorities permitting such a sale, if fair. Melin v. Melin, 189 Iowa 370, 178 N.W. 346; Whitely v. Whitely, 178 Md. 538, 84 A. 68.

22. Wilmington Trust Co. v. Carrow, 14 Del.Ch. 290, 125 A. 350; In re Gleeson's Will, 5 Ill.App.2d 61, 124 N.E.2d 624 (1955); Anderton v. Patterson, 363 Pa. 121, 69 A.2d 87 (1949).

claim against the trust property such as a mortgage [23] or the interests of beneficiaries under a liquidation trust.[24]

Other examples are found where the trustee sells his individual property to the trust as an investment,[25] or in the case of a corporate trustee holds or buys for the trust stock in the trustee corporation.[26] While the sale of the property of one trust to another trust having a common trustee involves possible conflicting interests,[27] the transaction is usually approved where the trustee can prove that it was fair to both trusts.[28]

It would seem that a strict application of the loyalty rule would make it illegal for a corporate trustee which has a banking department to deposit trust funds with itself. In choosing the safest and most advantageous bank of deposit for the trust funds it is not free to act solely for the interest of the beneficiaries, if it is allowed to consider a deposit with its own commercial department, where the interest of the bank is to secure the maximum of deposits on the most advantageous terms with regard to interest and withdrawals. A conflict of interest may thus be involved. Some authorities have accepted this view,[29] but there are also decisions supporting the transaction, at least if the bank accounts to the trust for any profit it makes on the money deposited.[30]

23. In re Franklin Bldg. Co., 178 F.2d 805 (7th Cir.1949), certiorari denied 339 U.S. 978, 70 S.Ct. 1023, 94 L.Ed. 1383 (1950); City Nat. Bk. & Tr. Co. of South Bend v. American Nat. Bk. at Indianapolis, 217 Ind. 305, 27 N.E.2d 764 (1940); Strickler's Estate, 328 Pa. 145, 195 A. 134 (1937); Dodge v. Stone, 76 R.I. 318, 69 A.2d 632 (1949).

24. In a liquidation trust the trustee holds the property of an insolvent corporation in trust for many bondholders. Frequently he or his agent buys the interests of some of the bondholders at a discount and retains them until the fund is distributed and then realizes a profit. This has generally held to be disloyal. Mosser v. Darrow, 341 U.S. 267, 71 S.Ct. 680, 95 L.Ed. 927 (1951); In re Bond & Mortgage Guarantee Co., 303 N.Y. 423, 103 N.E.2d 721 (1952); Dick & Reuteman Co. v. Doherty Realty Co., 16 Wis. 342, 114 N.W.2d 475 (1962). But see Victor v. Hillebrecht, 405 Ill. 264, 90 N.E.2d 751 (1950), certiorari denied 339 U.S. 980, 70 S.Ct. 1026, 94 L.Ed. 1384 (1950), *contra.*

25. In re Ryan's Will, 291 N.Y. 376, 52 N.E.2d 909 (1943); Marcellus v. First Tr. & Dep. Co., 291 N.Y. 372, 52 N.E.2d 907 (1943); In re Binder's Estate, 137 Ohio St. 26, 27 N.E.2d 939 (1940). There has recently been a tendency to permit corporate trustees to purchase investments with their own funds, earmark them for later allocation to their trusts, and from time to time sell them to the trusts at cost. First Nat. Bank v. Basham, 238 Ala. 500, 191 So. 873 (1939); Pike v. Camden Tr. Co., 128 N.J.Eq. 414, 16 A.2d 634 (1940); In re Coulter's Estate, 204 Misc. 473, 121 N.Y.S.2d 531 (1953), affirmed 283 App.Div. 691, 128 N.Y.S.2d 539 (1954); 7 Pa.C.S.A. §§ 819–1111.

26. In re Durston's Will, 297 N.Y. 64, 74 N.E.2d 310 (1947); City Bank Farmers Trust Co. v. Taylor, 76 R.I. 129, 69 A.2d 234. But see In re Riker's Estate, 125 N.J. Eq. 349, 5 A.2d 685 (1939), *contra,* as to retention.

27. Barker v. First Nat. Bank, 20 F.Supp. 185 (N.D.Ala.1937). The Uniform Trusts Act, § 6, treats the transaction as disloyal.

28. Bryan v. Security Tr. Co., 296 Ky. 95, 176 S.W.2d 104 (1943); French v. Hall, 198 Mass. 147, 84 N.E. 438, 16 L.R.A., N.S., 205; Roberts v. Michigan Trust Co., 273 Mich. 91, 262 N.W. 744 (1935) (voidable if a profit to the selling trust).

29. In re National Banks Acting as Fiduciaries, 30 Pa.Dist. 63; First Nat. Bank of Danville v. Commercial Bank & Tr. Co., 163 Va. 162, 175 S.E. 775 (1934); Restatement, Trusts, Second, § 170, Comment *m.*

30. Corbett v. Hospelhorn, 172 Md. 257, 191 A. 691 (1937); Herzog v. Title Guar. & Trust Co., 148 App.Div. 234, 132 N.Y.S. 1114, modified on another point in

The great convenience of deposits by corporate trustees with their own banking departments has led in recent years to their validation by statute, on the condition that the bank set aside as security for the total of the trust deposits a fund of high grade securities, and in some cases account for interest at market rates.[31] These statutes have been adopted in most states and afford trust beneficiaries greater protection than they would have if trustees were required to deposit in separate institutions where their claims would be unsecured. The statutes often except from their operation trust deposits which are insured by the Federal Deposit Insurance Corporation.

The lending of trust funds to the trustee individually, or of individual funds to the trust, has the vice of possible conflict of personal and fiduciary interests.[32]

If a trustee holds a leasehold interest in trust, he may not secure a renewal of the lease or a purchase of the reversion for himself, since he is thus competing with the trust for an advantage.[33]

It is sometimes held also that a trustee is guilty of disloyalty in employing himself to do work for the trust (for example, legal or real estate appraisal work),[34] or in voting stock held in trust in order to procure his election as an individual as an officer of the corporation.[35]

So too, the loyalty principle may be applied where a trustee of a business engages in a competing enterprise,[36] accepts a gift from one

210 N.Y. 531, 103 N.E. 885; Hayward v. Plant, 98 Conn. 374.

31. See Bogert, Trusts and Trustees (rev. 2d edit.), § 598.

32. Bogle v. Bogle, 51 N.M. 474, 188 P.2d 181 (1947). Statutes sometimes expressly make the transaction a breach of trust. Uniform Trusts Act, § 3. And see other references in Bogert, Trusts and Trustees, (rev. 2d edit.), § 543(J).

33. Washington Theatre Co. v. Marion Theatre Corp., 119 Ind.App. 114, 81 N.E.2d 688 (1948); Hamberg v. Barsky, 355 Pa. 462, 50 A.2d 345 (1947); Nicolai v. Desilets, 185 Wash. 435, 55 P.2d 604 (1936). "The cestui que trust has a right to the chance of renewal. . . . Such as it is, the trustee shall not take it to himself. . . ." Dwight, C., in Mitchell v. Reed, 61 N.Y. 123, 136.

34. In re Lair's Estate, 70 Cal.App.2d 330, 161 P.2d 288 (1945); Matter of Thompson's Estate, 50 Cal.2d 613, 328 P.2d 1 (1958) (settlor permitted payment); Gamble v. Gibson, 59 Mo. 585; Green v. Winter, 1 Johns.Ch.N.Y., 26; Fryberger v. Anderson, 125 Minn. 322, 147 N.W. 107. "The result therefore is, that no person in whom fiduciaries duties are vested shall make a profit of them by employing himself, because in doing this he cannot perform one

part of his trust, namely, that of seeing that no improper charges are made." Broughton v. Broughton, 5 De G.M. & G. 160, 164. But modern American cases and statutes often allow a trustee who is a lawyer to collect at least a reasonable sum for legal services rendered to the trust. Babcock v. Hubbard, 56 Conn. 284, 15 A. 791; Shelton v. McHaney, 343 Mo. 119, 119 S.W.2d 951 (1938); Norris v. Bishop, 207 Ky. 621, 269 S.W. 751 (1925); Willis v. Clymer, 66 N.J.Eq. 284, 57 A. 803.

35. In re Steinberg's Estate, 5 Cal.2d 674, 56 P.2d 202 (1936); Mangels v. Safe Deposit & Trust Co., 167 Md. 290, 173 A. 191 (1934); Taylor v. Errion, 140 N.J.Eq. 495, 55 A.2d 11 (1947). But see Sueske v. Schofield, 376 Ill. 431, 34 N.E.2d 399 (1941) (trustee-officer may keep salary when not excessive).

For a discussion of a possible breach of the corporate trustee's duty of loyalty to the trust beneficiaries by its retention of its own stock, see Bogert, Trusts and Trustees (rev. 2d edit.), § 543(G); and, as to whether a corporate trustee may vote its own stock held in one or more of its trust accounts, see § 543(N).

36. McKinstry v. Thomas, 258 Ala. 690, 64 So.2d 850 (1953). See Bogert, Trusts and Trustees (rev. 2d edit.), § 543(O).

with whom he deals while conducting the trust business,[37] or obtains an incidental benefit for himself while engaged in conducting the trust business.[38]

The penalties and remedies available in case of a breach of the duty of loyalty are in the discretion of the court. They may consist of imposing a constructive trust on property [39] in the hands of the trustee individually or on the profits [40] of a disloyal transaction, or of setting aside the objectionable act. The court may enjoin a threatened disloyal act.[41] Where a sale by the trustee constitutes a breach, the court may order a second sale to be held.[42] Removal from the trusteeship may also be decreed,[43] or forfeiture of interest [44] or compensation.[45] A decree against the disloyal trustee for the payment of money into the trust fund may also be granted.[46]

What would otherwise be a disloyal transaction may be validated by a provision of the trust instrument,[47] although the courts give a strict construction to clauses which allegedly permit such conduct.[48] If the beneficiaries are competent and are fully informed as to their rights and the facts, they may prevent themselves from objecting to the disloyal act by consenting in advance [49] or by ratification after the act.[50] For good cause shown the courts sometimes approve the doing of an act which would otherwise be objectionable as disloyal.[51] Occasionally legislatures relax the loyalty rules as to one or more acts of trust

37. Devers v. Greenwood, 139 Cal.App. 2d 345, 293 P.2d 834 (1956); Sherman v. Lanier, 39 N.J.Eq. 249.

38. Purchase v. Atlantic Safe Dep. & Tr. Co., 81 N.J.Eq. 344, 87 A. 444; East Side Mill & Lumber Co. v. Dwyer Logging Co., 155 Or. 339, 64 P.2d 89 (1937). See Bogert, Trusts and Trustees (rev. 2d edit.), § 543(q.)

39. Meade v. Vande Voorde, 139 Neb. 827, 299 N.W. 175, 137 A.L.R. 554 (1941). And see § 76, ante.

40. Pomeroy v. Bushong, 317 Pa. 439, 177 A. 10 (1935).

41. Shanley's Estate v. Fidelity Union Trust Co., 108 N.J.Eq. 564, 138 A. 388 (1927).

42. Staats v. Bergen, 17 N.J.Eq. 554.

43. See § 160, post.

44. In re Busby's Estate, 288 Ill.App. 500, 6 N.E.2d 451 (1937).

45. Continental Ill. Nat. Bank & Tr. Co. v. Kelley, 333 Ill.App. 119, 76 N.E.2d 820 (1948); George Washington Memorial Park Cemetery Ass'n v. Memorial Development Co., 141 N.J.Eq. 47, 55 A.2d 675 (1947).

46. Mosser v. Darrow, 341 U.S. 267, 71 S.Ct. 680, 95 L.Ed. 927 (1951); In re Comstock's Estate, 219 Minn. 325, 17 N.W.2d 656 (1945); Lewis' Estate, 349 Pa. 455, 37 A.2d 559 (1944).

47. In re Flagg's Estate, 365 Pa. 82, 73 A.2d 411 (1950); Steele's Estate, 377 Pa. 250, 103 A.2d 409 (1954) (appointment of trustee with knowledge of conflicting interest).

48. In re Anneke's Trust, 229 Minn. 60, 38 N.W.2d 177 (1949); In re Durston's Will, 297 N.Y. 64, 74 N.E.2d 310 (1947); City Bank Farmers Trust Co. v. Taylor, 76 R.I. 129, 69 A.2d 234 (1949).

49. For approval in advance, see Strudthoff v. Yates, 28 Cal.2d 602, 170 P.2d 873 (1946); Furrh v. Furrh, 251 S.W.2d 927 (Tex.Civ.App.1952). For confirmation, see State ex rel. Caulfield v. Sartorious, 344 Mo. 919, 130 S.W.2d 541 (1939); Honeywell v. Dominick, 223 S.C. 365, 76 S.E.2d 59 (1953).

50. James v. James, 55 Ala. 525; Hayward v. Ellis, 13 Pick., Mass., 272; Mulford v. Minch, 11 N.J.Eq. 16, 64 Am.Dec. 472; Boerum v. Schenck, 41 N.Y. 182; Beeson v. Beeson, 9 Pa. 279; Connolly v. Hammond, 51 Tex. 635; Lewis v. Hill, 61 Wash. 304, 112 P. 373.

51. Hayes v. Hall, 188 Mass. 510, 74 N.E. 935; Scholle v. Scholle, 101 N.Y. 167, 4 N.E. 334.

administration.[52]

 WESTLAW REFERENCES

trustee /s duty /2 loyalty

davoue +3 fanning

Illustrations of Applications of Loyalty Rule

71 sct 680

trustee /s duty /s loyalty /s purchas*** /s property

TRUSTEE'S DUTY IN TRANSACTIONS WITH BENEFICIARY [1]

§ 96. If a trustee enters into a transaction with a beneficiary relating to the interest of the beneficiary under the trust, the trustee owes the beneficiary a duty to display the utmost fairness, which ordinarily involves disclosure to the beneficiary of all relevant facts which are unknown to the beneficiary, a statement as to the legal rights of the beneficiary and the effect of the proposed dealing, and the payment of adequate consideration if no gift was involved. In addition there may be a duty to advise the beneficiary to secure independent counsel as to the wisdom of the transaction or to secure such advice for him.

The doctrine applies to all fiduciaries, and also to persons in a confidential relationship. The authorities are divided as to whether the existence of a confidential relation between donor and donee of itself causes a presumption of undue influence in the obtaining of the gift.

If the trustee does not convince the court that he exhibited the utmost fair play in the transaction, the beneficiary may procure a decree setting it aside or establishing a constructive trust as to a benefit obtained by the trustee.

Trustees are often superior to their beneficiaries in business experience and knowledge of trust affairs. They acquire information as to the character and financial situation of the beneficiaries, and the latter customarily impose confidence in the integrity of their trustees. There are often opportunities for trustees to procure advantages for themselves by reason of dealings with the persons whom they represent, and experience has shown that they sometimes acquire benefits from the beneficiaries by unfair means. On account of these facts the court of equity has established a doctrine applicable to all direct dealings between trustee and beneficiary, namely, that the trustee must display the utmost candor and fair play in order that the transaction shall stand against attack.[2] The rule is not, as in the case

52. See, for example, 7 Pa.C.S.A. § 403.

§ 96

1. Restatement, Trusts, Second, § 170 (2), Comment *w*.

2. Hardy v. Hardy, 217 Ark. 305, 230 S.W.2d 11 (1950); Papineau v. Security–First Nat. Bank, 6 Cal.2d 668, 59 P.2d 131 (1936); Van Gorp v. Van Gorp, 229 Iowa 1257, 296 N.W. 354 (1941); Dunn v. Dunn, 42 N.J.Eq. 431, 7 A. 842.

of disloyal transactions, that the dealing is absolutely voidable at the option of the beneficiary, regardless of its merits, but rather that it is conditionally voidable. It stands if the trustee proves its fairness. It falls if he fails to make such proof. No burden to prove unfairness rests upon the beneficiary. There is no duty on the part of the trustee to refrain from entering into a business transaction with the beneficiary regarding his interest in the trust, but there is an obligation to act with the utmost fairness if such an arrangement is made. Sometimes the courts express the doctrine by stating that in direct dealings between trustee and beneficiary there is a rebuttable presumption of fraud or undue influence. In some states the principle is set forth in a statute.[3]

The rule applies to transactions with regard to the interest of the beneficiary under the trust, but not to a dealing between trustee and beneficiary with reference to property of the latter which has no connection with the trust.[4] It governs during the trust relationship only, and not after the trust has terminated.[5] All fiduciaries are affected by the rule, for example, executors, guardians, and agents;[6] and in addition persons who occupy a confidential relation must comply with its terms.[7] Thus if a guardian purchases the interest of the ward for whom he is acting, or a gift is made by an aged, infirm person to a near relative who has been acting as business advisor, a burden will arise to prove the existence of fair play.

Any business transaction which concerns the interest of the beneficiary under the trust is controlled by the rule, for example, gifts inter vivos[8] or by will,[9] contracts,[10] sales,[11] releases,[12] surrenders,[13] consents,[14] and mortgages.[15] A trustee who acquires a benefit in any of

3. See, for example, West's Ann.Cal. Civ.Code § 2235; S.Dak.Codif.Laws § 55–2–8. See also Bogert, Trusts and Trustees (rev. 2d edit.), § 544.

4. Stone v. Stone, 407 Ill. 66, 94 N.E.2d 855 (1950); First Nat. Bank & Trust Co. v. Gold, 217 Wis. 522, 259 N.W. 260 (1935).

5. Laney v. Dean, 267 Ala. 129, 100 So. 2d 688 (1958); Halper v. Wolff, 82 Conn. 552, 74 A. 890.

6. Bradner v. Vasquez, 43 Cal.2d 147, 272 P.2d 11 (1954) (attorney and client); Maddox v. Maddox, 151 Neb. 626, 38 N.W.2d 547 (1949) (executor and legatee).

7. Staufenbiehl v. Staufenbiehl, 388 Ill. 511, 58 N.E.2d 569 (1944); Ostertag v. Donovan, 65 N.M. 6, 331 P.2d 355 (1958).

The rule is applied where the trustee procures a benefit in the name of a dummy or straw man, or his wife, or other person having an identity of interest. Burns v. Skogstad, 69 Idaho 227, 206 P.2d 765 (1949).

8. Edwards v. Collins, 207 Ga. 204, 60 S.E.2d 337 (1950); In re Randall's Estate, 64 Idaho 629, 132 P.2d 763 (1942), rehear-ing denied 64 Idaho 629, 135 P.2d 299 (1943).

9. Dial v. Welker, 328 Ill. 56, 159 N.E. 286 (1927).

10. Buder v. Fiske, 174 F.2d 260 (8th Cir.1949), rehearing denied 177 F.2d 907 (8th Cir.1949); In re Lee's Estate, 214 Minn. 448, 9 N.W.2d 245 (1943).

11. McNeill v. McNeill, 223 N.C. 178, 25 S.E.2d 615 (1943); Perpetual Royalty Syndicate v. Albritton, 149 S.W.2d 700 (Tex.Civ.App.1941).

12. Allen v. Moushegian, 320 Mass. 746, 71 N.E.2d 393 (1947); Wool Growers Service Corp. v. Ragan, 18 Wn.2d 655, 140 P.2d 512 (1943), rehearing denied 18 Wn.2d 655, 141 P.2d 975 (1943).

13. Zink v. Carlile, 126 Colo. 208, 248 P.2d 306 (1952).

14. Dalton v. Lawrence Nat. Bank, 169 Kan. 401, 219 P.2d 719 (1950); Bilton v. Lindell Tower Apts., 358 Mo. 209, 213 S.W.2d 952 (1948).

15. Assets Corp. v. Perrin Properties, 48 Cal.App.2d 220, 119 P.2d 375 (1941).

these ways must bear the burden of proving the fairness of the transaction, if the beneficiary seeks to have it set aside.

If the trustee is to uphold the transaction under attack, he must prove that the beneficiary was informed by the trustee of all the facts which would naturally influence the beneficiary to accept or reject the proposal,[16] or that the beneficiary had knowledge of the relevant facts which he had obtained from other sources.[17] In addition there must be proof that the beneficiary was informed of his legal rights and of the legal effect of the proposed arrangement.[18] If the transaction was a sale or other deal based on consideration, there must be evidence that some consideration was actually paid and that it was adequate and not merely nominal.[19] It will also greatly bolster the case of the trustee if he can prove that the beneficiary was advised by the trustee to secure independent advice before entering into the transaction and did so,[20] or that the beneficiary secured such counsel of his own accord.[21] While great stress is laid on the existence of independent advice,[22] it is generally held that the lack of it is not conclusive proof that the transaction was unfair, but instead is to be considered with other factors in determining whether the transaction should be allowed to stand.[23]

It will also be material to know who initiated the arrangement which is being attacked. If the trustee proposed it, and drew the papers needed, or employed a lawyer to consummate the deal, fair play is often regarded as unproven; [24] but if the beneficiary suggested the transaction and made the arrangements needed there is more apt to be a finding of fair play.[25]

If a gift was involved, it is material to consider whether it was

16. Shoup v. Dowsey, 134 N.J.Eq. 440, 36 A.2d 66 (1944); Wendt v. Fischer, 243 N.Y. 439, 154 N.E. 303 (1926) (where an agent to sell land organized a dummy corporation to buy and told his principal that the sale was to be a "client of the office", and Cardozo, J., said: "If dual interests are to be served, the disclosure to be effective must lay bare the truth without ambiguity or reservation, in all its stark significance".)

17. Herpolsheimer v. Michigan Tr. Co., 261 Mich. 209, 246 N.W. 81 (1933) (business trust; sale to trustee of interest of beneficiary who was employed in business and knew its situation).

18. United States Nat. Bank v. Guiss, 214 Or. 563, 331 P.2d 865 (1958).

19. In re Ferguson's Will, 193 Minn. 235, 258 N.W. 295 (1935); McElveen v. McElveen, 233 Miss. 672, 103 So.2d 439 (1958); Silvey v. Brixey, 112 S.W.2d 75 (Mo.App.1938).

20. Garrett v. First Nat. Bank, 233 Ala. 467, 172 So. 611 (1937); Woolwine v. Bryant, 244 Iowa 66, 54 N.W.2d 759 (1952); Woodson v. Raynolds, 42 N.M. 161, 76 P.2d 34 (1938).

21. Staude v. Heinlein, 414 Ill. 11, 110 N.E.2d 228 (1953); In re Haskell's Estate, 283 Mich. 513, 278 N.W. 668 (1938).

22. Overstreet v. Beadles, 151 Kan. 842, 101 P.2d 874 (1940); Turner v. Leathers, 191 Tenn. 292, 232 S.W.2d 269 (1950).

23. Barnum v. Fay, 320 Mass. 177, 69 N.E.2d 470 (1946); Graziano v. Graziano, 81 R.I. 215, 102 A.2d 243 (1954); Jardine v. Archibald, 3 Utah 2d 88, 279 P.2d 454 (1955).

24. Lynn v. Lynn, 21 Ill.2d 131, 171 N.E.2d 53 (1960); In re Day's Estate, 198 Or. 518, 257 P.2d 609 (1953).

25. Berigan v. Berrigan, 413 Ill. 204, 108 N.E.2d 438 (1952); Michaelson v. Wolf, 364 Mo. 356, 261 S.W.2d 918 (1953).

natural because of the relationship between the donee and donor,[26] or was unnatural because of superior claims by others on the generosity of the donor and the lack of any motive for making the gift.[27] Furthermore, great doubt may be cast on the fairness of the gift if it was made during the life of the donor and was highly improvident in that it would strip the donor of property needed for living expenses.[28]

In the case of a gift to a person in a confidential relation with the donor there has been a division of opinion among the courts as to whether the mere existence of the close relationship raised a presumption of undue influence and therefore cast a burden on the donee to prove that the donation was made in the exercise of the free will of the donor. Some courts have held that the confidential relation of itself caused a burden to be placed on the donee to prove fair play and freedom from undue influence;[29] but others have taken the position that there is no presumption of undue influence merely because of the confidential relation between donor and donee, and that in addition proof must be adduced that the donee suggested the gift or had a part in drawing up the papers which gave it effect.[30]

The relief generally accorded to the beneficiary when the trustee has received a benefit from a direct dealing with the beneficiary regarding the latter's interest under the trust, and the trustee has not been able to convince the court that he acted with fairness, is the setting aside of the transaction [31] or the creation of a constructive trust as to any property acquired by the trustee as a result of his breach of duty.[32] If the fiduciary has conveyed away the property obtained from the beneficiary, a money judgment for its value may be given.[33]

 WESTLAW REFERENCES

trustee /s act*** /5 fair**** /s beneficiary
find 345 p2d 724

---

26. McKinney v. Odom, 363 P.2d 272 (Okl.1961).

27. White v. Ross, 160 Ill. 56, 43 N.E. 336 (donee rich, donor poor); Kitts v. Kitts, 315 S.W.2d 617 (Ky.1958).

28. Miller v. Miller, 138 N.J.Eq. 225, 47 A.2d 32 (1946); Katz v. Lockman, 356 Pa. 196, 51 A.2d 619 (1947).

29. Davis v. Davis, 255 Ala. 215, 50 So. 2d 723 (1951); Igo v. Marshall, 140 Colo. 560, 345 P.2d 724 (1959); Hollinger's Estate, 351 Pa. 364, 41 A.2d 554 (1945).

30. Peters v. Florida Nat. Bank of Jacksonville, 155 Fla. 453, 20 So.2d 487 (1945); Clark v. Powell, 351 Mo. 1121, 175 S.W.2d 842 (1943); In re Livingston's Will, 5 N.J. 5, 73 A.2d 916 (1950).

31. Schneider v. Schneider, 125 Iowa 1, 98 N.W. 159.

32. Phillips v. Willis, 31 Del.Ch. 5, 63 A.2d 171 (1949); Hofert v. Latorri, 22 Ill.2d 126, 174 N.E.2d 866 (1961).

33. Howland v. Smith, 9 A.D.2d 197, 193 N.Y.S.2d 140 (1959), appeal dismissed 7 N.Y.2d 988, 199 N.Y.S.2d 495, 166 N.E.2d 503 (1960).

Chapter 11

DUTIES OF THE TRUSTEE—
POSSESSION AND PROTECTION

Table of Sections

DUTY TO TAKE POSSESSION OF TRUST PROPERTY [1]

§ 97. A trustee has a duty to secure possession of the tangible assets of the trust and the documents representing intangible assets as soon as is reasonably possible after he has become trustee. He should use reasonable skill and diligence to collect choses in action which are due the trust.

At the beginning of his administration the trustee has a duty to study the terms of the trust instrument in order to learn his duties and powers. He should ascertain who the beneficiaries are,[2] and should notify them of their interests.[3] He is obligated to inform himself as to the identity of the trust property so that he may proceed to take control of it and apply it to the trust purposes.

He has a duty to take possession of the trust property and may bring any action necessary in order to enable him to do so.[4] If the res is tangible property such as goods and chattels or cash, he should assume control thereof. If the subject matter of the trust is intangible property such as deeds to real estate, notes, bonds, or certificates for shares of stock, he should take possession of the documents represent-

§ 97

1. Bogert, Trusts and Trustees (rev. 2d edit.), § 581 et seq.; Restatement, Trusts, Second, §§ 175, 177.

2. Fast v. McPherson, 98 Ill. 496.

3. Birmingham Trust & Sav. Bank v. Ansley, 234 Ala. 674, 176 So. 465 (1937);

April v. April, 272 N.Y. 331, 6 N.E.2d 43 (1936).

4. Hogg v. Hoag, 154 Fed. 1003 (2d Cir. 1907); In re McLellan's Estate, 8 Cal.2d 49, 63 P.2d 1120 (1936); Speakman v. Tatem, 48 N.J.Eq. 136, 21 A. 466; April v. April, 272 N.Y. 331, 6 N.E.2d 43 (1936).

ing that type of property. In rare cases the beneficiary is permitted by the trust instrument to have possession of the trust property, as where a widow has been authorized to occupy a home rent-free. Here the trustee should take possession at the outset and then place the beneficiary in control.[5]

Possession will normally be obtained from either the settlor, or the executor of the settlor in the case of a trust created by will, or from a predecessor trustee or his representative where there has been a change in the trusteeship due to death, resignation, or removal of the predecessor trustee. If the settlor of a living trust has contracted to deliver certain property to the trustee but has failed to do so, the trustee should endeavor to enforce the obligation.[6] If the res of a testamentary trust was certain described stocks and bonds, these will come into possession of the executor, and in the course of his administration or at the end thereof he will be obligated to hand over to the trustee these securities; the trustee should keep in touch with the executorial administration and secure the property from the executor as soon as can be done in the exercise of ordinary skill and diligence.[7] Where the incoming trustee is a successor trustee who is taking over because his predecessor has for any reason ceased to be trustee, there will be a duty to be reasonably diligent and prudent in securing all trust assets from the retiring trustee or his representative.[8]

If the subject matter of the trust is described as property which has a certain value, the trustee is obligated to see that the property tendered to him has the requisite value at the time he takes it over.[9] Examples are found where the res is to be one-half of the residuary estate, or stock in a named corporation having a designated market value, or that portion of the residuary estate needed to produce an income of $5,000 a year.

For failure to act promptly and with reasonable skill in securing possession of the trust property, the trustee may be held liable for any loss caused thereby.[10] For example, if a testamentary trustee fails to demand the trust property from an executor for a long period, and during this time the executor embezzles the estate property, the trustee

5. Wade v. Powell, 20 Ga. 645; Root v. Yeomans, 15 Pick., 32 Mass. 488; Freeman v. Cook, 41 N.C. 373.

6. Parsons v. Boyd, 20 Ala. 112; Nagle v. Conard, 80 N.J.Eq. 253, 86 A. 1003; In re Hartje's Estate, 320 Pa. 76, 181 A. 497.

7. In re McClellan's Estate, 8 Cal.2d 49, 63 P.2d 1120 (1936); In re Ward's Estate, 121 N.J.Eq. 606, 191 A. 772 (1937). The trustee should see that the executor delivers property of the kind required by the trust instrument, and not property of another type which the executor deems of equivalent value.

8. Kinion v. Riley, 310 Mass. 338, 37 N.E.2d 984 (1941); Pfeffer v. Lehmann, 255 App.Div. 220, 7 N.Y.S.2d 275 (1938); In re Brown's Estate, 343 Pa. 19, 21 A.2d 898 (1941).

9. In re Marks' Estate, 102 So.2d 301 (Fla.App.1958); First Nat. Bank v. Truesdale Hospital, 288 Mass. 35, 192 N.E. 150 (1934); In re Brown's Estate, 112 N.J.Eq. 499, 164 A. 692 (1933). If the trustee is given power to fix the valuation of property to be received, he must act honestly and reasonably in fixing the value. In re Hansen's Estate, 344 Pa. 12, 23 A.2d 886 (1942).

10. Hunt v. Gontrum, 80 Md. 64, 30 A. 620; In re Brooke's Estate, 321 Pa. 529, 184 A. 54 (1936).

may be held liable for the value of the trust res.[11]

The amount and kind of property which is to be the subject matter of the trust may be described in a schedule affixed to a living trust instrument, or in the case of a testamentary trust may be ascertained from the terms of the will, the executor's inventory and his accounts presented in court and a distribution decree issued by the court, or in the case of a successor trustee by the court accounting of the predecessor and the decree of the court receiving this account. A trustee will be protected in depending on a court decree describing the trust property he is entitled to receive.[12]

A trustee who takes over a trust which has no cash, and who finds that expenditures are needed in order to ascertain the trust property or the liabilities of a predecessor trustee or his bondsmen, is under no duty to advance his own money for this purpose; but he does have an obligation to request the beneficiaries to pay such expenses, and if they refuse to contribute they may not complain of the failure of the trustee to collect the trust property.[13]

If a trustee finds at the outset of his administration that some of the property delivered to him is of no value, he should seek a court order permitting him to abandon it,[14] since the power to abandon on his own motion is doubtful.[15]

A trustee may find that part or all of the trust property consists of choses in action, for example, a claim against an executor, predecessor trustee, or third persons for some violation of their duties which has caused injury to the trust beneficiaries. The trustee has a duty to use reasonable diligence and skill in attempting to collect on these causes of action and to treat the proceeds as trust property.[16] Other choses may be notes, bonds, or mortgages which form part of the trust estate at the beginning. The trustee has a duty to use the skill and diligence of a reasonably prudent creditor in collecting these claims after their maturity,[17] and may be held liable for any loss occasioned by delay or inaction.[18] The power to arbitrate or compromise a claim is usually accorded a trustee of a chose by common law or by statute,[19] as is the

11. In re Kline's Estate, 280 Pa. 41, 124 A. 280, 32 A.L.R. 926 (1924).

12. Carr v. Bank of America Nat. Trust & Sav. Ass'n, 11 Cal.2d 366, 79 P.2d 1096 (1938); In re Gibson's Will, 40 N.Y.S.2d 727 (Sur.1943).

13. McClure v. Middletown Trust Co., 95 Conn. 148, 110 A. 838.

14. Hertz v. Miklowski, 326 Mich. 697, 40 N.W.2d 452 (1950); Fidelity Union Tr. Co. v. Sayre, 137 N.J.Eq. 179, 44 A.2d 25 (1945).

15. As denying the power to abandon without court permission, see Byrne v. Byrne, 124 N.J.Eq. 273, 1 A.2d 464 (1938); McKinnon v. Bradley, 178 Or. 45, 165 P.2d 286 (1946).

16. Smith v. Pettigrew, 34 N.J.Eq. 216; Tucker v. Brown, 20 Wn.2d 740, 150 P.2d 604 (1944).

17. Waterman v. Alden, 144 Ill. 90, 32 N.E. 972; Hunt v. Gontrum, 80 Md. 64, 30 A. 620; Speakman v. Tatem, 48 N.J.Eq. 136, 21 A. 466; Vilas v. Bundy, 106 Wis. 168, 81 N.W. 812.

18. Wasson v. Taylor, 191 Ark. 659, 87 S.W.2d 63 (1935); Buckle v. Marshall, 176 Va. 139, 10 S.E.2d 506 (1940); In re Church's Will, 221 Wis. 472, 266 N.W. 210 (1936).

19. Brower v. Osterhout, 7 Watts & S. 344; Purcell v. Robertson, 122 W.Va. 287, 8 S.E.2d 881 (1940). And see numerous statutes permitting the trustee to compro-

authority to enter into reorganizations or refinancing arrangements in the case of the failure of a corporate obligor.[20]

 WESTLAW REFERENCES

trustee /s duty /s possess*** /s "trust property"

380k182

moeller +3 english

DUTY TO DEFEND THE TRUST
AGAINST ATTACK [1]

§ 98.   A trustee has a duty to defend the trust and the interests of its beneficiaries against attack from the settlor or his successors or others who claim that the trust is invalid in whole or in part, where reasonable prudence would dictate a defense.   Generally, the court will not permit the trustee to attack the trust or to assert a title superior to that of the settlor.

The acceptance of a trust imposes on the trustee a duty to carry out the trust as prescribed in the trust instrument and to protect the beneficiaries in the enjoyment of the interests given them.   When an attempt is made by any person to destroy the trust in whole or in part, or to have it set aside or declared invalid, or otherwise to prejudice the interests of the beneficiaries, the trustee owes a duty to investigate and to form an opinion as to the merits of the claim of the person attacking the trust, and if the trustee becomes convinced that the claim is baseless or that there is reasonable ground for believing it is without foundation, he has a duty to use the skill and prudence of a reasonable man in opposing the claim.[2]   It is not his privilege to remain neutral and take the position of a mere stakeholder.

If the examination of the claim, and the advice received, indicate that the attack is well founded and that defense would be hopeless and so would involve unjustified expense, the trustee has no duty to defend but should accede to the claim.[3]   In doubtful cases he may be supported in compromising the claim and thus saving the trust from total destruction.[4]

The person attacking the trust may be the settlor who asserts that there was an invalidating cause in the act of trust creation, for

mise or arbitrate, or giving the court power to approve such conduct, cited in Bogert, Trusts and Trustees (rev. 2d edit.), § 592.

20.   Moeller v. English, 118 Conn. 509, 173 A. 389; Patterson v. Henrietta Mills, 219 N.C. 7, 12 S.E.2d 686 (1941).

§ 98

1.   Restatement, Trusts, Second, § 178.

2.   Rossi v. Davis, 345 Mo. 362, 133 S.W.2d 363 (1939); In re Lowe's Estate, 326 Pa. 375, 192 A. 405 (1937).

3.   Witherbee v. C.I.R., 70 F.2d 696 (2d Cir.1934); Bailey v. Buffalo Loan, Trust & Safe Dep. Co., 214 N.Y. 689, 108 N.E. 561.

4.   Burgess v. Nail, 103 F.2d 37 (10th Cir.1939); Jones v. Jones, 297 Mass. 198, 7 N.E.2d 1015 (1937).

example, fraud perpetrated on the settlor, or mistake.[5] Or the successors of a testator may attack the trust on the ground that the testator was of unsound mind when he executed his will.[6] In some instances third persons claim title to the property in the hands of the trustee.[7] Creditors of the beneficiaries may be seeking to take the beneficiaries' interests in order to collect debts, and the trustee may be obligated to defend by setting up protection under a spendthrift clause.[8] Or there may be an effort to terminate the trust, and where its purposes are not accomplished the trustee is under a duty to oppose.[9] There may be a claim that the trust is void because of a violation of the Rule against Perpetuities.[10]

The duty of the trustee to protect the trust extends to the case where there has been a court order or decree destroying the trust but the use of reasonable prudence under competent legal advice would indicate that the action of the court was unjustified. Here there may be a duty to appeal from the decision of the trial court.[11]

A failure to perform the duty to defend the interests of the beneficiaries will render the trustee liable for any damages caused. Thus where a trustee was served with an order, secured ex parte, to deliver the trust property to a receiver of the settlor and the trustee acquiesced in the order without appeal and delivered the property as ordered, he was held liable to the beneficiaries for the value of their interests in the trust property which were lost by his conduct.[12]

Expenses incurred by the trustee in performing his duty to defend the trust are payable from the trust property where the defense is successful.[13] And even if the trustee were unsuccessful, the court may allow counsel fees out of trust property where the result of the transaction had not been the total destruction of the trust and the trustee

5. Application of Corn Exchange Bank Trust Co., 87 N.Y.S.2d 675 (1948), modified on other grounds, 276 App.Div. 430, 95 N.Y.S.2d 210 (1950). And see Bullock v. Lloyd's Bank, (1954) 3 All Eng.R. 726 (unfairness to settlor and lack of independent advice).

6. Citizens Banking Co. v. Monticello State Bank, 143 F.2d 261 (8th Cir.1944) (receiver of settlor); Waterbury Trust Co. v. Porter, 130 Conn. 494, 35 A.2d 837 (1944) (heirs of settlor); Murphey v. Dalton, 314 S.W.2d 726 (Mo.1958) (claim testator of unsound mind).

7. Estate of Harvey, 164 Cal.App.2d 330, 330 P.2d 478 (1958) (widow of settlor claimed trust property was community property).

8. In re Gibbon's Estate, 132 Neb. 538, 272 N.W. 553 (1937).

9. Stein v. La Salle Nat. Bank, 328 Ill. App. 3, 65 N.E.2d 216 (1946).

10. Blackhurst v. Johnson, 72 F.2d 644 (8th Cir.1934).

11. Citizens Banking Co. v. Monticello State Bank, 143 F.2d 261 (8th Cir.1944); Chinnis v. Cobb, 210 N.C. 104, 185 S.E. 638 (1936); In re Trustees under the Will of Yost v. Moll, 102 Ohio App. 62, 141 N.E.2d 176 (1956) (power to appeal denied in particular case).

12. Republic Nat. Bank & Trust Co. v. Bruce, 130 Tex. 136, 105 S.W.2d 882 (1937) (erroneous delivery to receiver of settlor). And see People ex rel. Nelson v. Union Bank of Chicago, 306 Ill.App. 270, 28 N.E.2d 286 (1940) (trustee defaulted in suit to have trust set aside because trust instrument was a forgery).

13. Steinway v. Steinway, 112 App. Div. 18, 98 N.Y.S. 99, affirmed 197 N.Y. 522, 90 N.E. 1166; In re Lowe's Estate, 326 Pa. 375, 192 A. 405, 111 A.L.R. 518 (1937).

acted in good faith.[14] If the defense of the trustee was against a claim that the trust was void or voidable in its entirety, and the trustee failed in his effort, there will be no trust property out of which expenses can be paid, and the trustee can secure reimbursement only if the beneficiaries encouraged him in his defense and so rendered themselves equitably obligated to reimburse him.[15]

The costs of an action in which the trustee successfully or unsuccessfully defended the trust are allowed as the court in its discretion may determine, and are frequently made payable from trust property.[16]

The trustee is also under a duty not to attack the trust and claim that it is in whole or in part invalid,[17] as where the trustee sets up a claim that the testator who created the trust was incompetent and so the will void,[18] or that a trust for a widow was void because the settlor was not legally married to her and the marriage was bigamous.[19] The trustee will not be heard to set up a title in himself or a third person which is claimed to be superior to that of the settlor.[20] He is said to be estopped to assert a hostile title, a doctrine like that applied to tenants and bailees.[21]

As shown previously [22] where a trust is created for an illegal purpose (for example, to defraud creditors of the settlor), the settlor is generally denied aid of the court in enforcing rights as the beneficiary of a resulting or express trust. In such case the trustee has the power to set up a defect in the trust which prevents its enforcement.

  WESTLAW REFERENCES

trustee /s duty /3 defend /s trust

390k268 /p duty /2 defend

390k246

find 330 p2d 478

---

14. State v. United States Steel Co., 12 N.J. 51, 95 A.2d 740 (1953); First Nat. Bank of Wichita Falls v. Stricklin, 347 P.2d 652 (Okl.1959).

15. Hale v. Cox, 240 Ala. 622, 200 So. 772 (1941); Trautz v. Lemp, 334 Mo. 1085, 72 S.W.2d 104 (1934).

16. Eggert v. Pacific States Sav. & Loan Co., 53 Cal.App.2d 554, 127 P.2d 999 (1942).

17. Federal Trust Co. v. Damron, 124 Neb. 655, 247 N.W. 589 (1933); In re Strange's Estate, 7 Wis.2d 404, 97 N.W.2d 199 (1959).

18. Karner's Ex'r v. Monterey Christian Church, 304 Ky. 269, 200 S.W. 474.

19. Carter v. Carter, 321 Pa. 391, 184 A. 78.

20. Fellows v. Baas, 213 Miss. 346, 56 So.2d 831 (1952); In re Eustace's Estate, 198 Wash. 142, 87 P.2d 305 (1939).

21. Offic.Code Ga.Ann. 24–4–26.

22. See § 48, ante.

DUTY TO PROTECT AND PRESERVE
TRUST PROPERTY [1]

§ 99. A trustee has a duty to perform such acts as a reasonably prudent businessman would find necessary for the protection and preservation of the trust property.

The trustee has a duty to take whatever steps are necessary, in accordance with the skill and prudence of an ordinarily capable businessman managing his own property for like ends, to protect and preserve the trust property from loss or damage.[2] Among such acts are usually included recording a recordable document, such as a deed or mortgage under which the trustee has an interest, in order to prevent the cutting off of the interest of the trust by a conveyance or mortgage to a bona fide purchaser;[3] seeing that corporate shares are transferred to the name of the trustee or his nominee on the records of stock ownership;[4] giving notice of the ownership of a non-negotiable chose in action by the trustee to the obligor on such chose, in order to prevent payments being made to a prior owner;[5] the deposit of documents representing negotiable securities and other important papers in a safety deposit box;[6] the deposit of cash and commercial instruments like checks and drafts in a checking account in a bank having a good financial standing;[7] the securing of fire,[8] liability[9] and other insurance to the extent that customary good business practice would dictate; the bonding of employees of the trust who are to handle cash or negotiable paper;[10] making such repairs to buildings located on trust realty as are necessary to prevent deterioration;[11] in the case of life insurance held in trust, the payment of the premiums necessary to keep the insurance

§ 99

1. Bogert, Trusts and Trustees (rev. 2d edit.), § 582 et seq.; Restatement, Trusts, Second, § 176.

2. Morse v. Borough of Essex Falls, 116 N.J.Eq. 350, 173 A. 921; La–LSA–R.S. 9:2091.

3. Scherger v. Union Nat. Bank, 138 Kan. 239, 25 P.2d 588 (1933); Sprowles v. Eversole, 307 Ky. 191, 210 S.W.2d 346 (1948). And see Partridge v. American Tr. Co., 211 Mass. 194, 97 N.E. 925; Miller v. Parkhurst, 45 Hun 590, 9 N.Y.St.Rep. 759.

4. Letcher's Trustee v. German Nat. Bank, 134 Ky. 24, 119 S.W. 236.

5. Hobday v. Peters, 28 Beav. 603; Thompson v. Speirs, 13 Sim. 469.

6. Castree v. Shotwell, 3 N.J.L. 52; In re Boyle's Will, 99 Misc. 418, 163 N.Y.S. 1095. Recent legislation sanctions the renting of a box by co-trustees on terms permitting either trustee to have access. See Bogert, Trusts and Trustees (rev. 2d edit.), § 598.

7. Wagner v. Coen, 41 W.Va. 351, 23 S.E. 735; Watkins, 4 Mo.L.R. 332; Sothard, 15 Tenn.L.R. 669. There will be a breach if the trustee leaves excessive amounts on deposit, or permits the funds to be left in the bank unnecessarily long, or ignores warnings as to the solvency of the bank. Walsh v. Walsh, 231 Ala. 305, 164 So. 822 (1935); In re State Bank of Central City, 229 Iowa 195, 294 N.W. 260 (1940).

8. Willis v. Hendry, 127 Conn. 653, 20 A.2d 375 (1940).

9. United States Nat. Bank of Omaha v. Alexander, 140 Neb. 784, 1 N.W.2d 920 (1942); In re Reiff's Estate, 49 Pa.D. & C. 119.

10. Estate of Campbell, 36 Hawaii 631; Application of Brooklyn Trust Co., 174 Misc. 451, 20 N.Y.S.2d 974 (1940).

11. Annett-Mahnken Realty Co. v. Gollin, 110 N.J.Eq. 469, 160 A. 400 (1932); In re Farrell's Estate, 152 Misc. 118, 272 N.Y.S. 852 (1933).

from lapsing; [12] the cultivation and fertilization of farm lands held in trust; the paying of taxes and assessments levied by governmental agencies so that the trust property may be protected and not sold for non-payment of such obligations; [13] the payment of the principal and interest of mortgages on the trust property in order to prevent foreclosure; [14] and the payment of calls and assessments on corporate stock held by the trust.[15]

 WESTLAW REFERENCES

duty /3 protect preserve /5 "trust property"
390k182

DUTY TO SEPARATE AND EARMARK
TRUST PROPERTY [1]

§ 100. A trustee has a duty to keep trust property separate from his individual property and from the property held by him for other trusts.

He also has a duty to earmark or label the trust property as that of the trust in whatever way practicable. Recent statutes have very generally allowed trustees to hold some or all investments in the name of a nominee or in bulk form.

It is of great advantage to the trustee and the beneficiary to have trust property segregated from the individual property of the trustee and from all other property, and in addition to have it labelled or marked as the property of a given trust in whatever way is practicable. This line of conduct will assist an honest trustee in keeping his records of trust principal and income and in otherwise performing his duties as trustee. It will handicap a dishonest trustee in any effort he may make to juggle assets and to allot to the trust unsuccessful investments and keep for himself securities which have proved to be valuable, and will hinder him in any effort he may make to transfer the trust assets to a bona fide purchaser and thus cut off the beneficiary's interest. If the trustee becomes insolvent or dies, separation and earmarking will be of great advantage to the beneficiary in tracing trust property and in preventing individual creditors of the trustee from taking the trust property for the private debts of the trustee.[2]

12. Pearlman's Estate, 348 Pa. 488, 35 A.2d 418 (1944).

13. Appeal of Wordin, 71 Conn. 531, 42 A. 659; Merritt v. Jenkins, 17 Fla. 593; Disbrow v. Disbrow, 46 App.Div. 111, 61 N.Y.S. 614, affirmed 167 N.Y. 606, 60 N.E. 1110; In re Lueft, 129 Wis. 534, 109 N.W. 652.

14. Goldsborough v. De Witt, 171 Md. 225, 189 A. 226 (1937); Holbrook v. Stoddard, 283 Mass. 496, 186 N.E. 565 (1933).

15. See Restatement, Trusts, Second, §§ 265c, 277, Comments c and d. And see § 132, post.

§ 100

1. Bogert, Trusts and Trustees (rev. 2d edit.), § 596; Restatement, Trusts, Second, §§ 179, 180.

2. Chapter House Circle v. Hartford Nat. Bank & Tr. Co., 121 Conn. 558, 186 A. 543 (1936), contains an excellent discussion of the reasons for these rules. And see

Separation

On these bases equity has demanded of the trustee that he keep trust property physically separate from other property which he has in his possession either as bailee, owner, or as a holder in another fiduciary capacity.[3] Modern banking codes invariably declare such a duty.[4] Trust cash should be kept in a separate box, trust credit in a separate bank account, trust securities in a separate safety deposit box, and other trust assets should be segregated from the personal property of the trustee and from property which he holds under other trust or fiduciary relationships.[5]

If the trustee mixes the trust property with his own and there is difficulty in tracing it, the court may place upon him the burden of separating out the trust property or having the whole mass treated as trust property,[6] or of becoming a guarantor of its safety so that he is liable for its loss or shrinkage in value, even though the mingling of the funds had no causal connection with the damage.[7]

Earmarking

Under the law prevailing until the 1930's, a trustee was required by equity to earmark or label as property of a named trust all property held by him as trustee in whatever way was practicable for the type of property in question. Thus he had a duty to see that notes, mortgages, registered bonds, deeds and other evidences of ownership obtained by him during the course of his administration ran to him as trustee of an identified trust, and that stock certificates had such a label.[8] A bank account was required to be held in his name as trustee of a specific trust. An exception was and is still made in the case of bearer bonds which, due to great convenience, are allowed to be bought or retained by a trustee although they have no label of trust ownership on the face of the bonds.[9]

Ketcham, S., In Re Union Trust Co., 86 Misc. 392, 149 N.Y.S. 324, affirmed 219 N.Y. 514, 114 N.E. 1057.

3. Bird v. Stein, 258 F.2d 168 (5th Cir. 1958), certiorari denied 359 U.S. 926, 79 S.Ct. 608, 3 L.Ed.2d 628 (1959); McCook v. Harp, 81 Ga. 229, 7 S.E. 174; Moore v. McKenzie, 112 Me. 356, 92 A. 296; Wagner v. Coen, 41 W.Va. 351, 23 S.E. 735.

4. See Bogert, Trusts and Trustees (rev. 2d edit.), § 596.

5. Vincent v. Werner, 140 Kan. 599, 38 P.2d 687 (1934).

The modern tendency to permit mingling the funds of several trusts in a common trust fund or a participating mortgage is noticed later. See § 105, post.

6. Lupton v. White, 15 Ves.Jr. 432; Cook v. Addison, 7 Eq.Cas. 466.

7. Wangsness v. Berdahl, 69 S.D. 586, 13 N.W.2d 293 (1944). "A trustee who willfully and unnecessarily mingles the trust property with his own, so as to constitute himself in appearance its absolute owner, is liable for its safety in all events, and for the value of its use." West's Ann.Cal.Civ.Code, § 2236; followed in Mont., N.D. and S.D.

8. Mitchell v. Moore, 95 U.S. (5 Otto) 587, 24 L.Ed. 492 (1877); De Jarnette v. De Jarnette, 41 Ala. 708; Gilbert v. Welsch, 75 Ind. 557; Wolk v. Stefanowicz, 318 Pa. 197, 177 A. 821 (1935).

9. Matter of Halstead, 44 Misc. 176, 89 N.Y.S. 806, affirmed 110 App.Div. 909, 95 N.Y.S. 1131. But see In re Buckelew's Estate, 128 N.J.Eq. 81, 13 A.2d 855 (1940), decree affirmed 129 N.J.Eq. 383, 19 A.2d 779 (1941).

Under these older cases failure to earmark was deemed to make the trustee a guarantor of the safety of the trust property regardless of the cause of its loss.[10] For example, if he established a bank account for the deposit of trust funds, but allowed it to be entitled with his name without mention of any trust, and the bank failed, the trustee would be required to replace in the trust funds the amount of the loss; [11] and if he took a mortgage as a trust investment and had it run to himself individually with no mention of any trust, and the mortgage was foreclosed at a loss, the trustee would be required to pay into the trust funds from his individual property the amount of this loss.[12] Such was the result even though the failure to earmark had no causal connection with the loss. The rule was one of penalty and not of damages, and it is believed that it was a very salutary doctrine. It prevented a trustee from engaging in practices which were sometimes dangerous to the interests of the beneficiaries, and which were unnecessary and were often based on careless or ignorant methods of administration.

However, in comparatively recent years two influences have worked towards a marked relaxation of these common law doctrines. For many years prior to the depression of the 1930's, banks and trust companies had established the practice of holding mortgages and fee titles with no reference to the trust in the mortgage instrument or the deed. They had kept records of the ownership of the mortgages or titles in their corporate books but nothing appeared on the public records. This was for the purpose of facilitating transfer of the mortgages or titles, and of avoiding the necessity of making proof of authority to transfer. In the late 1920's and early 1930's beneficiaries discovered these violations of the earmarking rule and sought to make the banks liable for the shrinkage in value of the trust property which had come about through economic causes and not due to lack of earmarking. In view of the heavy impending possible losses to the corporate fiduciaries which would have resulted from the enforcement of the strict common law rule, and a consequent serious threat to the banking structure of the country, the courts held that they would change the rule to one of damages and that there was henceforth to be no liability unless the failure to earmark had caused a loss to the trust.[13] Thus, under this statement of the law, if a trustee lent trust funds and took a note and mortgage running to himself as a trust investment, with no mention of the trust in those instruments, and the investment was originally a legal one, but by reason of the shrinkage in

10. Freas' Estate, 231 Pa. 256, 79 A. 513; In re Fenelli's Estate, 323 Pa. 49, 185 A. 758 (1936).

11. Chancellor v. Chancellor, 177 Ala. 44, 58 So. 423, 45 L.R.A., N.S., 1; In re Arguello's Estate, 97 Cal. 196, 31 P. 937; McAllister v. Commonwealth, 30 Pa. 536.

12. In re Quest's Estate, 324 Pa. 230, 188 A. 137 (1936).

13. Chapter House Circle v. Hartford Nat. Bank & Trust Co., 124 Conn. 151, 199 A. 110 (1938); Voorhies v. Blood, 127 Fla. 337, 173 So. 705 (1937); Springfield Safe Deposit & Trust Co. v. First Unitarian Society, 293 Mass. 480, 200 N.E. 541 (1936); Rotzin v. Miller, 134 Neb. 8, 277 N.W. 811 (1938).

real estate values which occurred during the 1930's and a default in the mortgage there was a foreclosure at a loss, the trustee would not be liable for the loss, notwithstanding his breach of his duty to earmark the mortgage, since this violation did not cause the loss which was, instead, caused by adverse economic conditions in the country.[14]

In making these decisions the courts sometimes have cited the first Restatement of the Law of Trusts, which was approved in 1935 and which stated that while there was a duty to earmark there should be no liability for breach of it, except to the extent that damages could be proved to have been caused by the failure to earmark.[15] It would seem that the earmarking rule in 1935 was a rule of penalty, and that the Restatement did not set forth actually existing law but rather what was believed should be the law.[16]

Secondly, for many years prior to 1930, and for similar reasons of ease, speed, and lower costs of transfer, corporate trustees had built up a practice of holding corporate stock in the name of one or more nominees who were employees or officers of the banks, so that the trust did not appear on the stock certificate or the record of stock ownership.[17] The convenience of this, despite its doubtful legality, induced the corporate fiduciaries to propose legislation which would legalize the holding of stock and in many cases other investments in the name of nominees, provided correct records of ownership were kept in the office of the trustee and the trustee was liable for misconduct of the nominees. These proposed bills, and some others of like content,[18] have secured wide adoption.[19] Some apply to corporate trustees only, others to all trustees; some to trustees only, others to all fiduciaries; some to all trust investments, others to mortgages, stocks and other named investments only.

 WESTLAW REFERENCES

Separation

duty /5 separat*** /5 "trust property"

permit! /s mingl***

intermingl*** /s "trust property"

Earmarking

duty /5 earmark*** /5 "trust property"

---

14. Buckle v. Marshall, 176 Va. 139, 10 S.E.2d 506 (1940); In re Lefevre's Guardianship, 9 Wn.2d 145, 113 P.2d 1014 (1941).

15. § 179, Comment *d.*

16. See Bogert, 24 Tex.L.R. 417.

17. The delay and expense involved in procuring proof of the power of the trustee to transfer the stock was avoided where the records showed it registered in the name of one or more individuals.

18. Uniform Trusts Act, § 9.

19. Nearly all states have now adopted nominee statutes. For statutory references, see Bogert, Trusts and Trustees (rev. 2d edit.), § 596.

Chapter 12

DUTIES OF THE TRUSTEE— INVESTMENTS

Table of Sections

DUTY TO MAKE THE TRUST PROPERTY PRODUCTIVE [1]

§ 101. Generally a trustee is directed to collect and distribute income and therefore has, either expressly or impliedly, a duty to invest the trust property in income-producing assets as soon as he reasonably can.

In almost all cases [2] the settlor expressly or impliedly imposes on the trustee the duty to distribute income to one or more beneficiaries, and this obligation necessarily carries with it the duty to make the trust property produce income, which can normally be done only by continuing to hold property given to him by the settlor which is productive, or by buying for the trust assets which will bring in financial returns such as interest, rents, or dividends.[3]

§ 101

1. Bogert, Trusts and Trustees (rev. 2d edit.), § 611 et seq. (make trust fund productive; investments); Restatement, Trusts, Second, §§ 181, 379.

2. Occasionally the trustee is directed to permit the beneficiary to occupy land, or is to hold title and possession for distribu-tion purposes in the near future. Hinchman v. Fry, 89 Ind.App. 79, 147 N.E. 724; Walker v. Woodhouse, 178 N.C. 57, 100 S.E. 132. In these cases there is no duty to secure income from the property.

3. Linder v. Officer, 175 Tenn. 402, 135 S.W.2d 445 (1940); Moore v. Sanders, 106 S.W.2d 337 (Tex.Civ.App.1937).

Thus in the normal case there is a duty to consider what funds are available for investment, after laying aside cash for expenses and distributions to beneficiaries in the immediate future,[4] and to select within a reasonable time investments which meet the needs of the trust and are legal for it under the terms of the trust, any applicable court order, or the case or statutory law of the governing jurisdiction.[5] If there is an unreasonable delay in securing an investment, the trustee will be held liable for lost income. And if the cash is left on deposit an unreasonably long time and the bank fails, the trustee may be held liable for the loss.[6]

The authority of the trustee to invest the trust funds, and his corresponding duty, may be expressly set forth in the trust instrument or it may be inferred. If the proper administration of the trust requires investment, of course the duty to invest will be implied.[7] So, too, the power and duty to review and, possibly, change investments is one frequently implied. Where the trust administration is to last for some time, the production of a suitable income will frequently require the trustee to shift his investments. A power and duty to do this is liberally implied.[8] A direction to invest the "estate" will be construed to imply the duty to invest the accumulated income which is to be paid over to the beneficiaries on their majorities.[9] If interest is accumulating and will necessarily be held for some time in the hands of the trustee, he should invest it.[10]

Pending the discovery of a desirable investment, cash not currently needed or invested should be safeguarded by deposit in a checking account in a sound bank, as previously shown.[11] A New York court, in speaking of this duty of the trustee, has said that . . . "the deposit may be continued for so long a period as will enable the trustee, in the use of ordinary diligence, to obtain its secure and proper investment, or the exigencies of the estate may require. But where he fails by his neglect within a reasonable time to secure investments, and allows the money still to remain on deposit, and it is thereby lost, the law charges the trustee with the loss." [12] If the trustee can obtain interest on a call deposit, he should do so; but he should not place the funds of the trust on a time deposit without interest. Such a deposit is a loan to the bank

4. In re Whitney's Estate, 78 Cal.App. 2d 638, 248 P. 754 (1926).

5. In re Drake's Will, Sur., 132 N.Y.S.2d 259 (1954) (six months too long); In re D'Espinay-Durtal's Will, 4 A.D.2d 141, 163 N.Y.S.2d 309 (1957) (delay of four years a breach).

6. Barney v. Saunders, 57 U.S. (16 How.) 535, 14 L.Ed. 1047 (1853) (ten months); Woodley v. Holley, 111 N.C. 380, 16 S.E. 419 (three years).

7. Appeal of Grothe, 135 Pa. 585, 19 A. 1058.

8. Citizens' Nat. Bank v. Jefferson, 88 Ky. 651, 11 S.W. 767; Spencer v. Weber, 163 N.Y. 493, 57 N.E. 753.

9. In re Stewart, 30 App.Div. 368, 51 N.Y.S. 1050, affirmed 163 N.Y. 593, 57 N.E. 1125.

10. Fowler v. Colt, 22 N.J.Eq. 44.

11. Norwood v. Harness, 98 Ind. 134, 49 Am.Rep. 739; Jacobus v. Jacobus, 37 N.J.Eq. 17; In re Law's Estate, 144 Pa. 499, 22 A. 831, 14 L.R.A. 103; Crane v. Moses, 13 S.C. 561.

12. In re Knight's Estate, Sup., 4 N.Y.S. 412, 413.

without security and is not allowable. Funds on temporary deposit should be subject to immediate call by the trustee.[13] If a trustee fails to use reasonable care in selecting the bank in which to deposit trust funds,[14] or leaves the funds on deposit after he should have known that the bank was in a bad financial condition,[15] the trustee will be liable for any loss ensuing.

 WESTLAW REFERENCES

duty /5 "trust property" /5 productive

CONTROL BY THE SETTLOR, COURT, BENEFICIARY OR BY STATUTE [1]

§ 102. The trustee's investment duty may be controlled by

(a) Directions or authority of the settlor expressed in the trust instrument;

(b) Orders of the court of chancery;

(c) Conduct of the beneficiary in requesting, consenting to, or acquiescing in, investments;

(d) Statute.

In following the settlor's directions or authority the trustee is protected, unless there is clear evidence that such action would be harmful.

If the settlor gives the trustee discretion as to investments, the trustee is under a duty to use reasonable skill and judgment in making investment decisions.

Trust Provisions

In some trust instruments the settlor gives the trustee directions as to investments to be made, for example, that the trustee is to keep the trust funds invested in first mortgages on fee titles in a certain locality, or in seasoned securities of public utility corporations.[2] However the most common provision is that the trustee shall invest in his discretion for the best interests of the beneficiaries. There is no question as to the power of the settlor to give these instructions,[3] and the trustee is

13. Andrew v. Union Sav. Bank & Trust Co., 222 Iowa 881, 270 N.W. 465 (1936); Baer's Appeal, 127 Pa. 360, 38 A. 1. But see Smith v. Fuller, 86 Ohio St. 57, 99 N.E. 214, L.R.A. 1916C, 6 Ann.Cas. 1913D, 387.

Often statutes make savings accounts legal for trusts.

14. Caldwell v. Hicks, 15 F.Supp. 46 (S.D.Ga.1936); In re Howison's Estate, 49 Ohio App. 421, 197 N.E. 333 (1934).

15. In re Foster's Estate, 218 Iowa 1202, 256 N.W. 744 (1934).

§ 102

1. Restatement, Trusts, Second, § 227.

2. In re Jeffries' Estate, 393 Pa. 593, 143 A.2d 391 (1958); Crayton v. Fowler, 140 S.C. 517, 139 S.E. 161 (1927).

3. In re Reid, 170 App.Div. 631, 634, 156 N.Y.S. 500. The settlor may reserve the right to direct the investments after the commencement of the trust. Rice v. Halsey, 156 App.Div. 802, 142 N.Y.S. 58. He may prohibit investment in a named type of property. In re Jeffries' Estate,

obligated to follow them and is protected against liability in doing so [4] unless it clearly appears that such action would be injurious to the beneficiaries.

The settlor may express his wishes regarding investments in a permissive form, for example, by stating that the trustee *may* invest in preferred stocks having certain qualifications or in the bonds of a named corporation.[5] These clauses are given effect and protect the trustee who follows them, in the absence of special circumstances which make the purchase of the permitted investment clearly unwise.[6] If the settlor wishes to permit investments which would otherwise be non-legal, he should expressly say so, since ambiguous clauses of this type are sometimes given a strict construction.[7]

The most common type of investment clause is one granting *discretion* to the trustee to retain and make such investments as in his judgment seem best for the trust and its beneficiaries.[8] In such a case the trustee has a wide discretion. He is not required to make his selection from the securities and investments declared by equity or by statute to be legal investments for trust funds. He may choose reasonable investments outside statutory lists.[9] Thus where the trustee has discretion with respect to the investments, he may lawfully invest in railway and street railway bonds [10] and in real estate outside the state,[11] if such investments are reasonably prudent.

But the grant of discretion in the making of investments does not protect the trustee in *any* investment which he may make. He must use good faith and reasonable prudence in exercising his discretion.[12] Just because he may go outside a selected list of trust investments approved by the court or the legislature does not mean that he may

393 Pa. 593, 143 A.2d 391 (1958) (common stock).

4. MacGregor v. MacGregor, 9 Iowa 65; Worcester City Missionary Soc. v. Memorial Church, 186 Mass. 531, 72 N.E. 71; Vernon v. Marsh's Ex'rs, 3 N.J.Eq. 502.

5. In re Bartol's Estate, 182 Pa. 407, 38 A. 527.

6. In re Hirsch's Estate, 116 App.Div 367, 101 N.Y.S. 893, affirmed 188 N.Y. 584, 81 N.E. 1165; In re Ascher's Estate, 175 Misc. 943, 26 N.Y.S.2d 1000 (1941).

7. In re Franklin Trust Co., 84 Misc. 686, 147 N.Y.S. 885. Thus a direction to invest in "first-class interest-bearing real estate mortgage securities" does not authorize the purchase of bonds secured by a blanket mortgage protecting the whole issue. The trustee should obtain a mortgage for his benefit alone. In re Mendel's Will, 164 Wis. 136, 159 N.W. 806.

8. If it is intended that a grant of discretion should permit going outside a statutory list, it is best to state specifically that such is the settlor's desire. Otherwise

the words may be construed to mean merely an admonition to use good judgment in following the approved types. Matter of Carnell's Will, 260 App.Div. 287, 21 N.Y.S.2d 376 (1940), affirmed 284 N.Y. 624, 29 N.E.2d 935 (1940).

9. Lawton v. Lawton, 35 App.Div. 389, 54 N.Y.S. 760; Willis v. Braucher, 79 Ohio St. 290, 87 N.E. 185, 44 L.R.A., N.S., 873, 16 Ann.Cas. 66. In Lawson v. Cunningham, 275 Mo. 128, 204 S.W. 1100, under such a grant of discretion, an investment in land was sanctioned.

10. In re Allis' Estate, 123 Wis. 223, 101 N.W. 365.

11. Merchants' Loan & Trust Co. v. Northern Trust Co., 250 Ill. 86, 95 N.E. 59.

12. Appeal of Davis, 183 Mass. 499, 67 N.E. 604; Miller v. Pender, 93 N.H. 1, 34 A.2d 663, 150 A.L.R. 798 (1943); Marshall v. Frazier, 159 Or. 491, 80 P.2d 42 (1938). Thus a loan to the trustee is not warranted by the grant of discretion. Carrier v. Carrier, 226 N.Y. 114, 123 N.E. 135 (1919).

invest the trust funds in a speculative venture. He must select an investment which he honestly believes will be safe and productive,[13] and he must act with reasonable prudence and diligence.[14] The fact that the trustee has authority to exercise his discretion regarding investments has, for example, been held not to make it proper for him to invest in a manufacturing plant in another state, when he has little or no knowledge concerning the business,[15] or to invest in unseasoned stocks,[16] or to speculate in Western lands [17] with the trust funds.

In an opinion disapproving of an investment in the stock of an umbrella manufacturing company by a trustee having discretion concerning investments, the New York Court of Appeals has said: [18] "We concede that under the terms of the will the trustees were given a discretion as to the character of the investments they might make, and that they were not limited to the investments required by a court of equity in the absence of any directions from a testator. . ... But such a discretion, in the absence of words in the will giving greater authority, should not be held to authorize investment of the trust fund in new, speculative or hazardous ventures. If the trustees had invested in the stock of a railroad, manufacturing, banking, or even business corporation, which, by its successful conduct for a long period of time, had achieved a standing in commercial circles and acquired the confidence of investors their conduct would have been justified, although the investment proved unfortunate. But the distinction between such an investment and the one before us is very marked. Surely there is a mean between a government bond and the stock of an Alaska gold mine, and the fact that a trustee is not limited to the one does not authorize him to invest in the other."

A discretionary power to invest is subject to the restriction that it must not be abused, just as in the case of a grant of discretion to perform any other act.[19]

Duty Affected by Court Order

A court of equity, in appointing a trustee, may direct him as to the investments which he is to make. It also has power to permit or direct the trustee to ignore instructions of the settlor as to investments, when it appears that following these directions are impossible or are highly disadvantageous to the beneficiaries. In some cases trustees have applied to the court for permission to deviate from the investment

---

13. In re Smith, [1896] 1 Ch. 71.

14. Kimball v. Reding, 31 N.H. 352, 64 Am.Dec. 333; Clark v. Clark, 23 Misc. 272, 50 N.Y.S. 1041. The court will review the exercise of the discretion and will disapprove such investments as loans to a corporation in which the trustees are personally interested. In re Keane, 95 Misc. 25, 160 N.Y.S. 200.

15. In re Hart's Estate, 203 Pa. 480, 53 A. 364.

16. In re Hirsch's Estate, 116 App.Div. 367, 101 N.Y.S. 893, affirmed 188 N.Y. 584, 81 N.E. 1165.

17. In re Reed, 45 App.Div. 196, 61 N.Y.S. 50.

18. In re Hall, 164 N.Y. 196, 199, 200, 58 N.E. 11.

19. See § 89, ante.

provisions of the trust instrument and have been granted permission to do so.[20] For example, in a case where the settlor directed investment in real estate mortgages or bonds bearing interest at not less than 4%, and it appeared that such investments only produced from 2.6% to 3.5%, the trustee was allowed to buy other conservative investments which would yield 4%.[21] And where the settlor directed investment in savings bank accounts which at that time paid 4.1%, but later it appeared that the return was 1.9%, the court allowed investment in other legals.[22] However, no case for a deviation is made by proof that a change in investments would increase income if the directed investments would continue to produce the level of income which the settlor desired his beneficiaries to have.[23]

If the trustee is justifiably in doubt concerning the investments which the trust instrument authorizes him to make, he may apply to the court and succeed in inducing the court to advise or direct him,[24] although such a decision may be one not involving a question of law but rather of business judgment so that the court may refuse to assist the trustee regarding it.[25]

Court decrees regarding investments should protect the trustee, no matter what the result of the investment, if an investment made thereunder was made in accordance with the court order which was properly obtained.[26] Likewise, disobedience to a court order may render the trustee personally liable for losses. Thus where a trustee submitted the trust to the jurisdiction of the court and was ordered to invest the funds in government bonds, but instead left the money in a bank in which he was interested and the bank failed, the trustee was charged with the loss resulting to the trust estate.[27]

In a few states trustees had been required by statute to submit all

---

20. Lambertville Nat. Bank v. Bumster, 141 N.J.Eq. 396, 57 A.2d 525 (1948); Cutter v. American Tr. Co., 213 N.C. 686, 197 S.E. 542 (1938).

In a few cases it has been held that the court has no power to direct deviation from the settlor's investment provision unless the beneficiaries consent, but this is a minority view. Clark v. St. Louis A. & T.H.R. Co., 58 How.Prac., N.Y., 21; Burrill v. Sheil, 2 Barb., N.Y., 457; Snelling v. McCreary, 14 Rich.Eq., S.C., 291. Thus in International Trust Co. v. Preston, 24 Wyo. 163, 156 P. 1128, it was held that a court had no power to sanction an investment in Mexican bonds when the will directed investment in bonds of the United States or a state or municipality thereof.

21. St. Louis Union Trust Co. v. Ghio, 240 Mo.App. 1033, 222 S.W.2d 556 (1949).

22. Citizens Nat. Bank v. Morgan, 94 N.H. 284, 51 A.2d 841 (1947).

23. Porter v. Porter, 138 Me. 1, 20 A.2d 465 (1941); First Nat. Bank of Jersey City v. Stevens, 9 N.J.Super. 324, 74 A.2d 368 (1950).

24. Drake v. Crane, 127 Mo. 85, 29 S.W. 990, 27 L.R.A. 653; Tillinghast v. Coggeshall, 7 R.I. 383; Whitehead v. Whitehead, 85 Va. 870, 9 S.E. 10.

25. McCarthy v. Tierney, 116 Conn. 588, 165 A. 807 (1933).

26. Wheeler v. Perry, 18 N.H. 307; Wood v. Wood, 5 Paige, N.Y., 596, 28 Am. Dec. 451; In re Old's Estate, 176 Pa. 150, 34 A. 1022. In Hackett's Ex'rs v. Hackett's Devisees, 180 Ky. 406, 202 S.W. 864, the court stated that the testator's direction must be followed unless no such investment as is directed could be made or the safety of the investment directed had become doubtful by supervening circumstances. As showing the tendency of the English courts on this subject, see In re D'Epinoix's Settlement, [1914] 1 Ch. 890.

27. Whitehead v. Whitehead, 85 Va. 870, 9 S.E. 10.

proposed investments to the court for approval,[28] but this statutory requirement has been abandoned. If the court has jurisdiction to pass judgment on investments and does so conscientiously, its action would constitute a valuable check on the action of trustees, but too often it seems dubious whether more than a formal examination is given.

Request or Consent by Beneficiary

The trustee is not under a duty to obey the requests or instructions of a beneficiary as to how the trust fund shall be invested. The settlor has placed that responsibility on the trustee and impliedly taken it out of the control of the beneficiary.

However, if the trustee makes an improper investment at the request or direction or with the consent of a competent and fully informed beneficiary, he will not be liable for losses as a result of the improper investment.[29] And so, too, if the beneficiary acquiesces in or ratifies the unlawful investment after it has been made, he may not complain of losses resulting therefrom.[30] But the consent or ratification must be with full knowledge of the facts and of the legal rights of the beneficiaries in order to relieve the trustee from liability.[31] The beneficiary should be informed that the investment which he is approving is not legal for the trust or that there is doubt about its legality.[32] And the beneficiary must be of full age and sound mind, and must be under no other disability when he gives his consent or acquiescence, in order that the trustee may be protected.[33] Naturally a consent or

28. In re Nolan's Guardianship, 216 Iowa 903, 249 N.W. 648 (1933). See former Iowa and Nebraska statutes cited in Bogert, Trusts and Trustees (rev. 2d edit.), §§ 631, 643.

By statute or court rule, a trustee may be required to file an inventory or report of his investments with the court. See, for example, Kan.Stats.Ann. § 59–1603; Md. Rules of Procedure V74.

29. Campbell v. Miller, 38 Ga. 304, 95 Am.Dec. 389; In re Hoffman's Estate, 183 Mich. 67, 148 N.W. 268, 152 N.W. 952; In re Westerfield, 48 App.Div. 542, 63 N.Y.S. 10, appeal dismissed, 163 N.Y. 209, 57 N.E. 403; Hester v. Hester, 16 N.C. 328, 1 Dev. Eq. 328; Mills v. Swearingen, 67 Tex. 269, 3 S.W. 268. Thus where a portion of the trust assets is a claim against a mining company and the beneficiaries consent to the lending of more money to such company in an attempt to recover the sum already invested, they cannot afterward object to the investment. Mann v. Day, 199 Mich. 88, 165 N.W. 643. And acceptance by a beneficiary of securities on a distribution bars objection to them as improper investments. In re Kent, 173 App.Div. 563, 159 N.Y.S. 627.

30. See § 168, post. Backes v. Crane, 87 N.J.Eq. 229, 100 A. 900; In re Union Trust Co. of New York, 219 N.Y. 514, 114 N.E. 1057.

The mere sending of statements by the trustee to the beneficiary showing an investment, and a conversation between trustee and beneficiary about it after a default, do not show ratification. In re Johnston's Estate, 129 N.J.Eq. 104, 18 A.2d 274 (1941).

31. Appeal of Nichols, 157 Mass. 20, 31 N.E. 683; Adair v. Brimmer, 74 N.Y. 539; Appeal of Pray, 34 Pa. 100.

32. "The cestui que trust must be shown, in such case to have acted freely, deliberately, and advisedly, with the intention of confirming a transaction which he knew, or might or ought, with reasonable or proper diligence, to have known to be impeachable." White v. Sherman, 168 Ill. 589, 605, 606, 48 N.E. 128, 61 Am.St.Rep. 132.

33. Murray v. Feinour, 2 Md.Ch. 418.

A guardian of a minor beneficiary cannot acquiesce in a wrongful investment and bind the minor. International Tr. Co. v. Preston, 24 Wyo. 163, 156 P. 1128.

acquiescence obtained by fraud [34] or undue influence [35] will have no effect upon the beneficiary's rights. Obviously the beneficiaries who are in existence cannot consent or acquiesce in such a way as to affect the rights of beneficiaries not yet born.[36]

It is undesirable trust practice for a trustee to depend on consents and waivers by the beneficiaries to protect him against liability for investments. The settlor has placed the investment powers in the trustee, not in the beneficiaries. The trustee is, or ought to be, a person of judgment and capacity; often the beneficiaries are not skilled in investment work. The very purpose of the trust is to give the beneficiaries the benefits of the property without placing upon them the burdens of management. A trustee who submits every proposed investment to his beneficiaries and secures their written approval is attempting to shift his investment burden to the beneficiaries. Their approval does not often represent a considered opinion, but rather a merely formal act.

Statute

In most states, where the settlor or testator has not provided otherwise for investments of trust funds, the trustee's investment duties are governed by statute. A form of the prudent investor rule has been adopted by statute in 35 states.[37] In five states which have enacted the Uniform Probate Code, the general standard of care and performance made applicable to trustees by Code § 7–302 is the only statutory guide in the making of trust investments.[38] At this writing the statutory list type of statute is in effect only in Alabama, Kentucky, North Dakota (individual trustees only) and West Virginia,[39] although a number of other states maintain a statutory legal list, either for a specified portion of the trust assets [40] or in addition to a full or modified prudent investor statute.[41] In addition, all states make certain federal, state and local bonds or other obligations legal investments for trustees and other fiduciaries.

34. Zimmerman v. Fraley, 70 Md. 561, 17 A. 560; Appeal of Nichols, 157 Mass. 20, 31 N.E. 683.

35. Wieters v. Hart, 68 N.J.Eq. 796, 64 A. 1135.

36. Wood v. Wood, 5 Paige, N.Y., 596, 28 Am.Dec. 451. And life tenants cannot affect the rights of remaindermen. International Trust Co. v. Preston, 24 Wyo. 163, 156 P. 1128.

37. For statutory adoptions see Bogert, Trusts and Trustees (rev. 2d edit.), § 613. The rule has been adopted by rules of court in the Dist. of Col. and by court decision in Md., Mass., Mo., R.I. and Vt. For discussion of the rule, see § 106, post. In some states the statutes provide both a prudent man rule and a permissive list of investments, while in other states the prudent investor statute permits only a specified portion of the trust assets to be invested in nonlegals or in common stocks (N.H., N.D. as to corporate trustees, Ohio and Wis.). See § 106, post.

38. See the statutes of Alaska, Ariz., Fla., Me. and N.Mex., cited in ch. 30, Bogert, Trusts and Trustees (rev. 2d edit.).

39. See §§ 103–104, post.

40. See the statutes, post, this chapter, for N.H., N.D. (applicable to trust companies but not to individual trustees), Ohio and Wis.

41. Haw., Ida., Iowa, Md. (case law: no prudent man statute), N.J., Ohio (list combined with modified prudent man statute), R.I. (case law: no prudent man statute), Tenn. and Va.

WESTLAW REFERENCES

Trust Provisions

settlor /s direct*** /s investment /s trust

trust /s "investment clause"

Duty Affected by Court Order

court /s direct*** /s investment /s trust

Request or Consent by Beneficiary

trustee /s invest**** /s request consent /2 beneficiary

390k237

Statute

trust /s "prudent man" /3 statute

390k217.3(5) /p "prudent man"

legal permissive /2 list /s trust

390k217.3(4) /p "legal list"

DEVELOPMENT OF TRUST INVESTMENT LAW— STATUTORY LISTS [1]

§ 103. In early English law chancery prescribed types of investments which it would approve for trustees; but for many years there has been a statutory list which governs investments of a trustee.

Originally, in the United States, there were no statutes and trustees were guided by standards set by the courts, and this continues to be the case in a few states.

Later, many statutes were adopted which set forth a list of described types of investments in which a trustee might or must invest.

If a trustee follows a statutory list, he may be protected. If the list is permissive, the trustee may invest in securities outside the list if he sustains the burden of proving reasonable care and skill. If the list is mandatory, it would seem that an investment outside the list would be a breach of trust, no matter how great the care and judgment used.

In the earliest stage of the development of trust investment law there was no statutory control, and the courts of equity judged the propriety of the trustee's conduct in purchasing a particular investment in one of several ways: by following rules set up by the courts, for example, that only government obligations and first mortgages on realty would be approved; [2] or by holding that the standard was to be the skill and prudence of an ordinarily competent man seeking similar

---

§ 103

1. Restatement, Trusts, Second, § 227.

2. Ex parte Cathorpe, 1 Cox Eq.Cas. 182 (1785). For many years a statutory list of investments has existed in England. It was materially revised by the Trustee

Investments Act, 1961 (9 & 10 Eliz. 2, ch. 62). Some early American authorities followed the early English common law rule. Appeal of Hemphill, 18 Pa. 303; Simmons v. Oliver, 74 Wis. 633, 43 N.W. 561.

objectives;[3] or by passing on the merits of each investment without fixing any definite guide.

In the latter half of the nineteenth century and the early years of the twentieth century, many American legislatures set up lists of classes of investments from which a trustee was either required or permitted to make a choice. Due to the wide spread adoption of the so-called "prudent investor rule" during and since the 1940's, many of these statutory lists have been discarded as guides to the investing trustee, but they still exist in several states.[4] Most of these statutes provide that a trustee "may" invest in any assets on the statutory list,[5] but in a few states the word "shall" was used and thus the list was mandatory and not merely permissive.[6] The statutes describe the permitted or required investments, either by naming the entity whose obligations may be purchased (for example, those of the United States or any state thereof) or by setting forth the nature of the authorized assets (for example, first mortgages on lands within the state).[7]

The trustee in a state having a statutory list will normally buy securities on the legal list in his state, and nothing else, and in all probability he will then be protected against any claim of breach of trust. However, following the legal list does not insure protection to the trustee against liability. Whether the list is permissive or mandatory, the trustee must use reasonable care in following it.[8] Perhaps this care will be less than that required of a trustee who is selecting an investment on his own initiative and does not have any legal list to guide him. The trustee may assume that the investments on the legal list are in all probability safe and proper, but he must take at least some care to see that this is so and must not ignore plain warnings that securities on the list are not safe. Thus if it is generally known in the investment world that an obligor on a corporate bond has defaulted, or that a foreign government has been overthrown by a revolution, no trustee would be safe in investing in the bonds of the corporation or the foreign government even though they were on the legal list.

It is held that if the list is *permissive*, the legislature has merely stated that a trustee "may invest" in certain types of securities and the

---

3. This was the rule in Mass., Mich., Mo., N.C. and Vt. In a leading case the Massachusetts court expressed the rule as follows: "A trustee, to invest, is required to conduct himself faithfully and to exercise a sound discretion, observing how men of prudence, discretion and intelligence manage their own affairs, not in regard to speculation, but in regard to the permanent disposition of their funds, and considering the probable income as well as the probable safety of the capital involved." Creed v. McAleer, 275 Mass. 353, 175 N.E. 761, 762.

4. Ala., Ky., N.Dak. (individual trustees only) and W.Va. In N.H., Ohio, and Wis., the statutory list applies to a certain portion of the trust assets.

5. Ala., Ky., W.Va.

6. Prior law: Ala., Ga., Haw., Ia., Minn. (corporate trustees only), N.Y., N.Car., Ohio, R.I., W.Va.

7. For the wording of the statutes, see Bogert, Trusts and Trustees (rev. 2d edit.), §§ 616–666.

8. Indiana Tr. Co. v. Griffith, 176 Ind. 643, 95 N.E. 573, 44 L.R.A., N.S., 896, Ann. Cas. 1914A, 1023; In re Buckelew's Estate, 128 N.J.Eq. 81, 13 A.2d 855 (1940); In re Randolph, 134 N.Y.S. 1117 (Sur.), affirmed 150 App.Div. 902, 135 N.Y.S. 1138.

trustee is not limited to those on the legal list but may go outside it. But if he buys a security not on the list, he will be required to show that it was one which at that time would have been purchased by an ordinarily prudent man for the purposes of the trust.[9] Going outside the list puts a heavier burden on him than if he confines himself to the list.

If the list is *mandatory,* that is, the legislature has provided that a trustee "shall invest" in named securities, it would seem that the trustee is not at liberty to go outside the list to make investments which he thinks a reasonably prudent man would make. While the cases have been somewhat conflicting,[10] it would seem that the purchase of a nonlisted security is inevitably a breach of trust if the beneficiary elects to treat it as such.[11]

Where a trustee purchases an investment which is non-legal at the time it is made but which later becomes legal, he is liable only for the depreciation which occurred before it became a legal trust investment.[12] If the investment changes from a legal to a non-legal one, it may not be held.[13] The legality of the original investment is determined by the law then in existence and not by the investment law which controlled at the time the trust was established.[14]

 WESTLAW REFERENCES

"prudent investor rule"
legal /2 list /s trust
390k2173(5)
390k217.3(4)
statutory /2 list /s trust
mandatory /2 list /s trust

INVESTMENTS GENERALLY APPROVED [1]

§ **104. Statutory lists vary from state to state, but certain types of investments are generally approved, whether under a legal list or prudent investor statute, others are sanctioned in some states subject to certain limitations, and others are generally disapproved.**

9. Clark v. Beers, 61 Conn. 87, 23 A. 717; In re Cook's Trust Estate, 20 Del.Ch. 123, 171 A. 730 (1934); Buckle v. Marshall, 176 Va. 139, 10 S.E.2d 506 (1940). But see, *contra,* In re Jones' Trusteeship, 202 Minn. 187, 277 N.W. 899 (1938); Home Savings & Loan Co. v. Strain, 130 Ohio St. 53, 196 N.E. 770, 99 A.L.R. 903 (1935).

10. Delafield v. Barret, 270 N.Y. 43, 200 N.E. 67, 103 A.L.R. 941 (1936); 49 Harv.L.R. 821; 49 Yale L.J. 891.

11. It has been held that a court has no power to permit a trustee to invest outside the list of required investments. In re Jones' Trusteeship, 202 Minn. 187, 277 N.W. 899 (1938); In re Smith, 279 N.Y.

479, 18 N.E.2d 666 (1939), *dictum;* Humphries v. Manhattan Sav. Bank & Trust Co., 174 Tenn. 17, 122 S.W.2d 446 (1938).

12. Geldmacher v. New York, 175 Misc. 788, 25 N.Y.S.2d 380 (1940); Humphries v. Manhattan Sav. Bank & Tr. Co., 174 Tenn. 17, 122 S.W.2d 446 (1938).

13. See § 108, post.

14. In re Flynn's Estate, 205 Okl. 311, 237 P.2d 903 (1951).

§ 104

1. Restatement, Trusts, §§ 227–231. And see statutes and cases cited in Bogert, Trusts and Trustees (rev. 2d edit.), §§ 612–666.

Cases unaffected by statute also follow the same general lines with regard to approval or disapproval.

It is, of course, impossible in this work to describe fully the investments sanctioned by the legislatures in the lists which they have approved. They vary considerably from state to state and are subject to many qualifications. But an attempt will be made to give a broad outline of the types of securities on these lists.

It seems probable that investments permitted or directed by the statutory lists will probably qualify as reasonably prudent under the prudent investor rule,[2] and also that the latter rule is broader than the former so that, for example, common and preferred stocks may be purchased even though not on the statutory lists. Where a trustee is permitted to invest in his discretion, investments of the types mentioned in the statutory lists are apt to be approved.

Investments Generally Approved

It is generally recognized that the obligations of the United States, those guaranteed by it, and those of its instrumentalities, are the safest investments for trustees. Hence American statutes and court rules invariably have made them legal trust investments. Examples of obligations of federal agencies made legal by statute are bonds of the Home Owners Loan Corporation and of the Federal Home Loan Banks.

The statutory lists universally permit investment in the obligations of the state in question, and generally of the other states of the union, provided no default has occurred as to principal or interest for a certain period before the investment.

Municipal bonds have been very highly considered. Hence statutes generally permit investment by trustees in the bonds of cities, counties, school districts, and other municipal corporations. In most cases, however, the bonds must meet certain qualifications, intended to insure that there is adequate security, for example, that the total property liable for taxation has a certain valuation, or that the bonded debt does not exceed a certain proportion of the value of the taxable property, or that the municipality has a certain minimum population.

A type of security very highly regarded and always found on statutory investment lists is the first mortgage on a fee simple title to real property, where the debt secured does not exceed a certain proportion of the value of the mortgaged land. The margins required differ somewhat from state to state, and depend somewhat on whether the property is improved or unimproved, but a typical requirement is that the debt secured must not exceed fifty, or in some cases sixty, per cent of the value of the mortgaged land. In England, in the days before the investment statute, equity allowed a loan of two-thirds of the value of agricultural property but only fifty per cent of the value of residential or business property.[3] Land is fairly stable in value, but experience has

---

2. See § 106, post.   3. In re Salmon, 42 Ch.D. 351.

shown that it also fluctuates in value, and therefore security adequate when the loan is made may become inadequate when the loan becomes due, unless a considerable margin is allowed. It is common to require also that a loan on a real property mortgage is not to be made unless there is an independent valuation of the property which shows an adequate margin, unless an appropriate abstract of title or title guaranty policy is obtained, and unless any buildings on the mortgaged property are insured in favor of the mortgagee.

Certain corporate bonds secured by a mortgage to a trustee for the benefit of the bondholders are also commonly placed on the legal lists. The bonds of public utility corporations, such as electric light and power companies and telephone corporations are frequently made legal for trusts, as well as the bonds of industrial corporations, where prescribed qualifications are met.

Obligations of the International Bank for Reconstruction and Development are also frequently validated as trust investments.

Investments Approved to a Limited Extent or Occasionally

Other investments found on some statutory lists, and approved in some cases to a limited extent only, are bonds of the Dominion of Canada, of public housing authorities, and of railroads, equipment trust obligations of railroads secured by a lien on rolling stock, common or preferred stock, insurance policies on the lives of beneficiaries, notes secured by a pledge of high grade securities, interest bearing bank deposits to the extent to which they are covered by deposit insurance, ground rents, the purchase of real property after court approval, participating mortgages and mortgage pools, common trust funds, and investment trust obligations.

Investments Generally Disapproved

It is a general rule that investment of trust funds without proper security is a violation of the trust. The trustee should not lend trust moneys to an individual or a corporation and take in return only the bond or note of the borrower. A trustee making a loan without the security of some property will ordinarily be liable for any losses due to the failure of the debtor to repay,[4] even if he obtained one or more co-makers or endorsers on the note. The sale of trust property and the acceptance in return of unsecured notes of the buyer is seldom allowed by equity, and the trustee will be liable for a loss resulting from the failure of the maker of the notes.[5] A mortgage should be taken. In a

---

4. Cornet v. Cornet, 269 Mo. 298, 190 S.W. 333; Brewster v. Demarest, 48 N.J. Eq. 559, 23 A. 271; Deobold v. Oppermann, 111 N.Y. 531, 19 N.E. 94, 2 L.R.A. 644, 7 Am.St.Rep. 760; Collins v. Gooch, 97 N.C. 186, 1 S.E. 653, 2 Am.St.Rep. 284; Rowe v. Bentley, 29 Grat., Va., 756. In a few cases it has been held that trustees or persons in similar situations might invest upon per-

sonal security in extraordinary cases. Knowlton v. Bradley, 17 N.H. 458, 43 Am. Dec. 609; Scott v. Trustees of Marion Tp., 39 Ohio St. 153; Singleton v. Lowndes, 9 S.C. 465; Barney v. Parsons' Guardian, 54 Vt. 623, 41 Am.Rep. 858.

5. Miller v. Holcombe's Ex'r, 9 Grat., Va., 665.

few instances the taking of certificates of deposit, which amount to nothing more than loans to a bank without security, has been held a proper procedure for a trustee in the investment of the trust funds.[6] Interest-bearing savings bank accounts are often sanctioned by legislation, in view of the insurance of bank accounts (up to a limited amount) by the Federal Deposit Insurance Corporation.

With but few exceptions, the statutes do not sanction the use of trust funds in trade or business by the purchase of the interest of a sole trader or a partner, or the establishment of a new business by the trustee.[7] The hazards of buying and selling, manufacturing, and transporting goods are too great to render such operations proper for trustees. In addition, most trustees are not equipped by experience or time available to personally enter the field of business. The trustee may in breach of trust invest the trust moneys in business in any one of several ways. He may, for example, purchase land and engage in coal mining,[8] or buy a farm and engage in agricultural operations.[9] Neither one of these endeavors would be proper for the trustee to undertake. Or, although not buying directly the property necessary to engage in trade, the trustee may purchase with the trust funds a share in a partnership which is operating a business. Unless authorized by the trust instrument or by statute, this type of instrument is often held a breach of duty on the part of the trustee and renders him liable for losses.[10]

Equities

Perhaps the most common method adopted by trustees for investment of trust funds in business is that of the purchase of stocks of corporations engaged in business. In the early days a majority of the American courts passing upon such an investment condemned it as too hazardous and speculative.[11] In a few states there were constitutional provisions prohibiting statutory grants of power to buy stocks as fiduciary investments.[12] Corporate failures were at that time very common,

6. Hunt v. Appellant, 141 Mass. 515, 6 N.E. 554; St. Paul Trust Co. v. Kittson, 62 Minn. 408, 65 N.W. 74.

7. City of Bangor v. Beal, 85 Me. 129, 26 A. 1112; Windmuller v. Spirits Distributing Co., 83 N.J.Eq. 6, 90 A. 249; Nagle v. Von Rosenberg, 55 Tex.Civ.App. 354, 119 S.W. 706.

8. Butler v. Butler, 164 Ill. 171, 45 N.E. 426.

9. Wieters v. Hart, 68 N.J.Eq. 796, 64 A. 1135.

10. Penn v. Fogler, 182 Ill. 76, 55 N.E. 192; Trull v. Trull, 13 Allen, Mass., 407; In re Bannin, 142 App.Div. 436, 127 N.Y.S. 92.

In a few states a trustee is permitted to participate or hold an interest in a partnership if authorized by the trust instrument. See, for example, Ala. Code §§ 19–3–150 to 19–3–152; Colo.R.S. 15–1–701; Md. Rules of Procedure V77.

11. Tucker v. State, 72 Ind. 242; Kimball v. Reding, 31 N.H. 352, 64 Am.Dec. 333; King v. Talbot, 40 N.Y. 76; Appeal of Worrell, 23 Pa. 44. See, however, Costello v. Costello, 209 N.Y. 252, 103 N.E. 148, in which it was held that the statutory and court rules then in force in New York, while generally denying the trustee the right to invest in stock, did not invariably make such an investment illegal and that the trustees in that case were authorized to accept corporate stock in exchange for an interest in a partnership.

12. See, for example, Ala. Constitution, Art. 4, § 74.

and many enterprises were speculative.

In recent years, due to the lengthy and excellent dividend records of many well-established corporations, there has been an increasing effort to obtain legislative approval of corporate stocks as trust investments and much progress has been made in that direction.[13] The prudent investor rule has opened the door to a great increase in the purchase of shares of stock as trust investments.[14]

The older view regarding stocks was set forth in the opinion of the New York court in King v. Talbot, where the propriety of investments in railroad, canal company, and bank stocks was under consideration. The court said: [15] "It is not denied that the employment of the fund as capital in trade would be a clear departure from the duty of trustees. If it cannot be so employed under the management of a copartnership, I see no reason for saying that the incorporation of the partners tends, in any degree, to justify it. The moment the fund is invested in bank, or insurance, or railroad stock, it has left the control of the trustees; its safety, and the hazard or risk of loss, is no longer dependent upon their skill, care, or discretion, in its custody or management, and the terms of the investment do not contemplate that it will ever be returned to the trustees. If it be said that, at any time, the trustees may sell the stock (which is but another name for their interest in the property and business of the corporation), and so repossess themselves of the original capital, I reply that is necessarily contingent and uncertain; and so the fund has been voluntarily placed in a condition of uncertainty, dependent upon two contingencies: First, the practicability of making the business profitable; and, second, the judgment, skill, and fidelity of those who have the management of it for that purpose."

In those states where the prudent investor rule has been adopted by court decision, the courts have taken the position that investments in corporate stock are not necessarily improper and that their propriety is to be determined by the nature of the stock and the amount of the investment. If the stock is issued by a reputable company, of strong financial position, and the amount invested therein is not an unduly large proportion of the trust funds, the investment will be approved.[16] Thus in Dickinson, Appellant,[17] where a trustee first invested about $3,500 out of a $16,000 fund in stock of the Union Pacific Railroad

---

13. For earlier efforts to secure court approval of an investment in stocks, see Morris Community Chest v. Wilentz, 124 N.J.Eq. 580, 3 A.2d 808 (1939); Reiner v. Fidelity Union Trust Co., 127 N.J.Eq. 377, 13 A.2d 291, 128 A.L.R. 964 (1940). See the state trust investment statutes quoted in chapter 30, Bogert, Trusts and Trustees (rev. 2d edit.)

14. See statistics quoted in § 106, post, as showing the high percentage of common stock investments in personal trust investment portfolios of corporate fiduciaries. These statistics also show that common stocks comprised over 40% of the total assets of all pension fund plans administered by corporate fiduciaries.

15. 40 N.Y. 76, 88, 89 (1869).

16. McCoy v. Horwitz, 62 Md. 183; Appeal of Davis, 183 Mass. 499, 67 N.E. 604; In re Buhl's Estate, 211 Mich. 124, 178 N.W. 651 (preferred stock); Smyth v. Burns' Adm'rs, 25 Miss. 422; Peckham v. Newton, 15 R.I. 321, 4 A. 758; Scoville v. Brock, 81 Vt. 405, 70 A. 1014.

17. 152 Mass. 184, 25 N.E. 99, 9 L.R.A. 279.

Company, and then about three months later purchased about $2,500 more of the same stock, the court held that the first investment was to be approved but the second was a breach of trust on the ground that it was imprudent to place so much of the fund in a new venture. The court said: . . . "trustees in this Commonwealth are permitted to invest portions of trust funds in dividend paying stocks and interest bearing bonds of private business corporations, when the corporations have acquired by reason of the amount of their property, and the prudent management of their affairs, such a reputation that cautious and intelligent persons commonly invest their own money in such stocks and bonds as permanent investments." [18]

In many situations it is imprudent for the trustee to invest trust funds in real estate.[19] Real property may be productive or unproductive, dependent on many circumstances. Farm land will be productive, if the weather is good, the rainfall proper, and the farmer industrious and skillful. Business and residential property will be productive if the buildings are kept in good repair and are rentable, are not destroyed by fire, the trustee is diligent and skillful in the management of the property, and the neighborhood does not deteriorate. But often there are too many contingencies regarding the productivity of real property to make it a safe investment for a trustee. The ordinary trustee is not qualified to manage real estate. In addition real property is often difficult to sell. The trustee may find great trouble in converting the investment into cash when he is required to distribute the trust funds. Nor, unless authorized, should a trustee invest trust funds in a leasehold estate in real property.[20]

In some instances, however, courts have sanctioned a trust investment in real estate even though such property was outside the state in which the trust was to be administered, and some statutes recognize such a purchase as proper if prudent under the circumstances or if approved by the court on a showing of special reasons.[21] If unusual conditions render desirable an investment in land, the court may grant permission to use trust funds for such purpose,[22] or the trustee in rare cases may apply the trust funds without express court approval in advance.[23]

See also St. Louis Union Trust Co. v. Toberman, 235 Mo.App. 559, 140 S.W.2d 68 (1940).

18. 152 Mass. 184, 187, 188, 25 N.E. 99, 9 L.R.A. 279.

19. Bowman v. Pinkham, 71 Me. 295; West v. Robertson, 67 Miss. 213, 7 So. 224; Williams v. Williams, 35 N.J.Eq. 100; Baker v. Disbrow, 18 Hun, N.Y., 29; Morton's Ex'rs v. Adams, 1 Strob.Eq., S.C., 72; Stone v. Kahle, 22 Tex.Civ.App. 185, 54 S.W. 375.

20. In re Anderson, 211 N.Y. 136, 105 N.E. 79.

21. Merchants' Loan & Tr. Co. v. Northern Trust Co., 250 Ill. 86, 95 N.E. 59, 45 L.R.A.,N.S., 411; Thayer v. Dewey, 185 Mass. 68, 69 N.E. 1074.

Modern statutes authorize investments in real estate or interests therein. See § 106, post.

22. In re Bellah, 8 Del.Ch. 59, 67 A. 973; Ridley v. Dedman, 134 Ky. 146, 119 S.W. 756.

23. Bethea v. McColl, 5 Ala. 308; Troy Iron & Nail Factory v. Corning, 45 Barb., N.Y., 231.

It is obvious that the perishable and temporary character of chattels make them an investment highly unsuited to trusts. Thus, unless specifically authorized, it would be a clear violation of his common law duty, and his duty under all statutes, for a trustee to buy a herd of cattle or an elevator full of grain as a trust investment.

While loans secured by second mortgages on land are sometimes allowed, they are generally disapproved by courts of equity and by statutes.[24] The trustee should not place the trust funds in a position where they may be endangered by the foreclosure of a prior lien. If he holds a junior mortgage, he may be obliged to pay off the senior encumbrance in order to protect his investment. Such action might involve the investment of too great a proportion of the trust funds in one piece or type of property. In rare cases equity will sanction an investment secured by a second mortgage, but only when the security is adequate and unusual circumstances justify the trustee in taking this form of investment.[25]

Few decisions or statutes [26] approve an investment of the trust fund in a loan secured by a chattel mortgage or pledge or by a mortgage of a leasehold or life interest in realty.[27] The subject matter of the security is too temporary and evanescent in character.

 WESTLAW REFERENCES

Investments Generally Approved
legal   /2   list   /s   trust
trustee   /s   invest****   /s   obligations   /3   "united states"
trustee   /s   invest***   /s   obligations   /3   state
trustee   /s   invest****   /s   "municipal bonds"
trustee   /s   invest****   /s   "first mortgage"

Investments Approved to a Limited Extent or Occasionally
trustee   /s   invest****   /s   "dominion of canada"
trustee   /s   invest****   /s   railroad

Investments Generally Disapproved
knowlton   +3   bradley

Equities
king   +3   talbot

---

24. New Haven Trust Co. v. Doherty, 75 Conn. 555, 54 A. 209, 96 Am.St.Rep. 239; Gilbert v. Kolb, 85 Md. 627, 37 A. 423; Gilmore v. Tuttle, 32 N.J.Eq. 611; King v. Mackellar, 109 N.Y. 215, 16 N.E. 201.

25. Taft v. Smith, 186 Mass. 31, 70 N.E. 1031; Sherman v. Lanier, 39 N.J.Eq. 249; In re Bartol's Estate, 182 Pa. 407, 38 A. 527.

26. Some investment statutes approve of trust investments in mortgages on long term leaseholds, equipment trust obligations where the security is rolling stock of a railroad, or pledges of securities which themselves are legal for trust investment. See Bogert, Trusts and Trustees (rev. 2d edit.), §§ 616–666, for statutes in effect in most states and the District of Columbia.

27. Sherman v. Lanier, 39 N.J.Eq. 249.

MINGLING INVESTMENTS—PARTICIPATING MORTGAGES, COMMON TRUST FUNDS, AND INVESTMENT TRUSTS [1]

§ 105. At common law there was objection to the mixture of the funds of two or more trusts, or of trust and non-trust property, in a single investment or a group of investments, because such action violated the rules about segregation and earmarking of trust property and also involved conflicting interests and disloyalty.

However, in recent years the great advantages by way of diversification and ease of investment have induced the courts and legislatures to permit the mingling of two or more trust funds, or of trust funds and non-trust funds, in a single investment or group of investments. Examples are found in the participating mortgage or mortgage pool, the common trust fund and the mutual fund or investment trust.

Participating Mortgages

In recent times it has become customary for banks and trust companies to purchase a large mortgage and allot interests in it to various of its trusts which have funds for investment. The bank may originally advance its own funds and later reimburse itself for the price out of accumulated balances in its trusts, or it may make the original loan with combined trust funds. The mortgage and notes or bonds are made out to the bank and certificates of interest in the mortgage are executed by the bank and placed in the investment portfolios of the various contributing trusts; the books of the bank show at all times the exact status as to equitable ownerships of the mortgage.

These participating or contributory mortgages run counter to the strict rules of equity with regard to the segregation of the investments of each trust and their distinct earmarking.[2] There is also a possibility of a conflict of interest between the trusts which are involved, as to enforcement, extensions, renewals, reduction of interest, and similar matters, although generally an action good for one trust will be advantageous to the others.

The convenience of the participating mortgage is, however, very great. It furnishes a quick means of investing funds of all sizes, since the shares can be issued in small denominations. The securing of single mortgages tailored to fit the needs of each of many trusts is difficult. Banks, insurance companies, and savings and loan associations have been able to obtain most of the small mortgages. The corporate structure of modern business increases the number of large mortgages which cannot be financed by any single trust. The certifi-

---

§ 105

1. Restatement, Trusts, Second, § 227.

And see Bogert, Trusts and Trustees (rev. 2d edit.), §§ 675, 677, and 616–666.

2. Moore v. McKenzie, 112 Me. 356, 92 A. 296; Jones v. Harsha, 233 Mich. 499, 206 N.W. 979 (1926); Heaton v. Bartlett, 87 N.H. 357, 180 A. 244 (1935).

cates can be sold from trust to trust to meet the exigencies of the operation of each.

Although there was opposition to this form of trust investment in the beginning, and much contention between the advocates of strict trust law and the proponents of quick and convenient administration, the latter position won out in the courts,[3] and this result has been ratified in many states by statutes validating participating mortgages, provided certain prescribed conditions were met.[4]

These mortgages differ but little from the ordinary corporate bond issue, where a single mortgage is made to a trustee for bondholders, and the bonds are sold to the public while the security rests in a representative. The purchase of such bonds of well selected obligors has been generally approved for trusts and the mixture of trust investments with other funds has not been found objectionable. A trust having a bond of such an issue in effect also buys a share in the mortgage security, although it is not represented by any certificate of participation.

Mortgage Pools

In some states the participating mortgage concept has been carried further; a group of mortgages has been collected, interests in which have been sold to trusts exclusively, the whole set of mortgages being sometimes called a "pool". Here the arguments presented above, pro and con, apply, except that there is even greater diversification than in the case of the single mortgage. In Pennsylvania these pools have been highly regarded and are made the subject of special sanction and regulation.[5] It would seem that the arguments in favor of a participating mortgage also support the mortgage pool. Many common trust funds include mortgages, or are confined to that type of investment, and the common trust fund statutes would seem to support the mortgage pool.

The great practical advantages in mortgages participations and in pools of mortgages are distribution of risk and ease of investment. If a trust should have a small interest in many mortgages, instead of a large interest in one mortgage, the failure of one property or changes in the character of one neighborhood would not be extremely prejudicial to the trust. Small single mortgages are not easy to get. Interests in mortgages in denominations of $100 and $1,000 are very convenient for the investment of small balances or of the funds of small trusts.

3. First Nat. Bank of Birmingham v. Basham, 238 Ala. 500, 191 So. 873, 125 A.L.R. 656 (1939); In re Lalla's Estate, 362 Ill. 621, 1 N.E.2d 50 (1936); Springfield Safe Deposit & Tr. Co. v. First Unitarian Society, 293 Mass. 480, 200 N.E. 541 (1936); In re Union Tr. Co., 219 N.Y. 514, 114 N.E. 1057.

4. Gates v. Plainfield Tr. Co., 121 N.J. Eq. 460, 191 A. 304 (1937), affirmed 122 N.J.Eq. 366, 194 A. 65 (1937). And see 45 Yale L.J. 857. See state statutes quoted or cited in Bogert, Trusts and Trustees (rev. 2d edit.), §§ 616–666.

5. In re Rambo's Estate, 327 Pa. 258, 193 A. 1 (1937); In re Phillippi, 329 Pa. 581, 198 A. 16. And see Tannenbaum v. Seacoast Tr. Co., 125 N.J.Eq. 360, 5 A.2d 778 (1939).

Common Trust Funds

A third important development of more recent times has been the common trust fund. It is merely an extension of the idea of group investment illustrated by the participating mortgage and the mortgage pool. The bank or trust company purchases with the mingled funds of many of its trusts a large number of investments which are legal for all the participating trusts, consisting of bonds, stocks, or mortgages, and allots interests in the fund to the contributing trusts in proportion to the size of their payments. The denomination of shares is made small, so that trusts with small balances for investment can enter, and thus the bank can accept smaller trusts which it would otherwise find too burdensome for administration. Some corporate fiduciaries have two or more common trust funds, including in some instances one for investments by trustees where the trustee has been given discretion as to investments.

In recent years these common trust funds have received universal approval by statute [6] and many corporate trustees have made use of them. Some of the statutes or state banking department regulations prescribe detailed rules for the establishment and administration of the funds,[7] while other laws are mere enabling acts such as the Uniform Common Trust Fund Act [8] which permit the setting up of such funds and leave the methods of operation almost entirely to control by the regulations of the U.S. Comptroller of Currency, which must necessarily be followed.

This common trust fund met an obstacle in its early days in the shape of a decision that it was an "association" for federal income tax purposes and so subject to the corporate income tax.[9] To overcome this difficulty, which would have made it impractical to use the common trust fund because of the high income tax liabilities involved, the banks negotiated with the Treasury Department and secured passage of an Act of Congress to the effect that such common trust funds should not be treated as associations for income tax purposes if operated in accordance with rules to be laid down by the Federal Reserve Board, now by the U.S. Comptroller of the Currency. Extensive regulations have been issued by the Comptroller [10] and common trust funds which are maintained in harmony with them are not taxable as associations.

6. See, for example, Wis.S.A. 223.055. And see Bogert, Trusts and Trustees (rev. 2d edit.), § 677.

At the end of 1965 it was reported that there were 1,016 common trust funds with assets in excess of $7.5 billion. At the end of 1984 it was reported that there were 4,688 such funds administered by 877 banks and trust companies with assets of about 176 billion.

7. See Bogert, Trusts and Trustees (rev. 2d edit.), §§ 677, 616–666, including regulations issued in New York and North Carolina.

8. For the text and adoptions of this Act, see Bogert, Trusts and Trustees (rev. 2d edit.), § 677. See also 5 Law & Contemporary Problems 430, 439, 453.

9. Brooklyn Trust Co. v. Commissioner of Internal Revenue, 80 F.2d 865 (2d Cir. 1936).

10. Regulation 9, reprinted in Bogert, Trusts and Trustees (rev. 2d edit.), § 134. In 1962, Congress transferred authority over such matters from the Federal Reserve Board to the U.S. Comptroller of the Currency.

Instead the various participating trusts, or the beneficiaries thereof, are subject to the appropriate non-corporate income tax.

These common trust funds are being more widely used, especially by the larger banks and trust companies. They are operated under written plans, open for inspection at the office of the trustee, which, of course must be in accord with the federal regulations and with any relevant state law, and which give in great detail the rules about investments legal for the fund, entrances into and departures from it, valuations of the fund at regular intervals, etc. The institution receives no extra compensation for operating the common trust fund, its remuneration being received entirely as trustee of the various participating trusts.

In a few states [11] the common trust fund plan has been extended by statutes to permit the establishment of a mutual trust investment company, to hold a variety of securities, interests in which can be purchased for their trusts by banks and trust companies. Thus there is opportunity for a corporate trustee that does not wish to establish its own common trust fund, or is unable to do so, to obtain the advantages of such a fund for its trusts.

Investment Trusts

The so-called investment trusts, or investment companies, or mutual funds, have acquired a very important role in the investment world.[12] They are organizations, either in the form of corporations or of trusts, which buy with their own funds a variety of securities and offer interests in the combined investments to the public. Some make a charge for admission to the fund beyond the value of the share in the fund, and others deduct management fees from the distributions made to shareholders. The operators of the fund make sales and purchases, collect income, and distribute to the shareholders at frequent intervals their proportions of the net income and capital gains.

Investment by a trustee in one of these mutual funds is open to the same objections noted above with regard to participating mortgages and mortgage pools and other instances, namely, mingling the funds of one trust with those of another or with non-trust funds. In addition it may be argued that the purchase of an interest in an investment trust by a trustee involves a delegation by him to the managers of the investment trust of some of the powers of the investing trustee, in that he is required to use reasonable care in following the investment law with respect to his trust, but that buying shares in an investment trust

While the regulation technically applies to national banks only, as a practical matter state institutions must comply with it in order to avoid prohibitive income tax liabilities.

11. See, for example the statutes of Connecticut and New York, quoted in Bogert, Trusts and Trustees (rev. 2d edit.), §§ 622 and 648.

12. For a more detailed description of the operation of the investment trust, see Bogert, Trusts and Trustees (rev. 2d edit.), §§ 248, 249. A report of the Investment Company Institute showed that at the end of 1985, 1,531 mutual funds or investments trusts in the United States had assets of about $495.5 billion and about 35 million shareholder accounts.

leaves to the operators of that trust the discretion as to what security and income the beneficiaries of the investing trust will obtain.[13] Furthermore, the managers of the investment trust are paid in one way or another for their work, and if the trustee of the trust who buys shares in the investment trust is also paid a commission there is at least a possibility of unnecessarily high expense. Also, if, as is sometimes required, capital gains distributions by these mutual funds are to be allocated to the principal of the trust receiving them, there would seem to be a case of a violation of the duty of impartiality by the trustee who invests in the fund, since he is taking a sub-normal income for the purpose of securing additions to the principal of the trust, instead of getting normal income and mere maintenance of capital value.[14]

Notwithstanding these objections, in many states shares in investment trusts have been mentioned as valid trust investments.[15] It can be argued that they are a logical development of approval of trust fund mingling, such as participating mortgages, mortgage pools, and common trust funds. Since individual trustees do not have a chance to establish a common trust fund, they may resort to the investment trust in order to secure the advantages of diversification and ease of investment.

Although originally investment trusts held securities only, there has been a new development: creating a fund of real estate, held in fee or on leasehold, and selling interests in it. This plan has received statutory sanction and been given favorable income tax treatment though subject to federal regulations.[16] It is called a real estate investment trust.

 WESTLAW REFERENCES

Participating Mortgages

find 206 nw 979

"participating mortgage" /s trust

Mortgage Pools

"mortgage pools" /s trust

tannenbaum +3 seacoast

Common Trust Funds

"common trust fund"

find 80 f2d 865

13. Marshall v. Frazier, 159 Or. 491, 80 P.2d 42 (1938). But see, *contra*, In re Rees' Estate, 85 N.E.2d 563 (Ohio App. 1949).

14. Statistics published by the Investment Company Institute for 1985 showed that distributions from 1,071 equity, bond and income funds with 251.7 billion in assets were as follows: 12,864.2 billion in net investment income and 5,017.7 billion in net realized capital gains.

15. See statutes quoted in Bogert, Trusts and Trustees (rev. 2d edit.), §§ 616–666.

16. See Bogert, Trusts and Trustees (rev. 2d edit.), § 248. And see §§ 851 et seq., I.R.C., for federal income tax treatment.

THE PRUDENT INVESTOR RULE [1]

§ 106. In those states where there is no statutory list of permitted or required investments for trustees they are expected to use the care and skill of a reasonably prudent investor in retaining, buying, and selling trust investments. In most states this standard has been adopted in statutory form.

In applying this guide the trustee should maintain an equitable balance between the income beneficiaries and those who are ultimately to obtain the principal. The trustee should seek to obtain a steady flow of income consistent with reasonable assurance of safety of the capital fund invested.

In determining whether a trustee used the care and ability of a prudent investor, the courts will consider many factors, for example, the extent of the investigation made by the trustee before investing, ratings and the opinions of experts, the adaptability of the investment to the needs of the particular trust, diversification, protection against inflation, and the tax effects on the beneficiaries.

In some states which have not had a legislative declaration or court rule as to investments required of or permitted to trustees, the use of reasonable prudence, skill, and ability is the guide for the trustee. In Massachusetts, where this standard has long been applied, the court has stated its attitude as follows: "It has long been the rule in this commonwealth that in making investments, as well as in the general management of the trust, a trustee is held only to good faith and sound discretion, and hence that he cannot be held for the consequences of an error in judgment, unless the error is such as to show either that he acted in bad faith or failed to exercise sound discretion." [2]

Due largely to the efforts of banks and trust companies, there has been a strong trend since 1940 to abandon the statutory lists of investments and to require merely that the trustee use ordinary skill and diligence in retaining, buying, and selling trust investments. While the legal lists might have helped trustees in selecting investments and worked in the direction of certainty as to investment duties, it has been felt that it is very difficult to make up lists which will be fair and inclusive, that unless they are constantly reviewed and amended they lack needed flexibility, that corporate stocks and other investments can be added to the trust portfolios more easily under the prudent investor rule than by going to the legislatures, and that such additions are in line with current investment practices. Many of these prudent investor statutes permit a trustee to purchase for his trust any investment "which men of prudence, discretion and intelligence" would

§ 106
1. Restatement, Trusts, §§ 227, 228.

2. Taft v. Smith, 186 Mass. 31, 32, 70 N.E. 1031.

buy "in the management of their own affairs, not in regard to speculation, but in regard to the permanent disposition of their funds, considering the probable income, as well as the probable safety of their capital".[3] Since 1940 a prudent investor type of statute has been adopted in the vast majority of the states.[4]

In several states the prudent investor rule has been adopted to a limited extent and permits a trustee to use his discretion as to a certain percentage of his investments, but requires him to follow a statutory list as to the remainder of his purchases.[5]

In some states adopting the Uniform Probate Code (UPC) there is no trust investment statute as such; the general standard of care and performance applicable to trustees is the only investment guide.[6] In several other states both the UPC and a form of the prudent investor rule have been adopted.[7] In several other states a combination of a legal list of authorized investments and a prudent investor rule has been enacted by statute.[8]

There has also been a statutory tendency to permit a trustee to invest in additional categories of assets, such as mutual funds, real estate interests and businesses.[9]

The trust investment statutes differ as to whether the trustee, in considering and making trust investments, is to act as he would in managing his own affairs [10] or, possibly requiring a higher standard of

---

3. See, for example, Nev.R.S. 164.050.

4. This rule seems to be in force, either by statute or court decision, in Ark., Cal., Colo., Conn., Del., Fla., Ga., Haw., Idaho, Ill., Ind., Ia., Kan., La. (after 1962), Md., Mass. (judicial decision), Mich., Minn., Miss., Mo. (with permissive statutory list), Neb., Nev., N.J., N.Y., N.C., N.D. (corporate trustees) Okl., Or., Pa., R.I., S.C., S.D., Tenn., Tex., Utah, Vt., Va., Wash., Wis., Wyo.

See also Ky., Md., Nev., where the rule is modified or limited by a permissive statutory list.

In other states the trustee must select all or a part of the trust investments from a statutory list with the care of a prudent man. See Ala., Ky., N.D. (individual trustees only), W.Va.

See state statutes and cases set forth in Bogert, Trusts and Trustees (rev. 2d edit.), ch. 30.

5. N.H. (50%) and Ohio (60%). And see Wis.S.A. 881.01(2) (investments in common stocks limited to 50% of trust fund). For details of all state investment statutes, see Bogert, Trusts and Trustees (rev. 2d edit.), §§ 616–666.

6. Unif.Prob.Code § 7–302 provides that, except as provided by the terms of the trust, "the trustee shall observe the standards in dealing with the trust assets that would be observed by a prudent man dealing with the property of another." This language has been adopted by statute in Alaska, Arizona, Florida, Maine, Michigan, Nebraska, New Mexico, North Dakota (individual trustees), South Dakota and Utah.

7. See West's Fla.S.A. §§ 518.11, 737.302 (UPC); Mich.C.L.A. §§ 555.201, 700.813 (UPC); N.Dak.Cent.Code 6–05–15 (prudent investor rule; trust companies), 30.1–34–02 (UPC).

8. See, for example, Va.Code 1950, §§ 26.40, 26.40.1 and 26.45(1)(a) (prudent investor standard), and the trust investment statutes for Georgia, New Jersey and Ohio (limited prudent man rule).

9. As to investments in businesses, limited to a small portion of the portfolio, see Minn.Stat.Ann. § 501.66, subd. 6a ("growth enterprises"); West's RC Wash A 11.100.023.

10. Florida, Georgia, Minnesota, Nevada, New York, North Dakota, Virginia, Washington.

care, in managing the affairs of others.[11] Increasingly statutes require a trustee having special skills to exercise those skills.[12]

Perhaps in recognition of recent criticisms that the prudent investor rule gives little guidance or protection to trustees in making trust investments, and fails to allow for contemporary categories of investments and investment techniques, several states have recently adopted quite different versions of the prudent investor rule. Thus under the Minnesota enactment,[13] a trustee, "in determining the prudence of a particular investment, shall consider the role that the proposed investment or investment course of action plays within the overall portfolio of assets," and in "applying the total asset management approach, a trustee shall exercise the judgment and care under the circumstances then prevailing, which persons of prudence, discretion, and intelligence exercise in the management of their own affairs, not in regard to speculation but in regard to the permanent disposition of their funds." And so, in California,[14] the recent trust investment statute provides that a trustee is to act with "the care, skill, prudence and diligence under the circumstances then prevailing" and may consider general economic conditions as well as the anticipated needs of the trust and its beneficiaries. In Washington[15] the "total asset management approach" has also been adopted, and the trustee is to consider the effect the proposed investment would have on the "overall portfolio of assets."

In performing his investment duties a trustee should consider the purposes of the trust, which are normally the production of a constant flow of income consistent with maintenance of the safety of the principal of the fund, and the preservation of the principal of the trust.[16] He has no duty to make investments for the purpose of increasing the value of the trust assets. He is not permitted to speculate with the trust principal.[17]

The trustee should also take into account his obligation to act impartially between income and remainder beneficiaries,[18] and not to make an investment which will favor one at the expense of the other. Thus it might be held to be a breach of duty to place the whole trust fund in low yield government securities in order to secure for the remaindermen the maximum of safety, since the income beneficiaries would obtain a yield much less than could be obtained from other legal

---

11. Unif.Prob.Code § 7–302. See, for example, Mich.C.L.A. §§ 555.201, 700.813; N.J.S.A. 3B:20–13; N.Mex.Stats. 1978 45–7–302; N.Car.G.S. § 36A–2.

12. UPC § 7–302. And see, for example, N.J.S.A. 3B:20–13; N.Y.—McKinney's EPTL 11–2.2(a)(1) (fiduciary having "special investment skills"); N.Car.G.S. § 36A–2; Wash.—West's RC Wash A 11.100.020.

13. Minn.L.1986, ch. 442, enacting Minn.S.A. § 501.125, subd. 1.

14. West's Ann.Cal.Civ.Code § 2261.

15. West's RC Wash A 11.100.020.

16. Kimball v. Whitney, 233 Mass. 321, 123 N.E. 665; In re Buhl's Estate, 211 Mich. 124, 178 N.W. 651, 12 A.L.R. 569.

17. English v. McIntyre, 29 App.Div. 439, 51 N.Y.S. 697 (buying stock on margin); Davis v. Davis Tr. Co., 106 W.Va. 228, 145 S.E. 588 (1928).

18. Restatement Trusts, Second, § 183.

investments which would have adequate security.[19] And the making of an investment which had a slightly speculative character in order to acquire for the income beneficiary a higher than normal yield might well be subject to criticism by the remaindermen.

In deciding whether a trustee has used the reasonable skill and prudence required when he is governed by a statutory list or by the prudent investor rule, or when exercising discretionary powers, the courts consider many factors, dependent on the nature of the investment made, the needs of the particular trust, the trust investments already acquired, the investment market at the time, and the current practices of the ordinarily prudent investment public.

Diversification or spread of risk is desirable and, impliedly, seems to be required by legal list type statutes.[20] It would seem to be common prudence to place the trust funds in several types of investments and with several obligors, instead of concentrating the trust property in one security or enterprise. In some cases, where the investment in which too great concentration occurred had failed, the trustee who held liable for the loss on that portion of the investment which was excessive.[21] Other courts have voiced the view that lack of diversification alone is not a breach of trust.[22] If a beneficiary objects, he may be able to get a court order for greater diversification.[23]

If the trust is likely to need cash in the near future for expenses or distributions, the ready saleability of the trust property is a factor to be considered.[24] Seasoned issues will naturally be preferred to securities of new enterprises.[25] Stocks of a mining or other natural resource corporation may be undesirable because the corporation is "wasting", where no depreciation fund is set aside to take the place of minerals or resources being extracted.[26]

In the case of the loan of trust funds on a mortgage, reasonable prudence [27] will dictate consideration of the financial situation of the

19. Matter of Dwight's Trust, 204 Misc. 204, 128 N.Y.S.2d 23 (1952) (tax advantages to income beneficiaries at expense of remaindermen).

20. In re Dreier's Estate, 204 Wis. 221, 235 N.W. 439 (1931). See § 103, ante, and the statutes quoted in Bogert, Trusts and Trustees (rev. 2d edit.), §§ 616–666.

21. Appeal of Dickinson, 152 Mass. 184, 25 N.E. 99, 9 L.R.A. 279; In re Ward's Estate, 121 N.J.Eq. 555, 192 A. 68; Pennsylvania Co. for Ins. on Lives & Granting Annuities v. Gillmore, 142 N.J.Eq. 27, 59 A.2d 24 (1948) (breach so far as more than 25% of fund invested in real property mortgages in or near Philadelphia); Knox County v. Fourth & First Nat. Bank, 181 Tenn. 569, 182 S.W.2d 980 (1944).

22. Matter of Gottschalk's Estate, 167 Misc. 397, 4 N.Y.S.2d 13 (1938); In re First Nat. Bank of City of New York, Sup., 25

N.Y.S.2d 221 (1941); In re Romberger's Estate, 39 Pa.D. & C. 604; In re Saeger's Estate, 340 Pa. 73, 16 A.2d 19, 131 A.L.R. 1152 (1940). See 48 Harv.L.R. 347.

23. Mandel v. Cemetery Board, 185 Cal.App.2d 583, 8 Cal.Rptr. 342 (1960).

24. In re Lewis' Estate, 349 Pa. 455, 37 A.2d 559 (1944).

25. Aydelott v. Breeding, 111 Ky. 847, 64 S.W. 916.

26. Creed v. McAleer, 275 Mass. 353, 175 N.E. 761 (1931).

27. Where the statutory list exists the statute usually sets forth requirements in lending trust money on a mortgage. See §§ 103–104, ante, and Bogert, Trusts and Trustees (rev. 2d edit.), §§ 616–666, 674. See Liberty Title & Tr. Co. v. Plews, 6 N.J. 28, 77 A.2d 219 (1950) (no appraisal or examination of status of mortgagor); Fin-

mortgagor, the value of the property as determined by an independent appraisal, an abstract of title or title guaranty policy showing good title, the appearance of the property and its neighborhood as determined by an on-the-ground inspection, whether the property is income-producing and is special or general use property, whether the mortgage debt is in default or taxes unpaid, whether adequate insurance on buildings is provided, and whether the mortgage debt is due in a lump or is to be amortized over a period of years.[28] Some legal list statutes limited investments in mortgages to mortgages on land within the state or adjoining states, but in most statutes there is no such restriction.[29]

The investing trustee should consider the income tax effects on the beneficiaries in selecting an investment.[30]

The ordinarily skillful investor who is purchasing stocks or bonds will consider financial publications, corporate reports and balance sheets, and will consult investment experts.[31] If he is an individual trustee, he may be justified in employing an investment counsellor, but in the case of a corporate trustee it would not appear that this expense would be justified.[32]

The investing trustee should seek to secure the income yield which is normal for the types of property in which he is allowed to invest at the time of the investment.[33]

It would seem that the trustee may properly consider the possibilities of inflation and the consequent shrinkage in the purchasing power of the trust principal, and therefore may be led to buy stocks for the trust.[34]

ley v. Exchange Trust Co., 183 Okl. 167, 80 P.2d 296 (1938) (mortgagor dead); Driver v. Blakeley, 165 Or. 312, 107 P.2d 524 (1940) (mortgagee from whom trustee bought transferred his interest without recourse); In re Heyl's Estate, 331 Pa. 202, 200 A. 617 (1938) (unproductivity of mortgaged property not conclusive).

28. See treatment in Bogert, Trusts and Trustees (rev. 2d edit.), § 674.

29. As disapproving mortgages on land in other states, see McCullough's Ex'rs v. McCullough, 44 N.J.Eq. 313, 14 A. 642; Ormiston v. Olcott, 84 N.Y. 339; Collins v. Gooch, 97 N.C. 186, 1 S.E. 653, 2 Am.St. Rep. 284; Pabst v. Goodrich, 133 Wis. 43, 113 N.W. 398, 14 Ann.Cas. 824.

But the court sometimes makes an exception and approves a mortgage on foreign realty. Thayer v. Dewey, 185 Mass. 68, 70, 69 N.E. 1074.

30. Commercial Trust Co. of New Jersey v. Barnard, 27 N.J. 332, 142 A.2d 865 (1958).

31. Learoyd v. Whiteley, 12 A.C. 727; Matter of Clark's Will, 257 N.Y. 132, 177

N.E. 397, 77 A.L.R. 499 (1931); Miller v. Proctor, 20 Ohio St. 442.

Evidence as to the purchases of investors of a similar type is relevant, for example, insurance companies and universities. Chemical Bank & Tr. Co. v. Reynaud, 150 Misc. 821, 270 N.Y.S. 301 (1933), affirmed 239 App.Div. 904, 265 N.Y.S. 944 (1933).

Several recent statutes provide that the trustee will not be liable for investment losses by reason of acting, where authorized by the trust instrument, upon investment advice of an advisor or co-trustee or the settlor himself. See, for example, Colo. Rev.Stat. 15–1–307; 60 Okl.Stat.Ann. § 175.19. See Bogert, Trusts and Trustees (rev. 2d edit.), §§ 555, 701.

32. See Bogert, Trusts and Trustees (rev. 2d edit.), §§ 556, 612, 701.

33. Appeal of Graver, 50 Pa. 189; In re Whitecar's Estate, 147 Pa. 368, 23 A. 575.

34. See Lacovara, Effect of Inflation on Estate Planning, 98 Tr. & Est. 28. In a Minnesota case the court approved the purchase of stocks because of threatened

Recent statistics (1984) show that approximately 276 billion dollars worth of personal trust investments held by corporate fiduciaries with investment discretion were distributed as follows: common stocks, 48.7%; U.S. obligations, 12%; state and municipal obligations, 12.3%; other notes and bonds, 4.4%; cash and equivalents, 9.6%; balance consisting of mortgages, real estate, preferred stocks, etc.[35]

 WESTLAW REFERENCES

di(trustee /6 "sound discretion" "good faith")

"prudent investor statute"

390k217(3) /p "prudent investment statute"

prudent +2 man investor +2 standard rule

219k31 /p "prudent investor standard"

prudent /2 investor /9 diversif!

390k217.3(6) /p "prudent investor"

find 105 nw2d 900

DUTY TO EXAMINE AND REVIEW TRUST INVESTMENTS [1]

§ 107. On taking office a trustee has a duty to examine the investments delivered to him as the original trust assets and to decide whether they are proper for retention under the terms of the trust instrument and the applicable statute or common law. He cannot assume that the investments are legal.

During the course of his administration the trustee has a duty to review and reexamine the investments of his trust at reasonable intervals in order to determine whether they are proper for retention or should be sold.

When a trustee first receives the trust property from the settlor, the settlor's executor, a predecessor trustee, or another, he has a duty to examine it with reasonable care in the light of the investment provisions of the trust instrument, any relevant statute law, and prudent investment policy, in order to determine whether the property offered is that which he is entitled to receive and whether it is legal for retention by him. He cannot assume that what he is tendered is all that he is entitled to obtain, or that because the settlor purchased the property he desires it to be retained as trust property or considers it proper for trust holding, nor can he indulge in the presumption that a predecessor trustee has done his duty and purchased and retained

loss of purchasing power. In re Trusteeship of Mayo, 259 Minn. 291, 105 N.W.2d 900 (1960). But in Stanton v. Wells Fargo Bank & Union Tr. Co., 150 Cal.App.2d 763, 310 P.2d 1010 (1957), the court denied permission to deviate from the settlor's investment directions, notwithstanding the purchasing power argument.

35. 1984 figures reported by Federal Deposit Insurance Corporation.

§ 107

1. Restatement, Trusts, Second, §§ 230–231. Bogert, Trusts and Trustees (rev. 2d edit.), § 684.

nothing but proper trust investments.[2]

If a trustee makes a lawful investment for his trust, or receives such an investment from the settlor or a predecessor trustee, he cannot assume that it will continue indefinitely to be a proper investment. He cannot place the investment in his safety deposit box and ignore its status henceforth. He has a duty to examine all his trust investments at reasonable intervals, for example, in order to learn the condition of the obligor on bonds and mortgages, the condition of the property in which he holds a security interest, the status of the corporations whose stock he holds, and other facts bearing upon the legality of the investment for his trust.[3] He should look for defaults in payments of principal and interest, financial difficulties experienced by obligors, changes in the condition of real property, and similar matters. He should collect all relevant information through an examination of the property himself, reviewing corporate statements and reports, and reading financial services which give information regarding the business and finances of corporations.

The prudent investor statutes relieve the trustee from liability if he uses reasonable prudence in deciding to retain an investment.[4] This presupposes a duty to make a survey and inspection of the investments from time to time.

The trustee is charged with knowledge of what he could have learned by proper review and re-examination, and is liable for damages if he should have known of danger to the trust, could have protected the trust, but did not do so.[5] Thus where a corporate trustee in 1902 took over from a predecessor a mortgage on realty, knowing that the value of the mortgaged property was declining and difficulties in collection were experienced, foreclosed the mortgage in 1913, bought the property in on the foreclosure sale, and held it until several years later when it was sold at a loss, the trustee was held liable because of its duty to keep in touch with the facts regarding the mortgage and the property, the evidence that it knew or should have known of the undesirability of the mortgage as a trust investment, and the failure to take prompt action to foreclose.[6]

An individual trustee will do well to review the practice of corporate trustees and to conduct regular semi-annual or annual reviews when the trust investments are given a thorough examination.[7]

2. McClure v. Middletown Trust Co., 95 Conn. 148, 110 A. 838 (1920); Villard v. Villard, 219 N.Y. 482, 114 N.E. 789.

3. Re Stark's Estate, 15 N.Y.S. 729; Matter of Clark's Will, 257 N.Y. 132, 177 N.E. 397, 77 A.L.R. 499 (1931).

Even though the settlor permitted retention of an investment, it is the duty of the trustee to monitor it, and if he finds it unsatisfactory to apply to the court for permission to deviate from the settlor's permission. Johns v. Herbert, 2 App.D.C. 485.

4. See § 108, post, at nn. 18–20.

5. Tannenbaum v. Seacoast Trust Co., 125 N.J.Eq. 360, 5 A.2d 778 (Err. & App. 1939).

6. State Street Tr. Co. v. Walker, 259 Mass. 578, 157 N.E. 334.

7. As to examinations and review of the practices and procedures of corporate

WESTLAW REFERENCES

trustee /s duty /4 examine review /s trust

DUTY TO CHANGE TRUST INVESTMENTS [1]

§ 108. When, at the beginning of the trust, or thereafter, an investment becomes one not permitted under the terms of the trust or the law of the state in question, the trustee has a duty to sell it as soon as he reasonably can and to reinvest the proceeds.

If the trustee concludes that an investment delivered to him at the beginning of his administration is not lawful, he has a duty to sell it as soon as it is possible to do so, without too great sacrifice.[2] What is a reasonable period within which to make the sale depends upon many circumstances,[3] including the market there is for the investment [4] and the price at which it can be sold. For example, in a New Jersey case [5] a trustee received stock of an insurance company which was not legal for the trust and was producing about 1½% income on the market value of the stock. The trustee began selling the stock until the following year but did not complete the sale of it for five years. The court held in effect that the trustee should have sold the stock within five years and was liable for the difference between what it later received for the stock and what it could have obtained by a sale prior thereto.

This same duty to convert or sell investments arises where the trustee discovers that an investment originally legal, whether made by him or by a predecessor in title, has now become nonlegal or imprudent.[6] The reasons why the investment has become improper may be various, for example, that the property yields little or no income,[7] that its market price has greatly decreased,[8] or that it would be a breach of

trustees, see Bogert, Trusts and Trustees (rev. 2d edit.), § 962. See also Reg. § 9.9 (U.S. Comptroller of the Currency), by which a committee of a national bank's directors must audit its trust department at least once every twelve months and minutes are to be kept of review proceedings.

§ 108

1. Restatement, Trusts, Second, §§ 230–231. For fuller discussion see Bogert, Trusts and Trustees (rev. 2d edit.), §§ 685–686. And see 1 Univ. of Chi.L.R. 28.

2. Clark v. Clark, 167 Ga. 1, 144 S.E. 787 (1928); Creed v. McAleer, 275 Mass. 353, 175 N.E. 761, 80 A.L.R. 1117 (1931); In re Leitsch's Will, 185 Wis. 257, 201 N.W. 284, 37 A.L.R. 547 (1924).

3. McInnes v. Whitman, 313 Mass. 19, 46 N.E.2d 527 (1943) (liable for holding speculative securities more than a year); In re Casani's Estate, 342 Pa. 468, 21 A.2d

59, 135 A.L.R. 1513 (1941) (non-legals retained eight years in a declining market; burden on trustee to prove reasonable diligence).

4. Kinney v. Uglow, 163 Or. 539, 98 P.2d 1006 (1940) (no liability where trustee, after reasonable effort, could find no market for the non-legal).

5. Babbitt v. Fidelity Trust Co., 72 N.J. Eq. 745, 66 A. 1066.

6. Stephens' Ex'rs v. Milnor, 24 N.J. Eq. 358; State Street Trust Co. v. De Kalb, 259 Mass. 578, 157 N.E. 334 (1927) (unmistakable signs that security of mortgage was decreasing); In re Estate of Dreier, 204 Wis. 221, 235 N.W. 439 (1931).

7. Hubbell's Will, 302 N.Y. 246, 97 N.E.2d 888 (1951).

8. Dickerson v. Camden Trust Co., 1 N.J. 459, 64 A.2d 214 (1949).

the duty of loyalty to retain the investment.[9]

The courts have been inclined to be lenient with trustees who have failed to sell nonlegals during periods of war or depression, when it was very difficult to forecast the future.[10] But in some cases liability has been decreed.[11]

If a trustee does sell an improper investment, he is required to use reasonable care as to the time and terms of sale.[12] In some cases it has been held that a sale should have been made within one year from the time when the trustee should have decided that the investment was improper.[13]

In many trust instruments the settlor expressly *permits* the trustee to retain investments made by the settlor. This, of course, protects the trustee in such retention if he used reasonable care in so doing. It does not permit the trustee to retain the investment no matter how bad or risky it may become; he must use at least slight care in following the permissive clause.[14]

A permission to retain includes securities substituted for the original holdings, if they represent substantially the same investment, even though they differ in form. In cases of mergers, reorganizations, consolidations, and sales of corporations in which the trustee holds stock, he often receives new stock or bonds, and it becomes a question of fact whether the substituted securities are substantially equivalent,[15] or involve a change in the nature of the business, risk, security or

9. In re Durston's Will, 297 N.Y. 64, 74 N.E.2d 310 (1947); In re Trusteeship of Stone, 138 Ohio St. 293, 34 N.E.2d 755 (1941).

10. St. Louis Union Tr. Co. v. Stoffregen, 40 N.Y.S.2d 527 (1942), affirmed 266 App.Div. 832, 43 N.Y.S.2d 511 (1943).

11. In re Busby's Estate, 288 Ill.App. 500, 6 N.E.2d 451 (1937) (speculative stocks held on a narrow margin); Cameron Tr. Co. v. Leibrandt, 229 Mo.App. 450, 83 S.W.2d 234 (1935) (holding for seven years).

12. Braman v. Central Hanover Bank & Tr. Co., 138 N.J.Eq. 165, 47 A.2d 10 (1946).

13. Paul v. Girard Tr. Co., C.C.A.Ill., 124 F.2d 809 (1941).

14. See 20 Pa.C.S.A. § 7317 (fiduciary must use "due care and prudence in the disposition or retention of any such nonlegal instrument").

And see Fortune v. First Trust Co., 200 Minn. 367, 274 N.W. 524, 112 A.L.R. 346 (1937); Fairleigh v. Fidelity Nat. Bank & Trust Co., 335 Mo. 360, 73 S.W.2d 248 (1934); In re Dickinson's Estate, 318 Pa. 561, 179 A. 443 (1935). A Pennsylvania court has stated that trustees are protected by the settlor's permission to retain "un-less facts known to them, or which by ordinary watchfulness could have been known to them, rendered the holding of such securities an act of which it is inconceivable that one desiring to do his duty would, in the exercise of ordinary good business judgment or foresight, have been guilty." In re Linnard's Estate, 299 Pa. 32, 37, 148 A. 912, 914 (1930). A permission to retain the settlor's investments allows a corporate trustee to retain its own stock received from the settlor. In re Riding's Estate, 297 N.Y. 417, 79 N.E.2d 735 (1948). But see City Bank Farmers Tr. Co. v. Taylor, 76 R.I. 129, 69 A.2d 234 (1949) (clauses permitting disloyalty to be strictly construed).

15. Brown v. Fidelity Union Trust Co., 135 N.J.Eq. 404, 39 A.2d 120 (1944) (trustee authorized to retain stock in an investment trust; stock in another investment trust into which the first merged not equivalent); In re Cope's Estate, 351 Pa. 514, 41 A.2d 617 (1945) (trustee authorized to retain common stock of land title and trust company; it was merged with two others and conducted same business at same place; stock of new corporation an authorized investment).

priority.[16]

If the settlor *directs* a retention of his investments, or directs a sale of them, naturally this instruction will in the one case obligate the trustee to hold the investment unless very clear proof arises that the investment is unsound, or in the second instance to sell as soon as practicable at a reasonable price.[17]

In many states statutes permit the trustee to retain the settlor's investments without liability, but they have been construed to mean that retention is allowed unless an ordinarily prudent man would know that retention was highly dangerous to the beneficiaries,[18] and some of them expressly limit the power to retain to cases where the trustee uses reasonable prudence.[19]

The so-called "prudent investor statutes," which have been adopted in many states in recent years, apply that rule to the retention and sale of securities as well as to their purchase.[20]

Equity, under its power to permit deviation from the terms of a trust, sometimes allows a trustee to retain nonlegals,[21] or directs a sale even though the settlor gave power to retain.[22]

The duty of a trustee to sell a nonlegal or improper investment may be negatived by a request or consent of a beneficiary that the trustee retain the investment.[23]

 WESTLAW REFERENCES

trustee /s sell*** /s nonlegal

390k282 /p nonlegal

390k189 /p nonlegal

find 274 nw 524

390k179

---

16. Mertz v. Guaranty Tr. Co., 247 N.Y. 137, 159 N.E. 888 (1928); Matter of Olney's Estate, 255 App.Div. 195, 7 N.Y.S.2d 89 (1938) (capital structure different); In re Scott's Trust, 322 Pa. 1, 184 A. 245 (1936) (different maturity and interest rate).

17. Richardson v. Knight, 69 Me. 285; First Nat. Bank of Boston v. Truesdale Hospital, 288 Mass. 35, 192 N.E. 150 (1934); In re Bartol's Estate, 182 Pa. 407, 38 A. 527.

18. See, for example, Conn.G.S.A. § 45–89; Del.Code T. 12, § 3304; 20 Pa. C.S.A. § 7315 (even though not an "authorized investment"). And see People by Kerner v. Canton Nat. Bank, 288 Ill.App. 418, 6 N.E.2d 220 (1937); In re Riker's Estate, 125 N.J.Eq. 349, 350, 351, 5 A.2d 685 (1939).

19. See, for example, West's Ann.Cal. Civ.Code § 2261(b); N.Y.—McKinney's EPTL 11–2.2; 20 Pa.C.S.A. §§ 7315, 7317.

20. For references to these statutes, see Bogert, Trusts and Trustees (rev. 2d edit.), § 686. For the terms of these statutes see, ibid., §§ 616–664.

21. For cases, see Bogert, Trusts and Trustees (rev. 2d edit.), §§ 562, 687. Re Hazeldine, (1918) 1 Ch. 433.

22. Hawaiian Trust Co. v. Breault, 42 Haw. 268; Losa Estate, 86 Pa.D. & C. 572.

23. In re Ward's Estate, 350 Pa. 144, 38 A.2d 50 (1944). In re Bogert's Estate, Sur., 24 N.Y.S.2d 553 (1940).

Chapter 13

THE DUTIES OF THE TRUSTEE— RECEIPTS AND PAYMENTS— PRINCIPAL AND INCOME

Table of Sections

TRUSTEE'S DUTIES IN MAKING PAYMENTS TO BENEFICIARIES [1]

§ 109. **A trustee must follow the trust instrument as to the time, amount, form and destination of payments which he is directed or authorized to make from income or principal to the beneficiaries. It is usually held that his duties in this regard are absolute, and that he**

§ 109

1. Restatement, Trusts, Second, §§ 182, 226. Bogert, Trusts and Trustees (rev. 2d edit.), §§ 811–814.

is not excused from performing them correctly even though he may have used reasonable care and prudence.

The trustee is under a duty to make payments of income and distributions of trust principal as required or permitted by the trust instrument, unless he is otherwise directed by the court. He should follow the terms of the trust as to the time of payments, the persons to whom payments should be made, and their form. Under the rule generally in force, he is not excused for making an improper payment by proof that he acted honestly and used what he thought was reasonable care, or that the mispayment was based on ignorance or mistake or the forgery or fraud of the payee.[2] "It was the duty of the trustee, before making any payments whatsoever, to thoroughly and carefully examine the provisions of the trust instrument and also to determine as a fact whether the named beneficiaries be living or dead. A fiduciary cannot be relieved by a mistaken payment made in good faith to the wrong person."[3] Thus if a life beneficiary has died but the trustee does not know of the death, and continues to send checks payable to him after his death, and these are endorsed by the payee's wife for him and collected, the trustee will be liable.[4] Payments to the wrong person will render the trustee personally liable, although he will, of course, have a right to recover the improper payment from the payee.[5]

However, in recent years there has been a tendency to reduce the duty of the trustee in making payments to the standard of the care and prudence of a reasonable man.[6] This is the guide to trustees in nearly all their conduct. Why should they be held to a higher level of performance with respect to payments? The burden on trustees in keeping track of deaths, births, marriages, and incompetencies of beneficiaries is great. Where corporate trustees have a part in the drafting of trust instruments they often insist on a clause limiting their liability to lack of reasonable prudence. Some statutes are to a similar effect.[7] Thus where a trustee had a duty to pay income to a widow during her widowhood, and the trustee continued payments after her second marriage without knowledge of this marriage, it was held that there was no liability until the trustee received notice of the second marriage.[8]

The trustee is normally under a duty to make payments of income

2. Countiss v. Whiting, 306 Ill.App. 548, 29 N.E.2d 277 (1940); Baar v. Fidelity & Columbia Tr. Co., 302 Ky. 91, 193 S.W.2d 1011 (1946).

3. In re Blish Trust, 350 Pa. 311, 38 A.2d 9 (1944).

4. Darling Stores v. Fidelity-Bankers Trust Co., 178 Tenn. 165, 156 S.W.2d 419 (1941).

5. Prince De Bearn v. Winans, 111 Md. 434, 74 A. 626; Ellis v. Kelsey, 241 N.Y. 374, 150 N.E. 148 (1925); Moyer v. Norris-town-Penn Trust Co., 296 Pa. 26, 145 A. 682 (1929).

6. See § 93, ante. And see Cronheim v. Tennant, 30 N.J. 360, 153 A.2d 22 (1959); Application of Spitzmuller, 279 App.Div. 233, 109 N.Y.S.2d 1 (1951), affirmed 304 N.Y. 608, 107 N.E.2d 91 (1952).

7. See, for example, Wash.—RCWA 11.98.100. And see Bogert, Trusts and Trustees (rev. 2d edit.), § 814.

8. Rodgers v. Herron, 226 S.C. 317, 85 S.E.2d 104 (1954).

of a living trust from the date of its creation,[9] and in the case of a testamentary trust from the date of the death of the testator even though the trust was not funded until much later.[10] Unless directed as to the time of payments, he should make them at reasonable intervals,[11] whether monthly, quarterly or otherwise. He need not pay out all income, but may keep a reasonable reserve [12] to take care of future expenses and obligations of the trust. Usually he should not make advances of income which has not yet been collected [13] either from trust principal or from the personal funds of the trustee, but if he does so he will be allowed to reimburse himself or the trust principal account from later accruing income.[14]

If a trustee is directed or permitted to *apply* income to the benefit of a beneficiary, it is not his duty to pay it to the beneficiary or to his representative, if the beneficiary is under guardianship because of minority or incompetency.[15] But if his duty is to *pay* and the beneficiary is under age or of deficient mentality so that the income is subject to the control of his guardian, it would seem that payments by the trustee should be to the guardian.[16]

The manner or form in which a payment or distribution will depend on the terms of the trust. If a trustee is directed to pay in cash, he has no option to deliver bonds or stock of equivalent value.[17] But in many trusts the trustee is given discretion to pay in cash or in kind, and in some instances the distribution of securities instead of cash requiring a sale realizing a capital gain is prudent.[18] If a trustee is directed to buy an insurance company annuity for a beneficiary, or to purchase realty for him, some courts have allowed the beneficiary to elect to take the cost of the annuity or of the real estate.[19]

Many troublesome questions arise with regard to the construction of trust instruments and the consequent duties of trustees in making payments. For example, if the settlor directs that a certain sum shall

9. Jacks v. Monterey County Trust & Sav. Bank, 20 Cal.2d 494, 127 P.2d 532 (1942). See Bogert, Trusts and Trustees (rev. 2d edit.), § 817.

10. First Trust Co. of Wichita v. Varney, 142 Kan. 93, 45 P.2d 582 (1935); Bolles v. Boatmen's Nat. Bank, 363 Mo. 949, 255 S.W.2d 725 (1953).

11. In re Strome's Estate, 214 Or. 158, 327 P.2d 414 (1958).

12. Stempel v. Middletown Trust Co., 127 Conn. 206, 15 A.2d 305 (1940).

13. Rogers v. English, 130 Conn. 332, 33 A.2d 540 (1943).

14. In re Buckley's Estate, 4 Misc.2d 576, 150 N.Y.S.2d 337 (Sur.1956); In re Klein's Estate, 326 Pa. 393, 190 A. 882 (1937).

15. Moran v. Sutter, 360 Mo. 304, 228 S.W.2d 682 (1950).

16. Indian Head Nat. Bank v. Theriault, 97 N.H. 212, 84 A.2d 828 (1951); Bellinger v. Bellinger, 180 Misc. 948, 46 N.Y.S.2d 263 (1943).

17. Brown v. Fidelity Union Trust Co., 10 N.J.Misc. 555, 159 A. 809 (1932); Villard v. Villard, 219 N.Y. 482, 114 N.E. 789; In re Swindell's Estate, 332 Pa. 161, 3 A.2d 2 (1938).

18. In re Wellman's Will, 119 Vt. 426, 127 A.2d 279 (1956).

19. Ketcham v. International Trust Co., 117 Colo. 559, 192 P.2d 426 (1948); Hilton v. Sherman, 155 Ga. 624, 118 S.E. 356 (1923); Pasquay v. Pasquay, 235 Ill. 48, 85 N.E. 316; Title & Trust Co. v. United States Fidel. & Guar. Co., 147 Or. 255, 32 P.2d 1035 (1934).

be paid to the first beneficiary annually, but does not expressly state whether the payment is to be exclusively from income, or may be from principal if the income is inadequate to pay the prescribed sum, the courts are forced to make findings as to the probable intent of the settlor on the basis of the relationship of the settlor and beneficiary, the claims of others upon the generosity of the settlor, his financial situation, and the wording of the instrument. Sometimes they hold that the trustee may invade principal,[20] but in other decisions there is an opposite result.[21]

Where a settlor directs an *annuity* to be paid from trust income only, and the fund produces deficient income in some years, but later there is a surplus of income, are the surpluses of later years to be used to make up the deficiencies of prior years? The courts are obliged, often on very slender evidence, to determine the settlor's intent. The circumstances of the settlor and beneficiaries when the trust was created and the settlor's general objectives will be considered.[22]

Frequently a trustee is given discretion to use so much of the income as is necessary for the *support* of the beneficiary, either by paying it to him or applying it for him. "Support" includes not only food, clothing and housing for the beneficiary but also for his family to whom he owes a duty of support,[23] and also payments for medical care [24] and in satisfaction of his debts.[25] The courts have not agreed whether it also permits the paying of the funeral expenses of a life beneficiary.[26]

Many cases involving discretionary support trusts raise the problem whether, in deciding how much trust income or principal should be paid or expended for the support of the beneficiary, the trustee should take account of property owned by the beneficiary outside the trust and his other sources of support, or whether the trustee should ignore such additional financial means. For example, if the trust gives the trustee discretion to pay the settlor's son out of the income of the trust whatever sum is necessary to support him in comfort and according to the standard of living which he had maintained, and the trustee finds that $40,000 is required for this purpose, but that the son has an income of $20,000 a year from a salary and from his private investments, should the trustee pay the son $40,000 or $20,000? There is no easy rule for answering this question. The courts consider the situation of the settlor and his probable intent in the light of all the language of the instrument and its general objectives, the facts known

20. Duncan v. Elkins, 94 N.H. 13, 45 A.2d 297 (1946); Litcher v. Trust Co. of N.J., 11 N.J. 64, 93 A.2d 368 (1952).

21. First Nat. Bank in Oshkosh v. Barnes, 237 Wis. 627, 298 N.W. 215 (1941).

22. In re Platt's Estate, 21 Cal.2d 343, 131 P.2d 825 (1942); Bridgeport-City Trust Co. v. Leeds, 134 Conn. 133, 55 A.2d 869 (1947); In re Lowrie's Estate, 294 Mich. 298, 293 N.W. 656 (1940).

23. Reynolds v. Reynolds, 208 N.C. 254, 180 S.E. 70 (1935).

24. In re Surbeck's Estate, 185 Misc. 635, 56 N.Y.S.2d 487 (1944).

25. Orange First Nat. Bank v. Preiss, 2 N.J.Super. 486, 64 A.2d 475 (1949).

26. Delaware Trust Co. v. Tease, 36 Del.Ch. 43, 125 A.2d 169 (1956); In re Hafemann's Will, 265 Wis. 641, 62 N.W.2d 561 (1954).

to the settlor when he created the trust, and the relationship of the beneficiary to the settlor, and they sometimes find an intent to have the trustee ignore outside income,[27] and sometimes hold that he should consider it.[28]

 WESTLAW REFERENCES

trustee /s duty /s payment /s beneficiary
390k217.3(9)
find 192 p2d 426

DEVIATION FROM TRUST TERMS AS TO PAYMENTS [1]

§ 110. The settlor has no power to alter the provisions of the trust as to payments, unless he expressly reserved such power at the time of the trust creation.

The trustee has no power to change the trust terms as to payments, unless he can secure the approval of all the beneficiaries.

The court has power to permit the trustee to deviate from the provisions of the trust as to time and form of payments to beneficiaries, but not to change the relative size of their interests.

It frequently happens that the trustee or beneficiaries are dissatisfied with the terms of the trust with respect to the time, amount and form of payments of income or principal. Beneficiaries may be hard pressed for funds for living expenses or to enable them to buy a home. The trustee may believe that the directions which the settlor made regarding payments are unwise, in view of the settlor's purposes in creating the trust and the effect on the beneficiaries of strict application of distribution terms.

If the settlor is living, he may be able to remedy any injustice or undesirable result by amending the trust, if he expressly reserved the power to amend at the time he created the trust; if he did not reserve that power he cannot do so.[2]

The trustee cannot make such a change unless the settlor gave him this authority.[3] Thus if the instrument provides that the net income of the property shall be paid the settlor's widow during her life, and the principal divided among the settlor's children at the widow's death, and the income of the trust was adequate to support the widow at the beginning but due to her poor health and a decrease in trust income it

27. McClintock v. Smith, 238 Iowa 964, 29 N.W.2d 248 (1947); Winkel v. Streicher, 365 Mo. 1170, 295 S.W.2d 56 (1956).

28. Auchincloss v. City Bank Farmers Trust Co., 136 Conn. 266, 70 A.2d 105 (1949); Smith v. Gillikin, 201 Va. 149, 109 S.E.2d 121 (1959).

§ 110

1. Restatement, Trusts, Second, § 168, Bogert, Trusts and Trustees (rev. 2d edit.), §§ 562, 815.

2. § 145, post.

3. Longley v. Hall, 28 Mass. 120; In re Edward's Estate, 153 Or. 696, 58 P.2d 243 (1936).

has now become grossly inadequate so that she will be exposed to want and suffering if forced to live on trust income alone, the trustee has no power to make payments of principal to her even though he is convinced that the welfare of the widow was the chief concern of the settlor.[4] Nor could the trustee of his own initiative make greater payments of income than those provided by the instrument, or accelerate the payments, notwithstanding the happening of events which might make such action one naturally to be desired by the settlor. If the beneficiaries are all in existence and have vested interests and are competent, their consents that the trustee vary the terms as to payments will protect the trustee in acting accordingly.[5]

Attention has been called elsewhere [6] to the power of the court of chancery to authorize the trustee to deviate from the terms of the trust with respect to administration, when it is necessary or desirable to do so, in order to accomplish the fundamental objectives of the settlor. This power is frequently applied to payment clauses. If the court finds, due to a situation not contemplated by the settlor or a change in circumstances occurring since the trust was created, that the settlor's directions as to the time or form of payments are disadvantageous and threaten to frustrate achievement of the purposes of the trust, it will, on application of the trustee or beneficiaries, direct or permit the trustee to ignore the instructions of the settlor and to make payments in a different form or at a different time.[7]

For example, if the trust was for the benefit of a minor son of the testator and the trustee was directed to accumulate the income until the son reached twenty-one and then pay him the accumulations and the trust principal, and the evidence is that the son is in great need of funds for his education and support, the court may direct that the accumulation provision be disobeyed and that the trustee pay or apply all of the income to or for the minor son.[8] This is called "hastening the enjoyment" of the trust fund.

And a further illustration may be found in a case where the direction was to pay all the income of a trust to a son until he reached thirty, and then to pay him the principal of the trust. Here, if the son can prove great need for the principal before he reaches thirty due to a situation not contemplated by the settlor, he may be able to secure a decree advancing the time of payment of part or all of the trust principal.[9]

This power to advance the date of payments is sometimes provided

4. In re Welch, 23 L.J.Ch.N.S. 344; see § 145, post.

5. Hughes v. Federal Trust Co., 119 N.J.Eq. 502, 183 A. 299 (1936) (consents not effective where unborn persons may become beneficiaries).

6. See § 146, post.

7. Pearce v. Pearce, 199 Ala. 491, 74 So. 952; Suesens v. Daiker, 117 App.Div. 668, 102 N.Y.S. 919; Matter of Potts, 1 Ashm. 340. And see Bogert, Trusts and Trustees (rev. 2d ed.), § 815.

8. Bennett v. Nashville Tr. Co., 127 Tenn. 126, 153 S.W. 840.

9. Longwith v. Riggs, 123 Ill. 258, 14 N.E. 840; Tompkins v. Tompkins' Ex'rs, 18 N.J.Eq. 303.

by statute.[10] Most statutes granting the power involve minors,[11] but in some instances statutes permit advances to be made to adults as income beneficiaries.[12] It includes authority to direct delay of payments as well as a hastening of enjoyment.[13] Under it the court may direct a loan of trust property[14] as well as an absolute payment. And the court may ratify an unauthorized payment where it would have approved the payment if application had been made in advance.[15] The court may also permit a trustee to change the form (although not the size or value) of a payment, where such action will be highly advantageous to the beneficiary.[16]

The power of the court does not extend to remaking the settlor's gifts in the light of what the court thinks would have been done had the testator foreseen the future. Thus where the trust was to pay net income to the settlor's daughters for their lives and then deliver the principal to grandchildren, the court has no power to order advances of trust principal to the daughters, even though it believes they were the chief concern of the settlor and that the income of the trust has shrunk to an unexpected extent.[17] To do so would not be hastening enjoyment of property given to the daughters but taking property away from the grandchildren and giving it to the daughters.

The theory of the decisions approving deviations from payment directions is that the court is carrying out the fundamental objectives of the donor and disregarding merely minor directions as to time of payment. It is not remaking the settlor's gifts by giving property to A when the settlor directed it to be paid to B, but is directing the trustee to pay A's gift to him in a different form or at a different time. Naturally there must be some important reason for such alteration of the terms of the gift as to time and method of payment. This is usually found in a change of circumstances with respect to the beneficiaries or the trust principal or income, such that the trust as originally framed will not achieve the purposes which the settlor had reason to expect it would accomplish. "The court's action to the end sought would merely touch the management or mode of user, and would not proceed to even that limited extent if it were not made clearly to appear in proof that an exigency existed not contemplated by the creator of the trust, which, had it been in anticipation by him, would in likelihood have been

---

10. See, for example, Ala.Code 1975, § 35–4–253 (minor); N.Y.—McKinney's EPTL 7–1.6 (income beneficiary). And see Bogert, Trusts and Trustees (rev. 2d edit.), § 815.

11. See, for example, Ariz.R.S. § 33–253; West's Ann.Ind.Code 32–1–4–5.

12. See, for example, 20 Pa.C.S.A. § 6102(a); Wis.S.A. 701.13(2). And see Zinsmeister's Trustee v. Long, 250 Ky. 50, 61 S.W.2d 887 (1933); In re North's Estate, 242 Wis. 72, 7 N.W.2d 705 (1942).

13. First Nat. Bank v. Watters, 220 Ala. 356, 125 So. 222 (1929).

14. Hutchins v. Hutchins, 43 App.D.C. 544 (1834).

15. Dewey v. Burke, 246 Mass. 435, 141 N.E. 117 (1923).

16. Evans v. Grossi, 324 Mich. 297, 37 N.W.2d 111 (1949); Jacobs v. Bean, 99 N.H. 239, 108 A.2d 559 (1954).

17. In re Van Deusen's Estate, 30 Cal. 2d 285, 182 P.2d 565 (1947); Mills v. Michigan Trust Co., 124 Mich. 244, 82 N.W. 1046; Segelken v. Segelken, 26 N.J.Super. 178, 97 A.2d 501 (1953).

provided for. A court of equity, acting in *loco parentis* or occupying the place of the trust creator, in such case, does what it conceives would have been done by the creator had he foreseen the situation of his beneficiary in a substitution of another course of management in order to the completer realization of his purposed bounty." [18]

In order that a beneficiary may get the benefit of the court's power to advance payments, it must appear that he has a vested interest in the funds from which he is to be paid. If his interest is contingent, or vested but subject to divestment if a certain event happens, the court will not decree a payment to him since that might involve taking property of others and giving it to the claimant.[19] Thus if a trust is created to pay the income to three daughters during their minorities, with a gift of the principal to them, share and share alike, when the youngest reaches twenty-one, and if any dies before reaching twenty-one her share is to go to her issue, the court will not order the use of the principal for the three daughters during the trust since their interests in the principal are subject to the remote possibility of divestment.[20] They might all die before twenty-one, leaving issue, in which case the issue would get the trust principal. It is almost certain that the daughters will receive the trust principal in the future, but it is not absolutely certain.

However the rule about contingent interests is sometimes varied where the contingent gift of trust principal is to a class, the contingency relates to survivorship until a future date, and all members of the class have equal chances of survivorship. Here some courts have been induced to authorize advances of principal for the benefit of one member of the class, as in the case where principal is given to the children of the settlor who live until the youngest child reaches twenty-one.[21]

 WESTLAW REFERENCES

```
settlor trustor  /s  power  /s  modif! chang*** alter***  /s  trust
    /s  payment
390k59(2)
trustee  /s  power  /s  alter*** chang*** modif!  /s  trust
    /s  payment
"hastening the enjoyment"  /s  trust
power  /s  advanc***  /s  payment  /s  trust
find 182 p2d 565
```

---

18. Bennett v. Nashville Trust Co., 127 Tenn. 126, 153 S.W. 840, 46 L.R.A., N.S., 43.

19. Smith v. Guaranty Trust Co., 269 App.Div. 537, 56 N.Y.S.2d 330 (1945), affirmed 295 N.Y. 953, 8 N.E.2d 46 (1946); Boyle v. Marshall & Ilsley Bank, 242 Wis. 1, 6 N.W.2d 642 (1942).

20. Stewart v. Hamilton, 151 Tenn. (24 Thompson) 396, 270 S.W. 79, 39 A.L.R. 37 (1925).

21. Matter of Davison, 6 Paige 136; and see Wannamaker v. South Carolina State Bank, 176 S.C. 133, 179 S.E. 896 (1935).

ALLOCATION OF RECEIPTS TO INCOME
OR PRINCIPAL [1]

§ 111. Benefits received by a trustee for the use of trust property or as a profit produced by it are usually treated as trust income, while property received as a substitute for, or a change in the form of, the original trust property should generally be allocated by the trustee to the principal account.

The trustee's duties in this regard are set forth in detail in the Uniform (or Revised Uniform) Principal and Income Act, now in force in most states.

A settlor may direct the trustee as to the disposition of receipts, or give the trustee discretion to decide as to their allocation, in which case the determination of the trustee will control if made with due consideration of the purposes of the trust and with impartial attention to the interests of both the income and remainder beneficiaries.

Nearly all trustees act for two classes of beneficiaries, namely, income beneficiaries who are to receive the net income from the trust property for a period of years or lives, and remainder beneficiaries who at the termination of the income administration are given the capital or principal of the trust. The trustees receive money or other property in the course of their administration from a great variety of sources and for many different reasons. In each case they must decide whether to credit the receipt to the income or principal account of the trust.

The general rule for the guidance of the trustee is that money paid for the use of the trust property and any benefit received as a gain from the employment of that property is to be treated as trust income, while substitutes for the original trust res which are mere changes in form are to be considered trust principal. For example, subject to some qualifications and exceptions, interest, rents and ordinary cash dividends are to be regarded as trust income, but the proceeds of the sale of trust property and sums received on the collection of debts due the trust should be credited to the principal account of the trust. The application of this standard involves many difficulties and qualifications which are treated in later sections dealing with various types of receipts.

In at least 37 states, and in the absence of trust provisions to the contrary, the trustee will find that his duties as to most receipts and disbursements are governed by the Uniform Principal and Income Act or the Revised Uniform Principal and Income Act, and in the remaining states there are statutes covering at least some principal and income questions.[2] Or the trust instrument may give the trustee

---

§ 111

1. Restatement, Trusts, Second, §§ 232, 233. Bogert, Trusts and Trustees (rev. 2d ed.), § 816.

2. The Uniform Principal and Income Act, approved in 1930, is in effect (1986) in 14 states. See, for example, Ala.Code 1975, §§ 19–3–270 to 19–3–282; 20 Pa.C.S. A. §§ 8101–8112. The Revised Uniform

directions, or grant him discretion, to decide what receipts are to inure to the benefit of the income beneficiary and what receipts are to be added to trust principal.

While there has been some tendency to hold that such a discretionary clause permits a trustee to act only in cases where the law of the jurisdiction is in doubt or there is no controlling decision,[3] the better view is that under such a provision the trustee may act contrary to existing law if he makes his decision after serious consideration of the purposes of the trust, honestly and in good faith. In using his discretion the trustee must also keep in mind his duty to act impartially toward income and principal beneficiaries, and not to make an allocation which would be highly favorable to one and greatly disadvantageous to the other.[4]

Thus in one decision [5] a trustee with discretionary power was held justified in allocating to income relatively small gains from the sale of stock owned by the trust, although such receipts would normally go to trust principal, since the court found that the trustee had used "serious and responsible consideration, short of arbitrary or dishonest conduct or bad faith or fraud". And in another case the trustee was held justified in allocating to trust principal 27½% of oil royalties, even though all the royalties would otherwise have been payable to the income account.[6]

But in other cases a determination by the trustee, acting under a discretionary power, was held to be invalid because it was an abuse of

Principal and Income Act, approved in 1962, is in effect (1986) in 23 states. See, for example, Neb.R.S. §§ 30–3101 to 30–3115; N.Y.—McKinney's EPTL 11–2.1.

In nearly all of the states adopting the Uniform Act, amendments to that Act as originally proposed have been adopted. See, for example, Conn.Gen.Stats. § 45–113(1) (corporate dividends).

In some states, without either Uniform Act, the subject has been treated by statute. See, for example, Ia.Code Ann. § 633.103; N.J.S.A. 3B:19–1 to 3B:19–15.

For a discussion of the Uniform Act, see Nossaman, 28 Cal.L.R. 34; Bogert, 9 Univ. Chi.L.R. 30; 32 Col.L.R. 118. For a discussion of several important changes made by the Revised Uniform Act, see Bogert, 101 Tr. & Estates 787 (1962); Notre Dame Lawyer, Dec., 1962.

For references to adoptions of one or the other Uniform Act, see Bogert, Trusts and Trustees (rev. 2d edit.), §§ 802 and 816.

3. American Security & Trust Co. v. Frost, 73 App.D.C. 75, 117 F.2d 283 (1940), certiorari denied 312 U.S. 707, 61 S.Ct. 829, 85 L.Ed. 1139 (1941); Mercantile-Com-

merce Bank & Trust Co. v. Morse, 356 Mo. 336, 201 S.W.2d 915 (1947) (discretionary clause did not authorize departing from common law rules regarding premiums and discounts on bonds and profits from sales).

4. Parker's Estate, 17 Pa.D. & C. 38 (award of receipts to aged remote relatives who were remaindermen instead of to close relative who was income beneficiary). Restatement, Trusts, Second, § 183.

The trustee's discretionary power to decide whether receipts or accretions are to be treated as principal or income, and whether expenses are to be charged to principal or income, may not be used to shift beneficial interests between the income beneficiary and the charitable remainderman. Old Colony Trust Co. v. Silliman, 352 Mass. 6, 223 N.E.2d 504 (1967). For possible federal estate tax effects of such broad discretionary powers, see Bogert, Trusts and Trustees (rev. 2d edit.), § 275.5.

5. Dumaine v. Dumaine, 301 Mass. 214, 16 N.E.2d 625 (1938).

6. In re Bixby's Estate, 55 Cal.2d 819, 13 Cal.Rptr. 411, 362 P.2d 43 (1961).

discretion on account of its conflict with the trust purposes and variation from the law of the state.[7]

It is sometimes said that a legal life tenant is a trustee for the legal remainderman who is to follow him.[8] Undoubtedly the life tenant owes certain duties to the remainderman which are somewhat similar to those of trustees. The life tenant should preserve the property by the payment of taxes and mortgage interest,[9] he should refrain from waste or destruction of the property, and he should not buy in outstanding claims against the property for his sole benefit but should give the remainderman the benefit of such claims.[10] But the similarity to a trust is superficial.[11] The life tenant owns a separate interest. It is a case of successive interests in the same thing, usually both legal in nature. There is no simultaneous ownership of the same property interest, divided into legal and equitable parts. Life tenants are sometimes required to give bond to preserve the property for the remainderman.[12] This shows that they have power to injure the remainderman by abuse of the land or other property involved, but it does not show that the life tenant is a trustee.

WESTLAW REFERENCES

"uniform principal and income act"
allocat*** /s income principal /s trust
find 223 ne2d 504
390k177

PROBATE INCOME RECEIVED BY TESTAMENTARY TRUSTEE FROM EXECUTOR [1]

§ 112. A testamentary trustee generally receives, from the estate executor, income from some or all of the assets of the testator which had been collected during the period of executorial administration, which is called "probate income". The trustee must decide whether to treat probate income as income or principal of the trust.

If a sum of money is given by will to a trustee, in some states he is entitled to collect interest on that sum, and in other jurisdictions

7. In re Heard's Estate, 107 Cal.App. 2d 225, 236 P.2d 810 (1951) (entire stock dividend to trust principal although value of principal would not have been decreased by giving it to income); In re Watland, 211 Minn. 84, 300 N.W. 195 (1941) (proceeds of sale of stock given to trust income).

8. Buder v. Franz, 27 F.2d 101 (8th Cir.1928); In re Hamlin, 141 App.Div. 318, 126 N.Y.S. 396.

9. Grodsky v. Sipe, 30 F.Supp. 656 (E.D.Ill.1940).

10. Morrison v. Roehl, 215 Mo. 545, 114 S.W. 981.

11. Spring v. Hollander, 261 Mass. 373, 158 N.E. 791 (1927); Welsh's Estate, 239 Pa. 616, 86 A. 1091.

12. Scott v. Scott, 137 Iowa 239, 114 N.W. 881, 23 L.R.A.,N.S., 716, 126 Am.St. Rep. 277. In re Knowles' Estate, 148 N.C. 461, 62 S.E. 549.

§ 112

1. Restatement, Trusts, Second, § 234; Bogert, Trusts and Trustees (rev. 2d edit.), § 817; Bogert, 35 Notre Dame L. 175.

he may demand a proportionate part of the estate's income during its management by the executor. These payments should be allocated by the trustee to trust income.

If a testator gives specific property instead of cash to a trustee, the latter has a right to the income of that property collected during the executorial administration and should treat these payments as income of the trust.

If the will gives the residuary estate to a trustee, he is entitled to income received by the executor from property which was sold by the executor in order to raise funds to pay legacies, debts or taxes, and also to income collected by the executor from property ultimately turned over to the testamentary trustee; and by the majority rule both types of payments should be placed in the trustee's income account. If a part of the residuary estate is given to a trustee, the same rules are applied to a proportionate part of the income received by the executor.

The Uniform Principal and Income Act contains no provision specifically dealing with the problems of probate income, but they are covered by an amendment of the Act and by statute in several states. The Revised Uniform Principal and Income Act also covers the matter of probate income.

A testamentary trustee is generally entitled to probate income from the date of the testator's death.

The property of a decedent who left a will goes first into the hands of his executor who collects it, pays debts, funeral expenses, the costs of administration, taxes, and all other items, before paying legacies. This period of administration takes months, or perhaps several years, and during this time some of the property being held by the executor earns income which the executor collects. If one or more trusts have been created by the will, problems arise as to this income, sometimes called "probate income". What are the duties of the executor with regard to it, and what are the rights and duties of the trustees with relation to it? If the trustees have rights to all or part of the income, from what date do their rights accrue, and to whom shall they pay or credit any income collected from the executor, to the income or principal account of the trust?

Ordinarily, in the absence of statute, the inferred intent of the testator is that the beneficiaries of his trusts shall receive income from the date of his death.[2] Obviously they must be content with *net* income, after payment of expenses attributable to the trust property and general expenses of executorial administration.[3]

The court decree distributing the property of the estate to the

2. Cannon v. Cannon, 225 N.C. 611, 36 S.E.2d 17 (1945); Davidson v. Miners' & Mech. Sav. & Trust Co., 129 Ohio St. 418, 195 N.E. 845 (1935).

3. Estey v. Commerce Trust Co., 333 Mo. 977, 64 S.W.2d 608 (1933); Bonbright v. Bonbright, 142 N.J.Eq. 642, 61 A.2d 201 (1948).

trustee may provide answers to some questions.[4] The trustee may be given discretion as to the allocation of probate income, which will give him power to decide these questions if he is not guilty of an abuse of the discretion.[5]

If the will provides that the executor is to pay $100,000 to the testamentary trustee, which is to be held in trust for L for life, remainder to R, may the trustee insist on the payment of interest on the sum from the date of the testator's death to the date of payment of the legacy? In many cases, by statute or otherwise, the executor has a duty to pay interest at the legal or other rate;[6] in other states it is provided that the trustee is entitled to collect from the executor a proportionate part of the net income of the estate during its executorial administration, the fraction to be determined by a comparison of the value of the legacy to the trustee and the total value of the estate.[7] It is generally agreed that either type of payment received by the trustee from the executor should be treated as income of his trust.

The testator may give to a trustee 1,000 shares of the stock of A corporation, to be held for L for life, remainder to R. Here it is clear that the trustee is entitled to collect from the executor any dividends received on this stock while the executor was holding it, less an equitable share of administration expenses and any income taxes paid on the dividends; and the trustee should set aside the net payment from the executor as income of his trust.[8]

The will may give to a trustee all or a part of the residue of the estate which is to be determined after the payment of debts, expenses, taxes and other obligations. The executor may receive income on some of testator's property not specifically bequeathed, and thereafter he may be obliged to sell this property in order to raise funds with which to pay cash legacies, taxes, debts and expenses. If the property thus sold would have gone into the residue had liquidation not been required, the trustee of the residuary trust is entitled to the income from such property which the executor collected. Whether, after the trustee receives such income, he should regard it as income of his trust, or as principal, is a question on which the courts have differed. A large group of the older cases have held that such income should be regarded as trust principal since it was a part of the residue.[9] However other decisions and statutes, which now constitute the majority view, take the

4. In re De Laveaga's Estate, 50 Cal.2d 480, 326 P.2d 129 (1958).

5. Matter of Bixby, 158 Cal.App.2d 351, 322 P.2d 956 (1958).

6. First Nat. Bank & Trust Co. v. Baker, 124 Conn. 577, 1 A.2d 283 (1938); Gates v. Plainfield Tr. Co., 122 N.J.Eq. 366, 194 A. 65 (1937). N.J.S.A. 3B:23–11.

7. State Bank of Chicago v. Gross, 344 Ill. 512, 176 N.E. 739 (1931); In re Jackson's Estate, 318 Pa. 256, 178 A. 384 (1935). 20 Pa.C.S.A. § 8104.

8. Hale v. Anglim, 140 F.2d 235 (9th Cir.1944); Alig v. Levy, 219 Ind. 618, 39 N.E.2d 137 (1942); Dennison v. Lilley, 83 N.H. 422, 144 A. 523 (1928); In re Mead's Estate, 227 Wis. 311, 277 N.W. 694 (1938), rehearing denied 227 Wis. 311, 279 N.W. 18 (1938).

9. Proctor v. American Security & Trust Co., 69 App.D.C. 70, 98 F.2d 599 (1938); In re Feehely's Estate, 179 Or. 250, 170 P.2d 757, 166 A.L.R. 420 (1946); Rosenberger v. Rosenberger, 184 Va. 1024, 37 S.E.2d 55 (1946).

position that this income should be allocated to the income account of the testamentary trust.[10]

If as part of the residue the executor delivers assets to a trustee which have been held by him since the death of the testator and which have produced net probate income, it is generally agreed that such income should be placed by the trustee in the income account.[11] The same doctrine is applied to a trust of part of the residue, where the trustee is entitled to a proportionate part of the probate income of the property ultimately determined to be the residue.

While the original Uniform Principal and Income Act had no provision expressly concerned with probate income,[12] an amendment covering the matter was approved and adopted in a few states, and section 5 of the Revised Uniform Act enacts the provisions of the amendment.[13]

In recent years several states have enacted statutes covering the disposition of probate income.[14] Their tendency has been to favor the income beneficiaries of the testamentary trusts, on the ground that it is reasonable to infer such an intent on the part of the testator; the immediate recipients of the income of the trust are usually closer in relationship and interest to the testator than the remaindermen who are often removed from the testator by one or two generations or are collateral relatives or charities.

 WESTLAW REFERENCES

"probate income"

409k684.7 /p "probate income"

INTEREST—BONDS BOUGHT AT PREMIUM OR DISCOUNT [1]

§ 113. Interest on notes and bonds owned by the trust should ordinarily be treated by the trustee as income, since it is the price paid for the use of trust funds.

10. In re De Laveaga's Estate, 50 Cal. 2d 480, 326 P.2d 129 (1958); Whitman v. Lincoln Bank & Trust Co., 340 S.W.2d 608 (Ky.1960); Old Colony Trust Co. v. Smith, 266 Mass. 500, 165 N.E. 657 (1929); Wachovia Bank & Trust Co. v. Jones, 210 N.C. 339, 186 S.E. 335 (1936); American Nat. Bank v. Embry, 181 Tenn. 392, 181 S.W.2d 356 (1944); N.Y.—McKinney's EPTL 11–2.1.

11. Bridgeport-City Trust Co. v. Beach, 119 Conn. 131, 174 A. 308 (1934); In re Koffend's Will, 218 Minn. 206, 15 N.W.2d 590 (1944); Chrisman v. Cornell University, 132 N.J.Eq. 178, 27 A.2d 627 (1942).

12. Illinois, however, in adopting the Uniform Act, added a section regarding probate income. Ill.Rev.Stat. c. 30, ¶ 506.

13. For the text of this amendment which was approved in 1958, and for adoptions of the Revised Act, see Bogert, Trusts and Trustees (rev. 2d edit.), §§ 816, 817. The amendment was enacted in Colo. and Vt.

14. For current statutes as to probate income, see Fla.Stats.Ann. § 733.01; 18–A Me.R.S. § 8–202; Ill.Rev.Stat., c. 30, ¶ 506.

§ 113

1. Restatement, Trusts, Second, §§ 233, 239, 240.

Under case law the majority view is that if a bond is purchased by a trustee at a premium, he should amortize in order to prevent loss to the principal of the trust on the maturity of the bond, by deducting from the interest payments amounts which on the maturity of the bond will total the amount of the premium paid; but if a bond is purchased at a discount, the trustee is under no duty to pay to the income beneficiary the difference between the cost of the bond and the amount paid on it at maturity.

Under both the Uniform and the Revised Uniform Principal and Income Acts, all interest on bonds purchased by the trustee at a premium is trust income and the entire proceeds of the collection of a bond bought at a discount are trust principal. In several states the appreciation in the value of U.S. Savings Bonds at maturity is declared by statute to be trust income.

A large part of the receipts of the trustee may consist of interest on notes and bonds. This interest is received as the price for the use of the trust funds lent and, with the possible exceptions noted below, should be placed by the trustee in his income account.[2] It is a clear case of the product of trust property or gain from its use. And the proceeds from the collection of notes and bonds constitute a substitute for the original trust principal and are to be credited to the principal account.

In three cases, however, some doubt has been raised as to the propriety of treating all current returns from bonds as income and all the ultimate amount collected on their maturity as trust principal.

The first of these is the case of a premium, the amount paid for a bond in excess of its face value with accrued interest. For example, if the obligor on a bond agrees to pay $1,000 ten years from the date of the bond, with semi-annual interest at the rate of 5%, and a trustee purchases the bond for 105, he will pay $1,050 for it plus accrued interest. A principal amount of $1,050 will have been invested in an asset which at maturity of the bond will return to the trust only $1,000. Thus, unless parts of the interest payments are taken to make up this sum of $50, trust principal will suffer a loss of $50 when and if the bond is held to maturity and collected. Most courts have been impressed by the argument that the trustee should make periodic deductions from the interest payments so as to create a fund to make principal whole at the maturity of the bond. In the case put above, they would require the trustee to deduct $5 a year from the interest payments, or $2.50 from each semi-annual coupon, and add this amount to trust principal.[3]

2. Riggs v. Cragg, 26 Hun 89; Perry v. Terrel, 21 N.C. 441; Unif.Princ. & Inc.Act, § 3(1).

3. Estate of Gartenlaub, 185 Cal. 648, 198 P. 209 (1921); New England Trust Co. v. Eaton, 140 Mass. 532, 4 N.E. 69; Old Colony Trust Co. v. Comstock, 290 Mass. 377, 195 N.E. 389, 101 A.L.R. 1 (1935); Mercantile-Commerce Bank & Trust Co. v. Morse, 356 Mo. 336, 201 S.W.2d 915 (1947); Matter of Stevens, 187 N.Y. 471, 80 N.E. 358, 12 L.R.A.,N.S., 814.

For discussions of the premium and discount questions, see Edgerton, 31 Harv. L.R. 447; Black, 17 Mass.L.Q. 81, 21 Boston U.L.R. 305; Vierling, 5 St. Louis L.R. 1, 8 id. 1, 11 id. 266.

The reasons urged for this result are: (1) businessmen treat the coupon payments on premium bonds as part income and part return of the principal of the investment, and in computing "yield" they take into account the cost of the bond and not its face value; (2) a premium is paid for the benefit of the life tenant, since it is paid for a bond having an interest rate that is higher than normal; (3) a bond bought at a premium is a "wasting asset", unless amortization is employed, and should be treated as other assets of this type, discussed in a later section.[4]

The amortization rule does not apply where the *settlor* purchased the securities at a premium,[5] or where he expressly directed the trustee to buy the securities in question,[6] or when the settlor indicates in any way an intent that the entire income shall be paid to the income beneficiary.[7] In these instances the trustee may treat as income the entire interest received upon the securities.

The minority view is that the trustee is under no duty to accumulate a fund to care for the premium, that the entire interest upon the security should be paid to the beneficiary, and that the loss due to payment of the premium should fall on principal.[8]

Against amortization for premiums it can be argued: (1) the labor of computation is so great as to make undesirable the attempt to do exact justice between life tenant and remainderman; (2) premiums are not paid solely on account of unusually high interest rates but also because of greater security of payment of interest and principal; (3) for the purpose of ease of trust administration it is better to ignore both premiums and discounts and let them balance each other; (4) complications arise if the bond is not held to maturity but instead is called before that date or sold by the trustee; and (5) in many cases the amount of bonds purchased is small and the premium a relatively insignificant item.

The case of bonds bought at a discount has also caused argument and litigation. Thus if a bond calling for the payment of $1,000 ten years hence, and bearing 4% interest, is sold to the trustee for 95, or $950, and is held to maturity, the sum of $50 above the cost of the bond will be realized. The life tenant can argue that this amount should be paid to him as a return or gain on the investment, taking the place of interest, and that to give it to trust principal would be to award the remainderman an unjustified windfall.

The common law cases refused the plea of the life tenant in the discount cases and treated the gain on collection as belonging to trust

4. See § 122, post.

5. Hemenway v. Hemenway, 134 Mass. 446; Ballantine v. Young, 74 N.J.Eq. 572, 70 A. 668; McLouth v. Hunt, 154 N.Y. 179, 48 N.E. 548, 39 L.R.A. 230.

6. Shaw v. Cordis, 143 Mass. 443, 9 N.E. 794.

7. Morris v. Dosch, 194 Ark. 153, 106 S.W.2d 159 (1937).

8. American Security & Trust Co. v. Payne, 33 App.D.C. 178 (1834); Liberty Nat. Bank & Trust Co. v. Loomis, 275 Ky. 445, 121 S.W.2d 947, 131 A.L.R. 1419 (1938); In re Penn-Gaskell's Estate, 208 Pa. 346, 57 A. 715.

principal.[9] Against this result it might be urged: (1) if amortization for premiums is to take place, logically accumulations in favor of the life tenant for discounts should occur to afford impartiality of treatment between income and remainder beneficiaries; (2) bonds are sold at a discount on account of low interest rates and a part of the yield of such a bond is the discount to be collected at maturity; (3) if interest alone is to be given the income beneficiary, in the case of a bond bought at a discount the asset will be an underproductive one and should be handled in the manner described later with regard to other unproductive or underproductive trust investments where the income beneficiary gets part of the proceeds of the sale of the property.[10]

On the other hand it can be said: (1) the labor and expense involved in computing discounts is not justified by the results; (2) the advantages to the life tenant from premiums are balanced by the disadvantages from discounts, and *mutatis mutandis* with the remainderman; (3) the life tenant gets income at once from the amount of the discount, since it is invested in other property and earns income.

When the Uniform Principal and Income Act was drafted the arguments of convenience and ease of administration prevailed over a strict attempt to do exact justice between the two classes of beneficiaries, and it was provided that all the returns from premium bonds should be treated as income and the entire sum collected at the maturity of a discount bond should accrue to trust principal.[11]

In past years U.S. savings bonds sometimes have been a favored investment by trustees. They bear no interest but appreciate in value as they approach maturity. For example, $750 may be paid for such a bond, on the promise of the government that ten years later it can be redeemed for $1,000. Here the trustee realizes no interest as such during the ten year period, but at the end gains $250 which in form at least is principal. Several legislatures have recognized the injustice of allocating this entire sum to trust principal, have felt that it was in substance interest, although not called that, and have provided either that the appreciation should be treated as trust income when collected,[12] or that the annual amounts of the appreciation fixed by the terms of the bond should be regarded as income when accruing and should be advanced to income from the principal of the trust fund year by year.[13]

9. In re Gartenlaub's Estate, 198 Cal. 204, 244 P. 348 (1926); In re Houston's Will, 19 Del.Ch. 207, 165 A. 132 (1933); Townsend v. United States Trust Co., 3 Redf.Surr. 220; Mercantile-Commerce Bank & Trust Co. v. Morse, 356 Mo. 336, 201 S.W.2d 915 (1947).

10. See § 121, post, and the exceptions noted there with regard to interest due on defaulted bonds and the proceeds of salvage operations.

11. Unif.Princ. & Inc.Act, § 6. With one minor exception this rule was adopted in § 7 of the Revised Uniform Act.

12. See, for example, West's Ann.Cal. Civ.Code § 730.08; Conn.Gen.Stats.Ann. § 45–114. And see Bogert, Trusts and Trustees (rev. 2d edit.), § 826.

13. See, for example, Ill.Rev.Stat. c. 30, ¶ 508; N.Y.—McKinney's EPTL 11–2.1(f); 20 Pa.C.S.A. § 8106. See also In re Wehner's Will, 238 Wis. 557, 300 N.W. 241 (1941). A loss caused by redemption before maturity has been placed on trust income. In re Coulter's Estate, 204 Misc. 473, 121 N.Y.S.2d 531 (1953), affirmed 283 App.Div. 691, 128 N.Y.S.2d 539 (1954).

RENTS [1]

§ 114. Net rents are to be treated as trust income. From gross rents should be deducted such items as the cost of collecting the rent, insurance, and repairs, but not the expense of making improvements. Although in tax accounting practice a reserve for depreciation and obsolescence of buildings and other improvements to real estate is deducted from gross rents in computing taxable income, there is a split of authority as to whether a trustee is or is not allowed or required to follow this procedure for trust accounting purposes.

There is usually little difficulty with regard to the income and principal accounts as far as rents are concerned. Such receipts are clearly gains arising from the use of trust principal and should go to the income beneficiary.[2]

As will be shown later,[3] however, certain expenses should be deducted from gross rents, namely, such items as the cost of collecting the rent, insurance premiums on the real estate rented, taxes, interest on a mortgage on the trust realty, and repairs necessary to make the property safe and rentable. If the property is substantially altered or improved, however, the expense should not be taken from the rents but rather from the principal of the trust.

In recent years trustees have raised the question whether they should or may set up out of gross rents a sinking fund or reserve account to protect trust principal from depreciation and obsolescence of buildings located on realty owned by the trust. It has been urged that this practice has been followed in corporate bookkeeping and in the computation of income taxes. Even though the improvements to real estate are kept in repair from income, it is argued that they lose value due to depreciation or obsolescence. For example, a house may have greatly decreased in value due to the fact that there has been a change in the tastes of tenants which renders the building unrentable. It may be out of style and lack conveniences demanded by present day tenants.

Many of the cases which have considered the question have held

§ 114

1. Restatement, Trusts, Second, §§ 233, 239.

2. A bonus paid the trustee-lessor for extending the lease has been treated as trust income. Archambault's Estate, 232 Pa. 347, 81 A. 314. Where the trustee received a sum for permitting cancellation of the lease, it should be treated as rent and distributed to the income beneficiaries from time to time. Johnson v. Collamore, 271 Mass. 521, 171 N.E. 717 (1930); Lang v. Mississippi Valley Tr. Co., 343 Mo. 979, 124 S.W.2d 1198 (1938).

3. See § 124, post.

that there is neither a duty [4] nor a privilege [5] to set up a reserve for depreciation out of rents, and that any loss arising from depreciation or obsolescence of the building or other improvement must be borne by trust principal. Sometimes the settlor expressly permits or directs the maintenance of such a fund,[6] or a grant of discretion to decide income and principal questions has been held to permit the trustee to create a depreciation reserve.[7]

However there have been a number of recent cases in which the courts have directed the trustee to set aside a depreciation reserve without the authority of express language in the trust instrument or in a statute. In Minnesota [8] the Supreme Court, in a matter where the trustee held stock in a realty corporation owning apartment buildings, held that where depreciable buildings are acquired with trust funds after creation of the trust the trustee should deduct from the gross receipts a reasonable depreciation reserve. The California Supreme Court [9] directed the trustees to set aside depreciation reserves with respect to major renovations and repairs to a building upon the basis of section 7(3) of the Uniform Principal and Income Act then in effect in California. In a recent Maine decision,[10] the Supreme Court of that state found an implication that the trustee could create a depreciation reserve out of gross income, presumably to enable the trustee to borrow money to install an elevator in an office building held by the trustee. More recently, in an Illinois decision,[11] an appellate court held that the

---

4. Evans v. Ockershausen, 69 App.D.C. 285, 100 F.2d 695 (1938), certiorari denied 306 U.S. 633, 59 S.Ct. 462, 83 L.Ed. 1034 (1939); In re Davies' Estate, 197 Misc. 827, 96 N.Y.S.2d 191 (1950), affirmed 277 App. Div. 1021, 100 N.Y.S.2d 710 (1950). In re Hubbell's Will, 302 N.Y. 246, 97 N.E.2d 888 (1951) (court refused to pass on question of duty). But see In re Kaplan's Will, 195 Misc. 132, 88 N.Y.S.2d 851 (1949) (duty to create reserve for physical and material depreciation and obsolescence).

5. Hubbell v. Burnet, 46 F.2d 446 (8th Cir.1931); Laflin v. C.I.R., 69 F.2d 460 (7th Cir.1934); In re Roth's Estate, 139 N.J.Eq. 588, 52 A.2d 811 (1947); In re Ottman's Estate, 197 Misc. 645, 95 N.Y.S.2d 5 (1949); Chapin v. Collard, 29 Wn.2d 788, 189 P.2d 642 (1948).

But in some cases the existence of a privilege to set up such a fund has been asserted. Collins v. Tavares, 37 Hawaii 109; In re Girard's Estate, 49 Pa.D. & C. 217. This is particularly true where the improvements were owned by a trustee who was operating a business. In re Bailey's Trust, 241 Minn. 143, 62 N.W.2d 829 (1954) (nursery business); In re Ambrose's Will, 12 A.D.2d 687, 207 N.Y.S.2d 930 (1960).

And there has been some tendency to permit a trustee holding stock in a corporation which owned realty on which improvements were located to set aside out of dividends a depreciation reserve for obsolescence of the buildings. In re Clarke's Trust, 306 N.Y. 733, 117 N.E.2d 910 (1954) (per curiam opinion; Froessel, J., dissented and cited N.Y. cases disapproving a depreciation reserve). And see footnote 8, infra.

6. Fidelity Union Trust v. McGraw, 138 N.J.Eq. 415, 48 A.2d 279 (1946).

7. Rafferty v. Parker, 241 F.2d 594 (8th Cir.1957); In re Tynan's Estate, 129 Cal.App.2d 364, 276 P.2d 809 (1954).

8. In re Warner's Trust, 263 Minn. 449, 117 N.W.2d 224 (1962).

9. In re Kelley's Estate, 63 Cal.2d 679, 47 Cal.Rptr. 897, 408 P.2d 353 (1965).

10. Thaxter v. Fry, 222 A.2d 686 (Me. 1966).

11. Harris Trust and Savings Bank v. MacLeod, 4 Ill.App.3d 542, 281 N.E.2d 457 (1972). For current law see Ill.Rev.Stat. c. 30, ¶ 514(a)(2).

terms of the trust instrument impliedly authorized the trustees to set aside depreciation reserves.

Occasionally earlier statutes had authorized establishment of a depreciation reserve out of rents.[12] The Uniform Principal and Income Act provides that all rents are to be treated as trust income, and makes no exception with regard to a depreciation fund; another section providing for the protection of trust principal where the property is subject to "depletion" would seem inapplicable because that term refers to exhaustion by reason of the extraction of issues and profits in the case of oil or other mineral properties.[13]

The Restatement of Trusts (1935) contained no provision authorizing a depreciation reserve. In the Restatement of Trusts, Second,[14] published in 1957, a clause was inserted to the effect that the existence of a duty or privilege to create such a reserve depends on the circumstances of the trust in question, and a number of relevant considerations are mentioned. The Revised Uniform Principal and Income Act requires a charge against income for a reasonable allowance for depreciation under generally accepted accounting principles and permits depreciation of "extraordinary repairs or expenses incurred in making a capital improvement to principal".[15]

In support of a duty or privilege to create a depreciation reserve, it can be argued that such a practice is customary in corporate and tax accounting and that the federal income tax statute permits such a deduction. But it would not seem that this argument should be conclusive, since such practices do not involve an allocation of burdens and benefits between two owners of the same property but merely a recognition of the shrinkage in value in the case of a single owner. A further argument is that equity imputes to a settlor the intent that in the case of wasting property its original value shall be maintained out of the returns from it (as in the cases of mineral or timber lands held in trust), and that improvements to land are wasting assets. Yet the cases applying this doctrine have been instances in which the res was exhausted due to exploitation and use and not merely due to economic and social changes.

As supporting the position of those cases which deny a privilege or duty to create a depreciation reserve, it should be kept in mind that the settlor is regarded as primarily interested in the income beneficiaries who are closest to him, that the net rents of realty (after the usual deductions) are often inadequate for the support of the income beneficiaries, and that it is not natural to impute to the settlor an intent to require or permit a further deduction for a depreciation reserve. Further, the amount and rate of depreciation is somewhat speculative.

12. See, for example, Ala.Code T. 58, § 86(5).

13. §§ 3(1) and 10. The Revised Uniform Principal and Income Act of 1962 provides for a depreciation reserve out of rents, except in the case of realty occupied by a beneficiary.

14. § 239, Comment *h*.

15. §§ 13(a)(2), 13(c)(3).

The settlor may have expected the remaindermen to take the risk of such depreciation as well as to have the possibility of gains from appreciation. Ordinarily decreases and increases in the value of the trust property are concerns of the principal account of the trust.

 WESTLAW REFERENCES

rent /s "trust income"

find 117 nw2d 224

390k274(1) /p depreciation

"depreciation reserve" /s rent /p trust

CORPORATE DISTRIBUTIONS—CASH DIVIDENDS [1]

§ 115. At common law there were three principal rules regarding the allocation of benefits received by a trustee on account of ownership of corporate stock.

The Kentucky courts treated all benefits, whatever their form and source, as trust income. This rule was not followed elsewhere and has been replaced by a statute in Kentucky.

The Pennsylvania rule was based on the idea that a trustee receiving a corporate distribution should consider its source, that is, whether it came from corporate earnings which accrued during the trust's holding of the stock or prior thereto, and should also protect the original book or intact value of the trust's interest in the corporation by allocating to trust principal so much of any corporate distribution as was necessary for such preservation. This rule was followed in a number of states, but has been abandoned in Pennsylvania and other states.

The Massachusetts rule was based on ease of administration and substantial justice between income and remainder beneficiaries. It allotted cash dividends, whether ordinary or extraordinary, to trust income, on the theory that they were generally earned during the trustee's holding of the stock, and gave to trust principal those dividends payable in the stock of the declaring corporation, since they generally came in large part from surplus of the corporation created before the trust held the stock. This rule had a considerable following in the case law and in recent years the trend has been much in its favor.

While the Pennsylvania rule might have been applied to ordinary cash dividends, if strict logic were to have been followed, it was held to govern only cash dividends which were extraordinary in amount or time.

§ 115

1. Restatement, Trusts, Second, § 236.
Bogert, Trusts and Trustees (rev. 2d edit.),
§§ 843–844.

Special consideration is given to cash dividends payable upon the liquidation of the corporation or from a sale of part of its assets, and to dividends payable in "scrip" or in notes or bonds.

The Uniform Principal and Income Act adopted the Massachusetts rules with regard to all corporate distributions. The Revised Uniform Act also follows the Massachusetts rules in allocating corporate distributions in the form of stock dividends or stock splits of the distributing corporation to principal.

A trustee who holds corporate stock as a part of the trust principal is obliged to determine what to do with various benefits received by him from the corporation on account of his stock ownership. His problem is whether, in fairness and equity and in compliance with the expressed or inferred intent of the settlor, part or all of these benefits should be allocated to trust principal or to trust income.

Many settlors of large or complex trusts expressly provide as to the disposition of corporate benefits between income and principal accounts of the trusts, or grant to their trustees the power to allocate such benefits in their discretion.[2] A trustee is, of course, protected in following such instructions.

In early case law the American courts established three rules for the distribution of corporate benefits; the Kentucky, the Massachusetts, and the Pennsylvania rules. The Kentucky rule simply provided that all corporate benefits received by a trustee by virtue of his ownership of stock went to the income account. No inquiry was made as to the source of the benefit or the effect of its distribution, nor was its form considered. Hence cash and stock dividends, whether usual or extraordinary, went to the trust income account.[3] Later a statute was enacted to the effect that all dividends except those in the stock of the declaring corporation should be income,[4] and still later an amendment was made to the effect that dividends in stock of the declaring corporation that were less than 10% of the outstanding stock should be treated as trust income.[5]

The Pennsylvania courts sought to inquire into the effect of extraordinary cash and of all stock dividends, in order to determine the fairest distribution.[6] They argued that the income beneficiary should be equitably entitled to corporate income earned while he is a beneficiary, and that the remainderman should be equitably entitled to have the book or intact value of the stock maintained as it was when the

2. Lindau v. Community Fund of Baltimore, 188 Md. 474, 53 A.2d 409 (1947); In re Whitacre's Will, 208 Minn. 286, 293 N.W. 784 (1940).

3. Hite's Devisees v. Hite's Ex'r, 93 Ky. 257, 20 S.W. 778, 14 Ky.Law Rep. 385, 19 L.R.A. 173, 40 Am.St.Rep. 189. But see Bowles v. Stilley's Ex'r, 267 S.W.2d 707 (Ky.1954) (ordinary dividends are income, but extraordinary dividends in any form are capital).

4. Ky.R.S. § 386.020(4).

5. Ky.L.1954, c. 52. The present provisions are those of the Uniform Principal and Income Act; see Ky.Rev.Stats. § 386.230.

6. Earp's Appeal, 28 Pa. 368; Smith's Estate, 140 Pa. 344, 21 A. 438, 23 Am.St. Rep. 237.

trust first obtained the stock and to corporate income earned before the trust began to hold the stock but distributed by the corporation while the stock was in the hands of the trustee. They tried to distribute the benefits received from the corporation in such a way as to preserve original trust capital value. The intact or book value of one share of stock is the sum of corporate capital and surplus, divided by the number of shares of stock outstanding. Thus if a trustee bought one share of stock in a corporation at a time when the capital of the corporation was $10,000 and the surplus $5,000, and there were 100 shares outstanding, the book or intact value of the trust's investment in the stock would be $15,000 divided by 100, or $150. Under the Pennsylvania rule there was a duty on the part of the trustee to maintain this intact value of $150 and to use corporate dividends to preserve it to whatever extent was necessary.

The Pennsylvania rule was originally followed by many states,[7] but some of these jurisdictions have changed to the Massachusetts rule by adoption of the Uniform Principal and Income Act or other statute or by a shift in court decisions.[8] Pennsylvania has abandoned its rule by the adoption of the Uniform Act so that the rule now has a very limited effect. In two well-reasoned decisions it has been held that a statute substituting the Massachusetts for the Pennsylvania rule may constitutionally be made to have a retroactive effect, so that all trusts, no matter when created, are to be governed by the new rule,[9] since the Act is concerned with rules of administration and there is no property right in having corporate distributions allocated in any particular manner.

In a leading Pennsylvania case [10] the court held that it would not extend application of the original rule of apportionment to any new situations, since the complicated corporate financing techniques devised by accountants and lawyers to meet tax problems have rendered it impractical for the courts to go into the details of the sources and effects of these involved corporate distributions.

The Massachusetts rule is simple and is intended to ease the trustee's work and to accomplish approximate justice between income beneficiaries and remaindermen. The criterion is the form of the dividend. If the dividend is in cash, the trustee is entitled to treat it as

---

7. Cal., Del., Haw., Iowa, Md., Minn., Miss., N.J., N.H., N.Y., S.C., Tenn., Vt. and Wis.

8. See Bogert, Trusts and Trustees (rev. 2d edit.), § 848, for a discussion of changes and the present status of the Pennsylvania rule. By N.Y.L.1926, c. 843, it was provided that stock dividends thereafter received under trusts going into effect after May 17, 1926, should be treated as trust principal. The Pennsylvania rule was left in effect in New York as to trusts created before 1926.

9. In re Catherwood's Trust, 405 Pa. 61, 173 A.2d 86 (1961); In re Allis' Will, 6

Wis.2d 1, 94 N.W.2d 226 (1959). To the same effect see In re Warner's Trust, 263 Minn. 449, 117 N.W.2d 224 (1962).

10. Cunningham's Estate, 395 Pa. 1, 149 A.2d 72 (1959). For New York cases illustrating treatment of highly involved corporate financing problems, see In re Fosdick's Trust, 4 N.Y.2d 646, 176 N.Y.S.2d 966, 152 N.E.2d 228 (1958), reargument denied 5 N.Y.2d 861, 183 N.Y.S.2d 1025, 156 N.E.2d 923 (1958); In re Bingham's Will, 7 N.Y.2d 1, 194 N.Y.S.2d 465, 163 N.E.2d 301 (1959).

trust income without inquiry as to its source or effect or whether it is ordinary or extraordinary. If the dividend is payable in stock of the declaring corporation, the trustee should treat it as trust principal, but if the dividend is in the stock of a corporation other than the declaring corporation (for example, that of an affiliate or subsidiary corporation) it should be treated as trust income.[11] Cash dividends are usually declared out of current income accumulated during the time the trust has been holding the stock. Stock dividends are often declared out of undistributed earnings and surplus accumulated for some time and in many cases accruing in whole or in large part before the trust held the stock. A rough and ready rule which will do substantial justice is to be preferred to a more complex rule which strives for ideal justice but causes much trouble and expense. Giving stock dividends to trust principal is of benefit to the life tenant as well as the remainderman, since the life tenant immediately begins to receive income on such stock. The settlor can always expressly provide for the method of distribution of stock and cash dividends, if he does not like the rule fixed by law.

If the directors of the corporation declaring the dividend state in the resolution the source or purpose of the dividend, the trustee is entitled to rely on this statement, as where it is reported that the dividend is paid out of principal,[12] or is in payment of arrearages of dividends on cumulative preferred stock.[13]

Cash dividends are of two types, ordinary and extraordinary. The former are dividends payable in cash which are of the usual size and normally declared at regular intervals. Extraordinary dividends are larger or paid at less frequent intervals than those usually paid by the corporation.

Under the Pennsylvania rule, if a trustee bought in 1940 ten shares of stock in the X corporation, each share having a par value of $100, and the corporation then had a capital of $100,000 and a surplus of $100,000, the book value of each share of the stock, assuming there are 1,000 shares outstanding, would be $200. If the trustee held the stock until 1950, during which time ordinary cash dividends were paid and the capitalization remained the same but the surplus reached $150,000, and in 1950 the corporation issued an *extraordinary* cash dividend of $100 on each share of stock, it is evident that after this dividend has been paid the corporation will have a capitalization of $100,000 and a

11. Minot v. Paine, 99 Mass. 101, 96 Am.Dec. 705. See Mass.G.L. c. 203 § 21A. This rule has been followed by the courts in Ala., Conn., D.C., Ill., Ind., Ky., Me., Mich., Mo., Neb., N.H., N.Car., Ohio, R.I., S.D., Tex., Va., and W.Va., and it has been adopted in some 37 states which have enacted either the Uniform or the Revised Uniform Principal and Income Act or other statutes. See Bogert, Trusts and Trustees (rev. 2d edit.), § 850.

The Restatement of Trusts (1935) approved the Pennsylvania rule, but Restatement, Trusts, Second (1957) follows the Massachusetts rule.

12. Girard Trust Co. v. Mueller, 125 N.J.Eq. 597, 7 A.2d 413 (1939).

13. In re King's Estate, 349 Pa. 27, 36 A.2d 504, 153 A.L.R. 488 (1944).

surplus of $50,000, and that each share of stock will have a book value of $150. In order to maintain the book value of the trust's original investment in ten shares of this stock, namely, $2,000, the trustee who receives the $1,000 extraordinary cash dividend will be obliged to treat $500 of it as trust principal. His stock after the dividend will have a book value of $150 a share so that the ten shares will be worth $1,500. When bought it had a book value of $2,000. The $500 in book value lost by reason of this extraordinary cash dividend must be replaced by applying $500 of the extraordinary dividend to trust principal.[14] In those states following the Pennsylvania rule no inquiry was made as to the source or effect of *ordinary* cash dividends and they were considered trust income, although logical consistency would seem to have required otherwise.[15]

It is generally agreed that a dividend payable in stock or cash, as the trustee may elect, is to be treated as a cash dividend,[16] no matter whether the trustee elects to take stock or cash.

Sometimes a corporation does not have liquid assets from which to pay a cash dividend and issues a "scrip" dividend, that is, a promise to pay in cash or some other form of property at a later date. These dividends should be accorded the same treatment as the type of property in which they are ultimately payable.[17]

Sometimes a dividend is in the form of notes or bonds of the declaring corporation, in which case it is usually treated in the same way as a cash dividend would be under the Massachusetts rule, but its source and effect may have to be examined under the Pennsylvania rule.[18]

Where a trustee receives a dividend which is stated by the corporation declaring it to be based on a distribution of corporate capital,[19] or to be the result of total liquidation of the corporate assets,[20] he is usually required to treat it as trust principal, although logically under

---

14. Foard v. Safe Dep. & Tr. Co., 122 Md. 476, 89 A. 724; Lang v. Lang's Ex'r, 57 N.J.Eq. 325, 41 A. 705.

15. Opperman's Estate, 319 Pa. 455, 179 A. 729 (1935); In re Boyle's Estate, 235 Wis. 591, 294 N.W. 29, 130 A.L.R. 486 (1940).

16. Davis v. Jackson, 152 Mass. 58, 25 N.E. 21, 23 Am.St.Rep. 801; Newport Trust Co. v. Van Rensselaer, 32 R.I. 231, 78 A. 1009, 35 L.R.A.,N.S., 563; Uniform Principal and Income Act, § 5, Revised Uniform Act § 6(d). But see Ballantine v. Young, 79 N.J.Eq. 70, 81 A. 119; Thompson's Estate, 262 Pa. 278, 105 A. 273.

17. Hayes v. St. Louis Union Trust Co., 317 Mo. 1028, 298 S.W. 91 (1927); In re Robinson's Trust, 218 Pa. 481, 67 A. 775.

18. Humphrey v. Lang, 169 N.C. 601, 86 S.E. 526; Lueder's Estate, 337 Pa. 155, 10 A.2d 415 (1940).

19. Citizens & Southern Nat. Bank v. Fleming, 181 Ga. 116, 181 S.E. 768 (1935).

20. Powell v. Madison Safe Deposit and Trust Co., 208 Ind. 432, 196 N.E. 324 (1935); In re Etzel's Estate, 211 Iowa 700, 234 N.W. 210 (1931).

Capital gains distributions made by a mutual fund were allocable to principal under the then applicable principal and income statute. They were either a return of capital or profits realized on the sale of shares of the fund. In re Estate of Brock, 420 Pa. 454, 218 A.2d 281 (1966). See also Tait v. Peck, 346 Mass. 521, 194 N.E.2d 707 (1963).

§ 6(c) of the Revised Uniform Principal and Income Act provides that all distributions from capital gains, whether in the form of cash or an option to take new stock or cash or an option to purchase additional shares, are principal.

the former Pennsylvania rule it might have been apportionable.[21]

A dividend may be declared out of the proceeds of the sale of part of the assets of the corporation, in which case it might be called a partial liquidating dividend and so usually payable to trust principal.[22] But if the corporation is a trading corporation engaged regularly in buying and selling, maintains its assets at a relative stable figure, and declares a dividend out of the proceeds of the sale of part of its property, there is basis for holding that this is a distribution of the income of the corporation and therefore allocable by the trustee to trust income.[23]

Where a trustee holds shares in an investment trust or mutual fund which makes a distribution declared to be capital gains, that is, as the result of the sale of some of the securities in its portfolio at a profit, the majority view is that the distribution should be placed in the income account of the trust, on the ground that the investment trust is in reality running an investment business and that capital gains distributions are profits of that business.[24] Certainly investors in such trusts count on such distributions as income in computing the yield of their investments. Recent statistics show that the distributions by these investment trusts which are labelled income produced only about 2.8% on the investment, and that the capital gains distributions amounted to about 2.3%, so that to obtain a reasonable yield for the investor both distributions would have to be regarded as income. But the operators of the investment trusts argued strenuously that capital gains distributions should go to trust principal and they have had some success in convincing legislatures to take that position.[25]

 WESTLAW REFERENCES

dividend /s allocat! /s trust

"pennsylvania rule" /s dividend

"massachusetts rule" /s dividend

find 218 a2d 281

390k272.2(1)

390k272.3(11)

---

21. Lewis' Estate, 351 Pa. 576, 41 A.2d 683 (1945).

22. Curtis v. Osborn, 79 Conn. 555, 65 A. 968; Wilberding v. Miller, 90 Ohio St. 28, 106 N.E. 665.

23. Krug v. Mercantile Trust & Dep. Co., 133 Md. 110, 104 A. 414; Central Hanover Bank & Trust Co. v. Braman, 111 N.J. Eq. 191, 161 A. 674 (1932).

24. Rosenburg v. Lombardi, 222 Md. 346, 160 A.2d 601 (1960); In re Bailey's Will, 20 Misc.2d 539, 188 N.Y.S.2d 1005 (1959); Lovett Estate, 78 Pa.D. & C. 21.

25. See discussion in Bogert, Trusts and Trustees (rev. 2d edit.), § 858. § 6(c) of the Revised Uniform Principal and Income Act of 1962 takes this position.

STOCK DIVIDENDS [1]

§ 116. **Under the original Kentucky rule stock dividends were trust income, but this rule has been recently replaced by statute.**

Under the Massachusetts rule dividends in the stock of the declaring corporation are trust principal, but dividends in the stock of corporations other than the declaring corporation are trust income. Both the Uniform and the Revised Uniform Principal and Income Act follow this rule.

Under the Pennsylvania decisions stock dividends were trust principal to the extent necessary to preserve the value of the trust's original investment in the stock; and beyond that they were to be allocated to trust income or principal, dependent on the source of the corporate surplus on which they were based. This rule is no longer in effect in Pennsylvania.

Corporations quite often issue dividends in stock instead of in cash. Thus a corporation having $100,000 of capital stock of the par value of $100 a share outstanding may decide to double its stock and issue to each holder of one share of the old stock an additional share of the new stock. By way of corporate bookkeeping it will decrease its surplus account by the amount of $100,000 and increase its capital account by the same figure. If a trustee owned ten shares of the stock prior to the stock dividend, he will be given ten more shares and will have to decide whether in his accounts these ten new shares should be treated as income or principal of his trust, or should be allocated partly to one account and partly to another.

As previously suggested, under the common law Kentucky rule the current income account would be entitled to all benefits from corporate stock. Hence stock dividends of all corporations, whether of the issuing corporation or another, were to be considered trust income,[2] but this rule has been replaced by statute.[3]

The Massachusetts rule makes a distinction between stock of the corporation declaring the dividend and stock of another corporation. Thus if a trustee holds stock of X corporation and it declares a dividend in its own stock, the dividend is to be treated as principal of the trust.[4] However, if X corporation declares a dividend in stock of Y corporation, a subsidiary corporation the stock of which is all held by X corporation, then the trustee should treat the stock of Y corporation as trust income.[5] Stock of this type is usually based on an investment of

---

§ 116

1. Restatement, Trusts, Second, § 236; Bogert, Trusts and Trustees (rev. 2d edit.), §§ 845–852.

2. Goff v. Evans, 217 Ky. 664, 290 S.W. 490 (1927); Lightfoot v. Beard, 230 Ky. 488, 20 S.W.2d 90 (1929).

3. See § 115, ante.

4. Hyde v. Holmes, 198 Mass. 287, 84 N.E. 318; Lyman v. Pratt, 183 Mass. 58, 66 N.E. 423.

5. Gray v. Hemenway, 212 Mass. 239, 98 N.E. 789; Creed v. McAleer, 275 Mass. 353, 175 N.E. 761, 80 A.L.R. 1117 (1931). As to distributions which result from a court order, see Rev.Unif.Princ. & Inc.Act, 1962, § 6(b)(3).

surplus of the declaring corporation in the stock of the other corporation and hence its distribution is in substance a distribution of the earnings of the declaring corporation.

The Massachusetts court [6] has stated the rule as follows: "The rule for determining the respective rights of those entitled to the income and to the principal of trust funds established long ago in this commonwealth, and constantly followed, 'is to regard cash dividends however large, as income, and stock dividends, however made as capital.'" And in an early leading case [7] it explained the reason for the rule, as follows: "A trustee needs one plain principle to guide him; and the cestui que trust ought not to be subjected to the expense of going behind the action of the directors, and investigating the concerns of the corporation, especially if it is out of our jurisdiction."

The courts that have followed this Massachusetts rule have admitted that it is not logically perfect. "It was not pretended that this rule, which has been commonly known as the Massachusetts rule, was the ideal rule of reason; nor have the courts of high authority which have given their approval of it ever claimed it to be such, or one which would accomplish justice under all circumstances. What has been claimed for it is that its general application, at least if due regard be had for the substance and intent of the transaction, would prove more beneficent in its consequences, and on the whole lead to results more closely approximating to what was just and equitable, than would the application of any other rule or any attempt to go behind the declaration of the dividend to search out and discover the equities of each case according to some theoretical ideal." [8]

Both the Uniform and the Revised Uniform Principal and Income Acts follow the Massachusetts rule as to stock dividends. [9]

The Pennsylvania rule, as previously stated, called upon the trustee to investigate the effect of the stock dividend he receives, whether in the stock of the issuing or another corporation. His problem was to learn what the original book value of his interest in the corporation was, and what it was after the stock dividend had been paid. Thus if we assume that the trustee bought ten shares of stock in a corporation having 1,000 shares outstanding, the par value of each being $100, making its total capital account $100,000, and at the time of the purchase the surplus of the corporation was $100,000, the trustee would

---

6. Talbot v. Milliken, 221 Mass. 367, 368, 108 N.E. 1060.

7. Minot v. Paine, 99 Mass. 101, 108, 96 Am.Dec. 705.

8. Smith v. Dana, 77 Conn. 543, 548, 549, 60 A. 117, 69 L.R.A. 76, 107 Am.St. Rep. 51.

9. § 5, Uniform Act; § 6(a), Revised Uniform Act.

Where the corporation in which the trustee owns stock is reorganized, merged,

or consolidated, and shares of a succeeding corporation are issued in place of the old, the two corporations are considered as one for the purpose of applying stock dividend rules. Uniform Principal and Income Act, § 5(4). For cases of such types, see Matter of Hagen's Will, 262 N.Y. 301, 186 N.E. 792 (1933); In re King's Estate, 349 Pa. 27, 36 A.2d 504, 153 A.L.R. 488 (1944).

find that the original value of his holding in this corporation, from a bookkeeping and not a market point of view, was $200 a share, making a total of $2,000. If after some years the corporation has increased its surplus to $200,000, and decides to issue a stock dividend of 100%, it will award to the trustee ten shares of the new stock. The capital of the corporation will then be $200,000, its surplus $100,000, 2,000 shares will be outstanding, and the book value of each share will be $150. This will make the book value of the trustee's holding of twenty shares $150 times twenty, or $3,000. The trust's interest in the corporation has been increased from $2,000 to $3,000 as a result of the stock dividend. The trustee was required to maintain the original book value of the investment, namely, $2,000. The ten old shares now have a book value of $1,500, leaving a shrinkage in book value of $500 without taking into account the new stock. Hence new stock having a book value of $500 will have to be allocated to the trust principal account and this will amount to 3.33 shares of the ten shares of new stock.[10] As to the remaining 6.67 shares of new stock having a book value of $1,000, some of the Pennsylvania rule cases allocated them in their entirety to trust income,[11] but the most recent cases have held that this stock should be allocated according to the date of origin of the surplus on which it was based.[12] If investigation of the corporate books showed that the undistributed earnings which produced the surplus on which this portion of the stock dividend was based were all received by the corporation during the period while the trust had been holding the stock, the 6.67 shares should go to trust income, but if any part of those earnings had accrued before the trust received the stock, there should be an apportionment between income and principal of the trust.

This allocation required the trustee to ascertain what the book values of the trust's stock interest were at two dates. He could not rely with absolute confidence on the bookkeeping of the corporation which may have been erroneous. At his peril he must find out original book value and book value after the receipt of the stock dividend.[13] Either he must employ lawyers and accountants and take the chance their results are correct, or he must get an agreement between competent beneficiaries, or he must apply to the court of equity for instructions. The first method is expensive and hazardous, the second not often

---

10. Sloan's Estate, 258 Pa. 368, 102 A. 31; In re Harkness' Estate, 283 Pa. 464, 129 A. 458. And see In re Duffill's Estate, 180 Cal. 748, 183 P. 337; Bryan v. Aikin, 10 Del.Ch. 446, 86 A. 674, 45 L.R.A.,N.S., 477; Kalbach v. Clark, 133 Iowa 215, 110 N.W. 599, 12 L.R.A.,N.S., 801, 12 Ann.Cas. 647; Miller v. Safe Dep. & Trust Co. of Baltimore, 127 Md. 610, 96 A. 766; Goodwin v. McGaughey, 108 Minn. 248, 122 N.W. 6; Holbrook v. Holbrook, 74 N.H. 201, 66 A. 124, 12 L.R.A.,N.S., 768; Van Doren v. Olden, 19 N.J.Eq. 176, 97 Am.Dec. 650; Pritchitt v. Nashville Trust Co., 96 Tenn. 472, 36 S.W. 1064, 33 L.R.A. 856; In re Heaton's Estate, 89 Vt. 550, 96 A. 21, L.R.A.1916D, 201; In re Barron's Will, 163 Wis. 275, 155 N.W. 1087.

11. Mallory's Estate, 285 Pa. 186, 131 A. 714. For development of the rule, see 83 Univ. of Pa.L.R. 773, 86 Univ. of Pa.L.R. 765.

12. King's Estate, 361 Pa. 68, 66 A.2d 68 (1949); Harvey's Estate, 395 Pa. 62, 149 A.2d 104 (1959); In re Bingham's Will, 7 N.Y.2d 1, 194 N.Y.S.2d 465, 163 N.E.2d 301 (1959).

13. In re Flinn's Estate, 320 Pa. 15, 181 A. 492 (1935).

available, and the third is costly and time-consuming. Furthermore, it may be difficult to get a statement of the situation as to book value as of a given date not at the beginning of a month, quarter or year. And the books are apt to be located in a distant office. The Pennsylvania rule was idealistic but impractical. For these reasons,[14] and because of the clarity and simplicity of the Massachusetts rule, there has been a distinct shift to the latter rule in the last thirty years.[15]

A stock *dividend* should be distinguished from a stock *split* whereby an increased number of shares are issued to a stockholder without any change in the corporate capital or surplus accounts. The stockholder has an increased number of shares but the book value of his holding is not changed and there is no distribution of corporate property. Obviously stock splits should be allocated to trust principal.[16]

Very frequently the settlor provides in the trust instrument for the disposition of stock or other dividends, or grants discretion to his trustee to allocate them. These terms are effective but they have occasioned a great deal of litigation in their construction.[17]

In recent years many corporations have instituted a practice of declaring small stock dividends with some regularity in lieu of, or supplementary to, cash dividends. It would seem that the rule allocating all stock dividends to trust principal should not be applied to them, and that if the amount of stock issued does not exceed a certain small percentage of all the stock of the corporation of the same kind such dividends should be allocated to trust income.[18] For example, in Pennsylvania the maximum percentage has been fixed at 6%.[19]

14. See the Uniform and the Revised Uniform Principal and Income Acts adopted in at least 37 states. The statutory adoptions are cited in Bogert, Trusts and Trustees (rev. 2d edit.), § 816. Because the Uniform Principal and Income Act, as adopted in Pennsylvania, provided that it should apply to all questions arising after its adoption, regardless of the time of the origin of the trust, and thereafter the Supreme Court held such retroactive clause constitutional, the Pennsylvania rule as developed by case law is no longer applicable in that state. Catherwood's Trust, 405 Pa. 61, 173 A.2d 86 (1961).

15. For an early application of the complex Pennsylvania rule, see Appeal of Earp, 1857, 28 Pa. 368.

16. § 6(a) of the Revised Uniform Principal and Income Act states so specifically. And see Pentland v. Pentland, 113 So.2d 872 (Fla.App.1959), certiorari denied 119 So.2d 295 (1960); Trust Estate of Pew, 398 Pa. 523, 158 A.2d 552 (1960); Estate of Valiquette, 122 Vt. 350, 173 A.2d 832 (1961).

17. See Bogert, Trusts and Trustees (rev. 2d edit.), § 845.

18. Statutes to this effect have been adopted in New Jersey, New York and Pennsylvania, and in several other states the trustee is given discretion to allocate a corporate distribution to one or both of the income and principal accounts. See Bogert, Trusts and Trustees (rev. 2d edit.), § 859.

19. See 20 Pa.C.S.A. § 8105. In Catherwood's Trust, 405 Pa. 61, 173 A.2d 86 (1961), the court had stated that stock dividends not exceeding 6% of the outstanding stock should be treated as trust income under the Uniform Principal and Income Act. It would seem that under the Pennsylvania common law rule they might have been treated as ordinary dividends and allocated to income, but the Uniform Act made no exception for them. § 6 of the Revised Uniform Principal and Income Act of 1962 provides that small stock dividends shall be treated as trust principal, unless the declaring corporation stated they were issued in lieu of cash dividends.

WESTLAW REFERENCES

"kentucky rule" /s dividend

"massachusetts rule" /s dividend

"pennsylvania rule" /s dividend

"uniform principal and income act"

390k272.3(5)

find 173 a2d 86

STOCK SUBSCRIPTION RIGHTS [1]

§ 117. If a trustee who owns shares in a corporation receives a right to subscribe to new shares at a named price, he is required in most states to treat the right, or the proceeds of the sale of it, as trust principal. In a few cases following the former Pennsylvania rule the courts have followed the rules as to the maintenance of book value and apportionment.

Under the Uniform Principal and Income Act and the Revised Uniform Act, rights to subscribe to stock of the issuing corporation are trust principal, but rights to purchase the shares of another corporation are trust income.

Corporations sometimes issue to their stockholders rights to subscribe to new stock which is to be issued, the purpose being to raise new capital for the enterprise. It is customary to permit the old stockholders to subscribe to the new stock at a price lower than the market price of the new stock. When a trustee owning stock receives a stock subscription right he must decide whether to credit it to trust income or to trust principal. And also whether to sell it or to exercise it by investing trust funds in the new stock.

Suppose a trustee buys for $2,000 ten shares of stock in the X corporation, each having a par value of $100, the corporation being capitalized at $100,000 and having a $100,000 surplus. Assume that after the trustee has held the stock for some years and received ordinary cash dividends on it, and the surplus account has increased to $200,000, the corporation announces that it is going to increase its capital to $200,000, and that it is distributing to its old stockholders rights to subscribe at par to the same amount of new stock as the old stock which they hold. The trustee will receive a right to subscribe to ten new shares of stock which can be exercised by investing $1,000 more of trust principal, or he can probably sell his stock subscription right for at least $1,000, since the book value of the ten shares of new stock will be $2,000. There will be 2,000 shares of stock outstanding after the new issue is taken up, the capital will be $200,000, and the surplus will be $200,000, so that each share of stock will have a book value of $200.

§ 117

1. Restatement, Trusts, Second, § 236.

If the trustee exercises his subscription right and invests $1,000 more of trust principal, he will then have $3,000 invested, and will own twenty shares of stock of a book value of $200 each, making the interest of the trust in the corporation worth $4,000. Thus the trust will have gained $1,000 on the transaction and he must decide whether to allocate this gain to trust principal or to income.

If the trustee sells the subscription right for $1,000, he will then have approximately $1,000 in cash and ten shares of stock each of which has a book value of $200. The total amount of stock held by the trustee will have a book value of $2,000 and there will be $1,000 in cash, making a total value of $3,000, which shows a gain of $1,000, as in the case of the exercise of the right.

The great majority of the common law cases (whether adhering to the old Pennsylvania or to the Massachusetts rule) give the right or its proceeds to trust principal, usually stating merely that the right is an "incident" of the ownership of the stock or is "inherent" in it.[2] However, in a few jurisdictions that had followed the old Pennsylvania rule the right was subjected to the rule about maintenance of the intact value of the trust's investment in the stock, and any surplus gain after such maintenance has either been given to trust income or divided between income and principal, dependent on the time of the accrual of the benefits.[3]

The Uniform Principal and Income Act[4] allots rights to subscribe to the stock of the corporation issuing the rights to trust principal, but gives to trust income rights to subscribe to stock of a corporation other than the one which distributes the rights.

 WESTLAW REFERENCES

trust /s "stock subscription right"

---

2. De Koven v. Alsop, 205 Ill. 309, 68 N.E. 930, 63 L.R.A. 587; Lauman v. Foster, 157 Iowa 275, 135 N.W. 14; Girdwood v. Safe Dep. & Trust Co., 143 Md. 245, 122 A. 132 (1923); Chase v. Union Nat. Bank of Lowell, 275 Mass. 503, 176 N.E. 508 (1931); Baker v. Thompson, 181 App.Div. 469, 168 N.Y.S. 871, affirmed 224 N.Y. 592, 120 N.E. 858; In re Jenkins' Will, 199 Wis. 131, 225 N.W. 733 (1929).

Some cases have applied the same rule to rights to subscribe to the stock of an affiliate or subsidiary. Robertson v. De Brulatour, 188 N.Y. 301, 80 N.E. 938;

Plainfield Trust Co. v. Bowlby, 107 N.J.Eq. 68, 151 A. 545 (1930).

3. In re Schnur's Estate, 32 P.2d 970 (Cal.); Holbrook v. Holbrook, 74 N.H. 201, 66 A. 124, 12 L.R.A.,N.S., 768; In re Hostetter's Estate, 319 Pa. 572, 181 A. 567 (1935). See Neafie's Estate, 325 Pa. 561, 191 A. 56 (1937) (trust income and principal to share in benefit after maintenance of intact value).

4. § 5. To the same effect see § 6, Revised Uniform Principal and Income Act. And see Restatement, Trusts, Second, § 236.

PROFITS FROM MERCHANDISING OR AGRICULTURE [1]

§ 118. Occasionally a trustee is authorized to carry on a business, as where he is empowered to continue the settlor's merchandising, farming or stock–raising operations. The profits of such an enterprise, after deduction of operating expenses and the maintenance of inventory, should be allocated to trust income.

In a few instances a trustee is directed or permitted to continue the business of the settlor, or to use trust principal in business as a new enterprise. Here the trustee's duty as to receipts from the merchandising, farming, stock raising, or other business is clear. He should first pay operating expenses [2] and then maintain inventory as of the original value.[3] Thereafter he should treat the receipts as profits to be paid out as trust income.[4] In computing trust income he should follow the usual accounting practices with regard to business of the type which he is carrying on.

The special case of the development of natural resources, as in the case of timber, ores, oil and gas, will be discussed later [5] in connection with the subject of wasting assets.

Where a trustee running a business sells his equipment and stock for the purpose of going out of business, and devotes no portion of the proceeds to replacement, the transaction is similar to a liquidating dividend and the sum is ordinarily treated as trust principal.

 WESTLAW REFERENCES

280 sw2d 203

trustee /s continu*** /s business /s settlor trustor

---

§ 118

1. Restatement, Trusts, Second, § 233, Comments *a* and *c*; Uniform Principal and Income Act, §§ 7, 8; Revised Uniform Principal and Income Act, § 8.

2. In re Sulzer's Estate, 323 Pa. 1, 185 A. 793 (1936) (may advance principal to pay current expenses when income inadequate).

3. See Wright v. Markey, 280 S.W.2d 203 (Ky.1955) (racing and breeding farm held in trust; duty to replenish stock of horses from offspring).

4. Krug v. Mercantile Trust & Deposit Co., 133 Md. 110, 104 A. 414; Rossi v. Davis, 345 Mo. 362, 133 S.W.2d 363, 125 A.L.R. 1111 (1939); In re Hopson's Will, 213 App.Div. 395, 211 N.Y.S. 128 (1925).

And see First Nat. Bank of Mobile v. Wefel, 252 Ala. 212, 40 So.2d 434 (1949) (tree farm; proceeds, after maintaining the stand by replanting, income); Pool v. Rutherford, 336 Ill.App. 516, 84 N.E.2d 650 (1949) (crops); In re Ambrose's Will, 58 N.Y.S.2d 614 (Sur.1945) (fruit farm); Daugherty Estate, 3 Pa.D. & C.2d 781 (citrus crop maturing after beginning of trust is income).

5. § 122, post.

SUMS RECEIVED IN SETTLEMENT OF CLAIMS [1]

§ 119.   If a trustee receives an award based on the value of the trust property which has been taken in eminent domain proceedings, or a payment from an insurer based on the value of buildings destroyed or damaged, he should treat the receipt as trust principal since it is a substitute for the former trust property.

Where a claim against a trustee or third party is collected, the proceeds should be treated as trust income so far as the claim was based on an injury to the rights of the income beneficiary and the balance should be treated as trust principal.

When a trustee receives money in payment of a claim which he has against a third person, ordinarily the proper allocation of the payment to trust principal or income will be clear upon a consideration of the source of the claim and the theory of the payment. For example, if trust realty is condemned under eminent domain proceedings and the payment is based on the fee value of the land, it should be treated as a substituted trust principal asset.[2] If separate awards are made on account of damages to the interests of the income beneficiaries and to the principal fund of the trust, naturally the trustee should allocate the awards accordingly.

And if a house owned by the trustee is insured as to its entire value against fire and is destroyed, a payment made by the insurance company on account the loss will constitute a replacement of trust property, and hence such sum should be placed in the trust principal account.[3] If the trustee insures the income or remainder interest separately, a recovery will go to the income or principal account, as the case may be. If a trustee holds a life insurance policy as a trust res, the proceeds of its collection should be allocated to trust principal.[4]

A trustee sometimes has a cause of action against a predecessor trustee for breach of trust and a payment may be voluntarily or involuntarily made in satisfaction of the cause of action. Whether any part of the proceeds should go to trust income will depend on what interests under the trust were damaged by the breach. The wrongful act may have merely caused a loss of income or it may have produced a shrinkage in the value of the property which was the principal of the trust. For example, if the predecessor trustee placed the trust fund in a bank without interest, instead of investing it and obtaining income,

§ 119

1. Restatement, Trusts, Second, § 233; Uniform (and Revised Uniform) Principal and Income Act, § 3.

2. Gibson v. Cooke, 42 Mass. 75, 1 Metc. 75; City of Washington v. Ellsworth, 253 N.C. 25, 116 S.E. 167; Hostetter's Estate, 388 Pa. 339, 131 A.2d 360 (1957).

3. In re Petersen's Estate, 188 Cal. App.2d 414, 10 Cal.Rptr. 727 (1961); Hor-

ton v. Upham, 72 Conn. 29, 43 A. 492; Campbell v. Mansfield, 104 Miss. 533, 61 So. 593, 45 L.R.A.,N.S., 446. In re Mercereau's Estate, 15 Misc.2d 284, 180 N.Y.S.2d 598 (1958).

4. In re Lion's Will, 203 Misc. 30, 116 N.Y.S.2d 46 (1952); First Nat. Bank v. Barnes, 237 Wis. 627, 298 N.W. 215 (1941).

the injury is to the income beneficiary only, but if the predecessor embezzled negotiable securities constituting trust principal, and also a bank account in which trust income had been deposited, there has been injury to both principal and income and the recovery should be apportioned according to the respective amounts of income and principal involved.[5] And the same principles should apply where the cause of action is against the predecessor and a third person who participated with him in a breach of trust.

The proceeds of causes of action in favor of the trustee and against third persons should go to income or principal, dependent on which interest was injured. If a tenant of the trustee wrongfully injures the trust realty, the recovery should be treated as trust principal;[6] and if the trustee has a cause of action against a debtor on a note on account of default in the payment of interest and the principal of the debt the recovery should be divided.[7]

The special case of a cause of action for default on a mortgage or other security owned by the trust is considered later, in a separate section,[8] since it is a part of the unproductive property problem.

 WESTLAW REFERENCES

trustee /s money award /s payment settl**** /s claim

PROFITS AND LOSSES ON SALE OF TRUST ASSETS [1]

§ 120. The proceeds of the sale of trust property are ordinarily to be treated as trust principal, even though they include a profit in excess of cost price or inventory value. Losses on such sales fall on trust principal. The rule should govern sales of corporate stock where there is a gain in value due to undistributed earnings.

Where a trustee sells trust property, the proceeds should usually be placed in the principal account of the trust since they are the product of trust principal. This is true even though the proceeds include a profit over the cost price or original inventory value of the trust property sold. Such profits do not constitute earnings of the trust property. The principal account bears the risk of the trust property decreasing in value and should receive the benefit of its increase in value. Such profits are not treated as trust income,[2] even though they may be

---

5. In re Dashiell's Estate, 21 Del.Ch. 131, 181 A. 681 (1935); Rothenberg v. Franklin Washington Trust Co., 133 N.J. Eq. 261, 31 A.2d 831 (1943); Cate v. Hamilton Nat. Bank of Chattanooga, 178 Tenn. 249, 156 S.W.2d 812 (1941).

6. Amerige v. Goddard, 316 Mass. 566, 55 N.E.2d 919 (1944).

7. Veazie v. Forsaith, 76 Me. 172.

8. § 121, post.

§ 120

1. Restatement, Trusts, Second, § 233, Comment *b*.

2. In re Davis' Estate, 75 Cal.App.2d 528, 171 P.2d 463 (1946); Old Colony Trust Co. v. Walker, 319 Mass. 325, 65 N.E.2d 690 (1946); In re Koffend's Will, 218 Minn. 206, 15 N.W.2d 590 (1944).

capital gains and thus subject to income tax. The Uniform Principal and Income Act takes this view and makes no special case for corporate stock.[3] If the increase in the value of the trust asset is an unrealized gain, the income beneficiary has no right to it.[4]

If the property sold was held by the trustee as a part of a business conducted for the purpose of making profits by buying and selling, net profits from sales are to be treated as trust income.[5]

Of course, if the sale price includes a specific item for income owed but not paid on the item sold, as in the case of the sale of a bond with accrued interest, the price received is in part trust income.

There had been a tendency on the part of some courts to make a special case of the sale of corporate stock held by the trust, where it is sold at a profit, and where the reason for the increase in value was alleged to be in whole or in part the failure of the corporation to distribute earnings as dividends and the addition of such earnings to corporate surplus.[6] Such a dividend policy naturally increases the book and, probably, the market value of the stock. Some courts thought that the sale of such stock at a profit was an indirect way of getting dividends on the stock, and that the income beneficiary of the trust ought to receive such indirect distributions of corporate income. This view, however, has not received general favor [7] and is not believed to be sound. A practical objection to it is the extraordinary difficulty of learning what part of the sale price of the stock is due to the undistributed earnings of the corporation. In the Nirdlinger case [8] this amount was stipulated; apparently the remainderman was willing that the life tenant should have part of the price, but this does not often occur.

The beneficiary who is entitled to the income of the trust property obtains part of the benefit of a sale at a profit and reinvestment, for he obtains a greater income from the new trust fund than from the old. The principal of the estate, no matter what changes of form it undergoes, should be regarded as the same type of property. That the trust

3. § 3(2). The same rules apply under § 3 of the Revised Uniform Act.

4. In re Young's Will, 250 Iowa 126, 93 N.W.2d 74 (1958); In re Kilborn's Estate, 14 Misc.2d 1069, 181 N.Y.S.2d 613 (1958).

5. Holmes v. Hrobon, 93 Ohio App. 1, 103 N.E.2d 845 (1951), affirmed in part and reversed in part in 158 Ohio St. 508, 110 N.E.2d 574 (1953); Geyelin's Estate, 29 Pa. D. & C. 296; Hudson v. Clark, 200 Va. 325, 106 S.E.2d 133 (1958).

6. In re Sherman Trust, 190 Iowa 1385, 179 N.W. 109; Matter of United States Trust Co., 229 N.Y. 598, 129 N.E. 923, affirmed in memorandum opinion 190 App.Div. 494, 180 N.Y. 12; Nirdlinger's Estate, 290 Pa. 457, 139 A. 200, 56 A.L.R. 1303; Wallace v. Wallace, 90 S.C. 61, 72 S.E. 553. The adoption of the Uniform

Principal and Income Act changed the prior law in Pennsylvania, as to all trusts since the holding that the provision making the Act retroactive was valid.

7. Long v. Rike, 50 F.2d 124, 81 A.L.R. 521 (7th Cir.1931); In re Traung's Estate, 30 Cal.2d 811, 185 P.2d 801 (1947); Guthrie's Trustee v. Akers, 157 Ky. 649, 163 S.W. 1117; Safe Dep. & Trust Co. of Baltimore v. Bowen, 188 Md. 482, 53 A.2d 413 (1947); In re Clarke's Will, 204 Minn. 574, 284 N.W. 896; In re Fera's Estate, 26 N.J. 131, 139 A.2d 23 (1958); Matter of Schley's Will, 202 App.Div. 169, 195 N.Y.S. 871 (1922), affirmed 234 N.Y. 616, 138 N.E. 469 (1922); In re Roebken's Will, 230 Wis. 215, 283 N.W. 815 (1939).

8. 290 Pa. 457, 139 A. 200.

property is originally money, later becomes bonds, and still later real estate, ought not to affect the status of the property as the principal fund. A Pennsylvania court points out that the principal account bears losses which occur from investments, and should, therefore, be entitled to the benefit of gains which accrue. "If, then, in case of a loss by reason of an unfortunate investment, it falls on both the legatees for life and in remainder, it seems but equitable that, if there be a profit arising from the sale of a trust security, they should both participate in it in the same manner they would bear a loss, the former receiving more income from the increased corpus and the latter more corpus." [9]

Where there is a duty to sell trust property which has been wasting or unproductive, the proceeds are treated specially, as is shown in subsequent sections.[10] The statements in this section are based on the principle that the sale is made under a mere privilege to sell, or is made under a mandatory power of sale but the property is of an ordinarily productive type.

 WESTLAW REFERENCES

find 15 nw2d 590

trustee /s sale sell** trust /s property /s proceed profit
    loss /s income corpus principal

find 139 a. 200

390k273

PROCEEDS OF SALE OF UNPRODUCTIVE PROPERTY—MORTGAGE SALVAGE OPERATIONS [1]

§ 121. If a trustee holds unproductive or underproductive property and the sale of it is delayed, the trustee is under a duty to apportion the net proceeds of the sale between the income and principal accounts in such a way as to give trust income the amount it would have received had the property been sold as soon as the duty to sell arose and the proceeds had been then invested in normally productive property. The rule applies whether the sale produces more or less than the inventory value or cost of the property.

Where a trustee holds a mortgage, there is default, he forecloses and buys in the property, holds the property for a time, and then sells it, the transaction is sometimes called a "mortgage salvage operation". Some courts treat the case as merely one instance of a

9. In re Graham's Estate, 198 Pa. 216, 219, 47 A. 1108.

10. See §§ 121, 122, post.

§ 121

1. Bogert, Trusts and Trustees (rev. 2d edit.), §§ 824, 825; Restatement, Trusts, Second, §§ 240, 241.

See also Carey & Moodie, 33 Ill.L.R. 398; 89 Univ. of Pa.L.R. 1081; 58 Mich. L.R. 1049; 5 John Marshall L.Q. 9; Brandis, 9 N.C.L.R. 127.

delayed sale of unproductive property; others have divided the proceeds in proportion to the amount of interest and principal due on the mortgage.

The Uniform Principal and Income Act treats all unproductive property (including mortgages) under a single section and considerably modifies the common law rules, but only where the trustee had a duty to sell the property. The Revised Uniform Principal and Income Act requires allocation of a portion of the proceeds of mortgage salvage operations to trust income regardless of whether the trustee has a duty to sell.

It quite often happens that a trustee holds unproductive property or property which produces less than the average rate of return on trust investments. In this case he may be under a duty to retain the property because of directions in the trust instrument, or he may have a discretionary power to sell the property but no duty to sell, or he may be under a duty to sell either because of a direction of the settlor or because the investment is not a legal investment under state law. If the trustee sells such trust property after a delay during which he has been seeking a buyer, a problem arises as to whether part of the proceeds should be transferred to the trust income account to compensate for the lack of income received during the holding of the unproductive or underproductive property. Normally the proceeds of a sale of trust property belong to trust principal. Should an exception be made in this case?

If the trustee was directed to retain the investment in question, there will be no sale and no problem. If the trustee had no duty to sell but merely a discretionary power to sell, under the Uniform Act the entire proceeds of the sale are to go to trust principal, whether or not there has been a profit over cost price or inventory value.[2] The settlor is deemed to have intended that the income beneficiary should receive only the income which the property actually produced.

But if the trustee sold because of a *duty* to sell, most courts directed a division of the proceeds between trust income and principal. The settlor in such a case is deemed to have intended that the income beneficiary should have a constant flow of normal income, and to have intended that if such income did not come from some of the trust property for a period the deficiency should be made up later. The settlor is said to have a presumed intent that the income beneficiary should get "delayed income" out of the sale proceeds or, in other words, that upon sale the trustee should apportion the proceeds in such a way as to give the life tenant the income he would have had if the trustee had been able to carry out his duty to sell at once and had then invested the net proceeds of sale in normally productive trust property.[3]

2. See § 11 of the Uniform Principal and Income Act. And see Love v. Engelke, 368 Ill. 342, 14 N.E.2d 228 (1938); Lang v. Miss. Valley Trust Co., 359 Mo. 688, 223 S.W.2d 404 (1949); Dwight's Estate, 56 Pa. D. & C. 160.

3. Edwards v. Edwards, 183 Mass. 581, 67 N.E. 658; Lawrence v. Littlefield, 215

Thus if the trustee is given vacant suburban land which the settlor directs him to sell, or he has a duty to sell because it is not a proper trust investment, and after five years the trustee succeeds in selling, he should divide the net proceeds in such a way as to give the life beneficiary the delayed income described above. The trustee is to find what sum, if invested at the time the trustee's duty to sell arose, would have produced, at simple interest and at the average rate earned by trust investments in that vicinity, the net proceeds of the sale. This amount is subtracted from the net proceeds of the sale and the sum thus reached is called trust income, while the remainder of the proceeds is allotted to trust principal.

This computation can be made by the use of a simple formula. Let X equal the principal sum sought to be found. Let P equal the net proceeds of the sale, that is, the gross proceeds less the cost of selling and other proper deductions. Let T equal the time in years during which the property was held awaiting a sale. And let R equal the rate of trust income which is assumed to be normal or average, expressed in decimal form.

$$X = \frac{P}{1 + TR}$$

Thus if the unproductive suburban land were held five years and ultimately sold for $100,000 net, and the average trust income rate was 4%, the computation would be as follows:

$$X = \frac{\$100,000}{1 + (5 \times .04)} = \frac{\$100,000}{1.20} = \$83,333.33$$

Therefore the sum of $83,333.33 should be added to trust principal and the sum of $16,666.67 should be treated as trust income.

This rule is applied irrespective of the amount produced at the sale, that is, whether it was more or less than the cost of the property to the settlor or the trustee or the inventory value of the property when received by the trustee. The presumed intent of the settlor is to give the income beneficiary income during the period of delay necessary to make the sale, and not merely to give him a part of the profits of any sale.[4]

Costs of Sale, Income Pending Sale, and Carrying Charges

The costs of the sale, such as advertising and broker's commissions, should be deducted from the gross proceeds before making the computation above indicated.[5]

N.Y. 561, 109 N.E. 611; Patterson v. Old Dominion Trust Co., 149 Va. 597, 140 S.E. 810. *Contra*, Conner's Estate, 239 Pa. 449, 86 A. 1023; Mark's Estate, 38 Pa.D. & C. 489.

4. Lawrence v. Littlefield, 215 N.Y. 561, 109 N.E. 611.

5. Delaware Trust Co. v. Bradford, 30 Del.Ch. 277, 59 A.2d 212 (1948); Edwards v. Edwards, 183 Mass. 581, 67 N.E. 658.

If any net income is earned pending the sale, the property not being totally unproductive but merely underproductive, this income should be paid to the life tenant as collected, and the total amount thus paid should be deducted from that portion of the net proceeds of the sale which the life tenant would have obtained if the property had been wholly unproductive.[6]

Carrying charges pending the sale should be deducted from the proceeds of the sale before making an apportionment, or paid from trust principal if they are payable prior to the sale.[7] These include insurance premiums, taxes, and interest on any mortgage which may exist on the unproductive asset. In giving the income beneficiary the average trust yield, the court is deducting operating costs from his share, and it should not deduct them a second time by paying the carrying charges out of the part of the proceeds allocated to trust income.

If an income beneficiary dies during the period of delay in selling the unproductive property, his representative is entitled to that portion of the delayed income which had accrued up to the time of his death.[8]

The Uniform Principal and Income Act has a section [9] governing the disposition of the proceeds of the sale of unproductive property. It applies the apportionment rule only where the asset has not produced, for more than a year and until sold, an average net income of at least one per cent of its fair inventory value or cost, where there was a duty to sell, and where the net proceeds exceeded inventory value or cost. If these conditions are met, the rate applied in making the computation is five per cent. Costs of sale and carrying charges are to be deducted from gross proceeds. Income paid to the income beneficiary pending sale is to be debited to him when making any apportionment of the proceeds.

The Revised Uniform Principal and Income Act [10] has a similar section as to unproductive property but eliminates the "duty to sell" requirement as a condition to apportionment of sale proceeds, provides that the income beneficiary's share is determined from the date the asset becomes underproductive, uses a four per cent return on underproductive property, and eliminates the provision of the Uniform Act limiting the income beneficiary's share of the proceeds to the difference

6. Springfield Safe Dep. & Trust Co. v. Wade, 305 Mass. 36, 24 N.E.2d 764 (1940); In re Otis' Will, 276 N.Y. 101, 11 N.E.2d 556, 115 A.L.R. 875 (1937), reargument denied 277 N.Y. 650, 14 N.E.2d 203 (1938); In re Nirdlinger's Estate, 331 Pa. 135, 200 A. 656, 116 A.L.R. 1350 (1938).

7. Delaware Trust Co. v. Bradford, 30 Del.Ch. 277, 59 A.2d 212 (1948); Amerige v. Goddard, 316 Mass. 566, 55 N.E.2d 919 (1944); In re Des Forges' Will, 243 Wis. 178, 9 N.W.2d 609 (1943). In some cases it is stated that such charges should be paid out of trust principal: In re Bothwell's Estate, 65 Cal.App.2d 598, 151 P.2d 298 (1944), rehearing denied 65 Cal.App.2d 598, 151 P.2d 868 (1944); In re Rowland's Estate, 273 N.Y. 100, 6 N.E.2d 393 (1937).

8. In re Alston, 2 Ch. 584 (1901); Matter of Pinkney's Will, 208 App.Div. 181, 202 N.Y.S. 818 (1924), affirmed 238 N.Y. 602, 144 N.E. 909 (1924).

9. § 11. In Conn., Md., and Wis. the section was omitted, and in Ala., Colo., Ill., Kan., Tex. and Vt. it was amended.

10. § 12 ("Underproductive Property.")

between the sale price and inventory value of the underproductive property.

While most of the cases deal with unproductive land, the same doctrines should be applied to defaulted bonds and to stocks or other personal property which has been producing no income and where there is a duty to sell.[11]

Mortgage Salvage Operations

In past years trustees sometimes found that mortgages on real estate held by them became unproductive due to a default in the payment of interest or principal, and they have been obliged to foreclose and buy in the land, hold it for a time and then sell it at a loss over the amount of principal and income due on the mortgage and the costs of foreclosing and holding the property. Such a transaction is conveniently described as a "mortgage salvage operation".

Neither the Uniform Act nor the Revised Uniform Act contains a separate section regarding the results of collection on defaulted mortgages, but section 11 (and section 12 of the Revised Uniform Act) applies to all unproductive property and hence includes defaulted mortgages.

Some courts have treated these mortgage foreclosure operations as merely involving one type of unproductive property and have applied the formula given above to the net proceeds of the foreclosure transaction.[12] Other courts have divided the net proceeds between trust principal and trust income in the same proportion as the amount of trust income and trust principal due on the defaulted mortgage.[13] Thus, under this latter rule, if the amount of interest defaulted was $1,000 and the defaulted principal was $5,000, one-sixth of the net proceeds would be given to trust income and five-sixths to trust principal. These two rules produce the same results, except that the first gives the income beneficiary the current average trust yield on all legal trust investments, while the latter gives him income at the rate prescribed in the mortgage throughout the whole operation.

The costs of foreclosing the defaulted mortgage [14] and selling the property [15] after bidding it in should be deducted from the ultimate proceeds of the operation before apportionment. Carrying charges on the mortgaged property after the trustee acquires it should be deducted

---

11. In re Carr's Estate, 71 N.Y.S.2d 155 (Sur.1947); Quinn v. First Nat. Bank, 168 Tenn. 30, 73 S.W.2d 692 (1934).

12. Springfield Safe Dep. & Trust Co. v. Wade, 305 Mass. 36, 24 N.E.2d 764 (1940); Nirdlinger's Estate, 327 Pa. 171, 193 A. 30 (1937); Quinn v. First Nat. Bank, 168 Tenn. 30, 73 S.W.2d 692 (1934).

13. Bowen v. Safe Deposit & Trust Co., 188 Md. 490, 53 A.2d 416 (1947); Hudson County Nat. Bank v. Woodruff, 122 N.J.Eq. 444, 194 A. 266 (1937), modified 123 N.J.

Eq. 585, 199 A. 399 (1938); Matter of Chapal, 269 N.Y. 464, 199 N.E. 762, 103 A.L.R. 1268 (1936); Matter of Otis, 276 N.Y. 101, 11 N.E.2d 556, 115 A.L.R. 875 (1937), reargument denied 277 N.Y. 650, 14 N.E.2d 203 (1938); San Antonio Loan & Trust Co. v. Hamilton, 155 Tex. 52, 283 S.W.2d 19 (1955).

14. In re Easton's Estate, 13 N.Y.S.2d 295 (Sur.1939).

15. Matter of Chapal, 269 N.Y. 464, 199 N.E. 762 (1936).

from the proceeds of the salvaging operation when completed, and the rights of income beneficiary or remainderman who may have made payments with regard thereto should then be adjusted.[16]

In many cases the mortgage salvage operation becomes very complicated. If the trustee buys the property on foreclosure, he may be obliged to hold it for several years and take account of rents, repair bills, taxes and other expenses, and when he sells the property he is not apt to receive cash for all of the price, but rather some cash and a mortgage or bonds or other consideration.[17] The burdens of deciding doubtful questions and keeping records have induced several states to pass special statutes regarding the mortgage salvage process, instead of leaving the matter to the common law or the Uniform Principal and Income Act. Thus the Connecticut and Illinois statutes treat the entire proceeds as trust principal.[18] Massachusetts gives the trustee the discretion to apportion the net proceeds.[19] California[20] and New York[21] follow the rule in section 12 of the Revised Uniform Principal and Income Act, which states that the amount of net proceeds from the sale of underproductive property to be allocated as "delayed income is the difference between the net proceeds and the amount which, had it been invested at simple interest at 5% [4% in the Revised Act] per year while the property was unproductive, would have produced the net proceeds."

In Texas section 11 of the Uniform Act has been amended so that it expressly includes the salvaging of mortgages.[22] In Pennsylvania the rule of the Revised Act has been substantially adopted in dealing with mortgages and other interest-bearing obligations in default.[23]

 WESTLAW REFERENCES

find 223 sw2d 404

sale sell*** /s unproductive underproductive /s trust

Cost of Sale, Income Pending Sale, and Carrying Charges

"delaware trust" +5 bradford

16. Rutherford Nat. Bank v. Black, 133 N.J.Eq. 306, 32 A.2d 86 (1943); In re Haffen's Will, 155 Misc. 774, 280 N.Y.S. 357 (1935).

17. See Matter of Chapal, 269 N.Y. 464, 199 N.E. 762 (1936); Matter of Otis, 276 N.Y. 101, 11 N.E.2d 556 (1937), reargument denied 277 N.Y. 650, 14 N.E.2d 203 (1938).

18. Conn.G.S.A. § 45–91; Ill.Rev.Stat. c. 30 ¶ 513.

19. Mass.G.L.A., c. 203, §§ 24A and 24B.

20. West's Ann.Cal.Civ.Code, § 730.12.

21. N.Y.—McKinney's EPTL 11–2.1.

By N.Y.L.1940, c. 452, § 17–c(2) had been added to the Personal Property Law.

This subsection had provided that the foreclosure proceeds were to be created as trust principal but by rule the trustee could pay up to 3% of the principal amount of the mortgage to the income beneficiary out of income from the property during the salvage operation. The section had been declared constitutional in In re West's Estate, 289 N.Y. 423, 46 N.E.2d 501 (1943), affirmed sub nom. Demorest v. City Bank Farmers Trust Co., 321 U.S. 36, 64 S.Ct. 384, 88 L.Ed. 526 (1944).

22. Vernon's Ann.Tex.Prop. Code § 113.110.

23. 20 Pa. C.S.A. § 8110.

find 24 ne2d 764

409k684(4)

409k684(5)

Mortgages Salvage Operations

"mortgage salvage operation"　/s　trust

find 11 ne2d 556

RECEIPTS FROM PROPERTY SUBJECT TO DEPLETION—NATURAL RESOURCES [1]

§ 122. American case law is generally to the effect that if the settlor has not provided otherwise: (1) a trustee holding property other than natural resources subject to depletion should, where he has a duty to sell it, set up an amortization fund out of receipts to cover depletion in the value of the principal which occurs during the period before the sale is made; and (2) if he holds natural resources he should treat royalties and other payments for the development and severance of these resources as trust principal.

The subject is now governed by statute in many states. The Uniform and the Revised Uniform Principal and Income Acts to a large extent codify the common law rules, and recent amendments to the Uniform Act provide for apportionment of the receipts from natural resources.

Property other than Natural Resources

Sometimes a trustee finds that one of the assets of the trust is of such a character that, due either to the mere passage of time or the effect of the use of the property, it will have a limited life and gradually shrink in value. Examples are found in tangible personal property such as animals or household furniture,[2] the right to royalties on a copyrighted book [3] or play,[4] the right to renewal premium payments on insurance sold,[5] a lawyer's rights to future contingent fee payments,[6] the landlord's interest in a lease for years,[7] and the right to annuity payments during the life of a named person.[8] Thus if the trust asset is a right to royalty payments on a book, receipts will cease and the asset become valueless when the copyright runs out or the book ceases to sell.

---

§ 122

1. Restatement, Trusts, Second, §§ 239, 241. And see Barry, 21 Va.L.R. 611; 27 N.Y.U.L.R. 376.

2. Matter of Hopson's Estate, 213 App. Div. 395, 211 N.Y.S. 128 (1925). A racing and breeding farm is not wasting when the supply of animals is maintained by additions of colts. Wright v. Markey, 280 S.W.2d 203 (Ky.1955).

3. In re Elsner's Will, 210 App.Div. 575, 206 N.Y.S. 765 (1924).

4. In re Pipeson's Will, 147 N.Y.S.2d 198 (Sur.1955).

5. Industrial Trust Co. v. Parks, 57 R.I. 363, 190 A. 32 (1937).

6. In re Levinson's Will, 5 Misc.2d 979, 162 N.Y.S.2d 287 (1957).

7. Minot v. Thompson, 106 Mass. 583.

8. Porter v. Baddeley, L.R. 5 Ch.D. 542.

Such trust property is called "property subject to depletion" or "wasting property".

A trustee who obtains receipts on account of ownership of such assets must consider whether to treat them in their entirety as trust income, or whether his duty toward the remainder beneficiaries obligates him to set aside a portion of the payments as trust principal so that when the property becomes valueless and ceases to produce any returns there will be a fund which can be used to maintain the value of the trust principal as it existed at the beginning of the holding. Thus if a trustee holds a right to collect rents on a twenty year lease (and does not own the fee), and the rent is $1,000 a year, does the trustee have a duty to value the landlord's interest as it existed when he acquired it and to set aside from rents received such sums as will over the twenty year period equal the valuation?

In many of the cases discussing this problem the court found that the settlor had expressly [9] or impliedly [10] set forth an intent that all the receipts from the wasting property should be income of the trust, and a direction or permission that the trustee retain the property has been held to indicate such an intent.[11] Sometimes the trustee is given discretion to decide the income and principal questions involved and a reasonable decision is conclusive.[12] But if the settlor has not controlled the disposition of receipts in one of these ways, and there is a duty on the part of the trustee to sell the wasting asset as soon as possible without undue sacrifice, either because the settlor imposed such duty or because it existed by reason of the fact that the asset was not a legal trust investment, the courts have held that there is a duty on the part of the trustee to preserve the value of the trust's investment in the wasting asset as it existed at the time of acquisition of the asset by setting aside as trust principal a certain portion of the receipts from the wasting asset pending its sale.[13]

In making such a decision courts have reasoned that a settlor, who does not express himself otherwise, is deemed to intend that the trust property is to be preserved at its original value and that the income beneficiary is to have normal or average income on property of that value. To give the income beneficiary all the receipts from the wasting asset would give him abnormally high income and would subject the remaindermen to a reduction in the value of their interests as they existed when the trust began to hold the asset. Therefore the trustee should place a value on the wasting asset when he acquires it, and,

9. Dexter v. Dexter, 274 Mass. 273, 174 N.E. 493 (1931); Matter of James, 146 N.Y. 78, 40 N.E. 876.

10. Cadbury v. Parrish, 89 N.H. 464, 200 A. 791 (1938); Mitchell v. Mitchell, 151 Tex. 1, 244 S.W.2d 803 (1951).

11. Nelligan v. Long, 320 Mass. 439, 70 N.E.2d 175 (1946); In re Koffend's Will, 218 Minn. 206, 15 N.W.2d 590 (1944).

12. In re Bixby's Estate, 55 Cal.2d 819, 13 Cal.Rptr. 411, 362 P.2d 43 (1961).

13. Slade v. Chain, 1 Ch. 522 (1908); Burnett v. Lester, 53 Ill. 325; Ott v. Tewksbury, 75 N.J.Eq. 4, 71 A. 302. And see cases cited in footnotes 5–8, supra.

pending sale of it, should create an amortization fund out of receipts which will offset the loss in capital value up to the time of sale. If the asset is sold, the proceeds should be treated as trust principal, and from the two sources (the amortization fund and the sale proceeds) the value of the trust principal will be maintained. Any receipts remaining in the hands of the trustee after deducting for amortization should be treated as trust income.

Thus if a trustee finds that one of the assets given to him by the settlor was a right to collect rents for twenty years, that the annual rent is $1,000, and that the landlord's interest which he was given was at the time of its acquisition reasonably worth $18,000, the trustee should set aside out of each year's rent $900 so that in twenty years $18,000 will be realized, and treat $100 of the annual rents as trust income. If after holding the lease for five years, he sells it for $13,500, the capital of the trust will be maintained by use of the amortization fund then accumulated ($4,500) and the sale proceeds.

The Uniform Principal and Income Act gives all receipts from assets subject to depletion (other than natural resources) to trust income, unless the trustee was under a duty to sell the asset, in which case a sum not in excess of a fixed percentage of the value of the asset is to be treated as trust income and the rest as trust principal.[14] The percentage suggested in the Act is 5%, but in some states another rate has been fixed. Presumably this rule applies only to the period while a sale is delayed, but the section does not expressly so state.

The Revised Uniform Principal and Income Act[15] eliminates the "duty to sell" requirement and gives the income beneficiary a five per cent return on such assets. However the trustee has no power to subsequently revalue such assets if circumstances should warrant.

Receipts from Natural Resources

Where the trustee owns land from which natural resources can be extracted he holds a wasting asset. Oil and gas wells, mines, quarries, and timber lands will become exhausted and of little value in the course of a relatively short time.[16] The receipts will be temporarily very high, but in a short time the interest of the remaindermen in the property will have diminished greatly in value. It would seem on principle that the same rules and theories should be applied here as in the case of other assets which are subject to depletion, and that if the settlor expressly or impliedly allocated the receipts his direction should control.[17] If he directed or allowed retention of the natural resources he should be deemed to have expected that all receipts should go to

---

14. § 10. This section was omitted in Pa., and amended in Ill. so as to apply regardless of the absence of a duty to sell.

15. § 11.

16. See 18 Hastings Law Journal 391; Brigham, 86 U. of Pa.L.R. 471; 23 Temple L.Q. 74.

17. Eager's Guardian v. Pollard, 194 Ky. 276, 239 S.W. 39 (1922); Bedford's Appeal, 126 Pa. 117, 17 A. 538.

income of the trust;[18] but if there was a duty to sell the property the receipts from it pending sale should be apportioned so as to protect the remaindermen from loss by setting up an amortization fund. However, as will appear, the courts have not always treated receipts from natural resources in the same manner as returns from other wasting assets.

If the trust owns shares of stock in a corporation which is engaged in developing wasting property, whether the stock is a wasting asset of the trust should depend on whether the corporation is setting aside a depletion reserve out of its income.[19] If such a sinking fund has been created and is being replenished year by year, then the assets of the corporation are not wasting and the interest of the trust in the corporation through the ownership of its stock is not being depleted;[20] but if no such corporate reserve is being created both the property of the corporation and that of its stockholders are gradually shrinking in value.

Where the matter has not been controlled by an express or implied statement of the intent of the settlor as to the disposition of the receipts from natural resources, most of the common law cases have treated the returns as principal of the trust.[21] Where the trustee has granted a lease for development of the resources, he is said to have made a sale of part of the trust property,[22] and hence the usual rule that the proceeds of a sale are trust principal is to be applied.

There has been some tendency to apply the "open mine" doctrine, originating with regard to legal temporary and remainder interests. The doctrine is to the effect that if the donor of such interests had begun the exploitation of the natural resources prior to his gift, the tenant for life or years could extract benefits from the resources without limit and the remaindermen had no ground for complaint.[23] Applied to trust law this would give the receipts from natural resources to the income account, if the settlor had begun development or had authorized the trustee to exploit the resources, but otherwise to trust principal.[24]

18. Nelligan v. Long, 320 Mass. 439, 70 N.E.2d 175 (1946); In re Koffend's Will, 218 Minn. 206, 15 N.W.2d 590 (1944); Leach v. McCreary, 183 Tenn. 128, 191 S.W.2d 176 (1945).

19. Cadbury v. Parrish, 89 N.H. 464, 200 A. 791 (1938); Bonbright v. Bonbright, 142 N.J.Eq. 642, 61 A.2d 201 (1948); In re Knox's Estate, 328 Pa. 177, 195 A. 28 (1937).

20. First Nat. Bank v. Wefel, 252 Ala. 212, 40 So.2d 434 (1949) (tree farming; periodic reforestation; receipts income; property not wasting); Baldwin Galloway v. Julier, 154 Fla. 41, 16 So.2d 434 (1944).

21. Sternberg v. St. Louis Union Trust Co., 163 F.2d 714 (1947), certiorari denied 332 U.S. 843, 68 S.Ct. 267, 92 L.Ed. 414 (1947); Martin v. Eslick, 229 Miss. 234, 90 So.2d 635 (1956); Avis v. First Nat. Bank, 141 Tex. 489, 174 S.W.2d 255 (1943). But see Heyl v. Northern Trust Co., 312 Ill. App. 207, 38 N.E.2d 374 (1941) (where duty to sell, returns from oil lease apportionable).

22. Central Standard Life Ins. Co. v. Gardner, 17 Ill.2d 220, 161 N.E.2d 278 (1959); In re Bruner's Will, 363 Pa. 552, 70 A.2d 222 (1950).

23. Andrews v. Andrews, 31 Ind.App. 189, 67 N.E. 461; In re Blodgett's Estate, 254 Pa. 210, 98 A. 876; Cook v. Cook, 331 S.W.2d 77 (Tex.Civ.App.1959).

24. Pedroja v. Pedroja, 152 Kan. 82, 102 P.2d 1012 (1940); Poole v. Union Trust Co., 191 Mich. 162, 157 N.W. 430; Mairs v. Central Trust Co., 127 W.Va. 795, 34 S.E.2d 742 (1945).

The Uniform Principal and Income Act allocates receipts from natural resources, where the trustee is authorized by the instrument or by law to develop the resources, to trust income if a payment is received "as rent on a lease", but to trust principal if "received as consideration, whether as royalties or otherwise, for the permanent severance of such natural resources from the lands".[25] This section was omitted in one state in adopting the Uniform Act,[26] and was greatly amended in others.[27]

With regard to disposition of natural resources, the Revised Uniform Principal and Income Act [28] is substantially similar to section 9 of the Uniform Act but with several significant differences. Receipts from production payments are allocated between principal and income rather than entirely to principal, as provided in the Uniform Act. The first $27\frac{1}{2}\%$ of gross receipts from mineral royalties and similar payments is allocated to principal and the balance after expenses is allocated to income. Under the Revised Uniform Act the "open mine" doctrine, allowing the time for leasing or development to determine the allocation of receipts, and which had been adopted by section 9 of the Uniform Act, was abandoned.

 WESTLAW REFERENCES

Property Other Than Natural Resources
trust /3 property asset /s (subject /3 depletion) wasting
find 174 ne 493
409k684(3)
find 244 sw2d 803

Receipts from Natural Resources
wasting /2 asset property /s oil gas timber quarry mine "natural
    resource"
"open mine doctrine"
240k12
240k28 /p mine oil gas timber
373k22
260k79.1(3)

---

25. § 9. This was apparently intended to perpetuate the majority common law rule, based on the idea that a sale of a part interest in the lands was involved.

26. Maryland.

27. In Fla. and Ore. if the trustee is authorized to dispose of the natural resources all receipts are principal. In its adoption of the Uniform Act in 1941 Illinois followed § 9 of the Act, but no statement was made as to whether the trustee was or was not authorized to hold and develop; in 1961 a statute considerably altered the section as to future trusts and provided for apportionment and preservation of principal. See Ill.Rev.Stat. c. 30, ¶ 511. In Ala., Colo., Okl., Pa., and Tex. rentals were treated as income but payments for severance were apportioned by setting up an amortization fund based on the federal tax depletion allowance or a certain fraction of the receipts. In Cal. § 9 was harmonized with § 10 of the Uniform Act by giving all receipts to income if there was no duty to sell the natural resource, and giving the income account 5% of the value of the wasting asset if there was a duty to sell. See Bogert, Trusts and Trustees (rev. 2d edit.), § 827.

28. § 9.

APPORTIONMENT OF PERIODIC RECEIPTS—
SUCCESSIVE BENEFICIARIES [1]

§ 123. At common law interest is deemed to accrue day by day and a trustee is required to allot it to principal or income accordingly; but rents, dividends and all other receipts are regarded as accruing in a lump sum on the due day, so that a trustee should not apportion them between income and principal or successive income beneficiaries. The Uniform Principal and Income Act and other statutes require apportionment in the case of some receipts other than interest.

A problem which confronts every trustee is that of his duty as to the apportionment of income which is paid at regular intervals between successive beneficial interests. The trustee receives money which is ordinarily trust income, for example, rent, interest, or regular cash dividends on stock held, but during the period since the last periodic payment there has been a change with regard to ownership of the trust property or of interests under the trust which makes it doubtful to whom the latest payment should be delivered. If the settlor has included in his trust instrument a direction as to the apportionment of receipts, or has granted to the trustee discretion to decide questions of apportionment, there is no difficulty,[2] but otherwise problems arise which may be explained by illustrations. The criterion for deciding questions of apportionment is the date when the receipt accrued (that is, became payable), and not the date when the payment actually came into the hands of the trustee.[3]

Apportionment at Beginning of Trust

S owns three pieces of property: a bond of the X company for $1,000, bearing 4% interest, payable semi-annually on January 1st and July 1st; ten shares of stock in the Y company on which dividends of $30 are customarily declared on January 1st and July 1st; and the lessor's interest under a lease to Z by the terms of which Z is obligated to pay $100 a month rent to S on the first of each month for the preceding month. On January 15, 1986, S creates a living trust by which he gives the bond, stock, and leasehold interest to T, as trustee, to hold for W, the wife of S, for the life of W, and then to deliver the trust property to B, the son of S. T recognizes problems regarding the interest, rent, and dividends which he later receives. The first receipt he will obtain will naturally be the rent due on February 1, 1986, which was payable for the month of January, 1986. During half of January S

---

§ 123

1. Restatement, Trusts, Second, §§ 235, 235A, 238. Bogert, Trusts and Trustees (rev. 2d edit.), § 818.

See Hale, 16 Harv.L.R. 404; Harris, 9 Okl.L.R. 269; 12 Pa.B.A.Q. 84; Wis.L.R. 1942, 299.

2. In re McManus' Will, 282 N.Y. 420, 26 N.E.2d 960 (1940); Welch v. Welch, 235 Wis. 282, 290 N.W. 758 (1940).

3. Bouch v. Sproule, 12 A.C. 385; Dexter v. Phillips, 121 Mass. 178.

was the owner of the landlord's interest, and during the second half of that month, W was the equitable owner of the right to rent. Should one-half the $100 payment made on February 1 be treated as the property of S at the time the trust was created and half the property of W? The common law answered this question in the negative and decreed that the trustee should treat the entire $100 as income of the trust for W. It explained this result by stating that rent accrues in a lump sum on the rent day, and not day by day, and that therefore there was no rent due until February 1st and at that time the right to the rent was vested in W. This is a declaration that rent is not "apportionable".[4]

Secondly, the trustee will collect on July 1, 1986 the coupon on the X company bond amounting to $20, and will have to decide whether he is to divide this between the principal of the trust and the income account of the trust, or treat it all as income. It might be urged that one-twelfth of this $20 interest payment was for the period during which S owned the bond, namely, from January 1st to January 15th, and that this amount should be treated as a part of the principal of the trust which S gave to T as trustee, and that only eleven-twelfths of the $20 should be treated as trust income. This in fact is the view of the common law, explained by stating that interest accrues from day to day, not in a lump sum on the day when it is payable, and therefore is apportionable. One-twelfth of the interest had accrued as the property of S when he created the trust on January 15th.[5] Hence this one-twelfth should be treated by T as principal of the trust.

Thirdly, T probably will receive $30 on July 1, 1986, as the semi-annual regular dividend on the stock which he holds. Should he treat this as earned in part during the period when S owned the stock, and so as one-twelfth trust principal and eleven-twelfths trust income, or should he treat it all as trust income earned on the date when the dividend was paid to T, namely, July 1st, 1986. Here the common law refused apportionment and held that dividends do not accrue to stockholders until declared by the corporation. They are not paid for any particular period or accruable to the stockholder day by day or month by month. Therefore, at common law, T should treat the entire dividend as trust income as of July 1, 1976.[6]

If T had been given the right to an annuity, the result would have been the same as with dividends and rents. The annuity payments received by T would not have been apportionable, but would all have been treated as income of the trust as of the date they became due.[7]

4. Matter of Franklin, 26 Misc. 107, 56 N.Y.S. 858.

5. Bridgeport Trust Co. v. Marsh, 87 Conn. 384, 87 A. 865; Dexter v. Phillips, 121 Mass. 178, 23 Am.Rep. 261; Wilson's Appeal, 108 Pa. 344, 56 Am.Rep. 214.

6. Bates v. McKinley, 31 Beav. 280; Nutter v. Andrews, 246 Mass. 224, 142

N.E. 67. But see Bankers' Trust Co. of New York v. Lobdell, 116 N.J.Eq. 363, 173 A. 918, *contra.*

7. Heizer v. Heizer, 71 Ind. 526, 36 Am.Rep. 202; Nehls v. Sauer, 119 Iowa 440, 93 N.W. 346. In re Petit's Will, 246 Wis. 620, 18 N.W.2d 339 (1945). But see, *contra,* Savings Investment & Trust Co. v.

Apportionment During or at End of Trust

The problem of apportionment may arise not only at the beginning of the trust, but during its life, and at its termination. For example, the income may be directed to be paid first to W for life, and then to B for his life, and then the trust is to end and C is to receive the principal. If W dies during the period between periodic payments, the problem will arise as to whether part of a periodic payment later collected by the trustee is to go to the executor of W and the rest of it to B, or whether it all goes to B. And if B dies during the period between payments, the question will be whether the receipts after the death of B shall go partly to B's executor or administrator, or entirely to C.[8] The rules about apportionment are the same whether the trust begins or ends, or whether a shift in the right to trust income occurs in the middle of a periodic payment period. At common law the only payment apportioned was interest, because it was the only receipt which was regarded as accruing day by day.[9] Rents accrued in a lump sum on the rent day, dividends accrued on the day fixed in the resolution of the directors of the declaring corporation, and other receipts accrued in a similar manner.[10] Accrued interest was divided between the representative of the deceased life income beneficiary and the owner of the next interest under the trust, whether a second income beneficiary or a remainderman;[11] but there was usually no apportionment of rents, dividends or other receipts.[12]

If a periodic payment is not only accrued but also due, though uncollected, at the time the settlor creates the trust, and is later collected by his trustee, it is treated as a part of trust principal. Thus if S owns corporate stock on which a dividend has been declared as payable to him on certain date but he has not received the dividend during his lifetime and he dies leaving the stock to a trustee who later collects the dividend, the trustee should treat the dividend as a part of the principal of the trust and not as income.[13] And the same rule would be applied to interest, rents, and other receipts which were due the settlor. The same doctrine applies where the payment is due

Carhuff, 117 N.J.Eq. 235, 175 A. 190 (1934); Seattle-First Nat. Bank v. Brott, 15 Wn.2d 177, 130 P.2d 363 (1942).

8. Parker v. Ames, 121 Mass. 220; Kearney v. Cruikshank, 117 N.Y. 95, 22 N.E. 580; Rhode Island Hospital Trust Co. v. Noyes, 26 R.I. 323, 58 A. 999; In re Will of Barron, 163 Wis. 275, 155 N.W. 1087.

9. Kahn v. Wells Fargo Bank & Union Trust Co., 137 Cal.App.Supp. 775, 27 P.2d 672 (1933); Everhard v. Brown, 75 Ohio App. 451, 62 N.E.2d 901 (1945); Horlick v. Sidley, 241 Wis. 81, 3 N.W.2d 710 (1942).

10. In re Wuichet's Estate & Trusteeship, 138 Ohio St. 97, 33 N.E.2d 15 (1941). But see Graves v. Graves, 115 N.J.Eq. 547, 171 A. 681 (1934) (dividend apportioned between successive income beneficiaries); In re Wehrwane's Estate, 23 N.J. 205, 128 A.2d 681 (1934) (stock dividend apportioned).

11. In re Kuhn's Estate, 284 Mich. 450, 279 N.W. 893 (1938); In re Davidson's Estate, 287 Pa. 354, 135 A. 130 (1926).

12. Greene v. Huntington, 73 Conn. 106, 46 A. 883; Mann, Ex'x v. Anderson, 106 Ga. 818, 32 S.E. 870; Parker v. Ames, 121 Mass. 220; Marshall v. Moseley, 21 N.Y. 280.

13. In re Seller's Estate, 31 Del.Ch. 158, 67 A.2d 860 (1949); Matter of Kernochan, 104 N.Y. 618, 11 N.E. 149; In re Opperman's Estate, 319 Pa. 455, 179 A. 729 (1935).

during the life of B, a life beneficiary, but is not collected until after his death; B's executor should get the payment.[14] Thus if a trustee for B for life, remainder to C, holds as a trust asset a bond under which interest is payable on January 1 and July 1, and B dies on July 2, and on August 1 the trustee collects the interest which was due on July 1, the trustee should pay the interest to the personal representative of B.

If a trustee collects income of any sort but does not pay it to the income beneficiary until the trust for the latter has ended, due to the death of the beneficiary or other cause, the trustee has a duty to pay such income to the income beneficiary or to his successor in interest.[15]

In the case of dividends the declaration ordinarily states that they are payable to stockholders of record as of a certain date, and this is to control the duties of the trustee with regard to them, rather than the date of the declaration or the date of payment.[16]

In England the Apportionment Act of 1870 provided for the apportionment of all periodic payments, including dividends.[17] In several states legislation has been adopted requiring the apportionment of some payments other than interest.[18]

The Uniform Principal and Income Act requires apportionment at the beginning of a trust, between successive income beneficiaries, and at termination.[19] The Revised Uniform Act[20] has substantially the same provisions except that if the trust is inter vivos no apportionment is required at the beginning and all receipts partially accrued before commencement of the trust (and paid thereafter) are treated as income.

     WESTLAW REFERENCES

Apportionment of Beginning of Trust
apportion****   /s   beginning   /s   trust

Apportionment During or at End of Trust
apportion****   /s   end during   /s   trust
find 62 ne2d 901
"apportionment act of 1870"

---

14. Warner's Estate, 183 Cal.App.2d 846, 7 Cal.Rptr. 319 (1960); Green v. Green, 182 Md. 571, 35 A.2d 238 (1944); In re Keeney's Will; 22 Misc.2d 948, 198 N.Y.S.2d 879 (1960).

15. First Nat. Bank of Chicago v. Piaget, 2 Ill.App.2d 207, 119 N.E.2d 457 (1954); Thorndike v. Dexter, 340 Mass. 387, 164 N.E.2d 338 (1960); In re Bulis' Estate, 240 N.C. 529, 82 S.E.2d 750 (1954).

16. Wilmington Trust Co. v. Wilmington Trust Co., 25 Del.Ch. 193, 15 A.2d 665 (1940); Hackensack Trust Co. v. Ackerman, 138 N.J.Eq. 244, 47 A.2d 832 (1946).

17. 33 & 34 Vict. c. 35.

18. See, for example, Mass.G.L.A. c. 197 § 27; N.C.Gen.Stats. § 42–6. And see

Bogert, Trusts and Trustees (rev. 2d edit.), § 818.

19. § 4. Connecticut omitted § 4 when it adopted the Act. By Ill.Rev.Stat. c. 30 ¶ 505(c) income is not to be apportioned upon termination of an income interest, with a limited exception. In North Carolina and Virginia the legislature, in enacting the Uniform Principal and Income Act with its provision about apportionment, did not expressly repeal the pre-existing statutes in those states on the same subject. The Uniform Principal and Income Act, however, purports to repeal, upon adoption, all laws which are inconsistent with it.

20. § 4.

SOURCE FROM WHICH EXPENSES
SHOULD BE PAID [1]

§ 124. **The trustee should pay the ordinary, current and regularly recurring expenses of administration of the trust out of trust income, but should pay from trust principal any expenses which are extraordinary or are largely or wholly beneficial to the remainder interests under the trust. While no hard and fast rule can be laid down, in general the cost of keeping the trust property productive and secure is to be borne from trust income.**

In the administration of the trust the trustee must spend trust funds for many different kinds of expenses, and he must decide whether to charge these payments to trust income or to trust principal.

The decisions and statutes lay down the very general and vague rule that the ordinary and regularly recurring expenses of administration should be borne by trust income, and extraordinary expenditures should be charged to trust principal.[2] The theory is that the income beneficiaries should bear the responsibility for keeping the trust property safe and productive and for maintaining the status which existed when the trust began, but that expenditures which increase the value of the trust principal, or inure to the benefit of the remaindermen in particular, or are extraordinary in amount, should be paid from trust principal.

To a large extent the allocation of the burden of expenses is determined by the court before which an accounting is pending or in which litigation is occurring. This is particularly true with regard to costs, legal fees, and other expenses of legal proceedings which are often allowed to one or the other of the parties.[3] The court has power, under its general jurisdiction over trusts, to use its discretion in deciding such questions.

The following items have been held to be ordinary or current expenses and so payable from trust income: interest on a mortgage on the trust property,[4] real or personal property taxes,[5] the cost of repair

---

§ 124

1. Restatement, Trusts, Second, §§ 233, 237. Bogert, Trusts and Trustees (rev. 2d edit.), §§ 801–810.

See Matter of Eddy's Will, 207 App.Div. 162, 201 N.Y.S. 760 (1923).

2. Guthrie v. Wheeler, 51 Conn. 207; Rothschild v. Weinthel, 191 Ind. 85, 132 N.E. 687, 17 A.L.R. 1377 (1921); Cogswell v. Weston, 228 Mass. 219, 117 N.E. 37. See Hopkins v. Austin State Bank, 410 Ill. 67, 101 N.E.2d 536 (1951).

3. Atwood v. Kleberg, 163 F.2d 108 (5th Cir.1947), certiorari denied 332 U.S.

843, 68 S.Ct. 267, 92 L.Ed. 414 (1947); Page v. D'Amours, 99 N.H. 441, 113 A.2d 544 (1955); Trust Co. of N.J. v. Greenwood Cemetery, 21 N.J.Misc. 169, 32 A.2d 519 (1943) (even contrary to directions of settlor).

See, for example, the different methods of treating accounting costs: Perrine v. Newell, 49 N.J.Eq. 57, 23 A. 492.

4. Morton's Case, 74 N.J.Eq. 797, 70 A. 680.

5. Hagan v. Varney, 147 Ill. 281, 35 N.E. 219; In re Harris' Will, 170 Minn. 134, 212 N.W. 182 (1927).

of buildings on trust real estate,[6] rental of a safety deposit box,[7] insurance premiums in the case of fire or liability insurance,[8] premiums on the trustee's bond,[9] and costs of administering the trust, such as travelling expenses and disbursements for employing secretarial, accounting, legal or tax assistants.[10]

In the older cases the trustee's compensation was often taken from trust income,[11] but in some cases the expense was divided between income and principal.[12] In recent years there has been an increasing tendency to place part of the burden on principal, either by action of the court in the use of its discretion,[13] by the terms of the trust, or by statute.[14] The work of the trustee is often beneficial to both types of beneficiaries: low yields furnish a reason for relieving the income beneficiary to some extent; and appreciating values of principal assets will benefit the remaindermen.

The following expenses should normally be paid from trust principal: the principal debt in the case of a mortgage on trust property; [15] special assessments for public improvements or the cost of improvements made by the trustee where the improvement will probably last longer than the income beneficiary's interest; [16] costs of litigation which has as its object the enforcement or defense of the trust; [17] and

6. Alberts v. Steiner, 237 Mich. 143, 211 N.W. 46 (1926); Disbrow v. Disbrow, 46 App.Div. 111, 61 N.Y.S. 614, affirmed 167 N.Y. 606, 60 N.E. 1110. But the expense of repairing realty which is in an untenantable condition when acquired by the trustee is allocated to trust principal. In re Shurtz's Estate, 242 Iowa 448, 46 N.W.2d 559 (1951).

7. In re Kimber's Will, 172 Misc. 991, 16 N.Y.S.2d 786 (1939), affirmed 261 App. Div. 901, 26 N.Y.S.2d 492 (1941).

8. Prudential Ins. Co. of America v. Land Estates, 31 F.Supp. 845 (S.D.N.Y. 1939); Kingsley v. Spofford, 298 Mass. 469, 11 N.E.2d 487 (1937).

9. Butler v. Builders' Trust Co., 203 Minn. 555, 282 N.W. 462, 124 A.L.R. 1178 (1938).

10. Buder v. Fiske, 174 F.2d 260 (8th Cir.1949), rehearing denied 177 F.2d 907 (8th Cir.1949); In re Seller's Estate, 31 Del. Ch. 158, 67 A.2d 860 (1949); National Agric. College v. Lavenson, 55 N.M. 583, 237 P.2d 925 (1951); In re Kimber's Will, 261 App.Div. 901, 26 N.Y.S.2d 492 (1941).

11. Williamson v. Witkins, 14 Ga. 416; In re Spangler's Estate, 21 Pa. 335.

12. In re Hopson's Will, 213 App.Div. 395, 211 N.Y.S. 128 (1925); Miller v. Payne, 150 Wis. 354, 136 N.W. 811.

13. In re McMillin's Estate, 120 N.J. Eq. 432, 185 A. 913 (1936); McAfee v. Thomas, 121 Or. 351, 255 P. 333 (1927).

14. See statutes on compensation of the trustee, Bogert, Trusts and Trustees (2d edit.), § 975. And see In re Robert's Will Trusts, Ch. 274 (1937); Old Colony Trust Co. v. Townsend, 324 Mass. 298, 85 N.E.2d 784 (1949).

15. Ash v. Ash, 126 N.J.Eq. 531, 10 A.2d 150 (1940).

16. Plympton v. Boston Dispensary, 106 Mass. 544; Peltz v. Learned, 70 App. Div. 312, 75 N.Y.S. 104. Where the improvement is temporary, in that it will probably wear out before the income beneficiary's interest ends, it should be paid from trust income, or if paid from principal an amortization fund should be set up from income to replace the principal thus spent. In re Seller's Estate, 31 Del.Ch. 158, 67 A.2d 860 (1949); Jordan v. Jordan, 192 Mass. 337, 78 N.E. 459; In re Bohmert's Will, 102 N.Y.S.2d 394 (Sur.1950).

Section 12(4) of the Uniform Principal and Income Act provides for amortizing the cost of assessments for permanent improvements by deductions from income. § 13(c)(3) of the Revised Uniform Act authorizes amortization.

17. Carter v. Brownell, 95 Conn. 210, 111 A. 182; In re Estate of Cole, 102 Wis. 1, 78 N.W. 402, 72 Am.St.Rep. 854.

costs of investment and sale of trust property.[18]

Where real property is unproductive there has been a tendency in recent years to place the carrying charges such as mortgage interest and property taxes on the principal of the trust,[19] rather than to pay such charges out of the income of other trust property.

The Uniform Principal and Income Act[20] allocates the following expenses to trust income; ordinary expenses, including regularly recurring taxes, water rates, premiums on insurance, interest on mortgages, ordinary repairs, the trustee's compensation except commissions computed on principal, compensation of assistants, and court costs and attorney's and other fees on accountings. It places the burden of the following outlays on trust principal; commissions computed on principal, costs of investing or reinvesting, attorney's fees and other costs of maintaining actions to protect the trust property, costs of or assessments for improvements, carrying charges of unproductive property, and income taxes on capital gains.

The Revised Uniform Principal and Income Act[21] makes several important changes in the treatment of charges against income and principal. It requires a reasonable allowance for depreciation on improved realty (other than that used by a beneficiary as a residence), and provides that one-half of the expenses of periodic judicial accountings (unless otherwise directed by the court) and the trustee's regular compensation (whether based on principal or income) should be charged to income.

A trustee who foresees the necessity to meet a major expense out of trust income in the future may create a reserve fund to meet the expense by making deductions from income from time to time.[22]

Where expenditures occur at regular intervals, as in the case of property taxes, it would seem that their burden should be distributed between successive beneficiaries. Assume that a property tax is levied on January 1st for the preceding year, and that a trust exists for A for life, then for B for life, remainder to C. If A dies on June 1, 1986 and taxes are levied on January 1, 1986 for the year 1986, it would seem that this tax bill should not be met entirely out of the income due B, but that five-twelfths of it should be paid by A's estate, since he was life tenant for five months of the year 1986, and seven-twelfths of it should be paid by the trustee from income which has been accumulated for B,

18. McLean v. American Sec. & Trust Co., 113 F.Supp. 427 (D.D.C.1953); In re Schepp's Estate, Sur., 9 N.Y.S.2d 112 (1938).

19. In re Hill's Estate, 54 Cal.2d 39, 4 Cal.Rptr. 1, 351 P.2d 33 (1960); In re Danziger's Will, Sur., 58 N.Y.S.2d 790 (1945); Haas v. McGinn, 64 R.I. 133, 11 A.2d 284 (1940).

20. § 12. Changes in this section were made in California, Connecticut, Illinois, Maryland, Oklahoma, Oregon and Pennsylvania. See Bogert, Trusts and Trustees (rev. 2d edit.), § 802.

21. § 13.

22. In re Harris' Will, 170 Minn. 134, 212 N.W. 182 (1927); In re Parr, 45 Misc. 564, 92 N.Y.S. 990.

since B has been life tenant during seven months of the year 1986.[23]

 WESTLAW REFERENCES

390k274(3)

regular administrative /2 expense /s "trust income"

find 101 ne2d 536

expense /s "trust principal"

---

23. Taylor v. Bentinck-Smith, 304 Mass. 430, 24 N.E.2d 146, 126 A.L.R. 857 (1939); In re Daily's Estate, 117 Mont. 194, 159 P.2d 327 (1945); Phillips Exeter Academy v. Gleason, 102 N.H. 369, 157 A.2d 769 (1960).

Apportionment is provided by the Uniform Principal and Income Act, § 12(3), as to expenses payable out of income which represent regularly recurring charges. And see § 13(d) of the Revised Uniform Act.

Chapter 14

LIABILITIES FROM CONTRACTS, TORTS, AND PROPERTY OWNERSHIP

Table of Sections

PERSONAL LIABILITY OF TRUSTEES ON CONTRACTS [1]

§ 125. If a trustee makes a contract in the administration of the trust, he is personally liable unless the contract provides otherwise. If there is a breach of the contract by the trustee, the other party can recover a judgment against the trustee and collect it out of his individual property, but not out of the trust property, even though the person contracting with the trustee knew of the trust and knew that the trustee was making the contract for the benefit of the trust.

Trustees usually have express or implied authority to make many different kinds of contracts.[2] For example, a trustee of an office building may contract for the services of employees necessary to lease and run the building, and for fuel and light to make it usable, and a trustee of agricultural land may have power to borrow money to pay

---

§ 125

1. Bogert, Trusts and Trustees (rev. 2d edit.), § 711 et seq.; Restatement, Trusts, Second, §§ 262, 266–271, 271A, 275.

2. Shelby v. White, 158 Miss. 880, 131 So. 343 (1930); Ranzau v. Davis, 85 Or. 26, 158 P. 279.

operating costs during years of crop failure.[3] If the contract is one which the trustee is empowered to make, he will usually perform it and no difficulty will arise. He will pay the janitor and the coal supplier out of the income of the office building, or the bank loan out of the receipts from crops of later years. But occasionally the trustee makes contracts in his trust administration and fails to perform them. For example, he may hire a contractor to place a new roof on the office building and not pay the contract price and materials when due. The question then arises as to liability on such a contract and the remedies of the creditor.[4] Can the creditor get a judgment against the trustee as trustee, and collect it out of trust property, or must he sue the trustee in his individual capacity and collect by a levy or execution on the individual property of the trustee?

The question is decided by careful consideration of the views of the common law courts which enforce contracts as to the identity of the person who made the promise. The only legal person recognized by the court of law is the trustee as an individual, and not in his representative capacity. If Henry Smith is trustee under the will of John Brown, and Smith contracts for work and materials and promises to pay a certain sum therefor, the court of law regards Henry Smith as the person making the promise and liable upon it. It does not recognize Henry Smith, as trustee, as a distinct legal person at all. The trust estate or trust is not a person in the eye of the law,[5] and the beneficiaries of the trust did not make the contract. The trustee is not their agent and so it cannot be held that they should be bound because the trustee acted for them.[6] Nor are they liable on any other theory,[7] unless they assume the powers of management of the trust.[8] Smith is the legal entity who made the promise and hence he should be liable upon it. Whether his liability is permanent or will finally be shifted to the trust is of no concern to the law court. It leaves that matter to the court of equity.

Thus trustees are personally liable on the contracts they make during trust administration unless they expressly exclude such liability. For a breach of a contract where personal liability is not excluded, the third person as the promisee can sue the trustee at law and collect out of the trustee's individual property but not out of the property held in

3. Purdy v. Bank of Amer. Nat. Trust & Sav. Ass'n, 2 Cal.2d 298, 40 P.2d 481 (1935).

4. For valuable articles, see Brandeis, 15 Amer.L.R. 449; Stone, 22 Col.L.R. 527; Scott, 28 Harv.L.R. 725; Vanneman, 9 Univ. of Cinc.L.R. 1.

5. In some states by statute Massachusetts or business trusts are allowed to sue and be sued in the name of the trust. Alphonzo E. Bell Corp. v. Bell View Oil Syndicate, 46 Cal.App.2d 684, 116 P.2d 786

(1941); Ballentine v. Eaton, 297 Mass. 389, 8 N.E.2d 808 (1937).

6. Taylor v. Mayo, 110 U.S. 330, 4 S.Ct. 147, 28 L.Ed. 163 (1884); Everett v. Drew, 129 Mass. 150.

7. Rossman v. Marsh, 287 Mich. 720, 286 N.W. 83 (1939); Gates v. Avery, 112 Wis. 271, 87 N.W. 1091.

8. Otoe Co. Nat. Bank v. Delany, 88 F.2d 238 (8th Cir.1937).

trust.[9] The trustee's liability is not limited to the value of the trust property from which he may be able to secure indemnity.[10] An action at law cannot be maintained against the trustee as such, or in his representative capacity, and if he is described as a trustee in the plaintiff's pleading the reference to the trust is regarded as surplusage and as of no effect.[11]

It is immaterial that the person contracting with the trustee knew the trust existed, recognized that the trustee was acting in his fiduciary capacity, and knew that the contract was made in the course of the trust administration.[12] Nor is it relevant that the words "as trustee" followed the signature of the trustee on the contract.[13]

In some states, either as a result of court decisions or statute law, a contract creditor of the trustee may sue the trustee in his representative capacity in an action at law and collect his judgment from trust property.[14] A section of the Field Code of California,[15] also adopted in other states,[16] providing that a "trustee is a general agent for the trust property" and that his "acts, within the scope of his authority, bind the trust property to the same extent as the acts of an agent bind his principal", would seem intended to create representative liability and has been so construed in some cases.[17] But in other cases the individual liability of the trustee has also been enforced,[18] so that a choice between personal and representative liability is offered.[19] This tendency to recognize the trustee in his representative capacity as a juridical person is found in the Uniform Trusts Act which permits such an action if the beneficiaries have been notified and given an opportunity

9. Peyser v. American Security & Trust Co., 70 App.D.C. 349, 107 F.2d 625 (D.C.Cir.1939); Slatt v. Thomas, 95 Colo. 382, 36 P.2d 459 (1934); Bishop v. Bucklen, 390 Ill. 176, 60 N.E.2d 872 (1945); In re Gibbons' Estate, 132 Neb. 538, 272 N.W. 553 (1937).

10. Restatement, Trusts, Second, § 262, Comment b.

11. Zehnbar v. Spillman, 25 Fla. 591, 6 So. 214; O'Brien v. Jackson, 167 N.Y. 31, 60 N.E. 238; Smith v. Chambers, 117 W.Va. 204, 185 S.E. 211 (1936); Kincaid v. Hensel, 185 Wash. 503, 55 P.2d 1050 (1936).

12. Parker v. Parker, 282 Mich. 158, 275 N.W. 803 (1937); Breid v. Mintrup, 203 Mo.App. 567, 219 S.W. 703; Connally v. Lyons, 82 Tex. 664, 18 S.W. 799, 27 Am.St. Rep. 935.

13. Duvall v. Craig, 2 Wheat. 45; Dolben v. Gleason, 292 Mass. 511, 198 N.E. 762 (1935). But § 12(3) of the Uniform Trusts Act takes a contrary view.

14. See § 128, post. And see statutes of Ala., Conn., Ga., Ind., Mass., N.Dak., Okl., Pa., R.I. and Wash., cited in Bogert, Trusts and Trustees (rev. 2d edit.), § 712. See also Unif.Prob. Code § 7–306; Unif.

Trusts Act § 12. And see Cannon v. Robinson, 67 N.C. 53; Penn. Co. v. Wallace, 346 Pa. 532, 31 A.2d 71 (1943).

15. West's Ann.Cal.Civ.Code § 2267.

16. Mont.—R.C. § 72–23–307; N.Dak. C.C. 59–02–10; S.Dak.Codif.L. 55–3–7.

17. Irvine v. McGregor, 203 Cal. 583, 265 P. 218 (1928); Purdy v. Bank of America Nat. Trust & Sav. Ass'n, 2 Cal.2d 298, 40 P.2d 481 (1935).

18. Goldwater v. Oltman, 210 Cal. 408, 292 P. 624 (1930).

19. In a few states statutes provide that the plaintiff may either sue the trustee in his representative capacity or sue the trustee personally for contract liability. See S.Dak.Codif.Laws §§ 55–4–19 and 55–4–21 (presumption established that the word "trustee" after the trustee's name is evidence that personal liability was excluded). See also V.T.C.A., Prop.Code § 114.084. And see Wash.–RCWA 11.98.110. See 23 Cal.L.R. 538; 2 Hast.L.J. 58. But in Montana it has been held that the representative liability statute excludes personal liability. Tuttle v. Union Bank & Tr. Co., 112 Mont. 568, 119 P.2d 884 (1941).

to intervene,[20] as an alternative to an action against the trustee personally where he has not excluded personal liability.

A trustee is not personally liable on contracts made by the settlor with regard to trust property,[21] although, as shown later,[22] he may be affected in his representative capacity by such agreements.

Where there are co-trustees, a trustee who did not join in making a contract should not be liable on it.[23]

The trustee may be individually liable on contracts made for the trust by an authorized agent.[24]

A successor trustee is not liable on the contracts of his predecessor unless he assumed such responsibility.[25]

 WESTLAW REFERENCES

trustee /s implied express /2 authority /s contract
trustee /s personal** /2 liable liability /s contract
390k210 /p personal** /2 liable
390k171
find 98 ne 91

TRUSTEE'S POWER TO EXCLUDE PERSONAL AND INCLUDE REPRESENTATIVE LIABILITY [1]

§ 126. A trustee may exclude personal liability by inserting a clause to that effect in a contract, but the mere description of himself as trustee in the body of the contract or at the end with his signature is not generally held to show an agreement by the other party to forego personal liability of the trustee.

When a trustee makes a contract which is within his powers, he may provide for liability by himself in his representative capacity and consequent collection out of trust property. The express exclusion of personal liability implies an intent to create representative liability.

If the person contracting with the trustee is willing to deal with the trustee on such terms, the trustee may expressly provide in the contract against any personal liability upon his part, and if this is done, the trustee cannot be held individually liable for the performance of the contract.[2] In order to obtain this result the trustee should show a clear

20. § 12. The Act is in effect in Louisiana, Nevada, North Carolina, Oklahoma, South Dakota, Texas and Washington.

21. In re Jeffers' Estate, 272 Mich. 127, 261 N.W. 271 (1935); In re Glauser's Estate, 350 Pa. 192, 38 A.2d 64 (1944).

22. See § 132, post.

23. Markel v. Peck, 168 Mo.App. 358, 151 S.W. 772; Cornett v. West, 102 Wash. 254, 173 P. 44.

24. Blewitt v. Olin, 14 Daly 351.

25. King v. Stowell, 211 Mass. 246, 98 N.E. 91; United States Tr. Co. v. Stanton, 139 N.Y. 531, 34 N.E. 1098.

§ 126

1. Restatement, Trusts, Second, §§ 261–263, 266–267, 271–271A.

2. Schumann-Heink v. Folsom, 328 Ill. 321, 159 N.E. 250 (1927); State v. Thomas,

expression of intent in the contract. The best method is to state both in the body of the contract and in the signature that the trustee contracts as a trustee and not personally.[3]

It has been generally held that the mere description of the trustee as such, in the body of the contract, and the mere addition of the words "as trustee" following the trustee's signature, do not show an intent to contract against personal liability or an acceptance of such exclusion by the other party.[4] This seems a dubious construction; it is difficult to see what intent other than exclusion the words "as trustee" would connote. The Uniform Trusts Act provides that the use of these words is prima facie evidence of an intent to exclude personal liability.[5]

The courts are not agreed whether parol evidence may be used to prove an intent to exclude personal liability, where the contract was in writing and contained no express exclusion clause.[6]

Under the terms of the Uniform Negotiable Instruments Law [7] if a trustee signed a negotiable instrument "in a representative capacity" and on behalf of a named or described trust, he was not personally liable on the instrument but was liable in his representative capacity so that collection could be had out of the assets of the trust, assuming execution of the instrument was within the powers of the trustee.[8] This provision has been continued in the Uniform Commercial Code,[9] which has taken the place of the Uniform Negotiable Instruments Law in all states but Louisiana. If the name of the trust does not appear in the instrument, some courts have permitted oral evidence to explain that the name was stated orally to the payee by the maker.[10]

The fact that the trust instrument contains a clause providing that the trustee shall not be personally liable on contracts which he makes during the administration of the trust, but that all liabilities thereunder shall be satisfied out of trust property, should be effective to exclude personal liability of the trustee, if it was expressly or impliedly incorporated into the contract.[11] However the mere existence of such a

---

209 N.C. 722, 184 S.E. 529 (1936); Beggs v. Fite, 130 Tex. 46, 106 S.W.2d 1039 (1937).

Exclusion clauses are the rule and not the exception in well-drawn trusts.

3. Ballentine v. Eaton, 297 Mass. 389, 8 N.E.2d 808 (1937); Fowler v. Mutual Life Ins. Co., 28 Hun 195.

4. Duvall v. Craig, 15 U.S. (2 Wheat.) 45, 4 L.Ed. 180 (1817); Zimmer Constr. Co. v. White, 8 Cal.App.2d 672, 47 P.2d 1087 (1935); Dolben v. Gleason, 292 Mass. 511, 198 N.E. 762 (1935).

5. § 12(3). And see Ohio R.C. § 1339.65(A)(2); S.Dak.Codif.L. 55–4–21; Tex.Prop.Code §§ 114.063, 114.084; Wash. RCWA 11.98.110.

6. Woerter v. Mahler, 314 Ill.App. 324, 41 N.E.2d 230 (1942) (admissible); East River Sav. Bank v. Samuels, 284 N.Y. 470,

31 N.E.2d 906, 138 A.L.R. 149 (1940) (inadmissible); Pennsylvania Co. v. Wallace, 346 Pa. 532, 31 A.2d 71, 156 A.L.R. 1 (1943) (admissible).

7. § 20.

8. Cotton v. Courtright, 215 Ala. 474, 111 So. 7 (1926); Tebaldi Supply Co. v. MacMillan, 292 Mass. 384, 198 N.E. 651 (1935); First Nat. Bank of Pennsboro v. Delancey, 109 W.Va. 136, 153 S.E. 908 (1930).

9. § 3–403.

10. American Trust Co. v. Canevin, 184 Fed. 657 (3d Cir.1911); Magallen v. Gomes, 281 Mass. 383, 183 N.E. 833 (1933); Megowan v. Peterson, 173 N.Y. 1, 65 N.E. 738.

11. In some cases mere reference to a trust instrument with an exclusion clause

clause in a recorded trust instrument and consequent constructive notice thereof to the contracting party should not be held to show that he accepted the exclusion term and contracted on the basis of it.[12]

It is clear that the trustee has the power to give the contract creditor a direct remedy against the trustee in his representative capacity and thus to provide for collection of obligations out of the trust funds.[13] If this power did not exist the trustee would sometimes be handicapped in his administration and in the performance of his duty to make advantageous contracts, by reason of his inability to find a contracting party who would rely on the personal liability of the trustee because of his lack of personal funds, or because the trustee was unwilling to place initial contract responsibility on himself due to personal disadvantages that might ensue. Thus in Jessup v. Smith [14] a trustee employed an attorney to perform services beneficial to the estate and expressly stipulated that the estate alone should be liable. It was held that the trust property could be subjected to the payment of the debt, the court saying: [15] "A trustee, who pays his own money for services beneficial to the trust, has a lien for reimbursement. But if he is unable or unwilling to incur liability himself, the law does not leave him helpless. In such circumstances, he 'has the power, if other funds fail, to create a charge, equivalent to his own lien for reimbursement, in favor of another by whom the services are rendered' . . .."

A trustee has no duty to advance his own funds or pledge his own credit for the purpose of carrying out the trust. In those cases where the settlor has directed the carrying on by the trustee of a certain business, and the contract in question has been made by the trustee in connection with such business, the trustee has been held to have power to charge the trust estate by his contract.[16] The contract must be one which is beneficial to the beneficiaries and within the trustee's powers.[17] The cause of action under a provision for representative liability

in it has been held to show an intent to incorporate the exclusion clause in the contract. Bank of Topeka v. Eaton, 100 Fed. 8 (C.C.Mass.1900), affirmed 47 C.C.A. 140, 107 F. 1003 (1st Cir.1901); James Stewart & Co., Inc. v. National Shawmut Bank, C.C.A.Mass., 75 F.2d 148 (1st Cir.1935). See East River Savings Bank v. Samuels, 284 N.Y. 470, 31 N.E.2d 906, 138 A.L.R. 149 (1940), where trustees executed a bond and mortgage, and in the body of both instruments as well as at the end the words "as trustee" followed their names, and reference was made in the documents to the trust instrument, an intent to exclude personal liability was shown and it was held that exclusion occurred.

12. Allegheny Tank Car Co. v. Culbertson, 288 Fed. 406 (D.C.Tex.1923); Goldwater v. Oltman, 210 Cal. 408, 292 P. 624 (1930).

13. People ex rel. Nelson v. Home Bank & Trust Co., 300 Ill.App. 611, 21 N.E.2d 809 (1939); King v. Stowell, 211 Mass. 246, 98 N.E. 91; New v. Nicoll, 73 N.Y. 127, 29 Am.Rep. 111.

14. 223 N.Y. 203, 119 N.E. 403.

15. 223 N.Y. 203, 207, 119 N.E. 403, 404.

16. Gisborn v. Charter Oak Life Ins. Co., 142 U.S. 326, 12 S.Ct. 277, 35 L.Ed. 1029 (1892); Roberts v. Hale, 124 Iowa 296, 99 N.W. 1075, 1 Ann.Cas. 940; Cannon v. Robinson, 67 N.C. 53; Yerkes v. Richards, 170 Pa. 346, 32 A. 1089.

17. King v. Stowell, 211 Mass. 246, 98 N.E. 91; Murphey v. Dalton, 314 S.W.2d 726 (Mo.1958); Terminal Trading Co. v. Babbit, 7 Wn.2d 166, 109 P.2d 564 (1941).

is equitable in nature,[18] and gives the creditor a right to proceed against the trust estate directly, rather than a so-called derivative right to reach the trust property through the trustee's right of indemnity.

If the contract clearly states an intent to relieve the trustee of all personal liability but contains no express provision as to other liability, it would seem that a provision creating liability on the part of the trustee in his representative capacity should be implied,[19] since otherwise there would be no contract because of lack of mutuality of obligation. The trustee, as trustee, is the only other possible obligor.

If a trustee enters into a contract which it is not within his powers to create and excludes personal liability, he is not liable in his representative capacity, regardless of an express or implied provision that he shall be, and the contract creditor has no remedies except on the theory of a breach of warranty by the trustee of his power to make the contract,[20] or in quasi-contract where performance has increased the value of the trust estate.[21]

If a trustee attempts to make a contract on behalf of the trust but lacks power to do so, and he does not exclude personal liability,[22] the contract binds the trustee personally.[23]

 WESTLAW REFERENCES

trustee /s exclusion exclud*** /s personal** /2 liable liability

trustee /s liable liability /s representative /2 capacity

TRUSTEE'S RIGHT OF INDEMNITY AS TO CONTRACT LIABILITIES [1]

§ 127. A trustee who makes a contract which is within his powers and which is prudently made has a right that liability shall be satisfied out of trust property. The trustee may assert this right of indemnity by

(a) Paying the contract creditor out of trust property;

18. Williams v. Northern Tr. Co., 316 Ill.App. 148, 44 N.E.2d 333 (1942); O'Brien v. Jackson, 167 N.Y. 31, 60 N.E. 238.

19. Ballentine v. Eaton, 297 Mass. 389, 8 N.E.2d 808 (1937); Beggs v. Fite, 130 Tex. 46, 106 S.W.2d 1039 (1937).

20. Bagnell v. Ives, 184 Fed. 466 (C.C. Pa.1911). Such a warranty is implied in the case of an agent. In Equitable Tr. Co. v. Taylor, 330 Ill. 42, 161 N.E. 62 (1928), it was held that a creditor obtained no implied warranty of authority when he had seen the trust instrument and knew that it did not empower the trustee to make the contract.

21. Kirkwood v. Kidwell, 72 Ill.App. 492; In re Estate of Manning, 134 Iowa 165, 111 N.W. 409. See § 128, post.

22. For instances of effective exclusion of personal liability in ultra vires contracts, see Foster v. Featherston, 230 Ala. 268, 160 So. 689 (1935); Davis v. Holliday, 354 Mo. 10, 188 S.W.2d 40 (1945).

23. Downey Co. v. 282 Beacon St. Trust, 292 Mass. 175, 197 N.E. 643 (1935).

§ 127

1. Restatement, Trusts, Second, §§ 244–246, 249.

    (b) **Reimbursing himself out of trust property for advances he has made out of his own funds to meet liability under trust contracts;**

    (c) **Suing in equity to get a decree that initial liability rest on him as trustee, where he is sued at law individually on a contract which he made as trustee;**

    (d) **Requesting reimbursement for amounts paid from his own property to meet contract obligations, either on his accounting or in a suit to have trust property sold for that purpose; or**

    (e) **Retaining possession of trust property under a lien which the law gives him until he is repaid amounts which he has expended from his private funds for contract liability.**

There is a conflict as to whether the trustee is entitled to indemnity for contract obligations from the beneficiary when he cannot get full indemnity from the trust property.

A trustee has no right of indemnity from liability under a contract which the terms of the trust did not permit him to make. If the contract was within his powers but was imprudently made, his right of indemnity may be diminished, and his right may be extinguished or reduced by reason of damages which he has caused to the beneficiaries by breaches of trust.

It is obvious that ultimate liability for contracts made by the trustee in the proper administration of his trust should be satisfied out of the trust property. The trustee is only a representative. He personally does not gain from the trust administration. The benefits of the contract will go to the beneficiaries of the trust, and any burdens incident to it should be met from property equitably belonging to the beneficiaries, that is, from the trust property. While as a matter of contract law, and as between the contracting trustee and the third person, the liability of the trustee may be personal to the trustee, as a matter of equity that burden should ultimately be shifted to the trust property if the trustee had power to make the contract and made it with reasonable prudence.[2]

In recognition of this principle it is undoubted law that the trustee may meet such contract obligations in the first place out of trust property, that is, by self-help he may shift the burden from himself to the trust property. Or, if initially he meets the contract debt from his own pocket, by self-help he may later repay himself from trust property.[3]

Furthermore, if an action is pending at law against the trustee on a contract he made for the trust, and the trustee wants to avoid having a judgment recovered against him personally, he may sue in equity to have it decreed that the judgment shall be against him as trustee in the

2. United States v. Swope, 16 F.2d 215 (10th Cir.1926).

3. Hamlen v. Welch, C.C.A.Mass., 116 F.2d 413 (1st Cir.1940); In re Mathues' Estate, 322 Pa. 358, 185 A. 768 (1936).

first place, and he will succeed if he can prove that he made the contract lawfully and with ordinary prudence.[4] This is sometimes called the right of "exoneration" from liability.

It is also true that if the trustee has met the contract obligation out of his own funds he may claim reimbursement on his accounting as a trustee or by petitioning the court of equity to permit him to sell trust property in order to accomplish the reimbursement.[5]

In order to force the reimbursement to which he is entitled, the trustee may hold possession of the trust property. He is said to have a lien for that purpose,[6] that is, a right of retention until he is reimbursed or protected against future liability.

Although the English cases [7] hold that a trustee is entitled to indemnity for contract and other liabilities from the beneficiary, if the trust property is inadequate, the American authorities are not clear on the subject.[8]

The Restatement of Trusts [9] denies such a right, except where the beneficiary has agreed to it, or where the trustee has transferred trust property to the beneficiary without deducting the amount needed for indemnity and without an agreement to forego such right. In the latter case the right of indemnity is limited by the amount of the distribution made to the beneficiary.

The trustee has no right of indemnity against liability incurred by him in making a contract which was not lawful or proper under the terms of the trust instrument,[10] except to the extent that performance of the contract has increased the value of the trust estate.[11] And his right of indemnity is limited to the amount of liability that he might properly have incurred in the exercise of reasonable prudence.[12] Thus if he had power to buy real property but he agreed to pay an excessive price for it, and he has been held liable personally, he should be reimbursed from trust property to the extent of a reasonable price only.

4. Hobbs v. Wayet, 36 Ch.D. 256; In re National Financial Co., L.R. 3 Ch.App. 791.

5. Sorrels v. McNally, 94 Fla. 1174, 115 So. 540 (1927); Warner v. Tullis, 206 Iowa 680, 218 N.W. 575 (1928); Barrell v. Joy, 16 Mass. 221.

6. Woodard v. Wright, 82 Cal. 202, 22 P. 1118; Turton v. Grant, 86 N.J.Eq. 191, 96 A. 993; Percy v. Huyck, 252 N.Y. 168, 169 N.E. 127 (1929).

7. Hardoon v. Belilios, [1901] A.C. 118, noted in 14 Harv.L.R. 539; Mathews v. Ruggles-Brise, [1911] 1 Ch. 194. In some cases the beneficiary is liable because he agrees to reimburse the trustee. Cunniff v. McDonnell, 196 Mass. 7, 81 N.E. 879; Poland v. Beal, 192 Mass. 559, 78 N.E. 728.

8. As tending to deny the right, see Coffman v. Gates, 110 Mo.App. 475, 85 S.W. 657; Roger Williams Nat. Bank v. Groton Mfg. Co., 16 R.I. 504, 17 A. 170. But other cases seem to support the right: Darling v. Buddy, 318 Mo. 784, 1 S.W.2d 163 (1927) (business trust); Equitable Tr. Co. v. Kingsley, 119 Misc. 673, 197 N.Y.S. 267 (1922), affirmed 207 App.Div. 839, 201 N.Y.S. 900, 238 N.Y. 587, 144 N.E. 903 (1924); Wells-Stone Merc. Co. v. Aultman, Miller & Co., 9 N.D. 520, 84 N.W. 375.

9. (1935) § 249. And § 249 of the Restatement of Trusts, Second, affirms this position.

10. Sheets v. Security First Mtg. Co., 293 Ill.App. 222, 12 N.E.2d 324 (1937); Downey Co. v. 282 Beacon St. Trust, 292 Mass. 175, 197 N.E. 643 (1935).

11. Rathbun v. Colton, 15 Pick., 32 Mass., 471; Williams v. Smith, 10 R.I. 280.

12. Green v. Winter, 1 Johns.Ch. 26; Welsh v. Davis, 3 S.C. 110.

If co-trustees make a contract they are severally liable, and if one of them is obliged to bear the entire burden of a contract claim he may secure indemnity from the trust to the full extent of the liability.[13] He also has the right to secure contribution of their shares from the co-trustees who did not pay the claim.[14]

The trustee's right of indemnity may be reduced or totally extinguished by reason of a liability of the trustee to the beneficiaries for breach of trust.[15] Thus if a trustee has made a non-legal investment and damages in the amount of $5,000 have been incurred, and on his accounting the trustee claims the right to be reimbursed to the extent of $2,000 on account of a contract liability which he lawfully and prudently incurred for the trust and paid out of his own funds, the trustee will be denied indemnity. Because the trustee is indebted to the beneficiaries for wrongdoing does not prevent him, however, from paying a contract liability out of trust funds by self-help.[16]

 WESTLAW REFERENCES

find 185 a. 768

trustee /s contract /s indemnity

CONTRACT CREDITOR'S RIGHTS AGAINST THE TRUSTEE IN REPRESENTATIVE CAPACITY [1]

§ 128. Where a trustee makes a contract in the due course of his administration, a creditor under it can recover out of the trust property by suing the trustee in his representative capacity in equity, when

(a) **The trustee excluded personal liability and expressly contracted that the creditor might recover from trust property; or**

(b) **Although the trustee did not contract for collection out of trust property, the trustee has a right to indemnity against the claim, and it is impossible or extremely difficult for the creditor to collect from the trustee personally; or**

(c) **Although the contract was not properly made, performance of it has increased the value of the trust property.**

(d) **A statute permits.**

It has been shown in a previous section [2] that the trustee has the power to contract for collection by the contract creditor out of the trust

13. In re Frith, (1902) 1 Ch. 342.

14. In re Turner, (1897) 1 Ch. 536.

15. Re Johnson, 15 Ch.D. 548; Wilson v. Fridenburg, 21 Fla. 386; Clopton v. Gholson, 53 Miss. 466.

16. Staniar v. Evans, 34 Ch.D. 470; In re Blundell, 40 Ch.D. 370.

§ 128

1. Restatement, Trusts, Second, §§ 266–271A. See § 125, ante, for statutes changing the common law rule.

2. See § 126, ante.

property. In addition it is generally conceded that even though the trustee did not expressly or impliedly contract for representative liability, the creditor who has a claim against the trustee because of a proper contract is entitled to the benefit of the trustee's right of indemnity under some circumstances, and to bring a suit in equity to collect the debt based on the right of indemnity.[3] This is the so-called "derivative" right of the creditor. "The creditors may reach the trust property when the trustees are entitled to be indemnified therefrom, and . . . the creditors reach it by being substituted for the trustees, and standing in their place."[4] The courts have not clearly defined the circumstances in which this remedy is available. The large majority of cases in which the creditor has been allowed to step into the trustee's shoes and claim part of the trust property have been cases in which (a) the remedy against the trustee individually was worthless or difficult of enforcement; (b) the trust estate had had the benefit of the creditor's services or property; (c) the contract was one which the trustee could lawfully make;[5] and (d) the trustee was not in debt to the trust estate and so would have been entitled to reimbursement had he paid the claim.[6]

In cases where the trustee has had a right of indemnity and he has been a nonresident of the state where the creditor resided, the difficulty of pursuing the remedy against the trustee has induced some courts to allow the creditor to avail himself of the trustee's right of indemnity and to collect from the trust estate.[7] In other cases the insolvency of the trustee has been the moving cause for allowing direct action in equity by the creditor.[8] In some instances the fact that the settlor directed the carrying on of the business in which the contract was made was emphasized as a reason for allowing action against the estate, when the trustee was financially irresponsible.[9] No necessity for such emphasis is seen, since the question should be whether the contract was within the powers of the trustee, and not whether it was in the management of a continued business.

In some cases where the financial irresponsibility of the trustee is relied upon, proof of it must be made by an action at law against him, the recovery of judgment, and the return of an execution on that

---

3. Olson v. Foster, 42 Cal.App.2d 493, 109 P.2d 388 (1941); Willis v. Sharp, 113 N.Y. 586, 21 N.E. 705; Ranzau v. Davis, 85 Or. 26, 165 P. 1180.

But if the settlor devoted only part of the trust funds to the business in which the debt was contracted, the trustee's right, and hence the creditor's right of indemnity, relates to the property devoted to the business only and not to the general trust assets.

4. Mason v. Pomeroy, 151 Mass. 164.

5. Hewitt v. Phelps, 105 U.S. (15 Otto) 393, 26 L.Ed. 1072 (1881); Downey Co. v. 282 Beacon St. Tr., 292 Mass. 175, 197 N.E. 643 (1935).

6. Re Johnson, 15 Ch.D. 548; Clopton v. Gholson, 53 Miss. 466.

7. Gates v. McClenahan, 124 Iowa 593, 100 N.W. 479; Norton v. Phelps, 54 Miss. 467; Field v. Wilbur, 49 Vt. 157; Caflisch Lumber Co. v. Lake Lynn Lumber & Supply Co., 119 W.Va. 668, 195 S.E. 854 (1938).

8. Prudential Ins. Co. v. Land Estates, 31 F.Supp. 845 (S.D.N.Y.1939); Wells-Stone Mercantile Co. v. Aultman, Miller & Co., 9 N.D. 520, 84 N.W. 375; Henshaw v. Freer's Adm'rs, 1 Bailey Eq., S.C., 311.

9. Willis v. Sharp, 113 N.Y. 586, 21 N.E. 705, 4 L.R.A. 493; Wadsworth, Howland & Co. v. Arnold, 24 R.I. 32, 51 A. 1041.

judgment unsatisfied, which is the usual foundation for a creditor's bill.[10] In other decisions it has been held sufficient to prove the insolvency of the trustee by other means,[11] for example, by evidence that the trustee has become a bankrupt.[12]

If a contract is made by two or more trustees, each trustee has a right to indemnity, and the creditor can recover from the trust property if the right of one of the trustees to indemnity is intact, although the other trustees have defaulted and their right to indemnity has been wiped out. Thus if trustees A and B properly contract with X for a loan, the debt is not paid and X is unable to recover from A or B personally, and X sues A and B as trustees and seeks to recover from the trust property, and it appears that A owes the trust estate more than the amount of X's claim because of breaches of trust committed by A, but B has committed no breaches of trust and owes the trust estate nothing, X may recover through B by taking B's right of indemnity against liability on this contract.[13]

If the operator of a business dies and leaves it to trustees who continue the business and incur debts in such continuance, and a contest arises between the creditors of the deceased, who became such during his life, and the new creditors who contracted with the trustees, the result of a suit to recover from the trust property will depend upon whether the continuance of the business was with the consent of the old creditors. If they consented to it, otherwise than by merely failing to object, then they became in substance beneficiaries of the trust and must permit the new creditors to be satisfied out of all the trust property before the old creditors and other beneficiaries of the trust receive satisfaction. If, however, the old creditors did not consent, then they are entitled to be paid out of the property which the testator left at his death, in priority to the new creditors.[14]

Even in the case where the contract made by the trustee was without his powers, and normally his personal liability would be the only remedy available to the creditor, if the trust property has been increased in value by the performance of the contract the creditor may recover in equity the amount of such increase in value on quasi-contractual principles. It would seem that the trustee should have a right of indemnity to the extent of the benefit conferred on the beneficiaries,[15] but that irrespective of such right the creditor should be allowed recovery on quasi-contractual theories. Thus if a trustee has

10. Owen v. Dalamere, 15 Eq. 134; In re Morris, 23 L.R.Ir. 333.

11. Mason v. Pomeroy, 151 Mass. 164, 24 N.E. 202, 7 L.R.A. 771; King v. Stowell, 211 Mass. 246, 98 N.E. 91.

12. In re Richardson, (1911) 2 K.B. 705.

13. In re Frith, [1902] 1 Ch. 342; Mason v. Pomeroy, 151 Mass. 164, 24 N.E. 202, 7 L.R.A. 771.

14. Dowse v. Gorton, [1891] A.C. 190; In re Oxley, [1914] 1 Ch. 604; Adelman, 36 Mich.L.R. 185.

15. See West's Ann.Cal.Civ.Code, § 2273 (entitled to repayment of unlawful expenditures if productive of actual benefit to trust estate); Mont.—R.C. § 72–23–401; N.Dak.Cent.Code 59–02–14; S.Dak.Codif. Laws 55–3–13.

made a contract to improve trust real estate by the construction of a building thereon, but this contract was not proper or legal under the trust, and the builder has proceeded to perform the contract and to construct a building, the builder may recover in equity, in a suit against the trustee as such, an amount representing increase in the value of the trust property caused by his work and materials.[16]

 WESTLAW REFERENCES

```
mason  +3  pomeroy
225k18
di(trust  /2  property  /s  creditor)
```

LIABILITY OF TRUSTEE FOR TORTS [1]

§ 129. A trustee of a *private* trust is personally liable for torts committed by himself as trustee, or by his servants or agents when they are acting in the course of their work for him. There is some case and statutory authority permitting the person injured by the tort to sue the trustee in his representative capacity.

While many of the older cases limited the liability of trustees for *charity* to torts where they were personally at fault, and denied responsibility for torts of their servants or agents, other decisions held the trustees liable for acts of their employees in some instances and in a few states liability was enforced in all such cases. There has been a strong trend toward removal of the immunity of trustees for charity from liability for acts of their servants or agents. There has been a similar development where a charitable corporation was involved.

Private Trusts

Occasionally, while carrying on private trust activities, the trustee, or his agent or servant, commits a tort and injures a third person. Common examples are the cases where the trustee holds improved real estate in trust and negligently permits a part of the building within his control to become in a dangerous condition, or he entrusts the repair of stairs to a janitor employed by him, the janitor does his work carelessly, and a tenant is injured due to the defective condition of the premises. Here the common law courts, in which tort liability is enforced, recognize only one legal person as the one who committed the wrong. The trustee, as trustee, is not recognized by the court of law as a juristic

---

16. Brownfield v. McFadden, 21 Cal. App.2d 208, 68 P.2d 993 (1937); In re Manning's Estate, 134 Iowa 165, 111 N.W. 409; Henrietta Nat. Bank v. Barrett, Tex.Civ. App., 25 S.W. 456; Restatement, Trusts, Second, § 269. Some decisions to the contrary seem unsound: Johnson v. Leman, 131 Ill. 609, 23 N.E. 435, 7 L.R.A., 656, 19 Am.St.Rep. 63; Downey Co. v. 282 Beacon St. Trust, 292 Mass. 175, 197 N.E. 643 (1935).

§ 129

1. Bogert, Trusts and Trustees (rev. 2d edit.), § 731 et seq.; Restatement, Trusts, Second, §§ 264, 275, 402. See Fulda and Pond, 41 Col.L.R. 1332; McEniry, 31 Marq. L.R. 157; Feezer, 4 Ohio St.L.J. 289.

person, separate and apart from the trustee as an individual. If a trustee named John Doe committed the wrong in question either personally or through another acting for him, the law court held that John Doe was the tortfeasor. It did not admit the possibility of a tort by John Doe, as trustee.[2] It placed the liability on John Doe and left to a court of equity the question whether Doe should permanently bear this liability or should be able to shift it to the trust estate.[3] The liability of the trustee was not limited to the value of the trust property from which he possibly could secure indemnity.[4]

An action against a trustee who, personally or through an agent or servant, committed a tort, such as libel, slander, assault, negligence, or conversion, should therefore name John Doe as the defendant and omit all reference to his trusteeship,[5] and if judgment is recovered against Doe it may be satisfied out of Doe's own property in full, without regard to the amount of the trust property or the possiblity of recovery by Doe from the trust.[6]

A trustee is liable for the tortious acts of an agent or servant performed during the course of his employment.[7]

If by the terms of the trust the beneficiary is entitled to possession of the trust property and the trustee is a mere titleholder, the conduct of the beneficiary cannot be made a basis for tort liability of the trustee.[8]

In some states there has been a departure from the orthodox doctrine stated above and courts have allowed recovery at law in an action against the trustee in his representative capacity, and collection from the trust property on execution.[9] By statute, also, there has been

---

2. "In a court of law a trustee having legal title to real estate, together with the right of possession, is regarded as the owner of the property, having all the rights and subject to all the liabilities of ownership. . . . The duties of the trustee as owner make him personally liable for torts committed by him or by the agents or servants in his employ. . . . A trustee is not liable in his representative capacity for an injury caused by his negligence in the management of the property held in trust." Schmidt v. Kellner, 307 Ill. 331, 138 N.E. 604 (1923).

3. Shepard v. Creamer, 160 Mass. 496, 36 N.E. 475; Kirchner v. Muller, 280 N.Y. 23, 19 N.E.2d 665 (1939); Belvin's Ex'rs v. French, 84 Va. 81, 3 S.E. 891. Annotation, Liability of estate for tort of executor, administrator, or trustee, 82 A.L.R.3rd 892 (1978).

4. None of the cases mention any limitation of liability. And see Restatement, Trusts, Second, § 264, Comment *c*.

5. A description of the defendant as trustee in the pleadings may be treated as

surplusage, or the court may permit an amendment striking out the words "as trustee". Corso v. Dickson, 10 Ill.App.2d 343, 134 N.E. 644; Martin v. Talcott, 1 A.D.2d 679, 146 N.Y.S.2d 784 (1955).

6. Boston Beef Packing Co. v. Stevens, 12 F. 279 (C.C.N.Y.1882); Trani v. Gerard, 181 App.Div. 387, 168 N.Y.S. 808; Smith v. Rizzuto, 133 Neb. 655, 276 N.W. 406 (1937); In re Hodgson's Estate, 342 Pa. 250, 20 A.2d 294 (1941) (malicious prosecution).

7. Curtis v. Title Guaranty & Trust Co., 3 Cal.App.2d 612, 40 P.2d 562 (1935); Baker v. Tibbetts, 162 Mass. 468, 39 N.E. 350.

8. Pena v. Stewart, 78 Ariz. 272, 278 P.2d 892 (1955); Brazowski v. Chicago Title & Tr. Co., 280 Ill.App. 293.

9. Smith v. Coleman, 100 Fla. 1707, 132 So. 198 (1931); Miller v. Smythe, 92 Ga. 154, 18 S.E. 46; Wright v. Caney River Ry. Co., 151 N.C. 529, 66 S.E. 588; Ewing v. Wm. L. Foley, Inc., 115 Tex. 222, 280 S.W. 499, 44 A.L.R. 627 (1926). *Contra:* Wahl v. Schmidt, 307 Ill. 331, 138 N.E. 604; Keat-

some tendency to recognize the trustee, as a juristic person separate from the trustee as an individual, and to permit recovery out of the trust property through a law action against the trustee as trustee, as an alternative to personal liability of the trustee, if the beneficiaries were notified of the action and given an opportunity to intervene or take other action they deemed appropriate, and the tort was a common incident of the trustee's business activity, or the trustee was not personally at fault, or the tort increased the value of the trust property.[10]

Tort Liability of Trustees for Charity and of Charitable Corporations [11]

If the trustee is acting for charity, according to the older view, he is liable only for torts committed by himself personally,[12] and not for those committed by agents or servants in the course of their employment.[13] These rules applied to charitable corporations owning property absolutely and not in trust, so that the corporation was liable only for torts committed by its administrative officers. For example, if the trustee was operating a charitable hospital and he negligently selected an incompetent doctor or nurse who caused injury to a patient, the trustee was personally liable; but if the trustee used reasonable care in choosing his employees and in instructing and supervising them, and a nurse negligently caused injury to a patient, the trustee was not liable.

Some of the arguments advanced by the courts in support of the view that charitable corporations and trustees for charity should be immune from liability for torts committed by their agents and servants who were employed and supervised with reasonable care by the managers or trustees were: (1) liability would deplete the charitable trust fund and so defeat the intent of the settlor to bring social benefits to the community and discourage prospective donors from making charitable gifts; (2) the doctrine of respondeat superior should not apply where the employer is receiving no personal profit from the employment; (3) the analogy of immunity on the part of municipal corporations should

ing v. Stevenson, 21 App.Div. 604, 47 N.Y.S. 847; Parmenter v. Barstow, 22 R.I. 245, 47 A. 365, 63 L.R.A. 227. See also Johnston v. Long, 30 Cal.2d 54, 181 P.2d 645 (1947) (executor who has been discharged cannot be sued in his representative capacity for tort committed by servant prior to the discharge).

For other decisions see Bogert, Trusts and Trustees (rev. 2d edit.), § 732.

10. See §§ 13 and 14, Uniform Trusts Act, adopted in Louisiana, Nevada, North Carolina, Oklahoma, South Dakota and Texas. See also Unif.Prob.Code § 7–306, adopted in at least 12 states. For other statutes to the same effect, see Bogert, Trusts and Trustees (rev. 2d edit.), § 735. See, for example, V.Tex.C.A., Prop.Code § 114.062; Wash. RCWA 11.98.110.

11. Restatement, Trusts, Second, § 402. Bogert, Trusts and Trustees (rev. 2d edit.), § 401. And see McCaskill, 5 Cornell L.Q. 409, 6 Id. 56; Zollman, 19 Mich. L.R. 395 Taylor, 2 Cinc.L.R. 72; Feezer, 77 Pa.L.R. 191.

12. Farrigan v. Pevear, 193 Mass. 147, 78 N.E. 855, 7 L.R.A.,N.S., 481, 118 Am.St. Rep. 484, 8 Ann.Cas.1109; Herndon v. Massey, 217 N.C. 610, 8 S.E.2d 914 (1940).

13. Evans v. Lawrence & Mem. Assoc. Hospital, 133 Conn. 311, 50 A.2d 443 (1946); Webb v. Vought, 127 Kan. 799, 275 P. 170 (1929); Howard v. South Baltimore Gen. Hosp., 191 Md. 617, 62 A.2d 574 (1948).

be applied; and (4) in the case of persons receiving benefits directly from the charity there is an assumption of risk on their part when they accept the benefits.

In opposition to these reasons it can be stated: (1) the depletion argument is no argument at all, since the very question at issue is whether the fund should be depleted by tort liability; (2) as to the defeat of the settlor's intent, it may be that he expected his trust to bear its just burdens and expenses, and that if he did not, perhaps the law should not carry out his intent; (3) the possible discouragement of charitable gifts arising from liability is to be balanced against the social disadvantages of uncompensated injury suffered by persons who were themselves without fault; (4) unless there is liability on the part of the corporation or the trustees there will probably be no recovery, since the servants and employees probably will be judgment-proof; (5) any business enterprise, whether charitable or not, should bear the burdens and expenses of its operations and a certain amount of tortious conduct by agents and servants is an inevitable incident of any business; (6) immunity fosters careless conduct on the part of the subordinates in a charitable enterprise; (7) the public interest in seeing that persons who suffer financial loss and pain due to the fault of others is as great or greater than the social advantage of seeing the funds of the charity remain intact; and (8) if full liability is imposed insurance will be carried and the reduction in the amount of charitable funds kept to a minimum, and the burden of the liability will be spread among all who obtain benefits from the charity.

In a federal court decision [14] the late Judge Rutledge examined the state of the authorities and asserted that at the time eleven states adhered to full immunity,[15] three imposed unqualified liability,[16] seven held the charity liable to strangers and paying beneficiaries,[17] two imposed liability if the charity was protected by insurance,[18] and thirteen gave relief to strangers but denied recovery to beneficiaries of the charity.[19] The reasons for and against partial or complete immunity were set forth. In other opinions thorough consideration was given

---

14. President and Directors of Georgetown College v. Hughes, 76 U.S.App.D.C. 123, 130 F.2d 810 (1942).

15. As of 1942: Ark., Ill., Kan., Ky., Md., Mass., Mo., Or., Pa., Wis. For decisions applying the full immunity doctrine, see Martino v. Grace-New Haven Com. Hosp., 146 Conn. 735, 148 A.2d 259 (1959); St. Walburg Monastery v. Feltner's Adm'r, 275 S.W.2d 784 (Ky.1955); Williams v. Randolph Hosp. Inc., 237 N.C. 387, 75 S.E.2d 303 (1953).

16. As of 1942: Minn., N.H., N.Y. For the cases where full liability was decreed, see Dillon v. Rockaway Beach Hosp. & Disp., 284 N.Y. 176, 30 N.E.2d 373 (1940); Gable v. Salvation Army, 186 Okl. 687, 100 P.2d 244 (1940).

17. As of 1942: Ala., Cal., Fla., Ga., Ida., Okl., Utah. For illustrations of this rule, see Wheat v. Idaho Falls L.D.S. Hosp., 78 Idaho 60, 297 P.2d 1041 (1956); Sessions v. Thomas D. Dee Mem. Hosp. Ass'n, 94 Utah 460, 78 P.2d 645 (1938).

18. As of 1942; see, for example, Wendt v. Servite Fathers, 332 Ill.App. 618, 76 N.E.2d 342 (1947); Moore v. Moyle, 405 Ill. 555, 92 N.E.2d 81 (1950).

19. As of 1942; see, for example, Andrews v. Y.M.C.A., 226 Iowa 374, 284 N.W. 186 (1939); De Mello v. St. Thomas the Apostle Church Corp. of Warren, 91 R.I. 476, 165 A.2d 500 (1960).

to the problems involved and to the arguments pro and con.[20]

Some decisions have imposed liability on a charity in so far as it held property for income-producing purposes and not directly for carrying on its charitable work.[21]

In recent years there has been an effort to persuade the courts to abandon the charitable immunity doctrine on the ground that it is contrary to public policy, and these efforts have been successful in many states.[22] In a few states courts maintained the immunity doctrine on the ground that any change should come from the legislatures which should take account of public policy factors involved.[23]

Since 1942, in many states, the doctrine of charitable immunity from tort liability has undergone considerable change.[24] It appears that at the present time there are at least 35 states that have abolished the doctrine of charitable immunity from tort liability, either by statute or by court decision, that three other states have abolished the doctrine as to charitable hospitals (leaving it in effect as to religious institutions and other charities), that three states limit the immunity to recipients of the benefits of the charity, and that six states limit the immunity to the depletion of trust assets (thereby permitting recovery from other sources such as liability insurance). It appears that only New Mexico retains immunity from tort liability for charitable organizations.

The Restatement of Trusts (1935)[25] had declared that trustees for charity were personally liable for torts only if they were personally at fault, and that a tort creditor could not reach the trust property unless he was a beneficiary of the trust. The Restatement of Trusts, Second

---

20. Ray v. Tucson Med. Center, 72 Ariz. 22, 230 P.2d 220 (1951); Geiger v. Simpson Meth. Epis. Church, 174 Minn. 389, 219 N.W. 463 (1928); Foster v. Roman Cath. Diocese, 116 Vt. 124, 70 A.2d 230 (1950).

21. Michard v. Myron Stratton Home, 144 Colo. 251, 355 P.2d 1078 (1960); Blatt v. George H. Nettleton Home, 365 Mo. 30, 275 S.W.2d 344 (1955).

22. See, for example, Ray v. Tucson Med. Center, 72 Ariz. 22, 230 P.2d 220 (1951); Malloy v. Fong, 37 Cal.2d 356, 232 P.2d 241 (1951); Molitor v. Kaneland Com. Unit Dist., 18 Ill.2d 11, 163 N.E.2d 89 (1959); Noel v. Menninger Foundation, 175 Kan. 751, 267 P.2d 934 (1954); Parker v. Port Huron Hosp., 361 Mich. 1, 105 N.W.2d 1 (1960); Dalton v. St. Luke's Cath. Ch., 27 N.J. 22, 141 A.2d 273 (1958); Bing v. Thunig, 2 N.Y.2d 656, 163 N.Y.S.2d 3, 143 N.E.2d 3 (1957); Albritton v. Neighborhood Centers Association for Child Development, 12 Ohio St.3d 210, 466 N.E.2d 867 (1984); Fitzer v. Greater Greenville South Carolina Young Men's Christian Association, 277 S.C. 1, 282 S.E.2d 230 (1981); Howle v. Camp Amon Carter, 470 S.W.2d

629 (Tex.1971); Foster v. Roman Cath. Diocese, 116 Vt. 124, 70 A.2d 230 (1950); Pierce v. Yakima Vall. Mem. Hosp. Ass'n, 43 Wn.2d 162, 260 P.2d 765 (1953); Kojis v. Doctors Hosp., 12 Wis.2d 367, 107 N.W.2d 131 (1961).

Myers v. Drozda, 180 Neb. 183, 141 N.W.2d 852 (1966) (nonprofit charitable hospitals are not exempt from tort liability to their patients).

23. Simpson v. The Truesdale Hosp., 338 Mass. 787, 154 N.E.2d 357 (1958); Muller v. Nebraska Meth. Hosp., 160 Neb. 279, 70 N.W.2d 86 (1955); Springer v. Federated Church, 71 Nev. 177, 283 P.2d 1071 (1955); Landgraver v. Emanuel Luth. Char. Bd., 203 Or. 489, 280 P.2d 301 (1955); Knecht v. St. Mary's Hosp., 392 Pa. 75, 140 A.2d 30 (1958); Jones v. Baylor Hosp., 284 S.W.2d 929 (Tex.Civ.App.1955); Memorial Hosp. Inc. v. Oakes, 200 Va. 878, 108 S.E.2d 388 (1959).

24. For digests of the current statutes and decisions in all the states, see Bogert, Trusts and Trustees (rev. 2d edit.), § 401 (with pocket part supplement).

25. § 402.

(1957), provides that the trustee of a charitable trust is subject to personal tort liability only if the trustee was personally at fault, and that a person against whom a tort is committed in the course of a charitable trust can reach the trust property and apply it to the satisfaction of his claim, whether or not a beneficiary of the trust.[26] In the Restatement of the Law of Torts, Second, the American Law Institute supported abolition of the doctrine of charitable immunity from tort liability, on the grounds that "the interest of the public in proper care and treatment, and the compensation of harm done, may well outweigh in social importance the encouragement of donations."[27]

 WESTLAW REFERENCES

Private Trusts

trustee /s "tort liability"

390k235

272k50 /p trustee

find 138 ne 604

390k250

Tort Liability of Trustees for Charity and of Charitable Corporations

"tort liability" /s trustee /s charity

75k45(2)

"charitable immunity" /s "tort liability"

TRUSTEE'S RIGHT OF INDEMNITY AS TO TORT LIABILITY [1]

§ 130. A trustee is entitled to be indemnified out of trust property against liability for torts in the following cases:

(a) **Where he was not personally at fault;**

(b) **Where, even though the trustee was personally at fault, the tort occurred as a normal incident of the kind of activity in which the trustee was properly engaged;**

(c) **Where the commission of the tort increased the value of the trust property.**

While the amount of law on the topic is relatively small, it would appear that a trustee who has incurred tort liability is entitled to be indemnified by the trust in at least three instances.

If the tort was one which did not involve any personal blame or fault on the part of the trustee, it would seem fair and reasonable to permit the trustee to shift the burden to the trust.[2] Thus in a well

---

26. Also § 402.

27. § 895E.

§ 130

1. Restatement, Trusts, Second, §§ 247, 264, 278–279.

2. Benett v. Wyndham, 4 De G.F. & J. 259; Smith v. Rizzuto, 133 Neb. 655, 276 N.W. 406 (1937); Ewing v. William L. Foley, Inc., 115 Tex. 222, 280 S.W. 499, 44 A.L.R. 627 (1926). In Kellogg v. Church Charity Foundation, 128 App.Div. 214, 112

known English case,[3] the trustee of a coal mine had a duty to support the surface of the ground which was owned by another person and which was located above the mine. Although the trustee took reasonable precautions to support the surface, in fact the surface collapsed. This was a violation of an absolute duty imposed by the common law, but it was a tort without any personal fault on the part of the trustee. The court held that the trustee was entitled to indemnity against this tort liability.

A similar case arises where the tort liability occurs through the operation of the doctrine of respondeat superior. If the trustee with reasonable care engages, directs and supervises an employee who is doing work for the trust, and the employee commits a tort which causes the trustee to be liable, it would seem fair that the trustee should be able to shift the burden to the trust.[4]

So too, the law should recognize that the commission of occasional torts is an inevitable incident of the conduct of some trust business. Due to the fallibility of human beings, it is impossible to carry on certain activities without occasionally harming other persons. Thus if a trustee is conducting a newspaper, it is likely that he or his employees will at some time commit the tort of libel or negligence. Even the best conducted journals have these experiences. For these liabilities which are necessary incidents of the trust business, he should not bear permanent responsibility. The risks of the business should fall on the trust.[5]

Occasionally a trustee commits a tort which enhances the value of the trust estate. For example, if he converts the personal property of another and mixes it with the trust property, and he is sued in trover and a judgment collected from his personal property, the trust estate is enriched to the extent of the value of the converted property which it now owns as a result of the payment of the judgment in the trover action, and to the extent of such enrichment the trustee should be allowed reimbursement from the trust property. To hold otherwise would be to give a windfall to the trust estate.[6]

With the possible exception noted above regarding torts which are inevitable incidents of a business enterprise, a trustee should have no right of indemnity against liability for a tort *wilfully* committed.[7]

N.Y.S. 566, 570, Gaynor, J., stated: "The courts allow the judgment against him individually for damages to be paid out of the trust funds, if he was free from wilful misconduct in the tort." This would extend the right of indemnity beyond the usually held view.

3. In re Raybould, [1900] 1 Ch. 199.

4. Johnston v. Long, 30 Cal.2d 54, 181 P.2d 645 (1947); In re Lathers' Will, 137 Misc. 226, 243 N.Y.S. 366 (1930).

5. See § 13, Uniform Trusts Act. Cf. Restatement, Trusts, Second, § 247.

6. Willetts v. Schuyler, 3 Ind.App. 118, 29 N.E. 273; Leigh v. Lockwood, 15 N.C. 577; Morgan's Estate, 2 Pa.Dist. 816. Unif. Trusts Act, § 14.

7. In re Hodgson's Estate, 342 Pa. 250, 20 A.2d 294 (1941) (malicious prosecution).

It may be possible to support a right of indemnity from the *beneficiary* where he has received a distribution of trust property and the claim of the trustee is limited to the amount of such payment.[8]

Where the trustee has a right of indemnity he may use it in the ways discussed with regard to contracts.[9] He may pay the tort claim out of trust property by self-help, reimburse himself for the payment of the claim, secure a decree of exoneration from initial liability, or secure reimbursement through accounting or other proceedings.[10]

The rules as to the trustee's right to indemnity for tort liability would seem to be the same in the case of charitable trusts,[11] although the cases of liability of the trustee without personal fault will not be so numerous.

 WESTLAW REFERENCES

"re raybould"
trustee /s tort /s liability

TORT CREDITOR'S RIGHTS AGAINST THE TRUSTEE AS SUCH [1]

§ 131. Where a trustee of a trust is liable for a tort but collection cannot be had from him due to his insolvency or other cause, the injured party may sue the trustee in his representative capacity in equity and collect from trust property, if the trustee would have been entitled to reimbursement had he paid the claim out of his own pocket.

Although there is little authority on the subject, it seems clear that a tort creditor of a trustee who is unable to collect from the trustee out of his private property can sue in equity, making the trustee as such a defendant, and collect out of the trust property, if the trustee had a right of indemnity against liability in the case in question.[2] To recover in this way the person injured would have to prove inability to collect from the trustee by showing the unavailability of remedies at law, or at least great difficulty in collecting, as where the trustee is insolvent or a nonresident, that the tort was one for which the trustee had a right of indemnity, and that the trustee was not indebted to the trust estate in such a way as to destroy his right of indemnity. Thus if a trustee is

---

8. Herman v. Frank Martz Coach Co., 43 Pa.D. & C. 653; Restatement, Trusts, Second, § 249.

9. See § 127, ante.

10. Smith v. Rizzuto, 133 Neb. 655, 276 N.W. 406 (1937).

11. Powers v. Massachusetts Homeopathic Hosp., 47 C.C.A. 122, 109 Fed. 294 (1st Cir.1901); Kellogg v. Church Char. Foundation, 128 App.Div. 214, 112 N.Y.S. 566.

§ 131

1. Bogert, Trusts and Trustees (rev. 2d edit.), § 732; Restatement, Trusts, Second, §§ 267–269.

2. In re Raybould, [1900] 1 Ch. 199; Cook v. Holland, 575 S.W.2d 468 (Ky.App. 1978); Smith v. Rizzuto, 133 Neb. 655, 276 N.W. 406 (1937).

lawfully operating an apartment house for the trust, his servant is negligent and a tenant is injured thereby; and the tenant sues the trustee for damages and gets a judgment against him but finds his execution returned unsatisfied, the tenant could sue the trustee in his representative capacity in equity; and if he could prove that the trustee did not owe the trust estate money because of a breach of trust, the plaintiff could get a decree ordering the payment of his claim out of trust property. In this case the trustee had a right of indemnity and it had not been destroyed by his wrongful conduct. The trustee's right of indemnity, and the corresponding right of the creditor, might be extinguished or reduced by a breach of trust on the trustee's part which made him a debtor to the trust estate. This rule would seem applicable to both private and charitable trusts.

And, as in the case of contract liability, if the wrongful act of the trustee has resulted in an increase in the value of the trust property, there is a right of indemnity which the person injured by the tort should be able to use in equity for the purpose of securing satisfaction from trust property.[3]

In a few states, as previously noted, a direct action at law against the trustee in his representative capacity is allowed, and so it is unnecessary to rely on the derivative theory.[4]

 WESTLAW REFERENCES

smith +3 rizzuto
162k119

LIABILITY OF THE TRUSTEE AS
PROPERTY OWNER [1]

§ 132. The trustee's liabilities arising solely because of holding title to trust property are the same as if he owned the property absolutely. However he has a right of indemnity against personal liability incurred as titleholder.

Certain obligations arise from the mere ownership of property. They do not depend on contract or tort. They are obligations which are inherent in ownership of property of the type in question. For example, the ownership of real property, and sometimes the ownership of personalty, often involves liability for a property tax. And title to stock in a corporation carries with it liability to pay unpaid subscriptions for the stock and assessments in favor of creditors of the corporation.

Some tax statutes impose personal liability on the property owner, while others merely create an in rem claim against the property. If

---

3. See Unif. Trusts Act, § 14.

4. See § 129, ns. 9, 10, ante.

§ 132

1. Restatement, Trusts, Second, §§ 248, 265.

there is a personal obligation, it rests on the trustee individually.[2] And, apart from statute, a trustee owning corporate stock has a personal duty as owner to pay calls and assessments on the stock.[3] But very generally statutes have been adopted relieving a trustee from this personal obligation and providing for collection out of trust property, where the stock is registered in the name of the trustee as such on the records of the corporation or its agents.[4]

If a settlor has made a specifically enforceable contract to convey realty, and then gives the land to a trustee, the latter is subject to a suit for specific performance in his representative capacity,[5] although he is not personally liable for damages for nonperformance of the contract.

If a settlor as landlord or tenant has made covenants in a lease which run with the land, for example, covenants to pay rent or to make repairs, and later gives his interest in the land to a trustee the latter becomes personally liable for the performance of the covenants.[6]

A trustee who is personally liable as mere titleholder has a right to be indemnified out of the trust property. He may meet the liability in the first place from trust property, or may repay himself after he has satisfied the claim from his own funds.[7]

The question whether the trustee's personal liability as titleholder is unlimited in amount, or is restricted to the value of the trust property from which he can secure indemnity, is one on which there are differing views.[8] Normally, of course, the trust property will be adequate in value to give the trustee full protection.

 WESTLAW REFERENCES

trustee /s liable liability /s property /2 owner

find 255 nw 839

---

2. Thiebaud v. Tait, 138 Ind. 238, 36 N.E. 525; Dunham v. Lowell, 200 Mass. 468, 86 N.E. 951.

3. French v. Busch, 189 F. 480 (C.C. N.Y.1911); Union Savings Bank of San Jose v. Willard, 4 Cal.App. 690, 88 P. 1098; Commissioner of Banks v. Tremont Tr. Co., 259 Mass. 162, 156 N.E. 7.

4. See Bogert, Trusts and Trustees (rev. 2d edit.), § 720, for references to numerous statutes.

5. Hopkinson v. First Nat. Bank of Provincetown, 293 Mass. 570, 200 N.E. 381 (1936).

6. Irvine v. MacGregor, 203 Cal. 583, 265 P. 218 (1928); Board of Education v. Crilly, 312 Ill.App. 177, 37 N.E.2d 873 (1941); Rainault v. Evarts, 296 Mass. 590, 7

N.E.2d 145 (1937); McLaughlin v. Minnesota Loan & Trust Co., 192 Minn. 203, 255 N.W. 839 (1934).

7. Merritt v. Jenkins, 17 Fla. 593; Bourquin v. Bourquin, 120 Ga. 115, 47 S.E. 639.

8. As tending to show unlimited liability, see City of Bangor v. Peirce, 106 Me. 527, 76 A. 945, 29 L.R.A.,N.S., 770, 138 Am. St.Rep. 363; McLaughlin v. Minnesota Loan & Trust Co., 192 Minn. 203, 255 N.W. 839 (1934). An opposite view was expressed in Irvine v. MacGregor, 203 Cal. 583, 265 P. 218 (1928), and in Smith v. Rizzuto, 133 Neb. 655, 276 N.W. 406 (1937). Restatement, Second, Trusts, § 265, approves the rule of limited liability.

Chapter 15

SALES, MORTGAGES AND LEASES BY TRUSTEES

Table of Sections

TRUSTEE'S POWER TO SELL [1]

§ 133. The trust instrument usually gives the trustee a mandatory or discretionary power to sell the trust property. It may prohibit a sale or allow it only on condition.

A power of sale will be implied where it is reasonably necessary or highly convenient to accomplishing the settlor's purposes.

A power of sale may include a power to exchange and a power to give an option to buy when reasonably necessary.

The power to sell trust property may be and usually is expressly given by the settlor and by statute to the trustee.[2] No technical words are necessary to confer this authority upon him, it being sufficient that the settlor's intent is clear.[3] The power may be made mandatory, or

---

§ 133

1. Bogert, Trusts and Trustees (rev. 2d edit.), § 741 et seq.; Restatement, Trusts, Second, §§ 186, 190.

2. Blair v. Hazzard, 158 Cal. 721, 112 P. 298; Salisbury v. Bigelow, 20 Pick., Mass., 174; Shaw v. Bridgers, 161 N.C. 246, 76 S.E. 827. If an express power is given, no application to the court for permission to sell is necessary. Livermore v. Livermore, 231 Mass. 293, 121 N.E. 27.

In many states such as Colo., Ill., N.J., N.Y., Okl., Tex., Va., and Wash., where there are statutory grants of powers, a power of sale is always included. See also § 3(c)(7) of the Uniform Trustees Powers Act, adopted in Fla., Ida., Kan. Ky., Me., Miss., Mont., N.H., N.C., Oreg., Utah and Wyo. And see Bogert, Trusts and Trustees (rev. 2d edit.), § 551 (trustee's powers).

3. Holden v. Circleville Light & Power Co., 132 C.C.A. 550, 216 Fed. 490, Ann.Cas. 1916D, 443 (6th Cir.1914); Reeder v. Reeder, 184 Iowa 1, 168 N.W. 122.

the trustee may be given discretion to sell or retain.[4] It is commonly attached to the office of the trustee and not made personal to any particular trustee.[5]

In some states by statute, if a deed runs to one "as trustee" but there is no description of the beneficiaries or the terms of the trust, one buying the property from the trustee, or taking a mortgage on it as security for a loan, is protected if he takes in good faith.[6] The purchaser or mortgagee is entitled to rely on the existence of a power to sell or mortgage.

The settlor may prohibit the sale of certain trust property,[7] or provide that it shall be sold only if the settlor or a beneficiary consents,[8] or only to a particular buyer, but these provisions are subject to possible alteration by court order, as is shown later.[9]

Naturally, a power to sell includes a power to execute a contract for sale as well as to give a conveyance. If the law of the particular state requires a trustee to qualify by giving a bond, taking an oath, or securing letters of trusteeship, the trustee seeking to use his power of sale should be careful to complete qualification before making a contract or deed.[10]

While in some cases it has been held that a power of sale does not include a power to exchange the trust property for other property,[11] there are holdings to the contrary, for example, where such a method is reasonably necessary because of inability to sell for cash, or in the case of sale of realty to a corporation and taking of stock in the purchasing corporation in exchange.[12] A power to sell has been held to include a power to lease with an option to buy,[13] and to give oil and gas leases.[14]

In some cases it has been held that a trustee with a power of sale has no authority to grant options to buy, since he thereby surrenders his right to fix the price and terms of sale at the time of the sale,[15] but this statement is too broad; options may be granted if under the

4. Trust Co. of New Jersey v. Glunz, 121 N.J.Eq. 593, 191 A. 795 (1937); Peters v. Kanawha Banking & Trust Co., 118 W.Va. 484, 191 S.E. 581 (1937).

5. Weeks v. Frankel, 197 N.Y. 304, 90 N.E. 969. But occasionally it is made personal. Pippin v. Barker, 233 N.C. 549, 64 S.E.2d 830 (1951).

6. See statutory references in Bogert, Trusts and Trustees (rev. 2d edit.), § 893.

7. Garrott v. McConnell, 201 Ky. 61, 256 S.W. 14 (1923). But a prohibition of alienation may be void as constituting an invalid restraint on alienation for too long a period. Fox v. Burgher, 285 Ky. 470, 148 S.W.2d 342 (1941).

8. Palmer v. Williams, 24 Mich. 328; Sippy v. Colter, 347 Pa. 1, 31 A.2d 734 (1943).

9. See § 134, post.

10. Chappus v. Lucke, 246 Mich. 272, 224 N.W. 432 (1929).

11. Wilson v. Hamilton, 140 Ky. 327, 131 S.W. 32.

12. Ash v. Ash, 126 N.J.Eq. 531, 10 A.2d 150 (1940). And see Gray v. Corcoran, 127 Mont. 572, 269 P.2d 1091 (1954) (realty for other realty).

13. Connely v. Haggarty, 65 N.J.Eq. 596, 56 A. 371.

14. Franklin v. Margay Oil Corp., 194 Okl. 519, 153 P.2d 486 (1944).

And see Rockefeller v. First Nat. Bank, 213 Ga. 493, 100 S.E.2d 279 (1957) (sale of minerals in place).

15. Moore v. Trainer, 252 Pa. 367, 97 A. 462; 30 Col.L.R. 870. And see Equitable Tr. Co. v. Delaware Tr. Co., 30 Del.Ch. 118, 54 A.2d 733 (1947) (price to be fixed by appraisers; not necessary to give option).

circumstances a reasonably prudent seller would find it expedient so to do.[16] The length of the period for which the option is granted may well be an important factor.

A power of sale in favor of the trustee is implied in equity whenever such a power is necessary or useful in carrying out the trust, even though the trust instrument is silent on the subject of sale.[17] For example, where a trustee is directed to distribute trust real property at the termination of an income trust among numerous members of a class, the disadvantages of co-ownership and management by the distributees and the expenses of partition may reasonably lead to the implication of a power of sale and distribution of the proceeds.[18] "While it is true that under the original theory of a trust the powers and duties of the trustee were confined substantially to holding and caring for the property, it is equally true that the purposes of the modern trust are of a much broader character requiring ordinarily much greater powers on the part of the trustee, including a power of sale, which is generally expressly given. The power of sale, where not expressly given, will be implied from the fact that the trustee is charged with a duty which cannot be performed without a power of sale." [19]

In many cases where the question of the existence of such a power has arisen, the court has thought it necessary to the proper execution of the trust and has held that it existed,[20] while in others the court has considered a sale unessential and unauthorized.[21] The same principles govern the implication of powers of sale in charitable trusts.[22]

In some states statutes provide that every sale or other act of a trustee of real property is "void" if "in contravention of the trust." [23]

16. Loud v. St. Louis Union Tr. Co., 313 Mo. 552, 281 S.W. 744 (1925) (only way to sell mining stock was to give option to broker); Nelson v. American Trust Co., 104 N.J.Eq. 594, 146 A. 460 (1929).

17. Preston v. Safe Deposit & Trust Co., 116 Md. 211, 81 A. 523, Ann.Cas. 1913C, 975; Garesche v. Levering Inv. Co., 146 Mo. 436, 48 S.W. 653, 46 L.R.A. 232; Clark v. Fleischmann, 81 Neb. 445, 116 N.W. 290; Crown Co. v. Cohn, 88 Or. 642, 172 P. 804; Wisdom v. Wilson, 59 Tex.Civ. App. 593, 127 S.W. 1128.

Where a trust contains much real estate, part of which is unimproved, and the instrument gives the trustee all powers necessary for management and profitable use of the property, and directs payment of annuities to the settlor's relatives, a power of sale is to be implied. Revoc Co. v. Thomas, 179 Md. 101, 16 A.2d 847, 134 A.L.R. 373 (1940).

18. Heard v. Read, 169 Mass. 216, 47 N.E. 778; In re Bailey's Estate, 276 Pa. 147, 119 A. 907 (1923).

19. Robinson v. Robinson, 105 Me. 68, 71, 72 A. 883, 32 L.R.A.,N.S., 675, 134 Am. St.Rep. 537.

20. Pickering v. Loomis, 199 Ark. 720, 135 S.W.2d 833 (1940) (gift of land with unproductive residence on it, with direction to conserve and disburse); Penn v. Pennsylvania Co., 294 Ky. 271, 171 S.W.2d 437 (1943) (direction to "pay over" trust fund at end of lives to numerous remaindermen).

21. Goad v. Montgomery, 119 Cal. 552, 51 P. 681, 63 Am.St.Rep. 145; Robinson v. Ingram, 126 N.C. 327, 35 S.E. 612; Mundy v. Vawter, 3 Grat., Va., 518.

22. Tate v. Woodyard, 145 Ky. 613, 140 S.W. 1044. And see Bridgeport Public Library and Reading Room v. Burroughs Home, 85 Conn. 309, 82 A. 582.

23. See Bogert, Trusts and Trustees (rev. 2d edit.), § 893.

This puts a burden of inquiry on the purchaser from a trustee to ascertain the existence of a power of sale.

Unless the trust instrument makes consent by the beneficiaries to the sale a condition precedent,[24] their objection to a proposed sale will not be important unless they can convince a court of the impropriety of the sale.[25]

It is generally held that the lack of power on the part of the trustee to sell trust property may be remedied by showing the consent of the beneficiaries in advance that the sale take place, if they are competent and advised of the facts and their rights,[26] but in some instances such consent has been held insufficient to render the sale valid.[27] After the sale has taken place, the beneficiary may ratify[28] it, or estop himself from attacking its validity.[29] Thus acceptance of the proceeds of the sale with full knowledge of the facts may show an estoppel to assert that the sale was invalid.[30] Where the trustees are given power to sell land and distribute the proceeds among the beneficiaries of the trust, the beneficiaries may elect to take the land rather than the proceeds thereof.[31]

 WESTLAW REFERENCES

trustee /s power /2 sell
390k189 /p power /2 sell
trustee /s power /2 lease
find 38 a2d 101

COURT CONTROL OF TRUSTEES' SALES [1]

§ 134.   A court of equity has inherent power to order or forbid a sale of trust property, and to prescribe the method of sale, notwithstanding any direction of the settlor.   Statutes frequently set forth the power of probate or equity courts to control sales and to fix terms of sale.

24. Franklin Sav. Bank v. Taylor, 131 Ill. 376, 23 N.E. 397; Clemens v. Heckscher, 185 Pa. 476, 40 A. 80.

25. Boston Safe Dep. & Tr. Co. v. Hayward, 305 Mass. 536, 26 N.E.2d 342 (1940); In re Cope's Will, 347 Pa. 221, 32 A.2d 23 (1943).

26. Rogers v. Tyley, 144 Ill. 652, 32 N.E. 393; Turner v. Fryberger, 99 Minn. 236, 108 N.W. 1118, 109 N.W. 229.

27. Walton v. Follansbee, 165 Ill. 480, 46 N.E. 459; Mauldin v. Mauldin, 101 S.C. 1, 85 S.E. 60.

28. Long v. Long, 62 Md. 33; Swartz v. Duncan, 38 Neb. 782, 57 N.W. 543; In re Post, 13 R.I. 495.

29. Matthews v. Thompson, 186 Mass. 14, 71 N.E. 93, 66 L.R.A. 421, 104 Am.St. Rep. 550.

30. Shepherd v. Todd, 95 Ga. 19, 22 S.E. 32; Lawson v. Cunningham, 275 Mo. 128, 204 S.W. 1100.

31. Craig v. Leslie, 16 U.S. (3 Wheat.) 563, 4 L.Ed. 460 (1818); Harrison v. Prentice, 183 Md. 474, 38 A.2d 101 (1944); Smith v. A.D. Farmer Type Founding Co., 16 App.Div. 438, 45 N.Y.S. 192.

§ 134

1. Restatement, Trusts, Second, § 190. Bogert, Trusts and Trustees (rev. 2d edit.), §§ 743, 745.

The inherent power of the court of equity to enter whatever orders are necessary to carry out the settlor's purposes includes authority to direct or to prohibit sales of the trust property,[2] to decide the terms on which they are to be made,[3] and to approve a sale which a trustee has made that was contrary to the terms of the trust.[4] If the trust property is unproductive, for example, but can be sold and the proceeds invested in bonds or mortgages producing four or five per cent income, surely the trust purpose of the settlor that the beneficiaries receive support will be achieved better by a sale than by a retention.[5] If the trustee does not voluntarily make a sale, the court may order him to do so. It is usually immaterial whether the settlor directed a sale or a retention of the property, or whether the instrument gave the trustee a power of sale,[6] but some of the statutes regarding court control of sales make an exception of the case of an express direction by the settlor.[7] In most states equity has authority to override the settlor and make a decree which will be for the best interests of the beneficiaries, although it hesitates to do so unless a clear case of advantage to the beneficiaries and change of circumstances are shown. This is merely one illustration of the power of the court to permit deviation from the instrument, subsequently discussed.[8]

As a part of this same general control over trusts, chancery may forbid a sale even though a sale is directed by the settlor.[9] If, for example, the settlor directed the sale of all his assets and the investment of the proceeds in government bonds, and the court finds that some of the assets are safe, high-yield bonds, and that governments bear considerably less interest, and that the beneficiaries are greatly in need of all possible income, the court may ignore the settlor's command and direct the trustee not to sell.

Settlors of charitable trusts sometimes leave their homesteads or residential property to trustees for charity for operation as a home for the aged or an orphan asylum or similar institution and direct retention of the property forever. If, however, the neighborhood has changed, or other events make the original realty unsuited for the

---

2. Bibb v. Bibb, 204 Ala. 541, 86 So. 376 (1920) (property depreciated and subject to liens); Dallas Art League v. Weaver, 240 Ala. 432, 199 So. 831 (1941); Hewitt v. Beattie, 106 Conn. 602, 138 A. 795 (1927) (stone quarry could no longer be operated at a profit).

3. Roberts v. Roberts, 259 Ill. 115, 102 N.E. 239.

4. Faulk v. Rosecrans, 264 P.2d 300 (Okl.1953).

5. Fidelity Union Tr. Co. v. Sayre, 137 N.J.Eq. 179, 44 A.2d 25 (1945).

6. Suiter v. McWard, 328 Ill. 462, 159 N.E. 799 (1927); Young v. Young, 255

Mich. 173, 237 N.W. 535, 77 A.L.R. 963 (1931).

7. See terms of statutes digested in Bogert, Trusts and Trustees (rev. 2d edit.), § 743.

8. See § 146, post.

9. Bertron, Storrs & Griscom v. Polk, 101 Md. 686, 61 A. 616; Albright v. Albright, 91 N.C. 220. The court will not lightly override the settlor's directions as to sale or retention. There must be proof of serious loss to be occasioned by following the trust instrument. Stough v. Brach, 395 Ill. 544, 70 N.E.2d 585 (1946).

charitable object, the court may order a sale and a location elsewhere.[10]

This inherent power of the court of equity regarding sales is often expressed in statutes.[11] They may declare the existence of the power of the court or merely give procedures for its use. They are declaratory of well established equitable principles. Some of the statutes also provide for the regulation of trustee's sales by the probate court having jurisdiction over testamentary trusts.

 WESTLAW REFERENCES

di(equity court /s power /s order*** /s sale /s trustee)

390k1931/2

390k189 /p court /s order***

find 70 ne2d 585

390k58 /p court /s break modif! /s trust

CONDUCT OF SALES BY TRUSTEES [1]

§ 135. **In selling trust property the trustee should carefully follow any instructions of the settlor expressed in the trust instrument and the orders of any court which have been given to him. All important acts in connection with the contract to sell and the sale should be performed by co-trustees as a group and should not be delegated.**

If not controlled by the directions of the settlor or court, the trustee has a duty to use the skill and judgment of a reasonably prudent man in deciding whether and when to sell and in conducting negotiations and consummating the sale.

At common law a trustee's acceptance of an offer for property may be withdrawn before the conveyance is executed, if a higher offer is received, but there is recent statutory authority to the contrary.

In giving a bill of sale or a deed the trustee is not obliged to warrant or covenant except against his own acts. All warranties or covenants which he does make will bind him personally, unless he expressly excludes such liability.

Sales ordered by the court must be confirmed by the court, but otherwise, unless a statute or the trust instrument requires confirmation, there need be no application by the trustee to the court for approval of his sale. The court will not ordinarily refuse confirmation, unless there is gross inadequacy of price or other highly disadvantageous term.

10. Amory v. Attorney General, 179 Mass. 89, 60 N.E. 391; Rolfe & Rumford Asylum v. Lefebre, 69 N.H. 238, 45 A. 1087.

11. For digests of these statutes see Bogert, Trusts and Trustees (rev. 2d edit.), § 743.

§ 135

1. Restatement, Trusts, Second, § 190.

If a trustee has a power of sale, in deciding whether to sell and when and how to sell he should examine the trust instrument, any relevant statute, and any court order made with regard to the sale, and then follow closely any directions which he finds in these sources.[2] In these documents he may find instructions as to the time of sale, as to whether the sale shall be at public auction or at a private sale, and whether cash must be required or credit may be given.

As previously noted with regard to powers generally,[3] the trustee may not delegate to an employee the performance of important acts of discretion with regard to the sale[4] but may employ agents in other cases.[5]

The power of sale will normally be vested in co-trustees jointly. They must act together in all important transactions relating to the sale, such as signing a contract of sale or giving a deed.[6] Action in matters of this sort by one trustee alone will be void. But minor details of the sale may be delegated to one co-trustee.

If the trustee finds that there are no express directions regarding the manner of conducting the sale, he will then be bound to use the care and ability of an ordinarily prudent man in deciding when and how to sell and on what terms.[7] The nature of the property and the available market for it, as well as the purposes of the trust and the needs of the beneficiaries, will be the most important considerations in leading him to decisions. For example, corporate stock will be sold differently from land, and stock quoted on a stock exchange differently from stock of a family corporation. In the case of a tract of unimproved land it is a question of judgment whether better results can be achieved by offering it in lots or as a whole.[8]

Typical questions to which the standard of reasonable prudence must be applied are whether to sell at public or private sale,[9] if at auction whether subject to a reserve price,[10] whether for cash or on credit,[11] and whether subject to, or free of, incumbrances.[12] If he is not

---

2. Rooker v. Fidelity Tr. Co., 198 Ind. 207, 151 N.E. 610 (1926); Patterson v. Lanning, 62 Neb. 634, 87 N.W. 338.

3. See § 92, ante.

4. Saunders v. Webber, 39 Cal. 287; Grover v. Hale, 107 Ill. 638.

5. In re Duffy's Will, 230 Iowa 581, 298 N.W. 849 (1941) (if necessary for proper management of trust); Tyler v. Herring, 67 Miss. 169, 6 So. 840, 19 Am.St.Rep. 263; Gates v. Dudgeon, 173 N.Y. 426, 66 N.E. 116, 93 Am.St.Rep. 608. Some courts have felt it highly important that the trustee be present and guide the course of auction sales. Brickenkamp v. Rees, 69 Mo. 426; Fuller v. O'Neil, 69 Tex. 349.

6. Learned v. Welton, 40 Cal. 349; Page v. Gillett, 26 Colo.App. 204, 141 P. 866.

7. Reeder v. Lanahan, 111 Md. 372, 74 A. 575; Johnston v. Eason, 38 N.C. 330. Where a trustee holds realty near Washington, D.C. for sale, it is not reasonably prudent to fix an asking price on the basis of an appraisal by New York City appraisers. Webb & Knapp, Inc., v. Hanover Bank, 214 Md. 230, 133 A.2d 450 (1957).

8. Goode v. Comfort, 39 Mo. 313; Crown Co. v. Cohn, 88 Or. 642, 172 P. 804.

9. Asher v. Teter, 314 Ill.App. 200, 40 N.E.2d 803 (1942); Scott v. Scott, 291 S.W. 2d 551 (Ky.App.1956).

10. Re Payton's Settlement, 30 Beav. 242.

11. Woodruff v. Lounsberry, 40 N.J. Eq. 545, 5 A. 99; Bonham v. Coe, 249 App.

---

12. See note 12 on page 479.

to receive cash, the trustee will be influenced by the consideration whether the mortgage, stock or other property to be received in exchange is a legal investment for the trust.

At common law it has been held that a trustee who had received and accepted an offer for the trust property was under a duty to revoke his acceptance and accept a later higher offer, and was allowed to do so without liability to the first bidder.[13] This was justified on the ground that his duty to the beneficiaries was to obtain the maximum return for the property, and was an implied condition consequently in such contracts. The disadvantage of such a doctrine is evident. Bidders for trust property will be discouraged from bidding, making arrangements for buying, and putting up deposits, if they know their bargains are apt to be taken from them by subsequent higher bids. Furthermore, it may be argued that a trustee should respect his contracts, just as a non-trustee is required to do. In Pennsylvania, where the common law doctrine had most recognition, it has recently been abolished by statute.[14]

When the trustee comes to execute the instrument of conveyance evidencing his sale, for example, the bill of sale of goods or the deed of realty, he will have to decide whether to insert any warranties of the goods or any covenants as to the title to the land. The law requires him to do nothing more than to agree that the title to the thing conveyed has not been prejudiced by his own acts, that is, to execute a covenant against his own conduct.[15] But if the buyer demands further assurances, the trustee may insert warranties or covenants of other types. Since these are obligations contractual in nature, the trustee will incur personal liability for the truth of the warranties or covenants unless he includes in the bill of sale or deed a statement that the warranty or covenant is not to bind him personally.[16] A trustee selling part of trust realty may find it prudent to insert restrictive covenants in his deeds so as to protect the retained property.[17]

The settlor may direct the trustee to apply to the court of equity for confirmation of any sale he makes, and a court order or statute may make such a requirement, but if the trustee finds no duty to seek confirmation expressed in any of these ways, he will not be obliged to ask the court for confirmation of sales made on his own initiative.[18]

Div. 428, 292 N.Y.S. 423 (1937), affirmed 276 N.Y. 540, 12 N.E.2d 566 (1937).

12. Forshaw v. Higginson, 8 De G.M. & G. 827.

13. Kane v. Girard Tr. Co., 351 Pa. 191, 40 A.2d 466 (1945) (three justices dissenting); In re Herbert's Estate, 356 Pa. 107, 51 A.2d 753 (1947).

14. 20 Pa.C.S.A. §§ 3360(a), 7133. For construction see In re Brereton's Estate, 355 Pa. 45, 48 A.2d 868 (1946); In re Van Voorhis' Estate, 355 Pa. 82, 49 A.2d 257 (1946).

15. Bruneau v. Depositor's Trust Co., 144 Me. 142, 66 A.2d 86 (1949) (buyer no right to warranty deed unless expressly contracted for); Barnard v. Duncan, 38 Mo. 170, 90 Am.Dec. 416.

16. Bloom v. Wolfe, 50 Iowa 286; Glenn v. Allison, 58 Md. 527.

17. Dolan v. Brown, 338 Ill. 412, 170 N.E. 425 (1930).

18. Goodrich v. Proctor, 1 Gray, Mass., 567; Fleming v. Holt, 12 W.Va. 143.

Naturally in the case of sales ordered by the court confirmation will be needed.[19] Where court confirmation is necessary, it will be refused only where gross inadequacy of consideration or other unfairness is evident and not for slight disadvantages in the price or terms.[20] If the trust estate has had the benefit of the consideration paid by the purchaser, the sale will be set aside only upon the repayment of such consideration.

If the trustee had a power of sale and exercised it prudently, the remedies of seller and buyer are the same as if no trust were involved, and will include specific performance and an action for damages.[21]

If the trustee had no power of sale he may not enforce a contract to sell,[22] and the vendee may refuse to perform and sue the trustee personally on his contract or covenants.[23]

If the trustee had a power to sell but acted imprudently in exercising it, the beneficiary may be able to set aside the sale [24] or hold the trustee liable for damages.[25] The beneficiary in other cases may also secure an order that the trustee use his power of sale,[26] or may obtain an injunction against a wrongful sale.[27] The beneficiary, of course, may be estopped to question the validity of a sale, as when he accepts the proceeds of the sale with knowledge of the facts surrounding it.[28]

 WESTLAW REFERENCES

```
power  /2  sell***  sale  /s  vest***  /s  co-trustee
390k171
390k189
390k204  /p  set!  /2  aside  /4  sale
390k195
find 133 a2d 450
fiduciary trustee executor  /s  duty  /3  repudiate revoke
      /s  higher  /2  offer
390k191(3)  /p  power  /2  sell sale
find 4 a2d 132
390k203
```

19. Rader v. Bussey, 313 Ill. 226, 145 N.E. 192 (1924); Offutt v. Jones, 110 Md. 233, 73 A. 629.

20. Evans v. Hunold, 393 Ill. 195, 65 N.E.2d 373 (1946); Goode v. Comfort, 39 Mo. 313; Suarez v. De Montigny, 1 App. Div. 494, 37 N.Y.S. 503; Abernathy v. Phillips, 82 Va. 769, 1 S.E. 113.

21. Pleasants v. Wilson, 125 Md. 237, 93 A. 441; Barnard v. Duncan, 38 Mo. 170.

22. Rede v. Oakes, 4 De G.J. & Sm. 505.

23. Ball v. Safe Dep. & Tr. Co., 92 Md. 503, 48 A. 155; Harding Park Owners v.

Young, 146 N.Y.S.2d 718 (Sup.1955), affirmed 2 A.D.2d 884, 156 N.Y.S.2d 1007 (1956).

24. Gaver v. Gaver, 176 Md. 171, 4 A.2d 132 (1939); Brickenkamp v. Rees, 69 Mo. 426.

25. See § 154, post.

26. Fatjo v. Swasey, 111 Cal. 628, 44 P. 225.

27. In re Stone's Estate, 358 Pa. 335, 56 A.2d 664 (1948).

28. Childs v. Childs, 150 App.Div. 656, 135 N.Y.S. 972.

EXPRESS OR IMPLIED POWER TO BORROW
AND GIVE SECURITY [1]

§ 136. **A power to borrow and pledge or mortgage trust property as security is frequently expressly given to a trustee, either without qualification or to be used for a particular purpose only.**

Such a power is sometimes implied, for example, where there is an express power to sell in order to raise a particular sum or where there is an express power to manage and control. A power to sell does not generally include by implication a power to mortgage, but a power to buy may be found to include a power to give a purchase money mortgage. In each case the question is whether it is reasonable to assume that the settlor wanted to give the power to mortgage, considering the objectives of his trust.

Sometimes the trustee is given express authority to mortgage or pledge the trust property.[2] This power may be given without qualification, in which case it may be used for any lawful trust purpose, or exercise of it may be permitted only for a given purpose such as improving the trust property,[3] or paying off taxes or other encumbrances,[4] or only on the happening of a certain event such as the insufficiency of trust income to pay the living expenses of the beneficiary.[5] The settlor may also forbid encumbering the trust property.[6]

The power to borrow and mortgage or pledge may be given impliedly where it appears that the power is necessary or highly convenient in accomplishing the purposes the settlor desired to achieve.[7] A power of this type is not easily implied, however, since it sometimes involves speculation as to the effect of improvements, and a sale may be the preferable alternative.[8] In some cases where the trustee has been given the privilege or duty of raising a sum of money for a particular purpose (for example, in order to set up a beneficiary in business), a

---

§ 136

1. Bogert, Trusts and Trustees (rev. 2d edit.), § 751 et seq.; Restatement, Trusts, Second, § 191.

2. Bank of Visalia v. Dillonwood Lumber Co., 148 Cal. 18, 82 P. 374; Guilmartin v. Stevens, 55 Ga. 203; Boskowitz v. Held, 15 App.Div. 306, 44 N.Y.S. 136, affirmed 153 N.Y. 666, 48 N.E. 1104.

See Bogert, Trusts and Trustees (rev. 2d edit.), § 551, for references to numerous statutes giving the power to mortgage where not prohibited by the settlor.

3. Jones v. Harsha, 225 Mich. 416, 196 N.W. 624 (1923).

4. Nolen v. Witherspoon, 112 Tenn. 333, 187 S.W. 14.

5. Alexander v. Goellert, 153 Kan. 202, 109 P.2d 146 (1941). Heneage v. Federal Land Bank, 226 Miss. 250, 84 So.2d 137 (1955) (in case settlor determined mortgage necessary on account of emergency).

6. Spilman v. Mercer County Nat. Bank, 268 Ky. 761, 105 S.W.2d 1031 (1937).

7. Fergusson v. Fergusson, 148 Ark. 290, 229 S.W. 738 (1921); King v. Stowell, 211 Mass. 246, 98 N.E. 91. And see Breetz v. Hill, 293 Ky. 526, 169 S.W. 632 (property subject to taxes and other encumbrances; settlor expressed desire to keep property intact; sale would involve a sacrifice).

8. Purdy v. Bank of America Nat. Tr. & Sav. Ass'n, 2 Cal.2d 298, 40 P.2d 481 (1935).

power to borrow and mortgage has been implied.[9]

The express grant of a power to sell is ordinarily held not to include the power to mortgage,[10] nor does the power to change investments of the trust property ordinarily permit the trustee to mortgage the trust property.[11]

The trustee will be held to have an implied power to mortgage the trust property whenever the wording of the trust instrument or the necessities of the trust indicate that the settlor meant that such power should exist.[12] An example may be found where a mortgage is needed in order to prevent the wastage or loss of the trust property.[13] And, when a trustee is given broad power to take charge of, manage, and control property for a beneficiary, he has been held in some cases to have implied power to mortgage.[14] In such a case a court has said that "so long as it was deemed to the interest of the beneficiaries that the trustee should manage and control the property, the power to do so included the power to improve and repair, and if in the exercise of the discretion allowed him under the deed appointing him, he deemed it to the advantage of the beneficiaries that they procure the necessary funds by mortgaging the land he had the power and authority to do so."[15] In some cases a purchase-money mortgage by the trustee has been held impliedly authorized, where the trustee had power to buy property and inability to pay cash for it was reasonably to be expected.[16]

If the beneficiaries join with the trustee in the mortgage, or consent to it, or accept its benefits after it is executed, they may be estopped to assert its invalidity.[17]

9. Waterman v. Baldwin, 68 Iowa 255, 26 N.W. 435; Loebenthal v. Raleigh, 36 N.J.Eq. 169.

10. Townsend v. Wilson, 77 Conn. 411, 59 A. 417; Hamilton v. Hamilton, 149 Iowa, 321, 128 N.W. 380; Stengel v. Royal Realty Corp., 179 Md. 204, 17 A.2d 127 (1941); Loring v. Brodie, 134 Mass. 453; Stokes v. Payne, 58 Miss. 614; Potter v. Hodgman, 178 N.Y. 580, 70 N.E. 1107. A power to "dispose of" does not include a power to mortgage. Beakey v. Knutson, 90 Or. 574, 174 P. 1149. In Pennsylvania, where the conveyance theory of a mortgage prevails, a power to sell has been held to include a power to mortgage because a mortgage is a conditional sale. Davis v. Pennsylvania Co., 337 Pa. 456, 12 A.2d 66 (1940). And to the same effect, see 20 Pa. C.S.A. §§ 3354, 7133.

11. Griswold v. Caldwell, 65 App.Div. 371, 73 N.Y.S. 2.

12. Security Tr. Co. v. Merchants' & Clerks' Sav. Bank, 26 Ohio Cir.Ct.R. 381; Harding v. St. Louis Life Ins. Co., 2 Tenn. Ch. 465. In In re Billinger, [1898] 2 Ch. 534, a power to mortgage was implied from a power to carry on a real estate business.

13. Griley v. Marion Mtg. Co., 132 Fla. 299, 182 So. 297 (1937); Stengel v. Royal Realty Corp., 179 Md. 204, 17 A.2d 127 (1941).

14. Wechter v. Chicago Title & Tr. Co., 385 Ill. 111, 52 N.E.2d 157 (1943); Parks v. Central Life Assur. Soc., 181 Okl. 638, 75 P.2d 1111 (1938).

15. Ely v. Pike, 115 Ill.App. 284, 287.

16. Gernert v. Albert, 160 Pa. 95, 28 A. 576; Bomar v. Gist, 25 S.C. 340.

17. Boon v. Hall, 76 App.Div. 520, 78 N.Y.S. 557; Magraw v. Pennock, 2 Grant Cas., Pa., 89. As to joinder, see Massachusetts Mutual Life Ins. Co. v. Stout, 183 Ga. 649, 189 S.E. 248 (1936).

WESTLAW REFERENCES

trustee /s power authority /s pledge mortgage /s property

find 12 a2d 66

COURT CONTROL OVER BORROWING AND GIVING SECURITY [1]

§ 137. The court of chancery has inherent power to order or prohibit a mortgage by a trustee, regardless of the terms of the trust instrument. Statutes often declare this power and prescribe the procedure for its use. The court will ordinarily sanction a mortgage of trust property only for the purpose of conserving it or providing for its better management, and not to enable the trustee to enter into new business enterprises or speculative investments.

Chancery has inherent authority to permit the trustee to mortgage the trust property when such action is necessary to preserve the property or to enable the trustee to execute the trust as the settlor intended he should.[2] It is not necessary that such authority be declared in statutory form. The court may overrule a direction by the settlor that no mortgages are to be given, but a strong case must be made in order to induce the court to take such action.[3]

An example of this power may be found in a case in which a testator left all his property to his widow in trust for herself and her children. Debts of the testator were a lien upon certain land which he had devised to the trustee and the creditors were threatening suit. Equity authorized the trustee to mortgage the trust property to raise the money necessary to pay off the debts and thus preserve the trust property intact.[4] The power of the court is usually employed to enable the trustee to preserve the trust property, as where it is encumbered by tax or judgment liens, or where an emergency has occurred.[5] It is not usual for a court to permit a trustee to raise money by mortgage in order to repair or improve the trust property, unless the settlor has authorized improvements, since such action involves new risks and may involve somewhat speculative considerations,[6] although this is sometimes done.[7]

§ 137

1. Restatement, Trusts, Second, § 191. Bogert, Trusts and Trustees (rev. 2d edit.), §§ 762, 763.

2. Townsend v. Wilson, 77 Conn. 411, 59 A. 417; Long v. Simmons Female College, 218 Mass. 135, 105 N.E. 553; Butler v. Badger, 128 Minn. 99, 150 N.W. 233; In re Windsor Tr. Co., 142 App.Div. 772, 127 N.Y.S. 586; Shirkey v. Kirby, 110 Va. 455, 66 S.E. 40, 135 Am.St.Rep. 949.

3. Schramm v. United States Nat. Bank, 151 Or. 693, 52 P.2d 181 (1935).

4. Lyddane v. Lyddane, 144 Ky. 159, 137 S.W. 838.

5. Burroughs v. Gaither, 66 Md. 171, 7 A. 243; Butler v. Badger, 128 Minn. 99, 150 N.W. 233.

6. Schulting v. Schulting, 41 N.J.Eq. 130, 3 A. 526 (mortgage not permitted unless proof that land could not be sold without sacrifice); In re Stevenson's Estate, 186 Pa. 262, 40 A. 473.

7. Bond v. Tarboro, 217 N.C. 289, 7 S.E.2d 617, 127 A.L.R. 695 (1940); Smith v. Drake, 94 S.W.2d 236 (Tex.Civ.App.1936).

In many states the power of the court to sanction mortgages by trustees is stated in statutory form and the procedure regarding the application, proof, and confirmation of the mortgage is given.[8] These statutes are declaratory of a power already existing, so that the procedural rules are their most important parts. Some permit court sanction of mortgages without qualification; others state limited purposes for which the mortgages may be approved, or limit the power of the court to cases where the settlor has not prohibited a mortgage.

 WESTLAW REFERENCES

find 105 ne 553

court chancery /4 power authori** /5 trustee /6 borrow*** mortgag***

EFFECT OF LOANS AND GIVING SECURITY [1]

§ 138. If a trustee has no power to mortgage under any conditions, or has power to mortgage only on a condition which has not occurred, a mortgage or pledge by him is void; but if the money lent has been used to improve the property which the trustee purported to mortgage or used otherwise for the financial benefit of the beneficiaries, the lender may be given an equitable lien on the trust property.

A lender to a known trustee is ordinarily charged with knowledge of the facts regarding the trustee's power or lack of power to borrow and mortgage or pledge.

If a trustee had power to mortgage for a limited purpose only, or for general trust purposes, a mortgage by him is not invalidated by reason of an intent on his part to use the proceeds of the loan for an unlawful purpose and the actual use of them for an illegal object, unless the mortgagee had actual or constructive notice of the illegal object when he lent the money and took the mortgage. The mortgagee is not bound to see to the application of the loan proceeds.

The conduct of a trustee with regard to borrowing and mortgaging or pledging may be objectionable on any one of three grounds. In the first place, the trustee may seek to borrow and hypothecate the trust property when he has no power to do so, that is, when neither the express terms of his trust, its implied grants of power, nor a court order or statute permitted him to enter into the transaction. Here the mortgage given will be void.[2] The lender cannot object to such a holding since he is charged with knowledge of the powers of the trustee

---

8. See statutes digested in Bogert, Trusts and Trustees (rev. 2d edit.), §§ 743 and 763. Most statutes concern both sales and mortgages.

§ 138

1. Restatement, Trusts, Second, §§ 191, 296–297.

2. Taylor v. Clark, 56 Ga. 309; Tuttle v. First Nat. Bank of Greenfield, 187 Mass. 533, 73 N.E. 560, 105 Am.St.Rep. 420; Byron Reed Co. v. Klabunde, 76 Neb. 801, 108 N.W. 133.

when he deals with a known trustee. He should require proof of the trustee that in the existing fact situation the trustee can legally borrow and give security.[3]

Secondly, the trustee may have had a power to mortgage but only on the happening of a condition precedent, for example, the direction of the settlor or of a beneficiary. What is the result here if he mortgages but has not obtained the required direction? The mortgage is invalid.[4] The lender is bound to learn whether the condition precedent to the valid execution of the mortgage exists. He cannot safely rely on the assertions of the mortgagor-trustee.

However, if the mortgage is invalid and the money lent has been used by the trustee in such a way as to increase the value of the trust property covered by the invalid mortgage, or otherwise for the financial benefit of the beneficiaries, some cases hold that the lender should have a security interest in the property which was attempted to be mortgaged. Thus if a trustee represents that he has power to mortgage, and the lender foolishly believes him although an examination of the trust instrument would clearly have shown the opposite, and the trustee uses the money lent to build a house on the land described in the invalid mortgage, it may be fair that the lender have an equitable lien by way of security on the lot, to the extent that his money increased its value.[5]

Thirdly, although a trustee may have the power to mortgage, he may use it for an improper purpose. If he has power to mortgage to pay off tax liens or to repair real estate, but he in fact mortgages in order to use the money for his own personal purposes, the problem arises as to the effect of such a mortgage when the money lent has been improperly used by the trustee. If the lender actually knew of the improper purpose, he is a participant in a breach of trust in lending to the trustee, is liable for any damages flowing to the trust, and cannot enforce the mortgage against the trust property;[6] but if he did not have notice of the trustee's object the mortgage is valid, even though the trust got no benefit from the mortgage loan.[7] The lender is not bound to inquire into the trustee's motives and purposes, or to trace the money after the trustee gets it, or to see to the proper application of the money lent. The lender may assume that the trustee will use the proceeds of the loan for a legitimate purpose.[8]

3. Griley v. Marion Mtg. Co., 132 Fla. 299, 182 So. 297 (1937); O'Herron v. Gray, 168 Mass. 573, 47 N.E. 429, 40 L.R.A. 498; Snyder v. Collier, 85 Neb. 552, 558, 123 N.W. 1023, 1025, 133 Am.St.Rep. 682.

4. First Nat. Bank of Paterson v. National Broadway Bank, 150 N.Y. 459, 51 N.E. 398, 42 L.R.A. 139.

5. Griley v. Marion Mtg. Co., 132 Fla. 299, 182 So. 297 (1937), reversed 135 Fla. 824, 185 So. 734 (1939); Jones v. Swift, 300 Mass. 177, 15 N.E.2d 274 (1938).

6. See § 167, post.

7. Seaverns v. Presbyterian Hospital, 173 Ill. 414, 50 N.E. 1079, 64 Am.St.Rep. 125; McAuslan v. Union Tr. Co., 46 R.I. 176, 125 A. 296 (1924).

8. Parks v. Central Life Assur. Soc., 181 Okl. 638, 75 P.2d 1111 (1938). That the mortgage is being given to secure a personal debt of the trustee is, of course, clear notice that it is unauthorized. Ross v. Fitzgerald, 32 N.J.Eq. 838; Merriman v. Russell, 39 Tex. 278. See § 167, post, as to participation in a breach of trust.

The effect of notes and mortgages executed by trustees in performance of their trusts is governed by the general rules regarding contract obligations.[9] The trustee will be personally liable on promises and covenants in the notes and mortgages, unless he expressly excludes such liability.[10]

 WESTLAW REFERENCES

trustee   /s   mortgage   /s   "condition precedent"
merriman   +3   russell
390k189

LEASES BY TRUSTEES [1]

§ 139. If a trustee is to hold productive realty, he is usually given the express power to lease, and if such power is not directly mentioned by the settlor it is usually implied as necessary to the production of income for the beneficiaries.

The court of equity has inherent power to forbid, direct, or control the terms of leases to be made by a trustee, regardless of the terms of the trust instrument.

Statutes often govern the power of the trustee to lease and the term of a permissible lease, or set forth the power of the court to control leases and the procedure on applications for court authority.

In the absence of a direction by settlor, court or statute as to the duration and other terms of the lease, they should be such as a reasonably prudent man would provide. It is generally held that a trustee has no power to make a lease extending beyond the duration of the trust, but courts sometimes permit the making of leases which will or may extend beyond the life of the trust.

The trustee as landlord has a duty to perform his promises under the lease and to obey any common law or statutory rule regarding the obligations of lessors. He should secure performance of the tenant's obligations under the lease.

Power on the part of the trustee to lease the trust property is generally found in the trust instrument in plain terms.[2] Implied power to lease the trust property exists wherever it is necessary or desirable in order to enable the trustee to effectuate the purposes of the trust.

9. See §§ 125–128, ante.

10. Hamlen v. Welch, C.C.A.Mass., 116 F.2d 413 (1940); East River Sav. Bank v. Samuels, 284 N.Y. 470, 31 N.E.2d 906 (1940).

§ 139

1. Bogert, Trusts and Trustees (rev. 2d edit.), § 781 at seq.; Restatement, Trusts, Second, § 189.

2. Denegre v. Walker, 214 Ill. 113, 73 N.E. 409, 105 Am.St.Rep. 98, 2 Ann.Cas.

787; Ohio Oil Co. v. Daughetee, 240 Ill. 361, 88 N.E. 818, 36 L.R.A.,N.S., 1108. On the matters discussed in this section, see Kales, Powers in Trustees to Make Leases, 7 Ill.Law Rev. 427.

The statutory grants of numerous trustee powers in force in many states often include the power to lease. Bogert, Trusts and Trustees (rev. 2d edit.), §§ 551, 787.

The power to lease is generally a necessary incident of the management of trust real property.[3] If the trustee is to hold real estate and has the usual duty to make the trust property productive, he can generally obtain profits from it only by leasing it to others, since he would not normally be permitted or expected to engage in business and obtain profit from the land directly. The power to give oil and gas leases is frequently implied from powers of management[4] or of sale.[5] Trustees for charity may have an implied power to lease trust property, either to produce income or to enable the lessee to carry on the charitable work.[6] Thus in one case[7] a city was trustee of an auditorium to be used for education and entertainment, and it was held to have the power to lease part of the premises to the operator of a motion picture theatre who would pay rent and furnish public entertainment.

Courts of equity have inherent power to authorize a trustee to lease, and frequently exercise such authority upon proof of its necessity or desirability.[8] Their authority extends to overruling the settlor's directions about leases, where it is necessary in order to bring the intended benefits to the beneficiaries,[9] unless they are prevented by statute from making an order contrary to the terms of the trust. This is merely one example of the power of the court to permit deviation from the provisions of the instrument where it is necessary in order to accomplish the settlor's main objectives.[10]

In some states statutes declare when and for what term a trustee may lease trust property without court order,[11] and also set forth the circumstances in which a court may authorize a lease and the procedure for obtaining such authority.[12]

3. Smith v. Jones, 120 Fla. 237, 162 So. 496 (1935); Hutcheson v. Hodnett, 115 Ga. 990, 42 S.E. 422; First Nat. Bank in Wichita v. Magnolia Petroleum Co., 144 Kan. 645, 62 P.2d 891 (1936); Geer v. Traders' Bank of Canada, 132 Mich. 215, 93 N.W. 437.

4. Atwood v. Kleberg, 135 F.2d 452 (5th Cir.1943).

5. Layman v. Hodnett, 205 Ark. 367, 168 S.W.2d 819 (1943).

6. In re Clayton's Estate, 127 Colo. 592, 259 P.2d 617 (1953); Heffelfinger v. Scott, 142 Kan. 395, 47 P.2d 66 (1935).

7. John Wright & Associates v. Red Wing, 259 Minn. 111, 106 N.W.2d 205 (1960).

8. Packard v. Illinois Trust & Savings Bank, 261 Ill. 450, 104 N.E. 275; Pedroja v. Pedroja, 152 Kan. 82, 102 P.2d 1012 (1940). Equity may also validate a lease which was improper when made. Wilmer v. Philadelphia & Reading Coal & Iron Co., 130 Md. 666, 101 A. 588. The fact that the interests of all beneficiaries will be promoted must be shown before equity will authorize a lease. Schroeder v. Woodward, 116 Va. 506, 82 S.E. 192.

9. Adams v. Cook, 15 Cal.2d 352, 101 P.2d 484 (1940); Colonial Tr. Co. v. Brown, 105 Conn. 261, 135 A. 555 (1926) (settlor prohibited leases for longer than one year and construction of buildings higher than three stories).

10. See § 146, post.

11. Trustee may lease for five years without court approval. Minn.—M.S.A. § 501.22; N.Y.—McKinney's EPTL 11–1.1(b); Pa.—20 Pa.C.S.A. § 7142. Court approval is required for a longer lease. The five year leases are valid and bind the remaindermen even though the trust ends before the expiration of five years. 39 Cortlandt St. Corp. v. Lambert, 209 App. Div. 575, 205 N.Y.S. 161 (1924).

12. See statutes digested in Bogert, Trusts and Trustees (rev. 2d edit.), §§ 743, 787.

If a trustee finds no binding direction either in the trust instrument, a statute, or a court order, he may make such a lease as is reasonably prudent in view of the nature of the property and the real estate market.[13] He must use his discretion as to the selection of a tenant and the terms of the lease as to duration, amount of rent, and other terms.

Trustees sometimes find that it is advisable to make a long term lease, for example, one for fifty or ninety-nine years. In the case of property in a large city the proposed tenant is sometimes willing, if a long lease can be secured, to improve the land and pay a higher rent than could otherwise be obtained. The tenant will not be willing to construct an office or hotel building on the land leased unless he can have the use of the land for a long time and thus recover his investment. The life of the ordinary trust is limited to lives in being or a period of years not more than twenty-one, or to lives in being and twenty-one years. It is often doubtful, therefore, whether the trust will outlast a fifty or ninety-nine year lease, or perhaps it is certain that it will not. The trustee wants to make a long lease so as to get higher income and improvement of the land, but he doubts his power to lease for such a period. It may be urged that a trustee is limited as to the length of a lease which he can give by the size of the estate which he holds, and that the remaindermen at the end of the trust are entitled to a fee which they can use as they like and not merely to a fee encumbered by a lease.

The settlor may permit leases extending beyond the life of the income trust,[14] and if he does not expressly do so it has been found in a few cases that there was an implied power to give such leases where conditions made them highly advantageous.[15] However a majority of the courts have denied the existence of such an implied power [16] and have held that the lease was valid for the trust term only.[17]

The court of equity has inherent power to grant to the trustee authority to make a lease which will or may last beyond the trust, and it must be shown that the benefits to trust beneficiaries and to remaindermen justify the action and the remaindermen have no ground for complaint at losing control of their interests for a short period of time.[18] In some states statutes declare the existence of such a power in the

---

13. Russell v. Russell, 109 Conn. 187, 145 A. 648, 63 A.L.R. 783 (1929).

14. Collins v. Foley, 63 Md. 158.

15. Crown Co. v. Cohn, 88 Or. 642, 172 P. 804; Smith v. Widman Hotel Co., 74 S.D. 118, 49 N.W.2d 301 (1951); Upham v. Plankinton, 152 Wis. 275, 140 N.W. 5.

16. Campbell v. Kawananakoa, 31 Haw. 500; Bergengren v. Aldrich, 139 Mass. 259, 29 N.E. 667. See 21 Harv.L. Rev. 211; 21 So.Cal.L.R. 260.

17. Standard Metallic Paint Co. v. Prince Mfg. Co., 133 Pa. 474, 19 A. 411; In

re Will of Caswell, 197 Wis. 327, 222 N.W. 235 (1928).

18. Colonial Tr. Co. v. Brown, 105 Conn. 261, 135 A. 555 (1926); Russell v. Russell, 109 Conn. 187, 145 A. 648, 63 A.L.R. 783 (1929); Denegre v. Walker, 214 Ill. 113, 73 N.E. 409, 105 Am.St.Rep. 98; In re Hubbell Trust, 135 Iowa 637, 113 N.W. 512, 13 L.R.A.,N.S., 496, 14 Ann.Cas. 640; Nashville Tr. Co. v. Lebeck, 197 Tenn. 164, 270 S.W.2d 470 (1954); In re Caswell's Will, 197 Wis. 327, 222 N.W. 235, 61 A.L.R. 1359 (1928). That the settlor provided that leases should not exceed ten years does not

court.[19] There are examples of the grant of power by the court to the trustee to make a long term lease,[20] but in some instances permission has been denied.[21] If the matter is not settled by the trust instrument or a statute, the trustee should present the problem to the court,[22] and doubtless most prospective lessees would require such a procedure in view of the large financial interests involved.

An Iowa court, in denying permission to make a ninety-nine year lease because it was not reasonably necessary, since the trust had a probable duration of seventy-one years, summed up the law as follows: "(1) The trustees may lease for such reasonable terms as are customary and essential to the proper care of and to procure a reasonable income from the property. (2) Such terms should not, save on showing of reasonable necessity to effectuate the purposes of the trust, extend beyond the period the trust is likely to continue. (3) Should they extend unreasonably beyond such period, the excess only will be void. (4) Only upon a showing of such reasonable necessity, when not given such power by the instrument creating the trust, will the trustees be authorized to bind the estate so as to effectively deprive those ultimately entitled thereto of the property itself." [23]

While the earlier authorities denied that it was prudent to grant to a lessee an option to renew or to purchase the fee, on the ground that the trustee should not bind himself in advance as to a sale or new lease,[24] the better view seems to be that the reasonableness of such an option depends on the circumstances of each case and that it may be approved where in accordance with customary practices and where necessary in order to obtain a good tenant.[25]

The trustee is under a duty to enforce the lease, for example, to collect rents due and to enforce performance of any covenants the tenants may have made.[26] If he fails to collect rentals which he could have obtained by the use of ordinary care and diligence, he will be liable for it.[27] In so far as the lease and the law of landlord and tenant place upon the landlord the duty of keeping the leased buildings in

limit the court's power. Marsh v. Reed, 184 Ill. 263, 56 N.E. 306. The court may approve a long term lease after it has been made. Butler v. Topkis, Del.Ch., 63 A. 646.

19. See, for example, statutes of Cal. and La., quoted in Bogert, Trusts and Trustees (rev. 2d edit.), § 787.

20. Denegre v. Walker, 214 Ill. 113, 73 N.E. 409; Marsh v. Reed, 184 Ill. 263, 56 N.E. 306; Watland v. Good, 189 Iowa 1174, 179 N.W. 613; In re Menzel's Will, 247 Minn. 559, 77 N.W.2d 833 (1956); Nashville Tr. Co. v. Lebeck, 197 Tenn. 164, 270 S.W.2d 470 (1954).

21. In re Hubbell Trust, 135 Iowa 637, 113 N.W. 512 (proposed lease extending 28 years beyond probable trust term disapproved).

22. McCrory v. Beeler, 155 Md. 456, 142 A. 587 (1928).

23. In re Hubbell Trust, 135 Iowa 637, 664, 665, 113 N.W. 512, 522, 13 L.R.A.,N.S., 496, 14 Ann.Cas. 640.

24. In re Armory Board, 29 Misc. 174, 60 N.Y.S. 882; Hickok v. Still, 168 Pa. 155, 31 A. 1100, 47 Am.St.Rep. 880; Moore v. Trainer, 252 Pa. 367, 97 A. 462.

25. Raynolds v. Browning King & Co., 217 App.Div. 443, 217 N.Y.S. 15 (1926); Crown Co. v. Cohn, 88 Or. 642, 172 P. 804; Cardon's Estate, 278 Pa. 153, 122 A. 234 (1923).

26. City Bank Farmers Tr. Co. v. Smith, 263 N.Y. 292, 189 N.E. 222 (1934).

27. Kinney v. Uglow, 163 Or. 539, 98 P.2d 1006 (1940).

repair, the trustee has a duty to make repairs.[28] If statutes or ordinances require fire escapes or other safety measures, the trustee has a duty to comply.[29]

Except to the extent an improvement of real estate may be necessary and reasonably prudent for the purpose of making property tenantable,[30] that is, where the property cannot be rented without the improvement, the trustee has no duty or privilege to improve the premises in anticipation of, or after, a lease.[31] Thus, in a case where buildings are ancient, unsafe, and untenantable, and the property is in an unproductive condition, the trustee may be considered to have implied power to use a portion of the principal of the trust fund for the purpose of constructing new buildings on the land.[32] In other instances the peculiar conditions of the trust have made the expenditure for improvements unreasonable and the trustee has been held to have exceeded his powers in making them.[33] Thus the expenditure of $850,000 in erecting a new building upon land, when the value of the entire trust property was only $920,000, has been held to be unreasonable and not within the authority of the trustee.[34] The Massachusetts court stated its position regarding improvements in general in these words: "We have no doubt that a trustee under a Massachusetts trust would be justified in tearing down an old building owned by the trust and erecting a new one in its place, when a prudent business man would do so to secure a fair return by way of income, and at the same time to maintain the corpus of the portion of the principal so invested intact, having regard to the relation which such an investment, when made, would have to the amount of the principal of the trust fund as a whole." [35]

In some states statutes expressly authorize chancery to empower a trustee to sell or mortgage the trust property for the purpose of making repairs or improvements.[36]

  WESTLAW REFERENCES

    express /2 power /s trustee /s lease
    390k182 /p lease
    390k171 /p lease

28. Booth v. Bradford, 114 Iowa 562, 570, 87 N.W. 685, 688; Veazie v. Forsaith, 76 Me. 172; Sohier v. Eldredge, 103 Mass. 345; Kearney v. Kearney, 17 N.J.Eq. 59; Disbrow v. Disbrow, 46 App.Div. 111, 61 N.Y.S. 614, affirmed 167 N.Y. 606, 60 N.E. 1110.

29. In re Whittaker, (1929) 1 Ch. 662; City of Chicago v. Pielet, 342 Ill.App. 201, 95 N.E.2d 528 (1950).

30. Patterson v. Johnson, 113 Ill. 559; Stevens v. Stevens, 80 Hun, N.Y., 514, 30 N.Y.S. 625, 62 N.Y.St.Rep. 599.

31. Booth v. Bradford, 114 Iowa 562, 87 N.W. 685. And see § 99, ante.

32. Smith v. Keteltas, 62 App.Div. 174, 70 N.Y.S. 1065.

33. Green v. Winter, 1 Johns.Ch., N.Y., 26, 7 Am.Dec. 475; Killebrew v. Murphy, 3 Heisk., Tenn., 546; Hughes v. Williams, 99 Va. 312, 38 S.E. 138.

34. Warren v. Pazolt, 203 Mass. 328, 89 N.E. 381.

35. 203 Mass. 328, 345, 89 N.E. 381, 387.

36. See Bogert, Trusts and Trustees (rev. 2d edit.), §§ 743, 763.

implied /2 power /s lease /s trustee

390k205

chancery equity court /4 power authori** /4 trustee /s lease

390k1931/2 /p lease

collins +3 foley

"hubbell trust"

Chapter 16

ACCOUNTING AND COMPENSATION

Table of Sections

DUTY TO RETAIN TRUST DOCUMENTS AND VOUCHERS AND TO KEEP RECORDS [1]

§ 140. **In order that he may be able to present to the court and the beneficiaries an accurate history of his administration, the trustee is under a duty to retain trust documents, to secure and file vouchers for expenditures, and to keep records.**

Failure to perform his duties may cause the court considering his accounts to resolve doubts against him and otherwise to discipline him.

Ordinarily the management and control of the trust property is solely in the hands of the trustee. The beneficiary knows nothing of the trust business at first hand. The nature of the trust investments, the condition of the trust property, the income received, the expenditures made—these are all facts of which the beneficiary is usually ignorant, except as he obtains information regarding them from the trustee. And yet it is highly proper that the beneficiary should have knowledge of these matters, in order that he may know whether the trust is being properly administered. He is the owner of the trust property in equity, and is entitled to some or all of its benefits. It is obvious that he is entitled to know how the business of the trust is

§ 140
1. Restatement, Trusts, Second, § 172.
Bogert, Trusts and Trustees (rev. 2d edit.),
§ 961 et seq.

being carried on. This he cannot learn unless the trustee reduces to writing so far as possible the history of his administration, and retains such records and all documents which have come to him during the course of his administration. If all the trust business is conducted orally and left to the memory of the trustee, the beneficiary will be frustrated in his effort to secure adequate information.

From these principles arises the duty of the trustee to keep records of his transactions, to retain correspondence, to secure vouchers for all his expenditures and preserve them, and to procure and file all other documents which may shed light on the events which occur during the administration.[2]

In order to conduct himself as an ordinarily prudent business man operating a business for another, the trustee should also set up book-keeping entries according to an approved accounting system, so that there may be at all times available an orderly statement of the trust work, under such headings as receipts of principal and income and disbursements for the payment of expenses or as distributions to the beneficiaries.[3]

Failure to perform these duties may be ground for court removal of the trustee,[4] for denying or reducing his compensation,[5] or for charging him with the costs of an accounting proceeding.[6]

It is also stated by the courts that a breach of these duties will cause the court to "resolve all doubts against the trustee".[7] For example, claimed expenditures for which he has no receipt or voucher may be disallowed,[8] and where he kept no accurate account of his receipts he may be charged with estimated amounts.[9] It has been held that a settlor may relieve a trustee from the duty to keep formal records and account books, but not from the duty to account in a court of equity.[10]

The trust departments of corporate trustees are examined periodically by the U.S. Comptroller of the Currency, in the case of national banks, and representatives of the several Federal Reserve banks, the

2. Smallwood v. Lawson, 183 Ky. 189, 208 S.W. 808; Smith v. Tolverson, 190 Minn. 410, 252 N.W. 423 (1934).

3. Wylie v. Bushnell, 277 Ill. 484, 115 N.E. 618; In re Bailey's Trust, 241 Minn. 143, 62 N.W.2d 829 (1954) (no particular system required); Stockwell v. Stockwell's Estate, 92 Vt. 489, 105 A. 30.

4. Wylie v. Bushnell, 277 Ill. 484, 115 N.E. 618.

5. Dufford's Ex'r v. Smith, 46 N.J.Eq. 216, 18 A. 1052.

6. Appeal of Kilgore, 5 Sad.Pa., 306, 8 A. 441.

7. White v. Rankin, 18 App.Div. 293, 295, 46 N.Y.S. 228, affirmed 162 N.Y. 622, 57 N.E. 1128. And see State ex rel., Ras-

kin v. Schachat, 120 Conn. 337, 180 A. 502 (1935) (trustee of business could not show results; charged with compound interest); Long v. Earle, 277 Mich. 505, 269 N.W. 577 (1936) (trustee destroyed checks showing payees of trust funds; presumed that he embezzled funds).

8. McKibben v. Byers, 138 Kan. 216, 25 P.2d 357 (1933); McDowell v. Caldwell, 2 McCord Eq. 43.

9. In re Baldwin's Estate, 311 Mich. 288, 18 N.W.2d 827 (1945); American Nat. Bank of Portsmouth v. Ames, 169 Va. 711, 194 S.E. 784 (1938), cert. den. 304 U.S. 577, 58 S.Ct. 1046, 82 L.Ed. 1540.

10. Wood v. Honeyman, 178 Or. 484, 169 P.2d 131 (1946). See section 142, post.

Federal Deposit Insurance Corporation, and state banking authorities, who investigate the practices of such trustees with regard to the adequacy of records and accounts, as well as investment and other administrative procedures. In case of deficiencies or improper methods pressure is brought to bear for the purpose of securing proper methods of administration.[11]

 WESTLAW REFERENCES

trustee /s duty /s keep maintain /4 books records documents
326k30 /p trust
390k292

DUTY TO FURNISH INFORMATION TO THE BENEFICIARY [1]

§ 141. The trustee is under a duty to furnish to the beneficiary on demand all information regarding the trust and its execution which may be useful to the beneficiary in protecting his rights, and to give to the beneficiary facts which the trustee knows or ought to know would be important to the beneficiary.

The trustee also has a duty to permit the beneficiary to inspect trust records, documents, securities and other trust property.

The beneficiary is entitled to receive from his representative the full facts about the course of trust administration. It is not necessary that the beneficiary bring a bill in equity for an accounting in order to obtain information about the trust business. The trustee is under the duty of furnishing all pertinent information upon demand.[2] Thus in a leading English case it was held that a beneficiary was entitled to an order which would enable him to learn how the trust fund was invested, what encumbrances had been placed on any of the interests under the trust, and to inspect all deeds and documents relating to the trust. The court said: "The general rule, then, is what I have stated, that the trustee must give information to his cestui que trust as to the investment of the trust estate. Where a portion of the trust estate is invested in consols, it is not sufficient for the trustee merely to say that it is so invested, but his cestui que trust is entitled to an authority from the trustee to enable him to make proper application to the bank, as has been done in this case, in order that he may verify the trustee's own statement. . . ."[3] And in the case of a voting trust the beneficiary

---

11. See Bogert, Trusts and Trustees (rev. 2d edit.), § 962. And see Masters, 92 Tr. & Est. 170; Franklin, 94 Tr. & Est. 351; Scarborough, 104 Tr. & Est. 882; Tull, Jr., 106 Tr. & Est. 905.

§ 141

1. Restatement, Trusts, Second, § 173. Bogert, Trusts and Trustees (rev. 2d edit.), § 961.

2. Wylie v. Bushnell, 277 Ill. 484, 115 N.E. 618; Perrin v. Lepper, 72 Mich. 454, 40 N.W. 859; In re Scott's Estate, 202 Pa. 389, 51 A. 1023. The beneficiary is entitled to be informed in what securities the trust funds are invested. Baer v. Kahn, 131 Md. 17, 101 A. 596.

3. In re Tillott, 1 Ch. 86, 88, 89 (1892).

may be entitled to a list of the names and addresses of the beneficiaries.[4]

Where a trustee holds stock in a corporation, the beneficiary may obtain information from the trustee regarding the affairs of the corporation which comes to him by virtue of such ownership or because of the fact that he holds some stock as trustee and other stock as an individual.[5]

Furthermore, if reasonable regard for the interests of the beneficiary requires it, the trustee is under a duty to volunteer information to the beneficiary, and not merely to wait until the beneficiary asks for it.[6] For example, a trustee of a mortgage for bondholders has been held under a duty to inform the bondholders of a default by the mortgagor, so that the bondholders can unite to force foreclosure if they desire to do so,[7] and a trustee who knows that a beneficiary is considering selling his interest for less than its value has an obligation to inform the beneficiary of the facts.[8]

The duty to volunteer information is often performed by corporate trustees by rendering periodic statements to the beneficiaries, usually in the form of copies of the ledger sheets concerning the trust. For example, such condensed explanations of recent transactions may be mailed to the beneficiaries annually, semi-annually, or quarterly. The effect of their receipt and failure to object to them will be treated later.[9]

The general rule was well stated by a Michigan court: "The beneficiaries of a trust have the right to be kept informed at all times concerning the management of the trust, and it is the duty of the trustees to so inform them. It is not generally presumable that the beneficiaries have such information from independent sources."[10] An illustration of the enforcement of this same right is found in the cases holding that a beneficiary is entitled to examine legal opinions which the trustee obtains for the purpose of guiding him in carrying out the trust. The trustee is not, however, under the same obligation regarding opinions which he obtains for the purpose of defending himself from

---

4. Morris v. Broadview, Inc., 338 Ill. App. 99, 86 N.E.2d 863 (1949).

5. In re Hubbell's Will, 90 N.Y.S.2d 74 (Sur. 1948) affirmed 276 App.Div. 134, 93 N.Y.S.2d 555 (1949), reversed on other points in 302 N.Y. 246, 97 N.E.2d 888 (1950); In re Rappaport's Estate, 96 N.Y.S. 741 (citing Civ.Prac.Act, § 296, and Surr. Ct.Act, § 263); In re Shehan's Will, 285 App.Div. 785, 141 N.Y.S.2d 439 (1955), reargument denied 286 A.D. 953, 143 N.Y.S.2d 668 (1955).

6. Birmingham Trust & Sav. Co. v. Ansley, 234 Ala. 674, 176 So. 465 (1937); Hertz v. Miklowski, 326 Mich. 697, 40 N.W.2d 452 (1950) (danger of trust property being lost by enforcement of tax lien);

Moore v. Sanders, 106 S.W.2d 337 (Tex.Civ. App.1937) (duty to notify beneficiary of existence of the trust).

7. Lyman v. Stevens, 123 Conn. 591, 197 A. 313 (1938); First Trust Co. of Lincoln v. Carlsen, 129 Neb. 118, 261 N.W. 333 (1935). And see April v. April, 272 N.Y. 331, 6 N.E.2d 43 (1936) (duty to inform beneficiary of failure of settlor to perform promise to convey additional property).

8. Zottarelli v. Pacific States Sav. & Loan Co., 94 Cal.App.2d 480, 211 P.2d 23 (1949).

9. See § 143, post.

10. Loud v. Winchester, 52 Mich. 174, 183, 17 N.W. 784.

charges of misconduct.[11]

A trustee should not disclose to non-beneficiaries (for example, creditors of beneficiaries) facts regarding the trust. He should treat such information as confidential.[12] It would seem that a beneficiary has no right to information concerning the status of the interest of another beneficiary under the same trust.[13]

The beneficiary is also entitled to an inspection of all books and documents relating to the trust and of trust securities and other property held by the trustee.[14] He may personally examine the books or have an accountant or lawyer do it for him.[15] He is entitled to know from personal observation whether the trust papers, accounts, and documents are in the condition claimed by the trustee.

The privilege of obtaining information and of inspecting must be exercised at reasonable hours of the day and at reasonable intervals. The trustee cannot be required to give information and permit inspection outside of business hours or so frequently as to be unnecessary and unreasonable.

If one co-trustee excludes the others from access to trust books and papers, the court will order him to make the records available.[16]

WESTLAW REFERENCES

beneficiary /s entitle* /s inspect /s documents books records

duty /s trustee /s furnish*** /3 information /s beneficiary

find 40 nw2d 452

390k179

390k331

DUTY TO RENDER COURT ACCOUNTING [1]

§ 142. A trustee is under a duty to render a formal, written report or accounting in a court of equity when required by statute or ordered to do so by the court. Any person financially interested in the trust administration may bring a suit to obtain a decree for an accounting. The account may be upon termination of the trust (final), or during the course of administration (intermediate).

11. Wynne v. Humberston, 27 Beav. 421.

12. West's Ann.Cal.Fin.Code, § 1582; Mich.Comp.L.A. § 700.501. In In re First Trust & Dep. Co., 63 N.Y.S.2d 681 (1946), a beneficiary was allowed to examine a corporate trustee as to the average yield on all its trusts, but not as to the investments of other trusts.

13. In re Tillott, (1892) 1 Ch. 86.

14. Union Trust Co. of San Diego v. Superior Court, in and for San Diego County, 11 Cal.2d 449, 81 P.2d 150, 118 A.L.R. 259 (1938) (court order to permit inspection granted); Baydrop v. Second Nat. Bank, 120 Conn. 322, 180 A. 469 (1935).

15. Equitable Trust Co. v. Schwebel, 32 F.Supp. 241 (E.D.Pa.1940), affirmed 117 F.2d 738 (3d Cir.1941).

16. Wilson v. Board of Directors of City Trusts, 324 Pa. 545, 188 A. 588 (1936).

§ 142

1. Bogert, Trusts and Trustees (rev. 2d edit.), §§ 963–974; Restatement, Trusts, Second, §§ 172, 260.

See Judd, 42 Col.L.R. 207; Overstreet, 13 Mo.L.R. 255.

The trustee may also voluntarily present to the court or to the beneficiaries an account of his administration.

In many states, by statute or court rule, trustees are required to make accountings to the beneficiary or to a court at stated intervals and the procedure and effect of such accountings are fixed. In other states there are no statutes requiring periodic court accountings and the matter is left to the inherent jurisdiction of equity to permit or require accountings when requested or demanded.

It is elementary that a trustee is under an obligation to render an account of his dealings as trustee in a court having jurisdiction of the trust, when directed to account by that court or by the legislature.[2] General equitable jurisdiction extends to requiring accountings by all fiduciaries. This obligation is placed upon the trustee in order that the beneficiary may learn by a written, orderly statement what property has been received by the trustee, and what funds have been paid out and for what purposes, and may then object to the account, if he desires, and have the propriety of the trustee's actions passed upon by the court. The duty here is to give information in writing and under oath, in such manner that the beneficiaries and the court can scrutinize it, in advance of court action upon it, for breaches of trust.

The settlor may regulate the duty of the trustee to account by a provision in the trust instrument as to the time or form of the account,[3] but he cannot oust the court from its jurisdiction to order an account by a statement in the trust document that his trustee shall be under no duty to account to the beneficiaries.[4]

Failure to perform the duty to account may be punished by removal of the trustee [5] or by reducing or denying his compensation,[6] or by making him liable for the costs of the suit to obtain an accounting.

Not only may a court accounting be forced by a beneficiary or other interested party but it may be voluntarily rendered by a trustee.[7] Frequently trustees desire to present statements of their transactions and secure court approval of them in order that they may secure release from liability for the acts described in the account, and also to gain periodic payment of compensation and counsel fees.

2. Bone v. Hayes, 154 Cal. 759, 99 P. 172; Barnes v. Century Sav. Bank, 165 Iowa 141, 144 N.W. 367; Barnes v. Gardiner, 140 App.Div. 395, 125 N.Y.S. 433; Geisse v. Beall, 3 Wis. 367. An implied as well as an express trustee may be compelled to account. Tucker v. Weeks, 177 App.Div. 158, 163 N.Y.S. 595.

3. Pinckard v. Ledyard, 251 Ala. 648, 38 So.2d 580 (1949); Dunklee v. County Court of City and County of Denver, 106 Colo. 77, 103 P.2d 484 (1940); Application of Central Hanover Bank & Trust Co., 176 Misc. 183, 26 N.Y.S.2d 924 (1941), affirmed 263 App.Div. 809, 32 N.Y.S.2d 128, affirmed 288 N.Y. 608, 42 N.E.2d 610 (1942).

The trustor or settlor may expressly waive court accountings; see n. 24, post.

4. Ferguson v. Mueller, 115 Colo. 139, 169 P.2d 610 (1946); Wood v. Honeyman, 178 Or. 484, 169 P.2d 131, 171 A.L.R. 587 (1946).

5. In re McDougall's Estate, 189 Wis. 550, 208 N.W. 254 (1926). See § 160, post.

6. Gilbert v. Sutliff, 3 Ohio St. 129.

7. Arnold v. Alden, 173 Ill. 229, 50 N.E. 704.

The court in which the trustee may voluntarily account, or in which he may be compelled to account, is usually the court having general equitable jurisdiction. Quite frequently statutes give to the probate courts concurrent or exclusive jurisdiction over accountings by testamentary trustees.[8]

The statutes or court rules of those states with provisions governing trust accountings may be divided into three basic groups regarding the trustee's duty to account.[9] In some states, where no periodic court accountings are required, a court accounting may be secured only when the beneficiary or other interested party requests it or obtains a court order for it.[10] In a few states the statute provides that the beneficiary rather than the court is to receive the required periodic statements or accounts.[11] In many states, however, a statute requires formal court accountings by testamentary trustees, whether the beneficiaries have requested them or not, and this requirement is often extended to trustees of court-supervised trusts and to court-appointed trustees other than testamentary trustees.[12] In most of those states requiring court accountings annual as well as final accounts are required to be filed.[13] In some states a statute provides that a trustee who resigns or is removed by the court must file an account before receiving his discharge,[14] and an account may be required upon the death of the sole trustee.[15]

Although it appears that no state requires the filing of court accounts by a trustee of a *living trust*, by statute in many states a trustee of a living or testamentary trust may seek judicial settlement of his accounts.[16] In all states, nevertheless, a trustee always may be compelled by a court to account, upon petition of a beneficiary or other interested party,[17] and some statutes expressly provide that the court can require an accounting at any time.[18]

8. See Bogert, Trusts and Trustees (rev. 2d edit.), §§ 965–968.

9. For the wording of these statutes see Bogert, Trusts and Trustees (rev. 2d edit.), §§ 965–968. States without any comprehensive legislation on trustee accountings are Ark., Okl. and Tenn. (except for a trustee who resigns or is removed).

10. See Unif.Prob.Code § 7–303, adopted in Alas., Ariz., Colo., Fla., Haw., Idah., Ky., Me., Mich. (trusts not administered in probate), Minn., Mont., Neb., N.Mex., N.D., Utah.

To the same effect; Mo., Ore.

And see Vernon's Ann.Tex.Prop.Code § 113.151 (beneficiary may request; court may require).

11. Ill., La., Mont., Wash.

12. Ala., Conn., Del., D.C. (court rule), Ga., Ind., Ia., Kan., Ky. (court appointed trustee), Md. (court rule), Mass., Mich., Minn., Nev., N.H., N.J. (once, within one year of appointment), N.D., Ohio, S.Car., S.Dak. (court supervised trust), Vt., Va., W.Va., Wis.

13. Exceptions are Conn. (every three years), Del. (every two years), Ohio (two years).

14. Ky., Miss., N.Car., Ohio, Tenn., Va.

15. See, for example, Ohio R.C. § 2109.30.

16. Cal., Mont., N.J. (trustee of living trust), N.Y., Pa., R.I., S.Car., Wash.

17. See, for example, In re Estate of Paretta, 211 Cal.Rptr. 313, 165 Cal.App.3d 157 (1985). See Bogert, Trusts and Trustees (rev. 2d edit.), § 963.

18. N.J., N.Y., N.Dak. (trust company), Okl., Ore., Pa., Tex., Wash.

In many states the trustees of charitable trusts, including trusts in which the charity has a temporary or limited interest, are required to register and file periodic reports with the court or a designated state official,[19] and under federal law the trustees of an employee benefit plan must file annual reports with the U.S. Secretary of Labor and make copies available to plan participants.[20]

Increasingly statutes provide for nonjudicial settlement of trust accounts. Thus the Uniform Probate Code provides for informal accounting and barring of claims without judicial involvement unless the beneficiary or other interested party elects to go to court.[21] In several states where statutes do not require court or other accountings, trustees have used informal procedures in settling their accounts, whether or not the settlor has provided for such a procedure in the trust instrument. Thus quarterly or other periodic statements may have been furnished the beneficiaries and the trustee relies upon the approval of (or lack of objection to) these statements, together with receipts and releases of the beneficiaries, in distributing the trust assets and terminating the trust without liability.[22] In a few states the statute appears to authorize settlement of accounts by agreement between the trustee and beneficiaries without a court account.[23]

The trustee may be relieved from the duty of accounting in a number of ways. Under some trust accounting or trustee powers statutes the settlor may waive the requirement of a court accounting.[24] In other statutes it is provided that the beneficiary may relieve the trustee of the duty to account.[25] And in a few states the court itself may relieve the trustee of such duty.[26]

It can be argued that voluntary statements by trustees at regular intervals are customarily made and are much more economical than court accountings, which involve the employment of counsel and possibly accountants and the payment of large fees to guardians ad litem for minor or possible contingent beneficiaries. Yet it can be said in favor of compulsory court accountings that unless they are required carelessness will be encouraged and in some cases breaches of trust will be concealed for many years, and that the law should give the beneficiaries an opportunity to check on the results of the administration at

---

19. For references to statutes requiring registration and periodic reports of charitable organizations, see Bogert, Trusts and Trustees (rev. 2d edit.), §§ 411, 963 (n. 43).

20. 29 U.S.C.A. §§ 1023, 1024.

21. §§ 7–201, 7–307.

22. In Illinois, for example, the "receipt and release" method of accounting is customarily used.

23. See, for example, Ky.R.S. § 395.605, N.Y.—McKinney's SCPA 2202, 2203.

24. See Bogert, Trusts and Trustees (rev. 2d edit.), § 963, citing statutes for Conn., Ind., Ia., Kan., Ky., Mont., Wash. However, the settlor cannot oust the count of its inherent equitable jurisdiction to order an account. § 973.

25. For example, statutes in Mo., Mont., Nev., N.J., Wash.

26. See, for example, N.Car.G.S. § 36A–80.

frequent intervals so as to present claims in timely fashion and prevent further injury to their interests.

In a few states provision is made for the examination of the account by a court officer prior to its consideration by the court,[27] and thus an attempt is made to give expert aid to the court and the beneficiaries. But in most states the court merely acts on objections raised by the beneficiaries and provides no investigative service of its own. The court to which the account is presented has power to refer it to a master, referee, or auditor for consideration and report, and in some states express provision is made for this procedure.[28]

In order to fix the initial liability of trustees as to the amount of trust property received by them, it is required in some states that they file in the court having jurisdiction over the enforcement of the trust an inventory of the trust property they have obtained, within a short time after taking office.[29] In the case of testamentary trusts the distribution decree on the termination of the executor's work will serve the purpose of an inventory.

The suit or proceeding for a court accounting may be brought by any person having a contingent or vested, present or future, financial interest in the trust administration.[30] It is not necessary to allege or prove that the trustee is in default or that the petitioner is presently entitled to any trust property.[31] Thus the following are proper parties plaintiff: any beneficiary, whether his interest is present or future, vested or contingent;[32] a remainderman who is to take following the trust;[33] a surety on the bond of a trustee;[34] a sole trustee[35] or a co-trustee;[36] the executor of a deceased trustee;[37] and a successor trustee.[38] The settlor as such has no legal interest in the trust and cannot sue for an accounting.[39]

The action or proceedings to obtain an accounting may be brought against an express or a resulting or constructive trustee,[40] or his successor in interest after his death,[41] or against a trustee who has resigned or been removed.[42]

27. Md. (court rule), N.J. (court rule), Va., W.Va.

28. See statutes and court rules cited in Bogert, Trusts and Trustees (rev. 2d edit.), § 970.

29. Md. (court rule), Mo., Wis.

30. See Bogert, Trusts and Trustees (rev. 2d edit.), §§ 963, 970.

31. Barbour v. Cummings, 26 R.I. 201, 58 A. 660.

32. Brown v. Ricks, 30 Ga. 777; Savage v. Sherman, 87 N.Y. 277.

33. Franz v. Buder, 11 F.2d 854 (8th Cir.1926).

34. In re Holman's Estate, 216 Iowa 1186, 250 N.W. 498 (1933).

35. Arnold v. Alden, 173 Ill. 229, 50 N.E. 704.

36. Bermingham v. Wilcox, 120 Cal. 467, 52 P. 822.

37. In re Scott's Estate, 202 Pa. 389, 51 A. 1023.

38. Boreing v. Faris, 127 Ky. 67, 104 S.W. 1022.

39. Boone v. Davis, 64 Miss. 133, 8 So. 202. Marvin v. Smith, 46 N.Y. 571.

40. Tri-City Elec. Serv. Co. v. Jarvis, 206 Ind. 5, 185 N.E. 136 (1933).

41. In re Rothwell's Estate, 283 Mass. 563, 186 N.E. 662 (1933).

42. See § 31, ante, and § 160, post.

The beneficiary may be barred from obtaining an accounting or from objecting to an account in whole or in part, by his consent,[43] and laches on the part of the beneficiary in failing to demand an account may relieve the trustee of liability.[44]

 WESTLAW REFERENCES

trustee /s duty /3 account***

390k291

390k289

390k292

statute /s trust /3 account***

court /9 trust /3 account***

PROCEDURE ON COURT ACCOUNTING—EFFECT OF COURT APPROVAL [1]

§ 143. Where a court accounting is required or sought, the trustee has a duty to file a formal, verified statement of his transactions for the accounting period with the court, and to notify the beneficiaries of such filing and of the return day on which approval of the account will be requested.

The beneficiary may object to any item of the account and present evidence in support of his objections. The burden is on the trustee to justify his conduct with respect to the item in question. Failure to object may prevent the beneficiary from claiming later that a transaction described in the account was wrongful.

After hearing the evidence of the objectant and the trustee, or receiving a report with respect to it from an auditor or referee, the court will pass upon the propriety of the trustee's conduct and approve or disapprove the account in whole or in part or require its modification.

The approval by the court of a trustee's account prevents the beneficiaries from objecting later to any conduct of the trustee which was fairly stated in the account. Such approval does not prevent the beneficiary from applying for a reopening of the account if there has been fraud, concealment or mistake, and as to items affected by such wrongful acts the trustee may be held liable.

Many corporate trustees present voluntary written reports of their trust administration to their beneficiaries periodically out of court, and secure their approval by the beneficiaries. This protects the trustee against later complaint as to his administration, if it fully and fairly stated the facts and the beneficiaries were competent.

43. Amory v. Lowell, 104 Mass. 265 (1870); Butterfield v. Cowing, 112 N.Y. 486, 20 N.E. 369 (1889).

44. See McClane's Adm'x v. Shepherd's Ex'x, 21 N.J.Eq. 76; In re Rist's Estate, 192 Pa. 24, 43 A. 407.

§ 143

1. Restatement, Trusts, Second, § 220. Bogert, Trusts and Trustees (rev. 2d edit.), § 974.

Practice on Court Accountings

The practice upon trustees' accountings is so often governed by statute or court rules[2] that any general statement is difficult. The necessary parties are all those financially interested in the trust.[3] Where there are incompetents and unborn or unknown beneficiaries the court may appoint a guardian ad litem or such persons may be considered as represented by other parties of the same class.[4] Each party should be served with a copy of the petition or bill and given notice of the date and place at which the account will be brought up for consideration by the court. The account is filed with the court. In some states copies are required to be delivered to all parties, but in other jurisdictions it is sufficient to tender a copy for delivery on demand or to refer the parties to the copy filed in court. On the return day fixed in the account, when it is brought up for court approval, the beneficiaries are given the opportunity to object to any account item.[5]

If an objection is made by a party to an item in the account, the burden is on the trustee to justify it. The beneficiary does not have the burden of proving that the item should be disallowed.[6] A failure to object on the return day amounts to an approval of the account.[7] The trustee should present vouchers or receipts for all payments which he claims he has made,[8] but if satisfactory proof of the payment is made otherwise than by the presentation of a voucher, the claim may be allowed.[9] Where no voucher is presented and the charge seems questionable, the trustee may not be allowed the amount.[10] Obscurities and doubts in the account will be resolved against the trustee.[11] Some

2. For statutory details of the accounting procedures in the several states, see Bogert, Trusts and Trustees (rev. 2d edit.), §§ 965–968.

3. In the case of charitable trusts the Attorney General of the state is a necessary party.

4. Hale v. Hale, 146 Ill. 227, 33 N.E. 858; In re West's Estate, 231 Wis. 377, 284 N.W. 565 (1939).

5. Lycan v. Miller, 56 Mo.App. 79.

In re Mershon's Estate, 364 Pa. 549, 73 A.2d 686 (1950), an account showed that stock held by the trustee was worthless. The beneficiary was held to be charged with knowledge of what he could have discovered as to the reason for the stock becoming of no value, and to be prevented from claiming a breach of trust when he failed to object to the item in the account.

6. Mollohan v. Christy, 80 Ariz. 141, 294 P.2d 375 (1956); Bone v. Hayes, 154 Cal. 759, 99 P. 172; Chopelas v. Chopelas, 294 Mass. 327, 1 N.E.2d 374 (1936); Malcolmson v. Goodhue County Nat. Bank, 198 Minn. 562, 272 N.W. 157 (1936). But if the trustee submits evidence to back up his claims he may make out a prima facie case

and the burden of introducing evidence to rebut it may shift to the beneficiary. Conant v. Lansden, 341 Ill.App. 488, 94 N.E.2d 594 (1950), reversed in part on other grounds in 409 Ill. 149, 98 N.E.2d 773 (1951); In re Marlin's Estate, 140 Neb. 245, 299 N.W. 626 (1941).

7. Heinl v. French, 237 Iowa 232, 21 N.W.2d 591 (1946); In re First Account of Provident Tr. Co., 318 Pa. 529, 179 A. 86 (1935).

8. Smith v. Robinson, 83 N.J.Eq. 384, 90 A. 1063.

9. Brinkerhoff's Ex'rs v. Banta, 26 N.J.Eq. 157; In re United States Mortgage & Trust Co., 114 App.Div. 532, 100 N.Y.S. 12.

10. In re Quinn's Estate, 16 Misc. 651, 40 N.Y.S. 732.

11. Smith v. Robinson, 83 N.J.Eq. 384, 90 A. 1063; White v. Rankin, 18 App.Div. 293, 46 N.Y.S. 228, affirmed 162 N.Y. 622, 57 N.E. 1128; Landis v. Scott, 32 Pa. 495. And see In re McCabe's Estate, 87 Cal.App. 2d 430, 197 P.2d 35 (1948) (no books and no vouchers; expenditures claimed appeared excessive); Rugo v. Rugo, 325 Mass. 612, 91

statutes require that the securities owned by the trust be presented for inspection in court in connection with the accounting, and doubtless this may be ordered by the court without the aid of a statute.[12] The trustee is sometimes required to submit to examination under oath with respect to his acts during the period under review.

Some statutes or court rules prescribe rules as to the form and contents of the account.[13] It is customary to have separate schedules for income and principal on hand at the beginning of the period, for income and principal received during the accounting period, and for disbursements of income and principal.[14]

On the return day, after considering the objections and proof, and taking into consideration any report received from a master, auditor or other assistant to whom the matter has been referred, the court will take such action as is warranted by the evidence. It may approve or disapprove the account and the trustee's acts described in it in whole or in part, order the correction of the account, surcharge the trustee for breach of trust, direct payment of compensation earned since the last account, allow counsel fees for the preparation and submission of the account, and award costs in case of a contested proceeding. The approval of an account by the court to which it is presented prevents the beneficiaries from objecting later to the acts of the trustee which are fully and fairly stated in the account.[15] For example, if a trustee reports in his account that he has invested the trust fund in part in specified common stock that is not a lawful investment for his trust, but the beneficiary makes no objection to the investment when the matter is before the court, and the court approves the account, the investment will be validated and the beneficiary will not be allowed later to claim that the investment was a breach of trust.[16]

However, if in his account the trustee conceals or affirmatively misrepresents facts regarding his conduct, the approval of the account by the court will not grant him immunity from later action.[17] Thus

N.E.2d 826 (poor records kept and some destroyed).

12. See, for example, the accounting statutes in Kentucky and Ohio.

13. See, for example, the statutes in Dist. Col., Ga., Ind. and Ia. And see court rules in Md. and Mass.

14. Berlage v. Boyd, 206 Md. 521, 112 A.2d 461 (1955); In re Bailey's Trust, 241 Minn. 143, 62 N.W.2d 829 (1954).

15. Perry v. Perry, 339 Mass. 470, 160 N.E.2d 97 (1959); Shearman v. Cameron, 78 N.J.Eq. 532, 80 A. 545; Costello v. Costello, 209 N.Y. 252, 103 N.E. 148; In re Cooper's Estate, 39 Wn.2d 407, 235 P.2d 469 (1951). The statutes very often provide this result. Parties not served with notice of an accounting proceeding are not bound by an adjudication in it. In re Galli's Estate, 340 Pa. 561, 17 A.2d 899 (1941).

Usually the approval of an intermediate account has the same effect as approval of a final account. In re Genung's Estate, 161 Cal.App.2d 507, 326 P.2d 861 (1958); Roberts v. Michigan Trust Co., 273 Mich. 91, 262 N.W. 744 (1935); In re Pattison's Will, 190 Wis. 289, 207 N.W. 292 (1926). West's RCWash.A 11.106.080. But see, *contra*, Vincent v. Wener, 140 Kan. 599, 38 P.2d 687 (1934).

16. Harvard College v. Amory, 26 Mass. (9 Pick.) 446; Beam v. Patterson Safe Deposit & Tr. Co., 96 N.J.Eq. 141, 126 A. 25 (1924).

17. Henderson v. Segars, 28 Ala. 352; Wann v. Northwestern Tr. Co., 120 Minn. 493, 139 N.W. 1061.

where a trustee has purchased trust investments from himself, or a corporate trustee has bought them from an affiliated corporation, and the investment is stated in the account but not the identity of the seller to the trustee, and the court approves the account, there is no validation of the act of disloyalty by the trustee since that act was not disclosed in the account.[18] The decree of a court approving an account, like all court judgments and decrees, will be reopened by the court, on the application of an interested party, where it is shown that there was fraud, concealment, or mistake in the account or in the procuring of the court approval.[19]

In many states it is customary for corporate trustees to present to beneficiaries a written statement of the trust's receipts and disbursements at frequent intervals, perhaps every year or every six months. These reports are very brief, condensed outlines of the work of the trustee during the period and often merely copies of the records kept in the trust department. The practice is to request the beneficiaries to give express written approval of the accounts thus rendered, or to state that they will be considered approved if no objection is received within a limited period. Approvals by beneficiaries of full age and sound mind will relieve the trustee from liability for all acts fully described in these reports, if there was no misrepresentation or concealment or other unfair practice by the trustee.[20] These reports are often so condensed and abbreviated that it is doubtful whether they can be fully comprehended by the ordinary layman. It may be contended that a beneficiary who took no affirmative stand regarding them should not be regarded as approving them or the acts of the trustee set forth in them.[21]

On an accounting the trustee is charged with all principal and income received by him at the beginning of or during the accounting period, with all such property which he did not obtain but could have received if he had used ordinary diligence and care, and with all damages caused by his breaches of trust.[22] The trustee is credited with all sums expended by him from trust principal and income where the expenditure was lawful under the terms of the trust,[23] and with all allocations of receipts to the principal or income account when his acts

18. In re Cosgrove's Will, 236 Wis. 554, 295 N.W. 784, 132 A.L.R. 1514 (1941).

19. Beardsley v. Hall, 291 Mass. 411, 197 N.E. 35, 99 A.L.R. 1129 (1935); Richter v. Anderson, 56 Ohio App. 291, 10 N.E.2d 789 (1937).

20. Fleischmann v. Northwestern Nat. Bank & Trust Co., 194 Minn. 227, 260 N.W. 310 (1935); In re Kirby's Will, 90 N.Y.S.2d 324 (1949), modified on other grounds 93 N.Y.S.2d 898 (1949). See Westfall, 71 Harv.L.R. 40.

21. White v. Sherman, 168 Ill. 589, 48 N.E. 128. And see § 168, post. But see Harris Tr. & Sav. Bk. v. Wanner, 393 Ill.

598, 66 N.E.2d 867 (1946) (lack of objection held to prevent later complaint); In re Greenwalt's Estate, 343 Pa. 413, 21 A.2d 890 (1941) (remainderman who merely knew of statement made to life tenant and did not know of its contents held barred from objecting to investments).

22. Purdy v. Johnson, 174 Cal. 521, 163 P. 893; Farmers' Loan & Tr. Co. v. Pendleton, 179 N.Y. 486, 72 N.E. 508; In re Roach's Estate, 50 Or. 179, 92 P. 118.

23. United States v. Swope, 16 F.2d 215 (10th Cir.1926); Patterson v. Northern Trust Co., 286 Ill. 564, 122 N.E. 55.

were in compliance with the terms of the trust and the controlling legal rules. The latter includes disbursements for expenses of administration, for investment, and for paying the beneficiaries the amounts due them. What are proper debits and credits will be determined by the principles of law laid down in other sections of this work, for example, those dealing with receipts and payments, duties with regard to acquiring possession and protecting the trust property, expenses of the trust administration, contracts, torts, property ownership, sales, mortgages and leases.

The trustee has a lien to secure reimbursement for appropriate expenditures and this may be asserted at the time of the accounting settlement.[24]

 WESTLAW REFERENCES

Practice on Court Accountings
"trust accounting"   /s   "court rule"

find 272 nw 157

notice   /s   trust   /2   account***

COMPENSATION OF THE TRUSTEE [1]

§ 144. **A trustee is entitled to be compensated for his services, unless he has agreed to serve without charge.**

The amount of the compensation may be fixed by the trust instrument, or by agreement between the trustee and the settlor or beneficiaries.

The compensation of the trustee is covered by statute in many states, either by a provision that the trustee shall receive reasonable compensation or such compensation as the court may allow him, or by the establishment of a fee schedule.

If not controlled otherwise, the court will allow the trustee what it considers a reasonable sum for his services, taking into account the skill and diligence he has shown, the value and the nature of the trust property, and the results of his administration.

The trustee may lose his right to compensation by waiver of it. The court may reduce or deny compensation if the trustee has been guilty of a breach of trust.

Where there are co-trustees the total compensation due is divided among them in accordance with the value of the services each has performed.

24. Jones v. Dawson, 19 Ala. 672; King v. Cushman, 41 Ill. 31, 89 Am.Dec. 366; Feldman v. Preston, 194 Mich. 352, 160 N.W. 655; Matthews v. McPherson, 65 N.C. 189. In Bay Biscayne Co. v. Baile, 73 Fla. 1120, 75 So. 860, the trustee was given a lien on the trust property for costs, disbursements, and counsel fees in litigation in defense of the trust.

§ 144

1. Bogert, Trusts and Trustees (rev. 2d edit.), § 975; Restatement, Trusts, Second, §§ 242, 243.

Where there is a change in trustee personnel due to death or resignation, the court may award compensation to the retiring trustee and his successor on the basis of the work done by each.

Is a trustee entitled to compensation? Will chancery allow him compensation for his services in administering the trust?

It was the early rule in England that a trustee would be allowed no remuneration. In Robinson v. Pett [2] Lord Chancellor Talbot said: "It is an established rule that a trustee, executor, or administrator, shall have no allowance for his care and trouble; the reason of which seems to be, for that on these pretenses, if allowed, the trust estate might be loaded, and rendered of little value. Besides, the great difficulty there might be in settling and adjusting the quantum of such allowance, especially as one man's time may be more valuable than that of another; and there can be no hardship in this respect upon any trustee, who may choose whether he will accept the trust, or not." In England today a provision in the instrument for compensation will be respected, and the court may allow a trustee compensation.[3]

Some American courts of chancery were inclined, during the early history of the country, to follow the early English rule and to refuse compensation to trustees,[4] but the modern rule is to give the trustee reasonable compensation for his work.[5] In all American states the right to compensation is now established, either by rule of equity or by statute. A constructive trustee is usually entitled to no compensation, but may be awarded pay if he acted in good faith or greatly increased the value of the property.[6] It is not necessary, in order that a trustee obtain the right to compensation for his work, that there should be any stipulation to that effect in the trust instrument.[7] A trustee has a lien on the trust property for the amount due him for compensation for his services,[8] that is, he may retain possession of the property until he has been paid.

2. 3 P.Wms. 249, 251.

3. Re Thorley, [1891] 2 Ch. 613; Re Freeman, 37 Ch.D. 148; Trustee Act of 1925, § 42.

4. State v. Platt, 4 Har., Del., 154; Cook v. Gilmore, 133 Ill. 139, 24 N.E. 524; Miles v. Bacon, 4 J.J.Marsh., Ky., 457; Warbass v. Armstrong, 10 N.J.Eq. 263; Green v. Winter, 1 Johns.Ch., N.Y., 37, 7 Am.Dec. 475; Boyd v. Hawkins, 17 N.C. (2 Dev.Eq.) 195; Gilbert v. Sutliff, 3 Ohio St. 129. One argument for denying the trustee compensation was that a right to pay gave him conflicting interests and encouraged disloyalty. He would be tempted to operate the trust so as to magnify his fees instead of administering it solely with the interest of the beneficiary in mind.

5. Clark v. Platt, 30 Conn. 282; Compher v. Browning, 219 Ill. 429, 76 N.E. 678,

109 Am.St.Rep. 346; Devilbiss v. Bennett, 70 Md. 554, 17 A. 502; Rathbun v. Colton, 15 Mass.(Pick.) 471; Schwarz v. Wendell, Walk.Ch., Mich., 267; Olson v. Lamb, 56 Neb. 104, 76 N.W. 433, 71 Am.St.Rep. 670; Appeal of Heckert, 24 Pa. 482; Leach v. Cowan, 125 Tenn. 182, 140 S.W. 1070, Ann. Cas.1913C, 188. For a discussion of the abolition of the earlier rule and the reasons for such action, see Schriver v. Frommel, 183 Ky. 597, 210 S.W. 165.

6. See § 77, ante, and Hale v. Cox, 240 Ala. 622, 200 So. 772 (1941).

7. Bentley v. Shreve, 2 Md.Ch. 215; Sherrill v. Shuford, 41 N.C. (6 Ired.Eq.) 228.

8. Premier Steel Co. v. Yandes, 139 Ind. 307, 38 N.E. 849.

Compensation Fixed by Trust Instrument

The matter of compensation may be settled by express provisions in the trust instrument. If the settlor states that the trustee shall receive a certain amount for his services, the trustee will be deemed to have acquiesced in such provision if he accepts the trust.[9] In some states statutes provide that the trustee may renounce the compensation provided in the trust instrument and elect to take statutory commissions.[10] The trust instrument may prohibit any compensation.[11] If the settlor permits the trustee to fix his own compensation, his decision will be final unless extremely unreasonable.[12] Some courts have refused to increase the compensation of a trustee who had accepted a trust where the amount was set forth in the instrument,[13] but other courts have taken what seems a more reasonable attitude where there is proof of a serious, uncontemplated change in circumstances which makes it inequitable to hold the trustee to his agreement, since any other rule would keep an unwilling and probably inefficient trustee in office.[14]

A valid agreement inter vivos may, of course, be made between settlor and trustee with respect to the latter's compensation.[15] The trustee's compensation may likewise be fixed by contract between the trustee and the beneficiary.[16]

Corporate Trustee Fee Schedules

All large corporate trustees have fee schedules which they generally require settlors to accept unless a different fee is negotiated. While there are many variations with respect to particular types of property, for example, cash, securities, mortgages, common trust funds, and realty, the features usually found are a base charge plus an annual fee based on a percentage of the value of the trust principal, which is graduated from about two-thirds of 1% in the case of smaller trusts to lower percentage rates for large trusts, and often a distribution fee on the transfer of trust principal based on a percentage of the value of the property distributed. These schedules increasingly tend to place part

9. Biscoe v. State, 23 Ark. 592; In re Hanson's Estate, 159 Cal. 401, 114 P. 810; Jarrett v. Johnson, 216 Ill. 212, 74 N.E. 756; Thomas v. Thomas, 97 Miss. 697, 53 So. 630; Steinway v. Steinway, 197 N.Y. 522, 90 N.E. 1166; Southern Ry. Co. v. Glenn's Adm'r, 98 Va. 309, 36 S.E. 395.

10. See, for example, Mich.C.L.A. § 700.541. And see In re Andrus' Will, 4 Misc.2d 831, 158 N.Y.S.2d 536 (1956); In re Williams' Estate, 147 Wash. 381, 266 P. 137 (1928).

11. Wilson v. Biggama, 73 Wash. 444, 132 P. 43.

12. In re Bailey's Trust, 241 Minn. 143, 62 N.W.2d 829 (1954); In re Peabody's Estate, 218 Wis. 541, 260 N.W. 444 (1935).

13. In re Gifford's Estate, 139 N.J.Eq. 19, 48 A.2d 779 (1946); In re Loree's Estate, 24 N.J.Super. 604, 95 A.2d 435 (1953).

14. Kaiser v. Second Nat. Bank, 123 Conn. 248, 193 A. 761 (1937); Smith v. Stover, 262 Ill.App. 440.

15. In re Schell, 53 N.Y. 263.

16. Bowker v. Pierce, 130 Mass. 262; Ladd v. Pigott, 215 Mo. 361, 114 S.W. 984; Henry v. Hilliard, 157 N.C. 572, 73 S.E. 98. Where for thirteen years the beneficiaries have received statements showing the deduction of 10 per cent. commissions and have raised no objection, they will not be heard to object. American Colonization Soc. v. Latrobe, 132 Md. 524, 104 A. 120.

of the burden of annual commissions on trust principal.[17]

Control of Compensation by Court

In the absence of stipulation in the trust instrument, a binding contract between the parties, or statutory regulation, the amount of compensation is within the discretion of the court, whether it be the court of equity or, in the case of testamentary trusts in some states, the probate court.[18] The compensation is usually allowed at an accounting, at which time the trustee makes a request for an allowance for his work, which should be supported by proof of the value and type of property he has managed, the amount of time spent, the results of the administration and evidence as to special problems encountered.[19] The trustee should not deduct compensation in advance of court approval unless permitted to do so by statute.[20] While commissions for managing the trust so as to produce income will usually be allowed at the time of intermediate accountings, whether they are payable entirely from income or partly from income and partly from principal, it had often been the rule that principal commissions based on the safeguarding of the principal and maintenance of its value should not be allowed piecemeal but should be granted at the end of the trust when the results of the work of the trustee with respect to principal were known.[21]

In deciding what is reasonable compensation for a trustee the court will consider the amount of income and principal received and disbursed,[22] the pay customarily given agents or servants for similar work,[23] the success or failure of the work of the trustee,[24] any unusual skill which the trustee had and used,[25] the amount of risk and responsi-

---

17. For current schedules of typical fees set by corporate trustees, see Bogert, Trusts and Trustees (rev. 2d edit.), § 975 (with supplement).

18. Weiderhold v. Mathis, 204 Ill.App. 3; Taylor v. Denny, 118 Md. 124, 84 A. 369; White v. Ditson, 140 Mass. 351, 4 N.E. 606, 54 Am.Rep. 473; Appeal of Fidelity & Deposit Co. of Maryland, 172 Mich. 600, 138 N.W. 205; Marsh v. Marsh, 82 N.J.Eq. 176, 87 A. 91; Appeal of Heckert, 24 Pa. 482.

19. Robinson v. Tower, 95 Neb. 198, 145 N.W. 348; Lathrop v. Smalley's Ex'rs, 23 N.J.Eq. 192; Beard v. Beard, 140 N.Y. 260, 35 N.E. 488.

20. In re Mylin's Estate, 32 Pa.Super. 504. A withdrawal of compensation without order of court may constitute conversion. Robinson v. Tower, 95 Neb. 198, 145 N.W. 348.

By statute, in a number of states, a trustee is authorized to pay himself compensation and expenses without prior court approval. To this effect see Unif.Prob. Code § 7–205 (but their propriety and rea-

sonableness are subject to court review upon petition of a beneficiary). And see N.Y. SCPA § 2312 (corporate trustee entitled to reasonable commissions; subject to court review).

21. In re Williamson's Estate, 368 Pa. 343, 82 A.2d 49 (1951). By 20 Pa.S. § 7185, interim principal commissions may now be allowed. Colton's Estate, 11 Pa.D. & C.2d 538.

22. In re McLaughlin's Estate, 43 Cal. 2d 462, 274 P.2d 868 (1954); Waring v. Darnall, 10 Gill & J. 126.

23. In re Dorrance's Estate, 186 Pa. 64, 40 A. 149.

24. In re Patton's Estate, 170 Or. 186, 132 P.2d 402 (1942).

See 20 Pa.C.S.A. § 7185(a), where it is provided that the court "may take into account the market value of the trust at the time of the allowance".

25. In re Tuttle's Estate, 4 N.Y.2d 159, 173 N.Y.S.2d 279, 149 N.E.2d 715 (1958).

bility,[26] the time consumed,[27] the character of the work done (whether routine or of unusual difficulty),[28] and any other facts which prove the value of the trustee's services to the beneficiaries.

While the court may award the trustee a lump sum as compensation, it often bases its action on a percentage of the value of the property received and disbursed during the accounting period.[29]

The court has power to make extraordinary compensation allowances, but will not do so unless the trustee can prove that he has performed work beyond the ordinary duties of his office and has engaged in especially difficult work.[30]

Statutes—Reasonable Compensation

In many states statutes provide that the trustee is "entitled" to reasonable compensation, or that the court has the power to award reasonable remuneration, and no schedules of compensation are mentioned.[31] In other jurisdictions the statutes are silent but the court acts under its power to enforce and protect trusts.

Statutes Fixing Fee Schedules

In some states there are statutes fixing fee schedules which control where the settlor has made no provision on the subject.[32] The rates are generally graduated so that a higher percentage is charged on the smaller trusts. They customarily provide for annual income commissions, which in some cases are payable exclusively out of trust income but in others are divided between income and principal, or the court is given discretion to charge part of the commissions to trust principal.[33]

26. Burke's Appeal, 378 Pa. 616, 108 A.2d 58 (1954).

27. In re Peabody's Estate, 218 Wis. 541, 260 N.W. 444 (1935).

28. West Coast Hosp. Ass'n v. Florida Nat. Bank, 100 So.2d 807 (Fla.1958).

29. Marks v. Semple, 111 Ala. 637, 20 So. 791 (lump sum allowed); Abell v. Brady, 79 Md. 94, 28 A. 817 (5 per cent.); Berry v. Stigall, 125 Mo.App. 264, 102 S.W. 585 (5 per cent.); Babbitt v. Fidelity Trust Co., 72 N.J.Eq. 745, 66 A. 1076 (4 per cent.); Fisher v. Fisher, 170 N.C. 378, 87 S.E. 113 (5 per cent.); In re McKinney's Estate, 260 Pa. 123, 103 A. 590 (5 per cent.); Cobb v. Fant, 36 S.C. 1, 14 S.E. 959 (2½ per cent. for receiving and 2½ per cent. for paying over); Darling's Ex'r v. Cumming, 111 Va. 637, 69 S.E. 940 (5 per cent.).

30. Hardy v. Hardy, 222 Ark. 932, 263 S.W.2d 690 (1954); Baydrop v. Second Nat. Bank, 120 Conn. 322, 180 A. 469 (1935) (obliged to foreclose mortgage and bid in and manage property).

31. Under a statute of the first type (trustee "entitled"), the trustee may collect his compensation from the trust estate without prior court approval. See Unif. Prob.Code § 7–205 and the compensation statutes enacted in Illinois, Indiana, Louisiana and Rhode Island. And see N.Y. SCPA § 2312 (corporate trustee; subject to court review). Under the second type (allowance of reasonable compensation) the court awards compensation upon the trustee's application, usually on the trustee's accounting. See the compensation statutes enacted in California, Iowa, Kansas, Massachusetts and Pennsylvania, quoted in Bogert, Trusts and Trustees (rev. 2d edit.), § 975.

32. See Bogert, Trusts and Trustees (rev. 2d edit.), § 975, setting forth the statutes of Del., Ga., Haw., Ky., Md., N.J., N.Y., S.Car., Tenn., and Vt. (testamentary trustee).

33. See statutes of Del., N.H., N.Y., Ohio, Pa., and R.I. (as trustee determines). As shown in § 124, ante, originally all compensation was deducted from trust income, but in the Uniform Principal and Income Act, the Revised Uniform Act and in some other statutes there has been a

The statutes also sometimes give the trustee annual principal commissions, payable out of trust principal. The rates are based on a percentage of income and principal. There are also provisions for distribution commissions to be received when the trust principal is distributed, additional allowances for special work, and in some cases a rate is fixed for management of real estate or the collection of rents. A common income commission rate is 6% of income collected, with lower rates for trusts with substantial income. In a few states the legislature has given to trustees the same fees as awarded other named fiduciaries, for example, executors or guardians.[34]

Trustee's Waiver of Compensation

If the trustee has a right to compensation but voluntarily relinquishes his right, it may be held that he has "waived" his claim and may not thereafter secure from the court compensation for work done up to the time of the waiver. This may occur where the trustee pays trust income to the beneficiary without claiming any right to make a deduction for his work, or where on an accounting he asserts no right to pay and distributes the trust property accordingly.[35] "Where, through a long series of years, trustees voluntarily pay the net income from a trust fund to the beneficiary as the full net income thereon, it is a waiver by such trustees of their commissions." [36] "The statute allows commissions to executors and trustees; but they may waive them, if they wish, and, if there be any evidence of a waiver, their legal representatives are in no position to dispute it." [37] Where a trustee accounts and turns over the trust property without demanding commissions, even if he has not waived his claim, the Statute of Limitations begins to run on his right to collect compensation and may bar it.[38] An express waiver of commissions in the past is no bar to the recovery of present commissions.[39]

Power of Court to Reduce or Deny Compensation

The court has power to reduce the compensation of the trustee, or deny him all compensation, and it will exercise this power where the trustee has been guilty of a serious breach of trust.[40] This result can be explained on the theory that the court is adjusting the compensation to the results of the trustee's administration, that normal compensation is

strong tendency to permit part of the trustee's compensation to be charged to trust principal.

34. Ga., S.C., Tenn.

35. Barry v. Barry, 1 Md.Ch. 20; Ten Broeck v. Fidelity Trust & Safety Vault Co., 88 Ky. 242, 10 S.W. 798; Cook v. Stockwell, 206 N.Y. 481, 100 N.E. 131, Ann.Cas.1914B, 491. See Kinney v. Lindgren, 373 Ill. 415, 26 N.E.2d 471 (1940) (waiver in open court is binding).

36. Olcott v. Baldwin, 190 N.Y. 99, 109, 82 N.E. 748.

37. Cook v. Stockwell, 206 N.Y. 481, 484, 100 N.E. 131, Ann.Cas.1914B, 491.

38. Simmons v. Friday, 359 Mo. 812, 224 S.W.2d 90 (1949).

39. Denmead v. Denmead, 62 Md. 321.

40. Judge of Probate v. Jackson, 58 N.H. 458; Dufford's Ex'r v. Smith, 46 N.J. Eq. 216, 18 A. 1052; In re Welling's Estate, 51 App.Div. 355, 64 N.Y.S. 1025; In re Reich's Estate, 230 Pa. 55, 79 A. 151; Singleton v. Lowndes, 9 S.C. 465. See Bogert, Trusts and Trustees (rev. 2d edit.), § 980.

based on normal performance and that inferior work should receive something less. In addition it may be urged that the court is collecting damages from the trustee by denying him his usual pay. The court has discretion as to whether to employ this power and will not do so where the trustee acted under mistake or ignorance and the damage from the breach was slight,[41] but will be apt to forfeit the compensation in the case of an intentional breach of trust.[42]

Co-trustees

Two or more trustees are, in the absence of statute, entitled to one commission only. This commission should be divided between them in proportion to the amount of work done by each.[43] "It is, however, said they are joint trustees. Grant it, and how does it change the attitude of the parties? By becoming joint trustees, each, no doubt, became vested with a legal right to perform one-half of the labor with his entire skill, and, on performing one-half of the duties of the trust, as between him and his cotrustee, he would be entitled to one-half of the compensation. But where he performs but one-third of the duties, he can surely have no claim to more than one-third of the emoluments, unless conceded by the beneficiary as a gratuity; but he can, in justice, have no claim to the earnings of his cotrustee over and above the sum he has himself earned." [44] In New York provision is made for commissions to each of several trustees in cases of larger estates.[45]

Successor Trustees

Where two or more persons successively occupy the trusteeship, they should be compensated on a quantum meruit basis; each should be paid the reasonable value of his services during his term of office. "The practice of allowing a reasonable compensation to the estate of a deceased trustee, who dies before the completion of the trust, is well settled and sanctioned by authority." [46] The succeeding trustee receives compensation only for the work which he actually does.[47] Ordi-

41. In re Johnston's Estate, 129 N.J. Eq. 104, 18 A.2d 274 (1941); In re Blodgett's Estate, 261 App.Div. 878, 25 N.Y.2d 39; Appeal of Kilgore, Pa., 8 A. 441.

42. French v. Commercial Nat. Bank, 199 Ill. 213, 65 N.E. 252; Belknap v. Belknap, 5 Mass. (Allen) 468; McCulloch v. Tomkins, 62 N.J.Eq. 262, 49 A. 474.

43. In re McLaughlin's Estate, 43 Cal. 2d 462, 274 P.2d 868 (1954).

44. Huggins v. Rider, 77 Ill. 360, 364. And see Stevenson v. Moeller, 112 Conn. 491, 152 A. 889 (1931); Howard v. Hunt, 267 Mass. 185, 166 N.E. 568.

45. N.Y.—McKinney's SCPA 2308, 2309; N.Y.—McKinney's Civil Practice Law and Rules 8005, formerly N.Y. Civil Practice Act, § 1548a. If the estate equals or exceeds $200,000, each co-trustee re-

ceives a full annual commission if there are no more than three trustees. If there are four or more, three commissions are to be apportioned among the co-trustees on the basis of services rendered. N.Y.—McKinney's SCPA 2309.

For other statutes requiring apportionment, see Bogert, Trusts and Trustees (rev. 2d edit.), § 978.

46. Widener v. Fay, 51 Md. 273, 275.

See also In re Barker, 186 App.Div. 317, 174 N.Y.S. 230. But awarding compensation to the estate of the deceased trustee is discretionary with the court. In re Bushe, 227 N.Y. 85, 124 N.E. 154, 7 A.L.R. 1590 (1919).

47. In re Leavitt, 8 Cal.App. 756, 97 P. 916; Gibson's Case, 1 Bland, Md., 138, 17 Am.Dec. 257.

narily a trustee will not be compensated for the merely formal act of paying the trust funds over to a successor or receiving them from a predecessor.[48]

Compensation where Trustee is also Executor

It has been held that where the same person is named as executor and trustee, he is entitled to commissions in both capacities if he acted separately as to each fiduciary position [49] but not if the work was performed as a single function rather than two successive functions.[50] The question is sometimes decided by statute.[51] In New York and some other jurisdictions,[52] if the duties of the two offices are to be performed simultaneously and the work is inseparably blended, a single commission is allowed. The rule has been stated by the New York Court of Appeals as follows: [53] "Where by the terms of the will the two functions with their corresponding duties coexist and run from the death of the testator to the final discharge, interwoven, inseparable, and blended together so that no point of time is fixed or contemplated in the testamentary intention at which one function should end and the other begin, double commissions or compensation in both capacities cannot be properly allowed. But executors are entitled to commissions as executors and also as trustees where under the will their duties as executors and trustees are separable and their duties as executors having ended they take the estate as trustees and afterward act solely in that capacity."

It is frequently a difficult matter to determine just when the duties of the executorship have ended and those of the trusteeship begun. "In the absence of any direction in the will, or any evidence in relation thereto, the duties of the trustee named in the will, even though he be the person named therein as executor, would not begin until after the duties of the executor have terminated, . . . and until he commences to exercise his duties as trustee he is not entitled to compensation therefor." [54] The completion of the duties of the executorship may be shown in a variety of ways. "An accounting as executors and a

For a statute regarding compensation of a successor trustee, see N.Y.—McKinney's SCPA 1502(6).

48. Jenkins v. Whyte, 62 Md. 427; Young v. Barker, 141 App.Div. 801, 127 N.Y.S. 211.

49. Arnold v. Alden, 173 Ill. 229, 50 N.E. 704; In re Gloyd's Estate, 93 Iowa 303, 61 N.W. 975.

Hull v. Heimrich, 138 Or. 117, 3 P.2d 758 (1931); Tyler v. Reynolds, 120 W.Va. 232, 197 S.E. 735 (1938). See 44 Yale L.J. 523.

50. Judson v. Bennett, 233 Mo. 607, 136 S.W. 681.

51. By Pa. 20 P.S. 813 it had been provided that there should be a single com-

mission, but by a statute passed in 1945 double commissions were allowed. See 20 Pa.C.S.A. §§ 3274–3278. In re Williamson's Estate, 368 Pa. 343, 82 A.2d 49 (1951).

For current Pa.Law, see 20 Pa.C.S.A. §§ 3537 (executor) and 7185 (trustee).

52. In re Kelley's Estate, 91 Mont. 98, 5 P.2d 559 (1931); Parker v. Wright, 103 N.J.Eq. 535, 143 A. 870 (1928); In re Schliemann's Will, 259 N.Y. 497, 182 N.E. 153, 84 A.L.R. 662 (1932).

53. Chase, J., in Olcott v. Baldwin, 190 N.Y. 99, 105, 106, 82 N.E. 748.

54. Bemmerly v. Woodard, 136 Cal. 326, 331, 68 P. 1017.

transfer of the trust funds to the trustees pursuant to a decree of a court of competent jurisdiction is the most satisfactory proof of the completion of their duties in one capacity and the commencement of their duties in the other capacity; but such judicial decree is not the only means of proving that the transfer has actually been made." [55]

 WESTLAW REFERENCES

"english rule" /s trustee /s pay compensation

robinson +3 pett

di(trustee /4 compensation)

390k274(3)

390k330 /p compensation /5 trustee

Compensation Fixed by Trust Instrument

compensation /s trust /2 instrument

390k315 /p "trust instrument" /s compensation

390k316 /p "trust instrument" /s compensation

find 62 nw2d 829

Corporate Trustee Fee Schedules

corporate /3 trustee /6 fee /3 schedule

Control of Compensation by Court

court /s approv** /s trustee /3 compensation fee

trustee /3 fee compensation /s "lump sum"

trustee /3 fee compensation /s percentage

Statutes—Reasonable Compensation

statute /s trustee /s "reasonable compensation"

Statutes—Fixing Fee Schedules

statute /s trustee /s "fee schedule" commission

Trustee's Waiver of Compensation

trustee /s waive* /s compensation fee commission

Power of Court to Reduce or Deny Compensation

reduc! deny /4 compensation /5 trustee

390k315(2) /p "breach of trust"

390k321 /p "breach of trust"

Co-Trustees

find 274 p2d 868

Successor Trustees

successor /1 trustee /5 compensation

Compensation Where Trustee is Also Executor

find 50 ne 704

---

55. Olcott v. Baldwin, 190 N.Y. 99, 107, 82 N.E. 748. See also, Wylie v. Bushnell, 277 Ill. 484, 115 N.E. 618. Trustees may enter upon their duties before their final accounting as executors. In re McDowell, 178 App.Div. 243, 164 N.Y.S. 1024.

Chapter 17

ALTERATION OR TERMINATION
OF THE TRUST

Table of Sections

POWER OF TRUST PARTIES TO CHANGE THE TERMS OF A TRUST [1]

§ 145. Unless the trust instrument expressly provides for it, neither the settlor, trustee nor the beneficiaries can change the terms of the trust; but if competent beneficiaries consent to a change they may be barred from objecting to the execution of the trust as altered.

The settlor may reserve to himself, or create in another, the power to alter the provisions of the trust.

No Implied Power in Trust Parties to Modify

Once the trust instrument has been executed and delivered, its terms as to beneficiaries, investments, methods of administration, and all other matters are final, so far as they can be controlled by the trust parties, in the absence of any provision in the trust document for a change. There is no implied power to alter, nor does the law create any such power.[2] But, as later shown,[3] the court has the power to modify

---

§ 145

1. Bogert, Trusts and Trustees (rev. 2d edit.), §§ 992, 993; Restatement, Trusts, Second, §§ 331, 332, 367.

2. Childs v. Gross, 41 Cal.App.2d 680, 107 P.2d 424 (1940); Farwell v. Illinois

3. See note 3 on page 515.

the trust terms in some cases, and the settlor, trustee and beneficiaries may apply to the court for such action. Upon execution and delivery the trust transaction is a conveyance which is unchangeable by the trust parties.

It sometimes occurs that the *settlor* would like to remove one beneficiary and substitute another, or change the shares given to the various beneficiaries, or make new directions regarding investment policies, but he is unable to accomplish these results by his own efforts unless he retained such power in the trust instrument. These rules apply to charitable trusts as well as private trusts. Thus where land was given in trust for school purposes, the settlor cannot later add to the trust the restriction that the school should admit white children only.[4]

Nor is there any implied power in the *trustee* acting alone to modify the trust terms;[5] and the *beneficiaries* acting alone have no power to change the dispositive or administrative provisions,[6] although by disclaiming, surrendering or giving away their interests they can, of course, prevent the settlor's original intent from being achieved.[7] If the settlor, trustee, and all beneficiaries join in a modification, it would seem that thereafter no one can object to the execution of the changed trust,[8] but an agreement by the settlor and trustee will not be effective.[9]

If the settlor is the sole beneficiary, he should be allowed to alter the trust[10] even though he reserved no power to do so. If all the beneficiaries are competent and agree with the trustee on a change in the trust terms they will not be heard to complain of administration in accordance with the change,[11] although their consent may be withdrawn as to future transactions.[12] And if the beneficiaries acquiesce in

Merchants Trust Co., 264 Ill.App. 49; Bayless v. Wheller-Kelly-Hagny Tr. Co., 153 Kan. 81, 109 P.2d 108 (1941); Krause v. Jeannette Inv. Co., 333 Mo. 509, 62 S.W.2d 890 (1933); Werbelovsky v. Manufacturers Tr. Co., 12 A.D.2d 793, 209 N.Y.S.2d 564 (1961) (desire to increase benefits to one beneficiary because of his great need); Briggs v. Briggs, 162 Tex. 177, 346 S.W.2d 106 (1961).

"The party who makes a voluntary deed, whether of real or personal estate, without reserving a power to alter or revoke it, has no right to disturb it; and as against himself it is valid and binding, both in equity and at law." Stone v. King, 7 R.I. 358, 365.

3. See § 146, post.

4. Price v. School Directors, 58 Ill. 452.

5. Burling v. Newlands, 112 Cal. 476, 44 P. 810; Dahlgren v. Dahlgren, 55 App. D.C. 52, 1 F.2d 755 (1924).

6. Conant v. St. John, 233 Mass. 547, 124 N.E. 486 (1919). But an attempted amendment may be given effect as an as-

signment of a beneficiary's interest. Rappold v. Rappold, 224 Md. 131, 166 A.2d 897 (1961).

7. First Nat. Bank of Lincoln v. Cash, 220 Ala. 319, 125 So. 28 (1929); Simpkins v. Simpkins, 131 N.J.Eq. 227, 24 A.2d 821 (1942).

8. Burling v. Newlands, 112 Cal. 476, 44 P. 810; Sayers v. Baker, Tex.Civ.App., 171 S.W.2d 547 (1943).

For a statute authorizing such modification, see Wis.S.A. 701.12.

9. Green v. Gawne, 382 Ill. 363, 47 N.E.2d 86 (1943); Linder v. Nicholson Bank & Tr. Co., 170 S.C. 373, 170 S.E. 429 (1933).

10. Frentzel v. Siebrandt, 161 Neb. 505, 73 N.W.2d 652 (1955).

11. In re Newhouse's Estate, 29 Misc. 2d 1021, 212 N.Y.S.2d 2 (1960); Fry v. Stetson, 176 Pa.Super. 171, 106 A.2d 662 (1954).

12. In re Conner's Estate, 318 Pa. 145, 178 A. 12 (1935). And if a court is asked to

an attempt by the settlor to change the trust, they will not be allowed to question the validity of the alteration after the trustee has acted upon it.[13]

Power to Modify may be Reserved or Granted

The power to modify the trust may be, and frequently is, reserved to the settlor,[14] or vested in another person, for example, the trustee or one or more beneficiaries.[15] Such a power is frequently very desirable because of changes in financial situations and in relationships between the settlor and the beneficiaries, but the reservation of it to the settlor may subject him to income taxation on the trust income and his estate to inheritance or estate taxation on his death.[16]

A power to revoke, unless expressly or impliedly limited to changes short of destruction of the trust, includes a power to modify or amend the trust.[17] To hold otherwise would require a revocation first and then the creation of a new trust on the desired terms. And under a power to amend, an irrevocable trust may be made revocable [18] or a revocable trust made irrevocable.[19]

A power of alteration is not exhausted by a single use of it.[20] Provisions of the trust instrument regarding the method of execution of a reserved or granted power of alteration must be strictly obeyed.[21] The power may be relinquished by the holder of it, but not transferred.[22]

 WESTLAW REFERENCES

No Implied Power in Trust Parties to Modify
390k58

pass on the validity of the attempted change before it has been carried into effect, it will hold it invalid. In re Stanley's Will, 223 Wis. 345, 269 N.W. 550 (1936) (attempt to change trust to pay income from $50,000 to be invested to a trust to pay 6% on $50,000).

13. County Tr. Co. v. Young, 287 N.Y. 801, 40 N.E.2d 1019 (1942); Hurst v. Taubman, Okl., 275 P.2d 877 (1954).

14. Dingwell v. Seymour, 91 Cal.App. 483, 267 P. 327 (1928) (substitute other trust property); Helvering v. McIlvaine, 296 U.S. 488, 56 S.Ct. 332, 80 L.Ed. 345 (1936) (change a single trust into three trusts).

15. Olson v. Rossetter, 399 Ill. 232, 77 N.E.2d 652 (1948); Medwedeff v. Fisher, 179 Md. 192, 17 A.2d 141 (1941) (power in beneficiaries to extend life of trust). A power in trustees to change the beneficiaries does not include a power to make the settlor a beneficiary. Helvering v. Stuart, 317 U.S. 154, 63 S.Ct. 140, 87 L.Ed. 154 (1942).

16. As to federal and state tax effects, see Bogert, Trusts and Trustees (rev. 2d edit.), ch. 15.

17. Lit v. United States, 18 F.Supp. 435 (E.D.Pa.1937); Russell's Ex'rs v. Passmore, 127 Va. 475, 103 S.E. 652 (1920).

18. Stahler v. Sevinor, 324 Mass. 18, 84 N.E.2d 447 (1949).

19. Chicago Title & Tr. Co. v. Shellaberger, 399 Ill. 320, 77 N.E.2d 675 (1948).

20. Morton v. Commissioner, 109 F.2d 47 (7th Cir.1940); State Street Tr. Co. v. Crocker, 306 Mass. 257, 28 N.E.2d 5, 128 A.L.R. 1166 (1940).

21. Phelps v. State St. Tr. Co., 330 Mass. 511, 115 N.E.2d 382 (1953) (acknowledged writing required); In re Solomon's Estate, 332 Pa. 462, 2 A.2d 825 (1938) (power in two settlors held jointly and not exercisable by survivor).

22. Helvering v. Stuart, 317 U.S. 154, 63 S.Ct. 140, 87 L.Ed. 154 (1942).

```
implied  /1  power  /s  modif!  /s  trust
find 1 f2d 755
390k921  /2
find 166 a2d 897
```

Power to Modify May be Reserved or Granted

```
power  /2  modif!  /s  reserv***  /s  settlor trustor
390k58
power  /2  modif!  /s  trust  /s  grant***
power  /2  revoke  /s  trust
```

ALTERATION OF PRIVATE TRUSTS
BY THE COURT [1]

§ 146. The court of equity possesses the power to alter the administrative provisions of a private trust where, due to circumstances not known to the settlor or anticipated by him, or due to the unwisdom of the settlor's directions, a change is necessary or highly convenient to assure the accomplishment of the settlor's fundamental purposes. The court has no power to make other changes in administrative terms nor can it alter the respective beneficial interests of the beneficiaries or add new beneficiaries.

Sometimes a settlor gives instructions in the trust instrument with regard to the administration of the trust which turn out to be highly disadvantageous and to obstruct the trustee in carrying out the purposes which the settlor expressed. These difficulties are usually due to a change in conditions regarding the trust property or parties which have occurred since the trust was established and were not anticipated by the settlor.[2] In other instances they result from unwise and imprudent directions of the settlor as to methods of administration which he thought would be helpful but when put into practice proved an obstacle to the trustee in his efforts to secure for the beneficiaries the benefits which the settlor desired them to have.[3]

If the settlor or a trustee or beneficiary can prove to the court that such a situation exists, the court has power to allow the trustee to deviate from the administrative provisions laid down by the settlor, to ignore them, and to employ other methods in carrying out the trust.[4]

---

§ 146

1. Bogert, Trusts and Trustees (rev. 2d edit.), § 994; Restatement, Trusts, Second, §§ 166–167. See also Scott, 44 Harv.L.R. 1025; 28 Cal.L.R. 785; 35 Ill.B.J. 417.

2. Curtiss v. Brown, 29 Ill. 201; Hardy v. Bankers' Trust Co., 137 N.J.Eq. 352, 44 A.2d 839 (1945) (change in tax laws and in settlor's financial condition); Donnelly v. National Bank of Wash., 27 Wn.2d 622, 179 P.2d 333 (1947) (trust to educate grandson; his schooling interrupted by military service).

3. In re Fermer's Will, 177 Misc. 228, 30 N.Y.S.2d 248 (1941) (deposit funds in foreign bank); Industrial Trust Co. v. President and Fellows of Harvard College, 69 R.I. 317, 33 A.2d 167 (1943). And see Miller v. National Bank of Detroit, 325 Mich. 395, 38 N.W.2d 863 (1949) (mistaken view of settlor as to tax law).

4. Bolles v. Boatmen's Nat. Bk., 363 Mo. 949, 255 S.W.2d 725 (1953) (withholding of income to reimburse capital); United States Nat. Bk. v. First Nat. Bank, 172 Or. 683, 142 P.2d 785 (1943) (trustee to ignore provision regarding consultant).

The clauses of the instrument relating to the benefits to be conferred on the beneficiaries are primary and fundamental and are the principal concern of the court. The terms regarding methods and means of achieving these results are of secondary importance and equity will not permit them to interfere with the efforts of the trustee to bring to the beneficiaries the intended benefits.[5] Thus the settlor may have directed a sale of real estate, or the investment of the trust property in business, or may have prohibited leases by the trustee in excess of one year, or may have prohibited a mortgage by the trustee of the trust real estate, and a change in circumstances may have arisen which seriously handicaps the trustee in his administration if these provisions of the instrument must be followed. In such cases equity is ready to act and to direct a *deviation* from the settlor's directions to whatever extent is necessary to secure the results the settlor desired.[6]

The power to permit deviation will not be exercised merely to add to the convenience of the trustee, or to bring to the beneficiary more income than the settlor contemplated that he would obtain from the trust.[7]

Moreover, the court has no power to revise the settlor's conveyances or to enlarge or diminish his gifts. It cannot change the subject matter of the trust, or alter the shares of the beneficiaries, or add new beneficiaries to the list.[8] To do so would be to remake the deed or will of the settlor and to assume the power of distributing his property without his consent. Thus in a case where a trust to pay income to two daughters was insufficient to cover their living expenses and it was sought to secure the aid of equity in encroaching on the principal for the benefit of the life tenants, a California court said:[9] "A court of equity may modify a trust on a proper showing of changed conditions occurring after the creation of a trust if the rights of all beneficiaries are protected. . . . the order appealed from . . . provides for an

And see Hale v. Hale, 146 Ill. 227, 33 N.E. 858, 20 L.R.A. 247; Price v. Long, 87 N.J. Eq. 578, 101 A. 195; Cutter v. American Trust Co., 213 N.C. 686, 197 S.E. 542 (1938).

In many states statutes authorize the court to permit the trustee to deviate from trust terms. See, for example, West's Ann. Ind.Code 30–4–3–26; N.Y.—McKinney's EPTL 7–1.6, 11–1.1(c) (trustee powers). Other statutes authorize the court to modify a trust on a finding of impossibility or impracticality. See, for example, West's Ann.Ind.Code 30–4–3–28; La.R.S. 9:2026.

5. For a good statement of this theory, see Pennington v. Metropolitan Mus. of Art, 65 N.J.Eq. 11, 55 A. 468.

6. Illustrations of the operation of this power have previously been given in the sections on payments of trust income or principal, investments, sales, leases, and mortgages. See §§ 102, 110, 134, 137, and 139, ante; and see Hewitt v. Beattie, 106 Conn. 602, 138 A. 795 (1927) (direction to retain stone quarry; no market for stone); Marsh v. Reed, 184 Ill. 263, 56 N.E. 306 (prohibition of lease for longer than ten years disadvantageous).

7. Stanton v. Wells Fargo Bank & Union Tr. Co., 150 Cal.App.2d 763, 310 P.2d 1010 (1957); Porter v. Porter, 138 Me. 1, 20 A.2d 465 (1941). And see Johns v. Johns, 172 Ill. 472, 50 N.E. 337; First Methodist Episcopal Church of Ottumwa v. Hull, 225 Iowa 306, 280 N.W. 531 (1938).

8. Springfield Safe Dep. & Tr. Co. v. Friele, 304 Mass. 224, 23 N.E.2d 138 (1939); Stewart v. Hamilton, 151 Tenn. 396, 270 S.W. 79, 39 A.L.R. 37 (1925); In re Stanley's Will, 223 Wis. 345, 269 N.W. 550 (1936); In re Suhling's Will, 258 Wis. 215, 45 N.W.2d 608 (1951) (add a new beneficiary).

9. In re Van Deusen's Estate, 30 Cal. 2d 285, 182 P.2d 565 (1947).

invasion of the corpus of the trust contrary to the express provisions of the decree of distribution without any attempt to protect the interests of the residuary beneficiaries in that corpus . . .. To allow an invasion of the corpus without the consent of the residuary beneficiaries contrary to the provisions of the instrument is to take property from one without his consent and give it to another. . . . Sympathy for the needs of the respondents does not empower the court to deprive the residuary beneficiaries of their interests in the corpus of the trust without their consent."

Where all the beneficiaries are competent and request a change in the dispositive terms,[10] or where there has been litigation over a trust instrument and the parties request the court to approve a compromise agreement which would affect the interests of the beneficiaries,[11] the court has power to approve the desired change and sometimes does so.

Where it is proven that by mistake the trust instrument does not contain the terms intended by the settlor, the court may reform the instrument so that it will contain the terms the settlor and trustee actually agreed upon.[12] However reformation will not be granted where the mistake was as to the legal effect of the wording of the instrument.[13]

 WESTLAW REFERENCES

court equity chancery /s power /2 alter! change modif! /s trust
find 639 p2d 400
390k58 /p court equity chancery

POWER OF COURT TO ALTER CHARITABLE TRUSTS—CY PRES DOCTRINE [1]

§ 147. The court has power to change administrative provisions in charitable trusts where the settlor's directions hinder the trustee in accomplishing the trust purpose.

The court also has the power under the cy pres doctrine to order the trust funds to be applied to a charitable purpose different from that named by the settlor, where the settlor had an intent to benefit

10. Springfield Safe Dep. & Tr. Co. v. Stoop, 326 Mass. 363, 95 N.E.2d 161 (1950).

11. Gifford v. First Nat. Bank, 285 Mich. 58, 280 N.W. 108 (1938); In re O'Keeffe's Estate, 167 Misc. 148, 3 N.Y.S.2d 739 (1938); Reynolds v. Reynolds, 208 N.C. 578, 182 S.E. 341 (1935).

As to compromise settlements, see § 152, post.

12. Roos v. Roos, 42 Del.Ch. 40, 203 A.2d 140 (1964); Matter of Ikuta, 64 Hawaii 236, 639 P.2d 400 (1981). See West's Ann.Ind.Code 30–4–3–25. The evidence of mistake must be "clear, precise and convincing." In re Trust Estate of La Rocca, 411 Pa. 633, 192 A.2d 409 (1963).

13. Coolidge v. Loring, 235 Mass. 220, 126 N.E. 276 (1920); du Pont v. Southern National Bank of Houston, Texas, 771 F.2d 874 (5th Cir.1985), certiorari denied ___ U.S. ___, 106 S.Ct. 1467, 89 L.Ed.2d 723 (1986) (alleged mistake as to tax consequences of creating trust).

§ 147

1. Bogert, Trusts and Trustees (rev. 2d edit.), §§ 431–441; Restatement, Trusts, Second, §§ 381, 395–401.

charity generally and the accomplishment of the settlor's charitable purpose is or becomes impossible, impractical or inexpedient.

Changes in Administrative Provisions

The power of the court to strike out handicapping and obstructive administrative provisions is the same in the case of charitable trusts as with regard to private trusts. If a direction of the settlor as to method of operation of the charity is originally, or later becomes, highly disadvantageous to the accomplishment of the charitable objectives of the settlor, the court may and will direct the trustee to ignore the clause in question.[2] Examples are found in cases where the settlor directs that a charitable institution be set up in his residence and maintained there, and, due to changes in the neighborhood or the undesirable location of the home, the institution could much better be housed elsewhere. The court may order the real estate sold and the proceeds invested in a building at a more suitable location.[3] A further illustration may be found in the case where the founder of a home for retired clergymen directed that the wives of the residents should not be allowed to live with them in the home, and it was found that this provision greatly reduced the number of applicants for admission.[4] But this power does not include authority to change the testator's dispositive provisions.[5]

The Cy Pres Power

A much more important power, however, is one which is confined to charitable trusts, namely, the cy pres power. The original French phrase was "cy pres comme possible", meaning "as near as possible." Many American lawyers anglicize the word cy and pronounce it as if spelled "sigh," but do not anglicize pres but instead pronounce it as if spelled "pray". Others give a French pronunciation to the whole phrase as if it were spelled "see pray".

The courts have always been anxious to sustain and enforce charitable trusts and have given them very liberal and favorable construction in order to support their validity and to achieve the intended benefits to the public. Since such trusts are allowed to be perpetual, many are very ancient and often become obsolete or impossible or impracticable of execution due to changes in social, economic, political or other conditions. For example, a trust set up in 1790 to combat yellow fever in the United States may well be found of no value today,

---

2. Howard Savings Inst. v. Peep, 34 N.J. 494, 170 A.2d 39 (1961) (gift to Amherst College for loan fund to be limited to protestants and gentiles; charter of college prohibited discrimination; restriction to be ignored).

3. Gearhart v. Richardson, 109 Ohio St. 418, 142 N.E. 890 (1924).

4. Hamilton v. John C. Mercer Home, 228 Pa. 410, 77 A. 630.

5. Penick v. Bank of Wadesboro, 218 N.C. 686, 12 S.E.2d 253 (1940) (trustee had founded two charitable trusts; court could not transfer funds from one to the other charity).

due to the practical abolition of that disease in this country.[6] Also it is true that many settlors create charitable trusts which at the outset are unworkable due to the impracticality of the founders or their lack of foresight. These and similar reasons have led the courts to sanction the revision of charitable trusts to meet emergency conditions. No such remodeling of gifts would be possible in the case of a private trust.

Some courts explain the doctrine as being based on imputed or inferred intent of the settlor. "When the gift cannot be carried out in the precise mode prescribed by the donor, effect has been given to his general purpose by adopting a method which seemed to be as near his intention as existing conditions would permit. Such a construction is not the result of an arbitrary power exercised in disregard of the donor's wishes for the public benefit, but is as truly based upon a judicial finding of his intention as applied to new conditions as is the construction of a will, deed, or other written contract. The making of a gift for charitable purposes, which is unlimited as to the length of time it may continue, presupposes a knowledge on the part of the donor that material changes in the attending circumstances will occur which may render a literal compliance with the terms of the gift impracticable, if not impossible; and it is not unreasonable to infer that under such circumstances the nearest practicable approximation to his expressed wish in the management and development of the trust will promote his intention to make his charitable purpose reasonably effective; for it would be rash to infer that he intended that the trust fund should be used only in such a way that it could not result in a public benefit—in other words, that he wishes his general benevolent purpose to be defeated, if his method of administering the trust should become impracticable." [7]

Judicial and Prerogative Cy Pres

In England there are two kinds of cy pres power—the prerogative cy pres and the judicial cy pres. The former is based on the authority of the crown in England. As parens patriae the crown disposes of gifts made to charitable uses, where the purpose of the gift is unlawful, or where there is no intent indicated to have a trust and the gift is for charity in general or a particular charity. This power is exercised comparatively rarely. An illustration of the application of the prerogative cy pres is found in Cary v. Abbot,[8] where property was given to trustees "for the purpose of educating and bringing up poor children in the Roman Catholic faith." At the time of this gift it was unlawful in England because it was for the advancement of a religion other than the Church of England. The court held that the property involved was not to be given to the next of kin, but was to be applied to such charitable purposes as the king should direct. So, too, a gift to

---

6. Attorney General v. Earl of Craven, 21 Beav. 392 (pest house and burying ground for victims of the plague which had not occurred for 190 years).

7. Walker, J., in Keene v. Eastman, 75 N.H. 191, 193, 72 A. 213.

8. 7 Ves. 490.

establish readings of the Jewish law as an incident to that religion was applied by the prerogative cy pres power to providing a preacher of the Christian religion at a foundling home.[9] Obviously in the cases of religions held to be unlawful there was only a pretense of carrying out an object similar to that which the donor had desired. Since the toleration acts of the nineteenth century there has been little opportunity to apply prerogative cy pres to the case of a trust for an "illegal" religion.

The prerogative power has also been applied where the gift was to charity or to a particular type of charity without an expression of an intent to have a trust.[10]

It is generally held that the prerogative cy pres power does not exist in the United States. Neither national or state executives nor legislative persons or bodies possess it, nor can the courts exercise it.[11] The doctrine is founded on a monarchical system of government which is foreign to a republic. There is some discussion to the effect that the power rests in the legislatures,[12] but such a position seems of dubious soundness.[13] There has been no attempt to use the prerogative cy pres in the United States. Freedom in the choice of a religion removes any need for its use in that class of cases, and the lack of a trustee or expressed trust intent in the case of a gift to charity would normally not give rise to an occasion to employ the doctrine, since an implication of a trust intent would be usual and a trustee would be supplied.

In England the power of the court of chancery to alter charitable trusts has long been recognized, and in recent legislation the Charity Commissioners are granted such a power.[14] This is called the "judicial cy pres power" and is exercisable when a settlor has a broad, general charitable intent and his trust is or becomes impossible, inexpedient, or impracticable of fulfillment. The Charities Act, 1960,[15] gives an excellent analysis of the occasions for the application of cy pres which would probably appeal to most American courts as sound, but seems to enlarge the scope of the power somewhat in England.[16]

9. Da Costa v. De Pas, 1 Ambler 228.

10. Attorney General v. Syderfen, 1 Vern. 224; Kane v. Cosgrave, Ir.R., 10 Eq. 211.

11. Robbins v. Boulder County Com'rs, 50 Colo. 610, 115 P. 526; Kemmerer v. Kemmerer, 233 Ill. 327, 84 N.E. 256, 122 Am.St.Rep. 169; Erskine v. Whitehead, 84 Ind. 357; American Academy of Arts and Sciences v. President, etc., of Harvard College, 12 Gray, Mass., 582; In re Nilson's Estate, 81 Neb. 809, 116 N.W. 971; Reagh v. Dickey, 183 Wash. 564, 48 P.2d 941 (1935).

12. Mr. Justice Bradley, in Late Corporation of the Church of Jesus Christ of Latter-Day Saints v. United States, 136 U.S. 1, 51, 52, 56, 57, 10 S.Ct. 792, 34 L.Ed. 481 (1890).

13. See Opinion of the Justices, 101 N.H. 531, 133 A.2d 792 (1957); Puget Sound Nat. Bank v. Easterday, 56 Wn.2d 937, 354 P.2d 24 (1960).

14. Trustees of London Parochial Charities v. Attorney General, (1959) 1A. Eng. R. 1. 8 & 9 Eliz. 2, ch. 58.

15. 8 & 9 Eliz. 2, ch. 58.

16. Fulfillment or impossibility of fulfillment; trust property excessive; trust property can be advantageously combined with property of another charity; area or class ceased to exist or be suitable; original purposes covered by other means or have ceased to be charitable or have ceased to provide effective method of using the property.

In the United States judicial cy pres power has been very generally recognized and applied,[17] and is stated in statutory form in several states.[18] Although at one time the doctrine was rejected in some states (possibly because of its assumed connection with a monarchy and with arbitrary power),[19] this attitude has been changed by judicial or legislative action in some of these jurisdictions,[20] and the absence of the cy pres power has sometimes led the courts to apply a doctrine of liberal construction or "approximation" which has reached results similar to those which would have been produced by cy pres.[21]

Application of the Cy Pres Power

The cy pres doctrine is not used to turn a defective charitable trust into an effective one, as where a testator leaves money to print and circulate his writings on the theory that they will be of benefit to the public and the court finds that they are of no value and hence the trust is not charitable. If the trust had no other objects it will be held invalid and the property will not be applied to distribute other literature which will be of public benefit.[22]

A prerequisite to the use of cy pres is a finding that the settlor had a broad or general intent to aid charity as a whole, or some particular class of charitable objects, in the way chosen by him or in some other way. His intent must not have been narrow and particular. He must not have been concerned with one specific objective and a single method and nothing else. He must have intended that there should be some discretion in applying his gift to the public good. For example, if a donor provides a fund to construct a church of a particular denomination in the town where he was born, out of sentimental attachment to his birthplace and to the religion in which he believes, and the town has dwindled to a very small population and there are no followers of

17. In re Royer's Estate, 123 Cal. 614, 56 P. 461, 44 L.R.A. 364; Lewis v. Gaillard, 61 Fla. 819, 56 So. 281; Heuser v. Harris, 42 Ill. 425; Troutman v. De Boissiere Odd Fellows' Orphans' Home & Industrial School Ass'n, Kan., 64 P. 33, 5 L.R.A.,N.S., 692; Norris v. Loomis, 215 Mass. 344, 102 N.E. 419; Catron v. Scarritt Collegiate Institute, 264 Mo. 713, 175 S.W. 571; Nichols v. Newark Hospital, 71 N.J.Eq. 130, 63 A. 621; Utica Trust & Deposit Co. v. Thomson, 87 Misc. 31, 149 N.Y.S. 392; In re Kramph's Estate, 228 Pa. 455, 77 A. 814; Inglish v. Johnson, 42 Tex.Civ.App. 118, 95 S.W. 558.

The Supreme Court of Wisconsin has made it clear that judicial cy pres is in effect in Wisconsin. See In re Bletsch's Estate, 25 Wis.2d 40, 130 N.W.2d 275 (1964).

18. See, for example, Offic. Code of Ga. Ann. 53–12–77; La.R.S. 9:2331; Md. ET Law § 14–302; N.Y.—McKinney's EPTL 8–1.1(c); N.C.Gen.Stats. § 36A–53; 20 Pa. C.S.A. § 6110. For other statutes, see Bogert, Trusts and Trustees (rev. 2d edit.), § 433.

19. For example, Ala., Ariz., Del., D.C., Ky., N.C., S.C. and Tenn.; see Bogert, Trusts and Trustees (rev. 2d edit.), § 433.

20. See, for example, In re Bletsch's Estate, 25 Wis.2d 40, 130 N.W.2d 275 (1964); Va.Code § 55–31. And see other statutes and cases cited in Bogert, Trusts and Trustees (rev. 2d edit.), § 433.

21. See, for example, Mars v. Gilbert, 93 S.C. 455, 77 S.E. 131. And see S.Dak. Codif.L. 55–9–3.

For a decision applying the doctrine of equitable approximation under Virginia law, see Smith v. Moore, 343 F.2d 594 (4th Cir.1965) (fund insufficient to construct and operate a hospital was to be used to construct a new clinic as part of an existing hospital).

22. Wilber v. Owens, 2 N.J. 167, 65 A.2d 843 (1949).

his religion in the village, it may be held that his intent was narrow and local, and that he was concerned with the fostering of a particular religion in one town only and not with giving help to that religion or to religion in general in other localities, and hence that the fund should not be applied to aid the same religion in neighboring communities.[23] And where a gift was made to a town to aid it in constructing a home for the poor of the town, and the town refused the gift and the fund was wholly inadequate to build such a home, it has been held that the intent was to achieve one particular object, and that alone and by a single method, and when that became impossible, due to the refusal of the town to cooperate, the gift should not be applied to furnish food, shelter, or other necessaries to the poor of the town in other ways.[24]

If the settlor provides that the gift is to be used for the named charity and not otherwise,[25] or makes a gift over to another in case the charitable gift fails for any reason,[26] the court may readily find the intent narrow and refuse to apply cy pres. On the other hand if the testator expressly provided for cy pres if his charitable gift should be ineffective,[27] or gave his whole estate to various charities,[28] or did not provide a gift over in case the charitable gift failed,[29] the court may be induced to find the intent general and broad and to apply cy pres. The so-called community trusts established in many large cities give power to the managers to vary the original purposes of any gift when circumstances make a change expedient. This is an express grant of cy pres powers to the trustees which is effective.

If cy pres is not applied, either because the doctrine is not used in the state, or because the settlor had a narrow charitable intent, and the trust fails, there is a resulting trust for the settlor or his successors,[30] if the transfer in trust was gratuitous, or if the trustees paid consideration for the transfer to them they are allowed to retain the property on failure of the trust.[31]

The emergency which justifies the court in applying cy pres may be impossibility or impracticality or inexpediency. Thus where a trust

23. Teele v. Bishop of Derry, 168 Mass. 341, 47 N.E. 422, 38 L.R.A. 629.

24. 200 Mass. 269, 86 N.E. 351, 128 Am.St.Rep. 419. Similarly, a gift to use a farm for aiding needy unmarried women formerly employed in the straw industry indicated a specific and not a general charitable intent, and, the trust as planned being impracticable, cy pres could not be applied. Gilman v. Burnett, 116 Me. 382, 102 A. 108, L.R.A.1918A, 794.

25. Hampton v. O'Rear, 309 Ky. 1, 215 S.W.2d 539 (1948).

26. In re Fletcher, 280 N.Y. 86, 19 N.E.2d 794 (1939). But a general residuary clause, even in favor of charity, does not show an intent to exclude the use of cy pres. Attorney General v. Briggs, 164 Mass. 561, 42 N.E. 118.

27. Gardner v. Sisson, 49 R.I. 504, 144 A. 669 (1929).

28. Union Methodist Episcopal Church v. Equitable Tr. Co., 32 Del.Ch. 197, 83 A.2d 111 (1951); In re Stouffer's Trust, 188 Or. 218, 215 P.2d 374 (1950).

29. Worcester County Tr. Co. v. Grand Knight, 325 Mass. 748, 92 N.E.2d 579 (1950).

30. Waterbury Trust Co. v. Porter, 131 Conn. 206, 38 A.2d 598 (1944); Shannep v. Strong, 160 Kan. 206, 160 P.2d 683 (1945).

31. Trustees of M.E. Church v. Trustees of Jackson Square Evan. Luth. Church, 84 Md. 173, 35 A. 8.

was established to aid church members in securing admission to certain homes for the aged, and it appeared that there were no present or probable future vacancies in those homes, cy pres may be used.[32] There is also impossibility when the fund given to found and maintain a hospital is inadequate.[33] There is impracticality or inexpediency when at the time of the establishment of the charity its objects have already been achieved by other means,[34] as where property is given to construct a monument at a given location and when the gift became effective a monument of like purpose had already been built in that location.[35] If the trust fund proves to be excessively large, the surplus may be applied cy pres,[36] as where there is a subscription to aid the sufferers from a flood or other disaster and after all have been cared for a balance remains on hand.[37]

The cy pres doctrine is applied by equity to absolute gifts to charitable corporations or unincorporated associations, as well as to trusts for charity. Thus if a gift is made to a named home for the blind in a certain city, but at the time the will goes into effect there is no such institution there or in the neighborhood called by the name used, the court may apply the funds to aid other institutions intended to relieve and help blind persons.[38] And if an absolute gift to a charitable corporation fails because the institution has ceased to exist when the gift is supposed to take effect, the courts often use the cy pres power and in one way or another apply the property to accomplish the purposes of the extinct corporation or similar objectives.[39]

The meaning of the cy pres rule can best be explained by illustrations of its application. In the leading case of Jackson v. Phillips,[40] a testator provided for two trusts, the first to create a sentiment which would put an end to slavery, and the second for the aid of fugitive slaves. Shortly after the death of the testator slavery was abolished by the emancipation proclamation and a subsequent constitutional amendment, so that there was no need to agitate for the abolition of slavery and there were no fugitive slaves to be given help. The court held that the donor had in mind the broad purpose of aiding the Negro race, that the changed conditions warranted the court in applying the funds to purposes similar to those selected by the testator, and that the best substituted objects which had been suggested were the application of

---

32. Union M.E. Ch. v. Equitable Trust Co., 32 Del.Ch. 197, 83 A.2d 111 (1951).

33. In re Williams' Estate, 353 Pa. 638, 46 A.2d 237 (1946).

34. Jackson v. Phillips, 14 Allen 539 (trust to agitate for abolition of slavery; slaves emancipated); In re Neher's Estate, 279 N.Y. 370, 18 N.E.2d 625 (1939) (trust for village hospital; existing hospital adequate).

35. Society of California Pioneers v. McElroy, 63 Cal.App.2d 332, 146 P.2d 962 (1944).

36. Quinn v. Peoples Trust & Sav. Co., 223 Ind. 317, 60 N.E.2d 281 (1945) (trust for one scholarship; fund excessive).

37. Kerner v. Thompson, 293 Ill.App. 454, 13 N.E.2d 110 (1938).

38. Goree v. Georgia Industrial Home, 187 Ga. 368, 200 S.E. 684 (1938); New York City Mission Soc. v. Board of Pensions of Presbyterian Church, 261 App.Div. 823, 24 N.Y.S.2d 395 (1941).

39. Kentucky Children's Home v. Woods, 289 Ky. 20, 157 S.W.2d 473 (1941).

40. 14 Allen, Mass., 539.

the first trust fund to the education of freedmen in the South and the use of the second fund in aiding needy Negroes in the city where the testator had resided, giving preference to those who had formerly escaped from slavery. So too, in Ely v. Attorney General,[41] where the trust was for the founding of a home for deaf children to be located on the testator's land, but due to the inadequacy of the fund the exact intent of the testator could not be carried out, the court allowed the fund to be applied in assistance to a similar home already established a few miles distant from the testator's former residence.

Procedure in Applying Cy Pres

The cy pres power rests entirely with the court of equity and never in the trustees, unless expressly given to them by the donor. The trustees may not of their own volition apply the funds, except according to the terms of the trust, even though it seems to them obviously desirable.[42] The trustees may and should apply to the court for cy pres instructions when they think that an occasion for the use of the doctrine exists.

In order to bring cy pres into action a suit should be begun by the trustees, making the Attorney General of the state a party, as the representative of the people of the state, or the Attorney General should institute the suit. The court, if it finds conditions appropriate for the use of cy pres, may refer the matter to a master to take evidence, receive suggestions as to new plans, and recommend a substitute scheme for the charity, in which case the report of the master will be the basis for action by the court.[43]

The court has wide discretion in the framing of a "scheme" for the application of the charitable fund to a purpose as nearly like that of the donor as possible.[44] If the trust as drawn by the settlor was intended to aid the residents of a certain area, the substituted use will generally be confined to the same region;[45] and if the original trust was aimed at advancing one particular type of charity (for example, education), the court will probably apply the fund cy pres for the same kind of social benefit,[46] although it occasionally shifts to another type of charity.[47] If the settlor created several charitable trusts in his will, and one failed, often its property is distributed to the trusts for the other charities named by the testator.[48] If the occasion for using cy pres is that the institution to which the settlor made a gift has been dissolved, a common method of disposition is to award the property to another

41. 202 Mass. 545, 89 N.E. 166.

42. Lakatong Lodge, No. 114, of Quakertown, etc. v. Board of Education of Franklin Tp., 84 N.J.Eq. 112, 92 A. 870.

43. Bruce v. Maxwell, 311 Ill. 479, 143 N.E. 82 (1924); Jackson v. Phillips, 14 Allen, Mass., 539.

44. See Bogert, Trusts and Trustees (rev. 2d edit.), § 442.

45. In re Lawless' Will, 194 Misc. 844, 87 N.Y.S.2d 386 (1949).

46. Ford v. Thomas, 111 Ga. 493, 36 S.E. 841. Board of Education v. Rockford, 372 Ill. 442, 24 N.E.2d 366 (1939).

47. In re Campden Charities, 18 Ch.D. 310.

48. Miller v. Mercantile–Safe Dep. & Tr. Co., 224 Md. 380, 168 A.2d 184 (1961).

institution of a similar nature.[49]

 WESTLAW REFERENCES

Changes in Administrative Provisions
find 170 a2d 39
75k7 /p "cy pres"
75k37(1) /p "cy pres"
75k37(6) /p "cy pres"
75k37(8) /p "cy pres"
390k58 /p "charitable trust"

The Cy Pres Power
di cy pres
"cy pres comme possible"
75k37(1) /p "cy pres"
"cy pres power"
doctrine /s "cy pres"

Judicial and Prerogative Cy Pres
judicial /s "cy pres"
england /s "cy pres"
prerogative /s "cy pres"
find 343 f2d 594
75k37

Application of the Cy Pres Power
"cy pres" /s apply application
75k37 /p "cy pres" /s apply application
find 19 ne2d 794

Procedure in Applying Cy Pres
find 168 a2d 184
75k37 /p application apply /s "cy pres"

Power to Revoke or Terminate a Trust
power /2 revoke terminate /s trust
390k59(4)
390k25(3)
viney +3 abbott
find 2 a2d 825

POWER TO REVOKE OR TERMINATE A TRUST [1]

§ 148.   The settlor has no power to revoke the trust and secure the return of the trust property to him, whether the trust was created voluntarily or for consideration, unless he expressly reserved such a power, except where the settlor is also the sole beneficiary.

If the settlor directed that a power of revocation be inserted, but this was not done due to mistake or fraud on the part of the person

---

49. In re Women's Homeopathic Hospital of Phila., 393 Pa. 313, 142 A.2d 292 (1958).

§ 148

1. Bogert, Trusts and Trustees (rev. 2d edit.), §§ 998–1001; Restatement, Trusts, Second, §§ 330, 332, 367.

preparing the instrument for the settlor, he may have the instrument reformed to include the intended power of revocation. However, a mistake as to the law with regard to the necessity of inserting a power of revocation is of no effect.

In a few states by statute voluntary trusts are revocable, unless expressly made irrevocable, or are made revocable on the written consent of all beneficiaries.

The settlor may reserve to himself alone, or to himself jointly with others, or may grant to a third person, the power to revoke or terminate the trust. Such a power is personal and not transferable, but may be relinquished. It must be exercised in accordance with its terms.

The creation of a trust amounts to a conveyance of the settlor's property, usually by way of gift, and it may not be set aside or revoked at the option of the settlor because of a change of mind on his part, dissatisfaction with the operation of the trust, or for other reason, where the trust instrument made no provision for such revocation or resumption of ownership by the settlor.[2] Once the donor has transferred the equitable ownership to the beneficiaries, they are the unqualified owners of the trust property unless the trust document or oral statement of the trust retained control in the transferor. The power to rescind the act of trust creation because it was procured by fraud or other invalidating cause, or because of the incapacity of the settlor, has been discussed previously and has no relation to revocation.[3]

Thus if the settlor provided no power of revocation, the fact that he created a trust for his wife and later became estranged from her, or set up a trust for his children at a time when he was wealthy and later fell into financial reverses and hence needed the trust property for his own uses, does not give him opportunity to take it back and consider the trust at an end. There is no implied or law-given power of revocation.[4]

The case of Viney v. Abbott [5] is a good illustration of this rule. There Viney had transferred personal property to a trustee, to be held for the support of Viney during his life, and after his death for the benefit of certain relatives. No power of revocation was expressed in the instrument. Only a week after the creation of this trust Viney married, and sought to destroy the trust and retake the property. The court said: "It is immaterial whether there was any other consideration

2. Gray v. Union Trust Co. of San Francisco, 171 Cal. 637, 154 P. 306; Lovett v. Farnham, 169 Mass. 1, 47 N.E. 246; New Jersey Title Guarantee & Trust Co. v. Parker, 84 N.J.Eq. 351, 93 A. 196; Hammerstein v. Equitable Trust Co. of New York, 156 App.Div. 644, 141 N.Y.S. 1065; Fishblate v. Fishblate, 238 Pa. 450, 86 A. 469.

3. See § 9, ante.

4. Stipe v. First Nat. Bank, 208 Or. 251, 301 P.2d 175 (1956); Lamb v. First

Huntington Nat. Bank, 122 W.Va. 88, 7 S.E.2d 441 (1940). Some statutes provide that all trusts are irrevocable unless expressly made revocable. See, for example, Offic. Code of Ga.Ann. 53–12–3; Mont.C.A. 72–23–502. An exception exists in the case of the Totten or savings account trusts, where a power to revoke is generally implied. See § 20, ante.

5. 109 Mass. 300.

than appears upon the face of the indenture; for, even if the settlement was purely voluntary, the case falls within the doctrine, now well established in equity, that a voluntary settlement, completely executed, without any circumstances tending to show mental incapacity, mistake, fraud, or undue influence, is binding and will be enforced against the settlor and his representatives, and cannot be revoked, except so far as a power of revocation has been reserved in the deed of settlement, and that the fact that by the terms of the deed the income of the property is to be applied by the trustee to the benefit of the settlor during his lifetime does not impair the validity or effect of the further trusts declared in the instrument." [6]

One exception to this rule is found in the case where the settlor makes himself the sole beneficiary.[7] There he is allowed to change his mind as to how he will enjoy his property and to demand a return of the property from the trustee. Cases of this type are not uncommon, where the income is to be paid to the settlor for life and the principal distributed at his death to his appointees by will, or in default of appointment, to his heirs or next of kin.[8] Here, under the doctrine of "worthier title", the settlor is often held to be the sole beneficiary and his successors to have been intended to take by operation of the appointment or the law of intestacy, rather than by the trust instrument. In these cases courts often decree that the settlor may revoke, or the courts direct the termination of the trust on the request of the settlor-sole beneficiary.[9]

Under well known principles of equity with respect to granting relief where action has been taken under a mistake of fact or fraud, if the settlor directs his draftsman to insert in the trust instrument a power of revocation, but due to carelessness of the lawyer or stenographer, or due to intentional refusal by them to follow the instruction, the clause is omitted from the instrument, and the settlor signs it thinking that his orders have been obeyed, equity will decree a reformation of the instrument to include the omitted power.[10] But a mistaken belief as to the law of the state will not justify this relief, as where the settlor does not direct the inclusion of such a power because he erroneously thinks that the law implies such an authority and that the express insertion of it in the instrument is unnecessary.[11]

6. Gray, J., in Viney v. Abbott, 109 Mass. 300, 302, 303. For similar views see Kraft v. Neuffer, 202 Pa. 558, 52 A. 100. And see Harshaw v. McCombs, 63 N.C. 75, where a father created a trust for his only son who was sixteen, for the purpose of giving the son the income until he was of age and then having the principal transferred to him, with a gift to other relatives in case of the son's death, and the son shortly thereafter committed suicide. It was held there was no power of revocation.

7. Ampere Bank & Tr. Co. v. Esterly, 139 N.J.Eq. 33, 49 A.2d 769 (1946); Sack v. Chemical Bank & Tr. Co., 54 N.Y.S.2d 19 (1945); Wade v. McKeown, 193 Okl. 415, 145 P.2d 951 (1943).

8. In re Jackson's Estate, 351 Pa. 89, 40 A.2d 393 (1945).

9. Bixby v. California Tr. Co., 33 Cal. 2d 495, 202 P.2d 1018 (1949).

10. Garnsey v. Mundy, 24 N.J.Eq. 243; Bristor v. Tasker, 135 Pa. 110, 19 A. 851, 20 Am.St.Rep. 853.

11. Liberty Trust Co. v. Weber, 200 Md. 491, 90 A.2d 194 (1952); Coolidge v. Loring, 235 Mass. 220, 126 N.E. 276 (1920);

In a few decisions it has been held that the omission of a power of revocation in a voluntary trust is some evidence of a mistake of fact on the part of the settlor, since the inclusion of a power to revoke or terminate the trust in such a case is so common and so prudent.[12] But most courts do not regard this fact as creating any presumption of mistake.[13]

The fact that the trustee agrees with the settlor that the trust may be revoked,[14] or returns the trust property to him at his request,[15] does not show a revocation of the trust where no power to revoke had been reserved.

In recent years there has been a tendency in a few states to make all voluntary trusts revocable by the settlor, unless he expressly made them irrevocable, thus exactly reversing the common law.[16]

In New York voluntary trusts of both realty and personalty have been made revocable by the settlor, upon the written consent of "all persons beneficially interested",[17] and much litigation [18] has resulted concerning the meaning of the quoted phrase where the settlor was the life beneficiary and at his death the property was given to appointees or successors by intestacy. The problem was whether the appointees or next of kin or heirs were intended to take as remaindermen under the trust or the entire equitable interest was vested in the life tenant and his successors were to take from him. The controversy has been limited as to trusts which became operative on or after Sept. 1, 1951, by an amendment which declared that the heirs, next of kin, and distributees in this situation are not "beneficially interested".[19]

A power of revocation in the settlor alone,[20] or in him and others,[21]

Simon v. Reilly, 126 N.J.Eq. 546, 10 A.2d 474 (1940).

12. Aylsworth v. Whitcomb, 12 R.I. 298; but see Wallace v. Industrial Trust Co., 29 R.I. 550, 73 A. 25.

13. Patterson v. Johnson, 113 Ill. 559; Riddle v. Cutter, 49 Iowa 547; Rogers v. Rogers, 97 Md. 573, 55 A. 450; Sands v. Old Colony Trust Co., 195 Mass. 575, 81 N.E. 300, 12 Ann.Cas. 837; In re Curry, 390 Pa. 105, 134 A.2d 497 (1957); Findorff v. Findorff, 3 Wis.2d 215, 88 N.W.2d 327 (1958).

However, the absence of a power of revocation, coupled with facts as to the voluntary nature of the transaction and its improvidence, may be sufficient to make out a case of undue influence or other invalidating cause. Fidelity Union Trust Co. v. Parfner, 135 N.J.Eq. 133, 37 A.2d 675 (1944).

14. Colbo v. Buyer, 235 Ind. 518, 134 N.E.2d 45 (1956).

15. Hinton's Ex'r v. Hinton's Com., 256 Ky. 345, 76 S.W.2d 8 (1934).

16. West's Ann.Cal.Civ.Code § 2280 (applicable to voluntary trusts created after August 13, 1931); In re O'Brien's Trust Estate, 197 Okl. 436, 172 P.2d 607 (1946) (construing 60 Okl.S.A. § 175.41); V.Tex. C.A., Prop.Code § 112.051. N.C.—G.S. § 39–6 permits the revocation of a voluntary trust in so far as the interests of unborn persons are concerned. See 8 N.C.L.R. 92.

17. N.Y.—McKinney's EPTL 7–1.9. There is similar legislation in Okl. and Wis.; see 60 Okl.St.Ann. § 175.41, Wis.S.A. 701.12 (settlor and all beneficiaries may terminate).

18. For comments on the construction of the New York statutes, see 46 Col.L.R. 328; 60 Harv.L.R. 475; Payne, 9 St. Johns L.R. 24; Merrell, 14 N.Y.U.L.Q.R. 431; 48 Yale L.J. 874; Keating, 69 U.S.L.R. 412; 6 Fordham L.R. 242; Mariash, 16 Brookl. L.R. 41.

19. See N.Y.—McKinney's EPTL 7–1.9(b).

20. Hammerstein v. Equitable Tr. Co., 209 N.Y. 429, 103 N.E. 706.

or a power of termination in the trustee or others,[22] may be expressly provided in the trust instrument and will be effective. Such a clause does not make the instrument testamentary, even though the settlor is the life beneficiary,[23] but in such a case it may subject the property to the creditors of the settlor by virtue of statutes existing in a few states.[24]

The power of revocation is personal to the party in whom it is vested and may not be exercised by his successors, either by way of voluntary or involuntary transfer, for example, by his transferees or by his trustee in bankruptcy.[25] It can, however, be relinquished by notice from its holder to the trustee that such is the intent of the holder, and this practice has been followed in some cases in order to avoid adverse tax consequences from retention of the power.[26]

If the settlor provides that the power is to be exercised in a specific manner, or subject to certain conditions precedent, these directions are controlling.[27] Thus a power to be exercised by notice from the settlor delivered to the trustee has been held not exercisable by the will of the settlor;[28] and a power vested in two persons cannot be used by the survivor of them.[29] If no procedure for termination of the trust is prescribed, the power may be exercised in any reasonable manner, for example by written notice to the trustee.[30]

The settlor, in deciding whether to include a power of revocation in himself, must consider not only the vicissitudes of life which may cause him to want to take back or revamp his transfer, but also the tax consequences of inserting the power.[31] If the trust is made irrevocable,

21. Clark v. Freeman, 121 N.J.Eq. 35, 188 A. 493 (1936) (reserved to settlor and wife jointly and to survivor).

22. Farlow v. Farlow, 83 Md. 118, 34 A. 837; Falk v. Turner, 101 Mass. 494; Richardson v. Stephenson, 193 Wis. 89, 213 N.W. 673, 52 A.L.R. 681 (1927).

23. Hall v. Burkhan, 59 Ala. 349; Cribbs v. Walker, 74 Ark. 104, 85 S.W. 244. And see § 22, ante.

24. See, for example, Ala.Code § 35–4–290; West's Ann.Ind.Code 30–1–9–14; Kan. Stat.Ann. § 58–2414; Ohio Rev.Code § 1335.01; Wis.S.A. 701.07.

By statute in a number of states a settlor who reserves an unqualified power of revocation is deemed to be the owner of the trust assets so far as creditors are concerned. See Kan.Stat.Ann. 58–2414; Mich.C.L.A. § 556.128; Minn. Stat.Ann. § 502.76; N.Dak.Cent.Code 59–05–35; 60 Okl.St.Ann. § 299.15; S.Dak.Codif.L. 43–11–17.

25. Jones v. Clifton, 101 U.S. (11 Otto) 225, 25 L.Ed. 908 (1879); Murphey v. C.I.T. Corp., 347 Pa. 591, 33 A.2d 16 (1943); and see Chase Nat. Bank v. Ginnel, 50 N.Y.S.2d 345 (1944) (committee of incompetent set-

tlor cannot exercise power of revocation reserved to him, but may apply to the court for revocation).

26. Allen v. Trust Co. of Ga., 326 U.S. 630, 66 S.Ct. 389, 90 L.Ed. 367 (1946); Commissioner v. Prouty, 115 F.2d 331, 133 A.L.R. 977 (1st Cir.1940). See, as to tax consequences, Bogert, Trusts and Trustees (rev. 2d edit.), Chapter 15.

27. Worthington v. Rich, 77 Md. 265, 26 A. 403; Kelley v. Snow, 185 Mass. 288, 70 N.E. 89.

28. Gall v. Union Nat. Bank of Little Rock, 203 Ark. 1000, 159 S.W.2d 757 (1942).

29. In re Solomon's Estate, 332 Pa. 462, 2 A.2d 825 (1938).

30. Gifford Estate, 18 Pa.D. & C.2d 769.

31. As to the tax consequences, see Bogert, Trusts and Trustees (rev. 2d edit.), Ch. 15.

And see Shattuck, 26 Boston U.L.R. 437; King, 19 Rocky Mt.L.R. 1; Scott, 57 Harv.L.R. 362; Heffernan, Williams, 44 Cornell L.Q. 524.

a gift tax may ensue. If it is made revocable, he will be subject to taxation on the income of the trust; [32] and at his death the trust property will be a part of his estate for inheritance or estate tax purposes on the theory that possession and enjoyment of the corpus did not pass until the settlor's death.[33]

NORMAL TERMINATION OF THE TRUST— POWERS AND DUTIES OF TRUSTEE [1]

§ 149. The length of time for which the trust is to continue is usually fixed expressly in the trust instrument and the trust ends when this period expires.

If the instrument does not expressly fix the duration of the trust, it will be deemed to have been intended that the trust last until the settlor's purposes have been accomplished.

After the termination of the trust the trustee has such powers over the trust property as are necessary to enable him to preserve and administer it during the period required to wind up the trust affairs, make an accounting, obtain his discharge, and deliver the property to those who are entitled to it. The trustee has a duty to exercise these powers within a reasonable time.

Expiration of Trust Term

Usually the time of termination of the trust does not involve difficulty. Normally the term is fixed by the trust instrument or the oral settlement. Where the settlor states the period for which the trust is to continue, and this period is a lawful one, there can be little room for contention concerning expiration of the trust by its terms. The trust will last until the date set and then naturally cease.[2] Thus a period of years,[3] or the lives of one or more named persons,[4] may be fixed as the trust term. The settlor may prescribe that the trust shall last during a minority,[5] or until a beneficiary reaches an age beyond twenty one [6] or until the marriage of a given person.[7] Or the settlor may give the power to another to fix the trust term, for example, to the trustee.[8]

32. Richardson v. C.I.R., 121 F.2d 1 (2d Cir.1941).

33. Sanford's Estate v. Commissioner, 308 U.S. 39, 60 S.Ct. 51, 84 L.Ed. 20 (1939); In re Barber's Estate, 304 Pa. 235, 155 A. 565 (1931).

§ 149

1. Bogert, Trusts and Trustees (rev. 2d edit.), § 1010; Restatement, Trusts, Second, §§ 334, 344–347.

2. Yedor v. Chicago City Bank & Trust Co., 376 Ill. 121, 33 N.E.2d 220 (1941).

3. In re Hanson's Estate, 159 Cal. 401, 114 P. 810.

4. Embury v. Sheldon, 68 N.Y. 227; In re Wilson's Estate, 49 Pa. 241.

5. Mason v. Paschal, 98 Tenn. 41, 38 S.W. 92.

6. Anderson v. Messinger, 146 F. 929, 77 C.C.A. 179, 7 L.R.A.,N.S., 1094 (6th Cir. 1906).

7. In re Rose's Will, 156 Wis. 570, 146 N.W. 916.

8. Schreyer v. Schreyer, 101 App.Div. 456, 91 N.Y.S. 1065, affirmed 82 N.Y. 555, 75 N.E. 1134.

Although a settlor may not have expressly stated the trust term, or measured it by lives, years or similar standards, he may impliedly have fixed the duration of the trust by his statement of its purpose. It is rudimentary law that a trust will last no longer than necessary for the accomplishment of its purpose.[9] If the settlor has not otherwise fixed termination of the trust, he will be deemed to have intended that it should last until the trust purpose has been attained.[10] Thus a trust to educate grandchildren is terminated when their education is completed,[11] and a trust for a married woman, to protect her property from her then husband, may reasonably be construed to last during the marriage only.[12]

The rules regarding express or implied limits of the trust term have been stated by an Illinois court,[13] as follows:

"Where a testator by his will creates a trust and fixes the duration thereof, his direction will, if not in violation of the rule against perpetuities, be given effect and the trust will continue for the time indicated; but where a testator does not specifically indicate the time for which the trust is to continue, his intention must, if possible, be determined from the entire will. Where the evident purpose of a trust is the accomplishment of a particular object, the trust will terminate so soon as that object has been accomplished, and the fact that a fee is given to the trustee does not show the testator's intention that the trust estate shall continue after the active duties connected with the trust have been accomplished."

A trust is not like an agency, where the death of the principal revokes the relationship. The death of the settlor will, unless his life has been made a measuring life, have no effect on the continuance of the trust.[14] So too, under the application of the doctrine that equity never allows a trust to fail for want of a trustee, the death of the trustee will not extinguish the trust relationship.[15] A substitute trustee will be supplied. But if the powers of the deceased trustee were personal, that is, if an intention had been expressed by the settlor that the deceased trustee alone should exercise the powers, then his death will end the trust.[16]

The death of a beneficiary has no effect on the life of the trust,[17] unless the settlor made it a measuring life or terminating event. His interest, if transferable, passes to successors by intestacy or will.

9. See § 150, post. And see § 32, ante, for discussion of decisions to the effect that the size of the trustee's property interest is measured by the needs of the trust.

10. Edwards v. Edwards, 142 Ala. 267, 39 So. 82; Burke v. O'Brien, 115 App.Div. 574, 100 N.Y.S. 1048; Mackrell v. Walker, 172 Pa. 154, 33 A. 337.

11. In re Leto's Estate, 7 Misc.2d 400, 160 N.Y.S.2d 765 (1957).

12. Smith v. Metcalf, 1 Head, Tenn., 64.

13. Kohtz v. Eldred, 208 Ill. 60, 72, 60 N.E. 900.

14. Lyle v. Burke, 40 Mich. 499.

15. Shillinglaw v. Peterson, 184 Iowa 276, 167 N.W. 709.

16. Hadley v. Hadley, 147 Ind. 423, 46 N.E. 823.

17. Slevin v. Brown, 32 Mo. 176.

Powers and Duties of Trustee on Termination of Trust

When a trust terminates either because of the expiration of the trust term, or because of the exercise of a power of revocation or termination, or on account of a court decree or other cause, the powers and duties of the trustee do not immediately cease.[18] He has the power and duty to retain possession of the trust property, to safeguard and manage it, and to perform such other acts as are reasonably necessary to the winding up of the trust affairs during the period that is required to prepare his accounting, distribute the trust property and secure his discharge.[19]

In some cases his duty of distribution may be accomplished by a mere delivery of possession, as where the trust is revoked by the settlor or there is a legal remainder following the trust.[20] In other cases he may have an obligation to deliver possession and also execute and deliver an instrument of transfer, as where the distributee is an equitable remainderman and the trustee had full legal title.[21]

Unless the trustee has been so foolish as to agree to deliver cash upon termination of the trust,[22] he has a duty merely to deliver the trust property in its then existing form.[23]

The trustee has a duty to deliver the trust property and income earned during the winding up period with promptness.[24] If the property depreciates or is lost during the period when the trustee has unreasonably delayed the transfer, he may be held liable for its value at the time he should have delivered it.[25] If the trustee unnecessarily continues to hold and manage the trust property after the trust has ended, with the consent of those entitled to the property, he may become a de facto trustee for them under a new trust.[26]

 WESTLAW REFERENCES

Expiration of Trust Term
settlor trustor /s termination duration /5 trust
390k61
find 33 ne2d 220

18. Breen v. Breen, 411 Ill. 206, 103 N.E.2d 625 (1952).

19. C.I.R. v. Davis, 132 F.2d 644 (1st Cir.1943); Harlan v. Gleason, 180 Md. 24, 22 A.2d 579 (1941) (finish foreclosure suit); Neary v. City Bank Farmers Tr. Co., 260 App.Div. 791, 24 N.Y.S.2d 264 (1940); Mc-Neal v. Hauser, 202 Okl. 329, 213 P.2d 559 (1949); Saros v. Carlson, 244 Wis. 84, 11 N.W.2d 676 (1943) (power of sale necessary for distribution).

20. In re Jones' Will, 306 N.Y. 197, 117 N.E.2d 250 (1954).

21. Callahan v. Peltier, 121 Conn. 106, 183 A. 400 (1936); In re Rothwell's Estate, 283 Mass. 563, 186 N.E. 662 (1933). But see Trenton Banking Co. v. Howard, 121

N.J.Eq. 85, 187 A. 575 (1936) (on revocation by settlor trustee must execute instruments of conveyance).

22. For an instance of such an agreement, see Dickson v. Commonwealth Tr. Co., 361 Pa. 612, 65 A.2d 408 (1949).

23. In re Sentner's Estate, 344 Pa. 118, 23 A.2d 484 (1942).

24. In re Ducker's Will, 3 A.D.2d 852, 161 N.Y.S.2d 549 (1957).

25. McBride v. McBride, 262 Ky. 452, 90 S.W.2d 736 (1936); Surratt v. State to the Use of Bollinger, 167 Md. 357, 175 A. 191, 100 A.L.R. 1125 (1934).

26. Zuckman v. Freiermuth, 222 Minn. 172, 23 N.W.2d 541 (1946).

390k60
Powers and Duties of Trustee on Termination of Trust

duty /3 trustee /s termination /s trust

find 23 a2d 484

409k687(5)

PURPOSE ACCOMPLISHED OR BECOMES IMPOSSIBLE OF ACCOMPLISHMENT OR ILLEGAL [1]

§ 150. If the purpose of a private trust becomes accomplished before the date for normal termination of the trust, equity will consider the trust terminated, either because of the application of the Statute of Uses to a passive trust, or because equity will not compel the useless act of holding the property in trust for a longer period.

If it becomes impossible or illegal to accomplish the purposes of the settlor at a time before the normal date for trust termination, the court will terminate the trust or consider it terminated in the case of a private trust.

Accomplishment of Purpose

Not only may the trust terminate because of the expiration of the trust term fixed by the settlor, but also because the continuance of the trust would be useless. If the result sought to be reached by the establishment of the trust has been achieved by the trust, or otherwise, equity either will regard the trust as ended or will end it, and either will hold that title to the trust property automatically has passed to those entitled to it on termination of the trust, or will vest such persons with the title by virtue of its decree.[2] The court will not permit or require the continuance of a trust which will in no way accomplish the purposes sought by the settlor. The effect of the accomplishment of the objects of a charitable trust has been discussed elsewhere.[3]

"The duration of a trust depends upon the purposes of the trust. When the purposes have been accomplished the trust ceases."[4] In Koenig's Appeal[5] a trust for a married woman had been created and

---

§ 150

1. Bogert, Trusts and Trustees (rev. 2d edit.), §§ 1002, 1007; Restatement, Trusts, Second, §§ 165, 166, 335, 336, 398, 399.

2. Cherry v. Richardson, 120 Ala. 242, 24 So. 570; In re Hagerstown Trust Co., 119 Md. 224, 86 A. 982; Taylor v. Richards, 153 Mich. 667, 117 N.W. 208; Kahn v. Tierney, 135 App.Div. 897, 120 N.Y.S. 663, affirmed 201 N.Y. 516, 94 N.E. 1095; Packer's Estate, 246 Pa. 97, 92 A. 65; Temple v. Ferguson, 110 Tenn. 84, 72 S.W. 455, 100 Am.St.Rep. 791; Millsaps v. Johnson, Tex. Civ.App., 196 S.W. 202.

For statutes declaring the effect of fulfillment of purpose, impossibility or illegality, see West's Ann.Ind.Code 30–4–3–24; N.H.Rev.Stat.Ann. 564:15; 20 Pa.C.S.A. § 6102; Wis.S.A. 701.13(3). And see Bogert, Trusts and Trustees (rev. 2d edit.), § 1002.

3. See § 147, ante.

4. Winters v. March, 139 Tenn. 496, 501, 202 S.W. 73. For statutes to this effect, see Mich.C.L.A. § 555.23; Minn. Stat.Ann. § 501.40; S.Dak.Codif.L. 43–10–19.

5. 57 Pa. 352, 355.

divorce had later occurred. In discussing the termination of the trust the court said:

"But if the sole purpose of the trust was to protect the wife's estate against her husband, it is manifest that purpose was fully accomplished when the coverture ceased. The divorce of the parties terminated all possibility of the husband's interference with the property bequeathed and devised to the wife, as completely as his death would have done. Then why should the trust be continued after its exigencies have been met? It matters not what may be the nominal duration of an estate given by will to a trustee. It continues in equity no longer than the thing sought to be secured by the trust demands. Even a devise to trustees and their heirs will be cut down to an estate for life, or even for years, if such lesser estate be sufficient for the purpose of the trust."

Other examples are found where the only purpose of the trust was to support the settlor and pay her funeral expenses and she died and all bills were paid; [6] and where the sole object was to pay the debts of the settlor and they were later paid from a non-trust source.[7] But where a trust was created for one who happened to be an inebriate at the time of the commencement of the trust, but the object of the trust did not appear to have been to guard against improvidence arising from such habits, a change in the condition of the beneficiary to that of sobriety did not cause the trust to terminate.[8]

It would seem that in determining what the purpose of the settlor was with respect to the trust, the court considers not only the language of the instrument but also oral evidence as to the circumstances of the settlor, the beneficiaries and the settlor's family generally.[9] The courts have disagreed as to whether the parol evidence rule prevents the receipt of evidence of oral statements of the settlor as to his purpose, where there was a written trust instrument.[10]

Impossibility of Performance

The effect on private express trusts of imperfection in the declaration, illegality or impossibility in their creation, has been previously discussed.[11] If the imperfection, illegality or impossibility existed at the time it was sought to create the trust, the express trust never comes into being.[12] Legal title passes by virtue of the settlement, but the

And see Simmons v. Northwestern Tr. Co., 136 Minn. 357, 162 N.W. 450 (trust to protect a sister of the settlor in the enjoyment of property, free from interference by a worthless husband of the donee; beneficiary secured a divorce).

6. Murphy v. Westhoff, 386 Ill. 136, 53 N.E.2d 931 (1944).

7. Selden v. Vermilya, 3 N.Y. 525.

8. Anderson v. Kemper, 116 Ky. 339, 76 S.W. 122.

9. Carpenter v. Carpenter's Trustee, 119 Ky. 582, 84 S.W. 737.

10. Admitted in In re Easterday's Estate, 45 Cal.App.2d 598, 114 P.2d 669 (1941); Jordan v. Price, 49 N.E.2d 769 (Ohio App.1942). Not received in In re Roberts' Estate, 240 Iowa 160, 35 N.W.2d 756 (1949).

11. See § 75, ante. The trust may be destroyed if the trust property is destroyed or taken from the trustee under a right prior to that of the settlor. See Bogert, Trusts and Trustees (rev. 2d edit.), § 995.

12. First Nat. Bank v. Stewart, 215 Ga. 141, 109 S.E.2d 606 (1959).

trustee usually holds as a resulting trustee and not under the intended express trust.

If, however, the impossibility did not exist at the commencement of the trust but arose during its execution, a different question is presented. In this latter case the express trust has admittedly had existence. A change in circumstances causing impossibility of performance may result in court termination of the express trust.[13] For example, a family home is placed in trust as a residence for a group of children, but they will not live together; there is impossibility which terminates the trust.[14]

It has been previously shown that impossibility of performance has a different effect in charitable trusts from that given in private trusts.[15] Ordinarily, if a charitable trust becomes impossible of execution as directed by the settlor, equity will apply the cy pres doctrine and carry out the settlor's intention as nearly as possible.

Illegality

If the private trust is legal at its creation but, due to a change in the law, it becomes illegal during the course of its stated term, the trust terminates and the settlor or his successors are entitled to the property, unless the settlor has provided for other disposition.[16]

 WESTLAW REFERENCES

Accomplishment of Purpose
"koenig's appeal"
trust /s accomplish**** /s purpose
find 53 ne2d 931

Impossibility of Performance
di(trust /s impossib!)
75k37(3) /p impossib!
find 124 ne2d 226

---

13. For statutes to this effect, see West's Ann.Ind.Code 30–4–3–24; 20 Pa.C.S. A. § 6102. And, as to termination of small trusts, see West's Ann. Cal.Civ.Code § 2279.1, West's Ann.Cal.Prob.Code § 1120.6; Wis.S.A. 701.13(3) (where "continuation of the trust, in whole or in part, is impractical", due to change in circumstances such as size of trust).

By Wash.R.C.W.A. 11.09.070(32) a trustee is given the power to terminate the trust where the corpus is insufficient to implement the "intent" of the trust, and the power may not be exercised if the trustee is a grantor or beneficiary.

14. Gordon v. Gordon, 332 Mass. 193, 124 N.E.2d 226 (1955). If a trust is created for the purpose of selling realty, but a sale

after a certain date is prohibited, the trust ends on that date if the realty has not previously been sold since its objects could no longer be reached. Yedor v. Chicago City Bank & Trust Co., 376 Ill. 121, 33 N.E.2d 220 (1941).

15. See § 147, ante.

16. Schlessinger v. Mallard, 70 Cal. 326, 11 P. 728 (cemetery trust; use for that purpose illegal); In re Morse, 247 N.Y. 290, 160 N.E. 374 (1928) (trust of bank stock legal at first but became illegal because of later adoption of statute regarding voting trusts); In re Solbrig's Will, 7 Wis.2d 44, 96 N.W.2d 97 (1959) (trust for aliens; law provided for seizure of property in war time by Attorney General).

DESTRUCTION OF TRUST BY MERGER
OF INTERESTS [1]

§ 151. Where, after the trust has been created, the interests of all beneficiaries pass by operation of law or by conveyance to the trustee, the equitable and legal interests merge, no purpose of the settlor can thereafter be accomplished through the trust and it terminates. A beneficiary may surrender his interest to his trustee and thereby terminate the trust.

Where during the course of trust administration all beneficial interests under and following the trust come into the ownership of one person or group by sale, gift, or operation of law, these interests will merge and the trust will terminate, unless destruction of the trust would prevent the accomplishment of a purpose of the settlor or otherwise be inequitable.

The possible merger of the interests of trustees and beneficiaries at the beginning of the trust has been discussed previously.[2] It sometimes happens that the problem of merger arises during the course of the trust, although it did not exist at the beginning. Thus A may be made trustee for B, and later B may sell his interest to A; or A may be appointed trustee for A and B, and later B may die and the interest of B may pass to A by virtue of a gift in the will of B; or A and B may be created trustees for A and B for their lives, remainder to C, and C may die intestate and his property pass to A and B as his heirs. Here undoubtedly the legal and equitable interests in the same property become vested in the same person or group, and a suitable situation for the merger of the two interests arises.[3] No possible purpose of the settlor can be achieved by continuing the trust either as to the management of property for temporary beneficiaries, or as to conservation of principal for ultimate donees. Hence it would seem that the trust should be declared terminated.[4] If the trust is for L for life, remainder to R, and L's interest becomes vested in the trustee, a merger for the life of L may be decreed,[5] or a new trustee may be appointed to continue the trust for L.[6]

§ 151

1. Bogert, Trusts and Trustees (rev. 2d edit.), § 1003; Restatement, Trusts, Second, §§ 337, 341, 342, 343. For statutes regarding merger, see Offic.Code Ga.Ann. 53–12–4; N.Y.—McKinney's EPTL 7–1.1.

2. § 30, ante.

3. Wenzel v. Powder, 100 Md. 36, 59 A. 194, 108 Am.St.Rep. 380; Tifft v. Ireland, 273 Mass. 56, 172 N.E. 865 (1930).

4. Cunningham v. Bright, 228 Mass. 385, 117 N.E. 909. And as to conveyances by the trustee to the beneficiaries, see Healey v. Alston, 25 Miss. 190; Hickman v. Wood's Ex'r, 30 Mo. 199.

5. In re Richardson's Estate, 135 Misc. 726, 238 N.Y.S. 271 (1929).

6. In re Phipp's Will, 2 N.Y.2d 105, 157 N.Y.S.2d 14, 138 N.E.2d 341 (1956).

The beneficiary of a non-spendthrift trust may convey or surrender his interest to the trustee and thus extinguish the trust in whole or in part, since the trustee will then become the absolute owner.[7] It would seem that if real property is the subject of the trust which the beneficiary seeks to surrender, a careful examination of the Statute of Frauds should be made to determine whether the surrender must be in writing and signed by the beneficiary.[8] A surrender is not technically a "conveyance" but rather a release, yet it may be held to be within the spirit, although not the letter, of the Statute. Oral surrenders have been held valid in the case of many trusts of realty,[9] but in some cases a writing has been required.[10]

Another instance of possible merger and termination occurring during the existence of the trust is that of the union in one person or group of all the beneficial interests in the trust property. All equitable interests under the trust may be acquired by one person or group, or such equitable interests and all legal interests following the trust may come into the ownership of the same person or group. Identical ownership of successive equitable, or equitable and legal interests, in the same property gives an opportunity for the application of the doctrine of merger.[11]

Equity does not consider merger as a self-executing, automatic rule.[12] It refuses to apply the merger principle if the intent of the settlor would thereby be frustrated or an inequitable result would be produced.[13] It considers the practical effect of continuing the trust or of declaring it ended. Where no useful object which the settlor desired to achieve would be accomplished by keeping the trust alive, it will be decreed to be ended.[14] However if, notwithstanding the change in the ownership of the beneficial interests, one or more of the settlor's objectives could be furthered by the continuance of the trust, the court will refuse to hold that it is terminated by merger or is terminable.[15]

Thus if S created a trust to pay income to A for life and to deliver the principal to B at the death of A, and B conveyed his interest in

7. First Nat. Bank of Lincoln v. Cash, 220 Ala. 319, 125 So. 28 (1929); Keaton v. McGwier, 24 Ga. 217; Owings v. Owings, 3 Ind. 142.

8. See § 21, ante.

9. See Scott, Parol Extinguishment of Trusts in Land, 42 Harv.L.R. 849.

10. Coleman v. Coleman, 48 Ariz. 337, 61 P.2d 441, 106 A.L.R. 1309 (1936); Matthews v. Thompson, 186 Mass. 14, 71 N.E. 93, 66 L.R.A. 421, 104 Am.St.Rep. 550.

11. As to the attitude of equity toward merger, see Sherlock v. Thompson, 167 Iowa 1, 148 N.W. 1035; William D. Ray Co. v. Courtney, 250 N.Y. 271, 165 N.E. 289 (1929).

12. "Wherever it would work an injustice or defeat the intention of the donor, to

work a merger, the two estates will be kept alive although they come together in one person." In re Estate of Washburn, 11 Cal.App. 735, 106 P. 415.

13. Wechter v. Chicago Title & Tr. Co., 385 Ill. 311, 52 N.E.2d 157 (1943); In re Fitton's Will, 218 Wis. 63, 259 N.W. 718 (1935).

14. Dare v. New Brunswick Trust Co., 122 N.J.Eq. 349, 194 A. 61 (1937); Gillogly v. Campbell, 52 Ohio App. 43, 2 N.E.2d 620 (1935).

15. In re Easterday's Estate, 45 Cal. App.2d 598, 114 P.2d 669 (1941); In re Mowinkel's Estate, 130 Neb. 10, 263 N.W. 488 (1935).

remainder to A, if the sole object of the trust was to conserve the property for B termination might well be decreed, since keeping the property intact for B has now been rendered impossible.[16] But if the settlor is deemed to have had a second objective, namely, providing a manager of the property for A during his life, relieving him of the burdens of operating the property, and preventing him from suffering from his folly or misfortune, it may be decreed that merger should not be applied.[17] The existence of a spendthrift clause in the trust instrument may prevent merger.[18] For example, if a trust is for L for life with spendthrift provisions, remainder to R, L will be incapable of transferring his interest to R and laying a foundation for merger, and if R conveys to L no merger should occur since it would frustrate the intent of the settlor to protect L from folly or misfortune.[19]

 WESTLAW REFERENCES

merger /2 interest /s trust
390k154
find 61 p2d 441

TERMINATION OF TRUST BY COURT DECREE ON REQUEST OF BENEFICIARIES [1]

§ 152. Where the settlor and all the beneficiaries of a trust join in applying to the court for a termination of the trust, it will be ended even though the purposes which the settlor originally had in mind have not been accomplished.

Even though all the beneficiaries are competent and ascertained and they apply for a decree of termination, it will not be granted, according to the majority American rule, if one or more purposes which the settlor sought to accomplish by the trust may still be achieved by a continuance of the trust, and if the settlor does not join with the beneficiaries; but in England and some American jurisdictions such a decree will be allowed.

16. Ormsby v. Dumesnil, 91 Ky. 601, 16 S.W. 459, 13 Ky.Law Rep. 209; Brooks v. Davis, 82 N.J.Eq. 118, 88 A. 178; Simmons v. Northwestern Tr. Co., 136 Minn. 357, 162 N.W. 450; Brown v. Fidelity Union Tr. Co., 128 N.J.Eq. 197, 15 A.2d 788 (1940); Nichols v. First Nat. Bank, 199 Or. 659, 264 P.2d 451 (1953).

17. Bowlin v. Citizens' Bank & Tr. Co., 131 Ark. 97, 198 S.W. 288, 2 A.L.R. 575; Abbott v. Everett Tr. & Sav. Bank, 50 Wn. 2d 398, 312 P.2d 203 (1957).

18. There is no complication where the settlor is life beneficiary and there is a spendthrift clause, since the clause is invalid in that case and conveyance and merger can occur. In re Bowers' Trust Estate, 346 Pa. 85, 29 A.2d 519 (1943).

19. C.I.R. v. Ellis' Estate, 252 F.2d 109 (3d Cir.1958); In re Bosler's Estate, 378 Pa. 333, 107 A.2d 443 (1954). A 1945 statute permitted an income beneficiary of a spendthrift trust to release his interest in favor of a remainderman. In re Borsch's Estate, 362 Pa. 581, 67 A.2d 119 (1949) (statute held unconstitutional). For the current statute, see 20 Pa.C.S.A. § 6103.

§ 152

1. Bogert, Trusts and Trustees (rev. 2d edit.), §§ 1005–1008; Restatement, Trusts, Second, §§ 337–340. See also Scott, 65 Univ. of Pa.L.R. 632; Evans, 37 Yale L.J. 1070; Davis, 78 Univ. of Pa.L.R. 100; Cleary, 43 Yale L.J. 393.

In case of a bona fide dispute regarding the validity of a trust the courts sometimes approve a compromise settlement which terminates or modifies the trust, in order to put an end to litigation and family quarrels.

The disposition of some cases arising from applications by beneficiaries for court termination of trusts has already been discussed.[2] If the trust originally required no active duties of the trustee, or later became passive, it should be treated as terminable or as executed by operation of law.[3] Or if, after the origin of the trust, its purpose is accomplished, or becomes impossible of accomplishment or illegal, a decree of termination will be granted and a resulting trust declared for the settlor or his successors.[4] The Statute of Uses or a similar doctrine would apply, or the court would refuse to continue a useless trust. In a case involving this situation, a Pennsylvania court has said:[5]

"In the case now before us, all present and future interests in the trust property having been acquired by the remainderman, the 'thing sought to be secured,' i.e., the protection of the corpus pending the duration of the life estates, has become unessential. Under such circumstances, it is the right of a cestui que trust to have the legal estate of the trustee declared terminated. . . ."

In rare cases the court has terminated a trust where its administration has become extremely difficult[6] or the court found that termination was in the best interests of the beneficiaries.[7]

Active Trusts with Purpose Unaccomplished—Majority Rule

The cases which cause difficulty are those of active trusts where such objects as protection of temporary beneficiaries, delay in making payments, conservation of principal, and requiring a donee to enjoy his property through the management of another, have not been secured and are yet attainable through the trust. Many beneficiaries become impatient of the restrictions which the settlor put on his gifts to them; they want to get at and spend the property in the immediate present; and they consider that they are in substance the full owners of the property and should be able to decide for themselves how to enjoy it.

---

2. See §§ 150, 151, ante.

3. See § 46, ante, and Fox v. Fox, 250 Ill. 384, 95 N.E. 498; Root v. Blake, 14 Pick., Mass., 271; Supreme Lodge, Knights of Pythias v. Rutzler, 87 N.J.Eq. 342, 100 A. 189; McKenzie v. Sumner, 114 N.C. 425, 19 S.E. 375.

4. Sands v. Old Colony Tr. Co., 195 Mass. 575, 81 N.E. 300, 12 Ann.Cas. 837; Donaldson v. Allen, 182 Mo. 626, 81 S.W. 1151; Board of Directors v. First Nat. Bank, 33 N.J. 456, 165 A.2d 513 (1960) (trust for employees of corporation which had ceased to exist); In re Wood's Estate,

261 Pa. 480, 104 A. 673; Angell v. Angell, 28 R.I. 592, 68 A. 583; Armistead's Ex'rs v. Hartt, 97 Va. 316, 33 S.E. 616.

See § 150, ante.

5. In re Stafford's Estate, 258 Pa. 595, 598, 599, 102 A. 222.

6. Timmins Estate, 11 Pa.D. & C.2d 792. But see, *contra,* In re Stack's Will, 217 Wis. 94, 258 N.W. 324 (1935).

7. Schriver v. Frommel, 179 Ky. 228, 200 S.W. 327. But see, *contra,* Stephens v. Collison, 274 Ill. 389, 113 N.E. 691.

For these reasons applications by beneficiaries for a court decree of trust termination and distribution of the principal are very common.

In one type of case the law seems well settled. If the settlor is living and joins with all the beneficiaries in an application to end the trust and for distribution of the principal to the settlor or to the beneficiaries, or in part to each, the courts are inclined to grant the petition.[8] The principal concern of the courts in such cases is respect for the intent of the settlor and execution of his directions. In these instances it appears that the settlor has changed his mind. A decree of termination will secure the performance of the disposition which he now desires. Both donor and donees are willing that the gift be revoked or revised. There seems to be no reason why the courts should stand in their way. This rule will be applicable, of course, only in the case of living trusts, which constitute an increasingly significant portion of private trusts, and it may serve to settle a number of controversies. As previously shown,[9] this rule is applied where the settlor is the sole beneficiary and asks for a destruction of the trust.[10]

The case which has caused the greatest discussion and difference of opinion is that of the application by the beneficiaries in which the settlor does not join, either because he is dead or because he opposes destruction of the trust. Assuming that all the beneficiaries are in being, of full age and otherwise competent, and all request termination of the trust, should the court grant such relief if the settlor's objectives in setting up the trust are still unaccomplished and still could be attained by continuing the trust? For example, S creates a trust for his son B, a boy of twelve years, with directions to the trustee to pay to or for the son the net income until he reaches twenty-five, and then to turn over to him the trust principal. The son reaches twenty-one and is therefore able to give a binding release to the trustee; he applies to the court for an order that the trust be ended and the trustee hand over the trust property. Here the purposes of furnishing the son with a manager for his property and with support during his years of immaturity, and of delaying paying the principal to him until he reaches an age of some judgment and experience, are not fully accomplished and if the trust is allowed to run on until B is twenty-five these objectives will be forwarded.

In Claflin v. Claflin [11] the trustee was directed to pay the son of the testator $10,000 when he reached twenty-one, $10,000 when he arrived

---

8. Botzum v. Havana Nat. Bank, 367 Ill. 539, 12 N.E.2d 203 (1937); Stephens v. Moore, 298 Mo. 215, 249 S.W. 601 (1923); O'Brien v. Holden, 104 Vt. 338, 160 A. 192 (1932); Fowler v. Lanpher, 193 Wash. 308, 75 P.2d 132 (1939); Angle v. Marshall, 55 W.Va. 671, 47 S.E. 882. By West's Ann. Cal.Civ.Code § 771, added by Cal.L.1959, c. 470, the settlor and all beneficiaries can terminate a trust, even though the instrument declared it irrevocable. And see N.Y.—McKinney's EPTL 7–1.9; Wis.Stats.

Ann. § 701.12 (settlor and all beneficiaries may revoke, modify or terminate a trust without court approval).

9. See § 148, ante.

10. Sutliff v. Aydelott, 373 Ill. 633, 27 N.E.2d 529 (1940); Raffel v. Safe Dep. & Tr. Co., 100 Md. 141, 59 A. 702; Bottimore v. First & Merchants' Nat. Bank of Richmond, 170 Va. 221, 196 S.E. 593 (1938).

11. 149 Mass. 19, 20 N.E. 454, 3 L.R.A. 370.

at twenty-five, and the balance of the trust principal when the son became thirty. The trust instrument contained no spendthrift clause. After attaining his majority the son applied for the payment of the remainder of the principal. In refusing payment the court said:

"In the case at bar nothing has happened which the testator did not anticipate, and for which he has not made provision. It is plainly his will that neither the income nor any part of the principal should now be paid to the plaintiff. It is true that the plaintiff's interest is alienable by him, and can be taken by his creditors to pay his debts, but it does not follow that because the testator has not imposed all possible restrictions, the restrictions which he has imposed should not be carried into effect . . .. The restriction upon the plaintiff's possession and control is, we think, one that the testator had a right to make . . .."

In many other decisions the Claflin decision has been followed and the courts have denied the application for termination, on the ground that the donor had a right to frame his gift in accordance with his wishes and judgment and that it is the function of the courts to carry out the intent of those who make property transfers and not to alter or remake their gifts.[12] Where this doctrine is applied, the trust is said to be "indestructible". The attitude of the courts in these cases is harmonious with the views of those courts which have supported and enforced spendthrift trusts, where great emphasis has been laid on carrying out the intent of the donor.[13] The courts have a duty to respect the stated intent of donors when no conflict with public policy is involved.

If the trust in question is a spendthrift trust, then it would seem that there is always an unaccomplished purpose as long as the trust is to continue, namely, the protection of the beneficiary against misfortune and improvidence.[14]

---

12. Ramage v. First Farmers' & Merchants' Nat. Bank, 249 Ala. 240, 30 So.2d 706 (1947); Moxley v. Title Ins. & Tr. Co., 27 Cal.2d 457, 165 P.2d 15, 163 A.L.R. 838 (1946); DeLadson v. Crawford, 93 Conn. 402, 106 A. 326; Mohler v. Wesner, 382 Ill. 225, 47 N.E.2d 64 (1943); Lunt v. Van Gorden, 229 Iowa 263, 294 N.W. 351 (1940); Robbins v. Smith, 72 Ohio St. 1, 73 N.E. 1051; Hill v. Hill, 49 Okl. 424, 152 P. 1122; In re Yeager's Estate, 354 Pa. 463, 47 A.2d 813 (1946); Glasscock v. Tate, 107 Tenn. 486, 64 S.W. 715; Lanius v. Fletcher, 100 Tex. 550, 101 S.W. 1076; Fowler v. Lanpher, 193 Wash. 308, 75 P.2d 132 (1938); Bussell v. Wright, 133 Wis. 445, 113 N.W. 644.

For more recent cases to this effect, see Hopp v. Rain, 249 Iowa 891, 88 N.W.2d 39 (1958); Lafferty v. Sheets, 175 Kan. 741, 267 P.2d 962 (1954); Thomson v. Union Nat. Bank, 291 S.W.2d 178 (Mo.1956); In re Gardner's Will, 12 A.D.2d 477, 207 N.Y.S.2d 651 (1960); In re Bosler's Estate, 378 Pa. 333, 107 A.2d 443 (1954).

"The rule has its foundation in the well-established principle that within the limits of the law, every man may do as he pleases with his own property. He may, therefore, dispose of it in fee, or create estates therein in different persons, or grant or devise it on such conditions or under such restrictions as he may desire." In re Henderson's Estate, 258 Pa. 510, 515, 102 A. 217.

The payment of fees to the trustee is not a trust purpose, and therefore opposition on termination by the trustee on the ground that he will lose money is not material. In re Musser's Estate, 341 Pa. 1, 17 A.2d 411 (1941).

13. See § 40, ante.

14. Mason v. Rhode Island Hospital Tr. Co., 78 Conn. 81, 61 A. 57; Kirkland v. Merc. Safe Dep. & Tr. Co., 218 Md. 17, 145 A.2d 230 (1958); Rose v. Southern Michigan Nat. Bank, 255 Mich. 275, 238 N.W. 284 (1931); In re Smaltz' Estate, 329 Pa. 21, 195 A. 880 (1938). But see 20 Pa.C.S.A.

In some states statutes forbid the beneficiaries of trusts to collect and pay over the income and profits from alienating their interests. These statutes have been construed to prevent the abrogation of such trusts by act of the beneficiaries.[15]

A New York court, in considering the question, has said: [16]

"Whatever view may be taken of the general jurisdiction of courts of equity, in the absence of any statutory or legislative policy, to abrogate continuing trusts, created for the purpose of providing a sure support for the widow or children of a testator, or other beneficiary, the indestructibility of such trusts here, by judicial decree, results, we think, from the inalienable character impressed upon them by statute. The beneficiaries of trusts for the receipt of the rents and profits of land are prohibited from assigning or disposing of their interest, . . . and this provision is held to apply by force of other sections of the statute, to the interest of beneficiaries in similar trusts of personalty. . . . This legislative policy cannot, we think, be defeated by the action of the court permitting such alienation, or abrogating the trust."

That the trustee joins with the beneficiaries in applying for a decree of termination should not be material, since the trustee has no beneficial interest and his willingness to give up his representative position should not be controlling.[17] Thus in Young v. Snow, the trust was to keep the property in repair and to pay the income over for twenty years. All the beneficiaries and the trustee united in asking equity to end the trust before the expiration of the twenty years, but the court, following Claflin v. Claflin, declined.[18]

English and Minority American Rule

In England, on the other hand, the applicants are granted the decree of termination and the right to enjoy their property directly.[19] Since no one else has any interest in the property involved, it is held that there is no reason why the request should be denied. The donor, by assumption, retained no property interest in himself. He merely attempted to limit the donee's enjoyment by making it indirect and delayed. A minority of the American courts have followed this view, and the trusts have been ended although unaccomplished purposes remained.[20] This theory is exemplified by a Maine case [21] in which the trust was created for the aid of certain relatives in time of need. Obviously its purposes would not be rendered impossible of accomplish-

§ 6102(a) (termination regardless of spend-thrift provision).

15. Dale v. Guaranty Trust Co., 168 App.Div. 601, 153 N.Y.S. 1041, 1 Cornell Law Quarterly, 209. Patton v. Patrick, 123 Wis. 218, 101 N.W. 408. See § 51, ante.

16. Lent v. Howard, 89 N.Y. 169, 181.

17. Blackburn v. Blackburn, 167 Ky. 113, 180 S.W. 48; In re Simonin's Estate, 260 Pa. 395, 103 A. 927.

18. 167 Mass. 287, 45 N.E. 686.

19. Saunders v. Vautier, 4 Beav. 115; In re Weinter's Will Trusts, (1956) 2 All Eng.R. 482.

20. Spooner v. Dunlap, 87 N.H. 384, 180 A. 256; Newlin v. Girard Tr. Co., 116 N.J.Eq. 498, 174 A. 479 (1934). And see Mo.—V.A.M.S. § 456.590.

21. Dodge v. Dodge, 112 Me. 291, 92 A. 49.

ment until the beneficiaries had died, for they might at any time fall into need, but the court terminated the trust upon the written request of all the beneficiaries and allowed them to divide the property among themselves. In a New Jersey case it was held that where a trust to last for ten years was created for the benefit of a widow and children, with the beneficiaries to receive the principal at the end of the trust, the beneficiaries might demand the conveyance of the property to them prior to expiration of the trust.[22]

Some argument in favor of this minority position can be found in the fact that if the trust is not spendthrift and the court denies the beneficiaries a decree of termination, they can sell their interests and thus indirectly get the principal. Such a sale would ordinarily be at a sacrifice, since the purchaser might not be entitled to the principal until a future date and his interest might be subject to some contingencies. It may be argued that a rule which can be easily evaded is not of value.

It also has been urged in favor of the English rule that in other instances a donee has been held entitled to enjoy a gift according to his own preference, and has not been obliged to respect the desires of his donor with regard to the method and time of enjoyment, as where the direction is to provide a sum to purchase an annuity for a donee and he is held entitled to choose between taking the annuity and taking its purchase price;[23] or where the donor provided that realty should be bought for the donee, or realty sold and the proceeds turned over to the donee, and the beneficiary has been permitted to take the price of the realty in one case or the realty in the other.[24]

If some, but not all, of the beneficiaries come into court and request the termination of the trust and the distribution of the principal among all the beneficiaries, it seems clear that their demand should not be allowed. They are attempting to enforce their will on the other beneficiaries who prefer to take their benefits through the trust, and even if the English doctrine is followed it ought not to help the plaintiffs in such a case.[25]

22. Huber v. Donoghue, 49 N.J.Eq. 125, 23 A. 495.

23. Parker v. Cobe, 208 Mass. 260, 94 N.E. 476, 33 L.R.A.,N.S., 978; In re Bertuch's Will, 225 App.Div. 773, 232 N.Y.S. 36 (1928). But this rule is negated or qualified by some statutes and decisions: Ketcham v. International Tr. Co., 117 Colo. 559, 192 P.2d 426 (1948); Morgenthaler v. First Atl. Nat. Bank, 80 So.2d 446 (1955); American Bible Soc. v. Chase, 340 Ill.App. 548, 92 N.E.2d 332 (1950); See N.Y.—McKinney's EPTL 3–3.9.

24. Hilton v. Sherman, 155 Ga. 624, 118 S.E. 356 (1923); Pasquay v. Pasquay, 235 Ill. 48, 85 N.E. 316; Cravens' Exr. v. Cravens, 307 Ky. 83, 209 S.W.2d 827 (1948).

25. Schuster v. Schuster, 75 Ariz. 20, 251 P.2d 631 (1952); Rayhol Co. v. Holland, 110 Conn. 516, 148 A. 358 (1930); Allen v. Safe Dep. & Tr. Co., 177 Md. 26, 7 A.2d 180 (1939). *A fortiori*, the request will be denied if the applicants are trying to get all the property for themselves and deny any portion to other beneficiaries who may have contingent interests. In re Stack's Will, 217 Wis. 94, 258 N.W. 324, 97 A.L.R. 316 (1935). West's Ann.Cal.Civ.Code § 771, as added by L.1959, c. 470, allows a majority of the beneficiaries to request and obtain termination if the trust has lasted longer than lives in being and/or twenty one years.

If some, but not all, of the beneficiaries, alter their request, however, and urge the court to terminate the trust in part only, and to give them their share of the principal but leave the rest of the trust intact, a different case is presented. The attitude of the court should depend on the question whether it would terminate the whole trust if all beneficiaries requested it.[26] Partial extinction of the trust has been allowed where the trust purpose as to a portion of the beneficiaries has been accomplished and their interests could be severed.[27] Thus where a portion of the trust property was being held for the purpose of ascertaining whether a son of the settlor would have any afterborn children to share in the fund, and the son died childless, it was held that the trust object was achieved as to this property, and the property might be distributed to the beneficiaries entitled thereto free from the trust.[28] But the court is not apt to terminate the trust in part on the request of some of the beneficiaries where there is some result still to be achieved which was in the mind of the settlor as a trust purpose.[29]

In many cases there are incompetent beneficiaries, for example, infants or persons of unsound mind. If these parties are represented by guardians, or by other persons in the same class, or by the court, the case may well be treated as if all beneficiaries were fully competent and in court. But if such representation is not found to exist, then the trust should not be terminated as a whole even though the court follows the English doctrine.[30] The same idea would seem to be controlling if some of the beneficiaries have contingent interests,[31] or there is a possibility of persons who may be born later coming into the class of beneficiaries. The problem is whether they are so represented as to be parties to the same extent as if they were fully competent and in court.[32] Naturally if the guardians object to a termination of the trust the court will not permit the other beneficiaries to force a destruction of it.[33]

One difficulty in winding up a trust where there are contingent interests, so that the ultimate disposition of the fund cannot be settled

26. Atwood v. National Bank of Lima, 115 F.2d 861 (6th Cir.1940); Ames v. Hall, 313 Mass. 33, 46 N.E.2d 403 (1943); Fox v. Greene, 289 Mich. 179, 286 N.W. 203 (1939).

27. Williams v. Thacher, 186 Mass. 293, 71 N.E. 567; Welch v. Trustees of Episcopal Theological School, 189 Mass. 108, 75 N.E. 139; Latta v. Trustees of Gen. Assembly, 213 N.C. 462, 196 S.E. 862 (1938).

28. Wayman v. Follansbee, 253 Ill. 602, 98 N.E. 21.

29. McDonnell v. McDonnell, 72 App. D.C. 317, 114 F.2d 478 (1940); Fox v. Greene, 289 Mich. 179, 286 N.W. 203 (1939); Wachovia Bank & Tr. Co. v. Laws, 217 N.C. 171, 7 S.E.2d 470 (1940).

30. Randall v. Randall, 60 F.Supp. 308 (S.D.Fla.1944); Hills v. Traveler's Bank &

Tr. Co., 125 Conn. 640, 7 A.2d 652, 123 A.L.R. 1419 (1939).

31. Ramage v. First Farmers & Merch. Nat. Bank, 249 Ala. 240, 30 So.2d 706 (1947); Mohler v. Wesner, 382 Ill. 225, 47 N.E.2d 64 (1943).

32. Deal v. Wachovia Bank & Tr. Co., 218 N.C. 483, 11 S.E.2d 464 (1940); In re Kamerly's Estate, 348 Pa. 225, 35 A.2d 258 (1944). See Hills v. Travelers Bank & Tr. Co., 125 Conn. 640, 7 A.2d 652 (1939) (Attorney General not possible representative of contingent unborn beneficiaries).

See also Bogert, Trusts and Trustees (rev. 2d edit.), § 1007 (doctrine of "virtual representation").

33. Duffy v. Duffy, 221 N.C. 521, 20 S.E.2d 835 (1942).

until the contingencies have been resolved, is the necessity for impounding part or all of the fund for what may amount to a long period of years.

Court Approval of Compromise Settlements

In some jurisdictions the courts have power to approve compromise settlements of litigation regarding the validity or effect of trust instruments, and these agreements involve the modification of trusts or their complete destruction. Frequently some members of the family of the settlor bring suit to have the trust instrument declared void on the ground of the incapacity of the donor or other reason, or seek to have it construed in a way favorable to their interests, making as defendants the trustee and other relatives who contend that the trust is valid and should be carried out according to their notions of its meaning. In order to prevent long and expensive litigation and to restore peace and harmony to the family group, compromise agreements are sometimes drawn up and presented to the courts for approval. These involve a distribution of the property in ways different from those contemplated by the settlor, and frequently the destruction or modification of a trust. When satisfied that there is a bona fide dispute,[34] and not a mere moot case trumped up for the purpose of getting collusive destruction of the trust, the courts often sanction such settlements as being in accord with good public policy, if the compromise appears to the court to be fair toward the parties.[35] Thus courts sometimes terminate trusts which they would leave in existence if direct applications for termination had been made.

 WESTLAW REFERENCES

Active Trusts With Purpose Unaccomplished—Majority Rule
find 27 ne2d 529
390k61(3) /p termination
claflin +3 claflin /p trust
390k60
390k124
trust /s purpose /s unaccomplished

English and Minority American Rule
saunders +3 vautier
390k60
390k124
390k282
find 7 a2d 652

---

34. For a case of a controversy which was held not to be bona fide, see Altemeir v. Harris, 403 Ill. 345, 86 N.E.2d 229 (1949).

35. See West's Ann.Ind.Code 30–4–3–25 and other statutes authorizing such compromises, cited in Bogert, Trusts and Trustees (rev. 2d edit.), § 1009. And see Beede v. Old Colony Tr. Co., 321 Mass. 115,

71 N.E.2d 882 (1947); Gifford v. First Nat. Bank of Menominee, 285 Mich. 58, 280 N.W. 108 (1938); N.Y.—McKinney's EPTL 3–3.7; In re Wade's Will, 296 N.Y. 244, 72 N.E.2d 306 (1947); Redwine v. Clodfelter, 226 N.C. 366, 38 S.E.2d 203 (1946); 20 Pa.S. § 6102.

Court Approval of Compromise Settlements
390k61(1)
find 86 ne2d 229
390k61(3)   /p   terminat***

Chapter 18

REMEDIES OF BENEFICIARIES UNDER TRUSTS—LIABILITIES OF TRUSTEE AND THIRD PERSONS

Table of Sections

INSTRUCTION BY COURT OF EQUITY—COURT SUPERVISED TRUSTS [1]

§ 153. The trustee or a beneficiary may bring a suit in equity to secure the advice of the court as to the meaning of the trust instrument or as to questions of law affecting the trust administration.

It frequently occurs that the trust instrument is not clear in its meaning and there are reasonable doubts as to its construction concerning the rights of beneficiaries, the powers and duties of trustees, and similar matters. It is one function of the court of equity to remove these doubts and to advise the trust parties as to the proper methods of administering the trust with respect to the ambiguous clauses. A suit to obtain this relief may be brought by a trustee or a beneficiary.[2] The

§ 153

1. Bogert, Trusts and Trustees (rev. 2d edit.), §§ 559–560, 563, 861; Restatement, Trusts, Second, §§ 259, 394.

2. In re Van Deusen's Estate, 30 Cal. 2d 285, 182 P.2d 565 (1947); Gibault Home for Boys v. Terre Haute First Nat. Bank, 227 Ind. 410, 85 N.E.2d 824 (1949) (who are beneficiaries under trust); St. Louis Union Trust Co. v. Kaltenbach, 353 Mo. 1114, 186 S.W.2d 578 (1945).

modern action to obtain a declaratory judgment may be used.[3] In many states there are statutes setting forth the power of the court to give instruction and advice.[4]

Another example of the use of this remedy exists where a trust party finds that the law of the state is uncertain with respect to a problem of administration, and that there are no decisions or statutes covering the matter. Here the court will settle the doubt and instruct the trustee as to the rule to govern his conduct or the legal rights of the beneficiaries.[5]

Where a trustee is reasonably in doubt as to the meaning of the trust instrument or his duties thereunder, he has a duty to apply to the court for instructions.[6]

Even if the trust instrument gives the trustee power to construe it, his actions pursuant to the power will be subject to review by the court.[7]

This aid of the court may not be invoked to settle business problems or to advise the trustees how to use their discretionary powers.[8] For example, if they have power to select investments but disagree as to whether to purchase government bonds or to invest in real estate mortgages, the court will not give its opinion as to which would be the better selection.[9] And if the trustee has a discretionary power of sale, the court will not advise him whether to use it.[10] Nor will the court instruct as to problems which may come up in the future, where the situation which will then confront the trustee is uncertain and events may make it unnecessary ever to face the question.[11] It is no part of the court's duty to act as legal advisor to the trust parties on points where the law is clear and adequate information can be secured from members of the bar.[12]

3. See § 2, Uniform Declaratory Judgments Act, adopted in at least 37 states; Old Nat. Bank & Tr. Co. v. Hughes, 16 Wn. 2d 584, 134 P.2d 63 (1943).

4. See, for example, Idaho Code § 10–1204; Ohio Rev.Code § 2107.46; 60 Okl. S.A. § 175.23; 12 Pa.S. § 834. And see Bogert, Trusts and Trustees (rev. 2d edit.), § 559.

5. Smith v. Fowler, 301 Ky. 96, 190 S.W.2d 1015 (1945) (validity of trust in doubt); Huestis v. Manley, 110 Vt. 413, 8 A.2d 644 (1939) (effect of spendthrift trust).

6. Hungerford & Terry Inc. v. Geschwindt, 27 N.J.Super. 515, 99 A.2d 666 (1953).

7. Taylor v. McClave, 128 N.J.Eq. 109, 15 A.2d 213 (1940).

8. Richardson v. Hall, 124 Mass. 228; Caspari v. Cutcheon, 110 Mich. 86, 67 N.W. 1093.

9. McCarthy v. Tierney, 116 Conn. 588, 165 A. 807 (1933). And see Westport Bank & Tr. Co. v. Fable, 126 Conn. 665, 13 A.2d 862 (1940) (in a charitable trust the court will not select methods for trustees, but will advise whether purposes which the trustees have chosen are charitable).

10. Application of Smith, 133 Conn. 6, 47 A.2d 521 (1946).

11. Thomson v. First Nat. Bank, 212 Miss. 691, 55 So.2d 422 (1951); Boston Safe Dep. & Tr. Co. v. Northey, 332 Mass. 110, 123 N.E.2d 365 (1954) (who will be proper distributees of remainder interest at future time).

12. City Bank Farmers' Tr. Co. v. Smith, 263 N.Y. 292, 189 N.E. 222, 93 A.L.R. 598 (1934).

In a few states, upon application to the court, trusts may be taken under its supervision so that all acts of the trustee must thereafter be submitted to the court for approval, and consequently the court's power to advise and control is much broader than in the normal case.[13] The trustee in such court supervised trusts becomes similar to a receiver whose every act must be approved in advance or confirmed after the event.[14]

The settlor *as such* has no right to obtain a construction of the trust instrument by a court of equity.[15]

 WESTLAW REFERENCES

Supervised Trust
find 134 p2d 63
390k112
equity court chancery /s construction /s trust /s instrument

ENJOINING OR SETTING ASIDE WRONGFUL ACTS [1]

§ 154. If a trustee threatens to commit a breach of trust, the beneficiary may secure an injunction against the act; and if the breach has already occurred, the transaction may be set aside, if this action does not involve taking property from the hands of a bona fide purchaser.

If the trustee is preparing to commit a breach of trust, the beneficiary need not sit idly by and wait until damage has been done. He may sue in a court of equity for an injunction against the wrongful act.[2] The trustee will not be likely to violate the injunction and run the danger of punishment for contempt of court. Thus if the trustee is intending to sell the trust property for an unreasonably low price, or on improper conditions, or for an improper purpose, the beneficiary may receive the aid of the court in preventing this action.[3] If the trust

---

13. See Bogert, Trusts and Trustees (rev. 2d edit.), § 563 (court supervised trusts).

14. Smithson v. Callahan, 78 U.S.App. D.C. 355, 141 F.2d 13 (1944); Fla.St.Ann., §§ 737.01 to 737.28; Watts v. Watts, 158 Kan. 59, 145 P.2d 128 (1944); McCrory v. Beeler, 155 Md. 456, 142 A. 587 (1928); Minn.Stats.Ann. §§ 501.33 to 501.38. In re Bush's Trust, 249 Minn. 36, 81 N.W.2d 615 (1957); N.Dak.Cent.Code 59–04–1 to 59–04–31; In re Le Page's Trust, 67 N.D. 15, 269 N.W. 53 (1936); In re Eckhoff's Estate, 62 S.D. 110, 251 N.W. 892 (1933).

And see Art. VII, Uniform Probate Code, under which the concept of trust registration is intended to replace retained supervisory jurisdiction.

15. Carroll v. Smith, 99 Md. 653, 59 A. 131.

§ 154

1. Bogert, Trusts and Trustees (rev. 2d edit.), § 861; Restatement, Trusts, Second, § 199.

2. In re Atlantic City Amb. Hotel Corp., Sup., 62 N.Y.S.2d 62 (1946) (acting after expiration of trust); Wax v. Wax, 78 Pa.D. & C. 213 (payment of excessive salaries).

3. McCreary v. Gewinner, 103 Ga. 528, 29 S.E. 960; Beachey v. Heiple, 130 Md. 683, 101 A. 553; Cohen v. Mainthow, 182 App.Div. 613, 169 N.Y.S. 889.

funds are jeopardized, the trustee may be compelled to give a bond.[4] The trustee may also be directed to pay the funds into court pending litigation.[5]

Furthermore, even if the wrongful act of the trustee has been completed before the beneficiary has time to act, it may not be too late to receive the aid of the court in setting aside or avoiding the transaction.[6] Thus if the trustee releases a mortgage without receiving any consideration for the release, the beneficiary may have the mortgage reinstated where the property formerly subject to the mortgage is still in the hands of the mortgagor or his donees.[7] If an attempt is made by one of two trustees to release a mortgage belonging to the trustees, the beneficiary, co-trustee or a successor trustee may have a decree reinstating the mortgage on the records.[8] Naturally, as shown later,[9] if the trustee has conveyed trust property away in breach of trust to a bona fide purchaser, the deed cannot be set aside.

As shown earlier,[10] a beneficiary may secure a constructive trust as to trust property or its product and thus accomplish the same result as if a transaction were set aside, but the theories behind the two remedies are different. In the case of the constructive trust the transaction stands but the court fastens an equity on the transferee, while if the transaction is set aside the transferee loses his entire interest.

 WESTLAW REFERENCES

enjoin injunction /s breach /2 trust
390k368 /p breach /2 trust

DECREE FOR SPECIFIC PERFORMANCE OF PRIVATE TRUST [1]

§ 155. In the case of a private trust any beneficiary may sue in equity and obtain a decree that the trustee perform a certain act under the trust or carry out the trust in general. Such an action cannot be maintained by the settlor.

The beneficiary has a right to have the trustee carry out the trust as provided in the trust instrument and in accordance with the rules of equity. One of his most important remedies is to obtain a decree from equity directing specific performance of the duties of the trustee.[2] As

4. Starr v. Wiley, 89 N.J.Eq. 79, 103 A. 865.

5. Bullock v. Angleman, 82 N.J.Eq. 23, 87 A. 627.

6. Towle v. Ambs, 123 Ill. 410, 14 N.E. 689; Price v. Estill, 87 Mo. 378.

7. Locke v. Andrasko, 178 Wash. 145, 34 P.2d 444 (1934).

8. Coxe v. Kriebel, 323 Pa. 157, 185 A. 770, 106 A.L.R. 102 (1936).

9. See § 165, post.

10. See § 77, ante.

           § 155

1. Restatement, Trusts, Second, § 199.

2. Robinson v. Mauldin, 11 Ala. 977; Cooper v. McClun, 16 Ill. 435; Wyble v. McPheters, 52 Ind. 393; Goble v. Swobe, 64 Neb. 838, 90 N.W. 919; Attorney General ex rel. Bailey v. Moore's Ex'rs, 19 N.J.Eq. 503; Clark v. Brown, Tex.Civ.App., 108

shown previously,[3] persons having an incidental interest in the performance of a trust are not beneficiaries and may not sue for its enforcement. Examples are found in the case of a relative of the beneficiary,[4] or a town which looks to the trust to relieve it from the burden of supporting the pauper beneficiary.[5] The beneficiary may obtain a decree for the performance of a single act by the trustee, for example, the sale of the trust realty,[6] or for bringing the trust property into court,[7] or for conveyance to a new trustee,[8] or for specific investment;[9] or he may secure a decree for performance of all the duties of the trust in general terms.[10]

Unless the power is specifically reserved, the settlor has no power to obtain the enforcement of a private trust.[11] The creation of a trust does not involve a contract, even though the trustee may have made promises to carry it out, but rather amounts to a conveyance with equitable obligations. Naturally, if the settlor has an interest in the remainder following the trust, he can, after expiration of the trust, compel a reconveyance or delivery of possession by the trustee.[12] And if the trust is for the benefit of the settlor, he may enforce it; but here he occupies a double role, and enforcement is by him as beneficiary and not by him as settlor.[13]

 WESTLAW REFERENCES

di("specific performance" /s trust)

358k120 /p trust

padelford +3 "real estate"

ENFORCEMENT OF CHARITABLE TRUSTS [1]

§ 156. If the trustee of a charitable trust fails to carry it out, usually a suit to compel its enforcement must be brought by the Attorney General of the state as a representative of the public.

Ordinarily individual citizens who feel aggrieved at the breach of the charitable trust have no standing to sue for its enforcement.

S.W. 421; Harrigan v. Gilchrist, 121 Wis. 127, 99 N.W. 909.

3. See § 35, ante.

4. Autrey v. Stubenrauch, 63 Tex.Civ. App. 247, 133 S.W. 531.

5. Town of Sharon v. Simons, 30 Vt. 458.

6. Vrooman v. Virgil, 81 N.J.Eq. 301, 88 A. 372.

7. Bullock v. Angleman, 82 N.J.Eq. 23, 87 A. 627.

8. Nash v. Sutton, 117 N.C. 231, 23 S.E. 178.

9. Sherman v. Parish, 53 N.Y. 483.

10. Callis v. Ridout, Md., 7 Gill & J. 1.

11. Padelford v. Real Estate Land Title & Tr. Co., 121 Pa.Super. 193, 183 A. 442 (1936). But see Abbott v. Gregory, 39 Mich. 68, where the agreement of the trustee to carry out the trust was viewed as a contract apparently enforceable by either the beneficiary or the settlor.

12. Eaton v. Tillinghast, 4 R.I. 276.

13. Backes v. Crane, 87 N.J.Eq. 229, 100 A. 900; Hamilton v. Muncie, 182 App. Div. 630, 169 N.Y.S. 826.

§ 156

1. Bogert, Trusts and Trustees (rev. 2d edit.), § 411; Restatement, Trusts, Second, §§ 386, 391–394, 401.

Neither the settlor nor his successors are permitted to sue to enforce the charitable trust or to recover the trust property on account of a breach, unless the trustee's interest was determinable or subject to a condition subsequent.

At common law the founder of a charitable corporation and his heirs have the power of visitation by which the charity could be inspected and regulated. The power and duty to compel a charitable corporation to live up to its obligations rest in the Attorney General.

If a trustee for charity fails to carry out the trust or commits an act in breach of it, the power to secure enforcement or liability originally rested in the Attorney General in England since he was the legal representative of the crown,[2] but in recent years the Charity Commissioners have been given jurisdiction over the subject.[3] In the United States, in most states, the Attorney General, either by constitution, statute or rules of equity is empowered to enforce charitable trusts, because he is the law officer required to protect the people of the state and they are the beneficiaries.[4] But in a few states the power rests with a county law officer,[5] or is considered as being exercisable by either the Attorney General or the county officer.[6] "Courts of equity have jurisdiction to prevent a misuse or an abuse of charitable trusts . . . .. The Attorney General or a state's attorney representing the public is charged with the duty of preventing a breach of a trust for a public charity or to restore a trust fund after it has been diverted." [7]

In all suits brought by the trustee or others with respect to charitable trusts the Attorney General is usually regarded as a necessary party.[8]

The Attorney General may sue in his own name on his own initiative, or he may permit an interested individual to bring a suit in the name of the Attorney General but on the relation of the individual.[9] The main object of having a relator is to make him liable for the costs

2. Attorney General v. Kell, 2 Beav. 575.

3. Charities Act, 1960 (8 & 9 Eliz. 2, c. 58).

4. People ex rel. Ellert v. Cogswell, 113 Cal. 129, 45 P. 270, 35 L.R.A. 269; Attorney General v. Bedard, 218 Mass. 378, 105 N.E. 993; Longeor v. Red Wing, 206 Minn. 627, 289 N.W. 570 (1940); Tyree v. Bingham, 100 Mo. 451, 13 S.W. 952; Ewell v. Sneed, 136 Tenn. 602, 191 S.W. 131, 5 A.L.R. 303; State v. Taylor, 58 Wn.2d 252, 362 P.2d 247 (1961).

And see statutes cited in Bogert, Trusts and Trustees (rev. 2d edit.), § 411.

5. See, for example, Neb.Rev.St. § 30–240.

6. See People ex rel. Courtney v. Wilson, 327 Ill.App. 231, 63 N.E.2d 794 (1945); Mo.—V.A.M.S. § 71.120 (property held in trust by municipal corporation).

7. People ex rel. Smith v. Braucher, 258 Ill. 604, 608, 101 N.E. 944, 47 L.R.A.,N.S., 1015.

8. Stowell v. Prentiss, 323 Ill. 309, 154 N.E. 120 (1926); Passaic Nat. Bank & Tr. Co. v. East Ridgelawn Cemetery, 137 N.J. Eq. 603, 45 A.2d 814 (1946).

9. "A relator is a party in interest who is permitted to institute a proceeding in the name of the People or the Attorney General when the right to sue resides solely in that official." The consent of the Attorney General may be given informally. Brown v. Memorial Nat. Home Foundation, 162 Cal.App.2d 513, 329 P.2d 118 (1958).

of the suit if it is unsuccessful.[10]   Any person may act as a relator in a charitable information, regardless of personal financial interest in the enforcement of the trust.[11]

In recent years there has been an increasing appreciation of the fact that the Attorneys General and other enforcing officers have inadequate knowledge as to what charities exist within their several jurisdictions, and whether these trusts are being properly executed, and consequently there has been a movement to obtain this information in a systematic way and thereby increase the probability that the enforcing officer will act.[12]   Statutes have been adopted that provide for the furnishing of information by county recording officers as to wills and deeds creating charitable trusts, for having such trusts registered with the Attorney General, for the filing of reports as to trust administration with him, and for giving him the power to supervise, take testimony and issue orders.[13]   The effects of these statutes are that many neglected charities will be brought to light and some cases of breach will be discovered, and that a higher degree of enforcement will ensue.[14]

Where an absolute gift is made to a charitable corporation the Attorney General has the power and duty to see that the corporation applies the gift in accordance with the conditions on which it was made and with its charter, and he may bring suits to secure such results.[15]

Where property is given to trustees to support a charitable institution, the latter is allowed to sue for trust enforcement.[16]   It is a representative of the public which is benefited by the trust and is sometimes called a sub-trustee.

Occasionally individuals or groups located in the region where a charitable trust has been established and who seek to share in the social or economic benefits which enforcement would bring to the public have brought suits to compel the carrying out of the trust.   For example, in the case of a trust to operate a free school the parents of children who would be eligible to attend the school may seek a decree

10.   Attorney General v. Mayor of Dublin, 1 Bligh, N.S., 312; Attorney General v. Butler, 123 Mass. 304.

11.   Mackenzie v. Trustees of Presbytery of Jersey City, 67 N.J.Eq. 652, 61 A. 1027, 3 L.R.A.,N.S., 227.

12.   Forer, 105 U. of Pa.L.R. 1044; Brown, Coblentz, 30 Cal.S.B.J. 425; Bogert, 5 Hast.L.J. 95, 52 Mich.L.R. 633; 21 Univ. Chi.L.R. 118; 27 Boston U.L.R. 342; 32 Mass.L.Q. 14; 47 Col.L.R. 659; 23 Ind.L.J. 141.

13.   See, for example, Mass.G.L.A. c. 12, §§ 8–8M.   For references to similar statutes, see Bogert, Trusts and Trustees (rev. 2d edit.), § 411.   A Uniform Act relating to the supervision of charitable trusts was approved by the National Conference in 1954, and has been adopted in several states.   See, for example, Ill.Rev.Stat. c. 14, §§ 51–64; N.Y.—McKinney's EPTL 8–1.4. See also Charities Act, 1960, which continues supervisory powers in the Charity Commissioners in England.

14.   See Bogert, Trusts and Trustees (rev. 2d edit.), § 411.   For an early statement as to the benefits derived from the supervision act in New Hampshire, see an address by the Supervisor, Mr. D'Amours, 2 N.H.B.J. 161.

15.   St. Joseph's Hospital v. Bennett, 281 N.Y. 115, 22 N.E.2d 305 (1939).

16.   Sunday School Union v. Walden, 121 F.2d 719 (6th Cir.1941); Pratt v. Security Tr. & Sav. Bank, 15 Cal.App.2d 630, 59 P.2d 862 (1936); Northwestern University v. Wesley Mem. Hosp., 290 Ill. 205, 125 N.E. 13 (1919).

against the trustees that they establish and maintain the school.[17] In most instances the courts have refused to permit the maintenance of an action by such persons and have required that the proceeding be brought by the Attorney General.[18] However, in rare cases such parties have been successful in securing relief, possibly because the question of the proper party plaintiff was not raised.[19]

In the absence of special provisions in the trust instrument, neither the settlor nor his successors by will or intestacy may sue to enforce or to obtain a construction of a charitable trust.[20] They are not representatives of the public to be benefited. Nor may they secure a decree that the property be delivered to them when they can prove a violation of the trust.[21] They should bring pressure to bear on the Attorney General. Thus if T left property by will to trustees to establish and operate a hospital, and the trustees have failed in the performance of their duties, the successors of T may not maintain a bill for the enforcement of the hospital trust or for the return of the property to them on the ground of the failure of the trust.[22] If, however, the gift of T was framed in such a way as to create a possibility of reverter in T and his heirs in case of breach, the violation or neglect of the trust may give ground for a restoration of the property to T or his successors; and the same result would follow if the gift had been made on condition subsequent, with a power of termination in the donor or his heirs.[23] The gift might be to the trustees for the hospital "as long as a hospital is operated on the land", or "on condition that a hospital be established and operated on the land", with a reverter to the settlor or his heirs in case of breach.

If a gift was made to trustees for charity, and the settlor expressed a narrow and limited purpose so that cy pres would not be applied, there is a resulting trust for the settlor or his successors if the

---

17. Kolin v. Letich, 343 Ill.App. 622, 99 N.E.2d 685 (1951).

18. Pratt v. Security Trust and Sav. Bank, 15 Cal.App.2d 630, 59 P.2d 862 (1936) (park trust; even though Attorney General made a party defendant); Schaeffer v. Newberry, 227 Minn. 259, 35 N.W.2d 287 (1948) (American Legion sought to enforce park trust); Wiegand v. Barnes Foundation, 374 Pa. 149, 97 A.2d 81 (1953); Clevenger v. Rio Farms, 204 S.W.2d 40 (Tex.Civ.App.1947) (land settlement trust; farmers who wanted to buy land not allowed to sue to enforce).

19. Anderson v. Ryland, 232 Ark. 335, 336 S.W.2d 52 (1960) (taxpayer allowed to enforce school trust); Dominy v. Stanley, 162 Ga. 211, 133 S.E. 245 (1926); Seitzinger v. Becker, 257 Pa. 264, 101 A. 650; Howe v. School District No. 3, 43 Vt. 282.

As to the status of actual or prospective "beneficiaries" of a charitable trust to sue for its enforcement, see Bogert, Trusts and Trustees (rev. 2d edit.), § 414, citing recent cases in California, New Jersey and Texas permitting such suits.

20. Petition of Burnham, 74 N.H. 492, 494, 69 A. 720; Kemper v. Trustees of Lane Seminary, 17 Ohio 293; Strong v. Doty, 32 Wis. 381.

21. Anderson v. Richardson, 200 Va. 1, 104 S.E.2d 5 (1958).

22. Mills v. Montclair Tr. Co., 139 N.J. Eq. 56, 49 A.2d 889 (1946); Fairbanks v. Appleton, 249 Wis. 476, 24 N.W.2d 893 (1946).

23. Franks v. Sparks, 217 Ga. 117, 121 S.E.2d 27 (1961); Commercial Nat. Bank v. Martin, 185 Kan. 116, 340 P.2d 899 (1959); In re Randall's Estate, 341 Pa. 501, 19 A.2d 272 (1941); Town of Bristol v. Nolan, 72 R.I. 460, 53 A.2d 466 (1947).

charitable purpose becomes impossible of accomplishment.[24]

Power of Visitation

At common law the founder of a charitable corporation had a power of visitation of the institution by which he could make inspections, establish regulations, and procure information as to the status of the work, but this did not give him power to sue for the enforcement of the obligations of the corporation.[25] After his death his heirs could exercise the visitorial power. The founder could vest it in others named by him.[26] This power continues to exist.[27] In some states a power of visitation is held to exist in the courts,[28] or is granted to state boards of charities or other similar bodies.[29]

After considering the common law of England upon the subject of visitation, as expressed in Philips v. Bury [1 Ld.Raym. 5, 2 Term.R. 346], a Massachusetts court stated:

"By that law the visitor of all eleemosynary corporations is the founder or his heirs, unless he has given the power of visitation to some other person or body, which is generally the case; and to the visitor thus constituted belongs the right and power of inspecting the affairs of the corporation and superintending all officers who have the management of them, according to such regulations and restrictions as are prescribed by the founder in the statutes which he ordains, without any control or revision of any other person or body, except the judicial tribunals by whose authority and jurisdiction they may be restrained and kept within the limits of their granted powers, and made to regard the Constitution and general laws of the land." [30]

With respect to the possession of the power of visitation by chancery a New York court has said:

"While a court of equity never had visitorial power, yet it always assumed jurisdiction over the charity and its officers when a question arose as to the proper use and disposition of the funds. The power of visitation, therefore, pertained to the supervision and regulation of the work and purpose of the charity, while the court of equity, not as a visitor, but in its inherent power over trusts, assumed jurisdiction to determine whether the funds were being spent in accordance with the trust and purpose of the charity." [31]

24. First Univ. Soc. of Bath v. Swett, 148 Me. 142, 90 A.2d 812 (1952).

25. Allen v. McKean, 1 Sumn. 276, Fed.Cas. No. 229; Trustees of Auburn Academy v. Strong, 1 Hopk.Ch., N.Y., 278; Kolblitz v. Western Reserve University, 21 Ohio Cir.Ct.R. 144.

26. Trustees of Putnam Free School v. Attorney General, 320 Mass. 94, 67 N.E.2d 658 (1946).

27. State v. Taylor, 58 Wn.2d 252, 362 P.2d 247 (1961).

28. Leeds v. Harrison, 7 N.J.Super. 558, 72 A.2d 371 (1950); McKee's Estate, 378 Pa. 607, 108 A.2d 214 (1954).

29. See, for example, Minn.S.A. § 256.02; N.Y.—McKinney's Educ.Law § 4201. For other statutes, see Bogert, Trusts and Trustees (rev. 2d edit.), § 416.

30. In re Murdock, 7 Pick., Mass., 303, 321.

31. In re Norton, 97 Misc. 289, 299, 161 N.Y.S. 710.

WESTLAW REFERENCES

"attorney general" /s enforc**** /s "charitable trust"

75k49

england /s "charity commissioner"

Power of Visitation

power /2 visitation /s trustor settlor founder

phillips +3 borg-warner

find 362 p2d 247

390k171 /p charitable

75k50

DECREE AGAINST TRUSTEE FOR DAMAGES ON ACCOUNT OF BREACH OF TRUST [1]

§ 157. A trustee is liable in damages for losses to the beneficiaries caused by a breach of trust. The cause of action may be enforced by the beneficiaries, a co-trustee or a successor trustee. It was originally recognized in a court of equity only, and under modern codes is generally treated as having an equitable nature, but occasionally relief is granted on a legal theory.

The measure of damages is usually the difference between the values of the principal and income of the trust as they would have been if the trust had been performed and as they existed as a result of the wrongful conduct of the trustee.

In a few instances a trustee who has committed a breach of trust is held liable without regard to the amount of loss suffered by the beneficiary.

The claim against the trustee is general and not preferred.

Any liability of co-trustees is joint and several. Either may be held liable for the whole loss, but equity decrees contribution between co-trustees where the guilt is equal and indemnity against liability on the part of one trustee whose fault is not great.

It is elementary that a trustee who commits a breach of trust can be required to pay from his own pocket the damages caused to the trust beneficiaries. He can be compelled to replace the trust property lost by his wrongdoing and if he does not comply with the direction to make restoration a judgment can be collected out of his personal assets. A failure to perform any of the duties placed upon him by common law, statute or trust instrument, if loss is caused thereby, will give the beneficiaries, a co-trustee or a successor trustee a right to secure from the court of equity a decree that the wrongdoing trustee pay into the trust fund the amount of damages suffered.[2]

---

§ 157

1. Bogert, Trusts and Trustees (rev. 2d edit.), §§ 543(V), 862; Restatement, Trusts, Second, §§ 197–226 (Comment *a*).

2. Miller v. Butler, 121 Ga. 758, 49 S.E. 754; Burris v. Brooks, 118 N.C. 789, 24 S.E. 521; Silliman v. Gano, 90 Tex. 637, 39 S.W. 559, 40 S.W. 391. In the discretion of the court costs and counsel fees may also

This cause of action may be enforced by any of the injured beneficiaries, or by a successor trustee [3] acting on their behalf. It may be asserted in a separate suit or as a part of an accounting proceeding. Originally the court of equity was the only forum in which the claim could be advanced, and it continues to have jurisdiction over such demands; [4] it is often held that a suit in equity is the exclusive remedy.[5] Occasionally courts of law are asked to give relief and they sometimes acquiesce in cases where the amount due is either certain or easily ascertainable and no long and complicated accounting is required.[6] Under modern law it may be important that the cause of action is equitable in nature for the purpose of deciding such questions as the right to a jury trial.[7]

Perhaps the most common case in which the beneficiary may proceed at law against the trustee is where the trustee has promised to pay the beneficiary a definite sum; or the trust has been closed, the accounts settled, a definite sum fixed as that due, and the trustee has no further duty except to pay it to the beneficiary. In these cases courts of law have sometimes entertained jurisdiction in an action for money had and received or its equivalent and have not obliged the beneficiary to proceed in equity.[8] "It is well settled that a cestui que trust cannot bring an action at law against a trustee to recover for money had and received while the trust is still open; but when the trust has been closed and settled, the amount due the cestui que trust established and made certain, and nothing remains to be done but to pay over money, such an action may be maintained." [9]

A probate court may of course construe a will purporting to create a trust for the purpose of determining whether such trust was validly created,[10] and in some states probate courts have concurrent jurisdic-

be awarded against the trustee. Murphy v. Merchants' Nat. Bank of Mobile, 240 Ala. 688, 200 So. 894 (1941); Rothenberg v. Franklin Washington Trust Co., 131 N.J. Eq. 463, 25 A.2d 879 (1942).

Recovery may be had from the estate of the trustee, if he has died. Benson v. Liggett, 78 Ind. 452; Frank v. Morley's Estate, 106 Mich. 635, 64 N.W. 577; In re Spatz's Estate, 245 Pa. 334, 91 A. 492. The claim must be presented within the statutory time. Staley v. Kreinbihl, 152 Ohio St. 315, 89 N.E.2d 593 (1949); Smith v. Fitch, 25 Wn.2d 619, 171 P.2d 682 (1946).

3. Stewart v. Firemen's Ins. Co., 53 Md. 564.

4. Hopkins v. Granger, 52 Ill. 504; Wright v. Dame, 22 Pick., Mass., 55; Malone v. Malone, 151 Mich. 680, 115 N.W. 716; Husted v. Thomson, 158 N.Y. 328, 53 N.E. 20; McCoy v. McCoy, 30 Okl. 379, 121 P. 176, Ann.Cas.1913C, 146.

5. Goldschmidt v. Maier, 140 Cal. xvii, 73 P. 984; Robison v. Carey, 8 Ga. 527;

Upham v. Draper, 157 Mass. 292, 32 N.E. 2; Goupille v. Chaput, 43 Wash. 702, 86 P. 1058.

6. Clifford Banking Co. v. Donovan Commission Co., 195 Mo. 262, 94 S.W. 527; Hanford v. Duchastel, 87 N.J.L. 205, 93 A. 586.

7. Drake v. Rueckhaus, 68 N.M. 209, 360 P.2d 395 (1961).

8. Vincent v. Rogers, 30 Ala. 471; Daugherty v. Daugherty, 116 Iowa 245, 90 N.W. 65; O'Neil v. Epting, 82 Kan. 245, 108 P. 107; Nelson v. Howard, 5 Md. 327; Johnson v. Johnson, 120 Mass. 465; Pitcher v. Rogers' Estate, 199 Mich. 114, 165 N.W. 813; Van Camp v. Searle, 147 N.Y. 150, 41 N.E. 427; Parker v. Parker, 69 Vt. 352, 37 A. 1112.

9. Johnson v. Johnson, 120 Mass. 465, 466.

10. Carpenter v. Cook, 132 Cal. 621, 64 P. 997, 84 Am.St.Rep. 118.

tion with courts of equity over trusts created by will.[11]

It has sometimes been stated that equity will not take jurisdiction to enforce a trust where a complete and adequate remedy at law exists.[12] However the prevailing and better view is that the lack of a remedy at law is not a condition precedent to equitable relief, that originally all the remedies of the beneficiary were in chancery, and that he continues to be entitled to enforce all his rights in that court even though the courts of law may have given him certain remedies from time to time.[13] The statement of Lord Mansfield is applicable, although it was made with reference to another question: "This court will not allow itself to be ousted of any part of its original jurisdiction, because a court of law happens to have fallen in love with the same or a similar jurisdiction, and has attempted (the attempt for the most part is not very successful) to administer such relief as originally was to be had here and here only." [14]

The measure of liability is usually not a question of great difficulty. The beneficiaries are entitled to have the trustee restore to the trust the amount that the trust would not have lost if the trustee had properly performed his duty. They may demand that they be placed in the same financial situation as if the wrong had not been committed.[15] Thus if a trustee in breach of trust buys a nonlegal or improper investment, paying $10,000 for it from trust principal, holds it for a year during which time it earns no income, and at the end of the year the stock proves to have no market value, the principal account clearly has a claim for $10,000; and the income account is entitled to the amount of the average trust yield on $10,000 if that sum had been prudently invested in legal trust investments.[16] If the violation of the trust consisted of the embezzlement of $1,000 worth of bearer bonds, the decree will be for $1,000 in lost principal and the average trust yield or interest on $1,000 for the period between the taking of the bonds and the payment of the claim. Or if the trustee has breached his trust by leaving $5,000 uninvested in a checking account in a bank which bore no interest for a period of two years, instead of investing it

11. Green v. Gaskill, 175 Mass. 265, 56 N.E. 560. For numerous statutes on the matter, see Bogert, Trusts and Trustees (rev.2d edit.), § 870.

12. Langdon v. Blackburn, 109 Cal. 19, 41 P. 814; Coe v. Turner, 5 Conn. 86; Van Sciver v. Churchill, 215 Pa. 53, 64 A. 322; Downs v. Downs' Ex'r, 75 Vt. 383, 56 A. 9.

13. Camody v. Webster, 197 Ala. 290, 72 So. 622; Flye v. Hall, 224 Mass. 528, 113 N.E. 366; Gutch v. Fosdick, 48 N.J.Eq. 353, 22 A. 590, 27 Am.St.Rep. 473; Farrelly v. Skelly, 130 App.Div. 803, 115 N.Y.S. 522; Goldrick v. Roxana Petroleum Co., 74 Okl. 55, 176 P. 932; Borchert v. Borchert, 132 Wis. 593, 113 N.W. 35.

14. Eyre v. Everett, 2 Russell 381, 382. To the same effect, see Leaming, V.C., in

Hussong Dyeing Mach. Co. v. Morris, 89 A. 249.

15. For numerous illustrations, see Wright, Measure of trustee's liability for improper investments, 80 Univ. of Pa.L.R. 1105; Restatement, Trusts, Second, §§ 205–213.

In some states there are statutory rules regarding the measure of damages for some breaches of trust. West's Ann.Cal. Civ.Code §§ 2237, 2238; Mont.—Code Ann. 72–20–203, 72–20–210; N.D.—Cent.Code 59–01–10, 59–01–18; 23 Okl.St.Ann. § 63; S.Dak. Codif.L. 55–2–2, 55–2–10.

16. In re Dickinson, 152 Mass. 184, 25 N.E. 99, 9 L.R.A. 279.

promptly on its receipt, he might be held liable for the average trust yield on $5,000 for two years as the damage to the trust income account from failing to place the fund in legal trust investments of normal yield.[17]

In many cases the loss to the beneficiary is directly traceable to the trustee's breach of trust and the trustee is liable for the amount of loss plus interest. However, sometimes the causal connection between the breach of trust and the loss is less evident and the beneficiary may be required to establish not only a breach and loss to the trust but a causal connection between the breach and loss.[18] Implicit in this rule is the requirement that the loss would not have occurred but for the breach of trust. In several recent cases the courts have required proof of a direct causal connection between the breach and the trust's loss.[19]

In some situations there may be a breach of trust and an intervening cause or event which contributes to the loss. Thus if a trustee makes an unauthorized investment and a loss results, the trustee may be compelled to restore the amount paid for the investment even though the loss may not have been entirely due to the trustee's breach, such as a decline in the stock market or economy. In such a case the court usually declines to measure each of the various causes of the loss and requires the trustee to restore the full amount of loss (the amount paid for the investment) on the ground that the loss would not have occurred but for the trustee's breach.[20]

Another rule of damages provides that a trustee is liable for any profit he has made through his breach of trust even though the trust has suffered no loss.[21] Thus the trustee will be held liable for profits made through a prohibited dealing with trust property even though the trust paid fair market value for the property.[22]

A third measure of damages permits recovery of profit that would have accrued to the trust had there been no breach of trust. Thus

17. Wight v. Lee, 101 Conn. 401, 126 A. 218 (1924); Whitecar's Estate, 147 Pa. 368, 23 A. 575 (1892).

18. See Restatement, Trusts, Second, § 205, Comment *f*. And see cases cited in n. 19, post.

19. See, for example, Vale v. Union Bank, 88 Cal.App.3d 330, 151 Cal.Rptr. 784 (1979); Jefferson Nat. Bank of Miami Beach v. Central Nat. Bank of Chicago, 700 F.2d 1143 (7th Cir.1983); Pension Benefit Guaranty Corporation v. Greene, 570 F.Supp. 1483 (W.D.Pa.1983), affirmed 727 F.2d 1100 (3d Cir.1984), certiorari denied 469 U.S. 820, 105 S.Ct. 92, 83 L.Ed.2d 38 (1984).

20. See, for example, McAllister v. Commonwealth, 30 Pa. 536 (1858) (failure to earmark trust property); McBride v. McBride, 262 Ky. 452, 90 S.W.2d 736 (1936) (delay in turning over trust property to

beneficiaries); Meck v. Behrens, 141 Wash. 676, 252 P. 91 (1927) (unlawful delegation of trustee's discretionary powers).

And see Miller v. Pender, 93 N.H. 1, 34 A.2d 663 (1943); First National Bank of Boston v. Truesdale Hospital, 288 Mass. 35, 192 N.E. 150 (1934).

21. See In re Estate of Anderson, 149 Cal.App.3d 336, 196 Cal.Rptr. 782 (1983); Estate of Rothko, 84 Misc.2d 830, 379 N.Y.S.2d 923 (1975), decree modified on other grounds, 56 A.D.2d 499, 392 N.Y.S.2d 870 (1977), order affirmed 43 N.Y.2d 305, 401 N.Y.S.2d 449, 372 N.E.2d 291 (1977), on remand 95 Misc.2d 492, 407 N.Y.S.2d 954 (1978).

22. See, for example, Magruder v. Drury, 235 U.S. 106, 35 S.Ct. 77, 59 L.Ed. 151 (1914); Mosser v. Darrow, 341 U.S. 267, 71 S.Ct. 680, 95 L.Ed. 927 (1951); ERISA, 29 U.S.C.A. § 1109(a).

where the trustee's breach was his failure to purchase specified securities that subsequently appreciated, the court often surcharges the trustee for the amount of appreciation lost by the breach. Where the trustee sold property that he was directed to retain, the courts may measure his liability by the amount of subsequent appreciation in the property.[23]

In application of the measure of damages permitting recovery of the profit that would have accrued to the trust if there had been no breach of trust, some courts have applied the "benefit of the bargain" rule or a combination of rules in determining the trustee's liability.[24] In some cases the court has found the trustee acted negligently but in good faith and therefore has limited the trustee's liability for breach of trust to losses based upon inventory rather than appreciated values.[25]

In other cases, where the essence of the suit is the conversion of trust property, the beneficiary may be given the option of holding the trustee liable in damages for the value of the trust property at one time or another, or for the value of one item of property or another,[26] or, where the trustee has used the trust fund for his own benefit, recovering the property and holding the trustee liable for the actual income obtained from the trust property or for interest.[27]

In a few instances a trustee who has committed a breach of trust is held liable in money damages even though there is no proof that the beneficiary suffered a loss thereby, as where the trustee violates a duty

23. McKim v. Hibbard, 142 Mass. 422, 8 N.E. 152 (1886); McCord v. Nabours, 101 Tex. 494, 109 S.W. 913 (1908), modified, as to measure of recovery 101 Tex. 494, 111 S.W. 144 (1908); Estate of Rothko, 84 Misc. 2d 830, 379 N.Y.S.2d 923 (1975), decree modified on other grounds 56 A.D.2d 499, 392 N.Y.S.2d 870 (1977), order affirmed 43 N.Y.2d 305, 401 N.Y.S.2d 449, 372 N.E.2d 291 (1977), on remand 95 Misc.2d 492, 407 N.Y.S.2d 954 (1978) (executors).

And see Bogert, Trusts and Trustees (rev.2d Edit.), § 702.

24. See Bogert, Trusts & Trustees (rev. 2d Edit.), § 703.

25. See Estate of Talbot, 141 Cal.App. 2d 309, 296 P.2d 848 (1956).

By § 19 of the Uniform Trusts Act the court "may wholly or partly excuse a trustee who has acted honestly and reasonably from liability for violations of the provisions of this Act."

See Annotation, Measure of trustee's liability for breach of trust in selling investment property, or changing investments, in good faith, 58 A.L.R.2d 674 (1958).

And see Trustee, the stock market and the measure of damages. Tenney. 96

Trusts & Estates 824 (1957) (measure of liability for loss should be based on restoring original value rather than appreciated value, where trustee acted in good faith).

26. May v. LeClaire, 78 U.S. (11 Wall.) 217, 20 L.Ed. 50 (1870); Peabody v. Tarbell, 2 Cush. (56 Mass.) 226 (1848); Morse v. Hill, 136 Mass. 60 (1883) (proceeds of sale or actual value); Norris' Appeal, 71 Pa. 106 (1872) (amount wrongfully invested or value of such investment); Harrison v. Harrison, 2 Atk. 121 (1740).

See also duPont v. Delaware Trust Co., 364 A.2d 157 (Del.Ch.1975); Holmes v. Bateson, 434 F.Supp. 1365 (D.R.I.1977), affirmed on measure of damages 583 F.2d 542, 562 (1st Cir.1978).

And see, as to damages for conversion, Kan.Stat.Ann. 59–1704 (trustee converting trust property liable for double its value); 23 Okl.St.Ann. § 64; 42 Pa.C.S.A. § 8335.

27. Ball v. Hopkins, 268 Mass. 260, 167 N.E. 338 (1929); Docker v. Somes, 2 M. & K. 655 (1834).

See Restatement, Trusts, Second, § 206, Comment *c.*

of loyalty and is made liable for a profit he or an agent received therefrom,[28] or where the trustee has improperly sought to delegate the performance of the trust to another and is made a guarantor of the safety of the fund,[29] or where the trustee has failed to deliver the trust property to the beneficiary promptly on the termination of the trust and is made liable for shrinkages in value, although they were not caused by the acts of the trustee.[30] In these cases equity imposes a penalty in order to prevent certain breaches which are deemed to be highly prejudicial.

A trustee who has made two separate improper investments, on one of which there has been a profit and on the other of which there has been a loss, is not entitled to offset the profit against the loss. The beneficiary may insist on the profit as earned by his property, and may reject the unprofitable investment, and require the trustee to replace the cash invested and to retain the improper investment for himself.[31]

Where an improper investment has gone through several stages, the damages must be measured by the situations at the beginning and the end of the transactions, and the beneficiary may not use an intermediate value as a gauge. Thus if T invests $1,000 of trust funds in real estate illegally, sells it for $2,000, and invests the proceeds in corporate stock which is unlawful for him to buy and which depreciates in value to $500, if the beneficiary elects to hold the trustee liable in money for his improper conduct, he will be allowed to recover $1,000 plus the income which should have been earned by a proper trust investment of that amount and minus any income actually paid him from the improper investment. There is no option to hold the trustee liable for the $2,000 in value which this investment had at one stage, since that amount has been realized and expended for the trust in purchasing the last nonlegal investment. The series of nonlegal transactions must be ratified or rejected as a whole.[32]

In determining the damages suffered by the *income* beneficiary on account of the loss of the value of the use of trust property, either one of several methods of measurement may be employed, depending on the type of property and the circumstances of the case. Where the property, the use of which the beneficiary has been deprived, has produced a known income, this furnishes a more satisfactory basis for the award of damages than interest. Thus where the trustee mingles the trust funds with his own property, and the separate earnings of the trust property are known, recovery of such separate earnings is frequently allowed; [33]

28. Mosser v. Darrow, 341 U.S. 267, 71 S.Ct. 680, 95 L.Ed. 927 (1951).

29. Meck v. Behrens, 141 Wash. 676, 252 P. 91 (1927).

30. McBride v. McBride, 262 Ky. 452, 90 S.W.2d 736 (1936).

31. In re Deare, 11 T.L.R. 183; Creed v. McAleer, 275 Mass. 353, 175 N.E. 761, 80 A.L.R. 1117 (1931); In re Buck's Will, 55 N.Y.S.2d 841 (Sur.1945). Restatement, Trusts, Second, § 213; Harris, 23 Ky.L.J. 338.

32. Heathcote v. Hulme, 1 Jac. & Walker 122; Baker v. Disbrow, 18 Hun 29, affirmed 79 N.Y. 631.

33. Title Ins. & Trust Co. v. Ingersoll, 158 Cal. 474, 111 P. 360; Rainsford v. Rainsford, McMul.Eq., S.C., 335.

but the beneficiary may elect between such earnings and interest.[34] And so the actual rents received from real property used by the trustee for his personal purposes,[35] and the actual receipts from money unjustifiably left in a bank,[36] have been allowed as damages, rather than interest or estimated value. Occasionally, where the trustee has had the use of trust property, its rental value is used as the measure of damages.[37]

In many cases the loss to the income beneficiary is fixed by charging interest. Whether simple or compound interest is to be allowed rests in the discretion of the court. If simple interest will adequately compensate the beneficiary it will be charged. If compound interest will more accurately make the beneficiary whole, then that standard of computation will be followed. "Although as a general rule it may fairly be stated that, where the trustee is guilty of gross neglect or fraud, or mingles the money with his own, he should be charged with interest at the legal rate, with annual rests, and, if he is guilty of mere neglect, with simple interest only, this rule is subject to exceptions, and the real question is what the equities of the particular case demand." [38] If the trustee has converted the trust property to his own use, simple interest on the value of the property at the time of conversion is ordinarily allowed.[39] Simple interest has also been frequently charged when the trustee has failed to invest the funds though directed to do so by the trust instrument,[40] although the income loss might also be measured by applying the average yield on legal investments.

Compound interest will be allowed where it is necessary to compensate the beneficiary. It is not awarded as punishment. "The rule which makes an executor or other trustee chargeable with compound interest upon trust funds used by him in his own business is not adopted for the purpose of punishing him for any intentional wrongdoing in the use of such fund, but rather to carry into effect the principle, enforced by courts of equity, that the trustee shall not be permitted to make any profit from the unauthorized use of such funds." [41] Compound interest is sometimes allowed in case of fraud,[42] willful miscon-

34. Treacy v. Powers, 112 Minn. 226, 127 N.W. 936; City of Lincoln v. Morrison, 64 Neb. 822, 90 N.W. 905, 57 L.R.A. 885; In re Eisenlohr's Estate, 258 Pa. 431, 102 A. 115.

35. Percival-Porter Co. v. Oaks, 130 Iowa 212, 106 N.W. 626; Owens v. Williams, 130 N.C. 165, 41 S.E. 93; Thomson v. Peake, 38 S.C. 440, 17 S.E. 45.

36. Cornet v. Cornet, 269 Mo. 298, 190 S.W. 333; In re Wiley, 98 App.Div. 93, 91 N.Y.S. 661.

37. Johnson v. Richey, 5 Miss. 233, 4 How. 233; Weltner v. Thurmond, 17 Wyo. 268, 98 P. 590, 99 P. 1128, 129 Am.St.Rep. 1113.

38. Backes v. Crane, 87 N.J.Eq. 229, 100 A. 900, 904, 905.

39. Hall v. Glover, 47 Ala. 467; Stanley's Estate v. Pence, 160 Ind. 636, 66 N.E. 51, 67 N.E. 441; McKim v. Hibbard, 142 Mass. 422, 8 N.E. 152; Darling v. Potts, 118 Mo. 506, 24 S.W. 461; Mabie v. Bailey, 95 N.Y. 206.

40. Smith v. Darby, 39 Md. 268; In re Muller, 31 App.Div. 80, 52 N.Y.S. 565; Appeal of Stearly, 38 Pa. 525.

41. Miller v. Lux, 100 Cal. 609, 616, 35 P. 345, 639.

42. St. Paul Tr. Co. v. Strong, 85 Minn. 1, 88 N.W. 256.

duct,[43] or other gross delinquency.[44] Perhaps the most common instance of the collection of compound interest from the defaulting trustee is found where he has used the trust fund in his own business and the actual profits earned by the trust fund are not claimed or are impossible of computation,[45] or where there is a strong presumption that the trustee has used the funds in his own business because he renders no account and in no way shows the disposition of the trust money.[46] As Chancellor Walworth said: "Stating the account with periodical rests, and compounding interest, is only a convenient mode, adopted by the court, to charge the trustee with the amount of profits supposed to have been made by him in the use of the money; where the actual amount of profits, which he has made, beyond simple interest, cannot be ascertained." [47]

The claim of the beneficiary or successor trustee against the defaulting trustee is almost never a preferred claim, but instead gives a right to come in equally with the general creditors.[48] There has been a small amount of legislation creating a preference for such claims in special cases.[49] The case of a lien on the product or proceeds of the breach of trust is considered in a later section.[50] The situation now under consideration is that where the breach has not produced any property which is in the hands of the defaulting trustee, as where, for instance, he has embezzled the trust funds and wasted them in paying his own living expenses, and then dies or becomes insolvent while holding some property not connected with the trust.

Since co-trustees are joint tenants and hold their powers in joint control they are held jointly and severally liable for breaches of trust. Thus if A and B are trustees under the will of S and they have a duty to sell a nonlegal trust investment and reinvest in other securities, but they fail to do so and the nonlegal becomes valueless, they may be sued as co-defendants for the lost principal and income or one of them alone may be sued. Recovery may be collected entirely from the assets of either trustee, if both are sued.[51] The plaintiff is not required to split

---

43. Adams v. Lambard, 80 Cal. 426, 22 P. 180.

44. Mathewson v. Davis, 191 Ill. 391, 61 N.E. 68.

45. Bemmerly v. Woodward, 124 Cal. 568, 57 P. 561; State v. Howarth, 48 Conn. 207; Lehman v. Rothbarth, 159 Ill. 270, 42 N.E. 777; McKnight's Ex'rs v. Walsh, 23 N.J.Eq. 136; Cook v. Lowry, 95 N.Y. 103.

46. Voorhees' Adm'rs v. Stoothoff, 11 N.J.L. 145.

47. Utica Ins. Co. v. Lynch, 11 Paige, N.Y., 520, 524.

48. Wales v. Sammis & Scott, 120 Iowa 293, 94 N.W. 840; City of Lincoln v. Morrison, 64 Neb. 822, 90 N.W. 905, 57 L.R.A. 885; Mertens v. Schlemme, 68 N.J.Eq. 544, 59 A. 808.

49. In some states a claim against the estate of a deceased trustee for trust funds is made a preferred one by statute. See, for example, Colo.Rev.Stats. § 15–12–805; Ill.Rev.Stat. c. 110½, § 18–10. In several other states claims against insolvent or dissolved corporate fiduciaries are likewise preferred. See, for example, Md.Fin.Instits.L. § 3–804. See also Union Tr. Co. v. Ralston, 101 Ind.App. 548, 19 N.E. 94.

50. See § 158, post.

51. Furman v. Rapelje, 67 Ill.App. 31; Lose v. Lyman, 316 Mass. 271, 55 N.E.2d 433 (1944); Windmuller v. Spirits Distributing Co., 83 N.J.Eq. 6, 90 A. 249; In re Durston's Estate, 297 N.Y. 64, 74 N.E.2d 310 (1947); Harrigan v. Gilchrist, 121 Wis. 127, 99 N.W. 909.

his claim and enforce a proportionate part against each co-trustee, and in fact could not do so. But, as between co-trustees, equity will adjust their ultimate liabilities according to their degrees of blameworthiness. Thus if both are in equal guilt it may grant contribution to one who has paid the whole claim; [52] and if one is only slightly at fault and the other has been largely responsible for the wrongdoing the court may grant the comparatively innocent trustee indemnity and throw the whole loss on the other trustee.[53]

Criminal Liability of Trustee

Until the enactment of fairly recent statutes, a breach of trust by a trustee, even though fraudulent, was not a crime. The trustee had legal title and his original possession was lawful. In discussing a fraudulent appropriation of trust funds, a New York court said: [54] "The acts of the defendant were not larceny at common law, and not cognizable in a criminal prosecution. The underlying concept of larceny at common law was an initial *trespass* and *trover*. Where there was no trespass, there was no larceny, though trespass and trover in themselves were not necessarily larceny . . .. The defendant's conduct amounted to what was known formerly as 'a criminal breach of trust,' and until quite recent times was cognizable only in a court of equity and punishable only as contempt of court, where restitution was not made in obedience to a judgment so decreeing . . .. Nor did the defendant's act come within the scope of the early statutes creating the crime of embezzlement, which statutes were enacted to meet some of the deficiencies of the common-law rules as to larceny." But modern statutes frequently make the appropriation of the trust property by the trustee larceny or embezzlement, so that the beneficiary has the additional remedy of prosecuting the trustee for a crime, and in some cases collecting a fine from him under the criminal law.[55]

  WESTLAW REFERENCES

For Damages on Account of Breach of Trust
beneficiary /s damages /s "breach of trust"
390k166(2) /p "breach of trust"
"breach of trust" /s measure /3 liabiity damages
find 24 a2d 188

52. Jackson v. Dickinson, [1903] 1 Ch. 947; Buder v. Walsh, 314 S.W.2d 739 (Mo. 1958); Sherman v. Parish, 53 N.Y. 483.

See Berger, 9 Ind.L.J. 229; 22 Va.L.R. 804; Uniform Joint Tort Feasors Contribution Act.

53. Re Linsley, (1904) 2 Ch. 785; Overfield v. Pennroad Corp., 42 F.Supp. 586 (E.D.Pa.1941), affirmed 146 F.2d 889 (3d Cir.1944); Epworth Orphanage v. Long, 207 S.C. 384, 36 S.E.2d 37 (1945); Lockhart v. Reilly, 25 L.J.Ch. 697. In order that

questions of indemnity and contribution may be settled in the same action as that in which liability is determined it is desirable to make all co-trustees defendants. Spitz v. Dimond, 131 N.J.Eq. 186, 24 A.2d 188 (1942).

54. People v. Shears, 158 App.Div. 577, 580, 143 N.Y.S. 861.

55. For statutory references, see Bogert, Trusts and Trustees (rev.2d edit.), § 861. And see Mahla, 39 Col.L.R. 1004; Snyder, 11 Miss.L.J. 123, 368.

PERSONAL LIABILITY OF TRUSTEE WITH LIEN [1]

§ 158. If a trustee has committed a breach of trust and has in his possession and ownership the product of the breach, the beneficiary may be accorded a right to collect damages and to have a lien on the property which is the product of the breach.

In some cases the beneficiary is aided by the court of equity in the collection of his judgment against the trustee for breach of trust. He is given a lien or right to the use of specific property which is in the hands of the trustee for the purpose of collecting his claim, if this property is the product of the breach.[2] Thus if a trustee invests $10,000 of trust funds in speculative stock which is not a proper investment, and the stock declines in value to $2,000, it is the product of a wrongful disposition of trust funds, and if the beneficiary elects to hold the trustee liable for the $10,000 of trust principal he may have an equitable lien on the stock to aid him in collecting his judgment. He may treat the stock as belonging to the trustee personally, and not as trust property, but may claim that on account of the method by which the trustee acquired the stock it is fair that he hold it subject to a lien in favor of the beneficiary. Thus the stock will be sold under the supervision of the court, the proceeds will be applied on the $10,000 judgment, and the balance due will be collectible as an unsecured claim.[3]

This remedy should be distinguished from "tracing", an important right of the beneficiary which is discussed in a later section.[4] Under the lien theory the product is treated as the property of the trustee personally, while in tracing the product is treated as substitute trust property. A choice between the two methods of securing relief must be made by the injured beneficiary or his successor trustee.[5]

Where the product of a breach is of less value than the original trust property, and there is some chance of collecting out of the general assets of the trustee, the equitable method is preferable to tracing. On the other hand, if the product is greater in value than the original trust

---

§ 158

1. Restatement, Trusts, Second, § 202.

2. Citizens' Bank of Paso Robles v. Rucker, 138 Cal. 606, 72 P. 46; Hinsey v. Supreme Lodge K. of P., 138 Ill.App. 248; Newis v. Topfer, 121 Iowa 433, 96 N.W. 905; Bohle v. Hasselbroch, 64 N.J.Eq. 334, 51 A. 508, 61 L.R.A. 323; Finley v. Exchange Trust Co., 183 Okl. 167, 80 P.2d 296 (1938); In re Stopp's Estate, 330 Pa. 493, 199 A. 493 (1938).

A similar lien may be asserted against a third party who holds trust property or its proceeds and is not a bona fide purchaser. Day v. Rothy, 18 N.Y. 448.

3. Primeau v. Granfield, 184 Fed. 480 (S.D.N.Y.1911); Butler v. Commonwealth Tr. Co., 343 Pa. 143, 22 A.2d 718 (1941).

4. See § 161, post.

5. Shearer v. Barnes, 118 Minn. 179, 136 N.W. 861; Warsco v. Oshkosh Sav. & Tr. Co., 190 Wis. 87, 208 N.W. 886 (1926).

property, tracing will be a preferable remedy. Thus if $1,000 of trust funds has been wrongfully invested in land by the trustee, and the land has declined in value to $800, a money judgment plus a lien on the land will be advisable. But if the land has increased in value to $1,200, tracing into the land will give the beneficiary a more advantageous remedy.

In Will of Mendel, a trustee was directed to invest the funds in "first-class interest-bearing real estate mortgage securities." It being held that under this direction the securities actually purchased were improper investments, the beneficiaries were allowed to hold the trustee personally liable and to enforce an equitable lien upon the securities. The court said: [6] "This is not a case of following the trust fund into the property in which it has been improperly invested, and claiming such property, and, at the same time, claiming to recover the fund upon personal liability therefor . . .. The [successor] trustees do not claim the securities. They claim that, in equity, they are entitled to hold them as property of the wrongdoer, charged with a lien to make good, so far as practicable, the damage caused by the wrong. There can be no doubt but what the cestui que trust, in such circumstances as exist here, may retain the property and thereby ratify the wrong, or reject it and claim damages for the wrongful investment therein, or claim such damages and charge such property, as belonging to the wrongdoer, with a lien for the damages suffered."

 WESTLAW REFERENCES

beneficiary /s lien /s property /s "breach of trust"
find 22 a2d 718

RECOVERY FROM BONDSMAN OR GUARANTY FUND

§ 159. Where a trustee has given a bond with sureties and commits a breach of trust, the beneficiary or his representative may recover from the bondsman.

Where a corporate trustee is required by statute to make a deposit of a security fund with a state official as a guaranty of the faithful administration of its trusts, a beneficiary suffering from a breach of trust may secure satisfaction out of the security fund.

On a showing of necessity equity will require a bond where none has existed, or will order an increase in the size of the trustee's bond.

As has been previously shown,[1] the trustee often gives a bond for the faithful performance of his duties and is joined in this bond by sureties. The question when such a bond will afford a beneficiary a remedy against the surety depends partly upon the language of the

6. 164 Wis. 136, 143–144, 159 N.W. 806.

§ **159**

1. See § 33, ante.

bond. Ordinarily the misapplication of trust funds by the trustee,[2] the failure of the trustee to turn over the trust property to his successor [3] or to render an account required by statute,[4] or the mixture of trust and private funds by the trustee with consequent loss [5] is a default which will render the surety liable. Whether the surety becomes liable for defaults occurring before the execution of the bond depends upon the wording of the bond. In some cases the language has been broad enough to cover transactions occurring prior to the bond,[6] while in others the wording has been prospective and led to a decision that future acts of the trustee only were to be covered.[7]

In whose name the action against the surety should be brought depends upon the terms of the bond or upon statutory control.[8] Such bonds frequently run to the judge of the probate court,[9] the county judge,[10] or to the state.[11] The public officer or body, however, is merely the nominal plaintiff, and the beneficiaries are the real parties in interest,[12] as is illustrated where the Statute of Limitations is involved.[13] When the bond runs to the clerk or master of an equity court, the beneficiary cannot sue without leave of court.[14]

The nature of the surety's liability and the conditions precedent to fixing responsibility upon him are questions of the law of suretyship, not of trusts. Ordinarily the surety's liability is secondary to that of the trustee, and co-sureties are equally liable among themselves.[15] In pursuance of this rule the beneficiary has been required to prosecute an action against the trustee to have the amount of the default decreed before seeking recovery from the surety; [16] but in cases where the trustee is a nonresident,[17] or a bankrupt, a fugitive from justice and of unknown residence,[18] this requirement of prior action against the trustee has been dispensed with. The courts are not in harmony upon the effect to be given to a decree against the trustee adjudging him in default and fixing the amount of the defalcation. Some have held such decree merely prima facie evidence of the fact and amount of the

2. State v. Thresher, 77 Conn. 70, 58 A. 460; McIntire v. Linehan, 178 Mass. 263, 59 N.E. 767.

3. State v. Hunter, 73 Conn. 435, 47 A. 665; McKim v. Doane, 137 Mass. 195.

4. Prindle v. Holcomb, 45 Conn. 111.

5. Knowlton v. Bradley, 17 N.H. 458, 43 Am.Dec. 609.

6. Comegys v. State, 10 Gill. & J., Md., 175; Commonwealth v. Fidelity & Deposit Co. of Maryland, 224 Pa. 95, 73 A. 327, 132 Am.St.Rep. 755.

7. State v. Hunter, 73 Conn. 435, 47 A. 665; State v. Banks, 76 Md. 136, 24 A. 415; Thomson v. American Surety Co. of New York, 170 N.Y. 109, 62 N.E. 1073.

8. See statutes cited in Bogert, Trusts and Trustees (rev.2d edit.), § 864.

9. Bassett v. Granger, 136 Mass. 174.

10. Meyer v. Barth, 97 Wis. 352, 72 N.W. 748, 65 Am.St.Rep. 124.

11. Commonwealth v. Allen, 254 Pa. 474, 98 A. 1056; State v. Graham, 115 Md. 520, 81 A. 31.

12. Close v. Farmers' Loan & Trust Co., 195 N.Y. 92, 87 N.E. 1005.

13. Pearson v. McMillan, 37 Miss. 588.

14. Floyd v. Gilliam, 59 N.C. 183.

15. Clagett v. Worthington, 3 Gill., Md., 83.

16. Crane v. Moses, 13 S.C. 561.

17. Yates v. Thomas, 35 Misc. 552, 71 N.Y.S. 1113.

18. Commonwealth v. Allen, 254 Pa. 474, 98 A. 1056.

surety's liability,[19] but others have treated it as conclusive upon the surety.[20] Yet other courts have held that the surety was not at all bound by a proceeding against the trustee to which he was not a party,[21] or that he was bound only when he had agreed by his bond to be bound by such adjudication.[22]

If the court believes that a bond ought to be required, although one was not originally given by the trustee, or that the amount of the bond should be increased, on application of the beneficiary it will enter an order accordingly.[23] The beneficiary will be obliged to make a showing of a change in circumstances, for example, that the conduct of the trustee has given ground for apprehension as to the safety of the trust property, or that the size of the estate has increased.

Statutes quite commonly provide that a corporate trustee is excused from giving a bond but, as a condition precedent to accepting trusts, must deposit with a state official securities of a certain value as a guaranty fund for the faithful performance of its trusts. It is obvious that if such a fund is deposited and there is a breach of trust by the corporate trustee, the state official as pledgee of the fund may be required by the trust beneficiaries to use the fund for the purpose of satisfying the claim for damages.[24] These funds are not, however, of great importance since corporate fiduciaries are nearly always able to pay judgments obtained against them, and if they become insolvent the security deposits are not large enough to afford much help to trust beneficiaries.

 WESTLAW REFERENCES

find 59 ne 767

di(recovery /10 bond /s trustee)

find 68 f2d 795

---

19. Haddock v. Perham, 70 Ga. 572; Cully v. People, to Use of Dunlap, 73 Ill. App. 501.

20. Appeal of Glover, 167 Mass. 280, 45 N.E. 744; Commonwealth v. Fidelity & Deposit Co. of Maryland, 224 Pa. 95, 73 A. 327, 132 Am.St.Rep. 755; Meyer v. Barth, 97 Wis. 352, 72 N.W. 748, 65 Am.St.Rep. 124.

21. Thomson v. American Surety Co. of New York, 170 N.Y. 109, 62 N.E. 1073.

22. People ex rel. Collins v. Donohue, 70 Hun 317, 24 N.Y.S. 437.

23. McClernan v. McClernan, 73 Md. 283, 20 A. 908; Starr v. Wiley, 89 N.J.L. 79, 103 A. 865; Fidelity & Deposit Co. v. Wolfe, 100 Ohio St. 332, 126 N.E. 414 (1919).

24. Carcaba v. McNair, 68 F.2d 795 (5th Cir.1934), certiorari denied 292 U.S. 646, 54 S.Ct. 780, 78 L.Ed. 1497 (1934); In re Schmitt's Estate, 288 Ill.App. 250, 6 N.E.2d 444 (1937); Huntington Nat. Bank v. Fulton, 49 Ohio App. 268, 197 N.E. 204 (1934).

REMOVAL OF TRUSTEE—APPOINTMENT OF SUCCESSOR [1]

§ **160.** **If a beneficiary can prove that his financial interests will be seriously endangered by a continued operation of the trust by the trustee, he may be able to secure the trustee's removal by a court of equity.**

In rare cases, instead of removing the trustee and appointing a successor, the court will provide for the temporary conservation of the estate by the appointment of a receiver.

The court has power to remove a trustee and to appoint a successor trustee. In making an appointment it should consider the recommendations of the beneficiaries, and failure to do so may amount to an abuse of the discretion the court has in removal and appointments.

Power to Remove a Trustee

In many cases where breaches of trust have been committed or are threatened, or the trustee has become incompetent to continue his work, the beneficiaries desire to have him removed and to have a new administrator of the trust appointed in his place. The power to take such action rests in the court of equity by virtue of its inherent jurisdiction to enforce trusts and protect beneficiaries.[2] The power is often set forth in statutory form, but these statutes are merely declaratory of a common law authority resting in the court and are of principal importance on account of the rules of procedure which they prescribe for applications for removal.[3] In some states the court having probate jurisdiction is vested with power to remove trustees of testamentary trusts and appoint their successors.[4] The exercise of the power rests in the discretion of the court,[5] and appellate courts will not interfere with the decisions of the trial courts unless there has been a clear abuse of discretion.[6] The courts are reluctant to remove a trustee, because of the serious adverse effect of a removal on his reputation.[7] And if the trustee has been appointed by the settlor there is another ground for reluctance on the part of the court to change trustees, since it is reluctant to substitute its judgment for that of the creator of the trust.[8]

§ **160**

1. Restatement, Trusts, Second, §§ 107, 108, 199, 388, 397.

2. Waller v. Hosford, 152 Iowa 176, 130 N.W. 1093; City of St. Louis v. Wenneker, 145 Mo. 230, 47 S.W. 105, 68 Am.St. Rep. 561; In re McGillivray, 138 N.Y. 308, 33 N.E. 1077; Appeal of Piper, 20 Pa. 67.

3. For numerous statutory references, see Bogert, Trusts and Trustees (rev.2d edit.), § 519.

4. For references, see Bogert, Trusts and Trustees (rev.2d edit.), §§ 519, 870.

5. Scott v. Rand, 118 Mass. 215; Ward v. Dortch, 69 N.C. 277; Hodgson's Estate, 342 Pa. 250, 20 A.2d 294 (1941).

6. Jones v. Stubbs, 136 Cal.App.2d 490, 288 P.2d 939 (1955).

7. State ex rel. Caulfield v. Sartorius, 344 Mo. 919, 130 S.W.2d 541 (1939).

8. Shelton v. McHaney, 343 Mo. 119, 119 S.W.2d 951 (1938); In re Crawford's Estate, 340 Pa. 187, 16 A.2d 521 (1940).

If the application is for the removal of a court-appointed trustee, the court may feel it can exercise more latitude. The motive which actuates the court in ordering a removal is not punishment of an unfaithful or incompetent trustee, but rather protection of the beneficiaries from loss in the future administration of the trust.[9]

Where a municipal corporation is a trustee, the legislature has power to remove it from the trusteeship.[10]

The settlor may make provision for removal of his trustee by the beneficiaries, by the settlor himself, or by others.[11] These directions will control, both as to the holder of the power and as to the method of exercising it, but will not deprive the court of its inherent authority to remove.

Method of Removal

In the absence of statute the removal should be sought in a suit in equity,[12] but in some states more summary methods of removal are provided by legislation, as in the case of petitions, motions, and special proceedings.[13] Frequently removal takes place in connection with an accounting where the trustee is surcharged for wrongful conduct.[14]

The application for removal of the trustee may be made by any one having a financial interest in the execution of the trust.[15] It may be made by one or all of the beneficiaries,[16] whether their interests are vested or contingent,[17] or by a co-trustee.[18] The Attorney General is the proper party to apply for the removal of a trustee of a charitable trust.[19] The settlor as such does not have the requisite interest to enable him to apply for the removal of the trustee,[20] where he did not reserve the power in the trust instrument.

Normally all the beneficiaries should be made parties or their interests represented;[21] and all other persons interested in the trust should be joined in the action.[22] If one of several trustees is to be

9. Moore v. Bowes, 8 Cal.2d 162, 64 P.2d 423 (1937).

10. City of Philadelphia v. Fox, 64 Pa. 169.

11. Florida Nat. Bldg. Corp. v. Miami Beach First Nat. Bank, 151 Fla. 276, 9 So. 2d 563 (1942); In re Lowe's Estate, 68 Utah 49, 249 P. 128 (1926).

12. In re Denison's Will, 130 N.J.Eq. 72, 21 A.2d 304 (1941).

13. Zehnbar v. Spillman, 25 Fla. 591, 6 So. 214; Comegys v. State, 10 Gill & J. 175.

14. Estate of Holt, 33 Haw. 352; In re Cohen, 173 Misc. 878, 18 N.Y.S.2d 342 (1940).

15. There is a conflict as to whether the court may on its own motion remove a trustee. Cf. Wheeler v. Paddock, 293 Ill. App. 395, 12 N.E.2d 687 (1938), and Quincy

Trust Co. v. Taylor, 317 Mass. 195, 57 N.E.2d 573 (1944).

16. Barbour v. Weld, 201 Mass. 513, 87 N.E. 909; Goncelier v. Foret, 4 Minn. (13 Gil.) 1; Cooper v. Day, 1 Rich.Eq., S.C., 26.

17. Wilson v. Wilson, 145 Mass. 490, 14 N.E. 521, 1 Am.St.Rep. 477; In re Bartells' Will, 109 App.Div. 586, 96 N.Y.S. 579; Bailey v. Rice, 1 Tenn.Ch.App. 645.

18. Ingalls v. Ingalls, 257 Ala. 521, 59 So.2d 898 (1952).

19. State v. Fleming, 3 Del.Ch. 153.

20. Thompson v. Childress, 4 Baxt., Tenn., 327.

21. Butler v. Butler, 164 Ill. 171, 45 N.E. 426; Elias v. Schweyer, 13 App.Div. 336, 43 N.Y.S. 55.

22. Goodwin v. Goodwin, 69 Mo. 617.

removed, the co-trustees should be made defendants.[23] The trustee should be given notice of the proceeding to remove him in order that he may have the opportunity to defend himself.[24] It would be an abuse of discretion to remove him without notice to him, even assuming that the court had power to take such action.[25]

A trustee who unsuccessfully resists an application for his removal may be held liable for the costs of the proceeding;[26] but if he shows that there is no cause for his removal and that he has been performing his duties satisfactorily, the court may charge the costs of the proceeding to the trust estate or to the parties who sought his removal.[27]

Grounds for Removal

The party seeking removal must prove serious danger to the interests of the beneficiaries from the trustee's continuance in office,[28] either because of his condition and habits or on account of breaches of trust which he has committed or threatens to commit. In many states the statutes which recite the power to remove also set forth grounds which are to be deemed sufficient cause; such a list is not to be regarded as exclusive but merely illustrative. The power of the court exists in other cases where financial losses from the administration of the trustee are reasonably to be contemplated.[29]

Facts regarding the status of the trustee which have been held sufficient to warrant his removal are insanity,[30] habitual drunkenness,[31] extreme improvidence,[32] conviction of a crime involving dishonesty,[33] insolvency,[34] bankruptcy or receivership,[35] and absence from the jurisdiction.[36]

Breaches of trust which have been regarded by the courts as sufficiently serious to justify removal are disobedience to court orders[37]

23. Hamilton v. Faber, 33 Misc. 64, 68 N.Y.S. 144.

24. Hitch v. Stonebraker, 125 Mo. 128, 28 S.W. 443; Holcomb v. Kelly, Sup., 114 N.Y.S. 1048.

25. Ex parte Kilgore, 120 Ind. 94, 22 N.E. 104.

26. Lape's Adm'r v. Taylor's Trustee, Ky., 23 S.W. 960.

27. Ex parte Moots, 217 Ill.App. 518; Appeal of Bloomer, 83 Pa. 45.

28. Bouldin v. Alexander, 15 Wall. 131, 82 U.S. (15 Wall.) 131, 21 L.Ed. 69 (1872); Myers v. Trustees of Schools, 21 Ill. App. 223.

29. See collection of statutory references in Bogert, Trusts and Trustees (rev. 2d edit.), § 527.

30. In re Wadsworth, 2 Barb.Ch. 381.

31. Bayles v. Staats, 5 N.J.Eq. 313.

32. In re Cady's Estate, 103 N.Y. 678, 9 N.E. 442.

33. Rentschler's Estate, 392 Pa. 46, 139 A.2d 910 (1958), certiorari denied 358 U.S. 826, 79 S.Ct. 43, 3 L.Ed.2d 65 (1958), rehearing denied 358 U.S. 901, 79 S.Ct. 219, 3 L.Ed.2d 151 (1958).

34. In re Adams' Trust, 12 Ch.D. 634.

35. Tyronza Special School Dist. v. Speer, 94 F.2d 825 (8th Cir.1938).

36. Blumenstiel v. Morris, 207 Ark. 244, 180 S.W.2d 107 (1944) (must be danger to beneficiaries from out of state residence); Bergman v. Bergman, 323 Ill. 73, 153 N.E. 735 (1926). During the Second World War many states adopted statutes suspending the powers of a trustee who was absent on war service and permitting him to resume his work on return. See Bogert, Trusts and Trustees (rev.2d edit.), § 527, for statutory references.

37. Appeal of Morse, 92 Conn. 286, 102 A. 586; Attorney General v. Garrison, 101 Mass. 223.

or to directions in the trust instrument,[38] failure or refusal to act,[39] mingling the trust property with the trustee's individual property,[40] failure to account,[41] the acquisition of an interest adverse to that of the beneficiaries,[42] disloyalty,[43] the taking of unauthorized compensation,[44] the appropriation or attempted appropriation of the trust funds,[45] and breaches of trust causing large losses.[46]

A further cause for removal is sometimes found in a failure to cooperate with co-trustees, as where the defendant has been guilty of obstinate and obstructive conduct and a stalemate in the administration results.[47]

Disagreement and unpleasant personal relations between the trustee and beneficiaries are not usually enough to warrant removal.[48] The beneficiary often conceives that he could manage the trust better than the trustee, resents failure to follow his advice, is dissatisfied with returns, thinks that the trustee is too conservative in his investment policies, and otherwise finds fault with the trustee. Thus friction develops. But the settlor has entrusted the management to the trustee and not to the beneficiary. The very fact that he created a trust showed that he did not want the beneficiary to be the controlling factor in the management of the property. However, in some instances the hostile relations between trustee and beneficiary have gone so far that the court feels a new trustee should be appointed. Where the malicious or vindictive conduct of the trustee is the cause of disagreement and bitterness, removal is apt to be decreed.[49] If ill will exists and the trustee has discretion as to the benefits to be paid the beneficiary, the court may feel that it will be impossible for him to give an impartial and unbiased administration.[50]

Where a state, or an agency thereof, is named trustee, and the administration of the trust as directed by the settlor would be unconsti-

38. Cavender v. Cavender, 114 U.S. 464, 5 S.Ct. 955, 29 L.Ed. 212 (1885).

39. Lathrop v. Baubie, 106 Mo. 470, 17 S.W. 584.

40. Sparhawk v. Sparhawk, 114 Mass. 356.

41. In re Rutherford's Estate, 154 Kan. 361, 118 P.2d 553 (1941).

42. Lippard v. Parrish, 22 Del.Ch. 25, 191 A. 829 (1937); Matter of Townsend's Estate, 73 Misc. 481, 133 N.Y.S. 492 (trustee for life tenant with discretion as to income and duty to add unexpended income to principal became the owner of the remainder).

43. In re Hodgson's Estate, 342 Pa. 250, 20 A.2d 294 (1941).

44. Clark v. Clark, 167 Ga. 1, 144 S.E. 787 (1928).

45. Woods v. Chrissinger, 233 Ala. 575, 173 So. 57 (1937).

46. Davis v. Davis Tr. Co., 106 W.Va. 228, 145 S.E. 588 (1928).

47. In re Angell's Will, 268 App.Div. 338, 52 N.Y.S.2d 52 (1944), order affirmed 294 N.Y. 923, 63 N.E.2d 117 (1945).

48. Blumenstiel v. Morris, 207 Ark. 244, 180 S.W.2d 107 (1944); Broeker v. Ware, 27 Del.Ch. 8, 29 A.2d 591 (1942); Mathues' Estate, 322 Pa. 358, 185 A. 768 (1936).

49. Polk v. Linthicum, 100 Md. 615, 60 A. 455, 69 L.R.A. 920; Price's Estate, 209 Pa. 210, 58 A. 280 (trustee stated that one beneficiary was illegitimate child; if no basis, ground for removal); In re Hodgson's Estate, 342 Pa. 250, 20 A.2d 294 (1941).

50. Kadison v. Horton, 11 N.J.Super. 102, 78 A.2d 136 (1950), reversed on other points in 8 N.J. 506, 86 A.2d 238 (1951).

tutional in that it would constitute a denial of the equal protection of the law, the court may remove the trustee and appoint individuals and thus avoid a constitutional objection.[51] But if the settlor expressed an intent that the state or its agency should be the sole qualified trustee, and that the trust should be carried out exactly as directed, the court cannot avoid the difficulty by removing the trustee and appointing individuals or applying cy pres.[52]

There are instances of refusal to remove for mere errors of judgment,[53] misunderstanding of duties,[54] and breaches committed in good faith which did not cause large losses.[55]

Appointment of Successor

The power of the court of equity to fill vacancies in the trusteeship has been previously discussed.[56] It applies in case of a removal, if the court does not decide to use its discretion to permit the remaining trustees to administer the trust.[57]

The court should consult the beneficiaries and often will follow their recommendations in making an appointment. To fail to ask for and consider suggestions from the beneficiaries has in some cases been held an abuse of discretion which vitiates an appointment.[58]

Where trust duties are attached to the office of executor, and the executor is removed or resigns, he will also be treated as having been relieved of his duties as trustee,[59] but if the offices of executor and trustee are expressly made separate by the will and the same person occupies both offices, the revocation of the appointment as executor will not affect the trusteeship.[60]

51. Commonwealth v. Board of Directors, 353 U.S. 230, 77 S.Ct. 806, 1 L.Ed.2d 792 (1957), rehearing denied 353 U.S. 989, 77 S.Ct. 1281, 1 L.Ed.2d 1146 (1957) (attendance at school limited to white children).

But see Evans v. Newton, 382 U.S. 296, 86 S.Ct. 486, 15 L.Ed.2d 373 (1966) (appointment of private trustees did not transfer city park from the public to the private sector).

52. Evans v. Newton, 221 Ga. 870, 148 S.E.2d 329 (1966), affirmed, 90 S.Ct. 628, 396 U.S. 435, 24 L.Ed.2d 634 (1970); La Fond v. Detroit, 357 Mich. 362, 98 N.W.2d 530 (1959).

53. Shirk v. Walker, 298 Mass. 251, 10 N.E.2d 192, 125 A.L.R. 620 (1937); Monroe v. Winn, 16 Wn.2d 497, 133 P.2d 952 (1943).

54. Wiggins v. Burr, 54 Misc. 149, 105 N.Y.S. 649; Stewart's Estate, 48 Pa.D. & C. 526.

55. In re Comstock's Will, 219 Minn. 325, 17 N.W.2d 656 (1945); In re Barnes' Estate, 339 Pa. 88, 14 A.2d 274 (1940).

56. See § 32, ante.

57. McNair v. Montague, 260 Ill. 465, 103 N.E. 450; Petition of Pierce, 109 Me. 509, 84 A. 1070.

58. Central Trust Co. of Ill. v. Harvey, 297 Ill.App. 425, 17 N.E.2d 988 (1938); Hodgen's Ex'rs v. Sproul, 221 Iowa 1104, 267 N.W. 692 (1936); In re McCaskey's Estate, 293 Pa. 497, 143 A. 209 (1928). In re Labold's Will, 148 Ohio St. 332, 74 N.E.2d 251 (1947) (settlor gave third party controlling voice; abuse not to consult him).

59. Randall v. Gray, 80 N.J.Eq. 13, 83 A. 482; Cushman v. Cushman, 191 N.Y. 505, 84 N.E. 1112, affirming 116 App.Div. 763, 102 N.Y.S. 258.

60. Tuckerman v. Currier, 54 Colo. 25, 129 P. 210, Ann.Cas.1914C, 599.

Appointment of Receiver for Trusteeship

In rare cases, instead of removing a trustee and appointing a new one, the court appoints a receiver to manage and conserve the trust property. He is an officer of the court, subject to its order. This may well be done in case of a short unexpired term of the trust, or where a trust for business purposes is in financial difficulties.[61] "Besides it is an established rule of the Court of Chancery that, when a trust fund is in danger of being wasted or misapplied, it will interfere on the application of those interested in the fund, and by the appointment of a receiver, or in some other mode, secure the fund from loss." [62]

 WESTLAW REFERENCES

Power to Remove Trustee

beneficiary /s power /s remov*** /s trustee

390k167 /p trustee /s remov***

di(court equity chancery /s remov*** /s trustee)

390k166(2) /p power /s remov*** /s trustee

find 9 So2d 563

Method of Removal

di(application /s remov*** /s trustee)

find 59 so2d 898

390k165

390k166 /p remov*** /s trustee

390k167 /p remov*** /s trustee

Grounds for Removal

to (390) /p ground /10 remov*** /s trustee

remov*** /s trustee /s insan*** incapacitat!

remov*** /s trustee /s dr*nk!

remov*** /s trustee /s improviden!

remov*** /s trustee /s convict! charg! commission
    commit**** /4 crime criminal

remov*** /s trustee /s dishonesty misappropriat! misrepresent!

390k166

remov*** /5 trustee /5 bankrupt** insolven** receivership

remov*** /s trustee /s "breach of trust"

remov*** /s trustee /s disloyal**

find 10 ne2d 192

Appointment of Successor

di(appoint! /s successor /2 trustee)

Appointment of Receiver for Trusteeship

calhoun +3 king

di(appoint! /s receiver /s trust /2 fund property)

---

61. Calhoun v. King, 5 Ala. 523; Jones v. Dougherty, 10 Ga. 273; Gale v. Sulloway, 62 N.H. 57.

62. Jones v. Dougherty, 10 Ga. 273, 287, 288. And see Orphan Asylum Society v. McCartee, Hopk.Ch., N.Y., 429, 435.

Chapter 19

REMEDIES OF BENEFICIARIES— TRACING THE TRUST RES—THE BONA FIDE PURCHASER RULE

Table of Sections

RECOVERY OF THE TRUST RES OR ITS SUBSTITUTE—TRACING [1]

§ 161. The beneficiary, or a trustee representing him, may follow the trust res or its substitute into the hands of all persons except purchasers without notice of the trust, and may obtain a decree for the return of the trust property or its product to the trust fund.

An important remedy available to the beneficiary or a trustee representing him, is the recovery of the trust property or its product from one holding it after the trustee has committed a breach of trust.[2] This is called "following" or "tracing" the trust property. The right is sometimes declared by statute.[3] That this remedy exists, subject to qualifications to be explained, whether the property or its product is in the hands of the trustee [4] or his successor after his death,[5] or is held by

---

§ 161

1. Bogert, Trusts and Trustees (rev.2d edit.), §§ 865–868, 921; Restatement, Trusts, Second, § 202.

2. Oliver v. Piatt, 3 How. 333, 11 L.Ed. 622; Cooper v. Landis, 75 N.C. 526; In re Freas' Estate, 231 Pa. 256, 79 A. 513.

3. Ala.Code, § 19–3–106; West's Ann. Cal.Civ.Code § 2243; Offic.Code of Ga.Ann. 53–13–62, 53–13–63; Mont.—Code Ann.

72–20–301; N.Dak.—Cent.Code 59–01–06; S.Dak. Codif.Laws § 55–1–9.

4. Breit v. Yeaton, 101 Ill. 242; Clifford v. Farmer, 79 Ind. 529; Freeman v. Maxwell, 262 Mo. 13, 170 S.W. 1150; Lucia Mining Co. v. Evans, 146 App.Div. 416, 131 N.Y.S. 280; O'Neill v. O'Neill, 227 Pa. 334, 76 A. 26; Hubbard v. Burrell, 41 Wis. 365.

5. Edgerton v. Johnson, 178 F.2d 106 (7th Cir.1949).

a third person,[6] is unquestioned. The beneficiary naturally must elect to take one or the other, the original trust property or the substitute, where both are capable of identification.[7] He may also take income of the property which has been collected since the trust property was wrongfully acquired.[8] "The law is now well settled that as between the cestui que trust and trustee, and all parties claiming under the trustee otherwise than by purchase for a valuable consideration without notice, all property belonging to a trust, however much it may be changed or altered in its nature or character, and all the fruit of such property, whether in its original or altered state, continues to be subject to or affected by the trust."[9]

The beneficiary's right is not that of a lienholder or a preferred creditor. It is based on a property right in the res or its substitute. "The right of the beneficiary to pursue a fund and impose upon it the character of a trust is based on the principle that it is the property of the beneficiary, not upon any right of lien against the wrongdoer's general estate; and this, whether the property sought to be recovered is in the form in which the beneficiary parted with its possession or in a substituted form."[10]

The basic principles on which tracing is allowed are that ownership is not lost by a change in the form of the thing owned and that ownership includes the right to the products of the property owned. If a man owns standing timber which is cut down, made into lumber, and furniture fabricated from the wood, title to the products is the same as that to the original trees.[11] Similarly, ownership of a bond includes the interest which accrues on the obligation.

Assume A is trustee for B, and the original trust res is certain land, A violates the trust by selling the land to X, who knows of the breach, and A then deposits the proceeds of the sale in a bank to the credit of A personally. B may follow the original property into the hands of X and recover it on the theory that he treats the transfer as wrongful, or he may follow the proceeds of the original property into the bank account and take the claim against the bank as his property on the theory that he has exercised his election to consider the transfer of the real estate as rightful. By following and recovering the trust property or its substitute it is meant that the beneficiary, or a trustee acting for him, may obtain a decree that the property in question is subject to the trust

---

6. Chaves v. Myer, 13 N.M. 368, 85 P. 233, 6 L.R.A.,N.S., 793; Barnard v. Hawks, 111 N.C. 333, 16 S.E. 329.

7. Bonner v. Holland, 68 Ga. 718; Cadieux v. Sears, 258 Ill. 221, 101 N.E. 542.

8. Wilkins v. Wilkins, 144 Fla. 590, 198 So. 335 (1940) (not only realty but rental value of it recoverable); Schofield v. Rideout, 233 Wis. 550, 290 N.W. 155, 133 A.L.R. 834 (1940) (income of property into which trust funds traced).

9. Hill v. Fleming, 128 Ky. 201, 107 S.W. 764, 766, 16 Ann.Cas. 840. To the same effect see People v. California Safe Deposit & Tr. Co., 175 Cal. 756, 167 P. 388, 389, L.R.A.1918A, 1151.

10. Heidelbach v. Campbell, 95 Wash. 661, 665, 164 P. 247.

11. This doctrine may be subject to some qualification where the personalty is very greatly enhanced in value by the unintentional wrongdoing of the converter.

and is to be treated henceforth as a part of the trust property. This will involve delivery of it to the current trustee for the beneficiary.

This right to recover the property is, however, qualified. Its exercise depends upon two considerations: (a) the status of the holder of the property sought to be recovered; and (b) the ability of the beneficiary to identify the property in question as the original trust res or its substitute.

If the beneficiary is not sure whether there is trust property or its product which he can trace, he may bring a bill of discovery;[12] and if he is ignorant of the status of the trust, he is entitled to a decree compelling the trustee to give him information or to account.[13]

Where the suit is to recover the trust res or its substitute from a third person, and such third person has performed services or made expenditures which have enhanced the value of the property, reimbursement may in some cases be a prerequisite to relief.[14] For example, an action to recover the trust res from a taker who has paid no consideration will succeed only upon payment to the property holder of advances which he has made to cancel incumbrances on the property.[15] An attorney charged as a constructive trustee because he placed himself in a position of conflicting interest while acting for the plaintiff is entitled to be reimbursed for money spent to acquire titles adverse to those of the beneficiary.[16]

On principle it would seem that a purchaser of the trust property with notice of the trust ought not to be allowed to charge the beneficiary with the payment of the cost of improvements as a condition to the recovery of the property.[17] However the opposite view has sometimes found judicial approval.[18] Where the taker of title had constructive notice only, or acted in good faith, a basis for an allowance of the cost of improvements may be found.[19]

 WESTLAW REFERENCES

di(trace* tracing /s trust /2 res property)

12. Ferguson v. Rogers, 129 Ark. 197, 195 S.W. 22; Indian Land & Tr. Co. v. Owen, 63 Okl. 127, 162 P. 818.

13. Peters v. Rhodes, 157 Ala. 25, 47 So. 183; People v. Bordeaux, 242 Ill. 327, 89 N.E. 971; Taft v. Stow, 174 Mass. 171, 54 N.E. 506.

14. Wormley v. Wormley, 8 Wheat. 421, 5 L.Ed. 651; Bates v. Kelly, 80 Ala. 142.

15. Feingold v. Roeschlein, 276 Ill. 79, 114 N.E. 506.

16. Home Inv. Co. v. Strange, 109 Tex. 342, 195 S.W. 849.

17. Sketchley v. Lipkin, 99 Cal.App.2d 849, 222 P.2d 927 (1950); Hawley v. Tesch, 88 Wis. 213, 59 N.W. 670; Harrison v. Miller, 124 W.Va. 550, 21 S.E.2d 674 (1942).

18. Rines v. Bachelder, 62 Me. 95; Vocci v. Ambrosetti, 201 Md. 475, 94 A.2d 437 (1953); De Moss v. Rule, 194 Okl. 440, 152 P.2d 594 (1944).

19. Johnson v. Stull, 303 S.W.2d 110 (Mo.1957) (constructive notice only); Bechtel v. Bechtel, 162 Or. 211, 91 P. 529.

TRACING TRUST FUNDS—SUFFICIENCY OF IDENTIFICATION [1]

§ 162. In order that a beneficiary or a trustee representing him may recover the trust property or its proceeds he must identify the property claimed as the original trust res or as the product of it.

If the disposition of the original subject matter of the trust or its substitute is unknown, or it has been used by the trustee or a third person for non-trust purposes and in such a way that no product remains, for example, in paying a personal debt of the trustee, tracing is not available.

For the purpose of tracing trust property into the assets of a failed bank, cash, commercial paper, "cash items" and credit in another bank are treated as fungible items.

Where trust funds are traced into a fund or account which also contains items belonging to the trustee personally, it is presumed that withdrawals from the fund for the trustee's personal purposes or for unknown objectives are intended by the trustee to be from his portion of the account.

Where such a fund or account contains items belonging to two or more trusts, but contains no personal funds of the trustee, it should be presumed that withdrawals for the trustee's private benefit or for unknown purposes are to be charged to each of the trusts in proportion to the amount of credit they had in the mixed fund at that time. However some courts treat such wrongful removals as taken from the funds first deposited in the account, under the so-called "rule in Clayton's Case."

Where a fund or account contains the trustee's own property and trust property, the trustee purchases an investment from the account without designating its object or source, and later the trustee uses the remainder of account for his personal benefit, the majority view is that the beneficiary may treat the investment as made from the trust portion of the account.

Where a fund or account contains trust funds and the trustee's own property, part of the trust funds are wrongfully dissipated by the trustee, and later the trustee deposits his own money in the account without designating the purpose of such deposit, it is not presumed to be a replacement of the stolen trust funds unless the account was labelled a trust account.

The beneficiary is not aided by a presumption that trust funds traced into an account or mass of property remain there.

§ 162

1. Bogert, Trusts and Trustees (rev.2d edit.), §§ 866–868, 921–930; Restatement, Trusts, Second, § 202; Restatement, Restitution, §§ 205, 206, 215.

And see Williston, 2 Harv.L.R. 28; Ames, 19 Harv.L.R. 511; Scott, 27 Harv. L.R. 125.

Identification

The remedy of recovery of the trust property or its substitute is necessarily dependent on proof that the property claimed is the trust res or its product. The property which the beneficiary seeks to have equity decree to belong to him must be shown to be the original subject matter of the trust or something produced by it. If a claim is made that the realty or personalty in dispute was once in the hands of the trustee as trust property, the question of identification will not ordinarily be extremely difficult. But if the beneficiary seeks to show, for example, that certain land, securities, or a bank account are the avails of trust property, because the original trust property has, perhaps by means of several transactions, produced this land or these securities or this bank account, the problem is apt to be more difficult. The courts have not always agreed on what is sufficient identification.

Neither the number nor the character of the changes which have affected the trust property will prevent the beneficiary from following it, if he can make sufficient identification.[2]

The majority of the courts which have considered the degree of identification required have held strictly to the rule that to get the benefit of the tracing remedy the beneficiary must be able to follow the trust res to some particular piece of property, and that proof that the trust property claimed at one time was in the hands of the trustee or is located at some unknown place among the assets of the trustee is not satisfactory. For example, the trust fund must be traced into a particular bond, or tract of land, or bank account.[3] As said by Lewis, J., in Thompson's Appeal:[4] "Whenever a trust fund has been wrongfully converted into another species of property, if its identity can be traced, it will be held, in its new form, liable to the rights of the cestui que trust. No change in its state and form can divest it of such trust. So long as it can be identified either as the *original property* of the cestui que trust, or as the *product of it,* equity will follow it; and the right of reclamation attaches to it until detached by the superior equity of a bona fide purchaser, for a valuable consideration, without notice. The

2. Harrison v. Tierney, 254 Ill. 271, 98 N.E. 523. "It is a principle settled as far back as the Year Books that, whatever alteration of form any property may undergo, the true owner is entitled to seize it in its new shape if he can prove the identity of the original material." In re Oatway, (1903) 2 Ch. 356.

3. In re See, 126 C.C.A. 120, 209 Fed. 172 (2d Cir.1913); Lummus Cotton Gin Co. v. Walker, 195 Ala. 552, 70 So. 754; Hauk v. Van Ingen, 196 Ill. 20, 63 N.E. 705; Arnold Inv. Co. v. Citizens' State Bank of Chautauqua, 98 Kan. 412, 158 P. 68, L.R.A. 1916F, 822; Gault v. Hospital for Consumptives of Maryland, 121 Md. 591, 89 A. 105; Hewitt v. Hayes, 205 Mass. 356, 91 N.E. 332, 137 Am.St.Rep. 448; Watson v.

Wagner, 202 Mich. 397, 168 N.W. 428; Twohy Mercantile Co. v. Melbye, 83 Minn. 394, 86 N.W. 411; Phillips v. Overfield, 100 Mo. 466, 13 S.W. 705; Pierson v. Phillips, 85 N.J.Eq. 60, 95 A. 622; Brown v. Spohr, 180 N.Y. 201, 73 N.E. 14; Virginia-Carolina Chemical Co. v. McNair, 139 N.C. 326, 51 S.E. 949; Commonwealth v. Tradesmen's Tr. Co., 250 Pa. 372, 95 A. 574; Continental Nat. Bank v. Weems, 69 Tex. 489, 6 S.W. 802, 5 Am.St.Rep. 85; Watts v. Newberry, 107 Va. 233, 57 S.E. 657; Emigh v. Earling, 134 Wis. 565, 115 N.W. 128, 27 L.R.A.,N.S., 243.

4. 22 Pa. 16, 17. To the same effect see Little v. Chadwick, 151 Mass. 109, 110, 111, 23 N.E. 1005, 7 L.R.A. 570.

substitute for the original thing follows the nature of the thing itself so long as it can be ascertained to be such. But the right of pursuing it fails when the means of ascertainment fail."

In the following illustrative cases the courts have held, under the strict tracing rule, that the beneficiary identified the property sufficiently to enable him to follow it: where the beneficiary sent money to the bankrupt to enable the latter to buy cotton for the former, and the bankrupt bought some cotton, used some of the funds for his own purposes, employed some of his own funds to buy cotton for the beneficiary, and placed all the cotton in a warehouse belonging to the beneficiary;[5] where an agent to operate a store used the proceeds of sales to buy land, taking title in his own name;[6] and where trust money was used to purchase a drug store which was conducted by the trustee in his own name for four years, notwithstanding sales from the stock and replenishments of it.[7]

The beneficiary has been aided in tracing by holdings that money is fungible,[8] and that cash and commercial paper such as checks are equivalent, and that in the case of banks, cash, "cash items" and credit in another bank are equivalent. Thus if the beneficiary can prove that trust cash or commercial paper came into the hands of a bank as trustee, and that on the failure of the bank, cash, cash items, or credit in other banks was held by the bank in an amount greater than the trust claim, the requirements for tracing have been met.[9]

Where a trustee uses trust funds to pay insurance premiums on a policy of life insurance on his own life, payable to a member of his family, it has been held that the beneficiary can trace the trust funds into the proceeds of the policy upon the death of the trustee.[10] If trust money paid only part of the premiums, the trust can obtain only that proportion of the insurance purchased by its share of the premiums; but if all the premiums were paid by trust funds, then all the insurance proceeds should go to the trust, even though the amount of it is much larger than the amount of the trust money used to pay the premiums.[11]

5. Southern Cotton Oil Co. v. Elliotte, 134 C.C.A. 295, 218 Fed. 567 (6th Cir.1914).

6. Atkinson v. Ward, 47 Ark. 533, 2 S.W. 77.

7. Byrne v. McGrath, 130 Cal. 316, 62 P. 559, 80 Am.St.Rep. 127.

8. School Trustees v. Kirwin, 25 Ill. 62 (orig.ed. p. 73); Farmers' & Mechanics' Nat. Bank v. King, 57 Pa. 202, 98 Am.Dec. 215; Wulbern v. Timmons, 55 S.C. 456, 33 S.E. 568.

9. Erie Trust Company's Case, 326 Pa. 198, 191 A. 613 (1937). And see People ex rel. Auditor v. West Side Trust & Savings Bank, 376 Ill. 339, 33 N.E.2d 607 (1941); Chicago, M. St. P. & P. R. Co. v. Larabie Bros., 103 Mont. 126, 61 P.2d 823 (1936); State ex rel. Robertson v. Thomas W.

Wrenne & Co., 170 Tenn. 131, 92 S.W.2d 416 (1936).

10. Holmes v. Gilman, 138 N.Y. 369, 34 N.E. 205, 20 L.R.A. 566, 34 Am.St.Rep. 463.

11. Vorlander v. Keyes, 1 F.2d 67 (8th Cir.1924); Shaler v. Trowbridge, 28 N.J.Eq. 595; Truelsch v. Northwestern Mut. Life Ins. Co., 186 Wis. 239, 202 N.W. 352, 38 A.L.R. 914 (1925). But see, contra, and to the effect that the trust merely recovers the premiums paid: Summers v. Summers, 218 Ala. 420, 118 So. 912 (1928); Hubbard v. Stapp, 32 Ill.App. 541; Thum v. Wolstenholme, 21 Utah 446, 61 P. 537. And see Exchange State Bank v. Poindexter, 137 Kan. 101, 19 P.2d 705 (1933) (lien on insurance money for all trust funds embezzled, whether used to pay premiums or not).

Although the trust gets a windfall in this way, it is because it involuntarily invested in a profitable way. The insurance recovery is exclusively the product of trust funds. The beneficiary of the policy did not pay for the insurance and has no legal right to it.

Where trust funds are used to pay for improvements on real estate which belongs to the trustee individually, some courts have refused to permit tracing into the land or its proceeds on the theory that the improvement became the individual property of the trustee because of its attachment to his realty.[12] However it would seem that even though the title was not produced in whole or in part by trust funds, and so tracing is not possible, at least an equitable lien for the amount of the trust funds should be created by the court.[13]

Use of Trust Funds to Pay Trustee's Debts—"Swollen Assets" Theory

Many well reasoned decisions have held that the use of trust funds to pay the personal debts of the trustee produces no positive result on which to base a tracing claim against the assets of the trustee which he held at his death or insolvency.[14] They have expressly repudiated the "swollen assets" doctrine. The trustee is freed from a claim against him, but in return he acquires no property which could be described as the product of the trust property. Thus if T embezzles $1,000 of the trust funds and pays a personal creditor, there is no real change so far as the property of the trustee is concerned.

However some courts have held that the beneficiary may trace and recover his property if he can show that the assets in the hands of the trustee at his death or bankruptcy have been "swollen" or increased by the use of the trust property, even though no particular piece of property can be identified as the product of the trust res.[15] They argue that if the trust property had not been used to pay the personal creditors of the trustee, some of the trustee's personal assets would have been used for that purpose, and therefore the use of trust funds made the estate of the trustee at death or bankruptcy larger than it would otherwise have been. In many of the cases the trust claimant was the state or a municipal corporation and the court was anxious to

12. Appeal of Cross, 97 Pa. 471; Nichols v. Huffman, 121 W.Va. 615, 5 S.E.2d 789 (1939).

13. Lawson v. Ridgeway, 72 Ariz. 253, 233 P.2d 459 (1951); Mack v. Marvin, 211 Ark. 715, 202 S.W.2d 590 (1947); Fehn v. Schickling, 26 Tenn.App. 608, 175 S.W.2d 37 (1943).

14. Hoffman v. Rauch, 300 U.S. 255, 57 S.Ct. 446, 81 L.Ed. 629 (1937); First Nat. Bank v. Connolly, 172 Or. 434, 138 P.2d 613 (1943), rehearing denied 172 Or. 434, 143 P.2d 243 (1943); In re Royersford Trust Co., 317 Pa. 490, 178 A. 288 (1935); Want v. Alfred M. Best Co., 233 S.C. 460, 105 S.E.2d 678 (1958); Williams v. Weldon, 63 S.D. 377, 259 N.W. 272 (1935).

15. For leading cases see State v. Bruce, 17 Idaho 1; Peak v. Ellicott, 30 Kan. 156, 1 P. 499; Evangelical Synod v. Schoeneich, 143 Mo. 652, 45 S.W. 647. See Bogert, Trusts and Trustees (rev.2d edit.), § 922, for citations to decisions from Ala., Ark., Col., Fla., Ida., Ill., Ind., Iowa, Kan., Mich., Minn., Mo., Mont., Neb., N.D., Oh., Okl., Or., S.C., S.D., Utah, and Wis. However many of these decisions have been overruled by later decisions.

See Taft, 39 Col.L.R. 172.

protect the public, especially in times of depression and bank failure such as existed in the 1890's, late 1920's and 1930's.

The fallacy of the "swollen assets" theory lies in its failure to recognize that a trust requires specific property as its subject matter, and that the very essence of the beneficiary's right to trace is his ability to identify the trust res or its exact substitute. As a creditor a beneficiary is entitled to no preference over any other creditor. It is only as a property owner that he is entitled to take particular personalty or realty. The matter is illuminated by the court in Slater v. Oriental Mills: [16]

"While one who has been wronged may follow and take his own property, or its visible product, it is quite a different thing to say that he may take the property of somebody else. The general property of an insolvent debtor belongs to his creditors, as much as particular trust property belongs to a cestui que trust. Creditors have no right to share in that which is shown not to belong to the debtor, and conversely a claimant has no right to take from creditors that which he cannot show to be equitably his own. But right here comes the argument that it is equitably his own because the debtor has taken the claimant's money and mingled it with his estate, whereby it is swelled just so much. But, as applicable to all cases, the argument is not sound. Where the property or its substantial equivalent remains, we concede its force; but, where it is dissipated and gone, the appropriation of some other property in its stead simply takes from creditors that which clearly belongs to them. In the former case, as in Pennell v. Deffell, 4 De G., M. & G. 372, and In re Hallett's Estate, Knatchbull v. Hallett, L.R. 13 Ch.Div. 696, the illustration may be used of a debtor mingling trust funds with his own in a chest or bag. Though the particular money cannot be identified the amount is swelled just so much, and the amount added belongs to the cestui que trust. But in the latter case there is no swelling of the estate, for the money is spent and gone; or, as respondent's counsel pertinently suggests, 'Knight Bruce's chest, Jessel's bag, is empty.' Shall we therefore order a like amount to be taken out of some other chest or bag, or out of the debtor's general estate?"

A further fallacy in the swollen assets doctrine lies in its assumption that the use of the trust funds to pay the trustee's personal debts has swollen the estate which he leaves. As a matter of fact such use has the effect of paying one debt and at the same time creating another of exactly the same size, so that the estate is neither swollen nor diminished. Thus if T is trustee of the A trust, has in his hands $1,000 of trust money, and owes personally $500 to X and $1,000 to Y, and the only property which T owns personally is a bond worth $500, it is apparent that T is insolvent. He owes $1,500 and owns $500. The trust property does not count in the private affairs of T, either as an asset or a liability, as long as T is carrying out his trust. Now if T uses

16. 18 R.I. 352, 353, 27 A. 443.

the $1,000 of trust money to pay his creditor, Y, and dies, it cannot be said that the use of the trust money has "swollen" the estate left by T. The estate still has assets of $500 and liabilities of $1,500. Instead of owing Y $1,000, his estate owes the trust $1,000 on account of the misappropriated funds.[17]

Presumptions in Aid of Tracing

Due to the difficulties of proof in the cases of many deceased or insolvent trustees and many bank failures where constructive trust claims have been presented, the courts have adopted certain presumptions which are for the most part favorable to the trust claimant and disadvantageous to the general creditors of the person against whom tracing is sought. It would appear that these rules are not strictly presumptions, that is, inferences based on an observation of human conduct, but rather are fictions [18] invented by the courts to aid the tracing claimant in his contest with a dishonest trustee or his creditors or donees claiming through him during his life or at his death.

The types of cases in which the presumptions are applied are chiefly two, namely, the bank account cases and the decisions involving the assets of failed banks. Often trust funds can be traced into a checking account which the trustee held in his own name or as a trust account, and there have been over a long period many deposits and withdrawals, and ultimately the trustee dies insolvent or goes into bankruptcy and some credit remains in the bank deposit. The beneficiary of the trust seeks the deposit as the product of trust property. Instead of a checking account there may be a stock brokerage account or other similar asset. Secondly, in many cases efforts have been made to secure preferences on trust theories from the assets of insolvent banks, where the bank had been an express trustee or it was sought to charge the bank as a constructive trustee on account of its unlawful receipt of funds. An example of the latter kind is to be found where a public officer or a trustee wrongfully deposits cash or commercial paper in a bank which later fails.

No Presumption as to Continuance

If the beneficiary alleges that certain property is trust property, or that the proceeds of trust property have gone into it, the burden is on the beneficiary to prove that fact.[19] A few courts have held that proof of receipt of the property and the existence of similar property in the estate at insolvency or death raised a presumption that the trust property was among the trustee's assets, or in other words that the

---

17. See dissenting opinion of Cassoday, J., in Francis v. Evans, 69 Wis. 115, 122, 33 N.W. 93.

18. Swan, J., in In re Kountze Bros., 79 F.2d 98 (2d Cir.1935); Learned Hand, J., in Primeau v. Granfield, 184 Fed. 480 (S.D. N.Y.1911), reversed on another ground in 114 C.C.A. 549, 193 F. 911 (2d Cir.1911);

Mitchell v. Dunn, 211 Cal. 129, 294 P. 386 (1930).

19. Schuyler v. Littlefield, 232 U.S. 707, 34 S.Ct. 466, 58 L.Ed. 806 (1914); Waddell v. Waddell, 36 Utah 435, 104 P. 743; Chase & Baker Co. v. Olmsted, 93 Wash. 306, 160 P. 952.

burden was on the trustee or his representative to show that the property had been transferred or dissipated.[20] But the majority of courts considering this question have determined that the beneficiary is aided by no presumption of the retention of the trust property; he must show not only its receipt by the trustee but also that it remained among the assets of the trustee at the death or insolvency of the trustee, or on such other event fixing the rights of the parties.[21] Thus a beneficiary who merely proves that a bank collected trust moneys and does not show their disposition has not made out a case for following trust property.[22] He must show that such trust funds remained in the hands of the bank or its representative at the time he brought suit.

The beneficiary is occasionally aided in following trust property by a rule which may seem like a presumption of continuance but which really has reference to the doctrine of the loss of property by confusion of goods. If the trustee mingles trust funds with his own and the entire mingled fund is on hand, but the beneficiary cannot prove what particular items of property are the product of trust funds, the burden may be placed on the trustee to make a separation and to show the amount of his individual property in the mass,[23] and if the trustee cannot separate trust and private funds the whole fund or mass may be treated as trust property.[24]

Mixed Personal and Trust Funds—Presumption as to Withdrawals [25]

If personal funds of the trustee and trust funds are mixed in an account or fund of the sort described, is any presumption to be applied as to the source of withdrawals in determining whether a beneficiary can trace into the balance in the account? In such case the presumption that the trustee will perform his duty and act honestly and will not be guilty if a breach of trust enters into the situation. If funds are withdrawn from this mixed account for the personal use of the trustee, or for an unknown object, it is assumed that he would take out his own funds for these purposes before using the trust money. As long as any of the money of the trustee remains in the mixed fund, the withdrawals for his private benefit will be treated as being made from his private

---

20. Farnsworth v. Muscatine Produce & Pure Ice Co., 177 Iowa 20, 158 N.W. 741; State v. Bank of Commerce of Grand Island, 61 Neb. 181, 85 N.W. 43, 52 L.R.A. 858; Widman v. Kellogg, 22 N.D. 396, 133 N.W. 1020, 39 L.R.A.,N.S., 563.

21. Mathewson v. Wakelee, 83 Conn. 75, 75 A. 93; Shields v. Thomas, 71 Miss. 260, 14 So. 84, 42 Am.St.Rep. 458; Ellicott v. Kuhl, 60 N.J.Eq. 333, 46 A. 945; In re Hicks, 170 N.Y. 195, 63 N.E. 276.

22. Windstanley v. Second Nat. Bank of Louisville, 13 Ind.App. 544, 41 N.E. 956.

23. Bird v. Stein, 258 F.2d 168 (5th Cir.1958), certiorari denied 359 U.S. 926, 79 S.Ct. 608, 3 L.Ed.2d 628 (1959); Atkinson v.

Ward, 47 Ark. 533, 2 S.W. 77; Moore v. First Nat. Bank of Kansas City, 154 Mo. App. 516, 135 S.W. 1005; Yellowstone County v. First Tr. & Sav. Bank, 46 Mont. 439, 128 P. 596; Erman v. Erman, 101 Ohio App. 245, 136 N.E.2d 385 (1956).

24. Byrom v. Gunn, 102 Ga. 565, 31 S.E. 560; Ward v. Armstrong, 84 Ill. 151; Hunt v. Smith, 58 N.J.Eq. 25, 43 A. 428; Waddell v. Waddell, 36 Utah 435, 104 P. 743. And see Winger v. Chicago City Bank & Trust Co., 394 Ill. 94, 67 N.E.2d 265 (1946); Eaton v. Husted, 141 Tex. 349, 172 S.W.2d 493 (1943).

25. See Restatement, Restitution, §§ 209–214.

funds, and only after the private funds are exhausted will the trust funds be deemed to be invaded.[26] The leading case in establishing this rule is In re Hallett's Estate,[27] where the court referred to the principle "that, where a man does an act which may be rightfully performed, he cannot say that that act was intentionally and in fact done wrongly," and then said: "When we come to apply that principle to the case of a trustee who has blended trust moneys with his own, it seems to me perfectly plain that he cannot be heard to say that he took away the trust money when he had a right to take away his own money."

Thus, to put a simple case, if T mixed in his personal checking account $100 of trust money and $100 of his own funds, and while his credit stood at $200, he drew a check to his landlord for $100 to pay his rent, the courts may make a finding that the rent money was drawn from T's personal part of the account and that the $100 credit remaining belonged to the trust.

Mixed Trust Funds—Presumption as to Withdrawals [28]

Assume that T is trustee of two trusts and has a single bank account which serves both. In it he places $100 of A trust money on January 2d and on February 2d he deposits $100 of B money. On March 2d he draws a check against the account in his own favor in the amount of $100 to enable himself to pay his living expenses. There are no other credits or debits. There is a balance of $100. If the A and B beneficiaries both seek to trace into the balance, are they governed by any presumptions? Whose $100 was stolen by the March 2d check?

Here there has been a division of authority. Some courts have followed a rule of thumb laid down in a decision called "Clayton's Case",[29] which in fact was not concerned with trust law at all but rather with debits on a banking account, a question of debtor and creditor. The rule there enunciated has been called the "first in, first out" rule, that is, that in a case of this type the party making a withdrawal for personal or unknown purposes, is presumed to have intended to first take out of the mixed fund the monies first put into it until all of those monies are exhausted.[30] This is believed to be highly fictional and arbitrary, a rule which should not be used if any other

26. Covey v. Cannon, 104 Ark. 550, 149 S.W. 514; People v. California Safe Dep. & Tr. Co., 175 Cal. 756, 167 P. 388, L.R.A.1918A, 1151; Hewitt v. Hayes, 205 Mass. 356, 91 N.E. 332, 137 Am.St.Rep. 448; Board of Fire & Water Com'rs of City of Marquette v. Wilkinson, 119 Mich. 655, 78 N.W. 893, 44 L.R.A. 493; Harrison v. Smith, 83 Mo. 210, 53 Am.Rep. 571; Standish v. Babcock, 52 N.J.Eq. 628, 29 A. 327; Blair v. Hill, 50 App.Div. 33, 63 N.Y.S. 670, affirmed 165 N.Y. 672, 59 N.E. 1119; Continental Nat. Bank v. Weems, 69 Tex. 489, 6 S.W. 802, 5 Am.St.Rep. 85; Waddell v. Waddell, 36 Utah 435, 104 P. 743.

27. 13 Ch.Div. 696, 727, 728.

28. Niederlehner, 10 Univ. of Cinc. L.R. 278; 35 Mich.L.R. 1203.

29. 1 Meriv. 572, 608.

30. Spokane County v. First Nat. Bank, 16 C.C.A. 81, 68 Fed. 979 (9th Cir. 1895); Empire State Surety Co. v. Carroll County, 114 C.C.A. 435, 194 Fed. 593 (8th Cir.1912); In re A. Bolognesi & Co., 166 C.C.A. 216, 254 Fed. 770 (2d Cir.1918); In re Walter J. Schmidt & Co., D.C.N.Y., 298 Fed. 314 (S.D.N.Y.1923); Hewitt v. Hayes, 205 Mass. 356, 91 N.E. 332, 137 Am.St.Rep. 448; Cole v. Cole, 54 App.Div. 37, 66 N.Y.S. 314.

method of deciding the question on reason or principle can be discovered.

Other courts have applied what they claim is a doctrine founded on fair play and reason, namely, that the withdrawal should be deemed to have been made from each of the trust funds in proportion to the amount of credit each had in the account at the time of the check, assuming that the withdrawal cannot be proved to have been for the benefit of either of the trusts. Hence in the example above it would be presumed that half the stolen funds were A trust funds and half belonged to the B trust, since on March 2d A and B each had a credit of $100 in the account.[31] Of course, checks which were to the advantage of any participating trust should be charged to it. It seems fair to let all the trusts share the risk of the dishonesty of their fiduciary in proportion to the size of their interests. They all had the misfortune to have a faithless trustee. There is no reason why one set of beneficiaries should bear the loss any more than another set. There is no reason for presuming that the trustee would prefer to steal the older portion of the account. He would not care from what source the withdrawal was made.

Mixed Personal and Trust Funds—Investment

But the presumption of honesty declared in In re Hallett's Estate has not been followed to its logical conclusion in all cases. If a trustee has trust and private funds in a single account, and then withdraws a sum less than the amount of the private funds and invests it in securities in his own name without any express statement as to his intent, it would seem logical that the securities should be presumed to belong to the trustee personally since he would be presumed to use his own funds to make personal investments. But in many cases where such withdrawal and investment have been made, and later the trustee has withdrawn and dissipated the balance of the fund, the beneficiary has been allowed to take the investment made with the first withdrawal.[32] The leading case is In re Oatway.[33] In that case the trustee had paid for shares in the Oceana Company by a check on an account containing trust funds and sufficient private funds to meet the check. Later the trustee withdrew and dissipated the balance of the account. The beneficiary was allowed to take the Oceana stock, the court saying:

31. People v. Barrett, 405 Ill. 188, 90 N.E.2d 94 (1950); Andrew v. State Bank of New Hampton, 205 Iowa 1064, 217 N.W. 250 (1928); County Commissioners of Frederick County v. Page, 163 Md. 619, 164 A. 182 (1933); Yesner v. Commissioner of Banks, 252 Mass. 358, 148 N.E. 224 (1925). This is the rule applied in § 15 of the Uniform Trusts Act which has been adopted in eight states.

32. Brennan v. Tillinghast, 120 C.C.A. 37, 201 Fed. 609 (6th Cir.1913); Primeau v.

Granfield, 184 Fed. 480 (S.D.N.Y.1911), reversed on another ground in 193 F. 911 (2d Cir.1911); Mitchell v. Dunn, 211 Cal. 129, 294 P. 386 (1930); Glidden v. Gutelius, 96 Fla. 834, 119 So. 140; Petersen v. Swan, 239 Minn. 98, 57 N.W.2d 842 (1953); In re Erie Trust Co., 326 Pa. 198, 191 A. 613 (1937); City of Lincoln v. Morrison, 64 Neb. 822, 90 N.W. 905, 57 L.R.A. 885.

33. [1903] 2 Ch. 356, 360.

"It is, in my opinion, equally clear that when any of the money drawn out has been invested, and the investment remains in the name or under the control of the trustee, the rest of the balance having been afterwards dissipated by him, he cannot maintain that the investment which remains represents his own money alone, and that what has been spent and can no longer be traced and recovered was the money belonging to the trust. In other words, where the private money of the trustee and that which he held in a fiduciary capacity have been mixed in the same banking account, from which various payments have from time to time been made, then, in order to determine to whom any remaining balance or any investment that may have been paid for out of the account ought to be deemed to belong, the trustee must be debited with all the sums that have been withdrawn and applied to his own use, so as to be no longer recoverable, and the trust money in like manner debited with any sums taken out and duly invested in the names of the proper trustees."

There are, however, many holdings which do not follow the Oatway rule and permit the trustee or his successors to keep the investment made from the mixed funds.[34]

Presumption Regarding Deposits

It might be supposed that if the trustee reduces the mixed account below the amount of the trust funds by withdrawals for his own use, and later makes deposits of private moneys in the account, the trustee would be presumed to be restoring the trust funds, that the presumption of the performance of duty would again apply. But whether because the trustee has, in such a situation, already shown an express intent not to perform his duty, or for other reason, the courts have held that subsequent deposits of the personal funds of the trustee to the credit of an account which stands in the name of the trustee individually, but which contains trust funds as well as private funds, do not inure to the benefit of the beneficiary. The subsequent deposits are added to the private portion of the account. Hence if trustee A has a bank account entitled merely "A," and into such account $500 of trust moneys have entered, and at some time in the history of the account the balance is reduced below $500,[35] or the account is wholly exhaust-

34. Board of Com'rs of Crawford County, Ohio v. Strawn, 84 C.C.A. 553, 157 Fed. 49 (6th Cir.1907); Blackhurst v. Westfield, 111 Cal.App. 548, 295 P. 863 (1931); Farmers Bk. of White Plains v. Bailey, 221 Ky. 55, 297 S.W. 938 (1927); Phillips v. Overfield, 100 Mo. 466, 13 S.W. 705.

35. James Roscoe (Bolton), Ltd. v. Winder, [1915] 1 Ch. 62; Board of Com'rs of Crawford County, Ohio v. Strawn, 84 C.C.A. 553, 157 Fed. 49, 15 L.R.A.,N.S., 1100 (6th Cir.1907); In re M.E. Dunn & Co., 193 Fed. 212 (E.D.Ark.1912); Covey v. Cannon, 104 Ark. 550, 149 S.W. 514; Hewitt v. Hayes, 205 Mass. 356, 91 N.E. 332,

137 Am.St.Rep. 448. But see, *contra*, In re T.A. McIntyre & Co., 104 C.C.A. 424, 181 Fed. 960 (2d Cir.1910); Church v. Bailey, 90 Cal.App.2d 501, 203 P.2d 547 (1949) (presumption of restoration applied even though no trust label on the account); Myers v. Matusek, 98 Fla. 1126, 125 So. 360 (1929); State Sav. Bank v. Thompson, 88 Kan. 461, 128 P. 1120. Supreme Lodge of Portuguese Fraternity of United States v. Liberty Trust Co., 215 Mass. 27, 102 N.E. 96 (where the withdrawal was a mistake and the subsequent deposit was expressly made as a replacement) is a different case.

ed [36] by withdrawals of funds for the use of A personally, deposits by A after such reduction below $500, or after such exhaustion, when no express intent to make the deposit as a restoration is shown, will not operate as a restoration of the trust funds and will inure to the personal benefit of A. But if the account is entitled "A, Trustee," it has been held that subsequent deposits of the personal funds of the trustee, under the circumstances just given, will be credited to the trust funds.[37] It has been held that where a trustee has a mixed account, and has on hand trust funds not deposited, and later deposits in the mixed account an amount equal to the trust funds which he was holding, it will be presumed that the funds so deposited were trust funds or trust fund replacements.[38] And, of course, there may be a restoration of misapplied trust funds by express action, as where a defaulting trustee uses his own money to buy land in his own name but with the express intent of making a restoration.[39] All deposits of trust funds in the mixed account are, of course, credited to the trust. The principal doctrine regarding subsequent deposits was thus stated by the Supreme Court: [40] "Where one has deposited trust funds in his individual bank account, and the mingled fund is at any time wholly depleted, the trust fund is thereby dissipated, and cannot be treated as reappearing in sums subsequently deposited to the credit of the same account."

As a result of the presumptions regarding withdrawals and deposits which have just been discussed, it follows that the beneficiary can never recover from a mixed account held without trust label a sum greater than the lowest balance since the admixture of the funds. So, if trustee A has an account standing in his own name in a bank, containing $1,000 of his own funds, and he deposits $1,000 of trust funds in the account on January 1, makes deposits of his own moneys and withdrawals for his own benefit until July 1, when he is declared a bankrupt, and at that time the balance in the account is $1,500, the beneficiary's right to follow his money into the claim against the bank will depend upon the state of the account between January and July 1. If it appears that on March 1 the account reached its lowest level and had been reduced to $500 the beneficiary will be confined to the recovery of that amount. The sums added to the fund after March 1 do not benefit the beneficiary, for they are not deemed to be restorations of the trust money; and after the balance went below $1,000 it is obvious that the trustee must have been withdrawing and dissipating trust funds.

---

36. Schuyler v. Littlefield, 232 U.S. 707, 34 S.Ct. 466, 58 L.Ed. 806 (1914), affirming decrees in In re Brown, 113 C.C.A. 348, 193 Fed. 24 (2d Cir.1912), and In re A.O. Brown & Co., 113 C.C.A. 354, 193 Fed. 30 (2d Cir.1912).

37. Mitchell v. Dunn, 211 Cal. 129, 294 P. 386 (1930); Baker v. N.Y. Nat. Exch. Bank, 100 N.Y. 31, 2 N.E. 452; Cohnfield v. Tannenbaum, 176 N.Y. 126, 68 N.E. 141; United Nat. Bank of Troy v. Weatherby, 70 App.Div. 279, 75 N.Y.S. 3.

38. Jeffray v. Towar, 63 N.J.Eq. 530, 53 A. 182; Baker v. New York Nat. Exch. Bank, 100 N.Y. 31, 2 N.E. 452, 53 Am.Rep. 150.

39. Houghton v. Davenport, 74 Me. 590.

40. Schuyler v. Littlefield, 232 U.S. 707, 710, 34 S.Ct. 466, 58 L.Ed. 806 (1914).

WESTLAW REFERENCES

Identification

di(identif! /s trust /2 fund asset)

di(trace* tracing /s trust /s cash money)

find 233 p2d 459

Use of Trust Funds to Pay Trustee's Debts—"Swollen Assets" Theory

slater +3 "oriental mill"

pennell +3 deffell

knatchbull +3 hallett

Presumptions in Aid of Tracing

find 79 f2d 98

390k358(2)

No Presumptions as to Continuance

find 34 sct 466

Mixed Personal and Trust Funds—Presumptions as to Withdrawals

private personal individual /s trust /5 property fund /s mixed
   mingled co-mingled blended /s withdr*w**

390k358(2)

Mixed Personal and Trust Funds—Investment

personal individual /s trust /5 fund property /s mixed mingled
   co-mingled blended /s investment

Presumption Regarding Deposits

individual personal /s trust /3 fund property /s mixed mingled
   co-mingled blended /s deposit

NECESSITY OF ELECTION BETWEEN TRACING AND DAMAGES [1]

§ 163. Where the trustee or a third person has rendered himself personally liable to the beneficiary by committing or joining in a breach of trust, and the trust res involved, or its substitute, can be traced into the hands of one not a bona fide taker for value, the beneficiary must elect between the recovery of damages and tracing as to each transaction.

It frequently happens that the trustee has committed a breach of trust and rendered himself personally liable, and that the trust property affected by this breach of trust, or its substitute, can be traced into the hands of the trustee or a third person. A third person may make himself personally liable by a joinder in a breach of trust or by other tort, and the trust res or its substitute may likewise be available. For example, a trustee may have misappropriated trust funds and bought real estate in his own name, and later conveyed this land to X who

§ 163

1. Bogert, Trusts and Trustees (rev.2d edit.), §§ 867, 945, 946; Restatement, Trusts, Second, §§ 202, 208–212, 295. For a general treatment of election of remedies as affecting the rights of a beneficiary, see § 168, post.

knew of the breach of trust by the trustee. Here there is a possibility of recovering damages from the trustee or X, or taking from the trustee the consideration he received for his conveyance to X or taking the realty from X. The questions arising in these situations are whether the beneficiary is confined to a money decree against the trustee or third person, or whether he must pursue the trust property or its product, or whether he may have the benefit of both remedies, or whether he must make an election between the remedies.

It is universally held that the beneficiary must choose between taking a money judgment or tracing.[2] This choice exists whether the property involved is in the hands of the trustee[3] or of a third person,[4] so long as the third person is affected by notice of the trust or has not paid value for the property. The trustee cannot compel the beneficiary to resort to either remedy. The choice rests with the beneficiary and not with the trustee.[5] "Now it is well settled that, when a trustee uses the property of the trust for his own benefit, the true owner is not compelled to follow the property, even though he might be able, by proving notice, to follow it successfully. He has his option, in such a case, to sue the trustee or follow the property. It would be monstrous to permit the trustee, in such cases, to say: 'Yes; I have used the trust property; I have got the benefit of that use; but you can prove that the party now in possession had notice of your claim. He trusted, it is true, to my statements; but he ought to have known me better. Your remedy is on him.' The rule is well established that the cestui que trust may sue the trustee, even though it appear that he has a right also to sue the person dealing with the trustee."[6]

Examples of the exercise of this right of election are found in cases where the trustee has made an unlawful investment and the beneficiary has had the option of taking the investment or of holding the trustee for the trust money thus invested, with interest.[7] Similarly, where the trustee wrongfully withdraws money from the trust funds the beneficiary may sue for conversion or have the money or its product impounded in the hands of a third party.[8]

Where a trustee makes several separate wrongful investments, the beneficiary may elect to hold him for damages in one case and trace the trust funds into the unlawful investment in another case.[9] And where

2. Oliver v. Piatt, 44 U.S. (3 How.) 333, 11 L.Ed. 622 (1845); Lathrop v. Bampton, 31 Cal. 17, 89 Am.Dec. 141; Woodrum v. Washington Nat. Bank, 60 Kan. 44, 55 P. 333.

3. Small v. Hockinsmith, 158 Ala. 234, 48 So. 541; Phinizy v. Few, 19 Ga. 66; Peabody v. Tarbell, 2 Cush., Mass., 226; Prewitt v. Prewitt, 188 Mo. 675, 87 S.W. 1000; Shanks v. Edmondson, 28 Grat., Va., 804.

4. Roberts v. Mansfield, 38 Ga. 452; Treadwell v. McKeon, 7 Baxt., Tenn., 201;

D. Sullivan & Co. v. Ramsey, Tex.Civ.App., 155 S.W. 580.

5. Miller v. Belville, 98 Vt. 243, 126 A. 590 (1924).

6. Roberts v. Mansfield, 38 Ga. 452, 458, 459.

7. Clark v. Anderson, 13 Bush., Ky., 111; Baker v. Disbrow, 18 Hun N.Y., 29.

8. Robinson v. Tower, 95 Neb. 198, 145 N.W. 348.

9. Title Insurance & Trust Co. v. Ingersoll, 158 Cal. 474, 111 P. 360; Murphy-

there is a single breach and only part of the trust funds involved can be traced, the beneficiary may take the product into which he can follow that part and hold the trustee liable for the portion of the trust funds which cannot be traced, as where a trustee steals $10,000 of trust money, buys real estate with half of it and gambles away the other half.[10]

But where there are two inconsistent remedies for the same wrong there must be an election between them.[11] Otherwise the injured beneficiary would obtain double recovery and the wrongdoer would be held liable to an unjust extent. For example, if a trustee has stolen trust funds and invested them in land in his own name, the beneficiary must choose between a money judgment and tracing into the land. To permit him to recover the amount of the embezzled funds and also to take the realty in which they were invested would be obviously inequitable. It is true that he could claim a lien on the land as an auxiliary to collection of the money judgment, as previously shown, but that would be on the theory that the land was the property of the trustee. The Supreme Court of Oregon has stated the principle as follows: [12]

"When a trustee has violated the trust by purchasing property with trust funds and taking the title in his own name, the cestui que trust has the right to elect either to proceed to fasten the trust upon the purchased property, or to proceed against the trustee personally. When with knowledge of the facts he thus makes an election, it is binding upon him, and it cannot be revoked. When a cestui que trust, with knowledge of the facts, elects to proceed against the trustee personally, he waives all right to have the trust impressed upon property purchased with trust funds, but conveyed to the trustee . . .."

The authorities are not clear as to what amounts to an election to rely on a money claim and not to trace. Some hold that merely presenting a claim in bankruptcy or probate proceedings is a binding election.[13] In other instances the bringing of an action,[14] the obtaining of judgment,[15] or an effort to enforce such a judgment,[16] has been held to be conclusive against a later attempt at tracing.

The filing of any proceeding founded on tracing,[17] or accepting

Bolanz Land & Loan Co. v. McKibben, 236 S.W. 78 (Tex.Com.App.1922); Abell v. Howe, 43 Vt. 403.

10. Church v. Bailey, 90 Cal.App.2d 501, 203 P.2d 547 (1949); Van Blarcom v. Van Blarcom, 124 N.J.Eq. 19, 199 A. 383 (1938); Federal Tr. Co. v. Baxter, 128 Neb. 1, 257 N.W. 368 (1934).

11. Haxton v. McClaren, 132 Ind. 235; Robinson v. Robinson, 22 Iowa 427; Barker v. Barker, 14 Wis. 131.

12. Bettencourt v. Bettencourt, 70 Or. 384, 142 P. 326, 330.

13. Hewitt v. Hayes, 205 Mass. 356, 91 N.E. 332; Tierman's Ex'r v. Security Bldg. & Loan Ass'n, 152 Mo. 135, 53 S.W. 1072.

14. Clark v. Kirby, 204 App.Div. 447, 198 N.Y.S. 172 (1923).

15. Carter v. Gibson, 61 Neb. 207, 85 N.W. 45, 52 L.R.A. 468.

16. Hilborn v. Bonney, 28 Cal.App. 789, 154 P. 26.

17. Hayes v. Kerr, 40 App.Div. 348, 57 N.Y.S. 1114.

property as belonging to the trust,[18] may be held to be a bar to a later claim for money damages.

When the beneficiary is in doubt as to the status of the trust property and its products and so does not feel able to make a safe choice as to tracing or a money claim, he may sue for an accounting and postpone his election until the facts as to the property become clear; [19] or he may demand a return of the trust property or its substitute, if that is possible, and assert a money claim as a request for alternative relief if tracing proves to be unavailable.[20]

 WESTLAW REFERENCES

oliver +3 piatt
baker +3 disbrow

SUBROGATION AND MARSHALING [1]

§ 164. Where the trust property is used without the consent of the beneficiary to pay an unsecured debt of the trustee or a person not connected with the trust, the beneficiary is entitled to be subrogated to the rights of the creditor so paid.

Where against the will of the beneficiary trust property is used to discharge a debt secured by an encumbrance on property not belonging to the trust, the beneficiary is entitled to be subrogated to the rights of the creditor thus paid and to have the encumbrance restored for his benefit.

Where the beneficiary can trace trust funds into an asset owned by the trustee or another, and this asset is also subject to a prior lien in favor of another creditor, but the latter also has other property as security for his claim, the trust beneficiary may employ the marshaling of assets doctrine and compel the creditor having two sources of collection to resort first to that one which is open to him exclusively, and so leave to the beneficiary, as far as possible, the asset into which he can trace.

Sometimes a trustee unlawfully uses trust funds to pay his own debts or the debts of another person who is not a trust beneficiary. Here, according to the better view, there can be no tracing of trust property into any asset in the hands of the trustee or of the other party whose debt has been discharged. The discharge of a debt leaves no affirmative product. It has a negative result from the point of view of the debtor in that it relieves him of a burden but does not increase his

---

18. Deer v. Deer's Estate, Mo.App., 180 S.W. 572.

19. Kreinson v. Commercial Nat. Bank, 323 Pa. 332, 185 A. 756 (1936).

20. Allen v. Allen, 196 Ga. 736, 27 S.E.2d 679 (1943); Beaver County v. Home Indemnity Co., 88 Utah 1, 52 P.2d 435 (1935).

§ 164

1. Bogert, Trusts and Trustees (rev. 2d edit.), § 930; Restatement, Trusts, Second, § 202; Restatement, Restitution, §§ 207–208.

property. But the court of equity holds that on general equitable principles of fair play the beneficiaries of the trust, whose money has been used without their consents to pay the debt of another, should be permitted to stand in the place formerly occupied by the creditor who has been paid. The trust should have the cause of action and remedies which the creditor formerly had. It should be subrogated to the position of that creditor. This result is based on the benefit which the beneficiary has involuntarily conferred on the creditor who has been satisfied. Thus if a trustee uses trust money to pay an unsecured bank loan of his wife without the knowledge or consent of the trust beneficiaries, they may be subrogated to the position of the bank as a creditor of the wife and have a cause of action against her for the amount of the debt. This right of subrogation is of great help if the debtor is a solvent person.

An example of the application of the rule can be found in the cases where T is trustee of two trusts, the A trust and the B trust, and T uses money from the A trust funds to pay the debts of the B trust.[2] Here there can be no tracing of the A trust funds into the hands of the creditors of the B trust, since they are bona fide purchasers, but it is fair that the beneficiaries of the A trust, or a trustee who is a successor of T and acts for the A trust beneficiaries, should have the rights formerly held by the creditors of T as trustee of the B trust. If these creditors were secured and have released their security, the security should be restored for the benefit of the A trust. If the creditors were unsecured, the A trust should be able to sue T for the amount of the debt paid, and if it cannot recover from T personally it should be able to proceed in equity against T, as trustee of the B trust, and take his right to indemnity and collect out of the B trust funds, provided T could have collected from such funds if he had paid the debt from his own pocket. This result is reached in some cases, although there has been a tendency to ignore the fact that the A trust must take through T, and that its rights will be of no value if T was in default to the B trust to an amount greater than the claim of the A trust. If the A money was used to pay the beneficiaries of the B trust sums due them, then the beneficiaries of the A trust should be subrogated to the claims of the B beneficiaries for payment out of B trust property, and it would be immaterial whether T as trustee of the B trust was in default or not, since a shortage in his accounts would not diminish the claims of the B beneficiaries. Their claims are direct and not derivative.[3]

Secondly, trust funds are sometimes used illegally by a trustee to discharge an encumbrance on his own property, or on the property of one not a party to the trust. For example, the trustee may use trust

2. Newell v. Hadley, 206 Mass. 335, 92 N.E. 507, 20 L.R.A.,N.S., 908; Fidelity & Casualty Co. v. Maryland Casualty Co., 222 Wis. 174, 268 N.W. 226 (1936); Weston, 25 Harv.L.R. 602; Baker, 59 Pa.L.R. 225; Jacob, 25 Ill.L.R. 19.

3. Whiting v. Hudson Tr. Co., 234 N.Y. 394, 138 N.E. 33, 25 L.R.A. 1470 (1923). See 23 Col.L.R. 596; 36 Harv.L.R. 762; 21 Mich.L.R. 919; 32 Yale L.J. 293, 377, 744.

money to pay off a mortgage on his home. Here there can be no tracing in a strict sense into the assets of the trustee, since the result is the cancellation of a debt and the discharge of a mortgage, nor can there be tracing into the hands of the former mortgage since he was a bona fide purchaser. However equity, on subrogation theories, can and does restore the debt and mortgage in favor of the trust which has been injured, and permits it to enforce the mortgage on the trustee's home.[4] Other secured claims to which such a rule would be applied are tax liens[5] and pledgees' interests.[6]

Lastly, the doctrine of marshaling of assets is sometimes useful to a beneficiary whose trust property has been improperly used by the trustee.[7] This doctrine is one which runs all the way through the administration of the estates of debtors, whether trust claimants are involved or not. It is merely the rule that where there are two creditors, one of whom has a security interest in the A property, and the other of whom has a prior security interest in the A property and also a security interest in the B property, the second creditor can be compelled to exhaust the B property before he resorts to the A property.[8] It is immaterial, ordinarily, to the second creditor whether he uses A property or B property, but it makes a great difference to the first creditor. This renders it fair that the court force the second creditor to resort first to the security which is exclusively his.

For example, T is trustee for A and uses trust money to invest in land in the name of T without trust label. Then T mortgages the land to X as security for a loan which X makes to T, and X is a bona fide purchaser. X also takes as security for this loan a pledge of jewelry owned by T. T becomes insolvent and his creditors seek to enforce their claims. The beneficiaries of the A trust can compel X to resort first to the pledge of jewelry as a means of satisfying his claim, since that security is exclusively his, and to resort to the land mortgaged only secondarily and to the extent he is not satisfied from the pledged jewelry. As to the mortgaged land X would be superior to A because of the application of the bona fide purchaser rule. If X failed to obey his duty under this rule, and resorted first to his mortgage, and thus left part or all of the pledge security untouched, A would be entitled to be

---

4. Hall v. Hall, 241 Ala. 397, 2 So.2d 908 (1941); Shinn v. Macpherson, 58 Cal. 596; McCaslin v. Schouten, 294 Mich. 180, 292 N.W. 696 (1940); Title Guarantee & Tr. Co. v. Haven, 196 N.Y. 487, 89 N.E. 1082, 25 L.R.A.,N.S., 1308, 17 Ann.Cas. 1131; Erie County v. Lamberton, 297 Pa. 406, 147 A. 86 (1929).

5. Dillard v. Owens, 122 S.W.2d 76 (Mo.App.1938).

6. In re Franklin Saving & Loan Co., 34 F.Supp. 585 (E.D.Tenn.1940); Beaver County v. Home Indemnity Co., 88 Utah 1, 52 P.2d 435 (1935).

7. M'Mahon v. Featherstonhaugh, 1895, 1 Ir.R. 83; Metzger v. Emmel, 289 Ill. 52, 124 N.E. 360 (1919); Morgan v. Meacham, 279 Ky. 526, 130 S.W.2d 992 (1938); Broadway Nat. Bank v. Hayward, 285 Mass. 459, 189 N.E. 199 (1934); Farmers' Loan & Tr. Co. v. Kip, 192 N.Y. 266, 85 N.E. 59.

8. For a statement of the doctrine, see the opinion of Mr. Justice Stone in Sowell v. Federal Res. Bank, 268 U.S. 449, 456, 457, 45 S.Ct. 528, 530, 69 L.Ed. 1041 (1925).

placed in the same position as if the marshaling doctrine had been followed, and thus might get a security interest in the pledged jewelry.

 WESTLAW REFERENCES

marshaling marshalling /5 asset /s trust
254k7 /p trust
254k2 /p trust

THE BONA FIDE PURCHASER RULE [1]

§ 165. **One who acquires for value a legal interest in property without notice that there is an outstanding trust or other equitable interest in the property in question may hold it free of such equitable interest.** **This is the so-called "bona fide purchaser rule" which is similar to, but separate from, the holder in due course rule in the law of negotiable instruments and the recording acts rule regarding unrecorded documents.**

The purchaser must have both paid value and obtained his legal title without notice of the equity. **The purchaser of an equitable interest does not get the benefit of the rule, priority between equities being usually determined by priority in time of acquisition.**

"Giving value" includes the transfer of any property interest, a change in status, or taking property as security for, or in payment of, a preexisting debt; but it does not include a mere promise to pay or to do any other act. **One who has paid part of the price before notice of an equity and thereby acquires full legal title is protected to a partial extent.** **"Value" is a concept different from "consideration" in the law of contracts.**

Notice of an equity may be actual or constructive, and it may exist because the purchaser had knowledge of facts putting him on inquiry which, if investigated with reasonable care, would have disclosed the outstanding equity.

The Rule Stated

In his attempt to trace the trust property and recover it from one to whom the trustee has transferred it, the beneficiary or a substitute trustee acting for him is often blocked by application of the bona fide purchaser rule.

If the trust property, or its substitute or product, has passed into the hands of a party who obtained the legal title to it and paid value for it without notice of the existence of the trust and the consequent equitable interest of the beneficiary, the equitable interest is cut off and the legal title holder may retain the property free and clear of any duty

---

§ 165

1. Bogert, Trusts and Trustees (rev. 2d edit.), §§ 881–897; Restatement, Trusts,

Second, §§ 284–294, 316–320, 408; Restatement, Restitution, §§ 172–176.

toward the beneficiary.[2]

It will be noticed that the rule applies to cut off equities of any type, and not merely to the interests of beneficiaries under trusts. For example, it governs such equities as those of contract vendees in specifically enforceable contracts, and of defrauded vendors who have conveyed away the legal title, equitable lienors, and many others.[3]

The rule is similar to, but distinct from, the holder in due course rule in the law of negotiable instruments[4] and the rule under the recording acts that the rights of a taker under a document subject to those acts may be cut off if the document is not recorded and the property thereafter is sold by the same grantor to a bona fide purchaser.[5] The cases under these two other rules regarding title, value and notice are often helpful in interpreting the bona fide purchaser rule in the field of trusts.

Reasons for the Rule

The reasons for, and theories as to the origin of, the rule have been discussed by many writers.[6] It would seem that the most satisfactory explanation of the origin of the rule lies in the nature and theory of the jurisdiction of the court of chancery. It is a court of conscience and originally acted purely *in personam*. It did not control titles except through orders to the holders of those interests, and then only when the conscience of the holder was affected in such a way as to make it fair to direct him to make a conveyance. Thus if a complainant in equity asserted that he held a beneficial interest in property as beneficiary or otherwise, and claimed a right to possession and title against the defendant, he was in effect asking the court to direct the defendant to give a deed, and the court would inquire whether the continued holding of the property by the defendant would be unconscionable or unfair to the complainant. If the court found that the defendant had obtained the legal title innocently and paid a price for it, the chancellor did not consider that there was any basis for issuing a decree against him. Retention of his property interest would not shock the court of chancery.[7]

2. In re Lyon's Estate, 163 Cal. 803, 127 P. 75; Saunders v. Richard, 35 Fla. 28, 16 So. 679; Carrie v. Carnes, 145 Ga. 184, 88 S.E. 949; Prevo v. Walters, 5 Ill. 35, 4 Scam. 35; Dillon v. Farley, 114 Iowa 629, 87 N.W. 677; Curtis v. Brewer, 140 Mich. 139, 103 N.W. 579; Groye v. Robards' Heirs, 36 Mo. 523; Doremus v. Doremus, 66 Hun 111, 21 N.Y.S. 13; McClelland v. Myers, 7 Watts, Pa., 160; Schneider v. Sellers, 98 Tex. 380, 84 S.W. 417; Chancellor v. Ashby, 2 Pat. & H.Va., 26.

The rule is often stated in statutory form. See references in Bogert, Trusts and Trustees (rev. 2d edit.), § 881.

3. Pool v. Rutherford, 336 Ill.App. 516, 84 N.E.2d 650 (1949).

4. This rule cuts off legal as well as equitable interests. See Dearman v. Trimmier, 26 S.C. 506, 2 S.E. 501.

5. This rule also cuts off both legal and equitable interests.

6. See Langdell, Summary of Equity Pleading, 90; Jenks, 24 Law Quart.R. 147; Ames, 1 Harv.Law Rev. 3, 16; Kenneson, 23 Yale Law J. 193; Searey, 23 Yale Law J. 447; Ballantine, 6 Minn.L.R. 87; Costigan, 12 Cal.L.R. 356.

7. Boone v. Chiles, 35 U.S. (10 Pet.) 177, 9 L.Ed. 388 (1836); Dixon v. Caldwell, 15 Ohio St. 412; Langdell, Summary of Equity Pleading, 90.

Other grounds suggested for the rule have been: (1) estoppel against the beneficiary on the ground that he has held the trustee out as having power to give a clear title; (2) commercial expediency based upon the policy of making property freely alienable and permitting purchasers to rely on appearances; (3) the trustee is in substance, although not in fact, an agent for the beneficiary and hence his acts should bind the latter; and (4) the beneficiary has in some way been guilty of a fault in leaving in office a dishonest trustee who has wrongfully transferred the trust property to an innocent purchaser. The arguments for these possible bases for the rule do not seem persuasive, although commercial expediency is undoubtedly the principal foundation of the related holder in due course and recording act rules and may be a valid basis for application of the bona fide purchaser rule.

Burden of Proof

The cases are in conflict as to whether the burden of proof is on the holder of the equity or on the person who claims to be a bona fide purchaser. Some cases seem to require that the beneficiary or other owner of an equitable interest prove that the defendant lacks in some way the qualities of a bona fide purchaser;[8] others require the party claiming that he has acquired a legal interest for value and without notice to furnish facts to substantiate this assertion.[9]

Legal Title Required

While there has been some contention that the rule should, or does, apply to takers of equitable interests,[10] the prevalent view is that in order to qualify one must have obtained the legal title to the property in question. If the purchaser has merely obtained an equity or equitable interest, he cannot get the benefit of the rule.[11] Equity applies to him the general doctrine that where there are two equities in the same property, and if there is no other way of deciding their priority,[12] then

---

8. Lightsey v. Stone, 255 Ala. 541, 52 So.2d 376 (1951); Warnock v. Harlow, 96 Cal. 298, 31 P. 166, 31 Am.St.Rep. 209; Claxton v. Claxton, 214 Ga. 715, 107 S.E.2d 320 (1959); Harris v. Stone, 15 Iowa 273; Zier v. Osten, 135 Mont. 484, 342 P.2d 1076 (1959); Hall v. Wilson, 215 S.W.2d 204 (Tex.Civ.App.1948).

9. Wright-Blodgett Co. v. United States, 236 U.S. 397, 35 S.Ct. 339, 59 L.Ed. 637 (1915); Osten-Sacken v. Steiner, 356 Mich. 468, 97 N.W.2d 37 (1959); Goette v. Howe, 232 Minn. 168, 44 N.W.2d 734 (1950); Stevens v. Brennan, 79 N.Y. 254; Levy v. Cooke, 143 Pa. 607, 22 A. 857; North American Uranium v. Johnston, 77 Wyo. 332, 316 P.2d 325 (1957).

10. See Ames, 1 Harv.L.R. 1; Restatement, Trusts, Second, § 285.

11. Louisville & Nashville R.R. Co. v. Boykin, 76 Ala. 560; Dugan v. Vattier, 3 Blackf. 245, 25 Am.Dec. 105; Grimstone v. Carter, 3 Paige 421, 24 Am.Dec. 230. In a few cases where the purchaser has obtained an equitable interest plus a power on his own part or through an independent third person to acquire the legal title, the purchaser is protected by the rule. Examples are the cases where a deed has been deposited in escrow (Winlock v. Munday, 156 Ky. 806, 162 S.W. 76), or stock has been sold but registration not changed on the corporation's books (Otis v. Gardner, 105 Ill. 436), or the deed to the purchaser was ineffective only for lack of acknowledgment (Duff v. Randall, 116 Cal. 226, 48 P. 66, 58 Am.St.Rep. 158).

12. Sometimes a junior equity is held to have a higher quality than a senior

time of origin of the equities controls and the one which is prior in time of origin is superior.[13]

Cases of contending equities where most courts have refused to apply the bona fide purchaser rule are found where: (1) the holder of an equitable interest assigns it twice and the second assignee gives value and is without notice of the prior assignment; [14] (2) the owner of a property interest (legal or equitable) creates in succession distinct equities in the interest in favor of persons who give value and have no notice; [15] (3) a trustee holds an equitable interest and conveys it to a bona fide purchaser.[16]

If A owns the fee of a tract of land, and is induced by B to contract to sell the land to B on the basis of fraudulent representations by B to A, B acquires an equitable interest in the land because of the doctrine of specific performance. If B sells his rights under the contract to C, who knows nothing of B's fraud and pays B the full value of B's interest, C is not a "bona fide purchaser" so as to prevent A from avoiding the contract on account of B's fraud. C acquired in good faith and for value merely an equitable interest. A already had the legal title and an equity to avoid the contract between him and B. Even if A had no legal title, his prior equity would prevail over C's junior equity.[17]

So too, if A furnishes the money to pay for land and directs his agent, B, to buy the land in the name of A, but B uses his own money and buys the land in the name of B, A has a right to have B charged as a constructive trustee, and this right is an equitable interest. If B sells his legal title to C who buys it in good faith and for value, C will be superior to A, as a bona fide purchaser of the legal title; but if B merely contracts to sell his legal interest to C, who in good faith and for value makes the contract, and then the interest of A appears, A will be superior to C, since both have mere equities, and A's is earlier in time.[18]

It does not matter how the purchaser acquired the legal title, whether by purchase inter vivos, transfer by will or intestacy, patent from the government,[19] court decree,[20] or purchase on a judicial sale.[21] Mortgagees and pledgees, as well as buyers of full interests, are protect-

claim and to be preferred on that account, as where the holder of the senior right has been in some way blameworthy. Weston v. Dunlap, 50 Iowa 183 (senior equity holder failed to record); Hume v. Dixon, 37 Ohio St. 66 (creditor took vendor's lien rather than mortgage). See Storke, 8 Rocky Mt.L.R. 1.

13. Southern Bank of Fulton v. Nichols, 235 Mo. 401, 138 S.W. 881; Mayer v. Kane, 69 N.J.Eq. 733, 61 A. 374.

14. Here priorities would be decided on the basis of time of assignment, or time of notice to the person against whom the equitable claim existed, as indicated in § 38, ante.

15. Dupont v. Werthman, 10 Cal. 354; Cutts v. Guild, 57 N.Y. 229.

16. Woods v. Dille, 11 Ohio 455; Briscoe v. Ashby, 65 Va. 454.

17. Duncan Townsite Co. v. Lane, 245 U.S. 308, 38 S.Ct. 99, 62 L.Ed. 309 (1917).

18. Johnson v. Hayward, 74 Neb. 157, 103 N.W. 1058, 5 L.R.A.,N.S., 112, 12 Ann. Cas. 800.

19. Dixon v. Caldwell, 15 Ohio St. 412.

20. Eich v. Czervonko, 330 Ill. 455, 161 N.E. 864 (1928).

21. Aluminum Co. of America v. Mineral Holding Trusts, 157 Tex. 54, 299 S.W.2d 279 (1956).

ed by the rule.[22] Thus if T is trustee for B and holds legal title to land, and T in breach of trust mortgages the land to M and embezzles the money lent, if M had no notice of the trust and in good faith believed T to have been the full owner of the realty M will be protected under the bona fide purchaser rule, and he can enforce his mortgage against the realty. B will be entitled merely to any surplus money that may arise after payment of the mortgage.

Innocence at Time of Payment and Getting Title

In order that one may be a bona fide purchaser he must have been innocent of any knowledge of the outstanding equity, both at the time when he got his title and at the date when he gave value. If he has merely contracted to buy the trust res at the time he receives notice of the trust, he is bound by the trust even though he has paid part or all of the consideration.[23] And if he has received the title to the trust property but has not yet paid the consideration at the time he receives notice, he cannot hold the property against the beneficiary.[24] In the words of Chancellor Kent: [25]

"A plea of a purchase for a valuable consideration, without notice, must be *with the money actually paid;* or else, according to Lord Hardwicke, you are not hurt. The averment must be, not only that the purchaser had not notice, at or before the time of the execution of the deeds, but that the purchase money was paid before notice. There must not only be a denial of notice before the purchase, but a denial of notice before payment of the money."

The bona fide purchaser may hold the trust res against the beneficiary even though he purchased from a donee of the trustee,[26] or from a purchaser with notice of the trust; [27] and a purchaser with notice or a donee from a bona fide purchaser without notice is superior to the beneficiary.[28] If the title of the bona fide purchaser is good, it must be good for sale purposes as well as for use and occupation. Thus if T in

22. Rafftery v. Kirkpatrick, 29 Cal. App.2d 503, 85 P.2d 147 (1938); Roop Grocery Co. v. Gentry, 195 Ga. 736, 25 S.E.2d 705 (1943). This is true in both lien and conveyance theory states.

23. Louisville & N.R.R. Co. v. Boykin, 76 Ala. 560; Dugan v. Vattier, 3 Blackf., Ind., 246, 25 Am.Dec. 105; Corn v. Sims, 3 Metc., Ky., 391; Grimstone v. Carter, 3 Paige, N.Y., 421, 24 Am.Dec. 230; Hoover v. Donally, 3 Hen. & M., Va., 316.

24. Burgett v. Paxton, 99 Ill. 288; Kitteridge v. Chapman, 36 Iowa 348; Paul v. Fulton, 25 Mo. 156; Dean v. Anderson, 34 N.J.Eq. 496; Everts v. Agnes, 4 Wis. 343, 65 Am.Dec. 314.

25. Jewett v. Palmer, 7 Johns.Ch., N.Y., 65, 68, 11 Am.Dec. 401.

26. Richardson v. Haney, 76 Iowa 101, 40 N.W. 115.

27. Bartlett v. Varner's Ex'r, 56 Ala. 580; Hampson v. Fall, 64 Ind. 382; Hoffman Steam Coal Co. v. Cumberland Coal & Iron Co., 16 Md. 456, 77 Am.Dec. 311; Bracken v. Miller, 4 Watts & S., Pa., 102.

28. Lathrop v. White, 81 Ga. 29, 6 S.E. 834; St. Joseph Mfg. Co. v. Daggett, 84 Ill. 556; Bracken v. Miller, 4 Watts & S., Pa., 102. "Undoubtedly if a person, though with notice, purchases from one without notice, he is entitled to stand in his shoes, and take shelter under his bona fides. If it were not so the bona fide purchaser without notice might be unable to dispose of the property, and thus its value in his hands be materially deteriorated. But if the second purchaser in such case be the original trustee, who reacquires the estate, he will be fixed with the trust. . . ." Church v. Ruland, 64 Pa. 432, 444.

breach of trust transfers trust property to a bona fide purchaser, and later the violation of the trust becomes public, and thereafter X with knowledge of the breach buys the property from the bona fide purchaser or takes it as a gift from the latter, X can hold the property against the beneficiary of the trust.[29] But the wrongdoing trustee, himself, may not get good title from a bona fide purchaser.[30] If he could, the door would be open for fraud on his part through collusion with third parties. If the trustee wrongfully transfers the trust res and later purchases it from one who hold it innocently as a purchaser for value, the res will be affected with the trust in the hands of the trustee, just as it was originally.[31]

Who is a Purchaser? What is "Value"?

A purchaser is usually one paying money or money's worth for the property. Therefore a donee inter vivos,[32] conveyees in consideration of love and affection,[33] a legatee or devisee from the trustee,[34] one taking by operation of law from the trustee [35] or as a representative of the trustee for the benefit of his creditors,[36] is not entitled to protection, even though he may have taken the property innocently. "A person to whose hands a trust fund comes by conveyance from the original trustee is chargeable as a trustee in his turn, if he takes it without consideration, whether he has notice of the trust or not. This has been settled for three hundred years, since the time of uses." [37]

It has been held that the giving of a note for the price does not constitute the maker of the note a purchaser, unless the note has been negotiated by the payee so that the maker is absolutely bound upon it,[38] and that merely promising to pay money,[39] render services,[40] or do another act does not make the promisor a payor of value under the rule. Thus a bank which has taken trust property and in return

29. Jones v. Independent Title Co., 23 Cal.2d 859, 147 P.2d 542 (1944); Harper v. Over, 101 S.W.2d 830 (Tex.Civ.App.1937).

30. Oliver v. Piatt, 44 U.S. (3 How.) 333, 11 L.Ed. 622 (1845); Church v. Church, 25 Pa. 278; Church v. Ruland, 64 Pa. 432.

31. Neise v. Krumacker, 136 N.J.Eq. 75, 40 A.2d 552 (1945); Downing v. Jeffrey, 173 S.W.2d 241 (Tex.Civ.App.1943).

32. Lehnard v. Specht, 180 Ill. 208, 54 N.E. 315; Attorney General v. Bedard, 218 Mass. 378, 105 N.E. 993; Johnson v. Johnson, 51 Ohio St. 446, 38 N.E. 61; Metzger v. Lehigh Valley Tr. & Safe Deposit Co., 220 Pa. 535, 69 A. 1037.

33. Eaton v. Husted, 141 Tex. 349, 172 S.W.2d 493 (1943).

Nominal consideration is not sufficient to amount to "value". Smith County Oil Co. v. Jefcoat, 203 Miss. 404, 33 So.2d 629

(1948); Allaben v. Shelbourne, 357 Mo. 1205, 212 S.W.2d 719 (1948).

34. Evans v. Moore, 247 Ill. 60, 93 N.E. 118, 139 Am.St.Rep. 302; Kluender v. Fenske, 53 Wis. 118, 10 N.W. 370.

35. Derry v. Derry, 74 Ind. 560.

36. Janney v. Bell, 111 F.2d 103 (4th Cir.1940); Smith v. Equitable Tr. Co., 215 Pa. 418, 64 A. 594.

37. Holmes, J., in Otis v. Otis, 167 Mass. 245, 246, 45 N.E. 737.

38. Davis v. Ward, 109 Cal. 186, 41 P. 1010, 50 Am.St.Rep. 29; Partridge v. Chapman, 81 Ill. 137; Rush v. Mitchell, 71 Iowa 333, 32 N.W. 367; Freeman v. Deming, 3 Sandf.Ch., N.Y., 327.

39. Exchange Bank of Perry v. Nichols, 196 Okl. 283, 164 P.2d 867 (1945).

40. Kelly v. Grainey, 113 Mont. 520, 129 P.2d 619 (1942) (furnish support).

opened a credit in favor of the transferor on a checking account is not a purchaser unless the credit is checked out.[41] However, under the uniform commercial acts governing the transfer of negotiable instruments, documents of title and tangible personalty, "value" has been defined to include "any consideration sufficient to support a simple contract" and this would include the making of any promise.[42] But, apart from statute, giving value is not identical with furnishing consideration, but is instead a narrower term.

There has been a sharp division in the case law as to whether one who takes property as security for, or in payment of, an antecedent debt is a purchaser for value. The modern tendency is to treat him as such, since he has changed his position in an important way; he has been lulled into security for a time and will have to take action to be restored to his former status.[43] Under these cases, if a trustee transfers trust property to a personal creditor in return for the discharge of the debt, the taker, after cancellation of the debt, may hold it against the beneficiary, provided he knew nothing of the trust. But many common law cases deny him the position of a purchaser for value, claiming that he has not given up anything substantial but rather has improved his position.[44] The uniform commercial acts, in their definition of value, make cancelling a debt or taking property as security for it "giving value".[45] Hence as to transfers and negotiations of commercial paper and tangible personal property, the former conflict of authorities has been resolved, but with reference to realty and noncommercial intangibles the older case law still prevails. Obviously if the creditor cancels or releases security he holds, he is "giving value".

An assignee for the benefit of creditors or trustee in bankruptcy stands in the shoes of the debtor and takes subject to all equities which affected the property in the debtor's hands. He is not a purchaser.[46] In taking the property he has not changed his position or that of the creditors he represents for the worse.

41. Peoples' State Bank v. Caterpillar Tractor Co., 213 Ind. 235, 12 N.E.2d 123 (1938); Barnsdall State Bank v. Springer, 176 Okl. 479, 56 P.2d 390 (1936).

42. See Uniform Negotiable Instruments Law ("N.I.L."), § 25; Uniform Commercial Code, § 1–201(44); Uniform Sales Act, § 76.

43. Schluter v. Harvey, 65 Cal. 158, 3 P. 659; First Nat. Bank of Ottawa v. Kay Bee Co., 366 Ill. 202, 7 N.E.2d 860 (1937); Adams v. Vanderbeck, 148 Ind. 92, 45 N.E. 645, 62 Am.St.Rep. 497; Merchants' Ins. Co. of Providence v. Abbott, 131 Mass. 397; Payne v. Allen, 178 Okl. 328, 62 P.2d 1227 (1936); Akin v. Security Savings & Trust Co., 157 Or. 172, 68 P.2d 1047 (1937); W. Horace Williams Co., Inc. v. Vandaveer, Brown & Stoy, 84 S.W.2d 333 (Tex.Civ.App. 1935).

44. Aetna Life Ins. Co. of Hartford, Conn. v. Morlan, 221 Iowa 110, 264 N.W. 58 (1935); Geffen v. Paletz, 312 Mass. 48, 43 N.E.2d 133 (1942); Meier v. Geldis, 148 Neb. 304, 27 N.W.2d 215 (1947); Howells v. Hettrick, 160 N.Y. 308, 54 N.E. 677; Home Owners' Loan Corp. v. Tognoli, 127 N.J.Eq. 390, 13 A.2d 571 (1940); Tucker v. Brown, 20 Wn.2d 740, 150 P.2d 604 (1944).

45. See, for example, Uniform Negotiable Instruments Law § 25; Uniform Stock Transfer Act, § 22; Uniform Commercial Code, § 1–201(44).

46. Chace v. Chapin, 130 Mass. 128; Martin v. Bowen, 51 N.J.Eq. 452, 26 A. 823; Stainback v. Junk Bros. Lumber & Mfg. Co., 98 Tenn. 306, 39 S.W. 530.

A judgment creditor is not,[47] in the absence of a statute,[48] a purchaser. He gives up nothing. He merely changes his position in an advantageous way by getting his claim liquidated and securing a possible lien for its collection. Property seized by him will be held subject to equities attaching to it in the hands of his debtor.

Where an execution creditor purchases property of his debtor at an execution sale in return for the cancellation of his judgment, he would seem to qualify as giving value if the cancellation of an old debt is treated as value[49] but not otherwise;[50] and if the purchaser is one other than the execution creditor there will necessarily be the payment of value.[51]

A change of status is held to be giving value, as where one makes a promise of marriage in return for a conveyance of property. The mere act of becoming betrothed is treated as giving value.[52] *A fortiori* entering into a marriage amounts to giving value.[53]

If the consideration given was illegal, clearly the purchaser will not be protected, as in cases of transfers in payment of gambling debts[54] or conveyances in return for illicit sexual relations.[55]

If a purchaser from a trustee in breach of trust has received legal title but paid only part of the price before he receives notice of the trust and its breach, equity will protect him only in part. Whatever result is fairest in the circumstances will be directed by the court. Either the purchaser will be allowed to keep the legal title on paying into the trust the balance of the price, or the purchaser will be directed to reconvey to the trust his legal title on being reimbursed for the part of the price paid, or the purchaser will be given an interest in the property proportionate to the amount of the part payment made.[56] It will be important to learn whether the price contracted to be paid was reasonable, whether the property can be partitioned, what portion of the price has been paid, whether the purchaser has made improvements, and other surrounding circumstances.

What is Notice?

To affect a purchaser with notice it is not essential that he knew who the beneficiaries were or the precise terms of the trust. It is

47. Houghton v. Davenport, 74 Me. 590; Harney v. First Nat. Bank, 52 N.J.Eq. 697, 29 A. 221.

48. Guin v. Guin, 196 Ala. 221, 72 So. 74.

49. Pugh v. Highley, 152 Ind. 252, 53 N.E. 171.

50. Rexburg Lumber Co. v. Purrington, 62 Idaho 461, 113 P.2d 511 (1941).

51. Fahn v. Bleckley, 55 Ga. 81.

52. Smith v. Allen, 5 Allen, Mass. 454, 81 Am.Dec. 758; De Hierapolis v. Reilly, 44 App.Div. 22, 60 N.Y.S. 417.

53. Johnson v. Petersen, 101 Neb. 504, 163 N.W. 869, 1 A.L.R. 1235.

54. Lacey v. Bentley, 39 Colo. 449, 89 P. 789.

55. Baxter v. Wilburn, 172 Md. 160, 190 A. 773 (1937).

56. Henry v. Phillips, 163 Cal. 135, 124 P. 837, Ann.Cas.1914A, 39; Paul v. Fulton, 25 Mo. 156; Haughwout v. Murphy, 22 N.J.Eq. 531; Durst v. Daugherty, 81 Tex. 650, 17 S.W. 388.

sufficient that he knew there was a trust and, either actually or constructively, knew that the transfer was in breach of that trust.[57]

Notice acquired by an agent during the performance of his duties frequently binds his principal, as does notice to a corporate officer.[58] The limitations on this type of notice are considered in a later section.[59] Thus knowledge of a bank cashier may prevent a bank from being a purchaser in good faith;[60] but a corporation is not charged with the knowledge of its officer who acted solely for his own benefit in the transaction.[61]

If the trust property is represented by a document, for example, a bond, certificate of stock or note, and it appears on the face of such document that the holder owns it as trustee, it has been held in many cases that a purchaser will be held to have notice of the trust, a duty to inquire into the power of the trustee to sell the document, and notice of a breach if reasonable inquiry would have discovered it.[62] But the uniform legislation regarding commercial and investment paper and documents of title representing interests in tangibles expressly denies any duty to inquire and notice which might come from it.[63]

Constructive notice under the recording acts is sufficient to prevent a party from being a bona fide purchaser, as in the case of deeds, mortgages, judgments, wills, and notices of pendency of actions which have been properly recorded. Frequently the purchaser receives constructive notice as to the existence of a trust and the trustee's powers,[64] or is put on inquiry as to such matters,[65] by the record of a deed or other instrument in his chain of title; but a deed which is not a link in that chain will not act as constructive notice.[66] Lis pendens may prevent the purchaser of the trust res from being a purchaser in good faith.[67]

57. Mayfield v. Turner, 180 Ill. 332, 54 N.E. 418; Zuver v. Lyons, 40 Iowa 510; Jeffray v. Towar, 63 N.J.Eq. 530, 53 A. 182.

58. Chapman v. Hughes, 134 Cal. 641, 58 P. 298, 60 P. 974, 66 P. 982; Webber v. Clark, 136 Ill. 256, 26 N.E. 360, 32 N.E. 748; Stewart v. Greenfield, 16 Lea, Tenn., 13.

59. See § 167, post.

60. Duncan v. Jaudon, 82 U.S. (15 Wall.) 165, 21 L.Ed. 142 (1872); Gaston v. American Exch. Nat. Bank, 29 N.J.Eq. 98.

61. Weber v. Richardson, 76 Or. 286, 147 P. 522, 1199.

62. Eldridge v. Turner, 11 Ala. 1049; Watson v. Sutro, 86 Cal. 500, 24 P. 172, 25 P. 64; Turner v. Hoyle, 95 Mo. 337, 8 S.W. 157; Harrison v. Fleischman, 70 N.J.Eq. 301, 61 A. 1025; Swan v. Produce Bank, 24 Hun, N.Y., 277; Stoddard v. Smith, 11 Ohio St. 581; Clemens v. Heckscher, 185 Pa. 476, 40 A. 80; Simons v. Southwestern R. Bank, 5 Rich.Eq., S.C. 270.

63. See § 167, post, for discussion of the effect of the N.I.L., Uniform Fiduciaries Act and Uniform Commercial Code on this question.

64. Hagan v. Varney, 147 Ill. 281, 35 N.E. 219; Knowles v. Williams, 58 Kan. 221, 48 P. 856; Turner v. Edmonston, 210 Mo. 411, 109 S.W. 33, 124 Am.St.Rep. 739; Johnson v. Prairie, 91 N.C. 159; Barrett v. Bamber, 81 Pa. 247; Simmons v. Dinsmore, 56 Tex. 404; Morgan v. Fisher's Adm'r, 82 Va. 417.

65. Hassey v. Wilke, 55 Cal. 525; Webber v. Clark, 136 Ill. 256, 26 N.E. 360, 32 N.E. 748; Mercantile Nat. Bank of Cleveland v. Parsons, 54 Minn. 56, 55 N.W. 825, 40 Am.St.Rep. 299.

66. Moore v. Hunter, 6 Ill. 317, 1 Gilman 317; Murray v. Ballou, 1 Johns. Ch., N.Y., 566; Claiborne v. Holland, 88 Va. 1046, 14 S.E. 915.

67. Murray v. Ballou, 1 Johns.Ch., N.Y., 566.

In some states there are special recording statutes relating to conveyances to a trustee, either declaring that record of it is constructive notice of the existence of the trust,[68] or that if a grantee is described as trustee in a conveyance without further description of the trust or the trustee's powers, one dealing with the trustee as to the property is entitled to treat the words "as trustee" as of no effect or to assume that the trustee had a power of sale.[69]

Open, notorious and exclusive possession [70] of real property by a beneficiary or other owner of an equitable interest has been held to give a purchaser notice of the rights of the possessor,[71] or at least to put the purchaser on inquiry.[72] In the words of the Supreme Court of North Dakota: "An open, notorious, and adverse possession of real property is notice to the world of every right or interest owned or held by the person in possession, whether such right be legal or equitable." [73]

Facts Putting on Inquiry

If the purchaser learns of facts which, while not conclusively showing the existence of a trust with respect to the property in question, ought to arouse doubt regarding the title in the mind of an ordinarily prudent man, he will be charged with notice of such further facts as he could have ascertained by the use of reasonable diligence.[74] Gross inadequacy of the seller's asking price may amount to a fact putting the buyer on inquiry, since in such a case an ordinarily prudent man would be led to suspect that the title of his seller was defective or subject to an equity or burden.[75] There has been a difference of judicial opinion as to whether the refusal by the seller to give anything more than a quitclaim deed is a fact placing on the buyer a duty to inquire as to defects in the title.[76]

If the facts are such as to impose a duty of inquiry, information should be sought from other sources than the trustee, for he is not impartial.[77] If he was a trustee and intended wrongfully to transfer the

---

68. See statutes referred to in Bogert, Trusts and Trustees (rev. 2d edit.), § 893.

69. See statutes digested in Bogert, Trusts and Trustees (rev. 2d edit.), § 893. These acts are intended to facilitate the searching and clearing of titles.

70. Beaubien v. Hindman, 38 Kan. 471, 16 P. 796.

71. McVey v. McQuality, 97 Ill. 93; McDaniel v. Peabody, 54 Iowa 305, 6 N.W. 538; Ferrin v. Errol, 59 N.H. 234; Flaherty v. Cramer, 62 N.J.Eq. 758, 48 A. 565; Grimestone v. Carter, 3 Paige, N.Y., 421, 24 Am.Dec. 230; Ross v. Hendrix, 110 N.C. 403, 15 S.E. 4; Petrain v. Kiernan, 23 Or. 455, 32 P. 158.

72. Witter v. Dudley, 42 Ala. 616; Morrison v. Kelly, 22 Ill. 609, 74 Am.Dec. 169; Bowman v. Anderson, 82 Iowa 210, 47 N.W. 1087, 31 Am.St.Rep. 473.

73. Krause v. Krause, 30 N.D. 54, 151 N.W. 991, 996.

74. Condit v. Maxwell, 142 Mo. 266, 44 S.W. 467; Jeffray v. Towar, 63 N.J.Eq. 530, 53 A. 182; Federal Heating Co. v. City of Buffalo, 182 App.Div. 128, 170 N.Y.S. 515.

75. Storrs v. Wallace, 61 Mich. 437, 28 N.W. 662; Condit v. Bigalow, 64 N.J.Eq. 504, 54 A. 160; Hanrick v. Gurley, 93 Tex. 458, 54 S.W. 347, 55 S.W. 119, 56 S.W. 330.

76. To the effect that the form of the deed is not important, see Archer v. Kelley, 194 Ga. 117, 21 S.E.2d 51 (1942); Croak v. Witteman, 73 N.D. 592, 17 N.W.2d 542 (1945). But see, *contra,* Crump v. Knight, 256 Ala. 601, 56 So.2d 625 (1952); McAboy v. Packer, 353 Mo. 1219, 187 S.W.2d 207 (1945).

77. Jonathan Mills Mfg. Co. v. Whitehurst, 19 C.C.A. 130, 72 Fed. 496 (6th Cir.

trust property, or to commit another breach of trust, he would not be likely to admit it. "It is well established that one who has reason to believe that another is offering property for sale, which he holds either as trustee or agent for a third person, cannot become a bona fide purchaser of the property for value by reliance on the statements of the suspected trustee or agent, either as to his authority or as to his beneficial ownership of the thing sold. In such a case, inquiry must be made of some one other than the agent or trustee—of some one who will have a motive to tell the truth, in the interest of the cestui que trust or principal." [78]

 WESTLAW REFERENCES

The Rule Stated
"bona fide purchaser" /3 rule theory doctrine /s trust
390k356(1)
390k357(1)

Reasons for the Rule
boone +3 chiles
400k239
400k220
400k223
150k60

Burden of Proof
sy, di(burden /3 proof proving /s "bona fida purchaser")
400k242 /p "bona fide purchaser"

Legal Title Required
"equitable interest" /s "bona fide purchaser"
"legal interest" /s "bona fide purchaser"
400k220 /p "bona fide"
400k239 /p "bona fide" innocen***
find 299 sw2d 279

Innocence at Time of Payment and Getting Title
"bona fide purchaser" /s innocen**
390k357 /p innocent /s "bona fide purchaser"
156k76 /p innocent /s "bona fide purchaser"
jewett +3 palmer
400k240
400k226
400k227

Who is a Purchaser? What is Value?
"bona fide purchaser" /s consideration /s trust
400k235
400k236
di("bona fide purchaser" /s value /s trust)

1896); Golson v. Fielder, 2 Tex.Civ.App. 400, 21 S.W. 173.

78. Jonathan Mills Mfg. Co. v. Whitehurst, 19 C.C.A. 130, 72 Fed. 496, 502 (6th Cir.1896).

239k15 /p "bona fide purchaser"

390k357(1)

343k238

What is Notice?

di("bona fide purchaser" /s notice /s trust)

343k240

390k357(1)

400k233

400k228(2)

358k23 /p notice

di("bona fide purchaser" /s "constructive notice")

Facts Putting on Inquiry

"bona fide purchaser" /s duty /2 inquir*

400k229(10) /p duty /2 inquir*

343k235(3)

Chapter 20

REMEDIES OF BENEFICIARIES—PARTICIPATION IN A BREACH—BARRING OF REMEDIES

Table of Sections

ACTIONS AGAINST THIRD PERSONS FOR DAMAGING TRUST PROPERTY [1]

§ 166. **Where a third person alone does an act which causes damage to the trust property, he may be held liable therefor. The action should be brought by the trustee but the beneficiary may sue in equity if the trustee refuses or neglects to bring a suit.**

Where a third person joins with the trustee in committing a breach of trust, an action may be maintained against him, or against him and the trustee, by the wrongdoing trustee, a successor or cotrustee, or by the beneficiary.

Wrong by Third Party Alone

Every property owner, whether his interest is legal or equitable, has a right to have third persons refrain from injuring or appropriating the subject of his property right. It is therefore a truism that a trust beneficiary, being the owner of an equitable property right, has the support of the courts in his claim that strangers shall not cause damage to the trust res or prevent the application of it to the purposes of the trust.[2] For example, an elevated railroad company which erects structures injurious to the trust property may be held liable in damages.[3] If

---

§ 166

1. Bogert, Trusts and Trustees (rev. 2d edit.), §§ 868, 870, 901–912; Restatement, Trusts, Second, §§ 280–295, 321–326, 393.

2. Ripperger v. Schroder-Rockefeller Co., 37 F.Supp. 375 (S.D.N.Y.1940).

3. Roberts v. N.Y. El. R.R. Co., 155 N.Y. 31, 49 N.E. 262.

persons unconnected with the trust wrongfully retain possession of the trust property, replevin or ejectment or a similar possessory action will lie.[4]

Title to, and possession of, the trust property normally rest in the trustee. He is the owner in the courts of law. It is therefore natural that a cause of action in favor of the trustee is held to arise when a third person interferes with the possession of the trust property, or misappropriates or damages it. Ordinarily the trustee, and he alone, is permitted to sue the wrongdoer.[5] Thus an action to recover the trust property or for injury to it,[6] to restrain the wrongful taxation of the trust res,[7] or in ejectment,[8] must be brought by the trustee, in the absence of special circumstances. The beneficiary may not ordinarily sue a third person for injury to or recovery of the trust property, in the absence of one or more of the special facts hereinafter mentioned.[9] Thus the beneficiary has been denied relief against a third person in actions of trover,[10] ejectment,[11] and for the recovery of damages to the trust property.[12]

The trustee and beneficiary may unite in an action to recover the trust fund from a third person who wrongfully holds it, although the addition of the beneficiary as a party plaintiff is ordinarily unnecessary.[13]

If the purposes of the trust are accomplished, and the trust is therefore passive, the beneficiary has been allowed to maintain ejectment.[14] Likewise the beneficiary may bring ejectment, if by the terms of the trust he is entitled to the possession of the trust property, even though the trust is active.[15] And if the beneficiary is in lawful possession, he may recover at law for an injury to that possession,[16] or enjoin a disturbance of the possession by a third party.[17]

If the trustee refuses to bring an action against a third person who

4. Warren v. Howard, 99 N.C. 190, 5 S.E. 424.

5. Cruse v. Kidd, 195 Ala. 22, 70 So. 166; Snyder v. Snover, 56 N.J.L. 20, 27 A. 1013.

6. Robinson v. Adams, 81 App.Div. 20, 80 N.Y.S. 1098, affirmed 179 N.Y. 558, 71 N.E. 1139.

7. Western R. Co. v. Nolan, 48 N.Y. 513.

8. Simmons v. Richardson, 107 Ala. 697, 18 So. 245.

9. Handler v. Alpert, 331 Ill.App. 405, 73 N.E.2d 171 (1947) (forcible detainer against a tenant); Weetjen v. Vibbard, 5 Hun, N.Y., 265; Dameron v. Gold, 17 N.C. 17.

10. Myers v. Hale, 17 Mo.App. 204; Poage v. Bell, 8 Leigh, Va., 604.

11. Obert v. Bordine, 20 N.J.L. 394; Bruce v. Faucett, 49 N.C. 391.

12. Lindheim v. Manhattan Ry. Co., 68 Hun 122, 22 N.Y.S. 685; Pennsylvania R. Co. v. Duncan, 111 Pa. 352, 5 A. 742.

13. Jennings' Ex'rs v. Davis, 5 Dana, Ky., 127; Marble v. Whaley, 33 Miss. 157.

14. Schenck v. Salt Dome Oil Corp., 28 Del.Ch. 54, 37 A.2d 64 (1944); Cable v. Cable, 146 Pa. 451, 23 A. 223; Hopkins v. Ward, 6 Munf., Va., 38.

15. Glover v. Stamps, 73 Ga. 209, 54 Am.Rep. 870; Cape v. Plymouth Congregational Church, 117 Wis. 150, 93 N.W. 449.

16. Stearns v. Palmer, 10 Metc., Mass., 32.

17. Reed v. Harris, 30 N.Y.Super.Ct. 151.

has injured or misappropriated the trust property, after demand,[18] or fails to sue,[19] or the trusteeship is vacant,[20] or the trustee has been absent for many years [21] or has an adverse interest,[22] the beneficiary may maintain a suit in equity against the third person in which the trustee is made a party defendant.[23] To wait until a new trustee could be appointed, or until the present trustee saw fit to act or his disabilities were removed, would endanger the cause of action. The necessities of the case entitle the beneficiary to proceed directly, in place of the trustee, to enforce the cause of action which the trustee has.

The principle is illustrated by a New York case in which a bondholder-beneficiary was allowed to maintain a bill to foreclose a mortgage held by the trustee as security for the bonds because of the absence of the trustee in a foreign country. There was an additional allegation that the trustee was insane. The court, through Finch, J., said: [24]

"It is conceded that the beneficiary may sue where the trustee refuses, but that is because there is no other remedy, and the right of the bondholder, otherwise, will go unredressed. The doctrine does not rest rigidly upon a technical ground, but upon a substantial necessity . . .. What occurred in the present case was tantamount to and an equivalent of a refusal by the trustee. He had gone beyond the jurisdiction; the whole apprehended mischief would be consummated before he could be reached; and if reached there was sufficient reason to believe that he was incompetent . . .. The court, in such an action, takes hold of the trust, dictates and controls its performance, distributes the assets as it deems just, and it is not vitally important which of the two possible plaintiffs set the court in motion. The bondholders are the real parties in interest; it is their right which is to be redressed, and their loss which is to be prevented; and any emergency which makes a demand upon the trustee futile or impossible and leaves the right of the bondholder without other reasonable means of redress should justify his appearance as plaintiff in a court of equity for the purpose of foreclosure."

Third Party Joins with Trustee in Breach

A third person owes a duty to a trust beneficiary not to join with the trustee in committing a breach of trust or assist him therein, and

18. De Kay v. Hackensack Water Co., 38 N.J.Eq. 158; O'Beirne v. Allegheny & K.R. Co., 151 N.Y. 372, 45 N.E. 873; Phoebe v. Black, 76 N.C. 379.

19. Wheeler v. Brown, 26 Ill. 369; Manley v. Brattleboro Tr. Co., 116 Vt. 460, 78 A.2d 488 (1951).

20. Zimmerman v. Makepeace, 152 Ind. 199, 52 N.E. 992; Judd v. Dike, 30 Minn. 380, 15 N.W. 672.

21. Hemmerich v. Union Dime Sav. Inst., 144 App.Div. 413, 129 N.Y.S. 267.

22. Webb v. Vermont Cent. R. Co., 9 Fed. 793 (C.C.Vt.1881); Rowland v. Kable, 174 Va. 343, 6 S.E.2d 633 (1940).

23. Schweinler v. Manning, 88 F.Supp. 964 (D.N.J.1949); Locke v. Andrasko, 178 Wash. 145, 34 P.2d 444 (1934).

24. Ettlinger v. Persian Rug & Carpet Co., 142 N.Y. 189, 192, 193, 36 N.E. 1055, 40 Am.St.Rep. 587.

may be held liable in damages if he knowingly participates with the trustee in the breach.[25] If he innocently aids the wrongdoing trustee, he will not be liable in damages but may be required to give up property thus obtained, if not a bona fide purchaser. "There can be no dispute that as a general principle all persons who knowingly participate or aid in committing a breach of trust are responsible for the money and may be compelled to replace the fund which they have been instrumental in diverting."[26] Thus a beneficiary of a trust for creditors may maintain a bill in equity against a third person who has induced the trustees to transfer the trust assets to him;[27] and individual creditors of the trustee, who knowingly accept trust funds from the trustee in payment of their debts, are liable therefor to the beneficiary.[28] Other examples of liability for participation are found where the third person aids the trustee to deceive the beneficiaries,[29] unlawfully borrows the trust funds,[30] induces the trustee to make a nonlegal investment,[31] pays trust funds to the trustee with knowledge that he intends to misappropriate them,[32] or assists the trustee to buy real estate for himself with trust funds.[33]

Corporate directors and officers of a trustee may be held liable for participating in a breach which they aid the corporation to commit.[34]

The wrongdoing trustee, or his co-trustee or successor, may also maintain the action against the third person who has taken part in a breach of trust.[35] The wrongdoing trustee is allowed to repent and to try to remedy the wrong.[36]

The liability for knowing participation is undisputed. The principal problems in the field are concerned with the question whether certain acts proved a conscious participation in a breach. These questions will be considered in the next succeeding section.

The remedies available against a wrongdoing trustee are also open in an action against a participator in a breach, for example, the tracing of trust funds if the participator is not a bona fide purchaser,[37] money

---

25. See cases cited in § 167, post. The doctrine applies to persons dealing with any fiduciary. Cachules v. 116 East 57th St., Inc., 125 N.Y.S.2d 97 (1953); Bonham v. Coe, 249 App.Div. 428, 292 N.Y.S. 423 (1937), affirmed 276 N.Y. 540, 12 N.E.2d 566 (1937).

26. Duckett v. National Mechanics' Bank, 86 Md. 400, 403, 38 A. 983, 39 L.R.A. 84, 63 Am.St.Rep. 513.

27. Kentucky Wagon Mfg. Co. v. Jones & Hopkins Mfg. Co., 160 C.C.A. 350, 248 Fed. 272 (5th Cir.1918).

28. Stratton v. Stratton's Adm'r, 149 Ky. 473, 149 S.W. 900.

29. Whitford v. Reddeman, 196 Wis. 10, 219 N.W. 361 (1928).

30. Attorney General v. Corporation of Leicester, 7 Beav. 176.

31. Kinney v. Lindgren, 373 Ill. 415, 26 N.E.2d 471 (1940).

32. Emerado Farmers' El. Co. v. Farmers' Bank of Emerado, 20 N.D. 270, 127 N.W. 522, 29 L.R.A.,N.S., 567.

33. Tucker v. Weeks, 177 App.Div. 158, 163 N.Y.S. 595.

34. Masonic Bldg. Corp. v. Carlsen, 128 Neb. 108, 258 N.W. 44 (1934); Finley v. Exchange Tr. Co., 183 Okl. 167, 80 P.2d 296 (1938).

35. Loring v. Salisbury Mills, 125 Mass. 138.

36. Wetmore v. Porter, 92 N.Y. 76.

37. Vorlander v. Keyes, 1 F.2d 67 (8th Cir.1924); Pharr v. Fink, 151 Ark. 305, 237 S.W. 728 (1922).

damages,[38] or damages and a lien on the product of the breach.[39]

The liabilities of the trustee and the participant are joint and several.[40] They may be sued separately or joined in the same action.[41] If one of them pays the whole claim, he may have a right to contribution from the other; [42] and if one is more blameworthy than the other the latter may have a right to be indemnified by the former.[43] It has been held that an agreement by a fiduciary to indemnify a third person against liability for selling a non-legal investment to the fiduciary is not against public policy and will be enforced.[44] However it would seem that such a contract facilitates the commission of breaches of trust and should be denied enforcement.[45]

 WESTLAW REFERENCES

Wrong by Third Party Alone

cruse +3 kidd

find 88 fsupp 964

390k247

beneficiary /s sue* suit /s trustee /s refuse*

Third Party Joins with Trustee in Breach

find 125 nys2d 97

di(assist advanc! aid*** participat*** /10 "breach of trust")

bliss +3 collier

PARTICIPATION IN A BREACH OF TRUST [1]

§ 167. A person who aids a trustee to commit a breach of trust is liable only if he knew or should have known that the trust was being violated.

One who pays money or delivers property to a trustee is not under a duty to see that it is applied to trust purposes.

One who accepts a transfer from a trustee of property which he knows is trust property is under a duty to inquire as to the power of the trustee to make the transfer, and as to the propriety of the objects of the transfer in the case of non-negotiable property, but not in the case of negotiable property.

38. Olin Cem. Ass'n v. Citizens' Sav. Bank, 222 Iowa 1053, 270 N.W. 455, 112 A.L.R. 1205 (1936); Andrews v. Miguel, 303 Mass. 179, 22 N.E.2d 660 (1939).

39. Bliss v. Collier, 232 Mich. 221, 205 N.W. 81 (1925); Campbell v. Webb, 363 Mo. 1192, 258 S.W.2d 595 (1953).

40. Atlanta Trust Co. v. National Bondholders' Corp., 188 Ga. 761, 4 S.E.2d 644 (1939); State ex rel. North St. Louis Trust Co. v. Wolfe, 343 Mo. 580, 122 S.W.2d 909 (1938).

41. Sweet v. Montpelier Sav. Bank & Tr. Co., 69 Kan. 641, 77 P. 538; Barksdale v. Finney, 55 Va. 338.

42. Patteson v. Horsley, 29 Gratt. 263.

43. See § 157, ante.

44. Delafield v. Barret, 270 N.Y. 43, 200 N.E. 67.

45. See 3 Univ. of Chi.L.R. 675; 46 Yale L.J. 1085; 22 Cornell L.Q. 147.

§ 167

1. Bogert, Trusts and Trustees (rev. 2d edit.), §§ 901–912; Restatement, Trusts, Second, §§ 283–295, 321–326.

A person who takes known trust property in payment of the trustee's personal debt, or who assists the trustee in applying known trust property to the payment of the trustee's personal debt to another, is guilty of participating in a breach of trust.

Corporations and their transfer agents are not under a duty to inquire into the power of trustees to transfer corporate stock or the propriety of proposed transfers.

Where the signatures and indorsements on commercial paper indicate that it is or may be trust property and it is deposited to the credit of the trustee personally, the bank is not charged with notice that trust funds are being transferred to the personal account, and is not guilty of a wrong in crediting the item to the personal account.

A bank is not guilty of participation in a breach of trust because it permits known trust funds to be drawn out by the trustee for his individual benefit or in payment of his personal debts, unless the bank had actual knowledge of the breach of trust or knew of facts which made its act one of bad faith.

While the discussion here is confined to the case of the trustee, the same problems arise with regard to many other fiduciaries, for example, executors, administrators, guardians, receivers, agents, and officers of corporations, and the rules laid down apply to all fiduciaries alike.[2]

The rules as to what amounts to participation in a breach of trust have been codified in the Uniform Fiduciaries Act which is now in force in many jurisdictions.[3] In a general way the Act restricts the third person's liability to cases where he accepts trust property in satisfaction of the trustee's personal debt to him, or where he actually knows of an intended breach of trust or acts with knowledge of such facts about the trustee and his conduct that the third person's action amounts to bad faith. The bad faith test is honesty and not the use of ordinary care.

Innocent Assistance to Wrongdoing Trustee

If a third person has no knowledge of an intent on the part of the trustee to commit a breach of trust and at the request of the trustee performs an act which assists the trustee in accomplishing his wrongful purpose, the third party is not a participant in a breach of trust and is not liable in damages to the beneficiaries of the trust.[4] Thus if the trustee has a personal bank account in which he deposits cash belonging to the trust, and the bank has no knowledge that the funds

---

2. Boston Ins. Co. v. Wells Fargo Bank & Union Tr. Co., 80 Cal.App.2d 59, 181 P.2d 84 (1947) (corporate employee); Peoples Nat. Bank v. Guier, 284 Ky. 702, 145 S.W.2d 1042 (1940) (executor); Thomson v. New York Tr. Co., 293 N.Y. 58, 56 N.E.2d 32 (1944), motion denied 293 N.Y. 751, 56 N.E.2d 746 (1944) (agent).

3. Approved in 1922 and now in force in 23 states and the District of Columbia. In some states parts of the Act have been superseded by the Uniform Commercial Code. For the text of the Act, see 9 U.L.A.

For discussions of some of the problems raised in this section, see Scott, 34 Harv. L.R. 454; Thulin, 6 Cal.L.R. 171; McCollom, 11 Col.L.R. 428; Merrill, 40 Harv.L.R. 1077.

4. Holly v. Domestic & Foreign Missionary Soc., 180 U.S. 284, 21 S.Ct. 395, 45 L.Ed. 531 (1901); First Nat. Bank v. Byrnes, 61 Kan. 459, 59 P. 1056.

deposited are trust property, and the trustee draws a check on the account to pay a debt which the bank knows is a personal debt of the trustee and the bank honors this check, it is not liable for taking part in a breach of trust since it did not know or have reason to know that trust money was being spent for an improper purpose.

If the third person who innocently helps a trustee commit a breach himself obtains property through the breach, he will be able to retain it if he was a bona fide purchaser, but otherwise will be obliged to return it to the trust.[5]

Guilty Assistance in Breach of Trust

A person who realizes, or should know, that an act which the trustee is attempting to perform will be a breach of trust, and then cooperates with the trustee in carrying out the transaction, is a participant in the breach and will be held liable to the beneficiary for the damages which arise therefrom.[6] The principal problem is to decide under what circumstances the third party is to be regarded as knowing of the impending breach. When is he deemed to know that certain property is trust property or that a bank account contains trust funds? When is he put on notice of the trustee's wrongful purpose? To what extent must a person dealing with a known trustee investigate the legality of his conduct so that he is charged with notice of facts he could have obtained by a reasonable inquiry?

Paying Money or Delivering Other Property to a Trustee

In some early case law it was held that a purchaser of trust property was under a duty to see to the application of the purchase price which he paid to the trustee and to learn whether it was being put to proper trust purposes, and that he was a participant in a breach if he could have learned that the trustee intended to use the payment improperly and after the delivery of the price the trustee committed a breach regarding it.[7]

This doctrine has been repudiated in case [8] and statutory law,[9] so that now there is no such duty and there will be no participation in a

---

5. Vorlander v. Keyes, 1 F.2d 67 (8th Cir.1924); Clingman v. Hill, 113 Kan. 632, 215 P. 1013 (1923).

6. Malmud v. Blackman, 251 App.Div. 192, 295 N.Y.S. 398 (1937), affirmed 278 N.Y. 658, 16 N.E.2d 391 (1938); Bonham v. Coe, 249 App.Div. 428, 292 N.Y.S. 423 (1937), affirmed 276 N.Y. 540, 12 N.E.2d 566 (1937).

7. Larmer v. Price, 350 Ill. 401, 183 N.E. 230 (1932); Hughes v. Tabb, 78 Va. 313.

8. Dawson v. Ramser, 58 Ala. 573; Davis v. Freeman, 148 Ga. 117, 95 S.E. 980; Bevis v. Heflin, 63 Ind. 129; Burroughs v. Gaither, 66 Md. 171, 7 A. 243; Gate City Building & Loan Ass'n v. National Bank of Commerce, 126 Mo. 82, 28 S.W. 633, 27 L.R.A. 401, 47 Am.St.Rep. 633; Conover v. Stothoff, 38 N.J.Eq. 55; Doscher v. Wyckoff, 132 App.Div. 139, 116 N.Y.S. 389; Kadis v. Weil, 164 N.C. 84, 80 S.E. 229; In re Streater's Estate, 250 Pa. 328, 95 A. 459; Weakley v. Barrow, 137 Tenn. 224, 192 S.W. 927; Redford v. Clarke, 100 Va. 115, 40 S.E. 630.

9. By § 2 of the Uniform Fiduciaries Act there is no duty to see to the application of purchase money, and the same result is provided by other statutes in some states. See Bogert, Trusts and Trustees (rev. 2d edit.), § 902.

breach unless the buyer knew of the intended misuse or had knowledge of facts which made his action in making the payment one of bad faith.[10]   And the same rule is applied to third persons who deliver money or other property to a trustee for other purposes, for example, by way of loan.

Purchase of Non-Negotiable or Negotiable Property from Known Trustee

As shown previously [11] one who deals with a person whom he knows is a trustee is put on inquiry as to the powers of the trustee, and hence takes part in a breach of trust if he participates in a transaction which was beyond the powers of the trustee.[12]   This rule has been applied to the cases of real property and non-negotiable personalty. For example, if the trustee had no power to mortgage trust realty, a lender to the trustee who took a mortgage on it would be a participant in a breach of trust regardless of his actual knowledge of the powers of the trustee, since he would be charged with knowledge of them.[13]

But in the case of negotiable instruments the policy of facilitating transfers has led to the statutory adoption of a rule that there is no duty to inquire in the case of the purchase of negotiable notes, bonds, stocks and similar instruments which are known to be trust property, and that a purchaser of such property is not a participant in a breach of trust when the trustee had no power of negotiation or was negotiating for an unlawful purpose, unless the purchaser had actual knowledge of the wrongful act or knowledge of facts making his conduct an act of bad faith.[14]   Some early cases to the contrary must be regarded as obsolete.[15]

Accepting or Aiding in the Application of Trust Property toward the Payment of the Personal Debt of the Trustee

If a creditor actually knows that property which is tendered to him in payment of the personal debt of a trustee is trust property, he is a participant in a breach of trust if he accepts the payment.[16]   It would seem that only one construction can be placed on such an act.   And the same rule should apply if the alleged participator knowingly aids the trustee in paying his personal debt to a third person out of trust

---

10. Larmer v. Price, 350 Ill. 401, 183 N.E. 230 (1932); Darnaby v. Watts, 28 S.W. 338, 16 Ky.Law Rep. 321.

11. See §§ 133, 136, ante.

12. Trust Co. of Chicago v. Jackson Park Bldg. Corp., 303 Ill.App. 531, 25 N.E.2d 616 (1940).

13. McKinnon v. Bradley, 178 Or. 45, 165 P.2d 286 (1946).

14. Negotiable Instruments Law, § 56; Uniform Fiduciaries Act, § 4; Uniform Com.Code, § 3–304(2), (4)(e).

15. Owens v. Nagel, 334 Ill. 96, 165 N.E. 165 (1929); Third Nat. Bank of Baltimore v. Lange, 51 Md. 138.   They were decided before the adoption of the modern commercial legislation.

16. Jackson v. Jefferson, 171 Miss. 774, 158 So. 486 (1935); Grace v. Corn Exchange Bank Trust Co., 287 N.Y. 94, 38 N.E.2d 449, 145 A.L.R. 436 (1941); American Surety Co. v. Multnomah County, 171 Or. 287, 138 P.2d 597, 148 A.L.R. 926 (1943).

funds,[17] as in the case of a bank which knows that a bank account contains nothing but trust credit and yet it cooperates with the trustee in withdrawing that credit to pay the landlord of the trustee for rent due from the trustee personally. The rule is clear but its application is difficult because of the necessity for deciding under many different conditions whether the alleged participant knew that the property being used was trust property, or ought to be charged with knowledge.

The basis for liability in this class of cases has been clearly stated by the courts.

"The principle governing the defendant's liability is, that a banker who knows that a fund on deposit with him is a trust fund cannot appropriate that fund for his private benefit, or where charged with notice of the conversion join in assisting others to appropriate it for their personal benefit, without being liable to refund the money if the appropriation is a breach of the trust." [18]

One typical case is where a bank account is entitled "T, as trustee", and a check on it is presented to the bank itself in payment of T's personal debt to it, or a check on it is drawn in favor of one who is known by the bank to be a personal creditor of T and is presented by that creditor for collection. Here it would seem it ought to be held that the bank is charged with notice of a breach of trust on account of the label of the account, the signature on the check, and the known destination of the payment.[19]

So too, if commercial paper such as a check or note is drawn in favor of "T, as Trustee", or is indorsed to him in that capacity, it would seem that the creditor, or the bank assisting the creditor, should know that there was a breach of trust if the paper was used to pay the personal debt of T.[20]

If a bank actually knows that an account which is held in the name of "T", without trust label, contains trust credit, there is a basis for applying the same rule as if the account had been headed "T, as Trustee".[21] However a difficult and much debated question arises where the bank does not have actual knowledge that the account headed "T" contains trust funds, but a careful examination of the commercial paper which had been deposited in that account would have shown that it was or might be trust property, and the question becomes whether the bank should be charged with knowledge that the account

17. Cohnfield v. Tannenbaum, 176 N.Y. 126, 68 N.E. 141; Hill Syrup Co. v. Nat. City Bank, 129 Wash. 171, 224 P. 578 (1924).

18. Allen v. Puritan Tr. Co., 211 Mass. 409, 422, 97 N.E. 916, L.R.A.1915C, 518.

19. Shepard v. Meridian Nat. Bank, 149 Ind. 532, 48 N.E. 346; State Bank of St. Johns v. McCabe, 135 Mich. 479, 98 N.W. 20; Baker v. N.Y. Nat. Exch. Bank, 100 N.Y. 31, 2 N.E. 452.

20. Anacostia Bank v. United States Fidelity & Guar. Co., 119 F.2d 455, 73 App. D.C. 388 (1941); Owens v. Nagel, 334 Ill. 96, 165 N.E. 165 (1929); Hall v. Windsor Sav. Bank, 97 Vt. 125, 121 A. 582 (1923).

21. Globe Sav. Bank v. Nat. Bank of Commerce, 64 Neb. 413, 89 N.W. 1030; Interstate Nat. Bank v. Claxton, 97 Tex. 569, 80 S.W. 604.

contained trust funds. Some courts have charged the bank with notice of the source of the credit in the trustee's personal bank account;[22] others have held that such action would place an unreasonable burden on banks and have denied any duty to inquire and any notice.[23] The problem arises where T deposits in his personal account a check payable to "T, as Trustee" or if a check is drawn by "T, as Trustee" in favor of T.

The Uniform Fiduciaries Act [24] settles some conflict in the authorities on these questions and limits the liability of a bank to the case where the account is labelled a trust account and a check on it is taken by the bank in payment of, or as security for, the personal debt of the trustee to it. The Act denies liability of a creditor who collects his debt by the use of a negotiable instrument indorsed to the fiduciary as such, or a check drawn by the fiduciary to the creditor, unless the creditor had actual knowledge that trust property was being used; and in the case of a check drawn by a fiduciary to himself and indorsed to a creditor, it imposes liability only in case of actual knowledge or knowledge of facts making the action of the transferee an act of bad faith.

Duties of Corporations and Transfer Agents

Where a trustee holds stock in a corporation and he or a transferee from him presents to the corporation or its transfer agent the stock certificate with an indorsement, and requests a change in the registration of the stock to the name of the transferee, there is no duty on the part of the corporation or its transfer agent to inquire into the propriety and validity of the transfer.[25] It may assume that the trustee is making the transfer for a lawful purpose. There will be no participation in a breach of trust unless the corporation or agent either knows of a breach or knows such facts that its assistance in the transfer is an act of bad faith.[26] Thus if T holds stock in C corporation in his name as trustee, and sells it to X and indorses the certificate to X who presents it to the transfer agent of C corporation for transfer, neither C nor its agent is liable for completing the transfer to X, even though, unknown to C and its agent, T had no power to sell the stock or sold it for the purpose of misappropriating the proceeds. This result is provided by special statutes in many states,[27] by the Uniform Fiduciaries Act,[28] by the Uniform Act for the Simplification of Security Transfers (which

---

22. Bischoff v. Yorkville Bank, 218 N.Y. 106, 112 N.E. 759; Grace v. Corn Exchange Bank Trust Co., 287 N.Y. 94, 38 N.E.2d 449 (1941). The opposite position has been taken by L.1948, c. 866, adding § 359-*l* to N.Y.Gen.Bus.Law.

23. Kerner v. Kinsey, 316 Ill.App. 416, 45 N.E.2d 291 (1942), affirmed 384 Ill. 180, 51 N.E.2d 126 (1943); Western Surety Co. v. Farmers & Merch. State Bank, 241 Minn. 381, 63 N.W.2d 377 (1954).

24. §§ 4–8.

25. Geyser-Marion Gold Mining Co. v. Stark, 45 C.C.A. 467, 106 Fed. 558 (8th Cir. 1901); Baker v. Atlantic Coast Line R. Co., 173 N.C. 365, 92 S.E. 170.

26. Marbury v. Ehlen, 72 Md. 206, 19 A. 648, 20 Am.St.Rep. 467; In re Bohlen's Estate, 75 Pa. 304. There was a minority common law view to the contrary. Loring v. Salisbury Mills, 125 Mass. 138.

27. See statutory references in Bogert, Trusts and Trustees (rev. 2d edit.), § 905.

28. § 3.

supplants the Uniform Fiduciaries Act in this respect),[29] and by the Uniform Commercial Code.[30]

In dealing with liability for taking part in a transfer of securities by a fiduciary, the legislatures have approved the contentions of corporations, transfer agents, and stock brokers that it is unreasonable to put a duty of inquiry on the intermediary who effects the transfer, since he is not paid for that service, and to require it of him would be burdensome and expensive.

Bank Permitting Trustee to Deposit Trust Property in Personal Bank Account of Trustee

If T has a personal checking account in B bank entitled "T", and tenders to the bank for credit in this account cash or checks which are known to the bank to be the property of T as trustee, the bank may well be held to take part in a breach of trust if it credits the trust cash or checks to T's personal account,[31] since T, as trustee, has a duty to keep trust property separate from his individual property and to earmark it as trust property. No damage will flow from the mere acceptance of the deposit, but the bank's knowledge and its participation in the wrongful deposit may well affect its liability as to withdrawals.

Generally, however, the only evidence of knowledge by the bank that trust property was going into the personal account has been that checks or other commercial paper offered for deposit showed by their form that they were trust property, as in the case where T presented for credit to his personal account a check drawn by T, as trustee, and payable to T; or a check drawn by X to T, as trustee, and indorsed by T, as trustee, to T. As shown previously,[32] there has been a difference of judicial opinion as to whether the bank should be charged with knowledge of what it could have learned if it had made inquiry as to the ownership of the items tendered for deposit.[33] However the prevalent view [34] has been that there is no duty to inquire and so no notice of what could have been learned, and this position has been taken in the Uniform Fiduciaries Act.[35]

29. For the terms of the Act and its theory, see Bogert, Trusts and Trustees (rev. 2d edit.), § 905. It has been adopted in all states.

30. § 8–403, adopted in all states.

31. British American El. Co. v. Bank of British No. America, (1919) A.C. 658.

32. See this section, supra.

33. As requiring inquiry, see Bank of Hickory v. McPherson, 102 Miss. 582, 59

So. 934; United States Fidel. & Guar. Co. v. People's Bk., 127 Tenn. 720, 157 S.W. 414.

34. Ogden v. Atlantic Nat. Bank, 276 Mass. 130, 176 N.E. 799 (1931); Clarke v. Public Nat. Bank & Tr. Co., 259 N.Y. 285, 181 N.E. 574 (1932).

35. § 9.

Bank's Liability for Cashing Check from Trustee as such to Himself Individually

It is generally held that a bank is not put upon inquiry as to a breach of fiduciary duty when a trustee presents for cashing a check drawn by himself as trustee to himself individually or a check drawn by a third person to T, as trustee, and indorsed by T as trustee to T. The bank may cash the check and will not be liable even though T was misappropriating trust funds,[36] unless the bank had actual knowledge that such was the object of the transaction or had knowledge of facts making its conduct an act of bad faith. The Uniform Fiduciaries Act so provides.[37] The bank may assume that the trustee was transferring trust funds to himself for an honest purpose, for example, paying himself commissions or reimbursing himself for funds advanced to the trust. However the bank is not under a duty to inquire what the purpose of the transaction was.

Bank's Liability for Honoring Check by Trustee as such to his Personal Creditors

If a bank account is held in the name of T, as trustee, or, although labelled merely "T", is known by the bank to contain trust credit, the bank will be a participant in a breach of trust if it honors a check on the account in favor of a third person when it actually knows that the check was given for the personal purposes of the trustee and not for trust purposes,[38] or has knowledge of facts which make its conduct an act of bad faith, but not otherwise.[39] The bank is not put on inquiry as to the legality of the transaction merely by the form of the check as to signature and indorsements. It may assume that the check is drawn for a lawful trust purpose.

The bank is not paid for any investigative service in such matters. To impose such a duty on it would be bad commercial policy, since it would greatly increase the burdens and delay the handling of checks.[40] The concern of the employees of a bank in dealing with checks is merely with the genuineness of the signatures. From the time of its presentation until it is debited to the account on which it is drawn, the check passes through many hands and is put through machines.

The Uniform Fiduciaries Act [41] limits the liability of the bank in

36. American Surety Co. of New York v. First Nat. Bank in West Union, W.Va., 141 F.2d 411 (4th Cir.1944), certiorari denied 322 U.S. 754, 64 S.Ct. 1267, 88 L.Ed. 1583 (1944); Boston Note Brok. Co. v. Pilgrim Tr. Co., 318 Mass. 224, 61 N.E.2d 113 (1945).

37. §§ 6, 7, and 8.

38. Lawrence Warehouse Co. v. Twohig, 224 F.2d 493 (8th Cir.1955); Georgia Railroad Nat. Bank & Tr. Co. v. Liberty Nat. Bank & Tr. Co., 180 Ga. 4, 177 S.E. 803 (1934).

39. Massachusetts Bonding & Ins. Co. v. Standard Tr. & Sav. Bank, 334 Ill. 494, 166 N.E. 123 (1929); Bischoff v. Yorkville Bank, 218 N.Y. 106, 112 N.E. 759; Pennsylvania Title & Tr. Co. v. Meyer, 201 Pa. 299, 50 A. 998.

40. See New Amsterdam Cas. Co. v. National Newark & Essex Banking Co., 119 N.J.Eq. 540, 182 A. 824 (1936); Grace v. Corn Exch. Bank Tr. Co., 287 N.Y. 94, 38 N.E.2d 449 (1941).

41. §§ 7, 8, and 9.

this case to instances of actual knowledge of a breach of fiduciary duty or conduct by the bank amounting to bad faith.

Liability for Conduct Amounting to Bad Faith

Even though a person dealing with a trustee may not have had knowledge that he was taking part in a breach of trust, he may be liable if he had knowledge of such facts and circumstances that his conduct was deemed to be an act of "bad faith".[42] This doctrine is similar to the rule that knowledge of facts which would put a reasonable man on inquiry is equivalent to notice of the information which could be obtained by making a reasonable investigation.[43] In rare cases persons dealing with a trustee do not actually know that he is intending to commit a breach but they have brought to their attention such highly suspicious and suggestive circumstances that they cannot join with the trustee in the proposed transaction without being dishonest and so committing an act of "bad faith".[44]

Examples of cases of this type are to be found where a fiduciary deposits a check to himself as fiduciary for collection, and asks for secrecy in the transaction and for payment in $1,000 bills, and he is known by the bank to have issued bad checks in the past;[45] or where the fiduciary draws a check in favor of a concern known to the bank to be engaged in gambling on the stock market;[46] or where the fiduciary has a bad financial reputation.[47]

Knowledge of one Breach of Trust putting a Bank on Inquiry as to Legality of later Withdrawals

In a leading case[48] the New York Court of Appeals held that after a bank had accepted payment of its claim against a fiduciary in his individual capacity from known trust funds, and consequently knew that the trustee had violated his trust, it was put on inquiry as to the purposes for which later checks on the account were drawn and was liable for the amount of those drawn for the personal purposes of the trustee. Having discovered that the trustee was dishonest, it should have been put on guard against later illegal transactions and should

---

42. This principle is applied throughout the Uniform Fiduciaries Act.

43. See § 165, ante.

44. Kentucky Rock Asphalt Co. v. Mazza's Adm'r, 264 Ky. 158, 94 S.W.2d 316 (1936); Teas v. Third Nat. Bank & Tr. Co., 125 N.J.Eq. 224, 4 A.2d 64 (1939) (indorsement by attorney for fiduciary); Liffiton v. National Sav. Bank, 267 App.Div. 32, 44 N.Y.S.2d 770 (1943), affirmed 293 N.Y. 799, 59 N.E.2d 35 (1944) (bank charged with knowledge of legal requirements as to establishment of fiduciary account).

45. Drainage District No. 7 of Poinsett County v. Citizens' Bank of Jonesboro, 205 Ark. 435, 170 S.W.2d 60 (1943).

46. Pearce v. Dill, 149 Ind. 136, 48 N.E. 788.

47. Farmers' Loan & Tr. Co. v. Fidelity Tr. Co., 30 C.C.A. 247, 86 Fed. 541 (9th Cir. 1898).

48. Bischoff v. Yorkville Bank, 218 N.Y. 106, 112 N.E. 759. Accord: Grace v. Corn Exchange Bank Tr. Co., 287 N.Y. 94, 38 N.E.2d 449 (1941). § 359–*l* of the N.Y. Gen.Business Law, providing that a bank has no duty to take notice of the source of deposits, makes no express provision regarding the Bischoff rule.

have required proof that later withdrawals were for trust objects. This rule has been followed in some states,[49] but disapproved in others,[50] and is repudiated by the Uniform Fiduciaries Act.[51]

Duty of Bank where Co-Trustees have Joint Account

Where co-trustees have a bank account in their joint names, and the power to draw checks on the account has not been delegated to one trustee, it would be participation in a breach of trust for the bank to honor a check on the account signed by one trustee only.[52] But if the co-trustees have filed with the bank an authorization to one of their number to draw checks, the bank is under no duty to inquire whether this authorization was legally given, on the theory that the signing of checks was an act capable of being delegated.[53] It may assume that there is a proper delegation unless the circumstances are such that such an assumption is an act of bad faith because of exceptional and highly suspicious facts known to the bank.

Notice to Agent Binds Principal

Notice to an agent or employee of a fact which affects participation in a breach of trust binds the principal or employer, with the qualifications noted below.[54] Thus if an officer or employee of a bank learns in the course of his work that a trustee who has an account in the bank has been stealing trust funds and intends to use the bank account for his personal purposes, the bank may be charged with knowledge of a breach of trust with regard to the account and be made liable for participating in it.[55] It is the duty of an agent to inform his principal of all facts learned by him during the performance of his duties which concern the interests of the principal, and it is presumed that the agent performs his duty, and therefore that relevant information obtained by the agent in the course of his work actually comes to the principal.

For the doctrine to apply, the facts must have been learned while the agency existed and during the course of the agent's work.[56] And if the agent in the transaction in question was not acting in the interest

49. Fidelity & Dep. Co. v. Farmers' Bank, 44 F.2d 11 (8th Cir.1930); Martin v. First Nat. Bank of Rush City, 51 F.2d 840 (D.Minn.1931); Wichita Roy. Co. v. City Nat. Bank, 127 Tex. 158, 89 S.W.2d 394 (1935).

50. New Amsterdam Cas. Co. v. National Newark & Essex Banking Co., 119 N.J.Eq. 540, 182 A. 824 (1936); Dockstader v. Brown, 204 S.W.2d 352 (Tex.Civ.App. 1947).

51. §§ 7–9.

52. See § 92, ante.

53. § 10, Uniform Fiduciaries Act. See Tenn.Code Ann. § 35–2–110.

54. Lowndes v. City Nat. Bank of South Norwalk, 82 Conn. 8, 72 A. 150, 22 L.R.A.,N.S., 408; Tesene v. Iowa State Bank, 186 Iowa 1385, 173 N.W. 918; Atwood-Stone Co. v. Lake County Bank, 38 S.D. 377, 161 N.W. 539. See Restatement, Second, Agency, §§ 268–282; Merrill on Notice; Uniform Commercial Code, § 1–201(27) and (28); Seavey, 65 Univ. of Pa. L.R. 1, 35; Mechem, Agency, §§ 1802–1854.

55. Fidelity & Dep. Co. v. Citizens Nat. Bank of Somerset, 290 Ky. 306, 161 S.W.2d 62 (1942); Ryan Bros. v. Curwensville St. Bank, 382 Pa. 248, 114 A.2d 178 (1955).

56. Church v. Security-First Nat. Bank, 40 Cal.App.2d 529, 105 P.2d 148 (1940); First Denton Nat. Bank v. Kenney, 116 Md. 24, 81 A. 227, Ann.Cas.1913B, 1337.

of his principal, but rather for his own personal advantage and against the interest of the principal, and hence would not naturally pass on information to the principal, notice to the agent does not bind the principal.[57] For example, if an officer of a bank in which a trustee has an account is cooperating with the trustee in stealing the trust funds in order to enrich himself, in that he is to share in the proceeds of the embezzlement, the facts regarding these transactions will not generally be imputed to the bank since the officer would not naturally pass them on to other officials but would instead conceal his criminal conduct as long as possible.[58] But some courts have bound the principal by notice to an agent who was acting in his personal interest when he was the sole representative of the principal who had any part in the transaction,[59] as where the cashier of a bank is also trustee of a trust which has a deposit in the bank, and as trustee he transfers trust funds to himself as cashier in breach of trust in order to make up shortages in his accounts as cashier.[60]

 WESTLAW REFERENCES

Liab! /s participat*** /s "breach of trust"

"uniform fiduciaries act" /s participat***

Innocent Assistance to Wrongdoing Trustee

find 21 sct 395

vorlander +3 keyes

Guilty Assistance in Breach of Trust

bonham +3 coe /p trust

Paying Money or Delivering Other Property to a Trustee

larmer +3 price

390k202

purchaser /s trust /2 property /s application /s proceeds money price

Purchase of Non-Negotiable or Negotiable Property from Known Trustee

trustee /s sell*** creat*** /s mortgage /s trust /5 property

duty /2 inquir* /s note bond stock /s trust**

56k339 /p trust**

Accepting or Aiding in the Application of Trust Property Toward the Payment of the Personal Debt of the Trustee

find 287 ny 94

57. Montgomery v. Commercial Tr. & Sav. Bank, 286 Ill.App. 241, 3 N.E.2d 139 (1936); Galloway v. Security State Bank of Ellendale, 193 Minn. 104, 258 N.W. 10 (1934).

58. Neagle v. McMullen, 334 Ill. 168, 165 N.E. 605 (1929); Leach v. State Sav. Bank, 202 Iowa 265, 209 N.W. 422 (1926); Henry v. Allen, 151 N.Y. 1, 45 N.E. 355, 36 L.R.A. 658; Knobeloch v. Germania Sav. Bank, 50 S.C. 259, 27 S.E. 962.

59. Munroe v. Harriman, 85 F.2d 493 (2d Cir.1936); Fidelity & Dep. Co. v. Citizens Nat. Bank, 290 Ky. 306, 161 S.W.2d 62 (1942). But see, *contra*, Hummel v. Bank of Monroe, 75 Iowa 689, 37 N.W. 954; First Nat. Bank v. Foote, 12 Utah 157, 42 P. 205.

60. Schneider v. Thompson, 58 F.2d 94 (8th Cir.1932).

52k130(1)

390k221

390k348

find 119 f2d 455

sy, di(person individual bank /s participat! /s breach /2 trust
    (duty obligat! /2 fiduciary))

"uniform fiduciaries act" /s bank

Duties of Corporations and Transfer Agents

marbury +3 ehlen

101k134

Bank Permitting Trustee to Deposit Property in Personal Bank Account of Trustee

trustee /s deposit /s own personal individual private /2 account

52k134(7)

Bank's Liability for Cashing Check from Trustee as Such to Himself Individually

find 141 f2d 411

52k130(1)

Bank's Liability for Honoring Check by Trustee as Such to His Personal Creditors

find 224 f2d 493

390k348

find 287 ny 94

52k130(1)

390k221 /p trustee

390k233

Liability for Conduct Amounting to Bad Faith

find 4 a2d 64

find 86 f 541

Knowledge of One Breach of Trust Putting a Bank on Inquiry as to Legality of Later Withdrawals

find 287 ny 94

52k119

52k130(1)

390k221

390k223

Duty of Bank Where Co-Trustees Have Joint Account

"uniform fiduciaries act" /s bank

Notice to Agent Binds Principal

find 114 a2d 178

52k134(5)

52k116(3) /p knowledge notice

RIGHT OR REMEDY BARRED BY ACT
OF THE BENEFICIARY [1]

§ 168. An act of the beneficiary may prevent him from asserting that he is a beneficiary, or from claiming that a breach of trust has occurred, as where the beneficiary approves of the trustee's conduct in advance or after the breach has been committed, or releases the trustee or third person from a cause of action against him, or is estopped to assert that a trust exists, or is barred from one remedy because of having elected to make use of an inconsistent remedy.

The affirmative conduct of a beneficiary may prevent him from later asserting that a trust exists or that he has a remedy thereunder. A large number of ill-defined terms have come into use in connection with the barring or destruction of the rights of beneficiaries. Courts and textwriters have used in different senses such words as "release," "waiver," "election," "acquiescence," "adoption," "ratification," "confirmation," "estoppel," and "laches." The hopeless confusion in the use of the word "waiver" has been shown by an eminent author.[2] It is believed that the most apt words to define affirmative conduct which bars the beneficiaries are "consent", "ratification", "release", "estoppel", and "election", and that negative action having a similar effect can be classed as "laches" or the operation of the Statute of Limitations.

Consent to a Breach of Trust

The beneficiary may prevent a cause of action from arising by consenting to the alleged wrongful act in advance,[3] by requesting that the act of which he now complains be done,[4] or by joining with the trustee in the transaction.[5] Thus beneficiaries who agree in advance to the continuance of a business by a trustee,[6] or to the making of a wrongful investment,[7] or to an allocation of receipts to principal or income,[8] may not thereafter question the legality of the conduct of the trustee. This doctrine was stated by Lord Eldon as follows: "It is established by all the cases that if the cestui que trusts joins with the trustees in that which is a breach of the trust, knowing the circum-

---

§ 168

1. Bogert, Trusts and Trustees (rev. 2d edit.), §§ 941–946; Restatement, Trusts, Second, §§ 216–218, 295, 313–315.

2. Ewart, Waiver Distributed.

3. Turner v. Fryberger, 99 Minn. 236, 108 N.W. 1118.

4. Chirurg v. Ames, 138 Iowa 697, 116 N.W. 865; Richards v. Keyes, 195 Mass. 184, 80 N.E. 812; Woodbridge v. Bockes, 59 App.Div. 503, 69 N.Y.S. 417, affirmed 170 N.Y. 596, 63 N.E. 362.

5. Butler v. Gazzam, 81 Ala. 491, 1 So. 16; Fonda v. Gibbs, 75 Vt. 406, 56 A. 91.

6. Quimby v. Uhl, 130 Mich. 198, 89 N.W. 722.

7. In re Fidelity & Deposit Co. of Maryland, 172 Mich. 600, 138 N.W. 205. A beneficiary who recommends a non-legal investment (In re Mattison's Will, 17 N.Y.S.2d 735 (Sur.1940)), or agrees to indemnify the trustee against liability for the act (In re Wohl's Estate, 36 N.Y.S.2d 931 (Sur.1942)), cannot later hold the trustee liable.

8. Scullin v. Clark, 242 S.W.2d 542 (Mo.1951).

stances, such a cestui que trust can never complain of such a breach of trust. I go further, and agree that either concurrence in the act, or acquiescence without original concurrence, will release the trustees. . . .." [9] A consent to an unlawful act may be withdrawn before the trustee has acted upon it. [10]

There is, however, no duty on a beneficiary to take a position with regard to approval or disapproval of a proposed act of the trustee. The beneficiary may refuse to express an opinion and may leave the matter to the judgment of the trustee, [11] and his mere silence or failure to object when he is informed of the line of conduct which the trustee proposes to take should not be held to amount to a sanctioning of the transaction. [12]

Ratification of an Unlawful Act

After the commission of a breach of trust or other wrong to the beneficiary, the latter may approve of the act and thus prevent himself from asserting later than he has a cause of action. [13] This is generally called "ratification". It may occur by an express statement of the attitude of the beneficiary, [14] or it may be implied from his conduct as where he accepts the benefits of the transaction without a claim that there has been a violation of duty. [15] Thus a beneficiary who joins in a petition to a court to confirm a voidable act by the trustee will not be heard later to question the act. [16] Where the trustee has been guilty of neglect of duty in delaying to bring suit, approval of the suit when it is brought may prevent the beneficiary from holding the trustee liable. [17] Similarly a beneficiary who knows that an improper investment has been made, raises no objection, and accepts income on it, is often held to have ratified the investment. [18] A beneficiary may ratify a disloyal act of his trustee and thus prevent himself from later objection. [19]

9. Walker v. Symonds, 3 Swanst. 2, 64.

10. Hawaiian Tr. Co. v. Gonser, 40 Hawaii 245; Waterbury v. Nicol, 20 Or. 595, 296 P.2d 487 (1956) opinion modified on other grounds, on rehearing 207 Or. 595, 298 P.2d 211 (1956).

11. White v. Sherman, 168 Ill. 589, 48 N.E. 128 (trustee suggested non-legal investments; beneficiaries told trustee to use own judgment. "They did not choose and were not bound, to exercise any judgment upon the subject.").

12. Ferro v. Citizens Nat. Tr. & Sav. Bank, 44 Cal.2d 401, 282 P.2d 849 (1955); Robinson v. McWayne, 35 Hawaii 689.

13. Bennett v. Pierce, 188 Mass. 186, 74 N.E. 360.

14. In re Wildenburg's Estate, 177 Misc. 49, 29 N.Y.S.2d 896 (1941); In re Armitage's Estate, 195 Pa. 582, 46 A. 117.

15. Burnet v. First Nat. Bank, 12 Ill. App.2d 514, 140 N.E.2d 362 (1957); Holmes v. Hrobon, 93 Ohio App. 1, 103 N.E.2d 845

(1951), affirmed in part and reversed in part in 158 Ohio St. 508, 110 N.E.2d 574 (1953).

16. Richards v. Keyes, 195 Mass. 184, 80 N.E. 812.

17. Ellig v. Naglee, 9 Cal. 683.

18. Willis v. Holcomb, 83 Ohio St. 254, 94 N.E. 486; Farish v. Wayman, 91 Va. 430, 21 S.E. 810; Trethewey v. Horton, 71 Wash. 402, 128 P. 632. But there must be knowledge of the unlawful nature of the act when the benefits are accepted. St. Paul Trust Co. v. Strong, 85 Minn. 1, 88 N.W. 256.

19. City Bank Farmers Trust Co. v. Cannon, 264 App.Div. 429, 35 N.Y.S.2d 870 (1942), decision amended 265 App.Div. 863, 38 N.Y.S.2d 245 (1942). The Uniform Trusts Act renders invalid consents and ratifications of certain types of disloyal acts on the ground of policy, although it permits releases therefor.

It would seem that there should be no duty on the part of a beneficiary to inform the trustee whether he disapproves or approves an act of trust administration after the trustee has called the facts to the attention of the beneficiary. Silence or failure to object ought not to be construed as approval, but rather that the beneficiary may reserve decision or delay enforcement of his rights.[20] However, in some cases where the failure to object has continued for a long period, or the beneficiary knew or should have known that the trustee was acting on the theory that his conduct had been validated by the beneficiary, it has been held that silence amounted to ratification.[21]

Release

The most direct way in which a beneficiary can bar a remedy is to execute a release to the trustee or third person against whom he has the right of action. As any one having a cause of action may discharge it, so it is elementary that the beneficiary may cancel his cause of action, that is, may release it.[22] Thus where the beneficiary has filed a bill for an account, a compromise has been offered, and after an examination of the account with the aid of attorneys the offer of compromise is accepted and a release executed by the beneficiary to the trustee, the beneficiary's remedy is clearly destroyed.[23] Or if the trustee has presented a statement of his account to the beneficiary out of court, and the beneficiary has agreed that it is satisfactory and has accepted the property tendered to him as full performance of the trust, and has given a release, the beneficiary will be prevented from later questioning the acts of the trustee.[24] A release should be distinguished from a surrender of his interest by the beneficiary to the trustee which results in the trustee becoming the owner free of the trust.[25] The general rules as to form and consideration for releases apply to releases by a beneficiary.[26]

Co-trustees who have committed a breach are jointly liable, as are trustees and third persons who have participated in a violation of trust duties. At common law a release of one joint tortfeasor released all, since the cause of action was regarded as a single one and could not be

20. In re Cook's Trust Estate, 20 Del. Ch. 123, 171 A. 730 (1934) ("A trustee cannot relieve himself, of the responsibility of an investment by the simple expedient of informing the beneficiary that the investment has been made. The cestui que trust is under no duty to act as adviser to his trustee."); White v. Sherman, 168 Ill. 589, 48 N.E. 128.

21. Nelson v. Portland Tr. & Sav. Bank, 153 Or. 19, 53 P.2d 1051 (1936); Coulter's Estate, 379 Pa. 209, 108 A.2d 681 (1954).

22. Cocks v. Barlow, 5 Redf.Sur., N.Y., 406; Dearing v. Selvey, 50 W.Va. 4, 40 S.E. 478.

23. Forbes v. Forbes, 5 Gill., Md., 29.

24. Hagerty v. Clement, 195 La. 230, 196 So. 330 (1940); In re Schoenewerg's Estate, 277 N.Y. 424, 14 N.E.2d 777 (1938).

25. See § 96, ante.

26. In re Peck's Estate, 323 Mich. 11, 34 N.W.2d 533 (1948); Brereton's Estate, 388 Pa. 206, 130 A.2d 453 (1957). As to consideration, see Donovan v. Security-First Nat. Bank, 67 Cal.App.2d 845, 155 P.2d 856 (1945); Wool Growers' Service Corp. v. Ragan, 18 Wn.2d 655, 140 P.2d 512 (1943), rehearing denied 18 Wn.2d 655, 141 P.2d 875 (1943).

separated into parts.[27] On the other hand a covenant not to sue a party so jointly liable would not destroy remedies against the other tortfeasors.[28]

Conditions Precedent to Consent, Ratification, or Release [29]

In order that a consent, ratification, or release by a beneficiary may be effective, certain conditions precedent must be met, namely, that the beneficiary is furnished by the trustee or third party involved with full information as to the relevant facts, the rights of the beneficiary, and as to the legal effect of the transaction.[30] For example, if he is asked to consent to an improper investment in advance of its making, or to approve of it after it has been made, or to release the trustee from liability for making it, he must have details as to the character of the investment from both financial and legal points of view, namely, the facts as to its security and income-producing capacity, that it is improper under the law of the state or the terms of the trust (or that there is doubt as to its legality), and that if it is non-legal the beneficiary has a right to prevent it from being made or to hold the trustee in damages for losses caused by it.[31]

"To establish a ratification by a cestui que trust, the fact must not only be clearly proved, but it must be shown that the ratification was made with a full knowledge of all the material particulars and circumstances, and also in a case like the present that the cestui que trust was fully apprised of the effect of the acts ratified, and of his or her legal rights in the matter. Confirmation and ratification imply, to legal minds, knowledge of a defect in the act to be confirmed and of the right to reject or ratify it. The cestui que trust must therefore not only have been acquainted with the facts, but apprised of the law, how these facts would be dealt with by a court of equity." [32]

Obviously, if there are misrepresentations of facts or law by the trustee, or concealment when there is a duty to speak, the transaction is not binding on the beneficiary.[33]

27. Bryan v. Creaves, 138 F.2d 377 (7th Cir.1943), certiorari denied 321 U.S. 778, 64 S.Ct. 619, 88 L.Ed. 1071 (1944); First & Merchants' Nat. Bank of Richmond v. Bank of Waverly, 170 Va. 496, 197 S.E. 462, 116 A.L.R. 1156 (1938). For an abandonment of this rule, see Cal.L.1957, c. 1700, adding § 877 to the Code of Civ.Proc., and Fla.Stats.Ann. § 768.041.

28. Douglas v. Thompson, 206 Ark. 92, 176 S.W.2d 717 (1943); Ramsey v. Camp, 254 N.C. 443, 119 S.E.2d 209 (1961).

29. See § 96, ante, as the duties of the trustee engaging in direct dealing with the beneficiary.

30. Crutcher v. Joyce, 134 F.2d 809 (10th Cir.1943); Jones v. Lloyd, 117 Ill. 597, 7 N.E. 119; Barton v. Fuson, 81 Iowa 575,

47 N.W. 774; Appeal of Berryhill's Adm'x, 35 Pa. 245.

31. Pennsylvania Co. v. Gillmore, 142 N.J.Eq. 27, 59 A.2d 24 (1948); In re Hoyt's Estate, 294 N.Y. 373, 62 N.E.2d 609 (1945), motion denied 294 N.Y. 979, 63 N.E.2d 712 (1945); In re Trusteeship of Stone, 138 Ohio St. 293, 34 N.E.2d 755 (1941).

32. Adair v. Brimmer, 74 N.Y. 539, 553, 554. For similar cases, see In re Bender's Estate, 122 N.J.Eq. 192, 192 A. 718 (1937), affirmed 123 N.J.Eq. 171, 196 A. 677 (1938); Slay v. Burnett Trust, 143 Tex. 621, 187 S.W.2d 377 (1945).

33. Knox County v. Fourth & First Nat. Bank, 181 Tenn. 569, 182 S.W.2d 980 (1944).

The beneficiary must have full legal capacity. If he is an infant or is mentally unsound or is under guardianship his action will be void or voidable.[34]

One beneficiary cannot consent, ratify, or release for another. Life beneficiaries cannot affect the rights of remaindermen. A majority cannot bind a minority.[35]

Estoppel by Misrepresentation [36]

A beneficiary may be estopped to claim that he is a beneficiary or to assert claims under a trust. If he represents expressly or impliedly that there is no trust, or that no breach has occurred, and the person to whom the representation is made justifiably acts in reliance [37] on the statement in such a way that he cannot retreat without damage,[38] a court may hold that the beneficiary is estopped to assert a trust or a breach thereof.[39]

Examples of the application of this doctrine are found where the trust is not on the record and is unknown to the general public, and hence the trustee appears to have the beneficial ownership. Here if the beneficiary expressly states to a proposed purchaser of the property from the trustee, or to a proposed mortgagee, that there is no trust and that the titleholder is in fact the owner, the beneficiary may well be estopped from a later assertion of his equitable interest.[40] A similar result might be decreed where the beneficiary knew that the creditors of the concealed trustee were extending credit to him on the faith of his apparent ownership of the property and the beneficiary did not warn the creditors of the existence of the trust.[41]

The beneficiary's act may have caused the trustee to neglect his duty, as where a beneficiary assured a trustee that he would pay the taxes and water rents and as a result the trustee failed to pay them. The beneficiary's act barred his remedy against the trustee for neglect of duty in failing to pay these charges.[42]

34. Garrett v. Reid-Cashion Land & Cattle Co., 34 Ariz. 245, 270 P. 1044 (1928); Garrett v. First Nat. Bank, 233 Ala. 467, 172 So. 611 (1937); Parker v. Hayes' Adm'r, 39 N.J.Eq. 469; Clark v. Law, 22 How.Pr. 426.

35. Crews v. Willis, 195 Okl. 475, 159 P.2d 251 (1945); In re Quest's Estate, 324 Pa. 230, 188 A. 137 (1936); St. Germain v. Tuttle, 114 Vt. 263, 44 A.2d 137 (1945).

36. For discussion of the various types of estoppel, see Bigelow on Estoppel, and Ewart on Estoppel by Misrepresentation.

37. Fitch v. Double "U" Sales Corp., 212 Md. 324, 129 A.2d 93 (1957); Fallaw v. Oswald, 194 S.C. 387, 9 S.E.2d 793 (1940).

38. Bolles v. Boatmen's Nat. Bank, 363 Mo. 949, 255 S.W.2d 725 (1953).

39. Wolfe v. North Carolina Joint Stock Land Bank, 219 N.C. 313, 13 S.E.2d 533 (1941).

40. Bryant v. Klatt, 2 F.2d 167 (S.D. N.Y.1924); Rafftery v. Kirkpatrick, 29 Cal. App.2d 503, 85 P.2d 147 (1938); Day v. Maynard, 297 Ky. 317, 180 S.W.2d 80 (1944).

41. Dorminy v. Russell, 182 Ga. 635, 186 S.E. 679 (1936); Bergin v. Blackwood, 141 Minn. 325, 170 N.W. 508; Mertens v. Schlemme, 68 N.J.Eq. 544, 59 A. 808.

42. Vreeland v. Van Horn, 17 N.J.Eq. 137.

Election of Remedies

The beneficiary may also do an act which, while not intended by him as a bar to his remedies under the trust, will be so treated in equity because any other result would be unconscionable. In such a case the beneficiary has placed himself and his opponent in such positions that he cannot fairly ask equity to grant him the remedy in question. Thus the beneficiary may have an election between two inconsistent remedies, and if he enforces one remedy, or begins proceedings for its enforcement, he may be denied the right to enforce the other remedy thereafter.[43]

The remedies of holding the trustee liable in damages for a breach and tracing the trust property are inconsistent and a choice must be made between them.[44] If the beneficiary successfully enforces either of these remedies he cannot assert the other remedy,[45] and in many cases it has been held that if he takes formal action to enforce one remedy he is prevented from pursuing the other remedy even though he never completes enforcement of the first remedy.[46]

A beneficiary does not make an election when he thinks he has a choice of two remedies and attempts to pursue one of them, but discovers that he can secure no relief by the method he has chosen. He may later assert the remedy which is actually open to him. "An election of remedies presupposes a right to elect. . . . It 'is simply what its name imports; a choice shown by an overt act, between two inconsistent rights, either of which may be asserted at the will of the chooser alone'. . . . If in truth there is but one remedy, and not a choice between two, a fruitless recourse to a remedy withheld does not bar recourse thereafter to the remedy allowed." [47]

 WESTLAW REFERENCES

Consent to a Breach of Trust
beneficiary /s consent*** /s "breach of trust"
390k230 /p beneficiary /s consent*** /s "breach of trust"
walker +3 symonds

Ratification by Unlawful Act
ratif! /s "breach of trust"
390k237
find 35 nys2d 870

Release
"breach of trust" /s release
331k1 /p "breach of trust"

43. Wiswall v. Stewart, 32 Ala. 433, 70 Am.Dec. 549; Hyatt v. Vanneck, 82 Md. 465, 33 A. 972; Washburn v. Rainier, 149 App.Div. 800, 134 N.Y.S. 301.

44. See § 163, ante.

45. Deer v. Deer's Estate, Mo.App., 180 S.W. 572; Adams v. Mid-West Chev. Corp., 198 Okl. 461, 179 P.2d 147 (1946).

46. Armour & Co. v. Lambdin, 154 Fla. 86, 16 So.2d 805 (1944); Mulligan v. Amo, 211 App.Div. 498, 207 N.Y.S. 407 (1925); Bettencourt v. Bettencourt, 70 Or. 384, 142 P. 326.

47. Cardozo, J., in Schenck v. State Line Tel. Co., 238 N.Y. 308, 311, 144 N.E. 592, 35 A.L.R. 1149 (1924).

Conditions Precedent to Consent Ratification, or Release
find 134 f2d 809

390k237

adair +3 brimmer

Estoppel by Misrepresentation
find 129 a2d 93

390k343

di(beneficiary /s estop! /s trust)

vreeland +3 "van horn"

Election of Remedies
find 144 ne 592

INACTION OF THE BENEFICIARY—LACHES [1]

§ 169. Regardless of statutes of limitation, if the beneficiary, without reasonable excuse, fails to assert his right and seek his remedy for a long period, and because of this inaction it has been rendered difficult or impossible for the defendant to make an adequate defense, the beneficiary may be held guilty of laches and his remedy barred.

Remedy Barred by Inaction of the Beneficiary

The failure of the beneficiary to assert his rights for a long period of time may bar his remedy.[2]

"But there is a defense peculiar to courts of equity, founded on lapse of time and the staleness of the claim, where no statute of limitations governs the case. In such cases, courts of equity act upon their own inherent doctrine of discouraging, for the peace of society, antiquated demands, refuse to interfere where there has been gross laches in prosecuting the claim, or long acquiescence in the assertion of adverse rights."[3]

The defense of laches is independent of the Statute of Limitations. The fact that a statutory period for the barring of causes of action has been set, and that this period has not elapsed, does not prove that the beneficiary has not been guilty of laches. Delay for a period shorter than the statutory limit may be sufficient to destroy the beneficiary's remedy.[4] "Independently of any statute of limitations, courts of equity uniformly decline to assist a person who has slept upon his rights and shows no excuse for his laches in asserting them."[5]

Laches may bar the remedy in the case of resulting and construc-

§ 169

1. Bogert, Trusts and Trustees (rev. 2d edit.), §§ 948, 949; Restatement, Trusts, Second, §§ 219, 327, 409.

2. Laches may bar the remedy of the trustee against third persons. In re Grote's Estate, 390 Pa. 261, 135 A.2d 383 (1957).

3. Badger v. Badger, 69 U.S. (2 Wall.) 87, 94, 17 L.Ed. 836 (1864).

4. Nettles v. Nettles, 67 Ala. 599; Appeal of Evans, 81 Pa. 278.

5. Speidel v. Henrici, 120 U.S. 377, 387, 7 S.Ct. 610, 30 L.Ed. 718 (1887). Although originally laches was exclusively a

tive,[6] as well as express trusts,[7] but the courts are more reluctant to apply it to express than to implied trusts.[8] The courts are reluctant to apply the doctrine to charitable trusts.[9] Laches is a defense which usually must be pleaded,[10] but may be raised by demurrer where the bill shows on its face facts constituting laches,[11] and sometimes the court on its own motion will raise the defense.[12]

Basis for Laches Doctrine

Various reasons have been given by the courts for the laches principle, but they are founded on inexcusable, prejudicial delay. In a large number of cases it has been held that there must be something besides mere lapse of time in order to establish laches. One who is sought to be held as trustee, or the third party sued, must have changed his position in reliance on the delay, or his position must have changed from external causes.[13]

"Laches, in legal significance, is not delay, but delay that works a disadvantage to another. So long as parties are in the same condition, it matters little whether one presses a right promptly or slowly, within limits allowed by law; but when, knowing his rights, he takes no step to enforce them until the condition of the other party has, in good faith, become so changed that he cannot be restored to his former state, if the right be then enforced, delay becomes inequitable, and operates as estoppel against the assertion of the right." [14]

Thus if material witnesses have died during the period of delay,[15] and especially if the person who the beneficiary claims was trustee has died [16] or become insane,[17] or if important documentary evidence has

doctrine of the court of chancery, it is now applied in the case of legal causes of action.

6. Amory v. Trustees of Amherst College, 229 Mass. 374, 118 N.E. 933; Sprague v. Protestant Episcopal Church of Diocese of Michigan, 186 Mich. 554, 152 N.W. 996.

7. Preston v. Horwitz, 85 Md. 164, 36 A. 710.

8. Fellrath v. Peoria German School Ass'n, 66 Ill.App. 77; Jenkins v. Hammerschlag, 38 App.Div. 209, 56 N.Y.S. 534; Stephenson v. Stephenson, 351 Mo. 8, 171 S.W.2d 565 (1943).

9. Mt. Vernon Mtge. Corp. v. United States, 236 F.2d 724, 98 U.S.App.D.C. 429 (1956), certiorari denied 352 U.S. 988, 77 S.Ct. 386, 1 L.Ed.2d 367 (1957).

10. Davis v. Downer, 210 Mass. 573, 97 N.E. 90.

11. Wragg v. Montgomery, 245 Ala. 362, 17 So.2d 173 (1943).

12. Lewis v. Bowman, 113 Mont. 68, 121 P.2d 162 (1942).

13. Haney v. Legg, 129 Ala. 619, 30 So. 34, 87 Am.St.Rep. 81; Lasker-Morris Bank & Trust Co. v. Gans, 132 Ark. 402, 200 S.W. 1029; Woodruff v. Williams, 35 Colo. 28, 85 P. 90, 5 L.R.A.,N.S., 986; Evans v. Moore, 247 Ill. 60, 93 N.E. 118, 139 Am.St. Rep. 302; Jones v. Henderson, 149 Ind. 458, 49 N.E. 443; In re Mahin's Estate, 161 Iowa 459, 143 N.W. 420; Hudson v. Cahoon, 193 Mo. 547, 91 S.W. 72; Van Alstyne v. Brown, 77 N.J.Eq. 455, 78 A. 678; Bruner v. Finley, 187 Pa. 389, 41 A. 334.

14. Stiness, J., in Chase v. Chase, 20 R.I. 202, 203, 37 A. 804.

15. Elliott v. Clark, 5 Cal.App. 8, 89 P. 455; Smick's Adm'r v. Beswick's Adm'r, 113 Ky. 439, 68 S.W. 439; Streitz v. Hartman, 35 Neb. 406, 53 N.W. 215; Heinisch v. Pennington, 73 N.J.Eq. 456, 68 A. 233; Coxe v. Carson, 169 N.C. 132, 85 S.E. 224.

16. Veitch v. Woodward Iron Co., 200 Ala. 358, 76 So. 124; Benson v. Dempster, 183 Ill. 297, 55 N.E. 651; Love v. Rogers, 118 Md. 525, 85 A. 771; Reid v. Savage, 59 Or. 301, 117 P. 306; Groome v. Belt, 171 Pa. 74, 32 A. 1132; Pilcher v. Lotzgesell, 57

17. See note 17 on page 633.

been lost,[18] the courts will be apt to regard the inaction as amounting to laches. Furthermore, if the property in question has greatly increased in value,[19] or the rights of third parties have in the meantime attached,[20] or if the alleged beneficiary has recognized the legal title holder as the beneficial owner during the period of delay,[21] there will be a strong tendency to treat the delay of the beneficiary as laches which bars his remedy.

Other courts have laid stress on the inability of the courts to do certain justice where long delay has occurred, and have said that the basis of the doctrine is the inability to ascertain the truth after great lapse of time.[22] Thus a New Jersey court [23] has stated that delay will be "fatal when it is operative to render the court unable to feel confident of its ability to ascertain the truth as well as it could have done when the subject for investigation was recent and before the memories of those who had knowledge of the material facts had become faded and weakened by time." And a Pennsylvania court, in referring to an attempt to establish equities on facts which occurred fifty-two years before, has said: [24]

"Of the men who were then in active life, and capable of being witnesses, not one in twenty thousand is now living. Written documents whose production might have settled this dispute instantly, have been, in all human probability, destroyed, or lost, or thrown away as useless. The matter belongs to a past age of which we can have no knowledge, except what we derive from history, through whose medium we can dimly discern the outlines of great public events, but all that pertains to men's private affairs is wholly invisible, or only visible in such a sort as to confound the sense and mislead the judgment."

Still other courts have placed emphasis on the view that the doctrine of laches is founded on the public policy of encouraging repose.[25]

Some courts have given a presumption of abandonment or release as a reason for the application of laches.[26]

Wash. 471, 107 P. 340; Russell v. Fish, 149 Wis. 122, 135 N.W. 531.

17. Whitney v. Fox, 166 U.S. 637, 17 S.Ct. 713, 41 L.Ed. 1145 (1897).

18. Leggroan v. Zion's Sav. Bank & Tr. Co., 120 Utah 93, 232 P.2d 746 (1951).

19. Russell v. Miller, 26 Mich. 1; Delmoe v. Long, 35 Mont. 139, 88 P. 778; Graham v. Donaldson, 5 Watts, Pa., 451.

20. Butt v. McAlpine, 167 Ala. 521, 52 So. 420.

21. Havenor v. Pipher, 109 Wis. 108, 85 N.W. 203.

22. Monroe v. Gregory, 147 Ga. 340, 94 S.E. 219; Kellogg v. Kellogg, 169 App.Div.

395, 155 N.Y.S. 310; Harrison v. Gibson, 23 Grat., Va., 212.

23. Cox v. Brown, 87 N.J.Eq. 462, 464, 101 A. 260.

24. Strimpfler v. Roberts, 18 Pa. 283, 299, 57 Am.Dec. 606.

25. Veitch v. Woodward Iron Co., 200 Ala. 358, 76 So. 124; Kleinclaus v. Dutard, 147 Cal. 245, 81 P. 516; Sprinkle v. Holton, 146 N.C. 258, 59 S.E. 680.

26. Sanchez v. Dow, 23 Fla. 445, 2 So. 842; Newberry v. Winlock's Ex'x, 168 Ky. 822, 182 S.W. 949; Lafferty v. Turley, 3 Sneed, Tenn., 157.

Length of Period of Delay

The mere fact that a long period of time has elapsed between the date of the accrual of a right and the date of the commencement of an action to enforce the right will not alone show laches.[27] "It has long since been settled by this court that mere lapse of time, short of the period fixed by the Statute of Limitations, will not bar a claim to equitable relief, when the right is clear, and there are no countervailing circumstances."[28] But the passage of a long interval has led many courts to find laches without requiring strict proof of any specific prejudice arising from the delay.[29] The lapse of a long period must inevitably prove disadvantageous to the defendant. Delay for a short period, for example, two years,[30] has been held to be laches under certain circumstances. Each case must depend on its own peculiar facts, that is, on the reasons for and the effects of the delay.

Excuses for Delay

When laches is pleaded and the delay and prejudicial effects are shown, the beneficiary may be able to avoid the application of the doctrine of laches if he can prove that a reasonable excuse existed for his inaction.[31] This he may do by showing that he had no knowledge or reason to know of the existence of any cause of action until very shortly before the commencement of his suit.[32] If he did not know that he had been wronged, it would be inequitable to deprive him of a remedy. This situation sometimes exists where the trustee has concealed the facts as to a breach of trust.[33]

But mere proof of ignorance is not enough to excuse delay. The ignorance must have been reasonable—it must have existed despite the exercise of reasonable care to learn the facts and to protect the

27. Percival-Porter Co. v. Oaks, 130 Iowa 212, 106 N.W. 626; Reihl v. Likowski, 33 Kan. 515, 6 P. 886.

28. Cantwell v. Crawley, 188 Mo. 44, 57, 86 S.W. 251.

29. Ewald v. Kierulff, 175 Cal. 363, 165 P. 942 (43 years); Martin v. Martin, Del.Ch., 74 A. 864 (26 years); Rittenhouse v. Smith, 255 Ill. 493, 99 N.E. 657 (30 years); Cecil's Committee v. Cecil, 149 Ky. 605, 149 S.W. 965 (25 years); Chandler v. Lally, 308 Mass. 41, 31 N.E.2d 1 (1941) (25 years delay after trustee's refusal to account); Sprague v. Trustees of Protestant Episcopal Church of Diocese of Michigan, 186 Mich. 554, 152 N.W. 996 (30 years); Quairoli v. Italian Beneficial Society of Vineland, 64 N.J.Eq. 205, 53 A. 622 (20 years); Jackson v. Farmer, 151 N.C. 279, 65 S.E. 1008 (29 years); Stianson v. Stianson, 40 S.D. 322, 167 N.W. 237, 6 A.L.R. 280 (24 years); Spaulding v. Collins, 51 Wash. 488, 99 P. 306 (20 years). In many of these cases it would seem almost certain

that the Statute of Limitations would have barred the cause of action and that the discussion of laches was academic.

30. Curtis v. Lakin, 36 C.C.A. 222, 94 Fed. 251 (8th Cir.1899). In Cowan v. Union Trust Co. of San Francisco, 38 Cal. App. 203, 175 P. 799, the period was three years and four months.

31. Ewald v. Kierulff, 175 Cal. 363, 165 P. 942; Blaul v. Dalton, 264 Ill. 193, 106 N.E. 196; Sackman v. Campbell, 15 Wash. 57, 45 P. 895.

32. Mullen v. Walton, 142 Ala. 166, 39 So. 97; Anderson v. Northrop, 30 Fla. 612, 12 So. 318; Manning v. Manning, 135 Ga. 597, 69 S.E. 1126; Southern Bank of Fulton v. Nichols, 235 Mo. 401, 138 S.W. 881; Delmoe v. Long, 35 Mont. 139, 88 P. 778; In re Roney's Estate, 227 Pa. 127, 75 A. 1061.

33. Samia v. Central Oil Co., 339 Mass. 101, 158 N.E.2d 469 (1959).

beneficiary's rights.[34]   A beneficiary cannot sit idly by and close his eyes to what is going on around him.   "One who would repel the imputation of laches on the score of ignorance of his rights must be without fault in remaining so long in ignorance of those rights.   Indolent ignorance and indifference will no more avail than will voluntary ignorance of one's rights." [35]

If the beneficiary, throughout the period of alleged laches, has continuously asserted his rights,[36] for example, by maintaining exclusive possession of the trust res,[37] he will not be guilty of laches.   And joint possession by the beneficiary and trustee rebuts the idea of laches [38] since it shows a recognition of the interest of the beneficiary.   Payment of taxes by the beneficiary shows an assertion of his right and militates against laches.[39]

Strong evidence in contradiction of the allegation of laches is found in the continuous acknowledgment and fulfillment of the trust by the trustee during the period of alleged laches.   If the trustee admits the trust and performs it, either there is no breach or other wrong, or it is so concealed from the beneficiary that he may reasonably remain ignorant of it.[40]   Other facts excusing delay and rebutting the imputation of laches are family relationship between the alleged beneficiary and trustee, making a settlement of differences out of court natural,[41] and infancy or other legal incapacity of the beneficiary during the period of inaction.[42]

   WESTLAW REFERENCES

Remedy Barred by Inaction of the Beneficiary
di laches
390k256
390k296
find 135 a2d 383
"charitable trust"   /s   laches
75k50   /p   laches

34.   Weber v. Chicago & W.I.R. Co., 246 Ill. 464, 92 N.E. 931; Taylor v. Coggins, 244 Pa. 228, 90 A. 633; Redford v. Clarke, 100 Va. 115, 40 S.E. 630.

35.   Redford v. Clarke, 100 Va. 115, 122, 123, 40 S.E. 630.

36.   Grayson v. Bowlin, 70 Ark. 145, 66 S.W. 658; Howe v. Howe, 199 Mass. 598, 85 N.E. 945, 127 Am.St.Rep. 516.

37.   Dufour v. Weissberger, 172 Cal. 223, 155 P. 984; Flaherty v. Cramer, 62 N.J.Eq. 758, 48 A. 565; Houston, E. & W.T.R. Co. v. Charwaine, 30 Tex.Civ.App. 633, 71 S.W. 401.

38.   Doyle v. Doyle, 268 Ill. 96, 108 N.E. 796; Cox v. Brown, 87 N.J.Eq. 462, 101 A. 260.

39.   Johnson v. Bayley, 15 Vt. 595.

40.   Cooney v. Glynn, 157 Cal. 583, 108 P. 506; Snyder v. Snyder, 280 Ill. 467, 117 N.E. 465; Chadwick v. Chadwick, 59 Mich. 87, 26 N.W. 288; Lamberton v. Youmans, 84 Minn. 109, 86 N.W. 894; Gutch v. Fosdick, 48 N.J.Eq. 353, 22 A. 590, 27 Am.St. Rep. 473; Laughlin v. Laughlin, 219 Pa. 629, 69 A. 288; Goode v. Lowery, 70 Tex. 150, 8 S.W. 73; Hammond v. Ridley's Ex'rs, 116 Va. 393, 82 S.E. 102.

41.   Delkin v. McDuffie, 134 Ga. 517, 68 S.E. 93; Snyder v. Snyder, 280 Ill. 467, 117 N.E. 465; Cetenich v. Fuvich, 41 R.I. 107, 102 A. 817.

42.   In re Zech's Estate, 69 S.D. 51, 6 N.W.2d 432 (1942); Patrick v. Stark, 62 W.Va. 602, 59 S.E. 606.

Basis for Laches Doctrine

di(laches   /3   doctrine theory   /s   trust)

390k365(5)   /p   laches

150k84   /p   laches   /s   trust

390k365(2)   /p   laches

390k256

390k331   /p   laches

Length of Period of Day

length long   /s   period time   /s   laches   /s   trust

find 31 ne2d 1

390k365(2)

390k365(3)

241k103(3)

Excuses for Delay

ewald   +3   kierulff

390k365(2)

find 85 ne 945

cetenich   +3   fuvich

REMEDY BARRED BY COURT DECREE OR STATUTE OF LIMITATIONS [1]

§ 170. A court decree approving an account or discharging a trustee prevents a beneficiary from asserting a cause of action against the trustee on matters stated in the account as to which the beneficiary objected or had an opportunity to object.

A trustee or beneficiary may be barred from suing on a claim by reason of a judgment against him in prior litigation based on the same claim, under the principle of res adjudicata.

A discharge of a trustee in bankruptcy proceedings removes liability to the beneficiary, except for fraudulent conduct, embezzlement, misappropriation, or defalcation.

If a trustee has died, a money claim against his estate may be barred by a failure to present the claim within the time required by the probate law, but this does not apply to claims based on tracing trust property.

Statutes of Limitation bar suits to enforce express, resulting and constructive trusts after the expiration of a fixed period.

The Statute of Limitations runs against a cause of action in favor of the beneficiary and against the trustee of an express trust from the date when a breach or repudiation of the trust was known to the beneficiary or could have been known by the use of reasonable diligence.

§ 170

1. Bogert, Trusts and Trustees (rev. 2d edit.), §§ 950–956; Restatement, Trusts, Second, §§ 220, 221, 327, 409. Restatement, Judgments, Second, §§ 24–32, 41–42.

A cause of action against the trustee of a resulting trust is barred by the Statute of Limitations under the same conditions as in the case of an express trust.

One who may be charged as a constructive trustee holds wrongfully and adversely, and the Statute of Limitations operates to bar the remedy of the possible constructive trust beneficiary from the date when he knew, or should have known, the facts upon which the constructive trust might be based.

Causes of action in favor of the trustee or beneficiary and against third persons are subject to the normal operation of the Statute of Limitations. Disabilities of the beneficiaries do not toll the running of the Statute against the trustee.

Discharge of Trustee by Court Decree

It has previously been shown [2] that if a trustee renders a court accounting and his report is approved by the court and the court decree discharges him from liability for the acts set out in the account, after the beneficiary has objected to the account or had an opportunity to contest it, the trustee is relieved of all further liability with regard thereto.

If a trustee or beneficiary has litigated a claim and the result has been adverse to him, and a judgment or decree has been rendered to the effect that he has no cause of action, he is prevented from further assertion of the claim in the courts by reason of the application of the doctrine of res adjudicata.[3]

The federal Bankruptcy Code provides for discharges of the bankrupt from his obligations. If a trustee goes through bankruptcy proceedings and receives a discharge, ordinary claims against him based on breaches of trust will be destroyed and he will be relieved from further responsibility with regard thereto, but the discharge does not affect any debt based upon "fraud or defalcation" while acting in a fiduciary capacity.[4]

In England, by statute, the court has power to excuse a trustee from liability for a breach of trust where it finds that he acted "honestly and reasonably".[5] This provision is also found in the Uniform Trusts Act.[6] Without the aid of a statute the courts sometimes validate unlawful acts of the trustee after their occurrence when it

2. See § 143, ante.

3. See Restatement, Judgments, Second, §§ 17, 18–20 (claim preclusion), 17, 27–29 (issue preclusion).

And see Jordan Co. v. Sperry Bros., 141 Iowa 225, 119 N.W. 692; Second Nat. Bank & Tr. Co. v. Reid, 304 Mich. 376, 8 N.W.2d 104 (1943).

4. 11 U.S.C.A. § 523(a)(4) (1978); American Surety Co. v. Greenwald, 223 Minn. 37, 25 N.W.2d 681 (1946).

5. § 61, Trustee Act of 1925. See Perrins v. Bellamy, (1899) 1 Ch. 797 (trustee made a sale of trust property where he had no power to sell, after receiving advice from solicitor that there was a power of sale).

6. § 19. And see Ind.Code 30–3–1–1 (good faith). And see footnote 16, post, this section.

appears that the court would have authorized the act if application had been made in advance.[7]

Statutes of Limitation

While the original English Statute of Limitations covered common law actions only,[8] modern legislation applies to causes of action arising out of trusts.[9] In the United States statutes now universally limit the time within which an action to enforce an express, resulting, or constructive trust may be brought, although there is great diversity of treatment.[10] In many jurisdictions a final clause in the Statute, applying to all other causes of action not expressly mentioned, is held to govern suits to enforce trusts.

At times when there has been no statute controlling the bringing of suits in equity, chancery has followed the law and held that the statutory limitation on a similar legal cause of action should govern.[11] For example, if the statute allowed ten years for bringing an action of ejectment, a suit in equity to recover possession of realty would be held to be limited to a ten year period.

"But it is said that courts of equity are not within the statutes of limitations. This is true in one respect: They are not within the words of the statutes, because the words apply to particular legal remedies; but they are within the spirit and meaning of the statutes, and have been always so considered. . . . I think, therefore, courts of equity are bound to yield obedience to the statute of limitations upon all legal titles and legal demands, and cannot act contrary to the spirit of its provisions. I think the statute must be taken virtually to include courts of equity; for when the Legislature by statute limited the proceedings at law in certain cases, and provided no express limitations for proceedings in equity, it must be taken to have contemplated that equity followed the law, and therefore it must be taken to have virtually enacted in the same cases a limitation for courts of equity also." [12]

If the claim of the beneficiary is for money and is against the estate of a deceased trustee, it may be barred because of failure to present it within the short claims period allowed by the probate law,[13] but this does not apply to tracing claims where the trust property or its product is claimed and not money.[14]

7. Vickers v. Vickers, 189 Ky. 323, 225 S.W. 44; In re Catanach's Estate, 273 Pa. 368, 117 A. 178.

8. 21 James I, c. 16, 1623, as printed in 4 Chitty's Stats. 4th Ed. 85.

9. 2 & 3 Geo. VI, c. 21.

10. For a collection of statutory material, see Bogert, Trusts and Trustees (rev. 2d edit.), § 950.

11. Holloway v. Eagle, 135 Ark. 206, 205 S.W. 113; Appeal of Kutz, 40 Pa. 90; Redford v. Clarke, 100 Va. 115, 40 S.E. 630.

12. Hovenden v. Annesley, 2 Sch. & Lef. 607, 630, 631.

13. Staley v. Kreinbihl, 152 Ohio St. 315, 89 N.E.2d 593 (1949); Smith v. Fitch, 25 Wn.2d 619, 171 P.2d 682 (1946).

14. Simon v. Simon, 141 Neb. 839, 5 N.W.2d 140 (1942).

Express Trusts

The expression, "the Statute of Limitations has no application to express trusts," is frequently found in opinions.[15] From this one might be led to believe that no statute of limitations would ever bar the remedy of a beneficiary or trustee of an express trust; that after a breach of the trust by a trustee the beneficiary might sue at any time and would never be met by a statutory bar. But those using this expression have not intended to convey any such comprehensive meaning. They have merely meant that as long as the express trust continued to be recognized and enforced by the trustee there was no running of the Statute of Limitations. For example, that a trust had been in existence for forty years, during all of which time the trustee had held the trust property, collected the income, and turned it over to the beneficiary, would be no reason for barring the rights of the beneficiary to the trust property. If one had had adverse possession of property for forty years, he would, of course, be entitled to hold it as against all the world; however the trustee in the case put did not have adverse possession of the trust property, but had possession subject to the rights of the beneficiary. Hence the statement that the Statute of Limitations has no application to express trusts merely means that as long as the trust is continuing, recognized and enforced there is no cause of action in favor of the beneficiary and against the trustee, and the possession of the trustee is not adverse.

When the trustee violates any of his obligations under the trust, or denies the trust, repudiates all of his duties under it, and claims the trust property as his own, then a cause of action arises in favor of the beneficiary and the Statute of Limitations starts to run. It is well settled that in express trusts, and as between beneficiary and trustee, the Statute of Limitations runs from the date when the beneficiary knows or, by the use of ordinary care should have known, of a breach or a repudiation of the trust by the trustee.[16] If the situation is such that the beneficiary would have obtained information as to the breach or repudiation if he had used ordinary care and diligence, he is in the same legal situation as if he had had actual knowledge.[17]

15. Whetsler v. Sprague, 224 Ill. 461, 79 N.E. 667; Neilly v. Neilly, 23 Hun N.Y., 651; In re Passmore's Estate, 194 Pa. 632, 45 A. 417.

16. De Bardelaben v. Stoudenmire, 82 Ala. 574, 2 So. 488; Lamb v. Lamb, 171 Cal. 577, 153 P. 913; Warren v. Adams, 19 Colo. 515, 36 P. 604; Albretch v. Wolf, 58 Ill. 186; Parks v. Satterthwaite, 132 Ind. 411, 32 N.E. 82; Cooley v. Gilliam, 80 Kan. 278, 102 P. 1091; Owens v. Crow, 62 Md. 491; Second Religious Soc. of Boxford v. Harriman, 125 Mass. 321; Pitcher v. Roger's Estate, 199 Mich. 114, 165 N.W. 813; Johnston v. Johnston, 107 Minn. 109, 119 N.W. 652; Smith v. Combs, 49 N.J.Eq. 420, 24 A. 9; Woolley v. Stewart, 169 App.Div.

678, 155 N.Y.S. 169; Rouse v. Rouse, 176 N.C. 171, 96 S.E. 986; Paschall v. Hinderer, 28 Ohio St. 568; Davidson v. Davidson, 262 Pa. 520, 106 A. 64; Hunter v. Hubbard, 26 Tex. 537; Garvey v. Garvey, 52 Wash. 516, 101 P. 45; In re McClear's Estate, 147 Wis. 60, 132 N.W. 539.

By statute some states have provided for a Statute of Limitations as to actions arising out of trusts. See, for example, Ill. Rev.Stat. c. 83, § 27 (revocable inter vivos trusts to which addition made by pour-over will; seven months after will admitted to probate); Minn.Stat.Ann. § 541.05.

17. Wilkerson v. Seib, 20 Cal.2d 556, 127 P.2d 904 (1942); Leggroan v. Zion's

In all states the Statutes of Limitation provide that the Statute does not run against one who is under a disability, for example, infancy. Thus if a cause of action arises in favor of a boy of fourteen, the period of time allowed to bring the action would not start to run until he attained his majority. In applying these clauses in cases arising in connection with trusts the question is merely, in whom is the claim vested? The disability of a trustee has no effect on a right of action accruing to a beneficiary, but if the beneficiary is himself under disability the Statute will be tolled or prevented from running during the period of his disability as to a cause of action available to him.[18] And if the trustee is given a cause of action against third persons, it is unimportant that the beneficiary may be a minor or incompetent,[19] but the trustee's disabilities will toll the Statute.

Although a cause of action for recovery of charitable trust property from a third person would seem capable of being barred by the Statute of Limitations,[20] the courts have been very lenient in the application of the Statute to causes of action in favor of the public and against the trustee of the charity.[21]

What Amounts to Repudiation?

When conduct of the trustee amounts to a single breach of trust, even though the trustee has not abandoned the whole administration and claimed the property for himself, will normally not be so difficult of determination, as where the trustee fails to perform a statutory duty to account, or makes an improper investment. Whether a given act is consistent with recognition or continuance of the trust, or indicates an intent to repudiate the whole trust and claim adversely, may be more difficult to ascertain.[22] During the continuance and recognition of the trust the possession of the trustee is the possession of the beneficiary.[23] There is no adverse or hostile holding.[24] Where the beneficiary remains in possession of the trust property, acts of the trustee are not ordinarily construed as a repudiation of the trust, since he has so far

Sav. Bank & Tr. Co., 120 Utah 93, 232 P.2d 746 (1951) (no distributions for six years).

18. Kretzer v. Gross, 189 Ind. 455, 128 N.E. 355 (1920); Cary v. Cary, 159 Or. 578, 80 P.2d 886, 121 A.L.R. 1371 (1938).

19. Molton v. Henderson, 62 Ala. 426; Wilmerding v. Russ, 33 Conn. 67.

20. Strother v. Barrow, 246 Mo. 241, 151 S.W. 960; Remington v. Providence, 43 R.I. 484, 113 A. 791 (1921); Presbyterian Church v. Pendarvis, 227 S.C. 50, 86 S.E.2d 740 (1955).

21. Attorney General v. Old South Society, 13 Allen 474; William Buchanan Foundation v. Shepperd, 283 S.W.2d 325 (Tex.Civ.App.1955), reversed, 155 Tex. 406, 289 S.W.2d 553 (1956), to permit carrying out of compromise agreement.

22. For cases where it was held that repudiation was shown, see: Stonehill v. Swartz, 129 Ind. 310, 28 N.E. 620 (open and adverse possession of trust property); Adams v. Holden, 111 Iowa 54, 82 N.W. 468 (conveyance in violation of trust); Dewey v. Dewey, 163 Neb. 296, 79 N.W.2d 578 (1956) (trustee occupies, improves, and takes profits without accounting); Woolley v. Stewart, 222 N.Y. 347, 118 N.E. 847 (trustee took rents and claimed he had purchased land).

23. Anderson v. Dunn, 19 Ark. 650; Huntley v. Huntley, 43 N.C. 250; Marr's Heirs v. Gilliam, 1 Cold., Tenn., 488.

24. Cooper v. Cooper, 61 Miss. 676, 696.

recognized the trust as to allow the beneficial owner possession.[25]

The termination of the trust and retention of the trust property by the trustee thereafter, without any agreement between the former trustee and beneficiaries, would seem to amount to repudiation. Thus if the trustee effects a settlement and is discharged as trustee, his possession of the trust property, if he retains any, will be adverse to the beneficiary, and the Statute of Limitations will run against the right of the beneficiary to reclaim the property or to allege fraud or impropriety in the account.[26] In the words of Finch, J.: "In the case of a direct trust the statute will begin to run when it ends, and the trustee has no longer a right to hold the fund or property as such, but is bound to pay it over or transfer it discharged of the trust." [27] Where the death of the beneficiary causes termination of the trust, the holding by the trustee will be adverse after death and the Statute will operate against the persons equitably entitled to the property on death.[28]

The Statute of Limitations does not begin to run against a remainder beneficiary's cause of action to obtain the trust property until the expiration of the precedent estate.[29] Until his right to the use of the property accrues, the possession of the trustee will not be adverse to the remainder beneficiary, but will be adverse only to the owners of the preceding interest.

In a few cases questions have arisen regarding the application of a Statute of Limitations to a claim by the trustee against the beneficiary, as where the trustee has made advances from his own funds for the benefit of the beneficiary or has a claim for compensation. As long as the trust is being administered without opportunity or necessity to present such demands, and the beneficiary has not resisted the enforcement of the trustee's claim, the Statute does not run, but if there is an accounting or other occasion when the trustee would normally assert his rights and they are not urged, he may find himself barred by the operation of the statute from the date of his duty to present the claim.[30]

Resulting Trusts

Resulting trusts are based on an inferred or presumed intent that they shall exist. The most common example of them is found in the case of payment by one of the consideration for a conveyance and the taking of the title in the name of another, with the consent of the payor of the consideration. The question has frequently arisen whether the Statute of Limitations begins to run against the rights of the benefici-

25. American Mining Co. v. Trask, 28 Idaho 642, 156 P. 1136; Clark v. Clark, 21 Neb. 402, 32 N.W. 157.

26. Wellborn v. Rogers, 24 Ga. 558; Spallholz v. Sheldon, 216 N.Y. 205, 110 N.E. 431, Ann.Cas.1917C, 1017; Coleman v. Davis, 2 Strob.Eq., S.C., 334.

27. Gilmore v. Ham, 142 N.Y. 1, 10, 36 N.E. 826, 40 Am.St.Rep. 554.

28. Snodgrass v. Snodgrass, 185 Ala. 155, 64 So. 594.

29. Pritchard v. Williams, 175 N.C. 319, 95 S.E. 570; Stewart v. Conrad's Adm'r, 100 Va. 128, 40 S.E. 624.

30. In re Lunt, 235 Iowa 62, 16 N.W.2d 25 (1944); In re Rutherford's Estate, 154 Kan. 361, 118 P.2d 553 (1941); Simmons v. Friday, 359 Mo. 812, 224 S.W.2d 90 (1949).

ary of a resulting trust from the date when the trustee obtained title, on the theory of an adverse holding from that date, or only from the date of a repudiation by the resulting trustee of the trust, on the theory of a friendly holding until the appearance of a contrary intent. Most courts have taken the position that a resulting trustee is like an express trustee; his normal position is that of a holder in subordination to the rights of the beneficiary, and from the date of the event which makes possible the trust, until the contrary appears, he should be regarded as holding for the beneficiary and not adversely to him.[31] "But so long as the trustee recognizes the trust, the beneficiary may rely upon the recognition, and ordinarily will not be in fault for omitting to bring an action to enforce his rights. The case then resembles an express trust of a continuing nature, and is subject to the statute of limitations in like manner. If the trustee is in possession by permission of the cestui que trust, the possession will be that of the latter." [32]

If the resulting trustee has expressly recognized the trust or conferred benefits on the beneficiary under it, there is no running of the Statute; [33] but if the trustee has openly and clearly declined to recognize his obligations and has claimed the property for himself, and the beneficiary knows or has an opportunity to know of this conduct, there is a cause of action which should be affected by the Statute of Limitations.[34]

Constructive Trusts

The application of the Statute of Limitations to constructive trusts ought not to be difficult. These trusts are involuntary and are imposed upon the trustee because of wrongdoing, either in the original acquisition of the property or in its unconscionable retention after the rightful securing of title. There is a cause of action from the date when the trustee's wrongful holding begins, and the Statute of Limitations should begin to run against it from the time when the wronged party knows or should know of the inequitable conduct of the titleholder.[35] No express

---

31. Lasker-Morris Bank & Tr. Co. v. Gans, 132 Ark. 402, 200 S.W. 1029; Faylor v. Faylor, 136 Cal. 92, 68 P. 482; In re Mahin's Estate, 161 Iowa 459, 143 N.W. 420; Hanson v. Hanson, 78 Neb. 584, 111 N.W. 368; Guyer v. London, 187 Okl. 326, 102 P.2d 875 (1940); Davies v. Metropolitan Life Ins. Co., 189 Wash. 138, 63 P.2d 529 (1937).

32. Crowley v. Crowley, 72 N.H. 241, 245–246, 56 A. 190. See also, Lufkin v. Jakeman, 188 Mass. 528, 530, 531, 74 N.E. 933.

33. Appeal of Corr, 62 Conn. 403, 26 A. 478; Miller v. Saxton, 75 S.C. 237, 55 S.E. 310; Cole v. Noble, 63 Tex. 432.

34. Treager v. Friedman, 79 Cal.App. 2d 151, 179 P.2d 387 (1947).

35. Lide v. Park, 135 Ala. 131, 33 So. 175, 93 Am.St.Rep. 17; Benoist v. Benoist, 178 Cal. 234, 172 P. 1109; Washbon v. Linscott State Bank, 87 Kan. 698, 125 P. 17; Brawner v. Staup, 21 Md. 328; Hudson v. Cahoon, 193 Mo. 547, 91 S.W. 72; Markley v. Camden Safe Deposit & Tr. Co., 74 N.J.Eq. 279, 69 A. 1100; Lammer v. Stoddard, 103 N.Y. 672, 9 N.E. 328; Dunn v. Dunn, 137 N.C. 533, 50 S.E. 212; In re Marshall's Estate, 138 Pa. 285, 22 A. 24; Kennedy v. Baker, 59 Tex. 150; Sheppard v. Turpin, 3 Grat., Va., 373; Buttles v. De Baun, 116 Wis. 323, 93 N.W. 5.

Occasionally the view has been taken that the Statute does not run against a constructive trustee until he repudiates any obligation. Reynolds v. Sumner, 126 Ill. 58, 71, 18 N.E. 334, 1 L.R.A. 327, 9 Am.

repudiation by the constructive trustee of his obligations should be required to start the Statute running.

If the person who can be made a constructive trustee admits to the wronged party that there is an equitable obligation and states by words or other conduct that he intends to fulfill that obligation, the Statute does not run against the cause of action until the title-holder changes his attitude to one of hostility and this becomes known to the beneficiary.[36]

Thus where a trustee has wrongfully conveyed trust property to a third person, and the latter is sought to be held as a constructive trustee, the date of the conveyance will govern.[37] Where a trustee purchased the trust res at his own sale, the right to have a constructive trust declared arose at once and was barred in ten years from the date of the purchase.[38] Where one standing in a fiduciary relation, such as that of principal and agent, buys his principal's property, the Statute runs against the right to have a constructive trust declared from the date of the purchase.[39]

Knowledge of facts which would have led a reasonably prudent man to the discovery of the wrongful conduct is sufficient to start the Statute running.[40] If a person obtaining the property by fraud conceals his fraud,[41] or for any other reason not involving his own negligence the person claiming as beneficiary of a constructive trust is ignorant of the fraud, the Statute of Limitations does not operate.[42]

Causes of Action against Third Persons

An adverse possessor of the trust property for the statutory period may acquire title to it which will destroy both the legal interest of the trustee and the beneficial ownership of the beneficiary. Causes of action against third persons for the recovery of the trust res or for damages on account of its injury are subject to the ordinary statutes of limitation, the cause of action is vested in the trustee, and his delay or negligence in enforcing the causes of action will operate to bar the beneficiary's rights.[43]

St.Rep. 523; Newis v. Topfer, 121 Iowa 433, 96 N.W. 739.

36. Cash v. Cash, 258 Ala. 364, 63 So. 2d 27 (1953); Pagano v. Pagano, 207 Misc. 474, 139 N.Y.S.2d 219 (1955), affirmed 2 A.D.2d 756, 153 N.Y.S.2d 722 (1956).

37. Smith v. Dallas Compress Co., 195 Ala. 534, 70 So. 662.

38. Hubbell v. Medbury, 53 N.Y. 98.

39. McKean & Elk Land & Imp. Co. v. Clay, 149 Pa. 277, 24 A. 211; Ackerson v. Elliott, 97 Wash. 31, 165 P. 899.

40. Frost v. Bush, 195 Pa. 544, 46 A. 80; Cooper v. Lee, 75 Tex. 114, 12 S.W. 483.

41. Jacobs v. Snyder, 76 Iowa 522, 41 N.W. 207, 14 Am.St.Rep. 235; West v. Sloan, 56 N.C. 102.

42. Prewitt v. Prewitt, 188 Mo. 675, 87 S.W. 1000; Johnson v. Petersen, 100 Neb. 255, 159 N.W. 414; Wamburzee v. Kennedy, 4 Desaus, S.C., 474.

43. Cruse v. Kidd, 195 Ala. 22, 70 So. 166, 2 A.L.R. 36; Fleck v. Ellis, 144 Ga. 732, 87 S.E. 1055; Hart v. Citizens' Nat. Bank, 105 Kan. 434, 185 P. 1, 7 A.L.R. 933; Stoll v. Smith, 129 Md. 164, 98 A. 530.

"The rule in this court, that the Statute of Limitations does not bar a trust estate, holds only as between cestui que trust and trustee, not between cestui que trust and trustee on the one side and strangers on the other, for that would be to make the statute of no force at all, because there is hardly an estate of consequence without such trust, and so the act would never take place; therefore, where a cestui que trust and his trustee are both out of possession for the time limited, the party in possession has a good bar against them both." [44]

It is immaterial that the beneficiary has been an infant or otherwise under disability during part or all of the time when the Statute has been running against the trustee.[45] The power of enforcing the claim was not placed in his hands. The trustee was the proper plaintiff. It is true that if the trustee failed to act the beneficiary might have sued, but in that case he would be acting in place of the trustee and enforcing a cause of action owned by the trustee.

If a trustee and a third party knowingly join in a breach of trust, either the trustee (or his co-trustee or successor) may sue the participant,[46] or the beneficiary may maintain a suit.[47] In the case of action by the trustee the Statute will be tolled by disabilities of the trustee but not by those of the beneficiary;[48] while if the suit is brought by the beneficiary his disabilities alone will be important and his knowledge of the wrong will be a condition precedent to the running of the Statute.[49]

If the breach of trust in which the third party participated was committed because of mistake and without any actual wrongful intent, there are holdings that the only cause of action against the third party is vested in the trustee, that the time of his acquisition of knowledge of the breach is determinative, and that his disabilities, but not the lack of capacity on the part of the beneficiary, toll the Statute.[50] The distinction between collusive and mistaken breaches seems of doubtful soundness.[51]

 WESTLAW REFERENCES

Discharge of Trustee by Court Decree
find 8 nw2d 104
51k426(2) /p fiduciary trustee
perrins +3 bellamy

44. Lord Hardwicke in Lewellin v. Mackworth, as quoted in 2 Eq. Cases Abr. 579.

45. Crittenden v. Dorn, 274 F. 520 (9th Cir.1921), certiorari denied 257 U.S. 648, 42 S.Ct. 57, 66 L.Ed. 415 (1921); Molton v. Henderson, 62 Ala. 426; Wilmerding v. Russ, 33 Conn. 67.

46. Wetmore v. Porter, 92 N.Y. 76; Atwood v. Lester, 20 R.I. 660, 40 A. 866.

47. Squire v. Ordemann, 194 N.Y. 394, 87 N.E. 435; Neal v. Bleckley, 51 S.C. 506, 29 S.E. 249.

48. Franco v. Franco, 7 Ves.Jr. 75; Elliott v. Landis Mach. Co., 236 Mo. 546, 139 S.W. 356.

49. Marshall's Estate, 138 Pa. 285, 22 A. 24; Harris v. Smith, 98 Tenn. 286, 39 S.W. 343; Schofield v. Cleveland Tr. Co., 149 Ohio St. 133, 78 N.E.2d 167 (1948) (successor trustee representing beneficiaries not barred by delay of predecessor; Statute did not run until notice to successor of wrong).

50. Johnson v. Cook, 122 Ga. 524, 50 S.E. 367; Hayden v. Hayden, 178 N.C. 259, 100 S.E. 515.

51. See Evans, 17 Ky.L.J. 382.

Statute of Limitations

di(beneficiary　/s　trust　/s　"statute of limitation"　/3　bar　barred
　　commenc*** beginning beg*n run running apply! applied)

390k256

390k365(1)

241k100(7)　/p　trust

241k103(2)　/p　trust

241k103(4)　/p　trust

Express Trusts

di("express trust"　/s　"statute of limitation")

241k102(1)　/p　"express trust"

241k103(2)　/p　"express trust"

241k103(4)　/p　"express trust"

241k5(3)　/p　"express trust"

241k34(1)　/p　"express trust"

241k102(5)　/p　"express trust"

241k39(11)　/p　"express trust"

What Amounts to Repudiation?

390k365(3)

di(trust**　/s　beneficiary　/5　repudiat!)

241k103(2)　/p　trust　/s　repudiat!

241k103(4)　/p　trust　/s　repudiat!

di(repudiat!　/s　trust　/s　"statute of limitation"　/3　beg*n
　　beginning commenc*** run running bar barred apply! applied)

Resulting Trusts

di resulting trusts

di("resulting trust"　/s　"statute of limitation")

390k365(4)

241k103(4)　/p　"resulting trust"

repudiat!　/s　trust　/s　"statute of limitation"

241k103(2)　/p　"resulting trust"

241k102(6)

di("resulting trust"　/s　laches)

156k70(2)　/p　laches

390k365(2)

Constructive Trusts

390k365(5)

241k102(8)

241k13　/p　"constructive trust"

241k103(4)　/p　"constructive trust"

di("constructive trust"　/s　laches) & sy (trust**)

156k54　/p　"constructive trust"

390k365(2)　/p　"constructive trust"

118ak255　/p　"constructive trust"

156k58　/p　"constructive trust"

Causes of Action Against Third Persons

cruse　+3　kidd

lewellin　+3　mackworth

Appendix

WESTLAW REFERENCES

The WESTLAW System

WESTLAW is a computer-assisted legal research service of West Publishing Company. WESTLAW is accessible through a number of public communications networks. The materials available from WESTLAW are contained in databases stored at West Publishing Company's central computers in St. Paul, Minnesota.

The WESTLAW user sends a query, or message, to the computer where it is processed and documents are identified that satisfy the search request. The text of the retrieved documents is then stored on magnetic disks and transmitted to the user. The data moves through a telecommunication network. The user sees the documents on a video display terminal. When the documents appear on the terminal the user can decide whether further research is desired. If another search is necessary, the query may be recalled for editing, or an entirely new query may be sent to the computer. Documents displayed on the terminal may be printed out or, on some terminals, the text may be stored on its own magnetic disks.

In addition to the federal case law databases, WESTLAW provides access to state case law databases and many specialized databases. For example, WESTLAW contains separate topical databases for areas of the law such as federal tax, patents and copyrights, bankruptcy, communications, labor, securities, antitrust and business regulation, military justice, admiralty, and government contracts. WESTLAW also contains the text of the U.S. Code and the Code of Federal Regulations, West's INSTA–CITE®, Shepard's® Citations, Black's Law Dictionary, and many other legal sources.

Improving Legal Research with WESTLAW

Traditional legal research begins with the examination of texts, treatises, case digests, encyclopedias, citators, annotated law reports, looseleaf services, and periodicals. These secondary sources of the law provide compilations and summaries of authoritative material contained in primary legal sources. The goal of legal research is to analyze and interpret these primary sources.

In their familiar printed form, such primary sources appear in the state and regional reporters, federal reporters, and in statutory codes and administrative materials. In WESTLAW, these documents are extensively represented in electronic databases.

WESTLAW permits access to the many cases that do not get indexed or digested into manual systems of secondary legal sources. With WESTLAW it is possible to index any significant term or combination of terms in an almost unlimited variety of grammatical and numerical relationships by formulating a query composed of those terms.

WESTLAW queries may be made as broad or as specific as desired, depending upon the context of the legal issue to be researched.

WESTLAW queries add a dynamic aspect to the text of this hornbook. Since new cases are continuously being added to WESTLAW databases as they are decided by the courts, the addition of queries provides a type of self-contained updating service to the publication. Since a query may be addressed to the entire range of cases contained in the database designated for a search—from the earliest decisions to the most recent—the search results obtained from WESTLAW reflect the most current law available on any given issue.

In addition, WESTLAW queries augment the customary role of footnotes to the hornbook text by directing the user to a wider range of supporting authorities. Readers may use the preformulated queries supplied in this edition "as is" or formulate their own queries in order to retrieve cases relevant to the points of law discussed in the text.

Query Formulation:

(a) What is a WESTLAW Query?

The query is a message to WESTLAW. It instructs the computer to retrieve documents containing terms in the relationships specified by the query. The terms in a query are made up of words and/or numbers that pinpoint the legal issue to be researched.

An example of the kind of preformulated queries that appear in this publication is reproduced below. The queries corresponding to each section of the text are listed at the end of the section.

    bailment /s trust

This query is taken from chapter 2, section 13. The query, or question, that is directed to WESTLAW appears at the end of the section of the text. This query is asking WESTLAW to find documents containing the term BAILMENT within the same sentence as the term TRUST.

This query illustrates what a standard request to WESTLAW looks like—words or numbers describing an issue, tied together by connectors. These connectors tell WESTLAW in what relationships the terms must appear. WESTLAW will retrieve all documents from the database that contain the terms appearing in those relationships.

The material that follows explains the methods by which WESTLAW queries are formulated and shows how users can employ the preformulated queries in this publication in their research of the law of trusts. In addition, there are instructions that will enable readers to modify their queries to fit the particular needs of their research.

Query Formulation:

(b) Proximity Connectors

Proximity connectors allow search terms to be ordered so that relevant documents will be retrieved from WESTLAW. The connectors and their meanings appear below.

Space (or). A space between search terms means "or." Leaving a space between the query terms FIDUCIARY and TRUSTEE

    fiduciary trustee

instructs the computer to retrieve documents that contain either the word FIDUCIARY or the word TRUSTEE (or both).

& (and) or (ampersand). The & symbol means "and." Placing the & between two terms instructs the computer to retrieve documents that contain both of the terms. The terms on either side may be in reverse order. For example, if the & is inserted between the terms SETTLOR and TRUSTEE

    settlor & trustee

the computer will retrieve documents containing both the word SET-TLOR and TRUSTEE in the same document. In any such retrieved document, the word SETTLOR may either precede or follow the word TRUSTEE. The & may be placed between groups of alternative terms. For example, placing the & between SETTLOR or TRUSTOR and CAPACITY or INTENT

settlor trustor & capacity intent

instructs the computer to retrieve documents in which the terms SETTLOR or TRUSTOR (or both) and CAPACITY or INTENT (or both) appear in the same document.

/**p** (same paragraph). The /p symbol means "within the same paragraph." It requires that terms to the left of the /p appear within the same paragraph as terms to the right of the connector. For example, placing a /p between the terms SETTLOR and INTENT

settlor /p intent

will instruct the computer to retrieve documents in which SETTLOR and INTENT occur in the same paragraph. The terms on each side of the /p may appear in the document in any order within the paragraph. As with &, the /p connector may be placed between groups of alternative terms. Thus, the query

settlor trustor /p intent capacity

will command the retrieval of all documents in which the words SETTLOR or TRUSTOR (or both) occur in the same paragraph as the words CAPACITY or INTENT (or both).

/**s** (same sentence). The /s symbol requires that one or more search terms on each side of the /s appear in the same sentence. If a /s is placed between the words RES and TRUST

res /s trust

the computer is instructed to retrieve documents that have the word RES and the word TRUST in the same sentence, without regard to which of these words occur first in the sentence.

The /s may be placed between groups of alternative terms. Inserting a /s between the terms RES or CORPUS and TRUST or POUR–OVER

res corpus /s trust pour-over

instructs the computer to retrieve documents containing either the words RES or CORPUS (or both) within the same sentence as the words TRUST or POUR–OVER (or both), regardless of which terms appear first.

+**s** (precedes within sentence). The +s symbol requires that one or more terms to the left of the +s precede one or more terms to the right of the +s within the same sentence. The query

totten +s trust

instructs the computer to retrieve all documents in which the word TOTTEN precedes the word TRUST in the same sentence. The +s connector, like the other connectors, may be used between groups of alternative terms.

/**n** (numerical proximity-within n words). The /n symbol means "within n words," where n represents any whole number between 1 and 255, inclusive. It requires that terms to the left of the /n appear within the designated number of words as terms to the right of the connector. For example, placing a /2 between the terms SPEND–THRIFT and CLAUSE

SPEND-THRIFT   /2   CLAUSE

instructs the computer to retrieve all documents in which the term SPEND–THRIFT occurs within two words of the term CLAUSE. Numerical proximities may also be used between groups of alternative search terms. In addition, the +n symbol may be used to require that terms to the left of the numerical proximity symbol precede the terms to the right of the symbol. Thus, placing the +2 symbol between the words SPEND-THRIFT and CLAUSE or PROVISION

spend-thrift   +2   clause provision

instructs the computer to retrieve cases in which SPEND–THRIFT occurs within two words preceding either the word CLAUSE or the word PROVISION (or both).

"_____" (quotation marks/phrase). The "_____" (quotation marks/phrase) symbol can be thought of as the most rescrictive grammatical connector. Placing terms within quotation marks instructs the computer to retrieve all documents in which the terms appear in the precise proximity (i.e., contiguousness) and order that they have within the quotation marks. For example, placing the following terms within quotation marks

"charitable trust"

instructs the computer to retrieve all documents in which the term CHARITABLE appears adjacent to, and immediately preceding, the term TRUST. Phrases that are constructed with quotation marks may be used as alternatives by leaving a space between them. Thus, the query

"charitable trust" "ascertainable beneficiary"

instructs the computer to retrieve all documents in which the phrase CHARITABLE TRUST or ASCERTAINABLE BENEFICIARY (or both) occur.

This technique of query formulation is effective when used to search legal terms of art, legal concepts, or legal entities that occur together as multiple terms. Some examples are: "private trust", "rule against perpetuities", and "statute of frauds".

Phrase searching should be limited to those instances in which it is certain that the terms will always appear adjacent to each other and in the same order. For example, it would not be advisable to use the following query:

"a charitable trust must serve some public benefit"

These terms may occur in a different order and not be adjacent to each other. Therefore, a better query to use in searching for these terms would be:

charitable /2 trust /s social public /2 benefit interest

% (exclusion). The % symbol means "but not." It instructs the computer to exclude documents that contain terms appearing after the % symbol. For example, to retrieve documents containing the terms beneficiary and damages and "breach of trust" within the same sentence, but not the term co-ming!, the following query would be used:

beneficiary /s damages /s "breach of trust" % co-ming!

Query Formulation:

(c) A Recommended Strategy

There is no perfect methodology for query formulation. However, a systematic approach to query formulation will probably generate better search results. A step-by-step method is listed below and is suggested as a strategy for query formulation.

T Terms. After determining the legal issue to be researched, the first step in query formulation is to select the key terms from the issue that will be used as search terms in the query. Words, numbers, and various other symbols may be used as search terms.

The goal in choosing search terms is to select the most unique terms for the issue. In selecting such terms it is frequently helpful to conceptualize how the terms might appear in the language of the documents that will be searched by the query. Moreover, it is necessary to consider the grammatical and editorial structure of the document. This involves a consideration of how the writer of the document (i.e., judge or headnote and synopsis writer) has worded both the factual and legal components of the issues involved in the case.

While traditional book research generally starts with a consideration of the general legal concepts under which particular problems are subsumed, WESTLAW research starts with a consideration of specific terms that are likely to appear in documents that have addressed those problems. This is so because documents are retrieved from WESTLAW on the basis of the terms they contain. Accordingly, the more precisely terms that will single out the desired documents can be identified, the more relevant the search results will be.

A Alternative Terms. Once the initial search terms have been selected for a query, it is important to consider alternative terms and synonyms for those terms. The nature of the legal issue will determine which are desirable.

As an illustration, in formulating a query to research the issue of when the subject matter of a trust is certain, the researcher might first choose the following search terms (with appropriate root expansion or universal characters):

trust /s res /s certain

Clearly, the term ASCERTAINABLE would be a good alternative to certain. Similarly, the terms CORPUS, PROPERTY and PRINCIPAL could be added as synonyms for res. Adding these alternatives to the initial search terms produces the following terms:

trust /s res corpus principal property /s certain ascertainable

Note that a space, which means "or" in WESTLAW, should be left between search terms and their alternative.

R Root Expansion (!) and Universal Character (*). When constructing queries, it is necessary to consider various forms of the search terms that are selected. Derivative forms of words should be anticipated due to the variety of ways in which the language in a document may be worded. There are two devices available on WESTLAW for automatically generating alternative forms of search terms in a query.

One device is an unlimited root expansion. Placement of the ! symbol at the end of the root term generates other forms containing the root. For example, attaching the ! symbol to the root term REQUIR! in the following query:

trust /s requir!

instructs the computer to generate the words REQUIRE, REQUIRED, REQUIRING and REQUIREMENT as search terms for the query. This saves time and space that would otherwise be consumed in typing each of the alternative words in the query.

The other device permits the generation of all possible characters from a designated part of a term. This is done by placing one or more * symbols at the location of the term where universal character generation is desired. For example, placing two * symbols on the term TRUST in the following query

trust** /s duty

instructs the computer to generate all forms of the root term TRUST** with up to two additional characters. Thus, the words TRUST, TRUSTEE, TRUSTOR would be generated by this query. The * symbol may also be embedded inside a term as in the following query:

remov! /s trustee /s dr*nk!

This will generate the alternative terms drink and drunk; in addition drinking and drunken will be retrieved because of the use of the root expander.

WESTLAW automatically generates standard plural forms for search terms so it is generally unnecessary to use the root expansion devices to obtain plural forms of search terms.

Also note that WESTLAW will generate the various spellings for compound words. Whenever your search terms include a compound word, use a hyphen between the words. This way, the search will

generate the compound word's other forms. For example, inserting a
hyphen between the word SPEND and THRIFT

    spend-thrift

will generate spendthrift, spend thrift, and spend-thrift.

    C Connectors. The next step in query formulation is to consider
the appropriate grammatical context in which the search terms will
appear. Using the example provided in the preceding section

    trust /s res corpus principal property /s certain ascertainable

this query would instruct the computer to retrieve documents in which
TRUST appears within the same sentence as either RES or CORPUS or
PRINCIPAL or PROPERTY and also appears within the same sentence
as ASCERTAINABLE! or CERTAIN.

Query Formulation:

(d) General Principles of Query Formulation

    The art of query formulation is the heart of WESTLAW research.
Although the researcher can gain technical skills by using the terminal, there is no strict mechanical procedure for formulating queries.
One must first comprehend the meaning of the legal issue to be
researched before beginning a search on WESTLAW. Then, the user
will need to supply imagination, insight, and legal comprehension with
knowledge of the capabilities of WESTLAW to formulate a useful
query. Effective query formulation requires an alternative way of
thinking about the legal research process.

    Using WESTLAW is a constant balancing between generating too
many documents and missing important documents. In general, it is
better to look through a reasonable number of irrelevant documents
than it is to be too restrictive and miss important material. The
researcher should take into consideration at the initial query formulation stage what to do if too many, or not enough documents are
retrieved. Thought should be given as to how the query might be
narrowed or the search broadened, and what can be done if the initial
search retrieves zero documents.

    Some issues by their very nature will require more lengthy queries
than others; however, it is best to strive for efficiency in structuring
the query. Look for unique search terms that will eliminate the need
for a lengthy query. Keep in mind that WESTLAW is literal. Consider all possible alternative terms. Remember that searching is done by
syntactic structure and not by legal concepts.

    Always keep in mind database content and the parameters of the
system to date. Also, consider the inherent limitations of the computer. It does not think, create, or make analogies. The researcher must
do that for the computer. The computer simply looks for the terms in
the documents in the relationships specified in the query. The researcher should know what he or she is looking for, at least to the

extent of knowing how the terms are likely to show up in relevant documents.

The WESTLAW Reference Manual should be consulted for more information on query formulation and WESTLAW commands. The Reference Manual is updated periodically to reflect new enhancements of WESTLAW. It provides detailed and comprehensive instructions on all aspects of the WESTLAW system and offers numerous illustrative examples on the proper format for various types of queries. Material contained in the Reference Manual enables the user to benefit from all of the system's capabilities in an effective and efficient manner.

Search Techniques:

(a) Field Searching

Documents in WESTLAW are divided into separate sections called fields. The computer can be instructed to search for terms within designated fields. This technique is known as field searching. Moreover, in reviewing the documents that have been retrieved in a search, the user may instruct the computer to display specified fields. The fields available for WESTLAW case law databases are described below.

Title Field. The title field contains the title of the case (e.g., Community National Bank & Trust v. Rapaport).

Citation Field. The citation field contains the citation of the case (e.g., 213 So.2d 316).

Court Field. The court field contains abbreviations that allow searches for case law to be restricted to particular states, districts, or courts.

Judge Field. The judge field contains the name of the judge or justice who wrote the majority opinion.

Synopsis Field. The synopsis field contains the synopsis of the case, prepared by West editors.

Topic Field. The topic field contains the West Digest Topic name and number, the Key Number, and the text of the Key line for each digest paragraph.

Digest Field. The digest field contains digest paragraphs prepared by West editors. It includes headnotes, corresponding Digest Topics and Key Numbers, the title and citation of the case, court, and year of decision.

Headnote Field. The headnote field contains the language of the headnotes, exclusive of the Digest Topic and Key Number lines and case identification information.

Opinion Field. The opinion field contains the text of the case, court and docket numbers, names of attorneys appearing in the case, and judges participating in the decision.

The format for a query that will instruct the computer to search for terms only within a specified field consists of the field name followed by a set of parentheses containing the search terms and grammatical connectors, if any. For example, to retrieve the case appearing at 213 So.2d 316, the citation field, followed by a set of parentheses containing the volume and page numbers of the citation, separated by the +3 connector may be used:

    citation(213 +3 316)

    cite(213 +3 316)

Correspondingly, to retrieve the case entitled *Community National Bank & Trust v. Rapaport,* the title field, followed by a set of parentheses containing the names of the title, separated by the & connector may be used:

    title("community national" & rapaport)

Combination Field Searching. Fields may be combined in a query. For example, terms may be searched in the digest field and, at the same time, the query may be limited to search the court of a particular state. The following query illustrates this technique:

    digest(trust /s void /s "public policy") & court(mn)

This query instructs the computer to retrieve documents containing the words TRUST and VOID and "PUBLIC POLICY" within the digest field that were issued from Minnesota courts, as designated with the court field restriction. Any number of different fields may be combined with this method.

Moreover, terms may be searched in clusters of fields by joining any number of field names by commas. One application of this technique is to search for terms in the synopsis and digest fields. This technique is illustrated below:

    synopsis,digest(trust /s void /s "public policy") & court(mn)

In this example the terms TRUST and VOID and "PUBLIC POLICY" are searched in the synopsis and digest fields simultaneously.

The WESTLAW Reference Manual should be consulted for further instruction on how to perform searches using the field restrictions.

Search Techniques:

(b) Date Restriction

Queries may be restricted to retrieve documents appearing before, after, or on a specified date, or within a range of dates. The date restriction format consists of the word DATE followed by the appropriate restriction(s) within parentheses. The words BEFORE and AFTER may be used to designate the desired date relationships. Alternatively, the symbols < and > may be used. Moreover, the month and day and year may be spelled out (e.g., January 1, 1984) or they may be abbreviated as follows: 1–1–84, or 1/1/84. The date restriction is joined to the rest of the query by the & symbol. For example, to retrieve documents decided or issued after December 31, 1976, that discuss the doctrine of cy pres, any of the following formats could be used:

```
digest("cy pres"  /p  trust) & date(after 12/31/76)

digest("cy pres"  /p  trust) & date(>december 31, 1976)

digest("cy pres"  /p  trust) & date(>12-31-82)
```

To retrieve documents decided after December 31, 1976, and before March 15, 1983, the following format could be used:

```
digest("cy pres")  /p  trust) & date(after 12/31/76 and before 3/15/83)
```

Search Techniques:

(c) Digest Topic and Key Number Searching

Searches may be performed using West Digest Topic and Key Numbers as search terms. When this strategy is used, the search term consists of a West Digest Topic Number followed by the letter k, followed by a Key Number classified as a subheading under the Digest Topic. The computer will retrieve all cases that contain a headnote classified with the designated Digest Topic and Key Number. For example, to retrieve cases that contain the Digest Topic classification for TRUSTS (Digest Topic Number 390) and the Key Number for Interest Remaining in the Settlor or Creator of a Trust (Key Number 153), the following query would be used:

```
390k153
```

A related search technique employs Digest Topic classification numbers in conjunction with other search terms. Since the Digest Topic Numbers appear in the topic and digest fields of the cases, the numbers should be searched for only in these fields by using the field restriction method. For example, to retrieve cases classified under the Digest Topic for TRUSTS (Digest Topic Number 390) that deal with the Interest Remaining in the Settlor or Creator of a Trust, the following queries would be appropriate:

```
topic(390)  /p  interest control  /10  remain! balance  /10  creator settlor

digest(390)  /p  interest control  /10  remain! balance  /10  creator settlor
```

A complete list of Digest Topics and their numerical equivalents appears in the WESTLAW Reference Manual.

Using WESTLAW as a Citator

Legal Research frequently entails finding decisions that apply to specific sections of state statutes, or to other court decisions. WESTLAW can be used to retrieve documents that contain reference to such authority. Because citation styles are not always uniform, special care must be taken to identify variant forms of citations.

Retrieving Cases that Cite Codes and Statute Sections. Court decisions that cite to sections of state codes or to sections of state statutes are retrievable by including the section number in the query. For example, to retrieve cases that cite section 543.19 of the Minnesota Statutes, the following query could be used in the MN–CS database:

543.19

Since the section number is a unique term, it is unnecessary to use additional search terms in the query. The appearance of 543.19 in Minnesota case law is not likely to be anything other than a citation to that particular section. Using the number 543.19 as in the above query will retrieve all subsections of section 543.19 automatically.

Retrieving Cases that Cite Other Court Decisions. WESTLAW can be used as a citator of other court decisions if the title of the decision, its citation, or both, are known. When only the title of the case is known, use the following format:

matter re   +3   totten

This query instructs the computer to retrieve all documents that have cited the case of *In Re Totten.* The +3 numerical connector requires that the words MATTER or RE precede and occur within three words of the word TOTTEN.

If the citation of the case is known, a query may be constructed that will retrieve documents that have cited the case. This is done by using the numbers of the citation as search terms in the query. For example, to retrieve cases that have cited to Totten by its citation, 179 N.Y. 112, use the following format:

179   +3   112

If both the citation and the case title are known, the following format may be used:

totten   /s   179   +3   112

In the example above the computer is instructed to retrieve all documents that contain the terms TOTTEN, 179 and 112 within the number of words designated by the proximity connectors separating each term. This query would retrieve all documents that contain the full citation: *In Re Totten,* 179 N.Y. 112.

The date restriction may be utilized to retrieve documents that cite cases within a given year, range of years, or before or after a given date. For example, to retrieve all documents that have cited *In Re Totten* after the year 1982, this query could be used:

totten & date(after 1982)

Shepard's® Citations on WESTLAW

From any point in WESTLAW, case citations may be entered to retrieve Shepard's listings for those citations. To enter a citation to be Shepardized, the following formats can be used:

sh 179 n.y. 112

sh 179 ny 112

sh179ny112

When the citation is entered, Shepard's listings for the citation will be displayed. To Shepardize a citation it is not necessary to be in the same database as that of the citation. For example, a Supreme Court citation may be entered from the Pacific Reporter database.

West's INSTA–CITE

INSTA–CITE, West Publishing Company's case history system, allows users to quickly verify the accuracy of case citations and the validity of decisions. It contains prior and subsequent case histories in chronological listings, parallel citations, and precedential treatment.

Some examples of the kind of direct case history provided by INSTA–CITE are: "affirmed", "certiorari denied", "decision reversed and remanded", and "judgment vacated". A complete list of INSTA–CITE case history and precedential treatment notations appears in the WESTLAW Reference Manual.

An example of an INSTA–CITE reference from this hornbook appears below. The format to access the Insta-Cite display for a case citation consists of the letters IC followed by the citation, with or without spaces and periods:

    ic 179 n.y. 112
    ic 179 ny 112
    ic179ny112

FIND

The FIND command allows you to retrieve a case quickly from anywhere in WESTLAW without the need to run a separate search or change databases. If you know a case's citation, FIND will take you to that case in one step.

This command is especially useful when you are reading one case on WESTLAW and find another case cited which you want to view. The FIND command allows you to retrieve the cited case quickly without losing your place in the original case.

You can also use FIND to retrieve cases listed in a Shepard's or a Insta-Cite display or cases cited in other FOUND documents. You can FIND a case even if it is not cited anywhere, as long as you know its citation.

To use FIND enter the word **find** or **fi** followed by the citation and then press **ENTER**. You may enter either the West citation or any parallel citation. For example, you may use the U.S., S.Ct., or L.Ed.2d citation. Spacing and punctuation are optional. Any of the following examples are acceptable:

    find93sct880
    fi 93 s.ct. 880
    fi 93s.ct.880

When you are in the FIND system (e.g., if you are viewing a FOUND DOCUMENT, or have entered the word FIND), you can see a list of valid FIND publications and their acceptable abbreviations by typing **pubs** and pressing **ENTER**.

Black's Law Dictionary

WESTLAW contains an on-line version of Black's Law Dictionary. The dictionary incorporates definitions of terms and phrases of English and American law.

Included within the preformulated queries in this publication are references to Black's Law Dictionary for many important legal terms. The format of such commands is as follows:

di pour-over

The command consists of letters DI followed by the term to be defined. To see the definition of a phrase, enter the letters DI followed by the phrase (without quotation marks):

di corpus

If the precise spelling of a term to be defined is not known, or a list of dictionary terms is desired, a truncated form of the word may be entered with the root expansion symbol (!) attached to it:

di res!

di res ipsa!

The first example will produce a list of all dictionary terms that begin with RES. The second example will produce a list of dictionary terms, the first of which is RES IPSA LOQUITUR. From the list of terms a number corresponding to the desired term can be entered to obtain the appropriate definitions.

WESTLAW Case Law Databases

This section discusses the WESTLAW case law databases, in which the preformulated queries in this publication have been designed to be used. The case law databases consist of cases from the National Reporter System.

Cases in WESTLAW are in "full text plus." That is, they include the court's decision enhanced by a synopsis of the decision and headnotes stating the legal propositions for which the decision stands. The headnotes are classified to West's Key Number classification system.

WESTLAW contains many databases not discussed here. For example, there are databases that contain the entire United States Code, Code of Federal Regulations, and topical databases covering such areas as bankruptcy, patents and copyrights, federal tax, government contracts, communications, securities, labor, antitrust, admiralty, and military justice.

The case law databases are divided into two kinds: state and federal. WESTLAW has individual state databases containing decisions from specific states. The database identifier for an individual state database consists of the state's postal abbreviation followed by a hyphen and the letters CS (e.g. MN–CS for Minnesota cases). The available federal case law databases are: Supreme Court Reporter (SCT), U.S. Court of Appeals (CTA), and U.S. District Courts (DCT). WESTLAW also contains individual U.S. Court of Appeals databases.

The database identifier for an individual court of appeals database consists of the letters CTA followed by the number of the federal circuit (E.G. CTA8 for the Eighth Circuit Court of Appeals.)

The databases in which the queries in this publication will provide the most useful searches will vary depending upon research needs. For example, if the researcher is interested in the law of trusts of a particular state, these queries will yield the most useful information if used in the database that contains cases from that state. State cases can be found in individual state case law databases and in the regional reporter databases noted above.

Some issues to which the preformulated queries correspond will only appear in cases from the state databases, whereas other issues will be present only in the federal databases. However, some issues are sufficiently broad and have been so widely litigated that cases may be found with the queries in either the state or federal databases. Finally, some issues may have been litigated only in particular states and not in others, so that a given query may retrieve cases in one state but not in another.

In some instances, the query itself indicates which database it is to be used in. If a query contains a court restriction to a particular state or to a particular federal circuit, then that query can only be used in the database that contains that state or district. For example, the following query contains a court restriction for Texas cases:

112.035 & court(tx)

and therefore should be used in the Southwestern Reporter (SW) database, since that is the database in which Texas cases appear. Alternatively, the query could be used in the TX–CS database, without the court field restriction.

WESTLAW Hornbook Queries:

(a) Query Format

The queries that appear in this publication are intended to be illustrative. They are approximately as general as the material in the hornbook text to which they correspond.

Although all of the queries in this publication reflect proper format for use with WESTLAW, there is seldom only one "correct" way to formulate a query for a particular problem. This is so even though some techniques are clearly better than others. Therefore, the queries reflect a wide range of alternative ways that queries may be structured for effective research. Such variances in query style simply reflect the great flexibility that the WESTLAW system affords its users in formulating search strategies.

For some research problems, it may be necessary to make a series of refinements to the queries, such as the addition of search terms or the substitution of different grammatical connectors, to adequately fit the particular needs of the individual researcher's problem. The responsibility remains with the researcher to "fine tune" the WESTLAW queries in accordance with his or her own research requirements. The primary usefulness of the preformulated queries in this hornbook is in providing users with a foundation upon which further query construction can be built.

Individual queries in this hornbook may retrieve from one to over a hundred cases, depending on which database is utilized. If a query does not retrieve any cases in a given database, it is because there are no decisions in that database which satisfy the grammatical proximity requirements of the query. In this situation, to search another database with the same query, enter the letter S followed by the initials DB, followed by the new database identifier. Thus, if a query was initially addressed to the NE (Northeastern Reporter) database, but retrieved no documents, the user could then search the PAC (Pacific Reporter) database with same query by entering the following command:

s db pac

This command instructs WESTLAW to search the Pacific Reporter database with the same query that was previously used in the Northeastern Reporter database.

The maximum number of cases retrieved by a query in any given database will vary, depending on a variety of factors, including the relative generality of the search terms and grammatical connectors, the frequency of litigation or discussion of the issue in the courts, and the number of documents comprising the database.

WESTLAW Hornbook Queries:

(b) Textual Illustrations

This section explains how the queries provided in this hornbook may be used in researching actual problems in the law of contracts that a practitioner might encounter. Examples from the text of this edition have been selected to illustrate how the queries can be expanded, restricted, or altered to meet the specific needs of the reader's research.

A segment of the text from Chapter 4, section 39, of The Law of Trusts by Bogert appears below:

§ 39 Availability of Beneficiary's Interest to Creditors

If a trust is active, under early law it was natural that courts of law should not direct an execution against the equitable interest of the beneficiary, since they did not recognize that interest and regarded the trustee as the sole owner. However this attitude toward the unavailability of legal remedies has changed and increasingly statutes or the courts permit the interest of the beneficiary to be made subject to execution, attachment or other legal remedy without resort to equity proceedings.

Courts of equity will subject the interest of the beneficiary to the payment of his debts. This has been done by the so-called "creditor's bill" without the aid of statute, where reliance can be had on the doctrine that equity acts where the remedy at law is non-existent or inadequate; and in some states the right to maintain a creditor's bill has been provided by statute. In New York and several other states a judgment creditor is given the right by statute to obtain trust income in excess of the beneficiary's needs for support and education or a certain percentage or dollar amount. In some cases it has been held that a condition precedent to the maintenance of this suit is proof that an execution at law has issued and been returned unsatisfied, but in other jurisdictions it is sufficient to prove inadequacy of the legal remedy otherwise (for example, by showing insolvency or bankruptcy of the debtor), and in other states no showing of the lack of a legal remedy is demanded. The creditor secures an equitable lien on the interest of the beneficiary by starting his suit.

The text of this section discusses the circumstance when and under what circumstances a creditor has a right to reach the beneficiary's interest in a trust. In order to retrieve cases discussing this right, the following query

    beneficiary /2 interest /10 creditor

is given as a suggested search strategy on WESTLAW.

A headnote of a case that was retrieved from the ALLSTATES database appears below:

    R 6 OF 52   P 6 OF 20   ALLSTATES   T   419 So.2d 1370
[5]
307k26
POWERS
K. Rights and remedies of creditors.
Ala.1982.
Trust beneficiary did not own a fee simple absolute as to creditors due to operation of statute providing that in all cases where such absolute power of disposition is given, not accompanied by any trust, and no remainder is limited on the estate of the donee of the power, he has an absolute fee, since the remainder was limited to beneficiary's heirs should he fail to exercise his power of disposition. Code 1975, S 35–4–292(c).
Bynum v. Campbell
419 So.2d 1370

The relevant portion of the opinion that corresponds to this headnote appears below:

    R 6 OF 52   P 14 OF 20   ALLSTATES   T   419 So.2d 1370
On May 10, 1980, Bynum died, and Campbell moved to have Mark Scott Skelton, as administrator of Bynum's estate, substituted as a party defendant. The court granted this motion and ruled as follows on the parties' motions for summary judgment.
"The plaintiff's first contention is that the power of appointment given to H.O. Bynum, Jr. by Paragraph 9 of the trust instrument, coupled with his interest for life in the trust income, creates in H.O. Bynum, Jr. a fee absolute in the trust property against

which creditors can levy. At common law, one who took an estate less than a fee simple absolute in realty and who was also given an absolute power of disposition over such property was held to possess an absolute fee simple interest. See Robertson v. United States, 199 F.Supp. 78 (N.D.Ala.1961). Because the application of this common law rule frequently frustrated the intent of the grantor by defeating the interests of remaindermen, the rule has been modified by statute in this state. . . .''

The query can be altered to meet the needs of individual researchers. For example, a practitioner may wish to find cases involving when a creditor can reach the beneficiary's interest in a discretionary trust. In this situation, the preformulated query can be modified to retrieve documents relevant to the new issue as follows:

discretion! /s trust /s beneficiary /2 interest /10 creditor

The search terms discretion! and trust are added because they specifically refer to the new issue. Below is a portion of a case retrieved by this query from the ALLSTATES database:

R 3 OF 8   P 10 OF 14   ALLSTATES   T   31 Cal.Rptr. 281
In paragraph Six (6) of the trustor's will, as incorporated in the decree of distribution, the trustees are given the power 'in their discretion' to use the corpus of the trust for the benefit of the beneficiaries in the event of sickness or emergency, and in paragraph Six (6) the trustees, in making distribution, are authorized 'in their discretion' to determine values and to distribute in cash or in kind. In this portion of the instrument there can be no doubt that ordinary discretion only has been conferred upon the trustees. However, in the seventh paragraph of the trustor's will it is equally clear that he has conferred absolute discretion upon his trustees for they are there given the right to determine in their 'uncontrolled judgment' whether a beneficiary is mentally or physically incompetent, and if so determined, to expend payments due him in his behalf. In the same paragraph also, the trustor confers 'sole discretion' upon his trustees in making payments to any minor beneficiary, or to the parent Twelve of his will, the trustor conferred 'sole' discretion upon his trustees to terminate payments due to a beneficiary whose interests in the trust may be under attack by creditors. Sole discretion is the equivalent of absolute, unlimited or uncontrolled discretion, and simply indicates that the judgment of the trustees, exercised in good faith, shall control.

Ranking Documents Retrieved on WESTLAW: Age and Term Options

Documents retrieved by a query can be ordered in either of two ways. One way is to order retrieved documents by their dates, with the most recent documents displayed first. This is ranking by AGE. Using the AGE option is suggested when the user's highest priority is to retrieve the most recent decisions from a search.

Alternatively, documents can be ranked by the frequency of the appearance of query terms. This is ranking by TERMS. When a search is performed with the TERMS option, the cases containing the greatest number of different search terms will be displayed first.

When a database is accessed by entering a database identifier, WESTLAW responds with a screen requesting that the query be entered. At this point the user may select which type of ranking, AGE or TERMS, is desired.

The queries offered in this hornbook were formulated and tested for relevancy with use of the TERMS option. Accordingly, in certain instances use of the AGE option with the preformulated queries may display less relevant, yet more recent cases, first.

Conclusion

This appendix has reviewed methods that can be used to obtain the most effective legal research concerning the law of trusts. Bogert's Law of Trusts combines the familiar hornbook publication with a powerful and easily accessed computerized law library. The WESTLAW references at the end of each section of the hornbook text provide a basic framework upon which the lawyer can structure additional research on WESTLAW. The queries may be used as provided or they may be tailored to meet the needs of researcher's specific problems. The power and flexibility of WESTLAW affords users of this publication a unique opportunity to greatly enhance their access to and understanding of the law of trusts.

*

Table of Cases

A

A Bolognesi & Co., In re, 254 F. 770 (2nd Cir.1918)—§ **162, n. 30.**

A O Brown & Co., In re, 193 F. 30 (2nd Cir. 1912)—§ **162, n. 36.**

Abbot, In re, 39 Misc. 760, 80 N.Y.S. 1117—§ **31, n. 45.**

Abbott, In re, 55 Me. 580—§ **32, n. 68.**

Abbott v. Gregory, 39 Mich. 68—§ **155, n. 11.**

Abott v. Everett Trust and Sav. Bank, 50 Wash.2d 398, 312 P.2d 203 (1957)—§ **151, n. 17.**

Abell v. Brady, 79 Md. 94, 28 A. 817—§ **144, n. 29.**

Abell v. Howe, 43 Vt. 403—§ **163, n. 9.**

Abernathy v. Phillips, 82 Va. 769, 1 S.E. 113—§ **135, n. 20.**

Acadian Production Corporation of Louisiana v. McKendrick, 223 La. 79, 64 So.2d 850 (1953)—§ **95, n. 36.**

Ackerman v. Fichter, 179 Ind. 392, 101 N.E. 493, 46 L.R.A.,N.S., 221, Ann.Cas. 1915D, 1117—§ **58, n. 12.**

Ackers v. First Nat. Bank of Topeka, 192 Kan. 319, 387 P.2d 840 (1963)—§ **48, n. 3.**

Ackerson v. Elliott, 97 Wash. 31, 165 P. 899—§ **170, n. 39.**

Adair v. Brimmer, 74 N.Y. 539—§ **102, n. 31;** § **168, n. 32.**

Adams v. Adams, 14 Mass. (Allen) 65—§ **14, n. 13.**

Adams v. Adams, 64 N.H. 224, 9 A. 100—§ **31, n. 28.**

Adams v. Adams, 88 U.S. 185, 22 L.Ed. 504 (1874)—§ **23, n. 7;** § **31, n. 3, 32.**

Adams v. Adams, 213 Ga. 875, 102 S.E.2d 566 (1958)—§ **74, n. 41.**

Adams v. Adams, 348 Mo. 1041, 156 S.W.2d 610 (1941)—§ **74, n. 24.**

Adams v. Canutt, 66 Wash. 422, 119 P. 865—§ **21, n. 50.**

Adams v. Cook, 15 Cal.2d 352, 101 P.2d 484 (1940)—§ **139, n. 9.**

Adams v. Dugan, 196 Okl. 156, 163 P.2d 227 (1945)—§ **39, n. 26.**

Adams v. Holden, 111 Iowa 54, 82 N.W. 468—§ **170, n. 22.**

Adams v. Lambard, 80 Cal. 426, 22 P. 180—§ **157, n. 43.**

Adams v. Mid-West Chevrolet Corporation, 198 Okl. 461, 179 P.2d 147 (1946)—§ **168, n. 45.**

Adams v. Perry, 43 N.Y. 487—§ **35, n. 37.**

Adams v. Vanderbeck, 148 Ind. 92, 45 N.E. 645, 62 Am.St.Rep. 497—§ **165, n. 43.**

Adams' Trust, In re, 12 Ch.D. 634—§ **160, n. 34.**

Adamson v. Paonessa, 180 Cal. 157, 179 P. 880—§ **38, n. 60.**

Aetna Life Ins. Co. of Hartford, Conn. v. Morlan, 221 Iowa 110, 264 N.W. 58 (Iowa 1935)—§ **165, n. 44.**

Ahrens v. Simon, 101 Neb. 739, 164 N.W. 1051—§ **74, n. 33.**

Ahrens' Estate, Matter of, 272 A.D. 472, 71 N.Y.S.2d 462 (N.Y.A.D. 1 Dept.1947)—§ **89, n. 16.**

Akers v. Gillentine, 191 Tenn. 35, 231 S.W.2d 369 (1948)—§ **86, n. 3.**

Akin v. Akin, 276 Ill. 447, 114 N.E. 908—§ **74, n. 19.**

Akin v. Evans, 221 Md. 125, 156 A.2d 219 (1959)—§ **80, n. 4.**

Akin v. First Nat. Bank of Winston-Salem, 227 N.C. 453, 42 S.E. 518—§ **38, n. 11.**

Akin v. Security Savings & Trust Co., 157 Or. 172, 68 P.2d 1047 (1937)—§ **165, n. 43.**

Albergotti v. Summers, 203 S.C. 137, 26 S.E.2d 395 (1943)—§ **40, n. 17;** § **42, n. 5.**

Alberts v. Steiner, 237 Mich. 143, 211 N.W. 46 (1926)—§ **124, n. 6.**

Albretch v. Wolf, 58 Ill. 186—§ **170, n. 16.**

Albright v. Albright, 91 N.C. 220—§ **134, n. 9.**

Albritton v. Neighborhood Centers Ass'n for Child Development, 12 Ohio St.3d 210, 466 N.E.2d 867 (1984)—§ **129, n. 22.**

Alexander v. Goellert, 153 Kan. 202, 109 P.2d 146 (1941)—§ **136, n. 5.**

Alexander v. House, 133 Conn. 725, 54 A.2d 510 (1947)—§ **52, n. 2.**

Alexander v. Spaulding, 160 Ind. 176, 66 N.E. 694—§ **21, n. 8.**

Alexander v. Tams, 13 Ill. 221—§ **74, n. 66.**

Alexander v. Zion's Sav Bank & Trust Co., 2 Utah 2d 317, 273 P.2d 173 (1954)—§ **22, n. 17.**

Alford v. Bennett, 279 Ill. 375, 117 N.E. 89—§ **46, n. 10, 19.**

Alfred University v. Hancock, 69 N.J.Eq. 470, 46 A. 178—§ **60, n. 5.**

Alig v. Levey, 219 Ind. 618, 39 N.E.2d 137 (1942)—§ **112, n. 8.**

Allaben v. Shelbourne, 357 Mo. 1205, 212 S.W.2d 719 (1948)—§ **165, n. 33.**

Allegheny Tank Car Co. v. Culbertson, 288 F. 406 (D.C.Tex.1923)—§ **126, n. 12.**

B

F

G

H

Jones v. Carpenter, 90 Fla. 407, 106 So. 127—§ **77, n. 6.**

Jones v. Clifton, 101 U.S. 225, 25 L.Ed. 908 (1879)—§ **148, n. 25.**

Jones v. Coon, 229 Iowa 756, 295 N.W. 162 (1940)—§ **42, n. 2.**

Jones v. Dawson, 19 Ala. 672—§ **143, n. 24.**

Jones v. Dougherty, 10 Ga. 273—§ **160, n. 61, 62.**

Jones v. Glenn, 248 Ala. 452, 28 So.2d 198 (1946)—§ **38, n. 28.**

Jones v. Gore, 141 Cal.App.2d 667, 297 P.2d 474 (1956)—§ **74, n. 1.**

Jones v. Habersham, 107 U.S. 174, 2 S.Ct. 336, 27 L.Ed. 401 (1883)—§ **65, n. 16;** § **67, n. 25;** § **68, n. 19.**

Jones v. Harsha, 233 Mich. 499, 206 N.W. 979 (1926)—§ **105, n. 2.**

Jones v. Harsha, 225 Mich. 416, 196 N.W. 624 (1923)—§ **136, n. 3.**

Jones v. Henderson, 149 Ind. 458, 49 N.E. 443—§ **169, n. 13.**

Jones v. Independent Title Co., 23 Cal.2d 859, 147 P.2d 542 (1944)—§ **165, n. 29.**

Jones v. Jackson, 195 Or. 643, 246 P.2d 546 (1952)—§ **84, n. 14.**

Jones v. Jones, 111 Md. 700, 77 A. 270—§ **38, n. 38.**

Jones v. Jones, 223 Mo. 424, 123 S.W. 29, 25 L.R.A., N.S., 424—§ **46, n. 21.**

Jones v. Jones, 297 Mass. 198, 7 N.E.2d 1015 (1937)—§ **98, n. 4.**

Jones v. Jones, 344 Pa. 310, 25 A.2d 327 (1942)—§ **37, n. 18.**

Jones v. Jones' Ex'r, 96 Va. 749, 32 S.E. 463—§ **38, n. 23.**

Jones v. Lloyd, 117 Ill. 597, 7 N.E. 119—§ **168, n. 30.**

Jones v. Lynch, 137 S.W. 395 (Tex.Civ. App.)—§ **38, n. 15.**

Jones v. Stubbs, 136 Cal.App.2d 490, 288 P.2d 939 (1955)—§ **160, n. 6.**

Jones v. Swift, 300 Mass. 177, 15 N.E.2d 274 (1938)—§ **138, n. 5.**

Jones v. United States, 61 F.Supp. 406 (D.C.Mass.1945)—§ **48, n. 7.**

Jones v. Watford, 62 N.J.Eq. 339, 50 A. 180—§ **29, n. 8.**

Jones v. Weakley, 99 Ala. 441, 12 So. 420, 19 L.R.A. 700, 42 Am.St.Rep. 84—§ **32, n. 9.**

Jones v. Webster, 11 0.0. 184, 133 Ohio St. 492, 14 N.E.2d 928 (1938)—§ **55, n. 7.**

Jones v. Wright, 230 Ark. 567, 323 S.W.2d 932 (1959)—§ **74, n. 48.**

Jones' Trusteeship, In re, 202 Minn. 187, 277 N.W. 899 (1938)—§ **103, n. 9, 11.**

Jordan v. Jordan, 192 Mass. 337, 78 N.E. 459—§ **124, n. 16.**

Jordan v. Jordan, 193 Minn. 428, 259 N.W. 386—§ **76, n. 6.**

Jordan v. Price, 49 N.E.2d 769 (1942)—§ **150, n. 10.**

Jordan Co. v. Sperry Bros., 141 Iowa 225, 119 N.W. 692—§ **170, n. 3.**

Jordan's Estate, In re, 329 Pa. 427, 197 A. 150 (1938)—§ **55, n. 27.**

Jorgensen v. Pioneer Trust Co., 198 Or. 579, 258 P.2d 140 (1953)—§ **76, n. 4.**

Jose v. Lyman, 316 Mass. 271, 55 N.E.2d 433 (1944)—§ **157, n. 51.**

Joslin v. Astle, 59 R.I. 182, 194 A. 703—§ **86, n. 17.**

Jourdan v. Andrews, 258 Pa. 347, 102 A. 33—§ **21 n. 48;** § **36, n. 14.**

Judd v. Dike, 30 Minn. 380, 15 N.W. 672—§ **166, n. 20.**

Judge of Probate v. Jackson, 58 N.H. 458—§ **144, n. 40.**

Judson v. Bennett, 233 Mo. 607, 136 S.W. 681—§ **144, n. 50.**

Juilliard's Will, In re, 238 N.Y. 499, 144 N.E. 772 (1924)—§ **68, n. 15.**

Jurewicz v. Jurewicz, 317 Mass. 512, 58 N.E.2d 832 (1945)—§ **74, n. 30.**

K

Kadis v. Weil, 164 N.C. 84, 80 S.E. 229—§ **90, n. 11;** § **167, n. 8.**

Kadison v. Horton, 11 N.J.Super. 102, 78 A.2d 136 (1950)—§ **160, n. 50.**

Kager v. Brenneman, 47 App.Div. 63, 62 N.Y.S. 339—§ **32, n. 82.**

Kahn v. Rockhill, 28 A.2d 34 (N.J.Ch. 1942)—§ **38, n. 36.**

Kahn v. Tierney, 135 App.Div. 897, 120 N.Y.S. 663—§ **150, n. 2.**

Kahn v. Wells Fargo Bank & Union Trust Co., 137 Cal.App.Supp. 775, 27 P.2d 672 (1933)—§ **123, n. 9.**

Kain v. Gibboney, 101 U.S. 362, 25 L.Ed. 813 (1879)—§ **35, n. 40.**

Kaiser v. Second Nat. Bank of New Haven, 123 Conn. 248, 193 A. 761 (1937)—§ **144, n. 14.**

Kalbach v. Clark, 133 Iowa 215, 110 N.W. 599—§ **116, n. 10.**

Kalish v. Kalish, 166 N.Y. 368, 59 N.E. 917—§ **51, n. 22.**

Kamerly's Estate, In re, 348 Pa. 225, 35 A.2d 258 (1944)—§ **152, n. 32.**

Kane v. Cosgrave, Lr.R., 10 Eq. 211—§ **147, n. 10.**

Kane v. Girard Trust Co., 351 Pa. 191, 40 A.2d 466 (1945)—§ **135, n. 13.**

Kane Borough Park Lands Trustees' Appointment, In re, 177 Pa. 638, 35 A. 874—§ **32, n. 31.**

Kansas Pacific Ry. Co. v. Cutter, 16 Kan. 568—§ **15, n. 18.**

Kaplan's Will, Matter of, 88 N.Y.S.2d 851 (1949)—§ **114, n. 4.**

Karner, Ex'r v. Monterey Christian Church, 304 Ky. 269, 200 S.W. 474—§ **98, n. 18.**

L

M

Q

S

Index

CHARITABLE CORPORATION—Cont'd
Gift to, donor's intent, 54.

CHARITABLE FOUNDATION
Management for charity, 66.

CHARITABLE INTENT
Charitable trust gift, 54.

CHARITABLE TRUSTS
Accounts, 142.
Accumulations, income, 70.
Attorney General, enforcement, 156.
Cemeteries and monuments, 59.
Certainty as to purpose and beneficiaries, 55, 65.
Charitable and noncharitable purposes, 65.
Classes of persons benefited, 54.
Corporations,
    Capacity, act as trustee, 66.
    Gifts to, outright or in trust, 54, 66.
Court, powers,
    Alter administration, 147.
    Cy pres application, 147.
Creation,
    Acts required, 66.
    Mortmain statutes, 67.
    Rule against Perpetuities, 68.
    Suspension of power of alienation, 69.
Cy pres application by court, 147.
Definition, 54.
Deviation, authorized by court, 147.
Duration, 69.
Enforcement,
    Attorney General, 156.
    Individuals, 156.
    Power of visitation, 156.
England,
    Charitable Trusts (Validation) Act of 1954, 64.
    Charities Act of 1960, 56, 67.
    Law of Property Act, 70.
    Mortmain Statutes, 67.
    Statute of Charitable Uses, 56.
Failure, impossibility or impracticality, 147.
Federal regulation, 142.
Foundations, 66.
History, 56.
Masses, charitable purpose, 58.
Miscellaneous charitable and noncharitable purposes, 64.
Mixed trusts, 65.
Modification, 147.
Mortmain statutes, creation, 67.
Public benefits required, 54.
Purposes,
    Benevolent, 54.
    Community, 63.
    Definiteness, 55.
    Education, 60.
    Governmental, 63.
    Health, promotion of, 62.

CHARITABLE TRUSTS—Cont'd
    Masses, 58.
    Mixed, charitable and noncharitable, 65.
    Noncharitable, 64.
    Poverty, relief of, 61.
    Religious, 57.
Reports and accounts, 142.
Statute of Charitable Uses,
    English, 56.
    Similar American statutes, 56.
Statutes, regulation and enforcement, 142, 156.
Statutory restrictions,
    Accumulations, income, 70.
    Duration, 69.
    Mortmain statutes, 67.
    Remoteness of vesting, 68.
    Settlor, 66, 67.
    Suspension, power of alienation, 69.
    Trustee, 66, 67.
Supervision and enforcement, 156.
Termination,
    Court, 150.
    Failure, resulting trust, 147.
    Illegality, 150.
    Purposes accomplished or impossible, 150.
Tort liability of trustees, 129.
Uncertainty,
    Beneficiaries, 55.
    Purpose, 55.

CODIFICATION
See also Statutes; Uniform State Laws.
Law of trusts, 7.
Restatement, Second, Law of Trusts, 7.
State trust codes, 7.
Uniform state laws, 7.

COMMISSIONS
See Compensation of Trustee.

COMMON TRUST FUNDS
See Investments; Statutes.

COMMUNITY TRUSTS
Changing charitable needs, 147.
Defined, 66.

COMPENSATION OF TRUSTEE
Co-trustees, 144.
Court control, 144.
Double commissions, 144.
Forfeiture or reduction, 140, 144.
Statutes, 144.
Trust instrument controlling, 144.
Waiver by trustee, 144.

CONDITIONS
Changed, alteration or cy pres, 146, 147.
Charitable gift, 66.
Illegal purposes, 48.
Private trust, creation,
    Precedent, 48.
    Subsequent, 48.

CONFIDENTIAL RELATIONSHIP
Basis for constructive trust, 84, 86, 87, 96.
Gift, undue influence, 96.
Loyalty required, 96.

CONFLICT OF INTEREST
Trustee's duty of loyalty, 95.
Removal of trustee, 160.

CONFLICT OF LAWS
See also Charitable Trusts; Jurisdiction;
    Power of Appointment; Taxes and
    Taxation.
Restatement, Conflict of Laws, 7.

CONSENT OF BENEFICIARY
Barring remedies, 168.
Trust investments, 102.

CONSIDERATION
Creation of trusts, 24.

CONSTRUCTIVE TRUSTS
Bank, trustee's unauthorized deposit, 27.
Breach of trust, by trustee,
    Duty of fairness, dealing with benefi-
        ciaries, 96.
    Express trust, disloyalty, 86.
Confidential relationship, basis, 84, 86, 87,
    96.
Creation, theory, 77.
Duress, 80.
Evidence required, 78.
Fraud and concealment, 79, 85.
Homicide, property obtained by, 82.
Judicial sale, promise by buyer, 83.
Larceny or conversion, 87.
Mistake, 80.
Oral trust,
    Gift by will or intestacy, 85.
    Realty, breach of, 84.
Proof required, 78.
Remedy of beneficiary, 77.
Statute of Frauds, 78, 83, 84.
Statute of Limitations, 170.
Undue influence, 80.
Unenforceable contract to convey, breach
    of, 83.

CONTRACT
See also Contracts of Trustee.
In favor of trustee, creating trust, 10.
Subject matter of trust, 23, 25.
Unenforceable, breach, constructive trust,
    83.

CONTRACTS OF TRUSTEE
Exclusion of personal liability, 126.
Indemnity of trustee, 127.
Liability in representative capacity, 125,
    128.
Personal liability, 125.

CONVERSION OF PROPERTY
Basis for constructive trust, 81.
Investments, duty to convert, 108.

CORPORATE TRUSTEES
Foreign, qualification, 30.
Merger or consolidation, 32.
Qualification to act, 30.
Standard of care, 93.

CORPORATION, MUNICIPAL
As beneficiary, 35.
Capacity as trustee,
    Charitable, 66.
    Private, 30.

CORPORATION, PRIVATE
As beneficiary, 35.
Capacity as trustee,
    Charitable, 66, 67.
    Foreign, 30.
    Private, 30.
Duty, transfer of stock, 167.

CO-TRUSTEES
See also .Participation in Breach of
    Trust.
As joint tenants, 32.
Compensation, 144.
Delegation of powers, 92.
Disagreement, 89.
Inactive, 92.
Liabilities, 92, 125, 157, 168.
Powers of, 91.
Release by one, 168.
Right to indemnity, 127, 128, 157.

COURT SUPERVISION
Accounting, 142.
Appointment of trustee, 29, 32, 160.
Bond of trustee, 33.
Borrowing, 137.
Charitable trusts, 156.
Compensation, 144.
Discretionary powers of trustee, 89.
Express trusts, 153.
Investments, 102.
Qualification of trustee, 33.
Removal of trustee, 160.
Sales, 134.
Trusts, 153.

CREATION OF TRUST
Beneficiary,
    Necessity of, 34.
    Notice to and acceptance by, 36.
    Who may be, 35.
Charitable trusts, 66.
Clear proof required, 11.
Consideration not necessary, 24.
Expression of trust intent, 11.
Formalities,
    Delivery of possession, 32.

ELEEMOSYNARY
See Charitable Trusts; Education.

EMBEZZLEMENT
Agent of trustee, improper delegation of powers, 92.
Beneficiary's remedies, 157.
By trustee, recovery from bondsman, 159.
Constructive trust, ground for imposition, 81.

EMPLOYEE RETIREMENT INCOME SECURITY ACT OF 1974
Accounts of trustees, 142.
Exculpatory clauses, effect, 94.

ENFORCEMENT
See also Charitable Trusts; Remedies of Beneficiaries.
By beneficiary,
Enjoining or setting aside wrongful acts, 154.
Specific performance, 155.
By court, 153–155, 157.
Charitable trusts, 156.

EQUITABLE CHARGE
Distinguished from trust, 14.

EQUITABLE CONVERSION
Beneficiary's interest, settlor's direction, 37.

EQUITABLE INTERESTS
Nature of beneficiary's interest, 37.
Trust subject matter, 25.

EQUITABLE LIEN
Beneficiary, on product of trustee's breach, 158.

ESCHEAT
Interest of beneficiary to state, 38.

ESTOPPEL
Against trustee, Statute of Frauds, 21.
Barring beneficiary, 168.

EVIDENCE
See also Parol Evidence.
Constructive trusts, 78.
Creation of trust, 11.
Disclaimer by beneficiary, 36.
Resulting trusts, clear evidence required, 74.
Tracing trust funds, identification, 162.

EXCULPATORY CLAUSES
Acts of trustee, effect, 94.
Statutes, 94.

EXECUTION
See also Creditors; Remedies of Beneficiaries.
Creditors of beneficiary, remedy, 39.
Passive trust, beneficiary's interest, 39.

EXECUTORSHIP
Distinguished from trust, 15.

EXPECTANCIES
See Future Property.

EXPENSES OF TRUST
See Principal and Income.

EXPRESS TRUST
Meaning, 8.
Methods of creation, 10.
Who may create, 9.

FAILURE OF EXPRESS TRUST
See also Charitable Trusts; Resulting Trusts.
Charitable trust,
Cy pres application, 147, 150.
Resulting trust for settlor, 75, 147.
Resulting trust for settlor, 95.

FEES
See Compensation of Trustee.

FIDUCIARY RELATIONSHIP
See also Confidential Relationship.
Transactions between fiduciary and beneficiary, 96.
Trustees, duty of loyalty, 95.

FOREIGN CORPORATION
As trustee, 30.
Removal as trustee, 160.

FORMALITIES
Transfer of property interest to trustee, 32.
Wills Acts, testamentary dispositions, 22.
Writing, Statute of Frauds, 21.

FRAUD
See also Statute of Frauds.
Constructive trust, grounds, 79, 85.
Invalidate creation of trust, 9.

FRAUDULENT CONVEYANCES
Beneficiary's remedies, 161, 162.
Illegal trust, 48.

FUNCTIONS OF TRUSTS
Possible and common purposes, 47.

FUTURE PROPERTY
As trust subject matter, 25.

INDEFINITENESS —Cont'd
Intent of settlor, 11.
Subject matter of trust, 25.
Trust intent, precatory expressions, 19.

INDEMNITY
Co-trustees, 127, 128, 157.
Expenses of administration, right of trustee, 144.
Joint breach of trust, third person or trustee against the other, 166.
Right of trustee,
Contract liability, 127.
Property ownership liability, 132.
Tort liability, 130.

INFANTS
Capacity,
To be settlor, 9.
To be trustee, 30.

INFORMATION
See Trustee, Duties.

INJUNCTION
Remedy of beneficiary, breach of trust, 154.

INSPECTION
Right of beneficiary to inspect trust records, 141.

INSTRUCTIONS
Court, to trustee or beneficiaries, 153.
Trustee's duty to apply for, 153.

INSURANCE
Allocation to principal or income, expenses, 124.
Constructive trust of proceeds, homicide, 82.
Ownership, transfer to trustee, 32.
Premiums, paid from trust income, 124.
Proceeds, loss of property, trust principal, 119.
Rights of settlor's creditors, 47.
Subject matter of trust, 10, 25.

INSURANCE TRUSTS
Advantages, creditors and taxes, 47.
Defined, 10.
Pour over from will, 22.
Statutes, pour over, 22.
Trustee,
As beneficiary of policy, 10, 25.
Title, 32.
When purpose illegal, 48.
Wills Acts, applicability, 22.

INTENT
See also Creation of Trust.
Trust creation,

INTENT —Cont'd
Charitable trust, 66.
Private trust, expression of settlor, 11.

INTEREST
Allocation to income, 111.
Bonds bought at premium or discount, apportionment, 113.
Damages to include, trustee's breach, 157.

INTEREST OF BENEFICIARIES
See Beneficiary, Interest of.

INTERMEDIATE ACCOUNTING
See also Accounts of Trustee.
Conclusiveness as to matters covered, 143.

INVASION OF PRINCIPAL
Court authority, deviation from trust terms, 110, 146.
Discretionary trusts, 89, 109.
Power of trustee,
Discretionary, 89.
Mandatory, 109.

INVESTMENT TRUSTS
Distributions from, principal or income, 115.
Shares, as trust investments, 105.

INVESTMENTS
Breach of trustee's duty, 107, 108, 157.
Care and diligence required, 103, 106, 108.
Common stocks, 104, 106.
Common trust funds, 105.
Consent or request of beneficiary, 102.
Control by,
Beneficiary, 102.
Court, 102.
Settlor, 102.
Trust terms, 101, 102.
Court decree, protect trustee, 102.
Delegation of trustee's power, 92.
Development of American law, 103, 106.
Deviation from terms of trust, 108, 148.
Discretion in trustee, 102.
Disloyalty, purchases and sales, 95.
Diversification, 106.
Duties of trustee,
Change investments, 108.
Impartiality, 106.
Make trust productive, 101.
Reasonable care, 103, 106.
Review investments, 107.
Instructions from court, 102.
Legal list, 103.
Mingling of, 105.
Mortgage,
Participations, 105.
Pools, 105.
Nominee, holding trust assets in name of, 100.

MASSES
See Charitable Trusts.

MERGER
Beneficial interests, destruction of trust, 151.
Equitable and legal interests, no trust created, 30.

MISTAKE
Constructive trust, grounds for, 80.
Drafting, reformation, 148.
Settlor's, omission of power of revocation, 148.
Trustee's, exculpatory clauses, 94.

MIXED TRUSTS
Charitable and noncharitable purposes, 65.

MODIFICATION
See Alteration of Trust; Deviation from Terms of Trust.

MONUMENTS
See Cemeteries and Monuments.

MORTGAGE SALVAGING
See Principal and Income.

MORTGAGES
See also Borrowing and Mortgaging; Trustee, Powers.
Court control, 137.
Invalid, effect, 138.
Investments by trustee in, 104–106.
Power of trustee, 136.
Repairs and improvements, leased trust property, 139.
Salvage operations, principal and income, 121.

MORTMAIN ACTS
American statutes, charitable gifts, 67.
Charitable trusts, limiting creation, 67.
English restrictions, 67.

MUNICIPAL CORPORATION
Beneficiary, 35.
Trustee, 30.

MUTUAL FUNDS
See Investment Trusts.

NATIONAL BANKS
See Banks and Banking.

NEGLIGENCE
See also Remedies of Beneficiaries.
Trustee, improper payments to beneficiaries, 109.
Trustee's tort liability,
    Charitable trust, 129.
    Exculpatory clauses, 94.
    Private trust, 129.

NOMINEES
Holding trust property in name of, 100.

NONRESIDENTS
See also Aliens; Trustees.
Capacity to act as trustee,
    Corporate, 30.
    Individual, 30.
Removal as trustee, 160.

NOTICE
See also Bona Fide Purchaser.
Appointment of new trustee, proceedings, 32.
Assignment, beneficiary's interest, 39.
Breach of trust, Statute of Limitations, 170.
Constructive notice, recording acts, 165.
Of trust,
    To beneficiary, 36.
    To trustee, 31.
Recording acts, bona fide purchaser, 165.
Resignation, by trustee, 31.

OPTIONS
Power of trustee to grant, 133.
To renew lease, 139.

ORAL EVIDENCE
Creation of trust, when admissible, 21.
Formality in trust creation, Statute of Frauds, 21.
Promise by grantee, trust of realty, 84.

ORAL TRUST
See also Constructive Trusts.
Of realty, constructive trust, 84.
Statute of Frauds, 21.
Will or intestacy, gift on oral trust, 85.

ORIGIN
Uses and trusts, 2.

PAROL EVIDENCE
See Oral Evidence.

PART PERFORMANCE
Constructive trust, oral trust of realty, 84.
Statute of Frauds, bars defense of, 21.

PARTICIPATION IN BREACH OF TRUST
Bank, 167.
Defined, 167.
Liability of third person, 167.
Remedies, 167.

PASSIVE TRUSTS
Beneficiary's interest in, creditor's rights, 39.
Effect of passivity, 46.
Nature of, 46.
Statute of Uses,
    Application, 46.
    Effect, 5, 46.

†